PREFACE TO THE SECOND EDITION

In the scant three years since the First Edition of this casebook was published, developments have moved at a pace that has astonished even us. In the way that the present always reshapes interpretations of the past, nothing in the field looks the same after the watershed event of the 2000 presidential election dispute and the Supreme Court's decision in *Bush v. Gore*, 531 U.S. 28 (2000). The history of the relationship of constitutional law to democracy, and of the Supreme Court's decisions to intervene or not in other aspects of democratic politics, will inevitably come to be re-visited, by academics and students alike, in light of what is surely one of the most momentous events in the history of the Court. At the same time, major revision of national campaign-finance legislation, after years of dormancy, has become a genuine possibility with the passage in the Senate of the McCain-Feingold bill; as this book goes to press, we perhaps stand at the brink of the most dramatic revision of financing for national elections since the current system was created in the mid–1970s. And in moments less dramatic than *Bush v. Gore*, the Supreme Court continues to constitutionalize aspects of democratic politics; recently, for example, the Court endorsed the broadest conception it has ever recognized of the constitutional autonomy of political parties.

This substantially revised Second Edition, which is expanded fifty percent from the First Edition, seeks to take these and related developments into account. This edition also reflects the changing trajectory of our own interests in the field. The Second Edition includes two entirely new chapters. Chapter 4 presents the 2000 presidential election litigation in both its state and federal dimensions; this chapter also incorporates social-scientific analysis, academic commentary, and journalistic studies that have become available in the six months since the Court's decision in *Bush v. Gore*. Chapter 12 addresses a closely related set of issues: the law of remedies for flawed elections. Elections represent peculiar mixtures of private rights and public interests; even more than in many areas of law, the relationship of rights to remedies is unusually rich. These two new chapters can be taught as separate units or in conjunction with each other.

The other noteworthy major modifications include substantial development of the materials on political parties, now in Chapter 5, and those on campaign finance, now in Chapter 6. The new materials in these chapters reflect the increasing significance of the law of political parties and the increasing interest in campaign-finance alternatives. With respect to campaign finance, at the time of the First Edition, we sought merely to present enough material to enable an introduction to the topic in a course we envisioned as focusing more on other areas; campaign-finance legislation did not appear a live issue, and collectively we had limited expertise in an area that had not yet drawn our attention. Since then, interest in campaign-finance issues has exploded, both politically and academically; many states, often through voter initiatives, have enacted various campaign-finance changes, and major national legislation, for only the third time in the last hundred years, appears possible. Chapter 6 is a major expansion of the materials on this topic, designed to sustain several weeks of teaching; two of us indeed teach the subject at this length. The chapter includes extensive analysis of the problems of issue advocacy, soft money, and various reform proposals currently being considered. It also focuses the constitutional issues around the most recent Supreme Court pronouncements in the area and situates those issues more fully than before in the First Amendment materials within which the constitutional contests necessarily take place.

Chapter 5, on political parties, reflects our increasing recognition that analysis of the law of democracy must focus on the intermediate organizations that stand between voters and the state—with the most enduring and therefore important of these organizations being the political parties. American political culture has always reflected a far more ambivalent stance toward parties than that in European democracies; are strong parties to be feared as sources of corruption and threats to the individual choice and conscience that Americans seem to prize so highly, or are strong parties to be desired to ensure countervailing organizational powers capable of combating well-organized economic interests in the democratic arena? The materials in Chapter 5 reflect the complex and continuing history of this struggle in American law. At the same time that politics is expressing itself in new forms that abandon the conventional party structures—with the rise of serious third-party and independent candidacies, as well as the increasing use of the voter initiative to attack existing forms of politics—constitutional law is moving in the direction of affording political parties greater constitutional autonomy than they have ever received. We have also brought the materials on political parties in Chapter 5 side-by-side with the materials on campaign financing in Chapter 6, in the belief that the latter can best be understood only with a clear conception of the relationship—both as it currently is and as we might in theory want it to be—between parties, candidates, and individual voters.

Apart from these organizational changes, we have left intact the original structure and sequence of the First Edition. We have added new sections to several chapters to cover emerging questions, such as the constitutionality of the Voting Rights Act in light of the Supreme Court's recent decisions regarding the enforcement provisions of the Fourteenth Amend-

THE LAW OF DEMOCRACY

LEGAL STRUCTURE OF THE POLITICAL PROCESS

THIRD EDITION

by

SAMUEL ISSACHAROFF
Reiss Professor of Constitutional Law
New York University School of Law

PAMELA S. KARLAN
Kenneth and Harle Montgomery Professor of Public Interest Law
Stanford Law School

RICHARD H. PILDES
Sudler Family Professor of Constitutional Law
New York University School of Law

FOUNDATION PRESS

2007

THOMSON
™
WEST

© 1998, 2001, 2002 FOUNDATION PRESS
© 2007 By FOUNDATION PRESS
       395 Hudson Street
       New York, NY 10014
       Phone Toll Free 1–877–888–1330
       Fax (212) 367–6799
       foundation–press.com

Printed in the United States of America

ISBN 978–1–59941–167–5

TEXT IS PRINTED ON 10% POST CONSUMER RECYCLED PAPER

For my family — SI

For Beth and Art, Viola, Zadok, Edward, and Sofia — PSK

For my extraordinary and sustaining friends — RHP

*

PREFACE TO THE THIRD EDITION

Casebooks, like most of us, tend to get fatter as they age. This has been a particular risk for this casebook, which has functioned as both a teaching vehicle in the classroom and as a research treatise for judges, clerks, lawyers, and other practitioners who work in the field. We have put the Second Edition through a disciplined regimen this past year, though, and it has emerged leaner and more fit to face the coming years. Much of this revision consists of making note material more concise, reducing the coverage of cases that have become less important as the frontiers of the field have moved in new directions, and offering new integrative frameworks that were only dimly visible six years ago.

The most significant changes include the following: We have added a new chapter, entitled Race and Representation: A New Synthesis? We now see the *Shaw* cases on racial redistricting as linked to later doctrinal developments, such as the Court's interpretations of the Voting Rights Act in *Georgia v. Ashcroft* and *LULAC v. Perry*, and thus we have pulled this material together to ask whether a distinct vision of the relationship of race and political representation has been emerging since the mid–1990s. At the time of the previous edition, *Bush v. Gore* towered over all other issues, but in this edition, we have eliminated the separate chapter devoted to the 2000 Presidential election and instead integrated coverage of *Bush v. Gore* into the general issue of remedies for election disputes. We have turned the opening chapter into a general introduction that provides a broad opening perspective on theoretical, historical, and comparative aspects of the design of democratic institutions. Given the increasing importance in recent years of issues involving the constitutional status of political parties, we have given greater emphasis to these issues, including by moving the White Primary cases from Chapter 2 (The Right to Participate), to the opening of Chapter 4 (The Role of Political Parties). We have also focused more attention on issues of election administration, such as the Help America Vote Act, and taken full account of the most recent major developments in the field, including the 2006 renewal of the Voting Rights Act and the most recent developments in political gerrymandering.

Looking back over the Prefaces to previous editions, we are enormously gratified to see how many of those who have helped us earlier on, at the beginnings of their own careers, have gone on to enormous professional success, including as Senators and Presidential candidates, professors of law, officials at the Department of Justice, and lawyers involved in helping to shape the law of democracy. For this edition, we benefitted from work by the following students: Adam Jed, Matthew Miller, Dunia Dickey, Seth Endo, Ian Samuel, and Paul Hughes.

ment. In virtually every area, it is surprising how much development there has been even since the First Edition. Chapters 7, 9, and 10 bring the law of racial redistricting and the Voting Rights Act up to the end of the most recent Supreme Court Term. As we commence the process of redistricting for the first decade of the new century, these materials reflect the changing demographics of the United States as well as the current, still uncertain, state of the law that will apply nationwide to this massive process. Chapter 13, on alternative democratic structures, similarly reflects the quiet but dramatic expansion of alternative voting systems at the local level in more and more jurisdictions in the United States.

Some of us now teach this material as a four-credit course instead of the three-credit course with which we began. Some of us teach the material as a course in Advanced Constitutional Law and focus on the constitutional-law chapters in the book. Others of us teach it with a focus on voting rights and concentrate on Chapters 1, 2, 3, 7, 8, 9, and 10. Even as a four-credit course, it is not possible to cover all the chapters in this book, and there are many different ways of organizing a course around these materials. Chapter 4 can be (and has been) taught on its own as a seminar on the 2000 Election. We ourselves change from year to year the order in which we present material. We have provided syllabi to those who requested them to offer a few ways we have put the course together over the years.

The one thing that has not changed since the First Edition is the enormously enthusiastic response we get from our students and the extent to which that response has encouraged us to continue to pursue and expand upon these issues. Although we are all now at different institutions than we were when the First Edition was published, the student response remains similarly sustaining. Indeed, we now have the pleasure of seeing former students and research assistants who worked on the First Edition move into teaching positions themselves in which they are teaching these issues and writing important scholarship in the field. Nothing could be more gratifying; when we began the First Edition, we saw ourselves as trying to create a "field" of study that had not been conceived as a distinct subject of its own at all. Now a few years later, to watch students who participated in that process begin their teaching careers as scholars of law and the political process is a rare pleasure.

Students have also been extraordinarily generous in their willingness to support this book, in large and small ways, whether through the tedious labors of proof reading, through discrete research projects, or through major ongoing substantive work. We thank Kareem Crayton, Dina Hamerman, Jeff Hauser, Todd Lundell, Adam Morse, Tara Ragone, Paul Winke, and Saul Zipkin.

We have benefited tremendously from the rich conversations among legal scholars, other academics, and practitioners on the topics contained in this book. Many of the people we thanked in the First Edition have continued to enrich our thinking, and we have also benefitted from new colleagues who have contributed significantly to our work. In particular, we thank: Alex Aleinikoff, Jim Blacksher, Michelle Boardman, Richard Briffault, Bruce Cain, Viola Canales, Norman Chachkin, Chandler Davidson, Michael Dorf, Richard Engstrom, Cynthia Estlund, David Estlund, Beth Garrett, Heather Gerken, Tom Goldstein, Bernie Grofman, Lani Guinier, Penda Hair, Lisa Handley, Rick Hasen, Gerry Hebert, Rick Hills, Sherrilyn Ifill, Ellen Katz, Alex Keyssar, Morgan Kousser, Larry Kramer, Douglas Laycock, Daryl Levinson, Sandy Levinson, Allan Lichtman, Daniel Lowenstein, David Lublin, John Manning, Peyton McCrary, Eben Moglen, Burt Neuborne, Barack Obama, Dan Ortiz, Hew Pate, Nate Persily, Scot Powe, Bill Quigley, Jack Rakove, Judith Reed, Steve Ross, George Rutherglen, Rebecca J. Scott, Mike Seidman, Ed Still, David Strauss, Cass Sunstein, Henry Weinstein, Adam Winkler, and John Yoo.

Our deepest appreciation goes to Kristie Hart, without whom, in the most literal sense, this edition would not have appeared. Without her we would never have mastered the decidedly mixed blessing of camera-ready publication.

PREFACE TO THE FIRST EDITION

The foundations of democracy are being thrown open for examination today as they have been at only a few previous moments in political history. Internationally, more new democracies have been formed in the last decade than at any previous time, as countries ranging from South Africa, to the former Soviet Union, to Eastern and Central Europe, to less visible places like Nepal, are all moving to regimes of constitutional democracy. As democratic governments are constructed in diverse political, historical, and cultural contexts, the basic questions in democratic theory and practice are being confronted anew: what is the most appropriate conception of political representation, and should the answer vary depending on the specific contexts of different polities? What is the range of electoral structures different democracies might adopt, and what is at stake in the choice among them? How much can institutions shape a country's formal politics and political culture?

At the same time, assumptions about democratic structures long taken for granted in the United States are now facing pressure along several fronts. Some of these challenges stem from the way the Voting Rights Act, first enacted in 1965, has been reshaping the political process to seek greater inclusion of racial and ethnic minorities. Struggles over racial redistricting now regularly dominate the Supreme Court docket and are the site of some of the most contentious confrontations in constitutional law. In turn, these conflicts have raised questions about the most basic structures of American democracy, such as electing individual officeholders from geographically defined election districts. Technology has placed new pressures on the democratic process, where computers now allow a manipulation of district boundaries that no one foresaw at the outset of the Reapportionment Revolution. Alternative voting systems, such as cumulative voting, limited voting, and preference voting, are generating considerable interest as possible new directions for American democracy. How do these alternatives work; what are the advantages and disadvantages of each; what does experience show about how they work in practice? Other challenges stem from the role of money in politics. Agitation for campaign-finance reform is greater now than at any time since the 1970s, at least, and the possible directions for such reforms—as well as the constitutional constraints on possible reforms—differ dramatically. Still other challenges are emerging from the striking recent upsurge in the use of direct democracy to bypass the institutions of representative government. Does direct democracy contribute to good democratic politics or undermine it? If major policies are increasingly going to be adopted this way, are there techniques through which the process of direct citizen participation in politics can be improved?

Given the prevalence of these and similar questions—and given the longstanding centrality of democratic politics to all aspects of public law—it is something of a mystery that law schools have not typically taught courses in the law of democracy. Conceptions of democratic politics provide the backdrop for many courses, but that is where they remain. There is little systematic exploration of the historical struggles over the structure of democratic institutions, or of the theoretical principles that underlie the choice of different democratic forms, or of the practical consequences that follow from different institutional arrangements, or of the way in which the law shapes the kind of democratic politics we experience.

This casebook tries to address those absences. We examine an array of specific issues currently posing challenges to the practice of democratic politics in the United States: issues involving the individual right to vote, partisan and racial gerrymandering, the relationship of the state to political parties, campaign-finance reform, and the fair representation of minorities in democratic bodies. We look at both the constitutional framework for democratic politics and the approaches that have emerged through major legislative initiatives, such as the Voting Rights Act. Although we do not draw on the experiences of other democracies at each point in the book, we do also provide a comprehensive overview of alternatives to the traditional American approach for structuring electoral politics, including a look at consociational forms of democracy, proportional representation, and lottery voting. We attempt to bring historical perspective to the way specific issues have developed in the legal context of the United States. In addition, we develop certain theoretical themes that we believe run throughout nearly all the specific issues we explore, and that go to the foundational questions in the application of democratic theory to particular problems in democratic politics. If nothing else, our aim is to open the minds of readers to other ways of conceiving democratic institutions than those that are reflected in current arrangements.

The wealth of issues makes it unlikely that any one-semester course will cover the entire book. The tradeoff between breadth and depth might depend in part on the configuration of the course: a three-hour survey course for students with a relatively general interest in the political system might seek to expose students to a broad range of issues, while a weekly seminar might pick only a few topics for more extensive discussion. We have taught parts of these materials in settings ranging from seminars with a dozen students, where participants were expected to do substantial outside reading and short papers to focus the discussion, to large classes of 150; while the precise coverage varied, we found in each case that students were excited about discussing the doctrinal, philosophical, and practical aspects of voting rights law. There are a variety of ways to use this book. One course might concentrate on democratic theory and devote greater attention to Chapters 1, 4, 10, and 11. Another might focus more on questions relating to race, and accordingly spend more time with Chapters 2, 5, 6, 7, and 8. Yet another might focus more heavily on the regulation of partisan politics and campaigns; it would emphasize the materials in Chapters 3, 4, 8, and 9. Moreover, although each chapter works somewhat as a contained unit, the book's pervasive themes make it possible to "mix and match" materials from different chapters. For example, some professors might want to include the historical materials from Chapter 11 about the emergence of single-member congressional districts with earlier discussions of congressional districting in Chapter 3 (one person, one vote) or Chapter 8 (political gerrymandering and race-conscious redistricting); others might find it interesting to teach the materials on write-in voting and the development of the secret ballot that appear in Chapter 4 along with the materials in Chapter 2 on the formal right to participate. In working on this project, we found that the order in which the chapters appeared changed many times. One of the exciting aspects of this field is the multiplicity of connections among the materials; discussion can flow from one issue to another along many different paths, depending on the interests and expertise of the professor and students.

We would first like to express appreciation for our students who worked with earlier versions of this material in courses at the University of Chicago Law School, Harvard Law School, the University of Michigan Law School, New York University School of Law, Stanford Law School, the University of Texas School of Law, the University of Virginia School of Law, and Yale Law School. Not only did they offer numerous ideas we incorporated in terms of presentation of the material, but in many cases they wrote papers which deepened our understanding of the relevant issues and from which we borrowed in constructing this casebook. Their enthusiasm about the issues and material convinced us this book was worth doing.*

Over the years, our views on the issues discussed here have developed in conversation or collaboration with too many people to mention, but some of them include Alex Aleinikoff, Jim Blacksher, Richard Briffault, Bruce Cain, Norman Chachkin, Chandler Davidson, Richard Engstrom, Cynthia Estlund, David Estlund, Lani Guinier, Bernie Grofman, Gerry Hebert, Roderick Hills, Jr., Sherrilyn Ifill, Morgan Kousser, Douglas Laycock, Daryl Levinson, Sandy Levinson, Allan Lichtman, Daniel Lowenstein, David Lublin, Eben Moglen, Peyton McCrary, Dan Ortiz, Frank Parker, George Rutherglen, and Ed Still. Justice Holmes once stated that "it is required of a man that he should share the action and passion of his time at peril of

* In excerpting materials from cases and secondary sources, we have used the following conventions. Insertions are indicated with brackets and deletions with either ellipses or asterisks, depending on their length. We have not indicated the deletions of citation material or footnotes, but we have retained the original numbering of notes that we include. Notes that we have written are indicated by letters rather than numbers.

being judged not to have lived." Oliver Wendell Holmes, *Memorial Day* in The Occasional Speeches of Justice Oliver Wendell Holmes 6-7 (Mark Howe ed. 1962). Each of us has participated, not only as a scholar but also as a litigator, in shaping some of the legal doctrine covered in this book. We do not indicate at each point in the book when one of us has been involved in the underlying litigation, and instead rely on this general disclaimer to warn readers that we are not disinterested observers of all the events chronicled here. We would also like to thank our co-counsel, expert witnesses, even some of our opposing counsel, and, especially, our clients, for the many practical insights they provided into the operation and effects of the American law of democracy.

For reading or teaching sections of the manuscript and commenting, we would like to thank Cynthia Estlund, Elizabeth Garrett, Barack Obama, Dan Ortiz, Nate Persily, Scot Powe, Judith Reed, and David Strauss. For document assistance: David Gunn. For research assistance: Jeff Costello, Sally Dworak-Fisher, Alexandra Foster, Jeffrey Fisher, Gary Gansle, Jeff Gitchel, Tom Goldstein, Deborah Hamilton, Chris Herren, Chris Hoffman, David Horan, Bruce Itchkawitz, Daryl Levinson, Laura Mate, Alex Romain, Johanna Schneider, Anne Showalter, Paul Speaker, Sara Stadler, Elana Tyrangiel, and Heather Way. For copy editing: Ann Estlund. For manuscript production: Diane Cronk, Juli Martin, Sylvia Sexton. Finally, for a wealth of intellectual and material support, we thank the law schools at the Universities of Michigan, Texas, and Virginia, and our Deans: Jeffrey Lehman; Michael Sharlot; and Bob Scott.

SUMMARY OF CONTENTS

*

TABLE OF CONTENTS

TABLE OF CASES

Principal cases are in bold type. Non-principal cases are in roman type. References are to Pages.

*

THE LAW OF DEMOCRACY

LEGAL STRUCTURE OF THE POLITICAL PROCESS

*

CHAPTER 1

An Introduction to the Design of Democratic Institutions

Before the first vote is cast or the first ballot counted, the possibilities for democratic politics are already constrained and channeled. The election process is well underway before the formal stage of voting, for elections do not take place in a legal or institutional vacuum. Rather the election process emerges from previously fixed—and often carefully orchestrated—institutional arrangements that influence the range of possible outcomes that formal elections and subsequent policymaking can achieve. Thus a paradox rests at the core of democratic politics: this politics is in part a contest over the structure of state institutions, and yet those very institutions define the terms in which the contest of democratic politics proceeds.

The central focus of this book is this complex interaction between democratic politics and the formal institutions of the state. On one view of democracy, politics should be a domain autonomous of existing state institutions. Democratic politics provides the arena in which private preferences and collective deliberation should be free to develop without state interference or constraint; indeed, a democratic political system is largely defined by the relative liberty of citizens to criticize existing distributions of political power and institutional arrangements. This is probably the most conventional understanding of democracy: democratic deliberation *creates* public offices, officials, institutions, and policies, and these arrangements are justified to the extent they are responsive to democratic decisionmaking. In this view, democracy exists in some sense prior to and independent of the specific institutional forms in which it happens to be embodied at any particular time and place.

But this vision of democratic politics as autonomous from existing state institutions is, in our view, misconceived and perhaps even unintelligible. At the heart of a democratic political order lies a process of collective decisionmaking that must operate through pre-existing laws, rules, and institutions. The kind of democratic politics we have is always and inevitably itself a product of institutional forms and legal structures. There are many possible forms democracy can take, many different institutional embodiments of democratic politics. Should we have representative or direct democracy? If we employ electoral politics, should elections be from single-member geographical districts, through cumulative voting, or through one of the many forms of proportional representation? Who is eligible to participate in politics, and who decides that question? These institutional structures all limit and define the decisions available through democratic politics itself. In turn, these institutional arrangements are either the inherited product of prior democratic choice or of inertia—or perhaps some combination of the two. That is one central point we hope to convey: there is no "We the People" independent of the way the law constructs democracy.

That perspective leads to the second central point this book will emphasize throughout. Because democratic politics is not autonomous of existing law and institutions, those who control existing arrangements have the capacity to shape, manipulate, and distort democratic processes. Historical experience provides convincing reasons to believe that those who currently hold power will deploy that power to try to preserve their control. Thus, democratic politics constantly confronts the prospect of law being used to freeze existing political arrangements into place. Yet there is no way to take the law "out" of democracy. The question, then, is what the law might contribute to mediating or resolving this tension. Can institutional arrangements be developed that both reflect the inevitable role of law in shaping democracy and at the same time prevent that role from being manipulated by existing office holders for self-interested aims? That is the other side of the mutual relationship between law and democracy we stress: the need to find techniques and theories that prevent the capture of democratic politics by existing distributions of political power.

Any inquiry into institutional arrangements leads inevitably to issues concerning f the relationship among courts, legislatures, executive officials, and voters in overseeing democratic processes. At some points, we will see legislatures play a leading role, as when we explore Congress' enactment of the Voting Rights Act of 1965 and its subsequent amendments. At other points, the courts will assume center stage, invoking the tools of constitutional law. When courts become central players, that will raise some of the most difficult questions about institutional role in all of constitutional theory. On the one hand, courts will become embroiled in partisan political struggles not over specific enactments, but over the very political framework through which the electorate exercises its political will. The events of Florida in the 2000 Presidential Election provide a dramatic recent example. But the events of Florida, which now cast a shadow over all aspects of litigation in this area of law, only reflect in a most dramatic fashion the problem that is starkly posed whenever courts act to set aside the choices that emerge from pre-existing electoral arrangements. At that point, the pressure on the judiciary to articulate a coherent vision of properly functioning politics is most acute if the electoral will is to be deemed unlawful or unconstitutional. On the other hand, if the courts refuse to oversee the process, we risk leaving the power to shape the fundamental ground rules of politics in the largely unaccountable hands of existing officeholders. In many instances, we shall see that the judiciary emerges as the sole branch of government capable of destabilizing an apparently unshakable lock-up of the political process.

The central problematic of the tension between institutional constraints and some form of majoritarian choice goes to the heart of any constitutional democracy. The first three words in the United States Constitution, "We the People," purport to claim as a source of authority an already established background fact: an entity known as "the People" that has expressed its will in advance of the design of political institutions, including the institution of the Constitution itself. In this rhetorical structure, "the People" is a recognizable entity that can act as the creator of the Constitution. But many possible versions of "We the People" exist. Perhaps the most important task of any constitution is picking among these versions and giving effect, through specific institutions, to one version rather than another of "the People." Can "We the People" pre-exist the Constitution, as opposed to being created by it? Indeed, are not "the People" the most important legal creation of any constitution? Consider the following view:

> [Some theorists imagine that "democracy" involves] a collective will already in existence, lying in wait for democratic institutions to discover. Before institutions are formed, however, no such collective will exists. Political institutions and decision procedures must create the conditions out of which, for the first time, a political community can forge for itself a collective will. Those institutions and procedures specify whose views will be counted in determining the collective will and define the means by which the collective will can be recognized. No uniquely "rational" institutional architecture exists for constructing that will. Each bundle of institutions and practices represents a distinct social constitution of the collective will.

Richard H. Pildes and Elizabeth S. Anderson, *Slinging Arrows at Democracy: Social Choice Theory, Value Pluralism, and Democratic Politics*, 90 Colum. L. Rev. 2121, 2197–98 (1990). Is there some unique version of "We the People" that democracy itself or the Constitution should be understood to require? If not, what values and considerations should be looked to in determining which version of "We the People" to incorporate into the design of democratic political institutions?

A. A BRIEF COMPARATIVE VIEW

Consider the following questions about different voting systems. In each case, the institutional arrangement that underlie voting systems appear, at the very least, to color the likely consequences. Imagine yourself in the position of drafting the electoral rules for a newly established democracy. How would knowledge of the likely consequences on electoral outcomes influence your decisions on designing a voting system?

* * *

VOTING QUIZ

International Elections

1. Of the 36 democracies in the world with at least two million people and with a high human-rights rating of "Free" from the organization Freedom House, how many use a plurality, winner-take-all, single-member district election system such as in the United States? How many use forms of proportional representation?

2. In Tony Blair's first successful run for Prime Minister in the United Kingdom in 1997, where the Labour Party won a "landslide" and became the governing majority for the first time in 18 years, what percentage of the vote did Labour get? What percentage of the seats in the Parliament did Labour get? The second principal party is the Conservative Party, while a third party, the Liberal Party, regularly attracts votes in United Kingdom elections. What percent of the votes did this third party get in that same election? What percent of the seats in Parliament?

3. Germany and New Zealand use proportional representation to elect some of their legislators and a plurality, winner-take-all, single-member district system, as in the United States, to elect others. How much more likely is a woman to be elected under these proportional representation systems than in U.S-style districted elections?

4. How many times has a political party in the United Kingdom won a majority of the popular vote in elections since World War II?

5. In 1993, candidates for the Liberal Party in Canada won 53% of the popular vote in Ontario. What percentage of Ontario's 99 seats did they win? In 2004, the Conservatives won 93% of Saskatchewan's seats. What percentage of the vote did they win?

United States

6. Of 113 U.S. House Members who were first elected between 1980 and 1988 and who ran for re-election in 1996, how many won? How many won by a margin of more than 10%? How many won by more than 30%?

7. What percentage of Americans rate the job Congress does as excellent? What percentage approve of its job?

8. What percentage of the 6,129 state legislative seats elected in 2006 around the nation were contested?

9. Of 211 state legislative seats in New York, how many were won by margins of at least 10% in 2006? Of the 200 state legislative seats in Massachusetts, how many were contested by both major parties in 1996?

ANSWERS TO QUIZ

International

1. Only four of these 36 countries do not use proportional representation (PR) for at least some national elections. Those four countries are the United Kingdom and its former colonies Canada, Jamaica, and the United States.

2. In 1997, the Labour Party won the election with only 44.4% of the vote but gained 65.2% of the seats. Tony Blair captured only 0.5% more votes than Margaret Thatcher had in 1979, but his party won 12.2% more seats than her party had won in 1979. The Conservative Party gained 31.5% of the vote, but won only 25.7% of the seats. The Liberal Democrats gained 17.2% of vote but won only 7.2% of the seats.

3. In recent elections in Germany and New Zealand, women were three times as likely to be elected in the half of seats elected by PR than in the half elected from single-member districts. The ratio was 35% to 22% in Germany in 1998 and 45% to 15% in New Zealand in 1996. In Senegal, another mixed system, women won 20% of the PR seats but just 3% of the winner-take-all seats in 1998. Women consistently win more seats in PR elections than winner-take-all elections; for example, a study by Richard Vengroff, Lucy Creevey, and Henry Krisch found that the mean percentage of seats held by women was highest with PR, at 15%, and lowest in plurality-or-majority systems, at 8%.

4. No political party in the United Kingdom has won a majority of the popular vote in elections since World War II. The Conservative party never won more than 44% of the vote—which is less than the percentage won by Democratic presidential candidate Michael Dukakis in 1988—in its 18 years of government from 1979–1996. After receiving 43% of the vote in 1997, the Labour Party's vote share dropped to 41% in 2001 and 35% in 2005, though they have remained the governing party in Parliament throughout.

5. In 1993, candidates for the Liberal Party in Canada won 98 of 99 Ontario's seats with only 53% of the popular vote. The province-by-province results in the 1993 elections in Canada were classic examples of distortions of majority rule and minority representation. In 2004, the Conservatives won 93% of Saskatchewan's seats with only 41% of the vote.

United States

6. In 1996, of the 113 Members in the House of Representatives who were first elected in the 1980–1988: all 113 won; 109 won by at least 10% (e.g., more than 55%–45%); and 75 won by at least 30% (e.g., more than 65%–35%). Districts won by less than 10% are considered "competitive" districts that have some chance of changing hands in the next election.

7. In an April 1997 Harris poll, 2% of Americans rated the job of Congress as "excellent," with 32% approving overall. A decade later (after a switch in party control in the White House and both houses of Congress), "excellent"

ratings remained at 2% and the overall approval rating stood at 33%. (Harris Poll, Feb. 8, 2007).

8. Nationwide, a comprehensive study by McGlennon and Kaufman found that 2,175 candidates ran for state legislatures without major party opposition in 2006, approximately 35.5% of all seats. Their 2002 data are consistent with this, having found only 61% of state legislative seats contested that year.

9. In New York State's 62–member Senate, 3 races were decided by less than 10% in 2006. In the 150–member Assembly, 10 seats were decided by that margin in that year. As the New York Times editorialized, in state races, due to gerrymandered district lines, New Yorkers have "no more voting options than North Koreans have." As additional evidence of New York state's non-competitive elections, more than half of all U.S. House races in New York were won by more than 40% (e.g., 70%–30%) in elections from 1982 to 1996. Of the 200 state legislative seats in Massachusetts, only 63 (31.5%) were contested by both major parties in 1996.

* * *

The examples in the quiz are drawn largely from issues posed by the use of district-based legislative elections, rather than the proportional representation systems that are more widely used in democracies around the world. As the quiz illustrates, the choice of the basis for legislative representation has deep effects on the range of likely electoral outcomes, yet the use one or another form of legislative selection process is rarely questioned and almost never posed to the voters. This baseline condition nonetheless exerts a powerful pull on how any democracy operates and what choices are likely to be presented to the electorate.

How legislative selection is organized is only one out of many topics that has a similar impact on democratic choice. For example, how should the law view political parties? Should they be viewed with suspicion, as institutions that threaten to corrupt the relationship between citizens and elected officials? Or should they be viewed as organizations essential to effective democracy that deserve protection against state regulation? The way parties are organized, select their candidates, and are financed all have similar strong effects on the functioning of the political process and the prospects of successful challenges to the status quo. There are also questions of what rights the polity as a whole may claim to act directly through initiatives or referenda. And, of course, no discussion of democracy focused on the United States would be complete without recognition of the powerful role that race has had in defining the limits of participation and in pressing the question of guaranteeing minority rights against the majoritarian premises of all electoral systems. Each of these topics, and many others, will be developed in the Chapters that follow.

B. The Original Constitutional and Democracy

One of the striking features about this area of law is just how unsettled the main doctrines remain, in many cases even after decades of litigation. The opinions and the doctrines that emerge are, of course, simply the product of how questions are presented under the case and controversy requirements of Article III of the Constitution. Behind the cases lie deeply contested issues of democratic theory and political legitimacy, each of which tugs at reviewing courts and each of which challenge easy doctrinal resolution. Moreover, specific legal issues today arise within a framework of institutional structures and frameworks that were established many decades, and sometimes centuries, ago.

As you will soon discover, while the original Constitution devotes a great deal of attention to issues of governmental structure, it is largely silent with respect to the structure of democratic politics. The text does speak in about the terms of federal elected officials and even more generally about their necessary qualifications for election. But it omits explicit discussion of most other important issues regarding elections—from who gets to vote, to how ballots are to be cast, to the way the electoral system is to be structured for all public offices save the president and Senate, to issues of how elections are to be run and financed, and so forth.

The failure of the Constitution to offer much specific guidance reflects the pre-modern world of democratic practice and the long-since rejected assumptions of that world on which the Constitution rests. Most importantly for present purposes, the Constitutional structure was specifically intended to preclude the rise of political parties, which were considered the quintessential form of "faction."[1] Yet as we will examine in Chapter 4, political parties have long become the principal organizational form through which mass democracy can be mobilized and effectively pursued. No constitutional framework for enabling modern democratic self-government can neglect the role of political parties, yet the Constitution not only is silent about parties, it was designed to preclude their emergence.

---

1. As the classic study of shifting concepts of political representation in the 18th century puts it, "when [Madison] discussed the problem of interests in the tenth number of The Federalist, he was occupied immediately with the problem of so dividing the government as to resist the formation of political parties. No doubt influenced by his great Irish fellow-Whig, Burke, Madison anticipated the division of the country into conflicting and competing economic interests, and maintained that the chief cause of conflict would be between those with and those without property. The political organization of these interests he called factions, a disparaging name for parties—but he hoped that parties would merely come and go as their temporary objects dictated. By an irony which he cannot have either anticipated or enjoyed, Madison himself soon became one of the leading agents in the process by which interests were consolidated into parties...." J.R. Pole, Political Representation in England & the Origins of the American Republic 530–31 (1966).

Similarly, the original Constitution reflected a particularly elite conception of democratic politics.[2] But this more aristocratic conception of democracy was already being displaced by the 1790s, and was utterly supplanted as early as the Jacksonian era—developments that led virtually all the Framers who lived that long to a pervasive but underappreciated pessimism because democracy had fallen "into the hands of the young and ignorant and needy part of the community."[3] This transformation in the conception of democracy eventually culminates in certain structural changes, such as the Seventeenth Amendment's shift to direct senatorial elections, and the various franchise-expanding amendments. But these changes are layered onto a document and set of institutional structures that were built upon the pre-modern vision of democratic politics.[4] For example, while voting for

---

2. Gordon S. Wood, The Radicalism of the American Revolution 255 (1992). As Wood elaborates: "With the 'purest and noblest characters' of the society in power, Madison expected the new national government to play the same suprapolitical neutral role that the British king had been supposed to play in the empire." *Id.* Bernard Manin argues that the debate between Federalists and Anti–Federalists was, as the Anti–Federalists argued, essentially a debate over how aristocratic political leadership should be, or how much it should instead mirror the electorate. Bernard Manin, The Principles of Representative Government 121 (1997) ("The Federalists, however, all agreed that representatives should not be like their constituents. Whether the difference was expressed in terms of wisdom, virtue, talents, or sheer wealth and property, they all expected and wished the elected to stand higher than those who elected them.")

3. The characterization of pervasive pessimism is from Wood, *supra,* at 365; the complaint about commoner control of democracy is Benjamin Rush's, a signer of the Declaration of Independence, *id.,* at 366. Wood quotes a similar view of George Washington's from 1799, who bemoaned that the rising spirit of party politics had displaced character as the touchstone for electability: members of one party or another could "set up a broomstick" as a candidate, call it "a true son of Liberty," or a "Democrat" or "any other epithet that will suit their purpose," and the broomstick would still "command their votes in toto!" *Id.,* at 366. Similarly, J.R. Pole reports that in Virginia by the 1820s, "[t]he open electioneering of the candidates would certainly have struck anyone

bred in the habits of the eighteenth century as a debasement of the dignity of the legislature and a corruption of the freedom and purity of elections." J.R. Pole, Political Representation in England & the Origins of the American Republic 165 (1966).

4. In what Gordon Wood characterizes as "maybe the crucial moment" in "the history of American politics," Wood, *supra,* at 256, Wood recounts the attack on the first Bank of the United States launched by William Findley in 1786. Findley, an ex-weaver from Western Pennsylvania and defender of paper-money interests and debtor-relief laws, was the kind of common and backcountry legislator whom "gentry like Madison," *id.,* at 256, considered too narrowly self-interested to be worthy legislators. Findley argued not only that the elite political leaders were just as interested as anyone else in political outcomes, but that there was nothing wrong or suspect about the promotion of private interests through politics—indeed, that the promotion of private interests was exactly what democratic politics was about. As Wood sees it, Findley's attack on the Bank in 1786 anticipated "all of the modern democratic political developments of the *succeeding generation:* the increased electioneering and competitive politics, the open promotion of private interests in legislation, the emergence of parties, the extension of the actual and direct representation of particular groups in government, and the eventual weakening, if not the repudiation, of the classical republican ideal that legislators were supposed to be disinterested umpires above the play of private interests." *Id.,* at 258 (emphasis added). The point is that all these developments that

public officeholders was the quintessential attribute of representative government, the act of voting quickly changed its social meaning and significance from what the Framers originally envisioned. Initially, the open ballot played the role of ratifying social and political hierarchies; as another important historian notes, "leaders still assumed political office as their right and instructed the people as their duty."[5] Elections focused on personal qualities, not political issues; a striking example was that in the elections to the Virginia ratifying Convention for the Constitution, many districts would elect their two leading men—even though they held opposing opinions on whether the Constitution should be embraced.[6] Already by the early nineteenth century, though, the open ballot had come to symbolize a kind of political equality and independent choice of citizens, with genuine sovereign power, that had not been originally contemplated in the election-as-ratification conception.[7]

characterize modern conceptions of democratic politics and that emerge in the culture and politics of the early 19th century are at odds in the original vision of democracy which animated the Constitution's original design.

5. Robert H. Wiebe, Self–Rule: A Cultural History of American Democracy 29 (1995). For a similar view of the historical distinction between voting as the genuine collective choice between competing candidates in competitive contests, and voting as "a ritual of acclamation, a public act that recognizes (and reconstitutes) the superior status of the candidate," Don Herzog, Happy Slaves 197 (1989), see Mark Kishlansky, Parliamentary Selection: Social and Political Choice in Early Modern England (1986). For a similar view of the role of deference in English elections in the eighteenth century, see Bernard Manin, The Principles of Representative Government 96 (1997) ("[Before the English civil war] returning a Member was a way of honoring the 'natural leader' of the local community. Elections were seldom contested. It was seen as an affront to the man or to the family of the man who customarily held the seat for another person to compete for that honor. Electoral contests were then feared, and avoided as much as possible....) This distinctive feature of British political culture later came to be termed 'deference.' The term was coined by Walter Bagehot in the late nineteenth-century, but the phenomenon to which it referred had

long been typical of English social and political life."

6. Pole, *supra,* at 151. Referring to the colonial period, but in a pattern Pole argues continued after the Revolution, Pole concludes that "[i]ssues seldom entered elections, and even when they did it was often agreed that the natural leaders were the best men to entrust with the decisions." *Id.*

7. Wiebe, *supra,* at 29–30. Carrying on with the significance of the view of democratic politics and political representation he sees reflected in William Findley's speech from 1786, supra, Wood argues that within one generation following the Constitution's formation, the original views on these practices had changed dramatically: "In the generation following the formation of the Constitution, the Anti–Federalist conception of actual or interest representation in government—the William Findley conception of representation—came to dominate the realities, if not the rhetoric, of American political life.... Elected officials were to bring the partial, local interests of the society, and sometimes even their own interests, right into the workings of government. Partisanship and parties became legitimate activities in politics. And all adult white males, regardless of their property holdings or their independence, were to have the right to vote. By 1825, every state but Rhode Island, Virginia, and Louisiana had achieved universal white manhood suffrage." Wood, *supra,* at 294.

With respect to democratic politics, then, the American Constitution is a curious amalgam of textual silences, astute insights into the risks and temptations of political power, archaic assumptions that subsequent developments quickly undermined, and a small number of narrowly targeted more recent amendments that reflect more modern conceptions of politics. Particularly in this arena of democratic institutional design, the American Constitution reveals its age. More modern constitutions invariably devote considerable space to the institutional framework for politics and tend to reflect the structures now associated with democracy, such as political parties.

In light of this history, American courts facing contemporary questions of democratic principles today often have to construct a conception of democracy with less textual and historical foundation than in some other areas of constitutional law. Yet the pressure on courts to do so is great, given the self-interest existing power holders have in manipulating the ground rules of democracy in furtherance of their own partisan, ideological, and personal interests. Throughout, we will see the problems facing the Supreme Court as it struggles to work out a democratic theory of the Constitution to deal with numerous specific issues.To what extent should the Constitution's original assumptions preclude the Court from taking on this task itself? To what extent do those assumptions instead require that the Court play this role? As courts and the rest of us consider these specific issues, the questions that emerge will raise challenges both about the principles and ideas that underlie those background institutional structures of democracy, as well as about how to integrate these structures with the kinds of legal challenges that arise in contemporary circumstances.

CHAPTER 2

THE RIGHT TO PARTICIPATE

Constitutions are often viewed today as a way to constrain majority power to protect individual rights. But constitutions also provide the ground rules through which power is democratically attained. They set the terms on which political competition occurs.

Despite the centrality of this role for the American Constitution, however, there is paradoxically little that the text or its history offers in the way of directly relevant guidance. In part, this results from the great silences of the Constitution regarding the structure of electoral politics—silences that often reflects America's peculiar federal structure, in which so much regarding the ground rules of political competition was left to be settled at the state level. Thus, as the first cases in this Chapter will reveal, neither the original Constitution nor the Fourteenth Amendment secured even the basic right to vote.

In its original form, the Constitution contained scant mention of voting. The only organ of the national government that was elected directly was the House of Representatives, and Article I, section 2, clause 1 provided simply that "The House of Representatives shall be composed of Members chosen every second Year by the People of the several States, and the Electors in each State shall have the Qualifications requisite for Electors of the most numerous Branch of the State Legislature." Thus, the entitlement to vote in the only popular federal election was entirely dependent on a state's grant of the franchise, and all states limited the right to vote to only a subset of the population. The most widespread limitations involved age, sex, race, property ownership, and length of residence within the jurisdiction, but there were others as well. Nonetheless, the franchise was extended more widely among white males than in any other country at the time. *See* Chilton Williamson, American Suffrage: From Property to Democracy, 1760–1860, at 21–39 (1960) (American electorate in late 18th century included 50 to 75 percent of adult white males, as compared to 20 to 25 percent in England); see generally Alexander Keyssar, The Right to Vote: The Contested History of Democracy in the United States (2000). In a series of nineteenth century cases, the Supreme Court reiterated that "the Constitution of the United States has not conferred the right of suffrage upon any one," *United States v. Cruikshank*, 92 U.S. 542, 555 (1875). And yet, since the Civil War, a majority of the ratified constitutional amendments have dealt in whole or in part with voting and they have marked a consistent expansion of the franchise. Not only has voting come to occupy a more prominent place in the written Constitution; it has also come to be treated by the Supreme Court as a central, and fundamental, right of citizenship.

This Chapter looks at the development of the right to formal political participation in the election process. Who is entitled to cast a ballot, in which elections? What restrictions can states impose on the franchise? How and why does the Court generate answers to these questions in light of the Constitution's silence with respect to the right to vote?

A.   CONSTITUTIONAL TEXT

Most of the constitutional provisions dealing with the right to vote are phrased in the negative: they prohibit states from using specified grounds to deny the right to vote. The Fifteenth and Nineteenth Amendments, for example, provide that "the right of citizens of the United States to vote shall not be denied or abridged . . . on account of" race and sex, respectively, and the Twenty–Sixth Amendment contains parallel language regarding the right of citizens "who are eighteen years of age or older." Similarly, the Twenty–Fourth Amendment provides that the right to vote cannot be denied "by reason of failure to pay any poll tax or other tax," but it too simply identifies one forbidden basis for restricting the vote, potentially leaving all sorts of bases for disenfranchisement undisturbed. None of these amendments contains an affirmative grant of voting rights. Even the Seventeenth Amendment, which provides for the popular election of senators, directs only that states permit participation by voters who are qualified to vote for the most numerous branch of the state legislature, without explicitly regulating in any way who falls into that class.

With the exception of the Fifteenth Amendment, there has been little litigation over the amendments that explicitly regulate voting. The major source of constitutional voting rights litigation has been the Fourteenth Amendment. The amendment's specific voting rights provision—section 2, which provides that representation in Congress is to be apportioned among the states by population, but that a state shall lose a proportionate share of its seats if "the right to vote at any election [for federal or state office] is denied to any of the male inhabitants of the States, being twenty-one years of age, and citizens of the United States, or in any way abridged except for participation in rebellion, or other crime"—has been essentially a dead letter. *See Lampkin v. Connor*, 360 F.2d 505 (D.C.Cir. 1966). Instead, litigation has focused largely on section 1 of the Fourteenth Amendment, which prohibits states from abridging the privileges or immunities of citizens of the United States and from denying due process or equal protection to any person within their jurisdiction.

Although it is commonly thought that the franchise, once extended, is rarely retracted, particularly in a democratic culture such as that of the

United States, that has not always been so. See generally Keyssar, *supra*. The case of women and the vote provides one contrary example. When New Jersey adopted its post-American Revolution state constitution in 1776, and when it passed its election laws in 1890, those laws granted the vote to "all inhabitants" otherwise qualified; the breadth of this grant was intentional and it was understood to include property-holding women and black residents. New Jersey was the only state to enfranchise women for all elections. But by 1807, purportedly in response to women voting together and affecting election outcomes, Linda Kerber, No Constitutional Right to be Ladies 94 (1998), the New Jersey legislature withdrew the broad franchise and legislated that "no person shall vote in any state or county election for officers in the government of the United States or of this state, unless such person be a free, white male citizen."

Minor v. Happersett

88 U.S. 162 (1874).

■ THE CHIEF JUSTICE [WAITE] delivered the opinion of the court.

The question is presented in this case, whether, since the adoption of the fourteenth amendment, a woman, who is a citizen of the United States and of the State of Missouri, is a voter in that State, notwithstanding the provision of the constitution and laws of the State, which confine the right of suffrage to men alone. . . .

It is contended that the provisions of the constitution and laws of the State of Missouri which confine the right of suffrage and registration therefor to men, are in violation of the Constitution of the United States, and therefore void. The argument is, that as a woman, born or naturalized in the United States and subject to the jurisdiction thereof, is a citizen of the United States and of the State in which she resides, she has the right of suffrage as one of the privileges and immunities of her citizenship, which the State cannot by its laws or constitution abridge.

There is no doubt that women may be citizens. They are persons, and by the fourteenth amendment "all persons born or naturalized in the United States and subject to the jurisdiction thereof" are expressly declared to be "citizens of the United States and of the State wherein they reside." But, in our opinion, it did not need this amendment to give them that position. Before its adoption the Constitution of the United States did not in terms prescribe who should be citizens of the United States or of the several States, yet there were necessarily such citizens without such provision. There cannot be a nation without a people. The very idea of a political community, such as a nation is, implies an association of persons for the promotion of their general welfare. Each one of the persons associated becomes a member of the nation formed by the association. He owes it allegiance and is entitled to its protection. Allegiance and protection are, in this connection, reciprocal obligations. The one is a compensation for the other; allegiance for protection and protection for allegiance.

* * *

The Constitution does not, in words, say who shall be natural-born citizens. Resort must be had elsewhere to ascertain that. At common-law, with the nomenclature of which the framers of the Constitution were familiar, it was never doubted that all children born in a country of parents who were its citizens became themselves, upon their birth, citizens also. These were natives, or natural-born citizens, as distinguished from aliens or foreigners. . . . The words "all children" are certainly as comprehensive, when used in this connection, as "all persons," and if females are included in the last they must be in the first. That they are included in the last is not denied. In fact the whole argument of the plaintiffs proceeds upon that idea.

* * *

But if more is necessary to show that women have always been considered as citizens the same as men, abundant proof is to be found in the legislative and judicial history of the country. Thus, by the Constitution, the judicial power of the United States is made to extend to controversies between citizens of different States. Under this it has been uniformly held that the citizenship necessary to give the courts of the United States jurisdiction of a cause must be affirmatively shown on the record. Its existence as a fact may be put in issue and tried. If found not to exist the case must be dismissed. Notwithstanding this the records of the courts are full of cases in which the jurisdiction depends upon the citizenship of women, and not one can be found, we think, in which objection was made on that account.

* * *

Other proof of like character might be found, but certainly more cannot be necessary to establish the fact that sex has never been made one of the elements of citizenship in the United States. In this respect men have never had an advantage over women. The same laws precisely apply to both. The fourteenth amendment did not affect the citizenship of women any more than it did of men. In this particular, therefore, the rights of Mrs. Minor do not depend upon the amendment. She has always been a citizen from her birth, and entitled to all the privileges and immunities of citizenship. . . .

If the right of suffrage is one of the necessary privileges of a citizen of the United States, then the constitution and laws of Missouri confining it to men are in violation of the Constitution of the United States, as amended, and consequently void. The direct question is, therefore, presented whether all citizens are necessarily voters.

The Constitution does not define the privileges and immunities of citizens. For that definition we must look elsewhere. In this case we need not determine what they are, but only whether suffrage is necessarily one of them.

It certainly is nowhere made so in express terms. The United States has no voters in the States of its own creation. The elective officers of the United States are all elected directly or indirectly by State voters. The members of the House of Representatives are to be chosen by the people of the States, and the electors in each State must have the qualifications requisite for electors of the most numerous branch of the State legislature. Senators are to be chosen by the legislatures of the States, and necessarily the members of the legislature required to make the choice are elected by the voters of the State. Each State must appoint in such manner, as the legislature thereof may direct, the electors to elect the President and Vice–President....

The amendment did not add to the privileges and immunities of a citizen. It simply furnished an additional guaranty for the protection of such as he already had. No new voters were necessarily made by it. Indirectly it may have had that effect, because it may have increased the number of citizens entitled to suffrage under the constitution and laws of the States, but it operates for this purpose, if at all, through the States and the State laws, and not directly upon the citizen.

It is clear, therefore, we think, that the Constitution has not added the right of suffrage to the privileges and immunities of citizenship as they existed at the time it was adopted. This makes it proper to inquire whether suffrage was coextensive with the citizenship of the States at the time of its adoption. If it was, then it may with force be argued that suffrage was one of the rights which belonged to citizenship, and in the enjoyment of which every citizen must be protected. But if it was not, the contrary may with propriety be assumed.

When the Federal Constitution was adopted, all the States, with the exception of Rhode Island and Connecticut, had constitutions of their own. These two continued to act under their charters from the Crown. Upon an examination of those constitutions we find that in no State were all citizens permitted to vote. Each State determined for itself who should have that power. Thus, [for example,] in New Hampshire, "every male inhabitant of each town and parish with town privileges, and places unincorporated in the State, of twenty one years of age and upwards, excepting paupers and persons excused from paying taxes at their own request," were its voters; ... in New York "every male inhabitant of full age who shall have personally resided within one of the counties of the State for six months immediately preceding the day of election ... if during the time aforesaid he shall have been a freeholder, possessing a freehold of the value of twenty pounds within the county, or have rented a tenement therein of the yearly value of forty shillings, and been rated and actually paid taxes to the

State;" in New Jersey "all inhabitants ... of full age who are worth fifty pounds, proclamation-money, clear estate in the same, and have resided in the county in which they claim a vote for twelve months immediately preceding the election;" ... [and] in South Carolina "every free white man of the age of twenty-one years, being a citizen of the State and having resided therein two years previous to the day of election, and who hath a freehold of fifty acres of land, or a town lot of which he hath been legally seized and possessed at least six months before such election, or (not having such freehold or town lot), hath been a resident within the election district in which he offers to give his vote six months before said election, and hath paid a tax the preceding year of three shillings sterling towards the support of the government"....

In this condition of the law in respect to suffrage in the several States it cannot for a moment be doubted that if it had been intended to make all citizens of the United States voters, the framers of the Constitution would not have left it to implication. So important a change in the condition of citizenship as it actually existed, if intended, would have been expressly declared.

But if further proof is necessary to show that no such change was intended, it can easily be found both in and out of the Constitution.... [B]y the very terms of the amendment we have been considering (the fourteenth),

> "Representatives shall be apportioned among the several States according to their respective numbers, counting the whole number of persons in each State, excluding Indians not taxed. But when the right to vote at any election for the choice of electors for President and Vice–President of the United States, representatives in Congress, the executive and judicial officers of a State, or the members of the legislature thereof, is denied to any of the male inhabitants of such State, being twenty-one years of age and citizens of the United States, or in any way abridged, except for participation in the rebellion, or other crimes, the basis of representation therein shall be reduced in the proportion which the number of such male citizens shall bear to the whole number of male citizens twenty-one years of age in such State."

Why this, if it was not in the power of the legislature to deny the right of suffrage to some male inhabitants? And if suffrage was necessarily one of the absolute rights of citizenship, why confine the operation of the limitation to male inhabitants? Women and children are, as we have seen, "persons." They are counted in the enumeration upon which the apportionment is to be made, but if they were necessarily voters because of their citizenship unless clearly excluded, why inflict the penalty for the exclusion of males alone? Clearly, no such form of words would have been selected to express the idea here indicated if suffrage was the absolute right of all citizens.

And still again, after the adoption of the fourteenth amendment, it was deemed necessary to adopt a fifteenth.... The fourteenth amendment had already provided that no State should make or enforce any law which should abridge the privileges or immunities of citizens of the United States. If suffrage was one of these privileges or immunities, why amend the Constitution to prevent its being denied on account of race ...? Nothing is more evident than that the greater must include the less, and if all were already protected why go through with the form of amending the Constitution to protect a part?

It is true that the United States guarantees to every State a republican form of government.... The guaranty necessarily implies a duty on the part of the States themselves to provide such a government. All the States had governments when the Constitution was adopted. In all the people participated to some extent, through their representatives elected in the manner specially provided. These governments the Constitution did not change. They were accepted precisely as they were, and it is, therefore, to be presumed that they were such as it was the duty of the States to provide. Thus we have unmistakable evidence of what was republican in form, within the meaning of that term as employed in the Constitution.

As has been seen, all the citizens of the States were not invested with the right of suffrage. In all, save perhaps New Jersey, this right was only bestowed upon men and not upon all of them. Under these circumstances it is certainly now too late to contend that a government is not republican, within the meaning of this guaranty in the Constitution, because women are not made voters.

* * *

But we have already sufficiently considered the proof found upon the inside of the Constitution. That upon the outside is equally effective.

The Constitution was submitted to the States for adoption in 1787, and was ratified by nine States in 1788, and finally by the thirteen original States in 1790. Vermont was the first new State admitted to the Union, and it came in under a constitution which conferred the right of suffrage only upon men of the full age of twenty-one years, having resided in the State for the space of one whole year next before the election, and who were of quiet and peaceable behavior. This was in 1791. The next year, 1792, Kentucky followed with a constitution confining the right of suffrage to free male citizens of the age of twenty-one years who had resided in the State two years or in the county in which they offered to vote one year next before the election. Then followed Tennessee, in 1796, with voters of freemen of the age of twenty-one years and upwards, possessing a freehold in the county wherein they may vote, and being inhabitants of the State or freemen being inhabitants of any one county in the State six months immediately preceding the day of election. But we need not particularize further. No new State has ever been admitted to the Union which has conferred the right of suffrage upon women, and this has never been considered a valid objection to her admission. On the contrary, as is claimed in the argument, the right of suffrage was withdrawn from women as early as 1807 in the State of New Jersey, without any attempt to obtain the interference of the United States to prevent it. Since then the governments of the insurgent States have been reorganized under a requirement that before their representatives could be admitted to seats in Congress they must have adopted new constitutions, republican in form. In no one of these constitutions was suffrage conferred upon women, and yet the States have all been restored to their original position as States in the Union.

Besides this, citizenship has not in all cases been made a condition precedent to the enjoyment of the right of suffrage. Thus, in Missouri, persons of foreign birth, who have declared their intention to become citizens of the United States, may under certain circumstances vote. The same provision is to be found in the constitutions of Alabama, Arkansas, Florida, Georgia, Indiana, Kansas, Minnesota, and Texas.

Certainly, if the courts can consider any question settled, this is one. For nearly ninety years the people have acted upon the idea that the Constitution, when it conferred citizenship, did not necessarily confer the right of suffrage. If uniform practice long continued can settle the construction of so important an instrument as the Constitution of the United States confessedly is, most certainly it has been done here. Our province is to decide what the law is, not to declare what it should be.

We have given this case the careful consideration its importance demands. If the law is wrong, it ought to be changed; but the power for that is not with us. The arguments addressed to us bearing upon such a view of the subject may perhaps be sufficient to induce those having the power, to make the alteration, but they ought not to be permitted to influence our judgment in determining the present rights of the parties now litigating before us. No argument as to woman's need of suffrage can be considered. We can only act upon her rights as they exist. It is not for us to look at the hardship of withholding. Our duty is at an end if we find it is within the power of a State to withhold.

Being unanimously of the opinion that the Constitution of the United States does not confer the right of suffrage upon any one, and that the constitutions and laws of the several States which commit that important trust to men alone are not necessarily void, we affirm the judgment.

NOTES AND QUESTIONS

1. The insertion of the word "male" into Section 2 of the Fourteenth Amendment was the first textual reference to gender in the Constitution. The suffrage movement was quite alarmed by the proposed text of the amendment. As Elizabeth Cady Stanton put it, "If that word 'male' be inserted [into the Constitution], it will take us a century at least to get it out." She and Susan B. Anthony sparked a nationwide debate in newspapers and the floor of Congress. More than 10,000 supporters of women's rights wrote in protest to their Congressmen. Petitions protesting this aspect of Section 2 were presented on the floor of Congress on at least five occasions. Nonetheless, Congress adopted Section 2 with the word "male." According to Stanton, a friend with access to the congressional deliberations reported that when one committee member proposed substituting "persons" for "males," another replied, "That will never do, it would enfranchise wenches." Nina Morais, Note, *Sex Discrimination and the Fourteenth Amendment: Lost History*, 97 Yale L.J. 1153, 1159 (1988).

2. Following enactment of the amendment, suffragists sought to have Congress use its new powers under Section 5 of the Fourteenth Amendment to eliminate gender distinctions in state franchise laws. In 1870, supportive members in the House and Senate presented a memorial to Congress from the suffragist Victoria Woodhull, who testified on behalf of such legislation. The House and Senate Judiciary Committees issued reports, over dissenting views, concluding that denying women the vote did not violate the Fourteenth Amendment. To some, Woodhull's credibility was undermined because she was a well-known advocate of "free love." Part of the congressional response was to tell women suffragists that if they were right that the Fourteenth Amendment did grant the franchise, then they were already entitled to vote and could go to the courts to prove it.

3. Having lost these congressional battles, the suffrage movement then did turn to the courts. The plaintiff in *Minor*, Virginia L. Minor, had grown up in Charlottesville, Virginia, where she married a graduate of the University of Virginia School of Law. The couple moved to St. Louis in 1845; after being active in relief work during the Civil War, Mrs. Minor (a follower of Susan B. Anthony) had organized the Woman Suffrage Association of Missouri in 1867. Minor's husband, Francis, urged resort to the courts as a means of gaining credibility and supportive publicity for the Women's Suffrage Association. *See* The Oxford Companion to the Supreme Court of the United States 329 (ed. Kermit Hall 1992). Her petition, brought in the Circuit Court of St. Louis County, Missouri, had to be signed by her husband under Missouri law to be valid.

Minor's suit was not only rejected unanimously by the Court, but it was considered frivolous even in "progressive" circles. Consider the following editorial excerpt from The Nation, Oct. 14, 1875: "Considering the crowded condition of the Supreme Court docket, and the vast number of really important cases which are delayed by such suits as this," the editorial asked whether in "giving up precious time to the consideration of such arguments" the Court was not vulnerable to being charged with "delay of justice." In light of the context, is the most exceptional feature of Chief Justice Waite's opinion that it treats the claim with such respect and detailed analysis?

4. *Minor v. Happersett* completes the process begun in the *Slaughter–House Cases*, 83 U.S. 36 (1872), of essentially reading the privileges and immunities clause out of the Fourteenth Amendment. (Two years before *Minor*, the Court had decided its first case addressing issues of gender distinctions, *Bradwell v. Illinois*, 83 U.S. 130 (1872), in which the Court had found no violation of the privileges and immunities clause in Illinois' refusal to admit an otherwise qualified woman to the practice of law.) All subsequent Fourteenth Amendment cases depended on either the equal protection or due process clauses. As you read the later cases, consider whether the Court hasn't *sub silentio* revived a kind of privileges of citizenship analysis.

5. Note the different sorts of arguments in Chief Justice Waite's opinion. Waite appears to rely on the idea of a constitution as a fixed compact. But this approach could be applied with a central focus on either the actual text of the Constitution or on the original purposes of its adopters. To what extent does Chief Justice Waite's argument rest on the explicit text of the Constitution? What sorts of "originalist" arguments does Chief Justice Waite make?

In *A Revolution Too Soon: Woman Suffragists and the "Living Constitution," 1869–1875*, 76 N.Y.U. L. Rev. 1456 (2001), Adam Winkler documents the modes of constitutional arguments actually made in the *Minor* litigation. Winkler argues that the theory of constitutional interpretation deployed in *Minor* was the first major example of an "evolving jurisprudence" mode of argument. Throughout the nineteenth century, constitutional theory and practice emphasized originalist modes of interpretation. But because the original intent of the Fourteenth and Fifteenth Amendments, still so recent in time, were widely recognized not to support women's suffrage, Minor, Stanton, and others argued that the status of women had been evolving in law and that these changes should be read into the Fourteenth Amendment to make voting a right of citizenship that women too now possessed. Suffragists pointed out that, by the time of *Minor,* women in some states could sue and be sued; make contracts in their own name even though married; could do business in their own names; obtain passports; had the right to inherit property in their own name though married; and similar developments. They also attacked the premises of originalist jurisprudence.

Minor rejected these efforts to assert a more evolutionary approach to constitutional interpretation and re-asserted the conventional originalist methodology. Thus, this first effort to "evaluative interpretation" failed, in part because it was too close in time to the originalist history it sought to reject, and also in part, Winkler suggests, because suffragists sought to use the method to achieve a dramatic transformation for which no constitutional groundwork had been laid.

6. At the time of *Minor* and before, the relationship between citizenship and the franchise was more complicated than today. Consider, for example, the different perspectives taken in the notorious *Dred Scott v. Sandford*, 60 U.S. 393 (1856). As you may remember, the precise holding of the case was that African Americans could not bring suit in federal court because, enslaved or free, they could never become citizens.

Justice Curtis's dissent raised the argument that black enfranchisement in several states, including Massachusetts, New Hampshire, New York, New York and (suprisingly) North Carolina, at the time of the ratification of the Constitution proved their citizenship:

> Th[e] Constitution was ordained and established by the people of the United States, through the action, in each State, of those persons who were qualified by its laws to act thereon, in behalf of themselves and all other citizens of that State.... It would be strange, if we were to find in that instrument anything which deprived of their citizenship any part of the people of the United States who were among those by whom it was established.

To Justice Curtis, the fact that most of those states later restricted black enfranchisement—New York's 1820 Constitution required black voters to meet additional prerequisites not required of whites and New Jersey disenfranchised them entirely—was irrelevant.

By contrast, Chief Justice Taney downplayed entirely the relevance of the franchise to the question of citizenship. He pointed out that many individuals who were undoubtedly citizens—such as children or women—could not vote; nor could men who lacked qualifications such as property ownership. So the converse, he suggested, was also true:

> So, too, a person may be entitled to vote by the law of the State, who is not a citizen even of the State itself. And in some of the States of the Union foreigners not naturalized are allowed to vote. And the State may give the right to free negroes and mulattoes, but that does not make them citizens of the State, and still less of the United States.

7. Both *Minor* and *Dred Scott* mention restrictions on the franchise based on property. One of the seeming historical oddities in the movement toward broader suffrage rules was the exclusion of "paupers"—those receiving poor relief—from the vote. Many states amended their constitutions to add this exclusion during the nineteenth century; by the end of that century, 14 states excluded paupers. As of 1934, these states still excluded paupers from the vote. While these restrictions might be thought to be associated with more general property-holding qualifications on the franchise, the historical pattern is just the opposite: most states adopted "pauper" exclusions around the time those states were moving toward elimination of property qualifications.

An intriguing exploration of this phenomenon, which sheds much light on the relationship between conceptions of political community and the right to vote, can be found in Robert J. Steinfeld, *Property and Suffrage in the Early American Republic*, 41 Stan. L. Rev. 335 (1989). Steinfeld argues that pauper exclusions were integral to a new way of conceiving membership in a republican political community that emerged in the nineteenth century. As the franchise was extended and property qualifications replaced, American political thought still asserted that the "selves" with the requisite capacity for self-government had to have sufficient "independence;" those dependent on others would too easily be manipulated or corrupted in the exercise of the franchise. While before this time, that conception had been understood to require property holding to ensure independence, during this period wage earners succeeded in pressing their claim to the franchise. But the antithesis of such persons were those who had no legal right to dispose of their own labor. This included women, children, and paupers. As Steinfeld puts it, "[i]ncreasingly, political rights were being linked ... to self-ownership rather than to property ownership." *Id.* at 367. Paupers, whom towns were obligated to support with poor relief, were also legally obligated to work for the towns. Thus, the same reasons that justified expansion of the franchise to those without land, such as wage earners, were also used to justify denying the franchise to paupers. Note how a political theory of voting and "self-government" informed judgments on to whom the franchise should be extended.

8. *Minor* was overturned by the Nineteenth Amendment. The movement for women's equality is typically traced to the 1848 Woman's Rights Convention in Seneca Falls, New York, which issued the Declaration of Sentiments similar to the Declaration of Independence. The first item of proof of men's "tyranny" over women was: "He has never permitted her to exercise her inalienable right to the elective franchise." 1 History of Woman Suffrage 70 (Elizabeth Cady Stanton et al. eds., 1985) (reprinting Declaration of Sentiments). Women were first enfranchised in the Western territories, starting with Wyoming in 1869, Utah in 1870, Washington in 1883, and Colorado in 1893. The success of the suffrage movement in the West is sometimes attributed to the shared rigors of frontier life making men more willing to perceive women as legal equals. *See* Eleanor Flexner, Century of Struggle: The Woman's Rights Movement in the United States 159–66 (rev. ed. 1975). After victories in several states, the movement succeeded in having the Nineteenth Amendment ratified on August 26, 1920. The Amendment proclaims: "The right of citizens of the United States to vote shall not be denied or abridged by the United States or by any State on account of sex."

Recent years have seen an outpouring of legal and historical scholarship on the women's suffrage movement. For a fine, concise recent history, see Alexander Keyssar, The Right to Vote: The Contested History of Democracy in the United States 172–223 (2000). Keyssar notes that the women's suffrage movement was unusual in that it faced a strong counter movement of citizens opposed to their own enfranchisement. Women along with men argued that suffrage and political participation by women would deform natural gender roles and destroy family life. The demand for suffrage came centrally from middle-class women, women from families engaged in the professions, trade, commerce, and educated women. But many upper-class women became leaders of antisuffrage organizations and campaigns; rural women were also less responsive and difficult to organize; and urban working-class women did not embrace a movement that did not seem receptive to the foreign born and did not directly address economic issues. *Id.*, at 193.

By the mid–1900s, suffragists concluded that they had to move back toward a more inclusive vision of the franchise, and the turning point in the suffrage movement came around 1910 when working-class interest, expressed through organizations like the AFL, joined forces with the suffragist movement. The role of women in World War I gave a further legitimating push to the movement, and in 1918, Congress approved the Nineteenth Amendment and sent it for ratification to the states. Rejected through most of the South, the amendment was approved in the West, Northeast, Midwest (including Oklahoma), and Kentucky, Arkansas, Texas, and, by a margin of one vote, in Tennessee, which made Tennessee the thirty-sixth state necessary and made the Amendment law on August 18, 1920.

There was also a racist component to the argument for women's suffrage, which became more prevalent in the 1870s and 1880s, as well as strong elitist and class-based arguments that became even more pronounced later. As blacks became enfranchised and more immigrants arrived, women's suffrage was justified on the ground that white native-born women would ensure the political dominance of "Americans" against the potential power of blacks, Chinese, aliens, and transients. *Id.*, at 191. In the 1890s, there was a broad middle-and upper-class disenchantment with democracy that resulted in the emergence of various new restrictions on the franchise, such as literacy tests. Some suffragists, having moved away from the broad republican justification of the vote, endorsed this retrenchment and sought to fit women's suffrage within it. Thus, Stanton in an 1895 article entitled "Educated Suffrage" proposed doing away with the "ignorant foreign vote" by instituting tests for "intelligent reading and writing." *Id.*, at 199. Carrie Catt, head of the National Women's Suffrage Association, reflected the views of the Progressive Era when she similarly argued in the wake of the 1890 Census: "Today, there has arisen in America a class of men not intelligent, not patriotic, not moral, nor yet not pedigreed. In caucuses and conventions, it is they who nominate officials, at the polls through corrupt means, it is they who elect them and by bribery, it is they who secure passage of many a legislative measure." *Id.*, at 198.

Ironically, though the electorate nearly doubled in size between 1910 and 1920 as a result, voting patterns and partisan alignments do not appear to have been affected significantly. *Id.*, at 218. Political scientists have noted the "startling finding" that the influence of women's organizations over policies actually declined after women received the right to vote, a decline that lasted from the 1920s until the 1970s. See Anna L. Harvey,

Votes Without Leverage: Women in American Electoral Politics, 1920–1970, at 1 (1998).

9.   The Nineteenth Amendment has generated virtually no litigation. Like many political movements that culminate in specific legal change, there is a question as to how broadly or narrowly to interpret the specific legal manifestation of this larger political movement. Should the Nineteenth Amendment be seen as only a discrete legal change addressing the one specific issue of voting? Or as reflecting a broader principle of political equality—or even more general equality—for women? Might the courts have invoked this Amendment as a basis for reading the Fourteenth Amendment to require equal protection along gender lines much earlier than the 1970's, when the Court first began to strike down gender distinctions?

As Reva Siegel explains, courts have viewed the Nineteenth Amendment as a limited, discrete change to the constitutional system, rather than as expansive source of constitutional principle. Siegel contrasts this approach with the broader approach taken to race discrimination by the interpretations of the Fourteenth Amendment:

> The prevailing understanding of the Nineteenth and Fourteenth Amendments thus illustrates how the social memory of gender relations shapes and is shaped by acts of constitutional interpretation. In the quest for the vote, generations of American women resisted their pervasive legal disempowerment and raised core concerns about the organizing principles and institutions of American life. Their struggle provoked wide-ranging debate that explored the relations of the sexes, both in the family and in the state. This national, multigenerational debate about the norms that should structure public and private life ultimately produced a constitutional commitment to revise foundational structures of the Republic. During the 1920s, at least some courts responded to the ratification of the Nineteenth Amendment in ways that reflected the social meaning and institutional preoccupations of the women suffrage campaign. But this response was both hesitant and fleeting, and the meaning of the suffrage struggle soon faded from popular and legal consciousness. When, decades later, the Court finally began to develop a body of constitutional doctrine protecting women's rights under the Fourteenth Amendment, it did not build upon the memory of the woman suffrage campaign, but instead proceeded to elaborate a body of sex discrimination doctrine that is fundamentally indifferent to the history of women's struggles in the American legal system. Thus, the very body of law that currently protects women's rights is elaborated in terms that (1) efface the history of women's resistance to legal imposition and (2) obscure the specific institutional sites of that struggle.

Id. at 141. For an earlier version of this view, see also W. William Hodes, *Women and the Constitution: Some Legal History and a New Approach to*

the Nineteenth Amendment, 25 Rutgers L. Rev. 26, 50 (1970) (arguing that "the 19th amendment really had very little to do with the vote, but instead established the total equality of women with men. Under such an interpretation, there is a national right in all women to suffer no discrimination of any kind *because of their sex.*").

With respect to methods of constitutional interpretation, recall that the Fifteenth, Nineteenth, and Twenty-sixth Amendments are drafted in virtually identical language. They prohibit denial or abridgement of the right to vote on grounds of race, gender, and age over 18 years. If Professor Siegel's arguments are correct about the transformative reading of the Nineteenth Amendment, should that mean that the Fifteenth and Twenty-sixth Amendments should—or indeed, must—be interpreted in similarly transformative ways? Or if there is some difference in how these Amendments should be interpreted, must that difference be found in something outside their written texts, which speak in nearly identical language? The Supreme Court has never given the Fifteenth Amendment an expansive or transformative reading, nor has the Twenty-sixth Amendment been the font of significant constitutional development. Should we read these Amendments "intratextually," so that the words "the right to vote," "denied," and "abridged" are given the same meaning across the Amendments? For an argument in favor of such a method of interpretation, see Akhil R. Amar, *Intratextualism*, 112 Harv. L. Rev. 747, 748 (1999) ("In deploying this technique, the interpreter tries to read a contested word or phrase that appears in the Constitution in light of another passage in the Constitution featuring the same (or a very similar) word or phrase."). But in light of the Court's readings of the Fifteenth and Twenty-sixth Amendments, would intratextualism then not require rejection of Siegel's interpretive approach to the Nineteenth Amendment?

Richardson v. Ramirez

418 U.S. 24 (1974).

■ Mr. Justice Rehnquist delivered the opinion of the Court.

The three individual respondents in this case were convicted of felonies and have completed the service of their respective sentences and paroles. They filed a petition for a writ of mandate in the Supreme Court of California to compel California county election officials to register them as voters. They claimed, on behalf of themselves and others similarly situated, that application to them of the provisions of the California Constitution and implementing statutes which disenfranchised persons convicted of an "infamous crime" denied them the right to equal protection of the laws under the Federal Constitution.

Article XX, § 11, of the California Constitution has provided since its adoption in 1879 that "[l]aws shall be made" to exclude from voting persons convicted of bribery, perjury, forgery, malfeasance in office, "or other high crimes." At the time respondents were refused registration, former Art. II, § 1, of the California Constitution provided in part that "no alien ineligible to citizenship, no idiot, no insane person, no person convicted of any infamous crime, no person hereafter convicted of the embezzlement or misappropriation of public money, and no person who shall not be able to read the Constitution in the English language and write his or her name, shall ever exercise the privileges of an elector in this State."

* * *

II

Unlike most claims under the Equal Protection Clause, for the decision of which we have only the language of the Clause itself as it is embodied in the Fourteenth Amendment, respondents' claim implicates not merely the language of the Equal Protection Clause of § 1 of the Fourteenth Amendment, but also the provisions of the less familiar § 2 of the Amendment:

> "Representatives shall be apportioned among the several States according to their respective numbers, counting the whole number of persons in each State, excluding Indians not taxed. But when the right to vote at any election for the choice of electors for President and Vice President of the United States, Representatives in Congress, the Executive and Judicial officers of a State, or the members of the Legislature thereof, is denied to any of the male inhabitants of such State, being twenty-one years of age, and citizens of the United States, or in any way abridged, except for participation in rebellion, or other crime, the basis of representation therein shall be reduced in the proportion which the number of such male citizens shall bear to the whole number of male citizens twenty-one years of age in such State."

Petitioner contends that the ... language of § 2 expressly exempts from the sanction of that section disenfranchisement grounded on prior conviction of a felony. She goes on to argue that those who framed and adopted the Fourteenth Amendment could not have intended to prohibit outright in § 1 of that Amendment that which was expressly exempted from the lesser sanction of reduced representation imposed by § 2 of the Amendment. This argument seems to us a persuasive one unless it can be shown that the language of § 2, "except for participation in rebellion, or other crime," was intended to have a different meaning than would appear from its face.

The problem of interpreting the "intention" of a constitutional provision is, as countless cases of this Court recognize, a difficult one. . . . The legislative history bearing on the meaning of the relevant language of § 2 is scant indeed; the framers of the Amendment were primarily concerned with the effect of reduced representation upon the States, rather than with the two forms of disenfranchisement which were exempted from that consequence by the language with which we are concerned here. Nonetheless, what legislative history there is indicates that this language was intended by Congress to mean what it says.

* * *

Further light is shed on the understanding of those who framed and ratified the Fourteenth Amendment, and thus on the meaning of § 2, by the fact that at the time of the adoption of the Amendment, 29 States had provisions in their constitutions which prohibited, or authorized the legislature to prohibit, exercise of the franchise by persons convicted of felonies or infamous crimes.

More impressive than the mere existence of the state constitutional provisions disenfranchising felons at the time of the adoption of the Fourteenth Amendment is the congressional treatment of States readmitted to the Union following the Civil War. For every State thus readmitted, affirmative congressional action in the form of an enabling act was taken, and as a part of the readmission process the State seeking readmission was required to submit for the approval of the Congress its proposed state constitution.... [In readmitting the former Confederate states, the enabling legislation provided that each state was:]

> entitled and admitted to representation in Congress as one of the States of the Union upon the following fundamental condition: That [its] constitution ... shall never be so amended or changed as to deprive any citizen or class of citizens of the United States of the right to vote who are entitled to vote by the constitution herein recognized, except as a punishment for such crimes as are now felonies at common law, whereof they shall have been duly convicted, under laws equally applicable to all the inhabitants of said State....

The phrase "under laws equally applicable to all the inhabitants of said State" was introduced ... by Senator Drake of Missouri. Senator Drake's explanation of his reason for introducing his amendment is illuminating. He expressed concern that without that restriction, [the readmitted states] might misuse the exception for felons to disenfranchise Negroes.

* * *

This convincing evidence of the historical understanding of the Fourteenth Amendment is confirmed by the decisions of this Court which have discussed the constitutionality of provisions disenfranchising felons. Although the Court has never given plenary consideration to the precise question of whether a State may constitutionally exclude some or all convicted felons from the franchise, we have indicated approval of such exclusions on a number of occasions. In two cases decided toward the end of the last century, the Court approved exclusions of bigamists and polygamists from the franchise under territorial laws of Utah and Idaho. *Murphy v. Ramsey*, 114 U.S. 15 (1885); *Davis v. Beason*, 133 U.S. 333 (1890).

* * *

[T]he exclusion of felons from the vote has an affirmative sanction in § 2 of the Fourteenth Amendment, a sanction which was not present in the case of the other restrictions on the franchise which were invalidated in the cases on which respondents rely. We hold that the understanding of those who adopted the Fourteenth Amendment, as reflected in the express language of § 2 and in the historical and judicial interpretation of the Amendment's applicability to state laws disenfranchising felons, is of controlling significance in distinguishing such laws from those other state limitations on the franchise which have been held invalid under the Equal Protection Clause by this Court.

* * *

Pressed upon us by the respondents, and by amici curiae, are contentions that these notions are outmoded, and that the more modern view is that it is essential to the process of rehabilitating the ex-felon that he be returned to his role in society as a fully participating citizen when he has completed the serving of his term. We would by no means discount these arguments if addressed to the legislative forum which may properly weigh and balance them against those advanced in support of California's present constitutional provisions. But it is not for us to choose one set of values over the other. If respondents are correct, and the view which they advocate is indeed the more enlightened and sensible one, presumably the people of the State of California will ultimately come around to that view. And if they do not do so, their failure is some evidence, at least, of the fact that there are two sides to the argument.

* * *

NOTES AND QUESTIONS

1.   How persuasive is Justice Rehnquist's textual exegesis? Does the fact that section 2 exempts felon disenfranchisement from reducing a state's congressional seats necessarily mean that felon disenfranchisement cannot violate section 1 of the Amendment? *See* David Shapiro, *Mr. Justice Rehnquist: A Preliminary View*, 90 Harv. L. Rev. 293, 303 (1976) ("[T]here is not a word in the fourteenth amendment suggesting that the exemptions in section two's formula are in any way a barrier to the judicial application of section one in voting rights cases, whether or not they involve the rights of ex-convicts."). Is this simply an argument that a specific constitutional provision trumps a general one or something more?

For a different textual and structural approach, consider Gabriel J. Chin, *Reconstruction, Felon Disenfranchisement, and the Right to Vote: Did the Fifteenth Amendment Repeal Section 2 of the Fourteenth Amendment?*, 92 Geo. L.J. 259 (2004). Chin notes that section 2's reduction-of-representation clause has never actually been employed to deprive a state of congressional seats and points to what he terms the "fundamental explanation for Section 2's desuetude: It was repealed upon ratification of the Fifteenth

Amendment in 1870." Chin notes that even during the early part of Reconstruction, the reduction-of-representation clause failed to deter southern efforts to disenfranchise blacks. Thus, Congress abandoned section 2's "indirect approach" in favor of laws and policies "that actually granted African–Americans the right to vote," such as military enforcement of freedmen's voting rights, the franchise and a requirement that southern states seeking readmission guarantee nondiscrimination in the franchise. These efforts culminated in the passage of the Fifteenth Amendment. Chin draws the following implications with regard to the question of felon disenfranchisement: If section 2 was implicitly repealed by the Fifteenth Amendment, then it provides no affirmative textual warrant for felon disenfranchisement statutes; they should therefore be evaluated under the conventional equal protection and due process standards applied to other restrictions on the franchise—standards that are covered in the next section of this Chapter.

2. What are the arguments in favor of disenfranchising felons? Are they instrumental or expressive? Are these arguments unique to the disenfranchisement of felons or do they have similar force with regard to other groups? Are there countervailing arguments? *See generally* Note, *The Disenfranchisement of Ex–Felons: Citizenship, Criminality, and "the Purity of the Ballot Box"*, 102 Harv. L. Rev. 1300 (1989). The Note's author argues that ultimately the disenfranchisement of felons rests on two philosophical approaches: "Their predominant themes, contract and competence, correspond to the distinct conceptions of citizenship, community, and personal identity associated with the two main currents in American political thought—liberalism and civic republicanism.... The first is that ex-felons should be disenfranchised because they have broken the social contract; the second is that they should be excluded because only the virtuous are morally competent to participate in governing society."

In this light, consider Judge Henry Friendly's analysis in *Green v. Board of Elections*, 380 F.2d 445, 451–52 (2d Cir. 1967), *cert. denied*, 389 U.S. 1048 (1968):

> [I]t can scarcely be deemed unreasonable for a state to decide that perpetrators of serious crimes shall not take part in electing the legislators who make the laws, the executives who enforce these, the prosecutors who must try them for further violations, or the judges who are to consider their cases. This is especially so when account is taken of the heavy incidence of recidivism and the prevalence of organized crime.... A contention that the equal protection clause requires New York to allow convicted mafiosi to vote for district attorneys or judges would not only be without merit but as obviously so as anything can be.

How relevant ought it to be that Green's offense was not racketeering but conspiracy to organize the Communist party for the purpose of teaching and advocating the overthrow of the United States government? Compare

Judge Friendly's analysis with *Carrington v. Rash*, 380 U.S. 89, 94 (1965), discussed *infra*, which held that " 'fencing out' from the franchise a sector of the population because of the way they may vote is constitutionally impermissible."

How does *Green*'s approach differ from that taken in *Shepherd v. Trevino*, 575 F.2d 1110, 1115 (5th Cir. 1978), *cert. denied*, 439 U.S. 1129 (1979), which concluded that the state may exclude ex-offenders because they, "like insane persons, have raised questions about their ability to vote responsibly"?

3.   Scholars are not entirely in agreement about when offender disenfranchisement laws began to appear in the United States. A student note cites a provision in the Virginia constitution in 1776 as the first such law. See Douglas R. Tims, Note, *The Disenfranchisement of Ex–Felons: A Cruelly Excessive Punishment*, 7 Southwestern U.L. Rev. 124, 124 (1975). By contrast, a more recent study identifies the first provision as appearing sometime in the 1810's. See Christopher Uggen & Jeff Manza, Democratic Reversal?: Felon Disfranchisement and American Democracy 54 (Fig. 2) (2002) available online http://www.soc.umn.edu/=uggen/felon_dis enfranchisement.htm. According to Uggen & Manza, as late as the 1850's, a majority of states had no felon disenfranchisement. By the 1860's, however, two-thirds of the states had disenfranchisement provisions, id., and today, 49 states disenfranchise at least some offenders for at least some period of time. In any event, the complex history shows that "such provisions were neither universal nor uniform." Alexander Keyssar, The Right to Vote: The Contested History of Democracy in the United States 162 (2000).

All but one state—Vermont—disenfranchise offenders while they are actually serving time in prison. Many states disqualify individuals while they are on probation or parole, and several states continue to disenfranchise all persons convicted of a felony for life. For the most comprehensive recent studies of offender disenfranchisement, see Jeff Manza & Christopher Uggen, Locked Out: Felony Disenfranchisement and American Democracy (2006); *Developments in the Law—The Law of Prisons: One Person, No Vote: The Laws of Felon Disenfranchisement,* 115 Harv. L. Rev. 1939, 1942 (2002).

4.   The United States is an outlier with regard to its felon disenfranchisement practices. While some other democracies disenfranchise people serving criminal sentences, and a few restrict the vote for several years after completion of sentence in specific situations, even incarcerated individuals can vote in countries such as Canada, the Czech Republic, Denmark, France, Israel, Japan, Kenya, Netherlands, Norway, Peru, Poland, Romania, South Africa, Sweden and Zimbabwe. See generally Alec C. Ewald, *"Civil Death": The Ideological Paradox of Criminal Disenfranchisement Laws in the United States*, 200 Wis. L. Rev. 1045. In fact, German law requires prison authorities to encourage and assist prisoners in voting. See Nora V. Demleitner, *Continuing Payment on One's Debt to Society: The*

German Model of Felon Disenfranchisement as an Alternative, 84 Minn. L. Rev. 753 (2000).

Article 25 of the International Covenant on Civil and Political Rights (ICCPR) provides that all citizens shall have the "right and the opportunity" to vote "without unreasonable restrictions." International Covenant on Civil and Political Rights, Dec. 16, 1966, art. 25, 999 U.N.T.S. 171 (entered into force March 23, 1976). The United Nations Human Rights Committee, in a comment on Article 25, stated that "if conviction for an offence is a basis for suspending the right to vote, the period of such suspension should be proportionate to the offence and the sentence." General Comment Adopted by the Human Rights Committee under Article 40, Paragraph 4, of the ICCPR, General Comment No. 25(57), Annex V(1), UN Doc. CCPR/C/21/Rev.1/Add.7 (August 27, 1996).

Other nations' supreme courts have recently struck down restrictions on the franchise that burden prisoners. In *Sauve v. Canada (Chief Electoral Officer)*[2002] 3 S.C.R. 519 (Can.), the Canadian Supreme Court held that the disenfranchisement of all prisoners serving terms of more than two years—prisoners serving shorter sentences were already permitted to vote—violated the Canadian Charter of Rights and Liberties. In South Africa, the Constitutional Court issued an opinion in 1999, *August v. Electoral Comm'n*, 1999 (3) SA 1 (CC), holding as a matter of statutory construction that the government had to permit incarcerated individuals to register to vote without appearing at registration facilities. Following *August*, South Africa's Parliament enacted a statute that barred voting by incarcerated individuals, but the South African Constitutional Court held the statute unconstitutional. *See Minister of Home Affairs v. National Inst. for Crime Prevention and the Re–Integration of Offenders (NICRO)* (S. Afr. Const. Ct. Mar. 3, 2004), available at http://www.sentencingproject.org/pdfs/southafrica-decision.pdf.

What accounts for American exceptionalism with respect to the franchise?

5. A decade after *Ramirez*, the Supreme Court decided *Hunter v. Underwood*, 471 U.S. 222 (1985). There, Justice Rehnquist delivered a unanimous opinion for the Court striking down section 182 of the Alabama Constitution, which disenfranchised individuals convicted of "any crime . . . involving moral turpitude." Under administrative interpretations of the provision, some nonfelony offenses such as presenting a worthless check and petty larceny were covered while more serious misdemeanors such as second-degree manslaughter, assault on a police officer, and mailing pornography were not.

The basis for the Court's ruling was the finding that the crimes selected for inclusion in § 182 were believed by delegates to the 1901 Constitutional Convention that enacted § 182 to be more frequently committed by blacks than whites—and present-day evidence suggesting that blacks were at least 1.7 times as likely as whites to suffer disenfranchisement for the commission of nonprison offenses:

> Although understandably no "eyewitnesses" to the 1901 proceedings testified, testimony and opinions of historians were offered and received without objection. These showed that the Alabama Constitutional Convention of 1901 was part of a movement that swept the post-Reconstruction South to disenfranchise blacks. The delegates to the all-white convention were not secretive about their purpose. John B. Knox, president of the convention, stated in his opening address:
>
>> "And what is it that we want to do? Why it is within the limits imposed by the Federal Constitution, to establish white supremacy in this State."
>
> * * *
>
> In their brief to this Court, appellants maintain on the basis of their expert's testimony that the real purpose behind § 182 was to disenfranchise poor whites as well as blacks. The Southern Democrats, in their view, sought in this way to stem the resurgence of Populism which threatened their power.... Even were we to accept this explanation as correct, it hardly saves § 182 from invalidity. The explanation concedes both that discrimination against blacks, as well as against poor whites, was a motivating factor for the provision and that § 182 certainly would not have been adopted by the convention or ratified by the electorate in the absence of the racially discriminatory motivation.
>
> Appellants contend that the State has a legitimate interest in denying the franchise to those convicted of crimes involving moral turpitude, and that § 182 should be sustained on that ground. The Court of Appeals convincingly demonstrated that such a purpose simply was not a motivating factor of the 1901 convention. In addition to the general catchall phrase "crimes involving moral turpitude" the suffrage committee selected such crimes as vagrancy, living in adultery, and wife beating that were thought to be more commonly committed by blacks.

Is *Hunter* consistent with *Ramirez*? Does it turn on the felony/misdemeanor distinction, the state's inclusion of only some offenses on the list, or simply the presence of a racially discriminatory purpose? Is a state's choice of which crimes, or which criminals to disenfranchise, subject to anything other than cursory review? For example, Mississippi disenfranchises only individuals convicted of murder, rape, bribery, theft, arson, obtaining money or goods under false pretense, perjury, forgery, embezzlement or bigamy, *see* Miss. Const. art. 12, § 241, while New Hampshire law disenfranchises only those convicted of treason, bribery, or election offenses, *see* N.H. Const. Pt. I, art. 11. *See also McLaughlin v. City of Canton*, 947 F. Supp. 954 (S. D. Miss. 1995) (holding, *inter alia*, that Mississippi's disenfranchisement of misdemeanants violates the Fourteenth Amendment's equal protection clause).

6. Scholars have debated whether there are significant electoral and policy consequences as a result of felon disfranchisement laws. One study concludes, based on matching disenfranchised citizens with citizens of comparable socioeconomic status, age, and other factors, that, on average, thirty-two percent of disenfranchised voters would have voted in presidential elections, twenty-nine percent in senatorial elections held in presidential election years, and seventeen percent in senatorial elections held in non-presidential election years. *See* Christopher Uggen and Jeff Manza, *The Political Consequences of Felon Disfranchisement Laws in the United States*, 67 Am. Soc. Rev. 777 (2002). With few exceptions, these hypothetical voters would have strongly preferred Democratic to Republican candidates. What does this mean in terms of actual election results for either Senators or Presidents? Uggen and Manza speculate that if disenfranchised felons had been allowed to vote in senatorial elections, Democrats would have won seven senatorial seats that they had lost. Assuming that the Democrats elected in the absence of disenfranchisement would have held their seats as long as the Republicans who defeated them, the Democrats might well have held majority control of the Senate from 1986 to 2000.

By contrast, Thomas J. Miles, *Felon Disfranchisement and Voter Turnout*, 33 J. Leg. Studies 85 (2004), concludes, based on regression analyses, that felon disfranchisement laws have no discernible effect on state-level rates of voter turnout. Miles argues that those who become felons are unlikely to vote at significant rates beforehand; one state reported, for example, that only 10 percent of those who became felons had registered to vote before their incarceration. In more recent work, Uggen and Manza argue that once other demographic factors (such as race, education, and income level) are taken into account, ex-offenders and non-offenders are likely to participate at similar levels. See Jeff Manza & Christopher Uggen, *Punishment and Democracy: The Disenfranchisement of Nonincarcerated Felons in the United States*, 2 Perspectives on Politics 491, 497, 499 (2004).

Perhaps because of the massive increase in incarceration, the sense that offender disenfranchisement has outcome-determinative effects, or the heightened awareness of American exceptionalism, there has been a spate of scholarship regarding offender disenfranchisement in recent years. *See, e.g.*, Angela Behrens, Christopher Uggen & Jeff Manza, *Ballot Manipulation and the "Menace of Negro Domination": Racial Threat and Felon Disenfranchisement in the United States, 1850–2002*, 109 Am. J. Soc. 559 (2003); Gabriel J. Chin, *Race, The War on Drugs, and the Collateral Consequences of Criminal Conviction*, 6 J. Gender Race & Just. 253 (2002); Roger Clegg, *Who Should Vote?*, 6 Tex. Rev. L. & Pol. 159 (2001); Nora V. Demleitner, *Continuing Payment on One's Debt to Society: The German Model of Felon Disenfranchisement As an Alternative*, 84 Minn. L. Rev. 753 (2000); Alec C. Ewald, *"Civil Death": The Ideological Paradox of Criminal Disenfranchisement Laws in the United States*, 2003 Wis. L. Rev. 1045;

Daniel S. Goldman, *The Modern–Day Literacy Test?: Felon Disenfranchise-ment and Race Discrimination*, 57 Stan. L. Rev. 611 (2004); Afi S. Johnson–Parris, *Felon Disenfranchisement: The Unconscionable Social Contract Breached*, 89 Va. L. Rev. 109 (2003); Pamela S. Karlan, *Ballots and Bullets: The Exceptional History of the Right to Vote*, 71 U. Cin. L. Rev 1345 (2003); Pamela S. Karlan, *Convictions and Doubts: Retribution, Representation, and the Debate Over Felon Disenfranchisement*, 56 Sta. L. Rev. 1147 (2004); *One Person, No Vote: The Laws of Felon Disenfranchisement*, 115 Harv. L. Rev. 1939 (2002); Christopher Uggen & Jeff Manza, *Democratic Contrac-tion? The Political Consequences of Felon Disenfranchisement in the United States*, 67 Am. Soc. Rev. 777 (2002); Elena Saxonhouse, *Unequal Protection: Comparing Former Felons' Challenges to Disenfranchisement and Employ-ment Discrimination*, 56 Stan. L. Rev. 1597 (2004); Jill E. Simmons, *Beggars Can't Be Voters: Why Washington's Felon Re–Enfranchisement Law Violates the Equal Protection Clause*, 78 Wash. L. Rev. 297 (2003); Mark E. Thompson, *Don't Do the Crime If You Ever Intend to Vote Again: Challenging the Disenfranchisement of Ex–Felons as Cruel and Unusual Punishment*, 33 Seton Hall L. Rev. 167 (2002).

7. Arguments from constitutional structure have been used to justify the disenfranchisement of two other groups of U.S. citizens: D.C. residents and Puerto Ricans.

In *Adams v. Clinton*, 90 F. Supp. 2d 35 (D.D.C.) (three-judge court) (per curiam), *aff'd*, 531 U.S. 940 (2000), a three-judge court dismissed a lawsuit by seventy-five residents of the District of Columbia, as well as the district itself, challenging the failure to provide the District with congres-sional representation. The court found that the provisions governing con-gressional representation in Article I were "deeply . . . tied to the structure of statehood," and that the Constitution drew explicit distinctions between the "District" that was to serve as the "Seat of Government" and the "States" which were to be constructed and admitted to the union under very different provisions. The court also pointed to evidence that the founders foresaw that District residents would lack congressional represen-tation:

> At the New York ratifying convention, for example, Thomas Tredwell argued that "the plan of the federal city, sir, departs from every principle of freedom . . . subjecting the inhabitants of that district to the exclusive legislation of Congress, in whose appointment they have no share or vote." On the same day at that convention, Alexander Hamilton proposed that the Constitution be amended to provide: "When the Number of Persons in the District or Territory to be laid out for the Seat of the Government of the United States . . . amount to [an unspecified number] . . . Provision shall be made by Congress for having a District representation in that Body." The proposed amend-ment failed.

The court observed that the defendants had offered no policy-based justifi-cation for denying D.C. citizens the right to vote for a member of Congress:

The problem, however, is that strict scrutiny does not apply in this case. Although equal protection analysis scrutinizes the validity of classifications drawn by executive and legislative authorities, the classification complained of here is not the product of presidential, congressional, or state action. Instead, as we have just concluded, the voting qualification of which plaintiffs complain is one drawn by the Constitution itself. The Equal Protection Clause does not protect the right of all citizens to vote, but rather the right "of all *qualified* citizens to vote." *Reynolds v. Sims*, 377 U.S. 533 (1964) (emphasis added). "The right to vote in federal elections is conferred by Art. I, § 2, of the Constitution," *Harper v. Virginia Bd. of Elections*, 383 U.S. 663 (1966), and the right to equal protection cannot overcome the line explicitly drawn by that Article. . . .

Plaintiffs assert that, even if Article I were intended to deprive District residents of congressional representation . . . that deprivation cannot continue in light of the expansive application of the principle [of one person, one vote] in modern equal protection analysis.

But the one person, one vote cases themselves make clear that the structural provisions of the Constitution necessarily limit the principle's application in federal elections.

For discussions of D.C. enfranchisement, see Jamin B. Raskin, *Is This America? The District of Columbia and the Right to Vote*, 34 Harv. C.R.-C.L. L. Rev. 39 (1999); Peter Raven–Hansen, *Congressional Representation for the District of Columbia: A Constitutional Analysis*, 12 Harv. J. Legis. 167 (1975).

What are the implications of the Twenty–Third Amendment? That amendment, ratified in 1961, provides in pertinent part that the District will be entitled to three electoral votes in the presidential selection process and that those electors "shall be considered, for the purposes of the election of President and Vice President, to be electors appointed by a State." Courts and commentators have suggested that the amendment's affirmative conferral of an ability to vote in presidential elections for D.C. voters carries a negative inference: by failing to mention congressional elections for District residents, it implicitly condones the continuation of those exclusions. In this light, consider Professor Raskin's suggestion:

Reading the Twenty-third Amendment to preclude a constitutional claim for voting representation in Congress offends the dynamic of democratic enlargement that defines the Constitution. Consider for example the Twenty-fourth Amendment, added to the Constitution in 1964 to ban all poll taxes in federal elections. During the enactment and ratification debates, there was much discussion about whether the Amendment should extend to poll taxes in state elections as well, and a deliberate decision was made to limit the Amendment's scope. Just two years later, in *Harper v. Virginia Board of Elections*, the Supreme Court found that Virginia's state election poll tax violated the Equal

Protection Clause, although such a claim had been regarded as ridiculous by those who understood the Twenty-fourth Amendment's silence on the subject to imply that state poll taxes remained valid.

Raskin, *supra*, at 85.

Does Congress have the power to provide representation to District voters without a constitutional amendment? Note that in other electoral contexts, Congress has used its powers under the Fourteenth Amendment and the Seat of Government Clause to treat the District as though it were a state for both statutory and constitutional purposes. See, e.g., 2 U.S.C. § 431 (1994) (Federal Election Campaign Act); 42 U.S.C. § 1973ee-6(5) (1994) (voting accessibility for the elderly and handicapped); 42 U.S.C. § 1973ff-6(6) (1994) (Uniformed and Overseas Citizens Absentee Voting Act of 1986); 42 U.S.C. § 1973gg-1(4) (1994) (National Voter Registration Act of 1993). Could Congress simply provide that for purposes of the various provisions in 2 U.S.C. that deal with the apportionment of representatives among the states, the District is a state? Or would there be distinct vote dilution issues presented by an Act of Congress that would purport to grant representation to the District in the House (or Senate) without a constitutional amendment?

In a similar vein, courts have rejected claims by citizens living in Puerto Rico that the failure to provide the Commonwealth with presidential electoral votes violates the Constitution. In *Igartua De La Rosa v. United States*, 32 F.3d 8 (1st Cir. 1994), *cert. denied*, 514 U.S. 1049 (1995), the court of appeals held that Article II's express provision that the President of the United States shall be elected by electors who are chosen by the States, in such manner as each state's legislature may direct, foreclosed their claim since Puerto Rico was not a state. And unlike the District of Columbia, which had received electoral votes through ratification of the Twenty–Third Amendment, no such provision had been enacted with respect to Puerto Rico. The court of appeals subsequently reaffirmed that holding in *Igartua De La Rosa v. United States*, 229 F.3d 80 (1st Cir. 2000). In his concurrence, Judge Toruella observed that although the holding was "technically" correct as a legal matter, he felt "compelled to write separately because I can no longer remain silent to the subjacent question, because from my perspective, there are larger issues at stake." After reviewing the history of United States control over the island, he stated:

> The United States citizens residing in Puerto Rico are caught in an untenable Catch–22. The national disenfranchisement of these citizens ensures that they will never be able, through the political processes, to rectify the denial of their civil rights in those very political processes. This uninterrupted condition clearly provides solid basis for judicial intervention at some point, one for which there is resounding precedent.

One of the most neglected topics in American constitutionalism involves the constitutional issues surrounding the era of United States' "imperialism," the era in the late nineteenth and early twentieth centuries in which the United States acquired territories previously under the control of earlier "empires," such as Spain—including Puerto Rico, the Philippines, Guam, and to some extent Cuba. From the perspective of democratic principles and constitutional law, the potential acquisition or governance of these territories raised novel questions: could the United States hold territories in which the residents were denied the privileges of United States citizenship, particularly the right to vote? As a statutory matter, persons born in Puerto Rico are U.S. citizens. But as long as they reside in Puerto Rico (as opposed to living on the mainland), they cannot vote in presidential or congressional elections. For an introduction to these issues and their history, see Sanford Levinson, *Why the Canon Should Be Expanded to Include* The Insular Cases *and the Saga of American Expansionism*, 17 Const. Comm. 239 (2000). There is also a direct link between these issues and the disenfranchisement of black voters in the American South in the same period, discussed in later in this Chapter. A principal reason the federal government acquiesced so readily in the massive disfranchisement of black voters in the South was that the government (the Republican Party, then in control) as well as much northern opinion believed in restricting suffrage in these newly acquired territories—and justified that belief with arguments that strongly resembled those deployed by Southern defenders of black disfranchisement. *See* Richard H. Pildes, *Democracy, Anti–Democracy, and the Canon*, 17 Const. Comm. 293, 305 (2000). For further discussion of Puerto Rican suffrage, see Foreign in A Domestic Sense: Puerto Rico, American Expansion, and the Constitution (Christina Duffy Burnett and Burke Marshall eds. (2001)); Amber L. Cottle, Comment, Silent Citizens: United States Territorial Residents and the Right to Vote in Presidential Elections, 1995 U. Chi. Legal F. 315.

B.   THE MODERN CONSTITUTIONAL FRAMEWORK

In the decade between 1959 and 1969, the Supreme Court, which had addressed relatively few voting rights issues in the preceding half century not directly connected with black disenfranchisement (discussed later in this Chapter), entertained a steady stream of voting rights cases. In addition to the Reapportionment Revolution (discussed in Chapter 3), the Court also dramatically changed its approach to the formal right to participate. The following three cases illustrate that change.

Lassiter v. Northampton County Board of Elections
360 U.S. 45 (1959).

■ MR. JUSTICE DOUGLAS delivered the opinion of the Court.

* * *

[Lassiter, a "Negro citizen of North Carolina",] applied for registration as a voter. Her registration was denied by the registrar because she refused to submit to a literacy test as required by the North Carolina statute.

* * *

We come then to the question whether a State may consistently with the Fourteenth and Seventeenth Amendments apply a literacy test to all voters irrespective of race or color.... The States have long been held to have broad powers to determine the conditions under which the right of suffrage may be exercised, absent of course the discrimination which the Constitution condemns. Article I, § 2 of the Constitution in its provision for the election of members of the House of Representatives and the Seventeenth Amendment in its provision for the election of Senators provide that officials will be chosen "by the People." Each provision goes on to state that "the Electors in each State shall have the Qualifications requisite for Electors of the most numerous Branch of the State Legislature." So while the right of suffrage is established and guaranteed by the Constitution, it is subject to the imposition of state standards which are not discriminatory and which do not contravene any restriction that Congress, acting pursuant to its constitutional powers, has imposed....

We do not suggest that any standards which a State desires to adopt may be required of voters. But there is wide scope for exercise of its jurisdiction. Residence requirements, age, previous criminal record are obvious examples indicating factors which a State may take into consideration in determining the qualifications of voters. The ability to read and write likewise has some relation to standards designed to promote intelligent use of the ballot. Literacy and illiteracy are neutral on race, creed, color, and sex, as reports around the world show. Literacy and intelligence are obviously not synonymous. Illiterate people may be intelligent voters. Yet in our society where newspapers, periodicals, books, and other printed matter canvass and debate campaign issues, a State might conclude that only those who are literate should exercise the franchise. It was said last century in Massachusetts that a literacy test was designed to insure an "independent and intelligent" exercise of the right of suffrage.[7] North

---

7. Nineteen States, including North Carolina, have some sort of literacy requirement as a prerequisite to eligibility for voting. Five require that the voter be able to read a section of the State or Federal Constitution and write his own name. Five require that the elector be able to read and write a section of the Federal or State Constitution.... Two States require that the voter be able to read and write English.... [Two others] require that the voter read a constitutional provision in English, while [one] requires that the voting application be written in the applicant's hand before the registrar and without aid, suggestion or memoranda. [Another] has the requirement that the voter be able to read and speak the English language.

Georgia requires that the voter read intelligibly and write legibly a section of the State or Federal Constitution. If he is physically unable to do so, he may qualify if he can give a reasonable interpretation of a section read to him. An alternative means of qualifying is provided: if one has good character and

Carolina agrees. We do not sit in judgment on the wisdom of that policy. We cannot say, however, that it is not an allowable one measured by constitutional standards.

Of course a literacy test, fair on its face, may be employed to perpetuate that discrimination which the Fifteenth Amendment was designed to uproot. No such influence is charged here. On the other hand, a literacy test may be unconstitutional on its face. In *Davis v. Schnell*, 81 F. Supp. 872, aff'd 336 U.S. 933, the test was the citizen's ability to "understand and explain" an article of the Federal Constitution. The legislative setting of that provision and the great discretion it vested in the registrar made clear that a literacy requirement was merely a device to make racial discrimination easy. We cannot make the same inference here. The present requirement, applicable to members of all races, is that the prospective voter "be able to read and write any section of the Constitution of North Carolina in the English language." That seems to us to be one fair way of determining whether a person is literate, not a calculated scheme to lay springes for the citizen. Certainly we cannot condemn it on its face as a device unrelated to the desire of North Carolina to raise the standards for people of all races who cast the ballot.

Harper v. Virginia State Board of Elections

383 U.S. 663 (1966).

■ Mr. Justice Douglas delivered the opinion of the Court.

These are suits by Virginia residents to have declared unconstitutional Virginia's poll tax[1]....

understands the duties and obligations of citizenship under a republican government, and he can answer correctly 20 of 30 questions listed in the statute (e.g., How does the Constitution of Georgia provide that a county site may be changed?, what is treason against the State of Georgia?, who are the solicitor general and the judge of the State Judicial Circuit in which you live?) he is eligible to vote. Geo. Code Ann. §§ 34–117, 34–120. In Louisiana one qualifies if he can read and write English or his mother tongue, is of good character, and understands the duties and obligations of citizenship under a republican form of government. If he cannot read and write, he can qualify if he can give a reasonable interpretation of a section of the State or Federal Constitution when read to him, and if he is attached to the principles of the Federal and State Constitutions. La. Rev. Stat., Tit. 18, § 31. In Mississippi the applicant must be able to read and write a section of the State Constitution and give a reasonable interpretation of it. He must also demonstrate to the registrar a reasonable understanding of the duties and obligations of citizenship under a constitutional form of government. Miss. Code Ann. § 3213.

1. Section 173 of Virginia's Constitution directs the General Assembly to levy an annual poll tax not exceeding $1.50 on every resident of the State 21 years of age and over (with exceptions not relevant here). One dollar of the tax is to be used by state officials "exclusively in aid of the public free schools" and the remainder is to be returned to the counties for general purposes. Section 18 of the Constitution includes payment of poll taxes as a precondition for voting. Section 20 provides that a person must "personally" pay all state poll taxes for the three years preceding the year in which he applies for registra-

While the right to vote in federal elections is conferred by Art. I, § 2, of the Constitution, the right to vote in state elections is nowhere expressly mentioned. It is argued that the right to vote in state elections is implicit, particularly by reason of the First Amendment and that it may not constitutionally be conditioned upon the payment of a tax or fee. We do not stop to canvass the relation between voting and political expression. For it is enough to say that once the franchise is granted to the electorate, lines may not be drawn which are inconsistent with the Equal Protection Clause of the Fourteenth Amendment. But the *Lassiter* case does not govern the result here, because, unlike a poll tax, the "ability to read and write ... has some relation to standards designed to promote intelligent use of the ballot."

We conclude that a State violates the Equal Protection Clause of the Fourteenth Amendment whenever it makes the affluence of the voter or payment of any fee an electoral standard. Voter qualifications have no relation to wealth nor to paying or not paying this or any other tax. Our cases demonstrate that the Equal Protection Clause of the Fourteenth Amendment restrains the States from fixing voter qualifications which invidiously discriminate.... Previously we [have] said that neither home-site nor occupation "affords a permissible basis for distinguishing between qualified voters within the State." *Gray v. Sanders*, 372 U.S. 368, 380. We think the same must be true of requirements of wealth or affluence or payment of a fee.

Long ago, the Court referred to "the political franchise of voting" as a "fundamental political right, because preservative of all rights." Recently in *Reynolds v. Sims*, we said, "Undoubtedly, the right of suffrage is a fundamental matter in a free and democratic society. Especially since the right to exercise the franchise in a free and unimpaired manner is preservative of other basic civil and political rights, any alleged infringement of the right of citizens to vote must be carefully and meticulously scrutinized." There we were considering charges that voters in one part of the State had greater representation per person in the State Legislature than voters in another part of the State. We concluded:

> "A citizen, a qualified voter, is no more nor no less so because he lives in the city or on the farm. This is the clear and strong command of our Constitution's Equal Protection Clause. This is an essential part of the concept of a government of laws and not men. This is at the heart of Lincoln's vision of 'government of the people, by the people, [and] for

tion. By § 21 the poll tax must be paid at least six months prior to the election in which the voter seeks to vote.... The poll tax is often assessed along with the personal property tax. Those who do not pay a personal property tax are not assessed for a poll tax, it being their responsibility to take the initiative and request to be assessed. Va. Code

§ 58–1163. Enforcement of poll taxes takes the form of disenfranchisement of those who do not pay, § 22 of the Virginia Constitution providing that collection of delinquent poll taxes for a particular year may not be enforced by legal proceedings until the tax for that year has become three years delinquent.

the people.' The Equal Protection Clause demands no less than substantially equal state legislative representation for all citizens, of all places as well as of all races."

We say the same whether the citizen, otherwise qualified to vote, has $1.50 in his pocket or nothing at all, pays the fee or fails to pay it. The principle that denies the State the right to dilute a citizen's vote on account of his economic status or other such factors by analogy bars a system which excludes those unable to pay a fee to vote or who fail to pay.

It is argued that a State may exact fees from citizens for many different kinds of licenses; that if it can demand from all an equal fee for a driver's license, it can demand from all an equal poll tax for voting. But we must remember that the interest of the State, when it comes to voting, is limited to the power to fix qualifications. Wealth, like race, creed, or color, is not germane to one's ability to participate intelligently in the electoral process. Lines drawn on the basis of wealth or property, like those of race are traditionally disfavored. To introduce wealth or payment of a fee as a measure of a voter's qualifications is to introduce a capricious or irrelevant factor. The degree of the discrimination is irrelevant. In this context—that is, as a condition of obtaining a ballot—the requirement of fee paying causes an "invidious" discrimination that runs afoul of the Equal Protection Clause. . . .

We agree, of course, with Mr. Justice Holmes that the Due Process Clause of the Fourteenth Amendment "does not enact Mr. Herbert Spencer's Social Statics," *Lochner v. New York*, 198 U.S. 45, 75. Likewise, the Equal Protection Clause is not shackled to the political theory of a particular era. In determining what lines are unconstitutionally discriminatory, we have never been confined to historic notions of equality, any more than we have restricted due process to a fixed catalogue of what was at a given time deemed to be the limits of fundamental rights. [Accordingly, *Breedlove v. Suttles*, 302 U.S. 277 (1937), which upheld Georgia's use of a poll tax, is overruled.]

■ MR. JUSTICE BLACK, dissenting.

* * *

Since the *Breedlove* and *Butler* cases [upholding poll taxes against equal protection challenges] were decided the Federal Constitution has not been amended in the only way it could constitutionally have been, that is, as provided in Article V of the Constitution. I would adhere to the holding of those cases. The Court, however, overrules *Breedlove* in part, but its opinion reveals that it does so not by using its limited power to interpret the original meaning of the Equal Protection Clause, but by giving that clause a new meaning which it believes represents a better governmental policy. From this action I dissent.

* * *

I think the interpretation that this Court gave the Equal Protection Clause in *Breedlove* was correct.... All voting laws treat some persons differently from others in some respects. Some bar a person from voting who is under 21 years of age; others bar those under 18. Some bar convicted felons or the insane, and some have attached a freehold or other property qualification for voting. The *Breedlove* case upheld a poll tax which was imposed on men but was not equally imposed on women and minors, and the Court today does not overrule that part of *Breedlove* which approved those discriminatory provisions. And in *Lassiter v. Northampton Election Board*, this Court held that state laws which disqualified the illiterate from voting did not violate the Equal Protection Clause. From these cases and all the others decided by this Court interpreting the Equal Protection Clause it is clear that some discriminatory voting qualifications can be imposed without violating the Equal Protection Clause.

A study of our cases shows that this Court has refused to use the general language of the Equal Protection Clause as though it provided a handy instrument to strike down state laws which the Court feels are based on bad governmental policy. The equal protection cases carefully analyzed boil down to the principle that distinctions drawn and even discriminations imposed by state laws do not violate the Equal Protection Clause so long as these distinctions and discriminations are not "irrational," "irrelevant," "unreasonable," "arbitrary," or "invidious." ... [I]t would be difficult to say that the poll tax requirement is "irrational" or "arbitrary" or works "invidious discriminations." State poll tax legislation can "reasonably," "rationally" and without an "invidious" or evil purpose to injure anyone be found to rest on a number of state policies including (1) the State's desire to collect its revenue, and (2) its belief that voters who pay a poll tax will be interested in furthering the State's welfare when they vote. Certainly it is rational to believe that people may be more likely to pay taxes if payment is a prerequisite to voting. And if history can be a factor in determining the "rationality" of discrimination in a state law, then whatever may be our personal opinion, history is on the side of "rationality" of the State's poll tax policy. Property qualifications existed in the Colonies and were continued by many States after the Constitution was adopted. Although I join the Court in disliking the policy of the poll tax, this is not in my judgment a justifiable reason for holding this poll tax law unconstitutional. Such a holding on my part would, in my judgment, be an exercise of power which the Constitution does not confer upon me.

* * *

The Court's justification for consulting its own notions rather than following the original meaning of the Constitution, as I would, apparently is based on the belief of the majority of the Court that for this Court to be bound by the original meaning of the Constitution is an intolerable and debilitating evil; that our Constitution should not be "shackled to the political theory of a particular era," and that to save the country from the original Constitution the Court must have constant power to renew it and keep it abreast of this Court's more enlightened theories of what is best for our society. It seems to me that this is an attack not only on the great value of our Constitution itself but also on the concept of a written constitution which is to survive through the years as originally written unless changed through the amendment process which the Framers wisely provided. Moreover, when a "political theory" embodied in our Constitution becomes outdated, it seems to me that a majority of the nine members of this Court are not only without constitutional power but are far less qualified to choose a new constitutional political theory than the people of this country proceeding in the manner provided by Article V.

The people have not found it impossible to amend their Constitution to meet new conditions. The Equal Protection Clause itself is the product of the people's desire to use their constitutional power to amend the Constitution to meet new problems. Moreover, the people, in § 5 of the Fourteenth Amendment, designated the governmental tribunal they wanted to provide additional rules to enforce the guarantees of that Amendment. The branch of Government they chose was not the Judicial Branch but the Legislative. I have no doubt at all that Congress has the power under § 5 to pass legislation to abolish the poll tax in order to protect the citizens of this country if it believes that the poll tax is being used as a device to deny voters equal protection of the laws.

* * *

■ MR. JUSTICE HARLAN, whom MR. JUSTICE STEWART joins, dissenting.

* * *

Is there a rational basis for Virginia's poll tax as a voting qualification? I think the answer to that question is undoubtedly "yes."

Property qualifications and poll taxes have been a traditional part of our political structure. In the Colonies the franchise was generally a restricted one. Over the years these and other restrictions were gradually lifted, primarily because popular theories of political representation had changed. Often restrictions were lifted only after wide public debate. The issue of woman suffrage, for example, raised questions of family relationships, of participation in public affairs, of the very nature of the type of society in which Americans wished to live; eventually a consensus was reached, which culminated in the Nineteenth Amendment no more than 45 years ago.

Similarly with property qualifications, it is only by fiat that it can be said, especially in the context of American history, that there can be no rational debate as to their advisability. Most of the early Colonies had them; many of the States have had them during much of their histories; and, whether one agrees or not, arguments have been and still can be made in favor of them. For example, it is certainly a rational argument that payment of some minimal poll tax promotes civic responsibility, weeding out those who do not care enough about public affairs to pay $1.50 or thereabouts a year for the exercise of the franchise. It is also arguable, indeed it was probably accepted as sound political theory by a large percentage of Americans through most of our history, that people with some property have a deeper stake in community affairs, and are consequently more responsible, more educated, more knowledgeable, more worthy of confidence, than those without means, and that the community and Nation would be better managed if the franchise were restricted to such citizens. Nondiscriminatory and fairly applied literacy tests, upheld by this Court in *Lassiter v. Northampton Election Board*, 360 U.S. 45, find justification on very similar grounds.

These viewpoints, to be sure, ring hollow on most contemporary ears. Their lack of acceptance today is evidenced by the fact that nearly all of the States, left to their own devices, have eliminated property or poll-tax qualifications [and] by the cognate fact that Congress and three-quarters of the States quickly ratified the Twenty–Fourth Amendment. . . .

Kramer v. Union Free School District No. 15

395 U.S. 621 (1969).

■ MR. CHIEF JUSTICE WARREN delivered the opinion of the Court.

[N.Y. Educ. L. § 2012 limited the right to vote in certain school district elections to residents who were otherwise eligible to vote in state and federal elections if they also either (1) owned or leased taxable real property within the district, or (2) were parents or had custody of children enrolled in the local public schools.]

* * *

I

* * *

Appellant is a 31–year–old college-educated stockbroker who lives in his parents' home in the Union Free School District No. 15, a district to which § 2012 applies. He is a citizen of the United States and has voted in federal and state elections since 1959. However, since he has no children and neither owns nor leases taxable real property, appellant's attempts to register for and vote in the local school district elections have been unsuccessful. . . .

II

At the outset, it is important to note what is not at issue in this case. The requirements of § 2012 that school district voters must (1) be citizens of the United States, (2) be bona fide residents of the school district, and

(3) be at least 21 years of age are not challenged. Appellant agrees that the States have the power to impose reasonable citizenship, age, and residency requirements on the availability of the ballot. The sole issue in this case is whether the additional requirements of § 2012—requirements which prohibit some district residents who are otherwise qualified by age and citizenship from participating in district meetings and school board elections—violate the Fourteenth Amendment's command that no State shall deny persons equal protection of the laws.

"In determining whether or not a state law violates the Equal Protection Clause, we must consider the facts and circumstances behind the law, the interests which the State claims to be protecting, and the interests of those who are disadvantaged by the classification." *Williams v. Rhodes*, 393 U.S. 23, 30 (1968). And, in this case, we must give the statute a close and exacting examination. "Since the right to exercise the franchise in a free and unimpaired manner is preservative of other basic civil and political rights, any alleged infringement of the right of citizens to vote must be carefully and meticulously scrutinized." *Reynolds v. Sims*, 377 U.S. 533, 562 (1964). This careful examination is necessary because statutes distributing the franchise constitute the foundation of our representative society. Any unjustified discrimination in determining who may participate in political affairs or in the selection of public officials undermines the legitimacy of representative government.

* * *

[T]he deference usually given to the judgment of legislators does not extend to decisions concerning which resident citizens may participate in the election of legislators and other public officials. Those decisions must be carefully scrutinized by the Court to determine whether each resident citizen has, as far as is possible, an equal voice in the selections. Accordingly, when we are reviewing statutes which deny some residents the right to vote, the general presumption of constitutionality afforded state statutes and the traditional approval given state classifications if the Court can conceive of a "rational basis" for the distinctions made are not applicable. *See Harper v. Virginia Bd. of Elections*, 383 U.S. 663, 670 (1966). The presumption of constitutionality and the approval given "rational" classifications in other types of enactments[9] are based on an assumption that the institutions of state government are structured so as to represent fairly all the people. However, when the challenge to the statute is in effect a challenge of this basic assumption, the assumption can no longer serve as the basis for presuming constitutionality. And, the assumption is no less under attack because the legislature which decides who may participate at

---

9. Of course, we have long held that if the basis of classification is inherently suspect, such as race, the statute must be subjected to an exacting scrutiny, regardless of the subject matter of the legislation.

the various levels of political choice is fairly elected. Legislation which delegates decision making to bodies elected by only a portion of those eligible to vote for the legislature can cause unfair representation. Such legislation can exclude a minority of voters from any voice in the decisions just as effectively as if the decisions were made by legislators the minority had no voice in selecting.[10]

The need for exacting judicial scrutiny of statutes distributing the franchise is undiminished simply because, under a different statutory scheme, the offices subject to election might have been filled through appointment. States do have latitude in determining whether certain public officials shall be selected by election or chosen by appointment and whether various questions shall be submitted to the voters. In fact, we have held that where a county school board is an administrative, not legislative, body, its members need not be elected. However, "once the franchise is granted to the electorate, lines may not be drawn which are inconsistent with the Equal Protection Clause of the Fourteenth Amendment." *Harper v. Virginia Bd. of Elections*.

Nor is the need for close judicial examination affected because the district meetings and the school board do not have "general" legislative powers. Our exacting examination is not necessitated by the subject of the election; rather, it is required because some resident citizens are permitted to participate and some are not. . . .

III

Besides appellant and others who similarly live in their parents' homes, the statute also disenfranchises the following persons (unless they are parents or guardians of children enrolled in the district public school): senior citizens and others living with children or relatives; clergy, military personnel, and others who live on tax-exempt property; boarders and lodgers; parents who neither own nor lease qualifying property and whose children are too young to attend school; parents who neither own nor lease qualifying property and whose children attend private schools.

Appellant asserts that excluding him from participation in the district elections denies him equal protection of the laws. He contends that he and others of his class are substantially interested in and significantly affected by the school meeting decisions. All members of the community have an interest in the quality and structure of public education, appellant says, and he urges that "the decisions taken by local boards . . . may have grave consequences to the entire population." Appellant also argues that the level of property taxation affects him, even though he does not own property, as property tax levels affect the price of goods and services in the community.

---

10. Thus, statutes structuring local government units receive no less exacting an examination merely because the state legislature is fairly elected.

We turn therefore to question whether the exclusion is necessary to promote a compelling state interest. First, appellees argue that the State has a legitimate interest in limiting the franchise in school district elections to "members of the community of interest"—those "primarily interested in such elections." Second, appellees urge that the State may reasonably and permissibly conclude that "property taxpayers" (including lessees of taxable property who share the tax burden through rent payments) and parents of the children enrolled in the district's schools are those "primarily interested" in school affairs.

We do not understand appellees to argue that the State is attempting to limit the franchise to those "subjectively concerned" about school matters. Rather, they appear to argue that the State's legitimate interest is in restricting a voice in school matters to those "directly affected" by such decisions. The State apparently reasons that since the schools are financed in part by local property taxes, persons whose out-of-pocket expenses are "directly" affected by property tax changes should be allowed to vote. Similarly, parents of children in school are thought to have a "direct" stake in school affairs and are given a vote.

Appellees argue that it is necessary to limit the franchise to those "primarily interested" in school affairs because "the ever increasing complexity of the many interacting phases of the school system and structure make it extremely difficult for the electorate fully to understand the whys and wherefores of the detailed operations of the school system." Appellees say that many communications of school boards and school administrations are sent home to the parents through the district pupils and are "not broadcast to the general public"; thus, nonparents will be less informed than parents. Further, appellees argue, those who are assessed for local property taxes (either directly or indirectly through rent) will have enough of an interest "through the burden on their pocketbooks, to acquire such information as they may need."

We need express no opinion as to whether the State in some circumstances might limit the exercise of the franchise to those "primarily interested" or "primarily affected." ... [A]ssuming, arguendo, that New York legitimately might limit the franchise in these school district elections to those "primarily interested in school affairs," close scrutiny of the § 2012 classifications demonstrates that they do not accomplish this purpose with sufficient precision to justify denying appellant the franchise. . . .

[T]he classifications must be tailored so that the exclusion of appellant and members of his class is necessary to achieve the articulated state goal. Section 2012 does not meet the exacting standard of precision we require of statutes which selectively distribute the franchise. The classifications in § 2012 permit inclusion of many persons who have, at best, a remote and indirect interest in school affairs and, on the other hand, exclude others who have a distinct and direct interest in the school meeting decisions.[15]

Nor do appellees offer any justification for the exclusion of seemingly interested and informed residents—other than to argue that the § 2012 classifications include those "whom the State could understandably deem to be the most intimately interested in actions taken by the school board," and urge that "the task of . . . balancing the interest of the community in the maintenance of orderly school district elections against the interest of any individual in voting in such elections should clearly remain with the Legislature." But the issue is not whether the legislative judgments are rational. A more exacting standard obtains. The issue is whether the § 2012 requirements do in fact sufficiently further a compelling state interest to justify denying the franchise to appellant and members of his class. The requirements of § 2012 are not sufficiently tailored to limiting the franchise to those "primarily interested" in school affairs to justify the denial of the franchise to appellant and members of his class.

* * *

■ MR. JUSTICE STEWART, with whom MR. JUSTICE BLACK and MR. JUSTICE HARLAN join, dissenting.

* * *

Although at times variously phrased, the traditional test of a statute's validity under the Equal Protection Clause is a familiar one: a legislative classification is invalid only "if it rest[s] on grounds wholly irrelevant to achievement of the regulation's objectives." It was under just such a test that the literacy requirement involved in *Lassiter* [*v. Northampton County Bd. of Elections*, 360 U.S. 45 (1959)] was upheld. The premise of our decision in that case was that a State may constitutionally impose upon its citizens voting requirements reasonably "designed to promote intelligent use of the ballot." A similar premise underlies the proposition, consistently endorsed by this Court, that a State may exclude nonresidents from participation in its elections. Such residence requirements, designed to help ensure that voters have a substantial stake in the outcome of elections and an opportunity to become familiar with the candidates and issues voted upon, are entirely permissible exercises of state authority. Indeed, the appellant explicitly concedes, as he must, the validity of voting requirements relating to residence, literacy, and age. Yet he argues—and the Court accepts the argument—that the voting qualifications involved here somehow have a different constitutional status. I am unable to see the distinction.

15. For example, appellant resides with his parents in the school district, pays state and federal taxes and is interested in and affected by school board decisions; however, he has no vote. On the other hand, an unin-terested employed young man who pays not state federal taxes, but who rents an apartment in the district, can participate in the election.

Clearly a State may reasonably assume that its residents have a greater stake in the outcome of elections held within its boundaries than do other persons. Likewise, it is entirely rational for a state legislature to suppose that residents, being generally better informed regarding state affairs than are nonresidents, will be more likely than nonresidents to vote responsibly. And the same may be said of legislative assumptions regarding the electoral competence of adults and literate persons on the one hand, and of minors and illiterates on the other. It is clear, of course, that lines thus drawn cannot infallibly perform their intended legislative function. Just as "illiterate people may be intelligent voters," nonresidents or minors might also in some instances be interested, informed, and intelligent participants in the electoral process. Persons who commute across a state line to work may well have a great stake in the affairs of the State in which they are employed; some college students under 21 may be both better informed and more passionately interested in political affairs than many adults. But such discrepancies are the inevitable concomitant of the line drawing that is essential to law making. So long as the classification is rationally related to a permissible legislative end, therefore—as are residence, literacy, and age requirements imposed with respect to voting—there is no denial of equal protection.

Thus judged, the statutory classification involved here seems to me clearly to be valid. New York has made the judgment that local educational policy is best left to those persons who have certain direct and definable interests in that policy: those who are either immediately involved as parents of school children or who, as owners or lessees of taxable property, are burdened with the local cost of funding school district operations. True, persons outside those classes may be genuinely interested in the conduct of a school district's business—just as commuters from New Jersey may be genuinely interested in the outcome of a New York City election. But unless this Court is to claim a monopoly of wisdom regarding the sound operation of school systems in the 50 States, I see no way to justify the conclusion that the legislative classification involved here is not rationally related to a legitimate legislative purpose. . . .

With good reason, the Court does not really argue the contrary. Instead, it strikes down New York's statute by asserting that the traditional equal protection standard is inapt in this case, and that a considerably stricter standard—under which classifications relating to "the franchise" are to be subjected to "exacting judicial scrutiny"—should be applied. But the asserted justification for applying such a standard cannot withstand analysis.

* * *

I am at a loss to understand how such reasoning is at all relevant to the present case. The voting qualifications at issue have been promulgated, not by Union Free School District No. 15, but by the New York State Legislature, and the appellant is of course fully able to participate in the election of representatives in that body. There is simply no claim whatever here that the state government is not "structured so as to represent fairly all the people," including the appellant.

Nor is there any other justification for imposing the Court's "exacting" equal protection test. This case does not involve racial classifications, which in light of the genesis of the Fourteenth Amendment have traditionally been viewed as inherently "suspect." And this statute is not one that impinges upon a constitutionally protected right, and that consequently can be justified only by a "compelling" state interest. For "the Constitution of the United States does not confer the right of suffrage upon any one...." *Minor v. Happersett*, 21 Wall. 162, 178.

* * *

NOTES AND QUESTIONS

1. As you probably remember from constitutional law, modern equal protection law is often said to use three tiers of scrutiny. The most searching is "strict scrutiny," which requires that the government show that the challenged classification is necessary for the achievement of a compelling government interest; this standard has been applied over the years to distinctions based on "suspect classifications" such as race or nationality as well as to laws that impair the exercise of a fundamental right. The most lenient is "rational relationship" scrutiny, in which the court asks only whether the classification is reasonably connected to the achievement of some legitimate, albeit not necessarily compelling, interest. Most distinctions are reviewed using the rational relationship test. Somewhere in between lies "intermediate scrutiny": a distinction can be sustained if the government can show that it is actually and "substantially" related to an "important" purpose. This level of scrutiny has been used primarily to analyze distinctions based on sex. The conventional wisdom is that strict scrutiny is "strict in theory but fatal in fact," while virtually anything goes under rational relationship scrutiny. (The two most notable recent exceptions involve discrimination against retarded persons in *City of Cleburne v. Cleburne Living Center*, 473 U.S. 432 (1985), and the discrimination against gays, lesbians, and bisexuals involved in *Romer v. Evans*, 517 U.S. 620 (1996).)

Lassiter was decided under the rational relationship standard, while *Harper* and *Kramer* were decided using strict scrutiny. Does this factor alone explain their different outcomes? Could literacy tests survive strict scrutiny? Are the challenged distinctions in *Harper* and *Kramer* rationally related to the achievement of a legitimate government interest?

2. *Harper* does not examine whether the poll tax was adopted with the purpose and effect of disenfranchising black voters. Why does the Court not approach the case in that way?

The states were often quite explicit about the purpose of poll taxes and similar provisions when they were first adopted, in the late nineteenth and early twentieth centuries. For example:

> The Virginia poll tax was born of a desire to disenfranchise the Negro. At the Virginia Constitutional Convention of 1902, the sponsor of the suffrage plan of which the poll tax was an integral part frankly expressed the purpose of the suffrage proposal:
>
>> "Discrimination! Why, that is precisely what we propose; that, exactly, is what this Convention was elected for—to discriminate to the very extremity of permissible action under the limitations of the Federal Constitution, with a view to the elimination of every negro voter who can be gotten rid of, legally, without materially impairing the numerical strength of the white electorate."

Harman v. Forssenius, 380 U.S. 528 (1965). *See also United States v. State of Louisiana*, 225 F. Supp. 353 (E. D. La. 1963), *aff'd*, 380 U.S. 145 (1965) ("Judge Thomas J. Semmes, Chairman of the Judiciary Committee of the [1898 Louisiana Constitutional] Convention and a former president of the American Bar Association, described the purpose of the Convention: 'We [meet] here to establish the supremacy of the white race, and the white race constitutes the Democratic party of this State.' The Convention of 1898 'interpreted its mandate from the "people" to be, to disfranchise as many Negroes and as few whites as possible.' "). Consider also the account of Alabama's convention offered in *Hunter v. Underwood* earlier in this Chapter, where the architect of the clause disenfranchising persons convicted of misdemeanors of moral turpitude specified those crimes he thought blacks especially likely to commit.

3. For detailed information on the original context of the poll tax, see J. Morgan Kousser, The Shaping of Southern Politics: Suffrage Restrictions and the Establishment of the One–Party South, 1880–1910, at 63–72 (1974). By 1904, every ex-Confederate state had adopted the poll tax. How significant economically was a $1 or $2 poll tax at the time? The average per capita income, including non-cash income, in the eleven ex-Confederate states was $86 in 1880 and $100 in 1900; Kousser estimates that the bottom 76 percent of the population averaged only $55–$64 per person. In addition, those who worked the land tended to have little cash at all during the year until crops could be harvested and sold; by 1900 three-fourths of blacks in the South were sharecroppers or tenant farmers. Moreover, in many states the poll tax was cumulative—failure to pay in one year had to be made up in subsequent years (in Georgia and Alabama, the taxes could cumulate indefinitely). Note that the point of the tax was not so much to collect it as to bar voters who did not pay it; Kousser reports finding no recorded prosecutions of non-payers.

How effective was the poll tax in disenfranchising blacks? Historians have disagreed on this question. Kousser compares black turnout rates in Presidential elections in two states that had similar black populations during the 1880's: Georgia, when it had the poll tax, and Florida, when it did not. Turnout among black voters in Florida was consistently more than twice that in Georgia. Contemporaries certainly believed the poll tax enormously effective. One knowledgeable observer considered Georgia's cumulative poll tax "the most effective bar to Negro suffrage ever devised." A member of the Mississippi Constitutional Convention argued in 1902 that the tax had proven "the most effective instrumentality of Negro disenfranchisement;" similar statements from political actors can easily be found in other states.

Historians differ even more over whether the tax was intended to include whites as well. Some assert that the tax was a principal method for discouraging poorer whites, who tended to be Populists, from challenging the disenfranchisers' control of southern politics. For Alabama, one estimate is that nearly 25 percent of adult white men were disenfranchised solely as a result of the poll tax in 1904; the same figure is estimated for the effect of the Virginia poll tax between 1876 and 1882. Kousser notes that newspapers at the time warned of the effect on whites of the poll tax, but that no grandfather provisions or other means to exempt whites were attached. Although disenfranchising poor whites was far more difficult than disenfranchising blacks to defend publicly at the time, Kousser quotes numerous sources, such as a North Carolina Democratic party paper, which cast the campaign for suffrage restrictions as designed to rid the state of "the danger of the rule of Negroes and the lower classes of whites."

4. *Literacy and English-language competency.* Perhaps one reason the Supreme Court never revisited its holding in *Lassiter* is because Congress soon dealt with the permissibility of literacy tests legislatively. In section 4 of the Voting Rights Act of 1965, Congress temporarily suspended literacy and understanding tests in jurisdictions with low rates of voter participation and relieved individuals who had received their education in Spanish-language American-flag schools (largely Puerto Ricans) from the obligation to satisfy any English literacy requirement. When Congress amended the Voting Rights Act in 1970, it extended the temporary ban on literacy tests to the entire nation. The Court upheld that expansion in *Oregon v. Mitchell*, 400 U.S. 112 (1970). In 1975, when Congress once again amended and extended the Voting Rights Act, it permanently banned literacy tests throughout the nation. See 42 U.S.C. 1973aa (2000).

The 1975 amendments also changed the definition of literacy "test." In addition to the earlier meaning—which had covered any "requirement that a person as a prerequisite for voting or registration for voting (1) demonstrate the ability to read, write, understand, or interpret any matter," 42 U.S.C. § 1973b(c)—Congress also provided, in section 203 of the Act, that:

> [T]he term "test or device" shall also mean any practice or requirement by which any State or political subdivision provided any registration or voting notices, forms, instructions, assistance, or other materials or information relating to the electoral process, including ballots,

only in the English language, where the Director of the Census determines that more than five per centum of the citizens of voting age residing in such State or political subdivision are members of a single language minority.

42 U.S.C. § 1973b(f)(3). Jurisdictions that fall within this category must provide "any registration or voting notices, forms, instructions, assistance, or other materials or information relating to the electoral process, including ballots, ... in the language of the applicable language minority group as well as in the English language: *Provided,* That where the language of the applicable minority group is oral or unwritten or in the case of Alaskan Natives and American Indians, if the predominate language is historically unwritten, the State or political subdivision is only required to furnish oral instructions, assistance, or other information relating to registration and voting." 42 U.S.C. § 1973b(f)(4).

For discussion of the language-assistance provisions, see, e.g., Glenn D. Magpantay, *Asian American Access to the Vote: The Language Assistance Provisions (Section 203) of the Voting Rights Act and Beyond*, 11 Asian L.J. 31 (2004); Brenda Fathy Abdelall, Note, *Not Enough of a Minority?: Arab Americans and the Language Assistance Provisions (Section 203) of the Voting Rights Act*, 38 U. Mich. J.L. Ref. 911 (2005).

5. *Intelligent Use of the Ballot and Mental Competence.* Most states have constitutional provisions or statutes that explicitly declare people ineligible to vote because of various forms of mental incapacity, ranging from "insanity" to being under some form of legal guardianship to even less well-defined conditions. For a thorough survey of the law, see Sally Balch Hurme & Paul S. Appelbaum, *The Effect of Mental Impairment on the Rights of Voters*, ___ McGeorge L. Rev. ___ (2007). For a comparative discussion of competence-based disenfranchisment, see Louis Massicott, Andre Blais, & Antoine Yoshinaka, Establishing the Rules of the Game: Election Laws in Democracies (2003).

The question of voter competence may take on special salience given the interaction of several facts: there are 37 million U.S. residents over the age of 65 and 4 million over the age of 85; epidemiologic studies suggest that approximately 10 percent of the population of elderly people (those older than age 65), and nearly half of those older than 85, are more or less cognitively impaired; and voting rates tend to be correlated with age—for example, in the 2000 U.S. presidential election, the highest rate of voting among any age group involved persons aged 65 to 74 (72 percent). Two recent studies suggest substantial amounts of voting among potentially cognitively impaired adults. *See* Jason Karlawish et al., *Do Persons With Dementia Vote?*, 58 Neurology 1100 (2002) (finding that 69 percent of the patients in a dementia clinic at the University of Pennsylvania had voted— compared with 53.7 percent of the overall voting age population in Pennsylvania); Brian Ott et al., *A Survey of Voter Participation by Cognitively Impaired Elderly Patients*, 60 Neurology 1546 (2003) (finding that 60 percent of the patients in a Rhode Island clinic for patients with dementia had voted—as compared to 54.3 percent of the state's overall voting age population). *See generally* David A. Drachman, *Fading Minds and Hanging Chads: Alzheimer's Disease and the Right to Vote*, 6 Cerebrum: The Dana Forum on Brain Science 7 (2004); Jason Karlawish et al., *Addressing the Ethical, Legal and Social Issues Raised By Voting By Persons with Dementia*, 292 J.A.M.A 1345 (2004); B.D. Sales et al., *Voting Rights* in 1 Disabled Persons and the Law 99 (1982); K.K. Roy, *Sleeping Watchdogs of Personal Liberty: State Laws Disenfranchise the Elderly*, 2003 Elder L.J. 110.

In *Doe v. Rowe*, 156 F. Supp. 2d 35 (D. Me. 2001), the district court struck down a 1965 amendment to the Maine Constitution that prohibited persons "under guardianship for reasons of mental illness" from registering and voting. Three persons in that category (two with bipolar disorder and one with intermittent explosive disorder) challenged the provision under both the equal protection clause and the Americans With Disabilities Act. The court held that Maine's restriction bore no rational relationship to the legitimate objective of disqualifying people who lack the mental capacity to vote.

By contrast, in *Prye v. Carnahan*, 2006 WL 1888639 (W.D. Mo. 2006), the court upheld Missouri's practice of disenfranchising an individual "who has a guardian of his or her estate or person by reason of mental incapacity, appointed by a court of competent jurisdiction." Mo. Const. Art. 8, § 2. The district court recognized that elections are covered by the provision of the Americans with Disabilities Act, 42 U.S.C. § 12132, stating that "no qualified individual with a disability shall, by reason of such disability, be excluded from participation in or be denied the benefits of the services, programs or activities of a public entity," but it held that Missouri's competence process adequately differentiated between those mentally impaired individuals who were incapable of voting and those who were not. (For example, the individual plaintiff in *Prye* had been placed under an order of full incapacitation because of schizophrenia, but the order nonetheless provided that he was entitled to vote.) As this book went to press, the Eighth Circuit had just heard oral argument on an appeal in *Prye*.

What vision of voting underlies competence-based restrictions? How rational, or "intelligent," are most citizens in casting their ballots? *See* Boris Feldman, Note, *Mental Disability and the Right to Vote*, 88 Yale L.J. 1644 (1979) (discussing the disenfranchisement of various groups of mentally disabled voters and arguing that their incapacity to vote rationally provides no basis for barring them from the polls); cf. Daniel R. Ortiz, *The Engaged and the Inert: Theorizing Political Personality Under the First Amendment*, 81 Va. L. Rev. 1 (1995) (suggesting that most American voters are "civic slobs" whose votes are cast on the basis of emotion and absent much information). Is there a potential tradeoff between increasing the participation rates of individuals in institutional settings and the risk of undue influence or fraud? For extensive discussion of the voting rights of citizens with cognitive impairments, see Symposium, *Facilitating Voting as People Age: Implications of Cognitive Impairment*, ___ McGeorge L. Rev. ___ (2007).

6. Strict scrutiny comes into play either when a suspect classification is used or when a fundamental right is impaired. Which strand of strict scrutiny is responsible for *Harper*? Does *Kramer* follow from *Harper* or does it rest on a different rationale?

Given the tremendous evidence that poll taxes and literacy tests had been adopted and maintained for racially discriminatory purposes, why didn't the plaintiffs argue, or the Court decide, *Lassiter* and *Harper* as race discrimination cases? Note that the plaintiffs in both cases were black.

The case that *Harper* overruled, *Breedlove v. Suttles*, 302 U.S. 277 (1937), in which the Court had upheld poll taxes, contained a gender dimension not discussed in *Harper*. The $1 Georgia poll tax in *Breedlove* exempted women who did not register to vote as well as the blind. As part of the constitutional challenge to the poll tax, the ACLU challenged this gender-based exemption on behalf of a male plaintiff (Norman Breedlove, who cumulatively owed $13.50 in poll taxes) as both a violation of the Fourteenth and the Nineteenth Amendments. To the former, the Court responded that "discrimination in favor of all women being permissible," the selective exemption for a subset of women was constitutional. Women could "be exempted on the basis of special considerations to which they are naturally entitled. In view of burdens necessarily borne by them for the preservation of the race, the State reasonably may exempt them from poll taxes." *Id.* at 282 (citing, *inter alia, Muller v. Oregon*, 208 U.S. 412 (1908)). To the Nineteenth Amendment argument, the Court replied "[i]t is fanciful to suggest that the Georgia law is a mere disguise under which to deny or abridge the right of men to vote on account of their sex." *Id.* at 284. Poll taxes, of course, weighed more heavily on women than men, given that women's median income was substantially below that of men (unless the male paid the tax of, for example, his wife), and the "special treatment" provision of Georgia law might be thought to have encouraged women and men to think of a woman's going to the polls as an expensive luxury.

7. The *Kramer* Court notes that several aspects of the New York statute were not challenged, namely that school district voters be (1) citizens of the United States, (2) at least 21 years of age, and (3) bona fide residents of the school district. Could citizenship, age, and residency requirements withstand strict scrutiny? If not, what explains why they are subject to only rational relationship review?

8. *Citizenship.* For many years, citizenship was not an invariable requirement for voting. *See Minor v. Happersett*, 88 U.S. 162 (1874). In some jurisdictions today, resident aliens are permitted to vote in local elections. *See, e.g.,* Gerald L. Neuman, *"We Are the People": Alien Suffrage in German and American Perspective*, 13 Mich. J. Int'l L. 259 (1992); Jamin B. Raskin, *Legal Aliens, Local Citizens: The Historical, Constitutional, and*

Theoretical Meanings of Alien Suffrage, 141 U. Pa. L. Rev. 1391 (1993); Gerald M. Rosberg, *Aliens and Equal Protection: Why Not the Right to Vote?*, 75 Mich. L. Rev. 1092 (1977). For the Supreme Court's view that formal citizenship can be made a prerequisite to full rights of political participation, see *Cabell v. Chavez–Salido*, 454 U.S. 432, 439–40 (1982):

> The exclusion of aliens from basic governmental processes is not a deficiency in the democratic system but a necessary consequence of the community's process of political self-definition. Self-government, whether direct or through representatives, begins by defining the scope of the community of the governed and thus of the governors as well: aliens are by definition outside this community.

If school board positions are at issue, are resident aliens whose children attend public schools any less "interested" members of the community than Kramer was? In as mobile a society as ours what distinguishes citizens from aliens? Ought different rules apply to local as opposed to state or national elections?

For an interesting parallel set of problems from another constitutional system, consider two decisions in 1990 from the Constitutional Court of Germany. There, two states (or *Länder)*, had sought to permit foreign residents to vote in municipal elections, as long as their home country extended similar privileges to German nationals. In one, some seven thousand foreign residents, who had to have resided at least five years in the state, including Danes, Irish, Dutch, Norwegians, Swedes, and Swiss became eligible to vote. In the second, foreign nationals were required to have lived eight years in the relevant local government, and the extension added some ninety thousand persons to the voting rolls. The Constitutional Court held unconstitutional these decisions to extend the franchise in local elections, on the ground that the German Constitution *required* that only German citizens be permitted to vote in any election. When treaties of the European Union required that member states extend the franchise to all European Union citizens residing in a member state, the German Basic Law was amended in 1992 to nullify these court decisions and extend the franchise to resident foreign nationals. For discussion, see Donald P. Kommers, The Constitutional Jurisprudence of the Federal Republic of Germany 197–99 (1997).

9. *Age.* In *Oregon v. Mitchell*, 400 U.S. 112 (1970), the Supreme Court struck down a 1970 amendment to the Voting Rights Act which enfranchised 18–year–olds in state and local elections on the grounds that it was beyond Congress' power. (The Court did uphold their enfranchisement in elections for national office.) Soon after, the Twenty–Sixth Amendment was enacted. Section 1 provides:

> The right of citizens of the United States, who are eighteen years of age or older, to vote shall not be denied or abridged by the United States or by any State on account of age.

What, if any, implications does the amendment have for the claims of persons under eighteen? Does it forbid states from granting the right to vote to, for example, sixteen year-olds, who, after all are old enough in many states to drive, to be tried as adults, to consent on their own behalf to medical procedures, or to marry? Would giving them the vote dilute the voting rights of adults?

Does the Twenty–Sixth Amendment implicitly do to the claims of 17 year-olds what section 2 of the Fourteenth Amendment does to the claims of felons, namely, remove them from the ambit of strict scrutiny? Recall that in *Richardson v. Ramirez*, 418 U.S. 24 (1974), the Court held that felon disenfranchisement was contemplated by section 2 of the Fourteenth Amendment. See *Gaunt v. Brown*, 341 F. Supp. 1187 (S.D. Ohio 1972), *aff'd*, 409 U.S. 809 (1972) (holding that 17 year-olds who would turn 18 by the time of the general election had no right to vote in primary elections and that "in a case where a State is called on to justify its drawing the line for qualifications at 18 years of age no test is required").

Level of scrutiny aside, what is the justification for age restrictions on the franchise? Do such restrictions skew the policies adopted by governments towards short time horizons?

10. *Residency.* There has been relatively little litigation over citizenship and age restrictions. By contrast, residency restrictions of various sorts have engendered substantially more challenges.

Dunn v. Blumstein, 405 U.S. 330 (1972), involved a challenge to Tennessee's "durational residence" requirement. Durational residency requirements mandate that a citizen have lived in the jurisdiction for some extended period of time before being eligible to vote. *See generally* David Cocanower & David Rich, *Residency Requirements for Voting*, 12 Ariz. L. Rev. 477 (1970); John A. MacLeod & Merle F. Wilmerding, *State Voting Residency Requirements and Civil Rights*, 38 Geo. Wash. L. Rev. 93 (1969).

Tennessee law required that, in addition to being a resident, a would-be voter have been a resident for a year in the State and three months in the county before actually voting. Justice Marshall's opinion for the Court explained that "[a]n appropriately defined and uniformly applied requirement of bona fide residence may be necessary to preserve the basic conception of a political community, and therefore could withstand close constitutional scrutiny." But it held that the additional requirement of a substantial period of residence failed strict scrutiny.

Tennessee offered two justifications for its durational residence requirement: (1) preventing voting fraud through colonization and inability to identify persons offering to vote, and (2) making sure that a voter has "in fact, become a member of the community and that as such, he has a common interest in all matters pertaining to its government and is, therefore, more likely to exercise his right more intelligently."

With regard to the first interest, the Court held that Tennessee's requirement failed the means-ends test. Preventing fraud was clearly a compelling state interest. But durational requirements were not necessary to the achievement of that end: the state's failure to look behind voters' oaths meant that a person bent on fraud would simply swear to the length as well as the fact of his residence; moreover, the state should have ample time to check its registration rolls in the months leading up to an election.

As for the second interest, the Court largely rejected the premises on which it was based:

> The argument that durational residence requirements further the goal of having "knowledgeable voters" appears to involve three separate claims. The first is that such requirements "afford some surety that the voter has, in fact, become a member of the community." But here the State appears to confuse a bona fide residence requirement with a durational residence requirement. As already noted, a State does have an interest in limiting the franchise to bona fide members of the community. But this does not justify or explain the exclusion from the franchise of persons, not because their bona fide residence is questioned, but because they are recent rather than longtime residents.
>
> The second branch of the "knowledgeable voters" justification is that durational residence requirements assure that the voter "has a common interest in all matters pertaining to [the community's] government...." By this, presumably, the State means that it may require a period of residence sufficiently lengthy to impress upon its voters the local viewpoint. This is precisely the sort of argument this Court has repeatedly rejected ... Tennessee's hopes for voters with a "common interest in all matters pertaining to [the community's] government" is impermissible. The fact that newly arrived [Tennesseeans] may have a more national outlook than longtime residents, or even may retain a viewpoint characteristic of the region from which they have come, is a constitutionally impermissible reason for depriving them of their chance to influence the electoral vote of their new home State.[28]

---

28. Tennessee may be revealing this impermissible purpose when it observes:

"The fact that the voting privilege has been extended to 18 year old persons ... increases, rather than diminishes, the need for durational residency requirements.... It is so generally known, as to be judicially accepted, that there are many political subdivisions in this state, and other states, wherein there are colleges, universities and military installations with sufficient student body or military personnel over eighteen years of age, as would completely dominate elections in the district, county or municipality so located. This would offer the maximum of opportunity for fraud through colonization, and permit domination by those not knowledgeable or having a common interest in matters of government, as opposed to the interest and the knowledge of permanent members of the community. Upon completion of their schooling, or service tour, they move on, leaving the community bound to a course of political expediency not of its choice and, in fact, one over which its more permanent citizens, who will continue to be affected, had no control."

Finally, the State urges that a longtime resident is "more likely to exercise his right [to vote] more intelligently." [T]he State is apparently asserting an interest in limiting the franchise to voters who are knowledgeable about the issues. In this case, Tennessee argues that people who have been in the State less than a year and the county less than three months are likely to be unaware of the issues involved in the congressional, state, and local elections, and therefore can be barred from the franchise. We note that the criterion of "intelligent" voting is an elusive one, and susceptible of abuse. But without deciding as a general matter the extent to which a State can bar less knowledgeable or intelligent citizens from the franchise,[29] we conclude that durational residence requirements cannot be justified on this basis.

What vision of voting does the *Dunn v. Blumstein* Court embrace? Frank Michelman has argued that the Supreme Court's enfranchisement cases move back and forth between a deliberative, "republican" model of politics and a more strategic, "liberal" view. *See* Frank Michelman, *Conceptions of Democracy in American Constitutional Argument: Voting Rights,* 41 U.Fla.L.Rev. 443 (1989). Is the *Dunn* Court rejecting the idea that political activity will lead to commonly shared beliefs or simply the appropriateness of durational residency requirements in achieving republican ends?

11. *Who counts as a "bona fide resident"?* In *Carrington v. Rash,* 380 U.S. 89 (1965), the Supreme Court struck down a provision of the Texas Constitution that prohibited "any member of the Armed Forces of the United States" who moves his home to Texas during the course of his military duty from ever voting in any state election "so long as he or she is a member of the Armed Forces." Carrington had bought a house in El Paso—from which he commuted to a military post in New Mexico—and had opened a business in Texas as well. Texas defended its rule on two grounds: first, an interest in protecting local elections from bloc voting by military personnel that might overwhelm a small local civilian community and second, an assumption that most servicemen were transients and therefore not permanent members of the community.

The Court responded that although Texas undoubtedly had the power to restrict the franchise to bona fide residents, it could not " 'fenc[e] out' from the franchise a sector of the population because of the way they may vote. . . ." Thus, the fact that residents who were also in the armed services

---

29. In the 1970 Voting Rights Act, which added § 201, 42 U.S.C. § 1973aa, Congress provided that "no citizen shall be denied, because of his failure to comply with any test or device, the right to vote in any Federal, State, or local election. . . ." The term "test or device" was defined to include, in part, "any requirement that a person as a prerequisite for voting or registration for voting (1) demonstrate the ability to read, write, understand, or interpret any matter, (2) demonstrate any educational achievement or his knowledge of any particular subject. . . ." By prohibiting various "test[s]" and "device[s]" that would clearly assure knowledgeability on the part of voters in local elections, Congress declared federal policy that people should be allowed to vote even if they were not well informed about the issues. We upheld § 201 in *Oregon v. Mitchell.*

might have different viewpoints from civilian voters provided no basis for excluding them: "The exercise of rights so vital to the maintenance of democratic institutions ... cannot constitutionally be obliterated because of a fear of the political views of a particular group of bona fide residents." Moreover, although Texas could also deny the vote to transients, it had improperly singled out military personnel with essentially an irrebuttable presumption of nonresidence. The Court relied on *Gray v. Sanders*, 372 U.S. 368 (1963), for the proposition that "[t]here is no indication in the Constitution that ... occupation affords a permissible basis for distinguishing between qualified voters within the State." Instead of such an irrebuttable presumption, Texas would have to use a more finely crafted test of residence: "States may not casually deprive a class of individuals of the vote because of some remote administrative benefit to the State."

Notice that *Carrington* was decided before the Supreme Court explicitly applied strict scrutiny to restrictions on the franchise, but nonetheless used a somewhat heightened form of review. Charles Black has argued that the result in *Carrington* flows from the structure of the Constitution and the relationship among the federal government, the states, and individual citizens: states cannot disadvantage soldiers who are performing a national duty. See Charles L. Black, Jr., Structure and Relationship in Constitutional Law (1969).

Does Texas's first rationale—that military personnel might overwhelm the civilian community in which a large base is located—ring true with regard to other groups of voters? For example, consider "college towns," in which students, most of whom will likely remain in the community for around four years, outnumber non-student residents. Will students and nonstudents likely have distinctive political preferences? On what sorts of issues? Does it matter that the *average* American moves at least once each decade? What about untenured faculty members? Are they all that likely to remain in the same location?

A New York statute that identified certain categories of persons as particularly likely to include transients and subjected members of those classes "to the risk of a more searching inquiry than is applicable to prospective registrants generally" was upheld against a facial challenge in *Auerbach v. Rettaliata*, 765 F.2d 350 (2d Cir. 1985). But in *Williams v. Salerno*, 792 F.2d 323 (2d Cir. 1986), the Court of Appeals upheld an injunction that forbid the registrars in Westchester County from applying a more stringent substantive standard to the registration applications of students who lived in the dormitories of the State University campus at Purchase. The registrars had essentially determined that a dormitory room could never be a permanent domicile. The court disagreed with this erection of an irrebuttable presumption, since it would "have the effect of completely disenfranchising a person who abandons a former residence in a state other than New York with the intent of becoming a domiciliary of the community in New York where he or she attends school."

Ought it to matter that the decennial census counts college students as living where they attend school? Ought a state be permitted to charge nonresident tuition to persons who are qualified as residents for voting purposes?

12. *The Homeless.* The voting rights of homeless persons has also prompted both litigation and scholarship. *See, e.g.,* Patricia M. Hanrahan, *No Home? No Vote*, 21 Hum. Rts. 8 (Winter 1994); Edward J. Smith, *Disenfranchisement of Homeless Persons*, 31 Wash. U.J. Urb. & Contemp. L. 225 (1987); Suzie Turner, Note, *Recognition of the Voting Rights of the Homeless*, 3 J.L. & Pol. 103 (1986). A critical issue in obtaining the right to vote has been how to define a homeless person's "residence." Although many states allow homeless persons to vote, roughly two-thirds require that homeless persons provide mailing addresses.

In general, courts have held that a fixed address is unnecessary as long as a homeless person can provide sufficient information about his or her usual location to allow assignment to a precinct. *See, e.g., Pitts v. Black*, 608 F. Supp. 696 (S. D. N. Y. 1984) (striking down New York's requirement of a fixed address as a violation of the equal protection clause); *Collier v. Menzel*, 221 Cal.Rptr. 110 (Cal. App. 1985) (holding that a Santa Barbara city park could be a place of habitation for voting purposes); *Board of Election Commissioners v. Chicago/Gary Area Union of the Homeless*, No. 86–29 (Ill. Cir. Ct. Sept. 26, 1986) (permitting homeless persons to register if they provided two pieces of identification and an address or location description sufficient to enable assignment to an appropriate voting location).

13. *Nonresidents.* What about voting by nonresidents? Ought jurisdictions to extend the right to vote to persons who live outside their boundaries but are nonetheless affected by the government's decisions? Consider the following cases.

In *Brown v. Chattanooga Board of Commissioners*, 722 F. Supp. 380 (E. D. Tenn. 1989), black residents of Chattanooga challenged Tennessee Code Ann. § 2–2–107(a) and section 5.1 of the Chattanooga charter, which permitted nonresident "property qualification" as a basis for voting in municipal elections. The district court found that 547 nonresidents had registered to vote under these provisions, of whom 427 were known to be white (the others were black, other minorities, or of unknown race). About 32% of the city's population was black. Of the assessed real property in the city, 0.05% was owned by nonresidents. The district court began its analysis with the fact that the challenged provisions "expand rather than curtail the franchise." Thus, it determined that it should apply rational basis, rather than strict, scrutiny. Nonetheless, it concluded that the charter provision, although not the state law, was invalid:

> There is no question that city property owners, including nonresident property owners, have an interest in the conduct of municipal affairs, including property taxes, zoning, public services such as sewage and garbage disposal, and other matters that may affect their property. The

difficulty, however, with Chattanooga's charter provision is that it contains no limitation of the number of people who can "vote" on a piece of property or no limitation as to any minimum property value required for the exercise of the franchise. The record in this case shows that as many as 23 nonresidents have been registered to vote on a single piece of property in the city. By way of further example, 15 nonresidents are registered to vote as co-owners of one parcel of property which has an assessed value of $100.

The court offered as an example of the irrationality of the Chattanooga charter provision the possibility that "the law currently would permit Muammar el-Qaddafi to buy a parcel of land in Chattanooga and deed it to thousands of Libyans who would then be able to control the outcome of Chattanooga's elections." By contrast, other courts have upheld nonresident voting schemes using rational basis review. State law and the relevant municipal charter permitted nonresident property owners to vote in municipal elections in Savannah Beach, Georgia, a resort town, whose population at the time of the decisions in *Glisson v. Mayor and Councilmen of Savannah Beach*, 346 F.2d 135 (5th Cir. 1965), and *Spahos v. Mayor and Councilmen of Savannah Beach*, 207 F. Supp. 688 (S. D. Ga.), *aff'd*, 371 U.S. 206 (1962), was 1,385, with a summer population of 2,500. Nonresident property owners owned real estate with an assessed valuation of $2,852,040, while permanent residents owned property assessed at $1,586,485. Nonresident voters were limited to those who owned property in Savannah Beach and who resided in Chatham County. There were 712 resident voters and 467 property qualified nonresident voters. The Georgia legislation under these facts was found to have a "rational" objective and to make a reasonable classification with respect to the right to vote in municipal elections. In addition, Alabama has permitted residents of cities with independent school systems nonetheless to vote in county school board elections. *See Hogencamp v. Lee County Board of Education*, 722 F.2d 720 (11th Cir. 1984); *Phillips v. Andress*, 634 F.2d 947 (5th Cir. 1981); *Creel v. Freeman*, 531 F.2d 286 (5th Cir. 1976), *cert. denied*, 429 U.S. 1066 (1977). In these cases, the equal protection test of validity was whether the city residents had a "substantial interest" in the operation of the county school system.

Holt Civic Club v. City of Tuscaloosa, 439 U.S. 60 (1978), raised a converse claim. There, citizens who lived outside the municipal boundaries, but within the police jurisdiction, of Tuscaloosa, claimed that they were unconstitutionally barred from participating in Tuscaloosa's municipal elections. Justice Rehnquist's opinion for the Court centered on the appropriate standard of review:

> Appellants focus their equal protection attack on the statute fixing the limits of municipal police jurisdiction and giving extraterritorial effect to municipal police and sanitary ordinances. Citing *Kramer v. Union Free School Dist.*, and cases following in its wake, appellants argue that

the section creates a classification infringing on their right to participate in municipal elections. The State's denial of the franchise to police jurisdiction residents, appellants urge, can stand only if justified by a compelling state interest.

* * *

From [*Kramer*] and our other voting qualifications cases a common characteristic emerges: The challenged statute in each case denied the franchise to individuals who were physically resident within the geographic boundaries of the governmental entity concerned.... [O]ur cases have uniformly recognized that a government unit may legitimately restrict the right to participate in its political processes to those who reside within its borders....

Appellants' argument that extraterritorial extension of municipal powers requires concomitant extraterritorial extension of the franchise proves too much. The imaginary line defining a city's corporate limits cannot corral the influence of municipal actions. A city's decisions inescapably affect individuals living immediately outside its borders. The granting of building permits for high rise apartments, industrial plants, and the like on the city's fringe unavoidably contributes to problems of traffic congestion, school districting, and law enforcement immediately outside the city. A rate change in the city's sales or ad valorem tax could well have a significant impact on retailers and property values in areas bordering the city. The condemnation of real property on the city's edge for construction of a municipal garbage dump or waste treatment plant would have obvious implications for neighboring nonresidents. Indeed, the indirect extraterritorial effects of many purely internal municipal actions could conceivably have a heavier impact on surrounding environs than the direct regulation contemplated by Alabama's police jurisdiction statutes. Yet no one would suggest that nonresidents likely to be affected by this sort of municipal action have a constitutional right to participate in the political processes bringing it about.... The line heretofore marked by this Court's voting qualifications decisions coincides with the geographical boundary of the governmental unit at issue, and we hold that appellants' case, like their homes, falls on the farther side.

Thus stripped of its voting rights attire, the equal protection issue presented by appellants becomes whether the Alabama statutes giving extraterritorial force to certain municipal ordinances and powers bear some rational relationship to a legitimate state purpose....

Government, observed Mr. Justice Johnson, "is the science of experiment," *Anderson v. Dunn* (1821), and a State is afforded wide leeway when experimenting with the appropriate allocation of state legislative power....

The extraterritorial exercise of municipal powers is a governmental technique neither recent in origin nor unique to the State of Alabama. In this country 35 States authorize their municipal subdivisions to exercise governmental powers beyond their corporate limits. Although the extraterritorial municipal powers granted by these States vary widely, several States grant their cities more extensive or intrusive powers over bordering areas than those granted under the Alabama statutes.

In support of their equal protection claim, appellants suggest a number of "constitutionally preferable" governmental alternatives to Alabama's system of municipal police jurisdictions. For example, exclusive management of the police jurisdiction by county officials, appellants maintain, would be more "practical." From a political science standpoint, appellants' suggestions may be sound, but this Court does not sit to determine whether Alabama has chosen the soundest or most practical form of internal government possible. Authority to make those judgments resides in the state legislature, and Alabama citizens are free to urge their proposals to that body. Our inquiry is limited to the question whether "any state of facts reasonably may be conceived to justify" Alabama's system of police jurisdictions, *Salyer Land Co. v. Tulare Lake Basin Water Storage Dist.*, and in this case it takes but momentary reflection to arrive at an affirmative answer.

The Alabama Legislature could have decided that municipal corporations should have some measure of control over activities carried on just beyond their "city limit" signs, particularly since today's police jurisdiction may be tomorrow's annexation to the city proper. Nor need the city's interests have been the only concern of the legislature when it enacted the police jurisdiction statutes. Urbanization of any area brings with it a number of individuals who long both for the quiet of suburban or country living and for the career opportunities offered by the city's working environment. Unincorporated communities like Holt dot the rim of most major population centers in Alabama and elsewhere, and state legislatures have a legitimate interest in seeing that this substantial segment of the population does not go without basic municipal services such as police, fire, and health protection. Established cities are experienced in the delivery of such services, and the incremental cost of extending the city's responsibility in these areas to surrounding environs may be substantially less than the expense of establishing wholly new service organizations in each community.

Does *Holt* simply underscore that the standard of review is the entire ballgame?

What do you make of Justice Brennan's argument in dissent that geography was an "entirely arbitrary" basis for distinguishing between the enfranchised and the disenfranchised because the state provided no reason for defining the relevant political unit as the city of Tuscaloosa rather than the city together with its police jurisdiction?

Frank Michelman has argued that the disagreement in *Holt* turns on the majority and dissent's different "normative conception[s] of 'political community.' " Frank Michelman, *Conceptions of Democracy in American Constitutional Argument: Voting Rights*, 41 Fla. L. Rev. 443, 447 (1989).

C. THE STRUGGLE FOR BLACK ENFRANCHISEMENT

Unlike section 1 of the Fourteenth Amendment, the Fifteenth Amendment addresses voting explicitly. It provides, in section 1, that

> The right of citizens of the United States to vote shall not be denied or abridged by the United States or by any State on account of race, color, or previous condition of servitude.

During the Reconstruction period following the Civil War, and even during the first few years of Redemption—the period of reassertion of state autonomy and white supremacy beginning after the election of 1876—black male turnout (remember that the Reconstruction Amendments did nothing to enfranchise female voters) remained high: in all but two Southern states, a majority of adult black males voted in the presidential election of 1880. Nonetheless, by the first decade of the twentieth century, virtually all black voters had been eliminated from the rolls across the South, through a combination of force and the imposition of restrictive (and often fraudulently administered) voting qualifications. In Louisiana, for example, there were 127,923 black voters and 126,884 white voters on the registration rolls in 1888 (the population of the state was about fifty percent black); by 1910 only 730 blacks (less than 0.5 percent of the adult male population) were still registered. In 27 of the state's sixty parishes, no blacks were registered; in another nine, only one was registered. For extensive accounts of this process across the South, see Michael Perman, Struggle for Mastery: Disfranchisement in the South, 1888–1908 (2001); J. Morgan Kousser, The Shaping of Southern Politics: Suffrage Restrictions and the Establishment of the One–Party South, 1880–1910 (1974).

Part of the reason for the decline of black suffrage was Congress' inability or unwillingness to enforce the Reconstruction Amendments' guarantees. During the last decade of the nineteenth century, for example, although the Republican-controlled House refused to seat some southern Democrats on the grounds that their election had been procured by fraud, Congress declined to act on proposals to investigate allegations of black exclusion from the Alabama senatorial election of 1894 or to enforce the provisions of section 2 of the Fourteenth Amendment that provided for a reduction in the size of a state's House delegation if the state discriminated in voting. At the same time, there were a series of proposals by southern senators and representatives to repeal the Fifteenth Amendment outright.

The Supreme Court also played a pivotal role in invalidating national efforts to insure full citizenship to black citizens. The Court both struck down and eviscerated various federal protections of black voting rights, see, e.g., *United States v. Cruikshank*, 92 U.S. 542 (1875) (dismissing indictments arising out of the Colfax Massacre, in which a white mob murdered a group of black voters in Louisiana); *United States v. Reese*, 92 U.S. 214 (1875) (striking down other sections of the 1870 Enforcement Act as beyond congressional power), while upholding various state efforts to deny other aspects of citizenship to blacks, most centrally, the right to participate on juries. *See, e.g., Williams v. Mississippi*, 170 U.S. 213 (1898). Finally, the Court was asked to decide whether the blatant disfranchisement of black citizens through the new Southern constitutions could survive constitutional challenge under the Fourteenth and Fifteenth Amendments.

Giles v. Harris

189 U.S. 475 (1903).

■ MR. JUSTICE HOLMES delivered the opinion of the court.

This is a bill in equity brought by a colored man, on behalf of himself "and on behalf of more than five thousand negroes, citizens of the county of Montgomery, Alabama, similarly situated and circumstanced as himself," against the board of registrars of that county. . . .

The allegations of the bill may be summed up as follows. The plaintiff . . . applied in March, 1902, for registration as a voter, and was refused arbitrarily on the ground of his color, together with large numbers of other duly qualified negroes, while all white men were registered. The same thing was done all over the State. Under section 187 of article 8 of the Alabama constitution persons registered before January 1, 1903, remain electors for life unless they become disqualified by certain crimes, etc., while after that date severer tests come into play which would exclude, perhaps, a large part of the black race. Therefore, by the refusal, the plaintiff and the other negroes excluded were deprived not only of their votes at an election which has taken place since the bill was filed, but of the permanent advantage incident to registration before 1903. The white men generally are registered for good under the easy test and the black men are likely to be kept out in the future as in the past. This refusal to register the blacks was part of a general scheme to disfranchise them, to which the defendants and the State itself, according to the bill, were parties. The defendants accepted their office for the purpose of carrying out the scheme. The part taken by the State, that is, by the white population which framed the constitution, consisted in shaping that instrument so as to give opportunity and effect to the wholesale fraud which has been practised.

* * *

It seems to us impossible to grant the equitable relief which is asked.... The difficulties which we cannot overcome are two, and the first is this: The plaintiff alleges that the whole registration scheme of the Alabama constitution is a fraud upon the Constitution of the United States, and asks us to declare it void. But of course he could not maintain a bill for a mere declaration in the air. He does not try to do so, but asks to be registered as a party qualified under the void instrument. If then we accept the conclusion which it is the chief purpose of the bill to maintain, how can we make the court a party to the unlawful scheme by accepting it and adding another voter to its fraudulent lists? ... It is impossible simply to shut our eyes, put the plaintiff on the lists, be they honest or fraudulent, and leave the determination of the fundamental question for the future.... It is not an answer to say that if all the blacks who are qualified according to the letter of the instrument were registered, the fraud would be cured. In the first place, there is no probability that any way now is open by which more than a few could be registered, but if all could be the difficulty would not be overcome. If the sections of the constitution concerning registration were illegal in their inception, it would be a new doctrine in constitutional law that the original invalidity could be cured by an administration which defeated their intent. We express no opinion as to the alleged fact of their unconstitutionality beyond saying that we are not willing to assume that they are valid, in the face of the allegations and main object of the bill, for the purpose of granting the relief which it was necessary to pray in order that that object should be secured.

The other difficulty is of a different sort, and strikingly reinforces the argument that equity cannot undertake now, any more than it has in the past, to enforce political rights.... In determining whether a court of equity can take jurisdiction, one of the first questions is what it can do to enforce any order that it may make. This is alleged to be the conspiracy of a State.... The Circuit Court has no constitutional power to control its action by any direct means. And if we leave the State out of consideration, the court has as little practical power to deal with the people of the State in a body. The bill imports that the great mass of the white population intends to keep the blacks from voting. To meet such an intent something more than ordering the plaintiff's name to be inscribed upon the lists of 1902 will be needed. If the conspiracy and the intent exist, a name on a piece of paper will not defeat them. Unless we are prepared to supervise the voting in that State by officers of the court, it seems to us that all that the plaintiff could get from equity would be an empty form. Apart from damages to the individual, relief from a great political wrong, if done, as alleged, by the people of a state and the State itself, must be given by them or by the legislative and political department of the Government of the United States.

* * *

■ MR. JUSTICE BREWER dissenting.

* * *

[I cannot agree with] the proposition that the case presented by the plaintiff's bill is not strictly a legal one and entitling a party to a judicial hearing and decision. He alleges that he is a citizen of Alabama, entitled to vote; that he desired to vote at an election for representative in Congress; that without registration he could not vote, and that registration was wrongfully denied him by the defendants. That many others were similarly treated does not destroy his rights or deprive him of relief in the courts. That such relief will be given has been again and again affirmed in both National and state courts....

I refer to two recent cases which bear directly upon the present question. *Wiley v. Sinkler*, 179 U.S. 58, was an action brought in the Circuit Court of the United States by the plaintiff to recover damages of an election board for wilfully rejecting his vote for a member of the House of Representatives. We held that the court had jurisdiction, and said:

"This action is brought against election officers to recover damages for their rejection of the plaintiff's vote for a member of the House of Representatives of the United States. The complaint, by alleging that the plaintiff was at the time, under the constitution and laws of the State of South Carolina and the Constitution and laws of the United States, a duly qualified elector of the State, shows that the action is brought under the Constitution and laws of the United States. The damages are laid at the sum of $2500. What amount of damages the plaintiff shall recover in such an action is peculiarly appropriate for the determination of a jury, and no opinion of the court upon that subject can justify it in holding that the amount in controversy was insufficient to support the jurisdiction of the Circuit Court...."

Again, in *Swafford v. Templeton*, 185 U.S. 487, which, like the former case, was one brought in the Circuit Court of the United States to recover damages for the alleged wrongful refusal by the defendants as election officers to permit the plaintiff to vote at a national election for a member of the House of Representative, it was held that the court had jurisdiction.

* * *

It seems to me nothing need be added to these decisions, and unless they are to be considered as overruled they are decisive of this case.

■ MR. JUSTICE BROWN also dissents.

■ MR. JUSTICE HARLAN dissenting.

[Justice Harlan's primary argument was that the Supreme Court lacked jurisdiction over Giles's case because nothing in the record showed that the amount in dispute met the then-existing jurisdictional amount of $2000.] Upon this record, I will not formulate and discuss my views upon the merits of this case. But to avoid misapprehension, I may add that my conviction is that upon the facts alleged in the bill (if the record showed a sufficient value of the matter in dispute) the plaintiff is entitled to relief in respect of his right to be registered as a voter. I agree with Mr. Justice Brewer that it is competent for the courts to give relief in such cases as this.

NOTES AND QUESTIONS

1. *Giles* is an extremely important moment in the twentieth-century disenfranchisement of American blacks, for it signaled that, the Fifteenth Amendment notwithstanding, the Supreme Court would not intervene. A recent article by one of this casebook's authors notes that *Giles* is completely absent from modern sources that define "the canon" of American constitutional law: *Giles* is not even mentioned in the leading constitutional law casebooks, nor does it appear in Professor Tribe's important treatise, American Constitutional Law (3d. ed. 2000). What do you think accounts for this startling absence of a case dealing with such central issues of democratic citizenship and American constitutional law? Why should *Plessy v. Ferguson*, 163 U.S. 537 (1896), permitting segregated public facilities, be so well-known, yet *Giles v. Harris,* permitting the removal of black citizens from democracy, be so obscure? *See generally* Richard H. Pildes, *Democracy, Anti–Democracy, and the Canon*, 17 Const. Comm. 293 (2000).

2. Is Justice Holmes's opinion disingenuous? Note the Catch–22 he creates. Contemporary constitutional law has a variety of techniques for avoiding the problem he identifies, such as as-applied challenges and affirmative injunctions.

Justice Holmes' opinion might be read to turn on the distinction between equitable and legal relief. Near the end, Holmes suggests that "damages to the individual" for the alleged constitutional violations might be judicially available, even though "equity cannot undertake now, any more than it has in the past, to enforce political rights."

Giles, who had lived and voted in Montgomery for nearly 30 years before adoption of the 1901 Alabama Constitution, accepted this seeming invitation and brought a damages action on his own behalf against the board of registrars, seeking $5000 for their refusal to register him. He also brought a petition for mandamus, seeking that the courts order the board of registrars to register him and other eligible black voters.

The Alabama Supreme Court affirmed the dismissal of both complaints on two grounds: (1) that if Giles were right that the provisions of the Alabama Constitution violated the Fourteenth and Fifteenth Amendments, it then followed that the registrars had no authority to register him at all, and "their refusal to do so cannot be made the predicate for a recovery of damages against them;" (2) on the other hand, if the registrars did have authority to register voters, their decisions about who was qualified were judicial acts for which the registrars were legally immune.

In *Giles v. Teasley*, 193 U.S. 146 (1904), the Supreme Court affirmed. The Court held that the first ground cited by the Alabama Supreme Court constituted an independent and adequate state-law basis for dismissing Giles's federal claims. The Supreme Court in turn held that it had no jurisdiction to review these decisions of the Alabama Supreme Court. Justice Day's opinion acknowledged "the gravity of the statements" of Giles's complaints, but reminded him that *Giles v. Harris* had already explained "[t]he great difficulty of reaching the political action of a State through remedies afforded in the courts, state or federal." Thus, Giles's efforts to seek damages, injunctive relief, or mandamus were all judicially rejected.

3.   From another perspective, Holmes's opinion might be thought remarkable not for its disingenuousness, but for its candor. Holmes had several more technical legal grounds available which would have led to the same result of dismissing the complaint for lack of federal jurisdiction, but he chose not to rest on any of them: (1) the complaint failed to allege the requisite amount in controversy necessary for federal jurisdiction (at that time, $2,000)—this is the ground on which Justice Harlan would have dismissed; (2) the statute under which Giles sued protected federal rights against deprivations that arose from state "statutes" and "customs," but did not expressly include state constitutions—Holmes mentioned this problem but did not address it; (3) the claim might have been treated as moot, since the 1902 elections for which Giles sought registration had taken place already—the very approach the Court, before Holmes joined it, had taken in *Mills v. Green*, 159 U.S. 651 (1895), in which the Court dismissed as moot a challenge to South Carolina's disenfranchisement laws of the 1890's.

Instead, Holmes seemed determined to confront head on the problem of racial disenfranchisement—which his opinion itself called a "new and extraordinary situation"—only to proclaim judicial impotence in the face of it. Does *Giles* confirm the theory that "conformity of the law to the wishes of the dominant power in the community was the fundamental tenet of [Holmes'] legal theory?" Gary J. Aichele, Oliver Wendell Holmes, Jr. 145 (1989). Is *Giles* evidence of Holmes "viewing electoral majorities as unanswerable military victors?" David Luban, *Justice Holmes and the Metaphysics of Judicial Restraint*, 44 Duke L.J. 449, 515 (1994). Does it reflect a resigned moral relativism that some attribute to Holmes's experience fighting for the North in the Civil War, from which Holmes drew the lesson that "[d]eep seated preferences [could] not be argued about," Oliver Wendell Holmes, *Natural Law*, 32 Harv. L. Rev. 40 (1918), and that a judge must never "forget that what seem to him to be first principles [are] believed by half his fellow men to be wrong," Oliver Wendell Holmes, *Law and the Court* (1913), in The Essential Holmes 147 (Richard A. Posner, ed.,

1992)? Or does *Giles* reflect a belief that "adjudication should and must be result-oriented?" Thomas C. Grey, *Holmes and Legal Pragmatism*, 41 Stan. L. Rev. 787, 847 (1989). Or more starkly, that "[l]aw stands impotent before history?" Owen M. Fiss, History of the Supreme Court of the United States: The Troubled Beginnings of the Modern State, 1888–1910, at 373 (1993). *See generally* Eben Moglen, *Holmes' Legacy and the New Constitutional History*, 108 Harv. L. Rev. 2027, 2039–40, 2043–44 (1995) (suggesting the unexamined importance of the civil war experience to Holmes' social thought).

4. The dissents of Justices Brewer and Harlan might be seen as an early recognition of the view, not to be adopted by the Supreme Court until much later, that voting rights are constitutionally "fundamental" and warrant the strictest judicial scrutiny. These same justices wrote opinions upholding discrimination against black individuals in areas ranging from education to transportation. *See, e.g., Berea College v. Kentucky*, 211 U.S. 45 (1908); *Cumming v. Richmond County Board of Education*, 175 U.S. 528 (1899); *Louisville, New Orleans & Texas Railway v. Mississippi*, 133 U.S. 587 (1890).

5. Press reaction to the *Giles* decision recognized its sweep. One publication characterized the Fifteenth Amendment as "suspended in fact." *Recent Discussion of the Fifteenth Amendment*, Harper's Weekly, July 11, 1903, at 1144. A New York Times editorial termed *Giles* a "monstrous denial of justice and a humiliating admission of helplessness by the court," but concluded that "it is well that the court has decided as it has." *The Alabama Decision*, N.Y. Times, May 1, 1903, at 8.

6. *Giles* suggested that enforcement of voting rights was a political function to be handled by Congress. Within a month of the decision in *Giles v. Teasley*, however, Congress demonstrated yet another Catch–22 for black voters.

In the 1902 House elections, Asbury Lever had defeated Alexander Dantzler in South Carolina's Seventh District. Dantzler challenged the results, claiming that Lever's victory was illegitimate because South Carolina's new disenfranchising constitution violated the Reconstruction Act of June 25, 1868. In particular he claimed that "thousands of colored voters" had been disenfranchised under South Carolina's new constitution, in violation of both the 1868 Act and unspecified provisions of the federal constitution. But the House Committee on Elections confirmed Lever's victory, and declined "to put on record its opinion" of Dantzler's constitutional claim. Instead, it explained:

> However desirable it may be for a legislative body to retain control of the decision as to the election and qualification of its members, it is quite certain that a legislative body is not the ideal body to pass judicially upon the constitutionality of the enactments of other bodies. We have in this country a proper forum for the decision of constitutional and other judicial questions. If any citizen of South Carolina who

was entitled to vote under the constitution of that state in 1868 is now deprived by the provisions of the present constitution, he has the right to tender himself for registration and for voting, and in case his right is denied, to bring suit in a proper court for the purpose of enforcing his right or recovering damages for its denial.

That suit can be carried by him, if necessary to the Supreme Court of the United States. If the United States Supreme Court shall declare in such case that the "fundamental conditions" in the reconstruction acts were valid and constitutional and that the State constitutions are in violation of those acts, and hence invalid and unconstitutional, every State will be compelled to immediately bow in submission to the decision. The decision of the Supreme Court would be binding and would be a positive declaration of the law of the land which could not be denied or challenged.

H.R. Rep. No. 1740 at 3 (1904).

More broadly, what is the relationship between congressional power to control the shape of American democracy and the Supreme Court's power through constitutional decisionmaking?

7. *Giles* took place against the backdrop of Redemption, the failure to enforce federal civil rights legislation in the 1890's, and a pervasive effort across the South to disenfranchise black, and sometimes also poor white, voters. Given the rising tide of white supremacism, could the Court effectively have enfranchised black voters without federal legislative or executive support? With respect to whether a judicial remedy was available, consider the following plaintive editorial response to the decision from The New York Daily Tribune, April 29, 1908:

> Somewhere, somehow, there must be a way of passing on the constitutionality of State laws which plainly nullify the spirit of the federal Constitution, and it is no more an assumption of the administrative functions of a State government for the court to declare that State authorities cannot deprive negroes of a ballot on pretexts which do not exclude white men than it is for the court to overrule any other action of a State or its officers.

Note that the same paper reported the previous day that an unnamed Justice had asserted "that the legitimate outcome of the power [Giles asked the Court to assume] would be that the court of equity would take charge of the State government and administer it, which is an unheard of proposition." N.Y. Daily Tribune, April 28, 1908.

Giles raises enduring and fundamental questions about the power of courts to resist political repression or bring about effective change. *See* Richard H. Pildes, *Democracy, Anti–Democracy, and the Canon*, 17 Const. Comm. 293 (2000). Was Justice Holmes correct in his view that any Supreme Court decision holding unconstitutional Alabama's blatant circumvention of the Fifteenth Amendment would have been "an empty form" and that in the South of the late nineteenth and early twentieth centuries, "if the conspiracy [to disfranchise black voters] and the intent exist, a name on a piece of paper [that is, a court order] will not defeat them"? It is important not to romanticize the power of courts, or at the least, not to be anachronistic about how effective Supreme Court decisions in 1903 might have been, given the increasing legitimacy of the Supreme Court in the century since. *Giles* forces attention to the question of precisely where the power of courts in any political system, including that of the United States Supreme Court, comes from.

But just as judicial romanticism has its dangers, "realism" also can become a complacent and all-too-easy stance. Was Holmes appropriately "realistic" about his blatant political assessment of the likely effects of judicial intervention—or using "realism" as a way to excuse the Court's cowardice, or perhaps even to excuse his own personal agreement with black disfranchisement? By the time of *Giles*, many beacons of "enlightened" New England opinion had become disenchanted with the Fifteenth Amendment's implementation. In 1901, *The Atlantic Monthly*, for example, pronounced itself supportive in principle of political equality between races, but also proclaimed that black enfranchisement had been a "grave error" and a wrong-headed "short cut to equality" that had bestowed "the sudden gift of the ballot to men wholly unprepared to use it wisely." As a result, the Fifteenth Amendment had "proved disastrous." LXXXVIII, *The Atlantic Monthly* 433, 434, 436 (Oct. 1901). Given this position even from entities such as *The Atlantic Monthly*, perhaps Holmes' own views were similar.

From the perspective of the present, "realism" about the past also raises the danger of a false sense of historical necessity and determinism. There is surely a tendency to see what happened in the past as inevitable; the fact that black voters were disfranchised from *Giles* until the 1965 Voting Rights Act, can make it seem that black disenfranchisement was inevitable, no matter what Holmes and the Court did. Yet close attention to the social, legal, and political history of issues involving race can suggest much more contingency in the way the treatment of race developed in American law—and hence suggest that certain actions, at certain times, could indeed have influenced the subsequent path of race relations. Many in the present would no doubt be surprised to learn, for example, that on the very eve of disenfranchisment in North Carolina, there were still substantial, interracial political coalitions that allowed a fusion of political parties, with black and white support, to control the North Carolina legislature as late as 1894–1898. Yet in 1900, that State's disenfranchising Constitution was passed. *Giles* was only three years later.

Professor Pildes argues that the political context of disenfranchisement was more unpredictable, more fluid and up for grabs in many places, than would be suggested by the "realism" of Holmes' view that black disenfranchisement was inevitable and unstoppable. As evidence, Pildes notes that the disfranchising Constitutions were often passed with slim majorities, even though black voters were almost totally excluded from the vote. Thus, the 1900 North Carolina Constitution passed with 58.6% of the vote; in Alabama, only 57% of white voters supported the 1901 Constitution—and even that margin of victory almost certainly required overwhelming fraud in vote counting. Permanent disenfranchisement through constitutional means was resisted because it would disenfranchise many uneducated and poor whites, as well as blacks. Given the precariousness with which white supremacists managed to enshrine their position into state constitutions, is it actually "realistic" to think that a contrary Supreme Court decision in *Giles* would not have slowed the process of disenfranchisement down enough, at least in certain places, such as North Carolina, so as to have avoided permanent, constitutional, destruction of the suffrage for much of the twentieth century? For a contrary view, taking the position that a decision for Giles would have made no difference to the twentieth century development of black political participation see Michael J. Klarman, *The Plessy Era*, 1998 S. Ct. Rev. 303. For an extensive discussion of the *Giles* litigation, see R. Volney Riser, The Second *Dred Scott*: Disfranchisement, the Giles Cases, and Black Voting Rights Activism, 1891–1908 (forthcoming).

8. Also in this light, consider the Court's decision a decade later in *Guinn v. United States*, 238 U.S. 347 (1915). *Guinn* involved a federal prosecution of two Oklahoma election officers for having conspired to deprive certain black citizens, on account of their race, of the right to vote in the 1910 congressional election. The officials enforced a newly enacted state constitutional amendment that provided that:

> No person shall be registered as an elector of this State or be allowed to vote in any election herein, unless he be able to read and write any section of the constitution of the State of Oklahoma; but no person who was, on January 1, 1866, or at any time prior thereto, entitled to vote under any form of government, or who at that time resided in some foreign nation, and no lineal descendant of such person, shall be denied the right to register and vote because of his inability to so read and write sections of such constitution.

The United States argued that the so-called "Grandfather Clause," which exempted persons who were eligible to vote on January 1, 1866, and their lineal descendants from the literacy test, violated the Fifteenth Amendment: that date had been picked because it antedated passage of the Fifteenth Amendment and black enfranchisement; thus, virtually all whites, but virtually no blacks, would be exempt from the literacy test. The Supreme Court agreed:

> We have difficulty in finding words to more clearly demonstrate the conviction we entertain that this standard has the characteristics which the Government attributes to it than does the mere statement of the text. It is true it contains no express words of an exclusion from the standard which it establishes of any person on account of race,

color, or previous condition of servitude prohibited by the Fifteenth Amendment, but the standard itself inherently brings that result into existence since it is based purely upon a period of time before the enactment of the Fifteenth Amendment and makes that period the controlling and dominant test of the right of suffrage. In other words, we seek in vain for any ground which would sustain any other interpretation but that the provision, recurring to the conditions existing before the Fifteenth Amendment was adopted and the continuance of which the Fifteenth Amendment prohibited, proposed by in substance and effect lifting those conditions over to a period of time after the Amendment to make them the basis of the right to suffrage conferred in direct and positive disregard of the Fifteenth Amendment. And the same result, we are of opinion, is demonstrated by considering whether it is possible to discover any basis of reason for the standard thus fixed other than the purpose above stated. We say this because we are unable to discover how, unless the prohibiting of the Fifteenth Amendment were considered, the slightest reason was afforded for basing the classification upon a period of time prior to the Fifteenth Amendment. Certainly it cannot be said that there was any peculiar necromancy in the time named which engendered attributes affecting the qualification to vote which would not exist at another and different period unless the Fifteenth Amendment was in view.

Id. at 364–65. Can the result in *Guinn* be squared with the result in *Giles* by seeing *Guinn* as judicial enforcement of federal legislative and executive commands?

Is Justice Holmes's essential pessimism in *Giles* borne out by the post-*Guinn* experience? After the invalidation of the Grandfather Clause, the Oklahoma Legislature enacted a new registration scheme in 1916. Persons who had voted in the general election of 1914, which had been conducted under the amendment struck down in *Guinn*, automatically remained qualified voters but all other persons had to apply for registration between April 30, 1916 and May 11, 1916, if qualified at that time, or be forever barred from registering. Lane, a black citizen of Oklahoma, did not attempt to register until 1934, at which time registrars used the 1916 law to refuse his application. In *Lane v. Wilson*, 307 U.S. 268 (1939), the Supreme Court finally struck down Oklahoma's 1916 scheme. The state relied on *Giles*, arguing that Lane's claim that the Oklahoma scheme was invalid meant that there was no Oklahoma statute under which he could register and therefore that no right to registration has been denied. The Court distinguished *Giles* on the ground that Giles had raised an equitable claim, while Lane was advancing a legal one:

This case is very different from *Giles v. Harris*—the difference having been explicitly foreshadowed by *Giles v. Harris* itself. In that case this Court declared "we are not prepared to say that an action at law could not be maintained on the facts alleged in the bill." That is precisely the basis of the present action, brought under [the prior version of 42 U.S.C. § 1983].... Whosoever "under color of any statute" subjects another to such discrimination thereby deprives him of what the Fifteenth Amendment secures and, under § [1983] becomes "liable to the party injured in an action at law." The theory of the plaintiff's action is that the defendants, acting under color of [the Oklahoma statute] did discriminate against him because that Section inherently operates discriminatorily. If this claim is sustained his right to sue under [§ 1983] follows. The basis of this action is inequality of treatment though under color of law, not denial of the right to vote.

On the merits, the Court concluded that the 1916 law violated the Fifteenth Amendment:

> The Amendment nullifies sophisticated as well as simple-minded modes of discrimination. It hits onerous procedural requirements which effectively handicap exercise of the franchise by the colored race although the abstract right to vote may remain unrestricted as to race. When in *Guinn v. United States*, the Oklahoma "grandfather clause" was found violative of the Fifteenth Amendment, Oklahoma was confronted with the serious task of devising a new registration system consonant with her own political ideas but also consistent with the Federal Constitution. We are compelled to conclude, however reluctantly, that the legislation of 1916 partakes too much of the infirmity of the "grandfather clause" to be able to survive.

Only persons who were beneficiaries of the unconstitutional Grandfather Clause regime were exempted from the onerous 12–day registration window.

> We believe that the opportunity thus given negro voters to free themselves from the effects of discrimination to which they should never have been subjected was too cabined and confined. The restrictions imposed must be judged with reference to those for whom they were designed. It must be remembered that we are dealing with a body of citizens lacking the habits and traditions of political independence and otherwise living in circumstances which do not encourage initiative and enterprise.

Does Justice Frankfurter's distinction of *Giles* make sense? Compare his maneuvering around *Giles* here with his attempt in *Gomillion v. Lightfoot*, 364 U.S. 339 (1960), which appears later in this Chapter, to get around his view in *Colegrove v. Green*, 328 U.S. 549 (1946), that apportionment claims were nonjusticiable.

A NOTE ON LITERACY TESTS

Giles, *Guinn*, *Lane*, *Lassiter*, and *Harper* illustrate the major techniques for black disenfranchisement: force, restrictive and arbitrary registration practices, poll taxes, and literacy tests. Every state in the Deep South adopted a new constitution in the period between 1890 and 1908, and every constitution employed at least one, and often several, of these disenfranchising devices. *See* Michael Perman, Struggle for Mastery: Disfranchisement in the South, 1888–1908 (2001); J. Morgan Kousser, The Shaping of Southern Politics: Suffrage Restrictions and the Establishment of the One–Party South, 1880–1910 (1974); Armand Derfner, *Racial Discrimination and the Right To Vote*, 26 Vand. L. Rev. 523 (1973).

Literacy tests were one of the major disenfranchising devices used in the mid-twentieth century, during the period after the invalidation of the White Primary (which is covered in Chapter 4) and before passage of the Voting Rights Act of 1965, which provided a series of statutory protections of the right to vote that resulted in a dramatic upsurge in minority political participation (and which is covered in Chapters 6, 7, and 8.) Literacy tests might have served as a major barrier to black enfranchisement even if they had been administered fairly, given southern states' discriminatory educational systems, which often left black citizens functionally illiterate. But they were deployed in a discriminatory manner as well.

Consider Louisiana's provision. Under Louisiana law, a citizen was qualified to vote, if he or she could read and write English, was of good character, and could provide a reasonable interpretation of a section of the state constitution. The provision had been adopted at the state's 1898 disenfranchising convention. When black citizens attempted to register in significant numbers after World War II, the state deployed the interpretation provision to stop them in their tracks:

> The Louisiana Constitution contains 443 sections, as against 56 sections in the United States Constitution, and is the longest and the most detailed of all state constitutions. The printed copy published by the State, unannotated, contains 600 pages, not counting an index of 140 pages. The evidence clearly demonstrates great abuses in the selection of sections of the constitutions to be interpreted. Some registrars have favorite sections which they apparently use regardless of an applicant's race. Some open a volume containing the United States and Louisiana Constitutions and, like soothsayers seeking divine help from the random flight of birds, require an applicant to interpret the section on the page where the book opens. The Segregation Committee distributed to registrars sets of twenty-four cards, each containing three sections of the Constitution with instructions that they be used in administering the interpretation test....

> It is evident from the record that frequently the choice of difficult sections has made it impossible for many Negro applicants to pass. White applicants were more often given easy sections, many of which could be answered by short, stock phrases such as "freedom of speech", "freedom of religion", "States' rights", and so on. Negro

applicants, on the other hand, were given [extremely complex parts of the state constitution].

* * *

Registrars were easily satisfied with answers from white voters. In one instance "FRDUM FOOF SPETGH" was an acceptable response to the request to interpret Article 1, § 3 of the Louisiana Constitution [which guarantees freedom of speech].

On the other hand, the record shows that Negroes whose application forms and answers indicate that they are highly qualified by literacy standards and have a high degree of intelligence have been turned down although they had given a reasonable interpretation of fairly technical clauses of the constitution. For example the Louisiana Constitution, Article X, § 16 provides: "Rolling stock operated in this State, the owners of which have no domicile therein, shall be assessed by the Louisiana Tax Commission, and shall be taxed for State purposes only, at a rate not to exceed forty mills on the dollar assessed value." The rejected interpretation was: "My understanding is that it means if the owner of which does not have residence within the State, his rolling stock shall be taxed not to exceed forty mills on the dollar."

In another instance the registrar rejected the following interpretation of the Search and Seizure provision of the Fourth Amendment: "[Nobody] can just go into a person's house and take their belongings without a warrant from the law, and it had to specify in this warrant what they were to search and seize." Another rejected interpretation of the same Amendment by a Negro applicant was: "To search you would have to get an authorized authority to read a warrant." The Louisiana Constitution Article I, § 5 provides: "The people have the right peaceably to assemble." A registrar rejected the following interpretation: "That one may assemble or belong to any group, club, or organization he chooses as long as it is within the law."

Each of these incidents could conceivably be an isolated event, indicating personal dereliction by one registrar, regrettable, but basically trivial in the general administration of the interpretation test. However, the great number of these and other examples, illustrative of a conscious decision, show conclusively that the discriminatory acts were not isolated or accidental or peculiar to the individual registrar but were part of a pervasive pattern and practice of disfranchisement by discriminatory use of the interpretation test.

The State does not deny that unlimited discretion is vested in the registrars by the laws of Louisiana, but argues that officials must act reasonably and that their decisions are subject to review by district courts. Louisiana, however, provides no effective method whereby arbitrary and capricious action by registrars of voters may be prevented or redressed. Unreviewable discretion was built into the test.

* * *

The statistics demonstrate strikingly the effect of resurrection of the interpretation test. A report of the Louisiana Sovereignty Committee, December 14, 1960, boasts:

> "We would like to call your attention to the fact that, during this four year period of time, from 1956 until 1960, 81,241 colored people became of voting age, when the registration figures of colored people actually declined 2,377. Going further during this four year period, we had 114,529 white people who became of voting age and, during this four year period of time, the white registration increased 96,620."

United States v. State of Louisiana, 225 F. Supp. 353 (E. D. La. 1963), *aff'd*, 380 U.S. 145 (1965). Similarly, *Davis v. Schnell*, 81 F. Supp. 872 (S. D. Ala.), *aff'd*, 336 U.S. 933 (1949), struck down Alabama's Boswell Amendment, which limited registration to persons who could "understand and explain" any article of the Federal Constitution. The district court found that the test was both invalid on its face and invalid as applied:

> "[U]nderstand" may mean to interpret. This meaning requires an exceedingly high, if not impossible, standard. The distinguished Justices of the Supreme Court of the United States have frequently disagreed in their interpretations of various articles of the Constitution. We learn from history that many of the makers of the Constitution did not understand its provisions; many of them understood and believed that its provisions gave the Supreme Court no power to declare an act of Congress unconstitutional. An understanding or explanation given by the Supreme Court a few years ago as to the meaning of the commerce clause does not apply today. Among our most learned judges there are at least four different understandings and explanations of the Fourteenth Amendment to the Constitution as to whether it made the first eight Amendments applicable to state action. Such a rigorous standard . . . illustrates the completeness with which any individual or group of prospective electors, whether white or Negro, may be deprived of the right of franchise by boards of registrars inclined to apply this one of the innumerable meanings of such an indefinite phrase.

* * *

It, thus, clearly appears that [the Boswell] Amendment was intended to be, and is being used for the purpose of discriminating against applicants for the franchise on the basis of race or color. Therefore, we are necessarily brought to the conclusion that the

Amendment to the Constitution of Alabama, both in its object and the manner of its administration, is unconstitutional, because it violates the Fifteenth Amendment. While it is true that there is no mention of race or color in the Boswell Amendment, this does not save it.

The Alabama Literacy Test

The following example of a typical Alabama literacy test was reprinted in Howard Ball, Dale Krane & Thomas P. Lauth, Compromised Compliance 238–42 (1982). How many questions can you answer? Notice how some questions have ambiguous answers that allow for administrative discretion.

1.   Which of the following is a right guaranteed by the Bill of Rights?

___ Public Education   ___ Voting

___ Employment   ⤬ Trial by Jury

2.   The federal census of population is taken each five years. (True or false)

3.   If a person is indicted for a crime, name two rights which he has.

4.   A United States senator elected at the general election in November takes office the following year on what date?

5.   A President elected at the general election in November takes office the following year on what date?

6.   Which definition applies to the word "amendment?"

___ Proposed change, as in a Constitution

___ Making of peace between nations at war

___ A part of the government

7.   A person appointed to the United States Supreme Court is appointed for a term of ___

8.   When the Constitution was approved by the original colonies, how many states had to ratify it in order for it to be in effect?

9.   Does enumeration affect the income tax levied on citizens in various states?

10.   Persons opposed to swearing in an oath may say, instead: "I solemnly ___."

11.   To serve as President of the United States a person must have attained ___ 25, ___ 35, ___ 40, ___ 45 years.

12.   What words are required by law to be on all coins and paper currency of the United States?

13.   The Supreme Court is the chief lawmaking body of the state. (True or false)

14.   If a law passed by a state is contrary to provisions of the United States Constitution, which law prevails?

15. If a vacancy occurs in the United States Senate, the state must hold an election but, meanwhile, the place may be filled by a temporary appointment made by ___*Gov*

16. A United States senator is elected for a term of *6* years.

17. Appropriation of money for the armed services can be only for a period limited to *2* years.

18. The chief executive and the administrative officers make up the *Executive* branch of government.

19. Who passes laws dealing with piracy?

20. The number of representatives which a state is entitled to have in the House of Representatives is based on *Census*

21. The Constitution protects an individual against punishments which are *cruel* and *unusual*

22. When a jury has heard and rendered a verdict in a case, and the judgment on the verdict has become final, the defendant cannot again be brought to trial for the same case. (True or false)

23. Communism is the type of government in: ___ the United States, _✓_ Russia, ___ England.

24. Name two levels of government which can levy taxes. *Federal State*

25. Cases tried before a court of law are of two types, civil and *crim.*

26. By a majority vote of the members of the Congress, the Congress can change provisions of the Constitution of the United States. (True or false)

27. For security, each state has a right to form a *militia*

28. The electoral vote for President is counted in the presence of two bodies. Name them. *H of R Senate*

29. If no candidate for President receives a majority of the electoral vote, who decides who will become President? *H of R*

30. Of the original 13 states, the one with the largest representation in the first Congress was *VA*

31. Of which branch of state government is the Speaker of the House a part? ___ Executive _✓_ Legislative ___ Judicial

32. Capital punishment is the giving of a death sentence. (True) or false)

33. In case the President is unable to perform the duties of his office, who assumes them? *V P*

34. "Involuntary servitude" is permitted in the United States upon conviction of a crime. (True or false).

35. If a state is a party to a case, the Constitution provides that original jurisdiction shall be in *SC*

36. Congress passes laws regulating cases which are included in those over which the United States Supreme Court has ___ jurisdiction.

37. Which of the following is a right guaranteed by the Bill of Rights of the United States Constitution?

___ Public Housing   ___ Education

___ Voting   ✓ Trial by Jury

38. The Legislatures of the states decide how presidential electors may be chosen. (True or false)

39. If it were proposed to join Alabama and Mississippi to form one state, what groups would have to vote approval in order for this to be done?

40. The Vice President presides over _Senate_

41. The Constitution limits the size of the District of Columbia to ___.

42. The only laws which can be passed to apply to an area in a federal arsenal are those passed by ___ provided consent for the purchase of the land is given by the ___.

43. In which document or writing is the Bill of Rights found?

44. Of which branch of government is a Supreme Court justice a part? ___ Executive ___ Legislative ___ Judicial

45. If no person receives a majority of the electoral votes, the Vice President is chosen by the Senate. (True or false)

46. Name two things which the states are forbidden to do by the United States Constitution.

47. If election of the President becomes the duty of the United States House of Representatives it fails to act, who becomes President and when?
Speaker

48. How many votes must a person receive in order to become President if the election is decided by the United States House of Representatives?

49. How many states were required to approve the original Constitution in order for it to be in effect?

50. Check the offenses below which, if you are convicted of them, disqualify you for voting.

___ Murder   ___ Petty Larceny

___ Issuing worthless checks   ___ Manufacturing whiskey

51. The Congress decides in what manner states elect presidential electors. (True or false)

52. Name two of the purposes of the United States Constitution.

53. Congress is composed of ___.

54. All legislative powers granted in the United States Constitution may legally be used only by ___.

55. The population census is required to be made every _10_ years.

56. Impeachments of United States officials are tried by _Senater_

57. If an effort to impeach the President of the United States is made, who presides at the trial? _C J_

58. On the impeachment of the chief justice of the Supreme Court of the United States, who tries the case?

59. Money is coined by order of:

___ U.S. Congress

___ The President's Cabinet

___ State Legislatures

60. Persons elected to cast a state's vote for United States President and Vice President are called presidential ___.

61. Name one power which is exclusively legislative and is mentioned in one of the parts of the United States Constitution above.

62. If a person flees from justice into another state, who has authority to ask for his return?

63. Whose duty is it to keep Congress informed of the state of the Union?

64. If the two houses of Congress cannot agree on adjournment, who sets the time?

65. When the presidential electors meet to cast ballots for President, must all electors in a state vote for the same person for President or can they vote for different persons if they so choose? _anyone_

66. After the presidential electors have voted, to whom do they send the count of their votes?

67. The power to declare war is vested in ___.

68. Any power and rights not given to the United States or prohibited to the states by the United States Constitution are specified as belonging to whom? _The States_

Ultimately, as part of the Voting Rights Act of 1965, Congress abolished all literacy, understanding, and good character tests in the Deep South. In 1970, this ban was extended nationwide.

* * *

Perhaps the last gasp of disenfranchisement was the notorious Tuskegee gerrymander. Tuskegee was a majority black community in Macon County, Alabama. Blacks in Tuskegee were relatively well educated and independent of the local white power structure because of the presence of two nationally funded employers: the Tuskegee Institute, a black college, and a Veterans' Administration hospital. Beginning in the late 1950's, they sought to participate in the political process. They were met with three responses. First, the Macon County Board of Registrars engaged in a series of evasive maneuvers designed to prevent African Americans from registering to vote. *See United States v. Alabama*, 192 F. Supp. 677 (M. D. Ala. 1961), *aff'd*, 304 F.2d 583 (5th Cir.), *aff'd* 371 U.S. 37 (1962) (per curiam). Second, through a statewide referendum, Alabama adopted a constitutional amendment permitting the state to abolish Macon County altogether "if the uppity Negroes there continued pestering for the vote." Bernard Taper, Gomillion v. Lightfoot: Apartheid in Alabama 51 (1962). *See* Ala. Const. Amend. No. 132 (1957), *repealed* Ala. Const. Amend. No. 406 (1982). Third, the Alabama Legislature passed Local Act 140, which redrew Tuskegee's municipal boundaries.

The redrawn boundaries are reflected on the following map, taken from the Court's opinion. The pre-Act boundaries of Tuskegee consist of the entire square. The post-Act boundaries consist of the territory inside the heavy black line that begins approximately two-thirds of the way across the bottom of the square, heading roughly northwest.

Gomillion v. Lightfoot

364 U.S. 339 (1960).

■ MR. JUSTICE FRANKFURTER delivered the opinion of the Court.

This litigation challenges the validity, under the United States Constitution, of Local Act No. 140, passed by the Legislature of Alabama in 1957, redefining the boundaries of the City of Tuskegee. Petitioners, Negro citizens of Alabama who were, at the time of this redistricting measure, residents of the City of Tuskegee, brought an action in the United States District Court for the Middle District of Alabama for a declaratory judgment that Act 140 is unconstitutional.... Petitioners' claim is that enforcement of the statute, which alters the shape of Tuskegee from a square to an uncouth twenty-eight-sided figure, will constitute a discrimination against them in violation of the Due Process and Equal Protection Clauses of the Fourteenth Amendment to the Constitution and will deny them the right to vote in defiance of the Fifteenth Amendment.

* * *

At this stage of the litigation we are not concerned with the truth of the allegations, that is, the ability of petitioners to sustain their allegations by proof. The sole question is whether the allegations entitle them to make good on their claim that they are being denied rights under the United States Constitution. The complaint, charging that Act 140 is a device to disenfranchise Negro citizens, alleges the following facts: Prior to Act 140 the City of Tuskegee was square in shape; the Act transformed it into a strangely irregular twenty-eight-sided figure as indicated in the diagram appended to this opinion. The essential inevitable effect of this redefinition of Tuskegee's boundaries is to remove from the city all save only four or five of its 400 Negro voters while not removing a single white voter or resident. The result of the Act is to deprive the Negro petitioners discriminatorily of the benefits of residence in Tuskegee, including, inter alia, the right to vote in municipal elections.

These allegations, if proven, would abundantly establish that Act 140 was not an ordinary geographic redistricting measure even within familiar abuses of gerrymandering. If these allegations upon a trial remained uncontradicted or unqualified, the conclusion would be irresistible, tantamount for all practical purposes to a mathematical demonstration, that the legislation is solely concerned with segregating white and colored voters by fencing Negro citizens out of town so as to deprive them of their pre-existing municipal vote.

It is difficult to appreciate what stands in the way of adjudging a statute having this inevitable effect invalid in light of the principles by which this Court must judge, and uniformly has judged, statutes that, howsoever speciously defined, obviously discriminate against colored citizens. "The [Fifteenth] Amendment nullifies sophisticated as well as simple-minded modes of discrimination." *Lane v. Wilson.*

The complaint amply alleges a claim of racial discrimination. Against this claim the respondents have never suggested, either in their brief or in oral argument, any countervailing municipal function which Act 140 is designed to serve. The respondents invoke generalities expressing the State's unrestricted power—unlimited, that is, by the United States Constitution—to establish, destroy, or reorganize by contraction or expansion its political subdivisions, to wit, cities, counties, and other local units.

* * *

[A review of our cases] shows that the Court has never acknowledged that the States have power to do as they will with municipal corporations regardless of consequences. Legislative control of municipalities, no less than other state power, lies within the scope of relevant limitations imposed by the United States Constitution.

* * *

[A state's power to define municipal boundaries,] extensive though it is, is met and overcome by the Fifteenth Amendment to the Constitution of the United States, which forbids a State from passing any law which deprives a citizen of his vote because of his race. The opposite conclusion, urged upon us by respondents, would sanction the achievement by a State of any impairment of voting rights whatever so long as it was cloaked in the garb of the realignment of political subdivisions. "It is inconceivable that guaranties embedded in the Constitution of the United States may thus be manipulated out of existence."

The respondents find another barrier to the trial of this case in *Colegrove v. Green,* 328 U.S. 549. . . . [But t]he decisive facts in this case, which at this stage must be taken as proved, are wholly different from the considerations found controlling in *Colegrove.*

That case involved a complaint of discriminatory apportionment of congressional districts. The appellants in *Colegrove* complained only of a dilution of the strength of their votes as a result of legislative inaction over a course of many years. The petitioners here complain that affirmative legislative action deprives them of their votes and the consequent advantages that the ballot affords. When a legislature thus singles out a readily isolated segment of a racial minority for special discriminatory treatment, it violates the Fifteenth Amendment. In no case involving unequal weight in voting distribution that has come before the Court did the decision sanction a differentiation on racial lines whereby approval was given to unequivocal withdrawal of the vote solely from colored citizens. Apart from all else, these considerations lift this controversy out of the so-called "political" arena and into the conventional sphere of constitutional litigation.

In sum, as Mr. Justice Holmes remarked, when dealing with a related situation, in *Nixon v. Herndon*, "Of course the petition concerns political action," but "The objection that the subject matter of the suit is political is little more than a play upon words." A statute which is alleged to have worked unconstitutional deprivations of petitioners' rights is not immune to attack simply because the mechanism employed by the legislature is a redefinition of municipal boundaries. According to the allegations here made, the Alabama Legislature has not merely redrawn the Tuskegee city limits with incidental inconvenience to the petitioners; it is more accurate to say that it has deprived the petitioners of the municipal franchise and consequent rights and to that end it has incidentally changed the city's boundaries. While in form this is merely an act redefining metes and bounds, if the allegations are established, the inescapable human effect of this essay in geometry and geography is to despoil colored citizens, and only colored citizens, of their theretofore enjoyed voting rights. That was not *Colegrove v. Green*.

When a State exercises power wholly within the domain of state interest, it is insulated from federal judicial review. But such insulation is not carried over when state power is used as an instrument for circumventing a federally protected right.... "Acts generally lawful may become unlawful when done to accomplish an unlawful end, and a constitutional power cannot be used by way of condition to attain an unconstitutional result." The petitioners are entitled to prove their allegations at trial.

■ Mr. Justice Douglas, while joining the opinion of the Court, adheres to the dissents in *Colegrove v. Green*, 328 U.S. 549, and *South v. Peters*, 339 U.S. 276.

■ Mr. Justice Whitaker, concurring.

I concur in the Court's judgment, but not in the whole of its opinion. It seems to me that the decision should be rested not on the Fifteenth Amendment, but rather on the Equal Protection Clause of the Fourteenth Amendment to the Constitution. I am doubtful that the averments of the complaint, taken for present purposes to be true, show a purpose by Act No. 140 to abridge petitioners' "right ... to vote," in the Fifteenth Amendment sense. It seems to me that the "right ... to vote" that is guaranteed by the Fifteenth Amendment is but the same right to vote as is enjoyed by all others within the same election precinct, ward or other political division. And, inasmuch as no one has the right to vote in a political division, or in a local election concerning only an area in which he does not reside, it would seem to follow that one's right to vote in Division A is not abridged by a redistricting that places his residence in Division B if he there enjoys the same voting privileges as all others in that Division, even though the redistricting was done by the State for the purpose of placing a racial group of citizens in Division B rather than A.

But it does seem clear to me that accomplishment of a State's purpose—to use the Court's phrase—of "fencing Negro citizens out of" Division A and into Division B is an unlawful segregation of races of citizens, in violation of the Equal Protection Clause of the Fourteenth Amendment, *Brown v. Board of Education*, 347 U.S. 483; *Cooper v. Aaron*, 358 U.S. 1; and, as stated, I would think the decision should be rested on that ground—which, incidentally, clearly would not involve, just as the cited cases did not involve, the Colegrove problem.

NOTES AND QUESTIONS

1.   For detailed accounts of the political struggle in Tuskegee and its aftermath, see, e.g., Margaret Edds, Free At Last: What Really Happened When Civil Rights Came to Southern Politics (1987); Robert J. Norrell, Reaping the Whirlwind: Change and Conflict in Macon County, Alabama, 1941–1972 (1983); Bernard Taper, Gomillion v. Lightfoot: Apartheid in Alabama 51 (1962).

2.   Why does Justice Frankfurter rely on the Fifteenth Amendment rather than the Fourteenth? Consider the ways in which the scope of the former amendment is narrower than the scope of the latter.

3.   Were black voters actually disenfranchised or only placed into a "different" electoral jurisdiction—Macon County, rather than the city of Tuskegee? Does the police jurisdiction statute discussed in *Holt Civic Club, supra*, shed any light on this case? In recent years, the Supreme Court has treated *Gomillion* as if it were a Fourteenth Amendment case. *See, e.g., Shaw v. Reno*, 509 U.S. 630 (1993), discussed in greater depth in Chapter 9.

D.   VOTER REGISTRATION AND PARTICIPATION

Most Americans don't vote. In the 2002 elections, for example, only 37 percent of the voting-age population cast ballots. See Election Assistance Commission, Voter Registration and Turnout–2000 <http://www.eac.gov/election_resources/02to.htm>. Similarly, in the 2006 congressional midterm elections, only an estimated 40.5 percent of the "voting eligible population"—that is, citizens of voting age who were not ineligible because of criminal convictions—voted. *See* United States Election Project, 2006 Voting–Age and Voting–Eligible Population Estimates and Voter Turnout (2007), available at http://elections.gmu.edu/Voter_Turnout_2006.htm. In presidential election years, turnout is higher, but even then, large numbers of citizens don't show up at the polls. For example, in the 2004 presidential election, 60 percent of the voting-eligible population cast ballots. *See* United States Election Project, 2004 Voting–Age and Voting–Eligible Population Estimates and Voter Turnout (2006), available at http://elections.gmu.edu/Voter_Turnout_2004.htm. Surveys often suggests higher figures, but this data actually overestimate the level of participation. *See* Allen J. Lichtman & Samuel Issacharoff, *Black/White Voter Registration Disparities in Missis-*

sippi: Legal and Methodological Issues in Challenging Bureau of Census Data, 7 J. L. & Pol. 525 (1991).

The exceptionally low level of voter turnout in the United States for presidential elections compared to similar elections in other countries is often taken to raise serious questions about the state of American democracy. But note that while the United States does have the lowest turnout of any democracy, it is also true that the United States has more elections for more levels of government with more elective offices at each level than any other country in the world. *See* Michael Schudson, *Voting Rites: Why We Need a New Concept of Citizenship*, American Prospect, Fall 1994, at 62. For example, even the majority of judges in the United States are elected, rather than appointed, a fact traceable to the Jacksonian era's populist ideology. No other constitutional democracy elects judges on a similar scale; indeed, only Japan and Switzerland appear to have any form of electoral control over judges. Steven P. Croley, *The Majoritarian Difficulty: Elective Judiciaries and the Rule of Law*, 62 U. Chi. L. Rev. 689, 690–91 (1995).

What does the conjunction of these two facts—a multitude of elective offices but low voter turnout—suggest about the relationship between the rhetoric and practice of American democracy? One view might be that the ideology of popular sovereignty, understood as direct electoral participation, became so unchallengeable at various periods, such as the Jacksonian era, that American democracy now suffers from too many offices being elective. Might weak democracy—low turnout—stem, in part, from too much democracy—too many elections for too many offices? Is it clear that the best way to hold public officials accountable is through the electoral mechanism? Assuming it might be a good idea to change some currently elective offices to appointed ones, how politically likely is such a shift, given the power of popular sovereignty rhetoric in American culture? Note that commissions or bar associations in several states have recently proposed replacing elective state judiciaries with merit-selection systems, but none of these reforms has as yet been enacted. In general, what kinds of public offices should be controlled through popular vote as opposed to other selection methods?

At the same time, not only is voter participation in the United States low by comparison to turnout in other democracies; it is also low by historical standards. During the nineteenth century, turnout among eligible citizens (for much of the period white men over the age of 21) was dramatically higher. As a result of the same Jacksonian era changes that produced more elections, turnout shot up to 80 percent in the 1840 presidential election and even in midterm elections, over two-thirds of eligible citizens participated. *See* Voter Registration: Hearings on S. 352 and S. 472 Before the Senate Comm. on Post Office and Civil Serv., 93d Cong. 30 (1973) (presenting turnout data for presidential elections from 1824 to 1972).

Given the historical and comparative evidence, a number of commentators and critics have focused on structural aspects of the American political system that may depress turnout. Some have focused on features such as the system of geographic districting, often controlled by political parties and used to their own advantage, that have rendered many elections noncompetitive. (We focus on political gerrymandering and political competition in Chapter 10.) Others have focused on aspects of the system for financing campaigns. (That topic is covered in Chapter 5.) Here, we focus on a constellation of practices involving barriers faced by individual voters: the way in which elections are conducted and how citizens register to vote.

As an historical matter, Congress first set a single day for national elections in 1845, when it selected the first Tuesday after the first Monday in November as the date for choosing presidential electors. (That date was also designated for congressional elections in 1872. *See Foster v. Love*, 522 U.S. 67 (1997)). Part of the reason for choosing a uniform election day was to respond to the practice at the time of moving potential electors from one district to another to cast ballots in more than one jurisdiction. *See* Jack Rakove, *Butterflies, Chads, and History*, N.Y. Times, Nov. 29, 2000. During the mid-nineteenth century, there was no registration process as we now know it. Voter registration systems were adopted in the United States roughly around the time turnout began to decline—and in many states, particularly in the south and in northern states facing high amounts of immigration, were adopted for the purpose of barring blacks and immigrants from the polls. *See* Jason P.W. Halperin, *A Winner at the Polls: A Proposal for Mandatory Voter Registration*, 3 N.Y.U. J. Legis. & Pub. Pol'y 74–82 (1999/2000). Moreover, the United States is distinctive among western democracies in that the government takes virtually no affirmative responsibility for registering citizens. In most other nations, the government either automatically registers citizens in conjunction with national identity cards or other government data collection or conducts canvasses designed to register all eligible citizens. (In some countries, this registration process is reinforced by mandatory voting.)

Griffin v. Roupas

385 F.3d 1128 (7th Cir. 2004), *cert. denied*, 544 U.S. 923 (2005).

■ POSNER, CIRCUIT JUDGE.

The plaintiffs . . . are working mothers who contend that because it is a hardship for them to vote in person on election day, the U.S. Constitution requires Illinois to allow them to vote by absentee ballot. Illinois allows voting by absentee ballot only if the voter either "expects to be absent [on election day] from the county in which he is a qualified elector" or is unable to vote in person because of physical incapacity, religious observance, residing outside his precinct for attendance at a college or university, or having to perform specified official duties—election judge in another precinct, certain other election duties, or serving as a sequestered juror. Failing as they do to qualify for any of these exceptions, the plaintiffs ask us to order in the name of the Constitution weekend voting, all-mail voting, an unlimited right to an absentee ballot, a general hardship entitlement to such a ballot, or some other change in Illinois law (Internet voting from home, perhaps?) that would allow people who find it hard for whatever reason to get to the polling place on election day nevertheless to vote.

The procedural setting requires us to accept the allegation in the complaint that the plaintiffs, although they will not be out of the county in which they are registered to vote on election day, will be unable to get to the polling place even though the polls are open in Illinois from 6 a.m. to 7 p.m. on election day and employers are required to give employees two hours off work that day if they need the time for voting. Many people besides working mothers might find themselves in the same fix, such as emergency-room and other medical personnel, persons who work at the other end of a large county from their precinct, persons who work at two jobs, and those who are caring for a sick or disabled family member.

The Constitution does not in so many words confer a right to vote, though it has been held to do so implicitly. Rather, it confers on the states broad authority to regulate the conduct of elections, including federal ones. U.S. Const. art. I, § 4, cl. 1. Because of this grant of authority and because balancing the competing interests involved in the regulation of elections is difficult and an unregulated election system would be chaos, state legislatures may without transgressing the Constitution impose extensive restrictions on voting. Any such restriction is going to exclude, either de jure or de facto, some people from voting; the constitutional question is whether the restriction and resulting exclusion are reasonable given the interest the restriction serves. No greater precision in the articulation of the governing standard seems possible.

In essence the plaintiffs are claiming a blanket right of registered voters to vote by absentee ballot. For it is obvious that a federal court is not going to decree weekend voting, multi-day voting, all-mail voting, or Internet voting (and would it then have to buy everyone a laptop, or a Palm Pilot or Blackberry, and Internet access?). That leaves as the only alternative that will satisfy the plaintiffs a general hardship exemption from the requirement of in-person voting; and as a practical matter that means absentee voting at will. For "hardship" is a subjective category dependent on personal circumstances that cannot be codified but must be left to the judgment of each voter. It is hardly to be supposed that election officials would require proof of hardship or question claims of hardship; the necessary inquiry would be unmanageable.

So at bottom the plaintiffs are arguing that the Constitution requires all states to allow unlimited absentee voting, and the argument ignores a host of serious objections to judicially legislating so radical a reform in the name of the Constitution. Voting fraud is a serious problem in U.S.

elections generally and one with a particularly gamey history in Illinois, and it is facilitated by absentee voting. John C. Fortier & Norman J. Ornstein, "Symposium: The Absentee Ballot and the Secret Ballot: Challenges for Election Reform," 36 U. Mich. J.L. & Reform 483 (2003); William T. McCauley, "Florida Absentee Voter Fraud: Fashioning an Appropriate Judicial Remedy," 54 U. Miami L. Rev. 625, 631–32 (2000); Michael Moss, "Absentee Votes Worry Officials as Nov. 2 Nears," New York Times (late ed.), Sept. 13, 2004, p. A1. In this respect absentee voting is to voting in person as a take-home exam is to a proctored one. Absentee voters also are more prone to cast invalid ballots than voters who, being present at the polling place, may be able to get assistance from the election judges if they have a problem with the ballot. And because absentee voters vote before election day, often weeks before, they are deprived of any information pertinent to their vote that surfaces in the late stages of the election campaign. The major parties are reported to be encouraging their core supporters to vote by absentee ballot so that, having as it were put them in the bag, the parties can redirect their efforts and pitch to the waverers.

These and other problems created by absentee voting may be outweighed by the harm to voters who being unable to vote in person will lose their vote if they can't vote by absentee ballot. But the striking of the balance between discouraging fraud and other abuses and encouraging turnout is quintessentially a legislative judgment with which we judges should not interfere unless strongly convinced that the legislative judgment is grossly awry. Some states have decided, as the plaintiffs urge us to decide, that the drawbacks of absentee voting are so far outweighed by the interest in increasing voter turnout that every registered voter should be allowed to vote by absentee ballot. E.g., Cal. Election Code § 3003; Colo. Rev. Stat. § 1–8–102; Fla. Stat. Ann. § 101.662; Wash. Rev. Code Ann. § 29A.40.010. Oregon has gone the farthest in this direction by making *all* voting by mail. O.R.S. § 254.465. In Oregon, all ballots are absentee. (On whether the Oregon system is consistent with congressional legislation regulating federal elections, see *Voting Integrity Project, Inc. v. Keisling*, 259 F.3d 1169, 1174–76 (9th Cir. 2001).) Other states, including Illinois, have struck a compromise between concern with fraud and concern with turnout by allowing only certain classes of voter to cast an absentee ballot. E.g., Ala. Code 1975 §§ 17–10–3(a), (b); Ark. Code Ann. § 7–5–402; Md. Code Ann., Election Law § 9–304; Minn. St. § 203B.02; N.J. Stat. Ann. § 19:57–3; N.Y. Elec. Law § 8–400; Tex. Election Code Ann. § 82.001(a). The plaintiffs say this is not good enough; that the Constitution requires Illinois to go farther. But the states that have more liberal provisions for absentee voting may well have different political cultures from Illinois, cultures less hospitable to electoral fraud. One size need not fit all. The unfortunate experience with the "butterfly ballot" used in Palm Beach County, Florida in the 2000 Presidential election . . . illustrates the danger of unanticipated consequences from seemingly innocent alterations in election rules.

The plaintiffs contend alternatively that Illinois law is discriminatory and therefore denies them the equal protection of the laws because it bears more heavily on working mothers than on other classes in the community. The claim is belied by the complaint and briefs, where the hardships that prevent voting in person are illustrated with examples of people who are not working mothers—we mentioned some of those examples earlier. "Working mother" does not define a class that the election law singles out for adverse treatment.

The plaintiffs point out, also in an equal protection vein, that depending on where one lives in a county one might have farther to travel to the polling place than a person who plans to be just across the county line on election day, yet that person is allowed to vote by absentee ballot, no questions asked. But this turns out not to be true. To be entitled to vote by absentee ballot it's not enough that you're going to be out of the county on election day; you must certify that you are unable to vote in person.

Anyway, unavoidable inequalities in treatment, even if intended in the sense of being known to follow ineluctably from a deliberate policy, do not violate equal protection. . . .

The plaintiffs point out that anyone who wants to vote by absentee ballot has only to apply and check the box for being unable to vote in person because he is going to be out of the county on election day; no one is going to check up on whether he's telling the truth. Of course, that anyone might include the plaintiffs, but they say they're honest and won't lie on the application form though others will. This is ultimately a vote-dilution claim, and it will not fly, because it would amount to saying that any state election law that is enforced laxly, or perhaps is difficult to enforce at all, denies equal protection by hurting honest people.

The plaintiffs' final grievance concerns the length of the Illinois ballot. In 2000, the ballot for Cook County (the county that includes Chicago) "was twenty-one pages long, included the names of four hundred candidates and, for the first time in a presidential election year, had no simple mechanism to enable voters to cast a straight party-line vote. A combination of outdated technology and lengthy, confusing ballots undoubtedly led many voters to spoil their ballots and lose the right to have their vote counted." Paul S. Herrnson, Improving Technology and Administration: Toward a Larger Federal Role in Elections, 13 Stan. L. & Policy Rev. 147, 151 (2002). The longer and more confusing the ballot, the stronger the argument for allowing people to vote by mail, since then they can take their time trying to figure out the ballot, while when voting in person in a crowded polling place people are likely to feel rushed and as a result make more mistakes. But this argument has nothing to do with the problems faced by working mothers and other people who find it burdensome to vote in person. It applies to everyone. Its logic is that, Oregon-fashion, *everyone* should vote at home, at least in counties in which the ballot is long. If the plaintiffs got their way, Illinois would be forced to choose between shortening the ballot (and on a county-by-county basis?), which would mean reducing the number of offices filled by election, and allowing everyone to vote at home. The Constitution does not force such a choice on the states.

Crawford v. Marion County Election Board

472 F.3d 949 (7th Cir. 2007).

■ POSNER, CIRCUIT JUDGE.

* * *

[Indiana] law requires, with certain exceptions, that persons wanting to vote in person in either a primary or a general election must present at the polling place a government-issued photo ID, unless the person either wants to vote by absentee ballot (and is eligible to do so) or lives in a nursing home.

* * *

Even though it is exceedingly difficult to maneuver in today's America without a photo ID (try flying, or even entering a tall building such as the courthouse in which we sit, without one; see *United States v. Smith*, 426 F.3d 567 (2d Cir. 2005)), and as a consequence the vast majority of adults have such identification, the Indiana law will deter some people from voting. A great many people who are eligible to vote don't bother to do so. Many do not register, and many who do register still don't vote, or vote infrequently. The benefits of voting to the individual voter are elusive (a vote in a political election rarely has any *instrumental* value, since elections for political office at the state or federal level are never decided by just one vote), and even very slight costs in time or bother or out-of-pocket expense deter many people from voting, or at least from voting in elections they're not much interested in. So some people who have not bothered to obtain a photo ID will not bother to do so just to be allowed to vote, and a few who have a photo ID but forget to bring it to the polling place will say what the hell and not vote, rather than go home and get the ID and return to the polling place.

No doubt most people who don't have photo ID are low on the economic ladder and thus, if they do vote, are more likely to vote for Democratic than Republican candidates. Exit polls in the recent midterm elections show a strong negative correlation between income and voting Democratic, with the percentage voting Democratic rising from 45 percent for voters with an income of at least $200,000 to 67 percent for voters having an income below $15,000.

* * *

[The plaintiffs who brought this litigation were unable to find anyone interested in being a plaintiff who alleges that he or she would have voted but for the I.D. requirement. This] suggests that the motivation for the suit is simply that the law may require the Democratic Party and the other organizational plaintiffs to work harder to get every last one of their supporters to the polls.

The fewer the people who will actually disfranchise themselves rather than go to the bother and, if they are not indigent and don't have their birth certificate and so must order a copy and pay a fee, the expense of obtaining a photo ID, the less of a showing the state need make to justify the law. The fewer people harmed by a law, the less total harm there is to balance against whatever benefits the law might confer. The argument pressed by the plaintiffs that any burden on the right to vote, however slight it is or however meager the number of voters affected by it, cannot pass constitutional muster unless it is shown to serve a compelling state interest was rejected in *Burdick v. Takushi*, 504 U.S. 428, 433–34 (1992). The Court said that "election laws will invariably impose some burden upon individual voters.... [T]o subject every voting regulation to strict scrutiny and to require that the regulation be narrowly tailored to advance a compelling state interest, as petitioner suggests, would tie the hands of States seeking to assure that elections are operated equitably and efficiently."....

A strict standard would be especially inappropriate in a case such as this, in which the right to vote is on both sides of the ledger. See *Purcell v. Gonzalez*, 127 S. Ct. 5 (2006) (per curiam). The Indiana law is not like a poll tax, where on one side is the right to vote and on the other side the state's interest in defraying the cost of elections or in limiting the franchise to people who really care about voting or in excluding poor people or in discouraging people who are black. The purpose of the Indiana law is to reduce voting fraud, and voting fraud impairs the right of legitimate voters to vote by diluting their votes—dilution being recognized to be an impairment of the right to vote. On one side of the balance in this case is the effect of requiring a photo ID in inducing eligible voters to disfranchise themselves. That effect, so far as the record reveals, is slight....

On the other side of the balance is voting fraud, specifically the form of voting fraud in which a person shows up at the polls claiming to be someone else—someone who has left the district, or died, too recently to have been removed from the list of registered voters, or someone who has not voted yet on election day. Without requiring a photo ID, there is little if any chance of preventing this kind of fraud because busy poll workers are unlikely to scrutinize signatures carefully and argue with people who deny having forged someone else's signature. The plaintiffs ... note that as far as anyone knows, no one in Indiana, and not many people elsewhere, are known to have been prosecuted for impersonating a registered voter.

But the absence of prosecutions is explained by the endemic underenforcement of minor criminal laws (minor as they appear to the public and prosecutors, at all events) and by the extreme difficulty of apprehending a voter impersonator. He enters the polling place, gives a name that is not his own, votes, and leaves. If later it is discovered that the name he gave is that of a dead person, no one at the polling place will remember the face of the person who gave that name, and if someone did remember it, what would he do with the information? The impersonator and the person impersonated (if living) might show up at the polls at the same time and a confrontation might ensue that might lead to a citizen arrest or a call to the police who would arrive before the impersonator had fled, and arrest him. A more likely sequence would be for the impersonated person to have voted already when the impersonator arrived and tried to vote in his name. But in either case an arrest would be most unlikely (and likewise if the impersonation were discovered or suspected by comparing signatures, when that is done), as the resulting commotion would disrupt the voting. And anyway the impersonated voter is likely to be dead or in another district or precinct or to be acting in cahoots with the impersonator, rather than to be a neighbor (precincts are small, sometimes a single apartment house). One response, which has a parallel to littering, another crime the perpetrators of which are almost impossible to catch, would be to impose a very severe criminal penalty for voting fraud. Another, however, is to take preventive action, as Indiana has done by requiring a photo ID.

* * *

Indirect evidence of such fraud, or at least of an acute danger of such fraud, in Indiana is provided by the discrepancy between the number of people listed on the registered-voter rolls in the state and the substantially smaller number of people actually eligible to vote. The defendants' expert estimated that the registration rolls contained 1.3 million more names than the eligible voters in Indiana. This seems too high, but the plaintiffs' expert acknowledged that the rolls are inflated. How many impersonations there are we do not know, but the plaintiffs have not shown that there are fewer impersonations than there are eligible voters whom the new law will prevent from voting.

* * *

The plaintiffs complain that the new Indiana law is underinclusive because it fails to require absentee voters to present photo IDs. But how would that work? The voter could make a photocopy of his driver's license or passport or other government-issued identification and include it with his absentee ballot, but there would be no way for the state election officials to determine whether the photo ID actually belonged to the absentee voter, since he wouldn't be presenting his face at the polling place for comparison with the photo.

* * *

■ Evans, Circuit Judge, dissenting.

Let's not beat around the bush: The Indiana voter photo ID law is a not-too-thinly-veiled attempt to discourage election-day turnout by certain folks believed to skew Democratic. We should subject this law to strict scrutiny—or at least, in the wake of *Burdick v. Takushi*, 504 U.S. 428 (1992), something akin to "strict scrutiny light"—and strike it down as an undue burden on the fundamental right to vote.

The percentage of eligible voters participating in elections has, for many years, been on a downward trajectory. With that being the case, one would think states should be looking for creative ways (like allowing people to vote at places they frequent and are familiar with, like shopping malls rather than basements of fire stations) to increase voter participation. Yet, the Indiana law we sanction today does just the opposite. Constricting the franchise in a democratic society, when efforts should be instead undertaken to expand it, is not the way to go.

The fig leaf of respectability providing the motive behind this law is that it is necessary to prevent voter fraud—a person showing up at the polls pretending to be someone else. But where is the evidence of that kind of voter fraud in this record? Voting fraud is a crime (punishable by up to 3 years in prison and a fine of up to $10,000 in Indiana) and, at oral argument, the defenders of this law candidly acknowledged that no one—in the history of Indiana—had ever been charged with violating that law. Nationwide, a preliminary report to the U.S. Election Assistance Commission has found little evidence of the type of polling-place fraud that photo ID laws seek to stop. If that's the case, where is the justification for this law? Is it wise to use a sledgehammer to hit either a real or imaginary fly on a glass coffee table? I think not.

* * *

The real problem is that this law will make it significantly more difficult for some eligible voters—I have no idea how many, but 4 percent is a number that has been bandied about—to vote. And this group is mostly comprised of people who are poor, elderly, minorities, disabled, or some combination thereof. I would suspect that few, if any, in this class have passports (which cost in the neighborhood of $100), and most don't have drivers licenses (who needs a drivers license if you don't drive a car?) or state-issued ID cards which require valid (certified) birth certificates. And it's not particularly easy for a poor, elderly person who lives in South Bend, but was born in Arkansas, to get a certified copy of his birth certificate.

Now I certainly agree with my brother Posner that "it is exceedingly difficult to maneuver in today's America without a photo ID." But Indiana's law mostly affects those who, for various reasons, lack any real maneuverability at all. And lest one thinks that those who have maneuverability are immune from running into trouble with this law, consider this anecdotal tidbit.

The *Washington Post* (Nov. 3, 2006) reported that on Indiana's primary election day, Rep. Julia Carson shoved her congressional identification card in a pocket, ran out of her house and raced down the street to be at her polling site when it opened at 6 a.m. Carson, seeking to represent an Indianapolis district for a sixth term, showed the card to a poll worker, who said it was unacceptable under a new state law that requires every voter to show proof of identity with a certain type of photo ID. But Carson, after being turned away, went home and later returned to their polling places to cast her vote. Would most people, especially those without a vested interest in the system, do the same thing? I doubt it.

I believe that most of the problems with our voting system—like deceased persons or felons on registration rolls, machines that malfunction, and confusing ballots (think butterfly)—are suggestive of mismanagement, not electoral wrongdoing. And I recognize that there is, and perhaps there may always be, a fundamental tension between claims of voter fraud and fears of disenfranchisement. But Indiana's law, because it allows nothing except a passport or an Indiana ID card to prove that a potential voter is who he says he is, tips far too far in the wrong direction.

* * *

Common Cause/Georgia v. Billups

439 F. Supp. 2d 1294 (N. D. Ga. 2006).

■ Murphy, District Judge.

* * *

In 2005, the Georgia General Assembly adopted the 2005 Photo ID Act, which amended O.C.G.A. § 21–2–417 to require that all registered voters in Georgia who vote in person in all primary, special, or general elections for state, national, and local offices held on or after July 1, 2005, present a government-issued Photo ID to election officials as a condition of being admitted to the polls and before being issued a ballot and being allowed to vote. [In January 2006 in response to an earlier decision enjoining the 2005 law on a variety of grounds, including the fact that it involved an unconstitutional poll tax because of the cost of acquiring the necessary documents, the Georgia Legislature amended the voter ID law to authorize the provision of free voter ID cards to registered voters who presented to their county board of elections specified documents that established their identity.] . . . .

Secretary of State Cox informed the General Assembly and the Governor before the passage of the 2005 ID Act that the Act would ... [impose] a severe and unnecessary burden on the right to vote for hundreds of thousands of poor, elderly, and minority voters. She noted that there had been no documented cases of fraudulent voting by persons who obtained ballots unlawfully by misrepresenting their identities as registered voters to poll workers reported to her office during her nine years as Secretary of State and that the greatest concern about fraudulent voting was with respect to absentee voting. . . .

Twenty-six states do not require registered voters to present any form of identification as a condition of admission to the polls or to cast a ballot. Twenty-four states require voters to present some form of identification of the polls. Of those states requiring identification, only Georgia requires that voters present a Photo ID as the sole method of identification as a condition of voting, with no fail-safe alternative.

* * *

Governor Perdue estimated that 300,000 Georgians do not have a driver's license or other acceptable photo identification for voting. According to Plaintiffs, United States Department of Transportation data indicates that Georgia may have as many as 874,420 citizens of driving age who do not have driver's licenses. . . . [T]he AARP and the League of Women Voters estimated that over 152,000 Georgians who voted in the 2004 general election were over sixty years of age and did not have a Georgia driver's license.

* * *

Defendants argue that the Photo ID requirement simply regulates the manner of voting, and that requiring a Photo ID for in-person voting is a reasonable means of achieving the legitimate state interest of regulating voting and preventing in-person voter fraud. Defendants also contend again that the Photo ID requirement is not a severe restriction on voting because, in reality, it prevents no one from voting. Instead, according to Defendants, anyone may vote by absentee ballot under the new, more relaxed, absentee voting requirements. Defendants previously have argued that even voters who register by mail may vote for the first time via absentee ballot without showing a Photo ID, and that such voters simply must include a utility bill, a bank statement, or other form of identification permitted by [the Help America Vote Act] with their absentee ballots as a means of voter identification.

Defendants observe that, at most, the Photo ID requirement prevents some individuals who wish to vote in person from doing so until they obtain proper identification. Defendants also point out that those individuals who lack a Photo ID may obtain one free of charge from a State DDS Office, the State's GLOW Bus,[a] or from their county's registrar simply by appearing at those locations providing limited information.

a. The "GLOW" bus (Georgia Licensing on Wheels) is a mobile facility operated by the Georgia Department of Driver services that can travel to locations around the state to provide identification documents.

Defendants also observe that although opportunities for voter fraud via absentee ballot or fraudulent voter registrations may exist, the legislature may address one method of voting at a time. In this case, the legislature has chosen to address voter fraud via in-person voting first.

The Court finds that the appropriate standard of review for evaluating the 2006 Photo ID Act is the [*Burdick v. Takushi*, 504 U.S. 428 (1992)] sliding scale standard. Under that standard, the Court must weigh "the character and magnitude of the asserted injury to the rights protected by the First and Fourteenth Amendments that the plaintiff seeks to vindicate" against "the precise interests put forward by the State as justifications for the burden imposed by its rule," taking into consideration "the extent to which those interests make it necessary to burden the plaintiff's rights," *Burdick*, 504 U.S. at 433–34.

The Asserted Injury

For the reasons discussed below, the character and magnitude of the asserted injury to the right to vote is significant. Many voters who do not have driver's licenses, passports, or other forms of photographic identification have no transportation to a voter registrar's office or DDS service center, have impairments that preclude them from waiting in often-lengthy lines to obtain Voter ID cards or Photo ID cards, or cannot travel to a registrar's office or a DDS service center during those locations' usual hours of operation because the voters do not have transportation available. The evidence in the record demonstrates that many voters who lack an acceptable Photo ID for in-person voting are elderly, infirm, or poor, and lack reliable transportation to a county registrar's office. For those voters, requiring them to obtain a Voter ID card in the short period of time before the July 18, 2006, primary elections and the corresponding primary run-off elections is unduly burdensome. Indeed, those voters likely cannot obtain a Photo ID or Voter ID card before the July 18, 2006, primary elections and the corresponding run-off elections, resulting in their inability to vote in those elections. . . .

* * *

[T]he 2005 Photo ID Act also changed the law governing absentee voting to eliminate the conditions previously required for obtaining an absentee ballot, which had been in effect for some time. . . . Secretary of State Cox testified at the previous hearing that the absentee voting rules in effect prior to the passage of the 2005 Photo ID Act required voters to aver that they met one of several specified requirements to obtain an absentee ballot. Absent more information indicating that the State has made a further effort to inform Georgia voters concerning the new, relaxed absentee voting procedures, many Georgia voters simply may be unaware that the rules have changed. Those voters therefore still may believe that they must satisfy one of the former requirements to obtain an absentee ballot.

Voters who cannot satisfy the former requirements likely will not even attempt to obtain an absentee ballot.

* * *

As the Court previously noted, the absentee voting process also requires that voters plan sufficiently enough ahead to request an absentee ballot, to have the ballot delivered from the registrar's office via the United States Postal Service, to complete the ballot successfully, and to mail the absentee ballot to the registrar's office sufficiently early to allow the United States Postal Service to deliver the absentee ballot to the registrar by 7:00 p.m. on election day. The majority of voters—particularly those voters who lack Photo ID—would not plan sufficiently enough in advance of the July 18, 2006, primary elections to vote via mail-in absentee ballot successfully for those elections. In fact, most voters likely would not be giving serious consideration to the election or to the candidates until shortly before the election itself. Under those circumstances, and given the timing of the State's education efforts, it simply is unrealistic to expect that most of the voters who lack Photo IDs would take advantage of the opportunity to vote an absentee ballot by mail for the July 18, 2006, primary elections and the corresponding primary run-off elections.

Additionally, evidence submitted by Plaintiffs in connection with the 2006 Photo ID Act indicates that many Georgia voters have literacy skills that are below the level required to navigate the absentee voting process successfully without assistance. For those voters, absentee voting would not be an acceptable or reasonable alternative to in-person voting unless those voters could obtain help from someone else to negotiate the absentee voting process.

* * *

Additionally, the State argues that voters who do not have Photo ID will not be "turned away" from the polls; rather, those voters may vote a provisional ballot and return within forty-eight hours with a Voter ID card. Given the difficulty of obtaining a Voter ID card and Photo ID card discussed above, it is highly unlikely that many of the voters who lack Photo ID and who would vote via provisional ballots could obtain a Voter ID card or a Photo ID card and return to the polls or the registrar's office within the forty-eight hour period. Indeed, although many organizations are more than happy to transport individuals to polling places on election day, it is unlikely that those organizations or any other organization or individual would be able or willing to provide transportation to registrar's offices or DDS service centers to allow voters of provisional ballots to obtain Voter ID cards or Photo ID cards. The ability to vote a provisional ballot for the July 18, 2006, primary elections and the corresponding primary run-off elections thus is an illusion.

Further, many voters may not even attempt to vote a provisional ballot in person because they do not have a Photo ID, and they believe that they cannot make the necessary arrangements to obtain a Photo ID within forty-eight hours after casting their votes.

* * *

The right to vote is a delicate franchise. As the Court observed in its October 18, 2005, Order, a previous Plaintiff in the case, Plaintiff Tony Watkins, declined to pursue his claim concerning the 2005 Photo ID Act when he was informed that Defendants planned to depose him. Given the fragile nature of the right to vote, and the restrictions discussed above, the Court finds that the 2006 Photo ID Act imposes "severe" restrictions on the right to vote with respect to the July 18, 2006, primary elections and the corresponding primary run-off elections.

* * *

State Interest

The State and the State Defendants assert that the 2006 Photo ID Act's Photo ID requirement is designed to curb voting fraud. Undoubtedly, this interest is an important one. Unfortunately, the fact that the interest asserted is important and is legitimate does not end the Court's inquiry.

Extent to Which the State's Interest In Preventing Voter Fraud Makes It Necessary to Burden the Right to Vote

Finally, the Court must examine the extent to which the State's interest in preventing voter fraud makes it necessary to burden the right to vote. For the following reasons, the Court finds that the 2006 Photo ID Act's Photo ID requirement is not narrowly tailored to the State's proffered interest of preventing voter fraud. Secretary of State Cox testified at the previous hearing that her office has not received even one complaint of in-person voter fraud over the past nine years and that the possibility of someone voting under the name of a deceased person has been addressed by her Office's monthly removal of recently deceased persons from the voter roles. Additionally, although Defendants presented evidence from elections officials in connection with the 2005 Photo ID Act of fraud in the area of voting, all of that evidence addressed fraud in the area of voter registration and absentee voting, rather than in-person voting. The Photo ID requirement does not apply to voter registration, and any Georgia citizen of appropriate age may register to vote without showing a Photo ID. Indeed, individuals may register to vote by producing copies of bank statements or utility bills, or without even producing identification at all. The 2006 Photo ID statute, like its predecessor, thus does nothing to address the voter fraud issues that conceivably exist in Georgia.

Rather than drawing the 2006 Photo ID Act narrowly to attempt to prevent the most prevalent type of voter fraud, the State drafted its Photo ID requirement to apply only to in-person voters, and to apply only to absentee voters who had registered to vote by mail without providing identification and who were voting absentee for the first time. By doing so, the State, in theory, once again left the field wide open for voter fraud by absentee voting. Under those circumstances, the Photo ID requirement is not narrowly tailored to serve its stated purposes.

* * *

ACCORDINGLY, the Court GRANTS Plaintiffs' Second Motion for Preliminary Injunction with respect to the July 18, 2006, primary elections and the corresponding primary run-off elections, and ENJOINS and restricts Defendants individually and in their official capacities from enforcing or applying the 2006 Photo ID Act, which requires voters to present a Photo ID as a pre-condition to in-person voting in Georgia, to deny Plaintiffs or any other registered voter in Georgia admission to the polls, a ballot, or the right to cast their ballots and to have their ballots counted because of their failure or refusal to present a Photo ID with respect to the July 18, 2006, primary elections and the corresponding primary run-off elections. The Court will revisit this injunction with respect to the general elections to be held in November 2006.

NOTES AND QUESTIONS

1. What standard of scrutiny did the Seventh Circuit apply to the refusal to permit "no excuses" absentee voting? Is this consistent with *Harper* and *Kramer*, discussed earlier in this Chapter? In a similar vein, courts have never applied strict scrutiny to the requirement that voters register a substantial time before the general election. In *Marston v. Lewis*, 410 U.S. 679 (1973), the Supreme Court upheld closing the rolls in Arizona nearly two months before the election given the administrative necessities of obtaining accurate voting rolls in time for the election.

Notice that both the Seventh Circuit in *Crawford* and the district court in *Billups* applied the *Burdick* standard, but they reached dramatically different outcomes? Is this due to differences in the evidence before them or in the way the different judges balanced the various factors?

2. Precisely because the United States leaves voter registration and the conduct of elections largely up to the states—which themselves often devolve responsibility further, down to the county or local level—it is possible to compare practices used in different jurisdictions.

Spencer Overton, *Voter Identification*, 107 Mich. L. Rev. 631 (2007), the most comprehensive study of voter identification requirements, points out that only a few states require photo identification as an absolute prerequisite to voting. (Several others require either such identification or other documentation.) A majority of the U.S. population lies in the majority of states which do not require any documentary evidence at the polls except for those first-time voters required by the Help America Vote Act, 42 U.S.C. § 15483(b), to provide identification of some form after registering by mail.

Voters in those states may be required to sign affidavits, take oral oaths, provide other information orally that confirms their identity (such as birthdate), or sign a poll book that can be compared to the signature they provided when they registered.

Does this variety suggest that the most restrictive forms of identification cannot be justified?

In a similar vein, regarding registration requirements more generally, does the fact that one state—North Dakota—has no voter registration system at all, and that several states—for example, Idaho, Minnesota, New Hampshire, Wisconsin, and Wyoming—permit day-of-election registration shed any light on the justifiability of such registration requirements? Note that Minnesota, Wisconsin, and Wyoming rank among the top states in the percent of eligible voters registered.

Should the fact that some states permit all voters to cast absentee ballots—and that one state, Oregon, has moved entirely to voting by mail—be relevant to the question whether states have a justifiable interest in requiring voters to appear at the polls? Note that while the Seventh Circuit held in *Griffin* that voters have no right to cast an absentee ballot, the district court that heard the Indiana voter ID challenge relied on *Grifin* for the proposition that voters also enjoy no right to vote in person. *See Indiana Democratic Party v. Rokita*, 458 F. Supp. 2d 775, 813 n. 56 (S.D. Ind. 2006), aff'd sub nom. *Crawford v. Marion County Election Bd.*, 472 F.3d 949 (7th Cir. 2007), reh'g denied, 484 F.3d 436 (7th Cir. 2007).

3. The primary justifications given for restrictive registration and absentee voting regulations is the prevention of fraud.

In this light, consider the Supreme Court's opinion in *Purcell v. Gonzalez*, 127 S.Ct. 5 (2006), cited in *Crawford*. The case concerned a challenge to Arizona's new, and extremely restrictive, voter identification law. (The law resulted in nearly one-sixth of all voter registration forms being rejected over a two-year period in Arizona's largest county.). The Supreme Court, in the course of holding that the court of appeals had used the wrong legal standard in reversing the district court's denial of a preliminary injunction against the law, made the following observations:

> "A State indisputably has a compelling interest in preserving the integrity of its election process." *Eu v. San Francisco County Democratic Central Comm.*, 489 U.S. 214, 231 (1989). Confidence in the integrity of our electoral processes is essential to the functioning of our participatory democracy. Voter fraud drives honest citizens out of the democratic process and breeds distrust of our government. Voters who fear their legitimate votes will be outweighed by fraudulent ones will feel disenfranchised. "[T]he right of suffrage can be denied by a debasement or dilution of the weight of a citizen's vote just as effectively as by wholly prohibiting the free exercise of the franchise." *Reynolds v. Sims*, 377 U.S. 533, 555 (1964). Countering the State's

compelling interest in preventing voter fraud is the plaintiffs' strong interest in exercising the "fundamental political right" to vote. *Dunn v. Blumstein*, 405 U.S. 330, 336 (1972) (internal quotation marks omitted). Although the likely effects of Proposition 200 are much debated, the possibility that qualified voters might be turned away from the polls would caution any district judge to give careful consideration to the plaintiffs' challenges.

Professor Karlan observes that the Court's approach here—of framing what is a structural decision in terms of core principles regarding individual rights "represents a breathtaking expansion of the concept of vote dilution" that may shift the terms of future debate from a focus on "whether particular restrictive practices can be justified to one that presupposes that some level of vote denial or dilution is inherent in the system and the only question is which group of voters should be excluded." Pamela S. Karlan, *New Beginnings and Dead Ends in the Law of Democracy*, ___ Ohio St. L.J. ___ (2007).

Professor Overton notes that

No systematic, empirical study of the magnitude of voter fraud has been conducted at either the national level or in any state to date, but the best existing data suggests that a photo-identification requirement would do more harm than good. An estimated 6–11% of voting-age Americans do not possess a state-issued photo-identification card, and in states such as Wisconsin 78% of African–American men ages 18–24 lack a driver's license. By comparison, a study of 2.8 million ballots cast in 2004 in Washington State showed only 0.0009% of the ballots involved double voting or voting in the name of deceased individuals. If further study confirms that photo-identification requirements would deter over 6700 legitimate votes for every single fraudulent vote prevented, a photo-identification requirement would increase the likelihood of erroneous election outcomes.

Overton, *supra*, at 635. If Professor Overton is correct, does this affect the *Crawford* court's balancing?

For additional analysis of voter ID requirements, see Daniel P. Tokaji, *Early Returns on Election Reform: Discretion, Disenfranchisement, and the Help America Vote Act*, 73 Geo. Wash. L. Rev. 1206 (2005); Daniel P. Tokaji, *The New Vote Denial: Where Election Reform Meets the Voting Rights Act*, 57 S. Car. L. Rev. 689 (2006). Professor Tokaji's website contains a wide variety of primary source materials regarding voter ID, including his argument analogizing these forms of voter identification requirements to the poll tax. Even if, as in Indiana, the state agrees to provide that a photo ID will be issued without charge by the Bureau of Motor Vehicles to individuals who lack one:

requiring voters to stand in one line at the BMV for the privilege of possibly standing in another line once they go to vote effectively imposes a tax on the voters' time. It's a burden that many voters won't bear, which is presumably why the bill was passed on a straight party-line vote: Republican legislators are banking that Democrats are more likely to lack ID and won't go to the trouble of getting it . . . .

http://moritzlaw.osu.edu/blogs/tokaji/2005/04/indiana-photo-id-lawsuit.html. In thinking about the possibilities for discriminatory implementation of identification requirements, see, e.g., Glenn D. Magpantay, *Asian American Access to the Vote: The Language Assistance Provisions (Section 203) of the Voting Rights Act and Beyond*, 11 Asian L.J. 31, 46–47 (2004) (recounting such experiences in New York). For an extensive discussion of the variety of mechanisms that tend to reduce or suppress voter turnout, see Spencer Overton, Stealing Democracy: The New Politics of Voter Suppression (2006).

4. Did the *Crawford* court determine that prevention of fraud—rather than partisan advantage—was the actual motive behind passage of the ID requirement? Note that Republican legislators are far more likely than Democrats to support voter ID legislation. Is this relevant to determining a legislature's actual purpose? Note also that minority legislators are significantly less likely to support such legislation.

In determining whether preventing fraud is a legislature's actual motivation, to what extent should courts rely on hypotheses like the Seventh Circuit's—that the absence of actual evidence of fraud is irrelevant? Does this suggest that the Seventh Circuit was actually applying only the most deferential, rationality review standard rather than either the intermediate standard laid out in *Burdick* or some more searching standard?

5. The negative liberty aspect of voting has particular bite with respect to registration requirements. If voting were a positive entitlement, would the states bear more of a burden to assure registration? For example, would they be required to do affirmative outreach?

6. *Mail-in Voting.* Would voter participation—and more informed voting—be enhanced by doing away with voting at public polls on a single day and switching to a vote-by-mail system? For the first time in history, this system was used in the 2000 Presidential elections in one state. By statewide initiative, Oregon in 1998 enacted a statewide vote-by-mail system, after having used the system for several years in some local and special elections. In May 2000, Oregon became the first state to use an all-mail ballot for primary elections. For the presidential elections, ballots were mailed starting October 20, 2000—nearly three weeks before the rest of the country went to the polls on November 7th. Voters could vote anytime during that period; the ballot also included 26 initiatives and numerous candidate races in addition to the Presidency. There are no more polling places in Oregon. Voters filled in ballots at home and mailed them in or took them to drop boxes.

Proponents predicted that the system would increase turnout by at least 10 percent. The state also stands to save $3 million on election costs. Opponents argue that the system will be an invitation to fraud and that it will allow political consultants and interest groups to monitor the voting patterns and manipulate them more easily.

Does a system like Oregon's violate federal law that requires all federal elections to be conducted on the same day—since 1875, the first Tuesday after the first Monday in November, 2 U.S.C. § 7? The Supreme Court has held that certain forms of early congressional elections do conflict with the relevant federal statutes and hence are pre-empted. In *Foster v. Love*, 522 U.S. 67 (1997), the Court held that Louisiana's non-partisan primary structure (which the Court endorsed in other respects in *California Democratic Party v. Jones*, 530 U.S. 567 (2000)), violated these laws. Under Louisiana law, all candidates appeared on the same primary ballot, regardless of party; if any candidate received a majority of votes in the primary, he or she was elected without any further action on federal election day. Because the "final selection" of candidates could conclude (and 80 percent of the time, did) before federal election day, the system violated federal election law. By contrast, the Oregon system was upheld against a similar challenge. *See Voting Integrity Project v. Keisling*, 259 F.3d 1169 (9th Cir. 2001), cert. denied, 535 U.S. 986 (2002).

Texas recently established an early voting system that permits voting to begin seventeen days before federal election day. The Fifth Circuit upheld that system and distinguished *Foster* in *Voting Integrity Project v. Bomer*, 199 F.3d 773 (5th Cir. 2000). The court noted that absentee voting, which occurs in every state, would otherwise violate the "federal election day" law. For general discussion, see Edward B. Moreton, Jr., *Voting by Mail*, 58 S. Cal. L. Rev. 1261 (1985). Even if a candidate is not finally chosen until election day, as with the Oregon system, does the fact that Oregon's system permits voting for national elections to extend as far in advance of national election day as three weeks put the Oregon law in tension with the purposes of the federal "single-election day" statute?

7. In addition to traditional and quasi-traditional forms of remote voting, such as absentee voting and vote by mail, the question of internet voting has recently garnered some attention. For one extensive examination of the advantages and disadvantages of internet voting, see the California Internet Voting Task Force's 2000 report, A Report on the Feasibility of Internet Voting, http://www.ss.ca.gov/executive/ivote/final_report.htm. In 2000, the Arizona Democratic Party permitted voters to participate in the presidential primary by voting over the internet. The insights to be garnered from that experience may be limited somewhat by the fact that a week before the end of the voting period, one of the two major candidates, Bill Bradley, withdrew from the race. For a statistical analysis, see R. Michael Alvarez & Jonathan Nagler, *The Likely Consequences of Internet Voting for Political Representation*, 34 Loy. L.A.L. Rev. 1115 (2001).

Two sets of narrow questions regarding internet voting have occupied much of the attention so far: issues of potential fraud and the digital divide—that is, the fact that traditionally disadvantaged (and disenfranchised) social groups have less access to the internet. *See, e.g.,* National Telecommunications and Information Administration, Falling Through the Net: Defining the Digital Divide (1999), available from http://www. ntia.doc. gov/ ntiahome /fttn99/ contents.html.

Consider whether any of these problems is unique to internet-based voting:

> Socioeconomic disparities and differential access to "politically salient resources" have always affected the political prospects of minority voters. Consider, for example, the effects of the "literacy divide." In the nineteenth century, the introduction of the secret ballot had the effect (and arguably the purpose) of disenfranchising numbers of freedmen because they could not read and fill out officially issued ballots. In the twentieth century, literacy tests disenfranchised a disproportionate number of minority citizens, and English-language-only ballot materials deterred or prevented many others from voting. Today, the literacy divide means that many citizens, particular minorities, continue to lack effective access to information about candidates or issues; moreover, less well educated voters may often cast uninformed votes because they cannot understand ballot pamphlets. As the recent debacle in Florida showed, ballot spoilage rates are higher in minority areas, both because heavily nonwhite jurisdictions tend to use older and less reliable voting equipment and because less well-educated voters are more likely to cast invalid ballots. Finally, since educational levels are highly correlated with socioeconomic status, if minority voters are less well educated than their white or Anglo counterparts, socioeconomic disparities will often produce distinctive political interests. These differences will be reflected in racially polarized voting and the defeat of minority-preferred candidates in majority-white districts.
>
> Or, in a more narrowly mechanical vein, what about the little-noticed (at least outside the voting rights community) "vehicle divide"? The difference in access to an automobile is surprisingly important to political participation in rural areas: it can make it extremely difficult for minority voters to get to the polls and cast ballots. Many of the same voters who won't be able to vote on line already don't vote because they find it too difficult to get to the voting booth. In reality, online voting is essentially just a way of casting a ballot without going to a polling place, and there is little reason to think it won't have the same context-dependent effects as other forms of absentee voting.

Eben Moglen & Pamela S. Karlan, *The Soul of a New Political Machine: The Online, the Color Line, and Electronic Democracy*, 34 Loy. L.A.L. Rev. 1089 (2001).

Consider, finally, the more normative question whether remote voting is a good idea. In *Voting Alone: The Case Against Virtual Ballot Boxes*, http://www.tnr.com/archive/0999/091399/valelly091399.html, Professor Rick Vallely argues not only that voting over the internet will do little to combat voter apathy, but it will undermine voting's role as "a vital public ritual that increases social solidarity and binds citizens together." Vallely observes that voter turnout among the eligible electorate—white, property-owning male adults—was strikingly high during the nineteenth-century period of viva voce voting, when voters cast their votes publicly. For an extensive treatment of how "citizenship" has been experienced in different eras in the United States, which emphasizes the critical role of electoral practices in creating that experience, see Michael Schudson, The Good Citizen: A History of American Civic Life (1998). The advent of the secret ballot—which we discuss in more detail in Chapter 5—reduced corruption but it also "made voting much less of a collective enterprise, turning it into a solitary rite." Vallely argues that the very fact that voters cast their ballots in public polling places requires them to mingle with other voters who are quite different from them and reminds them that at least in this one respect, all citizens are equal. "E-voting," as he calls it, will replace civic ritual with individual anomie. Do you agree?

8. For the most part, voter registration and election administration is left to the states. There have, however, been some notable exceptions. The Voting Rights Act of 1965 provided for federal registrars and examiners in jurisdictions that had excluded minority voters. See 42 U.S.C. §§ 1973d, 1973e, 1973f. In the five years following the Act's passage, registrars appointed under the Act enrolled almost as many black voters in the South as had been registered in the entire preceding century. *See* Chandler Davidson, *The Voting Rights Act: A Brief History, in* Controversies in Minority Voting: The Voting Rights Act in Perspective 7, 21 (Bernard Grofman & Chandler Davidson eds. 1992).

More recently, the National Voter Registration Act of 1993, 42 U.S.C. §§ 1973gg to 1973gg–10 (the so-called "motor voter" law) marked a first, tentative attempt by Congress to create an affirmative government duty to register voters. The Act requires states to establish three sorts of registration procedures. First, they must enable individuals to register to vote simultaneously with their application for drivers' licenses. 42 U.S.C. § 1973gg–3. Second, states are required to provide for mail-in voter registration and the forms must be made readily available, essentially so groups can conduct registration drives. *See* 42 U.S.C. § 1973gg–4. Finally, states have to provide in-person registration at various agencies, including all public assistance agencies and agencies that serve primarily the disabled; they are encouraged to provide such assistance at other agencies, such as schools, libraries, and licensing bureaus. 42 U.S.C. § 1973gg–5.

The Act's requirements apply only to registration for federal elections. Why? Is a state's decision to maintain a dual registration system suspicious, particularly if the federal registration system achieves much higher registration among minority groups? In 1996, a state court judge ordered Illinois to abandon dual registration. *See* Sue Ellen Christian, *State Ordered To Stop 2–Step on Motor–Voter; Edgar Blasted for Dual System of Registration*, Chi. Trib., June 22, 1996, at 1 (requiring Illinois to let 160,000 voters who had been registered under the NVRA solely for federal elections to vote in state and local elections as well). *Cf. Harman v. Forssenius*, 380 U.S. 528 (1965); *Mississippi State Chapter, Operation Push v. Allain*, 674 F. Supp. 1245 (N. D. Miss. 1987) (holding that Mississippi's dual registration system violated section 2 of the Voting Rights Act because of its disproportionate impact on black citizens).

In addition to these affirmative obligations, the Act restricts states from engaging in certain actions that remove voters from the rolls. Perhaps the most important of these prohibitions is the Act's ban on removing voters simply for failure to vote. 42 U.S.C. § 1973gg–6(b)(2).

The Act has survived a variety of constitutional challenges raised by state governments. *See, e.g., Association of Community Organizations for Reform Now v. Edgar*, 56 F.3d 791 (7th Cir. 1995); *Voting Rights Coalition v. Wilson*, 60 F.3d 1411 (9th Cir. 1995), *cert. denied*, 516 U.S. 1093 (1996). But consider whether the NVRA is vulnerable in light of the Supreme Court's decision in *Printz v. United States*, 521 U.S. 898 (1997). *Printz* involved a challenge to the Brady Handgun Violence Prevention Act, which required local law enforcement agencies to conduct background checks of firearms buyers. In *Printz*, the Court held that the Federal Government cannot command State officers "to administer or enforce a federal regulatory program." Moreover, "no case-by-case weighing of the burdens or benefits is necessary; such commands are fundamentally incompatible with our constitutional system of dual sovereignty." The NVRA requires state officials in particular state agencies to provide forms permitting people to register to vote and to provide the same assistance in filling out those forms as they do in filling out their own agency's forms. How would you distinguish *Printz?* Note that subsequent to *Printz*, the Court upheld the Drivers Privacy Protection Act against a Tenth Amendment challenge, in part on the ground that Congress was regulating state officials directly, rather than seeking to control or influence the manner in which States regulated private parties directly. *Reno v. Condon*, 528 U.S. 141 (2000).

The Act took effect on January 1, 1995. Eleven million citizens either enrolled or updated their registrations during the Act's first year: 5.5 million registered in motor vehicle agencies, 1.3 registered in public assistance agencies, and 4.2 million registered by mail. Florida and Texas each registered over 1.2 million voters. *See* National Motor Voter Coalition, First Year Report on the Impact of the National Voter Registration Act, January 1, 1995–December 31, 1995 (1996).

What are the political consequences of increased registration? Initially, many Republicans opposed federal voter registration legislation (in fact,

President George H.W. Bush vetoed a precursor to the NVRA), in part on the assumption that making registration easier would disproportionately benefit the Democratic Party, since its supporters tended to be poorer and less well educated. At least so far, there is no persuasive evidence that the Act—or indeed, any of the other recent voting-related reforms—has significantly changed the partisan composition of the electorate. *See* Adam J. Berinsky, The Perverse Consequences of Electoral Reform in the United States, 33 Am. Pol. Research 471 (2005). A high percentage of new registrants are younger voters. In the last few presidential elections, voters under 30 made up the strongest age group supporting Republicans. *See* Cokie Roberts & Steven Roberts, *Young Voters Apathetic and Both Parties Like It That Way*, Dallas Morning News, July 7, 1996, at 5J. At the same time, some reports suggest that states have dragged their heels at implementing voter registration in public-assistance and other social service agencies, where the voters most prone to support Democrats are more likely to be found. *See, e.g., Condon v. Reno*, 913 F. Supp. 946 (D. S. C. 1995) (gubernatorial executive order required voter registration applications to be provided at the DMV but not at the Department of Social Services, the Department of Disabilities and Special Needs, the Commission for the Blind, the Department of Vocational Rehabilitation, or the Protection and Advocacy System for the Handicapped).

Most recently, provisions of the Help America Vote Act of 2002 have modified the NVRA. Of particular salience to the process of registering and receiving a ballot, HAVA requires states to upgrade and maintain statewide registration data bases, see 42 U.S.C. 15483(a), and requires voters who registered by mail and who have not previously voted in the jurisdiction to provide a specified form of identification, see *id.* § 15483(b). (HAVA also provides for "provisional ballots" to be given to individuals who appear at the polls but who are not otherwise permitted to vote. That provision is discussed more fully in Chapter 12.)

CHAPTER 3

THE REAPPORTIONMENT REVOLUTION

The right of individual citizens to vote freely is undoubtedly one of the defining features of democratic legitimacy. Unfortunately, the act of casting a ballot by itself is insufficient to guarantee a truly meaningful right of democratic participation. Because of the apparent legitimacy that the act of voting gives to government, it has been a hallmark of the twentieth century that repressive regimes of all sorts have claimed the mantle of elected representatives of their citizens. This has given rise to show elections in countries such as the former Soviet Union, in which citizens are not only allowed but oftentimes compelled to vote in state-sponsored elections. Such voting was an electoral device in name only, however, as the exclusive candidates for office were those on the state-approved slate. Clearly, something more than simply casting a ballot for a series of state-prescribed candidates is necessary to define democratic legitimacy.

In searching for a more robust understanding of voting in a democratic society, the inquiry must turn to the act of casting a *meaningful* vote. To be meaningful, a vote must matter in the sense that it is capable of being aggregated with those of like-minded voters in order to pursue common electoral objectives. As soon as the inquiry shifts to effectiveness in securing representation, therefore, our attention must move away from individuals to the capacity to aggregate effectively groups of votes. As expressed by Justice Lewis Powell, "[t]he concept of 'representation' necessarily applies to groups: groups of voters elect representatives, individual voters do not." *Davis v. Bandemer*, 478 U.S. 109, 167 (1986) (Powell, J., concurring in part and dissenting in part).

The search for meaningful electoral opportunity thrust the Supreme Court into one of the most difficult areas of policing the electoral system. In this Chapter, we shall explore the structural dimension of proper electoral opportunity, focusing on the emergence and application of the by now well-known one-person/one-vote rule.

A. THE POLITICAL THICKET

Colegrove v. Green

328 U.S. 549 (1946).

■ Mr. Justice Frankfurter announced the judgment of the Court and an opinion in which Mr. Justice Reed and Mr. Justice Burton concur.

[T]hree qualified voters in Illinois districts which have much larger populations than other Illinois Congressional districts ... brought this suit against the Governor, the Secretary of State, and the Auditor of the State of Illinois, as members ex officio of the Illinois Primary Certifying Board, to restrain them, in effect, from taking proceedings for an election in November 1946, under the provisions of Illinois law governing Congressional districts....

We are of opinion that the appellants ask of this Court what is beyond its competence to grant. This is one of those demands on judicial power which cannot be met by verbal fencing about "jurisdiction." It must be resolved by considerations on the basis of which this Court, from time to time, has refused to intervene in controversies. It has refused to do so because due regard for the effective working of our Government revealed this issue to be of a peculiarly political nature and therefore not meet for judicial determination.

This is not an action to recover for damage because of the discriminatory exclusion of a plaintiff from rights enjoyed by other citizens. The basis for the suit is not a private wrong, but a wrong suffered by Illinois as a polity. Compare *Nixon v. Herndon*, 273 U.S. 536 and *Lane v. Wilson*, 307 U.S. 268, with *Giles v. Harris*, 189 U.S. 475. In effect this is an appeal to the federal courts to reconstruct the electoral process of Illinois in order that it may be adequately represented in the councils of the Nation. Because the Illinois legislature has failed to revise its Congressional Representative districts in order to reflect great changes, during more than a generation, in the distribution of its population, we are asked to do this, as it were, for Illinois.

Of course no court can affirmatively re-map the Illinois districts so as to bring them more in conformity with the standards of fairness for a representative system. At best we could only declare the existing electoral system invalid. The result would be to leave Illinois undistricted and to bring into operation, if the Illinois legislature chose not to act, the choice of members for the House of Representatives on a state-wide ticket. The last stage may be worse than the first. The upshot of judicial action may defeat the vital political principle which led Congress, more than a hundred years ago, to require districting. This requirement, in the language of Chancellor Kent, "was recommended by the wisdom and justice of giving, as far as possible, to the local subdivisions of the people of each state, a due influence in the choice of representatives, so as not to leave the aggregate minority of the people in a state, though approaching perhaps to a majority, to be wholly overpowered by the combined action of the numerical majority, without any voice whatever in the national councils." 1 Kent, Commentaries (12th ed., 1873) * 230–31, n. (c). Assuming acquiescence on the part of the authorities of Illinois in the selection of its Representatives by a mode that defies the direction of Congress for selection by districts, the House of Representatives may not acquiesce. In the exercise of its power to judge the qualifications of its own members, the House may reject a delegation of Representatives-at-large. Article I, § 5, Cl. 1.... Nothing is clearer than that this controversy concerns matters that bring courts into immediate and active relations with party contests. From the determination of such issues this Court has traditionally held aloof. It is hostile to a democratic system to involve the judiciary in the politics of the people. And it is not less pernicious if such judicial intervention in an essentially political contest be dressed up in the abstract phrases of the law.

The appellants urge with great zeal that the conditions of which they complain are grave evils and offend public morality. The Constitution of the United States gives ample power to provide against these evils. But due regard for the Constitution as a viable system precludes judicial correction. Authority for dealing with such problems resides elsewhere. Article I, § 4 of the Constitution provides that "The Times, Places and Manner of holding Elections for ... Representatives, shall be prescribed in each State by the Legislature thereof; but the Congress may at any time by Law make or alter such Regulations...." The short of it is that the Constitution has conferred upon Congress exclusive authority to secure fair representation by the States in the popular House and left to that House determination whether States have fulfilled their responsibility. If Congress failed in exercising its powers, whereby standards of fairness are offended, the remedy ultimately lies with the people. Whether Congress faithfully discharges its duty or not, the subject has been committed to the exclusive control of Congress. An aspect of government from which the judiciary, in view of what is involved, has been excluded by the clear intention of the Constitution cannot be entered by the federal courts because Congress may have been in default in exacting from States obedience to its mandate.

The one stark fact that emerges from a study of the history of Congressional apportionment is its embroilment in politics, in the sense of party contests and party interests. The Constitution enjoins upon Congress the duty of apportioning Representatives "among the several States ... according to their respective Numbers...." Article I, § 2. Yet, Congress has at times been heedless of this command and not apportioned according to the requirements of the Census. It never occurred to anyone that this Court could issue mandamus to compel Congress to perform its mandatory duty to apportion.... Until 1842 there was the greatest diversity among the States in the manner of choosing Representatives because Congress had made no requirement for districting. 5 Stat. 491. Congress then provided for the election of Representatives by districts. Strangely enough, the power to do so was seriously questioned; it was still doubted by a Committee of Congress as late as 1901.... In 1850 Congress dropped the requirement. 9 Stat. 428, 432–33. The Reapportionment Act of 1862 required that the districts be of contiguous territory. 12 Stat. 572. In 1872 Congress added the requirement of substantial equality of inhabitants. 17 Stat. 28. This was reinforced in 1911. 37 Stat. 13, 14. But the 1929 Act, as we have seen, dropped these requirements. 46 Stat. 21. Throughout our history, whatever may have been the controlling Apportionment Act, the most glaring disparities have prevailed as to the contours and the population of districts....

To sustain this action would cut very deep into the very being of Congress. Courts ought not to enter this political thicket. The remedy for unfairness in districting is to secure State legislatures that will apportion properly, or to invoke the ample powers of Congress. The Constitution has many commands that are not enforceable by courts because they clearly fall outside the conditions and purposes that circumscribe judicial action.... The Constitution has left the performance of many duties in our governmental scheme to depend on the fidelity of the executive and legislative action and, ultimately, on the vigilance of the people in exercising their political rights.

Dismissal of the complaint is affirmed.

■ MR. JUSTICE BLACK, dissenting.

The complaint alleges the following facts essential to the position I take: Appellants, citizens and voters of Illinois, live in congressional election districts, the respective populations of which range from 612,000 to 914,000. Twenty other congressional election districts have populations that range from 112,116 to 385,207. In seven of these districts the population is below 200,000. The Illinois Legislature established these districts in 1901 on the basis of the Census of 1900. The Federal Census of 1910, of 1920, of 1930, and of 1940, each showed a growth of population in Illinois and a substantial shift in the distribution of population among the districts established in 1901. But up to date, attempts to have the State Legislature reapportion congressional election districts so as more nearly to equalize their population have been unsuccessful. A contributing cause of this situation, according to appellants, is the fact that the State Legislature is chosen on the basis of state election districts inequitably apportioned in a way similar to that of the 1901 congressional election districts. The implication is that the issues of state and congressional apportionment are thus so interdependent that it is to the interest of state legislators to perpetuate the inequitable apportionment of both state and congressional election districts. Prior to this proceeding a series of suits had been brought in the state courts challenging the State's local and federal apportionment system. In all these cases the Supreme Court of the State had denied effective relief....

It is difficult for me to see why the 1901 State Apportionment Act does not deny appellants equal protection of the laws. The failure of the Legislature to reapportion the congressional election districts for forty years, despite census figures indicating great changes in the distribution of the population, has resulted in election districts the populations of which range from 112,000 to 900,000. One of the appellants lives in a district of more than 900,000 people. His vote is consequently much less effective than that of each of the citizens living in the district of 112,000. And such a gross inequality in the voting power of citizens irrefutably demonstrates a complete lack of effort to make an equitable apportionment. The 1901 State Apportionment Act if applied to the next election would thus result in a wholly indefensible discrimination against appellants and all other voters in heavily populated districts. The equal protection clause of the Fourteenth Amendment forbids such discrimination. It does not permit the States to pick out certain qualified citizens or groups of citizens and deny them the right to vote at all. *See Nixon v. Herndon*, 273 U.S. 536, 541; *Nixon v. Condon*, 286 U.S. 73. No one would deny that the equal protection clause would also prohibit a law that would expressly give certain citizens a half-vote and others a full vote. The probable effect of the 1901 State Apportionment Act in the coming election will be that certain citizens, and among them the appellants, will in some instances have votes only one-ninth as effective in choosing representatives to Congress as the votes of other citizens. Such discriminatory legislation seems to me exactly the kind that the equal protection clause was intended to prohibit.

[. . .] While the Constitution contains no express provision requiring that congressional election districts established by the States must contain approximately equal populations, the constitutionally guaranteed right to vote and the right to have one's vote counted clearly imply the policy that state election systems, no matter what their form, should be designed to give approximately equal weight to each vote cast. To some extent this implication of Article I is expressly stated by § 2 of the Fourteenth Amendment which provides that "Representatives shall be apportioned among the several States according to their respective numbers. . . ." The purpose of this requirement is obvious: It is to make the votes of the citizens of the several States equally effective in the selection of members of Congress. It was intended to make illegal a nation-wide "rotten borough" system as between the States. The policy behind it is broader than that. It prohibits as well congressional "rotten boroughs" within the States, such as the ones here involved. The policy is that which is laid down by all the constitutional provisions regulating the election of members of the House of Representatives, including Article I which guarantees the right to vote and to have that vote effectively counted: All groups, classes, and individuals shall to the extent that it is practically feasible be given equal representation in the House of Representatives, which, in conjunction with the Senate, writes the laws affecting the life, liberty, and property of all the people. . . .

Had Illinois passed an Act requiring that all of its twenty-six Congressmen be elected by the citizens of one county, it would clearly have amounted to a denial to the citizens of the other counties of their constitutionally guaranteed right to vote. And I cannot imagine that an Act that would have apportioned twenty-five Congressmen to the State's smallest county and one Congressman to all the others, would have been sustained by any court. Such an Act would clearly have violated the constitutional policy of equal representation. The 1901 Apportionment Act here involved violates that policy in the same way. The policy with respect to federal elections laid down by the Constitution, while it does not mean that the courts can or should prescribe the precise methods to be followed by state legislatures and the invalidation of all Acts that do not embody those precise methods, does mean that state legislatures must make real efforts to bring about approximately equal representation of citizens in Congress. Here the Legislature of Illinois has not done so. Whether that was due to negligence or was a wilful effort to deprive some citizens of an effective vote, the admitted result is that the constitutional policy of equality of representation has been defeated. Under these circumstances it is the Court's duty to invalidate the state law....

■ Mr. Justice Douglas and Mr. Justice Murphy join in this dissent.

NOTES AND QUESTIONS

1. *Colegrove* is best remembered for Justice Frankfurter's evocative image of the "political thicket." Justice Frankfurter gives a number of justifications for the judiciary staying out of questions of political apportionment. These run a broad gamut from concerns over constitutional structure to the administrability of a potential remedy, should the Court immerse itself in deciding on proper forms of political governance. Among the concerns, we may identify: a) prudential limitations on the Court's jurisdiction (the "political question" doctrine); b) concerns over institutional competence (the Court has little expertise in redressing apportionment imbalances); c) administrability of remedies (embroilment in politics); and d) availability of alternative institutions to remedy any apportionment defects (such as Congress or the state legislature). How persuasive are any of these arguments individually?

2. Are there structural obstacles to the reform of malapportionment through the states' political process? Justice Black argues that congressional apportionment is conducted by the state legislature, which in turn is malapportioned along the same lines as the state congressional delegation. Would reform of the state's congressional delegation further the interests of state legislators from similarly malapportioned districts? Would it serve the interests of such legislators' constituents who would have otherwise enjoyed enhanced influence over the election of the state's congressional representatives?

3. Do similar problems present themselves in Congress? Why should representatives from one state be concerned about malapportionment in another state? Is there not reason to believe that the malapportionment found in Illinois was likely replicated in other states? Would this reduce the likelihood that other representatives would lend assistance to underrepresented citizens of Illinois?

4. The malapportionment in Illinois had a clear urban/rural division. The pattern of maldistribution of representatives generally resulted from the increasingly urban nature of American life through the twentieth century. The malapportionment tended to result from the distribution of representatives on a county-by-county basis. As urban areas grew, the malapportionment of representatives increased. Not surprisingly, rural representatives were unwilling to reapportion their states. Not only were rural constituents likely to be adversely affected by the consolidation of urban political power, but rural elected officials likely would be displaced from their jobs by reapportionment. Should rural interests be protected through independent representation even when the urban population is growing? May a state legitimately choose to represent regional interests on a non-population basis?

5. Consider the broader effects of malapportionment on a range of national policies. One observer remarked that "important secondary effect" of malapportionment was that cities turned to the federal government for solutions because state legislatures wouldn't help them. Anthony Lewis, Legislative Apportionment and the Federal Courts, 71 Harv. L. Rev. 1057, 1065 (1958). In making this point, Lewis quoted Illinois Senator Paul H. Douglas's observation that "those who complain most about Federal encroachment in the affairs of the States are most often the very ones who deny to the urban majorities in their States the opportunity to solve their problems through State action"—almost certainly a reference, given the context, to conservative members of Congress, including Southerners who opposed the Supreme Court's decision in *Brown v. Board of Education*. Id. at 1065 n.44 (internal quotation marks omitted).

Baker v. Carr

369 U.S. 186 (1962).

■ MR. JUSTICE BRENNAN delivered the opinion of the Court.

* * *

The General Assembly of Tennessee consists of the Senate with 33 members and the House of Representatives with 99 members.... [Under the Tennessee Constitution,] Tennessee's standard for allocating legislative representation among her counties is the total number of qualified voters resident in the respective counties, subject only to minor qualifications. Decennial reapportionment in compliance with the constitutional scheme was effected by the General Assembly each decade from 1871 to 1901.... In 1901 the General Assembly abandoned separate enumeration in favor of reliance upon the Federal Census and passed the Apportionment Act here in controversy. In the more than 60 years since that action, all proposals in both Houses of the General Assembly for reapportionment have failed to pass.

Between 1901 and 1961, Tennessee has experienced substantial growth and redistribution of her population. In 1901 the population was 2,020,616, of whom 487,380 were eligible to vote. The 1960 Federal Census reports the State's population at 3,567,089, of whom 2,092,891 are eligible to vote. The relative standings of the counties in terms of qualified voters have changed significantly. It is primarily the continued application of the 1901 Apportionment Act to this shifted and enlarged voting population which gives rise to the present controversy.

[T]he complaint alleges ... that "because of the population changes since 1900, and the failure of the Legislature to reapportion itself since 1901," the 1901 statute became "unconstitutional and obsolete." Appellants also argue that, because of the composition of the legislature effected by the 1901 Apportionment Act, redress in the form of a state constitutional amendment to change the entire mechanism for reapportioning, or any other change short of that, is difficult or impossible.[14] The complaint concludes that "these plaintiffs and others similarly situated, are denied the equal protection of the laws accorded them by the Fourteenth Amendment to the Constitution of the United States by virtue of the debasement of their votes."

* * *

IV

JUSTICIABILITY

In holding that the subject matter of this suit was not justiciable, the District Court relied on Colegrove v. Green, and subsequent per curiam

---

14. The appellants claim that no General Assembly constituted according to the 1901 Act will submit reapportionment proposals either to the people or to a Constitutional Convention. There is no provision for popular initiative in Tennessee. Amendments proposed in the Senate or House must first be approved by a majority of all members of each House and again by two-thirds of the members in the General Assembly next chosen. The proposals are then submitted to the people at the next general election in which a Governor is to be chosen. Alternatively, the legislature may submit to the people at any general election the question of calling a convention to consider specified proposals. Such as are adopted at a convention do not, however, become effective unless approved by a majority of the qualified voters voting separately on each proposed change or amendment at an election fixed by the convention. Conventions shall not be held oftener than once in six years.... [The enabling acts for the most recent conventions] ... provided that delegates ... were to be chosen from the counties and floterial districts just as are members of the State House of Representatives.

cases. . . . We hold that this challenge to an apportionment presents no nonjusticiable "political question." . . .

Of course the mere fact that the suit seeks protection of a political right does not mean it presents a political question. Such an objection "is little more than a play upon words." *Nixon v. Herndon,* 273 U.S. 536, 540. Rather, it is argued that apportionment cases, whatever the actual wording of the complaint, can involve no federal constitutional right except one resting on the guaranty of a republican form of government, and that complaints based on that clause have been held to present political questions which are nonjusticiable.

We hold that the claim pleaded here neither rests upon nor implicates the Guaranty Clause and that its justiciability is therefore not foreclosed by our decisions of cases involving that clause.

* * *

[. . . I]n the Guaranty Clause cases and in the other "political question" cases, it is the relationship between the judiciary and the coordinate branches of the Federal Government, and not the federal judiciary's relationship to the States, which gives rise to the "political question."

We have said that "In determining whether a question falls within [the political question] category, the appropriateness under our system of government of attributing finality to the action of the political departments and also the lack of satisfactory criteria for a judicial determination are dominant considerations." The nonjusticiability of a political question is primarily a function of the separation of powers.

* * *

It is apparent that several formulations which vary slightly according to the settings in which the questions arise may describe a political question, although each has one or more elements which identify it as essentially a function of the separation of powers. Prominent on the surface of any case held to involve a political question is found a textually demonstrable constitutional commitment of the issue to a coordinate political department; or a lack of judicially discoverable and manageable standards for resolving it; or the impossibility of deciding without an initial policy determination of a kind clearly for nonjudicial discretion; or the impossibility of a court's undertaking independent resolution without expressing lack of the respect due coordinate branches of government; or an unusual need for unquestioning adherence to a political decision already made; or the potentiality of embarrassment from multifarious pronouncements by various departments on one question.

Unless one of these formulations is inextricable from the case at bar, there should be no dismissal for nonjusticiability on the ground of a political question's presence. The doctrine of which we treat is one of "political questions," not one of "political cases." . . .

[Although] it is argued that this case shares the characteristics of . . . cases concerning the Constitution's guaranty, in Art. IV, § 4, of a republican form of government [. . . we believe] that the nonjusticiability of such claims has nothing to do with their touching upon matters of state governmental organization.

* * *

The question here is the consistency of state action with the Federal Constitution. We have no question decided, or to be decided, by a political branch of government coequal with this Court. Nor do we risk embarrassment of our government abroad, or grave disturbance at home if we take issue with Tennessee as to the constitutionality of her action here challenged. Nor need the appellants, in order to succeed in this action, ask the Court to enter upon policy determinations for which judicially manageable standards are lacking. Judicial standards under the Equal Protection Clause are well developed and familiar, and it has been open to courts since the enactment of the Fourteenth Amendment to determine, if on the particular facts they must, that a discrimination reflects no policy, but simply arbitrary and capricious action.

This case does, in one sense, involve the allocation of political power within a State, and the appellants might conceivably have added a claim under the Guaranty Clause. Of course . . . any reliance on that clause would be futile. But because any reliance on the Guaranty Clause could not have succeeded it does not follow that appellants may not be heard on the equal protection claim which in fact they tender. True, it must be clear that the Fourteenth Amendment claim is not so enmeshed with those political question elements which render Guaranty Clause claims nonjusticiable as actually to present a political question itself. But we have found that not to be the case here.

* * *

When challenges to state action respecting matters of "the administration of the affairs of the State and the officers through whom they are conducted" have rested on claims of constitutional deprivation which are amenable to judicial correction, this Court has acted upon its view of the merits of the claim. For example, . . . only last Term, in *Gomillion v. Lightfoot,* we applied the Fifteenth Amendment to strike down a redrafting of municipal boundaries which effected a discriminatory impairment of voting rights, in the face of what a majority of the Court of Appeals thought to be a sweeping commitment to state legislatures of the power to draw and redraw such boundaries.

* * *

We conclude that the complaint's allegations of a denial of equal protection present a justiciable constitutional cause of action upon which appellants are entitled to a trial and a decision. The right asserted is within the reach of judicial protection under the Fourteenth Amendment.

The judgment of the District Court is reversed and the cause is remanded for further proceedings consistent with this opinion.

■ MR. JUSTICE DOUGLAS, concurring.

[Omitted]

■ MR. JUSTICE CLARK, concurring.

One emerging from the rash of opinions with their accompanying clashing of views may well find himself suffering a mental blindness. The Court holds that the appellants have alleged a cause of action. However, it refuses to award relief here—although the facts are undisputed—and fails to give the District Court any guidance whatever.

* * *

II

The controlling facts cannot be disputed. It appears from the record that 37% of the voters of Tennessee elect 20 of the 33 Senators while 40% of the voters elect 63 of the 99 members of the House. But this might not on its face be an "invidious discrimination," for a statutory discrimination will not be set aside if any state of facts reasonably may be conceived to justify it.

[... T]he root of the trouble is not in Tennessee's Constitution, for admittedly its policy has not been followed. The discrimination lies in the action of Tennessee's Assembly in allocating legislative seats to counties or districts created by it. Try as one may, Tennessee's apportionment just cannot be made to fit the pattern cut by its Constitution.... The frequency and magnitude of the inequalities in the present districting admit of no policy whatever.... [T]he apportionment picture in Tennessee is a topsy-turvical of gigantic proportions. This is not to say that some of the disparity cannot be explained, but when the entire [system] is examined—comparing the voting strength of counties of like population as well as contrasting that of the smaller with the larger counties—it leaves but one conclusion, namely that Tennessee's apportionment is a crazy quilt without rational basis....

As is admitted, there is a wide disparity of voting strength between the large and small counties. Some samples are: Moore County has a total representation of two with a population (2,340) of only one-eleventh of Rutherford County (25,316) with the same representation; Decatur County (5,563) has the same representation as Carter (23,303) though the latter has four times the population; likewise, Loudon County (13,264), Houston

(3,084), and Anderson County (33,990) have the same representation, *i. e.*, 1.25 each.

* * *

The truth is that—although this case has been here for two years and has had over six hours' argument (three times the ordinary case) and has been most carefully considered over and over again by us in Conference and individually—no one, not even the State nor the dissenters, has come up with any rational basis for Tennessee's apportionment statute.

No one ... contends that mathematical equality among voters is required by the Equal Protection Clause. But certainly there must be some rational design to a State's districting. The discrimination here does not fit any pattern—as I have said, it is but a crazy quilt.

* * *

III

Although I find the Tennessee apportionment statute offends the Equal Protection Clause, I would not consider intervention by this Court into so delicate a field if there were any other relief available to the people of Tennessee. But the majority of the people of Tennessee have no "practical opportunities for exerting their political weight at the polls" to correct the existing "invidious discrimination." Tennessee has no initiative and referendum. I have searched diligently for other "practical opportunities" present under the law. I find none other than through the federal courts. The majority of the voters have been caught up in a legislative strait jacket. Tennessee has an "informed, civically militant electorate" and "an aroused popular conscience," but it does not sear "the conscience of the people's representatives." This is because the legislative policy has riveted the present seats in the Assembly to their respective constituencies, and by the votes of their incumbents a reapportionment of any kind is prevented. The people have been rebuffed at the hands of the Assembly; they have tried the constitutional convention route, but since the call must originate in the Assembly it, too, has been fruitless. They have tried Tennessee courts with the same result, and Governors have fought the tide only to flounder. It is said that there is recourse in Congress and perhaps that may be, but from a practical standpoint this is without substance. To date Congress has never undertaken such a task in any State. We therefore must conclude that the people of Tennessee are stymied and without judicial intervention will be saddled with the present discrimination in the affairs of their state government.

IV

* * *

In view of all this background I doubt if anything more can be offered or will be gained by the State on remand, other than time. Nevertheless, not being able to muster a court to dispose of the case on the merits, I concur in the opinion of the majority and acquiesce in the decision to remand. However, in fairness I do think that Tennessee is entitled to have my idea of what it faces on the record before us and the trial court some light as to how it might proceed.

* * *

■ MR. JUSTICE STEWART, concurring.

The separate writings of my dissenting and concurring Brothers stray so far from the subject of today's decision as to convey, I think, a distressingly inaccurate impression of what the Court decides. For that reason, I think it appropriate, in joining the opinion of the Court, to emphasize in a few words what the opinion does and does not say.

* * *

The complaint in this case asserts that Tennessee's system of apportionment is utterly arbitrary—without any possible justification in rationality. The District Court did not reach the merits of that claim, and this Court quite properly expresses no view on the subject. Contrary to the suggestion of my Brother Harlan, the Court does not say or imply that "state legislatures must be so structured as to reflect with approximate equality the voice of every voter." The Court does not say or imply that there is anything in the Federal Constitution "to prevent a State, acting not irrationally, from choosing any electoral legislative structure it thinks best suited to the interests, temper, and customs of its people." And contrary to the suggestion of my Brother Douglas, the Court most assuredly does not decide the question, "may a State weight the vote of one county or one district more heavily than it weights the vote in another?"

* * *

■ MR. JUSTICE FRANKFURTER, whom MR. JUSTICE HARLAN joins, dissenting.

The Court today reverses a uniform course of decision established by a dozen cases, including one by which the very claim now sustained was unanimously rejected only five years ago. The impressive body of rulings thus cast aside reflected the equally uniform course of our political history regarding the relationship between population and legislative representation—a wholly different matter from denial of the franchise to individuals because of race, color, religion or sex. Such a massive repudiation of the experience of our whole past in asserting destructively novel judicial power demands a detailed analysis of the role of this Court in our constitutional scheme. Disregard of inherent limits in the effective exercise of the Court's "judicial power" not only presages the futility of judicial intervention in the essentially political conflict of forces by which the relation between population and representation has time out of mind been and now is determined.

It may well impair the Court's position as the ultimate organ of "the supreme Law of the Land" in that vast range of legal problems, often strongly entangled in popular feeling, on which this Court must pronounce. The Court's authority—possessed of neither the purse nor the sword—ultimately rests on sustained public confidence in its moral sanction. Such feeling must be nourished by the Court's complete detachment, in fact and in appearance, from political entanglements and by abstention from injecting itself into the clash of political forces in political settlements.

* * *

We were soothingly told at the bar of this Court that we need not worry about the kind of remedy a court could effectively fashion once the abstract constitutional right to have courts pass on a state-wide system of electoral districting is recognized as a matter of judicial rhetoric, because legislatures would heed the Court's admonition. This is not only a euphoric hope. It implies a sorry confession of judicial impotence in place of a frank acknowledgment that there is not under our Constitution a judicial remedy for every political mischief, for every undesirable exercise of legislative power. The Framers carefully and with deliberate forethought refused so to enthrone the judiciary. In this situation, as in others of like nature, appeal for relief does not belong here. Appeal must be to an informed, civically militant electorate. In a democratic society like ours, relief must come through an aroused popular conscience that sears the conscience of the people's representatives. In any event there is nothing judicially more unseemly nor more self-defeating than for this Court to make in terrorem pronouncements, to indulge in merely empty rhetoric, sounding a word of promise to the ear, sure to be disappointing to the hope.

* * *

II

* * *

The Court has been particularly unwilling to intervene in matters concerning the structure and organization of the political institutions of the States. The abstention from judicial entry into such areas has been greater even than that which marks the Court's ordinary approach to issues of state power challenged under broad federal guarantees....

The cases involving Negro disfranchisement are no exception to the principle of avoiding federal judicial intervention into matters of state government in the absence of an explicit and clear constitutional imperative. For here the controlling command of Supreme Law is plain and unequivocal. An end of discrimination against the Negro was the compelling motive of the Civil War Amendments. The Fifteenth expresses this in terms, and it is no less true of the Equal Protection Clause of the Fourteenth.

* * *

The influence of these converging considerations—the caution not to undertake decision where standards meet for judicial judgment are lacking, the reluctance to interfere with matters of state government in the absence of an unquestionable and effectively enforceable mandate, the unwillingness to make courts arbiters of the broad issues of political organization historically committed to other institutions and for whose adjustment the judicial process is ill-adapted—has been decisive of the settled line of cases, reaching back more than a century, which holds that Art. IV, § 4, of the Constitution, guaranteeing to the States "a Republican Form of Government," is not enforceable through the courts.

* * *

III

The present case involves all of the elements that have made the Guarantee Clause cases non-justiciable. It is, in effect, a Guarantee Clause claim masquerading under a different label. But it cannot make the case more fit for judicial action that appellants invoke the Fourteenth Amendment rather than Art. IV, § 4, where, in fact, the gist of their complaint is the same—unless it can be found that the Fourteenth Amendment speaks with greater particularity to their situation.

* * *

Appellants invoke the right to vote and to have their votes counted. But they are permitted to vote and their votes are counted. They go to the polls, they cast their ballots, they send their representatives to the state councils. Their complaint is simply that the representatives are not sufficiently numerous or powerful—in short, that Tennessee has adopted a basis of representation with which they are dissatisfied. Talk of "debasement" or "dilution" is circular talk. One cannot speak of "debasement" or "dilution" of the value of a vote until there is first defined a standard of reference as to what a vote should be worth. What is actually asked of the Court in this case is to choose among competing bases of representation—ultimately, really, among competing theories of political philosophy—in order to establish an appropriate frame of government for the State of Tennessee and thereby for all the States of the Union.

In such a matter, abstract analogies which ignore the facts of history deal in unrealities; they betray reason. This is not a case in which a State has, through a device however oblique and sophisticated, denied Negroes or Jews or redheaded persons a vote, or given them only a third or a sixth of a vote.... What Tennessee illustrates is an old and still widespread method of representation—representation by local geographical division, only in part respective of population—in preference to others, others, forsooth, more appealing.

* * *

The notion that representation proportioned to the geographic spread of population is so universally accepted as a necessary element of equality between man and man that it must be taken to be the standard of a political equality preserved by the Fourteenth Amendment—that it is, in appellants' words "the basic principle of representative government"—is, to put it bluntly, not true. However desirable and however desired by some among the great political thinkers and framers of our government, it has never been generally practiced, today or in the past. It was not the English system, it was not the colonial system, it was not the system chosen for the national government by the Constitution, it was not the system exclusively or even predominantly practiced by the States at the time of adoption of the Fourteenth Amendment, it is not predominantly practiced by the States today. Unless judges, the judges of this Court, are to make their private views of political wisdom the measure of the Constitution—views which in all honesty cannot but give the appearance, if not reflect the reality, of involvement with the business of partisan politics so inescapably a part of apportionment controversies—the Fourteenth Amendment, "itself a historical product," ... provides no guide for judicial oversight of the representation problem.

* * *

Detailed recent studies are available to describe the present-day constitutional and statutory status of apportionment in the fifty States. They demonstrate a decided twentieth-century trend away from population as the exclusive base of representation. Today, only a dozen state constitutions provide for periodic legislative reapportionment of both houses by a substantially unqualified application of the population standard, and only about a dozen more prescribe such reapportionment for even a single chamber. "Specific provision for county representation in at least one house of the state legislature has been increasingly adopted since the end of the 19th century ..." More than twenty States now guarantee each county at least one seat in one of their houses regardless of population, and in nine others county or town units are given equal representation in one legislative branch, whatever the number of each unit's inhabitants. Of course, numerically considered, "These provisions invariably result in over-representation of the least populated areas...." And in an effort to curb the political dominance of metropolitan regions, at least ten States now limit the maximum entitlement of any single county (or, in some cases, city) to one legislative house—another source of substantial numerical disproportion.

* * *

The stark fact is that if among the numerous widely varying principles and practices that control state legislative apportionment today there is any generally prevailing feature, that feature is geographic inequality in relation to the population standard. Examples could be endlessly multiplied. In New Jersey, counties of thirty-five thousand and of more than nine hundred and five thousand inhabitants respectively each have a single senator. Representative districts in Minnesota range from 7,290 inhabitants to 107,246 inhabitants. Ratios of senatorial representation in California vary as much as two hundred and ninety-seven to one. In Oklahoma, the range is ten to one for House constituencies and roughly sixteen to one for Senate constituencies. Colebrook, Connecticut—population 592—elects two House representatives; Hartford—population 177,397—also elects two. The first, third and fifth of these examples are the products of constitutional provisions which subordinate population to regional considerations in apportionment; the second is the result of legislative inaction; the fourth derives from both constitutional and legislative sources. A survey made in 1955, in sum, reveals that less than thirty percent of the population inhabit districts sufficient to elect a House majority in thirteen States and a Senate majority in nineteen States. These figures show more than individual variations from a generally accepted standard of electoral equality. They show that there is not—as there has never been—a standard by which the place of equality as a factor in apportionment can be measured.

Manifestly, the Equal Protection Clause supplies no clearer guide for judicial examination of apportionment methods than would the Guarantee Clause itself. Apportionment, by its character, is a subject of extraordinary complexity, involving—even after the fundamental theoretical issues concerning what is to be represented in a representative legislature have been fought out or compromised—considerations of geography, demography, electoral convenience, economic and social cohesions or divergencies among particular local groups, communications, the practical effects of political institutions like the lobby and the city machine, ancient traditions and ties of settled usage, respect for proven incumbents of long experience and senior status, mathematical mechanics, censuses compiling relevant data, and a host of others. Legislative responses throughout the country to the reapportionment demands of the 1960 Census have glaringly confirmed that these are not factors that lend themselves to evaluations of a nature that are the staple of judicial determinations or for which judges are equipped to adjudicate by legal training or experience or native wit. And this is the more so true because in every strand of this complicated, intricate web of values meet the contending forces of partisan politics. The practical significance of apportionment is that the next election results may differ because of it. Apportionment battles are overwhelmingly party or intra-party contests. It will add a virulent source of friction and tension in federal-state relations to embroil the federal judiciary in them.

* * *

Dissenting opinion of MR. JUSTICE HARLAN, whom MR. JUSTICE FRANKFURT-ER joins.

* * *

II

The claim that Tennessee's system of apportionment is so unreasonable as to amount to a capricious classification of voting strength [fails] under dispassionate analysis.

* * *

What ... is the basis for the claim made in this case that the distribution of state senators and representatives is the product of capriciousness or of some constitutionally prohibited policy? It is not that Tennessee has arranged its electoral districts with a deliberate purpose to dilute the voting strength of one race ... or that some religious group is intentionally underrepresented. Nor is it a charge that the legislature has indulged in sheer caprice by allotting representatives to each county on the basis of a throw of the dice, or of some other determinant bearing no rational relation to the question of apportionment. Rather, the claim is that the State Legislature has unreasonably retained substantially the same allocation of senators and representatives as was established by statute in 1901, refusing to recognize the great shift in the population balance between urban and rural communities that has occurred in the meantime.

* * *

A Federal District Court is asked to say that the passage of time has rendered the 1901 apportionment obsolete to the point where its continuance becomes vulnerable under the Fourteenth Amendment. But is not this matter one that involves a classic legislative judgment? Surely it lies within the province of a state legislature to conclude that an existing allocation of senators and representatives constitutes a desirable balance of geographical and demographical representation, or that in the interest of stability of government it would be best to defer for some further time the redistribution of seats in the state legislature.

Indeed, I would hardly think it unconstitutional if a state legislature's expressed reason for establishing or maintaining an electoral imbalance between its rural and urban population were to protect the State's agricultural interests from the sheer weight of numbers of those residing in its cities. A State may, after all, take account of the interests of its rural population in the distribution of tax burdens, ... and recognition of the special problems of agricultural interests has repeatedly been reflected in federal legislation.... Does the Fourteenth Amendment impose a stricter limitation upon a State's apportionment of political representatives to its central government? I think not. These are matters of local policy, on the wisdom of which the federal judiciary is neither permitted nor qualified to sit in judgment.

* * *

These conclusions can hardly be escaped by suggesting that capricious state action might be found were it to appear that a majority of the Tennessee legislators, in refusing to consider reapportionment, had been actuated by self-interest in perpetuating their own political offices or by other unworthy or improper motives. Since *Fletcher v. Peck*, [6 Cranch 87, 3 L.Ed. 162 (1810)], was decided many years ago, it has repeatedly been pointed out that it is not the business of the federal courts to inquire into the personal motives of legislators.

* * *

NOTES AND QUESTIONS

1. Between *Colegrove* and *Baker*, the primary issues concerning whether malapportionment stated a cognizable cause of action had largely boiled down to a dispute over the manageability of a constitutional standard for evaluating apportionment systems. Although Justice Brennan is confident that there are no manageability problems in administering judicial review, *Baker* is curiously silent as to the exact contours of what courts should do. The opinion is far more noteworthy for its declarations of why the political question doctrine should not preclude judicial review than for what the nature of that review would be. The opinion does not respond to Justice Frankfurter's argument in dissent that there are no clear standards by which courts can navigate among the competing concerns present in apportionment.

2. What are the consequences of the Court's decision to rely on the equal protection clause, rather than the guaranty clause? One scholar has pointed out that Justice Brennan's explanation—that there was precedent suggesting the general nonjusticiability of the guaranty clause, while the equal protection clause had long been judicially enforceable—would make more sense if not for the fact that *Colegrove v. Green* was an also absolutely square precedent refusing to entertain malapportionment claims under the Fourteenth Amendment. If the Court had to overrule some precedent to review apportionment and the refusal to reapportion, why was overruling Fourteenth Amendment precedent—ultimately to develop a unique set of equal protection principles that apply nowhere else in constitutional law— better than addressing the problem as a matter of governmental structure? Perhaps the guaranty clause, which focuses on the structure of government, rather than individual rights, would have offered a better way of addressing the problem the Court identified. *See* Pamela S. Karlan, *Politics By Other Means*, 85 Va. L. Rev. 1697, 1717–18 (1999).

Judge Michael W. McConnell has also argued that the Court should have used the guaranty clause. In picking the equal protection clause, "the Court adopted a legal theory for addressing the issue that was wrong in principle and mischievous in its consequences. More careful attention to constitutional text and history would have produced a better solution." Michael W. McConnell, *The Redistricting Cases: Original Mistakes and Current Consequences*, 24 Harv. J.L. & Pub. Pol'y 103, 103 (2000):

> A districting scheme so malapportioned that a minority faction is in complete control, without regard to democratic sentiment, violates the basic norms of republican government. It would thus appear to raise a constitutional question under Article IV, Section 4, which states that "the United States shall guarantee to every State in this Union a Republican Form of Government." Constitutional standards under the Republican Form of Government Clause are ill-developed, but surely a government is not "republican" if a minority faction maintains control, and the majority has no means of overturning it.

> As of the early 1960s, however, Supreme Court precedent held that constitutional challenges based on the Republican Form of Government Clause present nonjusticiable "political questions." The basis for that holding was that the Clause does not provide "judicially manageable standards." Rather than addressing that dubious proposition directly, the Court side-stepped the issue by treating the case as arising under the Equal Protection Clause rather than the Republican Form of Government Clause. According to the Court, "judicial standards under the Equal Protection Clause are well developed and familiar," and thus do not present justiciability problems.

> As an interpretation of the political question doctrine, this was nonsense. At the time of *Baker*, the Equal Protection Clause had never been applied to the districting question, and there were any number of possible interpretations, with no judicially manageable means of choosing among them.... Conversely, if the Court were inclined to develop judicially manageable standards under the Equal Protection Clause, it could do so equally well under the Republican Form of Government Clause. The existence vel non of "judicially manageable standards" was inherent in the underlying issue, not in the constitutional label attached to it. Thus, it is hard to avoid the conclusion that the fateful decision to shift ground to equal protection was made for no reason other than to avoid the appearance of a departure from the nonjusticiability precedents.

> This was the worst of both worlds. The equal protection approach compounded the justiciability problem with a doctrinal problem. Not only did the Court find itself in the political thicket, as the dissenters warned, but also it was using the wrong tools to get out....

> Had the litigation proceeded under the Republican Form of Government Clause, it would have been quite different. The gravamen of a

> Republican Form of Government challenge is not that individual voters are treated unequally, but that the districting scheme systematically prevents effective majority rule. There are many systems of representation that would satisfy the Republicanism requirement. But at a minimum, the Clause must mean that a majority of the whole body of the people ultimately governs.

Id. at 105–07. Judge McConnell suggests a series of unintended consequences of the reliance on the equal protection clause that culminated in the aggressive political gerrymandering of the 1980's and 1990's discussed in Chapter 10. He suggests that these problems would be more tractable under a guaranty clause regime:

> One further implication of the Republican Form of Government theory should be noted. From the point of view of equal protection, partisan and racial gerrymandering appear to be two species of the same problem, with racial gerrymandering being the worse (since classification along racial lines is closest to the core concerns of the Fourteenth Amendment). From a Republicanism perspective, however, the two phenomena are distinguishable, and racial gerrymandering, if done for the purpose of bringing minority voting strength closer to what it would be under a system of proportional representation, is doctrinally unobjectionable. Partisan gerrymandering is designed to entrench a particular political faction against effective political challenge—sometimes even to give a political minority effective control. That is in obvious tension with the values of Republicanism. Racial gerrymanders of the sort we have seen in recent years, by contrast, do not threaten ultimate majority rule. To be sure, they have other consequences that may well be deemed undesirable—such as the exacerbation of racial polarization in elections—but they are not unrepublican. As long as the majority retains effective control, it is consistent with Republicanism for the majority to give greater influence to minority voices that would otherwise be submerged.

> Adopting the Republican Form of Government Clause and abandoning the Equal Protection Clause as the basis for evaluating electoral districting would thus be a practical and judicially manageable means of curbing gerrymandering abuses of all kinds, and it would put an end to the embarrassingly standardless line of cases that began with *Shaw v. Reno.*

Id. at 116.

3. *Baker* was perhaps the most profoundly destabilizing opinion in the Supreme Court's history. The patterns of malapportionment found in Tennessee were prevalent throughout the country. Within nine months of the Court's opinion in *Baker*, litigation was underway in 34 states challenging the constitutionality of state legislative apportionment schemes. *Reynolds v. Sims*, 377 U.S. 533, 556 n.30 (1964). The importance of *Baker* was quite apparent at the time. For example, in an interview conducted just before his retirement, Chief Justice Earl Warren explained that apportionment "is perhaps the most important issue we have had before the Supreme Court. If everyone in this country has the opportunity to participate on equal terms with everyone else and can share in electing representatives who will be representative of the entire community and not of some special interest, then most of these problems that we are now confronted with would be solved through the political process rather than through the courts." N.Y. Times, June 26, 1969 (city ed.), at 17, cols. 4,6,7.

4. Justice Clark in *Baker* offers alternative grounds for judicial intervention based upon process failure. His argument is that the prospect for political resolution of malapportionment, introduced by Justice Frankfurter in *Colegrove*, had effectively collapsed. He viewed the political system in Tennessee as essentially hostage to a self-interested political faction powerful enough to resist all legislative efforts at change. This form of political process failure resonates in the language of the *Carolene Products* footnote's rationale for judicial intervention. *United States v. Carolene Products,* 304 U.S. 144, 152 n.4 (1938). The famous *Carolene Products* footnote is generally remembered for its articulation of a theory of why judicial review needs be more exacting to combat "prejudice against discrete and insular minorities . . . which tends seriously to curtail the operation of the political processes ordinarily to be relied upon to protect minorities." However, the same footnote identified a broader rationale for judicial intervention in cases of what may be termed political process failure. Accordingly, court oversight is mandated not only where the political process might be infected by prejudice but also in the face of challenges to laws that "restrict[] those political processes which can ordinarily be expected to bring about repeal of undesirable legislation." This insight, in turn, draws from the concerns expressed by James Madison in The Federalist Papers of the need to provide mechanisms to check the effects of factionalism in the political process. *See* The Federalist No. 10 (James Madison). Does this provide a sounder basis for judicial intervention?

If the political process succumbs to capture by a self-interested faction, then a "process-failure" argument may be called upon to justify judicial intervention. Voting rights are therefore an arena in which deference to the legislative design is improper. On this view, voting cases "involve rights (1) that are essential to the democratic process and (2) whose dimensions cannot safely be left to our elected representatives, who have an obvious vested interest in the status quo." John Hart Ely, Democracy and Distrust 117 (1980). For example, Professor Michael Klarman argues that, "[i]t is difficult to imagine a more compelling case for judicial intervention on political process grounds than *Baker v. Carr*; Tennessee legislators had proven fiercely resistant to reapportioning themselves out of a job, and even a 'civically militant electorate' was not about to budge them." Michael J. Klarman, *The Puzzling Resistance to Political Process Theory,* 77 Va. L. Rev. 747, 757–58 (1991)(quoting *Baker,* 369 U.S. at 270 (Frankfurter, J., dissenting)).

Reynolds v. Sims

377 U.S. 533 (1964).

■ MR. CHIEF JUSTICE WARREN delivered the opinion of the Court.

* * *

Plaintiffs below alleged that the last apportionment of the Alabama Legislature was based on the 1900 federal census, despite the requirement of the State Constitution that the legislature be reapportioned decennially. They asserted that, since the population growth in the State from 1900 to 1960 had been uneven, Jefferson and other counties were now victims of serious discrimination with respect to the allocation of legislative representation. As a result of the failure of the legislature to reapportion itself, plaintiffs asserted, they were denied "equal suffrage in free and equal elections ... and the equal protection of the laws" in violation of the Alabama Constitution and the Fourteenth Amendment to the Federal Constitution. The complaint asserted that plaintiffs had no other adequate remedy, and that they had exhausted all forms of relief other than that available through the federal courts. They alleged that the Alabama Legislature had established a pattern of prolonged inaction from 1911 to the present which "clearly demonstrates that no reapportionment ... shall be effected"; that representation at any future constitutional convention would be established by the legislature, making it unlikely that the membership of any such convention would be fairly representative; and that, while the Alabama Supreme Court had found that the legislature had not complied with the State Constitution in failing to reapportion according to population decennially, that court had nevertheless indicated that it would not interfere with matters of legislative reapportionment.

* * *

III

A predominant consideration in determining whether a State's legislative apportionment scheme constitutes an invidious discrimination violative of rights asserted under the Equal Protection Clause is that the rights allegedly impaired are individual and personal in nature.... "[T]he right to vote is personal...." While the result of a court decision in a state legislative apportionment controversy may be to require the restructuring of the geographical distribution of seats in a state legislature, the judicial focus must be concentrated upon ascertaining whether there has been any discrimination against certain of the State's citizens which constitutes an impermissible impairment of their constitutionally protected right to vote.... Undoubtedly, the right of suffrage is a fundamental matter in a free and democratic society. Especially since the right to exercise the franchise in a free and unimpaired manner is preservative of other basic civil and political rights, any alleged infringement of the right of citizens to vote must be carefully and meticulously scrutinized....

Legislators represent people, not trees or acres. Legislators are elected by voters, not farms or cities or economic interests. As long as ours is a representative form of government, and our legislatures are those instruments of government elected directly by and directly representative of the people, the right to elect legislators in a free and unimpaired fashion is a bedrock of our political system. It could hardly be gainsaid that a constitutional claim had been asserted by an allegation that certain otherwise qualified voters had been entirely prohibited from voting for members of their state legislature. And, if a State should provide that the votes of citizens in one part of the State should be given two times, or five times, or 10 times the weight of votes of citizens in another part of the State, it could hardly be contended that the right to vote of those residing in the disfavored areas had not been effectively diluted. It would appear extraordinary to suggest that a State could be constitutionally permitted to enact a law providing that certain of the State's voters could vote two, five, or 10 times for their legislative representatives, while voters living elsewhere could vote only once. And it is inconceivable that a state law to the effect that, in counting votes for legislators, the votes of citizens in one part of the State would be multiplied by two, five, or 10, while the votes of persons in another area would be counted only at face value, could be constitutionally sustainable. Of course, the effect of state legislative districting schemes which give the same number of representatives to unequal numbers of constituents is identical. Overweighting and overvaluation of the votes of those living here has the certain effect of dilution and undervaluation of the votes of those living there. The resulting discrimination against those individual voters living in disfavored areas is easily demonstrable mathematically. Their right to vote is simply not the same right to vote as that of those living in a favored part of the State. Two, five, or 10 of them must vote before the effect of their voting is equivalent to that of their favored neighbor. Weighting the votes of citizens differently, by any method or means, merely because of where they happen to reside, hardly seems justifiable. One must be ever aware that the Constitution forbids "sophisticated as well as simple-minded modes of discrimination." *Lane v. Wilson*, 307 U.S. 268, 275; *Gomillion v. Lightfoot*, 364 U.S. 339, 342....

State legislatures are, historically, the fountainhead of representative government in this country.... But representative government is in essence self-government through the medium of elected representatives of the people, and each and every citizen has an inalienable right to full and effective participation in the political processes of his State's legislative bodies. Most citizens can achieve this participation only as qualified voters through the election of legislators to represent them. Full and effective participation by all citizens in state government requires, therefore, that each citizen have an equally effective voice in the election of members of his state legislature. Modern and viable state government needs, and the Constitution demands, no less.

Logically, in a society ostensibly grounded on representative government, it would seem reasonable that a majority of the people of a State could elect a majority of that State's legislators. To conclude differently, and to sanction minority control of state legislative bodies, would appear to deny majority rights in a way that far surpasses any possible denial of minority rights that might otherwise be thought to result. Since legislatures are responsible for enacting laws by which all citizens are to be governed, they should be bodies which are collectively responsive to the popular will. And the concept of equal protection has been traditionally viewed as requiring the uniform treatment of persons standing in the same relation to the governmental action questioned or challenged. With respect to the allocation of legislative representation, all voters, as citizens of a State, stand in the same relation regardless of where they live. Any suggested criteria for the differentiation of citizens are insufficient to justify any discrimination, as to the weight of their votes, unless relevant to the permissible purposes of legislative apportionment. Since the achieving of fair and effective representation for all citizens is concededly the basic aim of legislative apportionment, we conclude that the Equal Protection Clause guarantees the opportunity for equal participation by all voters in the election of state legislators.... Our constitutional system amply provides for the protection of minorities by means other than giving them majority control of state legislatures. And the democratic ideals of equality and majority rule, which have served this Nation so well in the past, are hardly of any less significance for the present and the future.

We are told that the matter of apportioning representation in a state legislature is a complex and many-faceted one. We are advised that States can rationally consider factors other than population in apportioning legislative representation. We are admonished not to restrict the power of the States to impose differing views as to political philosophy on their citizens. We are cautioned about the dangers of entering into political thickets and mathematical quagmires. Our answer is this: a denial of constitutionally protected rights demands judicial protection; our oath and our office require no less of us.... To the extent that a citizen's right to vote is debased, he is that much less a citizen. The fact that an individual lives here or there is not a legitimate reason for overweighting or diluting the efficacy of his vote. The complexions of societies and civilizations change, often with amazing rapidity. A nation once primarily rural in character becomes predominantly urban. Representation schemes once fair and equitable become archaic and outdated. But the basic principle of representative government remains, and must remain, unchanged—the weight of a citizen's vote cannot be made to depend on where he lives. Population is, of necessity, the starting point for consideration and the controlling criterion for judgment in legislative apportionment controversies. A citizen, a qualified voter, is no more nor no less so because he lives in the city or on the farm. This is the clear and strong command of our Constitution's Equal Protection Clause.

* * *

V

* * *

[W]e find the federal analogy inapposite and irrelevant to state legislative districting schemes. . . .

The system of representation in the two Houses of the Federal Congress is one ingrained in our Constitution, as part of the law of the land. It is one conceived out of compromise and concession indispensable to the establishment of our federal republic. Arising from unique historical circumstances, it is based on the consideration that in establishing our type of federalism a group of formerly independent States bound themselves together under one national government. Admittedly, the original 13 States surrendered some of their sovereignty in agreeing to join together "to form a more perfect Union." But at the heart of our constitutional system remains the concept of separate and distinct governmental entities which have delegated some, but not all, of their formerly held powers to the single national government. The fact that almost three-fourths of our present States were never in fact independently sovereign does not detract from our view that the so-called federal analogy is inapplicable as a sustaining precedent for state legislative apportionments. The developing history and growth of our republic cannot cloud the fact that, at the time of the inception of the system of representation in the Federal Congress, a compromise between the larger and smaller States on this matter averted a deadlock in the Constitutional Convention which had threatened to abort the birth of our Nation.

* * *

Political subdivisions of States—counties, cities, or whatever—never were and never have been considered as sovereign entities. Rather, they have been traditionally regarded as subordinate governmental instrumentalities created by the State to assist in the carrying out of state governmental functions.

* * *

Thus, we conclude that the plan contained in the 67–Senator Amendment for apportioning seats in the Alabama Legislature cannot be sustained by recourse to the so-called federal analogy. Nor can any other inequitable state legislative apportionment scheme be justified on such an asserted basis. This does not necessarily mean that such a plan is irrational or involves something other than a "republican form of government." We conclude simply that such a plan is impermissible for the States under the

Equal Protection Clause, since perforce resulting, in virtually every case, in submergence of the equal population principle in at least one house of a state legislature. Since we find the so-called federal analogy inapposite to a consideration of the constitutional validity of state legislative apportionment schemes, we necessarily hold that the Equal Protection Clause requires both houses of a state legislature to be apportioned on a population basis.

* * *

VI

By holding that as a federal constitutional requisite both houses of a state legislature must be apportioned on a population basis, we mean that the Equal Protection Clause requires that a State make an honest and good faith effort to construct districts, in both houses of its legislature, as nearly of equal population as is practicable. We realize that it is a practical impossibility to arrange legislative districts so that each one has an identical number of residents, or citizens, or voters. Mathematical exactness or precision is hardly a workable constitutional requirement.

In *Wesberry v. Sanders*, the Court stated that congressional representation must be based on population as nearly as is practicable. In implementing the basic constitutional principle of representative government as enunciated by the Court in *Wesberry*—equality of population among districts—some distinctions may well be made between congressional and state legislative representation. Since, almost invariably, there is a significantly larger number of seats in state legislative bodies to be distributed within a State than congressional seats, it may be feasible to use political subdivision lines to a greater extent in establishing state legislative districts than in congressional districting while still affording adequate representation to all parts of the State. To do so would be constitutionally valid, so long as the resulting apportionment was one based substantially on population and the equal-population principle was not diluted in any significant way. . . .

A State may legitimately desire to maintain the integrity of various political subdivisions, insofar as possible, and provide for compact districts of contiguous territory in designing a legislative apportionment scheme. Valid considerations may underlie such aims. Indiscriminate districting, without any regard for political subdivision or natural or historical boundary lines, may be little more than an open invitation to partisan gerrymandering. Single-member districts may be the rule in one State, while another State might desire to achieve some flexibility by creating multimember or floterial districts. Whatever the means of accomplishment, the overriding objective must be substantial equality of population among the various districts, so that the vote of any citizen is approximately equal in weight to that of any other citizen in the State.

History indicates, however, that many States have deviated, to a greater or lesser degree, from the equal-population principle in the apportionment of seats in at least one house of their legislatures. So long as the divergences from a strict population standard are based on legitimate considerations incident to the effectuation of a rational state policy, some deviations from the equal-population principle are constitutionally permissible with respect to the apportionment of seats in either or both of the two houses of a bicameral state legislature. But neither history alone, nor economic or other sorts of group interests, are permissible factors in attempting to justify disparities from population-based representation. Citizens, not history or economic interests, cast votes. Considerations of area alone provide an insufficient justification for deviations from the equal-population principle. Again, people, not land or trees or pastures, vote. Modern developments and improvements in transportation and communications make rather hollow, in the mid–1960's, most claims that deviations from population-based representation can validly be based solely on geographical considerations. Arguments for allowing such deviations in order to insure effective representation for sparsely settled areas and to prevent legislative districts from becoming so large that the availability of access of citizens to their representatives is impaired are today, for the most part, unconvincing.

A consideration that appears to be of more substance in justifying some deviations from population-based representation in state legislatures is that of insuring some voice to political subdivisions, as political subdivisions. Several factors make more than insubstantial claims that a State can rationally consider according political subdivisions some independent representation in at least one body of the state legislature, as long as the basic standard of equality of population among districts is maintained. Local governmental entities are frequently charged with various responsibilities incident to the operation of state government. In many States much of the legislature's activity involves the enactment of so-called local legislation, directed only to the concerns of particular political subdivisions. And a State may legitimately desire to construct districts along political subdivision lines to deter the possibilities of gerrymandering. However, permitting deviations from population-based representation does not mean that each local governmental unit or political subdivision can be given separate representation, regardless of population. Carried too far, a scheme of giving at least one seat in one house to each political subdivision (for example, to each county) could easily result, in many States, in a total subversion of the equal-population principle in that legislative body.

■ Mr. Justice Harlan, dissenting.

* * *

Preliminary Statement

Today's holding is that the Equal Protection Clause of the Fourteenth Amendment requires every State to structure its legislature so that all the members of each house represent substantially the same number of people; other factors may be given play only to the extent that they do not significantly encroach on this basic "population" principle. Whatever may be thought of this holding as a piece of political ideology—and even on that score the political history and practices of this country from its earliest beginnings leave wide room for debate . . .—I think it demonstrable that the Fourteenth Amendment does not impose this political tenet on the States or authorize this Court to do so.

The Court's constitutional discussion . . . is remarkable . . . for its failure to address itself at all to the Fourteenth Amendment as a whole or to the legislative history of the Amendment pertinent to the matter at hand. Stripped of aphorisms, the Court's argument boils down to the assertion that appellees' right to vote has been invidiously "debased" or "diluted" by systems of apportionment which entitle them to vote for fewer legislators than other voters, an assertion which is tied to the Equal Protection Clause only by the constitutionally frail tautology that "equal" means "equal."

Had the Court paused to probe more deeply into the matter, it would have found that the Equal Protection Clause was never intended to inhibit the States in choosing any democratic method they pleased for the apportionment of their legislatures. This is shown by the language of the Fourteenth Amendment taken as a whole, by the understanding of those who proposed and ratified it, and by the political practices of the States at the time the Amendment was adopted. It is confirmed by numerous state and congressional actions since the adoption of the Fourteenth Amendment, and by the common understanding of the Amendment as evidenced by subsequent constitutional amendments and decisions of this Court before *Baker v. Carr*, made an abrupt break with the past in 1962.

The failure of the Court to consider any of these matters cannot be excused or explained by any concept of "developing" constitutionalism. It is meaningless to speak of constitutional "development" when both the language and history of the controlling provisions of the Constitution are wholly ignored. Since it can, I think, be shown beyond doubt that state legislative apportionments, as such, are wholly free of constitutional limitations, save such as may be imposed by the Republican Form of Government Clause (Const., Art. IV, § 4), the Court's action now bringing them within the purview of the Fourteenth Amendment amounts to nothing less than an exercise of the amending power by this Court.

So far as the Federal Constitution is concerned, the complaints in these cases should all have been dismissed below for failure to state a cause of action, because what has been alleged or proved shows no violation of any constitutional right.

* * *

It should by now be obvious that these cases do not mark the end of reapportionment problems in the courts. Predictions once made that the courts would never have to face the problem of actually working out an apportionment have proved false. This Court, however, continues to avoid the consequences of its decisions, simply assuring us that the lower courts "can and . . . will work out more concrete and specific standards." Deeming it "expedient" not to spell out "precise constitutional tests," the Court contents itself with stating "only a few rather general considerations."

Generalities cannot obscure the cold truth that cases of this type are not amenable to the development of judicial standards. No set of standards can guide a court which has to decide how many legislative districts a State shall have, or what the shape of the districts shall be, or where to draw a particular district line. No judicially manageable standard can determine whether a State should have single-member districts or multimember districts or some combination of both. No such standard can control the balance between keeping up with population shifts and having stable districts. In all these respects, the courts will be called upon to make particular decisions with respect to which a principle of equally populated districts will be of no assistance whatsoever. Quite obviously, there are limitless possibilities for districting consistent with such a principle. Nor can these problems be avoided by judicial reliance on legislative judgments so far as possible. Reshaping or combining one or two districts, or modifying just a few district lines, is no less a matter of choosing among many possible solutions, with varying political consequences, than reapportionment broadside.

The Court ignores all this, saying only that "what is marginally permissible in one State may be unsatisfactory in another, depending on the particular circumstances of the case." It is well to remember that the product of today's decisions will not be readjustment of a few districts in a few States which most glaringly depart from the principle of equally populated districts. It will be a redetermination, extensive in many cases, of legislative districts in all but a few States.

Although the Court—necessarily, as I believe—provides only generalities in elaboration of its main thesis, its opinion nevertheless fully demonstrates how far removed these problems are from fields of judicial competence. Recognizing that "indiscriminate districting" is an invitation to "partisan gerrymandering," the Court nevertheless excludes virtually every basis for the formation of electoral districts other than "indiscriminate districting." In one or another of today's opinions, the Court declares it unconstitutional for a State to give effective consideration to any of the following in establishing legislative districts:

(1) history;

(2) "economic or other sorts of group interests"

(3) area;

(4) geographical considerations;

(5) a desire "to insure effective representation for sparsely settled areas";

(6) "availability of access of citizens to their representatives";

(7) theories of bicameralism (except those approved by the Court);

(8) occupation;

(9) "an attempt to balance urban and rural power"

(10) the preference of a majority of voters in the State

So far as presently appears, the only factor which a State may consider, apart from numbers, is political subdivisions. But even "a clearly rational state policy" recognizing this factor is unconstitutional if "population is submerged as the controlling consideration. . . . "

I know of no principle of logic or practical or theoretical politics, still less any constitutional principle, which establishes all or any of these exclusions. Certain it is that the Court's opinion does not establish them. So far as the Court says anything at all on this score, it says only that "legislators represent people, not trees or acres"; that "citizens, not history or economic interests, cast votes"; that "people, not land or trees or pastures, vote." All this may be conceded. But it is surely equally obvious, and, in the context of elections, more meaningful to note that people are not ciphers and that legislators can represent their electors only by speaking for their interests—economic, social, political—many of which do reflect the place where the electors live. The Court does not establish, or indeed even attempt to make a case for the proposition that conflicting interests within a State can only be adjusted by disregarding them when voters are grouped for purposes of representation.

NOTES AND QUESTIONS

1. *Reynolds* combined with *Wesberry v. Sanders*, 376 U.S. 1 (1964), to introduce the equipopulation principle to the constitutional law of reapportionment. *Reynolds* read the equal protection clause of the Fourteenth Amendment to impose the one-person/one-vote rule on state apportionment for its legislatures. *Wesberry* found a similar equipopulation principle in Art. I, § 2 of the Constitution, which provides:

The House of Representatives shall be composed of Members chosen every second Year by the people of the several States, and the Electors in each States shall have the Qualifications requisite for Electors of the most numerous Branch of the State Legislature.

Justice Harlan's dissent in *Reynolds* challenges the use of either constitutional provision as the basis for imposing the equipopulation rule. Does either source better justify judicial oversight of reapportionment? Should state authorities have greater latitude in departing from the equipopulation rule in congressional or state legislative apportionment?

2. How exacting should the equipopulation standard be? The Supreme Court has set different standards for state legislative and congressional redistricting plans. In the congressional context, the Court has long adhered to the principle that one person's vote be worth "as nearly as practicable" the equal of another's to the extent that a State must "make a good-faith effort to achieve precise mathematical equality." *Kirkpatrick v. Preisler*, 394 U.S. 526 (1969)(striking down "a State's preference for pleasingly shaped districts" that yielded districts up to 3.13 percent above and 2.84 percent below the ideal mathematical distribution of population per district). By contrast, in *Mahan v. Howell*, 410 U.S. 315 (1973), the Court upheld a Virginia state redistricting plan whose maximum percentage deviation from the ideal was 16.4 percent. (The maximum percentage deviation is derived by adding the percentage excess of the largest district above the ideal, in this case 6.8 percent, to the percentage under the ideal of the smallest district, in this case 9.6 percent). The Court, per Justice Rehnquist, seemingly retreated from *Reynolds* to find that the State interest in regional representation justified a broader deviation from the congressional standard. The Court grounded its opinion on a distinction between Article I, § 2 of the Constitution on the one hand, and the Equal Protection Clause on the other, as well as a recognition that: "there is a significantly larger number of seats in state legislative bodies to be distributed within a State than congressional seats, and that therefore it may be feasible for a State to use political subdivision lines to a greater extent in establishing state legislative districts than congressional districts while still affording statewide representation." As a result, the Court concluded that "the legislature's plan for apportionment of the House of Delegates may reasonably be said to advance the rational state policy of respecting the boundaries of political subdivisions." Does either the constitutional text or the policy argument justify a different standard for congressional as opposed to state legislative redistricting?

While congressional districts are increasingly held to a zero deviation standard (*see Karcher v. Daggett, infra*), state legislative plans with maximum population deviations in the vicinity of 10 percent were long considered presumptively valid, while the 16.4 percent figure in *Mahan* "approaches tolerable limits." Curiously, in *Brown v. Thomson*, 462 U.S. 835 (1983), the Court upheld a state legislative redistricting plan with a maximum deviation of 89 percent on the grounds that the complaint challenged only the apportionment of one district, rather than the statewide apportionment scheme. Does it make any sense to speak of a one-person/one-vote challenge to one district when the baseline must of necessity be the statewide apportionment?

Although the ten percent deviations were long treated as a safe harbor, in recent years, courts have struck down some plans that satisfied the ten percent rule on the grounds that the the deviations reflected no legitimate state policy. In *Cox v. Larios*, 542 U.S. 947 (2004), for example, the Supreme Court affirmed a district court judgment striking down a state legislative plan that had a deviation of 9.9 percent on the grounds that the plan reflected "blatantly partisan and discriminatory" attempts to protect Democratic incumbents while undermining Republican-held seats. (We return to this issue in this discussion of political gerrymandering in Chapter 10.)

3. How should population be measured for apportionment purposes? *Reynolds* appears to emphasize both equality of representation and the equal value of the ballot cast by all voters. Unfortunately, the two concepts are not identical. Simply counting persons does not yield equality of voting power to all voters, even were districts to be perfectly equipopulational. There are predictable groups who may not vote, including minors, convicted felons, immigrants. Should communities with large numbers of children be afforded the same amount of representation as those containing primarily senior citizens, even though the likely level of potential voters may be dramatically different? Is there not a paradox in counting voting-ineligible prisoners in maximum security facilities such as Parchman in Mississippi, or Huntsville in Texas, and then using their numbers to enhance the representation of local communities that will be heavily populated by prison guards and their families? Should undocumented aliens be counted among the total population in order to apportion representatives?

In *Burns v. Richardson*, 384 U.S. 73 (1966), the Supreme Court upheld a Hawaii districting plan based on registered voters. The state clearly intended to enhance the voting power of the permanent citizens of Hawaii, while excluding the largely transient but numerically overwhelming military population. The Court held that,

> [T]he Equal Protection Clause does not require the States to use total population figures derived from the federal census as the standard by which ... substantial population equality is to be measured.... Neither in *Reynolds v. Sims* nor in any other decision has this Court suggested that the States are required to include aliens, transients, short-term or temporary residents, or persons denied the vote for conviction of crime in the apportionment base by which their legislators are distributed and against which compliance with the Equal Protection Clause is to be measured.

Does *Burns* survive the subsequent development of voting rights law? Consider *Garza v. County of Los Angeles*, 918 F.2d 763 (9th Cir. 1990), *cert. denied*, 498 U.S. 1028 (1991). In a challenge to the drawing of county commissioner district lines, the County of Los Angeles defended in part on the grounds that the apparent underrepresentation of Hispanics was not legally cognizable since many were not eligible voters. The court rejected this argument based on:

[T]he standard enunciated in *Wesberry v. Sanders*, 376 U.S. 1 (1964) that "the fundamental principle of representative government is one of equal representation for equal numbers of people, without regard to race, sex, economic status, or place of residence within a state." This standard derives from the constitutional requirement that members of the House of Representatives are elected "by the people," *Reynolds*, 377 U.S. at 560, from districts "founded on the aggregate number of inhabitants of each state" (James Madison, The Federalist, No. 54 at 369 (J. Cooke ed. 1961)); U.S. Const. art. I, § 2. The framers were aware that this apportionment and representation base would include categories of persons who were ineligible to vote—women, children, bound servants, convicts, the insane, and, at a later time, aliens. *Fair v. Klutznick*, 486 F. Supp. 564, 576 (D. D. C. 1980). Nevertheless, they declared that government should represent all the people. In applying this principle, the *Reynolds* Court recognized that the people, including those who are ineligible to vote, form the basis for representative government. Thus population is an appropriate basis for state legislative apportionment.

In a separate dissent and concurrence, Judge Kozinski revisited *Reynolds* to find an equally compelling set of references to the need to preclude the disparate weighting of votes of defined sets of voters simply as a result of the happenstance of where they resided. He concluded that the Supreme Court's pronouncements supported both a principle of equal representation and a principle of equal voting power:

> While apportionment by population and apportionment by number of eligible electors normally yield precisely the same result, they are based on radically different premises and serve materially different purposes. Apportionment by raw population embodies the principle of equal representation; it assures that all persons living within a district—whether eligible to vote or not—have roughly equal representation in the governing body. A principle of equal representation serves important purposes: It assures that constituents have more or less equal access to their elected officials, by assuring that no official has a disproportionately large number of constituents to satisfy. Also, assuming that elected officials are able to obtain benefits for their districts in proportion to their share of the total membership of the governing body, it assures that constituents are not afforded unequal government services depending on the size of the population in their districts.

> Apportionment by proportion of eligible voters serves the principle of electoral equality. This principle recognizes that electors—persons eligible to vote—are the ones who hold the ultimate political power in our democracy. This is an important power reserved only to certain members of society; states are not required to bestow it upon aliens, transients, short-term residents, persons convicted of crime, or those

considered too young. *See* J. Nowak, R. Rotunda & J.N. Young, Constitutional Law § 14.31, at 722–23 (3d ed. 1986).

The principle of electoral equality assures that, regardless of the size of the whole body of constituents, political power, as defined by the number of those eligible to vote, is equalized as between districts holding the same number of representatives. It also assures that those eligible to vote do not suffer dilution of that important right by having their vote given less weight than that of electors in another location. Under this paradigm, the fourteenth amendment protects a right belonging to the individual elector and the key question is whether the votes of some electors are materially undercounted because of the manner in which districts are apportioned. . . .

When considered against the Supreme Court's repeated pronouncements that the right being protected by the one person one vote principle is personal and limited to citizens, the various arguments raised by the majority do not carry the day. Thus, the Court's passing reference in *Kirkpatrick v. Preisler*, 394 U.S. 526, 531 (1969), to "prevent[ing] debasement of voting power and diminution of access to elected representatives" suggests only that the Court did not consider the possibility that the twin goals might diverge in some cases. As *Kirkpatrick* contains no discussion of the issue, it provides no clue as to which principle has primacy where there is a conflict between the two.

In cases of conflict, which principle should govern? For a subtle reading of the variety of democratic values that can be seen reflected in the Court's opinion in *Baker v. Carr* and its progeny, see Guy–Uriel E. Charles, *Constitutional Pluralism and Democratic Pluralism: Reflections on the Interpretive Approach of* Baker v. Carr, 80 N.C.L. Rev. 1103 (2002).

4. In *Reynolds*, Chief Justice Warren was able to ground the claims in individual rights to equal treatment by the state. This was clearly facilitated by the remarkable disparities in the population-bases of various districts. In *Baker* for example, the divergences reached 23–to–1, while in *Reynolds* they were as high as 41–to–1. However, *Reynolds* expands the scope of the equipopulation principle by invoking the concept of *political fairness.* The Court claimed it was guaranteeing to each citizen "an *equally effective* voice" in the electoral process so as to yield "fair and effective representation" for the electorate as a whole. Since clearly there will always be winners and losers in contested elections, how does an individual voting for a losing candidate assess whether she has realized an "equally effective voice" and secured "fair and effective representation"? If the definition of fairness turns solely on the absence of malapportionment, what do the additional claims of *Reynolds* add? Or, if there is indeed some greater principle than simply equality in apportionment, what does *Reynolds* suggest it is? Can effective representation be measured in terms of individual voters?

One hint of the Court's thinking is its treatment of the comparisons to the U.S. Senate. The Court implies that, but for the original political compromise inherited in the Constitution, the constraints on the popular will involved in overrepresentation of small states should violate the principles of political fairness. Is the Court decidedly hostile to the argument that states or local jurisdictions may have their own political compromises that may in turn necessitate a Senate-like arrangement?

5.   While *Baker* introduced the concept of the justiciable claim of unconstitutional apportionment of legislative office, it fell to *Reynolds* and *Wesberry* to reduce the constitutional command to the equipopulation rule of one-person, one-vote. As conceived by the Supreme Court in the 1960's, the reliance on numerical standards of apportionment was to have served three purposes. First, numerical standards could be drawn from unassailable empirical data, specifically the decennial Census enumeration of population, and thus could provide an objective basis for measuring political equality. Second, the one-person, one-vote rule based on strict population equality could be readily managed by the courts and thus allowed a justiciable standard for judicial immersion into the "political thicket" of elected institutions. *See Karcher v. Daggett*, 462 U.S. 725, 732 (1983) (Justice Brennan invoking the justiciability argument in favor of strict numerical application of one-person, one-vote standard). Third, the existence of objective measures would defeat attempts to gerrymander districting schemes and would implement the constitutional guarantee that "each resident citizen has, as far as is possible, an equal voice" in the selection of public officials. *See Kramer v. Union Free School Dist.*, 395 U.S. 621, 627 (1969).

The third feature is untested in the early reapportionment cases. In *Reynolds*, the Court refers to the evils of an imprecise system "as an open invitation to partisan gerrymandering," 377 U.S. at 579, which the one person/one vote rule is intended to forestall. To what extent is gerrymandering consistent with an equipopulation scheme? An immediate problem is that districting always involves choices among competing apportionment schemes that may favor one or another political party, incumbent official, regional interest, minority group, etc. *Reynolds* offers very little to resolve these issues. Professor Dixon has commented that the problem is inherent to districting: "The primary difficulty is that in a generic sense all *districting is gerrymandering*. A near-infinite number of sets of "equal" districts may be drawn in any state; each set, however, having a quite different effect in terms of overall party balance and minority representation." Robert G. Dixon, Jr., Democratic Representation: Reapportionment in Law and Politics 462 (1968).

Lucas v. The Forty–Fourth General Assembly of the State of Colorado

377 U.S. 713 (1964).

■ MR. CHIEF JUSTICE WARREN delivered the opinion of the Court.

Involved in this case is an appeal from a decision of the Federal District Court for the District of Colorado upholding the validity, under the Equal Protection Clause of the Fourteenth Amendment to the Federal Constitution, of the apportionment of seats in the Colorado Legislature pursuant to the provisions of a constitutional amendment ["Amendment 7"] approved by the Colorado electorate in 1962.

* * *

II

[...] The 1953 apportionment scheme ... in effect immediately prior to the adoption of Amendment No. 7, was contained in several statutory provisions which provided for a 35–member Senate and a 65–member House of Representatives. Section 63–1–2 of the Colorado Revised Statutes established certain population "ratio" figures for the apportionment of Senate and House seats among the State's 63 counties. One Senate seat was to be allocated to each senatorial district for the first 19,000 population, with one additional senator for each senatorial district for each additional 50,000 persons or fraction over 48,000. One House seat was to be given to each representative district for the first 8,000 population, with one additional representative for each House district for each additional 25,000 persons or fraction over 22,400. Sections 63–1–3 and 63–1–6 established 25 senatorial districts and 35 representative districts, respectively, and allocated the 35 Senate seats and 65 House seats among them according to the prescribed population ratios. No counties were divided in the formation of senatorial or representative districts, in compliance with the constitutional proscription. Thus, senators and representatives in those counties entitled to more than one seat in one or both bodies were elected at large by all of the county's voters. The City and County of Denver was given eight Senate seats and 17 House seats, and Pueblo County was allocated two Senate seats and four House seats. Other populous counties were also given more than one Senate and House seat each. Certain counties were entitled to separate representation in either or both of the houses, and were given one seat each. Sparsely populated counties were combined in multicounty districts.

Under the 1953 apportionment scheme, applying 1960 census figures, 29.8% of the State's total population lived in districts electing a majority of the members of the Senate, and 32.1% resided in districts electing a majority of the House members. Maximum population-variance ratios of approximately 8–to–1 existed between the most populous and least populous districts in both the Senate and the House. One senator represented a district containing 127,520 persons, while another senator had only 17,481 people in his district. The smallest representative district had a population of only 7,867, while another district was given only two House seats for a population of 127,520. . . .

Amendment No. 7 provides for the establishment of a General Assembly composed of 39 senators and 65 representatives, with the State divided geographically into 39 senatorial and 65 representative districts, so that all seats in both houses are apportioned among single-member districts. Responsibility for creating House districts "as nearly equal in population as may be" is given to the legislature. Allocation of senators among the counties follows the existing scheme of districting and apportionment, except that one sparsely populated county is detached from populous Arapahoe County and joined with four others in forming a senatorial district, and one additional senator is apportioned to each of the counties of Adams, Arapahoe, Boulder and Jefferson. Within counties given more than one Senate seat, senatorial districts are to be established by the legislature "as nearly equal in population as may be." Amendment No. 7 also provides for a revision of representative districts, and of senatorial districts within counties given more than one Senate seat, after each federal census, in order to maintain conformity with the prescribed requirements. Pursuant to this constitutional mandate, the Colorado Legislature, in early 1963, enacted a statute establishing 65 representative districts and creating senatorial districts in counties given more than one Senate seat. Under the newly adopted House apportionment plan, districts in which about 45.1% of the State's total population reside are represented by a majority of the members of that body. The maximum population-variance ratio, between the most populous and least populous House districts, is approximately 1.7–to–1. The court below concluded that the House was apportioned as nearly on a population basis as was practicable, consistent with Amendment No. 7's requirement that "(n)o part of one county shall be added to another county or part of another county" in the formation of a legislative district, and directed its concern solely to the question of whether the deviations from a population basis in the apportionment of Senate seats were rationally justifiable.

Senatorial apportionment, under Amendment No. 7, involves little more than adding four new Senate seats and distributing them to four populous counties in the Denver area, and in substance perpetuates the existing senatorial apportionment scheme. Counties containing only 33.2% of the State's total population elect a majority of the 39–member Senate under the provisions of Amendment No. 7. Las Animas County, with a 1960 population of only 19,983, is given one Senate seat, while El Paso County, with 143,742 persons, is allotted only two Senate seats. Thus, the maximum population-variance ratio, under the revised senatorial apportionment, is about 3.6–to–1. Denver and the three adjacent suburban counties contain about one-half of the State's total 1960 population of 1,753,947, but are given only 14 out of 39 senators. The Denver, Pueblo, and Colorado Springs metropolitan areas, containing 1,191,832 persons, about 68%, or over two-thirds of Colorado's population, elect only 20 of the State's 39 senators, barely a majority. The average population of Denver's eight senatorial districts, under Amendment No. 7, is 61,736, while the five least populous districts contain less than 22,000 persons each. Divergences from population-based representation in the Senate are growing continually wider, since the underrepresented districts in the Denver, Pueblo, and Colorado Springs metropolitan areas are rapidly gaining in population, while many of the overrepresented rural districts have tended to decline in population continuously in recent years.

III

[. . . T]he Colorado scheme of legislative apportionment here attacked is one adopted by a majority vote of the Colorado electorate almost contemporaneously with the District Court's decision on the merits in this litigation. Thus, the plan at issue did not result from prolonged legislative inaction.

As appellees have correctly pointed out, a majority of the voters in every county of the State voted in favor of the apportionment scheme embodied in Amendment No. 7's provisions, in preference to that contained in proposed Amendment No. 8, which, subject to minor deviations, would have based the apportionment of seats in both houses on a population basis. However, the choice presented to the Colorado electorate, in voting on these two proposed constitutional amendments, was hardly as clear-cut as the court below regarded it. One of the most undesirable features of the existing apportionment scheme was the requirement that, in counties given more than one seat in either or both of the houses of the General Assembly, all legislators must be elected at large from the county as a whole. Thus, under the existing plan, each Denver voter was required to vote for eight senators and 17 representatives. Ballots were long and cumbersome, and an intelligent choice among candidates for seats in the legislature was made quite difficult. No identifiable constituencies within the populous counties resulted, and the residents of those areas had no single member of the Senate or House elected specifically to represent them. . . . Amendment No. 8 . . . would have perpetuated, for all practical purposes, this debatable feature of the existing scheme. . . . Thus, neither of the proposed plans was, in all probability, wholly acceptable to the voters in the populous counties, and the assumption of the court below that the Colorado voters made a definitive choice between two contrasting alternatives and indicated that "minority process in the Senate is what they want" does not appear to be factually justifiable.

Finally, . . . the initiative device provides a practicable political remedy to obtain relief against alleged legislative malapportionment in Colorado. An initiated measure proposing a constitutional amendment or a statutory enactment is entitled to be placed on the ballot if the signatures of 8% of those voting for the Secretary of State in the last election are obtained. No geographical distribution of petition signers is required. Initiative and referendum has been frequently utilized throughout Colorado's history. . . .

IV

[...] Except as an interim remedial procedure, justifying a court in staying its hand temporarily, we find no significance in the fact that a nonjudicial, political remedy may be available for the effectuation of asserted rights to equal representation in a state legislature. Courts sit to adjudicate controversies involving alleged denials of constitutional rights. While a court sitting as a court of equity might be justified in temporarily refraining from the issuance of injunctive relief in an apportionment case in order to allow for resort to an available political remedy, such as initiative and referendum, individual constitutional rights cannot be deprived, or denied judicial effectuation, because of the existence of a nonjudicial remedy through which relief against the alleged malapportionment, which the individual voters seek, might be achieved. An individual's constitutionally protected right to cast an equally weighted vote cannot be denied even by a vote of a majority of a State's electorate, if the apportionment scheme adopted by the voters fails to measure up to the requirements of the Equal Protection Clause. Manifestly, the fact that an apportionment plan is adopted in a popular referendum is insufficient to sustain its constitutionality or to induce a court of equity to refuse to act. As stated by this Court in *West Virginia State Bd. of Educ. v. Barnette,* 319 U.S. 624, 638 (1943), "One's right to life, liberty, and property ... and other fundamental rights may not be submitted to vote; they depend on the outcome of no elections." A citizen's constitutional rights can hardly be infringed simply because a majority of the people choose that it be. We hold that the fact that a challenged legislative apportionment plan was approved by the electorate is without federal constitutional significance, if the scheme adopted fails to satisfy the basic requirements of the Equal Protection Clause....

Since the apportionment of seats in the Colorado Legislature, under the provisions of Amendment No. 7, fails to comport with the requirements of the Equal Protection Clause, the decision below must be reversed....

Reversed and remanded.

■ Mr. Justice Clark, dissenting.

* * *

[...] I would refuse to interfere with this apportionment for several reasons. First, Colorado enjoys the initiative and referendum system which it often utilizes and which, indeed, produced the present apportionment. As a result of the action of the Legislature and the use of initiative and referendum, the State Assembly has been reapportioned eight times since 1881. This indicates the complete awareness of the people of Colorado to apportionment problems and their continuing efforts to solve them. The courts should not interfere in such a situation.... Next, as my Brother Stewart has pointed out, there are rational and most persuasive reasons for some deviations in the representation in the Colorado Assembly. The State has mountainous areas which divide it into four regions, some parts of which are almost impenetrable. There are also some depressed areas, diversified industry and varied climate, as well as enormous recreational regions and difficulties in transportation. These factors give rise to problems indigenous to Colorado, which only its people can intelligently solve. This they have done in the present apportionment.

Finally, I cannot agree to the arbitrary application of the "one man, one vote" principle for both houses of a State Legislature. In my view, if one house is fairly apportioned by population (as is admitted here) then the people should have some latitude in providing, on a rational basis, for representation in the other house. The Court seems to approve the federal arrangement of two Senators from each State on the ground that it was a compromise reached by the framers of our Constitution and is a part of the fabric of our national charter. But what the Court overlooks is that Colorado, by an overwhelming vote, has likewise written the organization of its legislative body into its Constitution, and our dual federalism requires that we give it recognition. After all, the Equal Protection Clause is not an algebraic formula. Equal protection does not rest on whether the practice assailed "results in some inequality" but rather on whether "any state of facts reasonably can be conceived that would sustain it".... Certainly Colorado's arrangement is not arbitrary. On the contrary, it rests on reasonable grounds which, as I have pointed out, are peculiar to that State. It is argued that the Colorado apportionment would lead only to a legislative stalemate between the two houses, but the experience of the Congress completely refutes this argument. Now in its 176th year, the federal plan has worked well. It is further said that in any event Colorado's apportionment would substitute compromise for the legislative process. But most legislation is the product of compromise between the various forces acting for and against its enactment.

In striking down Colorado's plan of apportionment, the Court, I believe, is exceeding its powers under the Equal Protection Clause; it is invading the valid functioning of the procedures of the States, and thereby is committing a grievous error which will do irreparable damage to our federal-state relationship. I dissent.

■ MR. JUSTICE STEWART, whom MR. JUSTICE CLARK joins, dissenting.

It is important to make clear at the outset what these cases are not about. They have nothing to do with the denial or impairment of any person's right to vote. Nobody's right to vote has been denied. Nobody's right to vote has been restricted. Nobody has been deprived of the right to have his vote counted.

[. . .] The question involved in these cases is quite a different one. Simply stated, the question is to what degree, if at all, the Equal Protection Clause of the Fourteenth Amendment limits each sovereign State's freedom to establish appropriate electoral constituencies from which representatives to the State's bicameral legislative assembly are to be chosen. The Court's answer is a blunt one, and, I think, woefully wrong. The Equal Protection Clause, says the Court, "requires that the seats in both houses of a bicameral state legislature must be apportioned on a population basis."

After searching carefully through the Court's opinions in these and their companion cases, I have been able to find but two reasons offered in support of this rule. First, says the Court, it is "established that the fundamental principle of representative government in this country is one of equal representation for equal numbers of people. . . ." With all respect, I think that this is not correct, simply as a matter of fact. It has been unanswerably demonstrated before now that this "was not the colonial system, it was not the system chosen for the national government by the Constitution, it was not the system exclusively or even predominantly practiced by the States at the time of adoption of the Fourteenth Amendment, it is not predominantly practiced by the States today." Secondly, says the Court, unless legislative districts are equal in population, voters in the more populous districts will suffer a "debasement" amounting to a constitutional injury. As the Court explains it, "To the extent that a citizen's right to vote is debased, he is that much less a citizen." We are not told how or why the vote of a person in a more populated legislative district is "debased," or how or why he is less a citizen, nor is the proposition self-evident. I find it impossible to understand how or why a voter in California, for instance, either feels or is less a citizen than a voter in Nevada, simply because, despite their population disparities, each of these States is represented by two United States Senators.

To put the matter plainly, there is nothing in all the history of this Court's decisions which supports this constitutional rule. The Court's draconian pronouncement, which makes unconstitutional the legislatures of most of the 50 States, finds no support in the words of the Constitution, in any prior decision of this Court, or in the 175–year political history of our Federal Union. . . . The rule announced today . . . stifles values of local individuality and initiative vital to the character of the Federal Union which it was the genius of our Constitution to create.

I

What the Court has done is to convert a particular political philosophy into a constitutional rule, binding upon each of the 50 States, from Maine to Hawaii, from Alaska to Texas, without regard and without respect for the many individualized and differentiated characteristics of each State, characteristics stemming from each State's distinct history, distinct geography, distinct distribution of population, and distinct political heritage. My own understanding of the various theories of representative government is that no one theory has ever commanded unanimous assent among political scientists, historians, or others who have considered the problem. But even if it were thought that the rule announced today by the Court is, as a matter of political theory, the most desirable general rule which can be devised as a basis for the make-up of the representative assembly of a typical State, I could not join in the fabrication of a constitutional mandate which imports and forever freezes one theory of political thought into our Constitution, and forever denies to every State any opportunity for enlightened and progressive innovation in the design of its democratic institutions, so as to accommodate within a system of representative government the interests and aspirations of diverse groups of people, without subjecting any group or class to absolute domination by a geographically concentrated or highly organized majority.

Representative government is a process of accommodating group interests through democratic institutional arrangements. Its function is to channel the numerous opinions, interests, and abilities of the people of a State into the making of the State's public policy. Appropriate legislative apportionment, therefore, should ideally be designed to insure effective representation in the State's legislature, in cooperation with other organs of political power, of the various groups and interests making up the electorate. In practice, of course, this ideal is approximated in the particular apportionment system of any State by a realistic accommodation of the diverse and often conflicting political forces operating within the State.

I do not pretend to any specialized knowledge of the myriad of individual characteristics of the several States, beyond the records in the cases before us today. But I do know enough to be aware that a system of legislative apportionment which might be best for South Dakota, might be unwise for Hawaii with its many islands, or Michigan with its Northern Peninsula. I do know enough to realize that Montana with its vast distances is not Rhode Island with its heavy concentrations of people. I do know enough to be aware of the great variations among the several States in their historic manner of distributing legislative power—of the Governors' Councils in New England, of the broad powers of initiative and referendum retained in some States by the people, of the legislative power which some States give to their Governors, by the right of veto or otherwise of the widely autonomous home rule which many States give to their cities. The Court today declines to give any recognition to these considerations and countless others, tangible and intangible, in holding unconstitutional the particular systems of legislative apportionment which these States have chosen. Instead, the Court says that the requirements of the Equal Protection Clause can be met in any State only by the uncritical, simplistic, and heavy-handed application of sixth-grade arithmetic.

But legislators do not represent faceless numbers. They represent people, or, more accurately, a majority of the voters in their districts—people with identifiable needs and interests which require legislative representation, and which can often be related to the geographical areas in which these people live. The very fact of geographic districting, the constitutional validity of which the Court does not question, carries with it an acceptance of the idea of legislative representation of regional needs and interests. Yet if geographical residence is irrelevant, as the Court suggests, and the goal is solely that of equally "weighted" votes, I do not understand why the Court's constitutional rule does not require the abolition of districts and the holding of all elections at large.

The fact is, of course, that population factors must often to some degree be subordinated in devising a legislative apportionment plan which is to achieve the important goal of ensuring a fair, effective, and balanced representation of the regional, social, and economic interests within a State. And the further fact is that throughout our history the apportionments of State Legislatures have reflected the strongly felt American tradition that the public interest is composed of many diverse interests, and that in the long run it can better be expressed by a medley of component voices than by the majority's monolithic command. What constitutes a rational plan reasonably designed to achieve this objective will vary from State to State, since each State is unique, in terms of topography, geography, demography, history, heterogeneity and concentration of population, variety of social and economic interests, and in the operation and interrelation of its political institutions. But so long as a State's apportionment plan reasonably achieves, in the light of the State's own characteristics, effective and balanced representation of all substantial interests, without sacrificing the principle of effective majority rule, that plan cannot be considered irrational.

II

This brings me to what I consider to be the proper constitutional standards to be applied in these cases.... I think that the Equal Protection Clause demands but two basic attributes of any plan of state legislative apportionment. First, it demands that, in the light of the State's own characteristics and needs, the plan must be a rational one. Secondly, it demands that the plan must be such as not to permit the systematic frustration of the will of a majority of the electorate of the State. I think it is apparent that any plan of legislative apportionment which could be shown to reflect no policy, but simply arbitrary and capricious action or inaction, and that any plan which could be shown systematically to prevent ultimate effective majority rule, would be invalid under accepted Equal Protection Clause standards. But, beyond this, I think there is nothing in the Federal Constitution to prevent a State from choosing any electoral legislative structure it thinks best suited to the interests, temper, and customs of its people.

* * *

NOTES AND QUESTIONS

1. Procedurally, which institutional arrangements should be used for resolving substantive questions as to what forms of representation are constitutionally tolerable? What considerations should determine whether the authority to resolve these substantive questions ought to lie with the current legislators of Colorado, or the voters of Colorado, or some administrative body, or, as *Lucas* concludes, with the judicial system? Several striking features stand out regarding the institutional and procedural context in which the plan challenged in *Lucas* was adopted: (a) the plan had been recently adopted; (b) it had been adopted by the voters, rather than the legislature; (c) it had been approved by a majority of voters in every county in the State, not just by a statewide majority. Given these particular features of the process in Colorado, does the Court make a persuasive case as to why "the fact that a challenged legislative apportionment plan was approved by the electorate is without federal constitutional significance?" Does the fact of recent popular enactment militate against judicial intervention?

2. Justice Stewart argues that "[r]epresentative government is a process of accommodating groups interests through democratic institutional arrangements." Why isn't this "group interest" vision of representation more accurate, or at least, an acceptable option for states to choose? Colorado's system recognizes distinct, minority political interests that the state (the majority of initiative voters) fears might get discounted in a strict majoritarian system. As Justice Stewart describes it, the purpose is to avoid subjecting "any group or class to absolute domination by a geographically concentrated or highly organized majority." In this case, the protected minority is rural voters. What is wrong with designing political institutions with these aims? Suppose Colorado had decided to design its senate to protect other kinds of minority interests, such as economic ones? Or, what if Colorado's objective had been to protect "discrete and insular" minority groups, such as racial or ethnic ones? Or consider still a broader justification, based on parallels to the United States Senate. If the existence of a distinctly elected upper branch of the legislature can be justified at the national level, why is that same type of justification not available here? Does the Court's decision hold, in effect, that strict majority rule is constitutionally required? Should courts be more willing to permit deviations from one-person, one-vote for the purpose of enhancing the ability of certain minority voters, i.e., black or Hispanic voters, to elect their preferred candidates? For example, if black-majority districts were permitted to have fewer residents than white-majority districts, it might be possible to create more black-majority districts than under the current one-vote, one-person regime. For an argument in favor of such a system, see Grant M. Hayden, *The Dilemma of Minority Representation*, 92 Calif. L. Rev. 1589 (2004).

3. Justice Stewart argues that the Court's decision in *Lucas* is inconsistent with "the very fact of geographic districting, the constitutional validity of which the Court does not question." Many American representative institutions, such as the United States House, use single-member geographic districts to elect legislators. This electoral structure first was mandated for congressional elections in 1842; that requirement lapsed in 1927, but was re-enacted by Congress in 1967 and remains in effect today. For the full history of territorial districting for Congress, see Chapter 13. Even during periods when no federal statute required single-member congressional districts, many states followed this practice. In what way is *Lucas* purportedly inconsistent with this long-established practice? Stewart argues that, like the Colorado Senate plan, the very *raison d'etre* of districting itself "carries with it an acceptance of the idea of legislative representation of regional needs and interests." Consider the possible purposes for basing elections to representative institutions on geographic districts. Are the purposes that motivate or justify the use of districted elections ultimately the same as those behind Colorado's Senate plan? If so, is Justice Stewart right that the rationale for invalidating that plan applies with as much force to the long-established practice of geographically-based election districts? If Justice Stewart is persuasive, which way should the tension be resolved: by concluding that *Lucas* is wrong, or by concluding that geographic-based districting is equally unconstitutional? If districting were abandoned, what would replace it? Consider the alternatives presented in Chapter 13.

4. What constitutional standard would the dissents have applied to evaluate the structure of democratic institutions? Justice Stewart would impose only two requirements: First, that the plan be a "rational one" in light of a particular State's characteristics and needs—it must reflect some intelligible policy. Second, the plan must not "systematically" prevent effective majority rule. Let us accept that legal rules need not be crystalline clear to perform the task asked of them; they need only be clear enough for the particular context. With that functional view of "clear" in mind, would the dissent's standards enable courts to apply these requirements appropriately? Do these two standards provide the right kind of guidance to those with the power in the first instance to design political institutions—typically, political actors, responsive to partisan pressures, who redistrict states every ten years? Is it relatively clear what kinds of redistricting plans the dissenters would rule out?

5. What latitude does the Constitution give to states seeking to protect minority rights? Does the Court actually object to the purposes the dissent offers to justify Colorado's Senate plan? Or is *Lucas* better understood as objecting to the means used to pursue these purposes? Perhaps the problem is not Colorado's aim of diffusing majoritarian power to enhance the political influence of minority interests, but rather pursuing that aim through the design of election districts. Why might the means chosen be particularly troubling? Consider possible alternative approaches to protecting minority voting power. One such approach might focus on voting rules. Colorado could require supermajority support to enact legislation, or to enact specific types of legislation that have particularly significant effects on certain minority interests. Or Colorado could give certain regions or interests in the state a legislative veto over some designated areas of legislation: for example, no legislation affecting water rights may be enacted without approval of representatives from the rural counties. Would these rules be equally effective at protecting the minority interests Colorado purports to care about? If so, would they be unconstitutional under *Lucas*? If not, what differs about building special concern for minority representation into voting rules rather than the underlying architecture of political institutions?

Perhaps voting rules embed these special protections in a more visible, and hence more publicly accountable, form. Unlike obscure features of institutional design, these kind of voting rules announce their presence each and every time policy is being made. Some political theorists have argued that the basic principles on which political power is organized must satisfy the condition of publicity: they must be capable of being publicly articulated and accepted. *See* John Rawls, A Theory of Justice 133, 177–83 (1971). Can a case be made that minority preferences in voting rules better satisfies this requirement than disproportional numbers of voters allocated to districts? That the voting rule preference is more likely to be continually revisited than the latter? Consider other means that might be available for Colorado to protect minority interests. Rather than manipulating numbers of voters per district, the state might manipulate the location of districts. For example, if the state wanted to assure some special voice for farmers in its legislature, it could place equal numbers of voters in districts, but draw certain districts so that they were dominated by farmers. Would this be unconstitutional under *Lucas*? How would it fare under the publicity standard?

6. What exactly is the underlying substantive injury in *Lucas*? The substantive concern might be that the Senate plan overrepresents the interests of smaller counties relative to their population; thus, it is voters in more urban areas that are disadvantaged by the apportionment plan. In some circumstances, that might raise troubling concerns. Here, however, the majority in each county voted to cede a bit of its power to voters in smaller counties. Is there any reason to distrust political processes in which majorities vote to give greater voice to the interests of political minorities? Notice the general attitude of skepticism the Court conveys about the initiative process, and the Court's willingness to discount the meaningfulness of the voters' approval of Amendment 7. Contrast this attitude with that in more recent cases we will examine concerning voter initiatives in Chapter 11.

7. The Court's response to the question of the exact nature of the constitutional injury ultimately appears to lie in its quotation of the magisterial flag salute case. In *West Virginia State Bd. of Educ. v. Barnette*, 319 U.S. 624, 638 (1943), the Court says: " 'One's right to life, liberty, and property . . . and other fundamental rights may not be submitted to vote; they depend on the outcome of no elections.' " Individual constitutional rights cannot be denied simply because political majorities desire to do so. Such a principle makes sense in contexts like *Barnette*; when personal constitutional liberties, such as the right to the integrity of one's own conscience, are at stake, the very nature of the constitutional right precludes political majorities from invading that right. These types of individual rights might well be understood as meriting protections from the temporary preferences of political majorities. *See* Ronald Dworkin, Taking Rights Seriously 184–205 (1977) (developing conception of legal rights as trumps over routine policy considerations). But is the aspect of "the right to vote" recognized in *Lucas* a personal or individual right in the same sense as the right to freedom of conscience? As Justice Stewart observes, no one in Colorado is denied the right to vote or to have that vote counted. And of course, no one has a right to have his or her preferred candidate elected. Instead, isn't the concern that the voters as a group in certain areas of the state have less overall political influence in the Senate than the same number of voters have as a group in other areas of the state? The question in *Lucas* is the relative distribution of political power within the state; but distributional questions require comparisons of the political power of different voting groups. As the Supreme Court subsequently noted, the right at issue in the reapportionment cases is not so much a question of casting a ballot, as "the right of qualified voters regardless of their political persuasion, to cast their votes effectively...." *Williams v. Rhodes*, 393 U.S. 23, 30 (1968). Consider the following argument, that the recognition of a right of effective participation takes the law of elections decidedly away from a conception of individual rights:

> [T]he right to cast an effective ballot implie[s] more than simply the equal weighting of all votes, as per the one-person, one-vote rule. To be effective, a voter's ballot must stand a meaningful chance of effective aggregation with those of like-minded voters to claim a just share of electoral results. For this reason, any sophisticated right to genuinely meaningful electoral participation must be evaluated and measured as a group right, that of groups of voters seeking the outcomes promised to them through the electoral system.

Samuel Issacharoff, *Groups and the Right to Vote*, 44 Emory L.J. 869, 883–84 (1995). Many aspects of voting rights are best understood in terms unfamiliar in other areas of constitutional law. For example, as we shall develop in later chapters, one of the inevitable effects and aims of apportionment is to treat voters as members of groups. That will raise questions about which dimensions of "group" identity should be considered relevant for this purpose, and which institutions should be empowered to decide that issue. Can economic interest provide a proper basis for attributions of group identity in the design of political institutions? Can racial or ethnic identity? Finally, legal regulation of the electoral process must recognize the unique blend of state action and constitutionally protected private conduct that voting implicates. *See* Pamela S. Karlan & Daryl J. Levinson, *Why Voting is Different*, 84 Cal. L. Rev. 1201 (1996). Accordingly, rather than being viewed through the prism of traditional personal or individual rights, voting rights are frequently better understood as group-based rights.

They focus on whether one group's political power is being inappropriately diluted or enhanced at the expense of other groups. If the "right to vote" in cases like *Lucas* is best understood as a group right, is the Court's reliance on *Barnette* justified? Or should the Court have been more willing to accept the contemporaneous decision of the majority in Colorado to grant its political minorities more influence than they otherwise would have had?

8. As the equipopulation command took hold, the intervening considerations identified by both Chief Justice Warren and Justice Harlan receded in importance. *Reynolds* itself left open the possibility that some intervening political considerations might justify departures from the equipopulation principle:

> So long as the divergences from a strict population standard are based on legitimate considerations incident to the effectuation of a rational state policy, some deviations from the equal-population principle are constitutionally permissible with respect to the apportionment of seats in either or both of the two houses of a bicameral state legislature.

However, as *Lucas* reveals, the Court refused to give any particular weight to the manner of adoption of the non-equipopulous system and held instead that the resulting apportionment violated one-person/one-vote. Consider the following early assessment of the reliance on numerical standards as the critical factor in reapportionment:

> The Warren Court's reliance on the one person, one vote principle without the development of other judicial restraints on the discretion of districting authorities threatened to transform the celebrated reapportionment revolution into a "gerrymandering revolution." . . . Not only had the Court failed to develop effective checks on the practice of gerrymandering, but in pursuing the goal of population equality to a point of satiety it had actually facilitated that practice. The Court rejected as justifications for even small population deviations the use of established political subdivision boundaries (such as those for counties) in designing districts and the construction of geographically "compact" districts. Although these non-population considerations, frequently required by state constitutions, did not prevent gerrymandering, they at least functioned as minimal restrictions on the cartographic flexibility of districting authorities. The absence of even these minimal restrictions in the districting process increased the already numerous options available for locating district boundaries. This expanded flexibility was conducive to the creation of politically self-serving representational designs.

Richard L. Engstrom, *The Supreme Court and Equipopulous Gerrymandering: A Remaining Obstacle in the Quest for Fair and Effective Representation*, 1976 Ariz. St. L.J. 277, 278–79. In the three decades since Professor Engstrom sounded this warning, the use of computers has transformed the process of redistricting. *See* Samuel Issacharoff, *Judging Politics: The Elusive Quest for Judicial Review of Political Fairness*, 71 Tex. L. Rev.

1643, 1695–1702 (1993); Michelle Browdy, Note, *Computer Models and Post*–Bandemer *Redistricting*, 99 Yale L.J. 1379, 1387–91 (1990). The increased availability of minutely detailed demographic information has allowed a proliferation of redistricting plans drawn by various interest constituents. It has also allowed for far greater flights of cartographic fancy as an increasingly elaborate set of districting designs could be constructed to accomplish specific political aims. *See* Richard H. Pildes & Richard G. Niemi, *Expressive Harms, "Bizarre Districts," the Voting Rights: Evaluating Elections District Appearances After* Shaw v. Reno, 92 Mich. L. Rev. 483 (1993)(documenting the greater irregularity of districts drawn after the 1990 Census to accommodate minority representation). The ability to create designer districts further increased in the post–2000 round of redistricting as more sophisticated computer programs were devised to include not only basic demographic and voting data, but projections of household income, magazine and cable television subscription patterns, car ownership and other socio-economic data deemed useful in projecting the likely voting trends of specific neighborhoods over the ten-year lifespan of a redistricting plan. *See* Nathaniel Persily The Real Y2k Problem: Census 2000 Data and Redistricting Technology (Brennan Center, 2000).

Karcher v. Daggett

462 U.S. 725 (1983).

■ JUSTICE BRENNAN delivered the opinion of the Court.

The question presented by this appeal is whether an apportionment plan [the "Feldman plan"] for congressional districts satisfies Art. I, § 2, of the Constitution without need for further justification if the population of the largest district is less than one percent greater than the population of the smallest district.

* * *

I

After the results of the 1980 decennial census had been tabulated, the Clerk of the United States House of Representatives notified the Governor of New Jersey that the number of Representatives to which the State was entitled had decreased from 15 to 14. [Ultimately, the New Jersey Legislature] ... passed a bill (S–711) introduced by Senator Feldman ... which created the apportionment plan at issue in this case....

Like every plan considered by the legislature, the Feldman Plan contained 14 districts, with an average population per district (as determined by the 1980 census) of 526,059. Each district did not have the same population. On the average, each district differed from the "ideal" figure by 0.1384%, or about 726 people. The largest district, the Fourth District, which includes Trenton, had a population of 527,472, and the smallest, the

Sixth District, embracing most of Middlesex County, a population of 523,-798. The difference between them was 3,674 people, or 0.6984% of the average district. The populations of the other districts also varied....

The legislature had before it other plans with appreciably smaller population deviations between the largest and smallest districts. The one receiving the most attention in the District Court was [one which] had a maximum population difference of 2,375, or 0.4514% of the average figure....

III

Appellants' principal argument in this case is addressed to the first question described above. They contend that the Feldman Plan should be regarded per se as the product of a good-faith effort to achieve population equality because the maximum population deviation among districts is smaller than the predictable undercount in available census data.

A

Kirkpatrick squarely rejected a nearly identical argument. "The whole thrust of the 'as nearly as practicable' approach is inconsistent with adoption of fixed numerical standards which excuse population variances without regard to the circumstances of each particular case." Adopting any standard other than population equality, using the best census data available, would subtly erode the Constitution's ideal of equal representation....

Any standard, including absolute equality, involves a certain artificiality. As appellants point out, even the census data are not perfect, and the well-known restlessness of the American people means that population counts for particular localities are outdated long before they are completed. Yet problems with the data at hand apply equally to any population-based standard we could choose.[] As between two standards—equality or something less than equality—only the former reflects the aspirations of Art. I, § 2.

To accept the legitimacy of unjustified, though small population deviations in this case would mean to reject the basic premise of *Kirkpatrick* and *Wesberry*. We decline appellants' invitation to go that far. The unusual rigor of their standard has been noted several times. Because of that rigor, we have required that absolute population equality be the paramount objective of apportionment only in the case of congressional districts, for which the command of Art. I, § 2, as regards the National Legislature outweighs the local interests that a State may deem relevant in apportioning districts for representatives to state and local legislatures, but we have not questioned the population equality standard for congressional districts. The principle of population equality for congressional districts has not proved unjust or socially or economically harmful in experience. If anything, this standard should cause less difficulty now for state legislatures than it did when we adopted it in *Wesberry*. The rapid advances in computer technology and education during the last two decades make it relatively simple to draw contiguous districts of equal population and at the same time to further whatever secondary goals the State has.... We thus reaffirm that there are no de minimis population variations, which could practically be avoided, but which nonetheless meet the standard of Art. I, § 2, without justification....

IV

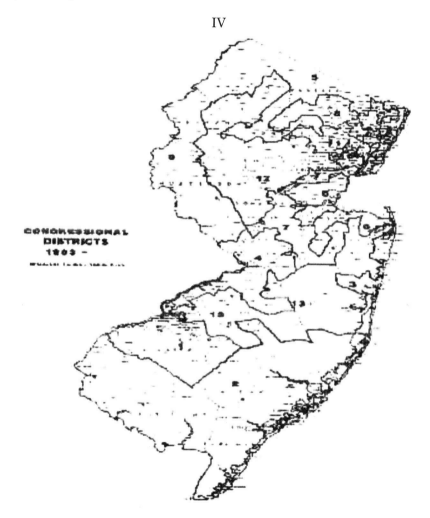

CONGRESSIONAL DISTRICTS 1983 -

By itself, the foregoing discussion does not establish that the Feldman Plan is unconstitutional. Rather, appellees' success in proving that the Feldman Plan was not the product of a good-faith effort to achieve population equality means only that the burden shifted to the State to prove that the population deviations in its plan were necessary to achieve some legitimate state objective ... [W]e are willing to defer to state legislative policies, so long as they are consistent with constitutional norms, even if they require small differences in the population of congressional districts. Any number of consistently applied legislative policies might justify some variance, including, for instance, making districts compact, respecting municipal boundaries, preserving the cores of prior districts, and avoiding contests between incumbent Representatives. As long as the criteria are nondiscriminatory, these are all legitimate objectives that on a proper showing could justify minor population deviations. The State must, however, show with some specificity that a particular objective required the specific deviations in its plan, rather than simply relying on general assertions. The showing required to justify population deviations is flexible, depending on the size of the deviations, the importance of the State's interests, the consistency with which the plan as a whole reflects those interests, and the availability of alternatives that might substantially vindicate those interests yet approximate population equality more closely. By necessity, whether deviations are justified requires case-by-case attention to these factors. . . .

■ JUSTICE WHITE, with whom the CHIEF JUSTICE, JUSTICE POWELL, and JUSTICE REHNQUIST join, dissenting.

* * *

II

[. . . T]here are many, including myself, who take issue with the Court's self-congratulatory assumption that *Kirkpatrick* has been a success. First, a decade of experience with *Kirkpatrick* has shown that "the rule of absolute equality is perfectly compatible with 'gerrymandering' of the worst sort." *Wells v. Rockefeller*, 394 U.S., at 551 (Harlan, J., dissenting). . . .

In addition to providing a patina of respectability for the equipopulous gerrymander, *Kirkpatrick's* regime assured extensive intrusion of the judiciary into legislative business. . . . More than a decade's experience with *Kirkpatrick* demonstrates that insistence on precise numerical equality only invites those who lost in the political arena to refight their battles in federal court. Consequently, "[most] estimates are that between 25 percent and 35 percent of current house district lines were drawn by the Courts." As I have already noted, by extending *Kirkpatrick* to deviations below even the 1% level, the redistricting plan in every State with more than a single Representative is rendered vulnerable to after-the-fact attack by anyone with a complaint and a calculator.

The Court ultimately seeks refuge in stare decisis. I do not slight the respect that doctrine is due, but is it not at least ironic to find stare decisis invoked to protect *Kirkpatrick* as the Court itself proceeds to overrule other holdings in that very decision? . . . [T]oday the Court—with no mention of the contrary holdings in *Kirkpatrick*—opines: "Any number of consistently applied legislative policies might justify some variance, including for instance, making districts compact, respecting municipal boundaries, preserving the cores of prior districts, and avoiding contests between incumbent Representatives." I, of course, welcome the Court's overruling of these ill-considered holdings of *Kirkpatrick*. There should be no question but that state legislatures may account for political and geographic boundaries in order to preserve traditional subdivisions and achieve compact and contiguous districts.

NOTES AND QUESTIONS

1. In many ways, Justice Brennan's opinion in *Karcher* marks the end of the road for the one-person/one-vote doctrine. The clear import of *Karcher* was a confrontation with a Democratic Party gerrymander that resulted in what was aptly termed "a flight of cartographic fancy." The only reason for the challenge was the inability of the equipopulation principle to constrain the partisan gerrymander of the New Jersey congressional delegation. While Justice Stevens in concurrence and Justice Powell in dissent would have reached the constitutionality of the gerrymander directly (we shall discuss this issue subsequently in Chapter 10), the plurality adhered only to an ever stricter application of numerical equality, all the while recognizing its increasing disutility in policing the political process. In response to the argument that the deviations were so trivial as to not only fall within the margin of error of the underlying Census enumeration, but so as to make any impact on individual voting strength meaningless, Justice Brennan argued:

> Adopting any standard other than population equality, using the best census data available, would subtly erode the Constitution's ideal of equal representation. If state legislators knew that a certain *de minimis* level of population differences was acceptable, they would doubtless strive to achieve that level rather than equality.... In this case, appellants argue that a maximum deviation of approximately 0.7% would be considered *de minimis*. If we accept that argument, how are we to regard deviations of 0.8%, 0.95%, 1%, or 1.1%?

Recall that the initial identified advantages of the equipopulation rule were its easy calculation, its administrability, and its prophylactic function against gerrymandering. What happens when there are real disputes about the underlying numbers and when the prophylactic effect is significantly diminished? Does administrability by itself justify the strict application of the equipopulation rule in *Karcher*? *See* John Hart Ely, Democracy and Distrust 121 (1980) (the equipopulation rule "is certainly administrable. In fact, administrability is its long suit, and the more troublesome question is what else it has to recommend it").

2. Paradoxically, strict adherence to the equipopulation principle has reemerged as a potential constraint of gerrymandering. The continuing interaction of one-person, one-vote litigation and partisanship is powerfully illustrated by the post–2000 round of congressional redistricting in Pennsylvania. Declining population entitled Pennsylvania to only 19 congressional seats, a decrease of two from the 1990s. The Republicans controlled both houses of the state legislature as well as the governorship. According to a three-judge federal district court that later reviewed the state's redistricting, prominent national figures in the Republican party ranging from the Speaker of the House to Karl Rove pressured state officials "to adopt a . . . redistricting plan as a punitive measure against Democrats for having enacted apparently pro-Democrat redistricting plans in other states. In response, Republican members of the state House and Senate. . . . ignored all Democratic members of the General Assembly" in drawing a new plan.

The ideal House district size in Pennsylvania at the time was 646,371.5 persons. The Republican plan came quite close: the most populous district had a population of 646,380 and the three least populous each had a population of 646,361, for a total deviation of nineteen people.

The political consequences of the plan were more significant. The plan targeted Democratic incumbents, pairing two sets against one another, and relocating a fifth Democrat into a decisively Republican district where he would have to face a Republican incumbent. In a state-court challenge, the court found that the plan would likely produce a congressional delegation with 13 or 14 Republicans and 5 or 6 Democrats, despite the fact that Democrats normally received more than half the votes cast for congressional candidates.

A three-judge federal district court heard the Democratic challenge and dismissed claims that the plan was an unconstitutional political gerrymander. *See Vieth v. Pennsylvania*, 188 F. Supp. 2d 532 (M. D. Pa. 2002) (three-judge court). But the same court upheld the claim that the plan violated one-person, one-vote. *Vieth v. Pennsylvania*, 195 F. Supp. 2d 672 (M. D. Pa. 2002) (three-judge court). The court found the nineteen-person deviation avoidable and rejected the state's justification for the deviation: while the state pointed to a variety of state interests to explain the overall contours of the plan, the court concluded that "since the focus of our inquiry in the justification phase is population deviation, the only justification submitted which deals with that issue is the policy objective of limiting voter precinct splits." The court found that because it was possible to draw a congressional district map with zero deviation and no precinct splits, the defendants' proffered justification was pretextual:

> Moreover, it is worth noting that of the maps presented at trial, Act 1 [the state's plan] is that which least comports with the neutral legislative policies that the *Karcher* Court stated would justify a Congressional redistricting plan with some deviations. Act 1 is the plan which contains the least compact districts. Act 1 splits the most counties (twenty-five) and municipalities (fifty-nine cities, townships, or boroughs) [and] . . . even splits the most precincts. To the extent that Act

1 retains the cores of prior districts, it does so only for districts containing Republican incumbents.

However, it is on *Karcher's* final endorsed neutral criteria—the avoidance of contests between incumbents—that Act 1 fails most miserably. Although Pennsylvania's loss of two congressional seats requires the pairing of only two sets of incumbents in the 2002 elections, Act 1 pits six incumbents against each other: two pairs of Democrats, and one Republican against one Democrat (the latter in a district that heavily favors Republican candidates). At the same time Act 1 pits more incumbents than necessary against one another, it also creates a new district, District 6, in which no incumbent resides. In the face of such evidence, it is clear that *Karcher*'s neutral criteria were not high on the priority list in enacting Act 1.

The General Assembly then redrew the plan. The new plan—Act 34—eliminated the minute population deviations. The federal district court then upheld this new plan, even as the court made clear that the new plan, like the one it replaced, was an obvious and extreme partisan gerrymander: "like its predecessor, Act 1, jettisons every other neutral non-discriminatory redistricting criteria that the Supreme Court has endorsed in one person-one vote cases. Despite an opportunity to improve upon the numerous deficiencies of Act 1, Defendants have returned to this court with essentially the same map. However, this map does not possess the same population deviations as Act 1." Thus, the court held that *Karcher* was satisfied and that there was no doctrinal basis for holding the partisan gerrymander unconstitutional simple as a partisan gerrymander. *Vieth v. Pennsylvania*, 241 F. Supp. 2d 478 (M.D. Pa. 2003) (three-judge court).

The Supreme Court accepted plaintiff's appeal of their partisan gerrymandering claim and then affirmed the lower court in the most important decision on partisan gerrymandering since the mid–1980s. See *Vieth v. Jubelirer*, 541 U.S. 267 (2004), discussed more fully in our treatment of partisan gerrymandering in Chapter 10. What are the consequences of this combination of a zero-tolerance doctrine on population deviations and virtually no doctrinal constraints on partisan gerrymandering?

3. Given the exacting quality of the equipopulation standard in *Karcher*, should not greater attention be paid to problems of miscounting in the Census enumeration? Although the Census has grown increasingly sophisticated, the Census Bureau estimates that millions of Americans are uncounted each decade. In addition, the undercounting is not random. Racial and ethnic minorities are significantly more likely than non-minorities to be left out of the enumeration. *See* Samuel Issacharoff & Allan J. Lichtman, *The Census Undercount and Minority Representation: The Constitutional Obligation of the States to Guarantee Equal Representation*, 13 Rev. of Litig. 1, 8 (1993) (reporting that percentage of black Americans missed in Census is steadily about 5 percentage points higher than percentage of white Americans missed from 1940 to 1980). Following the refusal of the

Census to statistically adjust the 1990 Census, several cities and states with heavy minority concentrations sued the Department of Commerce claiming that the persistent undercount was unconstitutional. In *Wisconsin v. City of New York*, 517 U.S. 1 (1996), the Supreme Court rejected this claim, primarily on the grounds that the Constitution vests Congress with essentially unreviewable authority to conduct an "actual Enumeration ... in such Manner as they shall by Law direct." Art. I, § 2, cl. 3. In addition, the Court credited the Secretary of Commerce's claim that "distributive accuracy" among the states was a more critical need than "numerical accuracy" in calculating the entire population: "Indeed, a preference for distributive accuracy (even at the expense of some numerical accuracy) would seem to follow from the constitutional purpose of the census, viz., to determine apportionment of the Representatives among the States." 517 U.S. at 19.

In January 1999, the Supreme Court decided the issue of statistical sampling for the 2000 Census in *Department of Commerce v. United States House of Representatives*, 525 U.S. 316 (1999). In an effort to address the growing problem of undercounting, the Census Bureau announced a plan to use statistical sampling for the purpose of apportioning Congressional seats to the States as part of the 2000 Census. However, the United States House of Representatives sought an injunction against the challenged sampling procedure. The case posed a significant constitutional question: whether the Census Clause prohibited the Census Bureau's use of statistical sampling methods by the Census Bureau. But the Court decided the case on statutory grounds, holding that the particular sampling method involved violated the Census Act, 13 U.S.C. § 195. The Court declined to hear the constitutional question presented. The Court interpreted the Act to allow for the use of sampling in gathering demographic data but read the statute to prohibit statistical sampling for the purpose of apportioning congressional seats. Thus, whether or not this use of statistical sampling would violate the Census Clause of the Constitution should a future amendment to the Census Act eliminate the statutory bar is still unclear.

The result in the Census Case is that sampling is not permitted for apportioning seats among the states for representation in the House of Representatives. But the Court also indicated that the Census Act permits—and might perhaps require—that sampling be used to compile the demographic data for the myriad other purposes for which the Census is used. This includes the state redistricting process, which is based on the Census data. Thus, the Secretary of Commerce currently plans to release the Census data in two forms: the first, without sampling, for apportionment of the House; the second, with sampling, for several other potential purposes. For a good, accessible summary of legal issues involving the 2000 Census, see Nathaniel Persily, *2000 Census Data: New Format and New Challenges*, in The Real Y2K Problem: Census 2000 Data and Redistricting Technology 1–27 (Brennan Center, 2000).

4. Should the protection of incumbents be a permissible grounds for departing from the equipopulation command? For arguments that this is an invitation to self-serving behavior by political insiders, *see* Kristen L. Silverberg, Note, *The Illegitimacy of the Incumbent Gerrymander*, 74 Tex. L. Rev. 913 (1996); Sally Dworak–Fisher, Note, *Drawing the Line on Incumbency Protection,* 2 Mich. J. of Race & Law 131 (1996).

5. Does the equipopulation principle require that a majority of voters be able to control electoral outcomes? Consider *Gordon v. Lance*, 403 U.S. 1 (1971), in which the Court reviewed West Virginia requirements that political subdivisions of the state not incur bonded indebtedness or increase tax rates without the approval of 60 percent of the voters in a referendum election. *Gordon* poses the *Baker/Reynolds* problem in reverse. Instead of an entrenched minority having the votes to affirmatively push through its desired legislative agenda, any minority of 40% plus 1 has effective veto power over the will of the majority. In any ensuing negotiations, it would be expected that such a minority would be able to secure significant concessions in order to allow the majority's preferred course of action to be realized. Nonetheless, in an opinion by Chief Justice Burger, the Court upheld the West Virginia supermajority requirements:

> Although West Virginia has not denied any group access to the ballot, it has indeed made it more difficult for some kinds of governmental actions to be taken. Certainly any departure from strict majority rule gives disproportionate power to the minority. But there is nothing in the language of the Constitution, our history, or our cases that requires that a majority always prevail on every issue. On the contrary, while we have recognized that state officials are normally chosen by a vote of the majority of the electorate, we have found no constitutional barrier to the selection of a Governor by a state legislature, after no candidate received a majority of the popular vote.
>
> The Federal Constitution itself provides that a simple majority vote is insufficient on some issues; the provisions on impeachment and ratification of treaties are but two examples. Moreover, the Bill of Rights removes entire areas of legislation from the concept of majoritarian supremacy. The constitutions of many States prohibit or severely limit the power of the legislature to levy new taxes or to create or increase bonded indebtedness, thereby insulating entire areas from majority control. Whether these matters of finance and taxation are to be considered as less "important" than matters of treaties, foreign policy, or impeachment of public officers is more properly left to the determination by the States and the people than to the courts operating under the broad mandate of the Fourteenth Amendment. It must be remembered that in voting to issue bonds voters are committing, in part, the credit of infants and of generations yet unborn, and some restriction on such commitment is not an unreasonable demand. That the bond issue may have the desirable objective of providing better education for

future generations goes to the wisdom of an indebtedness limitation: it does not alter the basic fact that the balancing of interests is one for the State to resolve.

Wisely or not, the people of the State of West Virginia have long since resolved to remove from a simple majority vote the choice on certain decisions as to what indebtedness may be incurred and what taxes their children will bear.

We conclude that so long as such provisions do not discriminate against or authorize discrimination against any identifiable class they do not violate the Equal Protection Clause. We see no meaningful distinction between such absolute provisions on debt, changeable only by constitutional amendment, and provisions that legislative decisions on the same issues require more than a majority vote in the legislature. On the contrary, these latter provisions may, in practice, be less burdensome than the amendment process. Moreover, the same considerations apply when the ultimate power, rather than being delegated to the legislature, remains with the people, by way of a referendum. Indeed, we see no constitutional distinction between the 60% requirement in the present case and a state requirement that a given issue be approved by a majority of all registered voters.

That West Virginia has adopted a rule of decision, applicable to all bond referenda, by which the strong consensus of three-fifths is required before indebtedness is authorized, does not violate the Equal Protection Clause or any other provision of the Constitution.

B.   LOCAL GOVERNANCE

As should be evident, there is a wide array of non-legislative elected offices in the United States. These range from local bodies that resemble smaller legislatures, such as county commissions or city councils, to specialized bodies, such as water district boards or parks commissions, to specific function bodies that are frequently not even elected, such as school boards. While there is no specific constitutional command that such bodies be elected, the applicability of the equipopulation principle to such bodies as were elected quickly came to occupy the courts. In *Avery v. Midland County*, 390 U.S. 474 (1968), the Court held that the election of the Commissioners Court of a Texas county must satisfy the *Reynolds* standard. Although the Commissioners Court performed functions that were both administrative/executive and legislative, the Court nonetheless found that one-person/one-vote applied because the Commissioner Court served as the immediate "unit of local government with general responsibility and power for local affairs." Should it have made any difference that the Texas Supreme Court had previously held that, "[t]he primary function of the commissioners court is the administration of the business affairs of the county. Its legislative functions are negligible and county government is not otherwise comparable to the legislature of the state"? *Avery v. Midland County*, 406 S.W.2d 422, 426 (Tex. 1966). Recall that *Kramer v. Union Free School District No. 15*, 395 U.S. 621 (1969), also rejected the attempted distinction between a school board and the state legislature.

By contrast, in *Sailors v. Board of Education of Kent County*, 387 U.S. 105 (1967), the Court upheld an appointive system of selecting members of a county school board, even though that system produced a board whose members each "represented" local school districts with disparate numbers of people. Although an argument could be made that the school board exercised some general responsibilities, the Court held that there was no constitutional requirement that school boards be elected and that the largely administrative function of the board permitted appointment of the county school board by delegates of local school boards.

In *Hadley v. Junior College District*, 397 U.S. 50 (1970), the Court confronted a case falling between the cracks of *Avery* and *Sailors*. Under Missouri law, eight school districts combined to form a Junior College District of Metropolitan Kansas City. The Trustees were apportioned on the basis of school age students residing in each of the eight school districts. Under this formula, the urban Kansas City school district elected 50 percent of the total number of trustees, although it contained 60 percent of the school age population. In order to reach the specific powers over junior colleges alone, however, the Court had to revisit the *Avery* rule that appeared to rely on the exercise of general powers to trigger one-person/one-vote scrutiny:

> Appellants in this case argue that the junior college trustees exercised general governmental powers over the entire district and that under *Avery* the State was thus required to apportion the trustees according to population on an equal basis, as far as practicable. Appellants argue that since the trustees can levy and collect taxes, issue bonds with certain restrictions, hire and fire teachers, make contracts, collect fees, supervise and discipline students, pass on petitions to annex school districts, acquire property by condemnation, and in general manage the operations of the junior college, ... their powers are equivalent, for apportionment purposes, to those exercised by the county commissioners in *Avery*. We feel that these powers, while not fully as broad as those of the Midland County Commissioners [], certainly show that the trustees perform important governmental functions within the districts, and we think these powers are general enough and have sufficient impact throughout the district to justify the conclusion that the principle which we applied in *Avery* should also be applied here.

What powers of government would not be considered "important governmental functions" after *Hadley*?

Board of Estimate v. Morris

489 U.S. 688 (1989).

■ JUSTICE WHITE delivered the opinion of the Court.

The Board of Estimate of the city of New York consists of three members elected citywide, plus the elected presidents of each of the city's five boroughs. Because the boroughs have widely disparate populations—yet each has equal representation on the board—the Court of Appeals for the Second Circuit held that this structure is inconsistent with the Equal Protection Clause of the Fourteenth Amendment. We affirm.

Appellees, residents and voters of Brooklyn, New York City's most populous borough, commenced this action against the city in December 1981. They charged that the city's charter sections that govern the composition of the Board of Estimate are inconsistent with the Equal Protection Clause of the Fourteenth Amendment as construed and applied in various decisions of this Court dealing with districting and apportionment for the purpose of electing legislative bodies.

* * *

As an initial matter, we reject the city's suggestion that because the Board of Estimate is a unique body wielding non-legislative powers, board membership elections are not subject to review under the prevailing reapportionment doctrine. The equal protection guarantee of "one-person, one-vote" extends not only to congressional districting plans, *see Wesberry v. Sanders*, not only to state legislative districting, see *Reynolds v. Sims*, but also to local government apportionment. Both state and local elections are subject to the general rule of population equality between electoral districts.

* * *

These cases are based on the propositions that in this country the people govern themselves through their elected representatives and that "each and every citizen has an inalienable right to full and effective participation in the political processes" of the legislative bodies of the Nation, State, or locality as the case may be. Since "most citizens can achieve this participation only as qualified voters through the election of legislators to represent them," full and effective participation requires "that each citizen have an equally effective voice in the election of members of his ... legislature." As Daniel Webster once said, "the right to choose a representative is every man's portion of sovereign power." Electoral systems should strive to make each citizen's portion equal. If districts of widely unequal population elect an equal number of representatives, the voting power of each citizen in the larger constituencies is debased and the citizens in those districts have a smaller share of representation than do those in the smaller districts. . . .

That the members of New York City's Board of Estimate trigger this constitutional safeguard is certain. All eight officials become members as a matter of law upon their various elections. The mayor, the comptroller, and the president of the city council, who comprise the board's citywide number, are elected by votes of the entire city electorate. Each of these three cast two votes, except that the mayor has no vote on the acceptance or modification of his budget proposal. Similarly, when residents of the city's five boroughs—the Bronx, Brooklyn, Manhattan, Queens, and Richmond (Staten Island)—elect their respective borough presidents, the elections decide each borough's representative on the board. These five members each have single votes on all board matters.

New York law assigns to the board a significant range of functions common to municipal governments. Fiscal responsibilities include calculating sewer and water rates, tax abatements, and property taxes on urban development projects. The board manages all city property; exercises plenary zoning authority; dispenses all franchises and leases on city property; fixes generally the salaries of all officers and persons compensated through city moneys; and grants all city contracts. This array of powers, which the board shares with no other part of the New York City government, are exercised through the aforementioned voting scheme: three citywide officials cast a total of six votes; their five borough counterparts, one vote each.

In addition, and of major significance, the board shares legislative functions with the city council with respect to modifying and approving the city's capital and expense budgets. The mayor submits a proposed city budget to the board and city council, but does not participate in board decisions to adopt or alter the proposal. Approval or modification of the proposed budget requires agreement between the board and the city council. Board votes on budget matters, therefore, consist of four votes cast by two at-large members; and five, by the borough presidents.

This considerable authority to formulate the city's budget, which last fiscal year surpassed $25 billion, as well as the board's land use, franchise, and contracting powers over the city's 7 million inhabitants, situate the board comfortably within the category of governmental bodies whose "powers are general enough and have sufficient impact throughout the district" to require that elections to the body comply with equal protection strictures.

The city also erroneously implies that the board's composition survives constitutional challenge because the citywide members cast a 6–to–5 majority of board votes and hence are in position to control the outcome of board actions. The at-large members, however, as the courts below observed, often do not vote together; and when they do not, the outcome is determined by the votes of the borough presidents, each having one vote. Two citywide members, with the help of the presidents of the two least populous boroughs, the Bronx and Staten Island, will prevail over a disagreeing coalition of the third citywide member and the presidents of the three boroughs that contain a large majority of the city's population. Furthermore, because the mayor has no vote on budget issues, the citywide members alone cannot control board budgetary decisions.

The city's primary argument is that the courts below erred in the methodology by which they determined whether, and to what extent, the method of electing the board members gives the voters in some boroughs more power than the voters in other boroughs. Specifically, the city focuses on the relative power of the voters in the various boroughs to affect board decisions, an approach which involves recognizing the weighted voting of the three citywide members.

[... T]he method urged by the city to determine an individual voter's power to affect the outcome of a board vote first calculates the power of each member of the board to affect a board vote, and then calculates voters' power to cast the determining vote in the election of that member. This method, termed the Banzhaf Index, applies as follows: 552 possible voting combinations exist in which any one member can affect the outcome of a board vote. Each borough president can cast the determining vote in 48 of these combinations (giving him a "voting power" of 8.7%), while each citywide member can determine the outcome in 104 of 552 combinations (18.8%). A citizen's voting power through each representative is calculated by dividing the representative's voting power by the square root of the population represented; a citizen's total voting power thus aggregates his power through each of his four representatives—borough president, mayor, comptroller, and council president. Deviation from ideal voting power is then calculated by comparing this figure with the figure arrived at when one considers an electoral district of ideal population. Calculated in this manner, the maximum deviation in the voting power to control board outcomes is 30.8% on nonbudget matters, and, because of the mayor's absence, a higher deviation on budget issues.

The Court of Appeals gave careful attention to and rejected this submission. We agree with the reasons given by the Court of Appeals that the population-based approach of our cases from *Reynolds* through *Abate* [*v. Mundt*, 403 U.S. 182 (1971)] should not be put aside in this litigation. We note also that we have once before, although in a different context, declined to accept the approach now urged by the city. *Whitcomb v. Chavis*, 403 U.S. 124 (1971). In that case we observed that the Banzhaf methodology "remains a theoretical one" and is unrealistic in not taking into account "any political or other factors which might affect the actual voting power of the residents, which might include party affiliation, race, previous voting characteristics or any other factors which go into the entire political voting situation."

The personal right to vote is a value in itself, and a citizen is, without more and without mathematically calculating his power to determine the outcome of an election, shortchanged if he may vote for only one representative when citizens in a neighboring district, of equal population, vote for two; or to put it another way, if he may vote for one representative and the voters in another district half the size also elect one representative. . . .

The Court of Appeals also thought that the city's approach . . . did not reflect the way the board actually works in practice; rather, the method is a theoretical explanation of each board member's power to affect the outcome of board actions. It may be that in terms of assuring fair and effective representation, the equal protection approach reflected in the *Reynolds v. Sims* line of cases is itself imperfect, but it does assure that legislators will be elected by, and represent citizens in, districts of substantially equal size. It does not attempt to inquire whether, in terms of how the legislature actually works in practice, the districts have equal power to affect a legislative outcome. This would be a difficult and ever-changing task, and its challenge is hardly met by a mathematical calculation that itself stops short of examining the actual day-to-day operations of the legislative body. . . .

Having decided to follow the established method of resolving equal protection issues in districting and apportionment cases, the Court of Appeals then inquired whether the presence of at-large members on the board should be factored into the process of determining the deviation between the more and less populous boroughs. The court decided that they need not be taken into account because the at-large members and the borough presidents respond to different constituencies. The three at-large members obviously represent citywide interests; but, in the Court of Appeals' judgment, the borough presidents represent and are responsive to their boroughs, yet each has one vote despite the dramatic inequalities in the boroughs' populations. Consideration of the citywide members might be different, the court explained, "If the at-large bloc was not simply a majority, but a majority such that it would always and necessarily control the governing body, and the district representatives play a decidedly subsidiary role. . . ."

The Court of Appeals then focused on the five boroughs as single-member districts, electing five representatives to the board, each with a single vote. Applying the formula that we have utilized without exception since 1971, the Court of Appeals agreed with the District Court that the maximum percentage deviation from the ideal population is 132.9%.

We do not agree with the Court of Appeals' approach. . . . Here the voters in each borough vote for the at-large members as well as their borough president, and they are also represented by those members. Hence in determining whether there is substantially equal voting power and representation, the citywide members are a major component in the calculation and should not be ignored.

Because of the approach followed by the District Court and the Court of Appeals, there was no judicial finding concerning the total deviation from the ideal that would be if the at-large members of the board are taken into account. In pleadings filed with the District Court, however, appellees indicated, and the city agreed, that the deviation would then be 78%. And as to budget matters, when only two citywide members participate, the deviation would be somewhat larger. We accept for purposes of this case the figure agreed upon by the parties.

We note that no case of ours has indicated that a deviation of some 78% could ever be justified. At the very least, the local government seeking to support such a difference between electoral districts would bear a very difficult burden, and we are not prepared to differ with the holding of the courts below that this burden has not been carried. The city presents in this Court nothing that was not considered below, arguing chiefly that the board, as presently structured, is essential to the successful government of a regional entity, the city of New York. The board, it is said, accommodates natural and political boundaries as well as local interests. Furthermore, because the board has been effective it should not be disturbed. All of this, the city urges, is supported by the city's history. The courts below, of course, are in a much better position than we to assess the weight of these arguments, and they concluded that the proffered governmental interests were either invalid or were not sufficient to justify a deviation of 132%.... Their analysis is equally applicable to a 78% deviation, and we conclude that the city's proffered governmental interests do not suffice to justify such a substantial departure from the one-person, one-vote ideal.

Accordingly the judgment of the Court of Appeals is

Affirmed.

NOTES AND QUESTIONS

1. In *Wells v. Edwards*, 347 F. Supp. 453 (M. D. La. 1972)(three-judge court), *aff'd*, 409 U.S. 1095 (1973) (per curiam), the court found the election of state court judges not to be governed by the one-person/one-vote rule. According to the court:

> The primary purpose of one-man, one-vote apportionment is to make sure that each official member of an elected body speaks for approximately the same number of constituents. But as stated in *Buchanan v. Rhodes*, [249 F. Supp. 860 (N.D. Ohio 1960), appeal dismissed, 385 U.S. 3]: "Judges do not represent people, they serve people." Thus, the rationale behind the one-man, one-vote principle, which evolved out of efforts to preserve a truly representative form of government, is simply not relevant to the makeup of the judiciary.

Wells involved the Louisiana Supreme Court, whose seven Justices were elected from judicial districts with widely varying populations—created directly by the Louisiana Constitution of 1921 and unchanged since that time. Is the equipopulation principle "simply not relevant" to the election of state court judges? Are elected judges truly less "representative" than elected Trustees of a Junior College District? For a discussion of the tension between judicial elections and judicial independence, *see* Hans A. Linde, *The Judge as Political Candidate*, 39 Clev. St. L. Rev. 1 (1991); Steven P. Croley, *The Majoritarian Difficulty: The Elective Judiciaries and the Rule of Law,* 62 U. Chi. L. Rev. 689 (1995).

2. *Morris* proved a significant tripwire in New York City. The Board of Estimate served to give enhanced power to the outlying boroughs of New York, primarily Staten Island. This arrangement allayed fears that the concentration of population and wealth in the largest boroughs would result in unfavorable treatment for residents without the same level of political clout. Although the modern borough-based Board of Estimate had not yet been created at the founding of New York City in 1898, it did emerge in 1901 and became a mainstay of the City's development. After *Morris*, strong secessionist sentiments surfaced in Staten Island. *See* Richard Briffault, *Voting Rights, Home Rule, and Metropolitan Governance: The Secession of Staten Island as a Case Study in the Dilemmas of Local Self–Determination*, 92 Colum. L. Rev. 775 (1992). Does regional representation to the least urbanized part of New York City fall within any of the recognized grounds for departure from the strict application of one-person/one-vote?

Ball v. James

451 U.S. 355 (1981).

■ JUSTICE STEWART delivered the opinion of the Court.

This appeal concerns the constitutionality of the system for electing the directors of a large water reclamation district in Arizona, a system which, in essence, limits voting eligibility to landowners and apportions voting power according to the amount of land a voter owns. The case requires us to consider whether the peculiarly narrow function of this local governmental body and the special relationship of one class of citizens to that body releases it from the strict demands of the one-person, one-vote principle of the Equal Protection Clause of the Fourteenth Amendment.

* * *

III

Reynolds v. Sims, supra, held that the Equal Protection Clause requires adherence to the principle of one-person, one-vote in elections of state legislators. *Avery v. Midland County,* 390 U.S. 474, extended the *Reynolds* rule to the election of officials of a county government, holding that the elected officials exercised "general governmental powers over the entire geographic area served by the body." 390 U.S., at 485. The Court, however, reserved any decision on the application of *Reynolds* to "a special-purpose unit of government assigned the performance of functions affecting definable groups of constituents more than other constituents." 390 U.S., at 483–484. In *Hadley v. Junior College District*, 397 U.S. 50, the Court extended *Reynolds* to the election of trustees of a community college district because those trustees "exercised general governmental powers" and "perform[ed] important governmental functions" that had significant effect on all citizens residing within the district. 397 U.S., at 53–54. But in that case the Court stated: "It is of course possible that there might be some case in which a State elects certain functionaries whose duties are so far removed from normal governmental activities and so disproportionately affect different groups that a popular election in compliance with *Reynolds* . . . might not be required. . . ."

The Court found such a case in *Salyer* [*Land Co. v. Tulare Lake Basin Water Storage District*, 410 U.S. 719 (1973)]. The Tulare Lake Basin Water Storage District involved there encompassed 193,000 acres, 85% of which were farmed by one or another of four corporations. . . . Under California law, public water districts could acquire, store, conserve, and distribute water, and though the Tulare Lake Basin Water Storage District had never chosen to do so, could generate and sell any form of power it saw fit to support its water operations. *Id.*, at 723–724. The costs of the project were assessed against each landowner according to the water benefits the landowner received. *Id.*, at 724. At issue in the case was the constitutionality of the scheme for electing the directors of the district, under which only landowners could vote, and voting power was apportioned according to the assessed valuation of the voting landowner's property. The Court recognized that the Tulare Lake Basin Water Storage District did exercise "some typical governmental powers," including the power to hire and fire workers, contract for construction of projects, condemn private property, and issue general obligation bonds. *Id.*, at 728, and n. 7. Nevertheless, the Court concluded that the district had "relatively limited authority," because "its primary purpose, indeed the reason for its existence, is to provide for the acquisition, storage, and distribution of water for farming in the Tulare Lake Basin." *Id.*, at 728. . . . The Court also noted that the financial burdens of the district could not but fall on the landowners, in proportion to the benefits they received from the district, and that the district's actions therefore disproportionately affected the voting landowners. *Id.*, at 729. The *Salyer* Court thus held that the strictures of *Reynolds* did not apply to the Tulare District, and proceeded to inquire simply whether the statutory voting scheme based on land valuation at least bore some relevancy to the statute's objectives. The Court concluded that the California Legislature could have reasonably assumed that without voting power apportioned according to the value of their land, the landowners might not have been willing to subject their lands to the lien of the very assessments which made the creation of the district possible. 410 U.S., at 731.

As noted by the Court of Appeals, the services currently provided by the Salt River District are more diverse and affect far more people than those of the Tulare Lake Basin Water Storage District. Whereas the Tulare

District included an area entirely devoted to agriculture and populated by only 77 persons, the Salt River District includes almost half the population of the State, including large parts of Phoenix and other cities. Moreover, the Salt River District, unlike the Tulare District, has exercised its statutory power to generate and sell electric power, and has become one of the largest suppliers of such power in the State. Further, whereas all the water delivered by the Tulare District went for agriculture, roughly 40% of the water delivered by the Salt River District goes to urban areas or is used for nonagricultural purposes in farming areas. Finally whereas all operating costs of the Tulare District were born by the voting landowners through assessments apportioned according to land value, most of the capital and operating costs of the Salt River District have been met through the revenues generated by the selling of electric power. Nevertheless, a careful examination of the Salt River District reveals that, under the principles of the *Avery, Hadley,* and *Salyer* cases, these distinctions do not amount to a constitutional difference.

First, the District simply does not exercise the sort of governmental powers that invoke the strict demands of *Reynolds.* The District cannot impose ad valorem property taxes or sales taxes. It cannot enact any laws governing the conduct of citizens, nor does it administer such normal functions of government as the maintenance of streets, the operation of schools, or sanitation, health, or welfare services.

Second, though they were characterized broadly by the Court of Appeals, even the District's water functions, which constitute the primary and originating purpose of the District, are relatively narrow. The District and Association do not own, sell, or buy water, nor do they control the use of any water they have delivered. The District simply stores water behind its dams, conserves it from loss, and delivers it through project canals. It is true, as the Court of Appeals noted, that as much as 40% of the water delivered by the District goes for nonagricultural purposes. But the distinction between agricultural and urban land is of no special constitutional significance in this context. The constitutionally relevant fact is that all water delivered by the Salt River District, like the water delivered by the Tulare Lake Basin Water Storage District, is distributed according to land ownership, and the District does not and cannot control the use to which the landowners who are entitled to the water choose to put it. As repeatedly recognized by the Arizona courts, though the state legislature has allowed water districts to become nominal public entities in order to obtain inexpensive bond financing, the districts remain essentially business enterprises, created by and chiefly benefiting a specific group of landowners.... As in *Salyer,* the nominal public character of such an entity cannot transform it into the type of governmental body for which the Fourteenth Amendment demands a one-person, one-vote system of election.

Finally, neither the existence nor size of the District's power business affects the legality of its property-based voting scheme. As this Court has noted in a different context, the provision of electricity is not a traditional element of governmental sovereignty, *Jackson v. Metropolitan Edison Co.*, 419 U.S. 345, 353 [(1974)], and so is not in itself the sort of general or important governmental function that would make the government provider subject to the doctrine of the *Reynolds* case. In any event, since the electric power functions were stipulated to be incidental to the water functions which are the District's primary purpose, they cannot change the character of that enterprise. The Arizona Legislature permitted the District to generate and sell electricity to subsidize the water operations which were the beneficiaries intended by the statute. A key part of the *Salyer* decision was that the voting scheme for a public entity like a water district may constitutionally reflect the narrow primary purpose for which the district is created. In this case, the parties have stipulated that the primary legislative purpose of the District is to store, conserve, and deliver water for use by District landowners, that the sole legislative reason for making water projects public entities was to enable them to raise revenue through interest-free bonds, and that the development and sale of electric power was undertaken not for the primary purpose of providing electricity to the public, but "to support the primary irrigation functions by supplying power for reclamation uses and by providing revenues which could be applied to increase the amount and reduce the cost of water to Association subscribed lands."

The appellees claim, and the Court of Appeals agreed, that the sheer size of the power operations and the great number of people they affect serve to transform the District into an entity of general governmental power. But no matter how great the number of nonvoting residents buying electricity from the District, the relationship between them and the District's power operations is essentially that between consumers and a business enterprise from which they buy. Nothing in the *Avery*, *Hadley*, or *Salyer* cases suggests that the volume of business or the breadth of economic effect of a venture undertaken by a government entity as an incident of its narrow and primary governmental public function can, of its own weight, subject the entity to the one-person, one-vote requirements of the *Reynolds* case.

The functions of the Salt River District are therefore of the narrow, special sort which justifies a departure from the popular-election requirement of the *Reynolds* case. And as in *Salyer*, an aspect of that limited purpose is the disproportionate relationship the District's functions bear to the specific class of people whom the system makes eligible to vote. The voting landowners are the only residents of the District whose lands are subject to liens to secure District bonds. Only these landowners are subject to the acreage-based taxing power of the District, and voting landowners are the only residents who have ever committed capital to the District through stock assessments charged by the Association. The *Salyer* opinion did not say that the selected class of voters for a special public entity must be the only parties at all affected by the operations of the entity, or that their entire economic well-being must depend on that entity. Rather, the question was whether the effect of the entity's operations on them was disproportionately greater than the effect on those seeking the vote.

As in the *Salyer* case, we conclude that the voting scheme for the District is constitutional because it bears a reasonable relationship to its statutory objectives. Here, according to the stipulation of the parties, the subscriptions of land which made the Association and then the District possible might well have never occurred had not the subscribing landowners been assured a special voice in the conduct of the District's business. Therefore, as in *Salyer*, the State could rationally limit the vote to landowners. Moreover, Arizona could rationally make the weight of their vote dependent upon the number of acres they own, since that number reasonably reflects the relative risks they incurred as landowners and the distribution of the benefits and the burdens of the District's water operations.

The judgment of the Court of Appeals is reversed, and the case is remanded for further proceedings consistent with this opinion.

■ JUSTICE POWELL, concurring.

Our cases have recognized the necessity of permitting experimentation with political communities. *E.g., Holt Civic Club v. Tuscaloosa*, 439 U.S. 60, 71–72 (1978). As this case illustrates, it may be difficult to decide when experimentation and political compromise have resulted in an impermissible delegation of those governmental powers that generally affect all of the people to a body with a selective electorate. But state legislatures, responsive to the interests of all the people, normally are better qualified to make this judgment than federal courts.... Given the broad reforms effected by *Reynolds v. Sims*, we should expect that a legislature elected on the rule of one person, one vote will be vigilant to prevent undue concentration of power in the hands of undemocratic bodies. The absence of just such a political safeguard was a major justification for the Court's role in requiring legislative reapportionment. *See Baker v. Carr*, 369 U.S. 186, 258–259 (1962) (Clark, J., concurring).

The Court's opinion convincingly demonstrates that the powers exercised by the Salt River District are not powers that always must be exercised by a popularly elected body.[] Both storage and delivery of water are functions that in other areas of the Nation are performed by private or administrative bodies. These tasks sometimes are performed by an elected government entity, because of the aridity of the Southwest, federal water policy, and the historical interest of Arizona landowners in irrigation, not because of their inherent character nor an insistent demand that the people as a whole decide how much water each will receive or how much each will pay for electricity.

Appellees argue that control of water is of prime importance in the Southwest and that many people purchase electricity from the District. These observations raise the question whether this Court should interfere with the constitution of the District, but do not answer it. The Arizona Legislature recently has demonstrated its control over the electoral processes of the District. It has reformed the District to increase the political voice of the small householder at the expense of the large landowner.[] This reform no doubt reflects political and demographic changes in Arizona since the District was established.

The authority and will of the Arizona Legislature to control the electoral composition of the District are decisive for me in this case. The District is large enough and the resources it manages are basic enough that the people will act through their elected legislature when further changes in the governance of the District are warranted. We should allow the political process to operate. For this Court to dictate how the Board of the District must be elected would detract from the democratic process we profess to protect.

NOTES AND QUESTIONS

1. Justice Powell's concurrence in *Ball* raises two important questions about the nature of judicial review of how the political process is constituted. He identifies the importance of the *Reynolds v. Sims* line of cases as destabilizing a locked-in legislative distribution of power that was structurally immune from being displaced by the electorate. This argument responds to Justice Frankfurter's initial argument in *Colegrove v. Green* that the resolution of the maldistribution of power should come from within the political process itself. Justice Powell also returns to the theme first encountered in *Kramer v. Union School District* that the justification for judicial intervention might turn on whether the voting rules in questions were of sufficient public moment to arouse concerted efforts at reform at the state legislative level. Thus, for Justice Powell, the fact that water issues are of undoubted public salience in the Southwest indicates that maldistributions of political power are remediable through the state legislature. It then follows that the courts should be leery of entrenching upon local decisions about how to order the political process.

There is, however, the real concern that Justice Powell may be substituting one area of judicial non-expertise for another. Do judges really possess the skills necessary to distinguish electoral arrangements over matters that "are basic enough" to elicit popular political mobilizations, from those that are not? Is the composition of water regulatory agencies more or less likely to fall into that category than electoral rules for selecting school boards? How can courts determine when sufficient political safeguards exist to leave claims of political distortion to the political process itself to remedy? Can a line be drawn that would reject remedies that must be directed to the political body that is itself under challenge, as with the redistricting powers of a state legislature over itself?

There is also a strong concern emanating from public choice theory. At its most basic, public choice theory would challenge the ability of a concerned but relatively diffuse majority of the electorate to force an issue squarely onto the legislative arena. Because of the greater investment of what are generally denominated special interest groups, self-interested minorities tend to do disproportionately well in the legislative arena. For example, though most polls routinely show a majority of Americans favoring some form of gun control, the National Rifle Association is relatively successful in frustrating efforts to limit access to firearms. While a majority of the electorate may favor such restrictions if the question were posed in a survey, few are willing to vote exclusively based on that preference. By contrast, the NRA is credibly able to threaten to deliver or withhold some non-trivial number of votes based exclusively on the gun control issue. For a politician therefore, a vote in favor of gun control by itself is unlikely to translate into any votes, but is rather certain to lose votes. There is also the funding, lobbyists, and public relations that come with this type of strong interest group involvement in the political process. Is it credible to argue, as does Justice Powell, that a political monopoly over water policies would be that easy to dislodge at the state legislative level? For an extensive discussion of public choice theory and the political process, see Daniel A. Farber & Philip P. Frickey, Law and Public Choice (1991).

2.   What is it that distinguishes the Salt River District from "the normal functions of government"? Can delivery of water to half the population of a parched state such as Arizona really be thought to be outside such normal governmental functions? After all, public works for the delivery of water have long been thought a major activity of government, going back to the Romans and even before. A history of the area under consideration in *Ball* raises questions about whether water management can properly be considered a non-central part of government:

> The land around Phoenix is martini-dry. The only reason a city exists there at all is that as long ago as the time of Christ, humans of the Hohokam tribe recognized that by the standards of the Sonoran desert, the Valley of the Sun can be made water rich. These native Americans built a 250–mile canal system that permitted an advanced civilization to support twenty thousand people. For reasons that remain a mystery, the Hohokam disappeared from the valley just before Columbus sailed. A century and a half later, the Spanish showed up and gave the name Rio Salado–Salt River–to the broad gravel bed from which the canals radiated. A miner, scout, and Confederate calvary veteran named Jack Swilling reintroduced canal building to the area in the late 1800s. Then, in 1902, President Teddy Roosevelt championed the National Reclamation Act, which provided government loans to "reclaim" Western lands with irrigation projects. Metropolitan Phoenix rose around the bed of the Salt River because, in 1903, the shadow government called the Salt River Project was born. . . .

> In the dry Southwest, water is the linchpin of the universe. With water you can create charming cities, fields of agricultural plenty, thriving industry, or wild rivers that charge the spirit. But there's not enough water to have all four. Who gets what is determined in a highly expensive, complex, and politicized fashion. And in central Arizona, that means the Salt River Project. An entity like the Salt River Project, which determines the price and availability of electricity, has the power of life and death. In Arizona in the summer, people without air conditioning die, just as surely as do people in Montana without winter heat. When the Salt River Project decides to encourage water conservation—or, conversely, subsidizes water use by making it artificially cheap—or decides to share the cost of a nuclear reactor forty miles upwind of Phoenix or builds a coal-fired generator whose pollution is accused of obscuring the Grand Canyon, it exercises more control over the Arizona environment than virtually any other player.

Joel Garreau, Edge City: Life on the Frontier 192–93 (1991). Consider an alternative analysis focusing on the difference between the proprietary and legislative functions of government:

> Local government as business enterprise gave the Court a new framework for considering questions of local government organization, thereby increasing the discretion accorded the states in the creation of locally representative public entities. If a local government is a business enterprise, then the organizing principles for political bodies—universal adult resident enfranchisement and equal population representation—need not apply. With the proprietary enterprise model as an option, a state may design a local government to be responsive and accountable to just a limited group within the locality without having to prove that the restriction on the franchise or the bias in local representation is narrowly focused on all those interested in the local government and necessary to the furtherance of a compelling state interest. Moreover, although based on the notion that the restrictive franchise is justified by the landowners' stake in the special district enterprise, proprietary governments are not, in turn, subject to a rigid requirement that votes actually reflect the extent of a landowner's potential liability. Proprietary governments may use assessment-based voting, acreage-based voting, or even one owner/one vote for qualified owners.

Richard Briffault, *Who Rules at Home?: One Person/One Vote and Local Governments*, 60 U. Chi. L. Rev. 339, 369 (1993).

3. Following *Ball*, a broad array of governmental bodies were found to be single purpose boards and therefore immune from one-person/one-vote challenge. *See, e.g., State v. Frontier Acres Community Development District Pasco County*, 472 So.2d 455 (Fla. 1985) (community development district); *Stelzel v. South Indian River Water Control District*, 486 So.2d 65 (Fla. App. 1986) (water control district); *Goldstein v. Mitchell*, 494 N.E.2d 914

(Ill. App. 1986) (drainage district); *Moores v. Edlebrock*, 276 Cal.Rptr. 320 (Cal. 1990) (water district); *Foster v. Sunnyside Valley Irrigation District*, 687 P.2d 841 (Wash. 1984) (irrigation district); *Porterfield v. Van Boening*, 744 P.2d 468 (Ariz. App. 1987) (irrigation district); *Arizona Farmworkers Union v. Agricultural Employment Relations Board*, 712 P.2d 960 (Ariz. App. 1985) (union representation district). *But see Lower Valley Water and Sanitation District v. Public Service Co. of N.M.*, 632 P.2d 1170 (N.M. 1981) (sanitation district not a single purpose body).

4. *Salyer* and *Ball* raise important issues about the nature of individual access to the ballot whenever jurisdictions limit the franchise to property owners, generally referred to as freeholders. For an example of cases upholding the franchise limited to freeholders, *see Lane v. Oyster Bay*, 603 N.Y.S.2d 53 (Sup. Ct. App. Div. 1993) (can limit vote on extension of sanitation collection district to freeholders). A number of issues follow from the restriction of the franchise. First, does the single purpose district ("SPD") exception make it permissible to limit the range of people who can sign the petition asking that a SPD be created in the first place? That is, do non-freeholders have any right to participate before the district exists? The general answer is that the petition can be limited. *See Gillard v. Estrella Dells I Improvement District*, 541 P.2d 932 (Ariz. App. 1975); *Lower Valley Water & Sanitation District v. Public Service Co. of N.M.*, 632 P.2d 1170 (N.M. 1981); *Humble v. Metropoilitan Transit Auth.*, 636 S.W.2d 484 (Tex. App. 1982); *Doenges v. Salt Lake City*, 614 P.2d 1237 (Utah 1980). There is, however, an exception to the general rule. If the result of a successful petition would be a vote by the full electorate, then the one-person/one-vote rule applies because one group cannot be allowed to control the full electorate's ability to vote. *See Hayward v. Clay*, 573 F.2d 187 (4th Cir.), *cert. denied*, 439 U.S. 959 (1978); *City of Seattle v. State*, 694 P.2d 641 (Wash. 1985).

A second outgrowth of the SPD cases is whether they recognize any affirmative right in the more directly affected group. For example, while it is clear that the vote in *Salyer* could be limited to freeholders, did it *have* to be limited to freeholders? The answer is no. *Collins v. Goshen*, 635 F.2d 954 (2d Cir. 1980); *Cantwell v. Hudnut*, 566 F.2d 30 (7th Cir. 1977), *cert. denied*, 439 U.S. 1114 (1979); *East Lake Water Assoc. v. Rogers*, 761 P.2d 627 (Wash. App. 1988). A similar question is whether, even if the directly affected group doesn't have the exclusive right to vote, does it have any right to vote at all? Again, the answer appears to be no. *See Collins v. Brennan*, 456 N.Y.S.2d 931 (Sup. Ct. Tompkins Cty. 1982) (referendum election on sewer project not required to include nonresident property owners).

A third question concerns the restriction of the franchise based on geography rather than property-holding, which is also generally upheld. *See Simi Valley Recreation & Park District v. Local Agency Formation Comm'n*, 124 Cal.Rptr. 635 (Cal. App. 1975) (permissible to exclude residents who don't live in area to be deannexed; special purpose district doesn't require strict scrutiny); *Moorman v. Wood*, 504 F. Supp. 467 (E. D. Ky. 1980) (permissible to limit franchise in deannexation to only those voters in area potentially to be deannexed); *New York v. State*, 556 N.Y.S.2d 823 (Sup. Ct.), *aff'd* 561 N.Y.S.2d 154 (Ct. App., N.Y., 1990) (permissible to limit vote on Staten Island secession to Staten Island residents); *King County Water District No. 54 v. King County Boundary Review Board*, 554 P.2d 1060 (Wash. 1976) (*en banc*) (in taking over water district, city can limit vote to city residents, who are most directly affected); *Provance v. Shawnee Mission Unified School District No. 512*, 648 P.2d 710 (Kan.), *aff'd* 683 P.2d 902 (Kan. 1984) (permissible to limit school closing election to residents in vicinity of affected school). *But see Fullerton Joint Union High School v. State Board of Educ.*, 654 P.2d 168 (Cal. 1982) (*en banc*) (cannot limit deannexation vote to voters in deannexation area).

Finally, courts have recognized a category of special purpose bodies that, like special purpose districts, have been held immune from one-person/one-vote challenge. These decisions include: *The Florida Bar re Amendments to the Rules Regulating the Florida Bar (Reapportionment)*, 518 So.2d 251 (Fla. 1987) (Florida Bar Association Board of Governors elected from circuits of varying population); *Opinion of the Justices*, 319 So.2d 699 (Ala. 1975) (electric company board); *Humane Society v. New Jersey State Fish & Game Council*, 362 A.2d 20 (N.J. 1976) (appointed board of state fish and game council); *Slisz v. Western Regional Off–Track Betting Corp.*, 382 F. Supp. 1231 (W. D. N. Y. 1974) (appointed board treated as "quasi-elective," but sustained because of limited powers); *Sullivan v. Farmers Home Administration*, 691 F. Supp. 927 (E. D. N. C. 1987) (FmHA County Loan Committees upheld despite borrowers and spouses not permitted on loan committees); *Hedge v. Lyng*, 689 F. Supp. 898 (D. Minn. 1988) (same); *Benner v. Oswald*, 444 F. Supp. 545 (M. D. Pa. 1978), *aff'd*, 592 F.2d 174 (3d Cir.), *cert. denied*, 444 U.S. 832 (1979) (university board of trustees); *Davis v. AT & T*, 478 F.2d 1375 (2d Cir. 1973) (assuming state action, corporation is a special purpose entity). *But see Quinn v. Millsap*, 491 U.S. 95 (1989) (striking down, under rational relation standard of review, a Missouri statute limiting membership to landholders for advisory board of freeholders appointed by governor); *Hellebust v. Brownback*, 824 F. Supp. 1511 (D. Kan. 1993), *aff'd* 42 F.3d 1331 (10th Cir. 1994) (striking down on one-person/one vote grounds a board that regulated milk and meat, had a right to inspect and seize, managed dams, and governed all weights and measures in state).

5.   One of the most important recent tests at the local-government level of the "one person, one vote" principle involves Business Improvement Districts ("BIDs"). BIDs are state-or locally-authorized entities established to promote business activity within a specific geographic sub-area of a city. A major example is New York City's Grand Central Business Improvement District (GCBID), established through state law in 1988, which includes 337 properties, including Grand Central Station, spread over 75 blocks in midtown Manhattan—an area approximately the size of downtown Los Angeles. GCBID is responsible for capital improvements and services, such as security, sanitation, social services for the homeless, maintenance, tourist information, and retail improvements. The city levies and collects an additional assessment from property owners within the district, in addition to ordinary municipal taxes. These funds are GCBID's primary source of revenue. The state-law established governing structure of BIDs deviate from the one person, one vote rule. Property owners and tenants within the district vote, but the authorizing statute requires that a majority of GCBID's members represent property owners. Property owners thus may vote for 31 board members, commercial tenants may elect 16 board members, and residential tenants may elect one board member.

Tenants of a cooperative apartment building in the district challenged the voting privilege property owners had over residents. The Second Circuit, in a two-to-one vote, rejected this challenge. *See Kessler v. Grand Central District Management Association, Inc.*, 158 F.3d 92 (2d Cir. 1998). The court concluded that GCBID was "a district that exists for a special, limited purpose, that [the governing board]'s activities have a disproportionate effect on property owners, and that [the governing board] has no primary responsibilities or general powers typical of a governmental agency." *Id.* at 108. In the court's view, the BID's purpose was to promote business in the district; this was a limited purpose that did not supplant the City's primary responsibility for providing traditional governmental services in the district. GCBID also lacked the traditional governmental power to impose taxes or enforce laws, and the City retained control over the BID's budget and scope of activities. Moreover, the burden of the special assessment fell disproportionately on property owners, for they were exclusively responsible for paying the assessment. The Second Circuit therefore applied the *Salyer–Ball* doctrine and required that the voting rules bear only "a reasonable relationship to the purposes of the GCBID." *Id.* at 108. That the district needed collective action of property owners to pursue the improvement projects, and that property owners might not agree to the additional assessment on their property absent principal control over how the money would be spent, was sufficient to meet this "reasonableness" standard.

The dissent found BIDs more analogous to the governmental units at issue in *Avery* and *Hadley*: "It is the importance of the government functions, and their applicability to a broad range of citizens, which makes the one person, one vote constitutional requirement applicable. Local government may not, by carving up its civic services and functions into a multitude of 'specializations,' each one subject to privatization, immunize the municipality from the strictures of one person, one vote." *Id.* at 126. GCBID provided an array of traditional governmental functions, its activities affected all those who lived and worked within its jurisdiction, and it enjoyed broad discretion over its activities. Hence, the dissent would have required one person, one vote.

Should BIDs be seen as essentially public entities, to which one person, one vote should apply? Or are they like the water districts in *Salyer* and *Ball*, which the Court characterized as "essentially business enterprises" and only of public character in a "nominal" sense? Are these the right terms in which the one vote, one person issue should be framed? Do these "innovative" structures of local government allow for the smuggling back in of property-based views of citizenship? In Richard Briffault, *A Government for Our Time? Business Improvement Districts and Urban Governance,* 99 Colum. L. Rev. 365, 373 (1999), Professor Briffault argues that BIDs reflect the uncertain state of contemporary ideas of governance:

> The conflict over BIDs mirrors the contemporary debate over the roles of the public and private sectors in American society. Yet, in its assumption of a sharp public-private divide, the argument about BIDs unintentionally reflects the limitations of that debate. Like many other aspects of governance in late-twentieth-century America, BIDs are neither wholly public nor fully private, but, rather, combine attributes of both public and private. BIDs are publicly created, they wield public powers, they provide public services, and they are subject to public control. Their empowerment of business and landowner interests and their provision of extra services to business districts based on special assessments paid within those districts, however, are distinctly "private" elements at odds with some of the basic features of public governance. Indeed, it is precisely because they are part of the public sector that the organization and financing of, and the enhanced services provided by, BIDs may seem so troubling. BIDs constitute a distinct challenge to the democratic accountability of public institutions and the equal treatment normally required in the provision of public services.

Yet Briffault concludes that the property-voter preference ought to be constitutional:

> Although the property owners paying BID assessments may be able to diffuse those costs throughout the district, the assessment payers do bear the costs of the BID in the first instance. Their support is typically critical for the establishment of the BID and for its continuation. A state could reasonably conclude that BIDs are a useful means of providing urban services and that property owner voting control would facilitate creation of the BID. As long as a BID's regulatory and fiscal powers are limited, and the city government has the capacity to oversee and control BID operations, property owner voting may be a constitutionally permissible component of local government innovation. *Id.,* at 444–45.

Even if constitutional, does this privatization of local government services undermine democratic values? For worries along those lines from the same author, see Richard Briffault, *The Rise of Sublocal Structures in Urban Governance,* 82 Minn. L. Rev. 503, 509 (1997) ("these structures may be able to improve the efficiency of local operations, but they are unlikely to improve the prospects for political participation by ordinary citizens in big-city governance.'').

6. Even if some elections are exempted from the requirements of one-person, one-vote, this does not necessarily exempt them from other constitutional and statutory commands. For example, judicial elections are not covered by one-person, one-vote, see *supra*, yet they are covered by provisions of the Voting Rights Act of 1965 that forbid racial discrimination in voting, see *Chisom v. Roemer*, 501 U.S. 380 (1991). *See also* Glenn P. Smith, Note, *Interest Exceptions to One–Resident, One–Vote: Better Results from the Voting Rights Act*, 74 Tex. L. Rev. 1153 (1996).

In *Rice v. Cayetano*, 528 U.S. 495 (2000), the Supreme Court confronted the question whether Hawaii could restrict the franchise for elections to choose the trustees of the Office of Hawaiian Affairs to persons who were descendants of people inhabiting the Hawaiian Islands in 1778. (The Office administered programs designed for the benefit of such individuals.) Hawaii argued that this limitation on the franchise was sustainable under the reasoning of *Salyer* and *Ball*. The Supreme Court rejected that analysis:

> We would not find those cases dispositive.... The question before us is not the one-person, one-vote requirement of the Fourteenth Amendment, but the race neutrality command of the Fifteenth Amendment. Our special purpose district cases have not suggested that compliance with the one-person, one-vote rule of the Fourteenth Amendment somehow excuses compliance with the Fifteenth Amendment. We reject that argument here.... The Fifteenth Amendment has independent meaning and force. A State may not deny or abridge the right to vote on account of race, and this law does so.

Fumalaro v. Chicago Board of Education

142 Ill.2d 54, 566 N.E.2d 1283 (1990).

■ JUSTICE WARD delivered the opinion of the court:

* * *

The record shows that, as in most large cities, Chicago has serious problems in its public school system. The Chicago School Reform Act was enacted in 1988 in an attempt to resolve certain of the problems. The Act makes significant changes in school governance and administration by decentralizing the school system and by imposing primary responsibility for local school governance on parents, community residents, teachers and school principals. The plaintiffs do not dispute the need for change in the Chicago public school system, but they challenge the constitutionality of the Act, arguing that sections of the statute violate the Federal and State constitutional assurances of equal protection and due process. The plaintiffs, who are registered voters and taxpayers in the City of Chicago, allege that the Act's voting scheme for electing members of the local school councils violates the equal protection clauses of the State and Federal Constitutions because it denies an equal vote in local school council elections to large portions of the electorate.

* * *

Local School Councils

Although the board of education retains many general administrative powers and responsibilities, its powers and responsibilities under the Act have been substantially altered. To place increased authority for individual school decisions at the individual school level, the Act provides for the creation of a local school council for each grammar school and each high school in the Chicago public school system (there are 539 schools in the Chicago public school system). (Ill.Rev.Stat.1989, ch. 122, par. 34–2.1.) The local school council is composed of the school principal and 10 elected members. The elected members are: six parents of currently enrolled students who are elected by parents of currently enrolled students, two residents of the attendance area served by the school who are elected by the residents of that area (except in multiarea districts—districts which draw and admit students from more than a single attendance area—where the community residents to be elected are elected by the parents of currently enrolled students, the principal of the multiarea school and the school staff and two teachers of the school who are elected by the school staff). Each local school council elects the principal who will serve at the school for a contract period of four years and may retain the principal for another four-year period when the contract expires. Should a principal not be retained, the local school council will select a new principal. The local school council also develops specific performance criteria for its principal and has responsibility for approving the budget plan drawn up and administered by the principal. In addition, the local school council has substantial advisory responsibilities.

Subdistrict Councils

The Act creates 11 subdistrict councils. Each local school council elects one of its parent or nonparent resident members to sit on a subdistrict council. Each subdistrict council performs various advisory functions (e.g., promoting and coordinating communication among local school councils, promoting and coordinating training of local school councils), elects and evaluates for retention the subdistrict school superintendent and is responsible for electing one of its members to sit on the school board nominating commission.

School Board Nominating Commission

The school board nominating commission is composed of 11 members elected from each subdistrict council and five members appointed by the mayor. The nominating commission, in an open public forum, interviews candidates for seats on the board of education and presents the mayor with a slate of three qualified candidates for each vacant seat on the board. The mayor selects one of the candidates for each seat from this list. The Act provides that there are to be 15 members on the board of education. An interim board of education was created by the Act until the mayor should appoint candidates as provided by the Act. A permanent board of education has now been selected under the Reform Act.

* * *

The plaintiffs argue that the Act's differentiated allocation of votes among parents, community residents and teachers in local school council elections impermissibly interferes with their fundamental right to have an equal voice in an election involving a governmental matter of general interest, namely, the operation of local schools. Under the Act, community residents who reside in multiarea districts and do not have children in attendance at the public schools are unable to vote for any local school council members. Community residents in single district attendance centers who do not have children in attendance in a public school are entitled to vote for only two members of the council. Parents, however, who have children in the school, are entitled to vote for six members of the council. The defendants, in response, contend that a voting scheme which results in differentiated treatment of voters will not be found to violate constitutional assurances of equal protection if the voters given the weighted vote have a greater interest in and are more greatly benefited by the particular activities of the governmental unit which is the subject of the election.... [Defendants' also argue] that strict scrutiny analysis should not be applied because the local school councils are subordinate panels of tightly limited authority which do not perform "general governmental functions." The local school councils cannot levy taxes, appropriate money, enter into contracts, issue bonds, acquire property, or set basic educational policy at the district level. All of these powers, the defendants point out, are retained by the board of education. The local school councils, the defendants argue, simply implement in the particular school, the district-wide policies set by the board.

* * *

The local school councils are readily distinguishable from the water districts at issue in *Ball* and *Salyer*. The local school councils are the cornerstone, in a real sense, of the operation of the city's schools and they play a significant role in the Act's scheme to improve education in the City of Chicago. They have important and multiple powers that affect the whole community.

The administration of education through the operation of our schools is a fundamental governmental activity in which all members of society have an interest. Furthermore, educational activities are financed by and affect virtually every resident. The local school councils perform an indispensable role in administering the board's educational policy at the local level and in carrying out the legislature's intent to create a dominant force at that level. We hold, therefore, that the local school councils exercise general governmental functions, as that term has been defined in *Hadley* and *Kramer*.

A second consideration in *Ball* and *Salyer* was whether the functions of the local water district disproportionately benefited those given the weighted votes. In *Ball* and *Salyer*, the functions performed by the water reclamation districts and the costs associated with the districts were directly linked to land ownership and directly and disproportionately benefited the landowners. Here, the cost of operating the community's schools falls directly or indirectly on virtually all community residents, e.g., property taxes are imposed on all residents regardless of whether they have children attending the schools, and the decisions of the local school council affect virtually every resident of the school's attendance area. The benefits resulting from the election of competent and efficient local school councils are far from limited to parents with children in the public schools. For example, nonparent residents are directly affected by the individual school's performance in that the quality of the community's schools often directly affects the value of their property; parents with children not yet of school age have a proper and direct interest in the quality and operation of the schools their children will soon enter; parents of children who attend private schools also have a direct interest in the school system (improved public schools would allow the parents to re-enroll their children in public school). Furthermore, it is clear that a community school is not judged solely on the basis of the general district-wide policy set by the board. The school is judged, instead, on its individual performance and on its ability to implement effectively general educational policy. Although a parent's interest in the quality of the school his or her child attends is clearly identifiable, it is not an exclusive interest. It simply cannot be said that the activities and the performance of the local school council have a sufficiently disproportionate effect on those parents with children in current attendance at the public school.

We hold, therefore, that because the local school councils perform a general governmental function which affects the entire community, the trial judge erred in applying the rational basis standard in determining whether the voting scheme of the Act violated equal protection. Absent a showing that an elected body serves a special limited purpose, a restriction which operates to dilute a citizen's vote must meet a strict scrutiny test of justification. (*Hill v. Stone*, 421 U.S. 289 (1975)). The Act creates a classification which dilutes the vote of those citizens who do not have children attending the public schools in the year of the local school council election. A rational basis will not justify the classification of voters created by the Act.

* * *

We hold that the Act does not meet the strict scrutiny standard and is violative of the equal protection clauses of the Federal and State Constitutions.

NOTES AND QUESTIONS

1. Do *Ball* and *Salyer* compel the conclusion in *Fumalaro*? Does *Morris* foreclose any possibility of enhancing parental representation in the governance of the educational system?

2. The Illinois Supreme Court relies on the broad impact of educational decisions in striking down the Chicago educational reforms. Recall, however, the discussion by Justice Powell in *Ball* that the broad impact of the electoral arrangement might yield viable political checks on any abuses of the franchise. Does the fact that the Chicago School Reform Act was passed by the state legislature as a response to a perceived crisis in the Chicago schools militate in favor of upholding the voting reforms?

C. The Senate, Republican Theory, and Interest Representation

The most salient feature of the equipopulation revolution in the Court's jurisprudence was its hostility to the claim that allocating representation in a specified manner was necessary to the protection of special interests that risked being numerically overwhelmed. Except in those areas deemed outside the one-person, one-vote rule—such as the special districts in *Salyer* and *Ball*—the demands of equal voting strength clearly outweighed local representational interests. Two issues nonetheless present themselves. The first, which will recur centrally in later chapters of this book, concerns how representational opportunity will be assigned even under the equipopulation principle. The second is to give a fuller accounting of the now anomolous position of the U.S. Senate as the one major elected institution in our political order that remains exempt from the constraints of equal representation.

The distinct features of the Senate emerged at the founding of the American Republic. American political thought in the constitutional period was strongly influenced by the English conception of the constitution as the embodiment of mixed government.

The Concept of Mixed Government at the Time of the Constitution: At the time of the American Revolution, the English political structure was widely considered the perfected form of representative government. Montesquieu called it "this beautiful systems." Even American revolutionaries, like John Adams and James Wilson, described the English system as "the best model of government that can be framed by Mortals." Gordon Wood, The Creation of the American Republic 11 (1969). The basis for this admiration was the exquisite "balance" the English constitution was thought to embody. This balance was exceptionally intricate, for it operated along two distinct dimensions: the English system of government was thought to incorporate the three principal *forms of government*, as well as the principal *social orders* within society. This system exerted great influence over the design of the American Constitution.

Since Aristotle, forms of government had been categorized into monarchy, aristocracy, and democracy. In monarchy, the entire ruling power was placed in the discretion of a single figure; in aristocracy, in the hands of a select wise elite; and in democracy, ruling power lay with the people as a whole. Each form was thought to have its own distinct virtues or capacities. For monarchy, it was order, strength, and energy; for aristocracy, it was wisdom; and for democracy, honesty and goodness. But each had dangers as well. Any one of these simple forms, if left to dominate, was thought prone to degenerate into extreme versions of itself as those with power sought to grab more.

Mixed government included each of these types of government within the overall constitutional structure. In "balancing" these simple forms, mixed government was thought to create a stable equilibrium of the virtues and vices of any one form taken in isolation. The King brought the benefits of monarchy; the House of Lords, of aristocracy, and the House of Commons, the benefits of democracy. This balance was the best security for liberty.

At the same time, the English system was thought to represent and balance the essential social elements or estates within that state. That is, mixed government was viewed as the political embodiment of society itself. By this period, the King no longer represented all of English society, but one of its distinct estates. The church had lost its status as a separate estate and was merged into the remaining two estates, the nobility and the people. These three orders—King, nobility, and the people—constituted all of English society, and corresponded perfectly to the three forms of government. "This marvelous coincidence between the society and the government, together with its relation to the three simple governments of antiquity, gave the English constitution its awareness and Parliament its sovereignty." Wood, *id.*, at 199.

The Transformation of Mixed Government into the United States Senate: But what mixed government meant for republican politics, in a society without a hereditary aristocracy and purportedly committed to egalitarian principles, posed vexing questions. Many of these focused on the issue of bicameral legislatures, particularly on the upper house or Senate. Should the states and the national government adopt a Senate at all, or should the legislature be unicameral? If a Senate was created, on what principles of representation should it be based?

As a general matter, democratic thought of the period was hostile to the representation of particular interests, and by extension to the use of electoral devices aimed at guaranteeing particularized interest representation. The most radical elements in the American Revolution, such as Thomas Paine, advocated unicameral elections. Thus, unicameral legislatures were established in those ex-colonies that were most under the sway of democratic theory: Georgia, Pennsylvania, and Vermont. The upper house of a bicameral legislature was generally associated by supporters and detractors with an aristocratic influence, present from the Roman Senate to the House of Lords; an upper house was thought necessary to check the proclivity for "passion" to hold sway in popular rule. For example, in The Federalist, No. 10, Madison discusses the dangers that might be posed by passion serving as the basis for confiscation of property should there not be institutional obstacles to direct majoritarian rule. *See also* Gordon S. Wood, *Interests and Disinterestedness in the Making of the Constitution*, in Beyond Confederation: Origins of the Constitution and American National Identity 69–103 (R. Beeman, S. Botein, and E. Carter II, eds. 1987)(describing Madison's aversion to his direct experience observing narrow interest-based legislation in the Virginia state legislature under the Articles of Confederation); Frank G. Bates & Oliver P. Field, State Government 151 (1939). Where large landed interests were able to check the exercise of democratic power, as in Maryland and South Carolina, the system of electors was supplemented by high property qualifications and long terms of office for the Senate. *See* Jackson Turner Main, The Upper House in Revolutionary America, 1763–1788 195–205 (1967). Their arguments were summarized by John Adams as providing six reasons why a single assembly was bad. It was "liable to all the vices, follies, and frailties of an individual; subject to fits of humor, starts of passion, flights of enthusiasm, partialities, or prejudice, and consequently productive of hasty results and absurd judgments. And all these errors ought to be corrected and defects applied by some controlling power." Moreover, he opined, "a single assembly is apt to be avaricious, and in time will not scruple to exempt itself from burdens, which it will lay, without compunction, on its constituents." *Id.* at 206, *quoting* Charles Francis Adams, ed. The Works of John Adams 195–196 (1858).

These issues were extensively debated on a state-by-state basis at the time of the Founding of the United States. For example, Thomas Jefferson, the most democratic of the Framers, proposed a draft constitution for Virginia in which he sought to ensure that the "wisest men" would be elected to the senate who would then be "perfectly independent of their electors." Thus he strongly resisted direct popular election and proposed term limits: a single nine-year term for state senators to avoid their "casting their eyes forward to the period of election (however distant) and be currying favor with the electors." *Id.* at 213. But in 1776, he lost this battle. The Virginia Constitution provided for direct popular election of the senate, with no special qualifications for either voters or candidates. In other states, higher property-holding requirements were sometimes imposed on candidates or, as Madison favored, on electors.

In struggling to apply the ideology of mixed government to America's republican setting, state constitution makers in the 1780s, the period leading up to the U.S. Constitution, gradually developed an alternative vision. Because America lacked any traditional aristocracy, a substitute was found in the criteria of property and wealth. Considered imperfect, these criteria nonetheless came to be viewed as proxies for eliciting the kind of "wisdom" and "steadiness" that justified the need for bicameralism and upper houses. In the process, the conception of representative government and of republicanism was dramatically transformed.

This transformation is best embodied in the Massachusetts Constitution of 1780. The theory justifying it quickly became widespread in debates over bicameralism. This theory was articulated in the famous *Essex Result*, the publication in 1778 of one county convention in Massachusetts that had met to consider what became the new state constitution:

> The only objects of legislation are the person and property of the individuals which compose the state. If the law affects only the persons of the members, the consent of a majority of any members is sufficient. If the law affects the property only, the consent of those who hold a majority of the property is enough. If it affects, (as it will very frequently, if not always) both the persons and property, the consent of a majority of the members, and of those members also, who hold a majority of the property is necessary.

Thus, upper houses were needed to protect distinct *interests*. One House represented persons; the other, the Senate, should represent property. This reflected a radical change in the way American society was coming to be conceived. First, republican thought had depended on a vision of a largely homogenous society, one with a unity of interests. This new vision acknowledged diverse and clashing economic interests; that vision would come to underlie the U.S. Constitution. Second, a conception of interest representation emerged. Equal *interests* among the society should have equal influence over government. As Madison put it, "persons and property being both essential objects of Government, the most that either can claim, is such a structure of it as will leave a reasonable security for the other." Gordon Wood, The Radicalism of the American Revolution 221(1992). Third, this conception was at odds with the crucial republican view that representatives should be disinterested; instead, it signaled an emerging view that all representatives were interested, and that the task of governmental design was to contain and balance the competing interests.

Thus, the classic ideal of mixed government, with honor and wisdom balancing goodness and honesty, was replaced with an ideal of different chambers representing different interests in a diverse society. Note that this view assumed a permanent, politically separate, and unified property interest in the society. Lest this view be too quickly dismissed as reactionary, recall that American representation was still extraordinarily popular by contemporary standards. When the Constitution was adopted in 1787, the states confined the franchise to property-owning white males. Yet what was seen as remarkable about the early American states was, in fact, the *breadth* of the franchise. By all accounts, the early American electorate was significantly more expansive than that of England. *See* Chilton Williamson, American Suffrage from Property to Democracy 21–39 (1960)(noting that the American states' electorate ranged from approximately 50 to 75 percent of adult white males as compared to 20–25 percent in England). That the House represented persons meant, in Massachusetts for example, that no property qualifications applied to those voting for House members; anyone could hold office as long as they had paid taxes for two years in the county; and representation was allocated exactly according to the population in each county. For the state Senate, voting became based on estates and representation was apportioned to counties on the basis of the taxes they paid.

Despite the initial popularity of the mixed governments, some made an argument that has since been often repeated but with little success: that bicameral legislatures and the entire idea of mixed government were unjustified in republican America. Consider the radical populist Thomas Paine, in Common Sense: the "exceedingly complex" English constitution was appropriate only "for the dark and slavish times in which it was erected," but not for the American republics. The English constitution reflected "two ancient tyrannies ... monarchical tyranny in the person of the king," and "aristocratical tyranny in the person of the peers," combined with "new Republican materials, in the persons of the Commons, on whose virtue depends the freedom of England." *Quoted in* Wood, *supra,* at 223–24. Even Alexander Hamilton agreed, at this time, in a "simple legislature" with equal-population based representation.

On this view, American institutions should therefore be pure applications of the republican principle of direct popular participation. In Pennsylvania, this experiment was adopted in the most radical constitution of the Revolutionary period. Pennsylvania abandoned the theory of mixed government altogether. The legislature was unicameral. Elections for offices took place every year. Term limits of four years were imposed. Suffrage rights were broader than in any other state. This was "simple" democracy in its most pure form. Its opponents attacked the system as "mob rule," and the Pennsylvania experiment quickly unraveled—whether through subversion by its opponents or its own defects remains unclear. This form of government has never since been adopted in any state in America. At present, only Nebraska has a unicameral legislature, and it adopted that format as a budget-saving measure during the Depression.

The debates at the Constitutional Convention brought directly to light the tension that had been building for many years between the emerging equality of republicanism and the inherited tradition of an upper house representing a distinct social class or economic interest. By the time of these debates, the justification for the Senate was obscure, even while virtually all of the participants agreed on the need for an upper chamber that would lend stability to government. Some wanted a Senate to reproduce the social balance of the English constitution; this view led Hamilton, for example, to argue that Senators should serve for life. Once this view was rejected out of recognition that in republican America the Senate could not be justified as representing a distinct social group, the question of the justification for the Senate became more acute. In the original Virginia Plan for the Constitution, drafted by Madison, Senators were to be elected by members of the House, in proportion to either the wealth or population of the states. Only after the Virginia Plan, was defeated and the Great Compromise (the Connecticut Compromise) was proposed, did a justification for the Senate finally emerge. Now the principle of representation for the upper chamber would be that each state would send two Senators, and the Senate became a means for ensuring that large states did not overrun the interests of the small states. In addition, bicamerialism became defended as simply yet another means of fragmenting and diffusing political power. Thus, the Senate became a "kind of perversion of the ancient theory of balanced government," an entity whose structure and justification was invented at the last stage to respond to the perceived need for bicameralism while completely transforming the reasons for it. Gordon S. Wood, The Creation of the American Republic 562 (1969).

In light of the history of the Senate, consider the Court's reasoning in striking down Georgia's county unit system by which votes for certain statewide offices were aggregated at the county level and then cast as county votes at the state level.

Gray v. Sanders

372 U.S. 368 (1963).

■ MR. JUSTICE DOUGLAS delivered the opinion of the Court:

* * *

This case . . . does not involve a question of the degree to which the Equal Protection Clause of the Fourteenth Amendment limits the authority of a State Legislature in designing the geographical districts from which representatives are chosen either for the State Legislature or for the Federal House of Representatives. Nor does it include the related problems of *Gomillion v. Lightfoot,* 364 U.S. 339, where 'gerrymandering' was used to exclude a minority group from participation in municipal affairs. Nor does it present the question, inherent in the bicameral form of our Federal Government, whether a State may have one house chosen without regard to population. The District Court, however, analogized Georgia's use of the county unit system in determining the results of a statewide election to phases of our federal system. It pointed out that under the electoral college, . . . required by Art. II, s 1, of the Constitution and the Twelfth Amendment in the election of the President, voting strength 'is not in exact proportion to population.... Recognizing that the electoral college was set up as a compromise to enable the formation of the Union among the several sovereign states, it still could hardly be said that such a system used in a state among its counties, assuming rationality and absence of arbitrariness in end result, could be termed invidious.'

Accordingly the District Court as already noted held that use of the county unit system in counting the votes in a statewide election was permissible 'if the disparity against any county is not in excess of the disparity that exists against any state in the most recent electoral college allocation.' Moreover the District Court held that use of the county unit system in counting the votes in a statewide election was permissible "if the disparity against any county is not in excess of the disparity that exists ... under the equal proportions formula for representation of the several states in the Congress." The assumption implicit in these conclusions is that since equality is not inherent in the electoral college and since precise equality among blocs of votes in one State or in the several States when it comes to the election of members of the House of Representatives is never possible, precise equality is not necessary in statewide elections.

We think the analogies to the electoral college, to districting and redistricting, and to other phases of the problems of representation in state or federal legislatures or conventions ... are inapposite. The inclusion of the electoral college in the Constitution, as the result of specific historical concerns, validated the collegiate principle despite its inherent numerical inequality, but implied nothing about the use of an analogous system by a State in a statewide election. No such specific accommodation of the latter was ever undertaken, and therefore no validation of its numerical inequality ensued. Nor does the question here have anything to do with the composition of the state or federal legislature.... The present case is only a voting case. Georgia gives every qualified voter one vote in a statewide election; but in counting those votes she employs the county unit system which in end result weights the rural vote more heavily than the urban vote and weights some small rural counties heavier than other larger rural counties.

NOTES AND QUESTIONS

1. In *Gray*, the Court began the process of narrowing the asserted justifications for malapportionment. Georgia's county unit system greatly enhanced the voting strength of the typical rural voter relative to urban voters living in more populous districts. Justice Douglas sweepingly proclaimed that, "The conception of political equality from the Declaration of Independence, to Lincoln's Gettysburg Address, to the Fifteenth, Seventeenth, and Nineteenth Amendments can mean only one thing—one person, one vote." Does this seem a credible reading of American constitutional history? Is there any difference between the use of the county-based system for state election purposes and the use of the states for elections to the U.S. Senate and in the Electoral College? For an argument that the current structure of the Electoral College, particularly the winner-take-all feature of state-by-state elections violates the Voting Rights Act, see Matthew M. Hoffman, *The Illegitimate President: Minority Vote Dilutions and the Electoral College*, 105 Yale L. J. 935 (1996).

2. Consider the Court's argument in *Gray* concerning the disparities in Georgia voting power in light of the following indictment of the Senate:

- The forty senators from the twenty smallest states represent a population base of 10 percent! In the Clinton era, this means even senators who represent 90 percent of the population are not enough by themselves to pass a bill. In the worst case lineup, a mere 10 percent of the population base could be enough to block a bill.

- The fifty senators from the twenty-five smallest states represent a population base of 16 percent. In the same worst case, senators representing just more than 16 percent of the population base could be enough to block a bill.

- Think of what they can *pass*. The sixty senators from the thirty smallest states represent a population base of only 24 percent. Yet senators representing 24 percent of the population have sixty votes. They can bring back the death penalty for sheep-stealing.

Hasn't it always been this bad?

No. In 1789, when the first Senate was sworn in, there were eighteen states, five newly admitted. The senators from the nine smallest states still represented 33 percent of the population. And there was no filibuster. So back then, to block a bill, it took senators representing a population based of 33 percent. Now, in the worst case lineup, it is merely 10 percent. One could also hope that in time the five new states would fill up. In 1789 they were practically empty (although back then, states like New York were pretty empty, too).

Thomas Geoghegan, *The Infernal Senate*, the New Republic (Nov. 21, 1995). For an analysis of the impact of the maldistribution of power in the Senate on federal expenditures at the state level, see Lynn A. Baker & Samuel H. Dinkin, *The Senate: An Institution Whose Time Has Gone?*, 13 J. L. & Politics 21, (Winter 1997). Baker and Dinkin argue that the existing allocation of representation in the Senate provides small population states disproportionately great coalition-building power relative to their shares of the nation's population, and injects a significant super-majoritarianism into the federal law-making process. Based on a sophisticated statistical model of the relative power of individual actors in being able to shape coalitions (the "Shapley–Shubik Index"), this article concludes that the current allocation of representation has:

three problematic effects on the structure of government. First, the Senate systematically and unjustifiably redistributes wealth from the large population states to the small ones. Second, it systematically and unjustifiably provides racial minorities a voice in the federal lawmaking process which is disproportionately small relative to their numbers. And finally, it systematically and unjustifiably affords large population states disproportionately little power, relative to their shares of the nation's population, to block federal homogenizing legislation that they consider disadvantageous.

Id. at 23. Do the critiques by Geoghegan and Baker & Dinkin call into question the legitimacy of the original constitutional compromise? Could alternative versions of a bicameral legislature serve the original Madisonian purposes without deviating so significantly from competing principles of popular representation?

CHAPTER 4

THE ROLE OF POLITICAL PARTIES

The preceding chapters have focused first on the individual's right to participate in the political process by casting a ballot and, second, on the structure of legislative institutions. But as we suggested at the outset of this book, a conception of politics that comprehends only atomistic individuals and governing bodies offers an impoverished account. It ignores the critical questions of how individuals aggregate their preferences to create governing bodies, and, just as important, how governments organize and constrain the political choices available to their citizens.

Since the time of De Tocqueville, observers of American politics have recognized the importance of voluntary intermediating institutions in a pluralist democracy. Most individuals participate in self-governance only through representatives; these organizations—ranging from churches to labor unions to neighborhood associations to contemporary mass-mailing ideological and affinity groups such as NOW, the AARP, and the National Rifle Association—both serve as a vehicle for making their members' voices more effective in the electoral process and, in many cases, help to shape their members' preferences.

Perhaps the most significant mediating institutions in the American political system are the political parties. For a comprehensive discussion, see Leon D. Epstein, Political Parties in the American Mold (1986). And as our dynamic account of the interaction between various actors in the system might suggest, American political parties are both the creators and the creatures of the existing political order. They thus stand in an ambiguous position vis-a-vis legal regulation. On the one hand, the Constitution sometimes constrains party behavior, as in the White Primary cases discussed in this Chapter. And sometimes the government is empowered to regulate party activity, as in the arena of campaign finance covered in the next chapter. On the other hand, the Constitution sometimes protects parties *against* governmental regulation. In this chapter, we focus on the ambiguous relationship among voters, parties and the state. To what extent can the government use parties or other mechanisms to channel individuals' expression of their political preferences? To what extent do individuals have rights as against political parties? And to what extent do political parties have rights as against individuals, or the state? That is, when do individuals have a right to participate in a party's processes and when does the party have a right to exclude them? And we focus as well on the way in which the electoral system enlists parties as an element of the electoral machinery. To what extent is such delegation permissible or desirable?

An Historical Note on Political Parties

Although today we consider political parties the quintessential organizational form through which democratic politics is structured, the Constitution did not expressly recognize their existence. But this omission did not reflect indifference to political parties or ignorance of their possible existence: the Constitution was expressly constructed to preclude the rise of parties. Indeed, this was one of the principal points of the entire constitutional framework. In this respect, then, the Constitution must be considered to have failed—although it is a failure rarely noticed because we now take for granted political parties as the embodiment of democratic politics.[a]

As we consider modern constitutional issues in the relationship of the state to political parties, it is worth keeping this deeper history in mind. How should originalist methods of constitutional interpretation deal with modern issues in state regulation of political parties, given that the Constitution itself was designed to avoid the very existence of parties? How should other methods of interpretation take into account, if at all, the original intent and early practices with respect to political parties? Note that the cases virtually never discuss these issues.

The Constitution was conceived as a "Constitution against parties." Richard Hofstadter, The Idea of a Party System: The Rise of Legitimate Opposition in the United States, 1780–1840, 40 (1969). When Madison wrote of the problem of "faction," as in Federalist No. 10, political parties were one of the paramount forms of faction he had in mind. Similarly, in his famous Farewell Address, George Washington warned against "the baneful effect" of parties:

> The common and continual mischiefs of the spirit of party are sufficient to make it the interest and duty of a wise people to discourage and restrain it.

> It serves always to distract the public councils and enfeeble the public administration. It agitates the community with ill-founded jealousies

---

a. More modern constitutions tend to embrace parties expressly as fundamental elements of democracy. Article 21 of the post-World War II German Constitution, or "Basic Law," for example, declares that "political parties shall participate in forming the political will of the people." For general discussion, see Donald P. Kommers, The Constitutional Jurisprudence of the Federal Republic of Germany, Ch. 5 (1997) (discussing Germany's creation of a "parteienstaat" or "party state"). Moreover, the German Constitution, according to its Court, has "raised [political parties] to the rank of constitutional institutions" and defines parties as "constitutionally integral of government." Id., at 200, 209. Therefore the Court has aggressively acted to protect the equality of political parties and their institutional integrity, and has emphasized the constitutional importance of ensuring, through judicial decision where necessary, meaningful party competition, which has often led the Court to protect the participatory rights of minor parties and the legislative positions of their members. Id., at 167, 169.

and false alarms; kindles the animosity of one part against another; foments occasionally riot and insurrection. It opens the door to foreign influence and corruption, which find a facilitated access to the government itself through the channels of party passion. Thus the policy and the will of one country are subjected to the policy and will of another.

George Washington, *Farewell Address,* in 1 A Compilation of the Messages and Papers of the Presidents 218–19 (James D. Richardson, ed. 1900).

The Framers viewed "faction" and "party" as interchangeable concepts. Republicanism was widely understood to imply popular sovereignty and the absence of government controlled by party. Party politics was considered the antithesis of the (elite) politics of "the common good" that the Constitution sought to enshrine. *See* Gordon Wood, The Creation of the American Republic 506–518 (1969). The hostility to the role that political parties were thought to play as permanent factions in turn helped shape the institutional forms of the American Republic. Many of the structural features of the new national government, such as bicameralism, separated powers, and federalism were designed to check the rise and effectiveness of party politics.

Despite these efforts, competing political philosophies rather quickly emerged; politicians came to be identified as Federalists or Republicans. But it is a mistake to see these early groupings as modern political parties. For even as the Jeffersonians in the early 1800's became the greatest party organizers that democratic politics had seen, their justification for party organization remained tied to the original Constitutional vision—and was radically different from the modern conception of parties. Thus, they argued their organization was an effort to *eliminate* parties; it was a temporary device made necessary by the corrupt efforts of their opponents to capture the government for party purposes.

This "antiparty" justification for nascent political organization dominated the early nineteenth century. Republicans, for example, did not conceive of themselves as defined through any specific policy commitments; they justified their organization as defined only through its commitment to preserving the constitutional structure and the principle of majority rule—as opposed to rule of the minority aristocratic interests to which, they alleged, their opponents aspired. In the view of some historians, it is not until after the Civil War that political parties come to be understood and justified in the form we now take for granted: as permanent features of democratic politics; as divided over competing policy views rather than standing for the "true" Constitution; as forms of loyal and desirable opposition. For a sophisticated and rich history of the shifting intellectual justifications for political parties, see Gerald Leonard, The Invention of Party Politics (2002).

The early hostility to political parties stands in rather stark contrast to contemporary political science. The Madisonian design for the early Republic hoped to avoid permanent non-governmental organizations standing between the citizenry and a representative government. Government, if properly functioning, would provide the vehicle for the expression of the sober popular will, channelled through the structures of checks and balances that would protect against rash decisions inflamed by "passion." Modern political scientists and legal scholars, by contrast, often argue that political parties are inevitable, given the need for political organization to aggregate the voices of individuals. Rather than seeing these intermediate institutions as antithetical to the ability of citizens to participate effectively in the political process, these scholars view such organizational vehicles as indispensable if lone individuals are to have any meaningful participation in the messy political marketplace. *See, e.g.*, E.E. Schattschneider, Party Government (1942); Maurice Duverger, Political Parties (3d. ed. 1963); Michael Fitts, *The Vices of Virtue: A Political Party Perspective on Civic Virtue Reforms of the Legislative Process*, 136 U. Pa. L. Rev. 1567 (1988); Jonathan R. Macey, *The Role of the Democratic and Republican Parties as Organizers of Shadow Interest Groups*, 89 Mich. L. Rev. 1 (1989). That might be so, but the question remains of how those organizations are justified and understood—particularly how they are reconciled with the constitutional framework. Throughout much of the nineteenth century, the conception of party we now take for granted—and that underlies modern constitutional doctrine—was considered antithetical to the Constitution.

The most extensive study of the history of ideas surrounding the rise and legitimation of political parties can be found in Nancy Rosenblum, On the Side of Angels: A Political Theory of Parties and Partisanship (forthcoming, Princeton University Press 2007). In addition to developing this intellectual and political history, Rosenblum argues forcefully for the value of strong parties and of strong partisanship in politics.

A. POLITICAL PARTIES AND STATE ACTION

1. THE BALLOT AND STATE GATEKEEPING

The physical act of voting differs rather dramatically from the way eighteenth and nineteenth century citizens indicated their choices, and with some corresponding implications for state regulation of political parties. Early voting was conducted viva voce, that is, by a voice vote from among the assembled electorate, or by a show of hands, the traditional European method. Contrary to contemporary mythology, in which the secret ballot occupies a sacred place, these early forms of voting represented a public statement by individual voters of their position. In *Burson v. Freeman*, 504 U.S. 191, 200–02 (1992), the Supreme Court offered the traditional account of the movement toward the secret ballot:

> Within 20 years of the formation of the Union, most States had incorporated the paper ballot into their electoral system. Initially, this paper ballot was a vast improvement. Individual voters made their own

handwritten ballots, marked them in the privacy of their homes, and then brought them to the polls for counting. But the effort of making out such a ballot became increasingly more complex and cumbersome.

Wishing to gain influence, political parties began to produce their own ballots for voters. These ballots were often printed with flamboyant colors, distinctive designs, and emblems so that they could be recognized at a distance. State attempts to standardize the ballots were easily thwarted—the vote-buyer could simply place a ballot in the hands of the bribed voter and watch until he placed it in the polling box. Thus, the evils associated with the earlier viva voce system reinfected the election process; the failure of the law to secure secrecy opened the door to bribery and intimidation.

Approaching the polling place under this system was akin to entering an open auction place. As the elector started his journey to the polls, he was met by various party ticket peddlers "who were only too anxious to supply him with their party tickets." Often the competition became heated when several such peddlers found an uncommitted or wavering voter. Sham battles were frequently engaged in to keep away elderly and timid voters of the opposition. In short, these early elections "were not a very pleasant spectacle for those who believed in democratic government."

The problems with voter intimidation and election fraud that the United States was experiencing were not unique. Several other countries were attempting to work out satisfactory solutions to these same problems. Some Australian provinces adopted a series of reforms intended to secure the secrecy of an elector's vote. The most famous feature of the Australian system was its provision for an official ballot, encompassing all candidates of all parties on the same ticket.

* * *

After several failed attempts to adopt the Australian system in Michigan and Wisconsin, the Louisville, Kentucky, municipal government, the Commonwealth of Massachusetts and the State of New York adopted the Australian system in 1888.... The success achieved through these reforms was immediately noticed and widely praised. One commentator remarked of the New York law of 1888:

"We have secured secrecy; and intimidation by employers, party bosses, police officers, saloonkeepers and others has come to an end.

"In earlier times our polling places were frequently, to quote the litany, 'scenes of battle, murder, and sudden death.' This also has come to an end, and until nightfall, when the jubilation begins, our election days are now as peaceful as our Sabbaths.

"The new legislation has also rendered impossible the old methods of frank, hardy, straightforward and shameless bribery of voters at the polls."

The triumphs of 1888 set off a rapid and widespread adoption of the Australian system in the United States. By 1896, almost 90 percent of the States had adopted the Australian system. This accounted for 92 percent of the national electorate.

For more extensive discussions of the history of ballots and voting, see Spencer D. Albright, The American Ballot (1942); Eldon C. Evans, A History of the Australian Ballot System in the United States (1917); L. E. Fredman, The Australian Ballot: The Story of an American Reform ix (1968).

But the traditional account, which views the secret ballot as an unambiguous improvement, may be at least somewhat incomplete. Morgan Kousser, for example, describes the movement to, and effect of, secret ballots rather differently:

> Until 1888, political parties printed and distributed the ballots in each of the United States. Besides discouraging split-ticket voting and encouraging strong party organization ... the party ballot insured illiterates the right to vote. Nevertheless, reformers, who were more concerned with eliminating fraud than safeguarding the rights of illiterates, instituted the secret ballot in eight Southern and 30 non-Southern states between 1888 and 1900.

> The publicly printed ticket required the voter, sometimes without any aid from anyone, to scurry quickly through a maze of names of candidates running for everything from presidential elector to county court clerk, a list which was often arranged by office rather than party. He then had to mark an "X" by the names of the candidates for whom he wished to vote, or, in some states, mark through or erase those he opposed. Such a task demanded not merely literacy, but fluency in the English language. An ingenious lawmaker could make voting all but impossible. Florida totally abolished party designations on the ballot. A Populist or Republican who wished to vote for his presidential electors had to count down five, ten, or fifteen unfamiliar names before starting to mark. Voters in one Virginia congressional district in 1894 confronted a ballot printed in the German Fraktur script.

J. Morgan Kousser, The Shaping of Southern Politics: Suffrage Restrictions and the Establishment of the One–Party South, 1880–1910, at 51–52 (1974). Kousser identifies the desire to exclude illiterate and foreign-born immigrants in the North, and blacks in the South, as a major consideration behind the adoption of standardized, pre-printed ballots. In this vein, consider the 1892 campaign song of the Arkansas Democratic Party, "Australian Ballot" (sung to the tune of "The Bonnie Blue Flag"):

> The Australian ballot works like a charm,
> It makes them think and scratch,

And when a negro gets a ballot
He has certainly got his match.

* * *

They go into the booth alone
Their ticket to prepare.
And as soon as five minutes are out
They have got to git from there.

John William Graves, *Negro Disfranchisement in Arkansas*, 26 Ark. Hist. Q. 199, 212–13 (1967). This element of the secret ballot is no longer with us. Today, as a statutory matter, a voter is entitled to assistance by the person of her choice, as long as that person is not her employer or an officer or agent of her union. *See* 42 U.S.C. § 1973aa–6 (1994). Nonetheless, in light of the historical context, it is worth at least thinking about the competing advantages and disadvantages of a system of non-anonymous or public voting. Voters who participate in municipal governance at town meetings, for example, still usually vote publicly. And many institutions—for example, many law school faculties—vote on important issues publicly (at least in the sense that the relevant electorate is aware of how each member voted).

One of the lasting effects of the secret ballot does remain. The standardized ballot does have the effect of introducing a strong measure of state regulation *prior to the election* in determining who shall be eligible for inclusion on the ballot. Notice that as soon as the state becomes involved in regulating even a function as simple as printing and distributing ballots, the problems the casebook raises throughout arise here too: will existing political forces, such as the dominant political parties, seek to capture the state processes and use them to perpetuate their hold on power? Is there some distinct role for courts and constitutional law to play in monitoring that process? Prior to the introduction of the standardized ballot, each voter could vote for whomever he preferred, regardless of the candidate's party, or even whether the candidate was publicly seeking a particular office, simply by preparing his personal ballot with that candidate's name on it. But the standardized ballot, at least in the first instance, constrained the voter's choices to the candidates whose names appeared on the ballot. Not until 1992 did the Supreme Court confront the question whether a state could constitutionally limit a voter's choice to a pre-set field of candidates in *Burdick v. Takushi*, 504 U.S. 428 (1992), a principal case later in this chapter.

2. THE WHITE PRIMARY CASES

Once the state assumed the burden of preparing a ballot, a series of obligations ensued. The state now had the power to determine who was on the ballot and the state had to organize a secure balloting environment distinct from the open town meeting that characterized the early days of the Republic. Initially, much of the administration of the election process was left to the parties themselves. That included the preparation of the printed ballots, but extended to some features that continue to be present (and problematic) in American elections, such as the use of party representatives to administer elections.

The increased role of state regulation of elections combined with the consolidated power of political parties to raise important issues concerning the integration of the parties into the state apparatus. In terms of formal constitutional doctrine, one of the most important manifestations of this tension was expressed through the "state action" doctrine. The basic question was the extent to which political parties were best conceptualized as mere appendages of the state, to whom constitutional constraints would attach, as opposed to being private organizations entitled to autonomy rights as against the state.

A series of cases from Texas, collectively known as the "White Primary" cases presented the state action question in its most direct form. Keep in mind while reading these cases that throughout the three decades they cover, Texas was effectively a one-party state, completely controlled by the Democratic Party. This further complicates the state action inquiry since, with respect to all regulations affecting rights of political participation, the regulator and the regulated entity were both in some fashion the Democratic Party.

Nixon v. Herndon

273 U.S. 536 (1927).

■ MR. JUSTICE HOLMES delivered the opinion of the Court.

[A Texas statute regulating primary elections provided that "in no event shall a negro be eligible to participate in a Democratic party primary election held in the State of Texas." Nixon brought suit against the Judges of Elections seeking damages of $5000.]

* * *

The petition alleges that the plaintiff is a negro, a citizen of the United States and of Texas and a resident of El Paso, and in every way qualified to vote, as set forth in detail, except that the statute . . . interferes with his right; . . . that the plaintiff, being a member of the Democratic party, sought to vote but was denied the right by defendants; and that [the Texas] statute is contrary to the Fourteenth and Fifteenth Amendments to the Constitution of the United States. The defendants moved to dismiss upon the ground that the subject matter of the suit was political and not within the jurisdiction of the Court and that no violation of the Amendments was shown. . . .

The objection that the subject matter of the suit is political is little more than a play upon words. Of course the petition concerns political action but it alleges and seeks to recover for private damage. That private damage may be caused by such political action and may be recovered for in a suit at law hardly has been doubted for over two hundred years. . . .

The important question is whether the statute can be sustained. But although we state it as a question the answer does not seem to us open to a doubt. We find it unnecessary to consider the Fifteenth Amendment, because it seems to us hard to imagine a more direct and obvious infringement of the Fourteenth. That Amendment, while it applies to all, was passed, as we know, with a special intent to protect the blacks from discrimination against them. That Amendment "not only gave citizenship and the privileges of citizenship to persons of color, but it denied to any State the power to withhold from them the equal protection of the laws. . . . What is this but declaring that the law in the States shall be the same for the black as for the white; that all persons, whether colored or white, shall stand equal before the laws of the States, and, in regard to the colored race, for whose protection the amendment was primarily designed, that no discrimination shall be made against them by law because of their color?" The statute of Texas in the teeth of the prohibitions referred to assumes to forbid negroes to take part in a primary election. . . . States may do a good deal of classifying that it is difficult to believe rational, but there are limits, and it is too clear for extended argument that color cannot be made the basis of a statutory classification affecting the right set up in this case.

NOTES AND QUESTIONS

1. In *Giles v. Harris,* discussed in Chapter 2, Justice Holmes had found that no claim could be brought to enjoin the operation of the Alabama voter registration laws designed to disenfranchise black voters. Can Justice Holmes's opinions in *Giles* and *Nixon v. Herndon* be reconciled?

2. Promptly after the decision in *Nixon v. Herndon*, Texas passed a new statute. This statute provided that "every political party in this State through its State Executive Committee shall have the power to prescribe the qualifications of its own members and shall in its own way determine who shall be qualified to vote or otherwise participate in such political party. . . ." The Democratic Party State Executive Committee then adopted a resolution providing that only "white democrats" could participate in the upcoming primaries. Once again, Nixon sued the election judges who refused to give him a ballot. In *Nixon v. Condon*, 286 U.S. 73 (1932), the Supreme Court struck down the new statute. The defendants argued that the Fourteenth Amendment did not apply because here the exclusion was the work of a private actor—the political party—rather than the state. Nixon responded that "if heed is to be given to the realities of political life," the party should be treated as "the instruments by which government becomes a living thing." The Court sidestepped the issue by resting its decision on a technicality: Texas law gave party executive committees, rather than party conventions, the power to regulate participation; the executive committee's power thus flowed from the state rather than the party membership:

> The pith of the matter is simply this, that when those agencies are invested with an authority independent of the will of the association in whose name they undertake to speak, they become to that extent the organs of the State itself, the repositories of official power.... What they do in that relation, they must do in submission to the mandates of equality and liberty that bind officials everywhere.... Whether in given circumstances parties or their committees are agencies of government within the Fourteenth or the Fifteenth Amendment is a question which this court will determine for itself....

> With the problem thus laid bare and its essentials exposed to view, the case is seen to be ruled by *Nixon v. Herndon*. Delegates of the State's power have discharged their official functions in such a way as to discriminate invidiously between white citizens and black. The Fourteenth Amendment, adopted as it was with special solicitude for the equal protection of members of the Negro race, lays a duty upon the court to level by its judgment these barriers of color.

But the Democrats did not give up in their efforts to bar Nixon and other blacks from primary elections. Three weeks after the decision in *Nixon v. Condon*, the State Democratic Convention passed a resolution "that all white citizens of the State of Texas who are qualified to vote under the Constitution and laws of the state shall be eligible to membership in the Democratic party and as such entitled to participate in its deliberations." Pursuant to this resolution, a county clerk refused to issue an absentee ballot to a black voter who sought to participate in the primary. The voter sued and in *Grovey v. Townsend*, 295 U.S. 45 (1935), the Supreme Court unanimously upheld his exclusion. Although the Court recognized that the use of nominating primaries was required by state law and was pervasively regulated by the state, it held that the party's exclusion of Grovey did not constitute state action subject to the Fourteenth Amendment. As a matter of state constitutional law, political parties possessed the right to determine their membership without state interference and thus Grovey's exclusion was the product of private, perhaps constitutionally protected, activity.

There, it seemed, the matter would rest: the Supreme Court had provided a roadmap for the continued exclusion of blacks from southern politics. But the Court's decision in *United States v. Classic*, 313 U.S. 299 (1941), opened the door to a renewed challenge to the white primary. *Classic* involved the prosecution of several Louisiana election officials who had stuffed ballot boxes and committed other sorts of fraud in a primary election. (As was true in the rest of the South, the primary election was the one that counted, since the state was overwhelmingly Democratic.) The statutes under which they were charged made it a felony either to conspire to interfere with the exercise of a federally protected right or to act under color of state law to deprive individuals of rights guaranteed by the Constitution or federal law. In *Classic*, the government alleged that the federally protected right with which the defendants had interfered was the right to vote. The district court dismissed the indictment on the grounds that the right to vote was not implicated since the defendants' actions occurred during a party primary election, rather than a general election. The Supreme Court disagreed. It held that "[t]he primary in Louisiana is an integral part of the procedure for the popular choice of Congressman. The right of qualified voters to vote at the Congressional primary in Louisiana and to have their ballots counted is thus the right to participate in that choice." Buoyed by *Classic*, black voters launched a new challenge to the Texas white primary.

Smith v. Allwright

321 U.S. 649 (1944).

■ MR. JUSTICE REED delivered the opinion of the Court.

* * *

We granted the petition for certiorari to resolve a claimed inconsistency between the decision in the *Grovey* case and that of *United States v. Classic*.

[... Under Texas law,] the Democratic party was required to hold the primary which was the occasion of the alleged wrong to petitioner....

[The state defends its refusal to provide Smith with a ballot for the Democratic primary] on the ground that the Democratic party of Texas is a voluntary organization with members banded together for the purpose of selecting individuals of the group representing the common political beliefs as candidates in the general election. As such a voluntary organization, it was claimed, the Democratic party is free to select its own membership and limit to whites participation in the party primary....

The right of a Negro to vote in the Texas primary has been considered heretofore by this Court [in *Nixon v. Herndon, Nixon v. Condon*, and *Grovey v. Townsend*.] ... Since *Grovey v. Townsend* and prior to the present suit, no case from Texas involving primary elections has been before this Court. We did decide, however, *United States v. Classic*. We there held that § 4 of Article I of the Constitution authorized Congress to regulate primary as well as general elections, "where the primary is by law made an integral part of the election machinery."... The Nixon Cases were decided under the equal protection clause of the Fourteenth Amendment without a determination of the status of the primary as a part of the electoral process. The exclusion of Negroes from the primaries by action of the State was held invalid under that Amendment. The fusing by the *Classic* case of the primary and general elections into a single instrumentality for choice of officers has a definite bearing on the permissibility under the Constitution of excluding Negroes from primaries. This is not to say that the *Classic* case cuts directly into the rationale of *Grovey v. Townsend*. This latter case was not mentioned in the opinion. *Classic* bears upon *Grovey v. Townsend* not because exclusion of Negroes from primaries is any more or less state action by reason of the unitary character of the electoral process but because the recognition of the place of the primary in the electoral scheme makes clear that state delegation to a party of the power to fix the qualifications of primary elections is delegation of a state function that may make the party's action the action of the State. When *Grovey v. Townsend* was written, the Court looked upon the denial of a vote in a primary as a mere refusal by a party of party membership.

* * *

The question as to whether the exclusionary action of the party was the action of the State persists as the determinative factor.

* * *

Texas requires electors in a primary to pay a poll tax. Every person who does so pay and who has the qualifications of age and residence is an acceptable voter for the primary.... [The state] directs the selection of all party officers.

Primary elections are conducted by the party under state statutory authority.

* * *

We think that this statutory system for the selection of party nominees for inclusion on the general election ballot makes the party which is required to follow these legislative directions an agency of the State in so far as it determines the participants in a primary election. The party takes its character as a state agency from the duties imposed upon it by state statutes; the duties do not become matters of private law because they are performed by a political party.... When primaries become a part of the machinery for choosing officials, state and national, as they have here, the same tests to determine the character of discrimination or abridgement should be applied to the primary as are applied to the general election. If the State requires a certain electoral procedure, prescribes a general election ballot made up of party nominees so chosen and limits the choice of the electorate in general elections for state offices, practically speaking, to those whose names appear on such a ballot, it endorses, adopts and enforces the discrimination against Negroes, practiced by a party entrusted by Texas law with the determination of the qualifications of participants in the primary. This is state action within the meaning of the Fifteenth Amendment.

The United States is a constitutional democracy. Its organic law grants to all citizens a right to participate in the choice of elected officials without restriction by any State because of race. This grant to the people of the opportunity for choice is not to be nullified by a State through casting its electoral process in a form which permits a private organization to practice racial discrimination in the election. Constitutional rights would be of little value if they could be thus indirectly denied.

The privilege of membership in a party may be, as this Court said in *Grovey v. Townsend* no concern of a State. But when, as here, that privilege is also the essential qualification for voting in a primary to select nominees for a general election, the State makes the action of the party the action of the State.... *Grovey v. Townsend* is overruled.

■ MR. JUSTICE ROBERTS, dissenting.

* * *

I believe it will not be gainsaid [that *Grovey v. Townsend*] received the attention and consideration which the questions involved demanded and the opinion represented the views of all the justices. It appears that those views do not now commend themselves to the court. I shall not restate them. They are exposed in the opinion and must stand or fall on their merits. Their soundness, however, is not a matter which presently concerns me.

The reason for my concern is that the instant decision, overruling that announced about nine years ago, tends to bring adjudications of this tribunal into the same class as a restricted railroad ticket, good for this day and train only. I have no assurance, in view of current decisions, that the opinion announced today may not shortly be repudiated and overruled by justices who deem they have new light on the subject.

* * *

It is regrettable that in an era marked by doubt and confusion, an era whose greatest need is steadfastness of thought and purpose, this court, which has been looked to as exhibiting consistency in adjudication, and a steadiness which would hold the balance even in the face of temporary ebbs and flows of opinion, should now itself become the breeder of fresh doubt and confusion in the public mind as to the stability of our institutions.

Terry v. Adams

345 U.S. 461 (1953).

■ MR. JUSTICE BLACK announced the judgment of the Court and an opinion in which MR. JUSTICE DOUGLAS and MR. JUSTICE BURTON join.

* * *

This case raises questions concerning the constitutional power of a Texas county political organization called the Jaybird Democratic Association or Jaybird Party to exclude Negroes from its primaries on racial grounds. The Jaybirds deny that their racial exclusions violate the Fifteenth Amendment. They contend that the Amendment applies only to elections or primaries held under state regulation, that their association is not regulated by the state at all, and that it is not a political party but a self-governing voluntary club. . . .

There was evidence that:

The Jaybird Association or Party was organized in 1889. Its membership was then and always has been limited to white people; they are automatically members if their names appear on the official list of county voters. It has been run like other political parties with an executive committee named from the county's voting precincts. Expenses of the party are paid by the assessment of candidates for office in its primaries. Candidates for county offices submit their names to the Jaybird Committee in accordance with the normal practice followed by regular political parties all over the country. Advertisements and posters proclaim that these candidates are running subject to the action of the Jaybird primary. While there is no legal compulsion on successful Jaybird candidates to enter Democratic primaries, they have nearly always done so and with few exceptions since 1889 have run and won without opposition in the Democratic primaries and the general elections that followed. Thus the party has been the dominant political group in the county since organization, having endorsed every county-wide official elected since 1889.

* * *

[The Fifteenth] Amendment bans racial discrimination in voting by both state and nation. It thus establishes a national policy, obviously applicable to the right of Negroes not to be discriminated against as voters in elections to determine public governmental policies or to select public officials, national, state, or local.

Clearly the Amendment includes any election in which public issues are decided or public officials selected. Just as clearly the Amendment excludes social or business clubs. And the statute shows the congressional mandate against discrimination whether the voting on public issues and officials is conducted in community, state or nation. Size is not a standard.

It is significant that precisely the same qualifications as those prescribed by Texas entitling electors to vote at county-operated primaries are adopted as the sole qualifications entitling electors to vote at the county-wide Jaybird primaries with a single proviso—Negroes are excluded. Everyone concedes that such a proviso in the county-operated primaries would be unconstitutional. The Jaybird Party thus brings into being and holds precisely the kind of election that the Fifteenth Amendment seeks to prevent. When it produces the equivalent of the prohibited election, the damage has been done.

For a state to permit such a duplication of its election processes is to permit a flagrant abuse of those processes to defeat the purposes of the

Fifteenth Amendment. The use of the county-operated primary to ratify the result of the prohibited election merely compounds the offense. It violates the Fifteenth Amendment for a state, by such circumvention, to permit within its borders the use of any device that produces an equivalent of the prohibited election.

The only election that has counted in this Texas county for more than fifty years has been that held by the Jaybirds from which Negroes were excluded. The Democratic primary and the general election have become no more than the perfunctory ratifiers of the choice that has already been made in Jaybird elections from which Negroes have been excluded. It is immaterial that the state does not control that part of this elective process which it leaves for the Jaybirds to manage. The Jaybird primary has become an integral part, indeed the only effective part, of the elective process that determines who shall rule and govern in the county. The effect of the whole procedure, Jaybird primary plus Democratic primary plus general election, is to do precisely that which the Fifteenth Amendment forbids—strip Negroes of every vestige of influence in selecting the officials who control the local county matters that intimately touch the daily lives of citizens.

We reverse the Court of Appeals' judgment reversing that of the District Court. We affirm the District Court's holding that the combined Jaybird–Democratic-general election machinery has deprived these petitioners of their right to vote on account of their race and color. The case is remanded to the District Court to enter such orders and decrees as are necessary and proper. . . . In exercising this jurisdiction, the Court is left free to hold hearings to consider and determine what provisions are essential to afford Negro citizens of Fort Bend County full protection from future discriminatory Jaybird–Democratic-general election practices which deprive citizens of voting rights because of their color.

* * *

■ MR. JUSTICE FRANKFURTER, [concurring]

* * *

The evidence, summarized by formal stipulation, shows that . . . formal State action, either by way of legislative recognition or official authorization, is wholly wanting.

* * *

This case is for me by no means free of difficulty.

* * *

[V]iolation of [the Fifteenth] Amendment and the enactments passed in enforcement of it must involve the United States or a State. In this case the conduct that is assailed pertains to the election of local Texas officials. To find a denial or abridgment of the guaranteed voting right to colored citizens of Texas solely because they are colored, one must find that the State has had a hand in it.

The State, in these situations, must mean not private citizens but those clothed with the authority and the influence which official position affords. The application of the prohibition of the Fifteenth Amendment to "any State" is translated by legal jargon to read "State action." This phrase gives rise to a false direction in that it implies some impressive machinery or deliberative conduct normally associated with what orators call a sovereign state. The vital requirement is State responsibility—that somewhere, somehow, to some extent, there be an infusion of conduct by officials, panoplied with State power, into any scheme by which colored citizens are denied voting rights merely because they are colored.

As the action of the entire white voting community, the Jaybird primary is as a practical matter the instrument of those few in this small county who are politically active—the officials of the local Democratic party and, we may assume, the elected officials of the county. As a matter of practical politics, those charged by State law with the duty of assuring all eligible voters an opportunity to participate in the selection of candidates at the primary—the county election officials who are normally leaders in their communities—participate by voting in the Jaybird primary. They join the white voting community in proceeding with elaborate formality, in almost all respects parallel to the procedures dictated by Texas law for the primary itself, to express their preferences in a wholly successful effort to withdraw significance from the State-prescribed primary, to subvert the operation of what is formally the law of the State for primaries in this county.

* * *

The State of Texas has entered into a comprehensive scheme of regulation of political primaries, including procedures by which election officials shall be chosen. The county election officials are thus clothed with the authority of the State to secure observance of the State's interest in "fair methods and a fair expression" of preferences in the selection of nominees. If the Jaybird Association, although not a political party, is a device to defeat the law of Texas regulating primaries, and if the electoral officials, clothed with State power in the county, share in that subversion, they cannot divest themselves of the State authority and help as participants in the scheme. . . .

This is not a case of occasional efforts to mass voting strength. Nor is this a case of boss-control, whether crudely or subtly exercised. Nor is this a case of spontaneous efforts by citizens to influence votes or even continued efforts by a fraction of the electorate in support of good government. This is a case in which county election officials have participated in and condoned a continued effort effectively to exclude Negroes from voting. Though the action of the Association as such may not be proscribed by the

Fifteenth amendment, its role in the entire scheme to subvert the operation of the official primary brings it within reach of the law.

* * *

It does not follow, however, that the relief granted below was proper. Since the vice of this situation is not that the Jaybird primary itself is the primary discriminatorily conducted under State law but is that the determination there made becomes, in fact, the determination in the Democratic primary by virtue of the participation and acquiescence of State authorities, a federal court cannot require that petitioners be allowed to vote in the Jaybird primary. The evil here is that the State, through the action and abdication of those whom it has clothed with authority, has permitted white voters to go through a procedure which predetermines the legally devised primary. . . . We cannot tell the State that it must participate in and regulate this primary; we cannot tell the State what machinery it will use. But a court of equity can free the lawful political agency from the combination that subverts its capacity to function. What must be done is that this county be rid of the means by which the unlawful "usage" in this case asserts itself.

■ MR. JUSTICE CLARK, with whom THE CHIEF JUSTICE, MR. JUSTICE REED, and MR. JUSTICE JACKSON join, concurring.

* * *

An old pattern in new guise is revealed by the record. The Jaybird Democratic Association of Fort Bend County was founded in 1889 to promote "good government" in the post-Reconstruction period. During its entire life span the Association has restricted membership to whites. In earlier years, the members at mass meetings determined their choice of candidates to support at forthcoming official elections. Subsequently the Association developed a system closely paralleling the structure of the Democratic Party.

* * *

The Fifteenth Amendment secures the franchise exercised by citizens of the United States against abridgment by any state on the basis of race or color. In Smith v. Allwright, 321 U.S. 649 (1944), this Court held that the Democratic Party of itself, and perforce any other political party, is prohibited by that Amendment from conducting a racially discriminatory primary election. By the rule of that case, any "part of the machinery for choosing officials" becomes subject to the Constitution's restraints. There, as here, we dealt with an organization that took the form of "voluntary association" of unofficial character. But because in fact it functioned as a part of the state's electoral machinery, we held it controlled by the same constitutional limitations that ruled the official general election. . . .

[T]he Jaybird Democratic Association is a political party whose activities fall within the Fifteenth Amendment's self-executing ban. Not every private club, association or league organized to influence public candidacies or political action must conform to the Constitution's restrictions on political parties. Certainly a large area of freedom permits peaceable assembly and concerted private action for political purposes to be exercised separately by white and colored citizens alike. More, however, is involved here.

The record discloses that the Jaybird Democratic Association operates as part and parcel of the Democratic Party, an organization existing under the auspices of Texas law.

* * *

Quite evidently the Jaybird Democratic Association operates as an auxiliary of the local Democratic Party organization, selecting its nominees and using its machinery for carrying out an admitted design of destroying the weight and effect of Negro ballots in Fort Bend County. To be sure, the Democratic primary and the general election are nominally open to the colored elector. But his must be an empty vote cast after the real decisions are made. And because the Jaybird-indorsed nominee meets no opposition in the Democratic primary, the Negro minority's vote is nullified at the sole stage of the local political process where the bargaining and interplay of rival political forces would make it count.

The Jaybird Democratic Association device, as a result, strikes to the core of the electoral process in Fort Bend County. Whether viewed as a separate political organization or as an adjunct of the local Democratic Party, the Jaybird Democratic Association is the decisive power in the county's recognized electoral process. Over the years its balloting has emerged as the locus of effective political choice. Consonant with the broad and lofty aims of its Framers, the Fifteenth Amendment, as the Fourteenth, "refers to exertions of state power in all forms." Shelley v. Kraemer, 334 U.S. 1, 20 (1948). Accordingly, when a state structures its electoral apparatus in a form which devolves upon a political organization the uncontested choice of public officials, that organization itself, in whatever disguise, takes on those attributes of government which draw the Constitution's safeguards into play.

In sum, we believe that the activities of the Jaybird Democratic Association fall within the broad principle laid down in Smith v. Allwright, supra. For that reason we join the judgment of the Court.

■ MR. JUSTICE MINTON, dissenting.

I am not concerned in the least as to what happens to the Jaybirds or their unworthy scheme. I am concerned about what this Court says is state action within the meaning of the Fifteenth Amendment to the Constitution.

[. . .] As I understand Mr. Justice Black's opinion, he would have this Court redress the wrong even if it was individual action alone. I can understand that praiseworthy position, but it seems to me it is not in accord with the Constitution. State action must be shown.

Mr. Justice Frankfurter recognizes that it must be state action but he seems to think it is enough to constitute state action if a state official participates in the Jaybird primary. That I cannot follow. For it seems clear to me that everything done by a person who is an official is not done officially and as a representative of the State. However, I find nothing in this record that shows the state or county officials participating in the Jaybird primary.

Mr. Justice Clark seems to recognize that state action must be shown. He finds state action in assumption, not in facts. This record will be searched in vain for one iota of state action sufficient to support an anemic inference that the Jaybird Association is in any way associated with or forms a part of or cooperates in any manner with the Democratic Party of the County or State, or with the State. It calls itself the Jaybird Democratic Association because its interest is only in the candidates of the Democratic Party in the county, a position understandable in Texas.

* * *

[S]urely white or colored members of any political faith or economic belief may hold caucuses. It is only when the State by action of its legislative bodies or action of some of its officials in their official capacity cooperates with such political party or gives it direction in its activities that the Federal Constitution may come into play. A political organization not using state machinery or depending upon state law to authorize what it does could not be within the ban of the Fifteenth Amendment.

* * *

This case does not hold that a group of Democrats, white, black, male, female, native-born or foreign, economic royalists or workingmen, may not caucus or conduct a straw vote. What the Jaybird Association did here was to conduct as individuals, separate and apart from the Democratic Party or the State, a straw vote as to who should receive the Association's endorsement for county and precinct offices. It has been successful in seeing that those who receive its endorsement are nominated and elected. That is true of concerted action by any group. In numbers there is strength. In organization there is effectiveness. Often a small minority of stockholders control a corporation. Indeed, it is almost an axiom of corporate management that a small, cohesive group may control, especially in the larger corporations where the holdings are widely diffused.

* * *

[T]he Jaybird Association's activities ... are confined to one County where a group of citizens have appointed themselves the censors of those who would run for public offices. Apparently so far they have succeeded in convincing the voters of this County in most instances that their supported candidates should win. This seems to differ very little from situations common in many other places far north of the Mason–Dixon line, such as areas where a candidate must obtain the approval of a religious group. In other localities, candidates are carefully selected by both parties to give proper weight to Jew, Protestant and Catholic, and certain posts are considered the sole possession of certain ethnic groups. The propriety of these practices is something the courts sensibly have left to the good or bad judgment of the electorate. It must be recognized that elections and other public business are influenced by all sorts of pressures from carefully organized groups. We have pressure from labor unions, from the National Association of Manufacturers, from the Silver Shirts, from the National Association for the Advancement of Colored People, from the Ku Klux Klan and others. Far from the activities of these groups being properly labeled as state action, under either the Fourteenth or the Fifteenth Amendment, they are to be considered as attempts to influence or obtain state action.

The courts do not normally pass upon these pressure groups, whether their causes are good or bad, highly successful or only so-so. It is difficult for me to see how this Jaybird Association is anything but such a pressure group. Apparently it is believed in by enough people in Fort Bend County to obtain a majority of the votes for its approved candidates. This differs little from the situation in many parts of the "Bible Belt" where a church stamp of approval or that of the Anti–Saloon League must be put on any candidate who does not want to lose the election.

The State of Texas in its elections and primaries takes no cognizance of this Jaybird Association. The State treats its decisions apparently with the same disdain as it would the approval or condemnation of judicial candidates by a bar association poll of its members.

In this case the majority have found that this pressure group's work does constitute state action. The basis of this conclusion is rather difficult to ascertain. Apparently it derives mainly from a dislike of the goals of the Jaybird Association. I share that dislike. I fail to see how it makes state action. I would affirm.

NOTES AND QUESTIONS

1. The following appraisal of the draft opinions in Terry was prepared by William H. Rehnquist, who was at the time Justice Robert Jackson's law clerk.

Re: Opinions of Black and FF in Terry v. Adams

If you are going to dissent, I should think you might combine the ideas which you expressed last week with an attack on the reasoning of the two "majority opinions."

(1) Black—simply assumes the whole point of the issue. The 15th Amendment requires state action, and certainly Congress under its

power to "enforce" the amendment cannot drastically enlarge its scope. Yet the Black opinion utterly fails to face the problem of state action. He says rather that the effect of the Fifteenth Amendment is to prevent the states from discriminating against Negroes in official elections; the result here is to accomplish that result "by indirection"; therefore that result is bad. Surely it should not take a quotation from Mr. Justice Holmes to establish the proposition that, especially in the field of constitutional law, differences will be ones of degree and the point at which the constitutional result changes will not be marked by any sharp turn in the road. Surely the justices of this Court do not sit here to ruthlessly frustrate results which they consider undesirable, regardless of the working of the Constitution.

(2) FF—places the weight of the decision on the rather skimpy support to be found in his discovery of "state action": the county election officials voted in the Jaybird primary. In the first place, they voted not in their capacity as election officials, but as private citizens. Secondly, it was not their voting which effected the discrimination; it was the previously adopted rules, with which they may have had nothing to do. Thirdly, if this is the vice why not simply enjoin the officials from voting? When one must strain this hard to reach a result, the chances are that something is the matter with the result....

(3) Your ideas—the Constitution does not prevent the majority from banding together, nor does it attaint success in the effort. It is about time the Court faced the fact that the white people in the South don't like colored people; the Supreme Court is not a watchdog to rear up every time private discrimination raises its admittedly ugly head. To the extent that this decision advances the frontier of state action and "social gain", it pushes back the frontier of freedom of association and majority rule. Liberals should be the first to realize, after the past twenty years, that it does not do to push blindly through towards one constitutional goal without paying attention to other equally desirable values that are being trampled on in the process.

This is a position that I am sure ought to be stated; but if stated by Vinson, Minton, or Reed it just won't sound the same way as if you state it.

How would you assess future Chief Justice Rehnquist's criticisms? Note that ultimately Justice Jackson joined Justice Clark's opinion. Also compare Justice Minton's dissent. Does it essentially adopt the Rehnquist position?

2. The state action issue in *Terry* can be approached by asking what remedial order the Court might frame. Does it follow from the decision that the Court should enjoin the Jaybirds from ever meeting and endorsing candidates? Should the Court enjoin state officials from participating in Jaybird meetings? If these orders seem problematic, what light does that shed on the state action analysis?

These questions generate a further, practical one: what happened after the Court's decision? There is a significant debate among legal academics and political scientists regarding how effective the Court's decisions have been. are or are not. In particular, do judicial court decisions change what practices are considered acceptable, even if the courts do not or cannot directly enforce their decisions? In that light, consider the aftermath of *Terry,* based on the account in Pauline Yelderman, The Jaybird Democratic Association of Fort Bend County (1979).

After *Terry* was handed down, blacks were allowed to vote in the Jaybird primary, whose successful nominees were still elected as nominees in the Democratic primary and, hence, became officeholders. A significant minority of the electorate was black, and they were able to swing some important contested races in succeeding elections (1954, 1956, 1958).

Public opinion as to the usefulness of the Jaybirds began to shift almost immediately. A newspaper poll of white citizens in Fort Bend County in 1958 asked, "Do you think the Jay Bird primary serves a useful purpose?" The newspaper headline trumpeted the results: OPINION POLL MAJORITY OKAYS JAY BIRDS. However, the article under the headline noted that a majority of those polled had declined to comment. In fact, only six persons expressed an opinion—of whom five argued for continuation of the Jay Birds. The following year, in October 1959, the executive committee met and voted to " 'suspend or recess' " the primary, and the remaining funds, roughly $1,000, were put into a savings account to be used if there were a future need for it. "Thus ended a seventy year old tradition," writes Yelderman. A decade later, the amount in the bank account, with accrued interested, had grown to $1,593.81. After consulting several former Jay Birds, the last secretary-treasurer asked the county judge to dispose of the funds by making a donation to the Fort Bend County Historical Museum "without any stipulation as to how the money should be used."

3. Is there any limit to the *Terry* position? Suppose that Fort Bend County was run, as a number of other Southern counties were, by a very few "bosses," who were also elected officials (for example, the sheriff and the probate judge). If those officials met every July at the local country club to pick a slate of candidates, and those candidates always won the election, could a voter claim the right to attend their annual lunch? Would it be different if the local Rotary Club or Chamber of Commerce did the picking?

In this regard, consider *Morse v. Republican Party of Virginia,* 517 U.S. 186 (1996). There, a five-justice majority, which was unable to coalesce behind a single opinion, held that the rules governing who could participate in the defendant party's nominating convention involved "voting" within the meaning of the Voting Rights Act of 1965, 42 U.S.C. §§ 1973 *et seq.* The Act's definitional provision defined the terms "vote" or "voting" to include "all action necessary to make a vote effective in any primary, special, or general election, including, but not limited to, . . . casting a ballot and having such ballot counted properly with respect to candidates for public or party office," 42 U.S.C. § 1973*l*(c)(1). The member of Congress who had drafted the provision explained that he had "recommended the addition of language which would extend the protections of the bill to the type of situation which arose last year when the regular Democratic delegation from Mississippi to the Democratic National Convention was chosen through a series of Party caucuses and conventions from which Negroes were excluded." 111 Cong. Rec. 16273 (July 9, 1965) (statement of Rep. Jonathan B. Bingham). *Morse* was a statutory interpretation case, but the application of the statute depended on there being state action, since only "states" and "political subdivisions" are bound by the Act.

4. What notion of political parties underlies *Smith* and *Terry*? Does the Court essentially view them as common carriers? How important is the fact that the Democratic or Jaybird winner always won? Would or should the Court's analysis be different for a smaller, or more ideological, party? For example, consider the Black Panther Party of Lowndes County, Alabama, founded in the wake of the 1965 march from Selma to Montgomery. Black voters sought to have a party responsive to their interests. Could white voters insist on participating in the party's nomination process?

5. Would the White Primary cases preclude parties not just from membership exclusions, but from imposing belief tests for participation? In fact, following the cases, several state parties did attempt to exclude black voters on the basis of belief. For example, after federal courts in South Carolina struck down the state's initial attempts to circumvent *Terry v. Adams*, "the party organized itself into clubs open only to white Democrats. Club members and blacks could vote in the primaries, but all voters were required to take an oath as follows: 'I ... solemnly swear that I understand, believe in and will support the principles of the Democratic Party of South Carolina, and that I believe in and will support the social (religious) and educational separation of the races.' Voters also were required to swear their belief in states' rights and their opposition to federal equal employment legislation." Laughlin McDonald, *The 1982 Extension of Section 5 of the Voting Rights Act of 1965: The Continued Need for Preclearance*, 51 Tenn. L. Rev. 1 (1983).

6. Would *Smith* and *Terry* extend beyond race? Suppose, for example, that a group of feminist separatists wished to found a local party that excluded men from its nomination process. Would the Nineteenth Amendment bar such discrimination? Similarly, could a party exclude voters based on their exercise of a fundamental right? For example, could a pro-life party open its nomination process only to voters who had never had abortions or who promised never to have or aid anyone else in obtaining one? In *Davis v. Beason*, 133 U.S. 333 (1890), the Supreme Court upheld a territorial statute that provided, among other things, that "No person ... who teaches, advises, counsels, or encourages any person or persons to become bigamists or polygamists, or to commit any other crime defined by law, ... is permitted to vote at any election, or to hold any position or office of honor, trust, or profit within this Territory." Idaho Rev. Stats. § 501. In order to cast a ballot, a voter had to swear that he or she "do[es] not and will not, publicly or privately, or in any manner whatever teach, advise, counsel or encourage any person to commit the crime of bigamy or polygamy, or any other crime defined by law, either as a religious duty or otherwise. . . ."

In *Romer v. Evans*, 517 U.S. 620, 634 (1996), the Court stated that "[t]o the extent *Davis* held that persons advocating a certain practice may be denied the right to vote, it is no longer good law. To the extent it held that the groups designated in the statute may be deprived of the right to vote because of their status, its ruling could not stand without surviving strict scrutiny, a most doubtful outcome." But the *Romer* Court seemed to be contemplating the formal right to register; it was not explicitly addressing the question whether political parties could restrict their membership for, as we shall see shortly, political parties *are* generally entitled to limit participation in their primaries to their own members.

7. The Texas Democratic Party cases from *Nixon* through *Terry* are collectively referred to as the "White Primary Cases" and generally stand for the proposition that forcible exclusion of black voters from the political process will not be tolerated. Is it possible, however, to distinguish among the cases on different grounds?

Consider an argument that focuses on the role of courts as preventing a lockup of the political process. One can begin by asking why it was so important to the Democratic Party to have the State of Texas forbid black voting in its primary elections. Perhaps the appeal to state intervention was a guarantee that no disgruntled elements of the party would seek to enhance their power by appealing to black voters. Historically, the Texas Democratic Party was a rather diverse and unstable mix of both conservative and populist currents that divided quite sharply over issues such as the New Deal. (This history is chronicled in Chandler Davidson, Race and Class in Texas Politics 155–79 (1990)). When such divisions were particularly sharp, what would discourage a sufficiently disgruntled faction from seeking to secure control of the Party by courting even the relatively small numbers of potential black voters? The answer was a precommitment among the varying factions that no one would appeal to black voters. The role of the state was guarantor of that agreement. In such circumstances, the agreements struck down in *Nixon v. Herndon, Nixon v. Condon*, and, although to a lesser extent, *Smith v. Allwright* all shared the critical feature of the Party using the state to secure the racial lockup of the political process. So long as the restrictive covenants of the Party were enshrined through state law, there was no prospect for black voters to serve as potential swing voters who could secure some measure of political redress in exchange for their votes.

Under these circumstances, judicial intervention can be justified as the necessary destabilizing element required in order to break the stranglehold on a political system unable to generate change from within. (We saw a variant of this same argument in the previous Chapter's discussion of the one-person, one-vote malapportionment cases.) Can the same be said of *Terry v. Adams*? By the time of *Terry*, the element of state enforcement had been removed. Certainly the Jaybirds were all white and held nearly complete power in the Democratic Party. But was this system stable? Was it as immune from change as those state-enforced arrangements struck down in the earlier White Primary Cases? Are competing values of freedom of political association more salient in *Terry* than in the other White Primary Cases? For a fuller analysis of the White Primary Cases as examples of political lockups, see Samuel Issacharoff and Richard Pildes, *Politics as Markets: Partisan Lockups of the Democratic Process*, 50 Stan. L. Rev. 643 (1998). For a rich historical account of these cases, which argues that they were among the few Court decisions that had significant practical effect on black political participation, see Michael J. Klarman, *The White Primary Rulings: A Case Study in the Consequences of Supreme Court Decisionmaking*, 29 Fla. St. U. L. Rev. 55 (2001). Professor Klarman argues more extensively that the white primary cases were decisive in shaping the Supreme Court's willingness to engage Jim Crow laws directly, and that they had more immediate practical effects than most of the more publicized desegregation rulings. Michael Klarman, From Jim Crow to Civil Rights: The Supreme Court and the Struggle for Racial Equality 458–60 (2004).

3. RESTRICTIONS ON WHOM VOTERS CAN VOTE FOR

Once the state action hurdle is bridged, as it was in the White Primary cases, then there are issues of constitutional dimension attaching to a claimed right of political expression by the voters and candidates denied their right to self-expression by appearing on the ballot or voting for a candidate of choice. Many of the current debates begin with the simple question whether there is a right of expression that attaches to the desire to participate in the political process in the way a voter or a candidate might wish.

Burdick v. Takushi

504 U.S. 428 (1992).

■ JUSTICE WHITE delivered the opinion of the Court.

The issue in this case is whether Hawaii's prohibition on write-in voting unreasonably infringes upon its citizens' rights under the First and Fourteenth Amendments.

* * *

I

Petitioner is a registered voter in the city and County of Honolulu. In 1986, only one candidate filed nominating papers to run for the seat representing petitioner's district in the Hawaii House of Representatives. Petitioner wrote to state officials inquiring about Hawaii's write-in voting policy and received a copy of an opinion letter issued by the Hawaii Attorney General's Office stating that the State's election law made no provision for write-in voting.

Petitioner then filed this lawsuit, claiming that he wished to vote in the primary and general elections for a person who had not filed nominating papers and that he wished to vote in future elections for other persons whose names were not and might not appear on the ballot.

* * *

II

Petitioner proceeds from the erroneous assumption that a law that imposes any burden upon the right to vote must be subject to strict scrutiny. Our cases do not so hold.

It is beyond cavil that "voting is of the most fundamental significance under our constitutional structure." It does not follow, however, that the right to vote in any manner and the right to associate for political purposes through the ballot are absolute. The Constitution provides that States may prescribe "the Times, Places and Manner of holding Elections for Senators and Representatives," Art. I, § 4, cl. 1, and the Court therefore has recognized that States retain the power to regulate their own elections. Common sense, as well as constitutional law, compels the conclusion that government must play an active role in structuring elections; "as a practical matter, there must be a substantial regulation of elections if they are to be fair and honest and if some sort of order, rather than chaos, is to accompany the democratic processes."

Election laws will invariably impose some burden upon individual voters. Each provision of a code, "whether it governs the registration and qualifications of voters, the selection and eligibility of candidates, or the voting process itself, inevitably affects—at least to some degree—the individual's right to vote and his right to associate with others for political ends." Consequently, to subject every voting regulation to strict scrutiny and to require that the regulation be narrowly tailored to advance a compelling state interest, as petitioner suggests, would tie the hands of States seeking to assure that elections are operated equitably and efficiently. Accordingly, the mere fact that a State's system "creates barriers ... tending to limit the field of candidates from which voters might choose ... does not of itself compel close scrutiny."

Instead ... a more flexible standard applies. A court considering a challenge to a state election law must weigh "the character and magnitude of the asserted injury to the rights protected by the First and Fourteenth Amendments that the plaintiff seeks to vindicate" against "the precise interests put forward by the State as justifications for the burden imposed by its rule," taking into consideration "the extent to which those interests make it necessary to burden the plaintiff's rights."

Under this standard, the rigorousness of our inquiry into the propriety of a state election law depends upon the extent to which a challenged regulation burdens First and Fourteenth Amendment rights. Thus, as we have recognized when those rights are subjected to "severe" restrictions, the regulation must be narrowly drawn to advance a state interest of compelling importance. "But when a state election law provision imposes only 'reasonable, nondiscriminatory restrictions' upon the First and Fourteenth Amendment rights of voters, 'the State's important regulatory interests are generally sufficient to justify' the restrictions." We apply this standard in considering petitioner's challenge to Hawaii's ban on write-in ballots.

A

There is no doubt that the Hawaii election laws, like all election regulations, have an impact on the right to vote, but it can hardly be said that the laws at issue here unconstitutionally limit access to the ballot by party or independent candidates or unreasonably interfere with the right of voters to associate and have candidates of their choice placed on the ballot. Indeed, petitioners understandably do not challenge the manner in which the State regulates candidate access to the ballot.

To obtain a position on the November general election ballot, a candidate must participate in Hawaii's open primary, "in which all registered voters may choose in which party primary to vote." *See* Haw. Rev. Stat. § 12–31 (1985). The State provides three mechanisms through which a voter's candidate-of-choice may appear on the primary ballot.

First, a party petition may be filed 150 days before the primary by any group of persons who obtain the signatures of one percent of the State's registered voters. Then, 60 days before the primary, candidates must file nominating papers certifying, among other things, that they will qualify for the office sought and that they are members of the party that they seek to represent in the general election. The nominating papers must contain the signatures of a specified number of registered voters: 25 for candidates for statewide or federal office; 15 for state legislative and county races. The winner in each party advances to the general election. Thus, if a party forms around the candidacy of a single individual and no one else runs on that party ticket, the individual will be elected at the primary and win a place on the November general election ballot.

The second method through which candidates may appear on the Hawaii primary ballot is the established party route. Established parties that have qualified by petition for three consecutive elections and received a specified percentage of the vote in the preceding election may avoid filing party petitions for 10 years. The Democratic, Republican, and Libertarian Parties currently meet Hawaii's criteria for established parties. Like new party candidates, established party contenders are required to file nominating papers 60 days before the primary.

The third mechanism by which a candidate may appear on the ballot is through the designated nonpartisan ballot. Nonpartisans may be placed on the nonpartisan primary ballot simply by filing nominating papers containing 15 to 25 signatures, depending upon the office sought, 60 days before the primary. To advance to the general election, a nonpartisan must receive 10 percent of the primary vote or the number of votes that was sufficient to nominate a partisan candidate, whichever number is lower. During the 10 years preceding the filing of this action, 8 of 26 nonpartisans who entered the primary obtained slots on the November ballot.

Although Hawaii makes no provision for write-in voting in its primary or general elections, the system outlined above provides for easy access to the ballot until the cutoff date for the filing of nominating petitions, two months before the primary. Consequently, any burden on voters' freedom of choice and association is borne only by those who fail to identify their candidate of choice until days before the primary. But [we have given] little weight to "the interest the candidate and his supporters may have in making a late rather than an early decision to seek independent ballot status." . . . [Thus,] any burden imposed by Hawaii's write-in vote prohibition is a very limited one. "To conclude otherwise might sacrifice the political stability of the system of the State, with profound consequences for the entire citizenry, merely in the interest of particular candidates and their supporters having instantaneous access to the ballot."

Because he has characterized this as a voting rights rather than ballot access case, petitioner submits that the write-in prohibition deprives him of the opportunity to cast a meaningful ballot, conditions his electoral participation upon the waiver of his First Amendment right to remain free from espousing positions that he does not support, and discriminates against him based on the content of the message he seeks to convey through his vote. At bottom, he claims that he is entitled to cast and Hawaii required to count a "protest vote" for Donald Duck, and that any impediment to this asserted "right" is unconstitutional.

Petitioner's argument is based on two flawed premises. First, [our prior cases have rejected the argument that] . . . voting rights cases are distinguishable from ballot access cases, stating that "the rights of voters and the rights of candidates do not lend themselves to neat separation." Second, the function of the election process is "to winnow out and finally reject all but the chosen candidates, not to provide a means of giving vent to 'short-range political goals, pique, or personal quarrels.'" Attributing to elections a more generalized expressive function would undermine the ability of States to operate elections fairly and efficiently.

Accordingly, we have repeatedly upheld reasonable, politically neutral regulations that have the effect of channeling expressive activity at the polls. Petitioner offers no persuasive reason to depart from these precedents. Reasonable regulation of elections does not require voters to espouse positions that they do not support; it does require them to act in a timely fashion if they wish to express their views in the voting booth. And there is nothing content based about a flat ban on all forms of write-in ballots....

[W]e conclude that, in light of the adequate ballot access afforded under Hawaii's election code, the State's ban on write-in voting imposes only a limited burden on voters' rights to make free choices and to associate politically through the vote.

B

We turn next to the interests asserted by Hawaii to justify the burden imposed by its prohibition of write-in voting. Because we have already concluded that the burden is slight, the State need not establish a compelling interest to tip the constitutional scales in its direction. Here, the State's interests outweigh petitioner's limited interest in waiting until the eleventh hour to choose his preferred candidate.

Hawaii's interest in "avoiding the possibility of unrestrained factionalism at the general election," provides adequate justification for its ban on write-in voting in November. The primary election is "an integral part of the entire election process," and the State is within its rights to reserve "the general election ballot ... for major struggles ... [and] not a forum for continuing intraparty feuds." The prohibition on write-in voting is a legitimate means of averting divisive sore-loser candidacies. Hawaii further promotes the two-stage, primary-general election process of winnowing out candidates, by permitting the unopposed victors in certain primaries to be designated office holders. This focuses the attention of voters upon contested races in the general election. This would not be possible, absent the write-in voting ban.

Hawaii also asserts that its ban on write-in voting at the primary stage is necessary to guard against "party raiding." Party raiding is generally defined as "the organized switching of blocs of voters from one party to another in order to manipulate the outcome of the other party's primary election." ... Hawaii's system could easily be ... frustrated at the general election by permitting write-in votes for a loser in a party primary or for an independent who had failed to get sufficient votes to make the general election ballot. The State has a legitimate interest in preventing these sorts of maneuvers, and the write-in voting ban is a reasonable way of accomplishing this goal.

We think these legitimate interests asserted by the State are sufficient to outweigh the limited burden that the write-in voting ban imposes upon Hawaii's voters.

III

Indeed, the foregoing leads us to conclude that when a State's ballot access laws pass constitutional muster as imposing only reasonable burdens on First and Fourteenth Amendment rights—as do Hawaii's election laws—a prohibition on write-in voting will be presumptively valid, since any burden on the right to vote for the candidate of one's choice will be light and normally will be counterbalanced by the very state interests supporting the ballot access scheme.

In such situations, the objection to the specific ban on write-in voting amounts to nothing more than the insistence that the State record, count, and publish individual protests against the election system or the choices presented on the ballot through the efforts of those who actively participate in the system. There are other means available, however, to voice such generalized dissension from the electoral process; and we discern no adequate basis for our requiring the State to provide and to finance a place on the ballot for recording protests against its constitutionally valid election laws.

"No right is more precious in a free country than that of having a voice in the election of those who make the laws under which, as good citizens, we must live." But the right to vote is the right to participate in an electoral process that is necessarily structured to maintain the integrity of the democratic system. We think that Hawaii's prohibition on write-in voting, considered as part of an electoral scheme that provides constitutionally sufficient ballot access, does not impose an unconstitutional burden upon the First and Fourteenth Amendment rights of the State's voters.

* * *

■ JUSTICE KENNEDY, with whom JUSTICE BLACKMUN and JUSTICE STEVENS join, dissenting.

* * *

In the election that triggered this lawsuit, petitioner did not wish to vote for the one candidate who ran for state representative in his district. Because he could not write in the name of a candidate he preferred, he had no way to cast a meaningful vote. Petitioner's dilemma is a recurring, frequent phenomenon in Hawaii because of the State's ballot access rules and the circumstance that one party, the Democratic Party, is predominant.

[. . .] Democratic candidates often run unopposed, especially in state legislative races. In the 1986 general election, 33 percent of the elections for state legislative offices involved single candidate races. The comparable figures for 1984 and 1982 were 39 percent and 37.5 percent. Large numbers of voters cast blank ballots in uncontested races, that is, they leave the ballots blank rather than vote for the single candidate listed. In 1990, 27 percent of voters who voted in other races did not cast votes in uncontested state Senate races. Twenty-nine percent of voters did not cast votes in uncontested state house races. Even in contested races in 1990, 12 to 13 percent of voters cast blank ballots.

Given that so many Hawaii voters are dissatisfied with the choices available to them, it is hard to avoid the conclusion that at least some voters would cast write-in votes for other candidates if given this option. The write-in ban thus prevents these voters from participating in Hawaii elections in a meaningful manner.

* * *

The dominance of the Democratic Party [creates a disincentive for voters to participate in Hawaii's ballot access scheme to generate candidates for specific offices] . . . because the primary election is dispositive in so many races. In effect, a Hawaii voter who wishes to vote for any independent candidate must choose between doing so and participating in what will be the dispositive election for many offices. This dilemma imposes a substantial burden on voter choice. It explains also why so few independent candidates secure enough primary votes to advance to the general election. As the majority notes, only eight independent candidates have succeeded in advancing to the general election in the past 10 years. That is, less than one independent candidate per year on average has in fact run in a general election in Hawaii.

The majority's approval of Hawaii's ban is ironic at a time when the new democracies in foreign countries strive to emerge from an era of sham elections in which the name of the ruling party candidate was the only one on the ballot. Hawaii does not impose as severe a restriction on the right to vote, but it imposes a restriction that has a haunting similarity in its tendency to exact severe penalties for one who does anything but vote the dominant party ballot.

Aside from constraints related to ballot access restrictions, the write-in ban limits voter choice in another way. Write-in voting can serve as an important safety mechanism in those instances where a late-developing issue arises or where new information is disclosed about a candidate late in the race. In these situations, voters may become disenchanted with the available candidates when it is too late for other candidates to come forward and qualify for the ballot. The prohibition on write-in voting imposes a significant burden on voters, forcing them either to vote for a candidate whom they no longer support, or to cast a blank ballot. Write-in voting provides a way out of the quandary, allowing voters to switch their support to candidates who are not on the official ballot. Even if there are other mechanisms to address the problem of late-breaking election developments (unsuitable candidates who win an election can be recalled), allowing write-in voting is the only way to preserve the voters' right to cast a meaningful vote in the general election.

* * *

Because Hawaii's write-in ban, when considered in conjunction with the State's ballot access laws, imposes a significant burden on voters such as petitioner, it must put forward the state interests which justify the burden so that we can assess them. I do not think it necessary here to specify the level of scrutiny that should then be applied because, in my view, the State has failed to justify the write-in ban under any level of scrutiny. The interests proffered by the State, some of which are puzzling, are not advanced to any significant degree by the write-in prohibition. I consider each of the interests in turn.

The interest that has the best potential for acceptance, in my view, is that of preserving the integrity of party primaries by preventing sore loser candidacies during the general election. . . . [But] a write-in ban is a very overinclusive means of addressing the problem; it bars legitimate candidacies as well as undesirable sore loser candidacies. If the State desires to prevent sore loser candidacies, it can implement a narrow provision aimed at that particular problem.

The second interest advanced by the State is enforcing its policy of permitting the unopposed victors in certain primaries to be designated as officeholders without having to go through the general election. The majority states that "this would not be possible, absent the write-in voting ban." This makes no sense. As petitioner's counsel acknowledged during oral argument, "to the degree that Hawaii has abolished general elections in these circumstances, there is no occasion to cast a write-in ballot." If anything, the argument cuts the other way because this provision makes it all the more important to allow write-in voting in the primary elections because primaries are often dispositive. . . .

The State also cites its interest in promoting the informed selection of candidates, an interest it claims is advanced by "flushing candidates into the open a reasonable time before the election." I think the State has it backwards. The fact that write-in candidates often do not conduct visible campaigns seems to me to make it more likely that voters who go to the trouble of seeking out these candidates and writing in their names are well informed. The state interest may well cut the other way.

The State cites interests in combating fraud and enforcing nomination requirements. But the State does not explain how write-in voting presents a risk of fraud in today's polling places. As to the State's interest in making sure that ineligible candidates are not elected, petitioner's counsel pointed out at argument that approximately 20 States require write-in candidates to file a declaration of candidacy and verify that they are eligible to hold office a few days before the election.

* * *

NOTES AND QUESTIONS

1. Most states permit write-in voting. In addition to Hawaii, only Nevada, Oklahoma, and South Dakota refuse to count write-in votes for any office. Several other states prohibit write-in votes for certain offices, or in primary or runoff elections, or in general elections for candidates who lost in the primary. And most states condition the tabulation of a candidate's votes upon his filing a declaration of candidacy prior to the election. *See generally* David Perney, Note, *The Dimensions of the Right to Vote: The Write–In Vote, Donald Duck, and Voting Booth Speech Written–Off*, 58 Mo. L. Rev. 945 (1993). Contrary to the U.S. Supreme Court's approach, most state courts to have faced the question have held that the "general concept of a right to vote" includes the right to cast a write-in ballot. *See id.* at 955.

2. To what extent does the ban on write-in voting entrench the existing political order? When is write-in voting most likely to affect the outcome of a particular election? What bearing, if any, should the fact that a large number of Hawaiian legislative elections had only one official candidate have on the Court's analysis? The Court's opinions make reference to the tremendous power of the state Democratic Party, including the fact that Democratic nomination for many offices is considered such a guarantee of electoral success that there is oftentimes no general election held. This fact pattern strongly implies that the prohibition on write-in votes serves to lock in the political power of the Democratic Party. After all, when the opinion speaks of "state policy" underlying the prohibition on write-in votes, who are the state policymakers other than those same Democratic Party elected officials who have reaped the benefits of the current system? Should courts assume some special role in more exacting oversight of the political process when incumbent powers appear to have designed electoral rules that serve to lock in their hold on power? Notice as well that the Court appears to hold out the prospect of forming independent parties as a sufficient vehicle for venting alternative political views. How does this argument compare with the original Madisonian skepticism toward constitutionally entrenching political parties? Should individual claims to self-expression in the political arena be dependent upon the creation of independent intermediate organizations? What if an individual voter wanted to express dissatisfaction with only one candidate in one specific election? Does the formation of an independent political party seem an efficient manner for such expression?

3. Note that the Court evaluates the burden of the write-in ban in isolation from other elements of the Hawaiian electoral structure as a whole. For a critique that argues ballot regulations should be assessed not in isolation from each other, but in terms of their cumulative effects on the right to meaningful participation, see Samuel Issacharoff and Richard H. Pildes, *Politics as Markets: Partisan Lockups of the Democratic Process*, 50 Stan. L. Rev. 643, 671 (1998):

> Moreover, this ban on write-in voting did not operate in isolation, nor are the stakes trivial. In addition to shutting down the write-in option, state laws make it exceptionally difficult for new parties and independent candidates to get on the ballot. For a candidate who wants to run as an independent, the difficulty does not lie in getting a place on the ballot, for only a handful of signatures are required. Rather, the

independent's real difficulty lies in the fact that voters who wish to vote for an independent must pay an enormous price. Hawaii law, in effect, requires primary voters to choose only a single ballot for all offices. In order to vote for an independent candidate for one office, for example, the voter loses the ability to vote in any other race. The same monopoly-enhancing restriction applies to voters who want to vote for a third-party candidate. These restrictions have even more bite in a one-party State in which the winner of the primary election, if a Democrat, is almost certainly going to win the general election. Consequently, the cumulative structure of Hawaii's laws eviscerates any nascent resistance to the Democratic monopoly.

Should courts take these cumulative effects into account in determining whether electoral burdens are undue? A panoply of regulations, each apparently defensible when considered alone, may nevertheless have the combined effect of severely restricting participation and competition. Even if each part of a regulatory regime might be upheld if challenged separately, one or another of these parts might have to fall if the overall scheme unreasonably curtails associational freedoms.

4. The Supreme Court's approach seems to reject the idea of voting as core political speech, since, under well-established doctrine, infringements of political speech are subject to strict scrutiny. Is the Court right? Is the fact that voters cast their ballots anonymously relevant here? In this regard, consider the Court's decision in *McIntyre v. Ohio Elections Commission*, 514 U.S. 334 (1995), striking down, on First Amendment grounds, Ohio's prohibition of anonymous campaign literature. The idea of locating a right to vote in the First Amendment guarantee of free speech has a distinguished pedigree. *See, e.g.,* Alexander Bickel, The Supreme Court and the Idea of Progress 59–61 (1978); Alexander Meiklejohn, Political Freedom 39–40 (1960). Nonetheless, the Supreme Court seems to have rejected that argument. Why?

5. More broadly, is the Court's conception of the right to vote unduly cramped? Why *shouldn't* at least one function of the election process be "to provide a means of giving vent to 'short-range political goals [or] pique' "? Isn't the kind of voter dissatisfaction that prompts casting a "protest vote" for Donald Duck an important piece of data for the political system? Donald Duck has a long and distinguished history as the exasperated voter's candidate of choice. In *Dixon v. Maryland Board of Elections*, 878 F.2d 776, 785 n.12 (4th Cir. 1989), for example, the court of appeals explained that "under appropriate circumstances" a write-in vote for Donald Duck should be constitutionally protected "as serious satirical criticism of the powers that be.... Correcting this problem through censorship of the vote is utterly inconsistent with the principles under which our form of government operates." Consider the argument that free speech jurisprudence could inform our understanding of the right to vote. Broadly speaking, there are two main justifications for free speech:

The first is instrumentalist: it views the freedom of speech as a tool for achieving certain societal objectives. Thus, philosophers and jurists have argued that free speech is valuable because it enables the search for truth in the marketplace of ideas or because it furthers the ability of the people to govern themselves by protecting political information. Under such theories, the freedom of speech is not valuable in itself but only for the results that unfettered dialogue can bring to society, in terms of either the "truth" or good self-government. The ends to which speech is directed determine whether the speech should be constitutionally protected.

The second major theoretical model for free speech focuses on the constitutive value of speech: it argues that freedom of speech is necessary because it is essential to one's dignity or self-fulfillment, vital aspects of one's identity. These aspects of identity are not objectives that can be separated from the underlying freedom but rather are inherently intertwined with it. Most importantly ..., constitutive approaches to the freedom of speech posit that the right has intrinsic value apart from the mere ability to use speech as a method of conveying ideas for external ends.

Adam Winkler, Note, *Expressive Voting*, 68 N.Y.U. L. Rev. 330, 339–40 (1993). Is the Supreme Court's view of voting in *Burdick* entirely instrumental? Does, or should, voting have any function beyond "the societal goal of gauging and institutionalizing the political will"? *Id.* at 331. Should voting be viewed as constitutive? What legal consequences might flow from such a stance?

4. RESTRICTIONS ON WHO APPEARS ON THE BALLOT

Although political parties no longer distribute the actual ballots voters use, they still perform a major function in determining who appears on the ballot. When the officially printed, Australian ballot was adopted, states necessarily needed some mechanism for determining who should appear on the ballot. As Professor Bradley Smith explains, "early laws were not restrictive, and there was a broad public consensus that ballot-access laws were not intended to be a substantive barrier;" indeed, some supporters of the Australian ballot had actually argued that it would increase the number of candidates, since it would relieve candidates or minor parties of the expense of printing ballots with their names on them and distributing them to voters. Bradley A. Smith, Note, *Judicial Protection of Ballot–Access Rights: Third Parties Need Not Apply*, 28 Harv. J. Legis. 167, 173 (1991).

Within a few decades, however, states began using restrictive ballot-access rules that drastically limited the number of candidates who could appear on the ballot. Every state provided essentially automatic access to the general election ballot for certain candidates, essentially those nominated by major political parties. Typically, the statute would place on the general election ballot the names of candidates nominated by parties that had received a specified share of the vote in a previous general election. *See, e.g.,* Mich. Stat. Ann. § 6.1560 (1996) (providing that a "political party the principal candidate of which received at the last preceding general election a vote equal to or more than 1% of the total number of votes cast for the successful candidate for secretary of state at the last preceding election in which a secretary of state was elected is qualified to have its name, party vignette, and candidates listed on the next general election ballot"); Va. Code Ann. § 24.2–101 (1996) (defining as a "political party," entitled to automatic ballot access for its candidates, "an organization of citizens of the Commonwealth which, at either of the two preceding statewide general elections, received at least ten percent of the total vote cast for any statewide office filled in that election"). In most states today, only the Democratic and Republican parties enjoy automatic ballot access; there are some states, however, where additional parties have automatic ballot lines.

Because appearance on the general election ballot is so tightly constrained—an issue to which we shall return later in the chapter—the major winnowing down of candidates occurs in primary elections. But here, too, a variety of regulations limit candidates' ability to get a spot. In general, these restrictions take two forms: filing fees and petition requirements.

Bullock v. Carter

405 U.S. 134 (1972).

■ MR. CHIEF JUSTICE BURGER delivered the opinion of the Court.

Under Texas law, a candidate must pay a filing fee as a condition to having his name placed on the ballot in a primary election....

Appellee Pate met all qualifications to be a candidate in the May 2, 1970, Democratic primary for the office of County Commissioner of Precinct Four for El Paso County, except that he was unable to pay the $1,424.60 assessment required of candidates in that primary. Appellee Wischkaemper sought to be placed on the Democratic primary ballot as a candidate for County Judge in Tarrant County, but he was unable to pay the $6,300 assessment for candidacy for that office. Appellee Carter wished to be a Democratic candidate for Commissioner of the General Land Office; his application was not accompanied by the required $1,000 filing fee.

* * *

Under the Texas statute, payment of the filing fee is an absolute prerequisite to a candidate's participation in a primary election. There is no alternative procedure by which a potential candidate who is unable to pay the fee can get on the primary ballot by way of petitioning voters,[5] and

---

5. Texas law does permit the names of independent candidates to appear on the offi- cial ballot in the general election if a proper application containing a voter petition is sub-

write-in votes are not permitted in primary elections for public office. Any person who is willing and able to pay the filing fee and who meets the basic eligibility requirements for holding the office sought can run in a primary.

Candidates for most district, county, and precinct offices must pay their filing fee to the county executive committee of the political party conducting the primary; the committee also determines the amount of the fee. The party committee must make an estimate of the total cost of the primary and apportion it among the various candidates "as in their judgment is just and equitable." ... In counties with populations of one million or more, candidates for offices of two-year terms can be assessed up to 10% of their aggregate annual salary, and candidates for offices of four-year terms can be assessed up to 15% of their aggregate annual salary. In smaller counties there are no such percentage limitations.[10]

The record shows that the fees required of the candidates in this case are far from exceptional in their magnitude. The size of the filing fees is plainly a natural consequence of a statutory system that places the burden of financing primary elections on candidates rather than on the governmental unit, and that imposes a particularly heavy burden on candidates for local office. The filing fees required of candidates seeking nomination for state offices and offices involving statewide primaries are more closely regulated by statute and tend to be appreciably smaller. The filing fees for candidates for State Representative range from $150 to $600, depending on the population of the county from which nomination is sought. Candidates for State Senator are subject to a maximum assessment of $1,000. Candidates for nominations requiring statewide primaries, including candidates for Governor and United States Senator, must pay a filing fee of $1,000 to the chairman of the state executive committee of the party conducting the primary.

* * *

(1)

* * *

mitted. The number of eligible voters required to sign the petition varies from 1% to 5% depending on the office sought. For district, county, and precinct offices, candidates must obtain the signatures of 5% of the eligible voters with a ceiling of 500 signatures. No person may sign the application of more than one person for the same office, and no person who has voted in a primary may sign the application of a candidate for an office for which a nomination.

10. The $6,300 fee required of appellee Wischkaemper, for example, amounts to 32% of the $19,700 annual salary for County Judge in Tarrant County. Similarly, in the May 2, 1970, Democratic primary, candidates for five county offices in Ward County were assessed $6,250 for a filing fee; this fee represented 76.6% of the $8,160 annual salary for four of these offices; for the fifth office, that of County Commissioner, it represented 99.7% of the annual salary of $6,270.

The threshold question to be resolved is whether the filing-fee system should be sustained if it can be shown to have some rational basis, or whether it must withstand a more rigid standard of review.

In *Harper v. Virginia Board of Elections,* 383 U.S. 663 (1966), the Court held that Virginia's imposition of an annual poll tax not exceeding $1.50 on residents over the age of 21 was a denial of equal protection. Subjecting the Virginia poll tax to close scrutiny, the Court concluded that the placing of even a minimal price on the exercise of the right to vote constituted an invidious discrimination. The problem presented by candidate filing fees is not the same, of course, and we must determine whether the strict standard of review of the Harper case should be applied.

The initial and direct impact of filing fees is felt by aspirants for office, rather than voters, and the Court has not heretofore attached such fundamental status to candidacy as to invoke a rigorous standard of review. However, the rights of voters and the rights of candidates do not lend themselves to neat separation; laws that affect candidates always have at least some theoretical, correlative effect on voters.... In approaching candidate restrictions, it is essential to examine in a realistic light the extent and nature of their impact on voters.

Unlike a filing-fee requirement that most candidates could be expected to fulfill from their own resources or at least through modest contributions, the very size of the fees imposed under the Texas system gives it a patently exclusionary character. Many potential office seekers lacking both personal wealth and affluent backers are in every practical sense precluded from seeking the nomination of their chosen party, no matter how qualified they might be, and no matter how broad or enthusiastic their popular support. The effect of this exclusionary mechanism on voters is neither incidental nor remote. Not only are voters substantially limited in their choice of candidates, but also there is the obvious likelihood that this limitation would fall more heavily on the less affluent segment of the community, whose favorites may be unable to pay the large costs required by the Texas system. To the extent that the system requires candidates to rely on contributions from voters in order to pay the assessments, a phenomenon that can hardly be rare in light of the size of the fees, it tends to deny some voters the opportunity to vote for a candidate of their choosing; at the same time it gives the affluent the power to place on the ballot their own names or the names of persons they favor. Appellants do not dispute that this is endemic to the system. This disparity in voting power based on wealth cannot be described by reference to discrete and precisely defined segments of the community as is typical of inequities challenged under the Equal Protection Clause, and there are doubtless some instances of candidates representing the views of voters of modest means who are able to pay the required fee. But we would ignore reality were we not to recognize that this system falls with unequal weight on voters, as well as candidates, according to their economic status.

Because the Texas filing-fee scheme has a real and appreciable impact on the exercise of the franchise, and because this impact is related to the resources of the voters supporting a particular candidate, we conclude, as in *Harper*, that the laws must be "closely scrutinized" and found reasonably necessary to the accomplishment of legitimate state objectives in order to pass constitutional muster.

(2)

Appellants contend that the filing fees required by the challenged statutes are necessary both to regulate the ballot in primary elections and to provide a means for financing such elections.

The Court has recognized that a State has a legitimate interest in regulating the number of candidates on the ballot. In so doing, the State understandably and properly seeks to prevent the clogging of its election machinery, avoid voter confusion, and assure that the winner is the choice of a majority, or at least a strong plurality, of those voting, without the expense and burden of runoff elections. Although we have no way of gauging the number of candidates who might enter primaries in Texas if access to the ballot were unimpeded by the large filing fees in question here, we are bound to respect the legitimate objectives of the State in avoiding overcrowded ballots. Moreover, a State has an interest, if not a duty, to protect the integrity of its political processes from frivolous or fraudulent candidacies.

There is no escape from the conclusion that the imposition of filing fees ranging as high as $8,900 tends to limit the number of candidates entering the primaries. However, even under conventional standards of review, a State cannot achieve its objectives by totally arbitrary means; the criterion for differing treatment must bear some relevance to the object of the legislation. To say that the filing fee requirement tends to limit the ballot to the more serious candidates is not enough. There may well be some rational relationship between a candidate's willingness to pay a filing fee and the seriousness with which he takes his candidacy, but the candidates in this case affirmatively alleged that they were unable, not simply unwilling, to pay the assessed fees, and there was no contrary evidence. It is uncontested that the filing fees exclude legitimate as well as frivolous candidates. And even assuming that every person paying the large fees required by Texas law takes his own candidacy seriously, that does not make him a "serious candidate" in the popular sense. If the Texas fee requirement is intended to regulate the ballot by weeding out spurious candidates, it is extraordinarily ill-fitted to that goal; other means to protect those valid interests are available.

Instead of arguing for the reasonableness of the exclusion of some candidates, appellants rely on the fact that the filing-fee requirement is applicable only to party primaries, and point out that a candidate can gain a place on the ballot in the general election without payment of fees by submitting a proper application accompanied by a voter petition. Apart from the fact that the primary election may be more crucial than the general election in certain parts of Texas, we can hardly accept as reasonable an alternative that requires candidates and voters to abandon their party affiliations in order to avoid the burdens of the filing fees imposed by state law. Appellants have not demonstrated that their present filing-fee scheme is a necessary or reasonable tool for regulating the ballot.

In addition to the State's purported interest in regulating the ballot, the filing fees serve to relieve the State treasury of the cost of conducting the primary elections, and this is a legitimate state objective; in this limited sense it cannot be said that the fee system lacks a rational basis. But under the standard of review we consider applicable to this case, there must be a showing of necessity. . . .

More importantly, the costs do not arise because candidates decide to enter a primary or because the parties decide to conduct one, but because the State has, as a matter of legislative choice, directed that party primaries be held. The State has presumably chosen this course more to benefit the voters than the candidates.

Appellants seem to place reliance on the self-evident fact that if the State must assume the cost, the voters, as taxpayers, will ultimately be burdened with the expense of the primaries. But it is far too late to make out a case that the party primary is such a lesser part of the democratic process that its cost must be shifted away from the taxpayers generally. The financial burden for general elections is carried by all taxpayers and appellants have not demonstrated a valid basis for distinguishing between these two legitimate costs of the democratic process. It seems appropriate that a primary system designed to give the voters some influence at the nominating stage should spread the cost among all of the voters in an attempt to distribute the influence without regard to wealth. Viewing the myriad governmental functions supported from general revenues, it is difficult to single out any of a higher order than the conduct of elections at all levels to bring forth those persons desired by their fellow citizens to govern. Without making light of the State's interest in husbanding its revenues, we fail to see such an element of necessity in the State's present means of financing primaries as to justify the resulting incursion on the prerogatives of voters.

(3)

Since the State has failed to establish the requisite justification for this filing-fee system, we hold that it results in a denial of equal protection of the laws. . . . By requiring candidates to shoulder the costs of conducting primary elections through filing fees and by providing no reasonable alternative means of access to the ballot, the State of Texas has erected a system that utilizes the criterion of ability to pay as a condition to being on the ballot, thus excluding some candidates otherwise qualified and denying an undetermined number of voters the opportunity to vote for candidates of their choice. These salient features of the Texas system are critical to our determination of constitutional invalidity.

NOTES AND QUESTIONS

1. Two years later, in *Lubin v. Panish*, 415 U.S. 709 (1974), the Supreme Court addressed California's filing fee regime. The California fees were far lower—representing either one or two percent of the annual salary of the office sought and ranging from $192 for State Assembly seats up to $982 for Governor. The Court noted that *Bullock* did not completely resolve the case because the Texas filing fees "were so patently exclusionary as to violate traditional equal protection concepts." Chief Justice Burger's opinion for the Court identified two conflicting "means of achieving an effective, representative political system"—the first being the "steady trend toward limiting the size of the ballot in order to 'concentrate the attention of the electorate on the selection of a much smaller number of officials and so afford to the voters the opportunity of exercising more discrimination in their use of the franchise,'" the second being the "increasing pressure" for "expansion of political opportunity" reflected in twentieth-century constitutional amendments, the Voting Rights Act, and the "gradual enlargement of the Fourteenth Amendment's equal protection provision in the area of voting rights." While the Court ultimately struck down California's scheme on equal protection grounds, it also seemed to recognize distinct categories of substantive rights involved in elections. First, the Court acknowledged the importance of weighing the burden on voters' associational rights: "The interests involved are not merely those of parties or individual candidates; the voters can assert their preferences only through candidates or parties or both and it is this broad interest that must be weighed in the balance." Second, the Court identified an independent right of candidates to be on the ballot: "Conversely, if the filing fee is more moderate, as here, impecunious but serious candidates may be prevented from running. Even in this day of high-budget political campaigns some candidates have demonstrated that direct contact with thousands of voters by 'walking tours' is a route to success. Whatever may be the political mood at any given time, our tradition has been one of hospitality toward all candidates without regard to their economic status." *Bullock* and *Lubin* taken together raise the question of precisely which constitutional rights (and whose constitutional rights) render filing fees so constitutionally suspect.

2. Does it seem plausible that someone like Lubin—who claimed he was unable to raise $701.60—is a "serious" candidate for a position on the Los Angeles County Board of Supervisors? If, realistically speaking, someone in his position has no chance of winning, or perhaps even affecting the outcome, what accounts for the Court's special solicitude for his claim? Is this consistent with the Court's perspective in *Burdick*?

3. The Court suggests that the fatal flaw in the filing fee regimes was their failure to provide any alternative mechanism by which indigent but serious candidates could get on the ballot. In *Lubin*, the Court suggested that "a candidate who establishes that he cannot pay the filing fee required for a place on the primary ballot may be required to demonstrate the 'seriousness' of his candidacy by persuading a substantial number of voters to sign a petition in his behalf."

Today, all states provide some petition mechanism for candidates to get on primary (and general election) ballots. Some of the petition requirements, such as Hawaii's (discussed in *Burdick*) are purely nominal, requiring only a few dozen signatures. Hawaii, you may recall, requires candidates seeking nominations for statewide office to submit petitions with the signatures of 25 registered voters and candidates for state legislative nominations to submit petitions with 15 signatures. It is hard to imagine that any "serious" candidate would be unable to meet such a requirement. But other petition requirements seem designed largely, if not entirely, to restrict the field to "insiders." In this regard, consider the New York system. New York Election Law § 6–136 provides, in pertinent part:

1. Petitions for any office to be filled by the voters of the entire state must be signed by not less than fifteen thousand or five per centum, whichever is less, of the then enrolled voters of the party in the state (excluding voters in inactive status), of whom not less than one hundred or five per centum, whichever is less, of such enrolled voters shall reside in each of one-half of the congressional districts of the state.

2. All other petitions must be signed by not less than five per centum, as determined by the preceding enrollment, of the then enrolled voters of the party residing within the political unit in which the office or position is to be voted for (excluding voters in inactive status), provided, however, that for the following public offices the number of signatures need not exceed the following limits:

* * *

(h) For any office to be filled by all the voters of any state senatorial district, one thousand signatures;

(i) For any office to be filled by all voters of any assembly district, five hundred signatures.

New York provides no filing fee alternative; thus, all candidates must obtain their ballot positions through indications of voter support. New York's law also contains a large number of technical requirements involving such things as how petitions should be collated and requirements for additional information by signatories. In recent years, New York has accounted for one-half of the ballot access challenges in the nation. *See* Katherine E. Schuelke, Note, *A Call for Reform of New York State's Ballot Access Laws*, 64 N.Y.U. L. Rev. 182 (1989).

Which candidates are benefitted or disadvantaged by New York's system? For one example of litigation involving the New York system, see *Rockefeller v. Powers*, 917 F.Supp. 155 (E. D. N. Y.), *aff'd*, 78 F.3d 44 (2d Cir.), *cert. denied*, 517 U.S. 1203 (1996), which involved the regulation of candidates on the state's Republican presidential primary ballot. Half of the candidates who ran in other states chose not even to attempt to appear on the New York ballot. Steve Forbes, who spent millions of dollars of his own money on his presidential bid, presumably could have met any filing fee requirement. But he was unable to meet the petition requirements in roughly half of the state's congressional districts. Only Bob Dole satisfied the ballot access requirements statewide. Interestingly, in 1988, when Dole was challenging George Bush (rather than occupying the front-runner's position), he had been unable to satisfy the same requirements.

To appear on the ballot in a particular congressional district (New York's scheme determines access district-by-district rather than statewide), a candidate needed to collect roughly 1250 signatures within the district during a 37–day period in the middle of the winter. Each candidate also faced a host of rules defining what was a valid signature, including rules as to the qualification of witnesses to signings and inclusion of the election or Assembly district numbers of signers. Moreover, a voter could sign only one petition. Can you think of reasons why a voter might want to sign more than one such petition? While the requirement of signatures from each congressional district undoubtedly would measure widespread support, it proved a close to insuperable obstacle to a candidate in districts where it was "easier to find a needle in haystack than an enrolled Republican," such as the 86 percent nonwhite Fifteenth Congressional District centered on Harlem. The district court and court of appeals held that the Republicans' system violated the due process clause because it placed an undue burden on the voting rights of Republicans in heavily Democratic districts; in those districts, the voters' choice was constrained.

Does it seem even remotely plausible that a candidate who cannot afford a filing fee would have the resources to get on the ballot under the sort of petitioning scheme at issue in *Rockefeller*? It turns out that many parties and candidates seeking spots on the ballot turn to paid signature gatherers, who charge fees like $3.50 per signature collected. *See* Rogers Worthington, *Perot Party Goes All Out in Ballot Drive*, Chi. Tribune, Oct. 23, 1995, at 3. Is Bradley Smith right that "[g]iven these numbers, it is ludicrous to suggest that a candidate who could not pay a one dollar filing fee, or even an $8,900 filing fee, could conduct a major petition drive to appear on the ballot"? Smith, *supra*, at 201; *cf. Andress v. Reed*, 880 F.2d 239 (9th Cir. 1989) (rejecting a potential candidate's claim that the cost to obtain the required 10,000 signatures would be more than the $1,702 filing fee he could not afford, and therefore violated the equal protection clause).

The Supreme Court has devoted substantial attention to the constitutionality of various petition schemes that determine when particular candidates can gain access to the ballot. We will return to this issue in the context of petitions to appear on the general election ballot and the question of entrenchment of the two-party system.

4. In a follow-up to *Rockefeller v. Powers*, the New York courts examined the proper standard of review for ballot access challenges. Even after the decision in *Rockefeller*, Senator John McCain faced almost insuperable obstacles to getting on the Republican Party primary ballot for the 2000 elections. He therefore challenged the post–1996 ballot access rules, and in *Molinari v. Powers*, 82 F. Supp. 2d 57 (E. D. N. Y. 2000), the same district judge that had invalidated the ballot access rules for the 1996 Presidential primary elections again invalidated the more recent rules. The "reformed" rules had required that primary candidates had to collect 5,000 signatures statewide and imposed a geographic distributional requirement that candidates also had to collect (under highly regulated circumstances) the signatures of at least 0.5% of the registered Republicans in each congressional district. The court found those regulations to be irrational and an undue burden on First Amendment rights:

> [T]he New York ballot access scheme as applied to the Primary poses an undue burden in its totality on the right to vote under the First Amendment.... Specifically, I am referring to the related requirements ... that (i) each witness to a designating petition must either be a registered Republican voter residing in the congressional district of the delegate candidate for whom he or she is witnessing signatures, or, in the alternative, must be a notary public or commissioner of deeds ... and (ii) the town/city "trap"....

> [T]o invalidate a petition [because of a failure to satisfy the second requirement] deprives the voter who signed the petition of the right to participate in the primary process by placing on the ballot candidates whom he or she supports. It also deprives the delegate candidates of a place on the ballot.... Moreover, it does this for no rational, much less compelling, reason....

> The proffered reasons for the residence requirement simply cannot justify the burden the residence requirement places on the petition gathering process. In essence, the residence requirement reduces by approximately 2.9 to 3 million voters the pool of Republicans available to volunteer to petition for signatures in any particular district.... While the effect of the residence requirement on a presidential candidate like Mr. Forbes or Senator McCain is significant ... the requirement poses no burden for the candidate supported by the Republican Party or the Republican State Committee.... Indeed, it is this fact that provides the only comprehensible reason for the residence requirement....

> The requirement in New York that witnesses reside in the same congressional district as the delegate candidates for whom they are

circulating petitions is even more burdensome to core political speech than the one at issue in [*Buckley v. American Constitutional Law Foundation, Inc.*, 525 U.S. 182 (1999)]. . . . My judgment is that the requirements that a witness reside in the congressional district in which he or she is witnessing a signature and that a witness or signer separately list the town or city in which he or she resides in addition to his or her residence address fail under any test.

Should courts sustain any rationally-based ballot qualification? Should the intent to restrict access be separately considered? How different is it from prior cases that the District Court evaluated "the scheme" in "its totality"—as opposed to assessing any one provision in isolation—in order to conclude that the scheme itself posed an undue burden? Compare this with the approach of the Supreme Court in *Burdick v. Takushi,* above, and the critique of that decision above in note 3 following that case.

5.   Before the *McCain* litigation, the New York Republican Party's presidential primary rules had been stunningly effective in keeping insurgent Republicans off the primary ballot. Never before had a candidate who was not the choice of the state party's leaders (such as Bush in 2000 or Dole in 1996) and who relied on federal matching funds (unlike Forbes, in 1996, who was self-financed) been able to surmount the ballot-access hurdles and create a competitive Republican primary. For a comprehensive study of the ballot-access struggles in New York, including a detailed history of the *McCain* litigation by one of the lawyers who represented McCain, see Nathaniel Persily, *Candidates v. Parties: The Constitutional Constraints on Primary Ballot Access Laws*, 88 Geo. L. J. 2181 (2001).

6.   A survey of ballot access cases shows that the trend in the lower federal courts is to uphold most state ballot access restrictions. *See, e.g., Wood v. Meadows*, 207 F.3d 708 (4th Cir. 2000) (holding that under a rational basis level of scrutiny, state interests in administrative convenience, limiting the number of candidates on general election ballot, requiring candidates to show a modicum of support, and designating the primary date as one where the full field of valid candidates is identified outweighed the burden imposed on independent candidates by law requiring them to file statements of candidacy signed by one-half of one percent of all registered Virginia voters with at least 200 signatures from each congressional district five months prior to general elections); *The Council of Alternative Political Parties v. Hooks*, 179 F.3d 64 (3d Cir. 1999) (upholding New Jersey election law denying independent and "alternative political party" gubernatorial candidates seeking general ballot access through primary nominations and requiring them to file nominating petitions with 800 signatures by the major parties' primary date); *Schulz v. Williams*, 44 F.3d 48 (2d Cir. 1994) (holding New York election law requiring independents wishing to nominate candidate for statewide office to gather the signatures of 15,000 registered voters, indicating their election district, assembly district and ward within a 42–day period from July 12 to August 23 to be constitutional under a rational basis level of scrutiny); *Socialist Workers Party v. Hechler*, 890 F.2d 1303 (4th Cir. 1989) (upholding West Virginia election law that barred voters signing nominating petition for minor party candidate from also participating in major party primary and requiring minor party candidate to file certificate of candidacy one month prior to major party primaries); *Libertarian Party of Virginia v. Davis*, 766 F.2d 865 (4th Cir. 1985) (upholding Virginia election law requiring minor party seeking general ballot access to submit petition signed by one-half of 1% of all registered voters, including at least 200 voters from each congressional district because justified by state interest in securing candidates with a modicum of numerical and geographic support); *Taman v. Illinois Board of Elections*, 2000 WL 521708 (N. D. Ill. 2000) (holding that a petition requirement of 2,131 signatures for judicial candidates cannot be considered an undue burden for a candidate seeking county-wide office in a county of over five million population); *Wood v. Quinn*, 104 F. Supp. 2d 611 (E. D. Va. 2000) (holding that law requiring independent senatorial candidates submit petitions containing 10,000 signatures, including 400 from each of 11 congressional districts witnessed by qualified voter from same congressional district is constitutional); *The Patriot Party of Pennsylvania v. Mitchell*, 826 F.Supp. 926 (E. D. Pa. 1993) (finding constitutional a Pennsylvania law requiring political party to obtain 15% of the registered vote in order to be deemed a "major political party" and that those who do not achieve such a threshold must repeatedly demonstrate voter support through nominating petitions or election support because the law serves to further the state's compelling interest in screening out frivolous candidates); *but see Tobin for Governor v. Illinois State Board of Elections*, 105 F. Supp. 2d 882 (N. D. Ill. 2000) (election law that requires that candidate nomination petition be signed by a registered voters is unconstitutional under *Buckley v. ACLF*); *Molinari v. Powers*, 82 F. Supp. 2d 57 (E. D. N. Y. 2000) (finding two aspects of Republican nominating requirements to be unconstitutional burdens on rights of candidates: (1) witness to petition must be registered Republican residing in congressional district of delegate candidate for whom he is witnessing signatures, and (2) petition signer must list larger town/city unit within which their village of residence is located).

For more information on ballot-access issues, check the Ballot Access News website maintained by Richard Winger: http://www.ballot-access.org.

B. Who Can Participate in a Party's Activities?

Since the mid–1800's, the United States has had two major political parties: the Democrats and the Republicans. For a history of the rise and fall of American political parties, see James L. Sundquist, Dynamics of the Party System (1983). Virtually all successful candidates for national office have been members of one party or the other; today, for example, and only a handful of Members of Congress at any given point are neither Republicans nor Democrats. And with a few notable and short-lived exceptions, virtually all state and local officials elected in partisan elections are affiliated with one (or sometimes both) of the major parties. For example, "of over 20,000 elections for state legislatures from 1982 to 1988, only three [were] won by members of a party other than the Democrats or Republicans." Bradley A. Smith, Note, *Judicial Protection of Ballot–Access Rights: Third Parties Need Not Apply*, 28 Harv. J. Legis. 167, 171 (1991).

Thus, as recognized in cases stretching as far back as *United States v. Classic*, 313 U.S. 299 (1941), primary elections and major party nomination processes are "an integral part of the procedure for the popular choice" of elected officials. States closely regulate major-party nomination processes, and a majority of states now require some form of primary elections. The Supreme Court has never squarely addressed the question whether a state can compel a party to use a particular nomination process, but as Professor Lowenstein has explained, it has been thought unlikely that the Court would strike down a mandatory primary law. *See* Daniel H. Lowenstein, *Political Parties: A Skeptical Inquiry*, 71 Tex. L. Rev. 1741, 1768–69 (1993). *See also Lightfoot v. Eu*, 964 F.2d 865, 872 (9th Cir. 1992) (rejecting a challenge to California's primary requirement), *cert. denied*, 507 U.S. 919 (1993). For an opposing view, see Arthur M. Weisburd, *Candidate-Making and the Constitution: Constitutional Restraints on and Protections of Party Nominating Methods*, 57 S. Cal. L. Rev. 213 (1984); Karl D. Cooper, Note, *Are State–Imposed Political Party Primaries Constitutional? The Constitutional Ramifications of the 1986 Illinois LaRouche Primary Victories*, 4 J.L. & Pol. 343 (1987).

The question of when particular individuals can participate in the nomination process implicates a variety of individual, party, and state interests. Bear in mind that since individual voters are free not to participate, no cases arise unless an individual seeks to take part. Although it is conceivable that some party members might object if both the party and the state agree to let an interested voter participate, it seems likely that courts would refuse to intervene in that sort of internecine debate. The most realistically possible legal questions can therefore be represented by the following three pairs of responses to the question: Can Citizen X participate in the "A" Party's nomination process?

Can Citizen X participate in the "A" Party's Nomination Process?		
	Party	*State*
1.	No	No
2.	No	Yes
3.	Yes	No

The following cases work through these permutations.

1.   Both the Party and the State Seek to Exclude Citizen X From Participating

Nader v. Schaffer

417 F.Supp. 837 (D. Conn.), *summarily aff'd*, 429 U.S. 989 (1976).

■ Robert P. Anderson, Circuit Judge:

[The plaintiffs in this case are registered voters who refused to register as members of a political party. Under Connecticut law, this precludes them from voting in any party primary. The case arises on a motion to dismiss by the named defendants: the Secretary of State of Connecticut, and the state Republican and Democratic parties.] Plaintiffs' principal argument is that participation in a primary election is an exercise of the constitutionally protected right to vote and of the constitutionally protected right to associate with others in support of a candidate. They also assert that to the latter there is a constitutionally protected correlative right not to associate, and to be free from coerced associations. They further claim a constitutionally protected right of privacy of association. Plaintiffs wish to exercise both of these claimed sets of rights, but [Connecticut law] limits them to one or the other; that is, in order to vote in a party's primary election, plaintiffs must enroll in the party, while on the other hand, if they maintain their stand against enrollment, they are precluded.

* * *

Plaintiffs argue that the alternative avenues of political activity open to them under Connecticut law [if they are unable to participate in primary elections] are ineffectual and unrealistic, since in most general elections, only the Democratic and Republican nominees have reasonable probabilities of success.... [But] any dominant position enjoyed by the Democratic and Republican Parties is not the result of improper support, or discrimination in their favor, by the State. Rather, the two Parties enjoy this position because, over a period of time, they have been successful in attracting the bulk of the electorate, so that they now have substantial followings.

* * *

Improper State support for the Democratic and Republican Parties cannot be inferred from the fact that their primary elections are closely regulated by statute. In the past, many political nominations were made by a process ... described as the "smoke-filled room." Many states, such as Connecticut, have enacted statutes calling for nomination by primary election, presumably because they find it beneficial to allow the general party membership a voice in the nominating process.

* * *

With regard to the claimed right not to associate, it is true that, in order to vote in a party's primary, plaintiffs must publicly affiliate with that party. But enrollment in Connecticut imposes absolutely no affirmative party obligations on the voter, in terms of time or money, and it does not even obligate him to vote for the party's positions or candidates or to vote at all. The voter's name, however, may be erased from the party's enrollment list on a proper showing that he does not support the party's principles or candidates. Conn. Gen. Stat. §§ 9–60, 9–61; but in actual practice these statutes are not used. Such limited public affiliation is simply not ... coerced orthodoxy imposed by government officials....

Plaintiffs also claim that the public nature of enrollment violates their right to privacy of association by potentially subjecting them to harassment because of their affiliations with a party. It is insufficient, however, for plaintiffs merely to raise the spectre of harassment; instead, they must make a detailed factual showing of actual threats or incidents of harassment. At least one form of potential harassment suggested by plaintiffs—loss of civil service employment due to political affiliation—cannot necessarily be considered a realistic threat since this practice was recently declared unconstitutional by the Supreme Court, at least as to patronage employees in non-policy-making positions. *Elrod v. Burns*, 427 U.S. 347 (1976).

* * *

Because the political party is formed for the purpose of engaging in political activities, constitutionally protected associational rights of its members are vitally essential to the candidate selection process.... [P]arty members also have a "right to organize a party in the way that will make it the most effective political organization." An attempt to interfere with a party's ability so to maintain itself is simultaneously an interference with the associational rights of its members. The rights of party members may to some extent offset the importance of claimed conflicting rights asserted by persons challenging some aspect of the candidate selection process. More importantly, party members are entitled to affirmative protection of their associational rights.... [T]he state has a legitimate interest in protecting party members' associational rights, by legislating to protect the party "from intrusion by those with adverse political principles."

In addition to protecting the associational rights of party members, a state has a more general, but equally legitimate, interest in protecting the overall integrity of the historic electoral process. This includes preserving parties as viable and identifiable interest groups; insuring that the results of primary elections, in a broad sense, accurately reflect the voting of party members. Parties should be able to avoid primary election outcomes which will confuse or mislead the general electorate to the extent it relies on party labels as representative of certain ideologies; and preventing fraudulent and deceptive conduct which mars the nominating process.

* * *

As we have noted, the phrase "preservation of the integrity of the electoral process" contemplates, in the nominating context, the assurance that primary election results reflect the will of party members, undistorted by the votes of those unconcerned with, if not actually hostile to, the principles, philosophies, and goals of the party. The phrase contemplates the prevention of fraud in the nominating process, and a candidacy determined by the votes of non-party members is arguably a fraudulent candidacy.

* * *

From the party's point of view, enrollment also serves an important housekeeping function. Candidates need to know who is in the electorate, so that they (the candidates) can attempt to persuade those individuals to vote for them. Party members who wish to establish, as party policy, a particular course of conduct through the election of a particular candidate, similarly need to know who their supporters are. It is common experience that direct solicitation of party members—by mail, telephone, or face-to-face contact, and by the candidates themselves or by their active supporters—is part of any primary election campaign. But, without the public list of party members which is provided by the enrollment process, such electioneering would become quite difficult.

* * *

[Plaintiffs' complaint is therefore dismissed.]

NOTES AND QUESTIONS

1.   Could a party require more of a voter than public affiliation with the party as a condition of participation in its nominating event? Consider the following state statutes. Ala. Code § 17–16–14(b) (1996) provides that:

> All poll lists for primary elections shall state at the top thereof that by participating in said primary election a voter shall indicate his preference for the party holding said primary, and will support the nominees of that party in the general election, and that he is qualified under the rules of such party to vote in its primary election. No person shall be eligible to participate in said primary unless he signs said poll list and thereby certifies to the truth of said statement.

Minn. Stat. § 200.02, subd. 17 (1996) defines a member of a political party as "an individual who:

> (a) Supports the general principles of that party's constitution;
>
> (b) Voted for a majority of that party's candidates in the last general election; or
>
> (c) Intends to vote for a majority of that party's candidates in the next general election."

Could a party limit voting in its primary to individuals who agree with these sorts of requirements? There are no reported cases involving enforcement of these types of provisions. *See* Arthur M. Weisburd, *Candidate-Making and the Constitution: Constitutional Restraints on and Protections of Party Nominating Methods*, 57 S. Cal. L. Rev. 213, 271 (1984). But if political parties enjoy associational freedom, as the Supreme Court has repeatedly held they do, why shouldn't they be able to exclude "those with adverse political principles"? In that case, who should decide whether an individual is really a member of the party?

Parties have enforced "loyalty oaths" in other nomination settings. Consider the following account of a Republican "firehouse primary" in Fairfax County, Virginia. (A "firehouse primary" is a polling process conducted by a party without state supervision. The Jaybird balloting described in *Terry v. Adams*, 345 U.S. 461 (1953), earlier in this Chapter, *see supra* Chapter 2, is an example of a firehouse primary.)

> Many were turned off by a requirement that they sign an "intent form" to support the Republican nominee regardless of yesterday's outcome.
>
> Shouting matches erupted at times, as Republican officials tried to block people who had refused to sign the form from voting.
>
> "My right to vote without coercion has been violated," said Thierry Gaudin, 45, of Reston. "It is a rigging of the game for the political power of a few at the cost of democracy."
>
> Gaudin pressed his point with a half-dozen Republican officials, including party Chairman Patrick Mullins, who had a simple response.
>
> "Sue us. Thank you," Mullins said.
>
> Police were called when Gaudin refused to leave. After an hour, he did so voluntarily.
>
> Supreme Court Justice Antonin Scalia, a Fairfax resident, at first questioned the legality of the oath, but signed after getting an explanation from a party official, said Steve Jennings Jr., who checked Scalia in.

Eric Lipton, *Democracy Can Stop Traffic*, Wash. Post, Jan. 8, 1995, at A1. Is Justice Scalia's deference to party wishes here consistent with his stance in *Tashjian v. Republican Party of Connecticut*, 479 U.S. 208 (1986), discussed *infra*?

2. In a related vein, are the two major political parties in this country organizations with clearly held ideological commitments to which individuals might actually be adverse? Consider Justice Powell's observations in his dissent in *Democratic Party of the United States v. LaFollette*, 450 U.S. 107 (1981), discussed *infra*:

> If [the national Democratic Party] were an organization with a particular ideological orientation or political mission, perhaps [permitting

individuals who did not profess this ideology would] . . . interfere with the associational rights of its founders.

The Democratic Party, however, is not organized around the achievement of defined ideological goals. Instead, the major parties in this country "have been characterized by a fluidity and overlap of philosophy and membership." It can hardly be denied that this Party generally has been composed of various elements reflecting most of the American political spectrum. The Party does take positions on public issues, but these positions vary from time to time, and there never has been a serious effort to establish for the Party a monolithic ideological identity by excluding all those with differing views.

3.   The court's opinion in *Nader* refers to the state's "interest in protecting the overall integrity of the historic electoral process." How should a court weigh such state declarations of public interest when a) the beneficiaries of the regulation are the two dominant political parties, and b) the decision is made by elected representatives from these two dominant political parties? Does it make sense to speak of a "state interest" in such circumstances? Are there any restrictions or limitations on such claims of "state interest" when the effect of state regulation is to restrict challenges to the preeminent position of the established political parties?

4.   Should parties have a greater right to exclude *candidates* from their nomination processes? In *Ray v. Blair*, 343 U.S. 214 (1952), the Supreme Court upheld the exclusion of Edmund Blair's name as a candidate for Democratic Presidential Elector because Blair refused to sign a pledge to aid and support "the nominees of the National Convention of the Democratic Party for President and Vice–President of the United States." Admittedly, the "office" of elector might be a special case; the only function an elector serves is to cast one of his state's votes in the Electoral College. It is inconceivable that more than a handful of voters are even aware of the *names* of the electors for whom they have voted; indeed, in many states the ballot simply allows voters to cast an undivided vote for the entire slate of electors pledged to a particular party's candidates for president and vice president. So Blair's implicit threat to bolt the party and refuse to support the Democratic candidate for president (a not insubstantial risk, perhaps, given the voting behavior of some arch-segregationist Democratic-pledged electors during the period) might be reframed as a threat to deny voters who cast ballots for the Democratic ticket *their* right to vote.

Two more recent examples of exclusion perhaps present the question more squarely.

Duke v. Massey

87 F.3d 1226 (11th Cir. 1996).

■ JOSEPH HATCHETT, CIRCUIT JUDGE:

David Duke, a controversial political figure, sought the Republican Party's nomination for President of the United States for the 1992 election. In pursuing the Republican Party nomination, Duke participated in presidential primaries in various states throughout the nation. In December 1991, Georgia's Secretary of State, Max Cleland, prepared and published a list of potential candidates for Georgia's presidential preference primary. Duke's name appeared on the Georgia list of presidential candidates for the Republican Party nomination. The Secretary submitted his initial list of presidential primary candidates to the presidential candidate selection committee (Committee) for the Republican Party....

On December 16, 1991, the Committee, consisting of Georgia's Republican Party Chairperson Alec Poitevint, Senate Minority Leader Tom Phillips, and House Minority Leader Paul Heard ... deleted Duke's name from the list of potential republican presidential candidates.[1]

* * *

Duke asserts that the Committee's decision and the Georgia statute severely burdened his rights of free speech and association under the First and Fourteenth Amendments to the United States Constitution. Duke contends that because the statute grants the committee members "unfettered discretion" to grant or deny ballot access it is unconstitutional in that it allows the Committee members to exclude candidates based on the content of their speech. Duke argues that the statute also infringes his right to freedom of association.

[...] Duke does not have a right to associate with an "unwilling partner," the Republican Party.... [T]he Republican Party has a right to "identify the people who constitute the association and to limit the association to those people only." ... Although Duke is correct in identifying his First and Fourteenth Amendment interests, those interests do not trump the Republican Party's right to identify its membership based on political beliefs nor the state's interests in protecting the Republican Party's right to define itself. Therefore, the Committee, acting as representatives of the Republican Party under O.C.G.A. § 21–2–193, did not heavily burden Duke's First Amendment and Fourteenth Amendment rights when it excluded him from the Republican Party's presidential primary ballot.

* * *

The voters, supporters of Duke, claim that O.C.G.A. § 21–2–193 burdens their associational rights and their right to vote for a candidate of their choice. The voters contend that the right to vote is "heavily burdened" when the choices of candidates on primary ballots are restricted

---

1. Under Georgia law, "each person designated by the Secretary of State as a presidential candidate shall appear upon the ballot of the appropriate political party or body unless all committee members of the same political party or body as the candidate agree to delete such candidate's name from the ballot." O.C.G.A. § 21–2–193(a).

and other persons are "clamoring" to be listed on the election ballot.... The Supreme Court has recognized that a free and open debate on the qualifications of candidates is "integral to the operation of the system of government established by our Constitution," and that burdens on candidate access to the ballot directly burden the voters' ability to voice preferences. In this case, however, the voters have failed to offer any authority suggesting that they have a right to vote for their candidate of choice as a Republican in a nonbinding primary.[7]

* * *

Although we do not believe that Duke and the voters' rights were heavily burdened as a result of the Committee's decision under O.C.G.A. § 21–2–193, we will apply strict scrutiny ... in order to err on the side of caution....

The state has a compelling interest in protecting political parties' right to define their membership.... We believe that O.C.G.A. § 21–2–193 is narrowly tailored to further Georgia's compelling state interests. Under the statute, three party leaders are appointed to serve on the Committee.[8] Although the Committee's decision to exclude a candidate from the presidential primary ballot is unreviewable by the entire membership of the party, these committee members are leaders in the Republican Party and are ultimately held accountable for their decisions by the membership of the Republican Party. Under the terms of O.C.G.A. § 21–2–193, a person cannot serve on the Committee unless the membership of the Republican Party has placed them in a key leadership position. Surely, these persons are aware of the principles and platform of the Republican Party and can decide what presidential candidates are aligned with the party's views. Therefore, as leaders the membership of the party elected, they have been entrusted with the authority to make decisions for the party, and O.C.G.A. § 21–2–193 recognizes that these party leaders are in the best position to decide who should appear on Georgia's Republican Party presidential primary ballot.

* * *

Duke and the voters argue that the operation of the Georgia statute actually undermined its purported interest in protecting a political party's ability to define itself because it allows the committee members to make decisions that the party membership may not review. This argument suggests that the full party should have the right to determine what names appear on the ballot for a presidential primary.... [But] a system that

---

7. Nothing precludes these voters from supporting Duke as an independent candidate or a third-party candidate in the general election.

8. It is difficult to imagine composing a committee of party leaders who are in a bet-

ter position to determine how a presidential candidate lines up with the views of the party than the State Chairperson of the party and the Majority and Minority leaders of both the state house and senate.

would require a full party vote to put candidates on the presidential primary ballot would likely duplicate the, results of the primary itself and also of the Committee. We hold that O.C.G.A. § 21–2–103 is narrowly tailored as it provides the state an efficient and effective means of furthering its compelling interest of protecting a political party's right to exclude persons with "adverse political principles."

Republican Party of Texas v. Dietz

940 S.W.2d 86 (Tex. Sup. Ct. 1997).

■ JUSTICE ABBOTT delivered the opinion of the Court.

* * *

I

The Log Cabin Republicans of Texas and the Texas Log Cabin Republicans, Inc. (collectively LCR) are Texas non-profit corporations of Republicans who support equal civil rights for gay and lesbian individuals. In April 1996, LCR applied for an exhibitor's booth at the 1996 Republican Party of Texas Convention which began on June 20. As part of the booth application, LCR agreed to abide by the rules and regulations issued by the Republican Party of Texas for the convention. One of these rules allowed the Republican Party "the right to restrict exhibits which, because of undue noise, method of operation, material, content, or any other reason, become objectionable."

The Exhibits Chairman for the convention orally informed LCR's President, Dale Carter, that the group's booth application was approved. The Republican Party also cashed the $400 check Carter submitted for the booth. On May 15, 1996, LCR submitted to the Republican Party an advertisement to be included in the convention program along with a $750 check for the cost of the advertisement. The advertisement asserted LCR's beliefs that equal rights should be provided for gay and lesbian individuals. On May 21, 1996, the Republican Party Executive Director sent a letter to LCR rejecting the advertisement and the booth request. The Party returned the $750 check and refunded the cost of the booth.

On May 30, 1996, LCR filed this lawsuit in Travis County seeking injunctive relief. LCR alleged that the Republican Party's actions unconstitutionally infringed upon LCR's rights to free speech, equal rights, and due course of law under the Texas Constitution. . . . [The district court granted a preliminary injunction essentially requiring the Party to let LCR participate.]

* * *

II

* * *

The district court's injunction was based on a finding that LCR would probably prevail on ... its free speech, equal rights, and due course of law claims under the Texas Constitution. The Republican Party urges that LCR's state constitutional claims cannot be maintained because the Party's conduct did not constitute "state action." ...

[We agree with the Party. S]everal decisions have considered the circumstances under which a political party (such as the Republican Party of Texas) is a state actor.

In the White Primary Cases, the Supreme Court ... declared that political parties were state actors when they held primary elections. While state action may exist when political parties exercise the "traditional government function" of conducting elections, it is not true that every act of a political party is state action. As one commentator has observed:

> The idea of parties as "public" is in tension not only with the everyday recognition that parties are not government agencies, but also with the need to assure that the party system maintains a basic autonomy from the state so that the parties may serve as vehicles for expressing the public's needs and sentiments. Such autonomy distinguishes democracies from authoritarian systems....

Daniel Lowenstein, *Associational Rights of Major Political Parties: A Skeptical Inquiry*, 71 Tex. L. Rev. 1741, 1750 (1993).

Accordingly, federal courts have held that some party activities, such as holding elections, are public state action, while other activities are private ... [T]he normal role of party leaders in conducting internal affairs of their party, other than primary or general elections, does not make their party offices governmental offices or the filling of these offices state action.... [For example, h]olding a presidential candidates' forum [is not state action] because the forum was not an integral part of the election process. Accordingly, the Democratic Party [has] the absolute right to exclude a Democratic presidential candidate from the forum, even [if] the candidate had originally been invited to participate.... [And t]he election of party ward chairmen [is similarly] not state action because there [is] no evidence that the chairmen [plays] an "integral part" in the election process.

[...] We hold that the actions of the Republican Party in denying LCR the booth and advertisement were mere internal party affairs. The stated purpose of LCR in attempting to obtain a booth and advertising space was to work toward changing the Party's internal platform. However, a Party's platform is not an element of the electoral process. Party candidates are free to accept in part and reject in part the platform, and there is no requirement that a party member adhere to all portions of the platform....

Because the Republican Party's conduct in denying LCR a booth and advertisement at the convention is an internal party affair rather than an integral part of the election process, the Republican Party is not a state actor under the undisputed facts of this case. Therefore, LCR cannot maintain its state constitutional claims against the Party, and the district court abused its discretion in issuing an injunction based on these claims.

* * *

■ SPECTOR, J., concurring in the judgment.

* * *

Even assuming a state action requirement should apply to the Log Cabin Republicans' claims, the majority does not offer a satisfactory justification for finding an absence of state action here....

Based only on the facts brought to light in a brief hearing on the temporary injunction, the trial court observed that a symbiotic relationship exists between the state and a major political party, and concluded that the Log Cabin Republicans could probably demonstrate a sufficient degree of state involvement to prevail on their constitutional claims....

Political speech, the type of speech that the Log Cabin Republicans sought to exercise at the Party's convention, is integral to our democratic form of government and receives the broadest protection under the First Amendment to assure an open debate on political issues. I cannot join an opinion that precipitately cuts off such a debate....

NOTES AND QUESTIONS

1. Must the Georgia Republican Party have an identifiable ideological character in order legitimately to exclude Duke, or can they exclude him for purely instrumental reasons, such as a belief that his running in the party's primary would repel some voters from the party? Does the court even care?

2. Could the Republican Party of Texas exclude gay people from holding party office? Could they exclude from nomination for public office gay people or persons who opposed discrimination on the basis of sexual orientation? Although no major party currently has such a policy, the Democratic Party's "Equal Division Rule," required party delegations to contain equal numbers of men and women, thereby excluding citizens on the basis of sex from some party positions. *See* Mary T. Boyle, Note, *Affirmative Action in the Democratic Party: An Analysis of the Equal Division Rule*, 7 J.L. & Pol. 559 (1991).

3.   If the Log Cabin Republicans are undeniably members of the Republican Party of Texas (and no one contested that fact), why don't they have a right to "work toward changing the Party's internal platform"?

4.   Who speaks for a party? Elected officials who have received the party's nomination? Party officials? Party members? How, if at all, can rank-and-file members of the Georgia Republican Party hold the party chairman accountable for the Commission's decision? What leverage do they have over the two elected Republican officials? As Professor Lowenstein colorfully observes, "Unlike a chair, or a planet, or a baked potato, a political party is not something that occupies a particular space at a particular time or that can be discerned with the senses. . . . Although there have been a great many typologies of the varying 'locations' and functions of parties, probably the most common identifies three: the party in the electorate, the party organization, and the party in or running for public office." Daniel H. Lowenstein, *Associational Rights of Major Political Parties: A Skeptical Inquiry*, 71 Tex. L. Rev. 1741, 1759, 1760 (1993); *see also* V. O. Key, Parties, Politics and Pressure Groups (5th ed. 1964); Frank J. Sorauf & Paul A. Beck, Party Politics in America (4th ed. 1980); Larry J. Sabato, The Party's Just Begun: Shaping Political Parties for America's Future (1988).

5.   Is *Duke* consistent with the Supreme Court's reasoning in *Nixon v. Condon*, 286 U.S. 73 (1932), the second of the White Primary cases. Leaving aside the question whether *Nixon v. Condon* and *Duke v. Massey* are simply products of different times, is there an intuitive difference between a party's excluding *voters* on the basis of their *race*—an immutable status—and a party's excluding *candidates* on the basis of their *beliefs*?

6.   The relationship between the White Primary cases and the constitutional associational rights of political parties is a complex one. For a sophisticated treatment of the interplay in light of the Voting Rights Act, see *LaRouche, Jr. v. Fowler,* 152 F.3d 974 (D.C. Cir. 1998) (per Garland, J.). Lyndon LaRouche sought the Democratic Party's nomination for President in 1996 and had allegedly won two delegates to the party's national convention through votes he had received in primary elections in two states. But applying an internal Democratic Party rule, the Chairman of the Party ruled that LaRouche was not a bona fide Democrat, was not to be treated as a qualified candidate, and that state parties should disregard any votes cast for him. This ruling was based on LaRouche's political beliefs, which the DNC Chairman characterized as "explicitly racist and anti-Semitic, and otherwise utterly contrary to the fundamental beliefs . . . of the Democratic Party." Concluding that viewpoint discrimination is "the *sine qua non* of a political party," the Court held that even if political parties were treated as state actors, they need only show that an internal party rule "rationally advance some legitimate interest of the party" to withstand constitutional scrutiny. The Court therefore rejected LaRouche's First Amendment challenge to the party's exclusion of his candidacy.

2.   THE PARTY SEEKS TO EXCLUDE CITIZEN X FROM PARTICIPATING BUT THE STATE DEMANDS THAT THE PARTY PERMIT HIM TO PARTICIPATE

California Democratic Party v. Jones

530 U.S. 567 (2000).

■ JUSTICE SCALIA delivered the opinion of the Court.

This case presents the question whether the State of California may, consistent with the First Amendment to the United States Constitution, use a so-called "blanket" primary to determine a political party's nominee for the general election.

* * *

In 1996 the citizens of California adopted by initiative Proposition 198. Promoted largely as a measure that would "weaken" party "hard-liners" and ease the way for "moderate problem-solvers," Proposition 198 changed California's partisan primary from a closed primary to a blanket primary. Under the new system, "all persons entitled to vote, including those not affiliated with any political party, shall have the right to vote . . . for any candidate regardless of the candidate's political affiliation." Cal. Elec. Code Ann. § 2001 (West Supp. 2000); *see also* § 2151. Whereas under the closed primary each voter received a ballot limited to candidates of his own party, as a result of Proposition 198 each voter's primary ballot now lists every candidate regardless of party affiliation and allows the voter to choose freely among them. It remains the case, however, that the candidate of each party who wins the greatest number of votes "is the nominee of that party at the ensuing general election." Cal. Elec. Code Ann. § 15451 (West 1996).

* * *

II

Respondents rest their defense of the blanket primary upon the proposition that primaries play an integral role in citizens' selection of public officials. As a consequence, they contend, primaries are public rather than private proceedings, and the States may and must play a role in ensuring that they serve the public interest. Proposition 198, respondents conclude, is simply a rather pedestrian example of a State's regulating its system of elections.

We have recognized, of course, that States have a major role to play in structuring and monitoring the election process, including primaries. . . . What we have not held, however, is that the processes by which political parties select their nominees are, as respondents would have it, wholly public affairs that States may regulate freely. To the contrary, we have continually stressed that when States regulate parties' internal processes they must act within limits imposed by the Constitution.

* * *

Representative democracy in any populous unit of governance is unimaginable without the ability of citizens to band together in promoting among the electorate candidates who espouse their political views. The formation of national political parties was almost concurrent with the formation of the Republic itself. Consistent with this tradition, the Court has recognized that the First Amendment protects "the freedom to join together in furtherance of common political beliefs," which "necessarily presupposes the freedom to identify the people who constitute the association, and to limit the association to those people only." That is to say, a corollary of the right to associate is the right not to associate. . . .

In no area is the political association's right to exclude more important than in the process of selecting its nominee. That process often determines the party's positions on the most significant public policy issues of the day, and even when those positions are predetermined it is the nominee who becomes the party's ambassador to the general electorate in winning it over to the party's views. . . .

Unsurprisingly, our cases vigorously affirm the special place the First Amendment reserves for, and the special protection it accords, the process by which a political party "selects a standard bearer who best represents the party's ideologies and preferences." The moment of choosing the party's nominee, we have said, is "the crucial juncture at which the appeal to common principles may be translated into concerted action, and hence to political power in the community."

* * *

California's blanket primary violates [these] principles. Proposition 198 forces political parties to associate with—to have their nominees, and hence their positions, determined by—those who, at best, have refused to affiliate with the party, and, at worst, have expressly affiliated with a rival. In this respect, it is qualitatively different from a closed primary. Under that system, even when it is made quite easy for a voter to change his party affiliation the day of the primary, and thus, in some sense, to "cross over," at least he must formally *become a member of the party;* and once he does so, he is limited to voting for candidates of that party.

The evidence in this case demonstrates that under California's blanket primary system, the prospect of having a party's nominee determined by adherents of an opposing party is far from remote—indeed, it is a clear and present danger. For example, in one 1997 survey of California voters 37 percent of Republicans said that they planned to vote in the 1998 Democratic gubernatorial primary, and 20 percent of Democrats said they planned to vote in the 1998 Republican United States Senate primary. . . .

The record also supports the obvious proposition that these substantial numbers of voters who help select the nominees of parties they have chosen not to join often have policy views that diverge from those of the party faithful. The 1997 survey of California voters revealed significantly different policy preferences between party members and primary voters who "crossed over" from another party. One expert went so far as to describe it as "inevitable [under Proposition 198] that parties will be forced in some circumstances to give their official designation to a candidate who's not preferred by a majority or even plurality of party members."

* * *

In any event, the deleterious effects of Proposition 198 are not limited to altering the identity of the nominee. Even when the person favored by a majority of the party members prevails, he will have prevailed by taking somewhat different positions—and, should he be elected, will continue to take somewhat different positions in order to be *re*nominated ... It is unnecessary to cumulate evidence of this phenomenon, since, after all, the whole *purpose* of Proposition 198 was to favor nominees with "moderate" positions. It encourages candidates—and officeholders who hope to be renominated—to curry favor with persons whose views are more "centrist" than those of the party base. In effect, Proposition 198 has simply moved the general election one step earlier in the process, at the expense of the parties' ability to perform the "basic function" of choosing their own leaders.

* * *

In sum, Proposition 198 forces petitioners to adulterate their candidate-selection process—the "basic function of a political party,"—by opening it up to persons wholly unaffiliated with the party. Such forced association has the likely outcome—indeed, in this case the *intended* outcome—of changing the parties' message. We can think of no heavier burden on a political party's associational freedom. Proposition 198 is therefore unconstitutional unless it is narrowly tailored to serve a compelling state interest. It is to that question which we now turn.

III

Respondents proffer seven state interests they claim are compelling. Two of them—producing elected officials who better represent the electorate and expanding candidate debate beyond the scope of partisan concerns—are simply circumlocution for producing nominees and nominee positions other than those the parties would choose if left to their own devices.... Both of these supposed interests, therefore, reduce to nothing more than a stark repudiation of freedom of political association: Parties should not be free to select their own nominees because those nominees, and the positions taken by those nominees, will not be congenial to the majority.

* * *

Respondents' third asserted compelling interest is that the blanket primary is the only way to ensure that disenfranchised persons enjoy the right to an effective vote. By "disenfranchised," respondents do not mean those who cannot vote; they mean simply independents and members of the minority party in "safe" districts. These persons are disenfranchised, according to respondents, because under a closed primary they are unable to participate in what amounts to the determinative election—the majority party's primary; the only way to ensure they have an "effective" vote is to force the party to open its primary to them. This also appears to be nothing more than reformulation of an asserted state interest we have already rejected—recharacterizing nonparty members' keen desire to participate in selection of the party's nominee as "disenfranchisement" if that desire is not fulfilled. We have said, however, that a "nonmember's desire to participate in the party's affairs is overborne by the countervailing and legitimate right of the party to determine its own membership qualifications."

* * *

Respondents' remaining four asserted state interests—promoting fairness, affording voters greater choice, increasing voter participation, and protecting privacy—are not, like the others, automatically out of the running; but neither are they, *in the circumstances of this case*, compelling. That determination is not to be made in the abstract, by asking whether fairness, privacy, etc., are highly significant values; but rather by asking whether the *aspect* of fairness, privacy, etc., addressed by the law at issue is highly significant. And for all four of these asserted interests, we find it not to be.

* * *

Finally, we may observe that even if all these state interests were compelling ones, Proposition 198 is not a narrowly tailored means of furthering them. Respondents could protect them all by resorting to a *nonpartisan* blanket primary. Generally speaking, under such a system, the State determines what qualifications it requires for a candidate to have a place on the primary ballot—which may include nomination by established parties and voter-petition requirements for independent candidates. Each voter, regardless of party affiliation, may then vote for any candidate, and the top two vote getters (or however many the State prescribes) then move on to the general election. This system has all the characteristics of the partisan blanket primary, save the constitutionally crucial one: Primary voters are not choosing a party's nominee. Under a nonpartisan blanket primary, a State may ensure more choice, greater participation, increased "privacy," and a sense of "fairness"—all without severely burdening a political party's First Amendment right of association.

* * *

Respondents' legitimate state interests and petitioners' First Amendment rights are not inherently incompatible. To the extent they are in this case, the State of California has made them so by forcing political parties to associate with those who do not share their beliefs. And it has done this at the "crucial juncture" at which party members traditionally find their collective voice and select their spokesman. The burden Proposition 198 places on petitioners' rights of political association is both severe and unnecessary. The judgment for the Court of Appeals for the Ninth Circuit is reversed.

■ JUSTICE STEVENS, with whom JUSTICE GINSBURG joins as to Part I, dissenting.

* * *

A State's power to determine how its officials are to be elected is a quintessential attribute of sovereignty. This case is about the State of California's power to decide who may vote in an election conducted, and paid for, by the State. The United States Constitution imposes constraints on the States' power to limit access to the polls, but we have never before held or suggested that it imposes any constraints on States' power to authorize additional citizens to participate in any state election for a state office. In my view, principles of federalism require us to respect the policy choice made by the State's voters in approving Proposition 198.

The blanket primary system instituted by Proposition 198 does not abridge "the ability of citizens to band together in promoting among the electorate candidates who espouse their political views." *Ante,* at 6. The Court's contrary conclusion rests on the premise that a political party's freedom of expressive association includes a "right not to associate," which in turn includes a right to exclude voters unaffiliated with the party from participating in the selection of that party's nominee in a primary election. In drawing this conclusion, however, the Court blurs two distinctions that are critical: (1) the distinction between a private organization's right to define itself and its messages, on the one hand, and the State's right to define the obligations of citizens and organizations performing public functions, on the other; and (2) the distinction between laws that abridge participation in the political process and those that encourage such participation.

* * *

[. . .] The reason a State may impose . . . significant restriction[s] on a party's associational freedoms is that both the general election and the primary are quintessential forms of state action. It is because the primary is state action that an organization—whether it calls itself a political party or just a "Jaybird" association—may not deny non-Caucasians the right to participate in the selection of its nominees. The Court is quite right in stating that those cases "do not stand for the proposition that party affairs are [*wholly*] public affairs, free of First Amendment protections." *Ante*, at 6. They do, however, stand for the proposition that primary elections, unlike most "party affairs," are state action. The protections that the First Amendment affords to the "internal processes" of a political party, *id.*, do not encompass a right to exclude nonmembers from voting in a state-required, state-financed primary election.

The so-called "right not to associate" that the Court relies upon, then, is simply inapplicable to participation in a state election. A political party, like any other association, may refuse to allow non-members to participate in the party's decisions when it is conducting its own affairs; California's blanket primary system does not infringe this principle. *Ante*, at 2–3, n. 2. But an election, unlike a convention or caucus, is a public affair. Although it is true that we have extended First Amendment protection to a party's right to invite independents to participate in its primaries ... [we have never] held or suggested that the "right not to associate" imposes a limit on the State's power to open up its primary elections to all voters eligible to vote in a general election. In my view, while state rules abridging participation in its elections should be closely scrutinized, the First Amendment does not inhibit the State from acting to broaden voter access to state-run, state-financed elections. When a State acts not to limit democratic participation but to expand the ability of individuals to participate in the democratic process, it is acting not as a foe of the First Amendment but as a friend and ally.

* * *

In my view, the First Amendment does not mandate that a putatively private association be granted the power to dictate the organizational structure of state-run, state-financed primary elections. It is not this Court's constitutional function to choose between the competing visions of what makes democracy work—party autonomy and discipline versus progressive inclusion of the entire electorate in the process of selecting their public officials—that are held by the litigants in this case.... That choice belongs to the people.

Even if the "right not to associate" did authorize the Court to review the State's policy choice, its evaluation of the competing interests at stake is seriously flawed. For example, the Court's conclusion that a blanket primary severely burdens the parties' associational interests in selecting their standard bearers does not appear to be borne out by experience with blanket primaries.... Following a bench trial and the receipt of expert witness reports, the District Court found that "there is little evidence that raiding [by members of an opposing party] will be a factor under the blanket primary. On this point there is almost unanimity among the political scientists who were called as experts by the plaintiffs and defendants." While the Court is entitled to test this finding by making an independent examination of the record, the evidence it cites—including the results of the June 1998 primaries, which should not be considered because they are not in the record—does not come close to demonstrating that the District Court's factual finding is clearly erroneous.

As to the Court's concern that benevolent crossover voting impinges on party associational interests, the District Court found that experience with a blanket primary in Washington and other evidence "suggested that there will be particular elections in which there will be a substantial amount of cross-over voting ... although the cross-over vote will rarely change the outcome of any election and in the typical contest will not be at significantly higher levels than in open primary states." In my view, an empirically debatable assumption about the relative number and effect of likely cross-over voters in a blanket primary, as opposed to an open primary or a nominally closed primary with only a brief pre-registration requirement, is too thin a reed to support a credible First Amendment distinction....

On the other side of the balance, I would rank as "substantial, indeed compelling," just as the District Court did, California's interest in fostering democratic government by "increasing the representativeness of elected officials, giving voters greater choice, and increasing voter turnout and participation in [electoral processes]." The Court's glib rejection of the State's interest in increasing voter participation is particularly regrettable. In an era of dramatically declining voter participation, States should be free to experiment with reforms designed to make the democratic process more robust by involving the entire electorate in the process of selecting those who will serve as government officials. Opening the nominating process to all and encouraging voters to participate in any election that draws their interest is one obvious means of achieving this goal. I would also give some weight to the First Amendment associational interests of nonmembers of a party seeking to participate in the primary process, to the fundamental right of such nonmembers to cast a meaningful vote for the candidate of their choice ... and to the preference of almost 60% of California voters—including a majority of registered Democrats and Republicans—for a blanket primary.... In my view, a State is unquestionably entitled to rely on this combination of interests in deciding who may vote in a primary election conducted by the State. It is indeed strange to find that the First Amendment forecloses this decision.

* * *

NOTES AND QUESTIONS

1. To what extent can the Court's sweeping First Amendment "right not to associate" be confined to the specific form of a blanket primary? Doesn't any state regulation of how candidates are nominated threaten to infringe the right to be free of unwanted associations? Ironically, this is the exact argument that was raised (unsuccessfully) by political parties to the initial imposition of primary nomination processes at the turn of the last century. *See generally* Adam Winkler, *Voters' Rights and Parties' Wrongs: Early Political Party Regulation in the State Courts, 1886–1915,* 100 Colum. L. Rev. 873 (2000). Don't all primary processes dilute the ability of the parties to define out those who are not deemed true partisans of the party's views?

2. Indeed, American political parties are distinct from political parties in other Western democracies precisely because, since the turn of the century with the rise of the mandatory primary elections, the law has regulated American parties, including their candidate selection processes, in a vastly more substantial and intrusive way than in European systems. British law banned party labels on parliamentary ballots before 1970, and since then, these labels are added when desired by individual candidates. Australia puts no party labels on ballots and simply treats parties as other private associations, subject to general laws rather than party-specific regulations. How much of the distinct American regulation of party nomination processes can or should be justified by American electoral rules, which provide the major parties special access to the ballot and permit the use of party labels on the ballot? Yet even those systems that provide for official ballot recognition of party labels do not have the regulation of party nominations that has long been characteristic of American politics. Only Germany, Turkey, and Norway regulate party candidate selection at all; yet even these regulations merely stipulate that dues-paying party members must be entitled to participate in what is essentially a selection process run by the parties themselves without regulation (these comparisons are as of 1986). This has led one of the leading studies of American political parties to pose the central question as being: "Why has the United States alone among democratic nations subjected *parties* to so much legal regulation and control?" Leon Epstein, Political Parties in the American Mold 158 (1986). Epstein goes on to show, in a fascinating historical study, what processes and arguments have led to the traditionally more extensive regulation of parties and candidate selection in the United States than elsewhere. Part of his answer is that Americans have long been more prone to view (and experience?) political parties as corrupt: "Nowhere else in the western democratic world did parties look so evil, at least to middle-class citizens, as they did in the United States." *Id.* at 159.

In light of both the longstanding legal tradition of party regulation in the United States, and the purportedly distinctive American concern for the venality of parties and their leaders, is *Jones* rightly decided? Does the Court adequately deal with this history and explain why the blanket primary, among all other forms of candidate-selection regulations in the twentieth 20th century, violates the associational rights of parties?

3. Given this history of party regulation in the United States, there is a long-standing argument that the party nomination processes are public functions—simply part of the electoral apparatus of the state. For an early form of this argument, see Alonzo H. Tuttle, *Limitations Upon the Power of the Legislature to Control Political Parties and Their Primaries,* 1 Mich. L. Rev. 466, 468 (1903) ("The right to nominate is as much a part of the franchise as the right to elect."). Justice Stevens' dissent follows upon this analytic approach. Thus, according to Stevens, the reason that a state may impose a particular form of candidate selection, even recognizing that it is a "significant restriction on a party's associational freedoms" is that "both the general election and the primary are quintessential forms of state action . . ." If this approach were to be followed, would there be any area of protection of the electoral activities of parties left protected from state regulation? For a challenge to the dissent's approach on this issue, see Samuel Issacharoff, *Private Parties with Public Purposes: Political Parties, Associational Freedoms, and Partisan Competition,* 101 Colum. L. Rev. 274 (2001).

4. Justice Scalia, the author of *Jones,* dissented from the Court's decisions holding patronage employment and contracting practices to violate First Amendment rights. *See Rutan v. Republican Party,* 497 U.S. 62 (1990) ("To the victor belong only those spoils that may be constitutionally obtained") (banning patronage decisions in transfer and promotion of public employees); *Board of County Comm'rs v. Umbehr,* 518 U.S. 668 (1996) (same for independent contractors). *See also Branti v. Finkel,* 445 U.S. 507 (1980) (banning patronge firing where party affiliation was not required for effective performance of office) and *Elrod v. Burns,* 427 U.S. 347 (1976) (banning patronage firing). Justice Scalia argued that the constitutional ban on patronage "reflects a naive vision of politics and an inadequate appreciation of the systemic effects of patronage in promoting political stability and facilitating the social and political integration of previously powerless groups." *Rutan,* 497 U.S., at 107 (Scalia, J., dissenting). He asserted that the ban on patronage had contributed to a decline of party strength in the United States and therefore to the growth of interest-group politics over the last decade. *See* Michael Fitts, *The Vice of Virtue,* 136 U. Pa. L. Rev. 1567, 1603–1607 (1988) (cited by Justice Scalia in support of this proposition). Justice Scalia went on to argue:

> [P]atronage stabilizes political parties and prevents excessive political fragmentation—both of which are results in which States have a strong governmental interest. Party strength requires the efforts of the rank and file, especially in the "dull periods between elections," to perform such tasks as organizing precincts, registering new voters, and providing constituent services. Even the most enthusiastic supporter of a party's program will shrink before such drudgery, and it is folly to think that ideological conviction alone will motivate sufficient numbers to keep the party going through the off years. Here is the judgment of one such politician, Jacob Avery (best known as the promoter of Adlai Stevenson): Patronage is a "necessary evil if you want a strong organization, because the patronage system permits of discipline, and without discipline, there's no party organization."

How much does the Court's *Jones* opinion depend upon the same view of the importance of strong, independent political parties reflected in Justice Scalia's dissents in the patronage cases? Yet those were dissents, after all. Does that suggest any fundamental inconsistency between the patronage decisions, which deny party autonomy, and *Jones*, which upholds the importance of party autonomy? For the view that the Court's decisions do indeed fail to offer any consistent normative understanding of democratic practices across different doctrinal problems in the law of politics, see Pamela S. Karlan, *Just Politics? Five Not So Easy Pieces of the 1995 Term*, 34 Hous. L. Rev. 289 (1997).

5.   The *Jones* litigation sparked renewed attention to the legal treatment of political parties. Consider the following summary of competing models of how the law should treat political parties:

The Managerial Paradigm

> Drawing on the fears of faction so central to the Constitution's creation, the Manager enforces a worldview on the party and electoral system that has as its primary goal the preservation of political order. That order finds its purest expression in the maintenance of the traditional two-party system.... Managers accord little importance to a political party's "freedom to associate." While there is something to be said for the Managerial paradigm, especially for its insight that parties serve important functions for and derive valuable resources from the state, its major weaknesses lie in its reification of the state and deceptively simple treatment of party ... it cannot effectively check the possible "tyranny" of the party as elected officials. It overlooks the fact that the party as elected officials controls the state, and hence, that actions the state takes can be manipulated to serve the interests of either elected officials generally or elected officials of the governing party specifically.

The Libertarian Paradigm

> Libertarians take the direct opposite view of the Managers regarding the electoral and party system. Far from instruments to serve the state, parties are merely a species of private, organized interest groups, which should thus be accorded maximal rights of association, privacy, expression, and freedom from state discrimination.... More specifically, parties should not receive any state benefits (e.g., public financing of party primaries) or be subject to state regulation (e.g., state law requiring parties to conduct primaries as the means of selecting general election candidates). However, like the Managerial paradigm, the Libertarian paradigm overlooks the heterogeneity of political parties: heterogeneity, that is, both in terms of type of party (i.e., major or minor) as well as the particular features of each state's laws that define and structure parties ... [J]ust as the Managers go too far in the state interest direction, the Libertarian paradigm goes too far in

the party rights direction.... If the danger of the first paradigm can be called the "tyranny of the party as elected officials," then the corresponding problem raised by the Libertarian approach is the "tyranny of the party as organization."

The Progressive Paradigm

[Progressives exhibit a] generalized hostility to parties ... [viewing them as] obstructive forces for the realization of the general will of the electorate. Progressives therefore tend to favor state regulations that vitiate party autonomy or freedom of association and make parties less relevant for electoral purposes.... [T]he real problem with the Progressive paradigm is that it does not recognize the essential role that parties play in brokering group interests and solving voters' collective action problems. A polity without parties places a greater cognitive burden on individual voters and weakens the collective responsibility of political agents.

Political Markets

Attempting to bring the virtues of law and economics and public choice analysis to the field of election law ... [f]or the Political Marketeer, the primary purpose of political parties is to offer voter-consumers electoral choices. For it is through unfettered partisan competition that an invisible political hand will operate to supply voter-consumers with goods (in this case, candidates and/or policy positions) that are purchased with votes at the polls. While there is much to be said for a paradigm that promotes electoral competition, this approach suffers from some important weaknesses. To begin with, it overlooks the role of "voice" in politics and relies far too heavily on "exit." ... Second, the Political Markets paradigm places its entire faith in the electorate. As consumers, they are sovereign. As such, it is a strongly populist approach that leaves little room for leadership, guidance, and assistance from the politically active.... The Political Markets paradigm merely allows for the articulation of and response to consumer preferences. It does not allow for deliberation and the transmission of information within party networks, particularly in a two-party system.

The Pluralist Paradigm

Pluralism takes as its point of departure the importance of organized groups in the political process.... American parties, according to the Pluralist, should be broader, decentralized coalitions of interest groups.... [This] represents a normative preference for a party system that can aggregate and account for the intensity of group preferences in the most politically, economically, and ethnically diverse country in the world.... However, Pluralists may exaggerate the representativeness of the interest group system. They tend to downplay the potential for autonomous party organizations to ignore large interest groups with dispersed interests and small groups outside the mainstream or without the resources to make their voice heard. Finally, given their weak ideological cohesion, Pluralist parties at the legislative level often prove ineffective as policy making bodies and can blur accountability such that no party ever appears "responsible" for anything.

Nathaniel Persily & Bruce E. Cain, *The Legal Status of Political Parties: A Reassessment of Competing Paradigms*, 100 Colum. L. Rev. 775 (2000).

6. An alternative approach would situate political parties more broadly within the intermediary institutions that collectively may be referred to as "civil society." This is the more ambiguous area that is not as intimate as the family, but not as fully public as the state. For the exponents of the importance of civil society, these intermediary institutions are among the central promoters and transmitters of a distinct set of civic values. As expressed by political theorist Nancy L. Rosenblum, in *Law and Political Parties, Political Parties as Membership Groups*, 100 Colum. L. Rev. 813 (2000):

> Parties are the groups people identify with, actively join, contribute to, work within, become officers of, and participate in setting agendas, goals, and strategies. Both the large-scale, long-term effects of parties on the political system and political culture overall and their capacity to shape the democratic dispositions and practices of citizens personally and individually are a function of their vitality as membership groups. Civil society theorists should grant parties a central place, and should be at least as solicitous of political parties as the many other associations that are objects of concern today. The justification I propose for valuing political parties, and for their centrality to democratic civil society, is based on their distinctive characteristics and effects as membership groups.

> In contrast to most interest and advocacy groups, parties must continuously seek to establish contact with the electorate in a fashion that elicits participation on a large scale. Parties do more than help recruit and support candidates for an extensive array of offices at every level of government. Indeed, the objective of contesting elections successfully involves more than campaign activities, registration drives, voter guides, and turn-out. It requires long-term development—establishing local presence, building cadres of activists, coordinating the support of social leaders, and seeking membership from every salient group. Parties raise and define public issues, engage in political education, choose officers, enact rules for process and representation, and decide on their purposes and policies as well as their strategies. They are distinctive sources of information and of experience in forming political judgments. They are forums for reasonably deliberative collective decision-making about public life. Potentially, they are the most important agenda-setting institution for the public interests of society as a whole. In all these respects, the value of parties is independent of particular

electoral successes, but strongly dependent on the vitality of parties as membership groups.

For a more skeptical examination of the capacity of parties to instill broader civic values, see James A. Gardner, *Can Party Politics Be Virtuous?*, 100 Colum. L. Rev. 667 (2000).

7. In light of *Jones*, suppose a state party adopts a rule that no candidate can appear under its label on a primary ballot unless he or she receives at least 15 percent of the votes cast at a party convention (held, obviously, before the electoral primary). This would be a means of party leaders and activists recapturing seeking to recapture some of the control that the mandatory primary law otherwise transfers to those who state law permits to vote in the actual primary. The Massachusetts Democratic Party did precisely this in the 1980s with the adoption of such a 15 percent rule. Massachusetts's primary-election structure permitted previously unenrolled voters to enter a party primary and declare their affiliation with that party on election day (voters could change their enrollment or become unenrolled again the next day). In contrast to the party rule, state law required that to be listed as a party candidate in the primary, a candidate only had to be an enrolled party member and have gathered a specified number of signatures (which did not have to come from party members).

In a conflict between state law and party-imposed primary-candidate requirements, does the Constitution require that state law or the party prevail? The Massachusetts courts concluded that, because the Constitution protected "party autonomy," the state law would be unconstitutional unless it was construed to permit the party to supplement the state-law candidate requirements. The Supreme Court, in a 6–3 vote with a lengthy dissent, dismissed the appeal for want of jurisdiction. Justice Stevens, who along with Justices Rehnquist and O'Connor dissented from the Court's refusal to hear the case on the merits, noted that the State Attorney General argued that the 15 percent rule and potentially similar internal party requirements "can permit the virtual nullification of the primary process." *Bellotti v. Connolly*, 460 U.S. 1057 (1983) (Stevens, J., dissenting).

Does *Jones* essentially also resolve the dispute within the Court over state-party conflicts such as that in *Connolly*? If so, why isn't the state right that *Jones* permits the "virtual nullification of the primary process?"

8. For a debate over the correctness of *Jones*, compare Richard L. Hasen, *Do the Parties or the People Own the Electoral Process?*, 149 U. Pa. L. Rev. 815 (2001) with Bruce E. Cain, *Party Autonomy and Two–Party Electoral Competition*, 149 U. Pa. L. Rev. 793 (2001). For an argument that the rights approach in *Jones* fails to take account of the institutional setting of democratic politics, including the generally protected position of the two major political parties, see Richard H. Pildes, *The Supreme Court, 2003 Term–Foreword: Constitutionalization of Democratic Politics*, 118 Harv. L. Rev. 28, 105–06 (2004).

9. In *Democratic Party of the United States v. LaFollette*, 450 U.S. 107 (1981), the Court confronted a conflict between a national party rule requiring voting for presidential delegates to be restricted to party members and a Wisconsin law requiring open primaries (i.e., not limited to party members). The case thus presented a conflict between a *national* party and a *state* rule. The Court sided with the national Democratic Party to the extent that the national party did not have to seat or accept the votes of the Wisconsin delegation. One way to understand the case would be to say that single states should not be able to unilaterally regulate nationwide activities. *Cf. Anderson v. Celebrezze,* 460 U.S. 780 (1983) (observing that "in the context of a Presidential election, state-imposed restrictions implicate a uniquely important national interest"). At the same time, the Court's observation that states have legitimate interests in conducting open primaries suggests that a state could mandate open primaries for the nomination of candidates for state and local office.

Justice Powell's dissent in *LaFollette* remarks on the fact that the state Democratic Party was aligned with Wisconsin against the national party. In a state like Wisconsin, where the Democratic Party was often in power, the state's laws regulating political parties will usually (although not inevitably) reflect the state party's view. If, therefore, we view the state of Wisconsin as essentially a placeholder for the state Democratic Party, then *Democratic Party* turns out to be a lawsuit between the national and state parties. Reconceptualized in this way, should the Court even entertain these sorts of internecine conflicts? *Cf. Cousins v. Wigoda*, 419 U.S. 477 (1975) (holding that the Illinois state courts had no power to force the National Democratic Party to seat an Illinois delegation that violated the party's delegate selection rules). Ought state parties have any associational rights that national parties are obligated to respect?

LaFollette also returns us to an ongoing question whether courts should consider if there are alternative fora available for the resolution of a conflict between state and national parties before deeming such conflicts justiciable. Consider the dispute between the Wisconsin and the national Democratic parties. Whatever the legal rule announced by the Supreme Court, it had relatively little effect at ground zero. In 1988, the national party revised its rules to permit Wisconsin to use an open primary. *See* Leon D. Epstein, *Will American Political Parties Be Privatized?*, 5 J.L. & Pol. 239, 255 n.69 (1989). For a more general account of national parties and "party reform," see Nelson W. Polsby, Consequences of Party Reform (1983).

10. More difficult than the problem of a conflict between the national and state parties is a direct confrontation between a state regulation and the official position of a party on party membership. Take, for example, the requirement that parties choose their candidates through primary elections rather than through conventions of nominations of the party executive committee. Clearly these are state impositions on the party that diminish the control of party insiders and make parties much more accountable to the electors broadly construed. What then happens when disputes arise over who the constituency of the party nomination process should be, but where the disputants are not the national versus state parties, but the state versus the state political parties? The next set of materials illustrates this issue.

3. THE PARTY WISHES TO PERMIT CITIZEN X TO PARTICIPATE BUT THE STATE DEMANDS HIS EXCLUSION

The Connecticut Republican Party that supported the state's defense of the closed primary in *Nader* executed an about-face a few years later. In 1984, the party's state convention adopted a party rule that would permit "[a]ny elector enrolled as a member of the Republican Party and any elector not enrolled as a member of a party," (that is, an independent voter) to vote in the party's primaries for Congress or statewide office. A major motivation behind the rule seemed to be the party's desire to gauge its candidates' attractiveness to independent voters. At the time, independents outnumbered Republicans roughly 5 to 4, and any successful Republican candidate would either have to appeal to independents or attract substantial Democratic crossover votes. The party's leadership in the state legislature proposed legislation to amend the closed primary law so that independents could vote in primaries when permitted by party rules. The first time the legislation came up for a vote, it was defeated in a party-line vote. In November 1984, the Republicans won a majority of the seats in both houses of the state legislature. This time the bill passed but the governor, who was a Democrat, vetoed the bill. So, the Republicans brought a lawsuit.

Tashjian v. Republican Party of Connecticut

479 U.S. 208 (1986).

■ JUSTICE MARSHALL delivered the opinion of the Court.

* * *

II

* * *

The nature of appellees' First Amendment interest is evident. "It is beyond debate that freedom to engage in association for the advancement of beliefs and ideas is an inseparable aspect of the 'liberty' assured by the Due Process Clause of the Fourteenth Amendment, which embraces freedom of speech." The freedom of association protected by the First and Fourteenth Amendments includes partisan political organization. "The right to associate with the political party of one's choice is an integral part of this basic constitutional freedom."

The Party here contends that [the Connecticut statute] impermissibly burdens the right of its members to determine for themselves with whom they will associate, and whose support they will seek, in their quest for political success. The Party's attempt to broaden the base of public participation in and support for its activities is conduct undeniably central to the exercise of the right of association. As we have said, the freedom to join together in furtherance of common political beliefs "necessarily presupposes the freedom to identify the people who constitute the association."

A major state political party necessarily includes individuals playing a broad spectrum of roles in the organization's activities. Some of the Party's members devote substantial portions of their lives to furthering its political and organizational goals, others provide substantial financial support, while still others limit their participation to casting their votes for some or all of the Party's candidates. Considered from the standpoint of the Party itself, the act of formal enrollment or public affiliation with the Party is merely one element in the continuum of participation in Party affairs, and need not be in any sense the most important.

Were the State to restrict by statute financial support of the Party's candidates to Party members, or to provide that only Party members might be selected as the Party's chosen nominees for public office, such a prohibition of potential association with nonmembers would clearly infringe upon the rights of the Party's members under the First Amendment to organize with like-minded citizens in support of common political goals.... The statute here places limits upon the group of registered voters whom the Party may invite to participate in the "basic function" of selecting the Party's candidates. The State thus limits the Party's associational opportunities at the crucial juncture at which the appeal to common principles may be translated into concerted action, and hence to political power in the community.

It is, of course, fundamental to appellant's defense of the State's statute that this impingement upon the associational rights of the Party and its members occurs at the ballot box, for the Constitution grants to the States a broad power to prescribe the "Times, Places and Manner of holding Elections for Senators and Representatives," Art. I, § 4, cl. 1, which power is matched by state control over the election process for state offices. But this authority does not extinguish the State's responsibility to observe the limits established by the First Amendment rights of the State's citizens. The power to regulate the time, place, and manner of elections does not justify, without more, the abridgment of fundamental rights.... We turn then to an examination of the interests which appellant asserts to justify the burden cast by the statute upon the associational rights of the Party and its members.

III

Appellant contends that [the Connecticut statute] is a narrowly tailored regulation which advances the State's compelling interests by ensuring the administrability of the primary system, preventing raiding, avoiding voter confusion, and protecting the responsibility of party government.

A

[...] Appellant contends that the Party's rule would require the purchase of additional voting machines, the training of additional poll workers, and potentially the printing of additional ballot materials specifically intended for independents voting in the Republican primary. In essence, appellant claims that the administration of the system contemplated by the Party rule would simply cost the State too much.

Even assuming the factual accuracy of these contentions, ... the possibility of future increases in the cost of administering the election system is not a sufficient basis here for infringing appellees' First Amendment rights.... While the State is of course entitled to take administrative and financial considerations into account in choosing whether or not to have a primary system at all, it can no more restrain the Republican Party's freedom of association for reasons of its own administrative convenience than it could on the same ground limit the ballot access of a new major party.

B

Appellant argues that [the Connecticut statute] is justified as a measure to prevent raiding, a practice "whereby voters in sympathy with one party designate themselves as voters of another party so as to influence or determine the results of the other party's primary." While we have recognized that "a State may have a legitimate interest in seeking to curtail 'raiding,' since that practice may affect the integrity of the electoral process," that interest is not implicated here. The statute as applied to the Party's rule prevents independents, who otherwise cannot vote in any primary, from participating in the Republican primary. Yet a raid on the Republican Party primary by independent voters, a curious concept ... is not impeded by [the statute]; the independent raiders need only register as Republicans ... as late as noon on the business day preceding the primary....

C

Appellant's next argument is that the closed primary system avoids voter confusion. Appellant contends that "[the] legislature could properly find that it would be difficult for the general public to understand what a candidate stood for who was nominated in part by an unknown amorphous body outside the party, while nevertheless using the party name." Appellees respond that the State is attempting to act as the ideological guarantor of the Republican Party's candidates, ensuring that voters are not misled by a "Republican" candidate who professes something other than what the State regards as true Republican principles.

As we have said, "[there] can be no question about the legitimacy of the State's interest in fostering informed and educated expressions of the popular will in a general election." To the extent that party labels provide a shorthand designation of the views of party candidates on matters of public concern, the identification of candidates with particular parties plays a role in the process by which voters inform themselves for the exercise of the franchise. Appellant's argument depends upon the belief that voters can be "misled" by party labels. But "[our] cases reflect a greater faith in the ability of individual voters to inform themselves about campaign issues." Moreover, appellant's concern that candidates selected under the Party rule will be the nominees of an "amorphous" group using the Party's name is inconsistent with the facts. The Party is not proposing that independents be allowed to choose the Party's nominee without Party participation; on the contrary, to be listed on the Party's primary ballot continues to require, under a statute not challenged here, that the primary candidate have obtained at least 20% of the vote at a Party convention, which only Party members may attend. . . .

In arguing that the Party rule interferes with educated decisions by voters, appellant also disregards the substantial benefit which the Party rule provides to the Party and its members in seeking to choose successful candidates. Given the numerical strength of independent voters in the State, one of the questions most likely to occur to Connecticut Republicans in selecting candidates for public office is how can the Party most effectively appeal to the independent voter? By inviting independents to assist in the choice at the polls between primary candidates selected at the Party convention, the Party rule is intended to produce the candidate and platform most likely to achieve that goal. The state statute is said to decrease voter confusion, yet it deprives the Party and its members of the opportunity to inform themselves as to the level of support for the Party's candidates among a critical group of electors. "A State's claim that it is enhancing the ability of its citizenry to make wise decisions by restricting the flow of information to them must be viewed with some skepticism." . . .

D

Finally, appellant contends that [the Connecticut statute] furthers the State's compelling interest in protecting the integrity of the two-party system and the responsibility of party government. . . .

The relative merits of closed and open primaries have been the subject of substantial debate since the beginning of this century, and no consensus has as yet emerged. Appellant invokes a long and distinguished line of political scientists and public officials who have been supporters of the closed primary. But our role is not to decide whether the state legislature was acting wisely in enacting the closed primary system in 1955, or whether the Republican Party makes a mistake in seeking to depart from the practice of the past 30 years.

[. . .] In the present case, the state statute is defended on the ground that it protects the integrity of the Party against the Party itself.

Under these circumstances, the views of the State, which to some extent represent the views of the one political party transiently enjoying majority power, as to the optimum methods for preserving party integrity lose much of their force. The State argues that its statute is well designed to save the Republican Party from undertaking a course of conduct destructive of its own interests. But on this point "even if the State were correct, a State, or a court, may not constitutionally substitute its own judgment for that of the Party." The Party's determination of the boundaries of its own association, and of the structure which best allows it to pursue its political goals, is protected by the Constitution. "And as is true of all expressions of First Amendment freedoms, the courts may not interfere on the ground that they view a particular expression as unwise or irrational."

* * *

■ JUSTICE SCALIA, with whom THE CHIEF JUSTICE and JUSTICE O'CONNOR join, dissenting.

* * *

In my view, the Court's opinion exaggerates the importance of the associational interest at issue, if indeed it does not see one where none exists. There is no question here of restricting the Republican Party's ability to recruit and enroll Party members by offering them the ability to select Party candidates; [Connecticut law] permits an independent voter to join the Party as late as the day before the primary. Nor is there any question of restricting the ability of the Party's members to select whatever candidate they desire. Appellees' only complaint is that the Party cannot leave the selection of its candidate to persons who are not members of the Party, and are unwilling to become members. It seems to me fanciful to refer to this as an interest in freedom of association between the members of the Republican Party and the putative independent voters. The Connecticut voter who, while steadfastly refusing to register as a Republican, casts a vote in the Republican primary, forms no more meaningful an "association" with the Party than does the independent or the registered Democrat who responds to questions by a Republican Party pollster. If the concept of freedom of association is extended to such casual contacts, it ceases to be of any analytic use.

The ability of the members of the Republican Party to select their own candidate, on the other hand, unquestionably implicates an associational freedom—but it can hardly be thought that that freedom is unconstitutionally impaired here. The Party is entirely free to put forward, if it wishes, that candidate who has the highest degree of support among Party members and independents combined. The State is under no obligation, however, to let its party primary be used, instead of a party-funded opinion poll, as the means by which the party identifies the relative popularity of its potential candidates among independents. Nor is there any reason apparent to me why the State cannot insist that this decision to support what might be called the independents' choice be taken by the party membership in a democratic fashion, rather than through a process that permits the members' votes to be diluted—and perhaps even absolutely outnumbered—by the votes of outsiders.

The Court's opinion characterizes this, disparagingly, as an attempt to "[protect] the integrity of the Party against the Party itself." There are two problems with this characterization. The first, and less important, is that it is not true. We have no way of knowing that a majority of the Party's members is in favor of allowing ultimate selection of its candidates for federal and statewide office to be determined by persons outside the Party. That decision was not made by democratic ballot, but by the Party's state convention—which, for all we know, may have been dominated by officeholders and office seekers whose evaluation of the merits of assuring election of the Party's candidates, vis-a-vis the merits of proposing candidates faithful to the Party's political philosophy, diverged significantly from the views of the Party's rank and file. I had always thought it was a major purpose of state-imposed party primary requirements to protect the general party membership against this sort of minority control. Second and more important, however, even if it were the fact that the majority of the Party's members wanted its candidates to be determined by outsiders, there is no reason why the State is bound to honor that desire—any more than it would be bound to honor a party's democratically expressed desire that its candidates henceforth be selected by convention rather than by primary, or by the party's executive committee in a smoke-filled room. In other words, the validity of the state-imposed primary requirement itself, which we have hitherto considered "too plain for argument," presupposes that the State has the right "to protect the Party against the Party itself." Connecticut may lawfully require that significant elements of the democratic election process be democratic—whether the Party wants that or not. It is beyond my understanding why the Republican Party's delegation of its democratic choice to a Republican Convention can be proscribed, but its delegation of that choice to nonmembers of the Party cannot.

* * *

NOTES AND QUESTIONS

1. After *LaFollete* and *Tashjian* is the rule that, in a conflict between a state and a party over who can participate in the party's nomination process, the party invariably wins? Must Connecticut now apply different rules for voting in the Democratic and Republican primaries, permitting only party members to vote in the former, while permitting party members and independents to vote in the latter? Consider an equal protection claim by an independent voter who argues that independents who want to vote in the Republican primary are able to vote but independents who want to vote in the Democratic primary cannot and thus that the state treats Democratic-leaning independents worse than Republican ones. Would the parties' First Amendment rights trump the voter's equal protection claim? What about a claim by a Republican voter that the state is treating him differently than a Democratic voter because it administers a system in which his primary vote is "diluted" by the votes of outsiders while the Democrat's vote is not? Note that in the White Primary Cases, black voters' equal protection/Fifteenth Amendment claims trumped party First Amendment associational rights. Is Justice Marshall's position as a justice in *Tashjian* entirely consistent with his position as counsel for the plaintiff in *Smith v. Allwright*?

2.   The Court places substantial weight on the fact that the Republican Party was not seeking to permit participation by voters who were registered members of other parties. Why is, or should, that fact be relevant? What would happen if the Court allowed part of the balance to be an individual voters' First Amendment interest in effective political participation? Put somewhat differently, is there any reason to suppose that the Republicans have less of an interest in associating with a Democratic voter who wishes to associate with them than with an independent voter?

3.   Professor Lowenstein argues that *Tashjian* represented "a significant and ... unwelcome step beyond the Court's earlier decisions" about the associational rights of parties. Daniel H. Lowenstein, *Associational Rights of Major Political Parties: A Skeptical Inquiry*, 71 Tex. L. Rev. 1741, 1742 (1993). A political party, he reminds us, is made up of three separate elements: (1) the party in the electorate, (2) the party organization, and (3) the party in or running for public office. *Id.* at 1760. He observes that "a party subject to state legislation operates under rules devised by the elected officials who make up the party in government. They are nominated by a process that, however imperfect, is vastly more democratic than is possible in the case of party officials, and their stake in the electoral success of the party is more immediate and personal than can be the case for party officials." *Id.* at 1770. If this is so, then many "party vs. the state" lawsuits can be recast as "party-organization vs. party-in-government" disputes, thereby lessening the justification for judicial deference to the party organization position. His general position is that "both the substance of the rules affecting parties and the question of who sets these rules should ordinarily be resolved in the give-and-take of the political process, and that extragovernmental party organizations should not enjoy a constitutional position that immunizes them from the results of that give-and-take." *Id.* at 1771.

4.   In *Rosario v. Rockefeller*, 410 U.S. 752 (1973), the Supreme Court upheld a New York law that required voters to enroll in the party of their choice at least 30 days before the general election in November in order to vote in the next subsequent, closed, party primary. The cutoff date for enrollment was thus roughly eight months before the presidential, and eleven months before a non-presidential, primary. The Court held that the statute was a permissible effort to prevent interparty "raiding" and did not unduly burden voters' ability to participate in the affairs of the party of their choice. Connecticut's statute seemed far less onerous, since it allowed voters to affiliate up until right before a party's primary. Thus, it both lowered the burden on voters and lowered its efficacy as a hedge on raiding.

5. *Blanket Primaries.* When *Jones* was decided, only two states in addition to California had blanket primaries. Those primary systems have since been declared unconstitutional. *See Democratic Party of Washington State v. Reed*, 343 F.3d 1198 (9th Cir. 2003) (declaring Washington's blanket primary unconstitutional per *Jones*), and *O'Callaghan v. State*, 6 P.3d 728 (Alaska 2000) (finding Alaska's blanket primary indistinguishable from *Jones* and hence unconstitutional). The territory of Guam was also using a blanket primary that has since been declared unconstitutional. *See* Steve Limtiaco, *Judge Rules Against Election Law*, Pacific Daily News, June 11, 2004.

Proponents of the blanket primary have not given up yet, however. In *Jones*, the Court not only expressly left open the question of the constitutionality of the open primary, *see California Democratic Party v. Jones*, 530 U.S. 567, 577 n.8 (2000), but also suggested that a state wishing to open its primary system more broadly could choose the non-partisan blanket primary, such as the system in use in Louisiana, *see id.*, at 585–86. In the Louisiana system, all qualified candidates, regardless of party affiliation, appear on the same ballot, and all voters, regardless of party affiliation, are entitled to vote. *See Love v. Foster*, 147 F.3d 383, 385–86 (5th Cir. 1998).

A major question raised by the Court's analysis in *Jones* is how a party's associational rights could be violated by the blanket primary, but not be violated by the non-partisan blanket primary.? As Professor Issacharoff has noted:

> While the Louisiana system does avoid allowing non-party members to forcibly participate in selecting the party's standard-bearer, it does so by denying the parties the right to ever select a standard-bearer at all.... If the justification for the Court's concern over the California blanket primary was that "[i]n no area is the political association's right to exclude more important than in the process of selecting its nominee," how could a coherent constitutional rule then endorse the denial of all party capacity to field a nominee in its own name?

Samuel Issacharoff, *Private Parties with Public Purposes: Political Parties, Associational Freedoms, and Partisan Competition*, 101 Colum. L. Rev. 274, 285 (2001). If non-partisan primaries do not violate the constitutional autonomy of parties recognized in *Jones*, is *Jones* a purely formalistic decision? Is the cost of this formalism the greater undermining of parties that would result from non-partisan primaries—in which all voters in the state choose candidates—than occurs in blanket primaries?

Does the question come down to the need to distinguish between the state's organizing the institutions of elections and the state's interfering in the internal organizations of groups like parties? Are rules regarding primary elections about the former or the latter? Suppose a state permitted parties to endorse whatever primary candidates they wanted, but required candidates to be chosen in blanket primaries. Would that protect the legitimate expressive rights of parties while also allowing states to regulate the institutional structures for elections, including primaries?

Note that Justice Scalia, while still a professor at the University of Chicago Law School, took much the same position on the undesirability of state regulation of primary-election structures that he did in *Jones*. Regarding whether any legislature, state or Congress, should be able to regulate the structure of primary elections, future-Justice Scalia wrote: "[a]s an original matter, I happen to think [any such legislation] *should* be invalidated. I see no reason why the government should be any more able to tell the Republican Party how to choose its leaders than to tell the Mormon Church how to select its elders."

But though these were his views in principle, he also argued that for the Court now to constitutionalize rights of autonomy for political parties would turn the Constitution into a momentary plaything. As he put it, "constitutional law is not an original matter.... We have an accepted governmental tradition of fairly extensive regulation in the latter field, dating from at least the days of La Follette (the *real* La Follette) in the 1900s. I doubt whether we are ready to repudiate such a long, significant, and not dishonorable portion of our political and constitutional history; or if we are, the Constitution has become a thing of the moment." Antonin Scalia, *The Legal Framework for Reform*, 4 Commonsense 49 (1982). Was Justice Scalia right in 1982 about whether the Constitution protected party autonomy—or in *Jones?*

6. The impact of *Jones* continues to be felt in regulation of primaries. For example, in California, voters passed Proposition 60 in the November 2004 elections; that proposition added a modified closed primary system to the state constitution. The proposition, which was added at the last minute by the state legislature to counter another ballot measure, Proposition 62 (which would have established an open primary system), passed with the support of 67.5% of the voters. In Oregon, the narrowly Democratic-dominated state senate passed SB 161 in late May, 2005, which would make several state offices non-partisan and eliminate partisan primary elections. If voters adopt such measures, should major parties receive constitutional protection from the courts against these modifications to primary-election structures?

In 2004, after its earlier blanket primary system was invalidated under *Jones*, Washington voters passed a ballot initiative that created a "Top Two" primary election system under which voters were permitted to select their favorite candidate for each office and the two candidates receiving the greatest number of votes would advance, all without regard for party affiliation. However, unlike the Louisiana non-partisan blanket primary system that contains no designation of party affiliation, Washington's primary system allowed candidate to list their "party preference" on the ballot. The Ninth Circuit found this feature to involve non-party members in creating a form of party sponsorship that violated the associational rights articulated in *Jones*. The Supreme Court has agreed to review this case. *Washington State Republican Party v. Washington*, 460 F.3d 1108 (9th Cir. 2006), *cert. granted*, 127 S.Ct. 1373 (2007). In response to the Ninth Circuit's decision, the Washington State Grange—an organization that spearheaded the development of the invalidated primary system—has moved to strike party designations altogether, creating a non-partisan blanket primary system that has been approved as narrowly tailored. Would such a result have the paradoxical effect of diminishing the associational rights of political parties?

7. *Semi-Closed Primaries.* At the time of *Jones*, eight states had semi-closed primary systems. In a semi-closed primary, independent and non-affiliated voters are permitted to participate in the primaries, but not members of the opposing party. In *Clingman v. Beaver,* 544 U.S. 581 (2005), the Court confronted the issue left open by *Tashjian* and, to a lesser extent, *Jones*. *Clingman* was a challenge by the Libertarian Party of Oklahoma to that State's semi-closed primary system, which prohibited members of other parties from participating in the primary of a different party. This is a mild variant of the fact pattern in *Tashjian,* in which the Court struck down a Connecticut rule barring independents from voting in a party primary. The critical difference in *Clingman* was that the Libertarian Party sought to enhance its base of support by inviting members of *other* parties to participate in its primary. Thus, according to Justice Thomas writing for the Court in a 6–3 opinion, the regulation did not implicate associational rights to join together with other like-minded partisans, the interest identified as controlling in *Jones*:

> [T]he Republican and Democratic voters who have brought this action do not want to associate with the LPO, at least not in any formal sense. They wish to remain registered with the Republican, Democratic, or Reform parties, and yet to assist in selecting the Libertarian Party's candidates for the general election. Their interest is in casting a vote for a Libertarian candidate in a particular primary election, rather than in banding together with fellow citizens committed to the LPO's political goals and ideas.

Ultimately, the Court found the burden on associational freedoms modest by comparison to others that had been upheld, including the prohibition on fusion candidacies upheld in *Timmons v. Twin Cities Area New Party*, 520 U.S. 351 (1997), a case discussed later in this Chapter. Nonetheless, the Court had to distinguish *Tashjian,* which had seemingly entrusted to the parties the ability to police their own borders free of state interference.

Justice Thomas redirected the inquiry from *Tashjian* to focus on the burden imposed on voters seeking to participate, rather than the party autonomy claims that had presumably been controlling not only in *Tashjian,* but in *Jones* as well. The critical distinction, therefore, was that the Oklahoma statute did not require voters "to affiliate publicly with a party to vote in its primary. . . . At issue here are voters who have *already* affiliated publicly with one of Oklahoma's political parties." Absent a clear burden on associational rights, the Court held the statute to be a mere regulatory encumbrance, entitled to no exacting scrutiny. The regulation was therefore a rational means of promoting the role of parties in the political system: "Oklahoma's semiclosed primary system, by retaining the importance of party affiliation, aids in parties' electioneering and party-building efforts."

Only three Justices joined Justice Thomas's opinion in its entirety. Concurring in the result and in parts of the opinion, Justice O'Connor, joined by Justice Breyer, cautioned that the Court may have given too much latitude to potentially self-serving political regulations, and insufficient attention to the "limited but important role of courts in reviewing electoral regulation."

> Although the State has a legitimate—and indeed critical—role to play in regulating elections, it must be recognized that it is not a wholly independent or neutral arbiter. Rather, the State is itself controlled by the political party or parties in power, which presumably have an incentive to shape the rules of the electoral game to their own benefit. Recognition of that basic reality need not render suspect most electoral regulations. Where the State imposes only reasonable and genuinely neutral restrictions on associational rights, there is no threat to the integrity of the electoral process and no apparent reason for judicial intervention. As such restrictions become more severe, however, and particularly where they have discriminatory effects, there is increasing cause for concern that those in power may be using electoral rules to erect barriers to electoral competition. In such cases, applying heightened scrutiny helps to ensure that such limitations are truly justified and that the State's asserted interests are not merely a pretext for exclusionary or anticompetitive restrictions.

Justice O'Connor was particularly concerned with a claim, not well presented below, "that Oklahoma's semiclosed primary law severely burdens their associational rights not through the law's own operation, but rather because *other* state laws make it quite difficult for voters to reregister as Independents or Libertarians so as to participate in the LPO primary." The O'Connor/Breyer concurrence thus redirects courts to inquire into the totality of the electoral process to determine whether it has been impermissibly closed off to political challenge:

> A panoply of regulations, each apparently defensible when considered alone, may nevertheless have the combined effect of severely restrict-

ing participation and competition. Even if each part of a regulatory regime might be upheld if challenged separately, one or another of these parts might have to fall if the overall scheme unreasonably curtails associational freedoms.

Justice Stevens, writing for the three dissenters, would have struck down the Oklahoma statute as evincing "a naked interest in protecting the two major parties." When combined with Justice O'Connor's concern for the openness of the entire political process, the Court appears to be redirecting its inquiry to examine more searchingly for the overall competitiveness of politics.

8. Before *Clingman*, in an action filed by the Libertarian Party, the Ninth Circuit struck down Arizona's semi-closed primary system, which allowed non-party members to participate in selecting not only the party's candidate, but also its party officials. *See Arizona Libertarian Party, Inc. v. Bayless*, 351 F.3d 1277 (9th Cir. 2003). However, the court remanded the case for a determination of whether non-members' selection of only party candidates, and not party officials, would also violate the party's First Amendment rights. Arizona's primary system allows any voter who is unaffiliated, registered as independent, or registered as a member of a party not appearing on the primary ballot to vote in the party primary of her choice. Voters registered with a party appearing on the primary ballot must vote in that party's primary. Is Arizona's system constitutional under *Tashjian*?

The lower courts have shown concern for minor parties in a semi-closed primary system in other cases. *See Cool Moose Party v. Rhode Island*, 183 F.3d 80 (1st Cir. 1999) (declaring unconstitutional a Rhode Island statute prohibiting members of one political party from voting in another party's primary when the bylaws of that party would otherwise permit such participation); *Van Allen v. Democratic State Committee of New York*, 771 N.Y.S.2d 285 (N.Y. 2003) (holding unconstitutional a New York state statute prohibiting non-members of a political party from voting in a party's primary elections where the party wants to allow unaffiliated voters). In contrast, when the challenger to the semi-closed system is an individual voter affiliated with a major party, the courts appear less concerned about associational rights. In *Neier v. State*, 565 S.E.2d 229 (N.C.App. 2002), the court upheld North Carolina's semi-closed party system permitting only party members and, at the party's option, independents to vote in a party's primary election against a challenge brought by a Republican party member who wished to vote in the Democratic primary where only the Democrats were fielding candidates for that particular office. And in *Hole v. North Carolina Bd. of Elections*, 112 F. Supp. 2d 475 (M. D. N. C. 2000), the court held that permitting unaffiliated voters to vote in a primary election if the party authorized it, did not violate a major party candidate's First Amendment right to free association. The candidate claimed that, if unaffiliated voters' votes were not counted, she might have won the primary election.

9. *Standing*. Who may challenge the state's regulation of a political party? The Eleventh Circuit has held that under *Jones*, only the party can bring a claim that its associational rights have been violated, and not individual voters. *See Osburn v. Cox*, 369 F.3d 1283 (11th Cir. 2004). Hence, the court determined that voters challenging the constitutionality of Georgia's open primary system lacked standing. In another case regarding standing, the court found that allowing non-party members to challenge the way a party has put forward its candidate would not violate the party's associational rights under *Jones*. *See Queens County Republican Committee v. New York State Board of Elections*, 222 F. Supp. 2d 341 (E. D. N. Y. 2002) (challenge by non-party member that candidate had violated signature-gathering requirements allowed).

C.   WHEN CAN THE GOVERNMENT REGULATE A PARTY'S INTERNAL AFFAIRS?

Parties do more than simply nominate candidates for discrete offices. For example, they promulgate platforms, collect and distribute campaign funds, appoint election judges, and set nomination policies. The party organization is thus in some senses the "intermediary's intermediary," interacting both with the party in the electorate and with the party in government. As we saw in the preceding section, to some extent, it may determine the membership of each of the other branches of the party. When can the other branches determine how the party organization is constituted?

Eu v. San Francisco County Democratic Central Committee

489 U.S. 214 (1989).

■ JUSTICE MARSHALL delivered the opinion of the Court.

* * *

I

A

The State of California heavily regulates its political parties. Although the laws vary in extent and detail from party to party, certain requirements apply to all "ballot-qualified" parties [which includes the Democratic, Republican, American Independent, and Peace and Freedom parties]. The California Elections Code (Code) provides that the "official governing bodies" for such a party are its "state convention," "state central committee," and "county central committees," and that these bodies are responsible for conducting the party's campaigns. At the same time, the Code provides that the official governing bodies "shall not endorse, support, or oppose, any candidate for nomination by that party for partisan office in the direct primary election." It is a misdemeanor for any primary candidate, or a person on her behalf, to claim that she is the officially endorsed candidate of the party.

Although the official governing bodies of political parties are barred from issuing endorsements, other groups are not. Political clubs affiliated with a party, labor organizations, political action committees, other politically active associations, and newspapers frequently endorse primary candidates. With the official party organizations silenced by the ban, it has been possible for a candidate with views antithetical to those of her party nevertheless to win its primary.[4]

In addition to restricting the primary activities of the official governing bodies of political parties, California also regulates their internal affairs. Separate statutory provisions dictate the size and composition of the state central committees; set forth rules governing the selection and removal of committee members; fix the maximum term of office for the chair of the state central committee; require that the chair rotate between residents of northern and southern California; specify the time and place of committee meetings; and limit the dues parties may impose on members. Violations of these provisions are criminal offenses punishable by fine and imprisonment.

* * *

II

A State's broad power to regulate the time, place, and manner of elections "does not extinguish the State's responsibility to observe the limits established by the First Amendment rights of the State's citizens." To assess the constitutionality of a state election law, we first examine whether it burdens rights protected by the First and Fourteenth Amendments. If the challenged law burdens the rights of political parties and their members, it can survive constitutional scrutiny only if the State shows that it advances a compelling state interest, and is narrowly tailored to serve that interest.

A

We first consider California's prohibition on primary endorsements by the official governing bodies of political parties. California concedes that its ban implicates the First Amendment, but contends that the burden is

---

4. In 1980, for example, Tom Metzger won the Democratic Party's nomination for United States House of Representative from the San Diego area, although he was a Grand Dragon of the Ku Klux Klan and held views antithetical to those of the Democratic Party.

"minuscule." We disagree. The ban directly affects speech which "is at the core of our electoral process and of the First Amendment freedoms." We have recognized repeatedly that "debate on the qualifications of candidates [is] integral to the operation of the system of government established by our Constitution." Indeed, the First Amendment "has its fullest and most urgent application" to speech uttered during a campaign for political office. Free discussion about candidates for public office is no less critical before a primary than before a general election. In both instances, the "election campaign is a means of disseminating ideas as well as attaining political office."

California's ban on primary endorsements, however, prevents party governing bodies from stating whether a candidate adheres to the tenets of the party or whether party officials believe that the candidate is qualified for the position sought. This prohibition directly hampers the ability of a party to spread its message and hamstrings voters seeking to inform themselves about the candidates and the campaign issues. A "highly paternalistic approach" limiting what people may hear is generally suspect, but it is particularly egregious where the State censors the political speech a political party shares with its members.

Barring political parties from endorsing and opposing candidates not only burdens their freedom of speech but also infringes upon their freedom of association. It is well settled that partisan political organizations enjoy freedom of association protected by the First and Fourteenth Amendments. Freedom of association means not only that an individual voter has the right to associate with the political party of her choice, but also that a political party has a right to "identify the people who constitute the association," and to select a "standard bearer who best represents the party's ideologies and preferences."

Depriving a political party of the power to endorse suffocates this right. The endorsement ban prevents parties from promoting candidates "at the crucial juncture at which the appeal to common principles may be translated into concerted action, and hence to political power in the community." Even though individual members of the state central committees and county central committees are free to issue endorsements, imposing limitations "on individuals wishing to band together to advance their views on a ballot measure, while placing none on individuals acting alone, is clearly a restraint on the right of association."

Because the ban burdens appellees' rights to free speech and free association, it can only survive constitutional scrutiny if it serves a compelling governmental interest. The State offers two: stable government and protecting voters from confusion and undue influence. Maintaining a stable political system is, unquestionably, a compelling state interest. California, however, never adequately explains how banning parties from endorsing or opposing primary candidates advances that interest. There is no showing, for example, that California's political system is any more stable now than it was in 1963, when the legislature enacted the ban. Nor does the State explain what makes the California system so peculiar that it is virtually the only State that has determined that such a ban is necessary.

The only explanation the State offers is that its compelling interest in stable government embraces a similar interest in party stability.... States may regulate elections to ensure that "some sort of order, rather than chaos ... accompanies the democratic processes." ... [But we have never held] that a State may enact election laws to mitigate intraparty factionalism during a primary campaign. To the contrary, [we have stated that] ... [a] primary is not hostile to intraparty feuds; rather it is an ideal forum in which to resolve them....

It is no answer to argue, as does the State, that a party that issues primary endorsements risks intraparty friction which may endanger the party's general election prospects. Presumably a party will be motivated by self-interest and not engage in acts or speech that run counter to its political success. However, even if a ban on endorsements saves a political party from pursuing self-destructive acts, that would not justify a State substituting its judgment for that of the party. Because preserving party unity during a primary is not a compelling state interest, we must look elsewhere to justify the challenged law.

The State's second justification for the ban on party endorsements and statements of opposition is that it is necessary to protect primary voters from confusion and undue influence. Certainly the State has a legitimate interest in fostering an informed electorate. However, "[a] State's claim that it is enhancing the ability of its citizenry to make wise decisions by restricting the flow of information to them must be viewed with some skepticism."

Because the ban on primary endorsements by political parties burdens political speech while serving no compelling governmental interest, we hold that [it] violate[s] the First and Fourteenth Amendment.

B

We turn next to California's restrictions on the organization and composition of official governing bodies, the limits on the term of office for state central committee chair, and the requirement that the chair rotate between residents of northern and southern California. These laws directly implicate the associational rights of political parties and their members....

The laws at issue burden these rights. By requiring parties to establish official governing bodies at the county level, California prevents the political parties from governing themselves with the structure they think best.[20] And by specifying who shall be the members of the parties' official governing bodies, California interferes with the parties' choice of leaders. A

---

20. For example, the Libertarian Party was forced to abandon its region-based organization in favor of the statutorily mandated county-based system.

party might decide, for example, that it will be more effective if a greater number of its official leaders are local activists rather than Washington-based elected officials. The Code prevents such a change. A party might also decide that the state central committee chair needs more than two years to successfully formulate and implement policy. The Code prevents such an extension of the chair's term of office. A party might find that a resident of northern California would be particularly effective in promoting the party's message and in unifying the party. The Code prevents her from chairing the state central committee unless the preceding chair was from the southern part of the State.

Each restriction thus limits a political party's discretion in how to organize itself, conduct its affairs, and select its leaders. Indeed, the associational rights at stake are much stronger than those we credited in *Tashjian*. There, we found that a party's right to free association embraces a right to allow registered voters who are not party members to vote in the party's primary. Here, party members do not seek to associate with nonparty members, but only with one another in freely choosing their party leaders.

Because the challenged laws burden the associational rights of political parties and their members, the question is whether they serve a compelling state interest. A State indisputably has a compelling interest in preserving the integrity of its election process. Toward that end, a State may enact laws that interfere with a party's internal affairs when necessary to ensure that elections are fair and honest. For example, . . . a State may impose restrictions that promote the integrity of primary elections. *See, e.g., American Party of Texas v. White* (limitation on voters' participation to one primary and bar on voters both voting in a party primary and signing a petition supporting an independent candidate); *Rosario v. Rockefeller* (waiting periods before voters may change party registration and participate in another party's primary). None of these restrictions, however, involved direct regulation of a party's leaders. Rather, the infringement on the associational rights of the parties and their members was the indirect consequence of laws necessary to the successful completion of a party's external responsibilities in ensuring the order and fairness of elections.

In the instant case, the State has not shown that its regulation of internal party governance is necessary to the integrity of the electoral process. Instead, it contends that the challenged laws serve a compelling "interest in the democratic management of the political party's internal affairs." This, however, is not a case where intervention is necessary to prevent the derogation of the civil rights of party adherents. *Cf. Smith v. Allwright*. Moreover, as we have observed, the State has no interest in "protecting the integrity of the Party against the Party itself." . . .

In sum, a State cannot justify regulating a party's internal affairs without showing that such regulation is necessary to ensure an election that is orderly and fair. Because California has made no such showing here, the challenged laws cannot be upheld.

* * *

NOTES AND QUESTIONS

1. California had argued that strict scrutiny was not required because the major political parties had "consented" to the statutory regime in that the parties could have achieved the statute's repeal through the legislative process had they wished to. Justice Marshall gave that argument short shrift:

> California's consent argument is contradicted by the simple fact that the official governing bodies of various political parties have joined this lawsuit....
>
> Simply because a legislator belongs to a political party does not make her at all times a representative of party interests. In supporting the endorsement ban, an individual legislator may be acting on her understanding of the public good or her interest in reelection. The independence of legislators from their parties is illustrated by the California Legislature's frequent refusal to amend the election laws in accordance with the wishes of political parties. Moreover, the State's argument ignores those parties with negligible, if any, representation in the legislature.

How persuasive is Justice Marshall's response? Why ought we assume that the particular officials who controlled the San Francisco County Democratic Central Committee at the time of this litigation were better "representatives" of the party? Are the legislators "independent" of their parties or simply more responsive to the "party in the electorate" than the "party organization"? In this respect, consider Professor Lowenstein's analysis:

> The question of who speaks for the party was especially embarrassing in *Eu*.... Only if the plaintiffs could speak for the Democratic and Republican parties was the posture of *Eu* comparable to that of *Tashjian*.

* * *

> Even if . . . one unrealistically exalts the legal status of the California central committees, the handful of county central committees that were plaintiffs in *Eu* cannot be regarded as speaking for the parties as a whole with regard to the statewide associational claims that were asserted. The Court simply swept under the rug the inconvenient fact that neither major-party state central committee was a plaintiff or otherwise had expressed a desire to assert the associational claims. Perhaps the Court believed the Ninth Circuit had dealt adequately with this fact. The lower court had asserted that legislators so dominated the membership of the state central committees that it was

wrong for the legislature to benefit from the committees' consequent unwillingness to challenge the constraints under which they labored. Perhaps under these circumstances the silence of the state central committees should not bar the claim that "the parties" seek freedom from legislative control, but nowhere in its opinion did the Ninth Circuit give any affirmative reason to believe that the scattered individual and county central committee plaintiffs spoke for "the Republicans" or "the Democrats." . . .

Daniel H. Lowenstein, *Associational Rights of Major Political Parties: A Skeptical Inquiry*, 71 Tex. L. Rev. 1741, 1781–82 (1993).

2. There are a variety of reasons why a party might embed particular rules in the law, rather than simply in party rules. Perhaps this represents a precommitment strategy in which the party binds its future self to avoid self-destructive acts. In this sense, a party's seeking statutory regulation might be akin to implanting a particular rule in the constitution rather than in an easy-to-modify or-repeal statute. *Eu* might be read to deprive parties of this hands-tying ability. Paradoxically, then, *Eu* might end up denying, rather than protecting, party autonomy. Would the validation of a party's precommitment strategy be consistent with the Court's decisions in the White Primary Cases?

3. Is Justice Marshall correct that California is not intervening "to prevent the derogation of the civil rights of party adherents"? Is racial discrimination the only way in which a party might deny its adherents their civil rights? The party's ambiguous stance as sometimes state actor and sometimes private, specially protected association makes this a difficult question. Suppose, for example, that a party imposed restrictions on its adherents that would, if imposed by the state directly, violate First Amendment rights. Would states be totally disempowered from protecting those members against retaliation for exercising their First Amendment rights?

4. In its discussion of the regulations of party structure, the Court seems to be giving parties heightened First Amendment associational protection. After all, a state could presumably regulate the composition of boards of directors of corporations chartered within the state. For example, many states require boards of directors to be elected by cumulative voting, a semi-proportional representation system. But *Eu* suggests this sort of regulation becomes unconstitutional if the corporation is a political party. Why?

5. As for the anti-endorsement provision, if a "party" picks its candidates through a primary election, how can the "party" endorse a candidate before it has indicated its preference? This paradox highlights the ambiguous definition of the "party." In a related area, after protracted litigation, a federal district court struck down California's ban on party endorsement of candidates in nonpartisan elections. *See California Democratic Party v. Lundgren*, 919 F.Supp. 1397 (N. D. Cal. 1996).

6. Is a political party's decision about how to finance its nomination process subject to governmental oversight? In *Morse v. Republican Party of Virginia*, 517 U.S. 186 (1996), the Supreme Court reviewed the defendants' decision to hold a nominating convention, rather than a primary, to select its candidate for United States Senate, and to charge individuals who wished to attend the convention a $45 registration fee. The Court held that these decisions were covered by section 5 of the Voting Rights Act of 1965, 42 U.S.C. § 1973c (2000), which forbids certain "states" from making any change in their voting laws without receiving prior approval from the Federal Government. (Section 5 is covered in Chapter 6 of this book.) Although the majority did not unite behind a single opinion, both Justice Stevens's opinion and Justice Breyer's found that the party was a state actor in performing its nominating function (relying on the White Primary Cases) and both opinions rejected the party's First Amendment claim. According to Justice Stevens, who was joined by Justice Ginsburg, the party never explained how "the registration fee at issue in this case . . . is itself protected by the First Amendment." He also rejected the argument that the requirement that a party obtain federal approval before implementing a new practice was "a 'classic prior restraint.' It imposes no restraint at all on speech. Given the past history of discrimination that gave rise to the preclearance remedy imposed by § 5, the minimal burden on the right of association implicated in this case is unquestionably justified." Similarly, Justice Breyer, joined by Justices O'Connor and Souter, found that the fee "lies . . . well outside the area of greatest 'associational concern.'" Suppose the Republican Party had proclaimed an ideological reason to requiring payment (e.g., because it wanted to measure participants' "commitment to the party"). Would, or should, the Court's response be different then? Moreover, does *Eu* suggest that the First Amendment rights attach to the party's right of self-governance, rather than to the speech value of its particular choices?

D. Does the Existing Legal Regime Improperly Entrench the Existing Two-Party System?

As we have already seen, every state limits, to some extent, which potential candidates' names appear on the ballot. Candidates nominated by the Democratic or Republican parties appear on the ballot in every state; often they are the *only* candidates on the general election ballot. For most of our history, American politics at the national level has been based on a two-party system. (In certain places, such as the Solid South of the early twentieth century, there is effectively only one political party.) But there is nothing inevitable about a two-party system. Two-party systems are the product of a series of conscious and unconscious choices about how electoral politics ought to be structured. Nor is the presence of two, and only two, parties necessary for a robust democracy. Countries such as Israel, the

Netherlands, and Finland all have multiparty democracies. We will turn to these issues more directly in Chapter 13.

While the United States' two-party politics may in part be the result of historical contingency, this by no means suggests that the survival of the two-party system is accidental. Once a two-party system is in place, the beneficiaries—namely, the parties who achieve electoral success—may engage in a variety of behaviors designed to perpetuate the privileged positions they won, perhaps fortuitously, during an earlier time. By contrast, a party whose candidates are not on the ballot is highly unlikely to win any elections. Concomitantly, a party whose candidates fail to attract substantial support may find its candidates excluded from the ballot in the future. Thus, access to the ballot is a critical juncture for the emergence of new parties. And it is at this juncture that American state legislatures, composed virtually entirely of partisans of the two established parties, have strenuously resisted the recognition of new parties.

1.   CHALLENGES TO BALLOT ACCESS BY INDEPENDENT AND THIRD-PARTY CANDIDATES

The Supreme Court first gave serious attention to the influence of ballot access laws in *Williams v. Rhodes*, 393 U.S. 23 (1968). The case concerned placement on the presidential election ballot. Parties whose candidate for governor at the last election received at least 10 percent of the votes cast were automatically given lines on the ballot. Other parties that wanted their candidates' names to appear were required to gather petition signatures from a number of voters equal to 15 percent of the ballots cast in the last gubernatorial election and to file those petitions by early February of the election year (substantially before the major parties had chosen their candidates).

In 1967, George Wallace decided to run for president as a third-party candidate. The Ohio American Independent Party was formed in January 1968, and during the next six months it obtained over 450,000 signatures, which easily exceeded the 15 percent requirement. But the Ohio secretary of state denied the party's request for a place on the ballot because the February deadline had expired. The Court held that Ohio's law violated the equal protection clause because it gave the two established parties a decided advantage over new parties. It found that Ohio's restrictive ballot access procedure heavily burdened the right of individuals to associate for the advancement of political beliefs and the right of qualified voters to cast their votes effectively, and that the state had shown no "compelling interest" justifying those burdens:

> [Ohio] claims that the State may validly promote a two-party system in order to encourage compromise and political stability. The fact is, however, that the Ohio system does not merely favor a "two-party system"; it favors two particular parties—the Republicans and the Democrats—and in effect tends to give them a complete monopoly.

There is, of course, no reason why two parties should retain a permanent monopoly on the right to have people vote for or against them. Competition in ideas and governmental policies is at the core of our electoral process and of the First Amendment freedoms. New parties struggling for their place must have the time and opportunity to organize in order to meet reasonable requirements for ballot position, just as the old parties have had in the past.

Ohio makes a variety of other arguments to support its very restrictive election laws. It points out, for example, that if three or more parties are on the ballot, it is possible that no one party would obtain 50% of the vote, and the runner-up might have been preferred to the plurality winner by a majority of the voters. Concededly, the State does have an interest in attempting to see that the election winner be the choice of a majority of its voters. But to grant the State power to keep all political parties off the ballot until they have enough members to win would stifle the growth of all new parties working to increase their strength from year to year. *Id.* at 31–32.

While the 15 percent requirement, coupled with the excessively early filing deadline might run afoul of the Constitution, less onerous requirements were permissible. In *Jenness v. Fortson*, 403 U.S. 431 (1971), the Court upheld Georgia's requirement that independent candidates secure supporting signatures amounting to 5 percent of the total registered voters in the last election for filling the office sought by the candidate.

In 1974, the Supreme Court decided another pair of ballot access cases, involving the rights of third-party and independent candidates. *Storer v. Brown*, 415 U.S. 724 (1974), concerned several provisions of the California Election Code. Section 6830 made independent candidates ineligible for placement on the ballot if they had voted in the immediately preceding primary or had been registered members of an existing political party within one year prior to the immediately preceding primary election. Section 6831 required independent candidates to file nomination papers signed by a number of voters between 5 and 6 percent of the entire vote cast in the preceding general election in the area served by the office they were seeking; these signatures had to be obtained during a 24-day period following the primary and ending 60 days prior to the general election, and none of the signatures could be from a person who voted in a primary.

The Court began its analysis by noting that although *Williams v. Rhodes* and the right-to-vote cases such as *Dunn v. Blumstein* and *Kramer v. Union Free School District* (covered in Chapter 2) had applied heightened scrutiny, not every "substantial restriction on the right to vote or to associate" required invalidation of a state statute. "[A]s a practical matter, there must be a substantial regulation of elections if they are to be fair and honest and if some sort of order, rather than chaos, is to accompany the democratic processes":

It is very unlikely that all or even a large portion of the state election laws would fail to pass muster under our cases; and the rule fashioned by the Court to pass on constitutional challenges to specific provisions of election laws provides no litmus-paper test for separating those restrictions that are valid from those that are invidious under the Equal Protection Clause. The rule is not self-executing and is no substitute for the hard judgments that must be made. Decision in this context, as in others, is very much a "matter of degree," very much a matter of "consider[ing] the facts and circumstances behind the law, the interests which the State claims to be protecting, and the interests of those who are disadvantaged by the classification." What the result of this process will be in any specific case may be very difficult to predict with great assurance. *Id.* at 730.

With regard to the "sore loser" statute, the Court found it legitimate in light of the integral role primary elections played in the state's overall electoral scheme:

The direct party primary in California is not merely an exercise or warm-up for the general election but an integral part of the entire election process, the initial stage in a two-stage process by which the people choose their public officers. It functions to winnow out and finally reject all but the chosen candidates. The State's general policy is to have contending forces within the party employ the primary campaign and primary election to finally settle their differences. The general election ballot is reserved for major struggles; it is not a forum for continuing intraparty feuds. The provision against defeated primary candidates running as independents effectuates this aim, the visible result being to prevent the losers from continuing the struggle and to limit the names on the ballot to those who have won the primaries and those independents who have properly qualified. The people, it is hoped, are presented with understandable choices and the winner in the general election with sufficient support to govern effectively.

[California's law] protects the direct primary process by refusing to recognize independent candidates who do not make early plans to leave a party and take the alternative course to the ballot. It works against independent candidacies prompted by short-range political goals, pique, or personal quarrel. It is also a substantial barrier to a party fielding an "independent" candidate to capture and bleed off votes in the general election that might well go to another party.

A State need not take the course California has, but California apparently believes with the Founding Fathers that splintered parties and unrestrained factionalism may do significant damage to the fabric of government. *See* The Federalist, No. 10 (Madison). It appears obvious to us that the one-year disaffiliation provision furthers the State's interest in the stability of its political system. We also consider that interest as not only permissible, but compelling and as outweighing the interest the candidate and his supporters may have in making a late rather than an early decision to seek independent ballot status. *Id.* at 735–36.

Note the extent to which the Court's opinion channels the acceptable forms of political sentiment. It puts "short-range political goals" and "pique" outside the boundaries of acceptable reasons for candidates to run and delegitimates these as sources to inform voter choice.

With respect to the signature requirement, the Court remanded for additional factfinding. The disqualification of voters who had participated in primaries was unproblematic. As the Court explained at greater length in another case decided the same day, *American Party of Texas v. White*, 415 U.S. 767 (1974), such a disqualification simply limited each voter to one nominating event for each office on the ballot. But its interaction with the 5 percent requirement might pose problems. In *Jenness*, the Court had intimated that 5 percent was near the high end of the range of permissible measures of support. If most voters had in fact voted in the primaries, then 5 percent of the pool of all voters might be closer to 10 percent of the pool of eligible signatories, and that might unreasonably freeze out new parties.

Storer's acknowledgment of the central indeterminacy of the Court's test was borne out over the next two decades. In *Anderson v. Celebrezze*, 460 U.S. 780 (1983), for example, the Court struck down Ohio's early filing deadline for independent presidential candidates. Although the Court recognized that the right of voters to express their choice for political office was "fundamental," the Court reiterated that "not all restrictions imposed by the States on candidates' eligibility for the ballot impose constitutionally suspect burdens on voters' rights to associate or to choose among candidates." A court faced with a challenge to the restriction of ballot access "must first consider the character and magnitude of the asserted injury to the rights protected by the First and Fourteenth Amendments that the plaintiff seeks to vindicate. It then must identify and evaluate the precise interests put forward by the State as justifications for the burden imposed by its rule. In passing judgment, the Court must not only determine the legitimacy and strength of each of those interests, it also must consider the extent to which those interests make it necessary to burden the plaintiff's rights. Only after weighing all these factors is the reviewing court in a position to decide whether the challenged provision is unconstitutional." *Anderson*, taken at its word, appears to impose a searching form of scrutiny on any state infringement on ballot access. It appears unlikely that any of the ballot restrictions covered in this Chapter could withstand a literal application of the standard of review set forth by Justice Stevens in *Anderson*. Perhaps for that reason, *Anderson* is largely disregarded in subsequent court opinions.

What explains the Court's inability to articulate a clear, easy-to-apply test to ballot restrictions? To what extent is the Court asking simply the sort of hypothetical question often at issue in rational-basis scrutiny cases, namely, "can we conceive of a way in which the challenged statute is rationally related to a legitimate governmental purpose"? To what extent is it demanding that the state provide empirical evidence to back up its claims? At what level of specificity or generality is the state's interest assessed? Everyone can agree that protecting the integrity of the electoral system is a compelling government interest, but the Court never defines what "integrity" consists of. Finally, on whose behalf does a state claim to articulate a specific interest in electoral rules? Since state governments are dominated by the two major parties, should courts be more suspicious of state claims to protect the integrity of the two-party system?

The Court's response to Washington State's ballot access scheme underscores these questions. Washington State did not use a filing fee or petition to winnow out nonserious candidates. Instead, the state conducted a "blanket primary" at which registered voters could vote for any candidate of their choice, irrespective of the candidates' political party affiliation. To be placed on the general election ballot, a candidate had to receive at least 1 percent of the votes cast for that office. Each candidate who was seeking a party's nomination had to declare his candidacy for that party's nomination. As to each party, only the name of the candidate who received a plurality of the votes cast for the candidates of his party would appear on the general election ballot.

Dean Peoples (yes, his real name) qualified to be placed on the primary election ballot for a U.S. Senate seat as the nominee of the Socialist Workers Party. Also appearing on that ballot were 32 other candidates seeking the nomination of a variety of other parties. Peoples received approximately 596 of the 681,690 votes cast in the primary (roughly .09 percent of the total), and thus the secretary of state refused to put his name on the general election ballot.

Munro v. Socialist Workers Party

479 U.S. 189 (1986).

■ JUSTICE WHITE delivered the opinion of the Court.

* * *

While there is no "litmus-paper test" for deciding a case like this, it is now clear that States may condition access to the general election ballot by a minor-party or independent candidate upon a showing of a modicum of support among the potential voters for the office.

* * *

[There] is surely an important state interest in requiring some preliminary showing of a significant modicum of support before printing the name of a political organization's candidate on the ballot—the interest, if no other, in avoiding confusion, deception, and even frustration of the democratic process at the general election.

* * *

The Court of Appeals determined that Washington's interest in insuring that candidates had sufficient community support did not justify the enactment of [this scheme] because "Washington's political history evidences no voter confusion from ballot overcrowding." We accept this historical fact, but it does not require invalidation of [the law.]

We have never required a State to make a particularized showing of the existence of voter confusion, ballot overcrowding, or the presence of frivolous candidacies prior to the imposition of reasonable restrictions on ballot access. In *Jenness v. Fortson*, [for example], we conducted no inquiry into the sufficiency and quantum of the data supporting the reasons for Georgia's 5% petition-signature requirement. In *American Party of Texas v. White*, we upheld the 1% petition-signature requirement, asserting that the "State's admittedly vital interests are sufficiently implicated to insist that political parties appearing on the general ballot demonstrate a significant, measurable quantum of community support." And, in *Storer v. Brown*, we upheld California's statutory provisions that denied ballot access to an independent candidate if the candidate had been affiliated with any political party within one year prior to the immediately preceding primary election. We recognized that California had a "compelling" interest in maintaining the integrity of its political processes, and that the disaffiliation requirement furthered this interest and was therefore valid, even though it was an absolute bar to attaining a ballot position. We asserted that "[it] appears obvious to us that the one-year disaffiliation provision furthers the State's interest in the stability of its political system." There is no indication that we held California to the burden of demonstrating empirically the objective effects on political stability that were produced by the 1–year disaffiliation requirement.

To require States to prove actual voter confusion, ballot overcrowding, or the presence of frivolous candidacies as a predicate to the imposition of reasonable ballot access restrictions would invariably lead to endless court battles over the sufficiency of the "evidence" marshaled by a State to prove the predicate. Such a requirement would necessitate that a State's political system sustain some level of damage before the legislature could take corrective action. Legislatures, we think, should be permitted to respond to potential deficiencies in the electoral process with foresight rather than reactively, provided that the response is reasonable and does not significantly impinge on constitutionally protected rights.

In any event, the record here suggests that revision of [the Washington ballot access regime] was, in fact, linked to the state legislature's perception that the general election ballot was becoming cluttered with candidates from minor parties who did not command significant voter support. In

1976, one year prior to [the revision,] the largest number of minor political parties in Washington's history—12—appeared on the general election ballot. The record demonstrates that at least part of the legislative impetus for revision . . . was concern about minor parties having such easy access to Washington's general election ballot.

The primary election in Washington . . . is "an integral part of the entire election process . . . [that] functions to winnow out and finally reject all but the chosen candidates." We think that the State can properly reserve the general election ballot "for major struggles," by conditioning access to that ballot on a showing of a modicum of voter support. In this respect, the fact that the State is willing to have a long and complicated ballot at the primary provides no measure of what it may require for access to the general election ballot. The State of Washington was clearly entitled to raise the ante for ballot access, to simplify the general election ballot, and to avoid the possibility of unrestrained factionalism at the general election.

Neither do we agree with the Court of Appeals and appellees that the burdens imposed on appellees' First Amendment rights by the 1977 amendments are far too severe to be justified by the State's interest in restricting access to the general ballot. Much is made of the fact that prior to 1977, virtually every minor-party candidate who sought general election ballot position so qualified, while since 1977 only 1 out of 12 minor-party candidates has appeared on that ballot. Such historical facts are relevant, but they prove very little in this case, other than the fact that [the statute] does not provide an insuperable barrier to minor-party ballot access.[11] It is hardly a surprise that minor parties appeared on the general election ballot before [the revision]; for, until then, there were virtually no restrictions on access. Under our cases, however, Washington was not required to afford such automatic access and would have been entitled to insist on a more substantial showing of voter support. Comparing the actual experience before and after 1977 tells us nothing about how minor parties would have fared in those earlier years had Washington conditioned ballot access to the maximum extent permitted by the Constitution.

* * *

We also observe that [Washington's system] is more accommodating of First Amendment rights and values than were the statutes we upheld in *Jenness*, *American Party*, and *Storer*. Under each scheme analyzed in those cases, if a candidate failed to satisfy the qualifying criteria, the State's voters had no opportunity to cast a ballot for that candidate and the candidate had no ballot-connected campaign platform from which to es-

---

11. [The law] apparently poses an insubstantial obstacle to minor-party candidates for nonstatewide offices and independent candidates for statewide offices. Since 1977, 36 out of 40 such minor-party candidates have qualified for the general election ballot and 4 out of 5 independent candidates for state-wide office have so qualified.

pouse his or her views; the unsatisfied qualifying criteria served as an absolute bar to ballot access. . . . Here, however, Washington virtually guarantees what the parties challenging the Georgia, Texas, and California election laws so vigorously sought—candidate access to a statewide ballot. This is a significant difference. Washington has chosen a vehicle by which minor-party candidates must demonstrate voter support that serves to promote the very First Amendment values that are threatened by overly burdensome ballot access restrictions. It can hardly be said that Washington's voters are denied freedom of association because they must channel their expressive activity into a campaign at the primary as opposed to the general election.

* * *

NOTES AND QUESTIONS

1.   Lurking in the Court's opinions on restrictions on ballot access is a concern for the state's interest in preventing unrestrained electoral factionalism. The contexts vary from the virtually uncontested elections in Hawaii in which the Democratic Party holds sway, to rules in Washington that attempt to restrict the election process to a "main arena" bout between the major parties. At what level of generality may a state assert an argument that expanded electoral participation risks "unrestrained factionalism"? Can an assertion that the state seeks to preserve a two-party monopoly suffice to meet the state's burden? Consider Minnesota's defense of ballot restrictions as restraining "factionalism" in *Timmons v. Twin Cities Area New Party*, which appears *infra*.

2.   Note that Justice White's opinion does not require empirical proof that a state's restrictions either respond to an actual problem or that they are the most reasonable way of avoiding voter confusion or ensuring the integrity of the process. In traditional terms, then, the Court seems to be applying a sort of rational relationship scrutiny—under which courts often hypothesize a relationship between the challenged classification and a legitimate governmental purpose, rather than requiring any actual proof—rather than any sort of heightened review.

By contrast, Justice Marshall's dissent suggested that some form of more searching judicial review was required because of the connection between the major parties and ballot access legislation: "The necessity for [a higher standard of review] becomes evident when we consider that major parties, which by definition are ordinarily in control of legislative institutions, may seek to perpetuate themselves at the expense of developing minor parties. The application of strict scrutiny to ballot access restrictions ensures that measures taken to further a State's interest in keeping frivolous candidates off the ballot do not incidentally impose an impermissible bar to minor-party access." Given the risk that elected legislators will almost always come from the two major parties, what standard of review should courts apply to regulations of ballot access?

3. *Munro* offers a noticeably constrained vision of the purpose of general elections: they serve "to winnow out and finally reject all but the chosen candidates" and thus the general election ballot is reserved "for major struggles." Under such a vision, most minor party candidates are irrelevant, since they have little chance of winning.

But suppose minor parties sponsor candidates for reasons beyond the (admittedly minuscule) chance of winning office. What was Peoples' and the SWP's aim in running? Does appearing on the primary ballot satisfy this aim? Consider Richard Hofstader's account of the distinctive aspirations and role of third parties. Hofstader points out that in the United States no third party has ever replaced one of the existing major parties and thus leaders of minor parties "must look for success in terms different from those that apply to the major parties, for in those terms third parties always fail." Richard Hofstader, The Age of Reform 89 (1955). In contrast to the two major parties, which are more concerned with patronage than principles, third parties are usually ideologically driven. "Their function has not been to win or govern, but to agitate, educate, generate new ideas and supply the dynamic element in our political life. When a third party's demands become popular enough, they are appropriated by one or both of the major parties and the third party disappears. Third parties are like bees; once they have stung, they die." *Id.*

4. *Munro* raises the possibility that the general election ballot may be limited essentially to ensure that the winning candidate receives a majority of the votes cast. Consider the ways in which such a practice secures stability in the electoral system. *See* Richard H. Pildes and Elizabeth S. Anderson, *Slinging Arrows at Democracy: Social Choice Theory, Value Pluralism, and Democratic Politics*, 90 Colum. L. Rev. 2121 (1990) (discussing the social choice theory arguments on behalf of a two-party political system: that such systems guarantee that the winning candidate has majority support, with no competing majority supporting an incompatible choice). What other aspects of the electoral system also strengthen the two-party system?

2.   The Interaction of Ballot Access and Other Electoral Regulations in Perpetuating the Two–Party System

Timmons v. Twin Cities Area New Party

520 U.S. 351 (1997).

■ Chief Justice Rehnquist delivered the opinion of the Court.

Most States prohibit multiple-party, or "fusion," candidacies for elected office.[1] The Minnesota laws challenged in this case prohibit a candidate

---

1. "Fusion," also called "cross-filing" or "multiple-party nomination," is "the electoral support of a single set of candidates by two or more parties." Fusion is "the nomina-tion by more than one political party of the same candidate for the same office in the same general election."

from appearing on the ballot as the candidate of more than one party. We hold that such a prohibition does not violate the First and Fourteenth Amendments to the United States Constitution.

Respondent is a chartered chapter of the national New Party. Petitioners are Minnesota election officials. In April 1994, Minnesota State Representative Andy Dawkins was running unopposed in the Minnesota Democratic–Farmer–Labor Party's (DFL) primary. That same month, New Party members chose Dawkins as their candidate for the same office in the November 1994 general election. Neither Dawkins nor the DFL objected, and Dawkins signed the required affidavit of candidacy for the New Party. Minnesota, however, prohibits fusion candidacies. Because Dawkins had already filed as a candidate for the DFL's nomination, local election officials refused to accept the New Party's nominating petition.

* * *

Fusion was a regular feature of Gilded Age American politics. Particularly in the West and Midwest, candidates of issue-oriented parties like the Grangers, Independents, Greenbackers, and Populists often succeeded through fusion with the Democrats, and vice versa. Republicans, for their part, sometimes arranged fusion candidacies in the South, as part of a general strategy of encouraging and exploiting divisions within the dominant Democratic Party.

Fusion was common in part because political parties, rather than local or state governments, printed and distributed their own ballots. . . . But after the 1888 presidential election, which was widely regarded as having been plagued by fraud, many States moved to the "Australian ballot system." . . . During the same period, many States enacted other election-related reforms, including bans on fusion candidacies. Minnesota banned fusion in 1901. This trend has continued and, in this century, fusion has become the exception, not the rule. Today, multiple-party candidacies are permitted in just a few States, and fusion plays a significant role only in New York.

* * *

The New Party's claim that it has a right to select its own candidate is uncontroversial, so far as it goes. That is, the New Party, and not someone else, has the right to select the New Party's "standard bearer." It does not follow, though, that a party is absolutely entitled to have its nominee appear on the ballot as that party's candidate. A particular candidate might be ineligible for office, unwilling to serve, or, as here, another party's candidate. That a particular individual may not appear on the ballot as a particular party's candidate does not severely burden that party's association rights. . . .

[Minnesota's ban on fusion does not involve] regulation of political parties' internal affairs and core associational activities. . . . The ban, which applies to major and minor parties alike, simply precludes one party's candidate from appearing on the ballot, as that party's candidate, if already nominated by another party. Respondent is free to try to convince Representative Dawkins to be the New Party's, not the DFL's, candidate. Whether the Party still wants to endorse a candidate who, because of the fusion ban, will not appear on the ballot as the Party's candidate, is up to the Party.

The Court of Appeals . . . held that Minnesota's laws "keep the New Party from developing consensual political alliances and thus broadening the base of public participation in and support for its activities." The burden on the Party was, the court held, severe because "history shows that minor parties have played a significant role in the electoral system where multiple party nomination is legal, but have no meaningful influence where multiple party nomination is banned." In the view of the Court of Appeals, Minnesota's fusion ban forces members of the new party to make a "no-win choice" between voting for "candidates with no realistic chance of winning, defecting from their party and voting for a major party candidate who does, or declining to vote at all."

But Minnesota has not directly precluded minor political parties from developing and organizing. Nor has Minnesota excluded a particular group of citizens, or a political party, from participation in the election process. The New Party remains free to endorse whom it likes, to ally itself with others, to nominate candidates for office, and to spread its message to all who will listen.

The Court of Appeals emphasized its belief that, without fusion-based alliances, minor parties cannot thrive. This is a predictive judgment which is by no means self-evident.[9] But, more importantly, the supposed benefits

---

9. Between the First and Second World Wars, for example, various radical, agrarian and labor-oriented parties thrived, without fusion, in the Midwest. One of these parties, Minnesota's Farmer–Labor Party, displaced the Democratic Party as the Republicans' primary opponent in Minnesota during the 1930's. As one historian has noted: "The Minnesota Farmer–Labor Party elected its candidates to the governorship on four occasions, to the U.S. Senate in five elections, and to the U.S. House in twenty-five campaigns. . . . Never less than Minnesota's second strongest party, in 1936 Farmer–Laborites dominated state politics. . . .

The Farmer–Labor Party was a success despite its independence of America's two dominant national parties and despite the sometimes bold anticapitalist rhetoric of its platform." It appears that factionalism within the Farmer–Labor Party, the popular successes of New Deal programs and ideology, and the gradual movement of political power from the states to the national government contributed to the Party's decline. Eventually, a much-weakened Farmer–Labor Party merged with the Democrats, forming what is now Minnesota's Democratic–Farmer–Labor Party, in 1944.

of fusion to minor parties does not require that Minnesota permit it. Many features of our political system—e.g., single-member districts, "first past the post" elections, and the high costs of campaigning—make it difficult for third parties to succeed in American politics. But the Constitution does not require States to permit fusion any more than it requires them to move to proportional-representation elections or public financing of campaigns.

* * *

[Because the burden on the New Party's associational rights is not very severe,] the State's asserted regulatory interests need only be "sufficiently weighty to justify the limitation" imposed on the Party's rights.... Minnesota argues here that its fusion ban is justified by its interests in avoiding voter confusion, promoting candidate competition (by reserving limited ballot space for opposing candidates), preventing electoral distortions and ballot manipulations, and discouraging party splintering and "unrestrained factionalism."

States certainly have an interest in protecting the integrity, fairness, and efficiency of their ballots and election processes as means for electing public officials. Petitioners contend that a candidate or party could easily exploit fusion as a way of associating his or its name with popular slogans and catchphrases. For example, members of a major party could decide that a powerful way of "sending a message" via the ballot would be for various factions of that party to nominate the major party's candidate as the candidate for the newly-formed "No New Taxes," "Conserve Our Environment," and "Stop Crime Now" parties. In response, an opposing major party would likely instruct its factions to nominate that party's candidate as the "Fiscal Responsibility," "Healthy Planet," and "Safe Streets" parties' candidate.

Whether or not the putative "fusion" candidates' names appeared on one or four ballot lines, such maneuvering would undermine the ballot's purpose by transforming it from a means of choosing candidates to a billboard for political advertising. The New Party responds to this concern, ironically enough, by insisting that the State could avoid such manipulation by adopting more demanding ballot-access standards rather than prohibiting multiple-party nomination. However, as we stated above, because the burdens the fusion ban imposes on the Party's associational rights are not severe, the State need not narrowly tailor the means it chooses to promote ballot integrity.

* * *

States also have a strong interest in the stability of their political systems. This interest does not permit a State to completely insulate the two-party system from minor parties' or independent candidates' competition and influence.... That said, the States' interest permits them to enact reasonable election regulations that may, in practice, favor the traditional two-party system, and that temper the destabilizing effects of party-splintering and excessive factionalism. The Constitution permits the Minnesota Legislature to decide that political stability is best served through a healthy two-party system. And while an interest in securing the perceived benefits of a stable two-party system will not justify unreasonably exclusionary restrictions, States need not remove all of the many hurdles third parties face in the American political arena today.

* * *

■ JUSTICE STEVENS, with whom JUSTICE GINSBURG joins, and with whom JUSTICE SOUTER joins as to Par[t] I . . . , dissenting.

* * *

I

The members of a recognized political party unquestionably have a constitutional right to select their nominees for public office and to communicate the identity of their nominees to the voting public. Both the right to choose and the right to advise voters of that choice are entitled to the highest respect.

The Minnesota statutes place a significant burden on both of those rights. . . . The fact that the Party may nominate its second choice surely does not diminish the significance of a restriction that denies it the right to have the name of its first choice appear on the ballot.

* * *

[A] party's choice of a candidate is the most effective way in which that party can communicate to the voters what the party represents and, thereby, attract voter interest and support.[1]

The State next argues that—instead of nominating a second-choice candidate—the Party could remove itself from the ballot altogether, and publicly endorse the candidate of another party. But the right to be on the election ballot is precisely what separates a political party from any other interest group.

---

1. The burden on the Party's right to nominate its first-choice candidates, by limiting the Party's ability to convey through its nominee what the Party represents, risks impinging on another core element of any political party's associational rights—the right to "broaden the base of public participation in and support for its activities." . . . A fusion ban burdens the right of a minor party to broaden its base of support because of the political reality that the dominance of the major party or independent candidate a "wasted" vote. When minor parties can nominate a candidate also nominated by a major party, they are able to present their members with an opportunity to cast a vote for a candidate who will actually be elected. Although this aspect of a party's effort to broaden support is distinct from the ability to nominate the candidate who best represents the party's views, it is important to note that the party's right to broaden the base of its support is burdened in both ways by the fusion ban.

The majority rejects as unimportant the limits that the fusion ban may impose on the Party's ability to express its political views, relying on our decision in *Burdick v. Takushi*, 504 U. S. 428, 445 (1992), in which we noted that "the purpose of casting, counting, and recording votes is to elect public officials, not to serve as a general forum for political expression." But in *Burdick* we concluded simply that an individual voter's interest in expressing his disapproval of the single candidate running for office in a particular election did not require the State to finance and provide a mechanism for tabulating write-in votes. Our conclusion that the ballot is not principally a forum for the individual expression of political sentiment through the casting of a vote does not justify the conclusion that the ballot serves no expressive purpose for the parties who place candidates on the ballot.

* * *

III

* * *

[I would also reject the majority's argument that the ban on fusion protects the state's interest in a healthy two-party system.] In most States, perhaps in all, there are two and only two major political parties. It is not surprising, therefore, that most States have enacted election laws that impose burdens on the development and growth of third parties. The law at issue in this case is undeniably such a law. The fact that the law was both intended to disadvantage minor parties and has had that effect is a matter that should weigh against, rather than in favor of, its constitutionality.

Our jurisprudence in this area reflects a certain tension: on the one hand, we have been clear that political stability is an important state interest and that incidental burdens on the formation of minor parties are reasonable to protect that interest; on the other, we have struck down state elections laws specifically because they give "the two old, established parties a decided advantage over any new parties struggling for existence." Between these boundaries, we have acknowledged that there is "no litmus-paper test for separating those restrictions that are valid from those that are invidious ... The rule is not self-executing and is no substitute for the hard judgments that must be made."

Nothing in the Constitution prohibits the States from maintaining single-member districts with winner-take-all voting arrangements. And these elements of an election system do make it significantly more difficult for third parties to thrive. But these laws are different in two respects from the fusion bans at issue here. First, the method by which they hamper third-party development is not one that impinges on the associational rights of those third parties; minor parties remain free to nominate candidates of their choice, and to rally support for those candidates. The small parties' relatively limited likelihood of ultimate success on election day does not deprive them of the right to try. Second, the establishment of single-member districts correlates directly with the States' interests in political stability. Systems of proportional representation, for example, may tend toward factionalism and fragile coalitions that diminish legislative effectiveness. In the context of fusion candidacies, the risks to political stability are extremely attenuated.[8] Of course, the reason minor parties so ardently support fusion politics is because it allows the parties to build up a greater base of support, as potential minor party members realize that a vote for the smaller party candidate is not necessarily a "wasted" vote. Eventually, a minor party might gather sufficient strength that—were its members so inclined—it could successfully run a candidate not endorsed by any major party, and legislative coalition-building will be made more difficult by the presence of third party legislators. But the risks to political stability in that scenario are speculative at best. . . . The fusion candidacy does not threaten to divide the legislature and create significant risks of factionalism, which is the principal risk proponents of the two-party system point to.

* * *

■ JUSTICE SOUTER, dissenting.

* * *

[I would leave open the question whether, in a different case, "preservation of the two-party system" would provide a permissible rationale.] There is considerable consensus that party loyalty among American voters has declined significantly in the past four decades, and that the overall influence of the parties in the political process has decreased considerably. In the wake of such studies, it may not be unreasonable to infer that the two-party system is in some jeopardy.

Surely the majority is right that States "have a strong interest in the stability of their political systems," that is, in preserving a political system capable of governing effectively. If it could be shown that the disappearance of the two-party system would undermine that interest, and that permitting fusion candidacies poses a substantial threat to the two-party scheme, there might well be a sufficient predicate for recognizing the constitutionality of the state action presented by this case. . . .

NOTES AND QUESTIONS

1. For discussions of fusion, see, e.g., Peter H. Argersinger, *"A Place on the Ballot": Fusion Politics and Antifusion Laws*, 85 Am. Hist. Rev. 287 (1980); William R. Kirschner, Note, *Fusion and the Associational Rights of*

---

8. Even in a system that allows fusion, a candidate for election must assemble majority support, so the State's concern cannot logically be about risks to political stability in the particular election in which the fusion candidate is running.

Minor Political Parties, 95 Colum. L. Rev. 683 (1995); Note, *Fusion Candidacies, Disaggregation, and Freedom of Association*, 109 Harv. L. Rev. 1302 (1996).

2. Does *Timmons* go even further than *Munro* in lifting any empirical burden from the state? The Chief Justice offers a set of quite fanciful hypotheticals. And there may be good reasons to suppose that the major parties will not fracture themselves into several ballot lines. In some states, for example, the party that received the highest number of votes in the last election gets the first spot on the ballot the next time around, with concomitant advantages. *See* Note, *California Ballot Position Statutes: An Unconstitutional Advantage to Incumbents*, 45 S. Cal. L. Rev. 365 (1972); Mark E. Dreyer, Comment, *Constitutional Problems with Statutes Regulating Ballot Position*, 23 Tulsa L. J. 123 (1987).

3. *Timmons* goes decidedly beyond earlier cases in its endorsement of the two-party system. Note how it links ballot access with other structural aspects of the electoral system, most notably single-member districts.

We shall return to questions of districting in later chapters, but it is worth at least understanding the dimensions of the Court's point. Single-member districts create a series of geographically based, winner-take-all contests. Only blocs of voters who constitute a plurality within a given constituency can elect the candidate they prefer. Thus, a voter who wishes to affect the outcome must vote for a candidate who has a realistic possibility of finishing first within her electoral district. This candidate is likely to be a centrist candidate (with the center being defined relative to the district's electorate). Voters closer to the ideological margins than to the center will not be able to join with like-minded voters in other constituencies.

The standard political science accounts suggest a strong propensity toward a two-party system in jurisdictions that use single-member districting systems. A simple analogy may clarify the point. Consider a town with a single main street one mile long whose residents are equally dispersed along this one-mile stretch. Assuming full choice, the first merchant who comes to town will open a store at the mid-point of the street; such a location is most efficient in terms of providing service to the largest number of customers. What would happen if there were two merchants, however? Ideally, each would open a store one-quarter of a mile from the town's borders; that too would maximize efficiency in providing customer access to shopping. Unfortunately, if one of the merchants were to choose such a location, the other would set up somewhere between the first merchant and the center of town. From that location, the second merchant could compete for some of the first merchant's market, while holding a preferred position for more than half the town. Because of this strategic dilemma, the resolution seen in markets around the world is for both merchants to establish stores in the center of town, usually across the street from each other. This classic illustration of markets may be found in

Harold Hotelling, *Stability in Competition,* 39 Econ. Journal 41 (1929), and Arthur Smithies, *Optimum Location in Spatial Competition,* 49 J. Pol. Con. 423. (1941)

The American single-member electoral district, also referred to as a "first-past-the-post" system, presents the same pressures toward centrism found in geographic markets. Imagine instead of a town whose population is dispersed along a one-mile stretch, an electorate comparably dispersed from left to right. If there were two political parties, the population's views would be most "efficiently" represented by each party's posturing itself one-quarter of the way in from an extreme pole. But each party faces an irresistible temptation to move towards the middle. If one party located itself one-quarter of the way in from the left, the other party would lay claim to the greatest number of potential voters by positioning itself only slightly to the right of the first party. The first party would be at a tremendous competitive disadvantage unless it were to move more to the center, with one perceived as the party of the center-left, and the other the party of the center-right. The analogy of political markets to the town merchants is first set out in Anthony Downs, An Economic Theory of Democracy 115–17 (1957).

Now consider the plight of a would-be third party. Imagine this party as a potential party of the right whose ideology would place it to the right of the center-right party. The new party would compete with the center-right party for those voters closest to the right pole. But such a strategy would rarely yield electoral success. The new party of the right and the center-right party would divide voters on the right part of the spectrum, leaving the center-left party in an ideal position. So long as elections were by plurality vote, the center-left party would prevail against the divided partisans of the right. As against charges of being "spoilers" "or 'guaranteeing' " the success of the center-left, the party of the right would be under tremendous pressure to return to the fold of the party of the center-right and agitate from within. Hence the pressure is not only toward centrist parties, but toward two and only two parties.

This then highlights the issues at stake in *Timmons.* As a general rule, there are two strategies available to third parties in a system structurally oriented toward two parties. The first is to displace one of the established parties, an event not successfully accomplished in American history. *See* James L. Sundquist, Dynamics of the Party System (1983). The second is to become a sufficiently credible political force so as to shift the balance of power within one of the established parties. As a historical matter, this has been the classic third party strategy in the U.S. for groups ranging from populists at the turn of the century to the Christian Coalition today. Because of the high cost of organizing a viable electoral vehicle in the face of first-past-the-post elections, ideological third party movements have had their greatest success in creating a sufficient base to influence the major political parties.

Should the Court in *Timmons* have distinguished electoral structures that have the incidental effect of entrenching the two-party system, such as single-member districts, from rules that have as their primary purpose restrictions on third parties, such as antifusion laws? Should the purpose of the restriction be a basis for judging the constitutionality of election laws?

The Supreme Court has been noticeably hostile to claims that districting constitutes impermissible entrenchment of the current two major parties. In *Gaffney v. Cummings*, 412 U.S. 735 (1973), for example, the Court confronted a challenge to Connecticut's "bipartisan gerrymander." In redrawing the state's legislative districts after the 1970 census, the Apportionment Board followed a policy of "political fairness" for the two major political parties and drew "what was thought to be a proportionate number of Republican and Democratic legislative seats." The Court rejected the claim that the bipartisan gerrymander unfairly diluted the voting strength of independent voters:

> [J]udicial interest should be at its lowest ebb when a State purports fairly to allocate political power to the parties in accordance with their voting strength and, within quite tolerable limits, succeeds in doing so. There is no doubt that there may be other reapportionment plans for Connecticut that would have different political consequences and that would also be constitutional.... [But we have no] constitutional warrant to invalidate a state plan, otherwise within tolerable population limits, because it undertakes, not to minimize or eliminate the political strength of any group or party, but to recognize it and, through districting, provide a rough sort of proportional representation in the legislative halls of the State.

Note that *Gaffney* presupposes that the decision to provide rough proportional representation to the two major parties does not minimize or cancel out the ability of other groups to elect their preferred candidates.

To what extent is Justice Stevens successful in distinguishing single-member districts from anti-fusion laws?

4. How much does *Timmons*—and the Court's other recent democracy cases, such as *Jones*, *supra*—reflect a consistent pattern of division among Justices, with that pattern reflecting deeper cultural attitudes towards democracy that differ among judges—and maybe among ourselves? For the view that such differences explain much of the rhetoric and imagery of *Timmons*, as well as the decision itself, consider the following:

> Whether democracy requires order, stability, and channeled, constrained forms of engagement, or whether it requires and even celebrates relatively wide-open competition that may appear tumultuous, partisan, or worse, has long been a struggle in democratic thought and practice (indeed, historically it was one of the defining set of oppositions in arguments about the desirability of democracy itself). Of course, the answer is that democracy requires a mix of both order (law,

structure, and constraint) and openness (politics, fluidity, and receptivity to novel forms). But people, including judges and political actors, regularly seem to group themselves into characteristic and recurring patterns of response to new challenges that arise. These patterned responses suggest that it is something beyond law, or facts, or narrow partisan politics in particular cases, that determine outcomes; it is, perhaps, cultural assumptions and historical interpretations, conscious or not, that inform or even determine these judgments. Whatever the analytical truth about the necessity of both order and openness to democracy, the cultural question is, from which direction do particular actors, such as judges, tend to perceive the greatest threat. Is the democratic order fragile and potentially destabilized easily? Or is the democratic order threatened by undue rigidity, in need of more robust competition and challenge? Does democratic politics contain within itself sufficient resources to be self-correcting? Or must legal institutions carefully oversee political processes to ensure their continued vitality?

Richard H. Pildes, *Democracy and Disorder*, 68 U. Chi. L. Rev. 695, 714 (2001).

3. THE INTERACTION OF ACCESS TO THE ELECTORAL ARENA AND THE PERPETUATION OF THE TWO PARTY SYSTEM

Third parties can suffer from exclusion not simply by being denied formal access to the ballot. Consider the effects of exclusion from the public arena in which candidates are presented to the electorate:

Arkansas Educational Television Commission v. Forbes
523 U.S. 666 (1998).

■ JUSTICE KENNEDY delivered the opinion of the Court.

* * *

I

Petitioner, the Arkansas Educational Television Commission (AETC), is an Arkansas state agency owning and operating a network of five noncommercial television stations (Arkansas Educational Television Network or AETN). . . .

In the spring of 1992, AETC staff began planning a series of debates between candidates for federal office in the November 1992 elections. AETC decided to televise a total of five debates, scheduling one for the Senate election and one for each of the four congressional elections in Arkansas. Working in close consultation with Bill Simmons, Arkansas Bureau Chief for the Associated Press, AETC staff developed a debate format allowing about 53 minutes during each 1–hour debate for questions to and answers by the candidates. Given the time constraint, the staff and Simmons "decided to limit participation in the debates to the major party candidates or any other candidate who had strong popular support."

On June 17, 1992, AETC invited the Republican and Democratic candidates for Arkansas' Third Congressional District to participate in the AETC debate for that seat. Two months later, after obtaining the 2,000 signatures required by Arkansas law, *see* Ark. Code Ann. § 7–7–103(c)(1) (1993), respondent Ralph Forbes was certified as an independent candidate qualified to appear on the ballot for the seat. Forbes was a perennial candidate who had sought, without success, a number of elected offices in Arkansas. On August 24, 1992, he wrote to AETC requesting permission to participate in the debate for his district, scheduled for October 22, 1992. On September 4, AETC Executive Director Susan Howarth denied Forbes' request, explaining that AETC had "made a bona fide journalistic judgement that our viewers would be best served by limiting the debate" to the candidates already invited.

On October 19, 1992, Forbes filed suit against AETC, seeking injunctive and declaratory relief as well as damages. Forbes claimed he was entitled to participate in the debate under both the First Amendment and 47 U.S.C. § 315, which affords political candidates a limited right of access to television air time. Forbes requested a preliminary injunction mandating his inclusion in the debate. The District Court denied the request, as did the United States Court of Appeals for the Eighth Circuit. The District Court later dismissed Forbes' action for failure to state a claim.

Sitting en banc, the Court of Appeals affirmed the dismissal of Forbes' statutory claim, holding that he had failed to exhaust his administrative remedies. The court reversed, however, the dismissal of Forbes' First Amendment claim. Observing that AETC is a state actor, the court held Forbes had "a qualified right of access created by AETN's sponsorship of a debate, and that AETN must have [had] a legitimate reason to exclude him strong enough to survive First Amendment scrutiny."

On remand, the District Court found as a matter of law that the debate was a nonpublic forum, and the issue became whether Forbes' views were the reason for his exclusion. . . . The District Court entered judgment for AETC. . . .

The Court of Appeals again reversed. The court acknowledged that AETC's decision to exclude Forbes "was made in good faith" and was "exactly the kind of journalistic judgment routinely made by newspeople." The court asserted, nevertheless, that AETC had "opened its facilities to a particular group—candidates running for the Third District Congressional seat." AETC's action, the court held, made the debate a public forum, to which all candidates "legally qualified to appear on the ballot" had a presumptive right of access. Applying strict scrutiny, the court determined that AETC's assessment of Forbes' "political viability" was neither a "compelling nor [a] narrowly tailored" reason for excluding him from the debate....

We now reverse.

II

* * *

At the outset ... it is instructive to ask whether public forum principles apply to the case at all.

Having first arisen in the context of streets and parks, the public forum doctrine should not be extended in a mechanical way to the very different context of public television broadcasting. In the case of streets and parks, the open access and viewpoint neutrality commanded by the doctrine is "compatible with the intended purpose of the property." In the case of television broadcasting, however, broad rights of access for outside speakers would be antithetical, as a general rule, to the discretion that stations and their editorial staff must exercise to fulfill their journalistic purpose and statutory obligations.

Congress has rejected the argument that "broadcast facilities should be open on a nonselective basis to all persons wishing to talk about public issues." ... Public and private broadcasters alike are not only permitted, but indeed required, to exercise substantial editorial discretion in the selection and presentation of their programming....

Claims of access under our public forum precedents could obstruct the legitimate purposes of television broadcasters. Were the doctrine given sweeping application in this context, courts "would be required to oversee far more of the day-to-day operations of broadcasters' conduct, deciding such questions as whether a particular individual or group has had sufficient opportunity to present its viewpoint and whether a particular viewpoint has already been sufficiently aired." "The result would be a further erosion of the journalistic discretion of broadcasters," transferring "control over the treatment of public issues from the licensees who are accountable for broadcast performance to private individuals" who bring suit under our forum precedents. In effect, we would "exchange 'public trustee' broadcasting, with all its limitations, for a system of self-appointed editorial commentators."

[...] This is not to say the First Amendment would bar the legislative imposition of neutral rules for access to public broadcasting. Instead, we say that, in most cases, the First Amendment of its own force does not compel public broadcasters to allow third parties access to their programming.

Although public broadcasting as a general matter does not lend itself to scrutiny under the forum doctrine, candidate debates present the narrow exception to the rule. For two reasons, a candidate debate like the one at issue here is different from other programming. First, unlike AETC's other broadcasts, the debate was by design a forum for political speech by the candidates. Consistent with the long tradition of candidate debates, the implicit representation of the broadcaster was that the views expressed were those of the candidates, not its own. The very purpose of the debate was to allow the candidates to express their views with minimal intrusion by the broadcaster. In this respect the debate differed even from a political talk show, whose host can express partisan views and then limit the discussion to those ideas.

Second, in our tradition, candidate debates are of exceptional significance in the electoral process. "It is of particular importance that candidates have the opportunity to make their views known so that the electorate may intelligently evaluate the candidates' personal qualities and their positions on vital public issues before choosing among them on election day." Deliberation on the positions and qualifications of candidates is integral to our system of government, and electoral speech may have its most profound and widespread impact when it is disseminated through televised debates. A majority of the population cites television as its primary source of election information, and debates are regarded as the "only occasion during a campaign when the attention of a large portion of the American public is focused on the election, as well as the only campaign information format which potentially offers sufficient time to explore issues and policies in depth in a neutral forum."

The special characteristics of candidate debates support the conclusion that the AETC debate was a forum of some type. The question of what type must be answered by reference to our public forum precedents, to which we now turn.

III

Forbes argues, and the Court of Appeals held, that the debate was a public forum to which he had a First Amendment right of access. Under our precedents, however, the debate was a nonpublic forum, from which AETC could exclude Forbes in the reasonable, viewpoint-neutral exercise of its journalistic discretion.

A

[. . .] "The Court [has] identified three types of fora: the traditional public forum, the public forum created by government designation, and the nonpublic forum." Traditional public fora are defined by the objective characteristics of the property, such as whether, "by long tradition or by government fiat," the property has been "devoted to assembly and debate." The government can exclude a speaker from a traditional public forum "only when the exclusion is necessary to serve a compelling state interest and the exclusion is narrowly drawn to achieve that interest."

Designated public fora, in contrast, are created by purposeful governmental action. "The government does not create a [designated] public forum by inaction or by permitting limited discourse, but only by intentionally opening a nontraditional public forum for public discourse." . . . "[T]he Court has looked to the policy and practice of the government to ascertain whether it intended to designate a place not traditionally open to assembly and debate as a public forum." If the government excludes a speaker who falls within the class to which a designated public forum is made generally available, its action is subject to strict scrutiny.

Other government properties are either nonpublic fora or not fora at all. The government can restrict access to a nonpublic forum "as long as the restrictions are reasonable and [are] not an effort to suppress expression merely because public officials oppose the speaker's view." . . .

B

The parties agree the AETC debate was not a traditional public forum . . . The issue, then, is whether the debate was a designated public forum or a nonpublic forum.

Under our precedents, the AETC debate was not a designated public forum. To create a forum of this type, the government must intend to make the property "generally available," to a class of speakers. A designated public forum is not created when the government allows selective access for individual speakers rather than general access for a class of speakers. . . .

[Our cases] illustrate the distinction between "general access," which indicates the property is a designated public forum, and "selective access," which indicates the property is a nonpublic forum. On one hand, the government creates a designated public forum when it makes its property generally available to a certain class of speakers. On the other hand, the government does not create a designated public forum when it does no more than reserve eligibility for access to the forum to a particular class of speakers, whose members must then, as individuals, "obtain permission."

[. . .] That this distinction turns on governmental intent does not render it unprotective of speech. Rather, it reflects the reality that, with the exception of traditional public fora, the government retains the choice of whether to designate its property as a forum for specified classes of speakers.

Here, the debate did not have an open-microphone format. . . . AETC reserved eligibility for participation in the debate to candidates for the Third Congressional District seat (as opposed to some other seat). . . . AETC made candidate-by-candidate determinations as to which of the eligible candidates would participate in the debate. "Such selective access, unsupported by evidence of a purposeful designation for public use, does not create a public forum." Thus the debate was a nonpublic forum.

In addition to being a misapplication of our precedents, the Court of Appeals' holding would result in less speech, not more. In ruling that the debate was a public forum open to all ballot-qualified candidates, the Court of Appeals would place a severe burden upon public broadcasters who air candidates' views. . . . On logistical grounds alone, a public television editor might, with reason, decide that the inclusion of all ballot-qualified candidates would "actually undermine the educational value and quality of debates."

Were it faced with the prospect of cacophony, on the one hand, and First Amendment liability, on the other, a public television broadcaster might choose not to air candidates' views at all. A broadcaster might decide " 'the safe course is to avoid controversy,' . . . and by so doing diminish the free flow of information and ideas." In this circumstance, a "government-enforced right of access inescapably 'dampens the vigor and limits the variety of public debate.' "

* * *

C

The debate's status as a nonpublic forum, however, did not give AETC unfettered power to exclude any candidate it wished. . . . To be consistent with the First Amendment, the exclusion of a speaker from a nonpublic forum must not be based on the speaker's viewpoint and must otherwise be reasonable in light of the purpose of the property.

In this case, the jury found Forbes' exclusion was not based on "objections or opposition to his views." The record provides ample support for this finding, demonstrating as well that AETC's decision to exclude him was reasonable. . . . It is, in short, beyond dispute that Forbes was excluded not because of his viewpoint but because he had generated no appreciable public interest.

There is no substance to Forbes' suggestion that he was excluded because his views were unpopular or out of the mainstream. His own objective lack of support, not his platform, was the criterion. Indeed, the very premise of Forbes' contention is mistaken. A candidate with unconventional views might well enjoy broad support by virtue of a compelling personality or an exemplary campaign organization. By the same token, a candidate with a traditional platform might enjoy little support due to an inept campaign or any number of other reasons.

The broadcaster's decision to exclude Forbes was a reasonable, viewpoint-neutral exercise of journalistic discretion consistent with the First Amendment. The judgment of the Court of Appeals is

Reversed.

■ JUSTICE STEVENS, with whom JUSTICE SOUTER and JUSTICE GINSBURG join, dissenting.

The judgment of the Court of Appeals should ... be affirmed. The official action that led to the exclusion of respondent Forbes from a debate with the two major-party candidates for election to one of Arkansas' four seats in Congress does not adhere to well-settled constitutional principles. The ad hoc decision of the staff of the Arkansas Educational Television Commission (AETC) raises precisely the concerns addressed by "the many decisions of this Court over the last 30 years, holding that a law subjecting the exercise of First Amendment freedoms to the prior restraint of a license, without narrow, objective, and definite standards to guide the licensing authority, is unconstitutional."

* * *

I

Two months before Forbes was officially certified as an independent candidate qualified to appear on the ballot under Arkansas law, the AETC staff had already concluded that he "should not be invited" to participate in the televised debates because he was "not a serious candidate as determined by the voters of Arkansas." He had, however, been a serious contender for the Republican nomination for Lieutenant Governor in 1986 and again in 1990. Although he was defeated in a run-off election, in the three-way primary race conducted in 1990—just two years before the AETC staff decision—he had received 46.88% of the statewide vote and had carried 15 of the 16 counties within the Third Congressional District by absolute majorities. Nevertheless, the staff concluded that Forbes did not have "strong popular support."

Given the fact that the Republican winner in the Third Congressional District race in 1992 received only 50.22% of the vote and the Democrat received 47.20%, it would have been necessary for Forbes, who had made a strong showing in recent Republican primaries, to divert only a handful of votes from the Republican candidate to cause his defeat. Thus, even though the AETC staff may have correctly concluded that Forbes was "not a serious candidate," their decision to exclude him from the debate may have determined the outcome of the election in the Third District ... The apparent flexibility of AETC's purported standard suggests the extent to which the staff had nearly limitless discretion to exclude Forbes from the debate based on ad hoc justifications. Thus, the Court of Appeals correctly concluded that the staff's appraisal of "political viability" was "so subjective, so arguable, so susceptible of variation in individual opinion, as to provide no secure basis for the exercise of governmental power consistent with the First Amendment."

AETC is a state agency whose actions "are fairly attributable to the State and subject to the Fourteenth Amendment, unlike the actions of privately owned broadcast licensees." ... The Court implicitly acknowledges these facts by subjecting the decision to exclude Forbes to constitutional analysis. Yet the Court seriously underestimates the importance of the difference between private and public ownership of broadcast facilities, despite the fact that Congress and this Court have repeatedly recognized that difference.

* * *

... Because AETC is owned by the State, deference to its interest in making ad hoc decisions about the political content of its programs necessarily increases the risk of government censorship and propaganda in a way that protection of privately owned broadcasters does not.

III

The Court recognizes that the debates sponsored by AETC were "by design a forum for political speech by the candidates." The Court also acknowledges the central importance of candidate debates in the electoral process. Thus, there is no need to review our cases expounding on the public forum doctrine to conclude that the First Amendment will not tolerate a state agency's arbitrary exclusion from a debate forum based, for example, on an expectation that the speaker might be critical of the Governor, or might hold unpopular views about abortion or the death penalty. Indeed, the Court so holds today.

It seems equally clear, however, that the First Amendment will not tolerate arbitrary definitions of the scope of the forum. We have recognized that "once it has opened a limited forum, ... the State must respect the lawful boundaries it has itself set." It follows, of course, that a State's failure to set any meaningful boundaries at all cannot insulate the State's action from First Amendment challenge. The dispositive issue in this case, then, is not whether AETC created a designated public forum or a nonpublic forum, as the Court concludes, but whether AETC defined the contours of the debate forum with sufficient specificity to justify the exclusion of a ballot-qualified candidate.

AETC asks that we reject Forbes' constitutional claim on the basis of entirely subjective, ad hoc judgments about the dimensions of its forum. The First Amendment demands more, however, when a state government effectively wields the power to eliminate a political candidate from all consideration by the voters. All stations must act as editors, and when state-owned stations participate in the broadcasting arena, their editorial decisions may impact the constitutional interests of individual speakers. A state-owned broadcaster need not plan, sponsor, and conduct political debates, however. When it chooses to do so, the First Amendment imposes important limitations on its control over access to the debate forum.

* * *

The televised debate forum at issue in this case may not squarely fit within our public forum analysis, but its importance cannot be denied. Given the special character of political speech, particularly during campaigns for elected office, the debate forum implicates constitutional concerns of the highest order, as the majority acknowledges. Indeed, the planning and management of political debates by state-owned broadcasters raise serious constitutional concerns that are seldom replicated when state-owned television networks engage in other types of programming. We have recognized that "speech concerning public affairs is . . . the essence of self-government." The First Amendment therefore "has its fullest and most urgent application precisely to the conduct of campaigns for political office." Surely the Constitution demands at least as much from the Government when it takes action that necessarily impacts democratic elections as when local officials issue parade permits.

The reasons that support the need for narrow, objective, and definite standards to guide licensing decisions apply directly to the wholly subjective access decisions made by the staff of AETC. The importance of avoiding arbitrary or viewpoint-based exclusions from political debates militates strongly in favor of requiring the controlling state agency to use (and adhere to) pre-established, objective criteria to determine who among qualified candidates may participate. When the demand for speaking facilities exceeds supply, the State must "ration or allocate the scarce resources on some acceptable neutral principle." A constitutional duty to use objective standards—*i.e.,* "neutral principles"—for determining whether and when to adjust a debate format would impose only a modest requirement that would fall far short of a duty to grant every multiple-party request. Such standards would also have the benefit of providing the public with some assurance that state-owned broadcasters cannot select debate participants on arbitrary grounds.

Like the Court, I do not endorse the view of the Court of Appeals that all candidates who qualify for a position on the ballot are necessarily entitled to access to any state-sponsored debate. I am convinced, however, that the constitutional imperatives that motivated our decisions in [other] cases . . . command that access to political debates planned and managed by state-owned entities be governed by pre-established, objective criteria. Requiring government employees to set out objective criteria by which they choose which candidates will benefit from the significant media exposure that results from state-sponsored political debates would alleviate some of the risk inherent in allowing government agencies—rather than private entities—to stage candidate debates.

Accordingly, I would affirm the judgment of the Court of Appeals.

NOTES AND QUESTIONS

1. Consider the risk in circularity of reasoning about who is a legitimate candidate. For example, it may be argued that the single most important factor in gaining legitimacy for a candidate, particularly a third-party candidate, is the ability to share the same stage with established candidates. Perhaps the clearest example of what that can mean to a third-party candidate is the gubernatorial election of Jesse Ventura in 1998 in Minnesota. By his own admission, Governor Ventura was not considered a serious candidate until "there were the three-way debates. Right at that point in the first debate, my numbers started rising very quickly . . . and they never changed." *ABC Good Morning America,* November 4, 1998. When asked about the possibility of having a minimum threshold of 15 percent in polls as a precondition for participating in the debates, Ventura opined, "I disagree with that 15 percent mark, because at the point in the primary here in Minnesota, which is six to seven weeks before the general election, I was only polling 10 percent. So if that criteria had been used here in Minnesota, I wouldn't be the governor today because I won the election because of debates and I don't think that that's a fair number to use. You should use the same number that you use to determine whether you have major party status." *Face The Nation*, April 2, 2000. How would Governor Ventura have fared under *Forbes* had he challenged exclusion from the Minnesota debates under a 15 percent threshold requirement for participation?

Moreover, unlike most other states, Minnesota's election laws also encouraged third-party candidacies like Ventura's. First, Minnesota is one of six states that permit same-day voter registration (post-election analyses indicate that Ventura would not have won without the votes of same-day registrants). Second, Minnesota has broad public financing of elections, including for third-party candidates; Ventura received a state contribution of $330,000, which was crucial because he raised little private money. Third, Minnesota has liberal ballot access laws for third parties. *See* Richard H. Pildes, *A Theory of Political Competition,* 85 Va. L. Rev. 1605, 1617–18 (1999). As this commentary concludes: "Had the more common and more anticompetitive rules and practices in other states been in place—regarding registration, financing, ballot access, and participation in candidate debates—Minnesota would likely be as rigidly a two-party state as most others. Election laws, combined with the right circumstances, can indeed matter." *Id.* at 1618.

2. What are the possible constitutional implications of *Forbes* for other areas of electoral regulation, such as campaign finance? Notice that *Forbes* holds that distinct constitutional rules apply to candidate-debates on public television because debates play a special role in the democratic process. What other aspects of electoral structures might be thought to play a similarly special role, thus justifying similar distinct constitutional treatment of regulation that would otherwise violate the Constitution were that regulation applied outside the electoral domain?

Notice the legal structure of the *Forbes* opinion: the Court first held that state-owned television programming was not subject to any of the First Amendment doctrines that would otherwise apply to what are known as public forums or even designated or limited public forums. Thus, the

Court first held that state-owned television was akin to private journalism and immune from First Amendment constraints that would apply to state action, particularly those prohibiting viewpoint discrimination. But then, the Court went on to hold that because one specific kind of public-television programming—candidate debates—played a special role in the democratic process, this special role required candidate debates to be treated as a constitutional exception to the principle that state television was akin to private journalism. As a result, the Court held that state-sponsored candidate debates—alone among state-television programming—*did* indeed have to meet constitutional requirements of viewpoint neutrality.

If special constitutional rules are to apply to state-sponsored candidate debates because of the "special role" such debates play in the electoral domain, might *Forbes* suggest that other regulations of electoral politics can be similarly excepted from the First Amendment doctrines that would otherwise apply were those regulations to govern speech activity outside the domain of elections? Perhaps the central issue in the constitutional assessment of campaign-finance regulation, for example, is whether the First Amendment should recognize a distinction between the "general domain of public discourse" and what we might call "the electoral domain." Only if these two domains can be legally distinguished from each other is it possible to envision various kinds of proposed reforms of electoral processes. In assessing whether *Forbes* does support such a distinction, consider the following:

> [After *Forbes*], the question is whether regulation should be permissible to remedy various perceived pathologies of current electoral discourse, *even if* that same degree of government intervention would be impermissible to remedy the parallel pathologies of non-electoral discourse in roughly comparable situations. Even more specifically, the question is whether such regulation ought to be permissible against the perceived distortions resulting from the undue influence of wealth, even if doing so would leave an imbalance in other sources of political influence. Accepting that position would require accepting the idea that elections can be demarcated, for First Amendment purposes, from the general domain of public discourse. This is both a normative question in First Amendment theory and a functional question of whether any regulatory approach can enforce this boundary with sufficient integrity.

Frederick Schauer and Richard H. Pildes, *Electoral Exceptionalism and the First Amendment,* 77 Tex. L. Rev. 1803, 1825 (1999). Would "excepting" elections from First Amendment rules that apply in other domains be a radical intrusion on First Amendment principles? This article argues not, for even with respect to core political speech, all regulations under current law are "already measured by domain-specific, institution-specific, sometimes media-specific, and generally context-specific First Amendment principles." *Id.,* at 1824. Thus, it is not "essentially" inconsistent with the First

Amendment to treat electoral politics as a distinct domain governed by its own First Amendment doctrines. For further elaboration, see Frederick Schauer, *Principles, Institutions, and the First Amendment*, 112 Harv. L. Rev. 84 (1998); for a partial critique of this view, see Robert Post, *Regulating Election Speech Under the First Amendment*, 77 Tex. L. Rev. 1837 (1999).

3. *Forbes* has generally been interpreted to allow state bodies to limit participation based on objective indicia of support, as opposed to a subjective assessment of the seriousness of the viewpoint being expressed. *See, e.g., Marcus v. Iowa Public Television*, 150 F.3d 924 (8th Cir. 1998) (approving the exclusion of third-party candidates since they were from minor parties and their exclusion was not based on their viewpoint); *Pryor v. Coats*, 203 F.3d 836 (10th Cir. 2000) (approving law school policy providing bulletin board space only to registered student groups who qualified for such registration by submitting applications containing at least 10 student members; the court followed *Forbes* in finding that an individual speaker could be excluded because of his "own objective lack of support" not because of his platform).

As we shall see, many areas of constitutional doctrine concerning the political process use the intent of state actors to demarcate what is constitutionally permissible from which is not, including such front-burner issues as campaign finance regulation and redistricting. Ferreting out the intent of official actors, particularly when the actor is a multi-headed entity such as a legislature, is oftentimes a daunting proposition. In trying to cabin the possibility of undetected unconstitutional motivation, courts may turn to rules of procedural regularity as a prophylactic screen against the presence of official bad faith. In *Forbes,* Justice Stevens identifies this as "a constitutional duty to use objective standards" that must be in place and publicly disclosed prior to the decision of which candidates to exclude. As Professor Owen Fiss explains,

> The appeal of the duty espoused by Stevens is manifold. For one thing, it would limit the ability of [television station] managers to use arbitrary standards, as the very construction of a list of objective criteria would produce an open discussion about the permissible grounds for exclusion. Every criterion would have to be openly defended and justified. Also, the duty to use objective, pre-announced standards would give the excluded candidate a better chance to prove that his or her exclusion was arbitrary or, under the rule of the majority [in *Forbes*], a form of viewpoint discrimination. As things currently stand, such proof can usually only be indirect; no manager is likely to create direct evidence that the candidate was excluded because of disagreement with his or her views. Once the standards for exclusion were promulgated, the manager would have to justify the exclusion in terms of one of the publicly announced criteria. The excluded candidate would then have a chance to show that this criterion had not been met,

which would create a powerful indication that viewpoint discrimination or some other arbitrary basis for exclusion had been used.

Owen M. Fiss, *The Censorship of Television*, 93 Nw. U. L. Rev. 1215, 1235 (1999).

4. The issue of how to choose "legitimate" candidates for purposes of candidate debates became a major one during the 2000 Presidential general election. Since 1988, the presidential debates have been overseen and structured by an entity called the Commission on Presidential Debates. This is established as an independent nonprofit group that is financially supported by corporate donations from major corporate entities. Although the Commission describes itself as "nonpartisan," its leadership is intentionally designed to have strong ties to the two major parties. One co-chair is a former Republican National Committee chairman; the other is a former Democratic National Committee chairman. In addition, various of the other members of the Commission's Board of Directors have been heavily involved in traditional partisan politics, including Caroline Kennedy, former Sen. John C. Danforth (R–Missouri), and Rep. Jennifer Dunn (R–Washington). *See* Karen Branch–Brioso, *"Nonpartisan" Board has Failed to Tame Debates*, St. Louis Post–Dispatch, Sept. 17, 2000, at A9.

The Commission adopted formal rules for candidate eligibility for debate participation in 2000 that imposed quite high thresholds for third-party candidates: (1) they had to qualify for the ballots in enough states to theoretically be able to win a majority of the Electoral College and (2) they had to receive 15% or more in 5 national polls prior to the debates. The leading third-party candidates, Ralph Nader of the Green Party and Patrick Buchanan of the Reform Party were not able to meet both criteria, and as a result, all three Presidential debates involved only the two major-party candidates. Nader and Buchanan met the first requirement but did not meet the second. A main point of contention raised by Nader and Buchanan was the role of televised debates in boosting Ross Perot's candidacy in 1992. After Perot's relative success in 1992, the Commission did not invite Perot to the debates in 1996. Criticizing the high threshold for the 2000 elections, some experts in presidential politics suggested that a 15% threshold was unfairly high and recommended a 5% hurdle to bring about a more competitive election; as Bruce Cain, a Berkeley political scientist put it, "we're homogenizing [the political dialogue]; keeping it safe, narrow" by limiting the debates to two candidates. *See* Eric Bailey, *Shut out of the Debates, Nader and Buchanan Have Plenty of Company,* L.A. Times, Sept. 30, 2000, at A13. Compare this view with Cain's endorsement of the Supreme Court's decision in *Jones, supra.* Are Cain's demands for more competitive elections and his endorsement of *Jones* consistent? For more information on the Commission and its policies, go to its website: Commission on Presidential Debates, *Candidate Selection Process,* (visited Oct. 16, 2000) at http://www.debates.org/pages/candsel.html.

5. After reviewing the way the Court treats novel democratic forms—third parties, fusion candidacies, blanket primaries, independent candidates—does the Court's jurisprudence seem overly concerned with the need for judicially-imposed order and stability to ensure the continuing vitality of American democracy? Is this concern realistic? Is there any fruitful comparison to be made between the economic sphere and the political sphere on these matters? For an argument that more competition, including some resulting instability, can well be tolerated by the relatively stable institutions of American democracy, see Richard H. Pildes, *Democracy and Disorder*, 68 U. Chi. L. Rev. 695, 717–18 (2001).

CHAPTER 5

MONEY AND POLITICS

One of the most salient features of the American political system is the sheer quantity of elective offices at all levels of government. At present, there are more than half a million government positions that are filled by popular election. Although candidates for these offices may be endorsed by a political party, they typically run for office as individuals independent of a formal party electoral slate. To be heard above the crowd, candidates need access to organization, paid publicity, and the media. These considerations point to the role of campaign financing as a determinant of who will serve in office. Correspondingly, the amount of money involved in electoral politics is striking. For example, the total bill for the 1996 presidential and congressional campaigns was estimated to be $1.6 billion, about the same as was spent in 2004. In 2006, a non-presidential year, over $1.4 billion was spent on federal elections. But these numbers tell only part of the story. Much of this chapter will address the problem of money being spent outside the control of the candidates and political actors by a dizzying array of entities that have emerged in the shadows of the campaign finance laws.

This chapter will address the difficult issues concerning the influence of money on the political system in general and on political speech in particular. Both the political and the legal dimensions of these issues are increasingly prominent; public pressure to reform the political system makes it likely that there will continue to be efforts to press Congress and state legislatures to pass campaign finance reform legislation of at least some form in the foreseeable future. Prospective legislation will be shaped not only by political forces, but by contestable views concerning the forms that the First Amendment and Supreme Court decisions permit such legislation to take.

The modern era of regulating the role of money in electoral politics dates from the period of reform following Watergate. Although the events themselves have left their mark mostly as a suffix appended to all manner of government misdeeds (e.g., Irangate, Travelgate), the break-in at the Democratic National Committee headquarters triggered a concerted effort to reform the political order. In turn, much of the reform effort was directed at the role of money—both as a potential source of corruption in politics and as a filter on which viewpoints could be effectively aired.

Since the time of Watergate, the issue of the role of contributions and money has taken on a life of its own in the law. This is an extremely complicated area of legal regulation because of the competing claims of the government's right to regulate the functions of the political marketplace, and the inevitable interaction between the right to contribute and the First Amendment rights of association and participation in politics. We will begin the chapter by discussing the most important of the regulatory efforts, the 1974 Amendments to the Federal Election Campaign Act of 1971, 2 U.S.C. § 441 *et seq.*, and then attempt to sort through the various concerns in contemporary campaign finance regulation. In order to do so, it is best to place the debates over campaign finance in context.

A. THE FIRST AMENDMENT BACKGROUND

The debates over the wisdom and permissibility of various campaign finance regulations are set in the context of difficult constitutional concerns over freedom of speech and association, as well as institutional considerations concerning the role of political parties and government regulators. Because many of the key debates and cases in this area are framed around arguments concerning freedom of expression, before turning to specific regulations and cases in this area, we consider the broad outlines of First Amendment law regarding speech and expression. The government's power to regulate speech depends largely upon the categorization of such regulation into one of the three following categories, each of which carries significantly different standards of constitutional scrutiny.

1. *Time, Place and Manner Regulation:* The government generally has broad power to regulate the time, place and manner of speech in a public forum. The general idea is that not everyone can speak at the same time or in the same place. Thus, government can require a parade permit for public gatherings or limit the hours in which megaphones may be used or similarly act to protect public safety or tranquility, so long as the regulation is not so onerous as to suppress speech or is not applied inconsistently depending on the identity or viewpoint of the speaker. Time, place and manner regulation is generally subject to a low level of scrutiny by courts, akin to what is termed "rationality review" in equal protection law, and there is considerable deference given to the means by which a government chooses to promote content-neutral concerns: "Content-neutral time, place, and manner restrictions are acceptable so long as they are designed to serve a *substantial governmental interest* and do not unreasonably limit alternative avenues of communication." *City of Renton v. Playtime Theatres, Inc.*, 475 U.S. 41 (1986) (emphasis added). Note that the state interest need not be compelling, and the government does not have to show a perfect fit between the means and the ends. Courts will often simply defer to the legislature as to what constitutes a substantial governmental interest and will have little trouble in finding that a regulation is sufficiently closely tailored to meet that interest. The classic example of such time, place and manner regulation is that upheld in *Ward v. Rock Against Racism*, 491 U.S. 781 (1989). New York City passed a law regulating the volume of

music played in an amphitheater in Central Park. The regulation also required performers to use equipment and technicians provided by the city. In overturning the lower court's ruling that this regulation was not the least restrictive alternative, the Supreme Court held that "a regulation of the time, place, or manner of protected speech must be narrowly tailored to serve the government's legitimate, content-neutral interests but that it need not be the least restrictive or least intrusive means of doing so. Rather, the requirement of narrow tailoring is satisfied 'so long as the . . . regulation promotes a substantial government interest that would be achieved less effectively absent the regulation.' " The Court went on to state that once these standards had been met courts should defer to the government's reasonable determination of the need for regulation.

2. *Content Regulation:* All government regulations inhibiting speech are subject to a fairly strict requirement of content neutrality. When regulations are related to the content of speech, the presumption of constitutionality that accompanies time, place and manner restrictions drops out. Instead, the First Amendment requires the government to show that the regulation is necessary to meet a "compelling state interest." Furthermore, the regulation must satisfy an independent test of "narrow tailoring" that requires the regulation to be drawn so as accomplish the stated permissible ends without unnecessarily infringing upon other protected speech. Thus, "the state action may be sustained only if the government can show that the regulation is a precisely drawn means of serving a compelling state interest." *Consolidated Edison Co. v. Public Service Comm'n*, 447 U.S. 530, 540 (1980). The differing presumptions on the constitutionality of content-based versus content-neutral regulations thus translate into differing standards of scrutiny when such regulations are challenged. Moreover, because the standard of scrutiny to be applied is so likely to determine the outcome of a challenge to a regulation of speech, the fate of regulations is often determined by whether it is construed by a court to be content-based or content-neutral.

The definition of content neutrality, however, is far from clear. For example, in 1989 the Supreme Court struck down a Texas flag burning statute as an impermissible content regulation because the statute effectively banned the burning of the flag only when used as part of an anti-government protest. *Texas v. Johnson*, 491 U.S. 397 (1989). Subsequently, Congress passed the Flag Protection Act, which prohibited all harm to the flag except when disposing of old flags. In reviewing the new statute, the Court split as to whether it constituted prohibited content-based regulation. The majority found that the government's expressed interest in preserving the flag as a national symbol was itself content-based: "Although Congress cast the Flag Protection Act in somewhat broader terms than the Texas statute at issue in *Johnson*, the Act still suffers from the same fundamental flaw: it suppresses expression out of concern for its likely communicative impact." The dissent was equally insistent that the regulation was content-neutral and was thus required only to meet a lower standard of scrutiny: "the Government may—indeed, it should—protect the symbolic value of the flag without regard to the specific content of the flag burner's speech." *United States v. Eichman*, 496 U.S. 310 (1990).

3. *Viewpoint Regulation:* Although much of the First Amendment caselaw treats content regulation as triggering the gravest form of scrutiny, that distinction should really be reserved for government regulation that not only is concerned with the content of the communication, but which seeks to advance or suppress a particular viewpoint on the subject matter. Accordingly, viewpoint regulation is the most disapproved category of speech regulation under the First Amendment, and approaches the standard of judicial scrutiny that is "strict in theory, fatal in fact." As expressed by the Court: "When the government targets not subject matter, but particular views taken by speakers on a subject, the violation of the First Amendment is all the more blatant. Viewpoint discrimination is thus an egregious form of content discrimination." *Rosenberger v. Rector & Visitors of the University of Virginia*, 515 U.S. 819, 829 (1995).

Not surprisingly, the demarcation between content and viewpoint considerations is imprecise. The general idea behind viewpoint discrimination is that government may not choose to promote or suppress only one side of an issue or debate. Consider, for example, Justice Scalia's opinion for the Court in *R.A.V. v. City of St. Paul*, 505 U.S. 377 (1992). St. Paul had passed a regulation prohibiting the display of any symbol known to "arouse[] anger, alarm or resentment in others on the basis of race, color, creed, religion or gender." In striking down this regulation, the Court held:

> In its practical operation, moreover, the ordinance goes even beyond mere content discrimination, to actual viewpoint discrimination. Displays containing some words—odious racial epithets, for example—would be prohibited to proponents of all views. But "fighting words" that do not themselves invoke race, color, creed, religion, or gender— aspersions upon a person's mother, for example—would seemingly be usable ad libitum in the placards of those arguing in favor of racial, color, etc., tolerance and equality, but could not be used by those speakers' opponents. One could hold up a sign saying, for example, that all "anti-Catholic bigots" are misbegotten; but not that all "papists" are, for that would insult and provoke violence "on the basis of religion." St. Paul has no such authority to license one side of a debate to fight freestyle, while requiring the other to follow Marquis of Queensberry rules.

While the Court saw this as a clear example of viewpoint discrimination, Justice Stevens in dissent vigorously contended the opposite: "In a battle between advocates of tolerance and advocates of intolerance, the ordinance does not prevent either side from hurling fighting words at the other on the basis of their conflicting ideas...." Although the Court often does not agree as to the substance of the regulation, the constitutional analysis is the same—does a particular statute limit one side of a debate while leaving the other side unregulated?

* * *

Much of the debate over campaign finance regulation maps directly onto the general contours of First Amendment law, with the same lines of demarcation between content neutral regulations and those concerned with the content and even the viewpoint of the regulated activity. Critics of campaign finance regulations argue that such restrictions on speech are not content neutral and therefore violate the basic First Amendment rights against government interference with speech. According to Professor Smith, this reflects the viewpoint bias of proponents of regulation:

> [T]he way in which campaign finance regulation favors certain elites raises First Amendment concerns. Traditional First Amendment jurisprudence requires most speech restrictions to be content-neutral, i.e., not to favor any particular viewpoint.... Many reformers, however, usually political liberals, view campaign finance reform favorably precisely because they assume that the targeted power base of money works mainly to the advantage of their political opponents. Once it is conceded that legislation is intended to hamper the expression of some ideas and not others, it is difficult to assert that the regulation is content-neutral.

Bradley A. Smith, *Faulty Assumptions and Undemocratic Consequences of Campaign Finance Reform*, 105 Yale L.J. 1049, 1080 (1996). Alternatively, Professor Sullivan advances a First Amendment argument that is concerned not so much with the political agenda of reformers but with the political content of the ideal of "uncorrupted" politics that would emerge in a more regulated campaign finance environment:

> [T]he "anti-corruption" argument for campaign finance reform claims the superiority of a particular conception of democracy as a ground for limiting speech. As a result, it runs squarely up against the presumptive ban on political view-point discrimination. Campaign finance reformers necessarily reject pluralist assumptions about the operation of democracy and would restrict speech in the form of political money to foster either of two alternative political theories. First, they might be thought to favor a Burkean or civic republic view, in which responsiveness to raw constituent preferences of any kind undermines the representative's obligation to deliberate with some detachment about the public good. Alternatively, they might be thought to favor a populist view in which the representative ought be as close as possible to a transparent vehicle for plebiscitary democracy, for the transmission of polling data into policy. Either way, they conceive democracy as something other than the aggregation of self-regarding interests, each of which is free to seek as much representation as possible. But surely the endorsement of civic republicanism or populism—or any other

vision of democracy—may not normally serve as a valid justification for limiting speech. Legislators may enforce an official conception of proper self-government through a variety of means, but not by prohibiting non-conforming expression.

Kathleen M. Sullivan, *Political Money and Freedom of Speech*, 30 U.C. Davis L. Rev. 663, 681–82 (1997). By contrast, for Professor Askin arguments that rest on the inevitability of regulations advancing normative views of the proper functioning of government go too far:

> Can there really be any serious doubt that our constitutional system favors popular government over a plutocracy? If we did not favor popular government, why not allow the rich to make direct payments to the poor in exchange for voting in a certain way? Indeed, why not allow individuals to actually sell their votes through proxy certificates? Are not such restrictions limitations on speech?
>
> The remarkable thing about Professor Sullivan's position is not that she considers it sound democratic policy, but that she believes it is constitutionally required. She would apparently find that the First Amendment forbids the majoritarian process from interfering with this plutocratic design. She obviously believes that when the sovereign people of the United States approved the First Amendment they were creating a society in which Congress could make no laws abridging the freedom of the moneyed classes to use their wealth for the political subjugation of society. Can anyone truly conceive that the Founders intended such a plan or that the people endorsed it?

Frank Askin, *Political Money and Freedom of Speech: Kathleen Sullivan's Seven Deadly Sins—An Antitoxin*, 31 U.C. Davis L. Rev. 1065, 1078 (1998).

Other scholars have similarly defended proposed campaign finance restrictions by placing them within the content-neutral category that should trigger the least First Amendment concern. For example, Professor Sunstein, although critical of the current form of campaign finance regulations, argues that "[w]e might ... think of campaign finance laws as viewpoint-neutral and even content-neutral restrictions on political speech. At least if the laws are fair, the particular content of the speech—the message that is being urged—is irrelevant to whether the campaign finance restriction attaches." Cass R. Sunstein, *Political Equality and Unintended Consequences,* 94 Colum. L. Rev. 1390, 1394 (1994). In response to the earlier argument that proponents of campaign finance reform support it because reform works to the advantage of their own political views, Professor Blasi similarly argues that campaign regulations in fact have no distributional impact on the ability of political parties to disseminate their message, and are accordingly also content neutral: "[I]n terms of the traditional canons of First Amendment doctrine, campaign spending limits ... should not be presumed to be unconstitutional. Spending limits are content neutral in form and indeterminate in political impact." Vincent Blasi, *Free Speech and the Widening Gyre of Fund–Raising: Why Campaign*

Spending Limits May Not Violate the First Amendment After All, 94 Colum. L. Rev. 1281, 1324 (1994).

Another possible defense of campaign finance regulation against First Amendment attack stems from an independent line of authority captured as the so-called "heckler's veto." The classic First Amendment concern for state infringement of the right to speak draws on the imagery of the policeman using his nightstick to suppress dissident speech. Much as this view of state censorship is the paradigmatic First Amendment concern, it does not end the inquiry. There are many situations in which injury may be perpetrated by a party other than the state and in which an individual citizen might seek assistance from the state in being allowed to enjoy the liberties of the society. Imagine a citizen who stands up in a public place to speak on a matter of public concern. Suppose that a heckler or an opponent tries to silence the speaker. At this point the speaker will seek recourse in the same policeman who had previously stood as the censorial villain. Should the policeman silence the heckler, the same apparent violation of rights of the heckler would appear to result. But the heckler's veto analysis would counter that the state is here furthering an objective of providing a forum for public discourse on matters of public concern and the coercive conduct furthers rather than frustrates freedom of expression.

The Supreme Court has held that a speaker's right to expression survives even if it provokes hostile reactions from a crowd. In *Terminiello v. Chicago*, 337 U.S. 1 (1949), a speaker was convicted of disorderly conduct when his audience became "angry and turbulent" over the words he expressed. In reversing Terminiello's conviction for disorderly conduct, the Court held that "a function of free speech under our system of government is to invite dispute" and the state may not restrict speakers' rights to expression simply because they provoke unrest or dissatisfaction from their audience. In other words, hostile audiences are prevented from interfering with the First Amendment rights of speakers. The Court further held, in a separate case, that the heckler's speech should be silenced before that of the speaker. *Kovacs v. Cooper*, 336 U.S. 77 (1949). The California Supreme Court interpreted this doctrine to afford the state a legitimate concern in "ensuring that some individuals' unruly assertion of their rights of free expression does not imperil other citizens' rights of free association and discussion." *In re Kay*, 1 Cal.3d 930, 941 (1970). Thus, courts have recognized that someone who speaks so loudly and belligerently as to drown out other speech cannot invoke his own First Amendment rights to be free from state restriction.

The extent of the application of this doctrine to the campaign finance context is uncertain. For many proponents of stricter campaign finance regulations, the presence of some speakers with vast amounts of money threatens to simply overpower other forms of communication. Instead of the antidote to speech being more speech, the analogy to the heckler's veto would cast well-heeled electoral participants in the mold of the obnoxious heckler drowning out the First Amendment rights of other speakers. Therefore, this argument would hold, when government acts to restrict the rights of the moneyed speaker, it is merely acting permissibly to silence the "crowd" and allow the other speakers their rights to free discussion. The moneyed speaker cannot invoke a First Amendment right to drown out the speech rights of others. The most sophisticated forms of this argument speak of "the silencing effect of speech," to invoke the terminology of, among others, Professor Fiss. *See* Owen M. Fiss, The Irony of Free Speech 5–26 (1996). This argument is strengthened to the extent that effective political speech relies almost exclusively on the main broadcast and print media, in which moneyed interests may saturate the means of communication, a premise that itself may be subject to dispute.

B.   Policy Considerations

Although this area is strewn with First Amendment concerns, we will also focus on the central issues of the legal and policy rationales for regulation of the political process. Three different approaches are central to the arguments over campaign finance regulation. For introductory purposes, these may be thought of as follows:

1. *Regulation of political markets:* There is a long tradition of viewing political speech from the vantage point of a marketplace of ideas. In the words of John Milton, "Let Truth and Falsehood grapple; whoever knew Truth put to the worse, in a free and open encounter." John Milton, *Areopagitica*, reprinted in The Tradition of Freedom 28 (Milton Mayer ed., 1957). The First Amendment has accordingly long been held to guarantee debate on public issues that is "uninhibited, robust, and wide-open." *New York Times v. Sullivan,* 376 U.S. 254, 270 (1964). As against the presumption of unfettered political speech, the argument for legal oversight of campaign finance incorporates the central features of arguments for regulatory oversight of markets generally. Viewing the political arena as a market for electoral gain implies a corresponding role for the state in preserving the openness of the market. By analogy to the role of antitrust regulation in commercial markets, the argument for regulation of campaign finance speaks to the dangers of monopoly concentration of power. Without some guarantee that competitors will be able to reach the consuming public, the argument runs, there is a danger that the political market will simply collapse. A second regulatory argument warns of the contamination of the political process not by the overbearing presence of a few political actors, but by the risk that such powerful market players may be able to extort special favors from vulnerable public officials. According to these arguments, campaign finance regulations preserve the functioning of an open political market either by limiting the concentration of economic power in the political arena, or by limiting the kinds of governmental decisions that concentrated economic power might induce.

2. *Equality*: Recall that in *Reynolds v. Sims*, the Court spoke of the Constitution as guaranteeing that "each citizen have an *equally effective* voice in the election of members of his [] legislature." 377 U.S. 533, 565 (1964)(emphasis added). While this guarantee of equality has not been fully elucidated in the one-person, one-vote arena, the same conception of effectiveness comes into play with campaign finances. An argument can be mounted that the post-*Baker/Reynolds* line of cases represents a democratic vision that would assure all citizens a meaningful, and indeed equal, chance to influence the political process. On this view, the regulation of the power of money is an indispensable part of the guarantee of meaningful equality in the electoral arena, lest the concentration of wealth simply drown out alternative voices. Professor Ronald Dworkin thus argues that, "each citizen must have a fair and equal opportunity not only to hear the views of others, as these are published or broadcast, but to command attention for his own views, either as a candidate for office or as a member of a politically active group committed to some program or convictions." Ronald Dworkin, *The Curse of American Politics*, New York Review of Books, Oct. 17, 1996, at 23.

3. *Liberty*: This view champions freedom from state restriction on expressive activity in the political arena. Regulations, directed either at speech or the expenditure of funds, necessarily implicate the state in restricting access to those who desire additional participation in electoral activity. Advocates of limiting state regulation typically compare campaign contributions and expenditures to other forms of protected political speech in arguing for a general First Amendment skepticism toward governmental restraints.

C.   BUCKLEY V. VALEO AND THE STATUTORY FRAMEWORK

Turning to the legal landscape proper, there is one inevitable starting point. The legal regulation of campaign finance is dominated by the great analytic divide created by *Buckley v. Valeo*, 424 U.S. 1 (1976)(per curiam). In reviewing the 1974 reforms to FECA, *Buckley* defined the current approach to legal regulation of campaign finance. The 1974 amendments tried to curb the perceived deleterious impact of money on elections through a variety of restrictions. The amendments limited the size of contributions that could be given in federal elections by individuals, political parties, or Political Action Committees ("PACs"). The amendments also placed ceilings on total spending by candidates in federal elections and limited personal spending by candidates. In exchange, the 1974 amendments created the first system of public funding for presidential elections through the use of matching funds for primary candidates and general federal funding of the presidential election. Finally, the amendments created elaborate reporting and disclosure requirements for candidates to federal office.

The entire regulatory structure was overseen by the Federal Election Commission, a federal agency comprised of six political appointees, no more than three from any one party, together with the House Clerk and Senate Secretary *ex oficio*. In practice, the FEC has always been comprised of three Democrats and three Republicans. The six commissioners serve as chairmen of the Commission on a one-year rotating basis. In order to act at all, four of the six commissioners must agree to any proposed regulatory undertaking. The Commission had no power to investigate anonymous complaints and was hamstrung by a number of odd procedural requirements. This unusual structure is hardly accidental. As well-chronicled by Brooks Jackson, the design was a willful effort by Congress to limit the power of an agency that would have authority to regulate and investigate congressional campaign activity. In Jackson's words, the agency was "born handicapped, then kidnaped." Brooks Jackson, Broken Promises: Why the Federal Election Commission Failed 26 (1990).

Even so, only part of the FECA regulatory regime survived Supreme Court review. In a long and oftentimes rambling opinion, the Supreme Court tried to distinguish between First Amendment protected political speech and permissible regulation by focusing on the form of campaign finance limitations. The Court openly acknowledged that all "contribution and expenditure limitations operate in an area of the most fundamental First Amendment activities." 424 U.S. at 14. Moreover, "The First Amendment denies government the power to determine that spending to promote one's political views is wasteful, excessive, or unwise. In the free society ordained by our Constitution it is not the government, but the people individually as citizens and candidates and collectively as associations and political committees who must retain control over the quantity and range of debate on public issues in a political campaign." *Id.* at 55.

However, the Court found a basic First Amendment distinction between expenditures by candidates who sought to advocate their positions and promote their aspirations for office, on the one hand, and contributions by supporters of these candidates or political positions, on the other:

> A restriction on the amount of money a person or group can spend on political communication during a campaign necessarily reduces the quantity of expression by restricting the number of issues discussed, the depth of their exploration, and the size of the audience reached. This is because virtually every means of communicating ideas in today's mass society requires the expenditure of money. The distribution of the humblest handbill or leaflet entails printing, paper, and circulation costs. Speeches and rallies generally necessitate hiring a hall and publicizing the event. The electorate's increasing dependence on television, radio, and other mass media for news and information has made these expensive modes of communication indispensable instruments of effective political speech. . . .

By contrast with a limitation upon expenditures for political expression, a limitation upon the amount that any one person or group may contribute to a candidate or political committee entails only a marginal restriction upon the contributor's ability to engage in free communication. A contribution serves as a general expression of support for the candidate and his views, but does not communicate the underlying basis for the support. The quantity of communication by the contributor does not increase perceptibly with the size of his contribution, since the expression rests solely on the undifferentiated, symbolic act of contributing. At most, the size of the contribution provides a very rough index of the intensity of the contributor's support for the candidate. A limitation on the amount of money a person may give to a candidate or campaign organization thus involves little direct restraint on his political communication, for it permits the symbolic expression of support evidenced by a contribution but does not in any way infringe the contributor's freedom to discuss candidates and issues. While contributions may result in political expression if spent by a candidate or an association to present views to the voters, the transformation of contributions into political debate involves speech by someone other than the contributor. . . .

It is unnecessary to look beyond the Act's primary purpose—to limit the actuality and appearance of corruption resulting from large individual financial contributions—in order to find a constitutionally sufficient justification for the $1,000 contribution limitation. Under a system of private financing of elections, a candidate lacking immense personal or family wealth must depend on financial contributions from others to provide the resources necessary to conduct a successful campaign. The increasing importance of the communications media and sophisticated mass-mailing and polling operations to effective campaigning make the raising of large sums of money an ever more essential ingredient of an effective candidacy. To the extent that large contributions are given to secure political quid pro quo's from current and potential office holders, the integrity of our system of representative democracy is undermined. Although the scope of such pernicious practices can never be reliably ascertained, the deeply disturbing examples surfacing after the 1972 election demonstrate that the problem is not an illusory one.

Of almost equal concern as the danger of actual quid pro quo arrangements is the impact of the appearance of corruption stemming from public awareness of the opportunities for abuse inherent in a regime of large individual financial contributions. In *CSC v. Letter Carriers,* [412 U.S. 548 (1973)], the Court found that the danger to "fair and effective government" posed by partisan political conduct on the part of federal employees charged with administering the law was a sufficiently important concern to justify broad restrictions on the employees' right of partisan political association. Here, as there, Congress could legitimately conclude that the avoidance of the appearance of improper influence "is also critical ... if confidence in the system of representative Government is not to be eroded to a disastrous extent."

Appellants contend that the contribution limitations must be invalidated because bribery laws and narrowly drawn disclosure requirements constitute a less restrictive means of dealing with "proven and suspected quid pro quo arrangements." But laws making criminal the giving and taking of bribes deal with only the most blatant and specific attempts of those with money to influence governmental action. And while disclosure requirements serve the many salutary purposes discussed elsewhere in this opinion, Congress was surely entitled to conclude that disclosure was only a partial measure, and that contribution ceilings were a necessary legislative concomitant to deal with the reality or appearance of corruption inherent in a system permitting unlimited financial contributions, even when the identities of the contributors and the amounts of their contributions are fully disclosed.

424 U.S. at 19–21, 26–28.

By contrast to the permissive arena of regulation for contributions, the Court has extended, as a general matter, broad constitutional protection to all expenditures by candidates for office. Reasoning that this form of "money is speech," the Court has applied strict scrutiny to any regulatory efforts aimed at limiting the use of money to express the views or positions of candidates. On the other hand, following the logic of *Buckley,* the Court has generally allowed content-neutral restrictions on campaign contributions. Contributions, unlike expenditures, have been viewed as standing at one remove from political speech and have accordingly been subject to lesser standards of judicial scrutiny. The result is an odd regulatory misalignment between the encumbered ability to raise money and the unfettered capacity to spend it. The resulting patchwork of regulation is summarized as follows:

> We shall never know what kind of regulatory regime the FECA amendments of 1974 created because they were so drastically altered by the Supreme Court in *Buckley v. Valeo.* What was intended to be a closed system in which the major flows of money into and out of campaigns were fully controlled emerged as an open system of uncontrolled outlets when the Court struck down all limits on direct spending in the campaign by candidates, PACs, and individuals. A tightly constrained regulatory system became a more relaxed, open-ended one. The modifications in *Buckley* meant that the original 1974 plan would never have to meet its two severest tests: the administration of spending limits in hundreds of races and the accommodation of excess money in a system with no effective outlets. Instead, the crippled FECA affected chiefly the recruitment of money, ending the freedom of the fat cats and encouraging the development of PACs.

Frank J. Sorauf, Inside Campaign Finance 238 (1992). After *Buckley,* campaign finance regulation survived in a form that no legislature ever voted to create and, one may surmise, no legislature would ever have voted to create. Nonetheless, the contributions/expenditures divide inherited from *Buckley* continues to be the key to current campaign finance regulation, despite increasing dissatisfaction by the Court over the central conceptual edifice inherited from *Buckley.*

D. THE CONTRIBUTION/EXPENDITURE DIVIDE

1. CONTRIBUTION LIMITS

Nixon v. Shrink Missouri Government PAC

528 U.S. 377 (2000).

■ JUSTICE SOUTER delivered the opinion of the Court.

The principal issues in this case are whether *Buckley v. Valeo* is authority for state limits on contributions to state political candidates and whether the federal limits approved in *Buckley*, with or without adjustment for inflation, define the scope of permissible state limitations today. We hold *Buckley* to be authority for comparable state regulation, which need not be pegged to *Buckley*'s dollars.

I.

In 1994, the Legislature of Missouri enacted Senate Bill 650 (SB650) to restrict the permissible amounts of contributions to candidates for state office. Mo. Rev. Stat. § 130.032 (1994). Before the statute became effective, however, Missouri voters approved a ballot initiative with even stricter contribution limits, effective immediately. The United States Court of Appeals for the Eighth Circuit then held the initiative's contribution limits unconstitutional under the First Amendment, with the upshot that the previously dormant 1994 statute took effect.

As amended in 1997, that statute imposes contribution limits ranging from $250 to $1,000, depending on specified state office or size of constituency. The particular provision [Mo. Rev. Stat. § 130.032] challenged here reads that:

> to elect an individual to the office of governor, lieutenant governor, secretary of state, state treasurer, state auditor or attorney general, [the amount of contributions made by or accepted from any person other than the candidate in any one election shall not exceed] one thousand dollars.

* * *

Respondents Shrink Missouri Government PAC, a political action committee, and Zev David Fredman, a candidate for the 1998 Republican nomination for state auditor, sought to enjoin enforcement of the contribution statute as violating their First and Fourteenth Amendment rights (presumably those of free speech, association, and equal protection, although the complaint did not so state). Shrink Missouri gave $1,025 to Fredman's candidate committee in 1997, and another $50 in 1998. Shrink Missouri represented that, without the limitation, it would contribute more to the Fredman campaign. Fredman alleged he could campaign effectively only with more generous contributions than § 130.032.1 allowed. On cross-motions for summary judgment, the District Court sustained the statute. Applying *Buckley v. Valeo* the court found adequate support for the law in the proposition that large contributions raise suspicions of influence peddling tending to undermine citizens' confidence "in the integrity of … government." The District Court rejected respondents' contention that inflation since *Buckley*'s approval of a federal $1000 restriction meant that the state limit of $1,075 for a statewide office could not be constitutional today.

The Court of Appeals for the Eighth Circuit nonetheless enjoined enforcement of the law pending appeal and ultimately reversed the District Court. Finding that *Buckley* had " 'articulated and applied a strict scrutiny standard of review,' " the Court of Appeals held that Missouri was bound to demonstrate "that it has a compelling interest and that the contribution limits at issue are narrowly drawn to serve that interest." The appeals court treated Missouri's claim of a compelling interest "in avoiding the corruption or the perception of corruption brought about when candidates for elective office accept large campaign contributions" as insufficient by itself to satisfy strict scrutiny.

* * *

Given the large number of States that limit political contributions, we granted certiorari to review the congruence of the Eighth Circuit's decision with *Buckley*. We reverse.

II.

A

* * *

B

In defending its own statute, Missouri espouses those same interests [that were addressed in *Buckley*] of preventing corruption and the appearance of it that flows from munificent campaign contributions. Even without the authority of *Buckley*, there would be no serious question about the legitimacy of the interests claimed, which, after all, underlie bribery and anti-gratuity statutes. While neither law nor morals equate all political contributions, without more, with bribes, we spoke in *Buckley* of the perception of corruption "inherent in a regime of large individual financial contributions" to candidates for public office as a source of concern "almost equal" to *quid pro quo* improbity. The public interest in countering that perception was, indeed, the entire answer to the overbreadth claim raised in the *Buckley* case. This made perfect sense. Leave the perception of impropriety unanswered, and the cynical assumption that large donors call the tune could jeopardize the willingness of voters to take part in democratic governance. Democracy works "only if the people have faith in those who govern, and that faith is bound to be shattered when high officials and their appointees engage in activities which arouse suspicions of malfeasance and corruption." *United States v. Mississippi Valley Generating Co.*, 364 U.S. 520 (1961).

Although respondents neither challenge the legitimacy of these objectives nor call for any reconsideration of *Buckley*, they take the State to task, as the Court of Appeals did, for failing to justify the invocation of those interests with empirical evidence of actually corrupt practices or of a perception among Missouri voters that unrestricted contributions must have been exerting a covertly corrosive influence. The state statute is not void, however, for want of evidence.

The quantum of empirical evidence needed to satisfy heightened judicial scrutiny of legislative judgments will vary up or down with the novelty and plausibility of the justification raised. *Buckley* demonstrates that the dangers of large, corrupt contributions and the suspicion that large contributions are corrupt are neither novel nor implausible. The opinion noted that "the deeply disturbing examples surfacing after the 1972 election demonstrate that the problem [of corruption] is not an illusory one." Although we did not ourselves marshal the evidence in support of the congressional concern, we referred to "a number of the abuses" detailed in the Court of Appeals's decision, which described how corporations, well-financed interest groups, and rich individuals had made large contributions, some of which were illegal under existing law, others of which reached at least the verge of bribery. The evidence before the Court of Appeals described public revelations by the parties in question more than sufficient to show why voters would tend to identify a big donation with a corrupt purpose.

* * *

In any event, this case does not present a close call requiring further definition of whatever the State's evidentiary obligation may be.... Although Missouri does not preserve legislative history, the State presented an affidavit from State Senator Wayne Goode, the co-chair of the state legislature's Interim Joint Committee on Campaign Finance Reform at the time the State enacted the contribution limits, who stated that large contributions have " 'the real potential to buy votes.' " The District Court cited newspaper accounts of large contributions supporting inferences of impropriety. One report questioned the state treasurer's decision to use a certain bank for most of Missouri's banking business after that institution contributed $20,000 to the treasurer's campaign. Another made much of the receipt by a candidate for state auditor of a $40,000 contribution from a brewery and one for $20,000 from a bank.... And although majority votes do not, as such, defeat First Amendment protections, the statewide vote on Proposition A certainly attested to the perception relied upon here: "An overwhelming 74 percent of the voters of Missouri determined that contribution limits are necessary to combat corruption and the appearance thereof."

[T]he closest respondents come to challenging these conclusions is their invocation of academic studies said to indicate that large contributions to public officials or candidates do not actually result in changes in candidates' positions. Brief for Respondents Shrink Missouri Government PAC et al. 41; Smith, *Money Talks Speech, Corruption, Equality, and Campaign Finance*, 86 Geo. L. J. 45, 58 (1997); Smith, *Faulty Assumptions and Undemocratic Consequences of Campaign Finance Reform*, 105 YALE L. J. 1049, 1067–1068 (1995). Other studies, however, point the other way. Reply Brief for Respondent Bray 4–5; F. Sorauf, Inside Campaign Finance 169 (1992); Hall & Wayman, *Buying Time: Moneyed Interests and the Mobilization of Bias in Congressional Committees*, 84 Am. Pol. Sci. Rev. 797 (1990); D. Magleby & C. Nelson, The Money Chase 78 (1990). Given the conflict among these publications, and the absence of any reason to think that public perception has been influenced by the studies cited by respondents, there is little reason to doubt that sometimes large contributions will work actual corruption of our political system, and no reason to question the existence of a corresponding suspicion among voters.

C

Nor do we see any support for respondents' various arguments that in spite of their striking resemblance to the limitations sustained in *Buckley*, those in Missouri are so different in kind as to raise essentially a new issue about the adequacy of the Missouri statute's tailoring to serve its purposes. Here, as in *Buckley*, "there is no indication ... that the contribution limitations imposed by the [law] would have any dramatically adverse effect on the funding of campaigns and political associations," and thus no showing that "the limitations prevented the candidates and political committees from amassing the resources necessary for effective advocacy." The District Court found here that in the period since the Missouri limits became effective, "candidates for state elected office [have been] quite able to raise funds sufficient to run effective campaigns," and that "candidates for political office in the state are still able to amass impressive campaign war chests." The plausibility of these conclusions is buttressed by petitioners' evidence that in the 1994 Missouri elections (before any relevant state limitations went into effect), 97.62 percent of all contributors to candidates for state auditor made contributions of $2,000 or less. Even if we were to assume that the contribution limits affected respondent Fredman's ability to wage a competitive campaign (no small assumption given that Fredman only identified one contributor, Shrink Missouri, that would have given him more than $1,075 per election), a showing of one affected individual does not point up a system of suppressed political advocacy that would be unconstitutional under *Buckley*.

* * *

D

The dissenters in this case think our reasoning evades the real issue. Justice Thomas chides us for "hiding behind" *Buckley*, and Justice Kennedy faults us for seeing this case as "a routine application of our analysis" in *Buckley* instead of facing up to what he describes as the consequences of *Buckley*. Each dissenter would overrule *Buckley* and thinks we should do the same.

The answer is that we are supposed to decide this case. Shrink and Fredman did not request that *Buckley* be overruled; the furthest reach of their arguments about the law was that subsequent decisions already on the books had enhanced the State's burden of justification beyond what *Buckley* required, a proposition we have rejected as mistaken.

III

There is no reason in logic or evidence to doubt the sufficiency of *Buckley* to govern this case in support of the Missouri statute. The judgment of the Court of Appeals is, accordingly, reversed, and the case is remanded for proceedings consistent with this opinion.

It is so ordered.

■ JUSTICE STEVENS, concurring.

[. . .] In response to [Justice Kennedy's] call for a new beginning, therefore, I make one simple point. Money is property; it is not speech.

Speech has the power to inspire volunteers to perform a multitude of tasks on a campaign trail, on a battleground, or even on a football field. Money, meanwhile, has the power to pay hired laborers to perform the same tasks. It does not follow, however, that the First Amendment provides the same measure of protection to the use of money to accomplish such goals as it provides to the use of ideas to achieve the same results.

* * *

■ JUSTICE BREYER, with whom JUSTICE GINSBURG joins, concurring.

The dissenters accuse the Court of weakening the First Amendment. They believe that failing to adopt a "strict scrutiny" standard "balances away First Amendment freedoms." But the principal dissent oversimplifies the problem faced in the campaign finance context. It takes a difficult constitutional problem and turns it into a lopsided dispute between political expression and government censorship. Under the cover of this fiction and its accompanying formula, the dissent would make the Court absolute arbiter of a difficult question best left, in the main, to the political branches. I write separately to address the critical question of how the Court ought to review this kind of problem, and to explain why I believe the Court's choice here is correct.

If the dissent believes that the Court diminishes the importance of the First Amendment interests before us, it is wrong. The Court's opinion does not question the constitutional importance of political speech or that its protection lies at the heart of the First Amendment. Nor does it question the need for particularly careful, precise, and independent judicial review where, as here, that protection is at issue. But this is a case where constitutionally protected interests lie on both sides of the legal equation. For that reason there is no place for a strong presumption against constitutionality, of the sort often thought to accompany the words "strict scrutiny." Nor can we expect that mechanical application of the tests associated with "strict scrutiny"—the tests of "compelling interests" and "least restrictive means"—will properly resolve the difficult constitutional problem that campaign finance statutes pose.

On the one hand, a decision to contribute money to a campaign is a matter of First Amendment concern—not because money is speech (it is not); but because it enables speech. Through contributions the contributor associates himself with the candidate's cause, helps the candidate communicate a political message with which the contributor agrees, and helps the candidate win by attracting the votes of similarly minded voters. Both political association and political communication are at stake.

On the other hand, restrictions upon the amount any one individual can contribute to a particular candidate seek to protect the integrity of the electoral process—the means through which a free society democratically translates political speech into concrete governmental action. Moreover, by limiting the size of the largest contributions, such restrictions aim to democratize the influence that money itself may bring to bear upon the electoral process. In doing so, they seek to build public confidence in that process and broaden the base of a candidate's meaningful financial support, encouraging the public participation and open discussion that the First Amendment itself presupposes.

In service of these objectives, the statute imposes restrictions of degree. It does not deny the contributor the opportunity to associate with the candidate through a contribution, though it limits a contribution's size. Nor does it prevent the contributor from using money (alone or with others) to pay for the expression of the same views in other ways. Instead, it permits all supporters to contribute the same amount of money, in an attempt to make the process fairer and more democratic.

Under these circumstances, a presumption against constitutionality is out of place. . . . In such circumstances—where a law significantly implicates competing constitutionally protected interests in complex ways—the

Court has closely scrutinized the statute's impact on those interests, but refrained from employing a simple test that effectively presumes unconstitutionality. Rather, it has balanced interests. And in practice that has meant asking whether the statute burdens any one such interest in a manner out of proportion to the statute's salutary effects upon the others (perhaps, but not necessarily, because of the existence of a clearly superior, less restrictive alternative). Where a legislature has significantly greater institutional expertise, as, for example, in the field of election regulation, the Court in practice defers to empirical legislative judgments—at least where that deference does not risk such constitutional evils as, say, permitting incumbents to insulate themselves from effective electoral challenge. This approach is that taken in fact by *Buckley* for contributions, and is found generally where competing constitutional interests are implicated, such as privacy, First Amendment interests of listeners or viewers, and the integrity of the electoral process. . . . For the dissenters to call the approach "sui generis" overstates their case.

* * *

But what if I am wrong about *Buckley*? Suppose *Buckley* denies the political branches sufficient leeway to enact comprehensive solutions to the problems posed by campaign finance. If so, like Justice Kennedy, I believe the Constitution would require us to reconsider *Buckley*. With that understanding I join the Court's opinion.

■ JUSTICE KENNEDY, dissenting.

* * *

I

Zev David Fredman asks us to evaluate his speech claim in the context of a system which favors candidates and officeholders whose campaigns are supported by soft money, usually funneled through political parties. The Court pays him no heed. The plain fact is that the compromise the Court invented in *Buckley* set the stage for a new kind of speech to enter the political system. It is covert speech. The Court has forced a substantial amount of political speech underground, as contributors and candidates devise ever more elaborate methods of avoiding contribution limits, limits which take no account of rising campaign costs. The preferred method has been to conceal the real purpose of the speech. Soft money may be contributed to political parties in unlimited amounts, and is used often to fund so-called issue advocacy, advertisements that promote or attack a candidate's positions without specifically urging his or her election or defeat. Issue advocacy, like soft money, is unrestricted, while straightforward speech in the form of financial contributions paid to a candidate, speech subject to full disclosure and prompt evaluation by the public, is not. Thus has the Court's decision given us covert speech. This mocks the First Amendment. The current system would be unfortunate, and suspect under the First Amendment, had it evolved from a deliberate legislative choice; but its unhappy origins are in our earlier decree in *Buckley*, which by accepting half of what Congress did (limiting contributions) but rejecting the other (limiting expenditures) created a misshapen system, one which distorts the meaning of speech.

The irony that we would impose this regime in the name of free speech ought to be sufficient ground to reject *Buckley's* wooden formula in the present case. The wrong goes deeper, however. By operation of the *Buckley* rule, a candidate cannot oppose this system in an effective way without selling out to it first. Soft money must be raised to attack the problem of soft money. In effect, the Court immunizes its own erroneous ruling from change. Rulings of this Court must never be viewed with more caution than when they provide immunity from their own correction in the political process and in the forum of unrestrained speech. The melancholy history of campaign finance in *Buckley's* wake shows what can happen when we intervene in the dynamics of speech and expression by inventing an artificial scheme of our own.

* * *

I would overrule *Buckley* and then free Congress or state legislatures to attempt some new reform, if, based upon their own considered view of the First Amendment, it is possible to do so. Until any reexamination takes place, however, the existing distortion of speech caused by the half-way house we created in *Buckley* ought to be eliminated. The First Amendment ought to be allowed to take its own course without further obstruction from the artificial system we have imposed. It suffices here to say that the law in question does not come even close to passing any serious scrutiny.

For these reasons, though I am in substantial agreement with what Justice Thomas says in his opinion, I have thought it necessary to file a separate dissent.

■ JUSTICE THOMAS, with whom JUSTICE SCALIA joins, dissenting.

[. . . O]ur decision in *Buckley* was in error, and I would overrule it. I would subject campaign contribution limitations to strict scrutiny, under which Missouri's contribution limits are patently unconstitutional.

I

I begin with a proposition that ought to be unassailable: Political speech is the primary object of First Amendment protection. The Founders sought to protect the rights of individuals to engage in political speech because a self-governing people depends upon the free exchange of political information. And that free exchange should receive the most protection when it matters the most—during campaigns for elective office. . . .

I do not start with these foundational principles because the Court openly disagrees with them—it could not, for they are solidly embedded in our precedents. Instead, I start with them because the Court today abandons them. For nearly half a century, this Court has extended First Amendment protection to a multitude of forms of "speech," such as making false defamatory statements, filing lawsuits, dancing nude, exhibiting drive-in movies with nudity, burning flags, and wearing military uniforms. Not surprisingly, the Courts of Appeals have followed our lead and concluded that the First Amendment protects, for example, begging, shouting obscenities, erecting tables on a sidewalk, and refusing to wear a necktie. In light of the many cases of this sort, today's decision is a most curious anomaly. Whatever the proper status of such activities under the First Amendment, I am confident that they are less integral to the functioning of our Republic than campaign contributions. Yet the majority today, rather than going out of its way to protect political speech, goes out of its way to avoid protecting it. As I explain below, contributions to political campaigns generate essential political speech. And contribution caps, which place a direct and substantial limit on core speech, should be met with the utmost skepticism and should receive the strictest scrutiny.

II

At bottom, the majority's refusal to apply strict scrutiny to contribution limits rests upon *Buckley's* discounting of the First Amendment interests at stake. The analytic foundation of *Buckley*, however, was tenuous from the very beginning and has only continued to erode in the intervening years. What remains of *Buckley* fails to provide an adequate justification for limiting individual contributions to political candidates.

A

To justify its decision upholding contribution limitations while striking down expenditure limitations, the Court in *Buckley* explained that expenditure limits "represent substantial rather than merely theoretical restraints on the quantity and diversity of political speech," while contribution limits "entail only a marginal restriction upon the contributor's ability to engage in free communication." In drawing this distinction, the Court in *Buckley* relied on the premise that contributing to a candidate differs qualitatively from directly spending money. It noted that "while contributions may result in political expression if spent by a candidate or an association to present views to the voters, the transformation of contributions into political debate involves speech by someone other than the contributor."
. . .

The decision of individuals to speak through contributions rather than through independent expenditures is entirely reasonable. Political campaigns are largely candidate focused and candidate driven. Citizens recognize that the best advocate for a candidate (and the policy positions he supports) tends to be the candidate himself. And candidate organizations also offer other advantages to citizens wishing to partake in political expression. Campaign organizations offer a ready-built, convenient means of communicating for donors wishing to support and amplify political messages. Furthermore, the leader of the organization—the candidate—has a strong self-interest in efficiently expending funds in a manner that maximizes the power of the messages the contributor seeks to disseminate....

In the end, *Buckley's* claim that contribution limits "do not in any way infringe the contributor's freedom to discuss candidates and issues," ignores the distinct role of candidate organizations as a means of individual participation in the Nation's civic dialogue. The result is simply the suppression of political speech. By depriving donors of their right to speak through the candidate, contribution limits relegate donors' points of view to less effective modes of communication. Additionally, limiting contributions curtails individual participation.... *Buckley* completely failed in its attempt to provide a basis for permitting government to second-guess the individual choices of citizens partaking in quintessentially democratic activities....

B

The Court in Buckley denigrated the speech interests not only of contributors, but also of candidates. Although the Court purported to be concerned about the plight of candidates, it nevertheless proceeded to disregard their interests without justification. The Court did not even attempt to claim that contribution limits do not suppress the speech of political candidates. It could not have, given the reality that donations "make a significant contribution to freedom of expression by enhancing the ability of candidates to present, and the public to receive, information necessary for the effective operation of the democratic process." *CBS, Inc. v. FCC*, 453 U.S. 367 (1981). Instead, the Court abstracted from a candidate's individual right to speak and focused exclusively on aggregate campaign funding.

The Court's flawed and unsupported aggregate approach [also] ignores both the rights and value of individual candidates. The First Amendment "is designed and intended to remove governmental restraints from the arena of public discussion, putting the decision as to what views shall be voiced largely into the hands of *each of us*, in the hope that use of such freedom will ultimately produce a more capable citizenry and more perfect polity and in the belief that no other approach would comport with the premise of *individual* dignity and choice upon which our political system rests." *Cohen v. California*, 403 U.S. 15 (1971). In short, the right to free speech is a right held by each American, not by Americans en masse. The Court in *Buckley* provided no basis for suppressing the speech of an individual candidate simply because other candidates (or candidates in the aggregate) may succeed in reaching the voting public. And any such reasoning would fly in the face of the premise of our political system—liberty vested in individual hands safeguards the functioning of our democracy. In the case at hand, the Missouri scheme has a clear and detrimental effect on a candidate such as petitioner Fredman, who lacks the advantages of incumbency, name recognition, or substantial personal wealth, but who has managed to attract the support of a relatively small number of dedicated supporters: It forbids his message from reaching the voters. And the silencing of a candidate has consequences for political debate and competition overall.

In my view, the Constitution leaves it entirely up to citizens and candidates to determine who shall speak, the means they will use, and the amount of speech sufficient to inform and persuade. *Buckley's* ratification of the government's attempt to wrest this fundamental right from citizens was error.

* * *

IV

In light of the importance of political speech to republican government, Missouri's substantial restriction of speech warrants strict scrutiny, which requires that contribution limits be narrowly tailored to a compelling governmental interest.

Missouri does assert that its contribution caps are aimed at preventing actual and apparent corruption. As we have noted, "preventing corruption or the appearance of corruption are the only legitimate and compelling government interests thus far identified for restricting campaign finances." *National Conservative Political Action Comm.*, 470 U.S. at 496–497. But the State's contribution limits are not narrowly tailored to that harm. The limits directly suppress the political speech of both contributors and candidates, and only clumsily further the governmental interests that they allegedly serve. They are crudely tailored because they are massively overinclusive, prohibiting all donors who wish to contribute in excess of the cap from doing so and restricting donations without regard to whether the donors pose any real corruption risk. Moreover, the government has less restrictive means of addressing its interest in curtailing corruption. Bribery laws bar precisely the *quid pro quo* arrangements that are targeted here. And disclosure laws "deter actual corruption and avoid the appearance of corruption by exposing large contributions and expenditures to the light of publicity." *Buckley v. Valeo.* In fact, Missouri has enacted strict disclosure laws.

* * *

V

Because the Court unjustifiably discounts the First Amendment interests of citizens and candidates, and consequently fails to strictly scrutinize the inhibition of political speech and competition, I respectfully dissent.

NOTES AND QUESTIONS

1. At the bottom of the Court's ongoing division over campaign finance regulation is the basic question posed twenty years ago by Judge J. Skelly Wright: "Is Money Speech?" J. Skelly Wright, *Politics and the Constitution: Is Money Speech?,* 85 Yale L.J. 1001 (1976). The court's basic approach in *Buckley* was to answer this question in the negative for contributions, but affirmatively for expenditures. In the initial post-*Buckley* cases, Justice White emerged as a strong advocate for treating money as unrelated to speech and challenging the Court's attempt to cordon off contributions from expenditures for First Amendment purposes. First, he challenged the analytic category that draws expenditures within the concept of speech:

> The First Amendment protects the right to speak, not the right to spend, and limitations on the amount of money that can be spent are not the same as restrictions on speaking. I agree with the majority that the expenditures in this case "produce" core First Amendment speech. But that is precisely the point: they produce such speech; they are not speech itself. At least in these circumstances, I cannot accept the identification of speech with its antecedents. Such a house-that-Jack-built approach could equally be used to find a First Amendment right to a job or to a minimum wage to "produce" the money to "produce" the speech.

FEC v. National Conservative Political Action Comm., 470 U.S. 480, 508–09 (1985) (White, J., dissenting). Second, Justice White challenged the administrability of the contributions/expenditures analytic scheme:

> Let us suppose that each of two brothers spends $1 million on TV spot announcements that he has individually prepared and in which he appears, urging the election of the same named candidate in identical words. One brother has sought and obtained the approval of the candidate; the other has not. The former may validly be prosecuted under § 608(e); under the Court's view, the latter may not, even though the candidate could scarcely help knowing about and appreciating the expensive favor. For constitutional purposes it is difficult to see the difference between the two situations. I would take the word of those who know that limiting independent expenditures is essential to prevent transparent and widespread evasion of the contribution limits.

Buckley v. Valeo, 424 U.S. 1, 261–62 (1976)(White, J., concurring in part and dissenting in part).

Insofar as a concern about corruption forms a major part of the Court's rationalization for upholding limits on contributions, is there any reason to believe a candidate will not be "just as beholden" to a supporter who purchases advertisements with private funds as one who contributes money to the candidate directly? Moreover, to the extent that donors may direct their contributions to party coffers that are, in turn, used to promote the party's candidate, does the knowledge by the candidate of such contributions not open the door to the same *quid pro quo* concerns that were used to uphold limits on contributions? This is an issue that will emerge directly in the next subsection.

2.   As applied, the contribution/expenditure distinction has faced rough sledding. In *California Medical Association v. Federal Election Commission*, 453 U.S. 182 (1981), the Court upheld a $5,000 contribution limit by individual and groups to PACs. The Court ran into difficulty with the argument that the California Medical Association would be free to expend as much money as it wished independently to promote its views, but faced restrictions only when it pooled its funds into a PAC for greater effectiveness. Only four members of the Court accepted that the fact of aggregating resources allowed for a contribution ceiling. Justice Blackmun provided the concurring fifth vote on the grounds that contributions have a greater capacity for corruption than do independent expenditures. The Court's attempt to segregate contributions from expenditures broke down in *Citizens Against Rent Control v. City of Berkeley*, 454 U.S. 290, 299 (1981), in which a clear majority of the Court held unconstitutional a limitation of $250 on contributions to committees formed to support or oppose ballot measures submitted to popular vote:

> Apart from the impermissible restraint on freedom of association, but virtually inseparable from it in this context, § 602 imposes a significant restraint on the freedom of expression of groups and those individuals who wish to express their views through committees. As we have noted, an individual may make expenditures without limit under § 602 on a ballot measure but may not contribute beyond the $250 limit when joining with others to advocate common views. The contribution limit thus automatically affects expenditures, and limits on expenditures operate as a direct restraint on freedom of expression of a group or committee desiring to engage in political dialogue concerning a ballot measure.

Subsequently, in *Federal Election Commission v. National Conservative Political Action Committee*, 470 U.S. 480 (1985), the Court struck down provisions of the Presidential Election Campaign Fund Act that used criminal sanctions to prohibit PACs from making contributions of more than $1,000 to any presidential candidate who had accepted public campaign financing. The Court, per then Justice Rehnquist, clearly indicated its frustration with the workability of the contributions/expenditures divide:

> The PACs in this case, of course, are not lone pamphleteers or street corner orators in the Tom Paine mold; they spend substantial amounts of money in order to communicate their political ideas through sophisticated media advertisements. And of course the criminal sanction in question is applied to the expenditure of money to propagate political views, rather than to the propagation of those views unaccompanied by the expenditure of money. But for purposes of presenting political

views in connection with a nationwide Presidential election, allowing the presentation of views while forbidding the expenditure of more than $1,000 to present them is much like allowing a speaker in a public hall to express his views while denying him the use of an amplifying system. 470 U.S. at 493.

3. Both Justice Breyer in concurrence and Justice Kennedy in dissent introduce a new element to the Court's debates over *Buckley*: is it working? Each appears willing to evaluate the constitutionality of various state regulations in terms of their efficacy in promoting healthy electoral practices and according to the incentives they give for vigorous electoral debate. Is this the proper framework for constitutional adjudication? Is the Court particularly adept at making such evaluations of the functioning of electoral regulations?

Beyond the institutional competence of the Court in administering a system of campaign finance regulation is a further concern about the unintended consequences of the regulatory enterprise. So long as the First Amendment imposes some limitations on how far speech in the public political arena may be regulated, the risk becomes that incomplete regulation creates two domains, one regulated and the other unregulated. The political campaign system may be thought of as being subject to "hydraulic" pressures whereby the tightening of controls in the regulated domain may not reduce the amount of or influence of money in the system overall, but rather in redirecting the flow of money toward less regulated enterprises and actors. Some argue that there is a "paradox involving the key claim that money has the capacity to command the will and distort the outcomes of the political process." In this view, "even if the reform advocates had their way, they would discover what the Corps of Engineers learned over the years in trying to redirect the Mississippi. Money, like water, will seek its own level. The price of apparent containment may be uncontrolled flood damage elsewhere." Thus the result may make matters decisively worse:

> Political actors spend money on politics because they care about political outcomes and think spending money makes it more likely their side will prevail. The money that reform squeezes out of the formal campaign process must go somewhere.

> We are particularly worried that reforms would exacerbate the already disturbing trend toward politics being divorced from the mediating influence of candidates and political parties. For all the influence that money may claim in the political process, votes are still channeled through candidates and political partes that have strong incentives to appeal more broadly than to a single issue or the desires of a single constituency. That money has influence is unquestionable. But the influence it has is profoundly qualified by the give and take of candidates who must stake out positions across a wide variety of issues and by political parties that have strong institutional interests in hewing to a middle course. Without mediating institutional buffers, money be-

comes the exclusive coin of the realm as politics pushes toward issue advocacy by groups not engaged in the give and take of party and coalitional politics.

Samuel Issacharoff & Pamela S. Karlan, *The Hydraulics of Campaign Finance Regulation,* 77 Tex. L. Rev. 1705, 1713–14 (1999). Some researchers have found such a displacement effect in states that have imposed significant contribution limits, such as Wisconsin. *See* Michael L. Malbin & Thomas L. Gais: The Day After Reform: Sobering Campaign Finance Lessons From The 50 American States 89–90 (1998).

4. How much of the constitutional debate regarding campaign-finance regulation is an empirical dispute over the measurable effects of such regulation? Note the kind of evidence the Court is prepared to find sufficient in *Shrink*. In particular, how much should it matter to constitutional analysis that campaign-finance regulation emerges from a voter initiative process, as opposed to legislation? In *Shrink*, the fact that the measure was voter-initiated *itself* seemed to provide, in part, the empirical evidence the First Amendment requires. Is that appropriate? In general, keep in mind the relationship between normative judgments and demands for empirical justification in constitutional cases involving democracy, particularly in the campaign-finance area. How much do disputes over purportedly empirical facts masquerade for what are really disputes about normative judgments?

2. EXPENDITURE LIMITS

Colorado Republican Federal Campaign Committee v. Federal Election Commission (Colorado Republican I)

518 U.S. 604 (1996).

■ JUSTICE BREYER announced the judgment of the Court and delivered an opinion, in which JUSTICE O'CONNOR and JUSTICE SOUTER join.

In April 1986, before the Colorado Republican Party had selected its senatorial candidate for the fall's election, that Party's Federal Campaign Committee bought radio advertisements attacking Timothy Wirth, the Democratic Party's likely candidate. The Federal Election Commission (FEC) charged that this "expenditure" exceeded the dollar limits that a provision of the Federal Election Campaign Act of 1971 (FECA) imposes upon political party "expenditure[s] in connection with" a "general election campaign" for congressional office. 90 Stat. 486, as amended, 2 U.S.C. § 441a(d)(3). This case focuses upon the constitutionality of those limits as applied to this case. We conclude that the First Amendment prohibits the application of this provision to the kind of expenditure at issue here—an expenditure that the political party has made independently, without coordination with any candidate.

To understand the issues and our holding, one must begin with FECA as it emerged from Congress in 1974. That Act sought both to remedy the appearance of a "corrupt" political process (one in which large contributions seem to buy legislative votes) and to level the electoral playing field by reducing campaign costs. *See Buckley v. Valeo.* It consequently imposed limits upon the amounts that individuals, corporations, "political committees" (such as political action committees, or PAC's), and political parties could contribute to candidates for federal office, and it also imposed limits upon the amounts that candidates, corporations, labor unions, political committees, and political parties could spend, even on their own, to help a candidate win election.

This Court subsequently examined several of the Act's provisions in light of the First Amendment's free speech and association protections.... Most of the provisions this Court found unconstitutional imposed expenditure limits. Those provisions limited candidates' rights to spend their own money, ... limited a candidate's campaign expenditures, ... limited the right of individuals to make "independent" expenditures (not coordinated with the candidate or candidate's campaign), ... and similarly limited the right of political committees to make "independent" expenditures.... The provisions that the Court found constitutional mostly imposed contribution limits—limits that apply both when an individual or political committee contributes money directly to a candidate and also when they indirectly contribute by making expenditures that they coordinate with the candidate, § 441a(a)(7)(B)(i).

Consequently, for present purposes, the Act now prohibits individuals and political committees from making direct, or indirect, contributions that exceed the following limits:

(a) For any "person": $1,000 to a candidate "with respect to any election"; $5,000 to any political committee in any year; $20,000 to the national committees of a political party in any year; but all within an overall limit (for any individual in any year) of $25,000. 2 U.S.C. §§ 441a(a)(1), (3).

(b) For any "multicandidate political committee": $5,000 to a candidate "with respect to any election"; $5,000 to any political committee in any year; and $15,000 to the national committees of a political party in any year. § 441a(a)(2).

FECA also has a special provision, directly at issue in this case, that governs contributions and expenditures by political parties. § 441a(d). This special provision creates, in part, an exception to the above contribution limits. That is, without special treatment, political parties ordinarily would be subject to the general limitation on contributions by a "multicandidate political committee" just described. See § 441a(a)(4). That provision, as we said in (b) above, limits annual contributions by a "multicandidate political committee" to no more than $5,000 to any candidate. And as also mentioned above, this contribution limit governs not only direct contributions but also indirect contributions that take the form of coordinated expenditures, defined as "expenditures made.... in cooperation, consultation, or concert, with, or at the request or suggestion of, a candidate, his authorized political committees, or their agents." § 441a(a)(7)(B)(i). Thus, ordinarily, a party's coordinated expenditures would be subject to the $5,000 limitation.

However, FECA's special provision, which we shall call the "Party Expenditure Provision," creates a general exception from this contribution limitation, and from any other limitation on expenditures. It says:

> Notwithstanding any other provision of law with respect to limitations on expenditures or limitations on contributions, ... political party [committees] ... may make expenditures in connection with the general election campaign of candidates for Federal office.... § 441a(d)(1).

After exempting political parties from the general contribution and expenditure limitations of the statute, the Party Expenditure Provision then imposes a substitute limitation upon party "expenditures" in a senatorial campaign equal to the greater of $20,000 or "2 cents multiplied by the voting age population of the State," § 441a(d)(3)(A)(i), adjusted for inflation since 1974, § 441a(c). The Provision permitted a political party in Colorado in 1986 to spend about $103,000 in connection with the general election campaign of a candidate for the United States Senate....

In January 1986, Timothy Wirth, then a Democratic Congressman, announced that he would run for an open Senate seat in November. In April, before either the Democratic primary or the Republican convention, the Colorado Republican Federal Campaign Committee (Colorado Party), the petitioner here, bought radio advertisements attacking Congressman Wirth. The State Democratic Party complained to the Federal Election Commission. It pointed out that the Colorado Party had previously assigned its $103,000 general election allotment to the National Republican Senatorial Committee, leaving it without any permissible spending balance. *See Federal Election Comm'n v. Democratic Senatorial Campaign Comm.*, 454 U.S. 27 (1981)(state party may appoint national senatorial campaign committee as agent to spend its Party Expenditure Provision allotment). It argued that the purchase of radio time was an "expenditure in connection with the general election campaign of a candidate for Federal office," § 441a(d)(3), which, consequently, exceeded the Party Expenditure Provision limits.

The FEC agreed with the Democratic Party....

II

The summary judgment record indicates that the expenditure in question is what this Court in *Buckley* called an "independent" expenditure, not a "coordinated" expenditure that other provisions of FECA treat as a kind of campaign "contribution".... So treated, the expenditure falls within the scope of the Court's precedents that extend First Amendment protection to independent expenditures. Beginning with *Buckley*, the

Court's cases have found a "fundamental constitutional difference between money spent to advertise one's views independently of the candidate's campaign and money contributed to the candidate to be spent on his campaign." *Federal Election Commission v. National Conservative Political Action Comm.*, 470 U.S. 480, 497 (1986)("*NCPAC*"). This difference has been grounded in the observation that restrictions on contributions impose "only a marginal restriction upon the contributor's ability to engage in free communication," *Buckley, supra,* at 20–21, because the symbolic communicative value of a contribution bears little relation to its size . . . and because such limits leave "persons free to engage in independent political expression, to associate actively through volunteering their services, and to assist to a limited but nonetheless substantial extent in supporting candidates and committees with financial resources." *Id.,* at 28. At the same time, reasonable contribution limits directly and materially advance the Government's interest in preventing exchanges of large financial contributions for political favors.

In contrast, the Court has said that restrictions on independent expenditures significantly impair the ability of individuals and groups to engage in direct political advocacy and "represent substantial . . . restraints on the quantity and diversity of political speech." *Id.,* at 19. And at the same time, the Court has concluded that limitations on independent expenditures are less directly related to preventing corruption, since "[t]he absence of prearrangement and coordination of an expenditure with the candidate . . . not only undermines the value of the expenditure to the candidate, but also alleviates the danger that expenditures will be given as a quid pro quo for improper commitments from the candidate." *Id.,* at 47.

Given these established principles, we do not see how a provision that limits a political party's independent expenditures can escape their controlling effect. A political party's independent expression not only reflects its members' views about the philosophical and governmental matters that bind them together, it also seeks to convince others to join those members in a practical democratic task, the task of creating a government that voters can instruct and hold responsible for subsequent success or failure. The independent expression of a political party's views is "core" First Amendment activity no less than is the independent expression of individuals, candidates, or other political committees.

We are not aware of any special dangers of corruption associated with political parties that tip the constitutional balance in a different direction. When this Court considered, and held unconstitutional, limits that FECA had set on certain independent expenditures by political action committees, it reiterated *Buckley*'s observation that "the absence of prearrangement and coordination" does not eliminate, but it does help to "alleviate," any "danger" that a candidate will understand the expenditure as an effort to obtain a "quid pro quo." The same is true of independent party expenditures.

III

The Government does not deny the force of the precedent we have discussed. Rather, it argued below, and the lower courts accepted, that the expenditure in this case should be treated under those precedents, not as an "independent expenditure," but rather as a "coordinated expenditure," which those cases have treated as "contributions," and which those cases have held Congress may constitutionally regulate.

While the District Court found that the expenditure in this case was "coordinated," it did not do so based on any factual finding that the Party had consulted with any candidate in the making or planning of the advertising campaign in question. Instead, the District Court accepted the Government's argument that all party expenditures should be treated as if they had been coordinated as a matter of law.... The question, instead, is whether the Court of Appeals erred as a legal matter in accepting the Government's conclusive presumption that all party expenditures are "coordinated." We believe it did.

■ JUSTICE KENNEDY, with whom THE CHIEF JUSTICE and JUSTICE SCALIA join, concurring in the judgment and dissenting in part.

* * *

We had no occasion in *Buckley* to consider possible First Amendment objections to limitations on spending by parties. While our cases uphold contribution limitations on individuals and associations, political party spending "in cooperation, consultation, or concert with" a candidate does not fit within our description of "contributions" in *Buckley*. In my view, we should not transplant the reasoning of cases upholding ordinary contribution limitations to a case involving FECA's restrictions on political party spending.

The First Amendment embodies a "profound national commitment to the principle that debate on public issues should be uninhibited, robust, and wide-open." *New York Times Co. v. Sullivan,* 376 U.S. 254, 270 (1964). Political parties have a unique role in serving this principle; they exist to advance their members' shared political beliefs. A party performs this function, in part, by "identify[ing] the people who constitute the association, and ... limit[ing] the association to those people only." *Democratic Party of United States v. Wisconsin ex rel. La Follette,* 450 U.S. 107, 122 (1981). Having identified its members, however, a party can give effect to their views only by selecting and supporting candidates. A political party has its own traditions and principles that transcend the interests of individual candidates and campaigns; but in the context of particular elections, candidates are necessary to make the party's message known and effective, and vice versa.

It makes no sense, therefore, to ask, as FECA does, whether a party's spending is made "in cooperation, consultation, or concert with" its candidate. The answer in most cases will be yes, but that provides more, not less, justification for holding unconstitutional the statute's attempt to control this type of party spending, which bears little resemblance to the contributions discussed in *Buckley*. Party spending "in cooperation, consultation, or concert with" its candidates of necessity "communicate[s] the underlying basis for the support," 424 U.S., at 21, i.e., the hope that he or she will be elected and will work to further the party's political agenda.

The problem is not just the absence of a basis in our First Amendment cases for treating the party's spending as contributions. The greater difficulty posed by the statute is its stifling effect on the ability of the party to do what it exists to do. It is fanciful to suppose that limiting party spending of the type at issue here "does not in any way infringe the contributor's freedom to discuss candidates and issues," *ibid.*, since it would be impractical and imprudent, to say the least, for a party to support its own candidates without some form of "cooperation" or "consultation." The party's speech, legitimate on its own behalf, cannot be separated from speech on the candidate's behalf without constraining the party in advocating its most essential positions and pursuing its most basic goals. The party's form of organization and the fact that its fate in an election is inextricably intertwined with that of its candidates cannot provide a basis for the restrictions imposed here.

We have a constitutional tradition of political parties and their candidates engaging in joint First Amendment activity; we also have a practical identity of interests between the two entities during an election. Party spending "in cooperation, consultation, or concert with" a candidate therefore is indistinguishable in substance from expenditures by the candidate or his campaign committee. We held in *Buckley* that the First Amendment does not permit regulation of the latter, and it should not permit this regulation of the former. Congress may have authority, consistent with the First Amendment, to restrict undifferentiated political party contributions which satisfy the constitutional criteria we discussed in *Buckley*, but that type of regulation is not at issue here.

I would resolve the Party's First Amendment claim in accord with these principles rather than remit the Party to further protracted proceedings. Because the principal opinion would do otherwise, I concur only in the judgment.

■ Justice Thomas, concurring in the judgment and dissenting in part, with whom The Chief Justice and Justice Scalia join in Parts I and III.

* * *

II

* * *

A

[. . .] Contributions and expenditures both involve core First Amendment expression because they further the "[d]iscussion of public issues and debate on the qualifications of candidates . . . integral to the operation of the system of government established by our Constitution." *Buckley*, 424 U.S. at 14. When an individual donates money to a candidate or to a partisan organization, he enhances the donee's ability to communicate a message and thereby adds to political debate, just as when that individual communicates the message himself. Indeed, the individual may add more to political discourse by giving rather than spending, if the donee is able to put the funds to more productive use than can the individual. . . .

I can discern only one potentially meaningful distinction between contributions and expenditures. In the former case, the funds pass through an intermediary—some individual or entity responsible for organizing and facilitating the dissemination of the message—whereas in the latter case they may not necessarily do so. But the practical judgment by a citizen that another person or an organization can more effectively deploy funds for the good of a common cause than he can ought not deprive that citizen of his First Amendment rights. Whether an individual donates money to a candidate or group who will use it to promote the candidate or whether the individual spends the money to promote the candidate himself, the individual seeks to engage in political expression and to associate with likeminded persons. A contribution is simply an indirect expenditure; though contributions and expenditures may thus differ in form, they do not differ in substance. As one commentator cautioned, "let us not lose sight of the speech." L. Powe, *Mass Speech and the Newer First Amendment*, 1982 S.Ct. Rev. 243, 258. . . .

The other justification in *Buckley* for the proposition that contribution caps only marginally restrict speech—that is, that a contribution signals only general support for the candidate but indicates nothing about the reasons for that support—is similarly unsatisfying. Assuming the assertion is descriptively accurate (which is certainly questionable), it still cannot mean that giving is less important than spending in terms of the First Amendment. A campaign poster that reads simply "We support candidate Smith" does not seem to me any less deserving of constitutional protection than one that reads "We support candidate Smith because we like his position on agriculture subsidies." Both express a political opinion. Even a pure message of support, unadorned with reasons, is valuable to the democratic process.

In sum, unlike the *Buckley* Court, I believe that contribution limits infringe as directly and as seriously upon freedom of political expression and association as do expenditure limits. The protections of the First Amendment do not depend upon so fine a line as that between spending money to support a candidate or group and giving money to the candidate or group to spend for the same purpose. In principle, people and groups give money to candidates and other groups for the same reason that they spend money in support of those candidates and groups: because they share social, economic, and political beliefs and seek to have those beliefs affect governmental policy. I think that the *Buckley* framework for analyzing the constitutionality of campaign finance laws is deeply flawed. Accordingly, I would not employ it, as JUSTICE BREYER and JUSTICE KENNEDY do.

B

Instead, I begin with the premise that there is no constitutionally significant difference between campaign contributions and expenditures: both forms of speech are central to the First Amendment. Curbs on protected speech, we have repeatedly said, must be strictly scrutinized....

The formula for strict scrutiny is, of course, well-established. It requires both a compelling governmental interest and legislative means narrowly tailored to serve that interest. In the context of campaign finance reform, the only governmental interest that we have accepted as compelling is the prevention of corruption or the appearance of corruption, *see NCPAC*, and we have narrowly defined "corruption" as a "financial quid pro quo: dollars for political favors," *id.,* at 497. As for the means-ends fit under strict scrutiny, we have specified that "[w]here at all possible, government must curtail speech only to the degree necessary to meet the particular problem at hand, and must avoid infringing on speech that does not pose the danger that has prompted regulation." *Federal Election Comm'n v. Massachusetts Citizens for Life,* 479 U.S. 238, 265 (1986).

* * *

Buckley's rationale for the contrary conclusion is faulty. That bribery laws are not completely effective in stamping out corruption is no justification for the conclusion that prophylactic controls on funding activity are narrowly tailored. The First Amendment limits Congress to legislative measures that do not abridge the Amendment's guaranteed freedoms, thereby constraining Congress' ability to accomplish certain goals. Similarly, that other modes of expression remain open to regulated individuals or groups does not mean that a statute is the least restrictive means of addressing a particular social problem. A statute could, of course, be more restrictive than necessary while still leaving open some avenues for speech.[9]

III

[... T]here is only a minimal threat of "corruption," as we have understood that term, when a political party spends to support its candi-

---

9. [...]There is good reason to think that campaign reform is an especially inappropriate area for judicial deference to legislative judgment. *See generally* L. BeVier, *Money and Politics: A Perspective on the First Amendment and Campaign Finance Reform*, 73 Cal. L. Rev. 1045, 1074–1081 (1985). What the argument for deference fails to acknowledge is the potential for legislators to set the rules of the electoral game so as to keep themselves in power and to keep potential challengers out of it.... Indeed, history demonstrates that the most significant effect of election reform has been not to purify public service, but to protect incumbents and increase the influence of special interest groups.

date or to oppose his competitor, whether or not that expenditure is made in concert with the candidate. Parties and candidates have traditionally worked together to achieve their common goals, and when they engage in that work, there is no risk to the Republic. To the contrary, the danger to the Republic lies in Government suppression of such activity. Under *Buckley* and our subsequent cases, § 441a(d)(3)'s heavy burden on First Amendment rights is not justified by the threat of corruption at which it is assertedly aimed.

* * *

■ JUSTICE STEVENS, with whom JUSTICE GINSBURG joins, dissenting.

In my opinion, all money spent by a political party to secure the election of its candidate for the office of United States Senator should be considered a "contribution" to his or her campaign. I therefore disagree with the conclusion reached in Part III of the Court's opinion.

I am persuaded that three interests provide a constitutionally sufficient predicate for federal limits on spending by political parties. First, such limits serve the interest in avoiding both the appearance and the reality of a corrupt political process. A party shares a unique relationship with the candidate it sponsors because their political fates are inextricably linked. That interdependency creates a special danger that the party—or the persons who control the party—will abuse the influence it has over the candidate by virtue of its power to spend. The provisions at issue are appropriately aimed at reducing that threat. The fact that the party in this case had not yet chosen its nominee at the time it broadcast the challenged advertisements is immaterial to the analysis. Although the Democratic and Republican nominees for the 1996 Presidential race will not be selected until this summer, current advertising expenditures by the two national parties are no less contributions to the campaigns of the respective front-runners than those that will be made in the fall.

Second, these restrictions supplement other spending limitations embodied in the Act, which are likewise designed to prevent corruption. Individuals and certain organizations are permitted to contribute up to $1,000 to a candidate. 2 U.S.C. § 441a(a)(1)(A). Since the same donors can give up to $5,000 to party committees, § 441a(a)(1)(C), if there were no limits on party spending, their contributions could be spent to benefit the candidate and thereby circumvent the $1,000 cap. We have recognized the legitimate interest in blocking similar attempts to undermine the policies of the Act.

Finally, I believe the Government has an important interest in leveling the electoral playing field by constraining the cost of federal campaigns. As Justice White pointed out in his opinion in *Buckley,* "money is not always equivalent to or used for speech, even in the context of political campaigns." 424 U.S. at 263. It is quite wrong to assume that the net effect of limits on contributions and expenditures—which tend to protect equal access to the political arena, to free candidates and their staffs from the interminable burden of fund-raising, and to diminish the importance of repetitive 30–second commercials—will be adverse to the interest in informed debate protected by the First Amendment.

Congress surely has both wisdom and experience in these matters that is far superior to ours. I would therefore accord special deference to its judgment on questions related to the extent and nature of limits on campaign spending.

NOTES AND QUESTIONS

1. The Court in *Colorado Republican I* finds that the independent expenditures of a political party are "core" activities that reflect the party's views on matters of philosophy and government. How convincing is the distinction between such expenditures by a political party and the contributions of a committed partisan to further a campaign reflecting his or her views on matters of philosophy and government? Should the Democratic or Republican parties have more right to spend funds to promote their views than private citizens? Does the Court identify a constitutional principle that would recognize such a distinction?

2. *Colorado Republican I* shows the tremendous tensions that resulted from the way that *Buckley* left in place only half of the regulatory regime created in FECA. The purpose behind the 1974 Amendments to FECA was to limit the overall impact of money on political campaigns. As the Act survived Court review, however, the combination of unrestricted expenditures and constrained contributions placed more pressure than ever on ingenious systems of fund-raising that did not run afoul of the Act. This pressure on "creative" fund-raising increased as a result of the introduction of public financing that attempted to condition the receipt of public funds on voluntary limitations on expenditures. In *Buckley*, the Supreme Court approved this regulatory device: "Congress may engage in public financing of election campaigns and may condition acceptance of public funds on an agreement by the candidate to abide by specified expenditure limitations. Just as a candidate may voluntarily limit the size of the contributions he chooses to accept, he may decide to forgo private fundraising and accept public funding." 424 U.S. at 25–51 n. 65. *Colorado Republican I* reflects the determined efforts of major parties to circumvent both contribution limitations and conditions for the receipt of public funding applicable to candidates by shifting an increased level of fundraising and campaign direction to nominally independent political parties. Whereas the candidate-controlled and more tightly regulated contributions and expenditures have been referred to as "hard money," the funds raised by political parties for such purposes as "party building" have been termed "soft money." Among the reasons for the emergence of soft money was the FECA restriction on corporations and unions making direct financial contributions. These groups can circumvent FECA by donating exempted soft money in the form of "get out the vote drives," volunteer travel expenses, consulting, polls, "ordinary course of business loans," and office construction expenses. As reflected in Table 1, the emerging strategy of shifting campaign activities to the uncontrolled arena has occasioned an explosion in the use of "soft money" between the 1992 and 1996 election cycles:

Table 1
Soft Money Spent by Major Parties—1991–2000
Source: Federal Election Commission

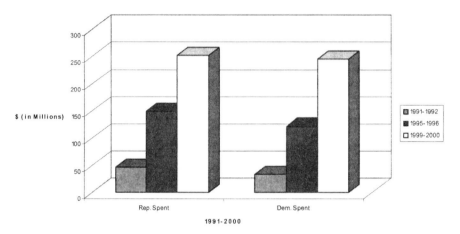

3. Does the distinction between "hard money" and "soft money" make sense? Is there a meaningful distinction in the risk of corruption posed by hard money as opposed to soft money contributions? In addition, the effect of soft money on campaigns must be considered. A series of studies by David Magleby on the role of soft money in recent elections demonstrate the significant impact this spending has had on the electoral process. David B. Magleby, The Other Campaign: Soft Money and Issue Advocacy in the 2000 Congressional Elections (2002); David B. Magleby, Outside Money (2000). The studies found that quality candidates are still crucially important, as even increased spending cannot help a bad candidate. In competitive elections, however, increased soft money spending resulted in a saturated media environment. In addition, soft money ads tend to increase the level of negativity in campaigns, which suppresses voter turnout and lowers participation levels. The studies found that "on the ground" efforts, including voter identification efforts through direct mail and phone banks were more effective than "in the air" efforts over television and radio and are being used more extensively. This increased spending allowed interest groups to set the issue agenda to a degree which they had not previously attained. The authors suggest that these trends indicate a fundamental shift in competitive congressional elections from a candidate-centered system of elections to an interest group and party-centered system.

4. To what extent has technology compromised the inherited regulatory structure of FECA? Michael Kang argues that the contemporary system of campaign regulation was aimed at limiting big money interests from dominating mass media advertising. He further argues that the break-up of television markets has made narrowcasting—defined as targeted, direct contact with voters—more relevant than broadcasting. Highlighting the impact of this fragmentation, Jim Margolis, a political advertising specialist who worked for John Kerry's presidential campaign, noted that he had to run commercials twice as often in 2004 as in the 1990s in order to cut through the clutter. Paul Farhi, *Voters Are Harder to Reach as Media Outlets Multiply*, Wash. Post, June 16, 2004, at A1. Kang concludes that, "narrowcasting represents a strategic modernization of old-fashioned politics that not only is difficult to regulate legally, but also makes the case for reform less compelling." Michael S. Kang, *From Broadcasting to Narrowcasting: The Emerging Challenge for Campaign Finance Law*, 73 Geo. Wash. L. Rev. 1070, 1095 (2005).

5. After *Colorado Republican I*, there was a clear majority of votes on the Supreme Court to overturn *Buckley*. These divided, however, between the group represented by Justice Thomas, who sought to overturn *Buckley's* restrictions on contributions, and the group represented by Justice Stevens, who would have overturned *Buckley's* protections of expenditures. Both of the anti-*Buckley* wings are united by rejecting the core insight of *Buckley* that different first amendment regimes govern the contributions and expenditures side of electoral regulation. But they are divided by an inability to agree on the direction in which the *Buckley* edifice should fall. Thus, it may be said that not only is the FECA regime as modified by *Buckley* one that no legislature ever envisioned as a policy matter, as Professor Sorauf argues, but that even the *Buckley* modification of FECA is not one that could command the consensus of the Court. Yet *Buckley* remains oddly stable because the antagonism of the dissenting views prevents the emergence of any majority coalition for overturning *Buckley*—at least thus far. For an account of the Court's inability to overturn *Buckley* despite diminishing doctrinal support for the core contribution/expenditure distinction, see Pamela S. Karlan, *Dead Ends and New Beginnings in the Law of Democracy*, ___ Ohio St. L. J. ___ (2007).

6. Justice Kennedy's opinion in *Colorado Republican I* directly ties concerns about campaign finance regulation to the ability of political parties to play their proper roles in a competitive democratic process. For Justice Kennedy, the result is an independent substantive ground for protecting political parties from the operation of FECA, regardless of the viability of the *Buckley* demarcation between regulation and expenditures. On this view, if parties are unable to advocate effectively for their chosen candidates, they lose their capacity for meaningful political expression, regardless of the characterization of their activities as contributions or expenditures. As discussed extensively in Chapter 4, this approach directs the inquiry back to the role that political parties are expected to play in maintaining the competitive vigor of the political process. Notice as well the striking similarity between the argument advanced by Justice Kennedy in the context of campaign finance regulation and that put forward by Justice Scalia in *California Democratic Party v. Jones,* in the context of direct regulation of party selection of candidates for office:

> In no area is the political association's right to exclude more important than in the process of selecting its nominee. That process often determines the party's positions on the most significant public policy issues of the day, and even when those positions are predetermined it is the nominee who becomes the party's ambassador to the general electorate in winning it over to the party's views. 530 U.S. at 574.

7. *Colorado Republican II:* The Supreme Court in *Colorado Republican* concluded that the advertisement in question was an independent expenditure protected by the First Amendment under *Buckley* but did not reach the issue of whether the First Amendment forbids limits on coordinated expenditures between political parties and their candidates, which are considered contributions under the FECA. However, on remand the federal district court held that the Party Expenditure Provision, which limits the amount of money a political party may spend in coordination with its candidates, violated the First Amendment, and the Tenth Circuit Court of Appeals affirmed. Despite the fact that the Supreme Court has typically upheld limitations on contributions, and has subjected them to a lower standard of scrutiny, the Tenth Circuit held that the labels "contribution" and "expenditure" did not decide the case at hand. In holding the limitations on coordinated expenditures unconstitutional, the court concluded:

> [T]he Party Expenditure Provision constitutes a "significant interference" with the First Amendment rights of political parties. This interference effects more than a "marginal restriction upon the [parties'] ability to engage in free communication." The FEC has not demonstrated on remand that coordinated spending by political parties corrupts, or creates the appearance of corrupting, the electoral process. Therefore, [the Party Expenditure Provision's] limit on party spending is not "closely drawn" to the recognized governmental interest but instead constitutes an "unnecessary abridgment" of First Amendment freedoms.

Federal Election Commission v. Colorado Republican Fed. Campaign Comm'n, 213 F.3d 1221 (10th Cir. 2000). As we turn to the Supreme Court's decision in *Colorado Republican II,* recall that the facts of the case concern the 1986 Colorado senatorial election. What does 14 years of legal review of the FEC's determination say about the efficacy of this approach to regulating electoral conduct in the heat of an election battle?

FEC v. Colorado Republican Federal Campaign Committee (Colorado Republican II)

533 U.S. 431 (2001).

■ JUSTICE SOUTER, delivered the opinion of the Court, in which STEVENS, O'CONNOR, GINSBURG, and BREYER, JJ., joined. THOMAS, J., filed a dissenting opinion, in which SCALIA and KENNEDY, JJ., joined, and in which REHNQUIST, C. J., joined as to Part II.

In *Colorado Federal Campaign Comm. v. Federal Election Comm'n*, 518 U.S. 604 (1996) (*Colorado I*), we held that spending limits set by the Federal Election Campaign Act were unconstitutional as applied to the Colorado Republican Party's independent expenditures in connection with a senatorial campaign. We remanded for consideration of the party's claim that all limits on expenditures by a political party in connection with congressional campaigns are facially unconstitutional and thus unenforceable even as to spending coordinated with a candidate. Today we reject that facial challenge to the limits on parties' coordinated expenditures.

I

Spending for political ends and contributing to political candidates both fall within the First Amendment's protection of speech and political association. But ever since we first reviewed the 1971 Act, we have understood that limits on political expenditures deserve closer scrutiny than restrictions on political contributions. Restraints on expenditures generally curb more expressive and associational activity than limits on contributions do. A further reason for the distinction is that limits on contributions are more clearly justified by a link to political corruption than limits on other kinds of unlimited political spending are (corruption being understood not only as quid pro quo agreements, but also as undue influence on an officeholder's judgment, and the appearance of such influence). At least this is so where the spending is not coordinated with a candidate or his campaign. In *Buckley* we said that:

> [u]nlike contributions, . . . independent expenditures may well provide little assistance to the candidate's campaign and indeed may prove counterproductive. The absence of prearrangement and coordination of an expenditure with the candidate or his agent not only undermines the value of the expenditure to the candidate, but also alleviates the danger that expenditures will be given as a quid pro quo for improper commitments from the candidate.

Given these differences, we have routinely struck down limitations on independent expenditures by candidates, other individuals, and groups, while repeatedly upholding contribution limits. . . .

The First Amendment line between spending and donating is easy to draw when it falls between independent expenditures by individuals or political action committees (PACs) without any candidate's approval (or wink or nod), and contributions in the form of cash gifts to candidates. But facts speak less clearly once the independence of the spending cannot be taken for granted, and money spent by an individual or PAC according to an arrangement with a candidate is therefore harder to classify. As already seen, Congress drew a functional, not a formal, line between contributions and expenditures when it provided that coordinated expenditures by individuals and nonparty groups are subject to the Act's contribution limits, 2 U. S. C. § 441a(a)(7)(B)(i). In *Buckley*, the Court acknowledged Congress's functional classification, 424 U. S., at 46–47, and n. 53, and observed that treating coordinated expenditures as contributions "prevent[s] attempts to circumvent the Act through prearranged or coordinated expenditures amounting to disguised contributions. . . ." *Buckley*, in fact, enhanced the significance of this functional treatment by striking down independent expenditure limits on First Amendment grounds while upholding limitations on contributions (by individuals and nonparty groups), as defined to include coordinated expenditures. *Colorado I* addressed the FEC's effort to stretch the functional treatment of coordinated expenditures further than the plain application of the statutory definition. . . .

But that still left the question whether the First Amendment allows coordinated election expenditures by parties to be treated functionally as contributions, the way coordinated expenditures by other entities are treated.

* * *

IV

* * *

A

* * *

1

The assertion that the party is so joined at the hip to candidates that most of its spending must necessarily be coordinated spending is a statement at odds with the history of nearly 30 years under the Act. It is well to remember that ever since the Act was amended in 1974, coordinated spending by a party committee in a given race has been limited by the provision challenged here (or its predecessor). It was not until 1996 and the decision in *Colorado I* that any spending was allowed above that amount, and since then only independent spending has been unlimited. As a consequence, the Party's claim that coordinated spending beyond the limit imposed by the Act is essential to its very function as a party amounts implicitly to saying that for almost three decades political parties have not been functional or have been functioning in systematic violation of the law. The Party, of course, does not in terms make either statement, and we cannot accept either implication. There is no question about the closeness of candidates to parties and no doubt that the Act affected parties' roles and their exercise of power. But the political scientists who have weighed in on this litigation observe that "there is little evidence to suggest that coordinated party spending limits adopted by Congress have frustrated the ability of political parties to exercise their First Amendment rights to support their candidates," and that "[i]n reality, political parties are dominant players, second only to the candidates themselves, in federal elections." Brief for Paul Allen Beck et al. as Amici Curiae. For the Party to claim after all these years of strictly limited coordinated spending that unlimited coordinated spending is essential to the nature and functioning of parties is in reality to assert just that "metaphysical identity," 518 U. S., at 623, between freespending party and candidate that we could not accept in *Colorado I.*

2

There is a different weakness in the seemingly unexceptionable premise that parties are organized for the purpose of electing candidates.... The fault here is not so much metaphysics as myopia, a refusal to see how the power of money actually works in the political structure.

When we look directly at a party's function in getting and spending money, it would ignore reality to think that the party role is adequately described by speaking generally of electing particular candidates. The money parties spend comes from contributors with their own personal interests.... Parties are thus necessarily the instruments of some contributors whose object is not to support the party's message or to elect party candidates across the board, but rather to support a specific candidate for the sake of a position on one, narrow issue, or even to support any candidate who will be obliged to the contributors.

Parties thus perform functions more complex than simply electing candidates; whether they like it or not, they act as agents for spending on behalf of those who seek to produce obligated officeholders. It is this party role, which functionally unites parties with other self-interested political actors, that the Party Expenditure Provision targets. This party role, accordingly, provides good reason to view limits on coordinated spending by parties through the same lens applied to such spending by donors, like PACs, that can use parties as conduits for contributions meant to place candidates under obligation.

* * *

5

The Party's arguments for being treated differently from other political actors subject to limitation on political spending under the Act do not pan out. Despite decades of limitation on coordinated spending, parties have not been rendered useless. In reality, parties continue to organize to elect candidates, and also function for the benefit of donors whose object is to place candidates under obligation, a fact that parties cannot escape. Indeed, parties' capacity to concentrate power to elect is the very capacity that apparently opens them to exploitation as channels for circumventing contribution and coordinated spending limits binding on other political players. And some of these players could marshal the same power and sophistication for the same electoral objectives as political parties themselves.

We accordingly apply to a party's coordinated spending limitation the same scrutiny we have applied to the other political actors, that is, scrutiny appropriate for a contribution limit, enquiring whether the restriction is "closely drawn" to match what we have recognized as the "sufficiently important" government interest in combating political corruption. With the standard thus settled, the issue remains whether adequate evidentiary grounds exist to sustain the limit under that standard, on the theory that unlimited coordinated spending by a party raises the risk of corruption (and its appearance) through circumvention of valid contribution limits. Indeed, all members of the Court agree that circumvention is a valid theory of corruption; the remaining bone of contention is evidentiary.

B

Since there is no recent experience with unlimited coordinated spending, the question is whether experience under the present law confirms a serious threat of abuse from the unlimited coordinated party spending as the Government contends. *Cf. Burson v. Freeman*, 504 U. S. 191, 208 (1992) (opinion of Blackmun, J.) (noting difficulty of mustering evidence to support long-enforced statutes). It clearly does. Despite years of enforcement of the challenged limits, substantial evidence demonstrates how candidates, donors, and parties test the limits of the current law, and it shows beyond serious doubt how contribution limits would be eroded if inducement to circumvent them were enhanced by declaring parties' coordinated spending wide open.

Under the Act, a donor is limited to $2,000 in contributions to one candidate in a given election cycle. The same donor may give as much as another $20,000 each year to a national party committee supporting the candidate. What a realist would expect to occur has occurred. Donors give to the party with the tacit understanding that the favored candidate will benefit. *See* App. 247 (Declaration of Robert Hickmott, former Democratic fundraiser and National Finance Director for Timothy Wirth's Senate campaign) ("We ... told contributors who had made the maximum allowable contribution to the Wirth campaign but who wanted to do more that they could raise money for the DSCC so that we could get our maximum [Party Expenditure Provision] allocation from the DSCC"); *id.*, at 274 (declaration of Timothy Wirth) ("I understood that when I raised funds for the DSCC, the donors expected that I would receive the amount of their donations multiplied by a certain number that the DSCC had determined in advance, assuming the DSCC has raised other funds"); *id.*, at 166 (declaration of Leon G. Billings, former Executive Director of the Democratic Senatorial Campaign Committee (DSCC)) ("People often contribute to party committees because they have given the maximum amount to a candidate, and want to help the candidate indirectly by contributing to the party"); *id.*, at 99–100 (fundraising letter from Congressman Wayne Allard, dated Aug. 27, 1996, explaining to contributor that "you are at the limit of what you can directly contribute to my campaign," but "you can further help my campaign by assisting the Colorado Party").

Although the understanding between donor and party may involve no definite commitment and may be tacit on the donor's part, the frequency of the practice and the volume of money involved has required some manner of informal bookkeeping by the recipient. In the Democratic Party, at least, the method is known as "tallying," a system that helps to connect donors to candidates through the accommodation of a party. *See* App. 246–247 (Hickmott declaration) ("[The tally system] is an informal agreement between the DSCC and the candidates' campaigns that if you help the DSCC raise contributions, we will turn around and help your campaign"); *id.*, at 268 (declaration of former Senator Paul Simon) ("Donors would be told the money they contributed could be credited to any Senate candidate. The callers would make clear that this was not a direct contribution, but it was fairly close to direct"); *id.*, at 165–166 (Billings declaration) ("There appeared to be an understanding between the DSCC and the Senators that the amount of money they received from the DSCC was related to how much they raised for the Committee").

Such is the state of affairs under the current law, which requires most party spending on a candidate's behalf to be done independently, and thus less desirably from the point of view of a donor and his favored candidate. If suddenly every dollar of spending could be coordinated with the candidate, the inducement to circumvent would almost certainly intensify. Indeed, if a candidate could be assured that donations through a party could result in funds passed through to him for spending on virtually identical items as his own campaign funds, a candidate enjoying the patronage of affluent contributors would have a strong incentive not merely to direct donors to his party, but to promote circumvention as a step toward reducing the number of donors requiring time-consuming cultivation. If a candidate could arrange for a party committee to foot his bills, to be paid with $20,000 contributions to the party by his supporters, the number of donors necessary to raise $1,000,000 could be reduced from 500 (at $2,000 per cycle) to 46 (at $2,000 to the candidate and $20,000 to the party, without regard to donations outside the election year).

V

* * *

[. . .] There is no significant functional difference between a party's coordinated expenditure and a direct party contribution to the candidate, and there is good reason to expect that a party's right of unlimited coordinated spending would attract increased contributions to parties to finance exactly that kind of spending. Coordinated expenditures of money donated to a party are tailor-made to undermine contribution limits. Therefore the choice here is not, as in *Buckley* and *Colorado I*, between a limit on pure contributions and pure expenditures. The choice is between limiting contributions and limiting expenditures whose special value as expenditures is also the source of their power to corrupt. Congress is entitled to its choice.

* * *

We hold that a party's coordinated expenditures, unlike expenditures truly independent, may be restricted to minimize circumvention of contribution limits. We therefore reject the Party's facial challenge and, accordingly, reverse the judgment of the United States Court of Appeals for the Tenth Circuit.

It is so ordered.

■ JUSTICE THOMAS, with whom JUSTICE SCALIA and JUSTICE KENNEDY join, and with whom THE CHIEF JUSTICE joins as to Part II, dissenting.

The Party Expenditure Provision, 2 U. S. C. § 441a(d)(3), severely limits the amount of money that a national or state committee of a political party can spend in coordination with its own candidate for the Senate or House of Representatives. Because this provision sweeps too broadly, interferes with the party-candidate relationship, and has not been proved necessary to combat corruption, I respectfully dissent.

I

As an initial matter, I continue to believe that *Buckley v. Valeo* should be overruled.... I remain baffled that this Court has extended the most generous First Amendment safeguards to filing lawsuits, wearing profane jackets, and exhibiting drive-in movies with nudity, but has offered only tepid protection to the core speech and associational rights that our Founders sought to defend.

* * *

II

* * *

2

Even if I were to ignore the breadth of the statutory text, and to assume that all coordinated expenditures are functionally equivalent to contributions, I still would strike down the Party Expenditure Provision.

The source of the "contribution" at issue is a political party, not an individual or a political committee, as in *Buckley* and *Shrink Missouri*. Restricting contributions by individuals and political committees may, under *Buckley*, entail only a "marginal restriction," but the same cannot be said about limitations on political parties.

Political parties and their candidates are "inextricably intertwined" in the conduct of an election. A party nominates its candidate; a candidate often is identified by party affiliation throughout the election and on the ballot; and a party's public image is largely defined by what its candidates say and do. . . .

As the District Court explained, to break this link between the party and its candidates would impose "additional costs and burdens to promote the party message." 41 F. Supp. 2d 1197, 1210 (D. Colo. 1999). This observation finds full support in the record. *See, e.g.*, App. 218 (statement of Anthony Corrado, Associate Professor of Government, Colby College) (explaining that, to ensure that expenditures were independent, party organizations had to establish legally separate entities, which in turn had to "rent and furnish an office, hire staff, and pay other administrative costs," as well as "engage additional consulting services" and "duplicate many of the functions already being undertaken by other party offices"); *id.*, at 52 (statement by Federal Election Commission admitting that national party established separate entities that made independent expenditures); *id.*, at 217 (statement of Anthony Corrado) (explaining that reliance on independent expenditures would increase fundraising demands on party organizations because independent expenditures are less effective means of communication). . . .

* * *

B

* * *

1

* * *

The dearth of evidence is unsurprising in light of the unique relationship between a political party and its candidates: "The very aim of a political party is to influence its candidate's stance on issues and, if the candidate takes office or is reelected, his votes." *Colorado I*, 518 U. S., at 646 (THOMAS, J., concurring in judgment and dissenting in part). If coordinated expenditures help achieve this aim, the achievement "does not . . . constitute 'a subversion of the political process.' " *Ibid.* (quoting *Federal Election Comm'n*, 470 U. S., at 497). It is simply the essence of our Nation's party system of government. One can speak of an individual citizen or a political action committee corrupting or coercing a candidate, but "[w]hat could it mean for a party to 'corrupt' its candidate or to exercise 'coercive' influence over him?'' 470 U. S, at 646.

* * *

2

Even if the Government had presented evidence that the Party Expenditure Provision affects corruption, the statute still would be unconstitutional, because there are better tailored alternatives for addressing the corruption. In addition to bribery laws and disclosure laws, the Government has two options that would not entail the restriction of political parties' First Amendment rights.

First, the Government could enforce the earmarking rule of 2 U. S. C. § 441a(a)(8), under which contributions that ''are in any way earmarked or otherwise directed through an intermediary or conduit to [a] candidate'' are treated as contributions to the candidate. Vigilant enforcement of this provision is a precise response to the Court's circumvention concerns. If a donor contributes $2,000 to a candidate (the maximum donation in an election cycle), he cannot direct the political party to funnel another dime to the candidate without confronting the Federal Election Campaign Act's civil and criminal penalties, see 2 U. S. C. § 437g(a)(6)(C) (civil); § 437g(d) (criminal). . . .

[T]here is a second, well-tailored option for combating corruption that does not entail the reduction of parties' First Amendment freedoms. The heart of the Court's circumvention argument is that, whereas individuals can donate only $2,000 to a candidate in a given election cycle, they can donate $20,000 to the national committees of a political party, an amount that is allegedly large enough to corrupt the candidate. If indeed $20,000 is enough to corrupt a candidate (an assumption that seems implausible on its face and is, in any event, unsupported by any evidence), the proper response is to lower the cap. That way, the speech restriction is directed at the source of the alleged corruption—the individual donor—and not the party. . . .

In my view, it makes no sense to contravene a political party's core First Amendment rights because of what a third party might unlawfully try to do. Instead of broadly restricting political parties' speech, the Government should have pursued better-tailored alternatives for combating the alleged corruption.

NOTES AND QUESTIONS

1. With *Colorado Republican II* and *Shrink Missouri*, the Court appeared to have entered a period of policing the contours of the application of the *Buckley* divide between contributions and expenditures. The divisions on the Court appear stable, with three members of the Court continuing to press for overturning even the contributions limitations of *Buckley*, and at least two of the Justices seeking to overturn *Buckley* in favor of regulating expenditures as well as contributions. Whatever the reservations of a majority of the Court about the wisdom of the original constitutional division drawn in *Buckley*, the core constitutional debates appear to have receded before the second-tier question of policing the application of the contributions/expenditures divide inherited from *Buckley*.

2. What explains the Court's determination in *Colorado II* to fold the treatment of political parties' coordinated expenditures into a more-or-less undifferentiated *Buckley* approach? Given the overlap in reasoning between Justice Kennedy's opinion in *Colorado Republican II* and the Court's strong endorsement of party First Amendment autonomy claims in *California Democratic Party v. Jones*, does the Court's decision not to afford special First Amendment protection to political parties come as a surprise?

3. In applying the *Buckley* approach in full, the salient question becomes the evidence of corruption or perception of corruption necessary to justify campaign finance regulation. The Court clearly divides on the assessment of the evidence in the record and in the scholarly literature on the actual threat of corruption posed by coordinated party expenditures. For the majority, such expenditures are shown to be means to circumvent contribution limitations and, as such, satisfy the government's burden for justifying the regulation. For the dissent, by contrast, there is no evidence of actual corruption flowing from contributions to parties which then in turn engage in coordinated campaign conduct.

E. ANTI-CORRUPTION AND THE STATE INTEREST

1. DO CONCERNS OVER CORRUPTION JUSTIFY CAMPAIGN FINANCE REGULATION?

After *Buckley* and its progeny, it appeared that the sole legitimate government interest in regulating campaign finance lay in removing the temptation for corruption. If so, could any governmental restriction on expenditures or contributions survive First Amendment scrutiny in referenda or initiatives? In such elections, the salient feature is that the decision is one of policy and not of candidate preference. Accordingly, there is no direct beneficiary of contributions who can provide some form of illicit *quid pro quo* service to the campaign contributor.

First National Bank of Boston v. Bellotti

435 U.S. 765 (1978).

■ JUSTICE POWELL delivered the opinion of the Court.

* * *

The statute at issue, Mass. Gen. Laws Ann., ch. 55, § 8 (West Supp. 1977), prohibits appellants, two national banking associations and three business corporations, from making contributions or expenditures "for the purpose of . . . influencing or affecting the vote on any question submitted to the voters, other than one materially affecting any of the property, business or assets of the corporation." The statute further specifies that "[n]o question submitted to the voters solely concerning the taxation of the income, property or transactions of individuals shall be deemed materially to affect the property, business or assets of the corporation." A corporation that violates § 8 may receive a maximum fine of $50,000; a corporate officer, director, or agent who violates the section may receive a maximum fine of $10,000 or imprisonment for up to one year, or both.

Appellants wanted to spend money to publicize their views on a proposed constitutional amendment that was to be submitted to the voters as a ballot question at a general election on November 2, 1976. The amendment would have permitted the legislature to impose a graduated tax on the income of individuals. After appellee, the Attorney General of Massachusetts, informed appellants that he intended to enforce § 8 against them, they brought this action seeking to have the statute declared unconstitutional. . . .

Appellants argued that § 8 violates the First Amendment, the Due Process and Equal Protection Clauses of the Fourteenth Amendment, and similar provisions of the Massachusetts Constitution. They prayed that the statute be declared unconstitutional on its face and as it would be applied to their proposed expenditures. The parties' statement of agreed facts reflected their disagreement as to the effect that the adoption of a personal income tax would have on appellants' business; it noted that "[t]here is a division of opinion among economists as to whether and to what extent a graduated income tax imposed solely on individuals would affect the business and assets of corporations." Appellee did not dispute that appellants' management believed that the tax would have a significant effect on their businesses.

* * *

III

The court below framed the principal question in this case as whether and to what extent corporations have First Amendment rights. We believe that the court posed the wrong question. The Constitution often protects interests broader than those of the party seeking their vindication. The First Amendment, in particular, serves significant societal interests. The proper question therefore is not whether corporations "have" First Amendment rights and, if so, whether they are coextensive with those of natural persons. Instead, the question must be whether § 8 abridges expression that the First Amendment was meant to protect. We hold that it does.

A

The speech proposed by appellants is at the heart of the First Amendment's protection.

> The freedom of speech and of the press guaranteed by the Constitution embraces at the least the liberty to discuss publicly and truthfully all matters of public concern without previous restraint or fear of subsequent punishment.... Freedom of discussion, if it would fulfill its historic function in this nation, must embrace all issues about which information is needed or appropriate to enable the members of society to cope with the exigencies of their period. *Thornhill v. Alabama*, 310 U.S. 88, 101–102 (1940).

The referendum issue that appellants wish to address falls squarely within this description. In appellants' view, the enactment of a graduated personal income tax, as proposed to be authorized by constitutional amendment, would have a seriously adverse effect on the economy of the State. The importance of the referendum issue to the people and government of Massachusetts is not disputed. Its merits, however, are the subject of sharp disagreement.

As the Court said in *Mills v. Alabama*, 384 U.S. 214, 218 (1966), "there is practically universal agreement that a major purpose of [the First] Amendment was to protect the free discussion of governmental affairs." If the speakers here were not corporations, no one would suggest that the State could silence their proposed speech. It is the type of speech indispensable to decisionmaking in a democracy, and this is no less true because the speech comes from a corporation rather than an individual. The inherent worth of the speech in terms of its capacity for informing the public does not depend upon the identity of its source, whether corporation, association, union, or individual.

The court below nevertheless held that corporate speech is protected by the First Amendment only when it pertains directly to the corporation's business interests. In deciding whether this novel and restrictive gloss on the First Amendment comports with the Constitution and the precedents of this Court, we need not survey the outer boundaries of the Amendment's protection of corporate speech, or address the abstract question whether corporations have the full measure of rights that individuals enjoy under the First Amendment. The question in this case, simply put, is whether the corporate identity of the speaker deprives this proposed speech of what otherwise would be its clear entitlement to protection. We turn now to that question. . . .

B

[A]ppellee suggests that First Amendment rights generally have been afforded only to corporations engaged in the communications business or through which individuals express themselves, and the court below apparently accepted the "materially affecting" theory as the conceptual common denominator between appellee's position and the precedents of this Court. It is true that the "materially affecting" requirement would have been satisfied in the Court's decisions affording protection to the speech of media corporations and corporations otherwise in the business of communication or entertainment, and to the commercial speech of business corporations. In such cases, the speech would be connected to the corporation's business almost by definition. But the effect on the business of the corporation was not the governing rationale in any of these decisions. None of them mentions, let alone attributes significance to, the fact that the subject of the challenged communication materially affected the corporation's business.

The press cases emphasize the special and constitutionally recognized role of that institution in informing and educating the public, offering criticism, and providing a forum for discussion and debate.... But the press does not have a monopoly on either the First Amendment or the ability to enlighten.... Similarly, the Court's decisions involving corporations in the business of communication or entertainment are based not only on the role of the First Amendment in fostering individual self-expression but also on its role in affording the public access to discussion, debate, and the dissemination of information and ideas.... Even decisions seemingly based exclusively on the individual's right to express himself acknowledge that the expression may contribute to society's edification....

Nor do our recent commercial speech cases lend support to appellee's business interest theory. They illustrate that the First Amendment goes beyond protection of the press and the self-expression of individuals to prohibit government from limiting the stock of information from which members of the public may draw. A commercial advertisement is constitutionally protected not so much because it pertains to the seller's business as because it furthers the societal interest in the "free flow of commercial information." *Virginia State Bd. of Pharmacy v. Virginia Citizens Consumer Council, Inc.,* 425 U.S. 748, 764 (1976)....

C

We thus find no support in the First or Fourteenth Amendment, or in the decisions of this Court, for the proposition that speech that otherwise would be within the protection of the First Amendment loses that protection simply because its source is a corporation that cannot prove, to the satisfaction of a court, a material effect on its business or property. The "materially affecting" requirement is not an identification of the boundaries of corporate speech etched by the Constitution itself. Rather, it amounts to an impermissible legislative prohibition of speech based on the identity of the interests that spokesmen may represent in public debate over controversial issues and a requirement that the speaker have a sufficiently great interest in the subject to justify communication.

Section 8 permits a corporation to communicate to the public its views on certain referendum subjects—those materially affecting its business—but not others. It also singles out one kind of ballot question—individual taxation—as a subject about which corporations may never make their ideas public. The legislature has drawn the line between permissible and impermissible speech according to whether there is a sufficient nexus, as defined by the legislature, between the issue presented to the voters and the business interests of the speaker.

In the realm of protected speech, the legislature is constitutionally disqualified from dictating the subjects about which persons may speak and the speakers who may address a public issue. . . . If a legislature may direct business corporations to "stick to business," it also may limit other corporations—religious, charitable, or civic—to their respective "business" when addressing the public. Such power in government to channel the expression of views is unacceptable under the First Amendment. Especially where, as here, the legislature's suppression of speech suggests an attempt to give one side of a debatable public question an advantage in expressing its views to the people, the First Amendment is plainly offended. Yet the State contends that its action is necessitated by governmental interests of the highest order. We next consider these asserted interests.

IV

The constitutionality of § 8's prohibition of the "exposition of ideas" by corporations turns on whether it can survive the exacting scrutiny necessitated by a state—imposed restriction of freedom of speech. Especially where, as here, a prohibition is directed at speech itself, and the speech is intimately related to the process of governing, "the State may prevail only upon showing a subordinating interest which is compelling," *Bates v. City of Little Rock*, 361 U.S. 516, 524 (1960). . . .

Appellee nevertheless advances two principal justifications for the prohibition of corporate speech. The first is the State's interest in sustaining the active role of the individual citizen in the electoral process and thereby preventing diminution of the citizen's confidence in government. The second is the interest in protecting the rights of shareholders whose views differ from those expressed by management on behalf of the corporation. However weighty these interests may be in the context of partisan candidate elections, they either are not implicated in this case or are not served at all, or in other than a random manner, by the prohibition in § 8.

A

* * *

Appellee advances a number of arguments in support of his view that these interests are endangered by corporate participation in discussion of a referendum issue. They hinge upon the assumption that such participation would exert an undue influence on the outcome of a referendum vote, and—in the end—destroy the confidence of the people in the democratic process and the integrity of government. According to appellee, corporations are wealthy and powerful and their views may drown out other points of view. If appellee's arguments were supported by record or legislative findings that corporate advocacy threatened imminently to undermine democratic processes, thereby denigrating rather than serving First Amendment interests, these arguments would merit our consideration.... But there has been no showing that the relative voice of corporations has been overwhelming or even significant in influencing referenda in Massachusetts, or that there has been any threat to the confidence of the citizenry in government....

Nor are appellee's arguments inherently persuasive or supported by the precedents of this Court. Referenda are held on issues, not candidates for public office. The risk of corruption perceived in cases involving candidate elections ... simply is not present in a popular vote on a public issue. To be sure, corporate advertising may influence the outcome of the vote; this would be its purpose. But the fact that advocacy may persuade the electorate is hardly a reason to suppress it: The Constitution "protects expression which is eloquent no less than that which is unconvincing." *Kingsley Int'l Pictures Corp. v. Regents,* 360 U.S. 684, 689 (1959). We noted only recently that "the concept that government may restrict the speech of some elements of our society in order to enhance the relative voice of others is wholly foreign to the First Amendment ..." *Buckley,* 424 U.S. at 48–49. Moreover, the people in our democracy are entrusted with the responsibility for judging and evaluating the relative merits of conflicting arguments. They may consider, in making their judgment, the source and credibility of the advocate. But if there be any danger that the people cannot evaluate the information and arguments advanced by appellants, it is a danger contemplated by the Framers of the First Amendment.... In sum, "[a] restriction so destructive of the right of public discussion [as § 8], without greater or more imminent danger to the public interest than existed in this case, is incompatible with the freedoms secured by the First Amendment."

B

Finally, appellee argues that § 8 protects corporate shareholders, an interest that is both legitimate and traditionally within the province of state law.... The statute is said to serve this interest by preventing the use of corporate resources in furtherance of views with which some shareholders may disagree. This purpose is belied, however, by the provisions of the statute, which are both underinclusive and overinclusive.

The underinclusiveness of the statute is self-evident. Corporate expenditures with respect to a referendum are prohibited, while corporate activity with respect to the passage or defeat of legislation is permitted, even though corporations may engage in lobbying more often than they take positions on ballot questions submitted to the voters. Nor does § 8 prohibit a corporation from expressing its views, by the expenditure of corporate funds, on any public issue until it becomes the subject of a referendum, though the displeasure of disapproving shareholders is unlikely to be any less.

The fact that a particular kind of ballot question has been singled out for special treatment undermines the likelihood of a genuine state interest in protecting shareholders. It suggests instead that the legislature may have been concerned with silencing corporations on a particular subject. Indeed, appellee has conceded that "the legislative and judicial history of the statute indicates . . . that the second crime was 'tailor-made' to prohibit corporate campaign contributions to oppose a graduated income tax amendment."

Nor is the fact that § 8 is limited to banks and business corporations without relevance. Excluded from its provisions and criminal sanctions are entities or organized groups in which numbers of persons may hold an interest or membership, and which often have resources comparable to those of large corporations. Minorities in such groups or entities may have interests with respect to institutional speech quite comparable to those of minority shareholders in a corporation. Thus the exclusion of Massachusetts business trusts, real estate investment trusts, labor unions, and other associations undermines the plausibility of the State's purported concern for the persons who happen to be shareholders in the banks and corporations covered by § 8.

The overinclusiveness of the statute is demonstrated by the fact that § 8 would prohibit a corporation from supporting or opposing a referendum proposal even if its shareholders unanimously authorized the contribution or expenditure. Ultimately shareholders may decide, through the procedures of corporate democracy, whether their corporation should engage in debate on public issues. Acting through their power to elect the board of directors or to insist upon protective provisions in the corporation's charter, shareholders normally are presumed competent to protect their own interests. In addition to intracorporate remedies, minority shareholders generally have access to the judicial remedy of a derivative suit to challenge corporate disbursements alleged to have been made for improper corporate purposes or merely to further the personal interests of management. . . .

V

Because that portion of § 8 challenged by appellants prohibits protected speech in a manner unjustified by a compelling state interest, it must be invalidated. The judgment of the Supreme Judicial Court is Reversed.

[Concurring opinion of CHIEF JUSTICE BURGER omitted.]

■ MR. JUSTICE WHITE, with whom MR. JUSTICE BRENNAN and MR. JUSTICE MARSHALL join, dissenting.

The Massachusetts statute challenged here forbids the use of corporate funds to publish views about referenda issues having no material effect on the business, property, or assets of the corporation. The legislative judgment that the personal income tax issue, which is the subject of the referendum out of which this case arose, has no such effect was sustained by the Supreme Judicial Court of Massachusetts and is not disapproved by this Court today. Hence, as this case comes to us, the issue is whether a State may prevent corporate management from using the corporate treasury to propagate views having no connection with the corporate business. The Court commendably enough squarely faces the issue but unfortunately errs in deciding it. The Court invalidates the Massachusetts statute and holds that the First Amendment guarantees corporate managers the right to use not only their personal funds, but also those of the corporation, to circulate fact and opinion irrelevant to the business placed in their charge and necessarily representing their own personal or collective views about political and social questions. I do not suggest for a moment that the First Amendment requires a State to forbid such use of corporate funds, but I do strongly disagree that the First Amendment forbids state interference with managerial decisions of this kind.

By holding that Massachusetts may not prohibit corporate expenditures or contributions made in connection with referenda involving issues having no material connection with the corporate business, the Court not only invalidates a statute which has been on the books in one form or another for many years, but also casts considerable doubt upon the constitutionality of legislation passed by some 31 States restricting corporate political activity, as well as upon the Federal Corrupt Practices Act, 2 U.S.C. § 441b. The Court's fundamental error is its failure to realize that the state regulatory interests in terms of which the alleged curtailment of First Amendment rights accomplished by the statute must be evaluated are themselves derived from the First Amendment. The question posed by this case, as approached by the Court, is whether the State has struck the best possible balance, i.e., the one which it would have chosen, between competing First Amendment interests. Although in my view the choice made by the State would survive even the most exacting scrutiny, perhaps a rational argument might be made to the contrary. What is inexplicable, is for the Court to substitute its judgment as to the proper balance for that of Massachusetts where the State has passed legislation reasonably designed to further First Amendment interests in the context of the political arena where the expertise of legislators is at its peak and that of judges is at its very lowest. Moreover, the result reached today in critical respects marks a drastic departure from the Court's prior decisions which have protected against governmental infringement of the very First Amendment interests which the Court now deems inadequate to justify the Massachusetts statute.

I

[...] The self-expression of the communicator is not the only value encompassed by the First Amendment. One of its functions, often referred to as the right to hear or receive information, is to protect the interchange of ideas. Any communication of ideas, and consequently any expenditure of funds which makes the communication of ideas possible, it can be argued, furthers the purposes of the First Amendment. This proposition does not establish, however, that the right of the general public to receive communications financed by means of corporate expenditures is of the same dimension as that to hear other forms of expression. In the first place, as discussed supra, corporate expenditures designed to further political causes lack the connection with individual self-expression which is one of the principal justifications for the constitutional protection of speech provided by the First Amendment. Ideas which are not a product of individual choice are entitled to less First Amendment protection. Secondly, the restriction of corporate speech concerned with political matters impinges much less severely upon the availability of ideas to the general public than do restrictions upon individual speech. Even the complete curtailment of corporate communications concerning political or ideological questions not integral to day-to-day business functions would leave individuals, including corporate shareholders, employees, and customers, free to communicate their thoughts. Moreover, it is unlikely that any significant communication would be lost by such a prohibition. These individuals would remain perfectly free to communicate any ideas which could be conveyed by means of the corporate form. Indeed, such individuals could even form associations for the very purpose of promoting political or ideological causes.

[...] The governmental interest in regulating corporate political communications, especially those relating to electoral matters, also raises considerations which differ significantly from those governing the regulation of individual speech. Corporations are artificial entities created by law for the purpose of furthering certain economic goals. In order to facilitate the achievement of such ends, special rules relating to such matters as limited liability, perpetual life, and the accumulation, distribution, and taxation of assets are normally applied to them. States have provided corporations with such attributes in order to increase their economic viability and thus strengthen the economy generally. It has long been recognized however, that the special status of corporations has placed them in a position to control vast amounts of economic power which may, if not regulated, dominate not only the economy but also the very heart of our democracy, the electoral process. Although *Buckley v. Valeo* provides support for the position that the desire to equalize the financial resources available to candidates does not justify the limitation upon the expression of support which a restriction upon individual contributions entails, the interest of Massachusetts and the many other States which have restricted corporate political activity is quite different. It is not one of equalizing the resources of opposing candidates or opposing positions, but rather of preventing institutions which have been permitted to amass wealth as a result of special advantages extended by the State for certain economic purposes from using that wealth to acquire an unfair advantage in the political process, especially where, as here, the issue involved has no material connection with the business of the corporation. The State need not permit its own creation to consume it. Massachusetts could permissibly conclude that not to impose limits upon the political activities of corporations would have placed it in a position of departing from neutrality and indirectly assisting the propagation of corporate views because of the advantages its laws give to the corporate acquisition of funds to finance such activities. Such expenditures may be viewed as seriously threatening the role of the First Amendment as a guarantor of a free marketplace of ideas. Ordinarily, the expenditure of funds to promote political causes may be assumed to bear some relation to the fervency with which they are held. Corporate political expression, however, is not only divorced from the convictions of individual corporate shareholders, but also, because of the ease with which corporations are permitted to accumulate capital, bears no relation to the conviction with which the ideas expressed are held by the communicator.

* * *

II

[...] In my view, the interests in protecting a system of freedom of expression, set forth supra, are sufficient to justify any incremental curtailment in the volume of expression which the Massachusetts statute might produce. I would hold that apart from corporate activities ... which are integrally related to corporate business operations, a State may prohibit corporate expenditures for political or ideological purposes. There can be no doubt that corporate expenditures in connection with referenda immaterial to corporate business affairs fall clearly into the category of corporate activities which may be barred. The electoral process, of course, is the essence of our democracy. It is an arena in which the public interest in preventing corporate domination and the coerced support by shareholders of causes with which they disagree is at its strongest and any claim that corporate expenditures are integral to the economic functioning of the corporation is at its weakest.

I would affirm the judgment of the Supreme Judicial Court for the Commonwealth of Massachusetts.

■ Mr. Justice Rehnquist, dissenting.

* * *

The question presented today, whether business corporations have a constitutionally protected liberty to engage in political activities, has never been squarely addressed by any previous decision of this Court. However, the General Court of the Commonwealth of Massachusetts, the Congress of the United States, and the legislatures of 30 other States of this Republic have considered the matter, and have concluded that restrictions upon the political activity of business corporations are both politically desirable and constitutionally permissible. The judgment of such a broad consensus of governmental bodies expressed over a period of many decades is entitled to considerable deference from this Court. . . .

There can be little doubt that when a State creates a corporation with the power to acquire and utilize property, it necessarily and implicitly guarantees that the corporation will not be deprived of that property absent due process of law. Likewise, when a State charters a corporation for the purpose of publishing a newspaper, it necessarily assumes that the corporation is entitled to the liberty of the press essential to the conduct of its business. . . .

It cannot be so readily concluded that the right of political expression is equally necessary to carry out the functions of a corporation organized for commercial purposes. A State grants to a business corporation the blessings of potentially perpetual life and limited liability to enhance its efficiency as an economic entity. It might reasonably be concluded that those properties, so beneficial in the economic sphere, pose special dangers in the political sphere. Furthermore, it might be argued that liberties of political expression are not at all necessary to effectuate the purposes for which States permit commercial corporations to exist. So long as the Judicial Branches of the State and Federal Governments remain open to protect the corporation's interest in its property, it has no need, though it may have the desire, to petition the political branches for similar protection. Indeed, the States might reasonably fear that the corporation would use its economic power to obtain further benefits beyond those already bestowed. I would think that any particular form of organization upon which the State confers special privileges or immunities different from those of natural persons would be subject to like regulation, whether the organization is a labor union, a partnership, a trade association, or a corporation. . . .

It is true, as the Court points out, that recent decisions of this Court have emphasized the interest of the public in receiving the information offered by the speaker seeking protection. The free flow of information is in no way diminished by the Commonwealth's decision to permit the operation of business corporations with limited rights of political expression. All natural persons, who owe their existence to a higher sovereign than the Commonwealth, remain as free as before to engage in political activity. . . .

I would affirm the judgment of the Supreme Judicial Court.

NOTES AND QUESTIONS

1. Should corporations be protected First Amendment speakers at all in the arena of democratic decisionmaking on candidates and issues? After all, the electorate or the political community with the power to make decisions in this area excludes corporations; with only a very few exceptions, such as the voting scheme involved in *Salyer v. Tulare Lake Basin*, 410 U.S. 719 (1973), discussed in Chapter 3, corporations and other artificial constructs of the law do not have the right to vote. The principles of "equal citizenship" recognized in cases like *Reynolds v. Sims* therefore cannot logically extend to corporate entities. For much of this century, it was taken for granted that corporate spending could be distinctly regulated; the first major national campaign-finance regulation, the Tillman Act of 1907 banned corporate contributions to federal candidates. Notice how Justice Powell's opinion justifies invalidating the Massachusetts ban on corporate spending; it is not because corporations have First Amendment rights of their own, but because "significant societal interests" will be served, in the Court's view, by treating corporate spending on ballot measures as protected by the First Amendment. If the Court is not enforcing individual rights here, but rather making judgments about what regulatory regime for democratic decisionmaking best serves "significant societal interests," is the Court the appropriate institution for those judgments?

The role of the corporation in democracy has been one of the most contentious subjects in American politics over the last hundred years or so. Election law over this time has treated the corporation in at least five different ways, some tolerating greater regulation of corporate spending on democracy, some tolerating less. For a chronicle of this history, see Adam Winkler, *"Other People's Money": Corporations, Agency Costs, and Campaign Finance Law*, 92 Geo. L.J. 871 (2004). For the argument from a leading corporate-law scholar that state regulation of corporate spending on democratic politics should be constitutionally permissible, given other state law regulation of corporate entities, see Victor Brudney, *Business Corporations and Stockholder's Rights Under the First Amendment*, 91 Yale L.J. 235 (1981).

2. The Supreme Court struck down the Massachusetts restriction on corporate speech, in part, because of the absence of clear legislative findings that corporate advocacy threatened the functioning of the democratic process. Given the Court's staunch hostility to a legislature's trying to give one side of a debate any electoral advantage, what would a legislative record that could satisfy the Court's scrutiny look like?

3. Should the prospect of corruption be the sole concern of campaign regulation—or even a concern at all? If corruption is "understood as implicit exchanges of campaign contributions for official actions," it is not clear that this should be a rationale for campaign finance reform. *See* David A. Strauss, *Corruption, Equality, and Campaign Finance Reform*, 94 Colum. L. Rev. 1369, 1389 (1994). Rather, Professor Strauss argues, campaign contributions are a way of cementing the bond between elected representatives and their constituents. If responsiveness to the interests of constituents is one mark of effective representation, then the difference between contributions and promise of votes in the future begins to blur. Strauss then argues that the real issue is a concern that certain groups have greater influence because of their greater wealth, a rationale for campaign finance regulation that is distinct from the narrower claim of corruption that the *Buckley* Court endorsed. *See also* Bruce E. Cain, *Moralism and Realism in Campaign Finance Reform*, 1995 U. Chi. Legal F. 111, 112 ("The core problem in campaign finance is not corruption in the traditional sense. Rather, it is how far equity considerations can and should be carried in a democracy").

4. Closely related to regulating the funding of political campaigns is the question of regulating the content of what candidates for office may say. The Court's concern for corruption does not carefully distinguish between the trade-off of legislative action for campaign money and the perhaps equally problematic trade-off of legislative action for votes during the campaign. In *Brown v. Hartlage,* 456 U.S. 45 (1982), the Court struck down the application to election promises of the Kentucky Corrupt Practices Act, which prohibited candidates from making an "expenditure, loan, promise, agreement, or contract as to action when elected, in consideration for a vote." In the context of a pledge of performance once in office, the Court ruled, "so long as the hoped for personal benefit is to be achieved through the normal processes of government, and not through some private arrangement, it has always been, and remains, a reputable basis upon which to cast one's ballot." *Id.* at 57. Under this rationale, should campaign contributions given in support of open public promises of anticipated legislative action be constitutionally protected? For the argument that actual promises made to voters during campaigns should be legally enforceable, see Stephen D. Sencer, Note, *Read My Lips: Examing False Campaign Promises,* 90 Mich. L. Rev. 428 (1991). On the question of vote buying, see Pamela S. Karlan, *Not by Money But by Virtue Won?: Vote Trafficking and the Voting Rights System,* 80 Va. L. Rev. (1994).

5. To what extent should the Court consider the effects that financial pressures have on the quality of governance, as opposed to the election process? The average cost of a successful Senate campaign has risen from just over $3 million in 1986 to over $7 million in 2000. Mark C. Alexander, *Let Them Do Their Jobs: The Compelling Government Interest in Protecting the Time of Candidates and Elected Officials,* 37 Loy. U. Chi. L.J. 669, 673 (2006). For an incumbent Senator to accrue this amount, she would have to raise more than $23,000 per week over her six-year term. As reported by former congressman Bob Edgar, even in an earlier era, "Eighty percent of my time, 80 percent of my staff's time, 80 percent of my events and meetings were fundraisers. Rather than go to a senior center, I would go to a party where I could raise $3,000 or $4,000." *Quoted in* Phillip M. Stern, Still the Best Congress Money Can Buy 119 (1992). Professor Vincent Blasi argues that "certain forms of campaign finance legislation can be justified, even against First Amendment challenge, by resort to the constitutionally ordained value of representation." Could legislative findings that the time of elected representatives is being redirected to endless fund raising satisfy the Supreme Court's invitation of actual evidence "that corporate advocacy threatened imminently to undermine democratic processes"? Consider the form of regulation that would follow from the argument put forward by Professor Blasi as an alternative to the narrow focus on anti-corruption:

> If candidate time protection is the objective, the principal regulatory measure must be a limit on the overall amount of money that can be spent in an election campaign. From this perspective, it is a matter of secondary importance what restrictions are placed on the size of contributions to candidates, parties, and political action committees; on the sources of funds collected by candidates; and on independent expenditures in support of candidates. Even the availability of public financing of some election expenses, or of a voucher system designed to equalize the opportunity to contribute, pales in significance compared to the need to limit overall spending. Candidates facing or fearing tight racers will be preoccupied with fund-raising (or voucher raising) under any system that does not restrict total spending. If candidates are permitted to spend vast amounts of money in pursuit of votes, they will inevitably spend vast amounts of time in pursuit of money. Spending limits are the sine qua non of candidate time protection.

> The centrality of candidate spending limits was not so apparent when Congress passed its major campaign finance reforms in 1971 and 1974, nor when the Supreme Court in 1976 held several provisions of that legislation unconstitutional, including the mandatory ceilings on overall campaign spending by congressional candidates. At that time, what has come to be known as the war chest mentality had not yet seized the congress.... One indication of how dramatically the war chest mentality has altered the regulatory landscape is the fact, startling in retrospect, that the Supreme Court in *Buckley* never considered how spending limits might be justified as a means of preventing candidates from spending excessive amounts of time on fund-raising. In 1976, candidate time protection was not seen as a major objective of campaign finance reform. Corruption, disproportionate influence, the fencing out of impecunious candidates, and the alienation of the electorate were the dominant concerns....

Vincent Blasi, *Free Speech and the Widening Gyre of Fund–Raising: Why Campaign Spending Limits May Not Violate the First Amendment After All*, 94 Colum. L. Rev. 1281, 1283 (1994). Is Professor Blasi correct in asserting that absent restrictions on expenditures, there can be no effective campaign finance regulation?

6. Justice White's dissents from the post-*Buckley* line of cases raise a separate issue concerning who should decide whether the structure of campaign financing threatens harm to the electoral process. The Court's decisions establish that campaign regulations potentially infringe upon critical First Amendment rights and must accordingly be subject to strict scrutiny. This in turn requires that governmental regulations be justified both by a compelling state interest and by a narrow tailoring to limit the scope of potential first amendment impact. Repeatedly, Justice White questions the capacity of the Court to second-guess Congress and state legislatures in determining both the extent of the compelling state interest and the precision of the fit between regulation and the state concern. For Justice White, beginning with *Buckley*, a critical issue is whether courts should defer to the superior fact-gathering abilities of legislatures in this arena:

> Despite its seeming struggle with the standard by which to judge this case, this is essentially the question the Court asks and answers in the affirmative with respect to the limitations on contributions which individuals and political committees are permitted to make to federal candidates. In the interest of preventing undue influence that large contributors would have or that the public might think they would have, the Court upholds the provision that an individual may not give to a candidate, or spend on his behalf if requested or authorized by the candidate to do so, more than $1,000 in any one election. This limitation is valid although it imposes a low ceiling on what individuals may deem to be their most effective means of supporting or speaking on behalf of the candidate, i.e., financial support given directly to the candidate. The Court thus accepts the congressional judgment that the evils of unlimited contributions are sufficiently threatening to warrant restriction regardless of the impact of the limits on the contributor's opportunity for effective speech and in turn on the total volume of the candidate's political communications by reason of his inability to accept large sums from those willing to give.

> The congressional judgment, which I would also accept, was that other steps must be taken to counter the corrosive effects of money in federal election campaigns. One of these steps is § 608(e), which, aside from those funds that are given to the candidate or spent at his request or with his approval or cooperation limits what a contributor may independently spend in support or denigration of one running for federal office. Congress was plainly of the view that these expenditures also have corruptive potential; but the Court strikes down the provision, strangely enough claiming more insight as to what may improperly influence candidates than is possessed by the majority of congress that passed this bill and the president who signed it. Those supporting the bill undeniably included many seasoned professionals who have been deeply involved in elective processes and who have viewed them at close range over many years.

Buckley v. Valeo, 424 U.S. 1, 260–61 (1976) (White, J., concurring in part and dissenting in part).

In *Citizens Against Rent Control v. City of Berkeley,* 454 U.S. 290, 310–11 (1981), Justice White applies the same rationale to state and local determinations of threats to the integrity of the political process:

> Perhaps, as I have said, neither the city of Berkeley nor the State of California can "prove" that elections have been or can be unfairly won by special interest groups spending large sums of money, but there is a widespread conviction in legislative halls, as well as among citizens, that the danger is real. I regret that the Court continues to disregard that hazard.

Does the First Amendment require independent judicial examination of both the compelling state interest and the specific tailoring of all campaign finance regulations? Should courts defer to the determinations of threats to the political process made by incumbent political powers?

2.   EQUALITY AND LIBERTY IN POLITICAL CAMPAIGNS

Buckley and its companion cases drew tremendous criticism as part of the *"Lochnerization"* of the First Amendment. *See* Morton J. Horwitz, *Foreword: The Constitution of Change: Legal Fundamentality Without Fundamentalism,* 107 Harv. L. Rev. 30, 111–16 (1993); Cass R. Sunstein, Democracy and the Problem of Free Speech 97 (1993). For critics of the campaign finance caselaw, this was a struggle in which "Capitalism almost always won." Owen M. Fiss, *Free Speech and Social Structure,* 71 Iowa L. Rev. 1405–07 (1986). Once the issue of campaign finance regulation is taken beyond the narrow rationale of preventing *quid pro quo* corruption of the political process, the difficulties in defining a coherent regulatory structure multiply. The inescapable question must be whether government can equalize the voices of all citizens consistent with a democratic ordering of politics. The Court's initial reaction was decidedly hostile. In *Buckley,* for example, the Court stated, "the concept that government may restrict the speech of some elements of our society in order to enhance the relative voice of others is wholly foreign to the First Amendment...." 424 U.S. at 48–49. Subsequently, the Court added a First Amendment freedom of association argument to its concerns about campaign finance regulation. In *Citizens Against Rent Control v. City of Berkeley,* 454 U.S. 290, 294 (1981), a case striking down a limitation of $250 on contributions to committees formed to support or oppose ballot measures submitted to a popular vote, the Court wrote:

> We begin by recalling that the practice of persons sharing common views banding together to achieve a common end is deeply embedded in the American political process. The 18th-century Committees of Correspondence and the pamphleteers were early examples of this phenomena and the Federalist Papers were perhaps the most significant and lasting example. The tradition of volunteer committees for collective action has manifested itself in myriad community and public activities; in the political process it can focus on a candidate or on a

ballot measure. Its value is that by collective effort individuals can make their views known, when, individually, their voices would be faint or lost.

However, this view was qualified even under the terms of *Buckley* itself in which the Court describes the First Amendment as having been "designed to secure the widest possible dissemination of information from diverse and antagonistic sources." 424 U.S. at 428–29. As Professor Julian Eule argued, the Court appeared to invite a requirement that the public be exposed to the widest possible diversity of views. Julian Eule, *Promoting Speaker Diversity: Austin and Metro Broadcasting*, 1990 Sup. Ct. Rev. 105, 109. In *Federal Election Commission v. Massachusetts Citizens for Life*, 479 U.S. 238, 257–58 (1986), the Court then took the critical step of allowing some restrictions of expenditures by distinguishing between funds amassed directly for purposes of political expression, and those that were generated as a byproduct of unrelated commercial activity:

> Political "free trade" does not necessarily require that all who participate in the political marketplace do so with exactly equal resources. Relative availability of funds is after all a rough barometer of public support. The resources in the treasury of a business corporation, however, are not an indication of popular support for the corporation's political ideas. They reflect instead the economically motivated decisions of investors and customers. The availability of these resources may make a corporation a formidable political presence, even though the power of the corporation may be no reflection of the power of its ideas.

This then set the stage for a much more expansive view of the power of the legislature to regulate the political marketplace. Professor Owen Fiss in turn argues that such an approach, far from being prohibited under the First Amendment analysis of *Buckley,* should be compelled:

> [W]hat the first amendment requires in these cases is not indifference, but a commitment on the part of the Court to do all that it can possibly do to support and encourage the state in efforts to enrich the public debate, to eliminate those restrictions of its subsidy programs that would narrow and restrict public debate, and if need be even to require the state to continue and embark on programs that enrich debate. 71 Iowa L. Rev. at 1424.

Austin v. Michigan Chamber of Commerce

494 U.S. 652 (1990).

■ Justice Marshall delivered the opinion of the Court.

* * *

I

Section 54(1) of the Michigan Campaign Finance Act prohibits corporations from making contributions and independent expenditures in connection with state candidate elections. The issue before us is only the constitutionality of the State's ban on independent expenditures. The Act defines "expenditure" as "a payment, donation, loan, pledge, or promise of payment of money or anything of ascertainable monetary value for goods, materials, services, or facilities in assistance of, or in opposition to, the nomination or election of a candidate." § 169.206(1). An expenditure is considered independent if it is "not made at the direction of, or under the control of, another person and if the expenditure is not a contribution to a committee." § 169.209(1); see § 169.203(4) (defining "committee" as a group that "receives contributions or makes expenditures for the purpose of influencing or attempting to influence the action of the voters for or against the nomination or election of a candidate"). The Act exempts from this general prohibition against corporate political spending any expenditure made from a segregated fund. § 169.255(1). A corporation may solicit contributions to its political fund only from an enumerated list of persons associated with the corporation. *See* §§ 169.255(2), (3).

The Chamber, a nonprofit Michigan corporation, challenges the constitutionality of this statutory scheme. The Chamber comprises more than 8,000 members, three-quarters of whom are for-profit corporations. The Chamber's general treasury is funded through annual dues required of all members. Its purposes, as set out in the bylaws, are to promote economic conditions favorable to private enterprise; to analyze, compile, and disseminate information about laws of interest to the business community and to publicize to the government the views of the business community on such matters; to train and educate its members; to foster ethical business practices; to collect data on, and investigate matters of, social, civic, and economic importance to the State; to receive contributions and to make expenditures for political purposes and to perform any other lawful political activity; and to coordinate activities with other similar organizations.

In June 1985 Michigan scheduled a special election to fill a vacancy in the Michigan House of Representatives. Although the Chamber had established and funded a separate political fund, it sought to use its general treasury funds to place in a local newspaper an advertisement supporting a specific candidate. As the Act made such an expenditure punishable as a felony, see § 169.254(5), the Chamber brought suit in District Court for injunctive relief against enforcement of the Act, arguing that the restriction on expenditures is unconstitutional under both the First and the Fourteenth Amendments.

* * *

C

We next turn to the question whether the Act is sufficiently narrowly tailored to achieve its goal. We find that the Act is precisely targeted to eliminate the distortion caused by corporate spending while also allowing corporations to express their political views. Contrary to the dissents' critical assumptions, ... the Act does not impose an absolute ban on all forms of corporate political spending but permits corporations to make independent political expenditures through separate segregated funds. Because persons contributing to such funds understand that their money will be used solely for political purposes, the speech generated accurately reflects contributors' support for the corporation's political views.

* * *

III

The Chamber contends that even if the Campaign Finance Act is constitutional with respect to for—profit corporations, it nonetheless cannot be applied to a nonprofit ideological corporation like a chamber of commerce. In [*FEC v. Massachusetts Citizens for Life, Inc. (MCFL)*, 479 U.S. 238 (1986)], we held that the nonprofit organization there had "features more akin to voluntary political associations than business firms, and therefore should not have to bear burdens on independent spending solely because of [its] incorporated status." 479 U.S. at 263. In reaching that conclusion, we enumerated three characteristics of the corporation that were "essential" to our holding. *Ibid.* Because the Chamber does not share these crucial features, the Constitution does not require that it be exempted from the generally applicable provisions of § 54(1).

The first characteristic of Massachusetts Citizens for Life, Inc., that distinguished it from ordinary business corporations was that the organization "was formed for the express purpose of promoting political ideas, and cannot engage in business activities." *Id.* at 264. Its articles of incorporation indicated that its purpose was "[t]o foster respect for human life and to defend the right to life of all human beings, born and unborn, through educational, political and other forms of activities," and all of the organization's activities were "designed to further its agenda," *id.* at 242. MCFL's narrow political focus thus "ensure[d] that [its] political resources reflect[ed] political support." *Id.* at 264.

In contrast, the Chamber's bylaws set forth more varied purposes, several of which are not inherently political. For instance, the Chamber compiles and disseminates information relating to social, civic, and economic conditions, trains and educates its members, and promotes ethical business practices. Unlike MCFL's, the Chamber's educational activities are not expressly tied to political goals; many of its seminars, conventions, and publications are politically neutral and focus on business and economic issues. . . .

We described the second feature of MCFL as the absence of "shareholders or other persons affiliated so as to have a claim on its assets or earnings. This ensures that persons connected with the organization will have no economic disincentive for disassociating with it if they disagree with its political activity." 479 U.S. at 264. Although the Chamber also lacks shareholders, many of its members may be similarly reluctant to withdraw as members even if they disagree with the Chamber's political expression, because they wish to benefit from the Chamber's nonpolitical programs and to establish contacts with other members of the business community. The Chamber's political agenda is sufficiently distinct from its educational and outreach programs that members who disagree with the former may continue to pay dues to participate in the latter. . . . Thus, we are persuaded that the Chamber's members are more similar to shareholders of a business corporation than to the members of MCFL in this respect.

The final characteristic upon which we relied in *MCFL* was the organization's independence from the influence of business corporations. On this score, the Chamber differs most greatly from the Massachusetts organization. MCFL was not established by, and had a policy of not accepting contributions from, business corporations. Thus it could not "serv[e] as [a] condui[t] for the type of direct spending that creates a threat to the political marketplace." 479 U.S. at 264. In striking contrast, more than three-quarters of the Chamber's members are business corporations, whose political contributions and expenditures can constitutionally be regulated by the State. . . . Business corporations therefore could circumvent the Act's restriction by funneling money through the Chamber's general treasury. Because the Chamber accepts money from for-profit corporations, it could, absent application of § 54(1), serve as a conduit for corporate political spending. In sum, the Chamber does not possess the features that would compel the State to exempt it from restriction on independent political expenditures.

IV

The Chamber also attacks § 54(1) as underinclusive because it does not regulate the independent expenditures of unincorporated labor unions. Whereas unincorporated unions, and indeed individuals, may be able to amass large treasuries, they do so without the significant state-conferred advantages of the corporate structure; corporations are "by far the most prominent example of entities that enjoy legal advantages enhancing their ability to accumulate wealth." *MCFL,* 479 U.S. at 258, n. 11. The desire to counterbalance those advantages unique to the corporate form is the State's compelling interest in this case; thus, excluding from the statute's coverage unincorporated entities that also have the capacity to accumulate wealth "does not undermine its justification for regulating corporations."

* * *

VI

Michigan identified as a serious danger the significant possibility that corporate political expenditures will undermine the integrity of the political process, and it has implemented a narrowly tailored solution to that problem. By requiring corporations to make all independent political expenditures through a separate fund made up of money solicited expressly for political purposes, the Michigan Campaign Finance Act reduces the threat that huge corporate treasuries amassed with the aid of favorable state laws will be used to influence unfairly the outcome of elections. The Michigan Chamber of Commerce does not exhibit the characteristics identified in *MCFL* that would require the State to exempt it from a generally applicable restriction on independent corporate expenditures. We therefore reverse the decision of the Court of Appeals.

It is so ordered.

[Concurring opinions of Justice Brennan and Justice Stevens, omitted.]

■ Justice Scalia, dissenting.

"Attention all citizens. To assure the fairness of elections by preventing disproportionate expression of the views of any single powerful group, your Government has decided that the following associations of persons shall be prohibited from speaking or writing in support of any candidate: ___." In permitting Michigan to make private corporations the first object of this Orwellian announcement, the Court today endorses the principle that too much speech is an evil that the democratic majority can proscribe. I dissent because that principle is contrary to our case law and incompatible with the absolutely central truth of the First Amendment: that government cannot be trusted to assure, through censorship, the "fairness" of political debate.

* * *

■ Justice Kennedy, with whom Justice O'Connor and Justice Scalia join, dissenting.

* * *

II

Our cases acknowledge the danger that corruption poses for the electoral process, but draw a line in permissible regulation between payments to candidates ("contributions") and payments or expenditures to express one's own views ("independent expenditures"). Today's decision abandons this distinction and threatens once-protected political speech. The Michigan statute prohibits independent expenditures by a nonprofit corporate speaker to express its own views about candidate qualifications. Independent expenditures are entitled to greater protection than campaign contributions. . . .

The majority almost admits that, in the case of independent expenditures, the danger of a political quid pro quo is insufficient to justify a restriction of this kind. Since the specter of corruption, which had been "the only legitimate and compelling government interest[s] thus far identified for restricting campaign finances," *NCPAC*, 470 U.S. at 496–497, is missing in this case, the majority invents a new interest: combating the "corrosive and distorting effects of immense aggregations of wealth," accumulated in corporate form without shareholder or public support. The majority styles this novel interest as simply a different kind of corruption, but has no support for its assertion. While it is questionable whether such imprecision would suffice to justify restricting political speech by for-profit corporations, it is certain that it does not apply to nonprofit entities....

With regard to nonprofit corporations in particular, there is no reason to assume that the corporate form has an intrinsic flaw that makes it corrupt, or that all corporations possess great wealth, or that all corporations can buy more media coverage for their views than can individuals or other groups. There is no reason to conclude that independent speech by a corporation is any more likely to dominate the political arena than speech by the wealthy individual, protected in *Buckley v. Valeo,* or by the well-funded PAC, protected in *NCPAC* (protecting speech rights of PAC's against expenditure limitations)....

The Act, as the State itself says, prevents a nonprofit corporate speaker from using its own funds to inform the voting public that a particular candidate has a good or bad voting record on issues of interest to the association's adherents. Though our era may not be alone in deploring the lack of mechanisms for holding candidates accountable for the votes they cast, that lack of accountability is one of the major concerns of our time. The speech suppressed in this case was directed to political qualifications. The fact that it was spoken by the Michigan Chamber of Commerce, and not a man or woman standing on a soapbox, detracts not a scintilla from its validity, its persuasiveness, or its contribution to the political dialogue.

* * *

IV

The Court's hostility to the corporate form used by the speaker in this case and its assertion that corporate wealth is the evil to be regulated is far too imprecise to justify the most severe restriction on political speech ever sanctioned by this Court....

By constructing a rationale for the jurisprudence of this Court that prevents distinguished organizations in public affairs from announcing that a candidate is qualified or not qualified for public office, the Court imposes its own model of speech, one far removed from economic and political reality. It is an unhappy paradox that this Court, which has the role of protecting speech and of barring censorship from all aspects of political life, now becomes itself the censor. In the course of doing so, the Court reveals a lack of concern for speech rights that have the full protection of the First Amendment. I would affirm the judgment.

NOTES AND QUESTIONS

1. In *Austin,* the Court identifies "a different type of corruption in the political arena" caused by disparities of wealth. Can this concern really be considered as a type of corruption at all? Professor Julian Eule argues to the contrary:

> Nobody ought to be fooled. This is simply a repackaging of the equalization goal. The corporate voice is being contained in order to "equalize the relative ability of all citizens to affect the outcome of elections." Once the definition of corruption is enlarged to encompass the corruption of the electoral process as well as the elected candidate, the distinction between the corruption rationale and the equalization one is obliterated.

Julian N. Eule, *Promoting Speaker Diversity: Austin and Metro Broadcasting,* 1990 S.Ct. Rev. 105, 109–10.

2. Can *Austin* be reconciled with the solicitude of prior cases for independence from state regulation? In *Meyer v. Grant,* 486 U.S. 414 (1988), for example, the Court struck down a Colorado law that made it a felony to use paid petition gatherers in conjunction with trying to get an initiative on a state-wide ballot. Writing for a unanimous Court, Justice Stevens held that the Colorado restriction unconstitutionally limited the right of political expression of groups seeking to leverage their resources by using paid petition gatherers:

> The circulation of an initiative petition of necessity involves both the expression of a desire for political change and a discussion of the merits of the proposed change. Although a petition circulator may not have to persuade potential signatories that a particular proposal should prevail to capture their signatures, he or she will at least have to persuade them that the matter is one deserving of the public scrutiny and debate that would attend its consideration by the whole electorate. This will in almost every case involve an explanation of the nature of the proposal and why its advocates support it. Thus, the circulation of a petition involves the type of interactive communication concerning political change that is appropriately described as "core political speech."

> The refusal to permit appellees to pay petition circulators restricts political expression in two ways: First, it limits the number of voices who will convey appellees' message and the hours they can speak and, therefore, limits the size of the audience they can reach. Second, it makes it less likely that appellees will garner the number of signatures necessary to place the matter on the ballot, thus limiting their ability to make the matter the focus of statewide discussion....

> That appellees remain free to employ other means to disseminate their ideas does not take their speech through petition circulators outside the bounds of First Amendment protection. Colorado's prohibition of

paid petition circulators restricts access to the most effective, fundamental, and perhaps economical avenue of political discourse, direct
one-on-one communication. That it leaves open "more burdensome"
avenues of communication, does not relieve its burden on First Amendment expression.... The First Amendment protects appellees' right
not only to advocate their cause but also to select what they believe to
be the most effective means for so doing.

Id. at 422–24. Does *Meyer* survive *Austin*? Can the Court's concern in
Austin over the distorting effect of wealth coexist with the general schema
from *Buckley,* which draws a First Amendment line between contributions
and expenditures? Consider the argument of Professor David Cole:

[*Austin* reflects] the Court's first serious acknowledgments of the
structural problem underlying the campaign spending issue: capitalism
and democracy are an uneasy mix. Free market capitalism threatens
the free marketplace of ideas by giving certain voices inordinate
influence, not because of the power of their ideas, but because of the
volume they can generate for their voices with dollars earned through
commercial activities. Because even "free speech" costs money, those
who succeed in the economic marketplace are able to purchase far
more speech opportunities than those who do not. Absent government
intervention of some kind, the marketplace of ideas, and in turn the
election of our representatives, threatens to go to the highest bidder.
The threat posed by concentrated wealth is not merely the aberration
of a bribed official, but the structural threat of a monopolized marketplace of ideas....

Where the laissez-faire model had focused almost exclusively on the
threats to free expression posed by public actors, the First Amendment
antitrust model recognized that a robust and wide-open debate could
also be undermined by powerful private actors. This recognition requires a wholesale rethinking of the role of the government in the
marketplace of ideas.... Once "corruption" is understood to encompass the systemic distorting effects of wealth, expenditures are just as
corrupting as contributions and referenda elections are just as subject
to being corrupted as candidate elections. Even the distinctions relied
upon in *Austin* are undermined by the "New Corruption": distortion
can be caused not only by for-profit corporations, but also by wealthy
individuals, nonprofit corporations, associations, and the media. Thus,
every distinction the Court has erected in the field of campaign finance
is called into question by the Court's belated recognition that economic
power can skew democratic speech.

David Cole, *First Amendment Antitrust: The End of Laissez–Faire in
Campaign Finance,* 9 Yale L. & Pol'y Rev. 236, 237, 266, 272 (1991); *see
also* Jamin Raskin & John Bonifaz, *The Constitutional Imperative and
Practical Superiority of Democratically Financed Elections,* 94 Colum. L.
Rev. 1160, 1163 (1994)(arguing that inequality of resources produces a

"massive structural bias in government which favors the parochial interests and personal wealth over the interests of those citizens lacking access to wealth"). Once down this path, however, there is no clear point of demarcation that separates disparities in wealth from other differential distribution of resources that bear on the political process. For example, Professor Lucas Powe argues that the logic of campaign finance reform pushes in two quite dramatic directions. L.A. Powe, Jr., *Mass Speech and the Newer First Amendment*, 1982 Sup. Ct. Rev. 243. First, the greatest potential concentration of extra-governmental power may be the mass media, whose extensive content regulation would run afoul of core First Amendment concerns. Second, if the real concern is the distortive effect of unequal wealth on the marketplace of ideas, would not the better argument be for attacking the source of the problem by redistributing all wealth? Do the market reform arguments of *Austin* offer a stopping point short of Professor Powe's slippery slope? Would Professor Powe's concern be met by a system that guaranteed each voter equal financial resources for the purpose of supporting or opposing any candidate or position in an election? *See* Edward B. Foley, *Equal-Dollars–Per–Voter: A Constitutional Principle of Campaign Finance*, 94 Colum. L. Rev. 1240 (1994).

3. The attempt to regulate campaign expenditures may also be criticized as encroaching on fundamental political liberties. For example, Professor Bradley Smith argues that the effect of regulation is to make it harder to challenge incumbents:

> Campaign finance reform measures, in particular limits on contributions and overall spending, insulate the political system from challenge by outsiders, and hinder the ability of challengers to compete on equal terms with those already in power.

> Contribution limits tend to favor incumbents by making it harder for challengers to raise money and thereby make credible runs for office. The lower the contribution limit, the more difficult it becomes for a candidate to raise money quickly from a small number of dedicated supporters. The consequent need to raise campaign cash from a large number of small contributors benefits those candidates who have in place a database of past contributors, an intact campaign organization, and the ability to raise funds on an ongoing basis from PACs. This latter group consists almost entirely of current officeholders. Thus, contribution limits hit political newcomers especially hard because of the difficulties candidates with low name recognition have in raising substantial sums of money from small contributors.

Bradley A. Smith, *Faulty Assumptions and Undemocratic Consequences of Campaign Finance Reform*, 105 Yale L. J. 1049, 1072–73 (1996).

4. On the other hand, the equality argument brings into sharp relief the unequal points of access to elected officials enjoyed by privileged sectors of American society. An important addition to the campaign finance debate ties the question of political contributions directly to the distribution of wealth in society, particularly the racial dimensions of socioeconomic status. In a series of pieces on this issue, Professor Spencer Overton has drawn attention to the emergence of a "donor class," which effectively controls the private funding of political campaigns. The most central of these articles is Spencer Overton, *The Donor Class: Campaign Finance, Democracy, and Participation,* 153 U. Pa. L. Rev. 73 (2004). For example, Overton reports that less than 2 percent of Americans contributed more than $200 to any federal candidate in 2004, yet contributions in excess of $200 made up roughly two-thirds of presidential elections funds. Analyzed differently, slightly more than 13 percent of American households made more than $100,000 in 2000, yet these households contributed over 85 percent of contributions over $200 collected by presidential candidates that year. Further, Professor Overton notes, 95.8 percent of this donor class is white. *Id.* At 102. Professor Terry Smith flips the inquiry by asking to what extent are minority candidates effectively dependent on non-minority financing. Terry Smith, *White Dollars, Black Candidates: Inequality and Agency in Campaign Finance Law,* 57 S.C.L. Rev. 735 (2006). Despite the fact that campaign contribution data are not coded by race, Professor Smith offers a striking observation about the predicament that this creates for black candidates. Thus, for example, "[d]uring the 2000 election cycle, a mere thirty zip codes gave twenty or more contributions to black candidates. Of those thirty zip codes, only six were majority black." *Id.* at 737. For further argument that American democracy is effectively stratified between a very small class of campaign funders, a bigger pool of election participants, and a sizeable pool of those who neither vote nor contribute and are thus presumably disregarded in the political process, see Burt Neuborne, *Democracy and the Poor,* in Law and Class in America (Paul Carrington and Trina Jones, eds.)(2006).

3.   SOFT MONEY AND THE REGULATORY GAP

Any regulation of campaign-related spending must confront the need to define a boundary between campaigns (the "electoral domain") and more general public debate over issues, ideas, and policies (the "domain of public discourse"). For general discussion of this important point, see C. Edwin Baker, *Campaign Expenditures and Free Speech,* 33 Harv. C.R.-C.L. L. Rev. 1 (1998). Even in the absence of *Buckley v. Valeo,* this task would be required as a matter of core First Amendment principles more deeply embedded, and less controversial, than *Buckley* itself. For the central concern of the First Amendment has long been understood to be a "profound national commitment to the principle that debate on public issues should be uninhibited, robust, and wide-open, and that it may well include vehement, caustic, and sometimes unpleasantly sharp attacks on government and public officials." *New York Times v. Sullivan,* 376 U.S. 254, 270 (1964). This principle is currently contested in discrete areas, like the regulation of hate speech or pornography, but it is not significantly disputed with respect to the ordinary issues of political debate and public discourse.

Long before *Buckley*, therefore, it was established that government could not regulate the domain of public discourse—most especially, political speech—for the purpose of establishing a greater "equality of voice" or "influence" among participants engaged in public debate. When large government and small government proponents are competing to control public opinion, for example, the First Amendment commitment to robust, wide-open debate does not permit government itself to favor either side—whether in the name of fairness, equality, or virtually any other justification. "As a general matter, the American First Amendment tradition requires that the financial, political, or rhetorical imbalance between the proponents of competing arguments is insufficient to justify government intervention to correct that imbalance." Frederick Schauer & Richard H. Pildes, *Electoral Exceptionalism and the First Amendment*, 77 Tex. L. Rev. 1803, 1825 (1999).

As a result, any form of campaign-finance regulation that implicates speech must meet at least two requirements: (1) in principle, there must be a theoretical distinction that can be justified between an arena that can be demarcated as "the electoral domain" and that which can be considered "the domain of public discourse;" and (2) in terms of practicable and administrative regulatory and constitutional doctrine, there must be a way of giving operational content to whatever boundary, in theory, can be offered to distinguish these two domains. Another way of putting this point is that when it comes to political participation, the governing principle is that of political equality among all citizens; the one-vote, one-person principle of Chapter 3 in the casebook reflects this principle. Yet when it comes to public discourse, the central governing principle is that of political liberty; each citizen should be able to express his or her opinions fully and without constraint. The First Amendment reflects *that* principle.

How does this relate to *Buckley v. Valeo*? At the time of *Buckley*, the landscape was essentially thought to include only campaign contributions and expenditures. By assumption, both these funding modes involve *campaigns* and hence the electoral domain. But by the 1996 elections, a major new form of influencing policy and elections came to the fore: this mode is known as issue advocacy. Issue advocacy is best understood by what it does *not* do—it is a communication that does not seek to advance the election of a clearly identified candidate (or perhaps group of candidates—such as Democrats). In its pure form, issue advocacy would involve advertising that sought to influence public opinion regarding political issues. An example would be the famous "Harry and Louise" advertisements, financed by the insurance industry, that successfully sought to build public opposition to President Clinton's health-care reform proposals. No national elections were pending; these advertisements were designed to change public opinion. As such, they were clearly in the "domain of public discourse" and entitled to the First Amendment protections that govern that domain.

But issue advertisements can easily merge into forms of electoral influence—and can be intentionally designed to do so. Imagine advertisements run two weeks before the 2000 Presidential election, financed by pharmaceutical companies, that urged voters not to support extending Medicare coverage to prescription drugs—when one of the major-party candidates had made support for such extension a central issue in his campaign and the other had strongly opposed it. Would/should this be an "issue ad?" Or an "electoral ad?" Should the law treat such an ad as part of the domain of public discourse—and hence unregulable? Or as part of the electoral domain—and hence subject to regulation as a form of campaign financing?

Buckley avoided coming to terms in any final way with the tension between equality and liberty and the tension between the electoral domain and the domain of public discourse. As Professor Kathleen Sullivan has put it, *Buckley* tried to "split the difference." It treated campaign expenditures as essentially unregulable speech, but campaign contributions as regulable electoral funding. Professor Sullivan nicely elaborates:

> *Buckley* involved nothing less than a choice between two of our most powerful traditions: equality in the realm of democratic polity, and liberty in the realm of political speech. The Court had to decide whether outlays of political money more resemble voting, on the one hand, or political debate, on the other. The norm in voting is equality: one person, one vote. The norm in political speech is negative liberty: freedom of exchange, against a backdrop of unequal distribution of resources (it has been said that freedom of the press belongs to those who own one). Faced with the question of which regime ought to govern regulation of political money, the Court in effect chose a little of both. It treated campaign contributions as more like voting, where individual efforts may be equalized, and campaign expenditures as more like speech, where they may not.

Kathleen M. Sullivan, *Political Money and Freedom of Speech*, 30 U.C. Davis L. Rev. 633, 667 (1997).

4.   THE COURT AND ISSUE ADVOCACY.

Among other features, the 1974 FECA legislation included broad regulation of what was arguably both issue and election advocacy. Congress regulated all spending "in connection with" or "for the purpose of influencing" a federal election, or "relative to" a federal candidate. Violation of the resulting regulations resulted in criminal penalties.

Based on First Amendment concerns, the Court in *Buckley* held these provisions unconstitutional. The Court held that the statutory definitions were so vague and overbroad that they failed to provide constitutionally adequate notice to persons the statute potentially regulated. According to the Court, "[t]he test is whether the language . . . affords the '[p]recision of regulation [that] must be the touchstone in an area so closely touching our most precious freedoms.' " Only what came to be known as express advocacy could constitutionally be regulated: that includes only "expenditures for communications that in express terms advocate the election or defeat of a clearly identified candidate." In an important footnote, the Court offered as a non-exclusive list of "express words of advocacy" the following examples: " 'vote for,' 'elect,' 'support,' 'cast your ballot for', 'Smith for Congress,' 'vote against,' 'defeat,' [and] 'reject.' " In time, these became known as *Buckley's* "magic words." the campaign finance equivalent of the "dirty words" that once upon a time dared not be broadcast.

Notice that this definition enables speech to be treated as express advocacy only if it can essentially pass through the eye of a needle. In the Court's second encounter with the problem, it suggested a slightly broader definition. *Federal Election Commission v. Massachusetts Citizens for Life, Inc.*, 479 U.S. 238 (1986), involved an anti-abortion group's "special edition" newsletter. This publication listed state and federal candidates in an upcoming primary; identified their positions on three key issues of concern to the group; provided photographs of those with one hundred percent favorable voting records, but not of others; and urged readers to vote for anti-abortion candidates. The Court concluded that the newsletter constituted express advocacy, even though it never explicitly called for votes for a particular candidate. Yet the newsletter could not "be regarded as a mere discussion of public issues that by their nature raise the names of certain politicians. Rather, it provides in effect an explicit directive: vote for these (named) candidates." 479 U.S. at 248–50.

The result of these doctrines, prior to the 2002 statutory overhaul that we shall turn to next, was that ads that were rather clearly aimed at influencing elections, at least in part, were treated to First Amendment protection and hence not reachable by campaign-finance regulation. Rather than contributing to a campaign, then, or engaging in "electoral" expenditures, those seeking to affect outcomes could simply finance the broadcasting of "issue" ads. The following example, taken from Richard Briffault, *Issue Advocacy: Redrawing the Elections/Politics Line*, 77 Tex. L. Rev. 1751 (1999), is of a television ad that was repeatedly run in the closing weeks of the 1996 state elections in Montana:

Who is Bill Yellowtail? He preaches family values, but he took a swing at his wife. Yellowtail's explanation? He "only slapped her," but her nose was broken. He talks law and order, but is himself a convicted criminal. And though he talks about protecting children, Yellowtail failed to make his own child support payments, then voted against child support enforcement. Call Bill Yellowtail and tell him we don't approve of his wrongful behavior. Call (406) 443-3620.

As Briffault described the then-existing state of the law:

> The anti-Yellowtail ad, financed by an organization cryptically named Citizens for Reform, was a classic instance of contemporary "issue advocacy." It was an issue ad not because it discussed any issues, but because it avoided "express advocacy" of either Democrat Yellowtail's defeat or the election of Rick Hill, Yellowtail's Republican opponent, in the race for Montana's seat in the House of Representatives. The ad featured harsh criticism of Yellowtail by name, was broadcast on the eve of the election, and was paid for by an organization that spent $2 million supporting Republican candidates in elections across the country. The ad contained an electioneering message but, because it carefully refrained from any call to vote against Yellowtail or for Hill, the ad fell short of express advocacy and was, instead, an issue ad. As a result, it was exempt from regulation under the Federal Election Campaign Act—even the provisions requiring the sponsor to disclose who paid for the ad.

By the time of the 1996 election cycle, campaigns and organizations learned to exploit the concept of issue advocacy. Recall that the Supreme Court had offered an extremely narrow conception of express advocacy, which meant that much of the terrain of election-related advertising fell within the category of issue advocacy. Moreover, because the Court had tried to create a bright-line rule for what constitutes "express advocacy," it had become easy to manipulate the presentation of ads to avoid having them considered express advocacy. Before 1996, reformers worried about the "soft money" problem. But by 1996, campaigns and organizations had learned that it was perhaps even easier to exploit the issue advocacy opening, and the 1996 elections saw a massive rise in "issue ads." Indeed, soft money could then be combined with so-called "issue ads" that were for all practical purposes forms of electoral advocacy; the result was a near perfect circumvention of the 1974 FECA. As the leading article on issue advocacy put it:

> Pragmatically, the current test is an open invitation for evasion. It is child's play for political advertisers and campaign professionals to develop ads that effectively advocate or oppose the cause of a candidate but stop short of the formal express advocacy that the courts permit to be regulated. The most common tactic for political advertisers is to include some language calling for the reader, viewer, or listener to respond to the message by doing something other than voting. In [one case], for example, the ad called on viewers to telephone the sponsor "for more information on traditional family values." Other ads urged voters to telephone the candidate targeted by the sponsor and ask him why he opposes tax cuts or term limits. . . . By combining sharp criticism of a candidate with an exhortation to call the sponsor or the candidate criticized, these ads can inoculate themselves from the charge that they constitute express advocacy.

Briffault, *supra*, at 1759. The scope of issue advocacy regulation emerged front and center as the key to subsequent regulatory efforts, only recast in the form of restrictions on "electioneering communication."

F. BCRA: The Second Round of Reform and Constitutional Challenge

The regulatory environment was significantly altered by the Bipartisan Campaign Reform Act of 2002, Pub. L. No. 107-155, known colloquially as BCRA, and sometimes as McCain–Feingold after the bill's principal sponsors. BCRA was intended to fill a perceived gap in the regulatory coverage of the post-*Buckley* FECA. The perception was that private funds that were meant to have been regulated had found other ways to enter the election system. The main objective of BCRA was to cabin two of the most notable loopholes in the regulatory scheme: the use of issue advertising and the rise of soft money activity by the political parties. There was a notable quid pro quo in BCRA that played a decidedly secondary role in the litigation, but may prove over time to be the most significant feature of the statute. In exchange for clamping down on soft money, BCRA allowed parties and candidates to raise more hard money—that is, money subject to federal contribution and disclosure requirements. Thus, for example, the maximum gift from an individual to a candidate has been increased from $1,000 to $2,000, a change that initially yielded a considerable immediate financial advantage to the Republican Party, but the long-term effect of which is still unclear.

The litigation so far has turned primarily on two features of BCRA. Title I of the Act contains a series of prohibitions on the use of soft money by political parties. Title II expands the concept of electioneering communication that was intended to stop the use of corporate and union money in pursuit of issue advocacy that influences candidate elections.

Title I: Restrictions on Political Party Soft Money. The main focus of this provision of BCRA was to reduce the ability of political parties to raise soft money and use it in ways that suggested coordination with federal campaigns. The various provisions of this Title, when taken together, would have eliminated the ability of the national political parties to raise or use soft money. The target here was events, such as the coffee gatherings at the White House under President Clinton, in which political incumbents would engage in fundraising that fell outside of FECA. In addition, BCRA enacted a ban on national and state political parties using nonfederal funds for issue advertisements that in any way involved issues identified with a federal election or candidates for federal office.

Title II: Regulating Electioneering Communication. In addition to the ban on the use of soft money for issue advocacy by the political parties, BCRA prohibited the use of any corporate or union funds for

"electioneering communication," as issue advocacy came to be characterized, and required disclosure of the sponsors of any electioneering communication. As discussed in the prior section of this Chapter, any attempt to
limit issue advocacy would run into tremendous definitional problems that
would immediately implicate traditional First Amendment concerns over
vagueness or overbreadth. BCRA attempted to avoid First Amendment
difficulties by confining its regulation to a clearly bounded electoral period
and by only covering communications with a reference to a candidate for
federal office—as opposed to the "magic words" of *Buckley*, such as "vote
for", "elect", etc.

We focus our discussion on these provisions of BCRA and the Court's
assessment of their constitutionality. We omit from this discussion the
various concurring and dissenting opinions, except for Justice Scalia's.
These opinions largely retrace the continued divisions on the Court over
the continued vitality of *Buckley,* something that the Court revisits in
Randall v. Sorrell, decided in 2006, to which we return later in this
Chapter.

McConnell et al. v. Federal Election Commission et al.

540 U.S. 93 (2003).

■ JUSTICES STEVENS and O'CONNOR delivered the opinion of the Court with
respect to BCRA Titles I and II. [Justices Souter, Ginsburg and Breyer
joined this opinion in its entirety].

* * *

I

More than a century ago the "sober-minded Elihu Root" advocated
legislation that would prohibit political contributions by corporations in
order to prevent " 'the great aggregations of wealth, from using their
corporate funds, directly or indirectly,' " to elect legislators who would
" 'vote for their protection and the advancement of their interests as
against those of the public.' " *United States v. Automobile Workers,* 352
U.S. 567, 571 (1957) (quoting E. Root, Addresses on Government and
Citizenship 143 (R. Bacon & J. Scott eds.1916)). In Root's opinion, such
legislation would " 'strik[e] at a constantly growing evil which has done
more to shake the confidence of the plain people of small means of this
country in our political institutions than any other practice which has ever
obtained since the foundation of our Government.' " 352 U.S., at 571. The
Congress of the United States has repeatedly enacted legislation endorsing
Root's judgment.

BCRA is the most recent federal enactment designed "to purge national politics of what was conceived to be the pernicious influence of 'big
money' campaign contributions." *Id.,* at 572. As Justice Frankfurter ex-

plained in his opinion for the Court in *Automobile Workers,* the first such enactment responded to President Theodore Roosevelt's call for legislation forbidding all contributions by corporations " 'to any political committee or for any political purpose.' " *Ibid.* (quoting 40 Cong. Rec. 96 (1906)). In his annual message to Congress in December 1905, President Roosevelt stated that " 'directors should not be permitted to use stockholders' money' " for political purposes, and he recommended that " 'a prohibition' " on corporate political contributions " 'would be, as far as it went, an effective method of stopping the evils aimed at in corrupt practices acts.' " 352 U.S., at 352. The resulting 1907 statute completely banned corporate contributions of "money ... in connection with" any federal election. Tillman Act, ch. 420, 34 Stat. 864. Congress soon amended the statute to require the public disclosure of certain contributions and expenditures and to place "maximum limits on the amounts that congressional candidates could spend in seeking nomination and election." *Automobile Workers, supra,* at 575–576.

In 1925 Congress extended the prohibition of "contributions" "to include 'anything of value,' and made acceptance of a corporate contribution as well as the giving of such a contribution a crime." *Federal Election Comm'n v. National Right to Work Comm.,* 459 U.S. 197, 209 (1982) (citing Federal Corrupt Practices Act, 1925, §§ 301, 313, 43 Stat. 1070, 1074). During the debates preceding that amendment, a leading Senator characterized " 'the apparent hold on political parties which business interests and certain organizations seek and sometimes obtain by reason of liberal campaign contributions' " as " 'one of the great political evils of the time.' " *Automobile Workers, supra,* at 576 (quoting 65 Cong. Rec. 9507–9508 (1924)). We upheld the amended statute against a constitutional challenge, observing that "[t]he power of Congress to protect the election of President and Vice President from corruption being clear, the choice of means to that end presents a question primarily addressed to the judgment of Congress." *Burroughs v. United States,* 290 U.S. 534, 547.

Congress' historical concern with the "political potentialities of wealth" and their "untoward consequences for the democratic process," *Automobile Workers, supra,* at 577–578, has long reached beyond corporate money. During and shortly after World War II, Congress reacted to the "enormous financial outlays" made by some unions in connection with national elections. 352 U.S., at 579. Congress first restricted union contributions in the Hatch Act, 18 U.S.C. § 610, and it later prohibited "union contributions in connection with federal elections ... altogether." *National Right to Work, supra,* at 209 (citing War Labor Disputes Act (Smith–Connally Anti–Strike Act), ch. 144, § 9, 57 Stat. 167). Congress subsequently extended that prohibition to cover unions' election-related expenditures as well as contributions, and it broadened the coverage of federal campaigns to include both primary and general elections. Labor Management Relations Act, 1947 (Taft–Hartley Act), 61 Stat. 136. During the consideration of those measures, legislators repeatedly voiced their concerns regarding the pernicious influence of large campaign contributions. . . .

In early 1972 Congress continued its steady improvement of the national election laws by enacting FECA, 86 Stat. 3. As first enacted, that statute required disclosure of all contributions exceeding $100 and of expenditures by candidates and political committees that spent more than $1,000 per year. It also prohibited contributions made in the name of another person and by Government contractors. The law ratified the earlier prohibition on the use of corporate and union general treasury funds for political contributions and expenditures, but it expressly permitted corporations and unions to establish and administer separate segregated funds (commonly known as political action committees, or PACs) for election-related contributions and expenditures.

As the 1972 presidential elections made clear, however, FECA's passage did not deter unseemly fundraising and campaign practices. Evidence of those practices persuaded Congress to enact the Federal Election Campaign Act Amendments of 1974, 88 Stat. 1263. . . .

The 1974 amendments closed the loophole that had allowed candidates to use an unlimited number of political committees for fundraising purposes and thereby to circumvent the limits on individual committees' receipts and disbursements. They also limited individual political contributions to any single candidate to $1,000 per election, with an overall annual limitation of $25,000 by any contributor; imposed ceilings on spending by candidates and political parties for national conventions; required reporting and public disclosure of contributions and expenditures exceeding certain limits; and established the Federal Election Commission (FEC) to administer and enforce the legislation. . . .

[In *Buckley,* this Court] concluded that each set of limitations raised serious—though different—concerns under the First Amendment. We treated the limitations on candidate and individual expenditures as direct restraints on speech, but we observed that the contribution limitations, in contrast, imposed only "a marginal restriction upon the contributor's ability to engage in free communication." Considering the "deeply disturbing examples" of corruption related to candidate contributions . . . , we determined that limiting contributions served an interest in protecting "the integrity of our system of representative democracy." In the end, the Act's primary purpose—"to limit the actuality and appearance of corruption resulting from large individual financial contributions"—provided "a constitutionally sufficient justification for the $1,000 contribution limitation." 424 U.S. at 26.

Three important developments in the years after our decision in *Buckley* persuaded Congress that further legislation was necessary to regulate the role that corporations, unions, and wealthy contributors play in the electoral process. As a preface to our discussion of the specific provisions of BCRA, we comment briefly on the increased importance of "soft money," the proliferation of "issue ads," and the disturbing findings of a Senate investigation into campaign practices related to the 1996 federal elections.

Soft Money

Under FECA, "contributions" must be made with funds that are subject to the Act's disclosure requirements and source and amount limitations. Such funds are known as "federal" or "hard" money. FECA defines the term "contribution," however, to include only the gift or advance of anything of value "made by any person for the purpose of influencing any election for *Federal* office." 2 U.S.C. § 431(8)(A)(i) (emphasis added). Donations made solely for the purpose of influencing state or local elections are therefore unaffected by FECA's requirements and prohibitions. As a result, prior to the enactment of BCRA, federal law permitted corporations and unions, as well as individuals who had already made the maximum permissible contributions to federal candidates, to contribute "nonfederal money"—also known as "soft money"—to political parties for activities intended to influence state or local elections.

Shortly after *Buckley* was decided, questions arose concerning the treatment of contributions intended to influence both federal and state elections. Although a literal reading of FECA's definition of "contribution" would have required such activities to be funded with hard money, the FEC ruled that political parties could fund mixed-purpose activities—including get-out-the-vote drives and generic party advertising—in part with soft money. In 1995 the FEC concluded that the parties could also use soft money to defray the costs of "legislative advocacy media advertisements," even if the ads mentioned the name of a federal candidate, so long as they did not expressly advocate the candidate's election or defeat. FEC Advisory Op. 1995–25.

As the permissible uses of soft money expanded, the amount of soft money raised and spent by the national political parties increased exponentially. Of the two major parties' total spending, soft money accounted for 5% ($21.6 million) in 1984, 11% ($45 million) in 1988, 16% ($80 million) in 1992, 30% ($272 million) in 1996, and 42% ($498 million) in 2000. The national parties transferred large amounts of their soft money to the state parties, which were allowed to use a larger percentage of soft money to finance mixed-purpose activities under FEC rules. In the year 2000, for example, the national parties diverted $280 million—more than half of their soft money—to state parties.

Many contributions of soft money were dramatically larger than the contributions of hard money permitted by FECA. For example, in 1996 the top five corporate soft-money donors gave, in total, more than $9 million in nonfederal funds to the two national party committees. In the most recent election cycle the political parties raised almost $300 million—60% of their total soft-money fundraising—from just 800 donors, each of which contributed a minimum of $120,000. Moreover, the largest corporate donors often made substantial contributions to both parties. Such practices corroborate evidence indicating that many corporate contributions were motivated by a desire for access to candidates and a fear of being placed at a disadvantage in the legislative process relative to other contributors, rather than by ideological support for the candidates and parties.

Not only were such soft-money contributions often designed to gain access to federal candidates, but they were in many cases solicited by the candidates themselves. Candidates often directed potential donors to party committees and tax-exempt organizations that could legally accept soft money. For example, a federal legislator running for reelection solicited soft money from a supporter by advising him that even though he had already "contributed the legal maximum" to the campaign committee, he could still make an additional contribution to a joint program supporting federal, state, and local candidates of his party. Such solicitations were not uncommon.

The solicitation, transfer, and use of soft money thus enabled parties and candidates to circumvent FECA's limitations on the source and amount of contributions in connection with federal elections.

Issue Advertising

In *Buckley* we construed FECA's disclosure and reporting requirements, as well as its expenditure limitations, "to reach only funds used for communications that expressly advocate the election or defeat of a clearly identified candidate." 424 U.S., at 80. As a result of that strict reading of the statute, the use or omission of "magic words" such as "Elect John Smith" or "Vote Against Jane Doe" marked a bright statutory line separating "express advocacy" from "issue advocacy." *See id.*, at 44, n. 52. Express advocacy was subject to FECA's limitations and could be financed only using hard money. The political parties, in other words, could not use soft money to sponsor ads that used any magic words, and corporations and unions could not fund such ads out of their general treasuries. So-called issue ads, on the other hand, not only could be financed with soft money, but could be aired without disclosing the identity of, or any other information about, their sponsors.

While the distinction between "issue" and express advocacy seemed neat in theory, the two categories of advertisements proved functionally identical in important respects. Both were used to advocate the election or defeat of clearly identified federal candidates, even though the so-called issue ads eschewed the use of magic words. Little difference existed, for example, between an ad that urged viewers to "vote against Jane Doe" and one that condemned Jane Doe's record on a particular issue before exhorting viewers to "call Jane Doe and tell her what you think."

Senate Committee Investigation

In 1998 the Senate Committee on Governmental Affairs issued a six-volume report summarizing the results of an extensive investigation into the campaign practices in the 1996 federal elections. The report gave particular attention to the effect of soft money on the American political system, including elected officials' practice of granting special access in return for political contributions.

The committee's principal findings relating to Democratic Party fundraising were set forth in the majority's report, while the minority report primarily described Republican practices. The two reports reached consensus, however, on certain central propositions. They agreed that the "soft money loophole" had led to a "meltdown" of the campaign finance system that had been intended "to keep corporate, union and large individual contributions from influencing the electoral process." One Senator stated that "the hearings provided overwhelming evidence that the twin loopholes of soft money and bogus issue advertising have virtually destroyed our campaign finance laws, leaving us with little more than a pile of legal rubble."

* * *

II

In BCRA, Congress enacted many of the committee's proposed reforms. BCRA's central provisions are designed to address Congress' concerns about the increasing use of soft money and issue advertising to influence federal elections. Title I regulates the use of soft money by political parties, officeholders, and candidates. Title II primarily prohibits corporations and labor unions from using general treasury funds for communications that are intended to, or have the effect of, influencing the outcome of federal elections.

* * *

III

Title I is Congress' effort to plug the soft-money loophole. The cornerstone of Title I is new FECA § 323(a), which prohibits national party committees and their agents from soliciting, receiving, directing, or spending any soft money. In short, § 323(a) takes national parties out of the soft-money business. . . .

A

* * *

Like the contribution limits we upheld in *Buckley,* § 323's restrictions have only a marginal impact on the ability of contributors, candidates, officeholders, and parties to engage in effective political speech. Complex as its provisions may be, § 323, in the main, does little more than regulate the ability of wealthy individuals, corporations, and unions to contribute large sums of money to influence federal elections, federal candidates, and federal officeholders.

Plaintiffs contend that we must apply strict scrutiny to § 323 because many of its provisions restrict not only contributions but also the spending and solicitation of funds raised outside of FECA's contribution limits. But for purposes of determining the level of scrutiny, it is irrelevant that Congress chose in § 323 to regulate contributions on the demand rather than the supply side. The relevant inquiry is whether the mechanism adopted to implement the contribution limit, or to prevent circumvention of that limit, burdens speech in a way that a direct restriction on the contribution itself would not. That is not the case here.

For example, while § 323(a) prohibits national parties from receiving or spending nonfederal money, and § 323(b) prohibits state party committees from spending nonfederal money on federal election activities, neither provision in any way limits the total amount of money parties can spend. Rather, they simply limit the source and individual amount of donations. That they do so by prohibiting the spending of soft money does not render them expenditure limitations.

[. . . P]laintiffs contend that the type of associational burdens that § 323 imposes are fundamentally different from the burdens that accompanied *Buckley's* contribution limits, and merit the type of strict scrutiny we have applied to attempts to regulate the internal processes of political parties. *E.g., California Democratic Party v. Jones*, 530 U.S. 567, 573–574 (2000). In making this argument, plaintiffs greatly exaggerate the effect of § 323, contending that it precludes *any* collaboration among national, state, and local committees of the same party in fundraising and electioneering activities. We do not read the provisions in that way. *See infra,* at 670. Section 323 merely subjects a greater percentage of contributions to parties and candidates to FECA's source and amount limitations. *Buckley* has already acknowledged that such limitations "leave the contributor free to become a member of any political association and to assist personally in the association's efforts on behalf of candidates." 424 U.S., at 22. The modest impact that § 323 has on the ability of committees within a party to associate with each other does not independently occasion strict scrutiny. None of this is to suggest that the alleged associational burdens imposed on parties by § 323 have no place in the First Amendment analysis; it is only that we account for them in the application, rather than the choice, of the appropriate level of scrutiny.

With these principles in mind, we apply the less rigorous scrutiny applicable to contribution limits to evaluate the constitutionality of new FECA § 323. Because the five challenged provisions of § 323 implicate different First Amendment concerns, we discuss them separately. We are mindful, however, that Congress enacted § 323 as an integrated whole to vindicate the Government's important interest in preventing corruption and the appearance of corruption.

New FECA § 323(a)'s Restrictions on National Party Committees

The core of Title I is new FECA § 323(a), which provides that "national committee[s] of a political party . . . may not solicit, receive, or direct to another person a contribution, donation, or transfer of funds or any other thing of value, or spend any funds, that are not subject to the limitations, prohibitions, and reporting requirements of this Act." The prohibition extends to "any officer or agent acting on behalf of such a national committee, and any entity that is directly or indirectly established, financed, or maintained, or controlled by such a national committee." § 441(a)(2).

The main goal of § 323(a) is modest. In large part, it simply effects a return to the scheme that was approved in *Buckley* and that was subverted by the creation of the FEC's allocation regime, which permitted the political parties to fund federal electioneering efforts with a combination of hard and soft money.

* * *

The Government defends § 323(a)'s ban on national parties' involvement with soft money as necessary to prevent the actual and apparent corruption of federal candidates and officeholders. Our cases have made clear that the prevention of corruption or its appearance constitutes a sufficiently important interest to justify political contribution limits. We have not limited that interest to the elimination of cash-for-votes exchanges. In *Buckley,* we expressly rejected the argument that antibribery laws provided a less restrictive alternative to FECA's contribution limits, noting that such laws "deal[t] with only the most blatant and specific attempts of those with money to influence government action." 424 U.S., at 28. Thus, "[i]n speaking of 'improper influence' and 'opportunities for abuse' in addition to '*quid pro quo* arrangements,' we [have] recognized a concern not confined to bribery of public officials, but extending to the broader threat from politicians too compliant with the wishes of large contributors." *Shrink Missouri,* 528 U.S., at 389; see also *Colorado II,* 533 U.S., at 441 (acknowledging that corruption extends beyond explicit cash-for-votes agreements to "undue influence on an officeholder's judgment").

Of "almost equal" importance has been the Government's interest in combating the appearance or perception of corruption engendered by large campaign contributions. *Buckley, supra,* at 27; see also *Shrink Missouri, supra,* at 390, *Federal Election Comm'n v. National Conservative Political Action Comm.,* 470 U.S. 480, 496–497 (1985). Take away Congress' authority to regulate the appearance of undue influence and "the cynical assumption that large donors call the tune could jeopardize the willingness of voters to take part in democratic governance." *Shrink Missouri,* 528 U.S., at 390; *see also id.,* at 40 (Breyer, J., concurring). And because the First Amendment does not require Congress to ignore the fact that "candidates, donors, and parties test the limits of the current law," *Colorado II,* 533 U.S., at 457, these interests have been sufficient to justify not only contribution limits themselves, but laws preventing the circumvention of such limits, *id.,* at 456 ("[A]ll Members of the Court agree that circumvention is a valid theory of corruption").

"The quantum of empirical evidence needed to satisfy heightened judicial scrutiny of legislative judgments will vary up or down with the novelty or the plausibility of the justification raised." *Shrink Missouri, supra,* at 391. The idea that large contributions to a national party can corrupt or, at the very least, create the appearance of corruption of federal candidates and officeholders is neither novel nor implausible. . . .

The question for present purposes is whether large *soft-money* contributions to national party committees have a corrupting influence or give rise to the appearance of corruption. Both common sense and the ample record in these cases confirm Congress' belief that they do. . . . [T]he FEC's allocation regime has invited widespread circumvention of FECA's limits on contributions to parties for the purpose of influencing federal elections. Under this system, corporate, union, and wealthy individual donors have been free to contribute substantial sums of soft money to the national parties, which the parties can spend for the specific purpose of influencing a particular candidate's federal election. It is not only plausible, but likely, that candidates would feel grateful for such donations and that donors would seek to exploit that gratitude.

The evidence in the record shows that candidates and donors alike have in fact exploited the soft-money loophole, the former to increase their prospects of election and the latter to create debt on the part of officeholders, with the national parties serving as willing intermediaries. Thus, despite FECA's hard-money limits on direct contributions to candidates, federal officeholders have commonly asked donors to make soft-money donations to national and state committees "solely in order to assist federal campaigns," including the officeholder's own. [citing district court findings]. . . .

For their part, lobbyists, CEOs, and wealthy individuals alike all have candidly admitted donating substantial sums of soft money to national committees not on ideological grounds, but for the express purpose of securing influence over federal officials. . . .

Particularly telling is the fact that, in 1996 and 2000, more than half of the top 50 soft-money donors gave substantial sums to *both* major national parties, leaving room for no other conclusion but that these donors were seeking influence, or avoiding retaliation, rather than promoting any particular ideology. . . .

The evidence from the federal officeholders' perspective is similar. For example, one former Senator described the influence purchased by nonfederal donations as follows:

"Too often, Members' first thought is not what is right or what they believe, but how it will affect fundraising. Who, after all, can seriously contend that a $100,000 donation does not alter the way one thinks about—and quite possibly votes on—an issue? ... When you don't pay the piper that finances your campaigns, you will never get any more money from that piper. Since money is the mother's milk of politics, you never want to be in that situation." 251 F. Supp. 2d, at 481 (Kollar–Kotelly, J.) (quoting declaration of former Sen. Alan Simpson ¶ 10).

Plaintiffs argue that without concrete evidence of an instance in which a federal officeholder has actually switched a vote (or, presumably, evidence of a specific instance where the public believes a vote was switched), Congress has not shown that there exists real or apparent corruption. But the record is to the contrary. The evidence connects soft money to manipulations of the legislative calendar, leading to Congress' failure to enact, among other things, generic drug legislation, tort reform, and tobacco legislation. [. . .]

In sum, there is substantial evidence to support Congress' determination that large soft-money contributions to national political parties give rise to corruption and the appearance of corruption.

* * *

IV

Title II of BCRA, entitled "Noncandidate Campaign Expenditures," is divided into two subtitles: "Electioneering Communications" and "Independent and Coordinated Expenditures." We consider each challenged section of these subtitles in turn.

BCRA § 201's Definition of "Electioneering Communication"

The first section of Title II, § 201, comprehensively amends FECA § 304, which requires political committees to file detailed periodic financial reports with the FEC. The amendment coins a new term, "electioneering communication," to replace the narrowing construction of FECA's disclosure provisions adopted by this Court in *Buckley*. As discussed further below, that construction limited the coverage of FECA's disclosure requirement to communications expressly advocating the election or defeat of particular candidates. By contrast, the term "electioneering communication" is not so limited, but is defined to encompass any "broadcast, cable, or satellite communication" that

(I) refers to a clearly identified candidate for Federal office;

(II) is made within—

(aa) 60 days before a general, special, or runoff election for the office sought by the candidate; or

(bb) 30 days before a primary or preference election, or a convention or caucus of a political party that has authority to nominate a candidate, for the office sought by the candidate; and

(III) in the case of a communication which refers to a candidate other than President or Vice President, is targeted to the relevant electorate.

New FECA § 304(f)(3)(C) further provides that a communication is " 'targeted to the relevant electorate' " if it "can be received by 50,000 or more persons" in the district or State the candidate seeks to represent.

In addition to setting forth this definition, BCRA's amendments to FECA § 304 specify significant disclosure requirements for persons who fund electioneering communications. BCRA's use of this new term is not, however, limited to the disclosure context: A later section of the Act (BCRA § 203, which amends FECA § 316(b)(2)) restricts corporations' and labor unions' funding of electioneering communications. Plaintiffs challenge the constitutionality of the new term as it applies in both the disclosure and the expenditure contexts.

The major premise of plaintiffs' challenge to BCRA's use of the term "electioneering communication" is that *Buckley* drew a constitutionally mandated line between express advocacy and so-called issue advocacy, and that speakers possess an inviolable First Amendment right to engage in the latter category of speech. Thus, plaintiffs maintain, Congress cannot constitutionally require disclosure of, or regulate expenditures for, "electioneering communications" without making an exception for those "communications" that do not meet *Buckley's* definition of express advocacy.

That position misapprehends our prior decisions, for the express advocacy restriction was an endpoint of statutory interpretation, not a first principle of constitutional law. . . .

Nor are we persuaded, independent of our precedents, that the First Amendment erects a rigid barrier between express advocacy and so-called issue advocacy. That notion cannot be squared with our longstanding recognition that the presence or absence of magic words cannot meaningfully distinguish electioneering speech from a true issue ad. Indeed, the unmistakable lesson from the record in this litigation is that *Buckley's* magic-words requirement is functionally meaningless. Not only can advertisers easily evade the line by eschewing the use of magic words, but they would seldom choose to use such words even if permitted. And although the resulting advertisements do not urge the viewer to vote for or against a candidate in so many words, they are no less clearly intended to influence the election. *Buckley's* express advocacy line, in short, has not aided the legislative effort to combat real or apparent corruption, and Congress enacted BCRA to correct the flaws it found in the existing system.

Finally we observe that new FECA § 304(f)(3)'s definition of "electioneering communication" raises none of the vagueness concerns that drove our analysis in *Buckley*. The term "electioneering communication" applies only (1) to a broadcast (2) clearly identifying a candidate for federal office, (3) aired within a specific time period, and (4) targeted to an identified audience of at least 50,000 viewers or listeners. These components are both easily understood and objectively determinable. Thus, the constitutional objection that persuaded the Court in *Buckley* to limit FECA's reach to express advocacy is simply inapposite here. [. . .]

BCRA § 203's Prohibition of Corporate and Labor Disbursements for Electioneering Communications

Since our decision in *Buckley*, Congress' power to prohibit corporations and unions from using funds in their treasuries to finance advertisements expressly advocating the election or defeat of candidates in federal elections has been firmly embedded in our law. The ability to form and administer separate segregated funds authorized by FECA, has provided corporations and unions with a constitutionally sufficient opportunity to engage in express advocacy. That has been this Court's unanimous view, and it is not challenged in this litigation.

Section 203 of BCRA amends FECA § 316(b)(2) to extend this rule, which previously applied only to express advocacy, to all "electioneering communications" covered by the definition of that term in amended FECA § 304(f)(3), discussed above. Thus, under BCRA, corporations and unions may not use their general treasury funds to finance electioneering communications, but they remain free to organize and administer segregated funds, or PACs, for that purpose. Because corporations can still fund electioneering communications with PAC money, it is "simply wrong" to view the provision as a "complete ban" on expression rather than a regulation.

* * *

V

Many years ago we observed that "[t]o say that Congress is without power to pass appropriate legislation to safeguard . . . an election from the improper use of money to influence the result is to deny to the nation in a vital particular the power of self protection." *Burroughs v. United States*, 290 U.S., at 545. We abide by that conviction in considering Congress' most recent effort to confine the ill effects of aggregated wealth on our political system. We are under no illusion that BCRA will be the last congressional statement on the matter. Money, like water, will always find an outlet. What problems will arise, and how Congress will respond, are concerns for another day. In the main we uphold BCRA's two principal, complementary features: the control of soft money and the regulation of electioneering communications. Accordingly, we affirm in part and reverse in part the District Court's judgment with respect to Titles I and II.

It is so ordered.

■ Chief Justice Rehnquist delivered the opinion of the Court with respect to BCRA Titles III and IV. Justice O'Connor, 'Justice Scalia, Justice Kennedy, and Justice Souter join this opinion in its entirety. Justice Stevens, Justice Ginsburg, and Justice Breyer join this opinion, except with respect to BCRA § 305. Justice Thomas joins this opinion with respect to BCRA §§ 304, 305, 307, 316, 319, and 403(b).

This opinion addresses issues involving miscellaneous Title III and IV provisions of the Bipartisan Campaign Reform Act of 2002 (BCRA), 116 Stat. 81. For the reasons discussed below, we affirm the judgment of the District Court with respect to these provisions.

* * *

BCRA § 307

BCRA § 307 . . . increases and indexes for inflation certain FECA contribution limits. The Adams and Paul plaintiffs challenge § 307 in this Court. Both groups contend that they have standing to sue. Again, we disagree.

The Adams plaintiffs, a group consisting of voters, organizations representing voters, and candidates, allege two injuries, and argue each is legally cognizable, "as established by case law outlawing electoral discrimination based on economic status . . . and upholding the right to an equally meaningful vote. . . ." Brief for Appellants.

First, they assert that the increases in hard money limits enacted by § 307 deprive them of an equal ability to participate in the election process based on their economic status. But, to satisfy our standing requirements, a plaintiff's alleged injury must be an invasion of a concrete and particularized legally protected interest. We have noted that "[a]lthough standing in no way depends on the merits of the plaintiff's contention that particular conduct is illegal, . . . it often turns on the nature and source of the claim asserted." *Warth v. Seldin,* 422 U.S. 490, 500, (1975). We have never recognized a legal right comparable to the broad and diffuse injury asserted by the Adams plaintiffs. Their reliance on this Court's voting rights cases is misplaced. They rely on cases requiring nondiscriminatory access to the ballot and a single, equal vote for each voter.

None of these plaintiffs claims a denial of equal access to the ballot or the right to vote. Instead, the plaintiffs allege a curtailment of the scope of their participation in the electoral process. But we have noted that "[p]olitical 'free trade' does not necessarily require that all who participate in the political marketplace do so with exactly equal resources." *Federal Election Comm'n v. Massachusetts Citizens for Life, Inc.,* 479 U.S. 238, 257 (1986);

see also *Buckley v. Valeo*, 424 U.S. 1, 48 (1976) (rejecting the asserted government interest of "equalizing the relative ability of individuals and groups to influence the outcome of elections" to justify the burden on speech presented by expenditure limits). This claim of injury by the Adams plaintiffs is, therefore, not to a legally cognizable right.

Second, the Adams plaintiffs-candidates contend that they have suffered a competitive injury. Their candidates "do not wish to solicit or accept large campaign contributions as permitted by BCRA" because "[t]hey believe such contributions create the appearance of unequal access and influence." Adams Complaint ¶ 53. As a result, they claim that BCRA § 307 puts them at a "fundraising disadvantage," making it more difficult for them to compete in elections.

The second claimed injury is based on the same premise as the first: BCRA § 307's increased hard money limits allow plaintiffs-candidates' opponents to raise more money, and, consequently, the plaintiffs-candidates' ability to compete or participate in the electoral process is diminished. But they cannot show that their alleged injury is "fairly traceable" to BCRA § 307. Their alleged inability to compete stems not from the operation of § 307, but from their own personal "wish" not to solicit or accept large contributions, *i.e.*, their personal choice. Accordingly, the Adams plaintiffs fail here to allege an injury in fact that is "fairly traceable" to BCRA.

* * *

BCRA § 318

BCRA § 318 . . . prohibits individuals "17 years old or younger" from making contributions to candidates and contributions or donations to political parties. The McConnell and Echols plaintiffs challenge the provision; they argue that § 318 violates the First Amendment rights of minors. We agree.

Minors enjoy the protection of the First Amendment. *See, e.g., Tinker v. Des Moines Independent Community School Dist.*, 393 U.S. 503, 511–513 (1969). Limitations on the amount that an individual may contribute to a candidate or political committee impinge on the protected freedoms of expression and association. When the Government burdens the right to contribute, we apply heightened scrutiny. We ask whether there is a "sufficiently important interest" and whether the statute is "closely drawn" to avoid unnecessary abridgment of First Amendment freedoms. The Government asserts that the provision protects against corruption by conduit; that is, donations by parents through their minor children to circumvent contribution limits applicable to the parents. But the Government offers scant evidence of this form of evasion. Perhaps the Government's slim evidence results from sufficient deterrence of such activities by § 320 of FECA, which prohibits any person from "mak[ing] a contribution in the name of another person" or "knowingly accept[ing] a contribution made by one person in the name of another," 2 U.S.C. § 441f. Absent a more convincing case of the claimed evil, this interest is simply too attenuated for § 318 to withstand heightened scrutiny. *See Nixon v. Shrink Missouri Government PAC,* 528 U.S. 377, 391 (2000) ("The quantum of empirical evidence needed to satisfy heightened judicial scrutiny of legislative judgments will vary up or down with the novelty and plausibility of the justification raised").

Even assuming, *arguendo,* the Government advances an important interest, the provision is overinclusive. The States have adopted a variety of more tailored approaches—*e.g.,* counting contributions by minors against the total permitted for a parent or family unit, imposing a lower cap on contributions by minors, and prohibiting contributions by very young children. Without deciding whether any of these alternatives is sufficiently tailored, we hold that the provision here sweeps too broadly. We therefore affirm the District Court's decision striking down § 318 as unconstitutional.

* * *

[Opinion of JUSTICES BREYER, KENNEDY, and THOMAS omitted].

■ JUSTICE SCALIA, concurring with respect to BCRA Titles III and IV, dissenting with respect to BCRA Titles I and V, and concurring in the judgment in part and dissenting in part with respect to BCRA Title II.

* * *

This is a sad day for the freedom of speech. Who could have imagined that the same Court which, within the past four years, has sternly disapproved of restrictions upon such inconsequential forms of expression as virtual child pornography, *Ashcroft v. Free Speech Coalition,* 535 U.S. 234 (2002), tobacco advertising, *Lorillard Tobacco Co. v. Reilly,* 533 U.S. 525 (2001), dissemination of illegally intercepted communications, *Bartnicki v. Vopper,* 532 U.S. 514 (2001), and sexually explicit cable programming, *United States v. Playboy Entertainment Group, Inc.,* 529 U.S. 803 (2000), would smile with favor upon a law that cuts to the heart of what the First Amendment is meant to protect: the right to criticize the government. For that is what the most offensive provisions of this legislation are all about. We are governed by Congress, and this legislation prohibits the criticism of Members of Congress by those entities most capable of giving such criticism loud voice: national political parties and corporations, both of the commercial and the not-for-profit sort. It forbids pre-election criticism of incumbents by corporations, even not-for-profit corporations, by use of their general funds; and forbids national-party use of "soft" money to fund "issue ads" that incumbents find so offensive.

To be sure, the legislation is evenhanded: It similarly prohibits criticism of the candidates who oppose Members of Congress in their reelection bids. But as everyone knows, this is an area in which evenhandedness is not fairness. If *all* electioneering were evenhandedly prohibited, incumbents would have an enormous advantage. Likewise, if incumbents and challengers are limited to the same quantity of electioneering, incumbents are favored. In other words, *any* restriction upon a type of campaign speech that is equally available to challengers and incumbents tends to favor incumbents.

Beyond that, however, the present legislation *targets* for prohibition certain categories of campaign speech that are particularly harmful to incumbents. Is it accidental, do you think, that incumbents raise about three times as much "hard money"—the sort of funding generally *not* restricted by this legislation—as do their challengers?

* * *

[Justice Scalia then discusses and rejects three rationales for treating campaign finance regulations outside First Amendment protection: "Money is Not Speech," "Pooling Money is Not Speech," and "Speech by Corporations Can Be Abridged." Justice Scalia concludes:]

Which brings me back to where I began: This litigation is about preventing criticism of the government. I cannot say for certain that many, or some, or even any, of the Members of Congress who voted for this legislation did so not to produce "fairer" campaigns, but to mute criticism of their records and facilitate reelection. Indeed, I will stipulate that all those who voted for the Act believed they were acting for the good of the country. There remains the problem of the Charlie Wilson Phenomenon, named after Charles Wilson, former president of General Motors, who is supposed to have said during the Senate hearing on his nomination as Secretary of Defense that "what's good for General Motors is good for the country." Those in power, even giving them the benefit of the greatest good will, are inclined to believe that what is good for them is good for the country. Whether in prescient recognition of the Charlie Wilson Phenomenon, or out of fear of good old-fashioned, malicious, self-interested manipulation, "[t]he fundamental approach of the First Amendment . . . was to assume the worst, and to rule the regulation of political speech 'for fairness' sake' simply out of bounds." *Austin,* 494 U.S., at 693 (Scalia, J., dissenting). Having abandoned that approach to a limited extent in *Buckley,* we abandon it much further today.

We will unquestionably be called upon to abandon it further still in the future. The most frightening passage in the lengthy floor debates on this legislation is the following assurance given by one of the cosponsoring Senators to his colleagues:

> This is a modest step, it is a first step, it is an essential step, but it does not even begin to address, in some ways, the fundamental problems that exist with the hard money aspect of the system. 148 Cong. Rec. S2101 (Mar. 20, 2002) (statement of Sen. Feingold).

The system indeed. The first instinct of power is the retention of power, and, under a Constitution that requires periodic elections, that is best achieved by the suppression of election-time speech. We have witnessed merely the second scene of Act I of what promises to be a lengthy tragedy. In scene 3 the Court, having abandoned most of the First Amendment weaponry that *Buckley* left intact, will be even less equipped to resist the incumbents' writing of the rules of political debate. The federal election campaign laws, which are already (as today's opinions show) so voluminous, so detailed, so complex, that no ordinary citizen dare run for office, or even contribute a significant sum, without hiring an expert advisor in the field, can be expected to grow more voluminous, more detailed, and more complex in the years to come—and always, always, with the objective of reducing the excessive amount of speech.

NOTES AND QUESTIONS

1. The primary inherited divide from *Buckley* concerned the different constitutional treatment of contributions and expenditures, with restrictions on the former facing relatively little constitutional scrutiny and those on the latter a heavy presumption of unconstitutionality. One of the main subjects addressed in *McConnell* was BCRA's restriction on political party uses of soft money. Previously the use of soft money for independent advocacy would have been considered an independent expenditure that likely could not be regulated. In *McConnell*, the Court for the first time treated the regulation of such expenditures as dependent on the source of the funds rather than the form of the regulation. The Court wrote that the challenged regulations "simply limit the source and individual amount of donations. That they do so by prohibiting the spending of soft money does not render them expenditure limitations." Is this consistent with the *Buckley* scheme? Once down this path, is it not possible to characterize all expenditure limits as contribution limits, since money to be spent must first have been amassed? Or conversely, could not all contribution limits be cast as expenditure limitations since the level of contributions will invariably affect the capacity to spend? Has *McConnell* thereby collapsed the remaining stands of the *Buckley* contributions/expenditures divide?

2. What is the definition of corruption that survives after *McConnell*? The dissents charge that until *McConnell*, corruption remained rooted in a quid pro quo exchange, even if the particulars of the exchange might be difficult to police or bring to the light of day. *McConnell* appears to move the inquiry much further beyond the difficulty of policing improper exchanges of money for influence. Part of the Court's frustration with bribery laws is that such direct payments of necessity operate in the shadows of political transactions. Regulations are unlikely to ferret out many overt exchanges of money for direct influence. *Buckley* focused essentially on the difficulty of enforcement and found that criminal antibribery laws were too unwieldy to effectively police the political process. *McConnell* shifts the concern with antibribery laws from their limited effectiveness to their limited range. The concern is now the "compliant" nature of politicians in the face of large donors and the appearance or perception of undue influence. The majority is careful to root this definition in the emerging case law since *Buckley*. But is this the same conception of corruption that animated *Buckley?*

3.   The Court's campaign finance cases return time and again to the issue of the weight of evidence adduced by Congress in support of regulations such as BCRA. At times the debate appears to be a matter of what presumption should apply to congressional action and what standard of review should follow. For example, the entire Court joins Chief Justice Rehnquist in striking down the ban on campaign contributions by minors on the grounds that Congress failed to provide sufficient evidence to overcome strict scrutiny. The Chief Justice notes that such limitations on contributions "impinge on the protected freedoms of expression and association." It is difficult to see why the appearance of corruption rationale that held sway for almost all of BCRA would not apply to minors making contributions, presumably with money that originated with their parents. What evidence would have been persuasive on the question whether contributions by minors were a form of circumvention?

More generally, what is the role of empirical evidence on such wide-ranging and contentious social issues? Do cases such as *McConnell* really turn on the level or proof or the perceived reasonableness of the legislative intuitions guiding the statutory initiatives? Again, it is useful to contrast the debate over the sufficiency of the evidence in *McConnell* to the treatment of evidentiary proof by the Canadian Supreme Court in *Harper*:

> The legislature is not required to provide scientific proof based on concrete evidence of the problem it seeks to address in every case. Where the court is faced with inconclusive or competing social science evidence relating the harm to the Legislature's measures, the court may rely on a reasoned apprehension of that harm. . . . [As previously established] "Discharge of the civil standard does not require scientific demonstration; the balance of probabilities may be established by the application of common sense to what is known, even though what is known may be deficient from a scientific point of view." (quoting *RJR-MacDonald Inc. v. Canada (Attorney General)*, 3 S.C.R. 199).

Attorney General of Canada v. Harper, 2004 S.C. 33. For further discussions of campaign finance rules in Canada and other countries, see K.D. Ewing and Samuel Issacharoff, Party Funding and Campaign Financing in International Perspective (2006). For an in depth examination of the unfolding confrontations with party funding in Britain since 1997, see Keith Ewing, The Cost of Democracy (2007).

4.   *Judging the Purposes of Election Laws.* Note Justice Scalia's argument that McCain–Feingold was an incumbent-protection scheme. Throughout this casebook, we have emphasized the omnipresent risk that election regulations enacted by self-interested legislatures can be a vehicle for incumbent or partisan protection. At the same time, that risk alone cannot be a justification for constitutional invalidation of such laws, lest all changes to election laws be stopped in place (and what about the risk that pre-existing election laws themselves reflect partisan or incumbent self-interest?). Given the nature of the problem, how can courts determine when a law serves incumbent-protection purposes or more public regarding ones? How should the Court have resolved this issue with respect to McCain–Feingold?

Some argue that the Court should have been more aggressive in scrutinizing whether the means in the law were sufficiently tailored to preventing corruption, as a way of determining whether the law was an illegitimate incumbent protection scheme. *See, e.g.*, Richard L. Hasen, Buckley *is Dead, Long Live* Buckley: *The New Campaign Finance Incoherence of* McConnell v. Federal Election Commission, 153 U. Pa. L. Rev. 31 (2004). But others argue that this sensible sounding demand cannot be meaningfully applied in the contexts of laws like McCain–Feingold; such scrutiny would require a firm anchor in proof of actual legislative "corruption." But, while one can show a correlation between contributions and votes, it is quite difficult to prove that those contributions *caused* those votes—which is what proof of corruption would require. Yet that something is difficult to prove does not mean it is not occurring. Nor are courts likely to be good at predicting whether laws like McCain–Feingold will turn out, in practice, to benefit incumbents dramatically. If this is all true, the question remains: how should courts go about judging whether such laws are incumbent protection schemes or not? Consider the following proposal:

> If courts lack an empirical anchor on which they can base conventional means-ends scrutiny, and if they also cannot credibly predict the likely effects on political competition of a law like BCRA, how can they judge whether campaign finance laws (or other electoral laws) are pretexts for self-entrenchment?
>
> General presumptions are also unavailing: presumptions of legitimacy associated with ordinary laws are not appropriate, given Congress's obvious self-interest in this context, but presumptions against legitimacy, in light of the risk of self-entrenchment, are also inappropriate, given that Congress should be able to regulate democratic processes when pursuing legitimate ends and not violating rights.
>
> In these circumstances courts can do little but rely on process-based assessments to judge the risk of impermissible self-entrenchment. Though academics regularly belittle process-based analysis, in many contexts involving democratic institutional design, such as *Georgia v. Ashcroft* and *McConnell*, the pragmatic constraints of judging make process-based reasoning almost inevitable.
>
> McCain–Feingold did not sneak through Congress on an unsuspecting public. Few legislative proposals in recent years have received as much sustained public commentary or news coverage. Political scientists and

academic experts on election financing were on both sides, but many, with no self-interest in incumbent protection, were central figures in pressing the case for BCRA. Far from being anxious to protect itself through passage of such a law, Congress manifested little desire to act. The political entrepreneurship of legislators with national support, like Senator McCain, was critical. The law required bipartisan support, including the signature of a Republican President not committed in advance to adoption of such a law. Many predicted that the ban on soft money would hurt the Democratic Party relative to the Republican Party, yet Democratic support was central to the law's passage.

Richard H. Pildes, *The Supreme Court, 2003 Term—Foreword: The Constitutionalization of Democratic Politics*, 118 Harv. L. Rev. 28, 137–38 (2004). Is this a credible solution? For a rejoinder arguing that BCRA's legislative history does not command this sort of deference and that the Court should balance rights and interests with a skeptical eye, see Richard L. Hasen, *Bad Legislative Intent*, 2006 Wisc. L. Rev. 843, 865–71.

5. As might be expected, *McConnell* unleashed a blizzard of commentary from academics and pundits. The best collection of essays ranging across the political spectrum is found in *Election Law Journal,* Vol. 3, No. 2, Spring 2004. Those seeking a full account of the various BCRA provisions and their treatment in *McConnell* should look particularly at Richard Briffault, McConnell v. FEC *and the Transformation of Campaign Finance Law*, 3 Election L. J. 147 (2004).

6. Some indication of the expansiveness of the Court's treatment of the anticorruption rationale came the year before *McConnell* in *Federal Election Commission v. Beaumont*, 539 U.S. 146 (2003). The issue in the case was the constitutionality of FEC regulations that barred nonprofit advocacy corporations from contributing directly to candidates for federal office. The case addressed an unresolved tension in the law following *Massachusetts Citizens for Life, Inc.,* because the regulated entities in question were both corporations and advocacy groups. As a result, any regulation could be cast within the framework of either ongoing regulation of corporate activity within the electoral domain or as a limitation on speech of a clearly political advocacy group which happened to operate under a corporate charter. Per Justice Souter, with Justice Kennedy concurring in the judgment, and over the dissent of Justice Thomas, in which Justice Scalia joined, the Court upheld the regulation of advocacy-oriented corporations, writing:

> Since 1907, there has been continual congressional attention to corporate political activity, sometimes resulting in refinement of the law, sometimes in overhaul. . . . Today, as in 1907, the law focuses on the "special characteristics of the corporate structure" that threaten the integrity of the political process.
>
> [. . .] In barring corporate earnings from conversion into political "war chests," the ban was and is intended to "preven[t] corruption or the appearance of corruption." *National Conservative Political Action*

Comm. But the ban has always done further duty in protecting "the individuals who have paid money into a corporation or union for purposes other than the support of candidates from having that money used to support political candidates to whom they may be opposed."

In sum, our cases on campaign finance regulation represent respect for the "legislative judgment that the special characteristics of the corporate structure require particularly careful regulation." And we have understood that such deference to legislative choice is warranted particularly when Congress regulates campaign contributions, carrying as they do a plain threat to political integrity and a plain warrant to counter the appearance and reality of corruption and the misuse of corporate advantages. . . .

[. . .] For present purposes, we will assume advocacy corporations are generally different from traditional business corporations in the improbability that contributions they might make would end up supporting causes that some of their members would not approve. But concern about the corrupting potential underlying the corporate ban may indeed be implicated by advocacy corporations. They, like their for-profit counterparts, benefit from significant "state-created advantages," *Austin*, and may well be able to amass substantial "political 'war chests.'" Not all corporations that qualify for favorable tax treatment under § 501(c)(4) of the Internal Revenue Code lack substantial resources, and the category covers some of the Nation's most politically powerful organizations, including the AARP, the National Rifle Association, and the Sierra Club. Nonprofit advocacy corporations are, moreover, no less susceptible than traditional business companies to misuse as conduits for circumventing the contribution limits imposed on individuals.

G.   JUDICIAL DEFERENCE AND ANTI-CORRUPTION

A passing reference in a footnote in *McConnell* appeared to imply that not only was the Court applying a more deferential standard of review for congressional determinations of the appearance of impropriety in the political process, but that the Court might get out of the business of as-applied challenges to the operation of campaign finance laws altogether. That footnote cryptically held that, with regard to the definition of electioneering communication, "We uphold all applications of the primary definition and accordingly have no occasion to discuss the backup definition." 540 U.S. at 190, n. 73. That reading was consistent with the general tenor of *McConnell* in ratcheting down the level of constitutional scrutiny applied to legislation in this area. *See generally* Samuel Issacharoff, *Throwing in the Towel: The Constitutional Morass of Campaign Finance*, 3 Election L.J. 259 (2004).

In *Wisconsin Right to Life, Inc. v. FEC,* 546 U.S. 410 (2006), a unanimous Court, including the new Chief Justice, quickly put to rest the premature accounts of the demise of constitutional scrutiny. In a per curiam opinion, the Court squarely rejected the idea that there could be no as-applied challenge to an FEC rule that prohibited communications that were claimed to be "grassroots lobbying advertisements."

The Court's unanimous holding that as-applied challenges were subject to judicial review did not indicate any cohering of opinions on the merits of *Buckley* or the Court's approach to campaign finance. Indeed, the first merits decision including Chief Justice Roberts and Justice Alito showed that the fractures may be deeper than ever. In *Randall v. Sorrell,* a review of Vermont's 1997 Campaign Finance Act, Act 64, which imposed mandatory contribution and expenditure limits, the Court managed six separate opinions, a thin plurality holding for the Court by Justice Breyer in which only Chief Justice Roberts joined in full, and perhaps the most direct indication that *Buckley* commands only fleeting support on the Court.

Randall v. Sorrell

___ U.S. ___, 126 S. Ct. 2479 (2006).

■ JUSTICE BREYER announced the judgment of the Court, and delivered an opinion in which THE CHIEF JUSTICE joins, and in which JUSTICE ALITO joins except as to Parts II–B–1 and II–B.

We here consider the constitutionality of a Vermont campaign finance statute that limits both (1) the amounts that candidates for state office may spend on their campaigns (expenditure limitations) and (2) the amounts that individuals, organizations, and political parties may contribute to those campaigns (contribution limitations). Vt. Stat. Ann., Tit. 17, § 2801 *et seq.* (2002). We hold that both sets of limitations are inconsistent with the First Amendment. Well-established precedent makes clear that the expenditure limits violate the First Amendment. *Buckley v. Valeo,* 424 U.S. 1, 54–58 (1976) *(per curiam).* The contribution limits are unconstitutional because in their specific details (involving low maximum levels and other restrictions) they fail to satisfy the First Amendment's requirement of careful tailoring. *Id.,* at 25–30. That is to say, they impose burdens upon First Amendment interests that (when viewed in light of the statute's legitimate objectives) are disproportionately severe.

I

A

Prior to 1997, Vermont's campaign finance law imposed no limit upon the amount a candidate for state office could spend. It did, however, impose limits upon the amounts that individuals, corporations, and political committees could contribute to the campaign of such a candidate. Individuals and corporations could contribute no more than $1,000 to any candidate for state office. Political committees, excluding political parties, could contribute no more than $3,000. The statute imposed no limit on the amount that political parties could contribute to candidates.

In 1997, Vermont enacted a more stringent campaign finance law, Pub. Act No. 64, the statute at issue here. Act 64, which took effect immediately after the 1998 elections, imposes mandatory expenditure limits on the total amount a candidate for state office can spend during a "two-year general election cycle," *i.e.*, the primary plus the general election, in approximately the following amounts: governor, $300,000; lieutenant governor, $100,000; other statewide offices, $45,000; state senator, $4,000 (plus an additional $2,500 for each additional seat in the district); state representative (two-member district), $3,000; and state representative (single member district), $2,000. These limits are adjusted for inflation in odd-numbered years based on the Consumer Price Index. Incumbents seeking reelection to statewide office may spend no more than 85% of the above amounts, and incumbents seeking reelection to the State Senate or House may spend no more than 90% of the above amounts. The Act defines "[e]xpenditure" broadly to mean the "payment, disbursement, distribution, advance, deposit, loan or gift of money or anything of value, paid or promised to be paid, for the purpose of influencing an election, advocating a position on a public question, or supporting or opposing one or more candidates."

With certain minor exceptions, expenditures over $50 made on a candidate's behalf by others count against the candidate's expenditure limit if those expenditures are "intentionally facilitated by, solicited by or approved by" the candidate's campaign. These provisions apply so as to count against a campaign's expenditure limit any spending by political parties or committees that is coordinated with the campaign and benefits the candidate. And any party expenditure that "primarily benefits six or fewer candidates who are associated with the political party" is "presumed" to be coordinated with the campaign and therefore to count against the campaign's expenditure limit.

Act 64 also imposes strict contribution limits. The amount any single individual can contribute to the campaign of a candidate for state office during a "two-year general election cycle" is limited as follows: governor, lieutenant governor, and other statewide offices, $400; state senator, $300; and state representative, $200. Unlike its expenditure limits, Act 64's contribution limits are not indexed for inflation.

A political committee is subject to these same limits. So is a political party, defined broadly to include "any subsidiary, branch or local unit" of a party, as well as any "national or regional affiliates" of a party (taken separately or together). Thus, for example, the statute treats the local, state, and national affiliates of the Democratic Party as if they were a single entity and limits their total contribution to a single candidate's campaign for governor (during the primary and the general election together) to $400.

* * *

II

We turn first to the Act's expenditure limits. Do those limits violate the First Amendment's free speech guarantees?

* * *

B

1

The respondents recognize that, in respect to expenditure limits, *Buckley* appears to be a controlling—and unfavorable—precedent. They seek to overcome that precedent in two ways. First, they ask us in effect to overrule *Buckley*. Post-*Buckley* experience, they believe, has shown that contribution limits (and disclosure requirements) alone cannot effectively deter corruption or its appearance; hence experience has undermined an assumption underlying that case. . . .

Second, in the alternative, they ask us to limit the scope of *Buckley* significantly by distinguishing *Buckley* from the present case. They advance as a ground for distinction a justification for expenditure limitations that, they say, *Buckley* did not consider, namely that such limits help to protect candidates from spending too much time raising money rather than devoting that time to campaigning among ordinary voters. We find neither argument persuasive.

* * *

3

[. . .] The sole basis on which the respondents seek to distinguish *Buckley* concerns a further supporting justification. They argue that expenditure limits are necessary in order to reduce the amount of time candidates must spend raising money. Increased campaign costs, together with the fear of a better-funded opponent, mean that, without expenditure limits, a candidate must spend too much time raising money instead of meeting the voters and engaging in public debate. *Buckley,* the respondents add, did not fully consider this justification. Had it done so, they say, the Court would have upheld, not struck down, FECA's expenditure limits.

In our view, it is highly unlikely that fuller consideration of this time protection rationale would have changed *Buckley's* result. The *Buckley* Court was aware of the connection between expenditure limits and a reduction in fundraising time. In a section of the opinion dealing with FECA's public financing provisions, it wrote that Congress was trying to "free candidates from the rigors of fundraising." 424 U.S. at 91. . . .

Under these circumstances, the respondents' argument amounts to no more than an invitation so to limit *Buckley's* holding as effectively to overrule it. For the reasons set forth above, we decline that invitation as well. And, given *Buckley's* continued authority, we must conclude that Act 64's expenditure limits violate the First Amendment.

III

We turn now to a more complex question, namely the constitutionality of Act 64's contribution limits. The parties, while accepting *Buckley's* approach, dispute whether, despite *Buckley's* general approval of statutes that limit campaign contributions, Act 64's contribution limits are so severe that in the circumstances its particular limits violate the First Amendment.

* * *

B

Following *Buckley,* we must determine whether Act 64's contribution limits prevent candidates from "amassing the resources necessary for effective [campaign] advocacy," 424 U.S. at 21; whether they magnify the advantages of incumbency to the point where they put challengers to a significant disadvantage; in a word, whether they are too low and too strict to survive First Amendment scrutiny. In answering these questions, we recognize, as *Buckley* stated, that we have "no scalpel to probe" each possible contribution level. *Id.* at 30. We cannot determine with any degree of exactitude the precise restriction necessary to carry out the statute's legitimate objectives. In practice, the legislature is better equipped to make such empirical judgments, as legislators have "particular expertise" in matters related to the costs and nature of running for office. . . . Thus ordinarily we have deferred to the legislature's determination of such matters.

Nonetheless, as *Buckley* acknowledged, we must recognize the existence of some lower bound. At some point the constitutional risks to the democratic electoral process become too great. . . . Yet that rationale does not simply mean "the lower the limit, the better." That is because contribution limits that are too low can also harm the electoral process by preventing challengers from mounting effective campaigns against incumbent officeholders, thereby reducing democratic accountability. Were we to ignore that fact, a statute that seeks to regulate campaign contributions could itself prove an obstacle to the very electoral fairness it seeks to promote. Thus, we see no alternative to the exercise of independent judicial judgment as a statute reaches those outer limits. . . .

[C]onsidered as a whole, Vermont's contribution limits are the lowest in the Nation. Act 64 limits contributions to candidates for statewide office (including governor) to $200 per candidate per election. We have found no State that imposes a lower per election limit. Indeed, we have found only seven States that impose limits on contributions to candidates for statewide office at or below $500 per election, more than twice Act 64's limit....

In sum, Act 64's contribution limits are substantially lower than both the limits we have previously upheld and comparable limits in other States. These are danger signs that Act 64's contribution limits may fall outside tolerable First Amendment limits. We consequently must examine the record independently and carefully to determine whether Act 64's contribution limits are "closely drawn" to match the State's interests.

C

Our examination of the record convinces us that, from a constitutional perspective, Act 64's contribution limits are too restrictive. We reach this conclusion based not merely on the low dollar amounts of the limits themselves, but also on the statute's effect on political parties and on volunteer activity in Vermont elections. *Taken together,* Act 64's substantial restrictions on the ability of candidates to raise the funds necessary to run a competitive election, on the ability of political parties to help their candidates get elected, and on the ability of individual citizens to volunteer their time to campaigns show that the Act is not closely drawn to meet its objectives. In particular, five factors together lead us to this decision.

First, the record suggests, though it does not conclusively prove, that Act 64's contribution limits will significantly restrict the amount of funding available for challengers to run competitive campaigns....

Second, Act 64's insistence that political parties abide by *exactly* the same low contribution limits that apply to other contributors threatens harm to a particularly important political right, the right to associate in a political party. *See, e.g., California Democratic Party v. Jones,* 530 U.S. 567, 574 (2000) (describing constitutional importance of associating in political parties to elect candidates); *Timmons v. Twin Cities Area New Party,* 520 U.S. 351, 357 (1997) (same); *Colorado I,* 518 U.S., at 616 (same); *Norman v. Reed,* 502 U.S. 279, 288 (1992) (same). Cf. *Buckley, supra,* at 20–22 (contribution limits constitute "only a marginal restriction" on First Amendment rights *because* contributor remains free to associate politically, *e.g.,* in a political party, and "assist personally" in the party's "efforts on behalf of candidates").

[...] We consequently agree with the District Court that the Act's contribution limits "would reduce the voice of political parties" in Vermont to a "whisper." And we count the special party-related harms that Act 64 threatens as a further factor weighing against the constitutional validity of the contribution limits.

Third, the Act's treatment of volunteer services aggravates the problem. Like its federal statutory counterpart, the Act excludes from its definition of "contribution" all "services provided without compensation by individuals volunteering their time on behalf of a candidate."

Fourth, unlike the contribution limits we upheld in *Shrink,* Act 64's contribution limits are not adjusted for inflation. . . .

Fifth, we have found nowhere in the record any special justification that might warrant a contribution limit so low or so restrictive as to bring about the serious associational and expressive problems that we have described. Rather, the basic justifications the State has advanced in support of such limits are those present in *Buckley.* The record contains no indication that, for example, corruption (or its appearance) in Vermont is significantly more serious a matter than elsewhere. Indeed, other things being equal, one might reasonably believe that a contribution of say, $250 (or $450) to a candidate's campaign was less likely to prove a corruptive force than the far larger contributions at issue in the other campaign finance cases we have considered.

These five sets of considerations, taken together, lead us to conclude that Act 64's contribution limits are not narrowly tailored. Rather, the Act burdens First Amendment interests by threatening to inhibit effective advocacy by those who seek election, particularly challengers; its contribution limits mute the voice of political parties; they hamper participation in campaigns through volunteer activities; and they are not indexed for inflation. Vermont does not point to a legitimate statutory objective that might justify these special burdens. We understand that many, though not all, campaign finance regulations impose certain of these burdens to some degree. We also understand the legitimate need for constitutional leeway in respect to legislative line-drawing. But our discussion indicates why we conclude that Act 64 in this respect nonetheless goes too far. It disproportionately burdens numerous First Amendment interests, and consequently, in our view, violates the First Amendment. . . .

IV

We conclude that Act 64's expenditure limits violate the First Amendment as interpreted in *Buckley v. Valeo.* We also conclude that the specific details of Act 64's contribution limits require us to hold that those limits violate the First Amendment, for they burden First Amendment interests in a manner that is disproportionate to the public purposes they were enacted to advance. Given our holding, we need not, and do not, examine the constitutionality of the statute's presumption that certain party expenditures are coordinated with a candidate. Accordingly, the judgment of the Court of Appeals is reversed, and the cases are remanded for further proceedings.

It is so ordered.

■ JUSTICE ALITO, concurring in part and concurring in the judgment.

I concur in the judgment and join in Justice BREYER's opinion except for Parts II–B–1 and II–B–2. Contrary to the suggestion of those sections, respondents' primary defense of Vermont's expenditure limits is that those limits are consistent with *Buckley v. Valeo. . . .*

Whether or not a case can be made for reexamining *Buckley* in whole or in part, what matters is that respondents do not do so here, and so I think it unnecessary to reach the issue.

■ JUSTICE KENNEDY, concurring in the judgment.

The Court decides the constitutionality of the limitations Vermont places on campaign expenditures and contributions. I agree that both limitations violate the First Amendment. . . .

The universe of campaign finance regulation is one this Court has in part created and in part permitted by its course of decisions. That new order may cause more problems than it solves. On a routine, operational level the present system requires us to explain why $200 is too restrictive a limit while $1,500 is not. Our own experience gives us little basis to make these judgments, and certainly no traditional or well-established body of law exists to offer guidance. On a broader, systemic level political parties have been denied basic First Amendment rights. . . . Entering to fill the void have been new entities such as political action committees, which are as much the creatures of law as of traditional forces of speech and association. Those entities can manipulate the system and attract their own elite power brokers, who operate in ways obscure to the ordinary citizen.

Viewed within the legal universe we have ratified and helped create, the result the plurality reaches is correct; given my own skepticism regarding that system and its operation, however, it seems to me appropriate to concur only in the judgment.

■ JUSTICE THOMAS, with whom JUSTICE SCALIA joins, concurring in the judgment.

* * *

II

* * *

The plurality recognizes that the burdens which lead it to invalidate Act 64's contribution limits are present under "many, though not all, campaign finance regulations." As a result, the plurality does not purport to offer any single touchstone for evaluating the constitutionality of such laws. Indeed, its discussion offers nothing resembling a rule at all. From all appearances, the plurality simply looked at these limits and said, in its "independent judicial judgment," that they are too low. The atmospherics—whether they vary with inflation, whether they are as high as those in other States or those in *Shrink* and *Buckley,* whether they apply to volunteer activities and parties—no doubt help contribute to the plurality's sentiment. But a feeling does not amount to a workable rule of law.

* * *

For these reasons, I concur only in the judgment.

■ JUSTICE STEVENS, dissenting.

Justice Breyer and Justice Souter debate whether the *per curiam* decision in *Buckley v. Valeo* forecloses any constitutional limitations on candidate expenditures. This is plainly an issue on which reasonable minds can disagree. The *Buckley* Court never explicitly addressed whether the pernicious effects of endless fundraising can serve as a compelling state interest that justifies expenditure limits, yet its silence, in light of the record before it, suggests that it implicitly treated this proposed interest insufficient. Assuming this to be true, however, I am convinced that *Buckley's* holding on expenditure limits is wrong, and that the time has come to overrule it. . . .

Buckley's conclusion to the contrary relied on the following oft-quoted metaphor:

> "Being free to engage in unlimited political expression subject to a ceiling on expenditures is like being free to drive an automobile as far and as often as one desires on a single tank of gasoline." 424 U.S. at 19, n. 18.

But, of course, while a car cannot run without fuel, a candidate can speak without spending money. And while a car can only travel so many miles per gallon, there is no limit on the number of speeches or interviews a candidate may give on a limited budget. Moreover, provided that this budget is above a certain threshold, a candidate can exercise due care to ensure that her message reaches all voters. Just as a driver need not use a Hummer to reach her destination, so a candidate need not flood the airways with ceaseless sound-bites of trivial information in order to provide voters with reasons to support her.

Indeed, the examples of effective speech in the political arena that did not depend on any significant expenditure by the campaigner are legion. It was the content of William Jennings Bryan's comments on the "Cross of Gold"—and William McKinley's responses delivered from his front porch in Canton, Ohio—rather than any expenditure of money that appealed to their cost-free audiences. Neither Abraham Lincoln nor John F. Kennedy paid for the opportunity to engage in the debates with Stephen Douglas and Richard Nixon that may well have determined the outcomes of Presidential elections. When the seasoned campaigners who were Members of the Congress that endorsed the expenditure limits in the Federal Election Campaign Act Amendments of 1974 concluded that a modest budget would not preclude them from effectively communicating with the electorate, they necessarily rejected the *Buckley* metaphor. . . .

For the foregoing reasons, I agree with Justice Souter that it would be entirely appropriate to allow further proceedings on expenditure limits to go forward in these cases. . . .

■ Justice Souter, with whom Justice Ginsburg joins, and with whom Justice Stevens joins as to Parts II and III, dissenting.

* * *

III

[Justice Souter addresses the four policy considerations raised by the plurality opinion for why the contribution limits should be found unconstitutionally low. The first two concern the requirement that a volunteer's expenses count against the person's contribution limit and the failure of the Vermont law to index its limits for inflation. Justice Souter argues that each is insubstantial.]

Third, subjecting political parties to the same contribution limits as individuals does not condemn the Vermont scheme. What we said in *Federal Election Comm'n v. Colorado Republican Federal Campaign Comm.*, 533 U.S. 431, 454–455 (2001), dealing with regulation of coordinated expenditures, goes here, too. The capacity and desire of parties to make large contributions to competitive candidates with uphill fights are shared by rich individuals, and the risk that large party contributions would be channels to evade individual limits cannot be eliminated. Nor are these reasons to support the party limits undercut by claims that the restrictions render parties impotent, for the parties are not precluded from uncoordinated spending to benefit their candidates. That said, I acknowledge the suggestions in the petitioners' briefs that such restrictions in synergy with other influences weakening party power would justify a wholesale reexamination of the situation of party organization today. But whether such a comprehensive reexamination belongs in courts or only in legislatures is not an issue presented by these cases.

Finally, there is the issue of Act 64's presumption of coordinated expenditures on the part of political parties. The plurality has no occasion to reach it; I do reach it, but find it insignificant. The Republican Party petitioners complain that the related expenditure provision imposes on both the candidate and the party the burden in some circumstances to prove that coordination of expenditure did not take place, thus threatening to charge against a candidate's spending limits some party expenditures that are in fact independent, with an ultimate consequence of chilling speech. On the contrary, however, we can safely take the presumption on the representation to this Court by the Attorney General of Vermont: the law imposes not a burden of persuasion but merely one of production, leaving the presumption easily rebuttable. . . . Requiring the party in possession of the pertinent facts to come forward with them, as easily as by executing an affidavit, does not rise to the level of a constitutionally offensive encumbrance here. . . .

IV

Because I would not pass upon the constitutionality of Vermont's expenditure limits prior to further enquiry into their fit with the problem of fundraising demands on candidates, and because I do not see the contribution limits as depressed to the level of political inaudibility, I respectfully dissent.

NOTES AND QUESTIONS

1. The addition of two new members of the Court has evidently done nothing to shore up the fragile status of the controlling rationale of *Buckley*. Only two Justices (Breyer and Roberts) are willing to endorse the *Buckley* rationale as such. Two Justices (Alito and Kennedy) endorse only the result in *Randall* but find that the question of overruling *Buckley* was not squarely presented. Three Justices (Scalia, Stevens, and Thomas) directly reject *Buckley,* albeit for different reasons. And, two Justices (Souter and Ginsburg) would read *Buckley* to permit expenditure limitations as well as contribution limitations. Less than two years after *McConnell,* the Court has seemingly abandoned its deferential stance toward legislative judgments in the campaign finance arena and signaled a renewed willingness to revisit the fundamentals of this area of law.

2. The dominant theme in the post-*Buckley* cases has been the tie between different contributions limitations and the question of corruption or potential corruption of public officials. As evident in *McConnell,* the Court's focus has largely been on how inferential the proof of corruption had to be in order to justify an expanding orbit of limitations on contributions. The Vermont contributions limitations were struck down in *Sorrell,* however, on the grounds that the amounts were too low, something which could not possibly implicate the corruption rationale that has animated the post-*Buckley* cases. Thus, the dispute between Justice Breyer's plurality opinion and Justice Souter's dissent turns on the weight that should be accorded to additional factors ranging from the indexing of limitations for inflation to the specific impact that limitations might have on political parties.

Significantly, none of these additional factors rests on either the rights claims of would-be contributors or on how compelling is the state interest in eliminating corruption or the perception of corruption—the standard exchange following *Buckley*. Rather, Justice Breyer's plurality opinion turns on questions of the structural integrity of the political process along such dimensions as the accountability of elected officials to the voters, the entrenchment of incumbents, and the overall competitiveness of elections. While the Court is clearly divided on how to approach campaign finance, *Randall* could signify a substantial erosion of the standard First Amendment analysis of campaign funding issues as a battle between the rights claims of potential donors and candidates on the one hand, and the claims of compelling interests by state regulators on the other. In particular, Justice Breyer's concern for the proper functioning of political parties emerges as a core concern in *Sorrell*. For an analysis of this shift in the

Court's approach to campaign finance regulation, see Pamela S. Karlan, *Dead Ends and New Beginnings in the Law of Democracy,* 68 Ohio St. L. J. ___ (2007).

3. Apart from its consistency with *Buckley,* it is possible to ask whether the anticorruption rationale can do the work assigned to it. Once corruption includes not simply the surreptitious agreement between two parties but the perception or appearance of such agreement in the eyes of outsiders, does the concept of corruption still encapsulate the perceived wrong?

Indeed, one need look no further than our neighbor to the north to see democratic elections conducted under such a regime. In *Libman v. Quebec (Attorney General),* 3 S.C.R. 569 (1997), the Supreme Court of Canada set forth three constitutional principles that it would apply in the campaign finance area:

> [1]   If the principle of fairness in the political sphere is to be preserved, it cannot be presumed that all persons have the same financial resources to communicate with the electorate. To ensure a right of equal participation in democratic government, laws limiting spending are needed to preserve the equality of democratic rights and ensure that one person's exercise of the freedom to spend does not hinder the communication opportunities of others. Owing to the competitive nature of elections, such spending limits are necessary to prevent the most affluent from monopolizing election discourse and consequently depriving their opponents of a reasonable opportunity to speak and be heard [equal dissemination of points of view].

> [2]   Spending limits are also necessary to guarantee the right of electors to be adequately informed of all the political positions advanced by the candidates and by the various political parties [free and informed vote]. . . .

> [3]   For spending limits to be fully effective, they must apply to all possible election expenses, including those of independent individuals and groups [applicability to all; effectiveness of spending limits generally]. . . .

In response, Parliament promulgated the Canada Elections Act of 2000, which set out rather restrictive spending limits, including on independent actors. Under the Act, no citizen could spend more than $3,000 in any election district or $150,000 nationally to promote or oppose a candidate for office. Even more stringent was a provision that extended the spending limit to any publicity concerning any issue with which a candidate might be "particularly associated." This is a far more intrusive restriction on speech than anything found in U.S. election laws.

In *Attorney General of Canada v. Harper,* 2004 SCC 33, the Canadian Supreme Court upheld the Act, first by relying on the logic of *Libman,* then by pursuing the role of equality as such:

> The Court's conception of electoral fairness as reflected in the foregoing principles [from *Libman*] is consistent with the egalitarian model of

elections adopted by Parliament as an essential component of our democratic society. This model is premised on the notion that individuals should have an equal opportunity to participate in the electoral process. Under this model, wealth is the main obstacle to equal participation; *see* C. Feasby, "Libman v. Quebec (A.G.) and the Administration of the Process of Democracy under the Charter: The Emerging Egalitarian Model" (1999), 44 McGill L.J. 5. Thus, the egalitarian model promotes an electoral process that requires the wealthy to be prevented from controlling the electoral process to the detriment of others with less economic power. The state can equalize participation in the electoral process in two ways; *see* O. M. Fiss, The Irony of Free Speech (1996), at p. 4. First, the State can provide a voice to those who might otherwise not be heard. The Act does so by reimbursing candidates and political parties and by providing broadcast time to political parties. Second, the State can restrict the voices which dominate the political discourse so that others may be heard as well. In Canada, electoral regulation has focused on the latter by regulating electoral spending through comprehensive election finance provisions. These provisions seek to create a level playing field for those who wish to engage in the electoral discourse. This, in turn, enables voters to be better informed; no one voice is overwhelmed by another. In contrast, the libertarian model of elections favours an electoral process subject to as few restrictions as possible.

The current third party election advertising regime is Parliament's response to this Court's decision in *Libman, supra*. The regime is clearly structured on the egalitarian model of elections. The overarching objective of the regime is to promote electoral fairness by creating equality in the political discourse. The regime promotes the equal dissemination of points of view by limiting the election advertising of third parties who, as this Court has recognized, are important and influential participants in the electoral process. The advancement of equality and fairness in elections ultimately encourages public confidence in the electoral system. Thus, broadly speaking, the third party election advertising regime is consistent with an egalitarian conception of elections and the principles endorsed by this Court in *Libman*.

H.   FRONTIERS OF REGULATION

1.   ISSUE ADVOCACY AND CORPORATIONS

Federal Election Comm'n v. Massachusetts Citizens for Life, Inc.

479 U.S. 238 (1986).

■ JUSTICE BRENNAN announced the judgment of the Court and delivered the opinion of the Court with respect to Parts I, II, III–B, and III–C, and an opinion with respect to Part III–A, in which JUSTICE MARSHALL, JUSTICE POWELL, and JUSTICE SCALIA join.

The questions for decision here arise under § 316 of the Federal Election Campaign Act (FECA or Act), 90 Stat. 490, as renumbered and amended, 2 U.S.C. § 441b. The first question is whether appellee Massachusetts Citizens for Life, Inc. (MCFL), a nonprofit, nonstock corporation, by financing certain activity with its treasury funds, has violated the restriction on independent spending contained in § 441b. That section prohibits corporations from using treasury funds to make an expenditure "in connection with" any federal election, and requires that any expenditure for such purpose be financed by voluntary contributions to a separate segregated fund. If appellee has violated § 441b, the next question is whether application of that section to MCFL's conduct is constitutional. We hold that the appellee's use of its treasury funds is prohibited by § 441b, but that § 441b is unconstitutional as applied to the activity of which the Federal Election Commission (FEC or Commission) complains.

I

A

MCFL was incorporated in January 1973 as a nonprofit, nonstock corporation under Massachusetts law. Its corporate purpose as stated in its articles of incorporation is:

> "To foster respect for human life and to defend the right to life of all human beings, born and unborn, through educational, political and other forms of activities and in addition to engage in any other lawful act or activity for which corporations may be organized...."

MCFL does not accept contributions from business corporations or unions. Its resources come from voluntary donations from "members," and from various fund-raising activities such as garage sales, bake sales, dances, raffles, and picnics. The corporation considers its "members" those persons who have either contributed to the organization in the past or indicated support for its activities.

* * *

In September 1978, MCFL prepared and distributed a "Special Edition" prior to the September 1978 primary elections. While the May 1978 newsletter had been mailed to 2,109 people and the October 1978 newsletter to 3,119 people, more than 100,000 copies of the "Special Edition" were printed for distribution. The front page of the publication was headlined "EVERYTHING YOU NEED TO KNOW TO VOTE PRO–LIFE," and readers were admonished that "[n]o pro-life candidate can win in November without your vote in September." "VOTE PRO–LIFE" was printed in large bold-faced letters on the back page, and a coupon was provided to be clipped and taken to the polls to remind voters of the name of the "pro-life" candidates. Next to the exhortation to vote "pro-life" was a disclaimer:" This special election edition does not represent an endorsement of any particular candidate."

To aid the reader in selecting candidates, the flyer listed the candidates for each state and federal office in every voting district in Massachusetts, and identified each one as either supporting or opposing what MCFL regarded as the correct position on three issues. A "y" indicated that a candidate supported the MCFL view on a particular issue and an "n" indicated that the candidate opposed it. An asterisk was placed next to the names of those incumbents who had made a "special contribution to the unborn in maintaining a 100% pro-life voting record in the state house by actively supporting MCFL legislation." While some 400 candidates were running for office in the primary, the "Special Edition" featured the photographs of only 13. These 13 had received a triple "y" rating, or were identified either as having a 100% favorable voting record or as having stated a position consistent with that of MCFL. No candidate whose photograph was featured had received even one "n" rating.

* * *

II

* * *

We ... hold that an expenditure must constitute "express advocacy" in order to be subject to the prohibition of § 441b. We also hold, however, that the publication of the "Special Edition" constitutes "express advocacy."

Buckley adopted the "express advocacy" requirement to distinguish discussion of issues and candidates from more pointed exhortations to vote for particular persons. We therefore concluded in that case that a finding of "express advocacy" depended upon the use of language such as "vote for," "elect," "support," etc., *Buckley,* 424 U.S. at 44, n. 52. Just such an exhortation appears in the "Special Edition." The publication not only urges voters to vote for "pro-life" candidates, but also identifies and provides photographs of specific candidates fitting that description. The Edition cannot be regarded as a mere discussion of public issues that by their nature raise the names of certain politicians. Rather, it provides in effect an explicit directive: vote for these (named) candidates. The fact that this message is marginally less direct than "Vote for Smith" does not change its essential nature. The Edition goes beyond issue discussion to express electoral advocacy. The disclaimer of endorsement cannot negate this fact. The "Special Edition" thus falls squarely within § 441b, for it represents express advocacy of the election of particular candidates distributed to members of the general public.

* * *

III

A

Independent expenditures constitute expression " 'at the core of our electoral process and of the First Amendment freedoms.' " *Buckley,* 424 U.S., at 39 (quoting *Williams v. Rhodes,* 393 U.S. 23, 32 (1968)). See also *FEC v. National Conservative Political Action Committee,* 470 U.S. 480 (1985) (*NCPAC*) (independent expenditures "produce speech at the core of the First Amendment"). We must therefore determine whether the prohibition of § 441b burdens political speech, and, if so, whether such a burden is justified by a compelling state interest. *Buckley, supra,* 424 U.S., at 44–45.

The FEC minimizes the impact of the legislation upon MCFL's First Amendment rights by emphasizing that the corporation remains free to establish a separate segregated fund, composed of contributions earmarked for that purpose by the donors, that may be used for unlimited campaign spending. However, the corporation is *not* free to use its general funds for campaign advocacy purposes. While that is not an absolute restriction on speech, it is a substantial one. Moreover, even to speak through a segregated fund, MCFL must make very significant efforts. . . .

Thus, while § 441b does not remove all opportunities for independent spending by organizations such as MCFL, the avenue it leaves open is more burdensome than the one it forecloses. The fact that the statute's practical effect may be to discourage protected speech is sufficient to characterize § 441b as an infringement on First Amendment activities.

* * *

B

When a statutory provision burdens First Amendment rights, it must be justified by a compelling state interest. The FEC first insists that justification for § 441b' s expenditure restriction is provided by this Court's acknowledgment that "the special characteristics of the corporate structure require particularly careful regulation." *National Right to Work Committee,* 459 U.S., at 209–210. The Commission thus relies on the long history of regulation of corporate political activity as support for the application of § 441b to MCFL. Evaluation of the Commission's argument requires close examination of the underlying rationale for this longstanding regulation.

We have described that rationale in recent opinions as the need to restrict "the influence of political war chests funneled through the corporate form," *NCPAC,* 470 U.S., at 501; to "eliminate the effect of aggregated wealth on federal elections," *Pipefitters,* 407 U.S., at 416; to curb the political influence of "those who exercise control over large aggregations of capital," *Automobile Workers,* 352 U.S., at 585; and to regulate the "substantial aggregations of wealth amassed by the special advantages which go with the corporate form of organization," *National Right to Work Committee,* 459 U.S., at 207.

This concern over the corrosive influence of concentrated corporate wealth reflects the conviction that it is important to protect the integrity of the marketplace of political ideas.

* * *

Direct corporate spending on political activity raises the prospect that resources amassed in the economic marketplace may be used to provide an unfair advantage in the political marketplace. Political "free trade" does not necessarily require that all who participate in the political marketplace do so with exactly equal resources. Relative availability of funds is after all a rough barometer of public support. The resources in the treasury of a business corporation, however, are not an indication of popular support for the corporation's political ideas. They reflect instead the economically motivated decisions of investors and customers. The availability of these resources may make a corporation a formidable political presence, even though the power of the corporation may be no reflection of the power of its ideas.

By requiring that corporate independent expenditures be financed through a political committee expressly established to engage in campaign spending, § 441b seeks to prevent this threat to the political marketplace. The resources available to *this* fund, as opposed to the corporate treasury, in fact reflect popular support for the political positions of the committee.... The expenditure restrictions of § 441b are thus meant to ensure that competition among actors in the political arena is truly competition among ideas.

Regulation of corporate political activity thus has reflected concern not about use of the corporate form *per se,* but about the potential for unfair deployment of wealth for political purposes.... Groups such as MCFL, however, do not pose that danger of corruption. MCFL was formed to disseminate political ideas, not to amass capital. The resources it has available are not a function of its success in the economic marketplace, but its popularity in the political marketplace. While MCFL may derive some advantages from its corporate form, those are advantages that redound to its benefit as a political organization, not as a profit-making enterprise. In short, MCFL is not the type of "traditional corporatio[n] organized for economic gain," *NCPAC, supra,* 470 U.S., at 500, that has been the focus of regulation of corporate political activity.

* * *

The Commission next argues in support of § 441b that it prevents an organization from using an individual's money for purposes that the individual may not support. We acknowledged the legitimacy of this concern as to the dissenting stockholder and union member in *National Right to Work Committee,* 459 U.S., at 208, and in *Pipefitters,* 407 U.S., at 414–415. But such persons, as noted, contribute investment funds or union dues for economic gain, and do not necessarily authorize the use of their money for political ends. Furthermore, because such individuals depend on the organization for income or for a job, it is not enough to tell them that any unhappiness with the use of their money can be redressed simply by leaving the corporation or the union. It was thus wholly reasonable for Congress to require the establishment of a separate political fund to which persons can make voluntary contributions.

This rationale for regulation is not compelling with respect to independent expenditures by appellee. Individuals who contribute to appellee are fully aware of its political purposes, and in fact contribute precisely because they support those purposes. It is true that a contributor may not be aware of the exact use to which his or her money ultimately may be put, or the specific candidate that it may be used to support. However, individuals contribute to a political organization in part because they regard such a contribution as a more effective means of advocacy than spending the money under their own personal direction. Any contribution therefore necessarily involves at least some degree of delegation of authority to use such funds in a manner that best serves the shared political purposes of the organization and contributor. In addition, an individual desiring more direct control over the use of his or her money can simply earmark the contribution for a specific purpose, an option whose availability does not depend on the applicability of § 441b. Cf. § 434(c)(2)(C) (entities other than political committees must disclose names of those persons making earmarked contributions over $200). Finally, a contributor dissatisfied with how funds are used can simply stop contributing.

* * *

Finally, the FEC maintains that the inapplicability of § 441b to MCFL would open the door to massive undisclosed political spending by similar entities, and to their use as conduits for undisclosed spending by business corporations and unions. We see no such danger. Even if § 441b is inapplicable, an independent expenditure of as little as $250 by MCFL will trigger the disclosure provisions of § 434(c). As a result, MCFL will be required to identify all contributors who annually provide in the aggregate $200 in funds intended to influence elections, will have to specify all recipients of independent spending amounting to more than $200, and will be bound to identify all persons making contributions over $200 who request that the money be used for independent expenditures. These reporting obligations provide precisely the information necessary to monitor MCFL's independent spending activity and its receipt of contributions. The state interest in disclosure therefore can be met in a manner less restrictive than imposing the full panoply of regulations that accompany status as a political committee under the Act.

* * *

C

Our conclusion is that § 441b's restriction of independent spending is unconstitutional as applied to MCFL, for it infringes protected speech without a compelling justification for such infringement. We acknowledge the legitimacy of Congress' concern that organizations that amass great wealth in the economic marketplace not gain unfair advantage in the political marketplace.

Regardless of whether that concern is adequate to support application of § 441b to commercial enterprises, a question not before us, that justification does not extend uniformly to all corporations. Some corporations have features more akin to voluntary political associations than business firms, and therefore should not have to bear burdens on independent spending solely because of their incorporated status.

In particular, MCFL has three features essential to our holding that it may not constitutionally be bound by § 441b's restriction on independent spending. *First,* it was formed for the express purpose of promoting political ideas, and cannot engage in business activities. If political fund-raising events are expressly denominated as requests for contributions that will be used for political purposes, including direct expenditures, these events cannot be considered business activities. This ensures that political resources reflect political support. *Second,* it has no shareholders or other persons affiliated so as to have a claim on its assets or earnings. This ensures that persons connected with the organization will have no economic disincentive for disassociating with it if they disagree with its political activity.... *Third,* MCFL was not established by a business corporation or a labor union, and it is its policy not to accept contributions from such entities. This prevents such corporations from serving as conduits for the type of direct spending that creates a threat to the political marketplace.

* * *

The judgment of the Court of Appeals is *affirmed.*

[Opinions omitted of Justice O'Connor, concurring in part and concurring in the judgment, and of Chief Justice Rehnquist, with whom Justice White, Justice Blackmun, and Justice Stevens joined, concurring in part and dissenting in part, and of Justice White, returning to his dissenting view in *Buckley* and its progeny.]

NOTES AND QUESTIONS

1. On remand from the Supreme Court, a three-judge district court for the District of Columbia once again revisited the distinctions drawn by *MCFL* in *Wisconsin Right To Life v. FEC,* 466 F. Supp. 2d 195 (D.D.C. 2006). In reviewing the as-applied challenge to BCRA's prohibition on electioneering communications, the court held that since WRTL's message was directed to items that were or could be on the legislative agenda, such communication was protected by the First Amendment and could not be shut down during the BCRA regulatory period. In 2007, the Supreme Court affirmed in an important decision. That decision can be found in the last appendix of this casebook.

2. CAMPAIGN FINANCE REFORM AND EXPENDITURES

Perhaps the most striking feature of the post-1974 campaign finance reform efforts has been the dramatic increase in election spending that accompanied the rise of federal regulation. Estimates of total spending on American elections topped $3 billion for the 1996 election cycle. This was an important background development for the Congress that enacted BCRA. As reflected in Table 2, campaigns for federal office, the most regulated area of elections, show an unmistakable rise in spending accompanying the post-reform period.

The failure of FECA reforms to check the escalating spiral of campaign spending has led to renewed calls for state funding of elections. This is already done in countries such as Japan, Germany, France, Spain and Belgium, in which public money is given to political parties in proportion to either their parliamentary representation or their percentage of votes obtained; Canada also reimburses parties and candidates for part of their campaign expenditures.

Because of the *Buckley* restriction on expenditure limitations, the substitution of public funds for private money must be accomplished in the form of a carrot rather than a stick. *Buckley* imposes a constitutional barrier to Congress simply mandating restrictions on expenditures. The alternative would be to induce candidates to forego expenditures beyond a set level as a condition of receiving public funds. This approach requires that there be a realistic offer of public funds at levels sufficiently high to induce candidates to swear off private financing. There are two major obstacles to this. First, there is a real concern that Americans will not accept public responsibility for campaign funding at levels adequate to sustain informed political debate. For example, less than 20 percent of Americans check off the box on their federal tax returns allowing for a three-dollar contribution to federal campaign funding. Second, even apart from the fiscal implications, the levels must be high enough to offer a meaningful alternative to private fundraising. The history of public funding of presidential elections is illustrative of this problem. The original levels of public funding under FECA were set substantially *below* the $30 million spent in the then most recent presidential election by George McGovern in one of the worst landslide *losses* in American history. *See* Justin A. Nelson, Note, *The Supply and Demand of Campaign Finance Reform*, 100 Colum. L. Rev. 524, 539 (2000). This is unlikely to be a level of accomplishment to which many candidates would aspire.

Table 2
Source: Federal Election Commission Congressional
Campaign Spending

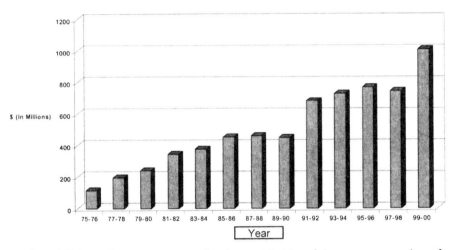

In addition, there are unresolved constitutional issues concerning the extent to which public funding may be used to limit private expenditures. So far, it is widely assumed that public funding may be conditioned on candidate acceptance of expenditure limitations. This is largely based on footnote 65 of *Buckley v. Valeo*, which states without elaboration, "Congress may engage in public financing of election campaigns and may condition acceptance of public funds on an agreement by the candidate to abide by specified expenditure limitations." This footnote does not address whether there are limits on what conditions might be imposed, a concept generally subsumed under notions of "unconstitutional conditions." *See* Richard A. Epstein, *The Supreme Court 1987 Term—Forward: Unconstitutional Conditions, State Power, and the Limits of Consent,* 102 Harv. L. Rev. 5 (1988); Kathleen M. Sullivan, *Unconstitutional Conditions,* 102 Harv. L. Rev. 1415 (1989); Seth F. Kreimer, *Allocational Sanctions: The Problem of Negative Rights in a Positive State,* 132 U. Pa. L. Rev. 1293 (1984). The question of what are the limitations on the receipt of public funds and what are the consequences of choosing not to receive such funds is emerging more prominently in challenges to state campaign finance regulation.

Apart from federal reform efforts, more than 20 states now provide at the state level for either public financing of campaigns or for conditioning campaign expenditures for state and local office. For examples of case law governing these regulatory schemes, see, e.g., the statutes discussed in the following cases: *Shrink Missouri Government v. Maupin,* 71 F.3d 1422, (8th Cir. 1995)(striking down a Missouri statute requiring candidates to sign an affidavit stating whether they will comply with certain spending limits; candidates who chose not to comply with the limits required to submit daily disclosure reports and only allowed to accept contributions from individuals, not PACs, corporations, etc.; the statute also prohibited the carryover of contributions between elections); *Day v. Holahan*, 34 F.3d 1356 (8th Cir. 1994)(striking down a Minnesota statute which provided an increase in a candidates' expenditure limit to the extent an expenditure is made expressly advocating defeat of the candidate or election of an opposing candidate; prohibited independent expenditures by certain corporations and limited contributions to PACs to $100); *Virginia Society for Human Life v. Caldwell*, 906 F. Supp. 1071 (W. D. Va. 1995)(certifying to state court an interpretation of a Virginia statute requiring individuals and PACs who contribute or expend more than $100 to file a statement of organization, maintain records, and file disclosure reports; but striking down a statutory provision requiring persons and PACs spending certain amounts to identify the person or group responsible for any campaign literature).

3.   "Clean Money"

The most far-reaching state initiative is the Maine Clean Elections Act of 1996. Under this Act, candidates are eligible for public funding once they have raised a threshold number of $5 contributions from constituents. If the candidate elects to follow the public funding route, she must turn over all these funds (referred to as "seed money") to the Clean Elections Fund and she is in turn barred from any further private fundraising. In exchange for giving up all collected funds and eschewing all further private fundraising, the Act holds out the promise of full public financing for state elections. The amount of funding is set by averaging the amount spent by candidates in the previous two elections. One of the central goals of the Act was to level the playing field for all candidates, particularly between incumbents and challengers. Another objective was to keep candidates who opted for public funding competitive with privately funded candidates by pegging the level of the state subsidy to the amounts that had previously been spent in prior elections for the same positions. Proponents of the Act argue that it survives *Colorado Republican I* and *NCPAC* by ensuring that participation is voluntary and that receipt of public funding is conditioned on the voluntary limitation on the acceptance of private funding. That argument in turn prompted a challenge arguing that the act offered, in essence, an offer "that could not be refused," which in turn constituted a distinct form of unconstitutional coercion of the right to expend resources for political aims.

Daggett v. Commission on Governmental Ethics and Election Practices

205 F.3d 445 (1st Cir. 2000).

■ Coffin, Senior Circuit Judge

This case involves a challenge to Maine's attempt to reconcile the state's interest in curbing the power of money in politics with the sweeping strictures of the First Amendment. In 1996, Maine voters passed via referendum An Act to Reform Campaign Finance, creating the Maine Clean Election Act, 21-A M.R.S.A. §§ 1121–1128, which introduced a public funding alternative to private fundraising for candidates for elective offices, and lowering the ceiling on campaign contributions, see id. §§ 1015(1) & (2), 1056(1).

Plaintiffs-appellants—legislative candidates, campaign contributors, political action committees (PACs), and the Maine Libertarian Party—challenged both the Act, asserting that the public funding mechanism unconstitutionally coerced candidates to participate, and the contribution limits, arguing that they infringed on the First Amendment rights of candidates as well as donors

* * *

IV.   PUBLIC FINANCING SYSTEM

Throughout this litigation, the Daggett appellants' overarching argument has been that the public funding scheme embodied in the Maine Clean Election Act is unconstitutional because it is impermissibly coercive—that is, it provides so many incentives to participate and so many detriments to foregoing participation that it leaves a candidate with no reasonable alternative but to seek qualification as a publicly funded candidate. We have already addressed the independent constitutionality of contribution limits and matching funds for independent expenditures, and now turn to consider whether the elements of the system, considered as a whole, create a situation where it is so beneficial to join up and so detrimental to eschew public funding that it creates coercion and renders a candidate's choice to pursue public funding essentially involuntary.

[. . .] In *Vote Choice*, this court's primary public funding case, we indicated that the appropriate benchmark of whether candidates' First Amendment rights are burdened by a public funding system is whether the system allows candidates to make a "voluntary" choice about whether to pursue public funding. See *Vote Choice, Inc. v. DiStefano*, 4 F.3d 26, 38 (1st Cir. 1993). ("Voluntariness has proven to be an important factor in judicial ratification of government-sponsored campaign financing schemes.") (citing *Buckley v. Valeo*, 424 U.S. 1, 95 (1976) (per curiam); *Republican Nat'l Comm. v. Federal Election Comm'n*, 487 F. Supp. 280, 285 (S.D.N.Y.), aff'd mem., 445 U.S. 955 (1980)); see also *Rosenstiel v. Rodriguez*, 101 F.3d 1544, 1552–53 (8th Cir. 1996) (upholding public funding system when it did not impose a burden on candidates because it was not coercive). We explained that the government may create incentives for candidates to participate in a public funding system in exchange for their agreement not to rely on private contributions. *See Vote Choice*, 4 F.3d at 38–9.

* * *

A. Matching Funds

* * *

Appellants argue that the matching funds provision is intended to thwart attempts by non-participating candidates to outspend their participating opponents. Appellants contend that non-participating candidates are unlikely to receive as many direct contributions because donors will not wish to give, knowing that their donations could result in additional funding for the participating opponent. They also complain about the fact that matching funds are allocated based on contributions to, as opposed to expenditures by, the non-participating opponent. They suggest that this is illegitimate for several reasons, all reflective of the fact that a non-participating candidate might spend contributions on something other than her campaign or create a reserve and the matching funds allegedly remove flexibility in the use of surplus funds. . . .

We cannot say, however, that the matching funds create an exceptional benefit for the participating candidate. Maine's Act does not provide an unlimited release of the expenditure ceiling—it allocates matching funds for the participating candidate of only two times the initial disbursement. Thus, a non-participating candidate retains the ability to outraise and outspend her participating opponent with abandon after that limit is reached. Further, the non-participating candidate holds the key as to how much and at what time the participant receives matching funds.

Although no two public funding schemes are identical, and thus no two evaluations of such systems are alike, we derive at least general support from other courts' evaluations of trigger provisions. In *Gable v. Patton*, 142 F.3d 940 (6th Cir. 1998), the Sixth Circuit upheld a Kentucky statute that was clearly more beneficial than Maine's-participating candidates received a two-for-one match for private contributions raised, without any limitation. Moreover, the Kentucky statute released a slate of publicly financed gubernatorial candidates from both expenditure limitations and a ban on accepting contributions within twenty-eight days of an election if non-participating opponents raised more than the initial expenditure limit for the participating candidates. Even though the trigger provision provided a "substantial advantage" for publicly funded candidates, the court concluded that it did not rise to the level of coerciveness. See *id.* at 948–49. ("Absent a clearer form of coercion, we decline to find that the incentives inherent in the Trigger provision are different in kind from clearly constitutional incentives.").

* * *

C. Cumulative Effect: Coerciveness

We now step back and look at the Maine public funding/matching funds/contribution limits system as a whole to see if the cumulative effect can be said to be impermissibly coercive. We have previously expressed that a "state need not be completely neutral on the matter of public financing of elections" and that a public funding scheme need not achieve an "exact balance" between benefits and detriments. See *Vote Choice*, 4 F.3d at 39. ("We suspect that very few campaign financing schemes ever achieve perfect equipoise."). In fact, "a voluntary campaign finance scheme must rely on incentives for participation, which, by definition, means structuring the scheme so that participation is usually the rational choice." *Gable*, 142 F.3d at 949. Nevertheless, "there is a point at which regulatory incentives stray beyond the pale, creating disparities so profound that they become impermissibly coercive." *Vote Choice*, 4 F.3d at 38, 39. ("Coerced compliance with any fundraising caps and other eligibility requirements would raise serious, perhaps fatal, objections to a system ...."). The question before us is whether the "tilt" rises to the level of a coercive penalty.

In determining whether the net advantage to a participating candidate is so great as to be impermissibly coercive, we look both to cases where coerciveness has been found and those where the funding and contribution limits system has been upheld. In *Wilkinson*, a district court enjoined the enforcement of contribution limits that were lower, by a ratio of five-to-one, for non-participating candidates than participating candidates because the limits were so low for non-participating candidates that they constituted an unacceptable penalty for foregoing public financing. See *Wilkinson v. Jones*, 876 F. Supp. 916, 929 (W.D. Ky. 1995). In *Shrink Missouri Government PAC v. Maupin*, 71 F.3d 1422 (8th Cir. 1995), the Eighth Circuit held that a ban on contributions from political action committees and other organizations to privately funded candidates was unconstitutional because it prevented privately funded candidates from gaining access to funding sources to which they would be entitled but for the choice to eschew public funding and its expenditure limitations. The statutes at issue in both of these cases, however, created much harsher repercussions for non-participating candidates than the MCEA.

On the other hand, statutes creating an array of benefits even more enticing to candidates than the MCEA have been upheld. In *Vote Choice*, Rhode Island's public funding system was upheld when it disbursed matching funds for private donations up to a given ceiling, it waived the expenditure ceiling to the extent that a non-participating candidate exceeded it, it allowed a participant to raise donations in increments double that allowed for a non-participant, and it granted a participant free air time on community television stations. In *Gable*, the court upheld Kentucky's arrangement, which granted participants a two-to-one match for all private dollars raised up to a certain expenditure limit and released the limit and continued to match funds at the two-to-one ratio after non-participating opponents collected more than the expenditure limit. In *Rosenstiel*, the Eighth Circuit upheld Minnesota's public funding system, which disbursed public subsidies for up to half of the expenditure ceiling, allowed taxpayer refunds of up to $50 for donations to participating candidates but not for donations to non-participating candidates, and completely released participants from expenditure limits after a non-participating opponent raised more than a certain percentage of the limit.

Turning to Maine's system, we first observe that the benefits for a participating candidate are accompanied by significant burdens. The benefits to the candidate include the release from the rigors of fundraising, the assurance that contributors will not have an opportunity to seek special access, and the avoidance of any appearance of corruption. More peripheral benefits include the ability to bypass a small number of additional reporting requirements ... and the opportunity to be free of the reduced contribution limits imposed on private contributions.

In order to gain these benefits, however, the candidate must go through the paces of demonstrating public support by obtaining seed money contributions as well as a substantial number of $5 qualifying contributions. Additional detriments include the limited amount of public funding granted in the initial disbursement; the uncertainty of whether and when additional funds will be received based on an opponent's fundraising; the ultimate cap on matching funds; and the foreclosure of the option of pursuing any private campaign funding or spending any monies above those disbursed by the Commission.

With regard to the contribution limits, we do not believe that they serve as a coercive penalty for non-participating candidates. Until the privately funded candidate reaches the funding level equivalent to the initial disbursement granted to his participating opponent, the contribution limits may serve to the disadvantage of the privately funded candidate. Nevertheless, once the privately funded candidate exceeds that initial disbursement level of his opponent and until he reaches the level at which his opponent's matching funds run out, the contribution limits work to the detriment of both candidates because the less the privately funded candidate raises the less his participating opponent receives in matching funds.

In conclusion, the incentives for a Maine candidate, as the district court characterized them, are "hardly overwhelming." Despite appellants' contention that a participating candidate cedes nothing in exchange for public funding, there are in fact significant encumbrances on participating candidates. The constraints on a publicly funded candidate, we think, would give significant pause to a candidate considering his options. In fact, appellant Representative Elaine Fuller has attested that she will not seek certification and appellant Senator Beverly Daggett has not yet decided. We also take note of the Commission figures that, as of February 8, halfway through the qualifying period, 27.5% of 142 legislative candidates have filed declarations of intent to seek public funding; on the other hand, at least 38, or roughly 26.7%, of the candidates have received contributions or made expenditures in excess of seed money limitations, signaling a desire not to seek certification. Thus, we hold that Maine's public financing scheme provides a roughly proportionate mix of benefits and detriments to candidates seeking public funding, such that it does not burden the First Amendment rights of candidates or contributors.

NOTES AND QUESTIONS

1. Could the Maine Clean Elections Act be applied to federal elections? Would the purposes of the Act be undermined if campaign reliance on soft money continued to escalate as projected in Table 1 of the Chapter? Would an accompanying restriction on soft money survive challenge under *Colorado Republican I* or *II?* As reflected in *Daggett,* thus far courts have upheld this form of "clean money" program. *See Citizens Clean Elections Commission v. Myers,* 1 P.3d 706 (Ariz. 2000), in which the Arizona Supreme Court upheld Arizona's Citizens Clean Elections Act against challenge on state law grounds.

2. The use of public funds has the paradoxical effect of putting more pressure on the need to control expenditures, particularly by political actors nominally independent of parties and candidates. The risk is that public funding could become an additional source of funds that supplements private funding rather than substitute for it. Consider the history of public financing of political conventions as a cautionary tale.

In 1974, as part of FECA, Congress mandated public funding of presidential nominating conventions and presidential elections as part of its post-Watergate reform effort. Congress was persuaded to prohibit private contributions to the parties' nominating conventions in the wake of a scandal in which ITT was believed to have donated $400,000 to the 1972 Republican National Convention in exchange for favorable treatment in an antitrust suit brought by the Department of Justice. Following the enactment of FECA, nominating conventions were treated as federal elections for the purposes of federal regulations. As such, nominating conventions fell under 1974 federal regulations prohibiting corporations and labor organizations from making contributions or expenditures in connection with a general election. 2 U.S.C. § 441b.

Under these regulations, each major party is now entitled to $4 million in public funding, plus a cost-of-living adjustment. Rather than serve as the cap on convention funding, however, public financing has served as the down payment on increasingly lavish affairs. Since 1974, the FEC has approved numerous exceptions that allow the Republican and Democratic Parties to circumvent the ban on private contributions to defray expenses from their nominating conventions, while still accepting full public funding. In a series of advisory opinions, the FEC progressively loosened restrictions on convention funding to "enable commercial vendors and local corporate and labor organizations to engage in various activities in connection with a Presidential nominating convention held in their city." In so doing, the FEC explicitly presumed that business and donors "are motivated by civic and commercial purposes rather than by election-influencing objectives" or policy-influencing objectives once the federal elections are decided. Federal Election Commission, *Presidential Nominating Conventions: Permissible Corporate/Labor Activity,* Record, February 1996, Vol. 22, No.2, 7–8. Federal election regulations now permit private individuals, corporations, and commercial vendors to contribute both to such municipal funds, set up by local government agencies and municipal corporations, and to non-profit funds managed by the convention city's "host committee" organizations.

But public funding was only part of the story. By 1996, the amount of private money filtering to the conventions dwarfed public funding. In 1996, the Chicago and San Diego Host Committees spent a combined $40.9 million on their respective conventions, over and above the $12.4 million in public funding each party received for its convention. Overall, the reports filed by these host committees with the Federal Election Commission reveal that the majority of funding comes from corporations that would otherwise be restricted in showing their largesse. The record further suggests that the presumption of disinterested private giving may not be warranted. For example, through promotional considerations, donated services, cash payments and the like, AT&T donated $2,653,226 to the Republican convention through the San Diego Host Committee and $558,741 to the Democratic convention through the Chicago Host Committee. As explained by J. Michael Brown, AT&T Vice President for Federal Legislation, the reason for the contributions was as follows:

> There's a political positioning that is important to us for our business. We are regulated at both the state and federal level. We participate actively in the government process. This year, in particular, as the communications industry is being restructured, we want to be present and visible and let people know we're a good company.

Congressional Quarterly, Vol. 54, Supp. to No. 31, August 3, 1996, at 31. Is this development predictable in light of the composition of the FEC as appointed representatives of the Democratic and Republican parties? Does the experience with convention financing call into question the claim by Justice White that the federal courts should adopt a deferential attitude toward the political branches in the regulation of campaign financing?

3. Consider a completely different form of regulation, one geared not so much to the contribution levels as such, but to the capacity to curry favor with candidates and officeholders. The most novel proposal is one championed by Professor Ian Ayres, most notably in his collaboration with Professor Bruce Ackerman. The heart of the Ackerman/Ayres proposal is that campaign finance regulations should keep the identity of donors secret from both the public and the candidates. Bruce Ackerman & Ian Ayres, *The Secret Refund Booth*, 73 U. Chi. L. Rev. 1107 (2006). This is exactly the opposite of strategies that focus on disclosure to inform the public of the source of campaign funds. Professors Ackerman and Ayres argue that mandatory disclosure does not provide a great benefit to the public because the public rarely polices the contributions and does not have access to other important information (for example, why the contribution was made or the amount of access that any given donor has to the candidate) that is held only by the candidate and the donor. As an alternative, Professors Ackerman and Ayres suggest that both politicians and the general public should operate under a "veil of ignorance" in which individuals could donate money to a candidate through a blind trust operated by the FEC, and then candidates would be informed of the aggregate amount of money in the account and be able to write checks on this sum for their campaigns. Professors Ackerman and Ayres hypothesize that this system would reduce incentives for special-interest donors to make contributions in exchange for political influence, leaving only public-spirited donors who wish to support a candidate without any expectation of receiving a special benefit.

Related to this aspect of the system, Professors Ackerman and Ayres propose granting fifty "Patriot dollars" to all registered voters, which could be applied to a political campaign during presidential election years. This initiative would allow all registered voters to contribute to campaigns, which Professors Ackerman and Ayres suggest is part of public citizenship. Bruce Ackerman & Ian Ayres, Voting with Dollars: A New Paradigm for Campaign Finance 14 (2002); *see also* Edward B. Foley, *Equal-Dollars–Per–Voter: A Constitutional Principle of Campaign Finance*, 94 Colum. L. Rev. 1240 (1994) (arguing that, as a constitutional principle, the electoral process should be wealth-neutral in order to be fair to rich and poor alike). So far, only Chile has experimented with an anonymous donation system, and Professors Ackerman and Ayres note that their proposal has been received coolly by leading public interest organizations and politicians in the United States. For an exchange over the Ackerman/Ayres proposal, including critical assessments by Professors Pamela Karlan and David Strauss, see *The Brennan Center Jorde Symposium on Constitutional Law*, 91 Cal. L. Rev. 641 (2003).

4.   527s AND PERIPHERAL POLITICAL ACTORS

Justices Stevens and O'Connor conclude their joint opinion in *McConnell* with the now familiar refrain about the hydraulic pressures that threaten circumvention of even the best intentioned campaign finance reforms: "Money, like water, will always find an outlet." The opinion goes on to identify the latest organizational vehicle for circumvention, the so-called "527 organizations," named after a provision of the Internal Revenue Code regulating political organizations:

> Experience under the current law demonstrates that Congress' concerns about circumvention are not merely hypothetical. Even without the added incentives created by Title I, national, state, and local parties already solicit unregulated soft-money donations to tax-exempt organizations for the purpose of supporting federal electioneering activity. *See, e.g.,* 3 1998 Senate Report 4013 ("In addition to direct contributions from the RNC to nonprofit groups, the senior leadership of the RNC helped to raise funds for many of the coalition's nonprofit

organizations''); *id.,* at 5983 (minority views) (''Tax-exempt 'issue advocacy' groups and other conduits were systematically used to circumvent federal campaign finance laws''); 251 F. Supp. 2d, at 517 (Kollar–Kotelly, J.); *id.,* at 848 (Leon, J.). Parties and candidates have also begun to take advantage of so-called ''politician 527s,'' which are little more than soft-money fronts for the promotion of particular federal officeholders and their interests. *See id.,* at 519 (Kollar–Kotelly, J.) ('' 'Virtually every member of Congress in a formal leadership position has his or her own 527 group.... In all, Public Citizen found 63 current members of Congress who have their own 527s' '' (quoting Public Citizen Congress Watch, Congressional Leaders' Soft Money Accounts Show Need for Campaign Finance Reform Bills, Feb. 26, 2002, p. 6)); 251 F.Supp. 2d, at 849–850 (Leon, J.). These 527s have been quite successful at raising substantial sums of soft money from corporate interests, as well as from the national parties themselves. *See id.,* at 519–520 (Kollar–Kotelly, J.) (finding that 27 industries had each donated over $100,000 in a single year to the top 25 politician 527 groups and that the DNC was the single largest contributor to politician 527 groups (citing Public Citizen Congress Watch, *supra,* at 10–11)); 251 F. Supp. 2d, at 850 (Leon, J.) (same). Given BCRA's tighter restrictions on the raising and spending of soft money, the incentives for parties to exploit such organizations will only increase.

In the 2004 election cycle, these new ''527 organizations'' emerged as the main source of soft-money infusions into the presidential campaign. As of July 5th, 2004—that is, before the party conventions—527 organizations had received over $180 million and had spent over $130 million of that money on federal elections, primarily on advertising and contributions to candidates, and also on activities such as voter registration drives, public events, and creation of campaign materials. (These data are collected on the website of the Center for Responsive Politics, http://www.opensecrets.org/527s/index.asp).

This expenditure was in the same range as that of the two leading candidates themselves, who at that time had spent $150 million (George W. Bush) and $120 million (John Kerry), respectively. In the months that followed, the activity of the 527s took on a life of its own. Most famous were the ads produced by the Swift Boat Veterans attacking the war record of John Kerry, and the heavy infusion of money from George Soros and groups such as MoveOn.org and the America Coming Together fund that basically carried the Democratic message during a period in which the Kerry campaign was short of funds. By the time the election was over, 527 organizations had spent over $400 million. More specifically, 527s accounted for about 10 percent of total campaign spending in 2004 and about 20 percent of the spending on the presidential election. About three-quarters of spending by 527s was by Democratic-leaning groups, with the Republicans relying more on hard money. But relatively little money can go a long way; for example, the Swift Boat ads cost just $546,000 but had a dramatic immediate effect on the campaign. *See* Richard Briffault, *The 527 Problem . . . and the Buckley Problem,* 73 Geo.Wash. L. Rev. 949 (2005).

This trend accelerated in 2006. As of July, 2006, four months before the general election, 527s had raised over $84 million and spent $101 million—an astonishing amount for a midterm election. The role of 527s became a focus for FEC review in the aftermath of *McConnell,* but remains unresolved. Although this failure of the FEC to regulate led to fears of a proliferation of 527 organizations and a major increase in their activities, the total amount of soft money in play in the 2004 presidential election was still less than at the same time in the 2000 cycle, most markedly with respect to corporate contributions. Part of this is no doubt the result of increases in the ability of individuals to give more hard money. But there seems no question that despite the rise of 527s as a potential mechanism to circumvent BCRA, more money stayed within the BCRA-modified FECA scheme than had been the case prior to BCRA's enactment. To the extent that BCRA set its sights on curtailing corporate contributions to election campaigns, the first election cycle under BCRA indicates success on that front.

At the same time, the 2008 presidential election season revealed another regulatory gap between federal and state limitations on contributions. In the two years before former Massachusetts Governor Mitt Romney launched his presidential exploratory committee, sixteen individuals contributed more than $100,000 each to his efforts, exploiting a crevice between federal and state law. Jeanne Cummings, *How Mitt Romney Avoided Campaign–Finance Rules,* Wall St. J., Jan. 30, 2007, at A1. Prior to officially entering the federal election fray, Mr. Romney was not subject to federal campaign finance regulations. His political team set up fundraising committees in three states—Michigan, Iowa, and Alabama—that did not have political contribution limits. Through such mechanisms, Mr. Romney's political action committees took in more than $7 million. Much of this money flowed to PACs based in states without contribution limits from out-of-state donors and these state committees were able to coordinate their activities, contributing to expenses such as rent and consulting costs incurred by the national campaign in Massachusetts.

On the other extreme from the presidential campaign of Governor Romney are the First Amendment implications of BCRA's ban on electioneering communications to the activities of private actors. For example, the FEC had to address allegations brought against filmmaker Michael Moore that claimed the production, distribution, and promotion of the film *Fahrenheit 9/11* constituted illegal corporate expenditures against President George W. Bush. The Commission determined that Moore's activities fell under an exemption for bona fide commercial activities. *In re Dog Eat Dog Films, Inc.,* Matter Under Review ("MUR") 5474 and *In re* Fahrenheit 9/11, Matter Under Review ("MUR") 5539.

Subsequently, a complaint was filed during the 2004 election against Kirk Shelmerdine, an unsuccessful National Association for Stock Car Auto Racing (NASCAR) team owner and driver, who placed a decal of the "Bush Cheney '04" logo on an unsold panel of the stock car that he drove in four races. The complaint charged that the decal on Mr. Shelmerdine's stock car failed to include a disclaimer stating who paid for the advertisement, 2 U.S.C. § 441, failed to report an independent expenditure, 2 U.S.C. § 434, and constituted an illegal corporate expenditure, 2 U.S.C. § 411b. The Commission determined that the decal was an independent expenditure worth more than $1,000 even though there was no actual market for the advertising space in the races in question. Nonetheless, the Commission exercised its prosecutorial discretion and chose to admonish Mr. Shelmerdine rather than impose a civil penalty based on the financial value of the violation. *In re Kirk Shelmerdine Racing LLC*, Matter Under Review ("MUR") 5563, Statement of Reasons ("SOR") of Comm'r Smith and Vice Chairman Toner (F.E.C. Aug. 8, 2005).

5.   Judicial Elections

Oddly related to campaign finance is the topic of judicial elections, another area in which the First Amendment has intersected heavily with the law of democracy. Recently, a distinct line of First Amendment case law has emerged concerning judicial elections, an area that had received relatively little attention except from reform groups seeking to supplant the election of judges altogether. Cases such as *Wells v. Edwards,* discussed in Chapter 3, allowed caseload demands to be considered in denying a strict application of one person, one vote to the election of judges. In *Chisom v. Roemer,* 501 U.S. 380 (1991), the Court allowed a statutory claim of minority vote dilution to be brought against Louisiana judicial elections under the Voting Rights Act. Although the statute assured minority voters an equal opportunity to elect "representatives" of their choice, the Court reasoned that "[a]ny abridgment of the opportunity of members of a protected class to participate in the political process inevitably impairs their ability to influence the outcome of an election." As a result, "[i]f the word 'representatives' did place a limit on the coverage of the Act for judicial elections, it would exclude all claims involving such elections from the protection of § 2"—a result the Court found contrary to the intent of Congress to provide broad remedies under the Voting Rights Act.

In any event, judicial elections have a number of distinctive features. Most significant for current purposes is the common practice of restricting the manner in which candidates for judicial office can campaign. The prospect of judges making routine campaign promises and engaging in the normal run of electioneering conduct appeared unseemly—even as judicial candidates were required to raise money to get themselves elected. In *Republican Party of Minnesota v. White,* 536 U.S. 765 (2002), the Court confronted a Minnesota ethical canon that required that a "candidate for a judicial office, including an incumbent judge," shall not "announce his or her views on disputed legal or political issues." The question for the Court was whether the restrictions would be viewed within the broad expressive mandates of the First Amendment, or whether they could be restricted to the specific requirements of judicial office. For example, one of the prohibited communications would have been seen as the mainstay of campaign speech in a contest for Congress or the state legislature: the lower courts had upheld the impropriety of a candidate announcing his view that "[t]he Minnesota Supreme Court has issued decisions which are marked by their disregard for the Legislature and a lack of common sense." The Supreme Court struck down the Minnesota ethical canon, reasoning that "the announce clause both prohibits speech on the basis of its content and burdens a category of speech that is 'at the core of our First Amendment freedoms'—speech about the qualifications of candidates for public office."

By placing the restriction on judicial electioneering squarely within the confines of the First Amendment, the Court required the State to come forward with a compelling interest in burdening speech—thereby raising a set of questions related to those presented in the campaign finance cases. The Court rejected the State's claimed interest in judicial impartiality, reasoning that judges must be impartial between parties, but could not be—and perhaps should not be—impartial as between all positions having to do with their office. But the most significant part of the opinion by Justice Scalia was the overwhelming presumption against any electoral regulation affecting speech:

> Moreover, the notion that the special context of electioneering justifies an abridgment of the right to speak out on disputed issues sets our First Amendment jurisprudence on its head. "[D]ebate on the qualifications of candidates" is "at the core of our electoral process and of the First Amendment freedoms," not at the edges. "The role that elected officials play in our society makes it all the more imperative that they be allowed freely to express themselves on matters of current public importance." "It is simply not the function of government to select which issues are worth discussing or debating in the course of a political campaign." We have never allowed the government to prohibit candidates from communicating relevant information to voters during an election.

White reaffirmed a stark divide between the deferential constitutional review of *elections*, which are seen as a matter of state administrative discretion, and *electoral speech,* which is held to exacting scrutiny that is unlikely to be satisfied. While Justice Scalia is quite dismissive of the claimed state interest in judicial impartiality, it is not clear what justification could have sufficed once the ethical canons were found to limit political speech. In two recent cases, the New York Court of Appeals tried to finesse the narrow spaces left open by *White*. First, in *In re Raab*, 793 N.E.2d 1287 (N.Y.2003), the Court of Appeals upheld a restriction on a judicial candidate raising money for other political candidates. The Court reasoned that unlike the speech restrictions in *White*, the New York regulations implicated the distinct interests in maintaining the integrity required for judicial office. Since the regulations affected the ability to raise money for others, the Court of Appeals found that "the interests the State seeks to advance in this case are not unlike those validated in *United States Civ. Serv. v. N.A. of Letter Carriers* (413 U.S. 548 [1973]). *Letter Carriers* involved a First Amendment challenge to the validity of the Hatch Act, which prohibits federal executive branch employees from engaging in various types of political activities, including holding office in a political party, organizing a political party or club and actively participating in fund-raising. The United States Supreme Court upheld the restrictions even though they limited the political activity of federal employees and prohibited them from engaging in conduct otherwise protected by the First Amendment."

More controversial may be *In re Watson*, 794 N.E.2d 1 (N.Y.2003), in which a judicial candidate was found to violate judicial conduct rules which prohibit "making pledges or promises of conduct in office other than the faithful and impartial performance of the duties of the office." The offending conduct was a campaign flyer in which the judicial candidate stated, "we are in desperate need of a Judge who will work with the police, not against them. We need a judge who will assist our law enforcement officers as they aggressively work towards cleaning up our city streets." In another communication, he added, "criminals from surrounding communities are flocking into Lockport. Once we gain a reputation for being tough, you'd be surprised how many will go elsewhere, making the caseload much more manageable." The New York court found the restriction distinguishable from the Minnesota rule struck down in *White* on the following grounds:

> New York's Rules Governing Judicial Conduct do not include a provision analogous to Minnesota's "announce clause." The pledges or promises clause in this case is significantly different from the announce clause in that it does not prohibit judicial candidates from articulating their views on legal issues....

> As its literal language suggests, the restriction is not a blanket ban on pledges or promises; a judicial candidate may promise future conduct provided such conduct is not inconsistent with the faithful and impartial performance of judicial duties.

> [The challenged Rule] furthers the State's interest in preventing party bias and promoting openmindedness, and the appearance of either, because it prohibits a judicial candidate from making promises that compromise the candidate's ability to behave impartially, or to be perceived as unbiased and openminded by the public, once on the bench. Such promises, even if they are not kept once the candidate is elected, damage the judicial system because the newly elected judge will have created a perception that will be difficult to dispel in the public mind. With all the uncertainties inherent in litigation, litigants and the bar are entitled to be free of the additional burden of

wondering whether the judge to whom their case is assigned will adjudicate it without bias or prejudice and with a mind that is open enough to allow reasonable consideration of the legal and factual issues presented.

A campaign pledge to favor one group over another if elected has the additional deleterious effect of miseducating voters about the role of the judiciary at a time when their attention is focused on filling judicial vacancies. Judges must apply the law faithfully and impartially—they are not elected to aid particular groups, be it the police, the prosecution or the defense bar. Campaign promises that suggest otherwise gravely risk distorting public perception of the judicial role.... The rule precludes only those statements of intention that single out a party or class of litigants for special treatment, be it favorable or unfavorable, or convey that the candidate will behave in a manner inconsistent with the faithful and impartial performance of judicial duties if elected.

Is this state interest sufficient under the standard of First Amendment scrutiny articulated in *White*? For a discussion of the kinds of judicial candidate speech that can be regulated, the interests that could justify regulation, and the question whether post-election recusal is more narrowly tailored to protect judicial impartiality, see Michelle T. Friedland, *Disqualification or Suppression: Due Process and the Response to Judicial Campaign Speech*, 104 Colum. L. Rev. 563 (2004).

Perhaps more centrally, does the presence of robust First Amendment scrutiny over the conduct of judicial elections further destabilize the precarious post-*Buckley,* post-*McConnell* regulation of campaign finance?

CHAPTER 6

PRECLEARANCE AND THE VOTING RIGHTS ACT

As the materials in Chapters 2 and 4 illustrate, the guarantees of the Fourteenth and Fifteenth Amendments were essentially disregarded in many states for roughly a century. To a substantial extent, nonenforcement of the amendments was a function of Southern legislators' control of Congress: attempts to eliminate the poll tax, for example, were stymied for decades by Southern senators and representatives, and no civil rights bill of any sort was passed until 1957, when a watered-down voting rights bill was enacted. Among other things, that bill created the Civil Rights Division of the Department of Justice and, along with the Civil Rights Act of 1960, authorized the Department to bring suits on behalf of citizens who were denied the right to vote on account of race.

These lawsuits, however, were extremely time-consuming and victories were often pyrrhic. The formal legal standard was hard to satisfy: in a jurisdiction with a literacy test, like Mississippi, for example, the United States had to prove that the applications of black applicants who had been denied registration were comparable to the applications of whites who had been registered. This meant going county by county, comparing literally thousands of applications. This analysis took hundreds, sometimes thousands, of hours. Local officials engaged in ingenious forms of resistance—''losing'' records, resigning (thereby vitiating injunctions against them of any force) and leaving registrar positions vacant so that no applicants could be registered, or purging black voters from the rolls shortly after their enfranchisement. *See, e.g., United States v. McElveen*, 180 F. Supp. 10 (E. D. La.), *aff'd sub nom. United States v. Thomas*, 362 U.S. 58 (1960). Perhaps just as importantly, several federal district court judges were almost equally resistant to the enfranchisement of black voters. Virtually every lawsuit required repeated trips to the Court of Appeals before any relief at all was granted.

Although the Department of Justice had filed 71 voting rights cases in the seven years following the 1957 Act, black registration in the South remained minuscule. Between 1958 and 1964, black registration in Alabama rose from 5.2 to 19.4 percent; in Mississippi, from 1954 to 1964 black registration rose from 4.4 percent to only 6.4 percent. Dallas County, Alabama—whose county seat, Selma, was soon to become nationally famous—offered a textbook illustration of the problems with case-by-case litigation of the disenfranchisement problem. The county had a voting-age population of approximately 29,500, including 15,000 blacks. Although roughly two-thirds of the county's eligible white citizens were registered to vote, only one percent of the black residents—156 out of 15,000—were registered. Nonetheless, it took thirteen months of procedural wrangling before the Department of Justice's lawsuit against the county registrars came to trial. By then, the registrars who had been in office when the suit had been filed had resigned and the district court refused to issue any injunction against the new registrars since it found that they had not discriminated against anyone. On appeal, the Fifth Circuit ordered the district court to enter an injunction against discriminatory practices, but it permitted the continued use of the literacy test. Although in the past, the test had been administered leniently—allowing essentially illiterate white applicants to register—it was now applied to black applicants with a vengeance: 175 black applicants with high-school diplomas were rejected, along with 21 applicants with college degrees and one who had a master's degree. Moreover, the board added an "understanding" requirement that demanded that applicants interpret an excerpt of the state constitution. As was true in other jurisdictions, black applicants were given far harder passages than their white counterparts; even if they were able to offer a plausible interpretation, the board would often reject them. After additional investigation, the Department of Justice filed a motion for further relief and, four years after the original lawsuit was filed, the district court finally issued a meaningful injunction. In the meantime, only 383 of the nearly 15,000 eligible black citizens had managed to register.

While the lawsuit was wending its way through the courts, grassroots civil rights organizations, such as the Southern Christian Leadership Conference (SCLC) and the Student Nonviolent Coordinating Committee (SNCC) had moved into Selma and launched a registration campaign. In part, they picked Selma because they knew that the Dallas County Sheriff, Jim Clark, was prone to the kind of overreaction that the national media would cover and which would garner support for their cause. *See* David J. Garrow, Protest at Selma: Martin Luther King, Jr., and the Voting Rights Act of 1965 (1978); Michael J. Klarman, Brown, *Racial Change and the Civil Rights Movement*, 80 Va. L. Rev. 7, 147–49 (1994). In February 1965, in nearby Perry County, Alabama, a nighttime voting-rights march was broken up by Alabama state troopers; in the ensuing assault, a trooper shot Jimmie Jackson, who was trying to protect his mother. A few weeks later, on March 7, 1965, SCLC and SNCC began a protest march from Selma to the state capital, Montgomery, to present Governor George Wallace with a list of their grievances. On the Edmund Pettis Bridge outside Selma, they were stopped by state troopers, sheriff's deputies, and "possemen" on horseback. The lawmen fired tear gas into the crowd and charged the marchers, trampling and injuring many of them. The entire scene was captured by television cameras and prompted nationwide revulsion. In the wake of "Bloody Sunday," Judge Frank M. Johnson issued an injunction permitting the march on the grounds that such a march provided one of the only available means for black citizens to petition their government for redress of grievances—since less dramatic political mechanisms such as voting were unavailable—and recognized that troops would be necessary to protect the marchers. *See Williams v. Wallace*, 240 F. Supp. 100 (M.D. Ala. 1965). In the wake of national outrage over the events in Selma, President Lyndon B. Johnson instructed the Department of Justice to propose a more expansive voting rights bill. That bill ultimately became the Voting Rights Act of 1965. Wilson Baker, at the time Selma's Director of Public Safety, later recalled asking then-Attorney General Nicholas Katzenbach, "What do you expect if the Voter [*sic*] Rights Bill passes?" Katzenbach replied, " 'What do you mean *if* it passes. You people passed that on that bridge. You people in Selma passed that on that bridge that Sunday.' He said, 'You can be sure it will pass, and because of that, if nothing else.' " Howell Raines, My Soul Is Rested: Movement Days in the Deep South Remembered 215 (1977). For an extensive account of how events and litigation in Alabama paved the way for the Voting Rights Act, see Brian K. Landsberg, Free At Last: The Alabama Origins of the Voting Rights Act (2007).

When he signed the Act into law in 1965, President Lyndon Johnson called it "one of the most monumental laws in the entire history of American freedom." In the ensuing decades, the Act transformed American politics in a variety of ways. This Chapter focuses primarily on one section of the Act—section 5—and how that section has been interpreted. The other major substantive provision in the Act—section 2—is covered in Chapter 8.

A. Congressional Power to Enact the Special Provisions of the Voting Rights Act

South Carolina v. Katzenbach

383 U.S. 301 (1966).

■ Mr. Chief Justice Warren delivered the opinion of the Court.

... South Carolina has filed a bill of complaint, seeking a declaration that selected provisions of the Voting Rights Act of 1965 violate the Federal Constitution, and asking for an injunction against enforcement of these provisions by the Attorney General.

* * *

The Voting Rights Act was designed by Congress to banish the blight of racial discrimination in voting, which has infected the electoral process in parts of our country for nearly a century. The Act creates stringent new remedies for voting discrimination where it persists on a pervasive scale, and in addition the statute strengthens existing remedies for pockets of voting discrimination elsewhere in the country. Congress assumed the power to prescribe these remedies from § 2 of the Fifteenth Amendment, which authorizes the National Legislature to effectuate by "appropriate" measures the constitutional prohibition against racial discrimination in voting. We hold that the sections of the Act which are properly before us are an appropriate means for carrying out Congress' constitutional responsibilities and are consonant with all other provisions of the Constitution. We therefore deny South Carolina's request that enforcement of these sections of the Act be enjoined.

I

The constitutional propriety of the Voting Rights Act of 1965 must be judged with reference to the historical experience which it reflects. Before enacting the measure, Congress explored with great care the problem of racial discrimination in voting.... Two points emerge vividly from the voluminous legislative history of the Act contained in the committee hearings and floor debates. First: Congress felt itself confronted by an insidious and pervasive evil which had been perpetuated in certain parts of our country through unremitting and ingenious defiance of the Constitution. Second: Congress concluded that the unsuccessful remedies which it had prescribed in the past would have to be replaced by sterner and more elaborate measures in order to satisfy the clear commands of the Fifteenth Amendment. We pause here to summarize the majority reports of the House and Senate Committees, which document in considerable detail the factual basis for these reactions by Congress.

* * *

The Fifteenth Amendment to the Constitution was ratified in 1870. Promptly thereafter Congress passed the Enforcement Act of 1870, which made it a crime for public officers and private persons to obstruct exercise of the right to vote. The statute was amended in the following year to provide for detailed federal supervision of the electoral process, from registration to the certification of returns. As the years passed and fervor for racial equality waned, enforcement of the laws became spotty and ineffective, and most of their provisions were repealed in 1894. The remnants have had little significance in the recently renewed battle against voting discrimination.

Meanwhile, beginning in 1890, the States of Alabama, Georgia, Louisiana, Mississippi, North Carolina, South Carolina, and Virginia enacted tests still in use which were specifically designed to prevent Negroes from voting.[1] Typically, they made the ability to read and write a registration

---

1. The South Carolina Constitutional Convention of 1895 was a leader in the widespread movement to disenfranchise Negroes. Senator Ben Tillman frankly explained to the state delegates the aim of the new literacy test: "[The] only thing we can do as patriots and as statesmen is to take from [the 'ignorant blacks'] every ballot that we can under

qualification and also required completion of a registration form. These laws were based on the fact that as of 1890 in each of the named States, more than two-thirds of the adult Negroes were illiterate while less than one-quarter of the adult whites were unable to read or write. At the same time, alternate tests were prescribed in all of the named States to assure that white illiterates would not be deprived of the franchise. These included grandfather clauses, property qualifications, "good character" tests, and the requirement that registrants "understand" or "interpret" certain matter.

* * *

According to the evidence in recent Justice Department voting suits, the latter stratagem is now the principal method used to bar Negroes from the polls. Discriminatory administration of voting qualifications has been found in all eight Alabama cases, in all nine Louisiana cases, and in all nine Mississippi cases which have gone to final judgment. Moreover, in almost all of these cases, the courts have held that the discrimination was pursuant to a widespread "pattern or practice." White applicants for registration have often been excused altogether from the literacy and understanding tests or have been given easy versions, have received extensive help from voting officials, and have been registered despite serious errors in their answers.[12] Negroes, on the other hand, have typically been required to pass difficult versions of all the tests, without any outside assistance and without the slightest error.[13] The good-morals requirement is so vague and subjective that it has constituted an open invitation to abuse at the hands of voting officials. Negroes obliged to obtain vouchers from registered voters have found it virtually impossible to comply in areas where almost no Negroes are on the rolls.

In recent years, Congress has repeatedly tried to cope with the problem by facilitating case-by-case litigation against voting discrimination. The

---

the laws of our national government." He was equally candid about the exemption from the literacy test for persons who could "understand" and "explain" a section of the state constitution: "There is no particle of fraud or illegality in it. It is just simply showing partiality, perhaps, [laughter,] or discriminating." He described the alternative exemption for persons paying state property taxes in the same vein: "By means of the $300 clause you simply reach out and take in some more white men and a few more colored men." Senator Tillman was the dominant political figure in the state convention, and his entire address merits examination.

12. A white applicant in Louisiana satisfied the registrar of his ability to interpret the state constitution by writing, "FRDUM FOOF SPETGH." *United States v. Louisiana*, 225 F. Supp. 353, 384. A white applicant in Alabama who had never completed the first grade of school was enrolled after the registrar filled out the entire form for him.

13. In Panola County, Mississippi, the registrar required Negroes to interpret the provision of the state constitution concerning "the rate of interest on the fund known as the 'Chickasaw School Fund.'" *United States v. Duke*, 332 F. 2d 759, 764. In Forrest County, Mississippi, the registrar rejected six Negroes with baccalaureate degrees, three of whom were also Masters of Arts. *United States v. Lynd*, 301 F. 2d 818, 821.

Civil Rights Act of 1957 authorized the Attorney General to seek injunctions against public and private interference with the right to vote on racial grounds. Perfecting amendments in the Civil Rights Act of 1960 permitted the joinder of States as parties defendant, gave the Attorney General access to local voting records, and authorized courts to register voters in areas of systematic discrimination. Title I of the Civil Rights Act of 1964 expedited the hearing of voting cases before three-judge courts and outlawed some of the tactics used to disqualify Negroes from voting in federal elections.

Despite the earnest efforts of the Justice Department and of many federal judges, these new laws have done little to cure the problem of voting discrimination.

* * *

II

The Voting Rights Act of 1965 reflects Congress' firm intention to rid the country of racial discrimination in voting. The heart of the Act is a complex scheme of stringent remedies aimed at areas where voting discrimination has been most flagrant. Section 4(a)–(d) lays down a formula defining the States and political subdivisions to which these new remedies apply. The first of the remedies, contained in § 4(a), is the suspension of literacy tests and similar voting qualifications for a period of five years from the last occurrence of substantial voting discrimination. Section 5 prescribes a second remedy, the suspension of all new voting regulations pending review by federal authorities to determine whether their use would perpetuate voting discrimination.

* * *

Coverage formula.

The remedial sections of the Act assailed by South Carolina automatically apply to any State, or to any separate political subdivision such as a county or parish, for which two findings have been made: (1) the Attorney General has determined that on November 1, 1964, it maintained a "test or device," and (2) the Director of the Census has determined that less than 50% of its voting-age residents were registered on November 1, 1964, or voted in the presidential election of November 1964. These findings are not reviewable in any court and are final upon publication in the Federal Register. § 4(b). As used throughout the Act, the phrase "test or device" means any requirement that a registrant or voter must "(1) demonstrate the ability to read, write, understand, or interpret any matter, (2) demonstrate any educational achievement or his knowledge of any particular subject, (3) possess good moral character, or (4) prove his qualifications by the voucher of registered voters or members of any other class." § 4(c).

* * *

South Carolina was brought within the coverage formula of the Act on August 7, 1965, pursuant to appropriate administrative determinations which have not been challenged in this proceeding. On the same day, coverage was also extended to Alabama, Alaska, Georgia, Louisiana, Mississippi, Virginia, 26 counties in North Carolina, and one county in Arizona. Two more counties in Arizona, one county in Hawaii, and one county in Idaho were added to the list on November 19, 1965. Thus far Alaska, the three Arizona counties, and the single county in Idaho have asked the District Court for the District of Columbia to grant a declaratory judgment terminating statutory coverage.

Suspension of tests.

In a State or political subdivision covered by § 4(b) of the Act, no person may be denied the right to vote in any election because of his failure to comply with a "test or device." § 4(a).

On account of this provision, South Carolina is temporarily barred from enforcing the portion of its voting laws which requires every applicant for registration to show that he:

> "Can both read and write any section of [the State] Constitution submitted to [him] by the registration officer or can show that he owns, and has paid all taxes collectible during the previous year on, property in this State assessed at three hundred dollars or more." S.C. Code Ann. § 23–62(4) (1965 Supp.).

The Attorney General has determined that the property qualification is inseparable from the literacy test, and South Carolina makes no objection to this finding. Similar tests and devices have been temporarily suspended in the other sections of the country listed above.

Review of new rules.

In a State or political subdivision covered by § 4(b) of the Act, no person may be denied the right to vote in any election because of his failure to comply with a voting qualification or procedure different from those in force on November 1, 1964. This suspension of new rules is terminated, however, under either of the following circumstances: (1) if the area has submitted the rules to the Attorney General, and he has not interposed an objection within 60 days, or (2) if the area has obtained a declaratory judgment from the District Court for the District of Columbia, determining that the rules will not abridge the franchise on racial grounds. These declaratory judgment actions are to be heard by a three-judge panel, with direct appeal to this Court. § 5.

South Carolina altered its voting laws in 1965 to extend the closing hour at polling places from 6 p.m. to 7 p.m. The State has not sought judicial review of this change in the District Court for the District of Columbia, nor has it submitted the new rule to the Attorney General for his scrutiny, although at our hearing the Attorney General announced that he does not challenge the amendment. There are indications in the record that other sections of the country listed above have also altered their voting laws since November 1, 1964.

* * *

III

These provisions of the Voting Rights Act of 1965 are challenged on the fundamental ground that they exceed the powers of Congress and encroach on an area reserved to the States by the Constitution.

* * *

[T]he basic question presented by the case [is]: Has Congress exercised its powers under the Fifteenth Amendment in an appropriate manner with relation to the States?

The ground rules for resolving this question are clear. The language and purpose of the Fifteenth Amendment, the prior decisions construing its several provisions, and the general doctrines of constitutional interpretation, all point to one fundamental principle. As against the reserved powers of the States, Congress may use any rational means to effectuate the constitutional prohibition of racial discrimination in voting.

* * *

Section 1 of the Fifteenth Amendment declares that "[the] right of citizens of the United States to vote shall not be denied or abridged by the United States or by any State on account of race, color, or previous condition of servitude." This declaration has always been treated as self-executing and has repeatedly been construed, without further legislative specification, to invalidate state voting qualifications or procedures which are discriminatory on their face or in practice.... The gist of the matter is that the Fifteenth Amendment supersedes contrary exertions of state power....

South Carolina contends that [only the judiciary can] strike down state statutes and procedures—that to allow an exercise of this authority by Congress would be to rob the courts of their rightful constitutional role. On the contrary, § 2 of the Fifteenth Amendment expressly declares that "Congress shall have power to enforce this article by appropriate legislation." By adding this authorization, the Framers indicated that Congress was to be chiefly responsible for implementing the rights created in § 1. "It is the power of Congress which has been enlarged. Congress is authorized to enforce the prohibitions by appropriate legislation. Some legislation is contemplated to make the [Civil War] amendments fully effective." *Ex parte Virginia*, 100 U.S. 339, 345. Accordingly, in addition to the courts, Congress has full remedial powers to effectuate the constitutional prohibition against racial discrimination in voting.

* * *

The basic test to be applied in a case involving § 2 of the Fifteenth Amendment is the same as in all cases concerning the express powers of Congress with relation to the reserved powers of the States. Chief Justice Marshall laid down the classic formulation, 50 years before the Fifteenth Amendment was ratified:

> Let the end be legitimate, let it be within the scope of the constitution, and all means which are appropriate, which are plainly adapted to that end, which are not prohibited, but consist with the letter and spirit of the constitution, are constitutional. *McCulloch v. Maryland,* 4 Wheat. 316, 421.

The Court has subsequently echoed his language in describing each of the Civil War Amendments:

> Whatever legislation is appropriate, that is, adapted to carry out the objects the amendments have in view, whatever tends to enforce submission to the prohibitions they contain, and to secure to all persons the enjoyment of perfect equality of civil rights and the equal protection of the laws against State denial or invasion, if not prohibited, is brought within the domain of congressional power. *Ex parte Virginia,* 100 U.S., at 345–346.

* * *

We therefore reject South Carolina's argument that Congress may appropriately do no more than to forbid violations of the Fifteenth Amendment in general terms—that the task of fashioning specific remedies or of applying them to particular localities must necessarily be left entirely to the courts. Congress is not circumscribed by any such artificial rules under § 2 of the Fifteenth Amendment.

* * *

IV

Congress exercised its authority under the Fifteenth Amendment in an inventive manner when it enacted the Voting Rights Act of 1965. First: The measure prescribes remedies for voting discrimination which go into effect without any need for prior adjudication. This was clearly a legitimate response to the problem, for which there is ample precedent under other constitutional provisions.... Congress had found that case-by-case litigation was inadequate to combat widespread and persistent discrimination in voting, because of the inordinate amount of time and energy required to overcome the obstructionist tactics invariably encountered in these lawsuits. After enduring nearly a century of systematic resistance to the Fifteenth Amendment, Congress might well decide to shift the advantage of time and inertia from the perpetrators of the evil to its victims.

* * *

Second: The Act intentionally confines these remedies to a small number of States and political subdivisions which in most instances were familiar to Congress by name. This, too, was a permissible method of dealing with the problem. Congress had learned that substantial voting discrimination presently occurs in certain sections of the country, and it knew no way of accurately forecasting whether the evil might spread elsewhere in the future. In acceptable legislative fashion, Congress chose to limit its attention to the geographic areas where immediate action seemed necessary.

* * *

Coverage formula.

[. . .] South Carolina contends that the coverage formula is awkwardly designed in a number of respects and that it disregards various local conditions which have nothing to do with racial discrimination. These arguments, however, are largely beside the point. Congress began work with reliable evidence of actual voting discrimination in a great majority of the States and political subdivisions affected by the new remedies of the Act. The formula eventually evolved to describe these areas was relevant to the problem of voting discrimination, and Congress was therefore entitled to infer a significant danger of the evil in the few remaining States and political subdivisions covered by § 4(b) of the Act. No more was required to justify the application to these areas of Congress' express powers under the Fifteenth Amendment. . . .

To be specific, the new remedies of the Act are imposed on three States—Alabama, Louisiana, and Mississippi—in which federal courts have repeatedly found substantial voting discrimination. Section 4(b) of the Act also embraces two other States—Georgia and South Carolina—plus large portions of a third State—North Carolina—for which there was more fragmentary evidence of recent voting discrimination mainly adduced by the Justice Department and the Civil Rights Commission. All of these areas were appropriately subjected to the new remedies. In identifying past evils, Congress obviously may avail itself of information from any probative source.

The areas listed above, for which there was evidence of actual voting discrimination, share two characteristics incorporated by Congress into the coverage formula: the use of tests and devices for voter registration, and a voting rate in the 1964 presidential election at least 12 points below the national average. Tests and devices are relevant to voting discrimination because of their long history as a tool for perpetrating the evil; a low voting rate is pertinent for the obvious reason that widespread disenfranchisement must inevitably affect the number of actual voters. Accordingly, the coverage formula is rational in both practice and theory. It was therefore permissible to impose the new remedies on the few remaining States and political subdivisions covered by the formula, at least in the absence of proof that they have been free of substantial voting discrimination in recent years.

* * *

Suspension of tests.

We now arrive at consideration of the specific remedies prescribed by the Act for areas included within the coverage formula. South Carolina assails the temporary suspension of existing voting qualifications, reciting the rule laid down by *Lassiter v. Northampton County Bd. of Elections,* 360 U.S. 45, that literacy tests and related devices are not in themselves contrary to the Fifteenth Amendment. In that very case, however, the Court went on to say, "Of course a literacy test, fair on its face, may be employed to perpetuate that discrimination which the Fifteenth Amendment was designed to uproot." *Id.,* at 53. The record shows that in most of the States covered by the Act, including South Carolina, various tests and devices have been instituted with the purpose of disenfranchising Negroes, have been framed in such a way as to facilitate this aim, and have been administered in a discriminatory fashion for many years. Under these circumstances, the Fifteenth Amendment has clearly been violated.

The Act suspends literacy tests and similar devices for a period of five years from the last occurrence of substantial voting discrimination. This was a legitimate response to the problem, for which there is ample precedent in Fifteenth Amendment cases. Underlying the response was the feeling that States and political subdivisions which had been allowing white illiterates to vote for years could not sincerely complain about "dilution" of their electorates through the registration of Negro illiterates. Congress knew that continuance of the tests and devices in use at the present time, no matter how fairly administered in the future, would freeze the effect of past discrimination in favor of unqualified white registrants. Congress permissibly rejected the alternative of requiring a complete re-registration of all voters, believing that this would be too harsh on many whites who had enjoyed the franchise for their entire adult lives.

Review of new rules.

The Act suspends new voting regulations pending scrutiny by federal authorities to determine whether their use would violate the Fifteenth Amendment. This may have been an uncommon exercise of congressional power, as South Carolina contends, but the Court has recognized that exceptional conditions can justify legislative measures not otherwise appropriate.... Congress knew that some of the States covered by § 4(b) of the Act had resorted to the extraordinary stratagem of contriving new rules of various kinds for the sole purpose of perpetuating voting discrimination in the face of adverse federal court decrees. Congress had reason to suppose that these States might try similar maneuvers in the future in order to evade the remedies for voting discrimination contained in the Act itself.

Under the compulsion of these unique circumstances, Congress responded in a permissibly decisive manner. . . .

[T]here was nothing inappropriate about limiting litigation under this provision to the District Court for the District of Columbia, and in putting the burden of proof on the areas seeking relief.

* * *

NOTES AND QUESTIONS

1. The core of the 1965 Act is the interaction of three provisions: the triggering formula, the suspension of tests and devices, and the preclearance requirement. The triggering formula is entirely mechanical. Although it was stated in formal, neutral terms, it managed to reach the Deep South and very few other jurisdictions. When the Act was amended and extended in 1970 and 1975, many other jurisdictions, most notably three boroughs of New York City in 1970, and the entire state of Texas in 1975, were brought within the special provisions of the Act.

Under the current version of section 4, which uses triggering dates in 1964, 1968, and 1972, nine states, 54 counties (including 40 in North Carolina), and twelve municipalities or townships are covered jurisdictions. *See* 28 C.F.R. Part 51, Appendix (2006).

Note that the special provisions did not reach either Texas or Arkansas in 1965. Those two states, like the states of the former Confederacy, had a long history of racial discrimination in voting. Remember, for example, the White Primary Cases discussed in Chapter 4. But neither state used a literacy test. Instead, the primary disenfranchising device in use by the 1960's in those two states was the poll tax.

Why didn't Congress use the poll tax as a triggering device as well? Some of the answer probably rests on then-raging arguments over Congress' authority to ban poll taxes through a statute rather than a constitutional amendment. The Twenty-Fourth Amendment, enacted in 1964, banned poll taxes as a qualification for voting in presidential and congressional elections. *See Harman v. Forssenius*, 380 U.S. 528 (1965). Moreover, as we have already seen in Chapter 2, the Supreme Court struck down the use of poll taxes under the Equal Protection Clause in *Harper v. Virginia State Board of Elections*, 383 U.S. 663 (1966). But some of the answer may depend on the identity of the two states involved: by omitting poll taxes from the list of "test[s] or device[s]," the Administration, presided over by a Texan, could sidestep determined opposition by Texas' and Arkansas's powerful legislative delegations.

In 1975, the definition of a "test or device" was amended to include the use of English-only election materials, including ballots, in areas with substantial numbers of non-English speakers. 42 U.S.C. § 1973b(f)(3). This amendment was designed in part to require Texas to provide bilingual election materials but largely to bring the state under the preclearance obligation. It also brought Arizona, New Mexico, and several counties, particularly in California and Colorado, under section 5 coverage.

2. *The identification of "covered jurisdictions."* The statutory formula applied to any "State or political subdivision" which satisfied the two elements of the trigger—use of a test or device and low voter turnout. The Act defined "political subdivision" to mean "any county or parish, except that where registration for voting is not conducted under the supervision of a county or parish, the term shall include any other subdivision of a State which conducts registration for voting." Voting Rights Act § 14(c)(2). Under the initial formulation, which looked at the practices in effect on November 1, 1964, seven full states—Alabama, Alaska, Georgia, Louisiana, Mississippi, South Carolina, and Virginia—were designated for coverage. In addition, 26 counties in North Carolina, three counties in Arizona, one county in Hawaii, and one county in Idaho were included.

The question of what jurisdictions beyond states and counties were covered was taken up in *United States v. Sheffield Board of Commissioners*, 435 U.S. 110 (1978). There, the Court held that the city of Sheffield, Alabama—a municipality within a covered state—was itself a covered jurisdiction despite the fact that the city did not conduct voter registration. The dispute arose in the context of a section 5 proceeding in which the city argued that it was not required to seek review of its new voting procedures because section 5 applied only to jurisdictions covered by section 4. The Court disagreed: "The language, structure, history, and purposes of the Act persuade us that § 5, like the constitutional provisions it is designed to implement, applies to all entities having power over any aspect of the electoral process within designated jurisdictions, not only to counties or to whatever units of state government perform the function of registering voters." *Id.* at 118. Thus, the city, as a state actor, was covered. Similarly, in *Dougherty County Board of Education v. White*, 439 U.S. 32 (1978), the Court held that a board of education was required to seek preclearance for a personnel rule that might affect candidates for public office.

3. The relationship between covered and non-covered jurisdictions creates some complications for determining the scope of section 5—the preclearance provision. In *Young v. Fordice*, 520 U.S. 273 (1997), the Court required Mississippi to seek preclearance of its system for registering voters even though the changes were made in an effort to comply with federal law, since the precise changes reflected policy choices made by state or local officials from covered jurisdictions. And in *Lopez v. Monterey County*, 525 U.S. 266 (1999), discussed later in this chapter, the Court confronted the question of how to deal with partially covered states, such as California. Only a few counties in California are covered jurisdictions. Here, the Court held that a "covered jurisdiction 'seeks to administer' a voting change," and thus must obtain preclearance even when "the jurisdiction implements a change required by the superior law of a noncovered State" and "exercises no discretion in giving effect to a state-mandated change."

4. Is coverage under sections 4 and 5 coterminous with the state action doctrine? Do they reach non-governmental entities engaged in state action, for example, political parties? *See Morse v. Republican Party of Virginia*, 517 U.S. 186 (1996) (holding that a state party's decisions about who could participate in its nominating conventions are covered by section 5).

Coverage of political parties, which the Department of Justice's regulations explicitly contemplates—*see* 28 C.F.R. § 51.7—raises a question about the interaction of constitutional concerns with statutory interpretation.

In *LaRouche v. Fowler*, 77 F. Supp. 2d 80 (D.D.C. 1999) (three-judge court) (per curiam), *pet. dism'd*, 529 U.S. 1035 (2000), for example, the court held that the Democratic Party's presidential nomination procedures were not subject to preclearance. First, the court held that the National Party was not a covered jurisdiction, and therefore was not itself required to seek preclearance. The National Party did not "exercis[e] delegated power over the electoral process" conferred by a covered jurisdiction. And while the court recognized that some state party rules in covered states would require preclearance, it held that applying that rule to the decisions to exclude LaRouche would infringe upon the parties' First Amendment associational rights to an impermissible extent:

> [T]he Supreme Court has consistently held that political party membership and governance implicate "core associational activities" constitutionally protected from government interference absent sufficient justification....

> [W]hile the Act is unarguably a statute of importance, it should not be read to extend coverage that would interfere with core associational rights; specifically here, internal national party rules as followed by state parties in a covered jurisdiction.

To what extent is *LaRouche* a straightforward application of the First Amendment principles regarding political parties' ideological autonomy described in Chapter 4? To what extent is the court's interpretation here driven by the idea that section 5's core purpose—to protect the voting rights of minority citizens—was not apparently implicated by the Democratic Party's decision to reject a fringe candidate? Consider historical context here: following the decision in *Terry v. Adams* (the final white primary case discussed in Chapter 4), the South Carolina Democratic Party in the mid-1950's enacted a rule that permitted anyone (including African Americans) to participate in the party's primary, but only if the individual swore that he or she "believe[d] in and will support the social (religious) and educational separation of the races." Would such a rule require preclearance? How would the *LaRouche* Court analyze this question?

5. When the Act was renewed in 1970, 1975, 1982, and 2006, the coverage period for jurisdictions already subject to the Act was extended. The Act, however, also permitted covered jurisdictions to "bail out," that is, to escape from the suspension of tests or devices under section 4 and the preclearance requirement of section 5, by bringing a declaratory judgment action in the United States District Court for the District of Columbia. In that action, the jurisdiction was required to show that no test or device had been used "during the five years preceding the filing of the action for the purpose or with the effect of denying or abridging the right to vote on account of race or color." Voting Rights Act § 4(a). In *Gaston County v. United States*, 395 U.S. 285 (1969), Gaston County, North Carolina, sought such a declaratory judgment. The district court and the Supreme Court denied bailout on the grounds that, regardless of whether the county had administered its literacy test impartially, its maintenance of a *de jure* segregated school system that provided black citizens with an inferior education "in turn deprived them of an equal chance to pass the literacy test." *Id.* at 291. Consider whether this rationale can be applied more broadly. For example, to what extent might racially polarized voting—discussed in Chapters 7 and 8—be legitimately treated as a product of prior *de jure* discrimination by the government, either because such discrimination contributed to socioeconomic differences that in turn create different political preferences or because the discrimination affected white voters' willingness to support black-sponsored candidates? *See, e.g.,* Pamela S. Karlan and Daryl J. Levinson, *Why Voting Is Different*, 84 Cal. L. Rev. 1201, 1229–30 (1996).

In 1982, the bailout provision was amended to provide more definite criteria: jurisdictions could be released if they could show compliance with the Act's requirements, the elimination of procedures that inhibited or diluted equal access, and "constructive efforts" to expand opportunities for political participation. 42 U.S.C. § 1973b(a)(1)(F) (2000). According to the Department of Justice, roughly a dozen jurisdictions have successfully used the bailout process. For discussions of bailout, see Paul F. Hancock & Lora L. Tredway, *The Bailout Standard of the Voting Rights Act: An Incentive to End Discrimination*, 17 Urb. Law. 379, 389–93 (1985); Richard A. Williamson, *The 1982 Amendments to the Voting Rights Act: A Statutory Analysis of the Revised Bailout Provisions*, 62 Wash. U. L.Q. 1, 6 (1984); Laughlin McDonald, *The 1982 Extension of Section 5 of the Voting Rights Act of 1965: The Continued Need for Preclearance*, 51 Tenn. L. Rev. 1, 77–79 (1983); Paul Winke, *Why the Preclearance and Bailout Provisions of the Voting Rights Act Are Still a Constitutionally Proportional Remedy*, 28 N.Y.U. Rev. L. & Soc. Change 69 (2003).

As this book went to press, a constitutional challenge had been filed to the continued coverage of section 5. *See Northwest Austin Municipal Utility Dist. No. 1 v. Gonzales*, No. 1:06–CV–01384 (D.D.C. Aug. 4, 2006), *available at* http://electionlawblog.org/archives/northwestaustin.pdf. (The constitutionality of section 5 is discussed in more detail *infra*.) One of the district's challenges rests on the fact that, as a subsidiary governmental unit within a covered jurisdiction, the utility district is barred from bailing out.

6. Internal congressional dynamics may explain another targeted provision of the 1965 Act: § 4(e), which provided in pertinent part that no person who had completed the sixth grade in a public school in, or a private school accredited by, the Commonwealth of Puerto Rico in which the language of instruction was other than English could be denied the right to vote in any election because of his inability to read or write English. (This section rested on Congress's enforcement power under section 5 of the Fourteenth Amendment rather than section 2 of the Fifteenth Amendment, perhaps because Congress did not see the problem as one of racial discrimination.) Representative Emanuel Cellar was chairman of the House Judiciary Subcommittee responsible for the 1965 Act.

New York maintained a literacy test. (Actually, it required that applicants for registration fill out a form which asked them questions regarding their place of residence, citizenship, and the like.) In *Katzenbach v. Morgan*, 384 U.S. 641 (1966), the Court upheld § 4(e). Justice Brennan's opinion for the Court offered the following analysis of congressional power:

A construction of § 5 [of the Fourteenth Amendment] that would require a judicial determination that the enforcement of the state law precluded by Congress violated the Amendment, as a condition of sustaining the congressional enactment, would depreciate both congressional resourcefulness and congressional responsibility for implementing the Amendment. It would confine the legislative power in this context to the insignificant role of abrogating only those state laws that the judicial branch was prepared to adjudge unconstitutional, or of merely informing the judgment of the judiciary by particularizing the "majestic generalities" of § 1 of the Amendment.

Thus our task in this case is not to determine whether the New York English literacy requirement as applied to deny the right to vote to a person who successfully completed the sixth grade in a Puerto Rican school violates the Equal Protection Clause. Accordingly, our decision in *Lassiter v. Northampton Election Bd.,* 360 U.S. 45, sustaining the North Carolina English literacy requirement as not in all circumstances prohibited by the first sections of the Fourteenth and Fifteenth Amendments, is inapposite.... *Lassiter* did not present the question before us here: Without regard to whether the judiciary would find that the Equal Protection Clause itself nullifies New York's English literacy requirement as so applied, could Congress prohibit the enforcement of the state law by legislating under § 5 of the Fourteenth Amendment? In answering this question, our task is limited to determining whether such legislation is, as required by § 5, appropriate legislation to enforce the Equal Protection Clause.

* * *

We therefore proceed to the consideration whether § 4(e) is "appropriate legislation" to enforce the Equal Protection Clause, that is, under the *McCulloch v. Maryland* standard, whether § 4(e) may be regarded as an enactment to enforce the Equal Protection Clause, whether it is "plainly adapted to that end" and whether it is not prohibited by but is consistent with "the letter and spirit of the constitution."[10]

There can be no doubt that § 4(e) may be regarded as an enactment to enforce the Equal Protection Clause.... [S]pecifically, § 4(e) may be viewed as a measure to secure for the Puerto Rican community residing in New York nondiscriminatory treatment by government—both in the imposition of voting qualifications and the provision or administration of governmental services, such as public schools, public housing and law enforcement.

Section 4(e) may be readily seen as "plainly adapted" to furthering these aims of the Equal Protection Clause. The practical effect of § 4(e) is to prohibit New York from denying the right to vote to large segments of its Puerto Rican community. Congress has thus prohibited the State from denying to that community the right that is "preservative of all rights." *Yick Wo v. Hopkins,* 118 U.S. 356, 370. This enhanced political power will be helpful in gaining nondiscriminatory treatment in public services for the entire Puerto Rican community. Section 4(e) thereby enables the Puerto Rican minority better to obtain "perfect equality of civil rights and the equal protection of the laws." It was well within congressional authority to say that this need of the Puerto Rican minority for the vote warranted federal intrusion upon any state interests served by the English literacy requirement. It was for Congress, as the branch that made this judgment, to assess and weigh the various conflicting considerations—the risk or pervasiveness of the discrimination in governmental services, the effectiveness of eliminating the state restriction on the right to vote as a means of dealing with the evil, the adequacy or availability of alternative remedies, and the nature and significance of the state interests that would be affected by the nullification of the English literacy requirement as applied to residents who have successfully completed the sixth grade in a Puerto Rican school. It is not for us to review the congressional resolution of these factors. It is enough that we be able to perceive a basis upon which the Congress might resolve the conflict as it did. There plainly was such a basis to support § 4(e) in the application in question in this case. Any contrary conclusion would require us to be blind to the realities familiar to the legislators.

10. Contrary to the suggestion of the dissent, ... § 5 does not grant Congress power to exercise discretion in the other direction and to enact "statutes so as in effect to dilute equal protection and due process decisions of this Court." We emphasize that Congress' power under § 5 is limited to adopting measures to enforce the guarantees of the Amendment; § 5 grants Congress no power to restrict, abrogate, or dilute these guarantees. Thus, for example, an enactment authorizing the States to establish racially segregated systems of education would not be—as required by § 5—a measure "to enforce" the Equal Protection Clause since that clause of its own force prohibits such state laws.

The result is no different if we confine our inquiry to the question whether § 4(e) was merely legislation aimed at the elimination of an invidious discrimination in establishing voter qualifications. We are told that New York's English literacy requirement originated in the desire to provide an incentive for non-English speaking immigrants to learn the English language and in order to assure the intelligent exercise of the franchise. Yet Congress might well have questioned, in light of the many exemptions provided, and some evidence suggesting that prejudice played a prominent role in the enactment of the requirement,[14] whether these were actually the interests being served. Congress might have also questioned whether denial of a right deemed so precious and fundamental in our society was a necessary or appropriate means of encouraging persons to learn English, or of furthering the goal of an intelligent exercise of the franchise. Finally, Congress might well have concluded that as a means of furthering the intelligent exercise of the franchise, an ability to read or understand Spanish is as effective as ability to read English for those to whom Spanish-language newspapers and Spanish-language radio and television programs are available to inform them of election issues and governmental affairs. Since Congress undertook to legislate so as to preclude the enforcement of the state law, and did so in the context of a general appraisal of literacy requirements for voting, . . . to which it brought a specially informed legislative competence, it was Congress' prerogative to weigh these competing considerations. Here again, it is enough that we perceive a basis upon which Congress might predicate a judgment that the application of New York's English literacy requirement to deny the right to vote to a person with a sixth grade education in Puerto Rican schools in which the language of instruction was other than English constituted an invidious discrimination in violation of the Equal Protection Clause.

What Fourteenth Amendment right, precisely, is section 4(e) designed to secure? Is it the right to vote or some more general interest in equal protection?

Footnote 10 of Justice Brennan's opinion offered his now-famous "ratchet theory" of constitutional law: Congress may expand, but not contract, the protections offered by a constitutional amendment. Does

---

14. This evidence consists in part of statements made in the Constitutional Convention first considering the English literacy requirement, such as the following made by the sponsor of the measure: "More precious even than the forms of government are the mental qualities of our race. While those stand unimpaired, all is safe. They are exposed to a single danger, and that is that by constantly changing our voting citizenship through the wholesale, but valuable and necessary infusion of Southern and Eastern European races. . . . The danger has begun. . . . We should check it."

This evidence was reinforced by an understanding of the cultural milieu at the time of proposal and enactment, spanning a period from 1915 to 1921—not one of the enlightened eras of our history. Congress was aware of this evidence.

Justice Brennan's theory make sense? Where does Congress' authority to go beyond the Court's interpretation of the Fourteenth or Fifteenth Amendments come from? If Congress can disagree with the Court's decision in *Lassiter*—and sections 4 and 5 of the Act did just that by bringing Northampton County within the list of covered jurisdictions whose literacy tests were suspended—why can't it disagree with other decisions? Moreover, is it entirely clear that congressional expansion under section 5 doesn't infringe on *other* constitutional rights or limits, like Article I, § 2's implicit conferral on the states of control over eligibility to vote; or the Tenth Amendment; or even the voting rights of individuals who *are* eligible to vote under New York's literacy requirement who now see their voting power diluted by the enfranchisement of a new class of individuals? Could Congress decide tomorrow that promoting a well-informed electorate was an important national interest and require a literacy or an understanding test like the ones required for naturalization?

The ratchet theory was rejected by the Supreme Court in *City of Boerne v. Flores*, 521 U.S. 507 (1997). There, the Court held that Congress' power under § 5 of the Fourteenth Amendment is essentially "remedial" and is thus "inconsistent with the suggestion that Congress has the power to decree the substance of the Fourteenth Amendment's restrictions on the States. . . . Congress does not enforce a constitutional right by changing what the right is. It has been given the power 'to enforce,' not the power to determine what constitutes a constitutional violation." Nonetheless, the Court reaffirmed the propriety of Congress' passage of § 4(e).

7. Originally, the Act suspended literacy tests only in "covered" jurisdictions, and only for a period of five years. In 1970, the Act was amended to ban all literacy tests nationwide. In *Oregon v. Mitchell*, 400 U.S. 112 (1970), the Supreme Court unanimously upheld the nationwide ban. Arizona challenged the ban on the grounds that its literacy test had always been administered fairly, and thus that the state was entitled to continue its use. (The case is captioned "Oregon v. Mitchell" because Oregon had challenged a different provision of the 1970 Act relating to the enfranchisement of eighteen–year–olds.) The challenge to other provisions of the Act produced a deeply fractured Court; thus, the Justices explained their views on the constitutionality of the literacy test suspension in separate opinions.

Justice Black, who had dissented in *South Carolina v. Katzenbach*, largely because he objected to Congress' singling out southern jurisdictions, upheld the nationwide ban on these terms:

> In enacting the literacy test ban . . . Congress had before it a long history of the discriminatory use of literacy tests to disfranchise voters on account of their race. . . . Moreover, Congress had before it striking evidence to show that the provisions of the 1965 Act had had in the span of four years a remarkable impact on minority group voter registration. Congress also had evidence to show that voter registration in areas with large Spanish-American populations was consistently

below the state and national averages. In Arizona, for example, only two counties out of eight with Spanish surname populations in excess of 15% showed a voter registration equal to the state-wide average. Arizona also has a serious problem of deficient voter registration among Indians. Congressional concern over the use of a literacy test to disfranchise Puerto Ricans in New York State is already a matter of record in this Court. *Katzenbach v. Morgan, supra.* And as to the Nation as a whole, Congress had before it statistics which demonstrate that voter registration and voter participation are consistently greater in States without literacy tests.

Congress also had before it this country's history of discriminatory educational opportunities in both the North and the South. The children who were denied an equivalent education by the "separate but equal" rule of *Plessy v. Ferguson*, 163 U.S. 537 (1896), overruled in *Brown v. Board of Education*, 347 U.S. 483 (1954), are now old enough to vote. There is substantial, if not overwhelming, evidence from which Congress could have concluded that it is a denial of equal protection to condition the political participation of children educated in a dual school system upon their educational achievement. Moreover, the history of this legislation suggests that concern with educational inequality was perhaps uppermost in the minds of the congressmen who sponsored the Act. The hearings are filled with references to educational inequality. Faced with this and other evidence that literacy tests reduce voter participation in a discriminatory manner not only in the South but throughout the Nation, Congress was supported by substantial evidence in concluding that a nationwide ban on literacy tests was appropriate to enforce the Civil War amendments.

Finally, there is yet another reason for upholding the literacy test provisions of this Act. In imposing a nationwide ban on literacy tests, Congress has recognized a national problem for what it is—a serious national dilemma that touches every corner of our land. In this legislation Congress has recognized that discrimination on account of color and racial origin is not confined to the South, but exists in various parts of the country. Congress has decided that the way to solve the problems of racial discrimination is to deal with nationwide discrimination with nationwide legislation.

Justice Brennan's opinion, joined by Justices White and Marshall, also focused on the denial of equal educational opportunity to minorities, as well as interstate movement:

The legislative history of the 1970 Amendments contains substantial information upon which Congress could have based a finding that the use of literacy tests in Arizona and in other States where their use was not proscribed by the 1965 Act has the effect of denying the vote to racial minorities whose illiteracy is the consequence of a previous, governmentally sponsored denial of equal educational opportunity. The

Attorney General of Arizona told the Senate Subcommittee on Constitutional Rights that many older Indians in the State were "never privileged to attend a formal school." Extensive testimony before both Houses indicated that racial minorities have long received inferior educational opportunities throughout the United States. And interstate migration of such persons, particularly of Negroes from the Southern States, has long been a matter of common knowledge.

Moreover, Congress was given testimony explicitly relating the denial of educational opportunity to inability to pass literacy tests in States not covered by the formula contained in the 1965 Act. The United States Commission on Civil Rights reported a survey of the Northern and Western States which concluded that literacy tests have a negative impact upon voter registration which "falls most heavily on blacks and persons of Spanish surname."

And Justice Stewart's opinion, joined by Chief Justice Burger and Justice Blackmun, focused on Congress' institutional competence to make the decision to ban nationwide:

Congress has now undertaken to extend the ban on literacy tests to the whole Nation. I see no constitutional impediment to its doing so. Nationwide application reduces the danger that federal intervention will be perceived as unreasonable discrimination against particular States or particular regions of the country. This in turn increases the likelihood of voluntary compliance with the letter and spirit of federal law. Nationwide application facilitates the free movement of citizens from one State to another, since it eliminates the prospect that a change in residence will mean the loss of a federally protected right. Nationwide application avoids the often difficult task of drawing a line between those States where a problem is pressing enough to warrant federal intervention and those where it is not. Such a line may well appear discriminatory to those who think themselves on the wrong side of it. Moreover the application of the line to particular States can entail a substantial burden on administrative and judicial machinery and a diversion of enforcement resources. Finally, nationwide application may be reasonably thought appropriate when Congress acts against an evil such as racial discrimination which in varying degrees manifests itself in every part of the country. A remedy for racial discrimination which applies in all the States underlines an awareness that the problem is a national one and reflects a national commitment to its solution.

Because the justification for extending the ban on literacy tests to the entire Nation need not turn on whether literacy tests unfairly discriminate against Negroes in every State in the Union, Congress was not required to make state-by-state findings concerning either the equality of educational opportunity or actual impact of literacy requirements on the Negro citizen's access to the ballot box. In the interests of uniformity, Congress may paint with a much broader brush than may this Court, which must confine itself to the judicial function of deciding individual cases and controversies upon individual records. *Cf. Lassiter v. Northampton Election Board, supra.* The findings that Congress made when it enacted the Voting Rights Act of 1965 would have supported a nationwide ban on literacy tests. Instead, at that time "Congress chose to limit its attention to the geographic areas where immediate action seemed necessary." *South Carolina v. Katzenbach,* 383 U.S., at 328. Experience gained under the 1965 Act has now led Congress to conclude that it should go the whole distance. This approach to the problem is a rational one; consequently it is within the constitutional power of Congress under § 2 of the Fifteenth Amendment.

Did *Katzenbach v. Morgan* and *Oregon v. Mitchell* essentially abandon any serious constitutional constraint on Congress's ability to regulate the right to vote? Under these decisions, when, if at all, might the Court doubt Congress' institutional competence to regulate the political process?

8.   Do recent changes in constitutional doctrine regarding congressional enforcement power cast light on the continued constitutionality of the Act? Starting with *City of Boerne v. Flores,* 521 U.S. 507 (1997), which rejected the ratchet theory of *Katzenbach v. Morgan,* the Supreme Court has suggested a more limited role for congressional power. *Boerne* involved the Religious Freedom Restoration Act of 1993 (RFRA), enacted in response to a Supreme Court decision, *Employment Division v. Smith,* 494 U.S. 872 (1990). *Smith* had rejected the respondents' claim that Oregon's denial of unemployment benefits to members of the Native American Church who had been fired for using peyote as part of a religious ceremony violated the free exercise clause.

An overwhelming bipartisan majority in Congress sought to reverse the result in *Smith* by enacting RFRA. Congress's power to enact RFRA rested on its claim to be using its Fourteenth Amendment section 5 powers to enforce the First Amendment's guarantee of free exercise of religion. (incorporated against the states through the due process clause).

The Court held RFRA unconstitutional for being beyond the scope of Congress's legitimate powers under section 5. The Court distinguished between legislation that provides remedies for acts that the Court would recognize violate the Fourteenth Amendment, and legislation that redefines the meaning of the Fourteenth Amendment. It held that the former was a valid exercise of Congress's powers under section 5 to "enforce" the Fourteenth Amendment but that the latter was invalid.

Notably, *Boerne* pointed to cases sustaining the Voting Rights Act's suspension of literacy tests as an appropriate use of congressional enforcement power, but it refrained from citing any of the post–1982 cases involving the preclearance provision of section 5. And in construing section 5 in *Reno v. Bossier Parish School Board,* 528 U.S. 320 (2000), the Court explained its narrow construction by referring to the constitutional difficulties the Act might otherwise raise.

Following *Boerne*, the Supreme Court has suggested that congressional enforcement power may be more extensive when Congress acts to protect a suspect or quasi-suspect class against discrimination, see *Nevada Dep't of Human Resources v. Hibbs*, 538 U.S. 721 (2003), or when Congress acts to safeguard a fundamental right, see *Tennessee v. Lane*, 541 U.S. 509 (2004).

In light of the line *Boerne* now recognizes between remedial and substantive uses of Congress's section 5 powers, reconsider the scope of Congress' power to legislate to protect the right to vote. Is it clear that the cases we just studied all present no more than remedial uses of Congress' powers under section 5? Are there principled grounds for distinguishing the provisions of the Voting Rights Act of 1965 from RFRA, or does the Court in *City of Boerne* simply treat these voting-rights precedents as sacrosanct, without giving persuasive grounds for doing so?

The Supreme Court has decided one post-*Boerne* case discussing in some detail the constitutionality of section 5. *Lopez v. Monterey County*, 525 U.S. 266 (1999), concerned the question of how section 5's preclearance requirements, which reached Monterey County, but did not apply to the state of California, should be applied to the county's implementation of a change in how its judges were elected that was mandated by state law. The Court held that the county was required to obtain preclearance:

> The State ... urges that requiring preclearance here would tread on rights constitutionally reserved to the States. The State contends, specifically, that § 5 could not withstand constitutional scrutiny if it were interpreted to apply to voting measures enacted by States that have not been designated as historical wrongdoers in the voting rights sphere. In the State's view, because California has not been designated as a covered jurisdiction, its laws are not subject to § 5 preclearance.
>
> We have recognized that the Act, which authorizes federal intrusion into sensitive areas of state and local policymaking, imposes substantial "federalism costs." The Act was passed pursuant to Congress' authority under the Fifteenth Amendment, however, and we have likewise acknowledged that the Reconstruction Amendments by their nature contemplate some intrusion into areas traditionally reserved to the States. As the Court recently observed with respect to Congress' power to legislate under the Fourteenth Amendment, "legislation which deters or remedies constitutional violations can fall within the sweep of Congress' enforcement power even if in the process it prohibits conduct which is not itself unconstitutional and intrudes into legislative spheres of autonomy previously reserved to the States." *City of Boerne v. Flores*, 521 U.S. 507 (1997).
>
> Moreover, we have specifically upheld the constitutionality of § 5 of the Act against a challenge that this provision usurps powers reserved

to the States. Nor does *Katzenbach* require a different result where, as here, § 5 is held to cover acts initiated by noncovered States. The Court in *Katzenbach* recognized that, once a jurisdiction has been designated, the Act may guard against both discriminatory animus and the potentially harmful effect of neutral laws in that jurisdiction. In *City of Rome [v. United States]*, we thus expressly reaffirmed that, "under the Fifteenth Amendment, Congress may prohibit voting practices that have only a discriminatory effect."

Recognizing that Congress has the constitutional authority to designate covered jurisdictions and to guard against changes that give rise to a discriminatory effect in those jurisdictions, we find no merit in the claim that Congress lacks Fifteenth Amendment authority to require federal approval before the implementation of a state law that may have just such an effect in a covered county. Section 5, as we interpret it today, burdens state law only to the extent that that law affects voting in jurisdictions properly designated for coverage. With respect to literacy tests, in fact, the Act already allows for the very action that the State claims would be unconstitutional here. At least until a 1970 amendment to the Act barring literacy tests nationwide, § 4 had been used to ban these tests in covered jurisdictions even where the tests had been enacted by a noncovered State. *See Gaston County v. United States*, 395 U.S. 285 (1969) (although State was not covered, "use of the State's literacy test within the county was ... suspended" when the county was designated a covered jurisdiction). Moreover, under § 4(b), a state-imposed literacy test may, as it did here, provide grounds for designating a county as a covered jurisdiction, notwithstanding the fact that the State as a whole is not covered.

* * *

In short, the Voting Rights Act, by its nature, intrudes on state sovereignty. The Fifteenth Amendment permits this intrusion, however, and our holding today adds nothing of constitutional moment to the burdens that the Act imposes....

Justice Thomas, in dissent, disagreed:

Section 5 is a unique requirement that exacts significant federalism costs, as we have recognized on more than one occasion. The section's interference with state sovereignty is quite drastic—covered States and political subdivisions may not give effect to their policy choices affecting voting without first obtaining the Federal Government's approval. As Justice Powell wrote in *City of Rome*, the section's "encroachment is especially troubling because it destroys local control of the means of self-government, one of the central values of our polity."

... [Thus,] we have taken great care to emphasize that Congress' enforcement power is remedial in nature. *See City of Boerne v. Flores*, 521 U.S. 507 (1997)....

There can be no remedy without a wrong....

There has been no legislative finding that the State of California has ever intentionally discriminated on the basis of race, color, or ethnicity with respect to voting. Nor has the State been found to run afoul of the Act's overbroad coverage formula. We recognized in *City of Boerne* that "preventive measures prohibiting certain types of laws may be appropriate when there is reason to believe that many of the laws affected by the congressional enactment have a significant likelihood of being unconstitutional." But I do not see any reason to think that California's laws discriminate in any way against voting or that the State's laws will be anything but constitutional. I therefore doubt that § 5 can be extended to require preclearance of the State's enactments and remain consistent with the Constitution.

Moreover, it is plain that the majority's reading of § 5 raises to new levels the federalism costs that the statute imposes. If preclearance of a State's voting law is denied when sought by a covered political subdivision, the State will be unable to develop a consistent statewide voting policy; its laws will be enforceable in noncovered subdivisions, but not in the covered subdivision....

I do not think ... that the suspension of tests and the preclearance remedy can be compared. The literacy test had a history as a "notorious means to deny and abridge voting rights on racial grounds." Literacy tests were unfairly administered; whites were given easy questions, blacks were given more difficult questions, such as "the number of bubbles in a soap bar, the news contained in a copy of the Peking Daily, the meaning of obscure passages in state constitutions, and the definition of terms such as habeas corpus." When we upheld the constitutionality of the suspension provision of the Voting Rights Act in *Katzenbach*, we indicated that the tests had actually been employed to disenfranchise black voters. Later in *Oregon v. Mitchell*, 400 U.S. 112 (1970), we upheld the national ban on the use of such tests—even though we recognized that they were not facially unconstitutional—as a proper means of preventing purposeful discrimination in the application of the tests and remedying prior constitutional violations by state and local governments in the education of minorities. Congress' suspension of tests, then, was a focused remedy directed at one particular prerequisite to voting. In contrast, the preclearance requirement presumes that a voting change—no matter how innocuous—is invalid, and prevents its enforcement until the Federal Government gives its approval....

Does *Lopez* resolve the question of section 5's continuing constitutionality? Does the fact that the Court extends section 5's coverage to acts that reflect the policy choices of uncovered entities, if those choices are ultimately implemented or enforced by covered jurisdictions, represent an expansion of the original rationale for section 5 in *South Carolina v. Katzenbach*, which focused on Congress' narrow tailoring of section 5's coverage?

9. Even if earlier versions of the Act are consistent with *City of Boerne*, does the 2006 renewal and extension, which continues the preclearance regime for an additional twenty-five years, raise constitutional difficulties?

The continued constitutionality of the section 5 raises a number of complex questions and has generated a substantial literature. For representative works, see, Richard L. Hasen, *Congressional Power to Renew the Preclearance Provisions of the Voting Rights Act After* Tennessee v. Lane, 66 Ohio St. L.J. 177, 183–88 (2005) (claiming that the Court's treatment of the preclearance regime in cases such as *City of Boerne v. Flores* is part of the "seismic shift in power from the federal government to the states" that may undermine the Act's constitutionality); Pamela S. Karlan, *Section 5 Squared: Congressional Power to Amend and Extend the Voting Rights Act*, 44 Houston L. Rev. 1 (2007) (arguing that the preclearance regime continues to satisfy the Supreme Court's construction of congressional enforcement powers under the Reconstruction Amendments and that the Court's decisions under the Elections Clause of Article I, § 4 and under the Equal Protection Clause with respect to political gerrymanders reinforce the Act's constitutionality); Pamela S. Karlan, *Two Section Twos and Two Section Fives: Voting Rights and Remedies After* Flores, 39 Wm. & Mary L. Rev. 725, 729–31 (1998) (arguing that section 5 remains constitutional under Rehnquist Court precedents); Ellen D. Katz, *Congressional Power to Extend Preclearance: A Response to Professor Karlan*, 44 Houston L. Rev. 33 (2007) (arguing that "Section 5's status as an operational statute, and not a wholly new one" is the factor most likely to support its continued constitutionality); Ellen D. Katz, *Not Like the South? Regional Variation and Political Participation Through the Lens of Section 2, in* Democracy, Participation and Power: Perspectives on Reauthorization of the Voting Rights Act (forthcoming 2007) (discussing the constitutional issues surrounding the Act); Richard H. Pildes, *The Future of Voting Rights Policy: From Anti–Discrimination to the Right to Vote* 20 (N.Y. Univ. School of Law Pub. Law & Legal Theory Research Paper Series, Working Paper No. 06–10, 2006), *available at* http://ssrn.com/abstract=900161 (commenting on constitutional questions regarding the limited geographic scope of Section 5); Daniel P. Tokaji, *Views on the 2006 Reauthorization of the Voting Rights Act: Intent and Its Alternatives: Defending the New Voting Rights Act*, 58 Ala. L. Rev. 349 (2006) (arguing that reauthorization may be upheld as an exercise of Congress's power over federal elections under the Elections Clause and that the Act might be upheld as an enforcement of the right to equal participation, rather than as a protection against intentional discrimination); Paul Winke, *Why the Preclearance and Bailout Provisions of the Voting Rights Act Are Still a Constitutionally Proportional Remedy*, 28 N.Y.U. Rev. L. & Soc. Change 69, 85–87 (2003) (noting the Justices' expressions of concern regarding section 5's constitutionality); Victor Andres Rodríguez, Comment, *Section 5 of the Voting Rights Act of 1965 After*

Boerne: *The Beginning of the End of Preclearance?*, 91 Cal. L. Rev. 769, 794–98 (2003) (identifying strands of Rehnquist Court jurisprudence that suggest difficulties with section 5).

In brief, much of the controversy centers on the question whether the special provisions continue to be justifiable more than forty years after their initial imposition. As is discussed in more depth in the discussion on race and representation, *see* Chapter 9, politics in the covered jurisdictions has changed in important ways over the ensuing two generations. For a discussion of changes within the covered jurisdictions and their implications for the continued desirability and constitutionality of section 5, see Samuel Issacharoff, *Is Section 5 of the Voting Rights Act a Victim of Its Own Success?*, 104 Colum. L. Rev. 1710 (2004).

Congress responded to the relevance of changes since the original passage of the Voting Rights Act by including the following findings in the 2006 amendments:

(1) Significant progress has been made in eliminating first generation barriers experienced by minority voters, including increased numbers of registered minority voters, minority voter turnout, and minority representation in Congress, State legislatures, and local elected offices. This progress is the direct result of the Voting Rights Act of 1965.

(2) However, vestiges of discrimination in voting continue to exist as demonstrated by second generation barriers constructed to prevent minority voters from fully participating in the electoral process.

(3) The continued evidence of racially polarized voting in each of the jurisdictions covered by the expiring provisions of the Voting Rights Act of 1965 demonstrates that racial and language minorities remain politically vulnerable, warranting the continued protection of the Voting Rights Act of 1965.

(4) Evidence of continued discrimination includes—

(A) the hundreds of objections interposed, requests for more information submitted followed by voting changes withdrawn from consideration by jurisdictions covered by the Voting Rights Act of 1965, and section 5 enforcement actions undertaken by the Department of Justice in covered jurisdictions since 1982 that prevented election practices, such as annexation, at-large voting, and the use of multi-member districts, from being enacted to dilute minority voting strength;

(B) the number of requests for declaratory judgments denied by the United States District Court for the District of Columbia;

(C) the continued filing of section 2 cases that originated in covered jurisdictions; and

(D) the litigation pursued by the Department of Justice since 1982 to enforce sections 4(e), 4(f)(4), and 203 of such Act to ensure that all language minority citizens have full access to the political process.

* * *

(7) Despite the progress made by minorities under the Voting Rights Act of 1965, the evidence before Congress reveals that 40 years has not been a sufficient amount of time to eliminate the vestiges of discrimination following nearly 100 years of disregard for the dictates of the 15th amendment and to ensure that the right of all citizens to vote is protected as guaranteed by the Constitution.

(8) Present day discrimination experienced by racial and language minority voters is contained in evidence, including the objections interposed by the Department of Justice in covered jurisdictions; the section 2 litigation filed to prevent dilutive techniques from adversely affecting minority voters; the enforcement actions filed to protect language minorities; and the tens of thousands of Federal observers dispatched to monitor polls in jurisdictions covered by the Voting Rights Act of 1965.

(9) The record compiled by Congress demonstrates that, without the continuation of the Voting Rights Act of 1965 protections, racial and language minority citizens will be deprived of the opportunity to exercise their right to vote, or will have their votes diluted, undermining the significant gains made by minorities in the last 40 years.

Fannie Lou Hamer, Rosa Parks, and Coretta Scott King Voting Rights Act Reauthorization and Amendments Act of 2006, § 2(b), Pub. L. No. 109–246, 120 Stat. 577. One question raised by the amendments is the extent to which courts must defer to such legislative findings.

The 2006 amendments to the Act retain the Act's basic structure, including its use of a coverage formula that rests on electoral turnout in the presidential elections of 1964, 1968, and 1972. Several scholars had suggested alternative formulas or processes for coverage. *See, e.g.*, Heather K. Gerken, *A Third Way for the Voting Rights Act: Section 5 and the Opt-In Approach*, 106 Colum. L. Rev. 708 (2006) (suggesting that the Act be amended to provide an "opt-in" in which community groups could invoke the preclearance process if negotiated resolution of election-law changes fails). For an extensive discussion of the decision to retain the formula, see Nathaniel Persily, *The Promises and Pitfalls of the New Voting Rights Act*, 117 Yale L.J. ___ (2007).

B. WHAT IS A "COVERED CHANGE"?

Although at first the suspension of literacy tests and the appointment of federal registrars in selected jurisdictions were the most significant aspects of the 1965 Act, once voters were registered attention turned to other electoral practices and to section 5 of the Act, which required covered jurisdictions to seek prior approval—"preclearance"—of any changes in voting practices in effect on the triggering date.

Many Southern jurisdictions responded to the explosive growth in black voter registration with a campaign of "massive resistance" akin to their attempts to evade the mandate of *Brown v. Board of Education*, 347 U.S. 483 (1954). Consider the first post-Act vote-dilution case, *Smith v. Paris*, 257 F. Supp. 901 (M.D. Ala. 1966), *modified*, 386 F.2d 979 (5th Cir. 1967). For over thirty years, elections to the Barbour County (Alabama) Democratic Executive Committee were held on a combined at-large and beat (that is, precinct) basis. Prior to the 1965 Act, only a minuscule number of blacks were registered to vote. Once federal examiners were sent to the county, however, black registration skyrocketed, and by March 1966, four beats in Barbour County had majority-black electorates. In each of these beats, black candidates filed to run. That month, the Committee "with little or no debate, without taking any minutes or making any record of its meetings or discussions, and, so far as the record reflects, with little or no discussion among the members of the community," changed the election method, requiring at-large (county-wide) elections for all positions. *Id.* at 904. The district court enjoined the new election method, finding that its purpose and effect "greatly diminish the effectiveness of the Negroes' right to vote." *Id. See also, e.g., Sims v. Baggett*, 247 F. Supp. 96 (M.D. Ala. 1965), the remedial stage of *Reynolds v. Sims*, where the district court rejected Alabama's state House reapportionment on the grounds that "the Legislature intentionally aggregated predominantly Negro counties with predominantly white counties for the sole purpose of preventing the election of Negroes to House membership." *Id.* at 109. *See generally* Frank R. Parker, Black Votes Count: Political Empowerment in Mississippi After 1965, at 34–77 (1990) (describing Mississippi legislation intended to neutralize black registration).

Section 5 of the Act provides, in pertinent part, that a jurisdiction must seek preclearance whenever it "shall enact or seek to administer any voting qualification or prerequisite to voting, or standard, practice, or procedure with respect to voting different from that in force or effect on [the date the jurisdiction became covered]."

To what extent does section 5 prevent attempts to circumvent the empowerment of minority voters? The following cases raise the question of when preclearance is required.

Allen v. State Board of Elections

393 U.S. 544 (1969).

■ Mr. Chief Justice Warren delivered the opinion of the Court.

These four cases, three from Mississippi and one from Virginia, involve the application of the Voting Rights Act of 1965 to state election laws and regulations.

* * *

In these four cases, the States have passed new laws or issued new regulations. The central issue is whether these provisions fall within the prohibition of § 5 that prevents the enforcement of "any voting qualification or prerequisite to voting, or standard, practice, or procedure with respect to voting" unless the State first complies with one of the section's approval procedures.

No. 25, *Fairley v. Patterson*, involves a 1966 amendment to § 2870 of the Mississippi Code of 1942. The amendment provides that the board of supervisors of each county may adopt an order providing that board members be elected at large by all qualified electors of the county. Prior to the 1966 amendment, all counties by law were divided into five districts; each district elected one member of the board of supervisors. After the amendment, Adams and Forrest Counties adopted the authorized orders, specifying that each candidate must run at large, but also requiring that each candidate be a resident of the county district he seeks to represent.

* * *

No. 26, *Bunton v. Patterson*, concerns a 1966 amendment to § 6271–08 of the Mississippi Code. The amendment provides that in 11 specified counties, the county superintendent of education shall be appointed by the board of education. Before the enactment of this amendment, all these counties had the option of electing or appointing the superintendent. . . .

No. 36, *Whitley v. Williams*, involves a 1966 amendment to § 3260 of the Mississippi Code, which changed the requirements for independent candidates running in general elections. The amendment makes four revisions: (1) it establishes a new rule that no person who has voted in a primary election may thereafter be placed on the ballot as an independent candidate in the general election; (2) the time for filing a petition as an independent candidate is changed to 60 days before the primary election from the previous 40 days before the general election; (3) the number of signatures of qualified electors needed for the independent qualifying petition is increased substantially; and (4) a new provision is added that each qualified elector who signs the independent qualifying petition must personally sign the petition and must include his polling precinct and county. Appellants are potential candidates whose nominating petitions for independent listing on the ballot were rejected for failure to comply with one or more of the amended provisions.

In . . . these cases, the three-judge District Court ruled that the amendments to the Mississippi Code did not come within the purview of and are not covered by § 5, and dismissed the complaints.

No. 3, *Allen v. State Board of Elections*, concerns a bulletin issued by the Virginia Board of Elections to all election judges. The bulletin was an attempt to modify the provisions of § 24–252 of the Code of Virginia of 1950 which provides, inter alia, that "any voter [may] place on the official ballot the name of any person in his own handwriting. . . ." The Virginia

Code (§ 24–251) further provides that voters with a physical incapacity may be assisted in preparing their ballots. For example, one who is blind may be aided in the preparation of his ballot by a person of his choice. Those unable to mark their ballots due to any other physical disability may be assisted by one of the election judges. However, no statutory provision is made for assistance to those who wish to write in a name, but who are unable to do so because of illiteracy. When Virginia was brought under the coverage of the Voting Rights Act of 1965, Virginia election officials apparently thought that the provision in § 24–252, requiring a voter to cast a write-in vote in the voter's own handwriting, was incompatible with the provisions of § 4(a) of the Act suspending the enforcement of any test or device as a prerequisite to voting. Therefore, the Board of Elections issued a bulletin to all election judges, instructing that the election judge could aid any qualified voter in the preparation of his ballot, if the voter so requests and if the voter is unable to mark his ballot due to illiteracy.

Appellants are functionally illiterate registered voters from the Fourth Congressional District of Virginia. . . . In the 1966 elections, appellants attempted to vote for a write-in candidate by sticking labels, printed with the name of their candidate, on the ballot. The election officials refused to count appellants' ballots, claiming that the Virginia election law did not authorize marking ballots with labels. As the election outcome would not have been changed had the disputed ballots been counted, appellants sought only prospective relief. . . . [Their complaint was also dismissed by a three-judge court.]

* * *

IV

* * *

[Section 5 applies] to "any voting qualification or prerequisite to voting, or standard, practice, or procedure with respect to voting. . . ." The Act further provides that the term "voting" "shall include all action necessary to make a vote effective in any primary, special, or general election, including, but not limited to, registration, listing . . . or other action required by law prerequisite to voting, casting a ballot, and having such ballot counted properly and included in the appropriate totals of votes cast with respect to candidates for public or party office and propositions for which votes are received in an election." § 14(c)(1). Appellees in the Mississippi cases maintain that § 5 covers only those state enactments which prescribe who may register to vote. While accepting that the Act is broad enough to insure that the votes of all citizens should be cast, appellees urge that § 5 does not cover state rules relating to the qualification of candidates or to state decisions as to which offices shall be elective....[29]

* * *

We must reject a narrow construction that appellees would give to § 5. The Voting Rights Act was aimed at the subtle, as well as the obvious, state regulations which have the effect of denying citizens their right to vote because of their race.... We are convinced that in passing the Voting Rights Act, Congress intended that state enactments such as those involved in the instant cases be subject to the § 5 approval requirements.

* * *

The weight of the legislative history and an analysis of the basic purposes of the Act indicate that the enactment in each of these cases constitutes a "voting qualification or prerequisite to voting, or standard, practice, or procedure with respect to voting" within the meaning of § 5.

No. 25 involves a change from district to at-large voting for county supervisors. The right to vote can be affected by a dilution of voting power as well as by an absolute prohibition on casting a ballot. *See Reynolds v. Sims.* Voters who are members of a racial minority might well be in the majority in one district, but in a decided minority in the county as a whole. This type of change could therefore nullify their ability to elect the candidate of their choice just as would prohibiting some of them from voting.

In No. 26 an important county officer in certain counties was made appointive instead of elective. The power of a citizen's vote is affected by this amendment; after the change, he is prohibited from electing an officer formerly subject to the approval of the voters. Such a change could be made either with or without a discriminatory purpose or effect; however, the purpose of § 5 was to submit such changes to scrutiny.

The changes in No. 36 appear aimed at increasing the difficulty for an independent candidate to gain a position on the general election ballot. These changes might also undermine the effectiveness of voters who wish to elect independent candidates. One change involved in No. 36 deserves special note. The amendment provides that no person who has voted in a primary election may thereafter be placed on the ballot as an independent candidate in the general election. This is a "procedure with respect to

---

29. Appellees in No. 3 also argue that § 5 does not apply to the regulation in their case, because that regulation was issued in an attempt to comply with the provisions of the Voting Rights Act. They argue that if § 5 applies to the Virginia regulation, covered States would be prohibited from quickly complying with the Act. We cannot accept this argument, however. A State is not exempted from the coverage of § 5 merely because its legislation is passed in an attempt to comply with the provisions of the Act. To hold otherwise would mean that legislation, allegedly passed to meet the requirements of the Act, would be exempted from § 5 coverage—even though it would have the effect of racial discrimination. It is precisely this situation Congress sought to avoid in passing § 5.

voting" with substantial impact. One must forgo his right to vote in his party primary if he thinks he might later wish to become an independent candidate.

The bulletin in No. 3 outlines new procedures for casting write-in votes. As in all these cases, we do not consider whether this change has a discriminatory purpose or effect. It is clear, however, that the new procedure with respect to voting is different from the procedure in effect when the State became subject to the Act; therefore, the enactment must meet the approval requirements of § 5 in order to be enforceable.

* * *

■ Mr. Justice Harlan, concurring in part and dissenting in part.

* * *

I

I shall first consider the Court's extremely broad construction of § 5. It is best to begin by delineating the precise area of difference between the position the majority adopts and the one which I consider represents the better view of the statute. We are in agreement that in requiring federal review of changes in any "standard, practice, or procedure with respect to voting," Congress intended to include all state laws that changed the process by which voters were registered and had their ballots counted. The Court, however, goes further to hold that a State covered by the Act must submit for federal approval all those laws that could arguably have an impact on Negro voting power, even though the manner in which the election is conducted remains unchanged. I believe that this reading of the statute should be rejected on several grounds. It ignores the place of § 5 in the larger structure of the Act; it is untrue to the statute's language; and it is unsupported by the legislative history.

A

First, and most important, the Court's construction ignores the structure of the complex regulatory scheme created by the Voting Rights Act. The Court's opinion assumes that § 5 may be considered apart from the rest of the Act. In fact, however, the provision is clearly designed to march in lock-step with § 4—the two sections cannot be understood apart from one another. Section 4 is one of the Act's central provisions, suspending the operation of all literacy tests and similar "devices" for at least five years in States whose low voter turnout indicated that these "tests" and "devices" had been used to exclude Negroes from the suffrage in the past. Section 5, moreover, reveals that it was not designed to implement new substantive policies but that it was structured to assure the effectiveness of the dramatic step that Congress had taken in § 4. The federal approval procedure found in § 5 only applies to those States whose literacy tests or similar "devices" have been suspended by § 4.

* * *

As soon as it is recognized that § 5 was designed solely to implement the policies of § 4, it becomes apparent that the Court's decision today permits the tail to wag the dog. For the Court has now construed § 5 to require a revolutionary innovation in American government that goes far beyond that which was accomplished by § 4. The fourth section of the Act had the profoundly important purpose of permitting the Negro people to gain access to the voting booths of the South once and for all. But the action taken by Congress in § 4 proceeded on the premise that once Negroes had gained free access to the ballot box, state governments would then be suitably responsive to their voice, and federal intervention would not be justified. In moving against "tests and devices" in § 4, Congress moved only against those techniques that prevented Negroes from voting at all. Congress did not attempt to restructure state governments. The Court now reads § 5, however, as vastly increasing the sphere of federal intervention beyond that contemplated by § 4, despite the fact that the two provisions were designed simply to interlock.

* * *

The difficulties with the Court's construction increase even further when the language of the statute is considered closely.... Immediately following the statute's description of the federal approval procedure, § 5 proceeds to describe the type of relief an aggrieved voter may obtain if a State enforces a new statute without obtaining the consent of the appropriate federal authorities: "no person shall be denied the right to vote for failure to comply with such qualification, prerequisite, standard, practice, or procedure." This remedy serves to delimit the meaning of the formula in question. Congress was clearly concerned with changes in procedure with which voters could comply. But a law, like that in *Fairley v. Patterson*, No. 25, which permits all members of the County Board of Supervisors to run in the entire county and not in smaller districts, does not require a voter to comply with anything at all, and so does not come within the scope of the language used by Congress....

B

While the Court's opinion does not confront the factors I have just canvassed, it does attempt to justify its holding on the basis of its understanding "of the legislative history and an analysis of the basic purposes of the Act." Turning first to consider the Act's basic purposes, the Court suggests that Congress intended to adopt the concept of voting articulated in *Reynolds v. Sims*, 377 U.S. 533 (1964), and protect Negroes against a dilution of their voting power.... [T]he fact is that Congress consciously refused to base § 5 of the Voting Rights Act on its powers under the

Fourteenth Amendment, upon which the reapportionment cases are grounded. The Act's preamble states that it is intended "to enforce the fifteenth amendment to the Constitution of the United States, and for other purposes." When Senator Fong of Hawaii suggested that the preamble include a citation to the Fourteenth Amendment as well, the Attorney General explained that he "would have quite a strong preference not to," because "I believe that S. 1564 as drafted can be squarely based on the 15th amendment."....

As the reapportionment cases rest upon the Equal Protection Clause, they cannot be cited to support the claim that Congress, in passing this Act, intended to proceed against state statutes regulating the nature of the constituencies legislators could properly represent. If Congress intended, as it clearly did, to ground § 5 on the Fifteenth Amendment, the leading voting case is not *Reynolds v. Sims*, but *Gomillion v. Lightfoot*, 364 U.S. 339 (1960). While that case establishes the proposition that redistricting done with the purpose of excluding Negroes from a municipality violates the Fifteenth Amendment, it also maintains the distinction between an attempt to exclude Negroes totally from the relevant constituency, and a statute that permits Negroes to vote but which uses the gerrymander to contain the impact of Negro suffrage.

* * *

C

Section 5, then, should properly be read to require federal approval only of those state laws that change either voter qualifications or the manner in which elections are conducted. This does not mean, however, that the District Courts in the four cases before us were right in unanimously concluding that the Voting Rights Act did not apply. Rather, it seems to me that only the judgment in *Fairley v. Patterson*, No. 25, should be affirmed, as that case involves a state statute which simply gives each county the right to elect its Board of Supervisors on an at-large basis.

In *Whitley v. Williams*, No. 36, however, Mississippi's new statute both imposes new qualifications on independent voters who wish to nominate a candidate by petition and alters the manner in which such nominations are made. Since the Voting Rights Act explicitly covers "primary" elections, *see* § 14(c)(1), the only significant question presented is whether a petitioning procedure should be considered a "primary" within the meaning of the Act. As the nominating petition is the functional equivalent of the political primary, I can perceive no good reason why it should not be included within the ambit of the Act.

The statute involved in *Bunton v. Patterson*, No. 26, raises a somewhat more difficult problem of statutory interpretation. If one looks to its impact on the voters, the State's law making the office of school superintendent appointive enacts a "voting qualification" of the most drastic kind. While under the old regime all registered voters could cast a ballot, now none are qualified. On the other hand, one can argue that the concept of a "voting qualification" presupposes that there will be a vote. On balance, I would hold that the statute comes within § 5....

Finally, Virginia has quite obviously altered the manner in which an election is conducted when for the first time it has been obliged to issue regulations concerning the way in which illiterate voters shall be processed at the polls. Consequently, I would reverse the lower court's decision in the *Allen* case, No. 3.

* * *

■ MR. JUSTICE BLACK, dissenting.

Assuming the validity of the Voting Rights Act of 1965, as the Court does, I would agree with its careful interpretation of the Act, and would further agree with its holding as to jurisdiction and with its disposition of the four cases now before us. But I am still of the opinion that ... a part of § 5 violates the United States Constitution. Section 5 provides that several Southern States cannot effectively amend either their constitutions or laws relating to voting without persuading the United States Attorney General or the United States District Court for the District of Columbia that the proposed changes in state laws do not have the purpose and will not have the effect of denying to citizens the right to vote on account of race or color. This is reminiscent of old Reconstruction days when soldiers controlled the South and when those States were compelled to make reports to military commanders of what they did. The Southern States were at that time deprived of their right to pass laws on the premise that they were not then a part of the Union and therefore could be treated with all the harshness meted out to conquered provinces. The constitutionality of that doctrine was certainly not clear at that time. And whether the doctrine was constitutional or not, I had thought that the whole Nation had long since repented of the application of this "conquered province" concept, even as to the time immediately following the bitter Civil War. I doubt that any of the 13 Colonies would have agreed to our Constitution if they had dreamed that the time might come when they would have to go to a United States Attorney General or a District of Columbia court with hat in hand begging for permission to change their laws.

* * *

NOTES AND QUESTIONS

1. In addition to deciding important questions about the scope of section 5, *Allen* also resolved a number of important procedural questions. First, it held that affected citizens had a private right of action under section 5: they could sue to enjoin voting practices or procedures that had not received preclearance. The Court recognized that these citizens could serve as "private attorneys general" to ensure compliance with section 5. Particularly in light of the Court's expansive reading of its scope, it was clear the Justice Department alone could not enforce section 5 adequately. Second, *Allen* held that private citizens could bring suit before local three-judge district courts, that is, courts in their home state, for an injunction ordering the jurisdiction seeking to use the new practice to obtain preclearance prior to implementation. (Private plaintiffs may also seek section 5 injunctions in state court. *See Hathorn v. Lovorn*, 457 U.S. 255 (1982).) By contrast, jurisdictions seeking preclearance were required to bring suit only in the United States District Court for the District of Columbia. Finally, *Allen* distinguished between the burden facing private plaintiffs in a so-called coverage lawsuit—simply to show that the defendant jurisdiction was seeking to use a new voting practice, standard, or procedure—and the burden facing plaintiff jurisdictions in so-called "preclearance" lawsuits—in which the jurisdiction was required to prove that the change has neither a discriminatory purpose nor a discriminatory effect. *See infra* section C.

2.   According to a study by the United States Commission on Civil Rights, the electoral changes from Mississippi at issue in *Allen* were only some of at least 30 bills introduced during regular and special legislative sessions in 1966, following passage of the Voting Rights Act in 1965. Twelve of these bills passed, making substantial alterations in the state's election laws. The bill at issue in *Allen* was sponsored by representatives from counties with either potential black majorities or at least one black-majority district. Abigail Thernstrom, Whose Votes Count: Affirmative Action and Minority Voting Rights 23–24 (1987). Why would white representatives from counties with potential black majorities favor at-large elections, if voting was polarized along racial lines in those counties? Would voter registration rates and turnout affect the outcome of at-large elections?

3.   What accounts for the difference between Chief Justice Warren's and Justice Harlan's approach? Notice that the Chief Justice's opinion focuses more heavily on the overall purpose of the Act while Justice Harlan concentrates on the Act's structure. Which approach do you find more persuasive? Does Justice Harlan have to stretch his own analysis to reach the result he clearly favors?

4.   Between 1965 and 1969, very few jurisdictions sought preclearance of any changes at all. Since then, the number of requests for preclearance has skyrocketed. Each year the Department receives an average of 17,000 preclearance submissions. The question remains, however, of what changes require preclearance. In *Perkins v. Matthews*, 400 U.S. 379 (1971), the Court held that changes in locations of the polling places, changes in municipal boundaries through annexations of adjacent areas which enlarged the number of eligible voters, and a change from ward to at-large election of aldermen were covered. Using the analysis from *Allen*, how would you explain the rationale? Similarly, in *Georgia v. United States*, 411 U.S. 526 (1973), the Court held that reapportionment involved a covered change. And in *Hadnott v. Amos*, 394 U.S. 358 (1969), and *NAACP v. Hampton County Election Commission*, 470 U.S. 166 (1985), the Court held that statutes relating to filing dates and special elections warranted section 5 scrutiny. Can you sketch out an account under which these types of measures would have a discriminatory purpose or effect? Are there any limits to the reach of section 5?

5. Perhaps the most expansive definition of covered changes came in the Supreme Court's decision in *Dougherty County Board of Education v. White*, 439 U.S. 32 (1978). The case involved a personnel rule promulgated by the school board ("Rule 58") that required any school board employee who became a candidate for political office to take an unpaid leave of absence, "such leave becoming effective upon the qualifying for such elective office and continuing for the duration of such political activity, and during the period of service in such office, if elected thereto." The rule was adopted under highly suggestive circumstances—less than a month after John White, a school board employee, became the first black candidate for the state legislature in roughly a century. As a result of the rule and his repeated candidacies, White lost a substantial amount of pay.

White filed suit, claiming that Rule 58 should be subject to section 5 preclearance. The Supreme Court, in an opinion by Justice Marshall, agreed. It gave "particular deference" to the Attorney General's regulations, which required preclearance of any "alteration affecting the eligibility of persons to become or remain candidates or obtain a position on the ballot in primary or general elections or to become or remain office-holders." 28 C.F.R. § 51.4(c)(4). And it rejected the board's contention that Rule 58 was simply a personnel rule:

> Rule 58 is not a neutral personnel practice governing all forms of absenteeism. Rather, it specifically addresses the electoral process, singling out candidacy for elective office as a disabling activity. Although not in form a filing fee, the Rule operates in precisely the same fashion. By imposing substantial economic disincentives on employees who wish to seek elective office, the Rule burdens entry into elective campaigns and, concomitantly, limits the choices available to Dougherty County voters.

The Court also pointed to the "circumstances surrounding [Rule 58's] adoption and its effect on the political process" as "sufficiently suggestive of the potential for discrimination to demonstrate the need for preclearance."

Justice Powell, joined in relevant part by Chief Justice Burger and Justices Rehnquist and Stewart, dissented, arguing that the Court had "torture[d] the language of the Act to conclude that this personnel regulation, having nothing to do with the conduct of elections as such, is state action 'with respect to voting.' No one is denied the right to vote; nor is anyone's exercise of the franchise impaired."

Presley v. Etowah County Commission

502 U.S. 491 (1992)

■ Justice Kennedy delivered the opinion of the Court.

In various Alabama counties voters elect members of county commissions whose principal function is to supervise and control the maintenance, repair, and construction of the county roads. *See* Ala. Code §§ 11–3–1, 11–3–10 (1975). [The case before us concerns] certain changes in the decision-making authority of the elected members on [the Etowah County Commission], and the question to be decided is whether these were changes "with respect to voting" within the meaning of § 5 of the Voting Rights Act of 1965.

* * *

I

To determine whether there have been changes with respect to voting, we must compare the challenged practices with those in existence before they were adopted. Absent relevant intervening changes, the Act requires us to use practices in existence on November 1, 1964, as our standard of comparison.

* * *

On November 1, 1964, commission members were elected at large under a "residency district" system. The entire electorate of Etowah County voted on candidates for each of the five seats. Four of the seats corresponded to the four residency districts of the county. Candidates were required to reside in the appropriate district. The fifth member, the chairman, was not subject to a district residency requirement, though residency in the county itself was a requirement.

Each of the four residency districts functioned as a road district. The commissioner residing in the district exercised control over a road shop, equipment, and road crew for that district. It was the practice of the commission to vote as a collective body on the division of funds among the road districts, but once funds were divided each commissioner exercised individual control over spending priorities within his district. The chairman was responsible for overseeing the solid waste authority, preparing the budget, and managing the courthouse building and grounds.

Under a consent decree issued in 1986, see *Dillard v. Crenshaw County*, No. 85–T–1332–N (M.D. Ala., Nov. 12, 1986), the commission is being restructured, so that after a transition period there will be a six-member commission, with each of the members elected by the voters of a different district. The changes required by the consent decree were precleared by the Attorney General. For present purposes, it suffices to say that when this litigation began the commission consisted of four holdover members who had been on the commission before the entry of the consent decree and two new members elected from new districts. Commissioner Williams, who is white, was elected from new district 6, and Commissioner Presley, who is black, was elected from new district 5. Presley is the principal appellant in the Etowah County case. His complaint relates not to the elections but to actions taken by the four holdover members when he and Williams first took office.

On August 25, 1987, the commission passed the "Road Supervision Resolution." It provided that each holdover commissioner would continue to control the workers and operations assigned to his respective road shop, which, it must be remembered, accounted for all the road shops the county had. It also gave the four holdovers joint responsibility for overseeing the repair, maintenance, and improvement of all the roads of Etowah County in order to pick up the roads in the districts where the new commissioners resided. The new commissioners, now foreclosed from exercising any authority over roads, were given other functions under the resolution. Presley was to oversee maintenance of the county courthouse and Williams the operation of the engineering department. The Road Supervision Resolution was passed by a 4–2 margin, with the two new commissioners dissenting.

The same day the Road Supervision Resolution was passed, the commission passed a second, the so-called "Common Fund Resolution." It provides in part that

> all monies earmarked and budgeted for repair, maintenance and improvement of the streets, roads and public ways of Etowah County [shall] be placed and maintained in common accounts, [shall] not be allocated, budgeted or designated for use in districts, and [shall] be used county-wide in accordance with need, for the repair, maintenance and improvement of all streets, roads and public ways in Etowah County which are under the jurisdiction of the Etowah County Commission.

This had the effect of altering the prior practice of allowing each commissioner full authority to determine how to spend the funds allocated to his own district. The Etowah County Commission did not seek judicial or administrative preclearance of either the Road Supervision Resolution or the Common Fund Resolution. The District Court held that the Road Supervision Resolution was subject to preclearance but that the Common Fund Resolution was not. No appeal was taken from the first ruling, so only the Common Fund Resolution is before us in the Etowah County case.

* * *

II

* * *

The principle that § 5 covers voting changes over a wide range is well illustrated by the separate cases we considered in the single opinion for the

Court in *Allen. Allen* involved four cases. The eponymous *Allen v. State Board of Elections* concerned a change in the procedures for the casting of write-in ballots. In *Whitley v. Williams*, there were changes in the requirements for independent candidates running in general elections. The challenged procedure in *Fairley v. Patterson* resulted in a change from single-district voting to at-large voting. The remaining case, *Bunton v. Patterson*, involved a statute which provided that officials who in previous years had been elected would be appointed. We held that the changes in each of the four cases were covered by § 5.

Our cases since *Allen* reveal a consistent requirement that changes subject to § 5 pertain only to voting. Without implying that the four typologies exhaust the statute's coverage, we can say these later cases fall within one of the four factual contexts presented in the *Allen* cases.

* * *

The first three categories involve changes in election procedures, while all the examples within the fourth category might be termed substantive changes as to which offices are elective. But whether the changes are of procedure or substance, each has a direct relation to voting and the election process.

III

A comparison of the changes at issue here with those in our prior decisions demonstrates that the present cas[e] do[es] not involve changes covered by the Act.

* * *

The Etowah County Commission's Common Fund Resolution is not a change within any of the categories recognized in *Allen* or our later cases. It has no connection to voting procedures: It does not affect the manner of holding elections, it alters or imposes no candidacy qualifications or requirements, and it leaves undisturbed the composition of the electorate. It also has no bearing on the substance of voting power, for it does not increase or diminish the number of officials for whom the electorate may vote. Rather, the Common Fund Resolution concerns the internal operations of an elected body.

* * *

Were we to accept the appellants' proffered reading of § 5, we would work an unconstrained expansion of its coverage. Innumerable state and local enactments having nothing to do with voting affect the power of elected officials. When a state or local body adopts a new governmental program or modifies an existing one it will often be the case that it changes the powers of elected officials. So too, when a state or local body alters its internal operating procedures, for example by modifying its subcommittee assignment system, it "implicates an elected official's decisionmaking authority."

Appellants and the United States fail to provide a workable standard for distinguishing between changes in rules governing voting and changes in the routine organization and functioning of government. Some standard is necessary, for in a real sense every decision taken by government implicates voting. This is but the felicitous consequence of democracy, in which power derives from the people. Yet no one would contend that when Congress enacted the Voting Rights Act it meant to subject all or even most decisions of government in covered jurisdictions to federal supervision. Rather, the Act by its terms covers any "voting qualification or prerequisite to voting, or standard, practice, or procedure with respect to voting." 42 U.S.C. § 1973c. A faithful effort to implement the design of the statute must begin by drawing lines between those governmental decisions that involve voting and those that do not.

A simple example shows the inadequacy of the line proffered by the appellants and the United States. Under the appellants' view, every time a covered jurisdiction passed a budget that differed from the previous year's budget it would be required to obtain preclearance. The amount of funds available to an elected official has a profound effect on the power exercised. A vote for an ill-funded official is less valuable than 'a vote for a well-funded one.

* * *

Under the view advanced by appellants and the United States, every time a state legislature acts to diminish or increase the power of local officials, preclearance would be required. Governmental action decreasing the power of local officials could carry with it a potential for discrimination against those who represent racial minorities at the local level. At the same time, increasing the power of local officials will entail a relative decrease in the power of state officials, and that too could carry with it a potential for discrimination against state officials who represent racial minorities at the state level. The all but limitless minor changes in the allocation of power among officials and the constant adjustments required for the efficient governance of every covered State illustrate the necessity for us to formulate workable rules to confine the coverage of § 5 to its legitimate sphere: voting.

Changes which affect only the distribution of power among officials are not subject to § 5 because such changes have no direct relation to, or impact on, voting. The Etowah County Commission's Common Fund Resolution was not subject to the preclearance requirement.

* * *

V

Nothing we say implies that the conduct at issue . . . is not actionable under a different remedial scheme. The Voting Rights Act is not an all-purpose antidiscrimination statute. The fact that the intrusive mechanisms of the Act do not apply to other forms of pernicious discrimination does not undermine its utility in combating the specific evils it was designed to address.

Our prior cases hold, and we reaffirm today, that every change in rules governing voting must be precleared. The legislative history we rehearsed in *South Carolina v. Katzenbach* was cited to demonstrate Congress' concern for the protection of voting rights. Neither the appellants nor the United States has pointed to anything we said there or in the statutes reenacting the Voting Rights Act to suggest that Congress meant other than what it said when it made § 5 applicable to changes "with respect to voting" rather than, say, changes "with respect to governance."

If federalism is to operate as a practical system of governance and not a mere poetic ideal, the States must be allowed both predictability and efficiency in structuring their governments. Constant minor adjustments in the allocation of power among state and local officials serve this elemental purpose.

* * *

NOTES AND QUESTIONS

1.   What accounts for the difference in result between *Dougherty County* and *Presley*? Is it simply a change in the Court's membership (note that three of the four Justices who were on the Court for both cases—Justices White, Blackmun, and Stevens—dissented in *Presley*), a change in the Court's attitude due to the passage of time, or something else?

2.   To what extent should evidence about the context in which a challenged provision is adopted inform the question whether it affects "voting"? Justice Marshall's opinion in *Dougherty County* seems to weigh these circumstances quite heavily while Justice Kennedy's opinion in *Presley* essentially disregards them. In dissent in *Presley*, Justice Stevens recognized the potential line-drawing problem identified by the majority but responded that "this is a case in which a few pages of history are far more illuminating than volumes of logic and hours of speculation about hypothetical line-drawing problems," and concluded that "[a]t the very least, I would hold that the reallocation of decisionmaking authority of an elective office that is taken (1) after the victory of a black candidate, and (2) after the entry of a consent decree designed to give black voters an opportunity to have representation on an elective body, is covered by § 5." On remand, this perspective prevailed: the district court concluded that the Commission's actions violated the 1986 consent decree. *See Presley v. Etowah County Commission*, 869 F. Supp. 1555 (M.D. Ala. 1994).

If context is considered, does this transform section 5 coverage litigation into a full-blown consideration of actual racial discrimination rather than simply an inquiry into whether, under some circumstances, a rule might be discriminatory?

3. The reliance on context poses another question: does the Court's decision in *Dougherty County* mean that *all* similar personnel rules—even if not adopted in similarly suspicious circumstances—require preclearance? One district court has held that "[w]hether a specific change made by a covered political jurisdiction constitutes a change in a 'voting qualification or prerequisite to voting, or standard, or practice, or procedure with respect to voting' that is subject to the preclearance requirement of Section 5 turns on whether such a change has the 'potential for discrimination' against black persons" in light of the facts presented by the plaintiffs in the case before it. *Greene County Racing Commission v. City of Birmingham*, 772 F. Supp. 1207, 1212 (N.D. Ala.1991) (three-judge court), *vacated and remanded sub nom. Harris v. City of Birmingham*, 505 U.S. 1201 (1992). Under this approach, for example, a personnel change in an all-white municipality would not require preclearance. Is that conclusion correct? Can any procedural rule, such as preclearance, function mechanically if it sometimes requires a substantive determination, such as the existence of a "potential for discrimination," to decide whether the procedural rule should apply?

Ultimately, this issue comes down to *who* should decide, and with what level of certainty, whether there is a potential for discrimination. Arguably, requiring plaintiffs in section 5 coverage cases to present facts regarding electoral circumstances in specific jurisdictions asks the local district court to do precisely what was forbidden by Congress—that is, to determine whether a change was actually discriminatory. The "potential for discrimination" inquiry may be simply a way of determining, with regard to a previously unaddressed type of statute, whether the change is a change "with respect to voting" (as opposed to a change affecting only things other than voting). *See, e.g., NAACP v. Hampton County Election Commission*, 470 U.S. 166 (1985) (declining to decide whether the change in the particular election date at issue was plausibly discriminatory because preclearance had been required of previous changes in election dates in other jurisdictions).

4. Note the *Dougherty County* Court's deference to the Department of Justice's interpretation of the scope of section 5. The current version of the Department's section 5 regulations, 28 C.F.R. § 51.13 (2006), provides the following examples of changes affecting voting:

(a) Any change in qualifications or eligibility for voting.

(b) Any change concerning registration, balloting, and the counting of votes and any change concerning publicity for or assistance in registration or voting.

(c) Any change with respect to the use of a language other than English in any aspect of the electoral process.

(d) Any change in the boundaries of voting precincts or in the location of polling places.

(e) Any change in the constituency of an official or the boundaries of a voting unit (e.g., through redistricting, annexation, deannexation, incorporation, reapportionment, changing to at-large elections from district elections, or changing to district elections from at-large elections).

(f) Any change in the method of determining the outcome of an election (e.g., by requiring a majority vote for election or the use of a designated post or place system).

(g) Any change affecting the eligibility of persons to become or remain candidates, to obtain a position on the ballot in primary or general elections, or to become or remain holders of elective offices.

(h) Any change in the eligibility and qualification procedures for independent candidates.

(i) Any change in the term of an elective office or an elected official or in the offices that are elective (e.g., by shortening the term of an office, changing from election to appointment or staggering the terms of offices).

(j) Any change affecting the necessity of or methods for offering issues and propositions for approval by referendum.

(k) Any change affecting the right or ability of persons to participate in political campaigns which is effected by a jurisdiction subject to the requirement of section 5.

5. In most cases, it will be clear whether a challenged practice involves a change: if it differs from the practices in effect on the triggering date for the jurisdiction's coverage, preclearance is required. Under some circumstances, however, the inquiry is slightly more complicated. In *Perkins v. Matthews*, 400 U.S. 379 (1971), for example, the plaintiffs sought an injunction against Canton, Mississippi's adoption of at-large elections. The change to at-large elections was mandated by a Mississippi statute enacted in 1962, which normally would have meant that at-large elections would have been the practice in effect on November 1, 1964, and their continued use would thus not require preclearance. But Canton ignored the statute in conducting its 1965 municipal elections and, as in 1961, elected aldermen by wards. The city argued that because it had no choice but to comply with the 1962 statute in the 1969 elections, it should not be enjoined from obeying the 1962 requirement. The Supreme Court disagreed, and ordered the city to seek preclearance:

> In our view, § 5's reference to the procedure "in force or effect on November 1, 1964," must be taken to mean the procedure that would

have been followed if the election had been held on that date. That judgment is necessarily a matter of inference in this case since Canton did not hold a municipal election on November 1, 1964. But in drawing that inference, there is little reason to blind ourselves to relevant evidence in the record by restricting our gaze to events that occurred before that date. Ordinarily we presume that officials will act in accordance with law. If the only available facts showed that Canton conducted its 1961 election by wards but that the Mississippi Legislature had subsequently enacted a statute in 1962 requiring future municipal elections to be held at large, Canton officials would be entitled to the weight of that presumption.

With the benefit of hindsight, however, we know that Canton elected its aldermen by wards in its June 1965 municipal election. The record reflects no relevant change between November 1964 and June 1965 to suggest that a different procedure would have been in effect if the elections had been held seven months earlier. Consequently, we conclude that the procedure in fact "in force or effect" in Canton on November 1, 1964, was to elect aldermen by wards. That sufficed to bring the 1969 change within § 5. . . . The bearing of the 1962 statute upon the change was for the Attorney General or the District Court for the District of Columbia to decide [in the course of deciding whether to grant preclearance.]

In *McCain v. Lybrand*, 465 U.S. 236, 256 (1984), the Court clarified that "[w]hen a jurisdiction adopts legislation that makes clearly defined changes in its election practices, sending that legislation to the Attorney General merely with a general request for preclearance pursuant to § 5 constitutes a submission of the changes made by the enactment and cannot be deemed a submission of changes made by previous legislation which themselves were independently subject to § 5 preclearance." Thus, in *Clark v. Roemer*, 500 U.S. 646 (1991), the Court reversed the district court's conclusion that preclearance of Louisiana's most recent round of additional judgeships within various at-large judicial electoral districts retroactively operated to preclear earlier increases in the number of positions on the grounds that "when an act provides for a certain number of judicial positions, approval of that act must include all of the judicial positions necessary to reach that number." Instead, those earlier judgeships required preclearance as well.

6. What does it mean to say that a *covered jurisdiction* is seeking to implement a change? *Connor v. Johnson*, 402 U.S. 690, 691 (1971), held that "[a] decree of the United States District Court is not within reach of Section 5 of the Voting Rights Act." The Court elaborated on this conclusion in *Lopez v. Monterey County*, 525 U.S. 266, 286–87 (1999): "[T]he exception grows largely from separation-of-powers concerns arising where a voting measure is the product of a federal court, specifically." Quoting from Justice Black's dissent in *Connor*, the Court continued that "[u]nder our constitutional system it would be strange indeed to construe § 5 . . . to require that actions of a federal court be stayed and reviewed by the Attorney General or the United States District Court for the District of Columbia."

But what happens when a federal judicial decree embodies a change proposed by a covered jurisdiction? In *McDaniel v. Sanchez*, 452 U.S. 130 (1981), the Supreme Court held that section 5 applies to a federal court's adoption of a reapportionment plan submitted by a legislative body as a proposed remedy for a judicial determination that the prior plan was unconstitutional.

> The preclearance procedure is designed to forestall the danger that local decisions to modify voting practices will impair minority access to the electoral process. The federal interest in preventing local jurisdictions from making changes that adversely affect the rights of minority voters is the same whether a change is required to remedy a constitutional violation or is merely the product of a community's perception of the desirability of responding to new social patterns.

> * * *

> [I]f covered jurisdictions could avoid the normal preclearance procedure by awaiting litigation challenging a refusal to redistrict after a census is completed, the statute might have the unintended effect of actually encouraging delay in making obviously needed changes in district boundaries. The federal interest in evenhanded review of all changes in covered jurisdictions is furthered by the application of the statute in cases such as this.

> * * *

> As we construe the congressional mandate, it requires that whenever a covered jurisdiction submits a proposal reflecting the policy choices of the elected representatives of the people—no matter what constraints have limited the choices available to them—the preclearance requirement of the Voting Rights Act is applicable.

And in *Branch v. Smith*, 538 U.S. 254 (2003), the Supreme Court confirmed that plans mandated by a *state* court in a covered jurisdiction require preclearance regardless of whether the plans also reflect a legislative choice.

McDaniel and related cases raise the question whether a federal court should defer to a jurisdiction's remedial choices as reflecting the will of the people even when the proposal flouts either procedural or substantive state law that normally would preclude such a choice. Isn't preclearance especially warranted as to remedial proposals since "the vindication of voting rights can hardly be trusted to the very representatives whose election is the result of the alleged vote dilution"? Samuel Issacharoff, Note, *Making the Violation Fit the Remedy: Intent and Equal Protection Law*, 92 Yale L.J. 328, 346 (1982).

C.   WHAT CONSTITUTES A DISCRIMINATORY PURPOSE OR EFFECT?

Assuming that preclearance is required because a jurisdiction has made a change with respect to voting, when ought preclearance to be denied? The vast majority of all preclearance decisions are made administratively within the Department of Justice. The standards the Department applies are supposed to mirror those that would be applied if the jurisdiction sought preclearance through a declaratory judgment action in the United States District Court for the District of Columbia. 28 C.F.R. § 51.52 (2006). Moreover, since the Department explains its position largely through relatively pro forma preclearance and objection letters to submitting jurisdictions, *see, e.g.*, Howard Ball, Dale Krane & Thomas Lauth, Compromised Compliance: Implementation of the 1965 Voting Rights Act 258 (1982) (providing an example of an objection letter); Hiroshi Motamura, *Preclearance Under Section 5 of the Voting Rights Act*, 61 N.C.L. Rev. 191, 192 (1983), the most general articulation of standards appears in the relatively sparse case law.

We start with the definition of discriminatory "effect," rather than discriminatory "purpose" both because the case law developed chronologically in that order and because the definition of "purpose" in section 5 may depend in some cases on the statute-specific notion of "effect."

1.   DISCRIMINATORY "EFFECT" AND THE CONCEPT OF RETROGRESSION

Beer v. United States
425 U.S. 130 (1976).

■ MR. JUSTICE STEWART delivered the opinion of the Court.

* * *

I

New Orleans is a city of almost 600,000 people. Some 55% of that population is white and the remaining 45% is Negro. Some 65% of the registered voters are white, and the remaining 35% are Negro [due both to differences in registration rates and to the different age profiles of the two groups.] In 1954, New Orleans adopted a mayor-council form of government. Since that time the municipal charter has provided that the city council is to consist of seven members, one to be elected from each of five councilmanic districts, and two to be elected by the voters of the city at large. The 1954 charter also requires an adjustment of the boundaries of the five single-member councilmanic districts following each decennial census to reflect population shifts among the districts.

In 1961, the city council redistricted the city based on the 1960 census figures. That reapportionment plan established four districts that stretched from the edge of Lake Pontchartrain on the north side of the city to the Mississippi River on the city's south side. The fifth district was wedge shaped and encompassed the city's downtown area. In one of these councilmanic districts, Negroes constituted a majority of the population, but only about half of the registered voters. In the other four districts white voters clearly outnumbered Negro voters. No Negro was elected to the New Orleans City Council during the decade from 1960 to 1970.

After receipt of the 1970 census figures the city council adopted a reapportionment plan (Plan I) that continued the basic north-to-south pattern of councilmanic districts combined with a wedge-shaped, downtown district. Under Plan I Negroes constituted a majority of the population in two districts, but they did not make up a majority of registered voters in any district. The largest percentage of Negro voters in a single district under Plan I was 45.2%. When the city submitted Plan I to the Attorney General pursuant to § 5, he objected to it, stating that it appeared to "dilute black voting strength by combining a number of black voters with a larger number of white voters in each of the five districts." He also expressed the view that "the district lines [were not] drawn as they [were] because of any compelling governmental need" and that the district lines did "not reflect numeric population configurations or considerations of district compactness or regularity of shape."

Even before the Attorney General objected to Plan I, the city authorities had commenced work on a second plan—Plan II. That plan followed the general north-to-south districting pattern common to the 1961 apportionment and Plan I. It produced Negro population majorities in two districts and a Negro voter majority (52.6%) in one district. When Plan II was submitted to the Attorney General, he posed the same objections to it that he had raised to Plan I. In addition, he noted that "the predominantly black neighborhoods in the city are located generally in an east to west progression," and pointed out that the use of north-to-south districts in such a situation almost inevitably would have the effect of diluting the maximum potential impact of the Negro vote. Following the rejection by the Attorney General of Plan II, the city brought this declaratory judgment action in the United States District Court for the District of Columbia.

The District Court concluded that Plan II would have the effect of abridging the right to vote on account of race or color. [It did not reach the question of discriminatory purpose.] It calculated that if Negroes could elect city councilmen in proportion to their share of the city's registered voters, they would be able to choose 2.42 of the city's seven councilmen, and, if in proportion to their share of the city's population, to choose 3.15 councilmen. But under Plan II the District Court concluded that, since New Orleans' elections had been marked by bloc voting along racial lines, Negroes would probably be able to elect only one councilman—the candidate from the one councilmanic district in which a majority of the voters were Negroes.

As a separate and independent ground for rejecting Plan II, the District Court held that the failure of the plan to alter the city charter provision establishing two at-large seats had the effect in itself of "abridging the right to vote . . . on account of race or color." As the court put it: "[T]he City has not supported the choice of at-large elections by any consideration which would satisfy the standard of compelling governmental interest, or the need to demonstrate the improbability of its realization through the use of single-member districts. These evaluations compel the conclusion that the feature of the city's electoral scheme by which two councilmen are selected at large has the effect of impermissibly minimizing the vote of its black citizens; and the further conclusion that for this additional reason the city's redistricting plan does not pass muster."

The District Court therefore refused to allow Plan II to go into effect. As a result there have been no councilmanic elections in New Orleans since 1970, and the councilmen elected at that time (or their appointed successors) have remained in office ever since.

II

A

The appellants urge, and the United States on reargument of this case has conceded, that the District Court was mistaken in holding that Plan II could be rejected under § 5 solely because it did not eliminate the two at-large councilmanic seats that had existed since 1954. The appellants and the United States are correct in their interpretation of the statute in this regard.

The language of § 5 clearly provides that it applies only to proposed changes in voting procedures. "[D]iscriminatory practices . . . instituted prior to November 1964 . . . are not subject to the requirement of preclearance [under § 5]." . . .

B

* * *

By prohibiting the enforcement of a voting-procedure change until it has been demonstrated to the United States Department of Justice or to a three-judge federal court that the change does not have a discriminatory effect, Congress desired to prevent States from "undo[ing] or defeat[ing] the rights recently won" by Negroes. Section 5 was intended "to insure that [the gains thus far achieved in minority political participation] shall not be destroyed through new [discriminatory] procedures and techniques." . . . . In other words the purpose of § 5 has always been to insure that no voting-procedure changes would be made that would lead to a retrogression in the position of racial minorities with respect to their effective exercise of the electoral franchise.

It is thus apparent that a legislative reapportionment that enhances the position of racial minorities with respect to their effective exercise of the electoral franchise can hardly have the "effect" of diluting or abridging the right to vote on account of race within the meaning of § 5. We conclude, therefore, that such an ameliorative new legislative apportionment cannot violate § 5 unless the new apportionment itself so discriminates on the basis of race or color as to violate the Constitution.

The application of this standard to the facts of the present case is straightforward. Under the apportionment of 1961 none of the five councilmanic districts had a clear Negro majority of registered voters, and no Negro has been elected to the New Orleans City Council while that apportionment system has been in effect. Under Plan II, by contrast, Negroes will constitute a majority of the population in two of the five districts and a clear majority of the registered voters in one of them. Thus, there is every reason to predict, upon the District Court's hypothesis of bloc voting, that at least one and perhaps two Negroes may well be elected to the council under Plan II. It was therefore error for the District Court to conclude that Plan II "will ... have the effect of denying or abridging the right to vote on account of race or color" within the meaning of § 5 of the Voting Rights Act.

* * *

NOTES AND QUESTIONS

1. The majority's opinion rests on a statutory reading that looks at whether the *change*, as opposed to the standard, practice, or procedure itself, has a discriminatory purpose or effect. Is that reading compelled by the statute itself? What are the arguments in favor of or against such a reading?

2. Note the consequences of drawn-out section 5 litigation: since the city could not implement an unprecleared plan, existing council members remained in office for six years while the case worked its way through the courts. This situation is not atypical. One person, one vote, combined with population shifts, surely rendered the pre-existing districts unconstitutional.

3. What do "retrogressive" and "ameliorative" mean? Consider the following questions posed by Justice Marshall in his dissent. What facts would a reviewing court, or the Department of Justice, need to know in order to resolve the question of preclearance? To what extent would resolution depend on questions of political philosophy rather than of fact?

> [T]he Court today finds that an increase in the size of the Negro majority in one district, with a concomitant increased likelihood of

electing a delegate, conclusively shows that Plan II is ameliorative. Will that always be so? Is it not as common for minorities to be gerrymandered into the same district as into separate ones? Is an increase in the size of an existing majority ameliorative or retrogressive? When the size of the majority increases in one district, Negro voting strength necessarily declines elsewhere. Is that decline retrogressive? Assuming that the shift from a 50.2% to a 52.6% majority in District B in this case is ameliorative, and is not outweighed by the simultaneous decrease in Negro voting strength in Districts A and C, when would an increase become retrogressive? As soon as the majority becomes "safe"? When the majority is achieved by dividing pre-existing concentrations of Negro voters?

Moreover, the Court implies . . . that this preliminary inquiry into the nature of the change is the proper approach to all § 5 cases. The Court's test will prove even more difficult of application outside the redistricting context. Some changes just do not lend themselves to comparison in positive or negative terms; others will always seem negative—or positive—no matter how good or bad the result. For instance, when a city goes from an appointed town manager to an elected council form of government, can the change ever be termed retrogressive, even if the new council is elected at large and Negroes are a minority? Or where a jurisdiction in which Negroes are a substantial minority switches from at-large to ward voting, can that change ever constitute a negative change, no matter how badly the wards are gerrymandered?

These observations are even more pressing in light of the Supreme Court's recent decision in *Georgia v. Ashcroft*, 539 U.S. 461 (2003). (The case appears as a principal case in Chapter 9, and is discussed more fully there.) In that case, the state legislature drew a new apportionment plan for the state senate that decreased the concentration of black voters in several districts in order to increase the number of seats controlled by Democrats. Supporters of the plan testified that this would increase the legislative influence of representatives elected from the majority-black districts, since it would enable them to hold powerful committee chairmanships. The Supreme Court held that the three-judge district court had applied the wrong legal standard in holding that the plan had a retrogressive effect:

> In assessing the totality of the circumstances, a court should not focus solely on the comparative ability of a minority group to elect a candidate of its choice. While this factor is an important one in the § 5 retrogression inquiry, it cannot be dispositive or exclusive.

* * *

> The State may choose, consistent with § 5, that it is better to risk having fewer minority representatives in order to achieve greater overall representation of a minority group by increasing the number of representatives sympathetic to the interests of minority voters.

In addition to influence districts, one other method of assessing the minority group's opportunity to participate in the political process is to examine the comparative position of legislative leadership, influence, and power for representatives of the benchmark majority-minority districts. A legislator, no less than a voter, is "not immune from the obligation to pull, haul, and trade to find common political ground." Indeed, in a representative democracy, the very purpose of voting is to delegate to chosen representatives the power to make and pass laws. The ability to exert more control over that process is at the core of exercising political power. A lawmaker with more legislative influence has more potential to set the agenda, to participate in closed-door meetings, to negotiate from a stronger position, and to shake hands on a deal. Maintaining or increasing legislative positions of power for minority voters' representatives of choice, while not dispositive by itself, can show the lack of retrogressive effect under § 5.

Scholars have described the approach in *Georgia v. Ashcroft* as far closer to the totality-of-the-circumstances analysis applied in section 2 vote-dilution cases than the conventional and relatively mechanical retrogression inquiry. *See* Samuel Issacharoff, *Is Section 5 of the Voting Rights Act a Victim of its Own Success?*, 104 Colum. L. Rev. 1710, 1719–20 (2004) (asking "whether anything like the totality-of-the-circumstances test was feasible in the statutory sixty days for review," suggesting that "the key challenge is whether such multifactored inquiries defy 'reviewable administration,'" and concluding that the Court "does not satisfactorily come to terms with this challenge"); Michael J. Pitts, *Georgia v. Ashcroft: It's the End of Section 5 As We Know It (And I Feel Fine)*, 32 Pepp. L. Rev. 265 (2005). Consider the extent to which the administrative process is suited for this more wide-ranging inquiry.

Is there a tension between the Court's decision and its earlier decision in *Presley v. Etowah County Commission*, 502 U.S. 491 (1992) (earlier in this Chapter)? There, the Court had held that changes "which affect only the distribution of power among officials are not subject to § 5 because such changes have no direct relation to, or impact on, voting." Although "in a real sense every decision taken by government implicates voting," the Court declared that "[a] faithful effort to implement the design of [section 5] must begin by drawing lines between those governmental decisions that involve voting and those that do not." Given *Presley*, a state legislature's decision to strip a representative from a majority-black district of her committee chairmanship would not be subject to section 5 review. But if decreasing or diminishing "legislative positions of power for minority voters' representatives of choice," cannot show the presence of retrogression in minority voters' "effective exercise of the electoral franchise," is there an inconsistency in treating the state's decision to maintain individual legislator's power as evidence of minority voting power? *See* Pamela S. Karlan, Georgia v. Ashcroft *and the Retrogression of Retrogression*, 3 Election L.J. (2004) (contrasting the two cases). In the Texas mid-decade redistricting discussed in Chapters 9 and 10, the career staff at the Department of Justice recommended an objection to the plan on the grounds that, although it preserved the number of minority districts, it resulted in retrogression under the more fluid *Georgia v. Ashcroft* standard. *See* Memorandum from the U.S. Dept. of Justice 71–72 (Dec. 12, 2003), *available at* http://www.washingtonpost.com/wp-srv/nation/documents/ texasDOJmemo.pdf (recommending that the Attorney General object to the Texas redistricting plan because it resulted in a retrogression in light of *Georgia v. Ashcroft*); *cf.* Recent Case, *Election Law—Voting Rights Act—District Court Holds that Section 2 Vote Dilution Claim Does Not Extend to the Protection of Influence Districts*—Session v. Perry, *298 F. Supp. 2d 451 (E.D. Tex. 2004)*, 117 Harv. L. Rev. 2433–35 (2004) (discussing the Texas plan).

In response to *Georgia v. Ashcroft*, Congress amended section 5 to add two new subsections to section 5. *See* Fannie Lou Hamer, Rosa Parks, and Coretta Scott King Voting Rights Act Reauthorization and Amendments Act of 2006, § 5, Pub. L. No. 109–246, 120 Stat. 577:

Section 5 of the Voting Rights Act of 1965 is amended—

* * *

(3) by adding at the end the following:

"(b) Any voting qualification or prerequisite to voting, or standard, practice, or procedure with respect to voting that has the purpose of or will have the effect of diminishing the ability of any citizens of the United States on account of race or color, or in contravention of the guarantees set forth in section 4(f)(2), to elect their preferred candidates of choice denies or abridges the right to vote within the meaning of subsection (a) of this section.

* * *

"(d) The purpose of subsection (b) of this section is to protect the ability of such citizens to elect their preferred candidates of choice.".

Do these amendments adequately clarify the relevant factors to be considered in performing a preclearance analysis? Under this test, how are reviewing authorities to determine whether the tradeoffs described by the Supreme Court are retrogressive? For an extensive discussion of the legislative history behind the *"Georgia v. Ashcroft* fix," see Nathaniel Persily, *The Promises and Pitfalls of the New Voting Rights Act*, 117 Yale L.J. ___ (2007).

2.   DISCRIMINATORY PURPOSE

Section 5 forbids covered jurisdictions from implementing voting changes unless they can show that the change has neither a discriminatory purpose nor a discriminatory effect. Just as the Court adopted a distinctive definition of discriminatory "effect" in section 5 cases, it also adopted a distinctive definition of discriminatory purpose—a definition subsequently rejected by Congress.

The Court first confronted the question of discriminatory purpose in a peculiarly tricky context—Richmond, Virginia's annexation of adjacent suburban territory. *City of Richmond v. United States*, 422 U.S. 358 (1975). An annexation of populated territory will always reduce the voting strength of members of the pre-annexation community. Moreover, unless the annexed territory has the same racial composition as the pre-annexation community, it will always alter the relative voting strength of racially identifiable groups. At the same time, although annexations have undeniable consequences for voting, they are often undertaken for reasons independent of those consequences.

In May 1969, Richmond annexed approximately 23 square miles of land adjacent to the city in Chesterfield County. Before the annexation, the city was 52 percent black; afterwards, the city was only 42 percent black. Richmond was governed by a nine-member city council, elected at large. In response to pressure from the Attorney General during the preclearance process, the city developed and submitted to the Attorney General a series of plans for establishing district-based elections. Ultimately, the city and the Attorney General settled on a nine ward proposal under which four of the wards would have substantial black majorities, four wards substantial white majorities, and the ninth a racial division of approximately 59 percent white and 41 percent black. The city and the Attorney General submitted this plan to the District Court for the District of Columbia in the form of a consent judgment in the pending lawsuit seeking judicial preclearance.

The district court, however, rejected the plan because it found that the annexation had had an invidious racial purpose—it was intended to prevent blacks from taking over control of the city. Furthermore, the ward system did not minimize the dilution of black voting power to the greatest possible extent, since it would easily have been possible to draw a plan with effective black voting majorities in five out of the nine wards.

In an opinion written by Justice White, the Supreme Court reversed the district court's rejection of the districting plan and remanded for further proceedings. With respect to the question of retrogressive effect, the Court held that as long as the plan "afford[ed black voters] representation reasonably equivalent to their political strength in the enlarged community," it would satisfy section 5.

With respect to the question of how preclearance authorities ought to treat questions of discriminatory purpose, as opposed to questions of effect, the Court's opinion took the following position:

> Accepting the findings . . . that the annexation, as it went forward in 1969, was infected by the impermissible purpose of denying the right to vote based on race through perpetuating white majority power to

> exclude Negroes from office through at-large elections, we are never-theless persuaded that if verifiable reasons are now demonstrable in support of the annexation, and the ward plan proposed is fairly designed, the city need do no more to satisfy the requirements of § 5.

Is this position defensible, particularly in light of *Beer*'s focus on the change itself? Is it consistent with the general constitutional law principle that strikes down acts taken with a discriminatory purpose? What if the city had mixed motives?

Consider the district court's account of the purpose behind the Richmond annexation:

> Richmond's focus in the negotiations was upon the number of new white voters it could obtain by annexation; it expressed no interest in economic or geographic considerations such as tax revenues, vacant land, utilities, or schools. The mayor required assurances from Chesterfield County officials that at least 44,000 additional white citizens would be obtained by the City before he would agree upon [the terms of the annexation].... And the mayor and one of the city councilmen conditioned final acceptance of the settlement agreement on the annexation going into effect in sufficient time to make citizens in the annexed area eligible to vote in the City Council elections of 1970.

If there is no discriminatory effect to an annexation, can a discriminatory purpose nonetheless taint the annexation? *See City of Pleasant Grove v. United States*, 479 U.S. 462 (1987), which involved an all-white municipality's annexation of two empty parcels of land. When the city sought preclearance it was denied, in large part because the Attorney General found that the city's refusal to annex an adjacent black community that had petitioned for inclusion showed that it had applied a wholly different and discriminatory annexation standard. The Supreme Court affirmed the denial of preclearance:

> [The city] relies on the fact that there were no black voters in Pleasant Grove at the time the relevant annexation decisions were made, so that the annexations did not reduce the proportion of black voters or deny existing black voters representation equivalent to their political strength in the enlarged community. [The city] contends that since the annexations could not possibly have caused an impermissible effect on black voting, it makes no sense to say that appellant had a discriminatory purpose. This argument is based on the incorrect assumption that an impermissible purpose under § 5 can relate only to present circumstances. Section 5 looks not only to the present effects of changes, but to their future effects as well, as shown by the fact that annexations of vacant land are subject to preclearance even though no one's right to vote is immediately affected. Likewise, an impermissible purpose under § 5 may relate to anticipated as well as present circumstances.

Is *Pleasant Grove* consistent with either *City of Richmond* or *Beer*? Perhaps relying on *Pleasant Grove*, the Department of Justice announced that:

> In those instances in which a plan is found to have a retrogressive effect, as well as in those cases in which a proposed plan is alleged to have a retrogressive effect but a functional analysis does not yield clear conclusions about the plan's effect, the Department of Justice will closely examine the process by which the plan was adopted to ascertain whether the plan was intended to reduce minority voting strength. This examination may include consideration of whether there is a purpose to retrogress in the future even though there is no retrogression at the time of the submission. If the jurisdiction has not provided sufficient evidence to demonstrate that the plan was not intended to reduce minority voting strength, either now or in the future, the proposed redistricting plan is subject to a Section 5 objection.

Guidance Concerning Redistricting and Retrogression Under Section 5 of the Voting Rights Act, as Amended, 42 U.S.C. 1973c, Fed. Reg., Jan. 18, 2001, at 5413–14. What does it mean to have an intent to retrogress in the future?

Reno v. Bossier Parish School Board (Bossier Parish II)

528 U.S. 320 (2000)

■ JUSTICE SCALIA delivered the opinion of the Court.

These cases present the question whether § 5 of the Voting Rights Act of 1965 prohibits preclearance of a redistricting plan enacted with a discriminatory but nonretrogressive purpose.

I

* * *

Bossier Parish is governed by a 12–member Police Jury elected from single-member districts for 4–year terms. In the early 1990s, the Police Jury set out to redraw its electoral districts in order to account for demographic changes reflected in the decennial census. In 1991, it adopted a redistricting plan which, like the plan then in effect, contained no majority-black districts, although blacks made up approximately 20% of the parish's population. On May 28, 1991, the Police Jury submitted its new districting plan to the Attorney General; two months later, the Attorney General granted preclearance.

The Bossier Parish School Board (Board) is constituted in the same fashion as the Police Jury, and it too undertook to redraw its districts after the 1990 census. During the course of that redistricting, appellant-intervenor George Price, president of the local chapter of the National Association for the Advancement of Colored People (NAACP), proposed that the Board adopt a plan with majority-black districts. In the fall of 1992, amid some controversy, the Board rejected Price's suggestion and adopted the Police Jury's 1991 redistricting plan as its own.

On January 4, 1993, the Board submitted its redistricting plan to the Attorney General for preclearance. Although the Attorney General had precleared the identical plan when submitted by the Police Jury, she interposed a formal objection to the Board's plan, asserting that "new information"—specifically, the NAACP plan proposed by appellant-intervenor Price—demonstrated that "black residents are sufficiently numerous and geographically compact so as to constitute a majority in two single-member districts." The Attorney General disclaimed any attempt to compel the Board to "adopt any particular plan," but maintained that the Board was "not free to adopt a plan that unnecessarily limits the opportunity for minority voters to elect their candidates of choice."

After the Attorney General denied the Board's request for reconsideration, the Board filed the present action for judicial preclearance of the 1992 plan in the United States District Court for the District of Columbia.... Before the District Court, appellants conceded that the Board's plan did not have a prohibited "effect" under § 5, since it did not worsen the position of minority voters.... [Nevertheless,] they contended that, although the Board's plan would have no retrogressive effect, it nonetheless violated § 5 because it was enacted for a discriminatory "purpose."

III

[W]hen considered in light of our longstanding interpretation of the "effect" prong of § 5 in its application to vote dilution claims, the language of § 5 leads to the conclusion that the "purpose" prong of § 5 covers only retrogressive dilution.

* * *

[In *Beer v. United States*, 425 U.S. 130 (1976),] we concluded that, in the context of a § 5 challenge, the phrase "denying or abridging the right to vote on account of race or color" ... limited the term it qualified, "effect," to retrogressive effects.

Appellants contend that in qualifying the term "purpose," the very same phrase does not impose a limitation to retrogression—i.e., that the phrase "abridging the right to vote on account of race or color" means retrogression when it modifies "effect," but means discrimination more generally when it modifies "purpose." We think this is simply an untenable construction of the text, in effect recasting the phrase "does not have the purpose and will not have the effect of x" to read "does not have the purpose of y and will not have the effect of x." As we have in the past, we refuse to adopt a construction that would attribute different meanings to the same phrase in the same sentence, depending on which object it is modifying.

Appellants point out that we did give the purpose prong of § 5 a broader meaning than the effect prong in *Richmond v. United States,* 422 U.S. 358 (1975)....

It must be acknowledged that *Richmond* created a discontinuity between the effect and purpose prongs of § 5. We regard that, however, as nothing more than an ex necessitate limitation upon the effect prong in the particular context of annexation—to avoid the invalidation of all annexations of areas with a lower proportion of minority voters than the annexing unit. The case certainly does not stand for the proposition that the purpose and effect prongs have fundamentally different meanings—the latter requiring retrogression, and the former not—which is what is urged here. The approved effect of the redistricting in Richmond, and the hypothetically disapproved purpose, were both retrogressive. We found it necessary to make an exception to normal retrogressive-effect principles, but not to normal retrogressive-purpose principles, in order to permit routine annexation. That sheds little light upon the issue before us here.

Appellants' only textual justification for giving the purpose and effect prongs different meanings is that to do otherwise "would reduce the purpose prong of Section 5 to a trivial matter"....

It is true enough that, whenever Congress enacts a statute that bars conduct having "the purpose or effect of x," the purpose prong has application entirely separate from that of the effect prong only with regard to unlikely conduct that has "the purpose of x" but fails to have "the effect of x"—in the present context, the conduct of a so-called "incompetent retrogressor." The purpose prong has value and effect, however, even when it does not cover additional conduct. With regard to conduct that has both "the purpose of x" and "the effect of x," the Government need only prove that the conduct at issue has "the purpose of x" in order to prevail. In the specific context of § 5, where the covered jurisdiction has the burden of persuasion, the Government need only refute the covered jurisdiction's prima facie showing that a proposed voting change does not have a retrogressive purpose in order for preclearance to be denied. When it can do so, it is spared the necessity of countering the jurisdiction's evidence regarding actual retrogressive effect—which, in vote-dilution cases, is often a complex undertaking. This advantage, plus the ability to reach malevolent incompetence, may not represent a massive addition to the effect prong, but it is enough to justify the separate existence of the purpose prong in this statute, and is no less than what justifies the separate existence of such a provision in many other laws.

At bottom, appellants' disagreement with our reading of § 5 rests not upon textual analysis, but upon their opposition to our holding in *Beer.* Although they do not explicitly contend that *Beer* should be overruled, they all but do so by arguing that it would be "untenable" to conclude (as we did in *Beer*) that the phrase "abridging the right to vote on account of race or color" refers only to retrogression in § 5, in light of the fact that virtually identical language ... in the Fifteenth Amendment—has never been read to refer only to retrogression. *See* ... U.S. Const. Amend. 15, § 1 ("The right of citizens of the United States to vote shall not be denied or abridged by the United States or by any State on account of race, color, or previous condition of servitude"). The term "abridge," however—whose core meaning is "shorten," see Webster's New International Dictionary 7 (2d ed. 1950); American Heritage Dictionary 6 (3d ed. 1992)—necessarily entails a comparison. It makes no sense to suggest that a voting practice "abridges" the right to vote without some baseline with which to compare the practice. In § 5 preclearance proceedings—which uniquely deal only and specifically with changes in voting procedures—the baseline is the status quo that is proposed to be changed: If the change "abridges the right to vote" relative to the status quo, preclearance is denied, and the status quo (however discriminatory it may be) remains in effect. In ... Fifteenth Amendment proceedings, by contrast, which involve not only changes but (much more commonly) the status quo itself, the comparison must be made with an hypothetical alternative....

In another argument that applies equally to our holding in *Beer*, appellants object that our reading of § 5 would require the District Court or Attorney General to preclear proposed voting changes with a discriminatory effect or purpose, or even with both. That strikes appellants as an inconceivable prospect only because they refuse to accept the limited meaning that we have said preclearance has in the vote-dilution context. It does not represent approval of the voting change; it is nothing more than a determination that the voting change is no more dilutive than what it replaces, and therefore cannot be stopped in advance under the extraordinary burden-shifting procedures of § 5, but must be attacked through the normal means of a § 2 action. As we have repeatedly noted, in vote-dilution cases § 5 prevents nothing but backsliding, and preclearance under § 5 affirms nothing but the absence of backsliding. This explains why the sole consequence of failing to obtain preclearance is continuation of the status quo. To deny preclearance to a plan that is not retrogressive—no matter how unconstitutional it may be—would risk leaving in effect a status quo that is even worse. For example, in the case of a voting change with a discriminatory but nonretrogressive purpose and a discriminatory but ameliorative effect, the result of denying preclearance would be to preserve a status quo with more discriminatory effect than the proposed change....

[B]y suggesting that § 5 extends to discriminatory but nonretrogressive vote-dilutive purposes, appellants ... would also exacerbate the "substantial" federalism costs that the preclearance procedure already exacts, *Lopez v. Monterey County*, 525 U.S. 266 (1999), perhaps to the extent of raising concerns about § 5's constitutionality. Most importantly, however, in light of our holding in Beer, appellants' reading finds no support in the language of § 5....

NOTES AND QUESTIONS

1. Consider the arguments put forward in the dissents of Justices Stevens, Souter, Ginsburg, and Breyer. Justice Stevens, joined by Justice Ginsburg, pointed out that "[i]n its administration of the voting rights statute for the past quarter century, the Department of Justice has consistently employed a construction of the Voting Rights Act of 1965 contrary to that imposed upon the Act by the Court today. Apart from the deference such constructions are always afforded, the Department's reading points us directly to the necessary starting point of any exercise in statutory interpretation—the plain language of the statute." He saw "nothing" in the word purpose "that would lead anyone to think that Congress had anything in mind but a present-tense, intentional effort to 'deny or abridge the right to vote on account of race.' Ergo, if a municipality intends to deny or abridge voting rights because of race, it may not obtain preclearance."

Justice Breyer argued that the Court's definition of purpose would have rendered the term largely irrelevant in 1965: "[S]ince at the time, in certain places, historical discrimination had left the number of black voters at close to zero, retrogression would have proved virtually impossible where § 5 was needed most." Thus the only imaginable discriminatory purpose would have been one to perpetuate existing levels of discrimination as changes were being made.

Justice Souter, joined by Justices Stevens and Ginsburg on this point, argued that "if today's decision achieves a symmetry with *Beer*, the achievement is merely one of well-matched error. The Court was mistaken in *Beer* when it restricted the effect prong of § 5 to retrogression, and the Court is even more wrong today when it limits the clear text of § 5 to the corresponding retrogressive purpose. Although I adhere to the strong policy of respecting precedent in statutory interpretation and so would not reexamine *Beer*, that policy does not demand that recognized error be compounded indefinitely, and the Court's prior mistake about the meaning of the effects requirement of § 5 should not be expanded by an even more erroneous interpretation of the scope of the section's purpose prong." He discussed at length the evidence of the school board's intentional racial discrimination. With respect to the question what the word "abridge" was intended to mean, he argued that it should be interpreted consistent with the Fifteenth Amendment:

> Since the Act is an exercise of congressional power under § 2 of that Amendment, *South Carolina v. Katzenbach*, the choice to follow the Amendment's terminology is most naturally read as carrying the meaning of the constitutional terms into the statute. Any construction of the statute, therefore, carries an implication about the meaning of the Amendment, absent some good reason to treat the parallel texts differently on some particular point, and a reading of the statute that would not fit the Constitution is presumptively wrong.

In each context, it is clear that abridgment necessarily means something more subtle and less drastic than the complete denial of the right to cast a ballot, denial being separately forbidden. Abridgment therefore must be a condition in between complete denial, on the one hand, and complete enjoyment of voting power, on the other. The principal concept of diminished voting strength recognized as actionable under our cases is vote dilution, defined as a regime that denies to minority voters the same opportunity to participate in the political process and to elect representatives of their choice that majority voters enjoy. The benchmark of dilution pure and simple is thus a system in which every minority voter has as good a chance at political participation and voting effectiveness as any other voter. Our cases have also recognized retrogression as a subspecies of dilution.... Although our cases have dealt with vote dilution only under the Fourteenth Amendment, I know of no reason in text or history that dilution is not equally violative of the Fifteenth Amendment guarantee against abridgement....

* * *

Giving purpose-to-abridge the broader, intended reading while preserving the erroneously truncated interpretation of effect would not even result in a facially irrational scheme. This is so because intent to dilute is conceptually simple, whereas a dilutive abridgment-in-fact is not readily defined and identified independently of dilutive intent. A purpose to dilute simply means to subordinate minority voting power; exact calibration is unnecessary to identify what is intended. Any purpose to give less weight to minority participation in the electoral process than to majority participation is a purpose to discriminate and thus to "abridge" the right to vote. No further baseline is needed because the enquiry goes to the direction of the majority's aim, without reference to details of the existing system.

2.   Why does the Court's opinion suggest that "extend[ing] § 5] to discriminatory but nonretrogressive vote-dilutive purposes, ... would also exacerbate the 'substantial' federalism costs that the preclearance procedure already exacts ... perhaps to the extent of raising concerns about § 5's constitutionality"? Isn't such activity precisely within the core of what the Fourteenth and Fifteenth Amendments prohibit in their self-executing provisions, namely, purposeful discrimination on the basis of race? Does this suggest a majority of the Court may think that the preclearance requirement itself comes close to exceeding congressional enforcement power?

3.   Congress expressly disapproved the Court's construction of "discriminatory purpose" in the 2006 amendments to section 5, declaring that "[t]he effectiveness of the Voting Rights Act of 1965 has been significantly weakened by the United States Supreme Court decisio[n] in Reno v. Bossier Parish II, ... which [has] misconstrued Congress' original intent in enacting the Voting Rights Act of 1965 and narrowed the protections afforded by Section 5 of the Act." Fannie Lou Hamer, Rosa Parks and Coretta Scott King Voting Rights Reauthorization and Amendments Act of 2006, § 2(b)(6).

The 2006 Act added a new subsection to the Act that provides, in pertinent part:

> The term "purpose" ... in subsections (a) and (b) of this section [which set out the preclearance requirement] shall include any discriminatory purpose.

42 U.S.C. § 1973c(c).

D. THE ADMINISTRATIVE PROCESS

As we have already seen, section 5 provides two alternative paths to preclearance: an administrative mechanism involving submission to the Attorney General and a declaratory judgment action in the United States District Court for the District of Columbia. The Attorney General has promulgated a set of extensive regulations for the administrative preclearance process. *See* 28 C.F.R. Part 51 (2006). In this section, we consider several issues raised by the administrative preclearance process.

The vast bulk of administrative submissions receive preclearance. Between 1965 and 1980, for example, the Attorney General objected to fewer than three percent of all submissions. *See* Richard Scher & James Button, *Voting Rights Act: Implementation and Impact*, in Implementation of Civil Rights Policy, 21, 34 (Charles S. Bullock, III, & Charles M. Lamb eds. 1984). The administrative process is initially handled by non-lawyer section 5 analysts, although their work is reviewed by attorneys before going to the Assistant Attorney General for Civil Rights, to whom the Attorney General has delegated preclearance authority. For general accounts of this process, see, e.g., Howard Ball, Dale Krane & Thomas Lauth, Compromised Compliance: Implementation of the 1965 Voting Rights Act (1982).

Section 5 provides explicitly that: "Neither an affirmative indication by the Attorney General that no objection will be made, nor the Attorney General's failure to object, nor a declaratory judgment entered under this section shall bar a subsequent action to enjoin enforcement of such qualification, prerequisite, standard, practice, or procedure." Thus, even if the Attorney General declines to object, a private party (or, in fact, the United States) may still sue to enjoin a precleared practice under any other constitutional or statutory provision. Such a lawsuit may differ, though, in several critical respects: the identity of the parties, venue, and the burden of proof. How might these affect the outcome? Can the Attorney General's failure to object be reviewed?

Morris v. Gressette

432 U.S. 491 (1977).

■ MR. JUSTICE POWELL delivered the opinion of the Court.

* * *

[In November 1971, South Carolina reapportioned its State Senate. It submitted the plan to the Attorney General for preclearance but while its submission was still pending, the local federal district court held that the plan violated one-person, one-vote. The court then ordered the state to develop a new plan. The state did, and the district court approved the new plan. The Attorney General then notified South Carolina that he would not interpose an objection to the new plan because he felt "constrained to defer to the . . . determination of the three-judge District Court." In light of the later decision in *Connor v. Waller*, 421 U.S. 656 (1975), such deference was not in fact required.

Objecting to that deference, another set of plaintiffs brought suit in the United States District Court for the District of Columbia challenging the Attorney General's failure to object to the new senate reapportionment plan. That suit was called *Harper v. Kleindienst*. Ultimately, the District Court directed the Attorney General to consider South Carolina's plan without regard to the decision by the South Carolina federal court. The next day the Attorney General interposed an objection because he was "unable to conclude that [the plan] does not have the effect of abridging voting rights on account of race." The Court of Appeals affirmed.]

Armed with the decision of the Court of Appeals and the belated objection interposed by the Attorney General, two South Carolina voters filed the present suit in the United States District Court for the District of South Carolina as a class action under § 5 of the Voting Rights Act. The plaintiffs, appellants here, sought an injunction against implementation of [the challenged plan] on the ground that the Attorney General had interposed an objection and the State had not subsequently obtained a favorable declaratory judgment from the United States District Court for the District of Columbia.

* * *

II

The ultimate issue in this case concerns the implementation of South Carolina's reapportionment plan for the State Senate. . . . It is conceded that no objection was entered within the 60–day period. But appellants insist that the Attorney General's nunc pro tunc objection of July 20, 1973, is effective under the Act and thus bars implementation of the reapportionment plan. Since that objection was interposed pursuant to the District Court's order in *Harper v. Kleindienst*, its validity depends on whether the

Harper court had jurisdiction under the Administrative Procedure Act to review the Attorney General's failure to object.

The Administrative Procedure Act stipulates that the provisions of that Act authorizing judicial review apply "except to the extent that—(1) statutes preclude judicial review; or (2) agency action is committed to agency discretion by law." 5 U.S.C. § 701(a). It is now well settled that "judicial review of a final agency action by an aggrieved person will not be cut off unless there is persuasive reason to believe that such was the purpose of Congress." The reviewing court must determine whether "Congress has in express or implied terms precluded judicial review or committed the challenged action entirely to administrative discretion."

As no provision of the Voting Rights Act expressly precludes judicial review of the Attorney General's actions under § 5, it is necessary to determine "whether nonreviewability can fairly be inferred." That inquiry must address the role played by the Attorney General within "the context of the entire legislative scheme."

The nature of the § 5 remedy, which this Court has characterized as an "unusual" and "severe" procedure, strongly suggests that Congress did not intend the Attorney General's actions under that provision to be subject to judicial review. Section 5 requires covered jurisdictions to delay implementation of validly enacted state legislation until federal authorities have had an opportunity to determine whether that legislation conforms to the Constitution and to the provisions of the Voting Rights Act. Section 5 establishes two alternative methods by which covered jurisdictions can comply with this severe requirement of federal preclearance review. First, a covered jurisdiction may file a declaratory judgment action in the District Court for the District of Columbia.... Second, a covered jurisdiction may submit a change in voting laws to the Attorney General and subsequently may enforce the change if "the Attorney General has not interposed an objection within sixty days after such submission."

According to the terms of § 5, a covered jurisdiction is in compliance pursuant to the latter alternative once it has (i) filed a complete submission with the Attorney General, and (ii) received no objection from that office within 60 days. This second method of compliance under § 5 is unlike the first in that implementation of changes in voting laws is not conditioned on an affirmative statement by the Attorney General that the change is without discriminatory purpose or effect. To the contrary, compliance with § 5 is measured solely by the absence, for whatever reason, of a timely objection on the part of the Attorney General....

Although there is no legislative history bearing directly on the issue of reviewability of the Attorney General's actions under § 5, the legislative materials do indicate a desire to provide a speedy alternative method of compliance to covered States....

In light of the potential severity of the § 5 remedy, the statutory language, and the legislative history, we think it clear that Congress intended to provide covered jurisdictions with an expeditious alternative to declaratory judgment actions. The congressional intent is plain: The extraordinary remedy of postponing the implementation of validly enacted state legislation was to come to an end when the Attorney General failed to interpose a timely objection based on a complete submission. Although there was to be no bar to subsequent constitutional challenges to the implemented legislation, there also was to be "no dragging out" of the extraordinary federal remedy beyond the period specified in the statute. . . .

Our conclusions in this respect are reinforced by the fact that the Attorney General's failure to object is not conclusive with respect to the constitutionality of the submitted state legislation. The statute expressly provides that neither "an affirmative indication by the Attorney General that no objection will be made, nor the Attorney General's failure to object . . . shall bar a subsequent action to enjoin enforcement" of the newly enacted legislation or voting regulation. . . . Where the discriminatory character of an enactment is not detected upon review by the Attorney General, it can be challenged in traditional constitutional litigation. But it cannot be questioned in a suit seeking judicial review of the Attorney General's exercise of discretion under § 5, or his failure to object within the statutory period.

* * *

■ Mr. Justice Marshall, with whom Mr. Justice Brennan joins, dissenting.

The Court holds today that an Attorney General's failure to object within 60 days to the implementation of a voting law that has been submitted to him under § 5 of the Voting Rights Act, as amended cannot be questioned in any court. Under the Court's ruling, it matters not whether the Attorney General fails to object because he misunderstands his legal duty, as in this case; because he loses the submission; or because he seeks to subvert the Voting Rights Act. Indeed, the Court today grants unreviewable discretion to a future Attorney General to bargain acquiescence in a discriminatory change in a covered State's voting laws in return for that State's electoral votes. *Cf.* J. Randall & D. Donald, The Civil War and Reconstruction 678–701 (2d ed. 1961) (settlement of the election of 1876).

* * *

II

Perhaps out of justifiable embarrassment, the majority never mentions the effect of its ruling. That effect is easy to describe: The Court today upholds a system of choosing members of the South Carolina Senate that has prevented the election of any black senators, despite the fact that 25% of South Carolina's population is black. Thus, South Carolina, which was a leader of the movement to deprive the former slaves of their federally guaranteed right to vote, *South Carolina v. Katzenbach,* is allowed to remain as one of the last successful members of that movement. It would take much more evidence than the Court can muster to convince me that this result is consistent with "Congress' firm intention to rid the country of racial discrimination in voting." . . . .

It is true that today's decision does not quite spell the end of all hope that the South Carolina Senate will someday be representative of the entire citizenry of South Carolina. If the Decennial Census in 1980 requires substantial reapportionment, and if the Voting Rights Act is still in effect when that reapportionment takes place, and if the then Attorney General is conscientious, the devices approved today will be rejected under the strict standards of § 5. This highly contingent possibility that the promise of the Fifteenth Amendment will be realized in South Carolina, some 110 years after that Amendment was ratified, is apparently sufficient in the eyes of the majority. It is not sufficient for me, as it was not for Congress, which wrote the Voting Rights Act in 1965 to put an end to what was then "nearly a century of widespread resistance to the Fifteenth Amendment." *South Carolina v. Katzenbach*.

* * *

NOTES AND QUESTIONS

1. Although the Attorney General's preclearance determination is not subject to judicial review, his objection may be overridden as a practical matter, since a jurisdiction may seek a declaratory judgment from the District of Columbia District Court without regard to whether an objection was interposed in the administrative process. That declaratory judgment is an entirely separate proceeding in which the administrative objection plays no role.

2. As a practical matter, few jurisdictions seek judicial preclearance after an administrative objection has been interposed. *See* Abigail M. Thernstrom, Whose Votes Count? Affirmative Action and Minority Voting Rights 158 (1987). Can you identify the practical reasons for this situation? The one repeated exception involves redistricting plans. Can you see why jurisdictions might be more inclined to fight the Department of Justice's decisions here than with respect to other voting changes?

3. To what extent does section 5 reflect public-choice notions of regulatory "capture" by special interest groups? *See* Abigail Thernstrom, Whose Votes Count? Affirmative Action and Minority Voting Rights 235 (1987). Might partisan concerns also affect the Department's use of its preclearance power? In this respect, consider to what extent Democrats or Republicans might embrace "max-black" strategies. *See* Pamela S. Karlan, *Loss and Redemption: Voting Rights at the Turn of a Century*, 50 Vand. L. Rev. 291, 302–03 (1997) (discussing the relationship between partisanship and the creation of black districts); Richard H. Pildes, *The Politics of Race*, 108 Harv. L. Rev. 1359 (1995) (same); *see* also Samuel Issacharoff, *Is Section 5 of the Voting Rights Act a Victim of Its Own Success?*, 104 Colum. L. Rev. 1710 (2004) (suggesting that the intersection of the section 5 preclearance process and partisanship is particularly likely, and has increased over time, in the redistricting process). Are any problems with regulatory capture or partisanship exacerbated by the more complex preclearance standard enunciated by the Court in *Georgia v. Ashcroft*?

CHAPTER 7

MAJORITY RULE AND MINORITY VOTE DILUTION: CONSTITUTIONAL AND LEGISLATIVE APPROACHES

To the extent that courts or others believed that the one-vote, one-person doctrine and the emergence of constitutional constraints on race discrimination in voting would fully integrate various minority groups into the political process, they were disappointed. Indeed, as a matter of political and constitutional theory, one-vote, one-person was distinctly focused on ensuring majority rule and reflected less concern with claims of relatively small, geographically discrete groups of voters. First, the doctrine rested on a strong presumption in favor of majoritarian control and a distrust of minority influence. Although that distrust was overtly directed at rural, largely conservative, white numerical minorities, the heavy presumption in favor of majority control evinced little concern with political minorities, be they defined racially, ethnically, geographically, or in partisan terms. Second, in its focus on abstract mathematical equality, one-vote one-person downplayed the importance of group representation in the governance process. *See* Lani Guinier and Pamela S. Karlan, *The Majoritarian Difficulty: One Person, One–Vote*, in Reason and Passion: Justice Brennan's Enduring Influence 207 (E. Joshua Rosenkranz & Bernard Schwartz eds. 1997). Ironically, *Reynolds v. Sims*, 377 U.S. 533 (1964), "stripped Alabama's rural, predominantly black counties of their legislative influence virtually on the eve of the massive black enfranchisement brought about by the Voting Rights Act of 1965. Had the 1901 apportionment remained in effect until 1982 [that is, if the state did not change its system as black participation increased], blacks would have controlled a higher percentage of the seats in the Alabama Legislature (18% of the House and 20% of the Senate in a state with a 25% black population) than they controlled as a result of the protections against dilution [under the pre–1982 Voting Rights Act.]" Pamela S. Karlan, *The Rights to Vote: Some Pessimism About Formalism*, 71 Tex. L. Rev. 1705, 1718 n. 54 (1993); *see* James U. Blacksher & Larry T. Menefee, *From* Reynolds v. Sims *to* City of Mobile v. Bolden: *Have the White Suburbs Commandeered the Fifteenth Amendment?*, 34 Hastings L.J. 1, 39 n.261 (1982).

In this chapter, we explore the rise and fall of constitutional doctrine to deal with the potential that, even after the franchise has been extended on fair terms, political majorities can leverage their power into a system that dilutes the political power of minorities. One way of thinking about these issues is that, in the first generation of constitutional litigation, attention focused on access to the ballot box and conditions under which the franchise could be regulated. At that stage, the questions could be framed as involving an individual right (although of course the motivations for disenfranchisement might turn on individuals' membership in a racial group and the desire to maintain white supremacy). Once the franchise was widely available, a second generation of litigation turned to the institutional structures through which these individual votes were aggregated. As you will see, there are many different ways in which election systems can be designed to aggregate the votes cast; the choice between these different structures can dramatically affect the distribution of political power between competing interests, and hence strongly influence the policies political bodies adopt. At this stage, the questions focus less on individual rights and more on the "proper" distribution of political power between competing groups.

This issue is one of the most difficult in political and constitutional theory: how to design political institutions that both reflect the right of "the people" to be self-governing and that also ensure appropriate integration of, and respect for, the interests of political minorities. In the context we examine, this question has an institutional aspect as well: what distinct role should different existing institutions, such as courts and legislatures, play in responding to the tension between majority rule and minority interest? There is a doctrinal aspect to the issue as well that will be a recurrent theme: should constitutional law address these issues by focusing on when the majority uses its power over institutions for discriminatory purposes, or should it also focus on when the majority uses this power in ways that have the effect, however inadvertent, of diminishing minority influence?

A. DEFINING THE HARM

We begin with constitutional approaches, then turn to Congress' intervention via the important 1982 amendments to the Voting Rights Act ("VRA"). The constitutional analysis starts with *Whitcomb v. Chavis,* 403 U.S. 124 (1971), and *White v. Regester,* 412 U.S. 755 (1973). Together, *Whitcomb* and *White v. Regester* are of great importance in defining the concept of minority vote dilution, which began to emerge in the 1970s after the VRA was enacted and the first generation litigation had begun to wind down. The cases are important not just for the content they give this concept under the Constitution but, as we will see in Chapter 8, they will also be central to the statutory definition of vote dilution. Congress will draw directly on these decisions in amending the Voting Rights Act. Thus, it becomes crucial to determine the content and theory of the line the Court draws between *Whitcomb*, in which the Court rejects the claim of racial vote dilution, and the two contexts in *White v. Regester*, in which the Court accepts such a claim.

Whitcomb v. Chavis

403 U.S. 124 (1971).

■ Mr. Justice White delivered the opinion of the Court with respect to the validity of the multi-member election district in Marion County, Indiana . . . and announced the judgment of the Court. . . .

Indiana has a bicameral general assembly consisting of a house of representatives of 100 members and a senate of 50 members. Eight of the 31 senatorial districts and 25 of the 39 house districts are multi-member districts, that is, districts that are represented by two or more legislators elected at large by the voters of the district. Under the statutes here challenged, Marion County is a multi-member district electing eight senators and 15 members of the house.

On January 9, 1969, six residents of Indiana, five of whom were residents of Marion County, filed a suit . . . [alleging] that the two statutes invidiously diluted the force and effect of the vote of Negroes and poor persons living within certain Marion County census tracts constituting what was termed "the ghetto area." Residents of the area were alleged to have particular demographic characteristics rendering them cognizable as a minority interest group with distinctive interests in specific areas of the substantive law. With single-member districting, it was said, the ghetto area would elect three members of the house and one senator, whereas under the present districting voters in the area "have almost no political force or control over legislators because the effect of their vote is cancelled out by other contrary interest groups" in Marion County. The mechanism of political party organization and the influence of party chairmen in nominating candidates were additional factors alleged to frustrate the exercise of power by residents of the ghetto area. . . .

The three-judge court . . . first determined that a racial minority group inhabited an identifiable ghetto area in Indianapolis. That area, located in the northern half of Center Township and termed the "Center Township ghetto," . . . contained a 1967 population of 97,000 nonwhites, over 99% of whom were Negro, and 35,000 whites. The court proceeded to compare [representative census tracts within the ghetto] . . . with tract 211, a predominantly white, relatively wealthy suburban census tract in Washington Township contiguous to the northwest corner of the court's ghetto area and with tract 220, also in Washington Township, a contiguous tract inhabited by middle class Negroes. Strong differences were found in terms of housing conditions, income and educational levels, rates of unemployment, juvenile crime, and welfare assistance. The contrasting characteristics between the . . . ghetto area and its inhabitants on the one hand and tracts 211 and 220 on the other indicated the ghetto's "compelling interests in such legislative areas as urban renewal and rehabilitation, health care, employment training and opportunities, welfare, and relief of the poor, law enforcement, quality of education, and anti-discrimination measures." These interests were in addition to those the ghetto shared with the rest of the county, such as metropolitan transportation, flood control, sewage disposal, and education.

The court then turned to evidence showing the residences of Marion County's representatives and senators in each of the five general assemblies elected during the period 1960 through 1968. Excluding tract 220, the middle class Negro district, Washington Township, the relatively wealthy suburban area in which tract 211 was located, with an average of 13.98% of Marion County's population, was the residence of 47.52% of its senators and 34.33% of its representatives. The court's Center Township ghetto area, with 17.8% of the population, had 4.75% of the senators and 5.97% of the representatives.... Also, tract 220 alone, the middle class Negro district, had only 0.66% of the county's population but had been the residence of more representatives than had the ghetto area. The ghetto area had been represented in the senate only once—in 1964 by one senator—and the house three times—with one representative in 1962 and 1964 and by two representatives in the 1968 general assembly. The court found the "Negro Center Township Ghetto population" to be sufficiently large to elect two representatives and one senator if the ghetto tracts "were specific single-member legislative districts" in Marion County....

The court's conclusions of law on the merits may be summarized as follows:

1.   There exists within Marion County an identifiable racial element, "the Negro residents of the Center Township Ghetto," with special interests in various areas of substantive law, diverging significantly from interests of nonresidents of the ghetto.

2.   The voting strength of this racial group has been minimized by Marion County's multi-member senate and house district because of the strong control exercised by political parties over the selection of candidates, the inability of the Negro voters to assure themselves the opportunity to vote for prospective legislators of their choice and the absence of any particular legislators who were accountable for their legislative record to Negro voters.

3.   Party control of nominations, the inability of voters to know the candidate and the responsibility of legislators to their party and the county at large make it difficult for any legislator to diverge from the majority of his delegation and to be an effective representative of minority ghetto interests.

4.   Although each legislator in Marion County is arguably responsible to all the voters, including those in the ghetto, "partial responsiveness of

all legislators is [not] ... equal [to] total responsiveness and the informed concern of a few specific legislators.''

5. The apportionment statutes of Indiana as they relate to Marion County operate to minimize and cancel out the voting strength of a minority racial group, namely Negroes residing in the Center Township ghetto, and to deprive them of the equal protection of the laws.

6. As a legislative district, Marion County is large as compared with the total number of legislators, it is not subdistricted to insure distribution of the legislators over the county and comprises a multi-member district for both the house and the senate....

9. ... [Plaintiff] Walker "probably has received less effective representation" than Marion County voters because "he votes for fewer legislators and, therefore, has fewer legislators to speak for him," and, since in theory voting power in multi-member districts does not vary inversely to the number of voters, Marion County voters had greater opportunity to cast tie-breaking or "critical" votes. But the court declined to hold that the latter ground had been proved, absent more evidence concerning Lake County....

III

[...] The question of the constitutional validity of multi-member districts has been pressed in this Court since the first of the modern reapportionment cases. These questions have focused not on population-based apportionment but on the quality of representation afforded by the multi-member district as compared with single-member districts. In *Lucas v. Colorado General Assembly*, 377 U.S. 713 (1964), decided with *Reynolds v. Sims*, we noted certain undesirable features of the multi-member district but expressly withheld any intimation "that apportionment schemes which provide for the at-large election of a number of legislators from a county, or any political subdivision, are constitutionally defective." Subsequently, when the validity of the multi-member district, as such, was squarely presented, we held that such a district is not per se illegal under the Equal Protection Clause. That voters in multi-member districts vote for and are represented by more legislators than voters in single-member districts has so far not demonstrated an invidious discrimination against the latter. But we have deemed the validity of multi-member district systems justiciable, recognizing also that they may be subject to challenge where the circumstances of a particular case may "operate to minimize or cancel out the voting strength of racial or political elements of the voting population." ... But we have insisted that the challenger carry the burden of proving that multi-member districts unconstitutionally operate to dilute or cancel the voting strength of racial or political elements. We have not yet sustained such an attack.

IV

Plaintiffs [allege] that the Marion County district, on the record of this case, illegally minimizes and cancels out the voting power of a cognizable racial minority in Marion County. . . .

[T]he trial court struck down Marion County's multi-member district because it found the scheme worked invidiously against a specific segment of the county's voters as compared with others. The court identified an area of the city as a ghetto, found it predominantly inhabited by poor Negroes with distinctive substantive-law interests and thought this group unconstitutionally underrepresented because the proportion of legislators with residences in the ghetto elected from 1960 to 1968 was less than the ghetto's proportion of the population, less than the proportion of legislators elected from Washington Township, a less populous district, and less than the ghetto would likely have elected had the county consisted of single-member districts. We find major deficiencies in this approach.

First, it needs no emphasis here that the Civil War Amendments were designed to protect the civil rights of Negroes and that the courts have been vigilant in scrutinizing schemes allegedly conceived or operated as purposeful devices to further racial discrimination. There has been no hesitation in striking down those contrivances that can fairly be said to infringe on Fourteenth Amendment rights. But there is no suggestion here that Marion County's multi-member district, or similar districts throughout the State, were conceived or operated as purposeful devices to further racial or economic discrimination. As plaintiffs concede, "there was no basis for asserting that the legislative districts in Indiana were designed to dilute the vote of minorities."

Nor does the fact that the number of ghetto residents who were legislators was not in proportion to ghetto population satisfactorily prove invidious discrimination absent evidence and findings that ghetto residents had less opportunity than did other Marion County residents to participate in the political processes and to elect legislators of their choice. We have discovered nothing in the record or in the court's findings indicating that poor Negroes were not allowed to register or vote, to choose the political party they desired to support, to participate in its affairs or to be equally represented on those occasions when legislative candidates were chosen. Nor did the evidence purport to show or the court find that inhabitants of the ghetto were regularly excluded from the slates of both major parties, thus denying them the chance of occupying legislative seats. It appears reasonably clear that the Republican Party won four of the five elections from 1960 to 1968, that Center Township ghetto voted heavily Democratic and that ghetto votes were critical to Democratic Party success. . . . [I]t seems unlikely that the Democratic Party could afford to overlook the ghetto in slating its candidates.[30] Clearly, in 1964—the one election that

---

30. . . . For the 1960–1968 period which concerned the District Court, . . . the Demo-   cratic Party slated one Negro representative in 1960; one in 1962; one senator and two

the Democrats won—the party slated and elected one senator and one representative from Center Township ghetto.... Nor is there any indication that the party failed to slate candidates satisfactory to the ghetto in other years. Absent evidence or findings we are not sure, but it seems reasonable to infer that had the Democrats won all of the elections or even most of them, the ghetto would have had no justifiable complaints about representation. The fact is, however, that four of the five elections were won by Republicans, which was not the party of the ghetto and which would not always slate ghetto candidates—although in 1962 it nominated and elected one representative and in 1968 two representatives from that area. If this is the proper view of this case, the failure of the ghetto to have legislative seats in proportion to its population emerges more as a function of losing elections than of built-in bias against poor Negroes. The voting power of ghetto residents may have been "cancelled out" as the District Court held, but this seems a mere euphemism for political defeat at the polls.

On the record before us plaintiffs' position comes to this: that although they have equal opportunity to participate in and influence the selection of candidates and legislators, and although the ghetto votes predominantly Democratic and that party slates candidates satisfactory to the ghetto, invidious discrimination nevertheless results when the ghetto, along with all other Democrats, suffers the disaster of losing too many elections. But typical American legislative elections are district-oriented, head-on races between candidates of two or more parties. As our system has it, one candidate wins, the others lose. Arguably the losing candidates' supporters are without representation since the men they voted for have been defeated; arguably they have been denied equal protection of the laws since they have no legislative voice of their own. This is true of both single-member and multi-member districts. But we have not yet deemed it a denial of equal protection to deny legislative seats to losing candidates, even in those so-called "safe" districts where the same party wins year after year.

Plainly, the District Court saw nothing unlawful about the impact of typical single-member district elections. The court's own plan created districts giving both Republicans and Democrats several predictably safe general assembly seats, with political, racial or economic minorities in those districts being "unrepresented" year after year. But similar consequences flowing from Marion County multi-member district elections were viewed differently. Conceding that all Marion County voters could fairly be said to be represented by the entire delegation, just as is each voter in a single-member district by the winning candidate, the District Court thought the ghetto voters' claim to the partial allegiance of eight senators and 15

representatives in 1964; three representatives in 1966; and one senator and two representatives in 1968. The Republican Party slated one Negro senator in 1960; two representatives in 1966; and three representatives in 1968....

representatives was not equivalent to the undivided allegiance of one senator and two representatives; nor was the ghetto voters' chance of influencing the election of an entire slate as significant as the guarantee of one ghetto senator and two ghetto representatives. As the trial court saw it, ghetto voters could not be adequately and equally represented unless some of Marion County's general assembly seats were reserved for ghetto residents serving the interests of the ghetto majority. But are poor Negroes of the ghetto any more underrepresented than poor ghetto whites who also voted Democratic and lost, or any more discriminated against than other interest groups or voters in Marion County with allegiance to the Democratic Party, or, conversely, any less represented than Republican areas or voters in years of Republican defeat? We think not. The mere fact that one interest group or another concerned with the outcome of Marion County elections has found itself outvoted and without legislative seats of its own provides no basis for invoking constitutional remedies where, as here, there is no indication that this segment of the population is being denied access to the political system. . . .

V

The District Court's holding, although on the facts of this case limited to guaranteeing one racial group representation, is not easily contained. It is expressive of the more general proposition that any group with distinctive interests must be represented in legislative halls if it is numerous enough to command at least one seat and represents a majority living in an area sufficiently compact to constitute a single-member district. This approach would make it difficult to reject claims of Democrats, Republicans, or members of any political organization in Marion County who live in what would be safe districts in a single-member district system but who in one year or another, or year after year, are submerged in a one-sided multi-member district vote. There are also union oriented workers, the university community, religious or ethnic groups occupying identifiable areas of our heterogeneous cities and urban areas. Indeed, it would be difficult for a great many, if not most, multi-member districts to survive analysis under the District Court's view unless combined with some voting arrangement such as proportional representation or cumulative voting aimed at providing representation for minority parties or interests. . . .

We are not insensitive to the objections long voiced to multi-member district plans. . . . Criticism is rooted in their winner-take-all aspects, their tendency to submerge minorities and to overrepresent the winning party as compared with the party's statewide electoral position, a general preference for legislatures reflecting community interests as closely as possible and disenchantment with political parties and elections as devices to settle policy differences between contending interests. The chance of winning or significantly influencing intraparty fights and issue-oriented elections has seemed to some inadequate protection to minorities, political, racial, or economic; rather, their voice, it is said, should also be heard in the legislative forum where public policy is finally fashioned. In our view, however, experience and insight have not yet demonstrated that multi-member districts are inherently invidious and violative of the Fourteenth Amendment.... [W]e are unprepared to hold that district-based elections decided by plurality vote are unconstitutional in either single-or multi-member districts simply because the supporters of losing candidates have no legislative seats assigned to them. As presently advised we hold that the District Court misconceived the Equal Protection Clause in applying it to invalidate the Marion County multi-member district....

■ Separate opinion of Mr. Justice Harlan.

Earlier this Term I remarked on "the evident malaise among the members of the Court" with prior decisions in the field of voter qualifications and reapportionment.... Today's opinio[n] ... confirm[s] that diagnosis.

I

[... P]ast decisions have suggested that multi-member constituencies would be unconstitutional if they could be shown "under the circumstances of a particular case ... to minimize or cancel out the voting strength of racial or political elements of the voting population." *Fortson v. Dorsey*, 379 U.S. 433, 439 (1965); *Burns v. Richardson*, 384 U.S. 73, 88 (1966). Today the Court holds that a three-judge District Court, which struck down an apportionment scheme for just this reason, "misconceived the Equal Protection Clause."

Prior opinions stated that "once the class of voters is chosen and their qualifications specified, we see no constitutional way by which equality of voting power may be evaded." *Gray v. Sanders*, 372 U.S. 368, 381 (1963); *Hadley v. Junior College District*, 397 U.S. 50, 59 (1970). Today the Court sustains a provision that gives opponents of school bond issues half again the voting power of proponents. *Gordon v. Lance* [403 U.S. 1 (1971)].

II

The Court justifies the wondrous results in these cases by relying on different combinations of factors.... *Gordon v. Lance* relies heavily on the "federal analogy" and the prevalence of similar anti-majoritarian elements in the constitutions of the several States.

To my mind the relevance of such considerations as the foregoing is undeniable and their cumulative effect is unanswerable. I can only marvel, therefore, that they were dismissed, singly and in combination, in a line of cases which began with *Gray v. Sanders*, 372 U.S. 368 (1963)....

That line of cases can best be understood, I think, as reflections of deep personal commitments by some members of the Court to the principles of pure majoritarian democracy.... If this philosophy of majoritarianism had been given its head, it would have led to different results in each of the cases decided today, for it is in the very nature of the principle that it regards majority rule as an imperative of social organization, not subject to compromise in furtherance of merely political ends. It is a philosophy which ignores or overcomes the fact that the scheme of the Constitution is one not of majoritarian democracy, but of federal republics, with equality of representation a value subordinate to many others, as both the body of the Constitution and the Fourteenth Amendment itself show on their face.

III

If majoritarianism is to be rejected as a rule of decision, as the Court implicitly rejects it today, then an alternative principle must be supplied if this earlier line of cases just referred to is still to be regarded as good law. The reapportionment opinions of this Court provide little help. They speak in conclusory terms of "debasement" or "dilution" of the "voting power" or "representation" of citizens without explanation of what these concepts are....

... [T]he Court in this case declines to embrace [any particular] measure of voting power.... it neither suggests an alternative nor considers the consequences of its inability to measure what it purports to be equalizing. Instead it becomes enmeshed in the haze of slogans and numerology which for 10 years has obscured its vision in this field....

This case is nothing short of a complete vindication of Mr. Justice Frankfurter's warning nine years ago "of the mathematical quagmire (apart from divers judicially inappropriate and elusive determinants) into which this Court today catapults the lower courts of the country." *Baker v. Carr*, 369 U.S. 186, 268 (1962) (dissenting opinion).... I would reverse the judgment below and remand the case to the District Court with directions to dismiss the complaint.

■ MR. JUSTICE DOUGLAS, with whom MR. JUSTICE BRENNAN and MR. JUSTICE MARSHALL concur, dissenting in part and concurring in the result in part....

The merits of the case go to the question ... whether a gerrymander can be "constitutionally impermissible." The question of the gerrymander is the other half of *Reynolds v. Sims*, 377 U.S. 533. Fair representation of voters in a legislative assembly—one man, one vote—would seem to require (1) substantial equality of population within each district and (2) the avoidance of district lines that weigh the power of one race more heavily than another. The latter can be done—and is done—by astute drawing of district lines that makes the district either heavily Democratic or heavily Republican as the case may be. Lines may be drawn so as to make the voice of one racial group weak or strong, as the case may be.

The problem of the gerrymander is how to defeat or circumvent the sentiments of the community. The problem of the law is how to prevent it. As MR. JUSTICE HARLAN once said "A computer may grind out district lines which can totally frustrate the popular will on an overwhelming number of critical issues." The easy device is the gerrymander. The District Court found that it operated in this case to dilute the vote of the blacks....

In *Gomillion v. Lightfoot*, 364 U.S. 339, we dealt with the problem of a State intentionally making a district smaller to exclude black voters. Here we have almost the converse problem. The State's districts surround the black voting area with white voters.

Gomillion, involving the turning of the city of Tuskegee from a geographical square "to an uncouth twenty-eight-sided figure," was only one of our cases which dealt with elevating the political interests of one identifiable group over those of another. Georgia's county unit system was similar, although race was not a factor. Under the Georgia system a farmer in a rural county could have up to 99 times the voting power of his urban-dwelling brother. *See Gray v. Sanders*, 372 U.S. 368. Here the districting plan operates to favor "upper-middle class and wealthy" suburbanites.

A showing of racial motivation is not necessary when dealing with multi-member districts.... In *Burns v. Richardson*, we ... stated that assuming the requirements of *Reynolds v. Sims*, 377 U.S. 533, were satisfied, multi-member districts are unconstitutional "only if it can be shown that 'designedly or otherwise' ... [such a district would operate] to minimize or cancel out the voting strength of racial or political elements of the voting population." 384 U.S., at 88.... [W]e demanded that the invidious effects of multi-member districts appear from evidence in the record. Here that demand is satisfied by (1) the showing of an identifiable voting group living in Center Township, (2) the severe discrepancies of residency of elected members of the general assembly between Center and Washington Townships, ... (3) the finding of pervasive influence of the county organizations of the political parties, and (4) the finding that legislators from the county maintain "common, undifferentiated" positions on political issues....

It is said that if we prevent racial gerrymandering today, we must prevent gerrymandering of any special interest group tomorrow, whether it be social, economic, or ideological. I do not agree. Our Constitution has a special thrust when it comes to voting; the Fifteenth Amendment says the right of citizens to vote shall not be "abridged" on account of "race, color, or previous condition of servitude."

Our cases since *Baker v. Carr* have never intimated that "one man, one vote" meant "one white man, one vote." Since "race" may not be gerrymandered, I think the Court emphasizes the irrelevant when it says that the effect on "the actual voting power" of the blacks should first be known. They may be all Democratic or all Republican; but once their identity is purposely washed out of the system, the system, as I see it, has a constitutional defect. It is asking the impossible for us to demand that the blacks first show that the effect of the scheme was to discourage or prevent poor blacks from voting or joining such party as they chose. On this record, the voting rights of the blacks have been "abridged," as I read the Constitution.

The District Court has done an outstanding job, bringing insight to the problems. One can always fault a lower court by stating theoretical aspects of apportionment plans that may not have been considered. This District Court acted earnestly and boldly to correct a festering electoral system. I would not even vacate and remand ... I would affirm the judgment.

White v. Regester

412 U.S. 755 (1973).

■ MR. JUSTICE WHITE delivered the opinion of the Court.

This case raises two questions concerning the validity of the reapportionment plan for the Texas House of Representatives adopted in 1970 by the State Legislative Redistricting Board: ... second, whether the multimember districts provided for Bexar and Dallas Counties were properly found to have been invidiously discriminatory against cognizable racial or ethnic groups in those counties. . . .

* * *

III

We affirm the District Court's judgment, however, insofar as it invalidated the multimember districts in Dallas and Bexar Counties and ordered those districts to be redrawn into single-member districts. Plainly, under our cases, multimember districts are not per se unconstitutional, nor are they necessarily unconstitutional when used in combination with single-member districts in other parts of the State. But we have entertained claims that multimember districts are being used invidiously to cancel out or minimize the voting strength of racial groups. To sustain such claims, it is not enough that the racial group allegedly discriminated against has not had legislative seats in proportion to its voting potential. The plaintiffs' burden is to produce evidence to support findings that the political processes leading to nomination and election were not equally open to participation by the group in question—that its members had less opportunity than did other residents in the district to participate in the political processes and to elect legislators of their choice.

With due regard for these standards, the District Court first referred to the history of official racial discrimination in Texas, which at times touched the right of Negroes to register and vote and to participate in the democratic processes. It referred also to the Texas rule requiring a majority vote as a prerequisite to nomination in a primary election and to the so-called "place" rule limiting candidacy for legislative office from a multimember district to a specified "place" on the ticket, with the result being the election of representatives from the Dallas multimember district reduced to a head-to-head contest for each position. These characteristics of the Texas electoral system, neither in themselves improper nor invidious, enhanced the opportunity for racial discrimination, the District Court thought. More fundamentally, it found that since Reconstruction days, there have been only two Negroes in the Dallas County delegation to the Texas House of Representatives and that these two were the only two Negroes ever slated by the Dallas Committee for Responsible Government (DCRG), a white-dominated organization that is in effective control of Democratic Party candidate slating in Dallas County. That organization, the District Court found, did not need the support of the Negro community to win elections in the county, and it did not therefore exhibit good-faith concern for the political and other needs and aspirations of the Negro community. The court found that as recently as 1970 the DCRG was relying upon "racial campaign tactics in white precincts to defeat candidates who had the overwhelming support of the black community." Based on the evidence before it, the District Court concluded that "the black community has been effectively excluded from participation in the Democratic primary selection process," and was therefore generally not permitted to enter into the political process in a reliable and meaningful manner. These findings and conclusions are sufficient to sustain the District Court's judgment with respect to the Dallas multimember district and, on this record, we have no reason to disturb them.

IV

The same is true of the order requiring disestablishment of the multimember district in Bexar County. Consistently with *Hernandez v. Texas*, 347 U.S. 475 (1954), the District Court considered the Mexican–Americans in Bexar County to be an identifiable class for Fourteenth Amendment purposes and proceeded to inquire whether the impact of the multimember district on this group constituted invidious discrimination. Surveying the historic and present condition of the Bexar County Mexican–American community, which is concentrated for the most part on the west side of the city of San Antonio, the court observed, based upon prior cases and the record before it, that the Bexar community, along with other Mexican–Americans in Texas, had long "suffered from, and continues to suffer from, the results and effects of invidious discrimination and treatment in the fields of education, employment, economics, health, politics and others." The bulk of the Mexican–American community in Bexar County occupied the Barrio, an area consisting of about 28 contiguous census tracts in the city of San Antonio. Over 78% of Barrio residents were Mexican–Americans, making up 29% of the county's total population. The Barrio is an area of poor housing; its residents have low income and a high rate of unemployment. The typical Mexican–American suffers a cultural and language barrier that makes his participation in community processes extremely difficult, particularly, the court thought, with respect to the political life of Bexar County. "[A] cultural incompatability . . . conjoined with the poll tax and the most restrictive voter registration procedures in the nation have operated to effectively deny Mexican–Americans access to the political processes in Texas even longer than the Blacks were formally denied access by the white primary.'' The residual impact of this history reflected itself in the fact that Mexican–American voting registration remained very poor in the county and that only five Mexican–Americans since 1880 have served in the Texas Legislature from Bexar County. Of these, only two were from the Barrio area. The District Court also concluded from the evidence that the Bexar County legislative delegation in the House was insufficiently responsive to Mexican–American interests.

Based on the totality of the circumstances, the District Court evolved its ultimate assessment of the multi-member district, overlaid, as it was, on the cultural and economic realities of the Mexican–American community in Bexar County and its relationship with the rest of the county. Its judgment was that Bexar County Mexican–Americans ''are effectively removed from the political processes of Bexar [County] in violation of all the *Whitcomb* standards, whatever their absolute numbers may total in that County.'' Single-member districts were thought required to remedy ''the effects of past and present discrimination against Mexican–Americans,'' and to bring the community into the full stream of political life of the county and State by encouraging their further registration, voting, and other political activities.

The District Court apparently paid due heed to *Whitcomb v. Chavis,* did not hold that every racial or political group has a constitutional right to be represented in the state legislature, but did, from its own special vantage point, conclude that the multimember district, as designed and operated in Bexar County, invidiously excluded Mexican–Americans from effective participation in political life, specifically in the election of representatives to the Texas House of Representatives. On the record before us, we are not inclined to overturn these findings, representing as they do a blend of history and an intensely local appraisal of the design and impact of the Bexar County multimember district in the light of past and present reality, political and otherwise.

Affirmed in part, reversed in part, and remanded. MR. JUSTICE BRENNAN, with whom MR. JUSTICE DOUGLAS and MR. JUSTICE MARSHALL join, concurred in this part of the opinion and dissented on other grounds not relevant here.

NOTES AND QUESTIONS

1. The first equal protection challenge to multi-member election districts was brought to the Court in the immediate aftermath of *Reynolds v. Sims.* In *Fortson v. Dorsey,* 379 U.S. 433 (1965), plaintiffs challenged Georgia's system for electing its 54 state senators, which was based on existing counties (compare Georgia's county-unit system struck down in *Gray v.*

Sanders, 372 U.S. 368 (1963) and discussed in Chapter 3). Smaller counties were banded together into one election district and elected one senator. The larger counties, however, used multi-member elections in which they elected more than one senator, up to seven in the largest county. The Court held that equal protection was not violated by this hybrid system in which some counties used multi-member elections and others elected only one senator; at the time, the Court was focused primarily on the one-vote, one-person principle and found no violation of it because approximately equal numbers of voters elected each senator throughout the State. The plaintiffs had also alleged that the multi-member elections had been devised to dilute the political strength of racial and political minorities in the populous urban counties. The Court left that question open for further litigation, suggesting that there might be a constitutional basis for challenging electoral structures that diluted the voting power of certain groups: "It might well be that, designedly or otherwise, a multi-member constituency apportionment scheme, under the circumstances of a particular case, would operate to minimize or cancel out the voting strength of racial or political elements of the voting population." *Id.* at 439.

Note that some state courts have struck down, on state constitutional grounds, hybrid districting systems that mix multimember and single-member districts. *See Stephenson v. Bartlett*, 562 S.E.2d 377 (N.C. 2002); *Kruidenier v. McCulloch*, 142 N.W.2d 355 (Iowa), *cert. denied*, 385 U.S. 851 (1966).

2. In *Whitcomb*, the Court appears concerned with drawing the line between ordinary interest-group struggles in democratic politics, in which some groups will inevitably lose, and the improper dilution of the voting power of racial or political minorities. Vote dilution under the Constitution cannot become "a mere euphemism for political defeat at the polls."

How is the line between losing fairly versus unconstitutionally to be understood conceptually? Does *Whitcomb* hold that as long as blacks and other ethnic or political minorities are fully able to register and cast a vote, and to participate in politics, then they cannot claim their voting power has been impermissibly diluted when they are unable to elect the candidates they prefer? If so, does the concept of vote dilution have much power or meaning?

The Court holds that black voters in Marion County are losing because they are Democrats, not because they are black. Does that mean that the Court refuses to recognize a concept of partisan vote dilution—that is, a claim that one party has cleverly designed the electoral system to diminish the power of the other party? If the Court is implying such a view, is that view correct, or should the Constitution protect against partisan vote dilution as well as racial vote dilution? And if the Court is drawing a distinction between partisan and racial motivations and effects, how coherent would this line be if black voters were also overwhelmingly Democratic voters—as they likely were in 1971 in Indiana and as they largely are today? Note that a later Indiana state legislative apportionment returned to the Supreme Court, where the Court held that claims of partisan vote dilution are justiciable. *Davis v. Bandemer*, 478 U.S. 109 (1986). (That issue is the focus of Chapter 10.)

Justice Harlan argues that *Whitcomb* implicitly rejects a philosophy of pure majoritarian democracy, but that the Court's earlier decisions, such as *Reynolds v. Sims*, 377 U.S. 533 (1964), embrace just that philosophy. Is Justice Harlan right to see a fundamental tension between the one-vote, one-person cases and constitutional protections against minority vote dilution?

The three dissenters would have found impermissible vote dilution in *Whitcomb*. Consider whether the four factors they point to as justifying this conclusion ought to be sufficient to find a constitutional violation. The majority asserts that to find vote dilution here would be to endorse the "general proposition that any group with distinctive interests must be represented in legislative halls if it is numerous enough to command at least one seat and represents a majority living in an area sufficiently compact to constitute a single-member district." Is that exactly the proposition underlying the dissent? Why is that general proposition troubling, if indeed it is?

3. *White v. Regester* involved two separate counties and two different minority groups. With respect to black voters in Dallas County, the Court referred to several specific electoral features internal to the electoral structure. Thus, the Court paid heed to majority-vote requirements, "place" rules, and the powerful slating role of a white-dominated political organization, the Dallas Committee for Responsible Government (recall the *White Primary Cases* from Texas discussed in Chapter 4). The Court also noted racial appeals in recent political campaigns, along with Texas' past history of racial discrimination in voting. With respect to Mexican-American voters in Bexar County, does the Court instead seem focused on factors external to the practice of voting itself—such as the "cultural and economic realities" of the county's Mexican-American community?

The Court refers to the vote dilution inquiry as one that focuses on "the totality of the circumstances." Does it consider the same *kind* of circumstances relevant to the decisions in Dallas and Bexar counties? More generally, do the Court's two decisions within *White v. Regester* provide a consistent and coherent approach to identifying unconstitutional vote dilution?

In another case, Justice Stevens argued that a "constitutional standard that gave special protection to political groups identified by racial characteristics would be inconsistent with the basic tenet of the Equal Protection clause." *Rogers v. Lodge*, 458 U.S. 613, 651 (1982) (Stevens, J., dissenting). Is that what the Court has done in *White v. Regester*?

4. How does *White v. Regester* square with *Whitcomb*? Does *White v. Regester* persuasively establish that vote dilution in the Texas counties was not "a mere euphemism for defeat at the polls?" Are you persuaded that there are significant differences of constitutional principle between *Whitcomb* and *Regester*? Do the differences have to do with the fact that *Whitcomb* involved Indiana, which did not have the same history of formal disenfranchisement (and was not a covered jurisdiction under Section 5 of the 1965 VRA) as did Texas? Are the courts, at least in the immediate aftermath of the VRA, simply going to examine electoral structures in the South with more skepticism? Or are there important factual differences that reflect a clear understanding of when vote dilution occurs?

5. In the lower court effort to apply the *Whitcomb/White v. Regester* principles, the most important touchstone became the en banc Fifth Circuit decision in *Zimmer v. McKeithen*, 485 F.2d 1297 (5th Cir. 1973), *aff'd sub nom. East Carroll Parish School Board v. Marshall*, 424 U.S. 636 (1976) (per curiam). *Zimmer* provided more analytical content to the vote dilution inquiry by providing a catalogue of factors that would be deemed relevant. These "*Zimmer* factors" were invoked by many lower courts and by Congress when it amended the VRA in 1982.

In *Zimmer*, black plaintiffs challenged the use of at-large elections for the school board and policy jury (the county legislature) in East Carroll Parish, Louisiana. While the parish's population was nearly 60 percent black, blacks were only 46 percent of registered voters as of 1971. Plaintiffs argued that the at-large election scheme, which had been adopted in 1968 by federal court order, had the effect of diluting black voting power compared to a district or ward-based system. In upholding this challenge, the Fifth Circuit identified a "panoply of factors" that aided the dilution inquiry:

> [W]here a minority can demonstrate a lack of access to the process of slating candidates, the unresponsiveness of legislators to their particularized interests, a tenuous state policy underlying the preference for multi-member or at-large districting, or that the existence of past discrimination in general precludes the effective participation in the election system, a strong case is made. Such proof is enhanced by a showing of the existence of large districts, majority vote requirements, anti-single shot voting provisions and the lack of provision for at-large candidates from running from particular geographical subdistricts.... [A]ll these factors need not be proved to obtain relief.

Applying these factors to strike down the at-large scheme, the Fifth Circuit emphasized that from 1922 to 1962, no black had been permitted to register to vote in the parish, that Louisiana had a general policy against the use of at-large elections from these political bodies up until 1967, and that the parish employed a majority-vote requirement, as Texas had in *White v. Regester*.

Consider the different *Zimmer* factors. What might make each of them relevant to a vote dilution inquiry? Are courts likely to have the capacity to decide whether each factor, taken in isolation, is politically significant in particular cases? If they can, are courts likely to be able to apply these factors, taken in combination, in a consistent and principled manner from case to case? If not, is there some alternative way to frame the constitutional inquiry into vote dilution? Should the Court simply read the Constitution to create a bright-line rule against the use of multi-member districts? While rejecting this view as a constitutional matter, Justice Stevens suggested in a 1982 opinion that "[i]t might indeed be wise policy to accelerate the transition of minority groups to a position of political power commensurate with their voting strength by amending the [VRA] to prohibit the use of multimember districts in all covered jurisdictions." *Rogers v. Lodge*, 458 U.S. 613, 632 (1982) (Stevens, J., dissenting).

6. Notice that neither *White v. Regester* nor *Zimmer* discusses the role of polarized voting. Instead, they address the context under which minority vote dilution most likely occurs (for example, against a backdrop of historic discrimination and in the presence of significant socioeconomic disparities) and the likely outcome of minority underrepresentation (specifically, nonresponsiveness of governmental actors). But neither decision explains *how* an electoral system undervalues minority voting rights. In the absence of a clear operational definition of how dilution worked, *White/Zimmer* invited a free flowing inquiry into the totality of a political jurisdiction's practices. If minority plaintiffs were to claim non-responsiveness in the provision of sanitation services to the black part of town, for example, why shouldn't the municipal defendant have been heard to show that fire services were indeed comparable across the entire town? On the other hand, perhaps the *White/Zimmer* approach was sufficient to resolve the cases before the courts in early voting rights challenges in deeply segregated cities such as Selma, Alabama and Jackson, Mississippi:

> We may speculate that, as an evolutionary matter, no great doctrinal clarity emerged from the early case law challenging Deep South, at-large elections because none was needed. Even the crude methodology of *White/Zimmer* sufficiently illustrated that something was wrong when, more than a century after the adoption of the Fifteenth Amendment, blacks were still clustered in great numbers in poverty-stricken neighborhoods, unable to secure any meaningful representation on the councils of state.

Samuel Issacharoff, *Supreme Court Destabilization of Single-Member Districts*, 1995 U. Chi. Legal F. 205, 219. Does this hypothesis explain the different outcomes?

7. What role, if any, did the question of discriminatory *purpose*—as opposed to simply the presence of a discriminatory *effect*—play in *Whitcomb* and *White v. Regester*? In *Whitcomb*, the Court notes that the plaintiffs did *not* allege that the multi-member election districts had been designed for the purpose of diluting minority voting power. Does the fact that the Court nonetheless goes on to analyze the challenge at length before rejecting it suggest that the Constitution permits vote dilution claims to be established merely by proving discriminatory effects, as long as the evidence of such effects is more compelling than that in *Whitcomb*? Note that the dissent wavers on this question too: initially, Justice Douglas strongly states that impermissible motivation is not required to prove vote dilution, but he concludes that the Indiana system is unconstitutional because it has "purposely washed out of the system" the voting power of Marion County's black voters.

When we turn to *White v. Regester*, some of the opinion's language suggests the Court is striking down the districts for reasons of discriminatory purpose, while other language might suggest that discriminatory effects alone are sufficient. Read the opinion carefully and ask whether the Court finds the districts to have been designed out of discriminatory purposes? Or does the Court conclude that the districts are invalid because of their racial effects, without regard to issues of purpose? In *Zimmer*, the Fifth Circuit held that plaintiffs could win a vote dilution claim under the Constitution by proving either discriminatory purpose or that the electoral scheme "would operate or cancel out the voting strength of racial or political elements of the voting population."

B. THE RISE OF THE INTENT REQUIREMENT

After *Whitcomb* and *Regester*, the next major confrontation in the Supreme Court over the constitutional concept of vote dilution was in a case challenging at-large city council elections in Mobile, Alabama. The Court's approach to the question spawned considerable political controversy, leading eventually to major congressional amendments to the VRA. Consider both the substantive issue of how majority rule and minority interests can be accommodated in democratic institutions, as well as the institutional processes by which these questions are decided, as we turn to that dramatic sequence of judicial and congressional interactions.

City of Mobile v. Bolden

446 U.S. 55 (1980).

■ MR. JUSTICE STEWART announced the judgment of the Court and delivered an opinion, in which THE CHIEF JUSTICE, MR. JUSTICE POWELL, and MR. JUSTICE REHNQUIST joined.

The city of Mobile, Ala., has since 1911 been governed by a City Commission consisting of three members elected by the voters of the city at large. The question in this case is whether this at-large system of municipal elections violates the rights of Mobile's Negro voters in contravention of federal statutory or constitutional law....

I

... The three Commissioners jointly exercise all legislative, executive, and administrative power in the municipality. They are required after election to designate one of their number as Mayor, a largely ceremonial office, but no formal provision is made for allocating specific executive or administrative duties among the three. As required by the state law enacted in 1911, each candidate for the Mobile City Commission runs for election in the city at large for a term of four years in one of three numbered posts, and may be elected only by a majority of the total vote. This is the same basic electoral system that is followed by literally thousands of municipalities and other local governmental units throughout the Nation.[6]

II

Although required by general principles of judicial administration to do so, neither the District Court nor the Court of Appeals addressed the complaint's statutory claim—that the Mobile electoral system violates § 2 of the Voting Rights Act of 1965. Even a cursory examination of that claim, however, clearly discloses that it adds nothing to the appellees' complaint.

Section 2 of the Voting Rights Act provides:

"No voting qualification or prerequisite to voting, or standard, practice, or procedure shall be imposed or applied by any State or political subdivision to deny or abridge the right of any citizen of the United States to vote on account of race or color."

Assuming, for present purposes, that there exists a private right of action to enforce this statutory provision, it is apparent that the language of § 2 no more than elaborates upon that of the Fifteenth Amendment, and the sparse legislative history of § 2 makes clear that it was intended to have an effect no different from that of the Fifteenth Amendment itself....

III

... Our decisions ... have made clear that action by a State that is racially neutral on its face violates the Fifteenth Amendment only if motivated by a discriminatory purpose.... In *Gomillion v. Lightfoot,* ... [t]he constitutional infirmity of the state law ... was that in drawing the municipal boundaries the legislature was "solely concerned with segregating white and colored voters by fencing Negro citizens out of town so as to deprive them of their pre-existing municipal vote." The Court made clear

---

6. According to the 1979 Municipal Year Book, most municipalities of over 25,000 people conducted at-large elections of their city commissioners or council members as of 1977. It is reasonable to suppose that an even larger majority of other municipalities did so.

that in the absence of such an invidious purpose, a State is constitutionally free to redraw political boundaries in any manner it chooses.

In *Wright v. Rockefeller*, the Court upheld by like reasoning a state congressional reapportionment statute against claims that district lines had been racially gerrymandered, because the plaintiffs failed to prove that the legislature "was either motivated by racial considerations or in fact drew the districts on racial lines"; or that the statute "was the product of a state contrivance to segregate on the basis of race or place of origin."

... The appellees have argued in this Court that *Smith v. Allwright* and *Terry v. Adams* support the conclusion that the at-large system of elections in Mobile is unconstitutional, reasoning that the effect of racially polarized voting in Mobile is the same as that of a racially exclusionary primary. The only characteristic, however, of the exclusionary primaries that offended the Fifteenth Amendment was that Negroes were not permitted to vote in them. The difficult question was whether the "State [had] had a hand in" the patent discrimination practiced by a nominally private organization.

... [Appellees'] freedom to vote has not been denied or abridged by anyone. The Fifteenth Amendment does not entail the right to have Negro candidates elected, and neither *Smith v. Allwright* nor *Terry v. Adams* contains any implication to the contrary. That Amendment prohibits only purposefully discriminatory denial or abridgment by government of the freedom to vote "on account of race, color, or previous condition of servitude." Having found that Negroes in Mobile "register and vote without hindrance," the District Court and Court of Appeals were in error in believing that the appellants invaded the protection of that Amendment in the present case.

IV

The Court of Appeals also agreed with the District Court that Mobile's at-large electoral system violates the Equal Protection Clause of the Fourteenth Amendment. There remains for consideration, therefore, the validity of its judgment on that score.

A

The claim that at-large electoral schemes unconstitutionally deny to some persons the equal protection of the laws has been advanced in numerous cases before this Court. That contention has been raised most often with regard to multimember constituencies within a state legislative apportionment system. The constitutional objection to multimember districts is not and cannot be that, as such, they depart from apportionment on a population basis in violation of *Reynolds v. Sims* and its progeny. Rather the focus in such cases has been on the lack of representation multimember districts afford various elements of the voting population in a system of representative legislative democracy....

Despite repeated constitutional attacks upon multimember legislative districts, the Court has consistently held that they are not unconstitutional per se. We have recognized, however, that such legislative apportionments could violate the Fourteenth Amendment if their purpose were invidiously to minimize or cancel out the voting potential of racial or ethnic minorities....

This burden of proof is simply one aspect of the basic principle that only if there is purposeful discrimination can there be a violation of the Equal Protection Clause of the Fourteenth Amendment. *See Washington v. Davis; Arlington Heights v. Metropolitan Housing Dev. Corp.; Personnel Administrator of Mass. v. Feeney*....

In only one case has the Court sustained a claim that multimember legislative districts unconstitutionally diluted the voting strength of a discrete group. That case was *White v. Regester.* There the Court upheld a constitutional challenge by Negroes and Mexican–Americans to parts of a legislative reapportionment plan adopted by the State of Texas. The plaintiffs alleged that the multimember districts for the two counties in which they resided minimized the effect of their votes in violation of the Fourteenth Amendment, and the Court held that the plaintiffs had been able to "produce evidence to support findings that the political processes leading to nomination and election were not equally open to participation by the [groups] in question." In so holding, the Court relied upon evidence in the record that included a long history of official discrimination against minorities as well as indifference to their needs and interests on the part of white elected officials. The Court also found in each county additional factors that restricted the access of minority groups to the political process. In one county, Negroes effectively were excluded from the process of slating candidates for the Democratic Party, while the plaintiffs in the other county were Mexican–Americans who "[suffered] a cultural and language barrier" that made "participation in community processes extremely difficult, particularly ... with respect to the political life" of the county.

White v. Regester is thus consistent with "the basic equal protection principle that the invidious quality of a law claimed to be racially discriminatory must ultimately be traced to a racially discriminatory purpose." The Court stated the constitutional question in *White* to be whether the "multimember districts [were] being used invidiously to cancel out or minimize the voting strength of racial groups," strongly indicating that only a purposeful dilution of the plaintiffs' vote would offend the Equal Protection Clause....

We may assume, for present purposes, that an at-large election of city officials with all the legislative, executive, and administrative power of the municipal government is constitutionally indistinguishable from the election of a few members of a state legislative body in multimember districts—

although this may be a rash assumption.[15] But even making this assumption, it is clear that the evidence in the present case fell far short of showing that the appellants "conceived or operated [a] purposeful [device] to further racial ... discrimination."

* * *

[T]he District Court based its conclusion of unconstitutionality primarily on the fact that no Negro had ever been elected to the City Commission, apparently because of the pervasiveness of racially polarized voting in Mobile. The trial court also found that city officials had not been as responsive to the interests of Negroes as to those of white persons. On the basis of these findings, the court concluded that the political processes in Mobile were not equally open to Negroes, despite its seemingly inconsistent findings that there were no inhibitions against Negroes becoming candidates, and that in fact Negroes had registered and voted without hindrance. Finally, with little additional discussion, the District Court held that Mobile's at-large electoral system was invidiously discriminating against Negroes in violation of the Equal Protection Clause.[17]

In affirming the District Court, the Court of Appeals acknowledged that the Equal Protection Clause of the Fourteenth Amendment reaches only purposeful discrimination, but held that one way a plaintiff may establish this illicit purpose is by adducing evidence that satisfies the [*White/Zimmer* criteria.] Thus, because the appellees had proved an "aggregate" of the Zimmer factors, the Court of Appeals concluded that a discriminatory purpose had been proved. That approach, however, is incon-

---

15. [...] It is noteworthy that a system of at-large city elections in place of elections of city officials by the voters of small geographic wards was universally heralded not many years ago as a praiseworthy and progressive reform of corrupt municipal government....

17. The only indication given by the District Court of an inference that there existed an invidious purpose was the following statement: "It is not a long step from the systematic exclusion of blacks from juries ... to [the] present purpose to dilute the black vote as evidenced in this case. There is a 'current' condition of dilution of the black vote resulting from intentional state legislative inaction...."

What the District Court may have meant by this statement is uncertain. In any event the analogy to the racially exclusionary jury cases appears mistaken. Those cases typically have involved a consistent pattern of discrete official actions that demonstrated almost to a mathematical certainty that Negroes were being excluded from juries because of their race.

If the District Court meant by its statement that the existence of the at-large electoral system was, like the systematic exclusion of Negroes from juries, unexplainable on grounds other than race, its inference is contradicted by the history of the adoption of that system in Mobile. Alternatively, if the District Court meant that the state legislature may be presumed to have "intended" that there would be no Negro Commissioners, simply because that was a foreseeable consequence of at-large voting, it applied an incorrect legal standard. "Discriminatory purpose ... implies more than intent as volition or intent as awareness of consequences.... It implies that the decisionmaker ... selected or reaffirmed a particular course of action at least in part 'because of,' not merely 'in spite of,' its adverse effects upon an identifiable group." *Personnel Administrator of Mass. v. Feeney.*

sistent with our decisions in *Washington v. Davis* and *Arlington Heights*. Although the presence of the indicia relied on in *Zimmer* may afford some evidence of a discriminatory purpose, satisfaction of those criteria is not of itself sufficient proof of such a purpose. The so-called *Zimmer* criteria upon which the District Court and the Court of Appeals relied were most assuredly insufficient to prove an unconstitutionally discriminatory purpose in the present case.

First, the two courts found it highly significant that no Negro had been elected to the Mobile City Commission. From this fact they concluded that the processes leading to nomination and election were not open equally to Negroes. But the District Court's findings of fact, unquestioned on appeal, make clear that Negroes register and vote in Mobile "without hindrance," and that there are no official obstacles in the way of Negroes who wish to become candidates for election to the Commission. Indeed, it was undisputed that the only active "slating" organization in the city is comprised of Negroes. It may be that Negro candidates have been defeated, but that fact alone does not work a constitutional deprivation.

Second, the District Court relied in part on its finding that the persons who were elected to the Commission discriminated against Negroes in municipal employment and in dispensing public services. If that is the case, those discriminated against may be entitled to relief under the Constitution, albeit of a sort quite different from that sought in the present case. The Equal Protection Clause proscribes purposeful discrimination because of race by any unit of state government, whatever the method of its election. But evidence of discrimination by white officials in Mobile is relevant only as the most tenuous and circumstantial evidence of the constitutional invalidity of the electoral system under which they attained their offices.[20]

Third, the District Court and the Court of Appeals supported their conclusion by drawing upon the substantial history of official racial discrimination in Alabama. But past discrimination cannot, in the manner of original sin, condemn governmental action that is not itself unlawful. The ultimate question remains whether a discriminatory intent has been proved in a given case. More distant instances of official discrimination in other cases are of limited help in resolving that question.

Finally, the District Court and the Court of Appeals pointed to the mechanics of the at-large electoral system itself as proof that the votes of Negroes were being invidiously canceled out. But those features of that

---

20. Among the difficulties with the District Court's view of the evidence was its failure to identify the state officials whose intent it considered relevant in assessing the invidiousness of Mobile's system of govern- ment. To the extent that the inquiry should properly focus on the state legislature, see n. 21, infra, the actions of unrelated governmental officials would be, of course, of questionable relevance.

electoral system, such as the majority vote requirement, tend naturally to disadvantage any voting minority. They are far from proof that the at-large electoral scheme represents purposeful discrimination against Negro voters.[21]

B

We turn finally to the arguments advanced in Part I of MR. JUSTICE MARSHALL's dissenting opinion. The theory of this dissenting opinion ... appears to be that every "political group," or at least every such group that is in the minority, has a federal constitutional right to elect candidates in proportion to its numbers.[22] Moreover, a political group's "right" to have its candidates elected is said to be a "fundamental interest," the infringement of which may be established without proof that a State has acted with the purpose of impairing anybody's access to the political process....

Whatever appeal the dissenting opinion's view may have as a matter of political theory, it is not the law. The Equal Protection Clause of the Fourteenth Amendment does not require proportional representation as an imperative of political organization. The entitlement that the dissenting opinion assumes to exist simply is not to be found in the Constitution of the United States.

It is of course true that a law that impinges upon a fundamental right explicitly or implicitly secured by the Constitution is presumptively unconstitutional. But plainly "[it] is not the province of this Court to create substantive constitutional rights in the name of guaranteeing equal protection of the laws." Accordingly, where a state law does not impair a right or liberty protected by the Constitution, there is no occasion to depart from "the settled mode of constitutional analysis of [legislation] ... involving questions of economic and social policy."

---

21. According to the District Court, voters in the city of Mobile are represented in the state legislature by three state senators, any one of whom can veto proposed local legislation under the existing courtesy rule.

Likewise, a majority of Mobile's 11–member House delegation can prevent a local bill from reaching the floor for debate. Unanimous approval of a local measure by the city delegation, on the other hand, virtually assures passage.

There was evidence in this case that several proposals that would have altered the form of Mobile's municipal government have been defeated in the state legislature, including at least one that would have permitted Mobile to govern itself through a Mayor and City Council with members elected from individual districts within the city. Whether it may be possible ultimately to prove that Mobile's present governmental and electoral system has been retained for a racially discrimi-

natory purpose, we are in no position now to say.

22. The dissenting opinion seeks to disclaim this description of its theory by suggesting that a claim of vote dilution may require, in addition to proof of electoral defeat, some evidence of "historical and social factors" indicating that the group in question is without political influence. Putting to the side the evident fact that these gauzy sociological considerations have no constitutional basis, it remains far from certain that they could, in any principled manner, exclude the claims of any discrete political group that happens, for whatever reason, to elect fewer of its candidates than arithmetic indicates it might. Indeed, the putative limits are bound to prove illusory if the express purpose informing their application would be, as the dissent assumes, to redress the "inequitable distribution of political influence."

. . . The dissenting opinion erroneously discovers the asserted entitlement to group representation within the "one person, one vote" principle of *Reynolds v. Sims* and its progeny.[25] Those cases established that the Equal Protection Clause guarantees the right of each voter to "have his vote weighted equally with those of all other citizens." The Court recognized that a voter's right to "have an equally effective voice" in the election of representatives is impaired where representation is not apportioned substantially on a population basis. In such cases, the votes of persons in more populous districts carry less weight than do those of persons in smaller districts. There can be, of course, no claim that the "one person, one vote" principle has been violated in this case, because the city of Mobile is a unitary electoral district and the Commission elections are conducted at large. It is therefore obvious that nobody's vote has been "diluted" in the sense in which that word was used in the *Reynolds* case.

The dissenting opinion places an extraordinary interpretation on these decisions, an interpretation not justified by *Reynolds v. Sims* itself or by any other decision of this Court. It is, of course, true that the right of a person to vote on an equal basis with other voters draws much of its significance from the political associations that its exercise reflects, but it is an altogether different matter to conclude that political groups themselves have an independent constitutional claim to representation.[26] And the Court's decisions hold squarely that they do not. . . .

25. The dissenting opinion also relies upon several decisions of this Court that have held constitutionally invalid various voter eligibility requirements: *Dunn v. Blumstein* (length of residence requirement); *Evans v. Cornman* (exclusion of residents of federal property); *Kramer v. Union School District* (property or status requirement); *Harper v. Virginia Bd. of Elections* (poll tax requirement). But there is in this case no attack whatever upon any of the voter eligibility requirements in Mobile. Nor do the cited cases contain implicit support for the position of the dissenting opinion. They stand simply for the proposition that "if a challenged state statute grants the right to vote to some bona fide residents of requisite age and citizenship and denies the franchise to others, the Court must determine whether the exclusions are necessary to promote a compelling state interest." It is difficult to perceive any similarity between the excluded person's right to equal electoral participation in the cited cases, and the right asserted by the dissenting opinion in the present case, aside from the fact that they both in some way involve voting.

26. It is difficult to perceive how the implications of the dissenting opinion's theory of group representation could rationally be cabined. Indeed, certain preliminary practical questions immediately come to mind: Can only members of a minority of the voting population in a particular municipality be members of a "political group"? How large must a "group" be to be a "political group"? Can any "group" call itself a "political group"? If not, who is to say which "groups" are "political groups"? Can a qualified voter belong to more than one "political group"? Can there be more than one "political group" among white voters (e. g., Irish–American, Italian–American, Polish–American, Jews, Catholics, Protestants)? Can there be more than one "political group" among nonwhite voters? Do the answers to any of these questions depend upon the particular demographic composition of a given city? Upon the total size of its voting population? Upon the size of its governing body? Upon its form of government? Upon its history? Its geographic location? The fact that even these preliminary questions may be largely unanswerable suggests some of the conceptual and practical

The judgment is reversed, and the case is remanded to the Court of Appeals for further proceedings.

■ MR. JUSTICE BLACKMUN, concurring in the result.

Assuming that proof of intent is a prerequisite to appellees' prevailing on their constitutional claim of vote dilution, I am inclined to agree with MR. JUSTICE WHITE that, in this case, "the findings of the District Court amply support an inference of purposeful discrimination." I concur in the Court's judgment of reversal, however, because I believe that the relief afforded appellees by the District Court was not commensurate with the sound exercise of judicial discretion.

It seems to me that the city of Mobile, and its citizenry, have a substantial interest in maintaining the commission form of government that has been in effect there for nearly 70 years. The District Court recognized that its remedial order, changing the form of the city's government to a mayor-council system, "raised serious constitutional issues." Nonetheless, the court was "unable to see how the impermissibly unconstitutional dilution can be effectively corrected by any other approach."

Contrary to the District Court, I do not believe that, in order to remedy the unconstitutional vote dilution it found, it was necessary to convert Mobile's city government to a mayor-council system. In my view, the District Court at least should have considered alternative remedial orders that would have maintained some of the basic elements of the commission system Mobile long ago had selected—joint exercise of legislative and executive power, and citywide representation. In the first place, I see no reason for the court to have separated legislative and executive power in the city of Mobile by creating the office of mayor. In the second place, the court could have, and in my view should have, considered expanding the size of the Mobile City Commission and providing for the election of at least some commissioners at large. Alternative plans might have retained at-large elections for all commissioners while imposing district residency requirements that would have insured the election of a commission that was a cross section of all of Mobile's neighborhoods, or a plurality-win system that would have provided the potential for the effective use of single-shot voting by black voters. In failing to consider such alternative plans, it appears to me that the District Court was perhaps overly concerned with the elimination of at-large elections per se, rather than with structuring an electoral system that provided an opportunity for black voters in Mobile to participate in the city's government on an equal footing with whites.

fallacies in the constitutional theory espoused by the dissenting opinion, putting to one side the total absence of support for that theory in the Constitution itself.

■ Mr. Justice Stevens, concurring in the judgment.

[...] While I agree with Mr. Justice Stewart that no violation of respondents' constitutional rights has been demonstrated, my analysis of the issue proceeds along somewhat different lines.

In my view, there is a fundamental distinction between state action that inhibits an individual's right to vote and state action that affects the political strength of various groups that compete for leadership in a democratically governed community. That distinction divides so-called vote dilution practices into two different categories "governed by entirely different constitutional considerations."

In the first category are practices such as poll taxes or literacy tests that deny individuals access to the ballot. Districting practices that make an individual's vote in a heavily populated district less significant than an individual's vote in a smaller district also belong in that category. Such practices must be tested by the strictest of constitutional standards, whether challenged under the Fifteenth Amendment or under the Equal Protection Clause of the Fourteenth Amendment.

This case does not fit within the first category. The District Court found that black citizens in Mobile "register and vote without hindrance" and there is no claim that any individual's vote is worth less than any other's. Rather, this case draws into question a political structure that treats all individuals as equals but adversely affects the political strength of a racially identifiable group. Although I am satisfied that such a structure may be challenged under the Fifteenth Amendment as well as under the Equal Protection Clause of the Fourteenth Amendment, I believe that under either provision it must be judged by a standard that allows the political process to function effectively....

[The equal protection standard to be applied to claims of group vote dilution must apply equally to racial, ethnic, political, religious, economic, and all other groups.] My conclusion that the same standard should be applied to racial groups as is applied to other groups leads me also to conclude that the standard cannot condemn every adverse impact on one or more political groups without spawning more dilution litigation than the judiciary can manage. Difficult as the issues engendered by *Baker v. Carr* may have been, nothing comparable to the mathematical yardstick used in apportionment cases is available to identify the difference between permissible and impermissible adverse impacts on the voting strength of political groups....

In my view, the proper standard is suggested by three characteristics of the gerrymander condemned in *Gomillion*: (1) the 28–sided configuration was, in the Court's word, "uncouth," that is to say, it was manifestly not the product of a routine or a traditional political decision; (2) it had a significant adverse impact on a minority group; and (3) it was unsupported by any neutral justification and thus was either totally irrational or entirely motivated by a desire to curtail the political strength of the minority. These characteristics suggest that a proper test should focus on the objective effects of the political decision rather than the subjective motivation of the decisionmaker. In this case, if the commission form of government in Mobile were extraordinary, or if it were nothing more than a vestige of history, with no greater justification than the grotesque figure in *Gomillion*, it would surely violate the Constitution. That conclusion would follow simply from its adverse impact on black voters plus the absence of any legitimate justification for the system, without reference to the subjective intent of the political body that has refused to alter it.

Conversely, I am also persuaded that a political decision that affects group voting rights may be valid even if it can be proved that irrational or invidious factors have played some part in its enactment or retention. The standard for testing the acceptability of such a decision must take into account the fact that the responsibility for drawing political boundaries is generally committed to the legislative process and that the process inevitably involves a series of compromises among different group interests. If the process is to work, it must reflect an awareness of group interests and it must tolerate some attempts to advantage or to disadvantage particular segments of the voting populace. Indeed, the same "group interest" may simultaneously support and oppose a particular boundary change. The standard cannot, therefore, be so strict that any evidence of a purpose to disadvantage a bloc of voters will justify a finding of "invidious discrimination"; otherwise, the facts of political life would deny legislatures the right to perform the districting function. Accordingly, a political decision that is supported by valid and articulable justifications cannot be invalid simply because some participants in the decisionmaking process were motivated by a purpose to disadvantage a minority group.

■ Mr. Justice Brennan, dissenting.

I dissent because I agree with Mr. Justice Marshall that proof of discriminatory impact is sufficient in these cases. I also dissent because, even accepting the plurality's premise that discriminatory purpose must be shown, I agree with Mr. Justice Marshall and Mr. Justice White that the appellees have clearly met that burden.

■ Mr. Justice White, dissenting.

* * *

II

In the instant case the District Court and the Court of Appeals faithfully applied the principles of *White v. Regester* in assessing whether the maintenance of a system of at-large elections for the selection of Mobile City Commissioners denied Mobile Negroes their Fourteenth and Fifteenth Amendment rights. Scrupulously adhering to our admonition that "[the] plaintiffs' burden is to produce evidence to support findings that the political processes leading to nomination and election were not equally open to participation by the group in question," the District Court conducted a detailed factual inquiry into the openness of the candidate selection process to blacks. The court noted that "Mobile blacks were subjected to massive official and private racial discrimination until the Voting Rights Act of 1965" and that "[the] pervasive effects of past discrimination still substantially [affect] black political participation." Although the District Court noted that "[since] the Voting Rights Act of 1965, blacks register and vote without hindrance," the court found that "local political processes are not equally open" to blacks. Despite the fact that Negroes constitute more than 35% of the population of Mobile, no Negro has ever been elected to the Mobile City Commission. The plaintiffs introduced extensive evidence of severe racial polarization in voting patterns during the 1960's and 1970's with "white voting for white and black for black if a white is opposed to a black," resulting in the defeat of the black candidate or, if two whites are running, the defeat of the white candidate most identified with blacks. Regression analyses covering every City Commission race in 1965, 1969, and 1973, both the primary and general election of the county commission in 1968 and 1972, selected school board races in 1962, 1966, 1970, 1972, and 1974, city referendums in 1963 and 1973, and a countywide legislative race in 1969 confirmed the existence of severe bloc voting. Nearly every active candidate for public office testified that because of racial polarization "it is highly unlikely that anytime in the foreseeable future, under the at-large system, ... a black can be elected against a white." After single-member districts were created in Mobile County for state legislative elections, "three blacks of the present fourteen member Mobile County delegation have been elected." Based on the foregoing evidence, the District Court found "that the structure of the at-large election of city commissioners combined with strong racial polarization of Mobile's electorate continues to effectively discourage qualified black citizens from seeking office or being elected thereby denying blacks equal access to the slating or candidate selection process."

The District Court also reviewed extensive evidence that the City Commissioners elected under the at-large system have not been responsive to the needs of the Negro community. The court found that city officials have been unresponsive to the interests of Mobile Negroes in municipal employment, appointments to boards and committees, and the provision of municipal services in part because of "the political fear of a white backlash vote when black citizens' needs are at stake." The court also found that there is no clear-cut state policy preference for at-large elections and that past discrimination affecting the ability of Negroes to register and to vote "has helped preclude the effective participation of blacks in the election system today." The adverse impact of the at-large election system on minorities was found to be enhanced by the large size of the citywide election district, the majority vote requirement, the provision that candidates run for positions by place or number, and the lack of any provision for at-large candidates to run from particular geographical subdistricts.

... After noting that "whenever a redistricting bill of any type is proposed by a county delegation member, a major concern has centered around how many, if any, blacks would be elected," the District Court concluded that there was "a present purpose to dilute the black vote ... resulting from intentional state legislative inaction." ...

[T]he Court of Appeals reviewed the District Court's findings of fact, found them not to be clearly erroneous and held that they "compel the inference that [Mobile's at-large] system has been maintained with the purpose of diluting the black vote, thus supplying the element of intent necessary to establish a violation of the fourteenth amendment." ... The court observed that the District Court's "finding that the legislature was acutely conscious of the racial consequences of its districting policies," coupled with the attempt to assign different functions to each of the three City Commissioners "to lock in the at-large feature of the scheme," constituted "direct evidence of the intent behind the maintenance of the at-large plan." ...

III

A plurality of the Court today agrees with the courts below that maintenance of Mobile's at-large system for election of City Commissioners violates the Fourteenth and Fifteenth Amendments only if it is motivated by a racially discriminatory purpose.... The plurality nonetheless casts aside the meticulous application of the principles of these cases by both the District Court and the Court of Appeals by concluding that the evidence they relied upon "fell far short of showing" purposeful discrimination.

The plurality erroneously suggests that the District Court erred by considering the factors articulated by the Court of Appeals in *Zimmer v. McKeithen* to determine whether purposeful discrimination has been shown. This remarkable suggestion ignores the facts that *Zimmer* articulated the very factors deemed relevant by *White v. Regester* ... —a lack of minority access to the candidate selection process, unresponsiveness of elected officials to minority interests, a history of discrimination, majority vote requirements, provisions that candidates run for positions by place or number, the lack of any provision for at-large candidates to run from particular geographical subdistricts—and that both the District Court and the Court of Appeals considered these factors with the recognition that they are relevant only with respect to the question whether purposeful discrimination can be inferred.

... The plurality apparently bases [its] conclusion on the fact that there are no official obstacles barring Negroes from registering, voting, and running for office, coupled with its conclusion that none of the factors relied upon by the courts below would alone be sufficient to support an inference of purposeful discrimination. The absence of official obstacles to registration, voting, and running for office heretofore has never been deemed to insulate an electoral system from attack under the Fourteenth and Fifteenth Amendments. In *White v. Regester*, there was no evidence that Negroes faced official obstacles to registration, voting, and running for office, yet we upheld a finding that they had been excluded from effective participation in the political process in violation of the Equal Protection Clause because a multimember districting scheme, in the context of racial voting at the polls, was being used invidiously to prevent Negroes from being elected to public office.... Thus, even though Mobile's Negro community may register and vote without hindrance, the system of at-large election of City Commissioners may violate the Fourteenth and Fifteenth Amendments if it is used purposefully to exclude Negroes from the political process....

Because I believe that the findings of the District Court amply support an inference of purposeful discrimination in violation of the Fourteenth and Fifteenth Amendments, I respectfully dissent.

■ MR. JUSTICE MARSHALL, dissenting.

... The plurality would require plaintiffs in vote-dilution cases to meet the stringent burden of establishing discriminatory intent within the meaning of *Washington v. Davis, Arlington Heights v. Metropolitan Housing Dev. Corp.,* and *Personnel Administrator of Mass. v. Feeney*. In my view, our vote-dilution decisions require only a showing of discriminatory impact to justify the invalidation of a multimember districting scheme, and, because they are premised on the fundamental interest in voting protected by the Fourteenth Amendment, the discriminatory-impact standard adopted by them is unaffected by *Washington v. Davis* and its progeny.... Even if, however, proof of discriminatory intent were necessary to support a vote-dilution claim, I would impose upon the plaintiffs a standard of proof less rigid than that provided by *Personnel Administrator of Mass. v. Feeney*.

I

A

[... I]n *White v. Regester*, we invalidated the challenged multimember districting plans because their characteristics, when combined with historical and social factors, had the discriminatory effect of denying the plaintiff Negroes and Mexican–Americans equal access to the political process....[7]

7. *White v. Regester* makes clear the distinction between the concepts of vote dilution and proportional representation. We have held that, in order to prove an allegation of vote dilution, the plaintiffs must show more than simply that they have been unable to elect candidates of their choice.... When all that is proved is mere lack of success at the polls, the Court will not presume that members of a political minority have suffered an impermissible dilution of political power. Rather, it is assumed that these persons have means available to them through which they can have some effect on governmental decisionmaking.

For example, many of these persons might belong to a variety of other political, social, and economic groups that have some impact on officials. In the absence of evidence to the contrary, it may be assumed that officials will not be improperly influenced by such factors as the race or place of residence

It is apparent that a showing of discriminatory intent in the creation or maintenance of multimember districts is as unnecessary after *White* as it was under our earlier vote-dilution decisions. Under this line of cases, an electoral districting plan is invalid if it has the effect of affording an electoral minority "less opportunity than . . . other residents in the district to participate in the political processes and to elect legislators of their choice." It is also apparent that the Court in *White* considered equal access to the political process as meaning more than merely allowing the minority the opportunity to vote. *White* stands for the proposition that an electoral system may not relegate an electoral minority to political impotence by diminishing the importance of its vote. The plurality's approach requiring proof of discriminatory purpose in the present cases is, then, squarely contrary to *White* and its predecessors. . . .

B

The plurality fails to apply the discriminatory-effect standard of *White v. Regester* because that approach conflicts with what the plurality takes to be an elementary principle of law. "[Only] if there is purposeful discrimination," announces the plurality, "can there be a violation of the Equal Protection Clause of the Fourteenth Amendment." That proposition is plainly overbroad. It fails to distinguish between two distinct lines of equal protection decisions: those involving suspect classifications, and those involving fundamental rights.

We have long recognized that under the Equal Protection Clause classifications based on race are "constitutionally suspect," and are subject to the "most rigid scrutiny," regardless of whether they infringe on an independently protected constitutional right. Under *Washington v. Davis*, a showing of discriminatory purpose is necessary to impose strict scrutiny on facially neutral classifications having a racially discriminatory impact. Perhaps because the plaintiffs in the present cases are Negro, the plurality assumes that their vote-dilution claims are premised on the suspect-classification branch of our equal protection cases, and that under *Washington v. Davis*, they are required to prove discriminatory intent. That assumption fails to recognize that our vote-dilution decisions are rooted in a different strand of equal protection jurisprudence.

Under the Equal Protection Clause, if a classification "impinges upon a fundamental right explicitly or implicitly protected by the Constitution, . . .

---

of persons seeking governmental action. Furthermore, political factions out of office often serve as watchdogs on the performance of the government, bind together into coalitions having enhanced influence, and have the respectability necessary to affect public policy.

Unconstitutional vote dilution occurs only when a discrete political minority whose voting strength is diminished by a districting scheme proves that historical and social factors render it largely incapable of effectively utilizing alternative avenues of influencing public policy. In these circumstances, the only means of breaking down the barriers encasing the political arena is to structure the electoral districting so that the minority has a fair opportunity to elect candidates of its choice. . . .

strict judicial scrutiny" is required, regardless of whether the infringement was intentional. As I will explain, our cases recognize a fundamental right to equal electoral participation that encompasses protection against vote dilution. Proof of discriminatory purpose is, therefore, not required to support a claim of vote dilution. The plurality's erroneous conclusion to the contrary is the result of a failure to recognize the central distinction between *White v. Regester* and *Washington v. Davis, supra*: the former involved an infringement of a constitutionally protected right, while the latter dealt with a claim of racially discriminatory distribution of an interest to which no citizen has a constitutional entitlement.

Nearly a century ago, the Court recognized the elementary proposition upon which our structure of civil rights is based: "[The] political franchise of voting is . . . a fundamental political right, because preservative of all rights." *Yick Wo v. Hopkins*. We reiterated that theme in our landmark decision in *Reynolds v. Sims*, and stated that, because "the right of suffrage is a fundamental matter in a free and democratic society[,] . . . any alleged infringement of the right of citizens to vote must be carefully and meticulously scrutinized." We realized that "the right of suffrage can be denied by a debasement or dilution of¦the weight of a citizen's vote just as effectively as by wholly prohibiting the free exercise of the franchise." Accordingly, we recognized that the Equal Protection Clause protects "[the] right of a citizen to equal representation and to have his vote weighted equally with those of all other citizens." . . .

Indeed, our vote-dilution cases have explicitly acknowledged that they are premised on the infringement of a fundamental right, not on the Equal Protection Clause's prohibition of racial discrimination. . . . If the Court had believed that the equal protection problem with alleged vote dilution was one of racial discrimination and not abridgment of the right to vote, it would not have accorded standing to the plaintiffs [in earlier dilution cases], who were simply registered voters . . . alleging that the state apportionment plan, as a theoretical matter, diluted their voting strength because of where they lived. . . .

Our vote-dilution decisions, then, involve the fundamental-interest branch, rather than the antidiscrimination branch, of our jurisprudence under the Equal Protection Clause. They recognize a substantive constitutional right to participate on an equal basis in the electoral process that cannot be denied or diminished for any reason, racial or otherwise, lacking quite substantial justification. They are premised on a rationale wholly apart from that underlying *Washington v. Davis*. . . .

* * *

III

If it is assumed that proof of discriminatory intent is necessary to support the vote-dilution claims in these cases, the question becomes what evidence will satisfy this requirement.[34]

The plurality assumes, without any analysis, that these cases are appropriate for the application of the rigid test developed in *Personnel Administrator of Mass. v. Feeney*, requiring that "the decisionmaker ... selected or reaffirmed a particular course of action at least in part 'because of,' not merely 'in spite of,' its adverse effects upon an identifiable group." In my view, the *Feeney* standard creates a burden of proof far too extreme to apply in vote-dilution cases.

This Court has acknowledged that the evidentiary inquiry involving discriminatory intent must necessarily vary depending upon the factual context. One useful evidentiary tool, long recognized by the common law, is the presumption that "[every] man must be taken to contemplate the probable consequences of the act he does." The Court in *Feeney* acknowledged that proof of foreseeability of discriminatory consequences could raise a "strong inference that the adverse effects were desired," but refused to treat this presumption as conclusive in cases alleging discriminatory distribution of constitutional gratuities.

I would apply the common-law foreseeability presumption to the present cases. The plaintiffs surely proved that maintenance of the challenged multimember districting would have the foreseeable effect of perpetuating the submerged electoral influence of Negroes, and that this discriminatory effect could be corrected by implementation of a single-member districting plan. Because the foreseeable disproportionate impact was so severe, the burden of proof should have shifted to the defendants, and they should have been required to show that they refused to modify the districting schemes in spite of, not because of, their severe discriminatory effect. Reallocation of the burden of proof is especially appropriate in these cases, where the challenged state action infringes the exercise of a fundamental right. The defendants would carry their burden of proof only if they showed that they considered submergence of the Negro vote a detriment, not a benefit, of the multimember systems, that they accorded minority citizens the same respect given to whites, and that they nevertheless decided to maintain the systems for legitimate reasons....

NOTES AND QUESTIONS

1. *The meaning of Bolden.* As evidenced by the fragmented and passionately expressed opinions within the Court, *Bolden* was a controversial decision. The question is what the proper focus of this controversy ought to

---

34. The statutes providing for at-large election of the members of the two governmental bodies involved in these cases, ... have been in effect since the days when Mobile Negroes were totally disenfranchised by the Alabama Constitution of 1901. The District Court in both cases found, therefore, that the at-large schemes could not have been adopted for discriminatory purposes. The issue is, then, whether officials have maintained these electoral systems for discriminatory purposes.

be. Several possibilities exist, all of which were invoked in subsequent academic and congressional responses to the decision.

a.   Some criticized *Bolden* as a dramatic change in the governing legal standard under the Fifteenth Amendment. By requiring proof of discriminatory purpose, *Bolden* was said to overturn the approach of cases like *Whitcomb* and *White v. Regester*, as well as to be inconsistent with well-established lower court decisions like *Zimmer*. Which side has the better of this argument about fidelity to precedent? Is there a clearly right answer?

Note that the District Court and the Court of Appeals, both of which found the at-large election system unconstitutional, had each applied a discriminatory purpose analysis.

b.   Instead of focusing on whether the Fifteenth Amendment standard ought to require proof of discriminatory purpose, the criticism might focus on the way the Court *applied* the purpose standard. Assuming that *White v. Regester* also required a finding of discriminatory purpose, is the Court consistent in the two cases with respect to what facts are necessary and sufficient to proving purpose? If the facts here are insufficient to establish discriminatory purpose, what factual findings would suffice? Does the Court's decision preclude development of a fuller factual record in the lower courts on Mobile's at-large elections? Note that Justice White, author of *Washington v. Davis,* 426 U.S. 229 (1976), the case that constitutionalized the intent standard for the Fourteenth Amendment, agrees in *Bolden* that the Fifteenth Amendment should similarly be interpreted to require proof of discriminatory purpose. But unlike the plurality, he believes a showing of that purpose has been made here.

Critics of *Bolden* would soon turn to Congress and seek to "overturn" the Court's decision through amendments to the VRA. That requires a judgment about what precisely was wrong with *Bolden* that Congress should overturn: the purpose requirement itself or the application of that requirement to the facts in *Bolden.*

c.   Four Justices would not find discriminatory purpose in *Bolden.* Four would. Justice Stevens thus becomes the decisive vote; his opinion is significant, however, not just here, but for the general jurisprudential approach it takes to political rights.

First, he argues that equal protection must apply the same way to all claims that the voting power of some identifiable group has been diluted—whether the group is defined racially, politically, religiously, or economically. Second, and as a result, adverse impact alone on the voting power of any group cannot be sufficient to establish a constitutional violation. Third, constitutional doctrine should not focus on the subjective motivations of decision makers, which is what discriminatory purposes often do. Fourth, the Court should instead focus on whether the political decision at issue (1) is consistent with traditional practices or aberrational; (2) whether it is supported by any neutral justification; (3) whether it has an adverse impact on an identifiable group.

This approach is one Justice Stevens takes consistently to cases involving vote dilution claims. Consider whether it provides a more appropriate framework than other alternatives for dealing with these issues. As we confront other problems involving political rights, such as racial and partisan gerrymandering claims, return to the Stevens approach and ask how it would deal with the particular issue. For an overview of Justice Stevens' jurisprudence in this area, which suggests the coherence of his general approach, see Pamela S. Karlan, *Cousins' Kin: Justice Stevens and Voting Rights*, 27 Rutgers L.J. 3 (1996).

d. The plurality argues that Justice Marshall's dissent would require that every political group, or every minority political group, have the right to elect candidates in proportion to its numbers. Is that correct? If so, is that troubling, and why?

2. *The reaction to Bolden.* Voting rights lawyers responded to *Bolden* with despair and outrage. The decision was said to be "devastating. Dilution cases came to a virtual standstill; existing cases were overturned and dismissed, while plans for new cases were abandoned." Armand Derfner, *Vote Dilution and the Voting Rights Act Amendments of 1982 in* Minority Vote Dilution 161 (Chandler Davidson ed. 1989).

Turning to academic forums, critics lambasted the decision. *Bolden* purportedly "broke with precedents in vote dilution cases, it failed to reflect traditional solicitude for the right to vote, it established a difficult discriminatory intent standard with little direction as to how it should be applied, and it mandated judicial inquiry into discriminatory intent of public bodies—an exercise which is inherently divisive." Frank R. Parker, *The "Results" Test of Section 2 of the Voting Rights Act: Abandoning the Intent Standard*, 69 Va. L. Rev. 715, 737 (1983). With respect to proving intent, "the *Bolden* plurality made the possibility of proving racial purpose by circumstantial evidence in vote dilution cases remote ... the *Bolden* plurality clearly implied that circumstantial evidence of discriminatory purpose would not suffice to prove discriminatory intent." *Id.* at 743.

Fortuitously, sections 4 and 5 of the VRA were due to expire in 1982, and Congress had to reauthorize them to keep the statute alive. This provided critics of *Bolden* with a vehicle for seeking amendments to the Act that would, in effect, overturn *Bolden.* The 1982 congressional hearings became a stage on which critics of *Bolden* could parade its failings before Congress. Thus, many witnesses testified as to how difficult, perhaps impossible, it now was to win vote dilution claims.

Benjamin Hooks, Executive Director of the NAACP, testified that "Congress never intended that an impossible burden of proving 'intent' to discriminate be placed on persons denied the right of franchise." Similarly, Robert Krueger, a former member of Congress, testified that "[m]odern discrimination against racial and ethnic minorities is likely to be subtle and unexpressed rather than stated in the press and in the chambers of government. As a result, it becomes extremely difficult and in some cases nearly impossible to prove subjective intent to discriminate, even where the facts fairly and clearly indicate that intentional discrimination might have been in the minds of the officials in charge of voting practices." Extension of the Voting Rights Act, 1981: Hearings Before the Subcommittee on Civil and Constitutional Rights of the House Comm. on the Judiciary, 97th Cong., 1st Sess. 906 (1981). The mayor of Richmond, Virginia, Henry Marsh, testified that "[s]hould the intent standard prevail, however, it would be extremely difficult to prove voter discrimination absent a confession of intent by a voter official." *Id.* at 365. Are these views reasonable interpretations of what *Bolden* required? Plausible ones? Exaggerated ones?

3.   *Subsequent judicial applications of Bolden.* In light of the outcry over *Bolden,* what should be made of the following decisions:

a.   On remand, the District Court held additional hearings and then struck down Mobile's at-large elections as having been originally adopted for racially discriminatory purposes. *Bolden v. City of Mobile,* 542 F. Supp. 1050 (S.D. Ala. 1982). The court held that while the move to at-large elections early in the century had been motivated, as in many local governments in the North, by the aim of placing the business and professional classes in control of city government and excluding the lower classes, invidious racial reasons had also "played a substantial and significant part." This original purpose, combined with the present effects of the at-large elections (primarily the failure of black candidates to be elected and the non-responsiveness of elected officials to the black community) were sufficient to strike down the at-large elections. *Compare Bolden with Hunter v. Underwood,* 471 U.S. 222 (1985) (striking down criminal disenfranchisement provisions dating back to 1901 Alabama Constitution).

The opinion is an extensive, and fascinating, history of local government in Mobile, aided by the expert testimony of professional historians. The significant amount of time and costs involved in litigating vote dilution cases based on such extensive historical inquiry are detailed in Peyton McCrary, *The Significance of Mobile v. Bolden, in* Minority Vote Dilution 47, 48–49 (Chandler Davidson ed. 1989). Conceptually, is the best understanding of policy or constitutional doctrine in this arena one in which dilution questions ought to turn on elaborate historical inquiries into events this long ago? If not, what is the best alternative?

b.   Another important application of *Bolden*'s intent standard came in *Rogers v. Lodge,* 458 U.S. 613, 651 (1982), handed down two days after enactment of the 1982 VRA Amendments. Blacks were 53.6 percent of the population of Burke County, Georgia and 38 percent of its registered voters. Since 1911, the county had been governed by a five-member Board of Commissioners elected at-large. Candidates had to run for designated seats, but could reside anywhere in the county, and had to receive a majority of votes in the primary or general election (with a runoff election if needed).

The Court found that voting was polarized along racial lines. Whites voted overwhelmingly for white candidates, while blacks did likewise for black candidates. As a result of the at-large election system, the cohesive white majority could get all its candidates elected to office and thereby control the entire Board of Commissioners. Consequently, no black candidate had ever been elected to the Board.

The lower courts found that the at-large system, which had been adopted in 1911, had not been adopted for a discriminatory purpose. But those courts found that it had been *maintained* for such purposes. Applying *Bolden*, the Supreme Court affirmed in an opinion by Justice White.

The Court noted that the District Court had found the presence of polarized voting, the absence of black elected officials, and the presence of many of the *Zimmer* factors. While these factors could not, standing alone, establish a violation, the Court held that they could be used as evidence to prove discriminatory purpose. The trial court had pointed to the county's history of discrimination in education and voting, the depressed socio-economic status of blacks in the county, and the nonresponsiveness of elected officials to the needs of the black community—manifested in infrequent appointment of black officials to public bodies and discriminatory patterns of road paving. The trial court also concluded that the large size of the county made it more difficult for blacks to get to polling places or campaign for office, and that the majority-vote requirement and the requirement that candidates run for specific seats further bolstered the conclusion that the at-large system was being maintained for discriminatory purposes. The Court thus upheld orders that the at-large system be replaced with five single-member districts.

Are these factual circumstances about Burke County, Georgia, sufficiently different from those in Mobile, Alabama, as understood by the Supreme Court based on the evidence before it in *Bolden* to produce such different constitutional results? In dissent, Justices Powell and Rehnquist argued that *Rogers* was flatly inconsistent with *Bolden*; in their view, *Bolden* had ruled out appeal to this kind of "sociological evidence" to prove vote dilution. Note that seven Justices considered the two cases to require the same result, though they differed on what that result was. Other critics argued that *Rogers* demonstrated that the Court itself could not adhere to the intent standard. Abigail M. Thernstrom, Whose Votes Count? Affirmative Action and Minority Voting Rights 76 (1987) (*Rogers* with a "new label" had rescued a discarded product.").

c. Do *Rogers* and the result on remand in *Bolden* suggest that *Bolden's* intent standard would not be so difficult to meet in practice? Or does it suggest that the outcry, bolstered by congressional action to reject *Bolden*, caused the Court to water down the intent standard? For the suggestion that *Rogers* was the product of the Court having been "stung by nationwide criticism of the *Mobile* decision," see Armand Derfner, *Vote Dilution and the Voting Rights Act Amendments of 1982, in* Minority Vote Dilution 161 (Chandler Davidson ed. 1989).

C. THE 1982 AMENDMENTS TO SECTION 2 OF THE VRA

In the wake of *Bolden*, Congress re-entered center stage in the development of voting-rights policy. One theme this book emphasizes is the dynamic and complex institutional relationships in the creation, interpretation, and implementation of civil-rights policy. Perhaps nowhere is the complexity of those relationships better displayed than in the political response to the Supreme Court's *Bolden* decision—and then in the next iteration of this process, covered in the following Chapter, in which the courts return to center stage as they assume the role of giving shape to Congress' response to the Court's decision.

We do not seek to approach these institutional issues through mere abstract and formal discussions of "institutional competence," the "proper role" of courts versus legislatures, and the like. One advantage of studying a specific field in depth, such as voting rights, is that it becomes possible to explore the fine-grained details of how the federal courts and Congress (and, to a lesser extent, the executive branch) respond concretely to these issues and to each other's responses. In addition, we can examine these institutional questions from the broader historical perspective that sustained examination of one area of policy offers. As you study the following materials, consider what light they and previous materials shed on these institutional issues. What moves Congress to act in this arena? When it does, is there anything characteristic about the forms that legislative action tends to take? What if anything tends to differ about the ways courts and Congress address voting-rights issues? More generally, how are one's views about the abstract issues that are the typical staple of theory about these institutional questions—issues of institutional competence, proper judicial role, the role of democratic politics—affected by knowledge of the concrete details of judicial and legislative action over long periods of time? Does historical experience undermine more "traditional" views about the role of courts? Or confirm those views?

One reason these questions are often discussed in ways that seem unduly formal is that course materials frequently present only enacted statutes. But focusing on statutory language alone leaves discussion too unmoored from the confused and contentious details of actual legislative processes. In 1982, Congress amended the VRA in dramatic ways. We take the unusual step here of including not just the enacted provisions, but also an extensive account of the legislative developments behind the 1982 amendments. We also include a particularly authoritative document from the legislative history, which the courts have relied on heavily in interpreting these amendments: the Senate Judiciary Committee Report. Presenting legislative history in a casebook is difficult. We do so here by including the following: (a) the amended version of section 2, the aspect of the 1982 amendments we will study; (b) a narrative of the legislative history; (c) the Senate Committee Report.

Before turning to these materials, a word about context: recall that a central element of the VRA—section 5—was first enacted in 1965 as a temporary provision scheduled to expire in 1970. When this provision came up for re-consideration, the statute was amended in 1970 and 1975 to extend and expand its reach. The 1975 amendments extended section 5 for seven additional years, until August 1982; seven years was chosen to avoid having section 5 up for re-consideration in the midst of the 1980s reapportionment. (In 2006, Congress extended section 5 for another 25 years; those amendments are covered in Chapter 6.) *Bolden* was decided close to the time when Congress would have to re-visit the VRA because section 5 would expire.

As you study these materials, focus on whether Congress had a clear and coherent conception of vote dilution in mind when it sought to "reverse" *Bolden*. What did Congress think it meant to "reverse" that decision? What did Congress think *Bolden* itself meant?

1. Statutory Text: Section 2 as Amended in 1982

(a) No voting qualification or prerequisite to voting or standard, practice, or procedure shall be imposed or applied by any State or political subdivision in a manner which results in a denial or abridgement of the right of any citizen of the United States to vote on account of race or color, or in contravention of the guarantees set forth in section 1973b(f)(2) of this title [which protects certain "language minorities"], as provided in subsection (b) of this section.

(b) A violation of subsection (a) of this section is established if, based on the totality of circumstances, it is shown that the political processes leading to nomination or election in the State or political subdivision are not equally open to participation by members of a class of citizens protected by subsection (a) of this section in that its member have less opportunity than other members of the electorate to participate in the political process and to elect representatives of their choice. The extent to which members of a protected class have been elected to office in the State or political subdivision is one circumstance which may be considered: *Provided,* That nothing in this section establishes a right to have members of a protected class elected in numbers equal to their proportion in the population.

42 U.S.C. § 1973 (2000).

2. The Legislative History: General Context

What follows is a summary of the legislative history behind the adoption of the 1982 Amendments to Section 2. This history is worth studying in detail not just for what it reveals about the ideas surrounding Section 2, but for what it reveals about the legislative process and the relationship of judicial decisions to politics. For other perspectives on the Section 2 amendments, see Abigail M. Thernstrom, Whose Votes Count? Affirmative Action and Minority Voting Rights (1987); Armand Derfner, *Vote Dilution and the Voting Rights Act Amendments of 1982, in* Minority Vote Dilution 161 (Chandler Davidson ed. 1989). These excerpts are taken from an extensive and balanced summary of the 1982 legislative process.

Thomas M. Boyd and Stephen J. Markman, *The 1982 Amendments to the Voting Rights Act: A Legislative History*, 40 Wash. & Lee L. Rev. 1347 (1983)

* * *

As the expiration date for the preclearance provisions neared, groups within the institutional civil rights community began to organize for what they anticipated would be a difficult political fight. The Leadership Conference on Civil Rights, to which 165 organizations belonged, hired its first full-time executive director in preparation for the legislative campaign which lay ahead. Moreover, elements of the Leadership Conference, most notably the National Urban League, began to mobilize their local affiliates for the purpose of contacting congressional offices in affected states and applying political and media pressure designed to achieve a voting majority on the House and Senate floors. Seventy-five percent of all League affiliates did so during 1981–82.

Two other members of the conference, the National Education Association (NEA) and the NAACP, would become instrumental in transmitting local sentiment to the Congress. For this purpose, the NEA organized mailings to two contact members in each of the country's 435 congressional districts, and the NAACP set up telephone banks so that local members could notify their representatives of their feelings. These banks were set up for a week prior to action in the House subcommittee, full committee, and on the floor. In all, the banks were available to local members for nearly nine months....

The portion of the Act that generated the most intense interest during congressional consideration of the 1982 amendments was section 2, a little-used provision that tracked the language of the Fifteenth Amendment. The nationwide applicability of section 2 was originally designed to appease Southerners who felt that their constituencies were being singled out for extraordinary federal action. Section 2, however, had never been successfully used as the basis for litigation. When the Supreme Court issued its 1980 plurality opinion in *Mobile v. Bolden* nine months preceding the start of the 97th Congress, new and important issues surrounding the Act came into focus for the first time....

II.   House of Representative Consideration

[As introduced in the House by Congressman Peter W. Rodino, Jr., the longtime chairman of the House Judiciary Committee, the bill to amend the VRA had three important provisions. The first extended the life of the Section 5 provisions another ten years; the second similarly extended the Act's bilingual requirements. The third proposed amending section 2 in response to *Mobile;* if adopted, it would have deleted the words "to deny or abridge" in the existing Section 2 and substituted in their place "in a manner which results in a denial or abridgement of."

In the House, the hearings and legislative debate focused almost exclusively on these first two issues, primarily on how the preclearance provisions should be structured and the conditions under which covered jurisdictions should be able to "bailout" of coverage once they had been included. In the House, very little attention was focused on Rodino's proposed amendment to Section 2. It was noteworthy that the Department of Justice and the White House did not get involved during the House proceedings, declining to appear before the Subcommittee to express its views on any of the bills being considered.]

* * *

On June 24, the Subcommittee gathered for the only day of hearings devoted exclusively to the section 2 issue. In preparation for this day, Mr. Edwards requested that Chairman Rodino and Congressman Hyde state their positions on section 2 before the witnesses appeared. Hyde's response, dated June 23, supported the intent standard articulated in *Mobile*, contending that it was totally consistent with the Court's earlier ruling in *White v. Regester*. Congressman Hyde also endorsed the *White* requirement that the political process be "equally open" to all and suggested a disclaimer which "specifically states that proportional representation is not necessarily required as a result of statistical imbalance and polarized voting.' " Rodino's original letter, in response to Edwards' request, was shelved in favor of another, dated July 14, after the Hyde submission and after the June 24 testimony. Chairman Rodino again claimed that what Congress had intended in 1965 was a broader standard than the Court had interpreted in *Mobile*. Rodino argued that the test for identifying discrimination in section 2 should be governed by the extent to which racial and language minority groups are denied "access" to the political process "through vote dilution and other discriminatory devices and practices." . . . The focus of much of the testimony was on the meaning of the Court's 1973 decision in *White v. Regester*.

* * *

[In the full Committee, an amendment added a disclaimer to the original Rodino language. The disclaimer provided that "[t]he fact that members of a minority group have not been elected in numbers equal to the group's proportion of the population shall not, in and of itself, constitute a violation of this section." The new language was intended to cool apprehensions about the use of proportional representation as a remedy for section 2 violations].

H.R. 3112 then was passed by the House of Representatives by the one-sided vote of 389 to twenty-four, with thirty members not voting. The extraordinary efforts of the civil rights lobby had achieved its purpose. The long hours of planning and congressional contact had borne fruit. As one NAACP representative said:

> Whatever I asked for that I needed I got: money, executive director's and staff time.... We normally have a variety of issues we work on, but in this case I had all my staff working on it.

Said another:

> [A]s long as I have been in Washington, this [has been] one of the most amazing, most historical events of my career.... It was beautiful, I'm happy I had the chance to participate and be instrumental in this; I'll never forget this in my life, never....

IV.   THE SENATE

A.   Pre–Committee

The Senate bill [originally S. 895, then changed to S.1992] was introduced by Senator Edward M. Kennedy of Massachusetts and Senator Charles Mathias, Jr. of Maryland.... Apart from the principal sponsors of S. 895, Senator Kennedy and Mathias, the key participants in the extension debate were conservative Senators, Strom Thurmond of South Carolina and Orrin Hatch of Utah. Both occupied leadership positions on the Judiciary Committee, with Thurmond serving as Chairman of the Committee and Hatch serving as Chairman of the Judiciary Subcommittee on the Constitution. S. 895 and related voting rights legislation had been referred to this Committee.

The civil rights records of Thurmond and Hatch differed considerably from those of Kennedy and Mathias. Senator Thurmond had only ascended to the chairmanship of the Judiciary Committee at the beginning of the year when the Republicans won control of the Senate. However, he had been in the Senate for nearly three decades and had developed a reputation in some quarters as an opponent of most federal civil rights legislation, although more recently he had cast a critical vote in support of a constitutional amendment providing for voting representation in Congress for the predominantly minority population of the District of Columbia. As one of the most dedicated advocates of the doctrine of state's rights, the South Carolinian had voted against the passage of the original Voting Rights Act in 1965, as well as the 1970 and 1975 amendments. Senator Hatch, in his first term of office, had never before cast a vote on the Voting Rights Act but already had acquired a reputation as an articulate critic of many of the initiatives of the civil rights leadership. He had been the leading congressional critic of "affirmative action" and racial quota programs on constitutional grounds, and had led a successful filibuster during the ninety-sixth Congress that blocked efforts to expand Title VIII of the Fair Housing Act of 1968. His objection had been to efforts to establish a standard of defining housing discrimination that focused upon the statistical "effects" of an allegedly discriminatory action rather than upon the motivation of the alleged discriminator. Kennedy and Mathias, on the other hand, had each been in Congress for approximately twenty years and had cast "aye" votes on the original Voting Rights Act and both extensions. Both consistently endorsed the legislative objectives of the civil rights leadership and often had led fights on their behalf.

Following final House action on H.R. 3112, the strategies of both sides began to emerge. The supporters' principle objective was the perpetuation of the momentum that had been built up in the House.... The most significant fact about S. 1992, however, was that it was co-sponsored by sixty-one Senators.

* * *

In the meantime, the strategy of those who had misgivings about HR 3112 included the enlistment of active participation by the Administration in the form of support for an alternative. They attempted to slow down the legislative process so that they could inform their colleagues about what they perceived as difficulties with the House version. To a far greater extent than is normally the case with congressional hearings, the Senate hearings on S. 1992 seemed designed to highlight defects in the legislation through debate between some of the most articulate civil rights academics and lawyers in the country.

Critics of H.R. 3112 were nearly as successful in achieving their short term objectives prior to the outset of Senate hearings as were proponents.... The Administration had played virtually no role in House deliberations on the extension of the Voting Rights Act....

On October 2, three days before the House vote, Attorney General William French Smith forwarded a private report to the President summarizing the development of the Voting Rights Act and setting forth five alternatives for consideration. In retrospect, the most striking aspect of the recommendations, which were prepared in close collaboration with the office of Assistant Attorney General for Civil Rights, William Bradford Reynolds, was its cursory reference to the issue of section 2. Under the heading "Other Considerations," a single paragraph in the twenty-one page report addressed the section 2 controversy. Most significantly, it concluded "we are opposed to including in the Administration proposal any amendment of section 2 that suggests the incorporation of an 'effects' test." The report focused almost exclusively on the issue of bailout.

On November 6, following more than a month of debate within the White House, President Reagan issued a highly ambiguous statement. The statement expressed support for a ten-year extension.... Finally, Reagan stated that the Act should retain the intent test rather than incorporating a "new and untested" effects or results standard.

The President's announcement served as a beacon for Senate skeptics of the House legislation, most of whom had been urging opposition to H.R. 3112, in its various forms, for many months. Critics quickly accelerated efforts to build a case in favor of alternatives to the House measure and to communicate them to their colleagues. Well before hearings even had been scheduled, large amounts of literature were distributed to Senate offices by both sides.

An imbalance in lobbying resources characterized the entire Senate debate on the Voting Rights Act much as it had in the House. On the proponents' side, an impressive array of organizations such as MALDEF, the NAACP, and the ACLU, coordinated efforts to secure Senate adoption of the House bill. Spearheaded by the Leadership Conference on Civil Rights, supporters of the House bill included virtually all significant civil rights, labor, civil liberties, public interest, and religious organizations. These organizations were effective in lobbying Senators, just as they had been in the House, communicating to them strong civil rights support for adoption of a mirror image of H.R. 3112.... The imbalance in lobbying resources was more apparent in the context of these amendments than in any major civil rights legislation to come before the Congress in recent years. The Administration proved not only to be the most valuable ally of those with apprehensions about the House bill, but virtually their only ally....

B.   The Subcommittee

On January 27, 1982, shortly after the start of the second session of Congress, and after several initial delays, the Subcommittee on the Constitution began the first of eight scheduled days of hearings; a ninth was later added. The opening statement of Chairman Hatch made clear that the focal point of Senate hearings would be the results test contained in the amended section 2. In a lengthy statement, Hatch sought to dispel what he referred to as "myths" surrounding the extension of the Act. He observed, "The debate beginning in the Senate today will focus upon a proposed change in the Act that involves one of the most important constitutional issues ever to come before this body. Involved in this debate will be the most fundamental issues involving the nature of American representative democracy, federalism, civil rights, and the separation of powers." Hatch went on to argue that the proposed change in section 2, from an intent test to a results test, would redefine the concept of "discrimination" and would "transform the Fifteenth Amendment and the Voting Rights Act from provisions designed to ensure equal access and equal opportunity in the electoral process to those designed to ensure equal outcome and equal success."

For the first time during congressional consideration of the Voting Rights Act extension, the issue of the proposed change to section 2 was moved to the forefront of debate. In this regard, Senators Thurmond and Hatch differed in their emphases during committee consideration. Thurmond, since he represented a state that had been covered since the inception of the Act in 1965, was now principally concerned with what he perceived as a need for a more effective bailout procedure for covered jurisdictions of the South. As a result, Senator Thurmond directed his primary attention toward a reform of section 5....

Senator Hatch, though, was preoccupied with section 2. Because of his involvement with the amendments to Title VIII of the 1968 Civil Rights Act, he had become sensitive to the abandonment of intent as a basis for identifying racial discrimination. His efforts in re-evaluating affirmative action programs represented similar apprehensions about the recent evolution of national civil rights policy.

The two leading Senatorial proponents of S. 1992, Mathias and Kennedy, delivered opening statements after Hatch, with Mathias speaking from the witness stand rather than from the committee podium. Hatch closely questioned both Senators.

Senator Mathias chose to concentrate his remarks on the question of section 2:

> The House amendment is needed to clarify the burden of proof in voting discrimination cases and to remove the uncertainty caused by the failure of the Supreme Court to articulate a clear standard in the *City of Mobile v. Bolden*.... We are not trying to overrule the Court. The Court seems to be in some error about what the legislative intent was.... Prior to *Bolden*, a violation in voting discrimination cases [could] be shown by reference to a variety of factors that, when taken together, added up to a finding of illegal discrimination. But in *Bolden,* the plurality appears to have abandoned this totality of circumstances approach and to have replaced it with a requirement of specific evidence of intent ... this is a requirement of a smoking gun, and I think it becomes a crippling blow to the overall effectiveness of the Act.

Hatch then initiated a line of questioning that was to be repeated on a number of occasions throughout the hearings. He requested that Mathias be more specific concerning the overall objectives of the new section 2 test:

> SENATOR MATHIAS: The purpose of the bill is to provide for fair and just access to the electoral process.

> SENATOR HATCH: Is [it] the most fair and just access—if 55% of Baltimore is black, that 55% ought to be represented as sole black districts or at least majority black districts.

> SENATOR MATHIAS: A fair and just operation of the electoral process is to give all citizens equal access to vote, run, or otherwise participate in the process.

SENATOR HATCH: What does "equal access" mean?

SENATOR MATHIAS: You are well aware of what it means.

SENATOR HATCH: I want to know what you think it means, because I know what it means under the effects test. I think it means, as the Attorney General of the United States does, proportional representation.

SENATOR MATHIAS: You look at the totality of circumstances; that is what we have been doing.

SENATOR HATCH: That is what we do under the intent standard. I am quite confused as to relevance of these circumstances that you are considering in their totality.... I do not understand what the question is that the court asks itself in evaluating the totality of circumstances under the results test? What precisely does the court ask itself after it has looked to the totality of circumstances and what is the standard for evaluation under the results test?

SENATOR MATHIAS: Look at the results.

SENATOR HATCH: That is all? And if there was absolutely no intent to discrimination, as they found in the *Mobile* case, if the results looked like discrimination, then would the court be able to come down on that jurisdiction—on Baltimore, for example?

Senator Hatch inquired throughout the hearings about the significance of the "totality of circumstances" description of the proposed results test. Hatch's chief goal seemed to create a distinction between the scope of permissible evidence under a test for discrimination and the standard for evaluating such evidence. The distinction normally was couched in terms of what threshold question should judges ask in attempting to evaluate evidence before them in a section 2 proceeding. It was not until much later in the hearing process that proponents of the House bill seemed prepared to respond to this query. In Hatch's view, however, a reasonable and comprehensible response was never forthcoming.

[...] The themes highlighted by Hatch, as well as by proponents of the House measure, were restated frequently during the remaining eight days of hearings. Although occasional discussion of the merits of the new bailout standard relating to section 5 occurred, the consistent focus of the hearings remained upon the meaning and wisdom of the proposed results test in section 2. The principle elements of controversy regarding section 2 were as follows:

(1) *Whether the results standard was respective of the law existing prior to the Mobile decision.* This question was important in determining whether Hatch's predictions of proportional representation were credible. If the results standard merely reflected the understanding of the law prior to *Mobile*, Hatch would have difficulty demonstrating that an explicit restatement of the results standard in section 2 to overturn *Mobile* would lead to

proportional representation. While Hatch occasionally argued that some of the decisions interpreting the effects standard of section 5 established a remedy of proportional representation, his principal argument was that the law on section 2, prior to *Mobile*, had never been anything other than an intent standard. Thus, the absence of proportional representation requirements in the past was largely irrelevant. In this regard, Hatch frequently quoted Justice Stewart's comments in *Mobile*....

To the extent that Hatch was successful in demonstrating that the results test represented a new test, one that had not existed prior to the *Mobile* decision, he was far more likely to be credible in suggesting that the impact of this test would be unwise public policy or, at best, uncertain.

In contrast, supporters of H.R. 3112 took issue with both Hatch and Justice Stewart. Laughlin McDonald, the Director of the Southern Regional Office of the American Civil Liberties Union, argued that *Mobile* required proof of intent and, therefore, was a "change in the law." McDonald continued, "Prior to *Mobile*, it was understood by lawyers trying these cases and by the judges who were hearing them that a violation of voting rights could be made out upon proof of a bad purpose or effect ... *Mobile* had a dramatic effect on our cases." ...

(2) *Whether the results standard would inevitably lead to proportional representation*. Although virtually all witnesses on both sides of the debate claimed to reject the notion of proportional representation as desirable public policy, the critical issue in the entire debate was whether the results test would lead to a political regime in which proportional representation of racial and ethnic groups became the standard on which voting rights violations would be predicated. Critics of H.R. 3112 repeatedly attacked the results test as one which could lead to such a situation. Assistant Attorney General for Civil Rights Reynolds remarked that the proposed amendment to section 2 might lead to the use of "quotas" in the election process, and that local units of government would be required to "present compelling justification for any voting system which does not lead to proportional representation." Dr. Berns similarly concluded that the amendment would reverse *Mobile* and authorize "[f]ederal courts to require States to change their laws to ensure that minorities will be elected in proportion to their numbers."

Defenders of the amendment assumed that the results test represented a restatement of the law prior to *Mobile*. They argued that proportional representation had not resulted from federal court decisions during this period. As McDonald observed, "I cannot ... think of a single case in which we have won, in which we have settled, in which the courts have ruled for us under the Constitution or under section 2 ... which have resulted in proportional representation.... As an actual matter, we have never gotten proportional representation." To a large extent, the common rejection of proportional representation by proponents and critics of H.R. 3112 masked more fundamental problems of definition.

(3) *What was meant by the results test if not proportional representation.* Hatch argued that the test either would lead to proportional representation or that the test had no comprehensible meaning. If the test had no such meaning, he felt it was likely to invest the federal courts with sharply enhanced authority to substitute their own policy preferences on voting practices and electoral structures for the policies of state legislatures and local elected bodies.

Hatch asked of witnesses what the "core value" was of the results test. In the absence of any clearly defined value, Hatch argued that the totality of circumstances response, relied on by proponents of the House measure, was "unsatisfactory." To speak of the scope of permissible evidence in the context of the totality of circumstances missed the point, in his judgement. Any test, including the intent test, encouraged consideration of the totality of circumstances. The crucial inquiry involved determining the threshold question asked by a court in evaluating evidence; in other words, the standard by which the totality of circumstances would be judged. [Hatch] further complained that efforts to elicit greater guidance on the meaning of the test had degenerated into "wholly uninstructive statements of the sort that 'you know discrimination when you see it,'" or else "increasingly explicit references to the numerical and statistical comparisons that are tools of proportional representation." Initial difficulties on the part of supporters in either understanding or responding to inquiries about the "core value" of the results test soon changed. Supporters responded to such inquiries by referring either to the specific factors outlined by the Court in *White v. Regester* or by the lower federal courts in *Zimmer v. McKeithen.* Professor Norman Dorsen, of the New York University School of Law and President of the American Civil Liberties Union, was among the first to concede that the totality of circumstances description of the results test was inadequate. He relied on Justice White's remarks in *White* to provide a more useful description of the new test. In *White*, Justice White stated that "[t]he plaintiffs burden is to produce evidence to support findings that the political processes leading to nomination and election were not equally open to participation by the group in question." Justice White's language eventually was debated in the context of the compromise offered as an alternative to the House language after the completion of Senate hearings.

(4) *Whether the disclaimer of proportional representation contained in the House proposal was effective.* Supporters of H.R. 3112 constantly argued that the amendment would not result in proportional representation because of the "disclaimer" in the new section 2.... Critics of the test were concerned that the disclaimer posed no serious barrier to a mandate of proportional representation. They, however, also recognized the internal political difficulties that the disclaimer posed. A casual observer of these amendments, several Senators noted, could not help but assume that the disclaimer language established at least some significant obstacle to the judicial transformation of the results test into a test of proportional representation....

(5) *The meaning of the intent test.* Just as critics and proponents differed on the proper meaning of the proposed results test, the two sides in the Voting Rights Amendments debate repeatedly disagreed about the meaning of the intent test, which Hatch, Thurmond and the Reagan Administration wished to preserve. Proponents of the results test repeatedly characterized the intent standard as requiring direct evidence of discriminatory purpose or intent such as overt statements of bigotry or evidence of a "smoking gun." Proponents also felt that the intent test required courts to "mind read" in order to discern the intentions of "long-dead" legislators. Dr. Arthur Fleming, Chairman of the United of States Commission on Civil Rights, and an outspoken opponent of the intent test, contended that "inquiries [into intent] can only be divisive, threatening to destroy any existing racial progress in a community. It is the intent test, not the results test, that would make it necessary to brand individuals as racist in order to obtain judicial relief." . . .

(6) *What was Congress' original intent in passing section 2 of the Voting Rights Act.* The final major issue related to whether Congress' intent in 1965 was compatible with the newly proposed results test. Critics of the test argued that even if the lower federal courts had adopted a results test in their pre-*Mobile* interpretation of section 2 (which they declined to concede), the original intent of Congress had been the establishment of a test in section 2 premised upon the traditional standard of intent or purpose. The Subcommittee Report found it particularly persuasive that Congress chose not to utilize the effects language in section 2 that Congress had expressly incorporated into sections 4 and 5. Congress also had exhaustively debated the concept of an effects standard in the context of sections 4 and 5, but had not in the context of section 2.

Proponents of the results test responded by pointing to the sparse legislative history existing on the meaning of section 2. Relying upon statements by former Attorney General Nicholas Katzenbach, they concluded that Congress was aware of the competing definitions of "discrimination" and intended that section 2 cover voting rights violations established under either. Ironically, critics of the results test also relied upon the former Attorney General's remarks in 1965 to establish their case as to the original legislative intent. . . .

Concluding the March 1 hearing, as well as the entire sequence of hearings on Voting Rights Act Amendments, Senator Hatch reaffirmed his commitment to the idea of nondiscrimination and perhaps in anticipation of forthcoming legislative events, remarked that:

> Whatever the outcome of this debate, I personally hope that we will be able to say a decade from now that we did what was right; I personally hope that we will not have to say a decade from now that no one really appreciated at the time what section 2 was all about.

[The Subcommittee then reported a version of the bill to the full Senate Judiciary Committee].

C.   The Full Committee

During a thirty day hiatus between Subcommittee and full Committee action, intensive lobbying and negotiations took place within the Judiciary Committee, much as it had in the House, between members and the Judiciary Committee and outside organizations, notably the Leadership staff of the Committee Administration and the leadership of the Conference on Civil Rights. . . .

As final Committee action approached, a general feeling seemed to exist among members of the Committee that they wished to remain supportive of the mass of outside organizations lobbying for the House version, while at the same time responding to the potentially explosive issue of proportional representation and electoral quotas.

On April 24, Senator Robert Dole of Kansas, one of the few remaining undecided members of the Committee, accorded them this opportunity by proposing a compromise on both sections 2 and 5 that was designed to reconcile the two competing viewpoints on the Committee. Formulated in coordination with representatives of the Leadership Conference, the new language on section 2 proposed to retain the results language of H.R. 3112, but to append a new subsection attempting to describe its parameters in greater detail. . . .

Since Senator Dole was in a politically critical position in the center of the Committee, the proposed compromise effectively resolved any remaining doubts about the fate of the Voting Rights Act in the Senate and in the entire Congress. . . .

Since the Dole compromise had been coordinated with leaders of the civil rights community, it carried with it the support of the original sponsors of S. 1992, Senators Kennedy and Mathias. In addition, the Dole compromise attracted the support of each of the other Committee co-sponsors as well as Senator Heflin. Faced with this show of bipartisan support, several Republican conservatives who had been leaning toward the Subcommittee version rather than the original also opted for the compromises.

On May 3, one day before the Judiciary Committee was finally to consider S. 1992, the Administration, unsuccessful in brokering alternative compromises, also joined in support of the compromise. President Reagan announced then that "the compromise would greatly strengthen the safeguards against proportional representation while also protecting the basic right to vote." Attorney General Smith and Assistant Attorney General Reynolds followed with similar statements.

The Dole proposal effectively supplied a political resolution to misgivings about section 2. It did not, however, put to rest the considerable confusion over what the compromise ultimately was intended to mean. During most of the remaining debate in the Senate, each side attempted to explain the reach of the Dole provision. When the full Committee commenced debate on the extension on April 28, Senator Dole explained the purpose of his language in the following manner:

> Proponents of the results standard in the Mathias–Kennedy bill persuasively argue that intentional discrimination is too difficult to prove to make enforcement of the law effective. Perhaps, more importantly, they have asked if the right to exercise a franchise has been denied or abridged, why should plaintiffs have to prove that the deprivation of this fundamental right was intentional. On the other hand, many on the Committee have expressed legitimate concerns that a results standard could be interpreted by the courts to mandate proportional representation.... The supporters of this compromise believe that a voting practice or procedure which is discriminatory in result should not be allowed to stand regardless of whether there exists a discriminatory purpose or intent.... However, we also feel that the legislation should be strengthened with additional language delineating what legal standard should apply under the results test and clarifying that it is not a mandate for proportional representation. Thus, our compromise adds a new subsection to section 2 which codifies language from the 1973 Supreme Court decision of *White v. Regester.*

The compromise was met with sharp criticism from Senator Hatch, who recognized that the Dole provision inevitably would replace the Subcommittee language. He raised a number of points designed to demonstrate that the Dole compromise was largely an "illusory" one, and that the impact of the provision was not likely to be different from the unamended House provision. Hatch made the following points with regard to the compromise: (1) the emphasis upon the totality of circumstances perpetuated the confusion that proponents of the results test had generated between the scope of the permissible evidence and the standard by which such evidence would be evaluated in a court; (2) in Hatch's view, no "core value" existed by which a results test could judge discriminatory conduct other than by a proportional representation analysis, and nothing in the compromise language established any alternative; (3) the compromise also perpetuated confusion between proportional representation as a right and proportional representation as a remedy; (4) as with the original results language, the flaw was not with an inadequately strong disclaimer of proportional representation, but with the central notion itself of a results test; (5) the concept of an "equally open" system did nothing to address the problem of legislative guidance to the courts; and (6) the concept of "protected groups" within the language of the compromise was inconsistent with the Act's original intent to protect the right of individuals, not groups, to cast their votes.

Immediately prior to final Judiciary Committee consideration of amendments to the Subcommittee bill, Hatch engaged Dole in a series of questions designed further to draw out Dole's intent in developing the compromise language.... When Hatch asked about the relationship between Dole's compromise and the *White v. Regester* test, Senator Dole said that the compromise carried forth the *White v. Regester* test. He argued that the *White v. Regester* test did not require proportional representation nor did it invalidate at-large election systems. Dole subsequently reiterated that the existence of an at-large system would not, in and of itself, give rise to a violation in circumstances where there would not otherwise have been a violation. Finally, in probably the most ambiguous exchange between the two, Senator Dole was asked whether the compromise was designed to preclude courts from imposing proportional representation as a remedy for a section 2 violation. After first responding that the compromise did not so prohibit a court, Dole stated that such concerns were unwarranted because "it is a well established legal principle that remedies must be commensurate with the violation established."

[The Committee approved the Dole compromise amendment, which became part of the enacted version of the VRA, and issued the Senate Committee Report, excerpts of which are printed below].

V. CONCLUSION

[. . .] The 1982 Amendments to the Voting Rights Act were significant in what they failed to say, in addition to what the new statute finally contained. The alterations to sections 5 and 2 will be litigated for years to come, with the apparent legislative intent to broaden both sections at the fulcrum of the debate.

[. . .] As so often happens in complex legislative matters, particularly where highly charged emotional issues are involved, the federal judiciary will ultimately have to tell Congress what it intended to achieve in its 1982 Amendments to sections 2 and 5. Indeed, the very constitutionality of these provisions will be the subject of considerable debate in the courts in the years ahead. While some compromises promote stability of the law, others merely postpone difficult policy decisions. The undeniably substantial controversies involved in the Voting Rights Act debate must finally be resolved; when they are, they will contribute in great measure toward a definition of the objectives of civil rights policy in the United States for the next generation. . . .

3. THE SENATE JUDICIARY COMMITTEE REPORT

Apart from the text of a statute itself, courts typically view the formal committee reports, which accompany the referral of a bill from committee to the full House or Senate, as the most authoritative documents concerning the purposes of legislation. Because Section 2 received so little focus in the House, and only became the center of attention in the Senate, the most extensive discussion from the legislative history on Section 2 was that provided in the Senate Judiciary Committee Report. This Report has been invoked frequently by courts construing Section 2, and we reproduce the most important excerpts, including majority, dissenting and concurring views.

S. Rep. No. 97-417 (1982)

S. 1992 amends Section 2 of the Voting Rights Act of 1965 to prohibit any voting practice, or procedure [that] results in discrimination. This amendment is designed to make clear that proof of discriminatory intent is not required to establish a violation of Section 2. It thereby restores the legal standards, based on the controlling Supreme Court precedents, which applied in voting discrimination claims prior to the litigation involved in *Mobile v. Bolden*. The amendment also adds a new subsection to Section 2 which delineates the legal standards under the results test by codifying the leading pre-*Bolden* vote dilution case, *White v. Regester*.

This new subsection provides that the issue to be decided under the results test is whether the political processes are equally open to minority voters. The new subsection also states that the section does not establish a right to proportional representation.

* * *

VI. AMENDMENT TO SECTION 2 OF THE VOTING RIGHTS ACT

A. Overview: Proposed Amendment to Section 2

The proposed amendment to Section 2 of the Voting Rights Act is designed to restore the legal standard that governed voting discrimination cases prior to the Supreme Court's decision in *Bolden*. . . .

In *Bolden*, a plurality of the Supreme Court broke with precedent and substantially increased the burden on plaintiffs in voting discrimination cases by requiring proof of discriminatory purpose. The Committee has concluded that this intent test places an unacceptably difficult burden on plaintiffs. It diverts the judicial inquiry from the crucial question of whether minorities have equal access to the electoral process to a historical question of individual motives.

In our view, proof of discriminatory purpose should not be a prerequisite to establishing a violation of Section 2 of the Voting Rights Act.

* * *

D. The Operation of Amended Section 2

The amendment to the language of Section 2 is designed to make clear that plaintiffs need not prove a discriminatory purpose in the adoption or maintenance of the challenged system of practice in order to establish a violation. Plaintiffs must either prove such intent, or, alternatively, must show that the challenged system or practice, in the context of all the circumstances in the jurisdiction in question, results in minorities being denied equal access to the political process.

The "results" standard is meant to restore the pre-*Mobile* legal standard which governed cases challenging election systems or practices as an illegal dilution of the minority vote. Specifically, subsection (b) embodies the test laid down by the Supreme Court in *White*.

If the plaintiff proceeds under the "results test," then the court would assess the impact of the challenged structure or practice on the basis of objective factors, rather than making a determination about the motivations which lay behind its adoption or maintenance.

As the Supreme Court has repeatedly noted, discriminatory election systems or practices which operate, designedly or otherwise, to minimize or cancel out the voting strength and political effectiveness of minority groups, are an impermissible denial of the right to have one's vote fully count, just as much as outright denial of access to the ballot box.

In adopting the "result standard" as articulated in *White v. Regester*, the Committee has codified the basic principle in that case as it was applied prior to the *Mobile* litigation.

The Committee has concluded that *White*, and the decisions following it, made no finding and required no proof as to the motivation or purpose behind the practice or structure in question. Regardless of differing interpretations of *White* and *Whitcomb*, however, and despite the plurality opinion in *Mobile* that *White* involves an "ultimate" requirement of proving discriminatory purpose, the specific intent of this amendment is that the plaintiffs may choose to establish discriminatory results without proving any kind of discriminatory purpose.

Section 2 protects the right of minority voters to be free from election practices, procedures or methods, that deny them the same opportunity to participate in the political process as other citizens enjoy.... To establish a violation, plaintiffs could show a variety of factors, depending upon the kind of rule, practice, or procedure called into question.

Typical factors include:

1. The extent of any history of official discrimination in the state or political subdivision that touched the right of the members of the minority group to register, to vote, or otherwise to participate in the democratic process;

2. The extent to which voting in the elections of the state or political subdivision is racially polarized;

3. The extent to which voting in the elections of the state or political subdivision has used unusually large election districts, majority vote requirements, anti-single shot provisions, or other voting practices or procedures that may enhance the opportunity for discrimination against the minority group;

4. If there is a candidate slating process, whether the members of the minority group have been denied access to that process;

5. The extent to which members of the minority group in the state or political subdivision bear the effects of discrimination in such areas as

education, employment and health, which hinder their ability to participate effectively in the political process;

6. Whether political campaigns have been characterized by overt or subtle racial appeals;

7. The extent to which members of the minority group have been elected to public office in the jurisdiction.

Additional factors that in some cases have had probative value as part of plaintiff's evidence to establish a violation are: whether there is a significant lack of responsiveness on the part of elected officials to the particularized needs of the members of the minority group, and whether the policy underlying the state or political subdivision's use of such voting qualification, prerequisite to voting, or standard, practice or procedure is tenuous. While these enumerated factors will often be the most relevant ones, in some cases other factors will be indicative of the alleged dilution.

The cases demonstrate, and the Committee intends, that there is no requirement that any particular number of factors be proved, or that a majority of them point one way or the other.

* * *

Disclaimer

When a federal judge is called upon to determine the validity of a practice challenged under Section 2, as amended, he or she is required to act in full accordance with the disclaimer in Section 2 which reads as follows:

The extent to which members of a protected class have been elected to office in the State or political subdivision is one "circumstance" which may be considered, provided that nothing in this section establishes a right to have members of a protected class elected in numbers equal to their proportion in the population.

Contrary to assertions made during the full Committee mark-up of the legislation, this provision is both clear and straightforward.

This disclaimer is entirely consistent with the above mentioned Supreme Court and Court of Appeals precedents, which contain similar statements regarding the absence of any right to proportional representation. It puts to rest any concerns that have been voiced about racial quotas.

The basic principle of equity that the remedy fashioned must be commensurate with the right that has been violated provides adequate assurance, without disturbing the prior case law or prescribing in the statute mechanistic rules for formulating remedies in cases which necessarily depend upon widely varied proof and local circumstances. The court should exercise its traditional equitable powers to fashion the relief so that it completely remedies the prior dilution of minority voting strength and fully provides equal opportunity for minority citizens to participate and to elect candidates of their choice.

* * *

E.   Responses to Questions Raised about the Results Test

Opponents of the "results test" codified by the Committee have made numerous allegations as to the potential dangers of its adoption. At bottom, all of these allegations proceed from two assumptions, both of which are demonstrably incorrect.

First, these allegations assume that the "results test" is a radically new and untested standard for voting discrimination suits, with unknown contours and unforeseeable consequences. Opponents nonetheless are somehow confident enough of the implications of this allegedly new standard to predict that it will: inevitably lead to a requirement of proportional representation for minority groups on elected bodies; make thousands of at-large election systems across the country either *per se* illegal or vulnerable on the basis of the slightest evidence of underrepresentation of minorities; and be a divisive factor in local communities by emphasizing the role of racial politics.

They specifically list a number of states and cities whose election systems they allege would be vulnerable under the Committee bill.

The second assumption, equally incorrect, is that the only way to safeguard against these dangers is to make proof of discriminatory intent an essential element of establishing violations of Section 2.

* * *

The Subcommittee Report claims that the results test *assumes* "that race is the predominant determinant of political preference." The Subcommittee Report notes that in many cases racial bloc voting is not so monolithic, and that minority voters do receive substantial support from white voters.

That statement is correct, but misses the point. It is true with respect to most communities, and in those communities it would be exceedingly difficult for plaintiffs to show that they were effectively excluded from fair access to the political process under the results test.

Unfortunately, however, there still are some communities in our Nation where racial politics do dominate the electoral process.

In the context of such racial bloc voting, and other factors, a particular election method can deny minority voters equal opportunity to participate meaningfully in elections.

To suggest that it is the results test, carefully applied by the courts, which is responsible for those instances of intensive racial politics, is like saying that it is the doctor's thermometer which causes high fever.

The results test *makes no assumptions one way or the other* about the role of racial political considerations in a particular community. If plaintiffs assert that they are denied fair access to the political process, in part, because of the racial bloc voting context within which the challenged election system works, they would have to prove it.

Proponents of the "intent standard" however, do presume that such racial politics no longer affect minority voters in America. This presumption ignores a regrettable reality established by overwhelming evidence at the Senate and House hearing.

These conclusions, based on a careful review of the existing track record under the "results test" in the Committee amendment have convinced us that the questions raised by some about that test are satisfactorily answered by that record.

F.   The Limitations of the Intent Test

The intent test is inappropriate as the exclusive standard for establishing a violation of Section 2. . . .

The main reason is that, simply put, the test asks the wrong questions. In the *Bolden* case on remand, the district court after a tremendous expenditure of resources by the parties and the court, concluded that officials had acted more than 100 years ago for discriminatory motives. However, if an electoral system operates today to exclude blacks or Hispanics from a fair chance to participate, then the matter of what motives were in an official's mind 100 years ago is of the most limited relevance. The standard under the Committee amendment is whether minorities have equal access to the process of electing their representative. If they are denied a fair opportunity to participate, the Committee believes that the system should be changed, regardless of what may or may not be provable about events which took place decades ago.

Second, the Committee has heard persuasive testimony that the intent test is unnecessarily divisive because it involves charges of racism on the part of individual officials or entire communities. . . . Third, the intent test will be an inordinately difficult burden for plaintiffs in most cases. In the case of laws enacted many decades ago, the legislators cannot be subpoenaed from their graves for testimony about the motive behind their actions. Further, whatever the uneven extent of the legislative records for State legislative session of 50 or 100 years ago, it is clear that most counties and smaller cities will not have available the kind of official records and newspaper files which the plaintiffs were able to procure for the retrial of *Mobile*.

In the case of more recent enactments, the courts may rule that plaintiffs face barriers of "legislative immunity," both as to the motives involved in the legislative process and as to the motives of the majority electorate when an election law has been adopted or maintained as the result of a referendum.

Moreover, recent enactments, and future ones, are those most likely to pose the fundamental defect of relying exclusively on an intent standard, namely, the defendant's ability to offer a non-racial rationalization as the result of a referendum.

This defect cannot be cured completely even though plaintiffs are allowed to establish discriminatory intent by use of a wide variety of circumstantial and indirect evidence, including proof of the same factors used to establish a discriminatory result. The inherent danger in exclusive reliance on proof of motivations lies not only in the difficulties of plaintiff establishing a prima facie case of discrimination, but also in the fact that the defendants can attempt to rebut that circumstantial evidence by planting a false trail of direct evidence in the form of official resolutions, sponsorship statements and other legislative history eschewing any racial motive, and advancing other governmental objectives. So long as the court must make a separate ultimate finding of intent, after accepting the proof of the factors involved in the *White* analysis, that danger remains and seriously clouds the prospects or eradicating the remaining instances of racial discrimination in American elections. . . .

ADDITIONAL VIEWS OF SENATOR ORRIN G. HATCH OF UTAH

Section 2 "Compromise"

The proposed amendment to section 2 contains two provisions. The first provision [adopts the results test]. . . . For all the reasons outlined in the subcommittee report, I believe this provision to be dangerously misconceived.

The question then is whether or not the second provision—a new disclaimer of proportional representation—would mitigate any of these difficulties and improve upon the House disclaimer provision. . . . The "compromise" disclaimer refers to violation being established on the basis of the "totality of circumstances." This, I gather, is supposed to be helpful language. It is not. There is little question that, under either a results or an intent test, a court would look to the "totality of circumstances." The difference is that under the intent standard, unlike under the results standard, there is some ultimate core value against which to evaluate this "totality." Under the intent standard, the totality of evidence is placed before the court which must ultimately ask itself whether or not such evidence raises an inference of intent or purpose to discriminate. Under the results standard, there is no comparable and workable threshold question for the court. As one witness observed during subcommittee hearings:

> Under the results test, once you have aggregated out those factors: what do you have? Where are you? You know it is the old thing we do

in law school: you balance and you balance, but ultimately how do you balance? What is the core value?

There is no core value under the results test other than election results. There is no core value that can lead anywhere other than toward proportional representation by race and ethnic group. There is no ultimate or threshold question that a court must ask under the results test that will lead in any other direction.

* * *

More fundamentally, however, the purported "disclaimer" language in the amended section 2 is illusory for other reasons as protection against proportional representation.... It is illusory because the precise "right" involved in the new section 2 is not to proportional representation *per se* but to political processes that are "equally open to participation by members of a class of citizens protected by subsection (a)." The problem, in short, is that *this* right is one that can be intelligently defined only in terms that partake largely of proportional representation. This specific right— political processes "equally open to participation"—is one violated where there is a lack of proportional representation *plus* the existence of what have been referred to as "objective factors of discrimination." Such factors are described in greater detail in the subcommittee report, but the most significant of these factors is clearly the at-large electoral system. The at-large system is viewed by some in the civil rights community as an "objective factor of discrimination" because they believe that it serves as a "barrier" to minority electoral participation.

* * *

I would note, however, that in one important respect the provision is even more objectionable than the House provision. It refers expressly to the "right" of racial and selected ethnic groups to "elect representatives of their choice." This is little more than a euphemistic reference to the idea of a right in such groups to the establishment of safe and secure political ghettoes so that they can be assured of some measure of proportional representation. In this regard, I note the recent statement of Georgia State Senator Julian Bond with reference to a redistricting proposal in that State,

> I want this cohesive black community to have an opportunity to elect a candidate *of their choice*. White people see nothing wrong with having a 95% white district. Why can't we have a 68% black district?

That ultimately is what the so-called right to "elect candidates of one's choice" amounts to—the right to have established racially homogenous districts to ensure proportional representation, through the election of specific number of Black, Hispanic, Indian, Aleutian, and Asian–American officeholders.

* * *

ADDITIONAL VIEWS OF SENATOR ROBERT DOLE

The Committee Report is an accurate statement of the intent of S. 1992, as reported by the Committee. However, I would like to add a few further comments concerning the language of the substitute amendment which I offered and the Committee adopted as it relates to Section 2 of the Voting Rights Act, and in particular, what I intended that the substitute accomplish and why it was needed.

* * *

While convinced of the inappropriateness of the "intent standard," however, I was also convinced that in order for this legislation to garner the broad bipartisan support which it deserved, the codification of the "results" test had to be accompanied by language which alleviated fears that the standard could be interpreted as granting a right of proportional representation. During the hearing, this was a concern expressed by many and opposition to the results test was based primarily on this fear. Yet, during the hearings a unanimous consensus was established, among both the opponents and proponents of the results test, that the test for Section 2 claims should not be whether members of a protected class have achieved proportional representation. It was generally agreed that the concept of certain identifiable groups having a right to be elected in proportion to their voting potential was repugnant to the democratic principle upon which our society is based. Citizens of all races are entitled to have an equal chance of electing candidates of their choice, but if they are fairly afforded that opportunity, and lose, the law should offer no redress.

NOTE ON THE SUBSTANCE OF THE 1982 AMENDMENTS

1. The 1982 amendments marked a significant shift in the nature of litigation under the Voting Rights Act. Between 1965 and 1982, virtually all litigation raised claims under section 5. Private plaintiffs challenged various measures on the grounds that they constituted changes "with respect to voting" and therefore could not be implemented unless and until they received preclearance from either the Department of Justice or the United States District Court for the District of Columbia. The objective of the litigation was thus to channel the assessment of the challenged practices into the administrative process. Section 2 was virtually never used. Prior to *Washington v. Davis*, 426 U.S. 229 (1976), and *Nevett v. Sides*, 571 F.2d 209 (5th Cir. 1978), *cert. denied*, 446 U.S. 951 (1980), there was little reason to suppose the statutory standard was more protective than the constitutional one, and the plurality opinion in *Bolden* found that section 2 merely restated the constitutional prohibition.

The 1982 amendments, however, squarely decoupled the statutory standard under section 2 from the constitutional standard under the Fourteenth or Fifteenth Amendments: the new section 2 rejected the requirement that plaintiffs show a discriminatory purpose. Since the 1982 amendments, more racial vote dilution litigation has taken place under section 2, rather than under either section 5 or the Constitution.

2. In the next chapter, we will see how courts gave content to the amended section 2 through the process of statutory interpretation. Before seeing that process, consider your own understanding of what Congress did in 1982.

Did Congress develop a clear conception of vote dilution or discriminatory "results" when enacting the 1982 Amendments? It does seem clear that Congress understood itself to be effectively "overturning" or rejecting *Mobile v. Bolden*. But was there a consensus within Congress as to what *Mobile* meant, or what it meant for Congress to overturn it?

Did Congress simply incorporate into the statute the prior judicial caselaw that had been developing, case by case, on this question? To the extent that is the way the 1982 Amendments should be seen, was that prior status quo itself clear enough to provide coherent content to the concept of vote dilution? Did Congress jump into the fray and seek to "codify" the judicial approach before the courts themselves had worked out a consistent and clear approach? Should Congress be seen as having essentially delegated the task to the courts of defining vote dilution and discriminatory "results" on a case-by-case basis? If so, would that be troubling or appropriate?

Some political scientists argue that congressmen are motivated to legislate in ways that enable them to gain credit among those who perceive legislation to be doing something good while avoiding responsibility for things that will be perceived as bad among other constituencies. *See generally* David Mayhew, Congress: The Electoral Connection (1974). Thus, Congress might enact "symbolic legislation:" legislation that signals something positive to some constituents while not actually imposing any concrete costs. Another manifestation is for Congress to enact broadly worded legislation that postpones the difficult decision-making to agencies or courts; Congress can then claim credit for having addressed an issue while blaming agencies or courts when they make the inevitable difficult decisions, which impose real costs, that filling in the blank statutory terms will entail. For work developing these views, see, for example, David Schoenbrod, Power Without Responsibility: How Congress Abuses the People Through Delegation (1993); Michael Hayes, Lobbyists and Legislators: A Theory of the Political Process (1981).

Are these general theoretical claims about the legislative process borne out by the 1982 Amendments? If so, what implications, if any, follow?

3. Consider the Senate Report and the seven factors it lays out as guideposts. Note that the Report then identifies two additional factors, and then concludes that "there is no requirement that any particular number of factors be proved, or that a majority of them point one way or the other."

First, consider each factor alone and what kinds of difficulties it might pose for courts seeking to implement the congressional mandate. Which particular factors are most likely to be ones courts are likely to find manageable? Second, when courts try to look at these factors in the aggregate, how would they go about putting them together? That is, what kind of guidance has Congress provided when it lists a multitude of factors for courts to consider, then goes on to state that no factor is necessary nor are some factors taken together sufficient? Are multi-factor tests like that in the Senate Report evidence that vote dilution can be determined only after a sophisticated, nuanced inquiry that will turn on subtle variables from case to case? Or are such tests evidence that Congress failed to develop any coherent concept of vote dilution, and simply threw a laundry list of factors at the courts?

Most importantly, recall the history of *Baker v. Carr* and the development of one-vote, one-person doctrine, discussed in Chapter 3. There the Court began doctrinal development with a recognition of the multitude of interests that districting might be thought to implicate; within a short time, however, the doctrine quickly came to make strict mathematical equality of district populations an absolute priority over any of these other interests (at least with respect to congressional districts). Recall the discussion about the institutional and intellectual forces that might drive courts to take complex social problems and devise simple, rigid, easy-to-administer formulas for resolving them. Should one anticipate that section 2 would spawn a similar process as courts seek to transform Congress' multi-factor approach into administrable judicial doctrine? If so, around what factors would judicial doctrine coalesce?

Note that one factor that emerges as central in the Senate Report is the extent to which voting is "racially polarized." This factor is nowhere directly mentioned in the *White/Zimmer* line of cases; it starts to rise in the Senate debates when proponents are forced to respond to Senator Hatch's argument that the amended section 2 will guarantee proportional representation along racial lines. Does the emergence of this factor (or others) in the Senate debates reveal that *White/Zimmer* lacked a clear operational core, and that Congress would have to provide that core in amending the statute? Or should this be seen as a signal to the courts that Congress found the pre-*Bolden* case law an insufficient guide to vote dilution?

4. Is section 2 constitutional? Under what source of constitutional power does Congress have the capacity to "overturn" *Mobile v. Bolden* and enact legislation that invalidates state and local electoral arrangements that have discriminatory "results" even if not motivated by discriminatory purposes? The Supreme Court has not squarely addressed the constitutionality of the amended section 2, although lower courts have been unanimous in finding it constitutional. *See, e.g., United States v. Marengo County Comm'n*, 731

F.2d 1546, 1556–1563 (11th Cir.), *cert. denied*, 469 U.S. 976 (1984); *Jones v. Lubbock*, 727 F.2d 364, 372–75 (5th Cir. 1984). Some Justices have raised this question explicitly as a reminder that the Court has not confronted it; these signals might suggest that at least some Justices view the constitutional question as open and difficult. *See, e.g., Chisom v. Roemer*, 501 U.S. 380, 418 (1991) (Kennedy, J., dissenting). For a fuller discussion, see *Bush v. Vera*, 517 U.S. 952 (1996) (O'Connor, J., concurring) (noting that political bodies are entitled to assume section 2 is constitutional "unless and until current lower court precedent is reversed and it is held unconstitutional").

The leading precedents on both the constitutionality of the VRA and on the general scope of Congress' powers to effectively "overturn" by statute Supreme Court decisions are *South Carolina v. Katzenbach*, 383 U.S. 301 (1966) (upholding the original VRA as a valid exercise of Congress' power under section 2 of the Fifteenth Amendment); *Katzenbach v. Morgan*, 384 U.S. 641 (1966); *Oregon v. Mitchell*, 400 U.S. 112 (1970) (which uphold Congress' ban on literacy tests despite *Lassiter*); and *City of Rome v. United States*, 446 U.S. 156 (1980) (upholding the section 5 "results" test). These cases are discussed both in Chapter 6 and in Chapters 8 and 9. Particularly in light of the decision in *City of Boerne v. Flores*, 521 U.S. 507 (1997)—discussed in more detail in Chapter 6—consider whether the "results" tests of amended section 2 is constitutional. Does amended section 2 raise the same issues as those involved in the earlier challenges to the 1965 version of the VRA? Or must the congressional justifications for using its Fourteenth Amendment enforcement power to enact the 1982 amendments rest on different kinds of arguments? Are the 1982 amendments exercises of Congress' "remedial" powers to enforce the Fourteenth Amendment, as the courts have construed the Amendment? Or are the 1982 amendments an attempt by Congress to redefine the "substantive meaning" of the Fourteenth or Fifteenth Amendments? In the area of voting rights, how is the Court to draw the line, which *City of Boerne* makes crucial, between remedial and substantive legislation when Congress regulates voting practices? *See generally* Pamela S. Karlan, *Two Section Twos and Two Section Fives: Voting Rights and Remedies After Boerne*, 39 Wm. & Mary L. Rev. 725 (1998).

NOTE ON THE POLITICAL PROCESS BEHIND THE 1982 AMENDMENTS

What more general insights into the political economy of civil-rights legislation might be drawn from the specific story of these major amendments? Consider the following:

1. A standard assumption of much post–1937 constitutional theory is that majoritarian political processes can systematically fail to protect or actively exploit the interests of "discrete and insular" minorities. The role of courts applying constitutional law is considered most justified when courts act to protect such groups. A further assumption is that racial minorities are the quintessential "discrete and insular" political group. Do the 1982 Amendments challenge that conventional wisdom?

a. In addition to the description of the lobbying dynamics surrounding the 1982 Amendments provided by Boyd and Markman, consider the following account from a larger study of congressional lobbying, taken from Michael Pertschuk, Giant Killers 148 (1986):

> In mobilizing grass roots; in structuring the media; in formulating and implementing legislative strategy; in substantive expertise and legislative draftsmanship; in building and sustaining a close and trusting relationship with its congressional leaders; in seeking out, packaging, and coaching a knockout array of witnesses at a hearing—the Leadership Conference was unmatched.... When the arms control community sought to organize to fight the MX missile, they turned to the Leadership Conference on Civil Rights as a model.

b. Why was there so little organized interest-group resistance to the 1982 Amendments? Those who have documented the legislative process consistently report "the absence of any organized opposition to the legislation." Abigail M. Thernstrom, Whose Votes Count? Affirmative Action and Minority Voting Rights 113 (1987). But note that the 1982 Amendments occur at the start of Ronald Reagan's first term as President; Reagan was skeptical of race-conscious public policies in other arenas. Is it odd that in such a political context the Congress should have overwhelmingly and with bipartisan support have adopted the "results" test of section 2? Why might there be less resistance to such policies in the voting arena than in other areas, such as employment or housing discrimination?

Consider the interests affected when policies such as these are adopted in different domains. If employment discrimination laws banned discriminatory "results," what interests or individuals would bear the most immediate burden of these heightened protections for minority workers? If voting-rights law incorporate a "results" test, are there comparable interests or individuals so palpably and immediately affected? The most obvious group made most directly worse off by the 1982 Amendments would probably be politicians who would be elected to office under the pre-1982 regime; indeed, one view is that white Democratic politicians, in particular, would be most disadvantaged by the changes the 1982 Amendments make.

If politicians are the principal "losers" from the 1982 Amendments, how easy is it likely to be to mobilize public opinion to resist those Amendments? If it is white Democratic politicians who pay the greatest personal cost, what additional complexities do they face in leading the charge to resist the Amendments?

What does all this suggest about the political economy of enacting civil-rights legislation in different domains? That the organization of interests is likely to vary dramatically from area to area? Should that affect the way courts interpret statutes or apply the Constitution with respect to different issues involving civil rights, or should the Courts nonetheless take the same approach across all areas of civil-rights policy?

c. Bruce Ackerman has suggested that the post–1937 consensus in constitutional law on the need for courts to protect "discrete and insular" minorities needs rethinking, in light of more sophisticated insights into the political economy behind the enactment of legislation. Thus, Ackerman argues it is often "discrete and insular" groups that have the *most* clout in politics:

> In fact, for all our *Carolene* talk about the powerlessness of insular groups, we are perfectly aware of the enormous power such voting blocs have in American politics. The story of the protective tariff is [the] classic illustration of insularity's power in American history. Over the past half-century, we have been treated to an enormous number of welfare-state variations on the theme of insularity by the farm bloc, the steel lobby, the auto lobby, and others too numerous to mention. In this standard scenario of pluralistic politics, it is precisely the diffuse character of the majority forced to pay the bill for tariffs, agricultural subsidies, and the like, that allows strategically located Congressmen to deliver the goods to their well-organized constituents. Given these familiar stories, it is really quite remarkable to hear lawyers profess concern that insular interests have too little influence in Congress.

Bruce Ackerman, *Beyond Carolene Products*, 98 Harv. L. Rev. 713, 728 (1985).

Does Ackerman's argument, along with the case study of the 1982 Amendments, suggest that racial minorities effectively have more political power than the *Carolene Products* approach assumes?

2. Abner Mikva, a former congressmen and federal judge (as well as White House counsel to the President), has offered informed and unconventional observations on the dynamic of judicial and congressional relationships. *See* Abner J. Mikva & Jeff Bleich, *Civil Rights Legislation in the 1990s: When Congress Overrules the Court*, 79 Cal. L. Rev. 729 (1991). Mikva and Bleich argue that when the Supreme Court interprets certainly highly visible statutes narrowly, such as civil-rights laws, Congress has a well-documented record of revisiting the issue and often overturning the Court. Moreover, when Congress is forced back into the policy arena, it not only reverses the Court, but enacts even more aggressive legislation than its initial efforts. Thus, as Mikva and Bleich put it:

> [P]arties who seek to win in the Court what they lost in Congress must be wary of what they pray for. Frequently, these parties win the battle but lose the war by galvanizing congressional forces to overrule the Court and advance to an even higher policy ground.... When Congress believes the Court is needlessly obstructing legislative policy, it tends to harden and harshen its position unnaturally.... [In the civil-rights area in general,] the Supreme Court's decisions seem to have produced a conservative defeat. Narrow civil rights decisions prompted

Washington lobbyists to assemble an aggressive campaign, which may have encouraged Congress to include stronger, less ambiguous language than the political process normally tolerates.

How well does Mikva and Bleich's account describe the relationship between *Mobile v. Bolden* and the 1982 Amendments to section 2?

3. How responsive is Congress to Supreme Court decisions, particularly those in the civil-rights area, whether they involve constitutional or statutory issues (recall that *Bolden* involved both)? Many commentators assume Congress is too inertial or too busy to be particularly responsive. But one study concludes that, at least in the modern era, Congress has been quite responsive to Supreme Court decisions, at least in the civil rights area. *See* William N. Eskridge, *Overriding Supreme Court Statutory Interpretation Decisions*, 101 Yale L.J. 331 (1991). Between 1967–1974, each Congress overrode on average about six Supreme Court decisions; between 1975–1990, each Congress overrode an average of twelve Supreme Court decisions. *Id.* at 338. According to Mikva and Bleich, *supra*, between 1982 and 1988, "Congress overruled seven Supreme Court decisions concerning interpretation of antidiscrimination provisions; in each instance, Congress increased the ability of plaintiffs to bring and prevail in suits compared to the rights recognized by the court." Mikva & Bleich, *supra*, at 740. The Eskridge study concludes that Congress was most likely to override the Court between 1967–1990 in criminal law areas, then antitrust, and then civil rights. In the 1991 Civil Rights Act, Congress overrode numerous Supreme Court decisions interpreting civil-rights statutes.

What does the pattern of congressional response to Court decisions in this area suggest, if anything, about how both the courts and Congress ought to understand their institutional roles in enacting and interpreting statutory provisions like section 2?

4. Eskridge also provides a provocative predictive theory, based on his study of past experience, of how courts and Congress will interact in the area of statutory interpretation. Consider whether this theory explains the pattern of institutional relationships in the development of voting-rights policy—and what it suggests about how the courts will interpret section 2. Eskridge argues that courts face incentives that drive them to be less responsive to the Congress that originally enacts legislation than to the Congress (and President) in power at the time the courts interpret the statute. Thus, "current legislative expectations are usually more important to the Court than original legislative expectations ... Congress should be aware that judicial interpretations of statutes it enacts are not going to be faithful to its original expectations...." Eskridge, *supra*, at 415. *See also* William M. Eskridge, *Reneging on History? Playing the Court/Congress/President Civil Rights Game*, 79 Cal. L. Rev. 613 (1991).

If this prediction is right, what does it suggest about how courts will interpret Section 2? If the prediction is right, what steps might Congress take to make it more likely that the judicial interpretation of section 2 will remain closer to the intent of the enacting Congress?

CHAPTER 8

RACIAL VOTE DILUTION UNDER THE VOTING RIGHTS ACT

As we saw in previous chapters, neither one-person, one-vote nor constitutional constraints on race discrimination in voting fully integrated racial minorities into the political process. One-person, one-vote was simultaneously too majoritarian and too individualistic. The majoritarian aspect of one-person, one-vote set ceilings on (numerical) minorities' political power. It did very little to provide a floor, especially given districting techniques (including the decision to use multimember districts or at-large elections) that allowed for winner-take-all elections. And while the Court's vision of voting as a fundamental, personal right reinforced the struggle for black enfranchisement described in Chapter 2, it focused on the formal right to participate, rather than on electoral outcomes.

As for the constitutional prohibition on racial vote dilution, the discriminatory purpose test delineated in *Washington v. Davis*, 426 U.S. 229 (1976), and applied to vote dilution claims beginning with *Nevett v. Sides*, 571 F.2d 209 (5th Cir.1978), *cert. denied*, 446 U.S. 951 (1980), and *City of Mobile v. Bolden*, 446 U.S. 55 (1980), threw a substantial obstacle in the path of minority plaintiffs. As we saw in the preceding chapter, proving intentional discrimination, particularly with regard to longstanding, widespread practices such as at-large elections, was time-consuming, costly, and often well-nigh impossible since it was hard to show that a particular election scheme was adopted precisely because it minimized minority voting strength rather than despite its dilutive effects. In the South, for example, at-large elections often came into being (or their enabling legislation came into being) as part of the post-Reconstruction legal overhaul. Often, at-large elections were adopted as part of a larger package. *See* J. Morgan Kousser, *The Undermining of the First Reconstruction: Lessons for the Second*, in Minority Vote Dilution 27, 32–33 (Chandler Davidson ed. 1984). Years later, it might be hard to distill out a specific intent with regard to the at-large provisions, and their continuing effect was masked for many years by the outright disenfranchisement of black voters.

After the Supreme Court decided *Bolden*, vote dilution litigation virtually shut down. *Bolden* was announced just as Congress was gearing up for hearings on whether to extend the temporary preclearance provisions of section 5 of the Voting Rights Act, which were scheduled to expire in 1982. As the materials at the end of the preceding chapter detail, in 1982,

Congress not only extended section 5—this time for 25 years—but also amended section 2 to prohibit voting practices or procedures that resulted in a denial of equal electoral opportunity, regardless of the intent behind the enactment or maintenance of the challenged system. But while this federal legislative process was underway, states reapportioned after the 1980 census, and obtained preclearance of new congressional and state legislative plans that once left minority citizens underrepresented in legislative bodies.

The 1982 amendments marked a significant shift in the nature of litigation under the Voting Rights Act. Between 1965 and 1982, virtually all the litigation raised claims under section 5. Private plaintiffs challenged a variety of measures on the grounds that they constituted changes "with respect to voting," and therefore that they could not be implemented unless and until they received preclearance from either the Department of Justice or the United States District Court for the District of Columbia. The objective of the litigation was thus to flush the actual assessment of the challenged practices into an essentially administrative process. Section 2 was virtually never used: prior to *Washington v. Davis* and *Nevett v. Sides*, there was little reason to suppose the statutory standard was more protective than the constitutional one, and the plurality opinion in *Bolden* found that section 2 merely restated the constitutional prohibition. The 1982 amendments, however, squarely decoupled the statutory standard under section 2 from the constitutional standard under the Fourteenth or Fifteenth Amendments, by rejecting the requirement that plaintiffs show a discriminatory purpose. In the years that followed, the bulk of racial vote dilution litigation took place under section 2, rather than under either section 5 or the Constitution.

A.   JUDICIAL MODULATION OF SECTION 2'S "RESULTS" STANDARD: THE *GINGLES* TEST

The first case under amended section 2 to receive plenary consideration from the Supreme Court involved the North Carolina General Assembly. In April 1982, the General Assembly enacted a legislative redistricting plan. That plan used a combination of single-member and multimember districts. Black voters in several of the multimember districts filed suit, claiming that within those districts there were concentrations of black citizens that were sufficiently large and contiguous to constitute effective voting majorities in single-member districts lying wholly within the boundaries of the multimember districts. (They also challenged the way in which the lines between two single-member state senatorial districts were drawn, but that issue was not addressed by the Supreme Court.) The relief they sought was the disaggregation of the multimember districts into single-member districts, some of which would have black effective voting majorities.

Thornburg v. Gingles

478 U.S. 30 (1986).

■ Justice Brennan announced the judgment of the Court and delivered the opinion of the Court with respect to Parts I, II, III–A, III–B, IV–A, and V, an opinion with respect to Part III–C, in which Justice Marshall, Justice Blackmun, and Justice Stevens join, and an opinion with respect to Part IV–B, in which Justice White joins.

* * *

I

* * *

The District Court applied the "totality of the circumstances" test set forth in § 2(b) to appellees' statutory claim, and, relying principally on the factors outlined in the Senate Report [that accompanied the 1982 amendments to the Voting Rights Act], held that the redistricting scheme violated § 2 because it resulted in the dilution of black citizens' votes in all seven disputed districts.

* * *

First, the court found that North Carolina had officially discriminated against its black citizens with respect to their exercise of the voting franchise from approximately 1900 to 1970 by employing at different times a poll tax, a literacy test, a prohibition against bullet (single-shot) voting, and designated seat plans for multimember districts. The court observed that even after the removal of direct barriers to black voter registration, such as the poll tax and literacy test, black voter registration remained relatively depressed; in 1982 only 52.7% of age-qualified blacks statewide were registered to vote, whereas 66.7% of whites were registered. The District Court found these statewide depressed levels of black voter registration to be present in all of the disputed districts and to be traceable, at least in part, to the historical pattern of statewide official discrimination.

Second, the court found that historic discrimination in education, housing, employment, and health services had resulted in a lower socioeconomic status for North Carolina blacks as a group than for whites. The court concluded that this lower status both gives rise to special group interests and hinders blacks' ability to participate effectively in the political process and to elect representatives of their choice.

Third, the court considered other voting procedures that may operate to lessen the opportunity of black voters to elect candidates of their choice. It noted that North Carolina has a majority vote requirement for primary elections.... The court also remarked on the fact that North Carolina does not have a subdistrict residency requirement for members of the General Assembly elected from multimember districts, a requirement which the court found could offset to some extent the disadvantages minority voters often experience in multimember districts.

Fourth, the court found that white candidates in North Carolina have encouraged voting along color lines by appealing to racial prejudice. It noted that the record is replete with specific examples of racial appeals, ranging in style from overt and blatant to subtle and furtive, and in date from the 1890s to the 1984 campaign for a seat in the United States Senate. . . .

Fifth, the court examined the extent to which blacks have been elected to office in North Carolina, both statewide and in the challenged districts. It found, among other things, that . . . the overall rate of black electoral success has been minimal in relation to the percentage of blacks in the total state population. . . .

With respect to the success in this century of black candidates in the contested districts, the court found that [there too, black electoral success had been quite minimal prior to 1982]. . . .

The court did acknowledge the improved success of black candidates in the 1982 elections, in which 11 blacks were elected to the State House of Representatives, including 5 blacks from the multimember districts at issue here. However, the court pointed out that the 1982 election was conducted after the commencement of this litigation. The court found the circumstances of the 1982 election sufficiently aberrational and the success by black candidates too minimal and too recent in relation to the long history of complete denial of elective opportunities to support the conclusion that black voters' opportunities to elect representatives of their choice were not impaired.

Finally, the court considered the extent to which voting in the challenged districts was racially polarized. Based on statistical evidence presented by expert witnesses, supplemented to some degree by the testimony of lay witnesses, the court found that all of the challenged districts exhibit severe and persistent racially polarized voting.

* * *

II

Section 2 and Vote Dilution Through Use of Multimember Districts

* * *

A

Section 2 and its Legislative History

* * *

The Senate Report which accompanied the 1982 amendments elaborates on the nature of § 2 violations and on the proof required to establish these violations. First and foremost, the Report dispositively rejects the position of the plurality in *Mobile v. Bolden,* 446 U.S. 55 (1980), which required proof that the contested electoral practice or mechanism was adopted or maintained with the intent to discriminate against minority voters. . . .

The Senate Report specifies factors which typically may be relevant to a § 2 claim: [1] the history of voting-related discrimination in the State or political subdivision; [2] the extent to which voting in the elections of the State or political subdivision is racially polarized; [3] the extent to which the State or political subdivision has used voting practices or procedures that tend to enhance the opportunity for discrimination against the minority group, such as unusually large election districts, majority vote requirements, and prohibitions against bullet voting; [4] the exclusion of members of the minority group from candidate slating processes; [5] the extent to which minority group members bear the effects of past discrimination in areas such as education, employment, and health, which hinder their ability to participate effectively in the political process; [6] the use of overt or subtle racial appeals in political campaigns; and [7] the extent to which members of the minority group have been elected to public office in the jurisdiction. The Report notes also that evidence demonstrating [8] that elected officials are unresponsive to the particularized needs of the members of the minority group and [9] that the policy underlying the State's or the political subdivision's use of the contested practice or structure is tenuous may have probative value. The Report stresses, however, that this list of typical factors is neither comprehensive nor exclusive. While the enumerated factors will often be pertinent to certain types of § 2 violations, particularly to vote dilution claims, other factors may also be relevant and may be considered. Furthermore, the Senate Committee observed that "there is no requirement that any particular number of factors be proved, or that a majority of them point one way or the other." Rather, the Committee determined that "the question whether the political processes are 'equally open' depends upon a searching practical evaluation of the 'past and present reality,' " and on a "functional" view of the political process.

* * *

B

Vote Dilution Through the Use of Multimember Districts

[The plaintiffs] contend that the legislative decision to employ multimember, rather than single-member, districts in the contested jurisdictions dilutes their votes by submerging them in a white majority, thus impairing their ability to elect representatives of their choice.[12]

The essence of a § 2 claim is that a certain electoral law, practice, or structure interacts with social and historical conditions to cause an inequality in the opportunities enjoyed by black and white voters to elect their

---

12. The claim we address in this opinion is one in which the plaintiffs alleged and attempted to prove that their ability to elect the representatives of their choice was im-

preferred representatives. This Court has long recognized that multimember districts and at-large voting schemes may "operate to minimize or cancel out the voting strength of racial [minorities in] the voting population." The theoretical basis for this type of impairment is that where minority and majority voters consistently prefer different candidates, the majority, by virtue of its numerical superiority, will regularly defeat the choices of minority voters. Multimember districts and at-large election schemes, however, are not per se violative of minority voters' rights. Minority voters who contend that the multimember form of districting violates § 2 must prove that the use of a multimember electoral structure operates to minimize or cancel out their ability to elect their preferred candidates.

While many or all of the factors listed in the Senate Report may be relevant to a claim of vote dilution through submergence in multimember districts, unless there is a conjunction of the following circumstances, the use of multimember districts generally will not impede the ability of minority voters to elect representatives of their choice.[15] Stated succinctly, a bloc voting majority must usually be able to defeat candidates supported by a politically cohesive, geographically insular minority group. These circumstances are necessary preconditions for multimember districts to

paired by the selection of a multimember electoral structure. We have no occasion to consider whether § 2 permits, and if it does, what standards should pertain to, a claim brought by a minority group, that is not sufficiently large and compact to constitute a majority in a single-member district, alleging that the use of a multimember district impairs its ability to influence elections. We note also that we have no occasion to consider whether the standards we apply to respondents' claim that multimember districts operate to dilute the vote of geographically cohesive minority groups that are large enough to constitute majorities in single-member districts and that are contained within the boundaries of the challenged multimember districts, are fully pertinent to other sorts of vote dilution claims, such as a claim alleging that the splitting of a large and geographically cohesive minority between two or more multimember or single-member districts resulted in the dilution of the minority vote.

15. Under a "functional" view of the political process mandated by § 2, the most important Senate Report factors bearing on § 2 challenges to multimember districts are the "extent to which minority group members have been elected to public office in the jurisdiction" and the "extent to which voting in the elections of the state or political subdivision is racially polarized." If present, the other factors, such as the lingering effects of past discrimination, the use of appeals to racial bias in election campaigns, and the use of electoral devices which enhance the dilutive effects of multimember districts when substantial white bloc voting exists—for example antibullet voting laws and majority vote requirements, are supportive of, but not essential to, a minority voter's claim. In recognizing that some Senate Report factors are more important to multimember district vote dilution claims than others, the Court effectuates the intent of Congress. It is obvious that unless minority group members experience substantial difficulty electing representatives of their choice, they cannot prove that a challenged electoral mechanism impairs their ability "to elect." § 2(b). And, where the contested electoral structure is a multimember district, commentators and courts agree that in the absence of significant white bloc voting it cannot be said that the ability of minority voters to elect their chosen representatives is inferior to that of

operate to impair minority voters' ability to elect representatives of their choice for the following reasons. First, the minority group must be able to demonstrate that it is sufficiently large and geographically compact to constitute a majority in a single-member district.[16] If it is not, as would be the case in a substantially integrated district, the multimember form of the district cannot be responsible for minority voters' inability to elect its candidates.[17] Second, the minority group must be able to show that it is politically cohesive. If the minority group is not politically cohesive, it cannot be said that the selection of a multimember electoral structure thwarts distinctive minority group interests. Third, the minority must be able to demonstrate that the white majority votes sufficiently as a bloc to enable it—in the absence of special circumstances, such as the minority candidate running unopposed—usually to defeat the minority's preferred candidate. In establishing this last circumstance, the minority group demonstrates that submergence in a white multimember district impedes its ability to elect its chosen representatives.

* * *

white voters. Consequently, if difficulty in electing and white bloc voting are not proved, minority voters have not established that the multimember structure interferes with their ability to elect their preferred candidates. Minority voters may be able to prove that they still suffer social and economic effects of past discrimination, that appeals to racial bias are employed in election campaigns, and that a majority vote is required to win a seat, but they have not demonstrated a substantial inability to elect caused by the use of a multi-member district. By recognizing the primacy of the history and extent of minority electoral success and of racial bloc voting, the Court simply requires that § 2 plaintiffs prove their claim before they may be awarded relief.

16. In this case appellees allege that within each contested multimember district there exists a minority group that is sufficiently large and compact to constitute a single-member district. In a different kind of case, for example a gerrymander case, plaintiffs might allege that the minority group that is sufficiently large and compact to constitute a single-member district has been split between two or more multimember or single-member districts, with the effect of diluting the potential strength of the minority vote.

17. The reason that a minority group making such a challenge must show, as a threshold matter, that it is sufficiently large and geographically compact to constitute a majority in a single-member district is this: Unless minority voters possess the potential to elect representatives in the absence of the challenged structure or practice, they cannot claim to have been injured by that structure or practice. The single-member district is generally the appropriate standard against which to measure minority group potential to elect because it is the smallest political unit from which representatives are elected. Thus, if the minority group is spread evenly throughout a multimember district, or if, although geographically compact, the minority group is so small in relation to the surrounding white population that it could not constitute a majority in a single-member district, these minority voters cannot maintain that they would have been able to elect representatives of their choice in the absence of the multimember electoral structure. . . .

III

Racially Polarized Voting

* * *

B

The Degree of Bloc Voting that is Legally Significant Under § 2

* * *

2

The Standard for Legally Significant Racial Bloc Voting

The Senate Report states that the "extent to which voting in the elections of the state or political subdivision is racially polarized" is relevant to a vote dilution claim. . . .

The purpose of inquiring into the existence of racially polarized voting is twofold: to ascertain whether minority group members constitute a politically cohesive unit and to determine whether whites vote sufficiently as a bloc usually to defeat the minority's preferred candidates. Thus, the question whether a given district experiences legally significant racially polarized voting requires discrete inquiries into minority and white voting practices. A showing that a significant number of minority group members usually vote for the same candidates is one way of proving the political cohesiveness necessary to a vote dilution claim, and, consequently, establishes minority bloc voting within the context of § 2. And, in general, a white bloc vote that normally will defeat the combined strength of minority support plus white "crossover" votes rises to the level of legally significant white bloc voting. The amount of white bloc voting that can generally "minimize or cancel" black voters' ability to elect representatives of their choice, however, will vary from district to district according to a number of factors, including the nature of the allegedly dilutive electoral mechanism; the presence or absence of other potentially dilutive electoral devices, such as majority vote requirements, designated posts, and prohibitions against bullet voting; the percentage of registered voters in the district who are members of the minority group; the size of the district; and, in multimember districts, the number of seats open and the number of candidates in the field.

Because loss of political power through vote dilution is distinct from the mere inability to win a particular election, a pattern of racial bloc voting that extends over a period of time is more probative of a claim that a district experiences legally significant polarization than are the results of a single election.[25]

* * *

25. [. . .] One important circumstance is the number of elections in which the minority group has sponsored candidates. Where a minority group has never been able to sponsor a candidate, courts must rely on other factors that tend to prove unequal access to the electoral process. Similarly, where a minority group has begun to sponsor candidates just recently, the fact that statistics

C

Evidence of Racially Polarized Voting

1

Appellants' Argument

* * *

[The State and the United States] argue that the term "racially polarized voting" must, as a matter of law, refer to voting patterns for which the principal cause is race. They contend that the District Court utilized a legally incorrect definition of racially polarized voting by relying on bivariate statistical analyses which merely demonstrated a correlation between the race of the voter and the level of voter support for certain candidates, but which did not prove that race was the primary determinant of voters' choices. According to appellants and the United States, only multiple regression analysis, which can take account of other variables which might also explain voters' choices, such as "party affiliation, age, religion, income[,] incumbency, education, campaign expenditures," "media use measured by cost, . . . name, identification, or distance that a candidate lived from a particular precinct," can prove that race was the primary determinant of voter behavior.

Whether appellants and the United States believe that it is the voter's race or the candidate's race that must be the primary determinant of the voter's choice is unclear; indeed, their catalogs of relevant variables suggest both. Age, religion, income, and education seem most relevant to the voter; incumbency, campaign expenditures, name identification, and media use are pertinent to the candidate; and party affiliation could refer both to the voter and the candidate. In either case, we disagree: For purposes of § 2, the legal concept of racially polarized voting incorporates neither causation nor intent. It means simply that the race of voters correlates with the selection of a certain candidate or candidates; that is, it refers to the situation where different races (or minority language groups) vote in blocs for different candidates. . . .

2

Causation Irrelevant to Section 2 Inquiry

The first reason we reject appellants' argument that racially polarized voting refers to voting patterns that are in some way caused by race, rather than to voting patterns that are merely correlated with the race of the voter, is that the reasons black and white voters vote differently have no relevance to the central inquiry of § 2. . . . It is the difference between the choices made by blacks and whites—not the reasons for that difference—that results in blacks having less opportunity than whites to elect their preferred representatives. Consequently, we conclude that under the "re-

from only one or a few elections are available for examination does not foreclose a vote dilution claim.

sults test" of § 2, only the correlation between race of voter and selection of certain candidates, not the causes of the correlation, matters.

* * *

3

Race of Voter as Primary Determinant of Voter Behavior

Appellants and the United States contend that the legal concept of "racially polarized voting" refers not to voting patterns that are merely correlated with the voter's race, but to voting patterns that are determined primarily by the voter's race, rather than by the voter's other socioeconomic characteristics.

The first problem with this argument is that it ignores the fact that members of geographically insular racial and ethnic groups frequently share socioeconomic characteristics, such as income level, employment status, amount of education, housing and other living conditions, religion, language, and so forth. Where such characteristics are shared, race or ethnic group not only denotes color or place of origin, it also functions as a shorthand notation for common social and economic characteristics. Appellants' definition of racially polarized voting is even more pernicious where shared characteristics are causally related to race or ethnicity. The opportunity to achieve high employment status and income, for example, is often influenced by the presence or absence of racial or ethnic discrimination. A definition of racially polarized voting which holds that black bloc voting does not exist when black voters' choice of certain candidates is most strongly influenced by the fact that the voters have low incomes and menial jobs—when the reason most of those voters have menial jobs and low incomes is attributable to past or present racial discrimination—runs counter to the Senate Report's instruction to conduct a searching and practical evaluation of past and present reality, and interferes with the purpose of the Voting Rights Act to eliminate the negative effects of past discrimination on the electoral opportunities of minorities.

* * *

Second, appellants' interpretation of "racially polarized voting" creates an irreconcilable tension between their proposed treatment of socioeconomic characteristics in the bloc voting context and the Senate Report's statement that "the extent to which members of the minority group . . . bear the effects of discrimination in such areas as education, employment and health" may be relevant to a § 2 claim. We can find no support in either logic or the legislative history for the anomalous conclusion to which appellants' position leads—that Congress intended, on the one hand, that proof that a minority group is predominately poor, uneducated, and unhealthy should be considered a factor tending to prove a § 2 violation; but that Congress intended, on the other hand, that proof that the same socioeconomic characteristics greatly influence black voters' choice of candidates should destroy these voters' ability to establish one of the most important elements of a vote dilution claim.

4

Race of Candidate as Primary Determinant of Voter Behavior

* * *

[B]oth minority and majority voters often select members of their own race as their preferred representatives.... Thus, as a matter of convenience, we ... may refer to the preferred representative of black voters as the "black candidate" and to the preferred representative of white voters as the "white candidate." Nonetheless, the fact that race of voter and race of candidate is often correlated is not directly pertinent to a § 2 inquiry. Under § 2, it is the status of the candidate as the chosen representative of a particular racial group, not the race of the candidate, that is important.

* * *

[A]ppellants' suggestion that racially polarized voting refers to voting patterns where whites vote for white candidates because they prefer members of their own race or are hostile to blacks, as opposed to voting patterns where whites vote for white candidates because the white candidates spent more on their campaigns, utilized more media coverage, and thus enjoyed greater name recognition than the black candidates, fails for another, independent reason. This argument, like the argument that the race of the voter must be the primary determinant of the voter's ballot, is inconsistent with the purposes of § 2 and would render meaningless the Senate Report factor that addresses the impact of low socioeconomic status on a minority group's level of political participation.

Congress intended that the Voting Rights Act eradicate inequalities in political opportunities that exist due to the vestigial effects of past purposeful discrimination. Both this Court and other federal courts have recognized that political participation by minorities tends to be depressed where minority group members suffer effects of prior discrimination such as inferior education, poor employment opportunities, and low incomes. The Senate Report acknowledges this tendency and instructs that "the extent to which members of the minority group ... bear the effects of discrimination in such areas as education, employment and health, which hinder their ability to participate effectively in the political process" is a factor which may be probative of unequal opportunity to participate in the political process and to elect representatives. Courts and commentators have recognized further that candidates generally must spend more money in order to win election in a multimember district than in a single-member district. If, because of inferior education and poor employment opportunities, blacks earn less than whites, they will not be able to provide the candidates of their choice with the same level of financial support that whites can provide theirs. Thus, electoral losses by candidates preferred by the black community may well be attributable in part to the fact that their white opponents outspent them. But, the fact is that, in this instance, the economic effects of prior discrimination have combined with the multimember electoral structure to afford blacks less opportunity than whites to participate in the political process and to elect representatives of their choice. It would be both anomalous and inconsistent with congressional intent to hold that, on the one hand, the effects of past discrimination which hinder blacks' ability to participate in the political process tend to prove a § 2 violation, while holding on the other hand that, where these same effects of past discrimination deter whites from voting for blacks, blacks cannot make out a crucial element of a vote dilution claim.

5

Racial Animosity as Primary Determinant of Voter Behavior

Finally, we reject the suggestion that racially polarized voting refers only to white bloc voting which is caused by white voters' racial hostility toward black candidates....

In amending § 2, Congress rejected the requirement announced by this Court in *Bolden* that § 2 plaintiffs must prove the discriminatory intent of state or local governments in adopting or maintaining the challenged electoral mechanism. Appellants' suggestion that the discriminatory intent of individual white voters must be proved in order to make out a § 2 claim must fail for the very reasons Congress rejected the intent test with respect to governmental bodies.

The Senate Report states that one reason the Senate Committee abandoned the intent test was that "the Committee ... heard persuasive testimony that the intent test is unnecessarily divisive because it involves charges of racism on the part of individual officials or entire communities."

* * *

The grave threat to racial progress and harmony which Congress perceived from requiring proof that racism caused the adoption or maintenance of a challenged electoral mechanism is present to a much greater degree in the proposed requirement that plaintiffs demonstrate that racial animosity determined white voting patterns. Under the old intent test, plaintiffs might succeed by proving only that a limited number of elected officials were racist; under the new intent test plaintiffs would be required to prove that most of the white community is racist in order to obtain judicial relief. It is difficult to imagine a more racially divisive requirement.

A second reason Congress rejected the old intent test was that in most cases it placed an "inordinately difficult burden" on § 2 plaintiffs. The new intent test would be equally, if not more, burdensome. In order to prove that a specific factor—racial hostility—determined white voters' ballots, it would be necessary to demonstrate that other potentially relevant causal factors, such as socioeconomic characteristics and candidate expenditures, do not correlate better than racial animosity with white voting behavior.

* * *

The final and most dispositive reason the Senate Report repudiated the old intent test was that it "asks the wrong question." Amended § 2 asks instead "whether minorities have equal access to the process of electing their representatives."

Focusing on the discriminatory intent of the voters, rather than the behavior of the voters, also asks the wrong question. All that matters under § 2 and under a functional theory of vote dilution is voter behavior, not its explanations. Moreover, as we have explained in detail, requiring proof that racial considerations actually caused voter behavior will result—contrary to congressional intent—in situations where a black minority that functionally has been totally excluded from the political process will be unable to establish a § 2 violation.

* * *

6

Summary

In sum, we would hold that the legal concept of racially polarized voting, as it relates to claims of vote dilution, refers only to the existence of a correlation between the race of voters and the selection of certain candidates. Plaintiffs need not prove causation or intent in order to prove a prima facie case of racial bloc voting and defendants may not rebut that case with evidence of causation or intent.

IV

The Legal Significance of Some Black Candidates' Success

A

North Carolina and the United States maintain that the District Court failed to accord the proper weight to the success of some black candidates in the challenged districts. Black residents of these districts, they point out, achieved improved representation in the 1982 General Assembly election. They also note that blacks in House District 23 have enjoyed proportional representation consistently since 1973 and that blacks in the other districts have occasionally enjoyed nearly proportional representation. This electoral success demonstrates conclusively, appellants and the United States argue, that blacks in those districts do not have "less opportunity than other members of the electorate to participate in the political process and to elect representatives of their choice." 42 U.S.C. § 1973(b). Essentially, appellants and the United States contend that if a racial minority gains proportional or nearly proportional representation in a single election, that fact alone precludes, as a matter of law, finding a § 2 violation.

Section 2(b) provides that "[the] extent to which members of a protected class have been elected to office . . . is one circumstance which may be considered." 42 U.S.C. § 1973(b). The Senate Committee Report also identifies the extent to which minority candidates have succeeded as a pertinent factor. However, the Senate Report expressly states that "the election of a few minority candidates does not 'necessarily foreclose the possibility of dilution of the black vote,'" noting that if it did, "the possibility exists that the majority citizens might evade [§ 2] by manipulating the election of a 'safe' minority candidate." . . .

[I]n conducting its "independent consideration of the record" and its "searching practical evaluation of the past and present reality," the District Court could appropriately take account of the circumstances surrounding recent black electoral success in deciding its significance to appellees' claim. In particular, . . . the court could properly notice the fact that black electoral success increased markedly in the 1982 election—an election that occurred after the instant lawsuit had been filed—and could properly consider to what extent "the pendency of this very litigation [might have] worked a one-time advantage for black candidates in the form of unusual organized political support by white leaders concerned to forestall single-member districting."

Nothing in the statute or its legislative history prohibited the court from viewing with some caution black candidates' success in the 1982 election, and from deciding on the basis of all the relevant circumstances to accord greater weight to blacks' relative lack of success over the course of several recent elections. Consequently, we hold that the District Court did not err, as a matter of law, in refusing to treat the fact that some black candidates have succeeded as dispositive of appellees' § 2 claim. Where multimember districting generally works to dilute the minority vote, it cannot be defended on the ground that it sporadically and serendipitously benefits minority voters.

B

The District Court did err, however, in ignoring the significance of the sustained success black voters have experienced in House District 23. In that district, the last six elections have resulted in proportional representation for black residents. This persistent proportional representation is inconsistent with appellees' allegation that the ability of black voters in District 23 to elect representatives of their choice is not equal to that enjoyed by the white majority.

In some situations, it may be possible for § 2 plaintiffs to demonstrate that such sustained success does not accurately reflect the minority group's ability to elect its preferred representatives, but appellees have not done so here. Appellees presented evidence relating to black electoral success in the last three elections; they failed utterly, though, to offer any explanation for the success of black candidates in the previous three elections. Consequently, we believe that the District Court erred, as a matter of law, in ignoring the sustained success black voters have enjoyed in House District 23, and would reverse with respect to that District.

V

Ultimate Determination of Vote Dilution

* * *

A

[. . .] Appellants and the United States argue that because a finding of vote dilution under amended § 2 requires the application of a rule of law to a particular set of facts it constitutes a legal, rather than factual, determination. Neither appellants nor the United States cite our several precedents in which we have treated the ultimate finding of vote dilution as a question of fact subject to the clearly-erroneous standard of Rule 52(a). *See, e.g., Rogers v. Lodge*, 458 U.S. [613 (1982)]; *City of Rome v. United States*, 446 U.S. 156 (1980); *White v. Regester*, 412 U.S. [755 (1973)].

* * *

We reaffirm our view that the clearly-erroneous test of Rule 52(a) is the appropriate standard for appellate review of a finding of vote dilution. . . .

B

The District Court in this case carefully considered the totality of the circumstances and found that in each district racially polarized voting; the legacy of official discrimination in voting matters, education, housing, employment, and health services; and the persistence of campaign appeals to racial prejudice acted in concert with the multimember districting scheme to impair the ability of geographically insular and politically cohesive groups of black voters to participate equally in the political process and to elect candidates of their choice. It found that the success a few black candidates have enjoyed in these districts is too recent, too limited, and, with regard to the 1982 elections, perhaps too aberrational, to disprove its conclusion. Excepting House District 23, with respect to which the District Court committed legal error, we affirm the District Court's judgment. We cannot say that the District Court, composed of local judges who are well acquainted with the political realities of the State, clearly erred in concluding that use of a multimember electoral structure has caused black voters in the districts other than House District 23 to have less opportunity than white voters to elect representatives of their choice.

* * *

■ JUSTICE WHITE, concurring.

I join Parts I, II, III–A, III–B, IV–A, and V of the Court's opinion and agree with Justice Brennan's opinion as to Part IV–B. I disagree with Part III–C of Justice Brennan's opinion.

Justice Brennan states in Part III–C that the crucial factor in identifying polarized voting is the race of the voter and that the race of the candidate is irrelevant. Under this test, there is polarized voting if the majority of white voters vote for different candidates than the majority of the blacks, regardless of the race of the candidates. I do not agree. Suppose an eight-member multimember district that is 60% white and 40% black, the blacks being geographically located so that two safe black single-member districts could be drawn. Suppose further that there are six white and two black Democrats running against six white and two black Republicans. Under Justice Brennan's test, there would be polarized voting and a likely § 2 violation if all the Republicans, including the two blacks, are elected, and 80% of the blacks in the predominantly black areas vote Democratic. I take it that there would also be a violation in a single-member district that is 60% black, but enough of the blacks vote with the whites to elect a black candidate who is not the choice of the majority of black voters. This is interest-group politics rather than a rule hedging against racial discrimination. I doubt that this is what Congress had in mind in amending § 2 as it did, and it seems quite at odds with the discussion in *Whitcomb v. Chavis*. Furthermore, on the facts of this case, there is no need to draw the voter/candidate distinction. The District Court did not and reached the correct result except, in my view, with respect to District 23.

■ JUSTICE O'CONNOR, with whom THE CHIEF JUSTICE, JUSTICE POWELL, and JUSTICE REHNQUIST join, concurring in the judgment.

* * *

In construing this compromise legislation, we must make every effort to be faithful to the balance Congress struck. This is not an easy task. We know that Congress intended to allow vote dilution claims to be brought under § 2, but we also know that Congress did not intend to create a right to proportional representation for minority voters. There is an inherent tension between what Congress wished to do and what it wished to avoid, because any theory of vote dilution must necessarily rely to some extent on a measure of minority voting strength that makes some reference to the proportion between the minority group and the electorate at large.

* * *

I

In order to explain my disagreement with the Court's interpretation of § 2, it is useful to illustrate the impact that alternative districting plans or types of districts typically have on the likelihood that a minority group will be able to elect candidates it prefers, and then to set out the critical elements of a vote dilution claim as they emerge in the Court's opinion.

Consider a town of 1,000 voters that is governed by a council of four representatives, in which 30% of the voters are black, and in which the black voters are concentrated in one section of the city and tend to vote as a bloc. It would be possible to draw four single-member districts, in one of which blacks would constitute an overwhelming majority. The black voters in this district would be assured of electing a representative of their choice, while any remaining black voters in the other districts would be submerged in large white majorities. This option would give the minority group roughly proportional representation.

Alternatively, it would usually be possible to draw four single-member districts in two of which black voters constituted much narrower majorities of about 60%. The black voters in these districts would often be able to elect the representative of their choice in each of these two districts, but if even 20% of the black voters supported the candidate favored by the white minority in those districts the candidates preferred by the majority of black voters might lose. This option would, depending on the circumstances of a particular election, sometimes give the minority group more than proportional representation, but would increase the risk that the group would not achieve even roughly proportional representation.

It would also usually be possible to draw four single-member districts in each of which black voters constituted a minority. In the extreme case, black voters would constitute 30% of the voters in each district. Unless approximately 30% of the white voters in this extreme case backed the minority candidate, black voters in such a district would be unable to elect the candidate of their choice in an election between only two candidates even if they unanimously supported him. This option would make it difficult for black voters to elect candidates of their choice even with significant white support, and all but impossible without such support.

Finally, it would be possible to elect all four representatives in a single at-large election in which each voter could vote for four candidates. Under this scheme, white voters could elect all the representatives even if black voters turned out in large numbers and voted for one and only one candidate. To illustrate, if only four white candidates ran, and each received approximately equal support from white voters, each would receive about 700 votes, whereas black voters could cast no more than 300 votes for any one candidate. If, on the other hand, eight white candidates ran, and white votes were distributed less evenly, so that the five least favored white candidates received fewer than 300 votes while three others received 400 or more, it would be feasible for blacks to elect one representative with 300 votes even without substantial white support. If even 25% of the white voters backed a particular minority candidate, and black voters voted only for that candidate, the candidate would receive a total of 475 votes, which would ensure victory unless white voters also concentrated their votes on four of the eight remaining candidates, so that each received the support of almost 70% of white voters.

* * *

Although § 2 does not speak in terms of "vote dilution," I agree with the Court that proof of vote dilution can establish a violation of § 2 as amended. The phrase "vote dilution," in the legal sense, simply refers to the impermissible discriminatory effect that a multimember or other districting plan has when it operates "to cancel out or minimize the voting strength of racial groups." *White [v. Regester].* This definition, however, conceals some very formidable difficulties. Is the "voting strength" of a racial group to be assessed solely with reference to its prospects for electoral success, or should courts look at other avenues of political influence open to the racial group? Insofar as minority voting strength is assessed with reference to electoral success, how should undiluted minority voting strength be measured? How much of an impairment of minority voting strength is necessary to prove a violation of § 2? What constitutes racial bloc voting and how is it proved? What weight is to be given to evidence of actual electoral success by minority candidates in the face of evidence of racial bloc voting?

The Court resolves the first question summarily: minority voting strength is to be assessed solely in terms of the minority group's ability to elect candidates it prefers. . . .

In order to evaluate a claim that a particular multimember district or single-member district has diluted the minority group's voting strength to a degree that violates § 2, however, it is also necessary to construct a measure of "undiluted" minority voting strength. "[The] phrase [vote dilution] itself suggests a norm with respect to which the fact of dilution may be ascertained." Put simply, in order to decide whether an electoral system has made it harder for minority voters to elect the candidates they prefer, a court must have an idea in mind of how hard it "should" be for minority voters to elect their preferred candidates under an acceptable system.

Several possible measures of "undiluted" minority voting strength suggest themselves. First, a court could simply use proportionality as its guide. . . . Second, a court could posit some alternative districting plan as a "normal" or "fair" electoral scheme and attempt to calculate how many candidates preferred by the minority group would probably be elected under that scheme. There are, as we have seen, a variety of ways in which even single-member districts could be drawn, and each will present the minority group with its own array of electoral risks and benefits; the court might, therefore, consider a range of acceptable plans in attempting to estimate "undiluted" minority voting strength by this method. Third, the court could attempt to arrive at a plan that would maximize feasible minority electoral success, and use this degree of predicted success as its measure of "undiluted" minority voting strength. If a court were to employ this third alternative, it would often face hard choices about what would truly "maximize" minority electoral success. An example is the scenario described above, in which a minority group could be concentrated in one completely safe district or divided among two districts in each of which its members would constitute a somewhat precarious majority.

The Court today has adopted a variant of the third approach, to wit, undiluted minority voting strength means the maximum feasible minority voting strength. In explaining the elements of a vote dilution claim, the Court first states that "the minority group must be able to demonstrate that it is sufficiently large and geographically compact to constitute a majority in a single-member district." If not, apparently the minority group has no cognizable claim that its ability to elect the representatives of its choice has been impaired.[1] Second, "the minority group must be able to show that it is politically cohesive," that is, that a significant proportion of the minority group supports the same candidates. Third, the Court requires the minority group to "demonstrate that the white majority votes sufficiently as a bloc to enable it—in the absence of special circumstances . . .— usually to defeat the minority's preferred candidate." If these three requirements are met, "the minority group demonstrates that submergence in a white multimember district impedes its ability to elect its chosen representatives." That is to say, the minority group has proved vote dilution in violation of § 2.

The Court's definition of the elements of a vote dilution claim is simple and invariable: a court should calculate minority voting strength by assuming that the minority group is concentrated in a single-member district in which it constitutes a voting majority. . . . If this is indeed the single, universal standard for evaluating undiluted minority voting strength for

---

1. I express no view as to whether the ability of a minority group to constitute a majority in a single-member district should constitute a threshold requirement for a claim that the use of multimember districts impairs the ability of minority voters to participate in the political processes and to elect representatives of their choice. Because the plaintiffs in this case would meet that requirement, if indeed it exists, I need not decide whether it is imposed by § 2. I note, however, the artificiality of the Court's distinction between claims that a minority group's "ability to elect the representatives of [its] choice" has been impaired and claims that "its ability to influence elections" has been impaired. *Ante*, n.12. It is true that a minority group that could constitute a majority in a single-member district ordinarily has the potential ability to elect representatives without white support, and that a minority that could not constitute such a majority ordinarily does not. But the Court recognizes that when the candidates preferred by a minority group are elected in a multimember district, the minority group has elected those candidates, even if white support was indispensable to these victories. On the same reasoning, if a minority group that is not large enough to constitute a voting majority in a single-member district can show that white support would probably be forthcoming in some such district to an extent that would enable the election of the candidates its members prefer, that minority group would appear to have demonstrated that, at least under this measure of its voting strength, it would be able to elect some candidates of its choice.

vote dilution purposes, the standard is applicable whether what is challenged is a multimember district or a particular single-member districting scheme.

* * *

To appreciate the implications of this approach, it is useful to return to the illustration of a town with four council representatives given above. Under the Court's approach, if the black voters who constitute 30% of the town's voting population do not usually succeed in electing one representative of their choice, then regardless of whether the town employs at-large elections or is divided into four single-member districts, its electoral system violates § 2. Moreover, if the town had a black voting population of 40%, on the Court's reasoning the black minority, so long as it was geographically and politically cohesive, would be entitled usually to elect two of the four representatives, since it would normally be possible to create two districts in which black voters constituted safe majorities of approximately 80%.

To be sure, the Court also requires that plaintiffs prove that racial bloc voting by the white majority interacts with the challenged districting plan so as usually to defeat the minority's preferred candidate. In fact, however, this requirement adds little that is not already contained in the Court's requirements that the minority group be politically cohesive and that its preferred candidates usually lose....

As shaped by the Court today, then, the basic contours of a vote dilution claim require no reference to most of the *"Zimmer* factors" that were developed by the Fifth Circuit to implement *White [v. Regester]*'s results test and which were highlighted in the Senate Report.... Of course, these other factors may be supportive of such a claim, because they may strengthen a court's confidence that minority voters will be unable to overcome the relative disadvantage at which they are placed by a particular districting plan, or suggest a more general lack of opportunity to participate in the political process. But the fact remains that electoral success has now emerged, under the Court's standard, as the linchpin of vote dilution claims, and that the elements of a vote dilution claim create an entitlement to roughly proportional representation within the framework of single-member districts.

II

* * *

I would reject the Court's test for vote dilution.... The Court's standard for vote dilution, when combined with its test for undiluted minority voting strength, makes actionable every deviation from usual, rough proportionality in representation for any cohesive minority group as to which this degree of proportionality is feasible within the framework of single-member districts. Requiring that every minority group that could possibly constitute a majority in a single-member district be assigned to such a district would approach a requirement of proportional representation as nearly as is possible within the framework of single-member districts. . . . This approach is inconsistent with the results test and with § 2's disclaimer of a right to proportional representation. . . .

[The results test] requires an inquiry into the extent of the minority group's opportunities to participate in the political processes. While electoral success is a central part of the vote dilution inquiry, . . . "it is not enough that the racial group allegedly discriminated against has not had legislative seats in proportion to its voting potential" and [we have] flatly rejected the proposition that "any group with distinctive interests must be represented in legislative halls if it is numerous enough to command at least one seat and represents a majority living in an area sufficiently compact to constitute a single member district." To the contrary, the results test . . . requires plaintiffs to establish "that the political processes leading to nomination and election were not equally open to participation by the group in question—that its members had less opportunity than did other residents in the district to participate in the political processes and to elect legislators of their choice."

* * *

I would adhere to the approach outlined in *Whitcomb* and *White* and followed, with some elaboration, in *Zimmer* and other cases in the Courts of Appeals prior to *Bolden*. Under that approach, a court should consider all relevant factors bearing on whether the minority group has "less opportunity than other members of the electorate to participate in the political process and to elect representatives of their choice." 42 U.S.C. § 1973. The court should not focus solely on the minority group's ability to elect representatives of its choice. Whatever measure of undiluted minority voting strength the court employs in connection with evaluating the presence or absence of minority electoral success, it should also bear in mind that "the power to influence the political process is not limited to winning elections." *Davis v. Bandemer* [478 U.S. 109 (1986), a case decided the same day] . . . .

III

Only three Justices of the Court join Part III–C of Justice Brennan's opinion, which addresses the validity of the statistical evidence on which the District Court relied in finding racially polarized voting in each of the challenged districts. Insofar as statistical evidence of divergent racial voting patterns is admitted solely to establish that the minority group is politically cohesive and to assess its prospects for electoral success, I agree that defendants cannot rebut this showing by offering evidence that the divergent racial voting patterns may be explained in part by causes other than race, such as an underlying divergence in the interests of minority and white voters. I do not agree, however, that such evidence can never affect the overall vote dilution inquiry. Evidence that a candidate preferred by the minority group in a particular election was rejected by white voters for reasons other than those which made that candidate the preferred choice of the minority group would seem clearly relevant in answering the question whether bloc voting by white voters will consistently defeat minority candidates. Such evidence would suggest that another candidate, equally preferred by the minority group, might be able to attract greater white support in future elections.

I believe Congress also intended that explanations of the reasons why white voters rejected minority candidates would be probative of the likelihood that candidates elected without decisive minority support would be willing to take the minority's interests into account. In a community that is polarized along racial lines, racial hostility may bar these and other indirect avenues of political influence to a much greater extent than in a community where racial animosity is absent although the interests of racial groups diverge.... Similarly, I agree with Justice White that Justice Brennan's conclusion that the race of the candidate is always irrelevant in identifying racially polarized voting conflicts with *Whitcomb* and is not necessary to the disposition of this case.

In this case, ... in view of the specific evidence from each district [regarding the refusal of white voters to support black candidates], ... I cannot say that its conclusion that there was severe racial bloc voting was clearly erroneous with regard to any of the challenged districts. Except in House District 23, where racial bloc voting did not prevent sustained and virtually proportional minority electoral success, I would accordingly leave undisturbed the District Court's decision to give great weight to racial bloc voting in each of the challenged districts.

IV

* * *

I agree with Justice Brennan that consistent and sustained success by candidates preferred by minority voters is presumptively inconsistent with the existence of a § 2 violation. Moreover, I agree that this case presents no occasion for determining what would constitute proof that such success did not accurately reflect the minority group's actual voting strength in a challenged district or districts.

* * *

V

When members of a racial minority challenge a multimember district on the grounds that it dilutes their voting strength, I agree with the Court that they must show that they possess such strength and that the multimember district impairs it. A court must therefore appraise the minority group's undiluted voting strength in order to assess the effects of the multimember district. I would reserve the question of the proper method or methods for making this assessment. But once such an assessment is made, in my view the evaluation of an alleged impairment of voting strength requires consideration of the minority group's access to the political processes generally, not solely consideration of the chances that its preferred candidates will actually be elected. Proof that white voters withhold their support from minority-preferred candidates to an extent that consistently ensures their defeat is entitled to significant weight in plaintiffs' favor. However, if plaintiffs direct their proof solely towards the minority group's prospects for electoral success, they must show that substantial minority success will be highly infrequent under the challenged plan in order to establish that the plan operates to "cancel out or minimize" their voting strength.

Compromise is essential to much if not most major federal legislation, and confidence that the federal courts will enforce such compromises is indispensable to their creation. I believe that the Court today strikes a different balance than Congress intended to when it codified the results test and disclaimed any right to proportional representation under § 2. For that reason, I join the Court's judgment but not its opinion.

■ JUSTICE STEVENS, with whom JUSTICE MARSHALL and JUSTICE BLACKMUN join, concurring in part and dissenting in part.

In my opinion, the findings of the District Court, which the Court fairly summarizes, adequately support the District Court's judgment concerning House District 23 as well as the balance of that judgment.

I, of course, agree that the election of one black candidate in each election since 1972 provides significant support for the State's position. The notion that this evidence creates some sort of a conclusive, legal presumption is not, however, supported by the language of the statute or by its legislative history. I therefore cannot agree with the Court's view that the District Court committed error by failing to apply a rule of law that emerges today without statutory support. The evidence of candidate success in District 23 is merely one part of an extremely large record which the District Court carefully considered before making its ultimate findings of fact, all of which should be upheld under a normal application of the "clearly erroneous" standard that the Court traditionally applies.

* * *

To paraphrase the Court's conclusion about the other districts, I cannot say that the District Court, composed of local judges who are well acquainted with the political realities of the State, clearly erred in concluding that use of a multimember electoral structure has caused black voters in House District 23 to have less opportunity than white voters to elect representatives of their choice. Accordingly, I concur in the Court's opinion except Part IV–B and except insofar as it explains why it reverses the judgment respecting House District 23.

NOTES AND QUESTIONS

1. The lead appellant in *Gingles* was Lacy Thornburg, the elected attorney general of North Carolina. Thornburg was a Democrat. James G. Martin, the governor, filed an *amicus* brief in support of the black appellees. *See Gingles*, 478 U.S. at 34. Martin was a Republican. Democrats had controlled both houses of the General Assembly during the reapportionment process; the lack of a veto left the governor a bystander to the apportionment process. Consider the ways in which racial and partisan politics might overlap in the decision whether to draw majority-black districts in areas where blacks are the most reliable Democratic voters. Compare the litigation postures taken by state officials in *Gingles* with the approaches taken by various players in the post–1990 North Carolina congressional reapportionment litigation, *Shaw v. Reno*, discussed in Chapter 9. The interaction of racial and political factors in North Carolina's reapportionment process is hardly a new phenomenon. For a detailed historical account, see J. Morgan Kousser, Shaw v. Reno *and the Real World of Redistricting and Representation*, 26 Rutgers L.J. 625, 670–91 (1995).

2. In general, Justice Brennan was one of the justices most solicitous of voting rights claims by racial minorities. In *Gingles*, though, he parts company with Justices Marshall, Blackmun, and Stevens on whether to strike down House District 23. To what extent was his decision strategic? If he had not voted to uphold the district, Justice O'Connor would have announced the judgment of the Court. Would that have given her opinion more influence than his? Might a desire to keep Justice White on board for most of his opinion also have played a role?

3. Justice Brennan derives the three-part test he announces for determining dilution through submergence neither from the legislative history of section 2, nor even from pre-amendment cases (since, as both he and Justice O'Connor point out, the factors identified in the Senate Report are distilled from the case law, specifically *White v. Regester*, 412 U.S. 755 (1973), and *Zimmer v. McKeithen*, 485 F.2d 1297 (5th Cir.1973) (en banc), *aff'd on other grounds sub nom. East Carroll Parish School Bd. v. Marshall*, 424 U.S. 636 (1976)). Instead, he distilled the test from several scholarly articles, most notably James U. Blacksher & Larry T. Menefee, *From* Reynolds v. Sims *to* City of Mobile v. Bolden: *Have the White Suburbs Commandeered the Fifteenth Amendment?*, 34 Hastings L.J. 1 (1982). Blacksher and Menefee were the lawyers for the plaintiffs in *Mobile v. Bolden*.

What accounts for the Court's substitution of the three-pronged "*Gingles* test" (as it has come to be known)—which looks at (1) the size and geographic location of the minority group; (2) its political cohesion and (3) the level of white bloc voting—for the nine "typical factors" identified in the Senate Report? Are the three *Gingles* factors more "objective" in some sense than the Senate Report factors? If they are, is *Gingles* yet another manifestation of the Court's preference for bright-line tests? Consider the following observation by a court of appeals:

> *Gingles* is a reasonable exercise of the Court's authority in statutory interpretation. The Court's approach, by focusing up front on whether there is an effective remedy for the claimed injury, promotes ease of application without distorting the statute or the intent underlying it. It reins in the almost unbridled discretion that section 2 gives the courts, focusing the inquiry so that plaintiffs with promising claims can develop a full record. The creation of preconditions—a choice of clear rules over muddy efforts to discern equity—shields the courts from meritless claims and ensures that clearly meritorious claims will survive summary judgment. That might not always have been true had courts been allowed to consider all of the *White/Zimmer* factors at the early stages of the proceedings. Thus, although ... the *Gingles* criteria might conceivably foreclose a meritorious claim, in general they will ensure that violations for which an effective remedy exists will be considered while appropriately closing the courthouse to marginal cases. In making that trade-off, the *Gingles* majority justifiably sacrificed some claims to protect stronger claims and promote judicial economy. The Voting Rights Act is a crucially important piece of national legislation, but it is subject to the same considerations of effective administration as other similar statutes.

McNeil v. Springfield Park District, 851 F.2d 937 (7th Cir. 1988), *cert. denied*, 490 U.S. 1031 (1989). *See also*, Samuel Issacharoff, *Polarized Voting and the Political Process: The Transformation of Voting Rights Jurisprudence*, 90 Mich. L. Rev. 1833 (1992); Blacksher & Menefee, *supra*, at 14 (contrasting the Court's willingness to intervene to prohibit malapportionment, where there was an easily quantifiable standard, with its reluctance to protect racial minorities from qualitative vote dilution through the use of at-large elections); Jan G. Deutsch, *Neutrality, Legitimacy, and the Supreme Court: Some Intersections Between Law and Political Science*, 20 Stan. L. Rev. 169, 248 (1968) (claiming that a formula like one-person, one-vote was virtually inevitable given the Court's institutional constraints and its desire for apparent neutrality); *cf.* Sanford Levinson, *Gerrymandering and the Brooding Omnipresence of Proportional Representation: Why Won't It Go Away?*, 33 UCLA L. Rev. 257 (1985) (claiming that a similar simplifying imperative would drive the Court toward a mathematical proportionality measure in gerrymandering cases).

4. "*Gingles* brought the racially polarized voting inquiry into the undisputed and unchallenged center of the Voting Rights Act," making proof of racial bloc voting the touchstone of a section 2 claim of dilution through submergence. Issacharoff, *supra*, at 1851. Later in the chapter, we shall return to one central area of disagreement among Justices Brennan, White, and O'Connor—namely, when legally sufficient racial bloc voting exists. But it is worth understanding throughout our consideration of the post-

Gingles case law how social scientists and courts go about estimating voter behavior. For more extensive discussions of the social science methodologies, *see generally* Bernard Grofman, *A Primer on Racial Bloc Voting Analysis*, in The Real Y2K Problem Census 2000 Data and Redistricting Technology 43–80 (N. Persily ed. 2000); Bernard Grofman, Lisa Handley, & Richard G. Niemi, Minority Representation and the Quest for Voting Equality 82–108 (1992); Richard L. Engstrom & Michael McDonald, *Quantitative Evidence in Vote Dilution Litigation: Political Participation and Polarized Voting*, 17 Urb. Law. 369 (Summer 1985); Wendy K. Tam Cho & Albert H. Yoon, *Statistical Expert Testimony in Voting Rights Cases*, 10 Cornell J.L. & Pub. Pol'y 237, 252–261 (2001). For a comprehensive discussion of the general issues posed by attempting to estimate individual voter behavior, see Gary King, A Solution to the Ecological Inference Problem: Reconstructing Individual Behavior from Aggregate Data (1997).

The concept of racial bloc voting had long played some role in judicial review of election systems, although the more empirical emphasis did not emerge until the 1980s. For example, in *United States v. Louisiana,* 225 F. Supp. 353 (E.D. La. 1963), *aff'd*, 380 U.S. 145 (1965), a case challenging Louisiana's discriminatory use of a literacy test, the court recounted the white supremacist Citizens' Council's drive to purge the registration rolls "of 'the great numbers of unqualified voters who have been illegally registered,' " and who "invariably vote in blocks and constitute a menace to the community." *Cf. United States v. Association of Citizens Councils of Louisiana*, 196 F. Supp. 908 (W.D. La. 1961) (noting that "[i]n elections held prior to [1956], the Negro voters [in Bienville Parish, Louisiana, where 86% of the white community but only 13% of the black community were registered to vote] had engaged in the reprehensible practice of 'bloc voting,' i.e., all or most of their votes were cast one way or another."). The concept of racial bloc voting often played out in racial appeals in campaigns, as with the claim by white candidates who played on the linguistic similarity between "bloc" voting and "black voting" to make the point that black voters would prefer different candidates, and that if enough black voters managed to cast ballots, those candidates would prevail.

The first reported racial vote dilution case, *Smith v. Paris*, 257 F. Supp. 901 (M.D. Ala. 1966), *modified*, 386 F.2d 979 (5th Cir.1967), struck down a switch from districted to at-large elections for the Barbour County, Alabama, Democratic Executive Committee as intentionally discriminatory because the change responded to racial bloc voting by submerging the votes of the black community. Blacks had been entirely disenfranchised prior to the passage of the Voting Rights Act, but a massive post-Act registration effort made them the majority in four of the county's sixteen "beats" (i.e., districts). Six black candidates ran for election to the committee:

> The tabulation of the election returns reflects that if the election had been held under the [single-member district] system that had previously been in force ... three of the plaintiffs would very likely have been

elected [since they received a majority of the votes cast in the predominantly black beats]. Under the county-wide vote system established by this resolution, all plaintiffs were defeated by substantial majorities. The district court noted "the anomalous twist that predominantly Negro beats now have their representatives determined for them by the predominantly white majority of voters in the county as a whole."

In these early cases, the courts' allusions to bloc voting were largely anecdotal or commonsensical. They simply assumed, based on their familiarity with local politics, that voting was racially polarized. Not until *City of Petersburg v. United States*, 354 F. Supp. 1021 (D.D.C. 1972), *aff'd*, 410 U.S. 962 (1973), did a court "appl[y] the concepts of 'block voting' and 'polarization' as part of a formal analysis of evidentiary data." Joseph P. Viteritti, *Unapportioned Justice: Local Elections, Social Science, and the Evolution of the Voting Rights Act*, 4 Cornell J.L. & Pub. Pol'y 199, 232 (1994). The *Petersburg* court used a relatively simple methodological approach—"homogeneous precinct analysis" (referred to in *Gingles* as "extreme case analysis"). Basically, homogeneous precinct analysis looks at the returns from precincts whose population is overwhelmingly (more than 90 percent) of one race. In *Petersburg*, the court found that "[i]n recent Council elections, in which both black and white candidates have participated, the vote in [the four] precincts which are racially identifiable as being almost completely black or white has been overwhelmingly along racial lines." From this the court inferred "that the same type of voting occurs throughout the City of Petersburg in elections affecting local issues."

Homogeneous precinct analysis remains a widespread tool in voting rights cases. It is easy to perform: it requires only census data (or voter registration data in jurisdictions that keep registration statistics by race) and a set of election returns. It is also conceptually easy to understand: if one precinct contains only black voters, while two others contain only white ones, then the election returns will definitively reveal whether voters of different races prefer different candidates.

There are two potential problems with homogeneous precinct analysis, however. The first is practical: in many jurisdictions, most of the precincts will not be racially homogeneous (even if they are racially identifiable); thus, a homogeneous precinct analysis will have to ignore much of the available data. In some jurisdictions, homogeneous precinct analysis may be impossible; even if there are, for example, a few 90 percent-or-more white precincts, there may be no comparable black ones. The second problem involves the sort of inference made by the *Petersburg* court—that the behavior of voters in racially homogeneous communities is typical of the behavior of voters in more racially mixed ones. There may be reasons to doubt an exact correspondence: blacks in overwhelmingly black precincts, for example, may often have lower income and education levels than blacks who live in integrated settings and thus may have different political preferences; whites who choose to live in racially integrated neighborhoods may be more open to crossover voting and biracial coalition building than those who choose to live in all-white communities. *Cf. Major v. Treen*, 574 F.Supp. 325 (E.D.La.1983) (three-judge court) (finding, with regard to the racial bloc voting inquiry, that whites who had fled from New Orleans to overwhelmingly white suburbs to avoid school integration were less likely than whites within New Orleans to support black candidates in congressional races for seats containing both the city and suburbs). Thus, homogeneous precinct analysis might overestimate the overall level of racial bloc voting within a jurisdiction, particularly if voters living in homogeneous precincts are a relatively small share of the overall population.

The other common social science technique for estimating voter behavior is bivariate ecological regression. The word "bivariate" refers to the fact that the analysis looks at two variables: the racial composition of the precincts and the votes garnered by particular candidates. The adjective "ecological" refers to the kind of data used in the analysis: election returns reflect aggregate activity (they are usually reported on a precinct-by-precinct basis), rather than the direct observation of individual behavior. "Regression" is a statistical technique for measuring the relationship between two or more variables: it determines how much one variable changes as the other variable (or variables, in a "multivariate" analysis) changes. In the context of section 2 cases, the two variables are the racial composition of a precinct and the share of the vote received by a given candidate. To understand how the process works, let us consider the data in a hypothetical community where all the voters are either black or white and there are two candidates running for election, one black candidate and one white candidate. Some data can be acquired directly: census or registration data can give a pretty good idea of how many black voters and how many white voters there are in each precinct. (This represents a slight simplification, since often the data are not quite this precise. The least precise data set would be one providing only the overall number of black and white residents within each precinct. If that were the data being used, adjustments would be necessary to account for the fact that a higher percentage of the minority population is likely to be ineligible to vote because of youth and, in the case of Asian–Americans and Hispanics, noncitizenship, as well as for the fact that minority turnout is often significantly lower than white turnout. *See* Grofman, Handley & Niemi, *supra*, at 88.) Election returns will tell us how many votes each candidate received in each precinct. The information we wish to derive involves the percentage of black voters and white voters who voted for each candidate. Secret ballots prevent us from obtaining that information directly, and exit polls, particularly in racially charged election contests, may be inaccurate. *See, e.g.,* Leslie Phillips, *Sick of Polls? There's Just One More*, USA Today, Nov. 3, 1992, at 12A (reporting that "[r]aces with minority candidates have confounded exit pollsters, because some respondents seem to believe revealing their vote says something about their racial bias"; in 1989, for example, in the Virginia governor's race and the New York mayor's race, exit polls showed black candidates Douglas Wilder and David Dinkins holding significant leads but both candidates actually won by only a tiny margin).

Ecological regression tries to get around these problems by inferring individual behavior from the observed data. To understand how the technique works, imagine a scattergram. The horizontal axis measures the independent variable, the percentage of voters in each precinct who are black. The vertical axis measures the dependent variable, the percentage of votes received by the "black" candidate. As *Gingles* itself illustrates, that candidate is often himself or herself black.

The following figure is a scattergram generated from a 1980 Norfolk, Virginia, city councilmanic election studied by Engstrom & MacDonald, *supra*.

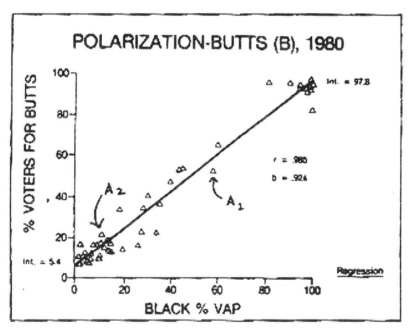

Every precinct within the community can be located on the scattergram. For example, a precinct that is 58 percent black and where the black candidate received 50 percent of the votes cast would be located at point A_1. A precinct that is 10 percent black and where the black candidate received 22 percent of the vote would be located at point A_2.

Regression is a technique for fitting a straight line through the data points. The regression line is the straight line that best fits the observed data points, meaning the line that minimizes the combined distances between each of the points and the line. It is also referred to as the "least squares" method because it seeks to minimize the aggregate distance of all the points on the graph to the regression line—as measured by squaring all the distances from the line and then adding them together. The slope and intercepts of the line enable us to draw some important conclusions about voting behavior. The slope of the line tells us how strongly the two variables are related: the greater the slope the stronger the relationship. If the regression coefficient (normally referred to as "b") is, for example, .924, then "it is estimated that every increase of 1.0 percent in the black portion of the [voting age population] across precincts tended to result in a .924 increase in the percentage of voters supporting [the black candidate]. In other words, if the black proportion of the [voting age population] in one precinct was 50 percentage points higher than in a second precinct, the percentage of voters supporting [the black candidate] in that precinct would be expected to be about 46.2 percentage points higher (50 x .924) than in the second precinct." *Id.* at 376.

Where the regression line intercepts the two vertical axes enables an estimation of the actual percentage of black and white voters who supported the black candidate. The left vertical axis of the scattergram represents the percentage of white votes received by the black candidate; the right axis represents the percentage of black votes she received. In our scattergram, the left intercept is 5.4; this means that the regression technique estimates that 5.4 percent of the white voters supported the black candidate. The right intercept is 97.8; thus, it is estimated that 97.8 percent of black voters voted for the black candidate. In the current double regression technique, statisticians perform a second regression to determine voting behavior with regard to the white candidate as well. Notice, however, that in communities with significant residential segregation the regression analysis is heavily determined by the extreme precincts that "anchor" the regression line. For example, in Norfolk, notice how many of the precincts are heavily segregated. In such communities, extreme case analysis and bivariate regression analysis can generally be expected to produce comparable estimates of black and white voting patterns.

In addition to deriving the regression coefficient, regression analysis can also provide both a correlation coefficient (commonly reported as "r"), which measures how consistently the scores for the dependent variable vary with the independent variable, and a measure of statistical significance, that is, how likely a pattern that looks like a straight line is simply the product of chance. The correlation coefficient tells us how close to the line the various data points fall. An "r" of + 1.0 would indicate a perfectly consistent positive relationship; an "r" of –1.0 would indicate a perfectly consistent negative relationship; and an "r" of 0 would indicate no relationship whatsoever between the two variables. An "r" above 0.5 is normally viewed as indicative of a real positive relationship; an "r" of 0.9 would be viewed as extremely high. The correlation coefficients for the elections studied in *Gingles* ranged from .70 to .98, meaning that between 70 and 98 percent of the variation in support for the black candidate could be ascribed to the racial composition of the electorate. In the 1980 Norfolk contest, the value of r is quite high: .985, meaning that 98.5 percent of the variation in how Butts fared in different precincts can be explained by the racial composition of the precincts.

Justice Brennan's opinion in *Gingles* endorsed a *bivariate* regression analysis, that is, one that looked at *two* variables: race of the voters and share of the votes received by each candidate. Justice O'Connor's approach, by contrast, seemed more hospitable to a *multivariate* analysis—one that looked at additional factors. We shall return to the issue below. For summaries of the various arguments that have raged in the social science literature over regression analysis, see, e.g., Grofman, Handley, & Niemi, *supra*; Bernard Grofman, *The Use of Ecological Regression to Estimate Racial Bloc Voting*, 27 U.S.F. L. Rev. 593 (1993).

In recent years, the social-scientific tools on which voting-rights litigation depends have grown substantially more sophisticated. A major development was the technical advances offered in Gary King, A Solution to the Ecological Inference Problem (1997). As one of the leading expert witnesses and social scientists concerning voting-rights litigation writes, the new tools reflected in King's work and others is "in the process of revolutionizing the analysis of [racial bloc voting]. . . ." Bernard Grofman, *A Primer on Racial Bloc Voting Analysis*, in The Real Y2K Problem Census 2000 Data and Redistricting Technology 43–80 (N. Persily ed. 2000). Grofman's article is an excellent, accessible synthesis of the different methods of assessing racial voting patterns, the approaches reflected in the latest techniques, and the extent to which different methods do or do not tend to converge on similar legal conclusions regarding racial-polarization patterns.

5. As a textual matter, section 2 prohibits "denial or abridgement of the right of any citizen of the United States to vote on account of race or color, or in contravention of the guarantees set forth in section 4(f)(2)." Section 4(f)(2), in turn, provides that "[n]o voting qualification or prerequisite to voting, or standard, practice, or procedure shall be imposed or applied by any State or political subdivision to deny or abridge the right of any citizen of the United States to vote because he is a member of a language minority group." Section 14(c)(3) of the Act provides that the term " 'language minority group' means persons who are American Indian, Asian American, Alaskan Natives or of Spanish heritage."

With only a handful of exceptions, section 2 cases have been brought by citizens who are black or who are members of language minority groups. White voters in Birmingham, Alabama challenged the city's continued use of at-large elections, see *White Minority Wins Right to Challenge At–Large Voting*, Chi. Trib., June 18, 1988, at 7, but the case was never tried to a judgment. More recently, in 2005, the Department of Justice filed a section 2 case, *United States v. Brown*, alleging that the practices of local election officials in Noxubee County, Mississippi, discriminated against whites. (Roughly two-thirds of the county's population is black.) Various county officials entered into a consent decree agreeing to avoid a range of electoral practices, but parts of the case remain to be tried. For a copy of the complaint, see http://www.usdoj.gov/crt/voting/sec_2/noxubee_comp.pdf.

How likely are white voters to be able to establish the various factors leading to section 2 liability?

NOTES AND QUESTIONS ON THE GINGLES FIRST PRONG

1. *Gingles* held that "the minority group must be able to demonstrate that it is sufficiently large and geographically compact to constitute a majority in a single-member district." Precisely how large is large enough?

Suppose that plaintiffs show that it would be possible to draw a district that is 51 percent black in total population. For a variety of demographic and sociological reasons, it is unlikely that such a district's actual electorate on election day will be majority black. First, nonwhite populations tend to be disproportionately young. According to the 2000 census, while 77.3 percent of the non-Hispanic white population was of voting age, only 68.5 percent of blacks and 65.0 percent of Hispanics were. This disparity may be exacerbated in cases involving Hispanic communities, where many of the adults will be ineligible to vote because they are not U.S. citizens. *Cf. Garza v. Los Angeles County Board of Supervisors*, 918 F.2d 763 (9th Cir. 1990), *cert. denied*, 498 U.S. 1028 (1991) (describing how districts with less than 0.7% deviations in total population varied from 707,651 to 1,098,663 in the number of voting age citizens they contained). Second, minority communities also historically have had lower voter registration and turnout characteristics than white communities. And there is some evidence that nonwhite voters tend to overreport registration and participation at a greater rate than whites. *See* Allan J. Lichtman & Samuel Issacharoff, *Black/White Voter Registration Disparities in Mississippi: Legal and Methodological Issues in Challenging Bureau of Census Data*, 7 J.L. & Pol. 525 (1991) (explaining the methodological flaws in census surveys that tend to overestimate registration and turnout). Thus, plaintiffs may realistically be no more likely to elect a candidate of their choice from a 51 percent black district than from a 40 percent one.

While *Gingles* did not expressly hold that plaintiffs must show that blacks are a majority of the voting-age population, the lower courts have generally adopted this requirement. *See, e.g., Romero v. City of Pomona*, 883 F.2d 1418 (9th Cir. 1989); *Overton v. City of Austin*, 871 F.2d 529 (5th Cir. 1989); *McNeil v. Springfield Park District*, 851 F.2d 937 (7th Cir. 1988), *cert. denied*, 490 U.S. 1031 (1989); *Latino Political Action Committee v. City of Boston*, 609 F. Supp. 739 (D. Mass. 1985), *aff'd*, 784 F.2d 409 (1st Cir. 1986). As the Fifth Circuit explained in *Overton*:

> [T]he raison d'etre of *Thornburg* and of amended § 2 is to facilitate participation by minorities in our political processes, by preventing dilution of their votes. Only voting age persons can vote. It would be a *Pyrrhic* victory for a court to create a single-member district in which a

minority population dominant in absolute, but not in voting age numbers, continued to be defeated at the polls. *Thornburg* implicitly recognized this fact:

> Unless minority voters possess the potential to elect representatives in the absence of the challenged structure or practice, they cannot claim to have been injured by that practice.

Is this reasoning entirely correct? Note that the North Carolina electoral scheme at issue in *Gingles* contained a majority-vote requirement. Thus, a group had to constitute a majority of the electorate to win an election. In jurisdictions with first-past-the-post, plurality-win systems, should the plaintiffs still be required to constitute an electoral *majority*? Suppose, for example, that a city council is elected in nonpartisan elections (as many are), that there are usually three candidates running for each available seat, and that the winning candidate normally garners 45 percent of the vote. Should a minority group be able to satisfy the first prong of *Gingles* by showing that it could constitute 45 percent of the electorate in a fairly drawn single-member district?

In cases involving Latino plaintiffs, courts have generally required plaintiffs to show the possibility of creating a district that is majority Latino in citizens of voting age. *See, e.g., Barnett v. City of Chicago*, 141 F.3d 699 (7th Cir. 1998) *Campos v. City of Houston*, 113 F.3d 544 (5th Cir. 1997); *Negron v. City of Miami Beach*, 113 F.3d 1563 (11th Cir. 1997).

2. Some plaintiffs have sought to escape *Gingles'* first prong by relying on footnote 12 of Justice Brennan's opinion, which expressly reserved the question "whether § 2 permits, and if it does, what standards should pertain to, a claim brought by a minority group, that is not sufficiently large and compact to constitute a majority in a single-member district, alleging that the use of a multimember district impairs its ability to influence elections." The Supreme Court has repeatedly sidestepped the question whether, and how, such "influence district" claims can be brought. *See Johnson v. De Grandy*, 512 U.S. 997, 1009 (1994); *Voinovich v. Quilter*, 507 U.S. 146, 152 (1993); *Growe v. Emison*, 507 U.S. 25, 40 n. 5 (1993). In *LULAC v. Perry*, 126 S.Ct. 2594 (2006), discussed in detail in Chapter 9, Justice Kennedy, in an opinion joined by Chief Justice Roberts and Justice Alito, rejected a section 2-based challenge to the elimination of a congressional district whose voting-age population was 20.8 percent black and that had elected a white candidate consistently supported by black voters: "That African–Americans had influence in the district, does not suffice to state a § 2 claim.... The opportunity 'to elect representatives of their choice' requires more than the ability to influence the outcome between some candidates, none of whom is their candidate of choice. There is no doubt African–Americans preferred Martin Frost to the Republicans who opposed him. The fact that African–Americans preferred Frost to some others does not, however, make him their candidate of choice. Accordingly, the ability to aid in Frost's election does not make the old District 24 an African–American opportunity district for purposes of § 2.''

Most lower courts have rejected claims that section 2 entitles minority groups to an influence district even if they cannot satisfy the first *Gingles* precondition. *See, e.g. Latino Political Action Committee v. Boston*, 784 F.2d 409 (1st Cir. 1986); *DeBaca v. County of San Diego*, 794 F. Supp. 990 (S.D. Cal. 1992), *aff'd*, 5 F.3d 535 (9th Cir. 1993); *Hastert v. State Bd. of Elections*, 777 F. Supp. 634 (N.D. Ill. 1991).

In a later case, however, the First Circuit took a different position. In *Metts v. Murphy*, 363 F.3d 8 (1st Cir. 2004) (*en banc*), the court of appeals reinstated a section 2 challenge to the Rhode Island state senate redistricting. Prior to the 2002 redistricting, State Senate District 9 in Providence was 25.69 percent black and 41.08 percent Hispanic and had been represented by a black legislator for many years. After the redistricting, much of the black population lay within a new district which was 21.42 percent black and 46.74 percent Hispanic. A Latino challenger defeated the incumbent black legislator in the primary election.

In finding that the plaintiffs—black voters—had stated a claim, the court of appeals referred to the ''Delphic language'' of the 1982 amendments and the opacity of the Supreme Court's caselaw:

> *Gingles* was directed to a particular practice—multi-member districts—which the Court suggested was particularly problematic, and the decision did not purport to offer a general or exclusive gloss on section 2 for all situations. But the concreteness of the *Gingles* test, set against the vagueness of the statute and plethora of criteria, has made it a focus in subsequent cases dealing with quite different problems. Indeed, the Supreme Court has said several times that *Gingles* applies to vote dilution claims directed against single member districts, but it has effectively qualified this statement in two different ways.
>
> First, several Supreme Court opinions after *Gingles* have offered the prospect, or at least clearly reserved the possibility, that *Gingles'* first precondition—that a racial minority must be able to constitute a ''majority'' in a single-member district—could extend to a group that was a numerical minority but had predictable cross-over support from other groups. *DeGrandy*, 512 U.S. at 1008–09; *Voinovich*, 507 U.S. at 158 (''The first *Gingles* precondition, the requirement that the group be sufficiently large to constitute a majority in a single district, would have to be modified or eliminated when analyzing the influence-dilution claim we assume, arguendo, to be actionable today.''). Further, the Court has so far reserved judgment on a second-cousin question: whether dilution of a minority racial group's influence, as opposed to the power to elect, could violate section 2—a position that would require substantial modification of *Gingles'* first-prong ''majority'' precondition.

Second, where single member districts are at issue—as in our case—opinions have increasingly emphasized the open-ended, multi-factor inquiry that Congress intended for section 2 claims. To say that *Gingles* applies as a precondition to section 2 liability may not tell one very much if *Gingles* itself is no longer to be "mechanically" applied. . . .

We are thus unwilling at the complaint stage to foreclose the possibility that a section 2 claim can ever be made out where the African–American population of a single member district is reduced in redistricting legislation from 26 to 21 percent. Yes, one would ordinarily expect the consequences to be small, but not always, and arguably not here (based on past history). At this point we know practically nothing about the motive for the change in district or the selection of the present configuration, the contours of the district chosen or the feasible alternatives, the impact of alternative districts on other minorities, or anything else that would help gauge how mechanically or flexibly the *Gingles* factors should be applied. . . .

As the district court correctly pointed out, there is tension in this case for plaintiffs in any effort to satisfy both the first and third prong of *Gingles*. To the extent that African–American voters have to rely on cross-over voting to prove they have the "ability to elect" a candidate of their choosing, their argument that the majority votes as a bloc against their preferred candidate is undercut. But it is not clear on the pleadings alone how many cross-over votes are needed to win an election—unlike in *Gingles*, Rhode Island law allows a candidate to win with less than an absolute majority—nor do we have any evidence at this stage about how vigorously the majority votes as a bloc over time, nor the impact of the fact that the "majority" here is made up of both Hispanics and whites. . . .

In dissent, Judges Selya and Toruella argued that the plaintiffs' claim "depends upon a radical premise: that a minority group whose members cannot conceivably comprise anything close to a numerical majority, even in what is from their point of view an ideally configured single-member district, can mount a vote dilution claim. Given the small size of the identified minority group in this case and the magnitude of the crossover voting on which it must rely, the claim necessarily fails."

Ultimately, the case was settled when Rhode Island redrew state senate district boundaries to create two open districts in the Providence area, one of which was 50 percent Hispanic and the other of which provided black voters with a good chance of nominating and electing a candidate of choice. *See* Liz Anderson, *Carcieri Signs into Law Redrawn Senate Districts*, Providence Journal, June 9, 2004, at B6.

For more extensive discussion of the relationship between the minority's ability to elect, white crossover voting, and the first prong of *Gingles*, see J. Morgan Kousser, *Beyond* Gingles: *Influence Districts and the Prag-*

matic Tradition in Voting Rights Law, 27 U.S.F. L. Rev. 551 (1993); Stanley Pierre Louise, Comment, *The Politics of Influence: Recognizing Influence Dilution Claims Under Section 2 of the Voting Rights Act*, 62 U.Chi.L.Rev. 1215 (1995).

3. A more limited recognition of influence district claims appears in *Garza v. Los Angeles County Board of Supervisors*, 918 F.2d 763 (9th Cir. 1990), *cert. denied*, 498 U.S. 1028 (1991). The plaintiffs in *Garza*, Hispanic voters in Los Angeles, challenged the district boundaries created in the 1981 decennial reapportionment. At the time the districts were drawn, it was arguably impossible to have drawn a district with a majority of Hispanic voters, although by the time the case was filed, such a district could be drawn. The county argued as a matter of law that the 1981 districts were lawful, "regardless of any intentional or unintentional dilution of minority voting strength, because at the time they were drawn there could be no single-member district with a majority of minority voters." The court of appeals disagreed, on the grounds that the first prong of *Gingles* was irrelevant in light of the district court's finding of *intentional* vote dilution. Is *Garza*'s implicit distinction between intent and non-intent claims faithful to section 2? Given Congress' rejection of a discriminatory purpose requirement for statutory claims, should a showing of discriminatory purpose nonetheless have special weight?

4. As Judge Kozinski's concurrence in *Garza* noted, there was a marked difference in citizenship rates between supervisory districts. This thus raised interesting questions about whether to equalize the number of citizens eligible to vote or the number of constituents within each district. As you will recall from Chapter 3, the equal protection clause requires equipopulous districting.

Would loosening that restriction enhance or diminish minority voting strength? Consider the situation in Canada. Roughly eleven percent of Canada's population are members of "visible-minority groups." Those individuals live overwhelmingly in urban areas. As a constitutional matter, Canada guarantees each province a minimum number of seats. Combined with limits on the overall size of the House of Commons, this creates malapportionment between provinces. More significantly for minority voters, within provinces, rural areas are overrepresented.

The constitutionality of this practice was upheld by the Supreme Court of Canada in Reference re Provincial Electoral Boundaries (the *Carter* decision), in which the court found that the right to vote guaranteed by section 3 of the Canadian Charter of Rights and Freedoms is a right to "effective representation," not "parity of voting power."

Michael Pal & Sujit Choudhry, *Is Every Ballot Equal? Visible–Minority Vote Dilution in Canada*, 13 IRPP Choices No. 1 (2007) (available at http:// ssrn.com/abstract=958057). Pal and Choudhry discuss the degree to which minority voters live in overpopulated districts ("ridings") and conclude:

Reform to alleviate the problem of visible minority vote dilution could proceed in a number of ways. The allowable variance under the *Electoral Boundaries Representation Act* should be reduced to 10 or 5 percent from the current 25 percent. Electoral boundary commissions should be pressed to consider the consequences upon visible minority voters of their decisions to overrepresent rural areas. Provincially, legislation should be amended so that variances are reduced to the 5–percent level. Most importantly, the various reform processes occurring throughout the country offer an unprecedented opportunity to remedy visible minority vote dilution. A move to a proportional representation system that maintains some geographically based constituencies would not eliminate the problem; it would simply apply to a smaller number of seats. Increasing the number of seats in the House of Commons while holding constant the minimum guarantees of seats, regardless of population, for the smallest provinces is a promising reform possibility. It should be given full consideration as a viable alternative to the status quo that balances representation by population with provincial representation.

5. To what extent is it relevant that the minority community is "large" in a physical sense, as opposed to a numerical one? How common is the Court's model of a large, geographically discrete and isolated minority community? Particularly in the rural and small-town south, residential patterns may be racially identifiable without producing sizeable concentrations or "ghettos" of the northern urban variety. *See* Chandler Davidson, Biracial Politics: Conflict and Coalition in the Metropolitan South 19–20 (1972) (explaining three types of racial residential patterns: (1) "back yard"—where black residences are scattered throughout the city; (2) the "ghetto" involving a "single intense concentration of Negro residences"; and (3) " 'urban clusters' involving one to three large concentrations of Negroes, as well as up to twenty smaller clusters scattered across the city").

Washington County, Florida, the jurisdiction involved in *Potter v. Washington County*, 653 F.Supp. 121 (N.D.Fla.1986), offers an example of the potential disjunction between size and segregation. Washington County was a rural county whose voting-age population was 13.1 percent black. The black community lived largely in three distinct neighborhoods, but those neighborhoods were so separated that they could not easily be combined into one geographic district. Still, by stringing some of the neighborhoods together it was possible to create a 55.8 percent black district. The district court rejected that option, even though the defendants conceded liability under section 2, because the district "arbitrarily cuts diagonally through the center of the county." *Potter* rests on a distinction between black communities that are sufficiently large and *contiguous* to form majority-black single-member districts and black communities that are geographically large and *compact*. (The proposed district would have included roughly 70 percent of Washington County's black residents in the

55.8 percent black district.) Thus, although the *district* was perhaps not compact, in that it extended from one end of the county to the other, the black *community* was fairly concentrated.

6. The second aspect of *Gingles'* first prong is the requirement that the minority group be "compact." *Gingles* seems to treat the compactness inquiry as entirely causal in nature—stating that "in a substantially integrated district, the multimember form of the district cannot be responsible for minority voters' inability to elect its candidates". But consider whether the compactness prong of *Gingles* is also related to the concept of "discrete and insular" minority groups introduced in *Carolene Products'* footnote 4 and lying at the heart of contemporary process theory. Does the compactness of a minority group increase the likelihood that officeholders will ignore its distinctive interests?

Gingles nowhere defines "compactness." There are a variety of different definitions used in social science literature, statutes, and judicial opinions. Some of these definitions are quite quantitative and look at the physical configuration of a district. *See, e.g.,* Colo. Const. art. V, § 47 (defining compactness in terms of the sum of the perimeters of district boundaries); Iowa Code Ann. § 42.4(1)(c) (West 1991) (defining compactness as "the ratio of dispersion of population about the population center of the district to the dispersion of population about the geographic center of the district"). By contrast, in *Dillard v. Baldwin County Board of Education*, 686 F. Supp. 1459 (M.D. Ala. 1988), the district court found section 2 liability on the basis of the plaintiffs' claim that it would have been possible to draw a majority-black district stretching down the county's western border. It rejected the defendant's claim that the plaintiffs' plan

> is unacceptable because it is too elongated and curvaceous and thus fails to meet the requirement of "compactness." By compactness, *Thornburg* does not mean that a proposed district must meet, or attempt to achieve, some aesthetic absolute, such as symmetry or attractiveness. An aesthetic norm, by itself, would be not only unrelated to the legal and social issues presented under § 2, it would be an unworkable concept, resulting in arbitrary and capricious results, because it offers no guidance as to when it is met. It is apparent from the *Thornburg* opinion that compactness is a relative term tied to certain practical objectives under § 2; the requirement is not that a district be compact, but that it be "sufficiently" compact under § 2. The term is a "practical" or "functional" concept, which must be considered in relation to § 2's laudatory national mission of opening up the political process to those minorities that have been historically denied such. . . . The degree of geographical symmetry or attractiveness is therefore a desirable consideration for districting, but only to the extent it aids or facilitates the political process, and only as one among many considerations a court should include, the principal one

being § 2's vote dilution prohibition, in determining whether there is sufficient compactness for a majority black district.

The court therefore believes, especially in light of § 2's strong national mandate, that a district is sufficiently geographically compact if it allows for effective representation. For example, a district would not be sufficiently compact if it was so spread out that there was no sense of community, that is, if its members and its representative could not effectively and efficiently stay in touch with each other; or if it was so convoluted that there was no sense of community, that is, if its members and its representative could not easily tell who actually lived within the district. Also of importance, of course, is the compactness of neighboring districts; obviously, if, because of the configuration of a district, its neighboring districts so lacked compactness that they could not be effectively represented, the *Thornburg* standard of compactness would not be met. These are not, however, the only factors a court should consider in assessing a proposed district; because compactness is a functional concept, the number and kinds of factors a court should consider may vary with each case, depending on the local geographical, political, and socio-economic characteristics of the jurisdiction being sued.

The . . . plan proposed by the plaintiffs meets this functional standard. In response to direct questions from the court, the superintendent of the Baldwin County Board of Education testified that he saw no administrative or other problems with the configuration of the proposed majority-black district in the plaintiffs' plan, and that the district could be effectively represented; in his words, the district is "manageable." The evidence also reflected that there would be a strong sense of community within the proposed black district.

For more thorough discussions of compactness, see Bernard Grofman, *Criteria for Districting: A Social Science Perspective*, 33 UCLA L. Rev. 77 (1985); Richard H. Pildes & Richard G. Niemi, *Expressive Harms, "Bizarre Districts," and Voting Rights: Evaluating Election–District Appearances After* Shaw v. Reno, 92 Mich. L. Rev. 483 (1993).

7. The question of compactness assumed greater importance during the 1990s because of the Court's *Shaw* jurisprudence. That case law is treated in depth in Chapter 9. For present purposes, suffice it to say that *Shaw v. Reno*, 509 U.S. 630 (1993), and its progeny forbid states from relying too heavily on race in drawing electoral districts. A central question in *Shaw* cases, given the Court's recognition that line drawers are always *aware* of the racial and demographic characteristics of their plans, is when race has played too great a role. In making that decision, the Court's jurisprudence essentially triple counted geographic compactness. First, in deciding whether to apply strict scrutiny at all, courts rely heavily on district shape: a district that flouts what courts think of as "traditional" standards of compactness raises suspicion. Second, in deciding whether compliance with section 2 provides a compelling interest for race-conscious districting, courts perform the standard first prong of the *Gingles* analysis. Finally, compactness is relevant to the question whether the challenged district that is "narrowly tailored." If it would have been possible to comply with section 2 without drawing so irregularly shaped a district, then a bizarrely shaped district is not "necessary."

8. Does compactness have a different meaning in the context of local elections with relatively small districts than in congressional elections with districts that often stretch across counties or contain more than 500,000 people? That is, what does it mean to say that a congressional district, outside of one contained entirely within an urban area, is "compact"?

9. Does compactness have normative force? That is, are there independent reasons for wanting districts to be compact? Professor Briffault has offered a somewhat mixed analysis:

> [A]lthough there are significant prudential reasons for utilizing territorial factors in the election of representatives, such as the representation of place-based interests or the asserted connection between territorial districts and popular political participation, they do not provide a constitutional basis for compelling states and localities to abide by the traditional territorial districting criteria.

> Certainly, "geographic boundaries have served traditionally, and perhaps intuitively, as the most common basis" for political representation, because "there is a spatial dimension to human organization." Many of the most important interests and concerns people have relate to their homes, their neighbors, the adjacent streets and roads, and their immediate geographic environment. Attention to territory—to the interests of people in compact and contiguous areas, and to the interests of people living in preexisting geographically defined neighborhoods or within local political subdivisions—can, thus, advance the political interests of residents that are linked to territory.

> * * *

> The appropriate role for place-based factors in the election of representatives may vary according to what the representative body in question does, or, more normatively, what we wish it would do. Where the principal function of the government in question is to address place-specific interests—garbage collection, street repair, and local recreation—then close attention to territoriality may be appropriate. Where, however, the representative body in question is not involved in providing services to particular places, in allocating limited resources to the conflicting demands of territorial communities, or in granting powers to, or overseeing the activities of, subordinate governments, there is less need to attend to place-based factors in framing the mechanism for the election of representatives. The differences among people in a state with respect to the actions the United States Congress ought to take on

such federal matters as international trade policy, health-care reform, welfare policy, deficit reduction, or the Internal Revenue Code, may have less to do with place within the state than with ideology, ethnicity, partisanship, or other nonterritorial interests. Indeed, there might be a positive value in reducing the role of territoriality in congressional elections if we thought Congress ought to devote less time to place specific pork-barrel projects and meddling in local affairs and more effort to setting policy on matters of national significance.

Besides representing interests that are connected to specific areas, territorial districting may promote popular political participation and facilitate citizen oversight of elected representatives. Voters may be more likely to engage with their neighbors in the discussion, debate, and deliberative interaction so necessary to democratic life than with people who are physically distant from them.

* * *

Moreover, the one-person, one-vote doctrine's stringent requirement of population equality inevitably constrains the role territorial factors may play in districting. Indeed, one person, one-vote exemplifies the primacy of the value of voter equality over the representation of discrete territories. The one-person, one-vote doctrine has downgraded compactness and congruence of district lines with political subdivision borders to a distant second place, behind population equality, in the criteria for legislative districting. Taken together, the requirements of population equality, decennial redistricting, and the use of increasingly sophisticated computer technologies that allow redistricting bodies swiftly to shift wards and census tracts across an array of potential apportionment schemes, have over the past three decades eroded the significance of traditional districting criteria.

Richard Briffault, *Race and Redistricting After* Miller v. Johnson, 1995 U. Chi. Legal F. 23, 40–44. Professor Gerken has suggested that reliance on compactness underscores the essentially group-based underpinnings of dilution analysis:

Redistricting practices plainly reflect the relevance of groups to a representational system. One of the main purposes of redistricting is to facilitate vote aggregation by grouping individuals together on the basis of shared interests. Redistricters do so to enable individuals to communicate their needs to their representatives and to help legislators represent their districts effectively.

Compact districts themselves reflect an effort to group individuals together in this fashion. Redistricters draw compact districts based in part on the assumption that keeping neighborhoods together will ensure a homogeneous district. In short, even when drawing districts solely along preexisting geographical boundaries, redistricters do not, in the words of Justice Ginsburg, "treat people as individuals" but "assemble people in groups."

Heather K. Gerken, *Understanding the Right to an Undiluted Vote*, 114 Harv. L. Rev. 1663, 1679 (2001).

10. Does *Gingles'* first prong require some particular level of concentration of minority voters within the illustrative districts? Consider *Gomez v. City of Watsonville*, 863 F.2d 1407 (9th Cir. 1988) *cert. denied*, 489 U.S. 1080 (1989). Watsonville was governed by a six-member city council and mayor. According to the 1980 census, 48.9 percent of the City's population was Hispanic, although due to demography and differential rates of citizenship, only 37.0 percent of Watsonville's voting-age citizens were.

Roughly two-thirds of the city's Hispanic population lived in three census tracts. But the district court held that that Watsonville's Hispanics were not sufficiently compact because the illustrative plans offered by the plaintiffs to meet the first prong of *Gingles* placed only one-third of the Hispanic electorate in the two majority-Hispanic districts. (The remainder of the Hispanic community was dispersed among the five majority non-Hispanic districts.)

The court of appeals reversed:

The district court erred in considering that approximately 60% of the Hispanics eligible to vote in Watsonville would reside in five districts outside the two single-member, heavily Hispanic districts in appellants' plan. Districting plans with some members of the minority group outside the minority-controlled districts are valid.... The fact that the proposed remedy does not benefit all of the Hispanics in the City does not justify denying any remedy at all.

The appellants' plan proposes two districts in which Hispanics would constitute a majority of the voters and would be able to elect representatives of their choice. It is sadly ironic that the district court concluded that because many Hispanic voters would still not be able to elect representatives of their choice under the proposed plan, no Section 2 claim could be maintained, thereby relegating all Hispanic voters to having no political effectiveness. The district court's finding is premised on a misunderstanding of the applicable legal standard.

Ought plan drawers seek to maximize the number of nonwhite voters placed in majority nonwhite districts in order to increase the number of individual voters who are able to elect a candidate of their choice? Remember, in a jurisdiction with severe racial bloc voting, voters who are in the racial minority within a district will essentially waste their votes. To what extent does increasing each *individual*'s ability to vote for a winning candidate decrease the influence of the *group* to which that voter belongs on the overall composition of the legislature? Is there simply an inherent tension between maximizing individual voters' influence and dilutive "packing"?

NOTES AND QUESTIONS ON THE GINGLES' SECOND PRONG

1. For the most part, *Gingles'* second prong—that "the minority group . . . show that it is politically cohesive"—has occasioned little litigation. In part, this is a function of the ease with which cohesion can be shown. As Justice Brennan's opinion explained it, "[a] showing that a significant number of minority group members usually vote for the same candidates is one way of proving the political cohesiveness necessary to a vote dilution claim, and, consequently, establishes minority bloc voting within the context of § 2." Thus, the statistical techniques discussed above can easily show that the minority community throws overwhelming support behind a few candidates. In part, the paucity of reported cases may also be a function of litigation decisions. Lawyers may be reluctant to bring suit on behalf of deeply divided minority communities because the benefits from victory would be so illusory: if the minority community is unable to unite behind a candidate, even a majority-black district may be unable to elect a minority-preferred candidate. And to the extent that voting rights lawyers rely on community involvement in the litigation process, the time and trouble of litigating a case on behalf of a fractured community may be too high.

Gingles presented a textbook example of one sort of racial politics: the black-white split of the Deep South. Litigation regarding political cohesiveness has focused largely on a quite different context: the multi-racial, multi-ethnic jurisdictions of the Southwest, Florida, and the urban north. In these jurisdictions, courts must confront a definitional problem absent from *Gingles*, namely, what counts as a minority "group." Must all the members share a single racial, ethnic, or linguistic identification or can minority groups be "aggregated"? When the Supreme Court was presented with this issue, in *Growe v. Emison*, 507 U.S. 25, 41 (1993), it sidestepped the question by assuming the permissibility of combining distinct ethnic and language groups—in that case, African and Native Americans in Minneapolis—but observing that there was no statistical or anecdotal evidence in the record to show minority political cohesion. The lower courts have been sharply divided.

Initially, most courts had either assumed without deciding or had explicitly permitted coalition suits under section 2. *See, e.g., Badillo v. City of Stockton*, 956 F.2d 884 (9th Cir. 1992); *Concerned Citizens v. Hardee County*, 906 F.2d 524 (11th Cir. 1990); *Campos v. City of Baytown*, 840 F.2d 1240 (5th Cir.), *cert. denied*, 492 U.S. 905 (1989); *Knox v. Milwaukee County Bd. of Election Comm'rs*, 607 F. Supp. 1112 (E.D. Wis. 1985). By contrast, the scholarly commentary on coalition lawsuits was largely negative. *See, e.g.,* Katharine I. Butler & Richard Murray, *Minority Vote Dilution Suits and the Problem of Two Minority Groups: Can a "Rainbow Coalition" Claim the Protection of the Voting Rights Act?*, 21 Pac. L.J. 619 (1990); Rick G. Strange, *Application of Voting Rights Act to Communities Containing Two or More Minority Groups—When is the Whole Greater*

Than the Sum of the Parts?, 20 Tex. Tech L. Rev. 95 (1989); Sebastian Geraci, Comment, *The Case Against Allowing Coalitions to File Section 2 Dilution Claims*, 1995 U. Chi. Leg. For. 389. *But see* Aylon M. Schulte, Note, *Minority Aggregation Under Section 2 of the Voting Rights Act: Toward Just Representation in Ethnically Diverse Communities*, 1995 U. Ill. L. Rev. 441.

In more recent decisions, however, several courts of appeals have rejected coalition claims. In *Nixon v. Kent County*, 76 F.3d 1381 (6th Cir. 1996) (en banc), a divided court of appeals rejected a section 2 claim by black and Hispanic voters in Kent County, Michigan, who together constituted 9.2 percent of the county's voting-age population, seeking the creation of two majority-minority districts on the county's Board of Commissioners. Similarly, in *Frank v. Forest County*, 336 F.3d 570 (7th Cir. 2003), *cert. denied*, 540 U.S. 1106 (2004), the Seventh Circuit rejected the claim that section 2 required aggregating Indian and black voters in drawing districts for a county board of supervisors.

2. There are many jurisdictions in which two distinctive ethnic groups are *not* cohesive. For example, African Americans and Cuban Americans have fought bitterly over how to allocate political power in South Florida. *See, e.g., Johnson v. De Grandy*, 512 U.S. 997 (1994) (a principal case later in this Chapter); *Meek v. Metropolitan Dade County,* 908 F.2d 1540 (11th Cir. 1990), *cert. denied*, 499 U.S. 907 (1991); Larry Rohter, *A Black–Hispanic Struggle Over Florida Redistricting*, N.Y. Times, May 30, 1992 (quoting a black state representative from Miami as saying "if the basis of an extra minority seat is the Voting Rights Act, then we ought to look and see who it was standing on the Edmund Pettus Bridge in Selma getting trampled.").

Moreover, there are even some jurisdictions which experience conflict within groups that are aggregated by the statutory language of the Voting Rights Act. The definitional provision of the Act, section 14(c)(3) contains the following provision:

> The term "language minorities" or "language minority group" means persons who are American Indian, Asian American, Alaskan Natives, or of Spanish heritage.

42 U.S.C. § 1973l(c)(3). For example, in *Arizonans for Fair Representation v. Symington*, 828 F. Supp. 684 (D. Ariz. 1992), *aff'd*, 507 U.S. 981 (1993), the three-judge court recognized a conflict between Navajo and Hopi tribes in Arizona that resulted placing them in separate congressional districts. *See also Guy v. Hickel*, Case No. A–92–494 CIV (JKS) (D. Alaska 1995) (rejecting a claim by Yupiq Eskimos who sued under § 2 because Eskimos as a whole were fairly represented within the Alaskan legislature); Frank J. Macchiarola & Joseph G. Diaz, *The 1990 New York City Districting Commission: Renewed Opportunity for Participation in Local Government or Race–Based Gerrymandering?*, 14 Cardozo L. Rev. 1175 (1993) (discussing councilmanic redistricting in New York and the conflict between Domini-

cans and Puerto Ricans in upper Manhattan and between American-born and Caribbean-born blacks in Brooklyn).

Is the answer to such internecine conflicts to conclude that the minority group is not sufficiently "politically cohesive" or should claims by distinctive subgroups be cognizable under the Voting Rights Act?

League of United Latin American Citizens (LULAC) v. Clements

999 F.2d 831 (5th Cir.) (en banc), *cert. denied*, 510 U.S. 1071 (1994).

■ Patrick Higginbotham, Circuit Judge:

Over the past fifty years, the steady march of civil rights has been to New Orleans and this court. It continues but the demands have changed. Relatively clear lines of legality and morality have become more difficult to locate as demands for outcomes have followed the cutting away of obstacles to full participation. With our diverse ethnic makeup, this demand for results in voting has surfaced profound questions of a democratic political order such as the limits on rearranging state structures to alter election outcomes, and majority rule at the ballot box and even in legislative halls, questions Congress has provoked but not answered. All this can make a simple voting rights case seem difficult, certainly so with state judges elected on a partisan ballot. . . .

I. Facts

On July 11, 1988, ten individual voters and the League of United Latin American Citizens sued in federal district court alleging that Texas' system of electing state trial judges violated § 2 of the Voting Rights Act and the Fourteenth and Fifteenth Amendments in several Texas counties. . . .

As they have throughout Texas history, Texas voters elect their trial judges in county-wide elections. A voter may vote for all of the trial courts of general jurisdiction in her county. At the same time, each trial court is a distinct court, such as the 134th judicial district court of Dallas County, with county-wide jurisdiction and its own history of incumbents. A candidate runs for a particular court. Plaintiffs contend that electing trial judges county-wide violates § 2 of the Voting Rights Act by impermissibly diluting the voting power of Hispanics and blacks. Plaintiffs proceed on behalf of language and ethnic minorities in different combinations in different counties. Depending on the county—more specifically, the numbers—they argue that Hispanic voters, black voters, or the combination of both Hispanic and black voters "have less opportunity than other members of the electorate to participate in the political process and elect representatives of their choice."

* * *

III.   Racial Bloc Voting

* * *

A central issue here, one that divided the panel and one over which the parties vigorously disagree, concerns *Gingles'* white bloc voting inquiry and the closely related *Zimmer* factor directing courts to examine "the extent to which voting . . . is racially polarized." . . . As the Court in *Gingles* held, the question here is not whether white residents tend to vote as a bloc, but whether such bloc voting is "legally significant." In finding a violation of § 2 in each of the nine challenged counties, the district court held that plaintiffs need only demonstrate that whites and blacks generally support different candidates to establish legally significant white bloc voting. Because "it is the difference between choices made by blacks and whites alone . . . that is the central inquiry of § 2," the court excluded evidence tending to prove that these divergent voting patterns were attributable to factors other than race as "irrelevant" and "legally incompetent."

On appeal, defendants contend that the district court erred in refusing to consider the nonracial causes of voting preferences they offered at trial. Unless the tendency among minorities and whites to support different candidates, and the accompanying losses by minority groups at the polls, are somehow tied to race, defendants argue, plaintiffs' attempt to establish legally significant white bloc voting, and thus their vote dilution claim under § 2, must fail. When the record indisputably proves that partisan affiliation, not race, best explains the divergent voting patterns among minority and white citizens in the contested counties, defendants conclude, the district court's judgment must be reversed.

We agree. The scope of the Voting Rights Act is indeed quite broad, but its rigorous protections, as the text of § 2 suggests, extend only to defeats experienced by voters "on account of race or color." Without an inquiry into the circumstances underlying unfavorable election returns, courts lack the tools to discern results that are in any sense "discriminatory," and any distinction between deprivation and mere losses at the polls becomes untenable. In holding that the failure of minority-preferred candidates to receive support from a majority of whites on a regular basis, without more, sufficed to prove legally significant racial bloc voting, the district court loosed § 2 from its racial tether and fused illegal vote dilution and political defeat.

* * *

The principles announced and applied in *Whitcomb [v. Chavis]* and *White [v. Regester]* are instructive and, we believe, controlling. As Justice White, the author of these opinions, recently indicated, the central "theme" of *Whitcomb* and *White* is "that it is not mere suffering at the polls but discrimination in the polity with which the Constitution is concerned." . . . [F]ailures of a minority group to elect representatives of its choice that are attributable to "partisan politics" provide no grounds for relief. Section 2 is "a balm for racial minorities, not political ones—even though the two often coincide." ... Rather, § 2 is implicated only where Democrats lose because they are black, not where blacks lose because they are Democrats.

* * *

Justice Brennan's discussion of the first and second *Gingles* factors received majority support. With respect to the third element, however, five justices rejected Justice Brennan's proposed standard for proving racial bloc voting. For this reason, we believe that it is to [Justice White's and Justice O'Connor's concurrences], not Justice Brennan's [opinion], that we should look in attempting to define the contours of the inquiry into legally significant bloc voting.

* * *

As courts and commentators alike have noted, Justice White and Justice O'Connor were united in their fidelity to *Whitcomb's* distinction between vote dilution and partisan politics and in their opposition to Justice Brennan's attempt to expunge this teaching from the bloc voting inquiry.

* * *

Both Justice Brennan and Justice O'Connor recognized that racial bloc voting is intimately related to the responsiveness of elected officials to the interests of minorities, one of the factors considered as part of the "totality of circumstances." ... The close tie between bloc voting and representatives' responsiveness ... rests on common sense: Public officials need not address concerns expressed by minorities so long as white bloc voting ensures that they will remain minority concerns.... [But] this close identification [is] warranted only where racial political considerations [are] present, that is, where white bloc voting cause[s] "minority candidates [to] lose elections solely because of their race." Justice Brennan's approach, [however], assumes that political leaders may safely ignore minority concerns even where black and white voters are separated only by differing interests. Put another way, Justice Brennan's bloc voting test accords governing majorities linked only by the perception of common interests the same permanence and thus relevance under § 2 as white blocs cemented by racial prejudice.

Justice O'Connor not only rejected Justice Brennan's polarized voting standard but was also unwilling to join in the questionable assumption that minorities are unable to influence elections and secure the attention of public officials where these groups have been unsuccessful in their efforts to elect their preferred representatives. Unlike Justice Brennan, she argued that "Congress also intended that explanations of the reasons why white voters rejected minority candidates would be probative of the likelihood that candidates elected without decisive minority support would be willing to take the minority's interests into account."... Justice O'Connor believed that a minority group's prospects for future electoral success and the likelihood that elected officials will take account of their interests differ materially "in a community where racial animosity is absent although the interests of racial groups diverge." A tendency among whites to cast their votes on the basis of race presents a far more durable obstacle to the coalition-building upon which minority electoral success depends than disagreements over ideology for, as Professor Ely observes, "prejudice blinds us to overlapping interests that in fact exist." John Hart Ely, Democracy and Distrust 153 (1980). Representatives who owe their office to the support of majorities bound by prejudice need not attend to the interests of minorities, since the bias uniting their constituents ensures that these issues will remain minority concerns. Where, on the other hand, voting patterns correlate with partisan affiliation or perceived interest, the open channels of communication facilitate a recognition of points of common ground that might otherwise go undetected. Elected officials in these communities cannot ignore minority interests because this group might be part of the winning coalition that votes them out of office.

* * *

[T]here are many other possible non-racial causes of voter behavior beyond partisan affiliation. A rule conditioning relief under § 2 upon proof of the existence of racial animus in the electorate would require plaintiffs to establish the absence of not only partisan voting, but also all other potentially innocent explanations for white voters' rejection of minority-preferred candidates. Factors that might legitimately lead white voters to withhold support from particular minority candidates include, for example, limited campaign funds, inexperience, or a reputation besmirched by scandal. Because these additional factors map only imperfectly onto partisan affiliation, detailed multivariate analysis might then be the evidence of choice....

This argument possesses considerable force.... [But today we need not decide whether additional factors are relevant, since our conclusion rests on] the fundamental division between "partisan politics" and "racial vote dilution" set out by the Court in *Whitcomb* and *White* and confirmed by Congress.

* * *

[The evidence in this case shows that] white voters constitute the majority of not only the Republican Party, but also the Democratic Party, even in several of the counties in which the former dominates. In Dallas County, for example, 30–40% of white voters consistently support Democrats, making white Democrats more numerous than all of the minority Democratic voters combined. The suggestion that Republican voters are galvanized by a "white" or "anti-minority" agenda is plausible only to the extent that the Democratic Party can be viewed as a vehicle for advancing distinctively minority interests, which clearly is not the case. At the same time, white Democrats have in recent years experienced the same electoral defeats as minority voters. If we are to hold that these losses at the polls, without more, give rise to a racial vote dilution claim warranting special relief for minority voters, a principle by which we might justify withholding similar relief from white Democrats is not readily apparent.

Second, both political parties, and especially the Republicans, aggressively recruited minority lawyers to run on their party's ticket. Consequently, white as well as minority voters found themselves not infrequently voting against candidates sharing their respective racial or ethnic backgrounds in favor of their party's nominee. In particular, the undisputed evidence discloses that white voters in most counties, both Republican and Democratic, without fail supported the minority candidates slated by their parties at levels equal to or greater than those enjoyed by white candidates, even where the minority candidate was opposed by a white candidate.

* * *

■ CAROLYN KING, CIRCUIT JUDGE, with whom HENRY POLITZ, CHIEF JUDGE, joins, dissenting:

* * *

Social science problems

Even without the legal problems inherent in the majority's approach to legally significant white bloc voting and racially polarized voting, the majority's approach is severely flawed from a social science perspective. Regardless of whether the majority requires a multivariate regression analysis, which would seek to eliminate all causes of voting behavior other than race, or only a trivariate regression analysis, which would attempt to eliminate partisan affiliation, there is a problem with requiring this type of evidence as an integral part of the vote dilution inquiry: it ignores the critical distinction between experimental research and non-experimental research. Specifically, it ignores the warning of most respected social scientists, including the experts who testified in this case, that the causes of voting behavior cannot be determined from the use of any kind of regression analysis—whether bivariate, trivariate, or multivariate.

It is important to recognize that the kind of evidence that the majority requires minority plaintiffs to introduce will involve no experimental manipulation of independent variables. The plaintiffs will not be able to manipulate the race or party affiliation of the candidate to determine which one had the greater effect on election outcomes. Rather, the plaintiffs will have to take existing election results and work backwards. This kind of real world research has been labelled "non-experimental research" by social scientists. . . .

[One critical problem with inferring causation on the basis of regression analyses is that] variables in nonexperimental research tend to be intercorrelated. Since more often than not researchers neither understand the causes of the interrelations nor attempt to study them, implications of regression coefficients for policy decisions are questionable.

Requiring minority plaintiffs to come forward with a multivariate regression analysis to determine the causes of racially divergent voting patterns [suffers from this problem]. . . . The independent variables listed by Judge Higginbotham—including incumbency, campaign expenditures, party identification, income, media use measured by cost, religion—"tend to be correlated, sometimes substantially." Therefore, "it [becomes] difficult, if not impossible, to untangle the effects of each variable." By inferring causation from such analysis, we would undoubtedly be engaging in what amounts to an "almost mindless interpretation[] of regression analysis in nonexperimental research." In short, we would be importing "junk science" into the Voting Rights Act while rejecting it in other contexts.

Requiring minority plaintiffs to only come forward with a trivariate regression analysis, as the majority seems to do in this case, does not alleviate the social science problems; it only multiplies them. Not only does such a requirement ignore the fact that the two independent variables (i.e., race and partisan affiliation) are substantially correlated, it also runs the risk that the two variables being studied are only proxies for causal variables that are not included in the regression equation. . . .

The trivariate regression analyses offered in this case undoubtedly demonstrate that the party affiliation of a candidate is a better predictor of electoral success than the race of the candidate. Because we are dealing with non-experimental research, however, I cannot take the leap that the majority makes—namely, that the party affiliation of a candidate is the best, or the single most powerful, explanation of electoral success. The evidence in this case also demonstrates that, in many of the counties, race is substantially correlated with party affiliation, and the trivariate regression analyses offered in this case did not determine, and could not have determined, why people join certain parties. In my view, then, they can no more explain why people vote the way they do than a bivariate regression analysis. Significantly, for purposes of the Voting Rights Act, they could not negate "race or color" as an explanation for election outcomes.

The practical problem

The majority's approach to legally significant white bloc voting and racially polarized voting places an almost insurmountable hurdle in front of minority groups proceeding under section 2. Unless minority plaintiffs can successfully establish that voters in the controlling political party are racially motivated—either through the use of questionable voting statistics or by calling people from that party and asking them why they voted the way they did[58]—their claim will fail. In fact, they will not even be able to make out a prima facie case.

The typical section 2 vote dilution case ... has two prominent features: One is a politically cohesive minority group (e.g., blacks or Hispanics) whose members share political interests and vote together, usually in a single political party that also includes whites. The other is the existence of a white majority, generally in a different political party, whose voting strength is sufficient usually to defeat the combined strength of minority votes plus white "crossover" votes. The problem for minority voters in the typical section 2 case is that they have been submerged in a white majority—unable to forge a coalition with enough whites to elect representatives of their choice. Thus, the Voting Rights Act, as interpreted in *Gingles* and succeeding cases, presupposes partisan voting and asks whether politically cohesive minority voters have an unequal opportunity to participate in the political process—a partisan political process—and to elect representatives of their choice on account of race or color.

Under the majority's reasoning, this typical scenario, the scenario specifically contemplated by the *Gingles* framework, will now preclude a finding of vote dilution. As long as some whites vote with minorities in the Democratic Party, partisan affiliation will always be a better predictor of election outcomes than race (even if a few minorities vote Republican). Such circumstances, under the majority's framework, will preclude a finding of vote dilution. In short, the majority has effectively eviscerated section 2 of the Voting Rights Act in communities where there is any measurable crossover voting by whites.[60]

* * *

NOTES AND QUESTIONS

1.   Does *LULAC*'s approach reinstate a requirement that plaintiffs prove a racially discriminatory intent, this time of individual voters? In an earlier

---

58.   *But see Kirksey v. City of Jackson*, 663 F.2d 659, 662 (5th Cir. Unit A Dec.1981) (holding that, because of First Amendment concerns, voters' motivations are not subject to searching scrutiny by plaintiffs in a voting rights case), *clarified*, 669 F.2d 316 (5th Cir. 1982).

60.   The majority implies that interest group politics did not begin in Texas until the 1980s, when the Republican Party emerged as a force to be reckoned with. The majority ignores that, even when Texas was a one party state, there were still different factions, or interest groups, within the Democratic party. Thus, partisan or interest group poli-

tics has always been a feature of Texas' colorful political landscape. To hold otherwise is to ignore the past reality. As noted previously, the evidence in this case reflects that, before 1980, minority-preferred candidates lost in Democratic primary elections, generally to white Democrats; after 1980, minority-preferred candidates may make it to the general election, but only to lose to white Republicans. "From the vantage point of minority voters—which is the vantage point of section 2—it is difficult to see how the arrival of a two party system in Texas has altered their ability to participate in the political process and elect candidates of their choice."

case, the Fifth Circuit had held that First Amendment concerns precluded the plaintiffs in a vote-dilution lawsuit from inquiring directly into the motivation behind individual citizens' votes. *Kirksey v. City of Jackson*, 663 F.2d 659, 662 (5th Cir. 1981).

2. *LULAC* marks a reinvigoration of the *Whitcomb v. Chavis* analysis of partisanship, discussed in Chapter 7. It should be noted that the early challenges to at-large elections (except for *Whitcomb*) were either in the one-party Democratic South or in one-party Democratic cities. *LULAC* grew out of a relatively recent phenomenon: the emergence of a heavily white southern Republican Party. *See* Pamela S. Karlan, *Loss and Redemption: Voting Rights at the Turn of a Century*, 50 Vand. L. Rev. 291, 314–20 (1997) (discussing the relationship between the Voting Rights Act and the rise of Southern Republicanism).

3.   The Second Circuit took a somewhat different tack on the question of the relationship among discriminatory purpose, partisan voting patterns, racial polarization, and section 2. *Goosby v. Town of Hempstead*, 180 F.3d 476 (2d Cir. 1999), involved a challenge to at-large elections for the Town Council, which has six members. (The Town has a population of over 725,000 people, making it more populous than six states and all but thirteen cities.) Since the inception of Town government in 1907, a member of the Republican Party had won every Town-wide election.

African Americans constituted 12.1 percent of the Town's 725,639 residents, and lived for the most part in a set of relatively segregated neighborhoods. Among white registered voters, 51 percent registered as Republicans, 26 percent as Democrats and 23 percent in another party or in no party. Among black registered voters, however, only 22 percent registered as Republicans, while 68 percent registered as Democrats and 10 percent in another party or expressed no party affiliation.

At trial, the plaintiffs concededly met the first two prongs of *Gingles*. They also concededly showed that white voters and black voters preferred different candidates and that the candidates preferred by white voters invariably won. The district court rejected the Town's contention that the strong correlation between race and party precluded it from finding "legally significant white bloc voting" unless it first found that partisan politics was a proxy for racial animus, and instead considered the evidence of partisanship under the "totality of the circumstances" test. Ultimately, it found a violation of section 2 and ordered a single-member district remedy.

On appeal, the court of appeals affirmed. It agreed with the Fourth Circuit's decision in *Lewis v. Alamance County*, 99 F.3d 600 (4th Cir. 1996), that causation—that is, the reason for divergent voting patterns—is irrelevant in the inquiry into the three *Gingles* preconditions, but relevant in the totality of circumstances inquiry, a position that had been taken by several other circuits as well.

Nonetheless, the court of appeals rejected the Town's argument that "blacks have lost as Democrats, not as 'blacks' ":

> The Town's argument implies that if blacks registered and voted as Republicans, they would be able to elect the candidates they prefer. But they are not able to elect preferred candidates under the Republican Party regime that rules in the Town. Moreover, blacks should not be constrained to vote for Republicans who are not their preferred candidates.
>
> The Supreme Court instructs that a Voting Rights Act violation occurs when "a certain electoral law, practice, or structure interacts with social and historical conditions to cause an inequality in the opportunities enjoyed by black and white voters to elect their preferred representatives." *Gingles*, 478 U.S. at 47. The electoral law at issue provides for at-large voting for Town Board members. The historical conditions implicated are the Republican Party's hegemony over the Town of Hempstead since the Town's inception over 90 years ago, the slating process by which candidates are selected by the Republican Party, and the predilection of the great majority of blacks to vote for Democrat candidates. The concatenation of these conditions has resulted in the vote dilution of which the plaintiff class complains and the consequent inability of blacks to elect their preferred candidates.
>
> The Republican slating process in the Town is unique. Although the Republican Committee members in the Town of Hempstead theoretically are empowered to choose a slate of candidates for the Town Board, the actual selection process has been much different. The Committee members have ceded their authority to the County Chairman, who designates the Town slate. The choice of candidates is his alone, although any number of people may suggest potential candidates. The present Nassau County Chairman, Joseph Mondello, has served in that capacity for some fifteen years. While black Republicans could mount a primary campaign to secure the Republican nomination for Town Board for a preferred candidate, it would be futile to do so. The Chairman-preferred candidate would always win in a Town-wide primary election, due to the overwhelming strength of the monolithic Republican organization.... [O]ne-man, no-vote ... prevails in the Republican Party in the Town of Hempstead and in the County of Nassau....

180 F.3d at 495–97. To what extent is the unique slating process relevant given that the overwhelming majority of black voters in Hempstead do not participate in Republican politics in the first place?

Judge Leval filed a thought-provoking concurrence on the question of the role of discriminatory intent or racial animus in section 2 cases. He offered a hypothetical jurisdiction, one in which the election rules were set many years ago, before members of a protected class moved into the area. In Judge Leval's view, "the more deeply judicial intervention would intrude into the political process, the more reluctant courts should be to find a violation without a finding of racial motivation." *Id.* at 501–02. So, for example, section 2 "might require the establishment of a polling place near a new concentration of protected class members, even though the location of polling places had not been racially motivated, if the inaccessibility of the polling place lessened the opportunity of class members to cast ballots. Such a remedy involves little judicial intrusion into the political process." But, he felt very differently about the question of districting. Suppose an electoral district's boundaries were

> set long ago and ha[ve] since been maintained without any racial motivation. In recent years, a cluster of members of a protected class develops around the dividing line, with a substantial percentage of the cluster falling on both sides of the line. If the members of that class could not elect their preferred representative in the districts on either side of the line, but could elect a representative if the line were shifted so that the entire community fell into one district, then plaintiffs from that class could argue that the maintenance of the line deprived them of the opportunity to elect a representative of their choice. In such a circumstance, the notion that courts could invalidate an election and require revision of election districts, without any showing of discriminatory intent, seems to me alarming and far beyond the probable contemplation of Congress.

Id. at 501 n.3. Judge Leval also suggested that

> In deciding whether or not discriminatory intent is necessary to a section 2 violation, another factor that may be relevant is whether the alleged violation appears more concerned with process or outcomes. The accessible location of polling places, for example, is necessary to a fair process in which all persons can cast a vote. The law may plausibly guarantee a fair process regardless whether the unfairness to be remedied is the product of discriminatory intent. But where plaintiffs allege that they are unable to elect representatives of their choice, their complaint, at least on its face, is that the outcome is unfavorable to them. Ordinarily, American law guarantees equal electoral opportunity, not equal electoral results. *See Davis v. Bandemer*, 478 U.S. 109 (1986). If courts are to police electoral outcomes, it is reasonable that they first require that discrimination, within the electorate if not the state, have infected the election. When discrimination is present, it can be said that the process also was not fair, in the sense that it was marred by illegitimate animus.

Id. at 502 n.4. Is there any warrant for Judge Leval's proposal in the text or structure of section 2?

Despite his disagreement with the majority's framework, Judge Leval agreed with the result. In his view, proof of the three *Gingles* factors "sufficiently supports an inference that race may have been a factor" to shift the burden to defendants to disprove the presumption of discriminatory purpose by government officials or the electorate. *Id.* at 502–03. In this case, based on the district court's factual findings, Judge Leval did not think the Town had carried its burden of disproving racial motivation. In reaching this conclusion, Judge Leval pointed to the fact that "[r]acial appeals have been features of Town elections on more than one occasion, [t]own law enforcement officers have engaged in race-conscious polic-ing,.... [a]gencies of the Town government have committed acts of racial discrimination to which the Town has made no response, ... [and the Town] has a history of indifference to the economic and social needs of the black communities within Hempstead...." Moreover, until "litigation be-gan, the Republican Party in Hempstead had never recruited an African–American candidate for the Town Board" and "a majority of white voters in Hempstead had never supported a black candidate for the Board." *Id.* at 503.

As a policy matter, is Judge Leval's approach actually less intrusive? Moreover, on whose discriminatory intent is he relying?

4. It is important to recognize that arguments over racial bloc voting involve both normative and empirical premises, and to keep clear whether particular arguments are prescriptive or descriptive. In particular, "[i]n the freighted arena of race and public policy, abstract principles often founder on uncomfortable facts." Richard H. Pildes, *The Politics of Race*, 108 Harv. L. Rev. 1359, 1381 (1995). In the *Shaw* cases discussed in Chapter 9, the Supreme Court has declared that the assumption that black voters "think alike, share the same political interests, and will prefer the same candidates at the polls" is "offensive and demeaning." *Miller v. Johnson*, 515 U.S. 900, 912 (1995); *Shaw v. Reno*, 509 U.S. 630, 647–48 (1993).

Often, courts adopt a prescriptive position—that is, they are making a value judgment, rather than saying that the assumption of shared interests is factually false. There is substantial evidence of systematic racial differ-ences in political attitudes, policy preferences, and actual voting behavior. For extensive documentation of these differences, see Donald R. Kinder and Lynn M. Sanders, Divided by Color: Racial Politics and Democratic Ideals (1996) and David Lublin, The Paradox of Representation 72–78 (1997). For example, between 1964 and 1992, no Democratic candidate for President won a majority of white votes, while every Democratic candidate received a majority of the black vote cast. *See* Pildes, *supra*, at 1379 n.84. In House elections from 1980 to 1994, on average 87% of blacks voted Democratic, whereas 49% of whites did so. This racial disparity in partisan preferences has increased in recent years. Between 1990 and 1994, the Democratic Party's share of the white vote in the South declined 15 points (from 50% to 35%), although its share of the black vote increased 11 points (from 80% to 91%). *See Portrait of the Electorate: Who Voted for Whom in the House*, N.Y. Times, Nov. 13, 1994, at 24. For disparities with regard to policy preferences, see, e.g., Lee Sigelman & Susan Welch, Black Americans' Views of Racial Inequality 143 (1991) (reaching the general conclusion that, "on issues where government action is contemplated, blacks as a group are more activist than whites"); *see also* An American Profile—Opinions and Behavior, 1972–1989, at 572, 710, 729 (Floris W. Wood ed. 1990) (showing differences in white and black responses over time to questions concerning the responsibility of government for aiding the poor, providing welfare, and solving big-city problems).

5.   Does a distinction between racial and political motivations make sense? To what extent do such attempts muddy the distinction between correlation and causation? Public opinion surveys consistently reveal that race in contemporary America is highly correlated with views on a number of politically salient issues. For some issues, race may be only a proxy for other shared characteristics such as residence, religion, or socioeconomic status. But what if race is a causal factor in disparities regarding these characteristics? For example, suppose black voters in a particular city all voted for candidates who vowed not to approve a dumpsite in a particular neighborhood, while white voters supported candidates in favor of the siting. If blacks live in the affected neighborhood in part as a result of intentional government-sponsored or-condoned racial discrimination in the housing market, is voting racially polarized? If the discrimination were more attenuated, and blacks lived in the neighborhood not because of discrimination in the housing market, but because their relatively lower incomes restricted their housing choices, would the disparity in voting behavior be purely political? For some issues, race may be more of a causal factor. For example, suppose black voters all supported a candidate who pledged to sponsor fair housing legislation while whites backed her opponent. *Cf. Hunter v. Erickson*, 393 U.S. 385 (1969) (striking down a city charter provision that required approval by referendum of any housing ordinance that sought to regulate discrimination on "the basis of race, color, religion, national origin or ancestry" but not other housing ordinances on the ground that the provision was racially discriminatory).

6.   There is yet another problem with an attempt to require something beyond simple correlation:

> The many difficulties with [the] attempt to disaggregate race and politics . . . all result from the fact that race and political affiliation are, in fact, substantially correlated. It is thus impossible to determine which of the two is a better *explanation*—as opposed to a *predictor*—of voting patterns. A hypothetical example may clarify this point. Suppose that the two dominant political parties were the Antiblacks and the Problacks, each advocating a platform consistent with its name. If, as we might expect, virtually all black voters were members of the Problack party and voted for Problack candidates, then political affiliation would be nothing more than a proxy for race. Race clearly would be a better explanation of voting patterns than political affiliation, and there would hardly be room for doubt as to the existence of racial bloc voting. In contemporary American politics a similar (though, of course,

weaker) causal relationship obtains between race and political party, with most blacks finding their interests better represented by the Democratic party. As a consequence, statistical tests such as the multivariate regression analyses of voting patterns offered by the *LULAC* defendants will necessarily be indeterminate with respect to the causal role of race in affecting voting behavior.... [A] typical section 2 scenario involves a politically cohesive group of nonwhite voters, usually Democrats, who have been unable to elect their preferred candidates because their votes, combined with white Democratic "crossover" votes, have consistently been submerged by the votes of an overwhelmingly white, largely Republican majority. In other words, the black or Hispanic voters have not been able to form a coalition with enough white voters to overcome the white majority bloc vote. In this scenario, as long as some whites vote with minorities for the Democratic candidate, political affiliation will *always* be a better predictor of election outcome than will race; accordingly, under Judge Higginbotham's approach, the nonwhite voters will have no remedy. Yet this is precisely the sort of racial exclusion that section 2 and *Gingles* sought to remedy.

Pamela S. Karlan & Daryl J. Levinson, *Why Voting Is Different*, 84 Cal. L. Rev. 1201, 1223–24 (1996).

7. Several recent court of appeals decisions have given additional consideration to the third *Gingles* factor. In *Old Person v. Cooney*, 230 F.3d 1113 (9th Cir. 2000), American Indians challenged Montana's state house apportionment under section 2. In remanding the case for further proceedings, the Ninth Circuit held that the district court had erred in relying on white voting behavior within majority-Indian electoral districts to conclude that white voters did not usually (that is, more often than not) vote to defeat the preferred candidate of Indian voters. The Court of Appeals relied in part on the Court's decision in *Johnson v. De Grandy*, 512 U.S. 997 (1994)—a principal case in the next section of this Chapter—which reflected "a post-*Gingles* phenomenon, a § 2 challenge to a plan that already included some majority-minority districts." *DeGrandy* had found racial bloc voting in the "tendency of non-Hispanic whites to vote as a bloc to bar minority groups from electing their chosen candidates *except in a district where a given minority makes up a voting majority*." *Id.* at 1003–04 (emphasis added). Thus, the Ninth Circuit concluded that it should "consider Indian electoral success in majority-Indian districts only in the inquiry into the totality of the circumstances," but not in deciding whether Indian voters had satisfied the third prong of *Gingles*. "To do otherwise would permit white bloc voting in a majority-white district to be washed clean by electoral success in neighboring majority-Indian districts. Such an approach would be antithetical to the directive in *Gingles* that legally significant white bloc voting be determined on a fact-specific 'district to district' basis." What is the underlying rationale for excluding white voting behavior in majority-minority districts? Is it that white voters' behavior under these circumstances may be colored by the knowledge that they are the numerical minority and thus they may be more willing to support coalitions with nonwhite voters? The Ninth Circuit also rejected the state's argument that whatever white bloc voting existed was not legally significant somewhere between 22 and 38 percent of white voters crossed over to vote for Indian preferred candidates.

Finally, the Court of Appeals rejected the state's alternative rationale for the observed behavior of white voters, namely partisan politics. The state argued that losses by Indian candidates could fairly be ascribed to partisan politics and not race when Democratic Indian candidates lose in majority Republican districts. But the court of appeals found that Indian (Indian-preferred) candidates generally received a lower percentage of white votes than did white Indian-preferred candidates in the same district and thus refused to attribute white bloc voting to "mere" partisan politics.

In *Rural West Tennessee African–American Affairs Council v. Sundquist*, 209 F.3d 835 (6th Cir. 2000), the court of appeals confronted the question of the weight to give so-called white-on-white elections in addressing the third *Gingles* factor. It held that while courts could consider electoral contests involving only white candidates, those elections might be less probative than contests that involved black candidates as well. See also *Nipper v. Smith*, 39 F.3d 1494, 1540 (11th Cir. 1994) (en banc) (holding that white-white elections may be considered, but are less probative than those involving black candidates); *Smith v. Clinton*, 687 F.Supp. 1310, 1318 (E.D. Ark.) (three judge court) (observing that § 2's guarantee of equal opportunity is not met when "candidates favored by blacks can win, but only if the candidates are white"), *aff'd*, 488 U.S. 988 (1988). In *Rural West*, the court of appeals noted that white voter cohesion in rural west Tennessee increased from 59% in white-white elections to 86% in black-white elections: "In view of such evidence that a white voting bloc coalesces to frustrate African–American candidacies, the district court properly considered the race of candidates in its § 2 analysis, and accorded greater weight to the results of black-white elections." 209 F.3d at 840–41.

8. The first section 2 case involving the post–2000 round of redistricting, *Page v. Bartels*, 144 F. Supp. 2d 346 (D.N.J. 2001) (three-judge court) (per curiam), offers an interesting glimpse into the interaction of race and politics. New Jersey's Apportionment Commission, composed of five Democrats, five Republicans, and one court-appointed neutral, adopted a plan for the state General Assembly that tracked quite closely the Democrats' proposal. (The plan was adopted by a vote of 6–1, at a meeting where only one of the five Republicans was present and that member was the sole "no" vote.)

The plan substantially reconfigured four districts in northern New Jersey: Districts 27, 28, 29, and 34. Under the 1991 plan, the racial compositions of the district were as follows (WVAP is white voting age population; BVAP is black voting age population; HVAP is Hispanic voting age population; and MVAP is minority voting age population)

District	WVAP	BAVAP	HVAP	MVAP
27	31.4%	52.8%	9.4%	68.6%
28	20.4%	57.4%	16.8%	79.6%
29	20.9%	48.2%	26.2%	79.1%
34	76.8%	3.9%	11.3%	23.2%

Under the 2001 plan, the districts' demographic compositions were:

District	WVAP	BAVAP	HVAP	MVAP
27	58.0%	27.5%	6.6%	42.0%
28	30.3%	48.3%	14.0%	69.7%
29	22.5%	39.2%	33.2%	77.5%
34	48.2%	35.3%	9.8%	51.8%

The plaintiffs in *Page*—several individual African–American registered voters and residents of Essex County, several individual Hispanic registered voters and residents of Essex Hudson Counties, and the Republican members of the New Jersey Senate and General Assembly—filed suit under section 2. They claimed that the reduction of the African–American voting age population in District 27 from 53% to 27% would deny African Americans in that district the ability to elect their preferred representatives and that new District 34, with a 35% African–American voting age population, would not afford sufficient opportunities for minorities to elect their preferred candidates in that district. (Each district elects two members of the General Assembly.) The plaintiffs also alleged that the interests of Hispanic and African Americans were so different they could not be considered members of the same voting bloc.

The defendants—various state officials and the six members of the Apportionment Committee who had voted in favor of the challenged plan—argued that voting within the assembly districts was not racially polarized and that minority representation would actually increase:

> In essence, the defendants seem to suggest that, although the "old" Districts 27, 28, and 29 have elected African–American representatives, some of these votes are being "wasted" under the 1991 plan, because those representatives would have been elected in any event with a much diminished minority population. Hence, if the "wasted" excess was diverted to the new districts (such as the new District 34), even more avenues for the election of minority representatives would be opened up.

The three-judge court agreed with the defendants and denied the plaintiffs' motion to enjoin use of the new districts. It credited testimony by Democratic state legislators that coalition building within the districts would lead to significant minority representation and testimony by defendants' expert witness that voting patterns within the districts, including white cross-over voting and black and Hispanic voters' support for other-minority candidates, would enable minority voters to elect their preferred candidates.

The district court found both that coalition-building made MVAP the relevant demographic figure and that white bloc voting would not prevent minority electoral success.

> Though we recognize and respect that the African–American and Hispanic communities have several differing sociological and political interests, the evidence of minority candidate coalitions and testimony about cross-over support by both Hispanic and African–American legislators strongly suggests, and we so find, that the African–American and Hispanic communities often vote as a bloc—a fact which may be considered in assessing the ability of either community to elect the candidate of its choice.

* * *

> We hold that plaintiffs have not satisfied their burden under the third *Gingles* element, in other words, they have not proved that the Bartels plan will impair minorities' ability to elect their preferred candidate. Drawing all the threads of the evidence together, we are satisfied that the Bartels plan is designed not to prevent or interfere with the election of minority representatives but rather will enhance and expand the opportunity for African Americans and Hispanics to participate in a meaningful way in the political process. We have found that even the reduction of the African–American voting age population in District 27 from 53% under the 1991 plan to 27% will not impair or prevent minorities from electing their preferred candidates from that district to the New Jersey Senate or General Assembly. Moreover, we have also found, based on the voluminous record produced, that minorities will be elected and constitute a significant voting force in the new District 34. Hence, rather than diluting the franchise participation of minorities, as plaintiffs claim, the Bartels plan will ensure that the minority voting age population remains an effective political force.

For all its trappings as a section 2 case, is *Page v. Bartels* really best understood as a case pitting Republicans against Democrats? Note that the plaintiffs included the Republican members of the state legislature and that the defendants were represented by a law firm that generally represents the Democratic Party in redistricting litigation.

9. The relationship between race and politics is also illustrated by *Osburn v. Cox*, 369 F.3d 1283 (11th Cir. 2004), which concerned the contested 2002 Democratic primary in Georgia's Fourth Congressional District. The two candidates, challenger Denise Majette and incumbent Cynthia McKinney, were both African–American women. Majette defeated incumbent McKinney by over 15,000 votes.

Five registered voters sued, raising various challenges to Georgia's primary election system, which does not require voters to register by party affiliation. Once registered to vote, a voter may choose in which political party's primary to vote on the day of the election by requesting the appropriate ballot. In other words, a Republican voter can lawfully vote in a Democratic primary and vice versa.

The central factual assertion in the plaintiffs' complaint was that Republican party members conceived a plan to run a candidate (Majette) in the Democratic Primary, funded that candidate, and then encouraged Republican voters to cross over and vote for her. The plaintiffs alleged, among other things, that the crossover voting of the Republicans diluted the voting strength of African–American voters in the Fourth Congressional District in violation of section 2. The court of appeals rejected that claim, holding that the fact that Republican voters crossed over did not show that black voters had been excluded from meaningful access to the political process due to the interaction of racial bias in the community with the challenged voting system.

The relationship between the structure of primary elections and minority voters' political power has recently become a subject of extensive scholarly attention. *See, e.g.*, Bernard Grofman, Lisa Handley, & David Lublin, *Drawing Effective Minority Districts*, 79 N.C. L. Rev. 1384 (2001); Ellen Katz, *Resurrecting the White Primary*, 153 U. Pa. L. Rev. 325 (2004); Richard Pildes, *Is Voting–Rights Law Now At War With Itself? Social Science and Voting Rights in the 2000s*, 80 N.C. L. Rev. 1523 (2002).

Professor Katz, in particular, notes how the tension between the right of voters to participate in the only meaningful election within a district— the right at the heart of the White Primary Cases (discussed in Chapter 4)—and the right of parties under *California Democratic Party v. Jones* (also discussed in Chapter 4) plays out in the context of minority voting rights:

> After *Jones*, political parties may exclude nonmembers from party primaries, even when the primary functions as the sole locus of meaningful electoral decisionmaking. So too, *Jones* offers a political party, and the Democratic Party in particular, the power to manipulate the racial composition of its primary electorate through use of the majority-minority primary.
>
> A century ago, the Democratic Party used similar authority to exclude black voters from its primary in order to keep them from influencing debate and forming bi-racial coalitions. Today, the party views black voting strength as an asset that it seeks to exploit to maximum partisan gain. Without doubt, the spirit propelling this endeavor differs dramatically from that which implemented the white primary. Remarkably, however, the legal regimes that authorize both efforts are strikingly similar, leaving one political party in charge of defining the racial make-up of a determinative party primary.

10. In light of the various limiting doctrines federal courts have developed in section 2 cases, consider the California Voting Rights Act of 2001. Cal. Elec. Code § 14025 et seq. The Act protects the same groups protected by the federal act, namely racial groups and specified language minorities. Section 14027 provides that "[a]n at-large method of election may not be imposed or applied in a manner that impairs the ability of a protected class to elect candidates of its choice or its ability to influence the outcome of an election, as a result of the dilution or the abridgment of the rights of voters who are members of a protected class." Section 14028 marks a substantial departure from the federal section 2 standard:

(a) A violation of Section 14027 is established if it is shown that racially polarized voting occurs in elections for members of the governing body of the political subdivision or in elections incorporating other electoral choices by the voters of the political subdivision. Elections conducted prior to the filing of an action pursuant to Section 14027 and this section are more probative to establish the existence of racially polarized voting than elections conducted after the filing of the action.

(b) The occurrence of racially polarized voting shall be determined from examining results of elections in which at least one candidate is a member of a protected class or elections involving ballot measures, or other electoral choices that affect the rights and privileges of members of a protected class. One circumstance that may be considered in determining a violation of Section 14027 and this section is the extent to which candidates who are members of a protected class and who are preferred by voters of the protected class, as determined by an analysis of voting behavior, have been elected to the governing body of a political subdivision that is the subject of an action based on Section 14027 and this section. In multiseat at-large election districts, where the number of candidates who are members of a protected class is fewer than the number of seats available, the relative groupwide support received by candidates from members of a protected class shall be the basis for the racial polarization analysis.

(c) The fact that members of a protected class are not geographically compact or concentrated may not preclude a finding of racially polarized voting, or a violation of Section 14027 and this section, but may be a factor in determining an appropriate remedy.

(d) Proof of an intent on the part of the voters or elected officials to discriminate against a protected class is not required.

(e) Other factors such as the history of discrimination, the use of electoral devices or other voting practices or procedures that may enhance the dilutive effects of at-large elections, denial of access to those processes determining which groups of candidates will receive financial or other support in a given election, the extent to which members of a protected class bear the effects of past discrimination in areas such as education, employment, and health, which hinder their ability to participate effectively in the political process, and the use of overt or subtle racial appeals in political campaigns are probative, but not necessary factors to establish a violation of Section 14027 and this section.

The California Act was upheld against federal and state constitutional challenges in Sanchez v. City of Modesto, 145 Cal.App.4th 660 (2006), *review den.*, 2007 Cal. LEXIS 2772 (Mar. 21, 2007).

In which of the cases you have read would application of the CVRA standard have resulted in a different outcome? A different remedy?

B. Reemergence of a "Totality of the Circumstances" Approach

After *Gingles*, there was some disagreement in the lower courts about the extent to which the three *Gingles* factors supplanted the Senate factors altogether, as opposed to simply providing a threshold inquiry. *See, e.g., Solomon v. Liberty County*, 899 F.2d 1012 (11th Cir. 1990) (en banc), *cert. denied*, 498 U.S. 1023 (1991), where the Eleventh Circuit was evenly split on the issue. As a practical matter, however, much section 2 litigation became routine. Plaintiffs would present some illustrative proposed districts to satisfy the first prong of the *Gingles* test; the testimony of an expert witness who had examined election returns to satisfy the two other prongs; census data, judicial opinions, and statutes to show the presence of many of the relatively cut-and-dried Senate Report factors such as a prior history of discrimination, socioeconomic differences, the presence of electoral features that enhanced the dilutive effect of at-large elections; and some lay testimony to round out the picture. Much of the litigation involved municipal and county governments which were both financially and functionally ill-equipped to defend the lawsuits: they lacked access to the expertise developed by the small but specialized plaintiffs'-side voting rights bar. For a description of that bar, see Gregory A. Caldeira, *Litigation, Lobbying, and the Voting Rights Law*, in Controversies in Minority Voting 230 (Bernard Grofman & Chandler Davidson eds. 1992). For a sweeping empirical account of the effectiveness of revised Section 2 as a litigation tool, see Ellen Katz et al., Documenting Discrimination in Voting: Judicial Findings Under Section 2 of the Voting Rights Act Since 1982, 39 U. Mich. J. L. Reform 643 (2006).

The section 2 lawsuits that followed the 1990 census differed in some important respects. With respect to black communities, much of the "easy" litigation had been accomplished in the half-decade between *Gingles* and the enactment of the new plans. There were far fewer lawsuits involving jurisdictions with large, geographically compact black communities, at-large elections, and virtually no minority elected officials. Such claims still continued to be brought in areas with large concentrations of Latino or Native American voters. In part, this was a function of substantial population growth among Latinos: in a number of communities, the Latino population was large enough after the 1990 census—a similar phenomenon appeared after the 2000 census—to create a district that was majority Latino where that had been impossible before. (Nearly all of the Department of Justice's current section 2 litigation involves the voting rights of Latinos.) *See* U.S. Dept. of Justice, Civil Rights Division, Voting Section Homepage, Cases Raising Claims Under Section 2 of the Voting Rights Act. <*available at* http://www.usdoj.gov/crt/voting/litigation/recent_sec2.htm.> In part, this is due to the fact that, until recently, few lawyers had devoted their attention to the voting rights of Native Americans. *See* Laughlin McDonald, *The Voting Rights Act in Indian Country: South Dakota, A Case Study*, 29 Am. Indian L. Rev. 43 (2004/2005).

In place of the challenges to at-large elections litigated between *Gingles* and the release of the census figures in 1991, plaintiffs brought challenges to single-member districting plans and lawsuits in jurisdictions where minorities had achieved some representation. Moreover, many of the lawsuits involved statewide apportionment schemes, and the defendants were better financed and had access to lawyers with greater expertise.

Johnson v. De Grandy

512 U.S. 997 (1994).

■ Justice Souter delivered the opinion of the Court.

* * *

I

[In April 1992, the Florida legislature adopted Senate Joint Resolution 2–G (SJR 2–G). SJR 2–G divided Florida into 40 single-member Senate, and 120 single-member House, districts based on population data from the 1990 census.] The De Grandy and NAACP plaintiffs [who had previously challenged the post–1980 plan on one-person, one-vote grounds] responded to SJR 2–G by amending their federal complaints to charge the new reapportionment plan with violating § 2. They claimed that SJR 2–G " 'unlawfully fragments cohesive minority communities and otherwise impermissibly submerges their right to vote and to participate in the electoral process,' " and they pointed to areas around the State where black or Hispanic populations could have formed a voting majority in a politically cohesive, reasonably compact district (or in more than one), if SJR 2–G had not fragmented each group among several districts or packed it into just a few.

The Department of Justice filed a similar complaint, naming the State of Florida and several elected officials as defendants and claiming that SJR

2–G diluted the voting strength of . . . the Hispanic population in an area largely covered by Dade County (including Miami). . . .

[The District Court] held the plan's provisions for state House districts to be in violation of § 2 because "more than [SJR 2–G's] nine Hispanic districts may be drawn without having or creating a regressive effect upon black voters," and it imposed a remedial plan offered by the De Grandy plaintiffs calling for 11 majority-Hispanic House districts. As to the Senate, the court found that a fourth majority-Hispanic district could be drawn in addition to the three provided by SJR 2–G, but only at the expense of black voters in the area. The court was of two minds about the implication of this finding, once observing that it meant the legislature's plan for the Senate was a violation of § 2 but without a remedy, once saying the Plan did not violate § 2 at all. In any event, it ordered elections to be held using SJR 2–G's senatorial districts.

In a later, expanded opinion the court reviewed the totality of circumstances as required by § 2 and *Thornburg v. Gingles*. In explaining Dade County's "tripartite politics," in which "ethnic factors . . . predominate over all others . . . ," the court found political cohesion within each of the Hispanic and black populations but none between the two, and a tendency of non-Hispanic whites to vote as a bloc to bar minority groups from electing their chosen candidates except in a district where a given minority makes up a voting majority. The court further found that the nearly one million Hispanics in the Dade County area could be combined into 4 Senate and 11 House districts, each one relatively compact and with a functional majority of Hispanic voters, whereas SJR 2–G created fewer majority-Hispanic districts; and that one more Senate district with a black voting majority could have been drawn. Noting that Florida's minorities bore the social, economic, and political effects of past discrimination, the court concluded that SJR 2–G impermissibly diluted the voting strength of Hispanics in its House districts and of both Hispanics and blacks in its Senate districts. The findings of vote dilution in the senatorial districts had no practical effect, however, because the court held that remedies for the blacks and the Hispanics were mutually exclusive; it consequently deferred to the state legislature's work as the "fairest" accommodation of all the ethnic communities in South Florida.

* * *

III

On the merits of the vote dilution claims covering the House districts, the crux of the State's argument is the power of Hispanics under SJR 2–G to elect candidates of their choice in a number of districts that mirrors their share of the Dade County area's voting-age population (i.e., 9 out of 20 House districts); this power, according to the State, bars any finding that the plan dilutes Hispanic voting strength. . . .

The State's argument takes us back to ground covered last Term in two cases challenging single-member districts. *See Voinovich v. Quilter*; *Growe v. Emison*. In *Growe*, we held that a claim of vote dilution in a single-member district requires proof meeting the same three threshold conditions for a dilution challenge to a multimember district [announced in *Gingles*]. . . .

In *Voinovich* we explained how manipulation of district lines can dilute the voting strength of politically cohesive minority group members, whether by fragmenting the minority voters among several districts where a bloc-voting majority can routinely out-vote them, or by packing them into one or a small number of districts to minimize their influence in the districts next door. Section 2 prohibits either sort of line-drawing where its result, " 'interacting with social and historical conditions,' impairs the ability of a protected class to elect its candidate of choice on an equal basis with other voters." . . . .

[T]he District Court found, and the State does not challenge, the presence of both th[e] Gingles preconditions [relating to racial bloc voting]. The dispute in this litigation centers . . . [instead on] whether, even with all three *Gingles* conditions satisfied, the circumstances in totality support a finding of vote dilution when Hispanics can be expected to elect their chosen representatives in substantial proportion to their percentage of the area's population.

* * *

B

We . . . part company from the District Court in assessing the totality of circumstances. The District Court found that the three *Gingles* preconditions were satisfied, and that Hispanics had suffered historically from official discrimination, the social, economic, and political effects of which they generally continued to feel. Without more, and on the apparent assumption that what could have been done to create additional Hispanic super-majority districts should have been done, the District Court found a violation of § 2. But the assumption was erroneous, and more is required, as a review of *Gingles* will show.

1

* * *

Gingles provided some structure to the statute's "totality of circumstances" test in a case challenging multimember legislative districts. . . . But if *Gingles* so clearly identified [three preconditions] as generally necessary to prove a § 2 claim, it just as clearly declined to hold them sufficient in combination, either in the sense that a court's examination of relevant circumstances was complete once the three factors were found to exist, or in the sense that the three in combination necessarily and in all circumstances demonstrated dilution.... To be sure, some § 2 plaintiffs may have easy cases, but although lack of equal electoral opportunity may be readily imagined and unsurprising when demonstrated under circumstances that include the three essential *Gingles* factors, that conclusion must still be addressed explicitly, and without isolating any other arguably relevant facts from the act of judgment.

2

If the three *Gingles* factors may not be isolated as sufficient, standing alone, to prove dilution in every multimember district challenge, *a fortiori* they must not be when the challenge goes to a series of single-member districts, where dilution may be more difficult to grasp. Plaintiffs challenging single-member districts may claim, not total submergence, but partial submergence; not the chance for some electoral success in place of none, but the chance for more success in place of some. When the question thus comes down to the reasonableness of drawing a series of district lines in one combination of places rather than another, judgments about inequality may become closer calls. As facts beyond the ambit of the three *Gingles* factors loom correspondingly larger, factfinders cannot rest uncritically on assumptions about the force of the *Gingles* factors in pointing to dilution.

* * *

[In this case,] the District Court was not critical enough in asking whether a history of persistent discrimination reflected in the larger society and its bloc-voting behavior portended any dilutive effect from a newly proposed districting scheme, whose pertinent features were majority-minority districts in substantial proportion to the minority's share of voting-age population. The court failed to ask whether the totality of facts, including those pointing to proportionality,[11] showed that the new scheme would deny minority voters equal political opportunity.

Treating equal political opportunity as the focus of the enquiry, we do not see how these district lines, apparently providing political effectiveness in proportion to voting-age numbers, deny equal political opportunity. The record establishes that Hispanics constitute 50 percent of the voting-age population in Dade County and under SJR 2–G would make up supermajorities in 9 of the 18 House districts located primarily within the

---

11. "Proportionality" as the term is used here links the number of majority-minority voting districts to minority members' share of the relevant population. The concept is distinct from the subject of the proportional representation clause of § 2, which provides that "nothing in this section establishes a right to have members of a protected class elected in numbers equal to their proportion in the population." 42 U.S.C. § 1973b. This proviso speaks to the success of minority candidates, as distinct from the political or electoral power of minority voters. And the proviso also confirms what is otherwise clear from the text of the statute, namely that the ultimate right of § 2 is equality of opportunity, not a guarantee of electoral success for minority-preferred candidates of whatever race.

county. Likewise, if one considers the 20 House districts located at least in part within Dade County, the record indicates that Hispanics would be an effective voting majority in 45 percent of them (i.e., nine), and would constitute 47 percent of the voting-age population in the area. In other words, under SJR 2–G Hispanics in the Dade County area would enjoy substantial proportionality. On this evidence, we think the State's scheme would thwart the historical tendency to exclude Hispanics, not encourage or perpetuate it. Thus in spite of that history and its legacy, including the racial cleavages that characterize Dade County politics today, we see no grounds for holding in this case that SJR 2–G's district lines diluted the votes cast by Hispanic voters.

* * *

3

It may be that the significance of the facts under § 2 was obscured by the rule of thumb apparently adopted by the District Court, that anything short of the maximum number of majority-minority districts consistent with the *Gingles* conditions would violate § 2.... But reading the first Gingles condition [this way] ... causes its own dangers, and they are not to be courted.

Assume a hypothetical jurisdiction of 1,000 voters divided into 10 districts of 100 each, where members of a minority group make up 40 percent of the voting population and voting is totally polarized along racial lines. With the right geographic dispersion to satisfy the compactness requirement, and with careful manipulation of district lines, the minority voters might be placed in control of as many as 7 of the 10 districts. Each such district could be drawn with at least 51 members of the minority group, and whether the remaining minority voters were added to the groupings of 51 for safety or scattered in the other three districts, minority voters would be able to elect candidates of their choice in all seven districts.[12] The point of the hypothetical is not, of course, that any given district is likely to be open to such extreme manipulation, or that bare majorities are likely to vote in full force and strictly along racial lines, but that reading § 2 to define dilution as any failure to maximize tends to obscure the very object of the statute and to run counter to its textually stated purpose. One may suspect vote dilution from political famine, but one is not entitled to suspect (much less infer) dilution from mere failure to guarantee a political feast. However prejudiced a society might be, it would be absurd to suggest that the failure of a districting scheme to provide a minority group with effective political power 75 percent above its numerical

---

12. Minority voters might instead be denied control over a single seat, of course. Each district would need to include merely 51 members of the majority group; minority vot- ers fragmented among the 10 districts could be denied power to affect the result in any district.

strength indicates a denial of equal participation in the political process. Failure to maximize cannot be the measure of § 2.

4

* * *

[On the other hand, an] inflexible rule [that proportionality is always a defense to a section 2 claim] would run counter to the textual command of § 2, that the presence or absence of a violation be assessed "based on the totality of circumstances." 42 U.S.C. § 1973(b).

* * *

Even if the State's safe harbor were open only in cases of alleged dilution by the manipulation of district lines, however, it would rest on an unexplored premise of highly suspect validity: that in any given voting jurisdiction (or portion of that jurisdiction under consideration), the rights of some minority voters under § 2 may be traded off against the rights of other members of the same minority class. Under the State's view, the most blatant racial gerrymandering in half of a county's single member districts would be irrelevant under § 2 if offset by political gerrymandering in the other half, so long as proportionality was the bottom line....

Finally, we reject the safe harbor rule because of a tendency the State would itself certainly condemn, a tendency to promote and perpetuate efforts to devise majority-minority districts even in circumstances where they may not be necessary to achieve equal political and electoral opportunity. Because in its simplest form the State's rule would shield from § 2 challenge a districting scheme in which the number of majority-minority districts reflected the minority's share of the relevant population, the conclusiveness of the rule might be an irresistible inducement to create such districts. It bears recalling, however, that for all the virtues of majority-minority districts as remedial devices, they rely on a quintessentially race-conscious calculus aptly described as the "politics of second best." If the lesson of *Gingles* is that society's racial and ethnic cleavages sometimes necessitate majority-minority districts to ensure equal political and electoral opportunity, that should not obscure the fact that there are communities in which minority citizens are able to form coalitions with voters from other racial and ethnic groups, having no need to be a majority within a single district in order to elect candidates of their choice. Those candidates may not represent perfection to every minority voter, but minority voters are not immune from the obligation to pull, haul, and trade to find common political ground, the virtue of which is not to be slighted in applying a statute meant to hasten the waning of racism in American politics.

* * *

IV

* * *

SJR 2–G creates 40 single-member Senate districts, five of them wholly within Dade County. Of these five, three have Hispanic super-majorities of at least 64 percent, and one has a clear majority of black voters. Two more Senate districts crossing county lines include substantial numbers of Dade County voters, and in one of these, black voters, although not close to a majority, are able to elect representatives of their choice with the aid of cross-over votes.

Within this seven-district Dade County area, both minority groups enjoy rough proportionality. The voting-age population in the seven-district area is 44.8 percent Hispanic and 15.8 percent black. Hispanics predominate in 42.9 percent of the districts (three out of seven), as do blacks in 14.3 percent of them (one out of seven). While these numbers indicate something just short of perfect proportionality (42.9 percent against 44.8; 14.3 percent against 15.8), the opposite is true of the five districts located wholly within Dade County.[19]

The District Court concentrated not on these facts but on whether additional districts could be drawn in which either Hispanics or blacks would constitute an effective majority. The court found that indeed a fourth senatorial district with an Hispanic super-majority could be drawn, or that an additional district could be created with a black majority, in each case employing reasonably compact districts. Having previously established that each minority group was politically cohesive, that each labored under a legacy of official discrimination, and that whites voted as a bloc, the District Court believed it faced "two independent, viable Section 2 claims." Because the court did not, however, think it was possible to create both another Hispanic district and another black district on the same map, it concluded that no remedy for either violation was practical and, deferring to the State's plan as a compromise policy, imposed SJR 2–G's senatorial districts.

We affirm the District Court's decision to leave the State's plan for Florida State Senate districts undisturbed. As in the case of the House districts, the totality of circumstances appears not to support a finding of vote dilution here, where both minority groups constitute effective voting majorities in a number of state Senate districts substantially proportional to their share in the population, and where plaintiffs have not produced evidence otherwise indicating that under SJR 2–G voters in either minority

---

19. In the five districts wholly within Dade County, where Hispanics are concentrated, the voting-age population is 53.9 percent Hispanic and 13.5 percent black. Sixty percent of the districts are Hispanic-majority (three out of five), and 20 percent are black-majority (one out of five), so that each minority group protected by § 2 enjoys an effective voting majority in marginally more districts than proportionality would indicate (60 percent over 53.9; 20 percent over 13.5).

group have "less opportunity than other members of the electorate to participate in the political process and to elect representatives of their choice."

* * *

NOTES AND QUESTIONS

1. The *Gingles* test responded well to "classical" claims of racial vote dilution—those brought by black voters challenging the use of at-large elections in predominantly white jurisdictions. The context in which *De Grandy* arose differed in at least two salient respects. First, it raised a challenge to an existing single-member district plan; second, it involved a three-way struggle for electoral power among Anglo whites, Cuban Americans, and African Americans. Consider the argument that both of these differences exposed difficulties with the *Gingles* test:

> *Gingles* proved tremendously useful in challenges to at-large electoral systems because of the confined nature of the inquiry.... The choice of districting arrangement, should the plaintiffs prevail, was left to a highly obscure remedial process in which district courts were directed to yield as much as possible to the policy choices of the affected jurisdiction.... The liability determination was therefore a straightforward binary inquiry: the at-large status quo or some potential alternative. The ultimate resolution of a successful plaintiffs' claim—the actual shape of the new voting scheme in a successful VRA action—was left to vaguely worded remedial standards under the highly discretionary authority of a district court judge.

* * *

Since the majority of voting rights challenges were initially brought in circumstances where blacks had not been elected to office since the demise of Reconstruction, the vote dilution inquiry could presume under-representation without having to define a baseline of proportionality. Under such circumstances, "dilution" was a functional proxy for exclusion, plain and simple.

Constructing a model of minority vote dilution in the redistricting context is far more problematic. To begin with, the choice of electoral alternatives, particularly after the computer revolution of the 1980s made the process accessible to all interested parties, was anything but binary.... In the redistricting context ... the issue inherited from *Gingles*—whether a superior arrangement could have been selected— does not answer the question whether it should have been selected. This, in turn, implicates the ultimate question of what should serve as the baseline in determining whether minority voting strength has been "diluted" through the choice of one or another redistricting configuration.

* * *

It is not only the *Gingles* presumption that fails with regard to Cuban–Americans, but the entire *Carolene Products* edifice. The *Carolene Products* premise that discreteness and insularity in the political process should be disabling has been significantly challenged by the emergence of public choice theory. Under public choice theory, the combination of freerider problems in holding together broad coalitions, together with transactions costs in drawing together broad, diffuse majorities, should provide cohesive minorities with superordinate power in the political arena.

* * *

What happens, however, when the presumptions underlying *Gingles* and *Carolene Products* are wrong? What happens if the insularity of Cuban–Americans is simply a reflection of normal patterns of healthy immigration, ones that bespeak no long-term disabilities? Shouldn't the cohesiveness of the community provide preferential access into the halls of political power, as occurred in prior periods with, for example, the Irish of Boston or the Eastern European immigrants of Chicago? If that is the case, then we should see evidence of political muscle in the Cuban–American community as the rate of citizenship and eligibility for voting increases.

In fact, every indication is that this is precisely the pattern of Cuban–American political participation. Not only are there no significant indicators of Cuban–Americans being systematically shut out of the political or economic processes of Dade County, but precisely the opposite seems to be the case. . . .

Without a palpable claim of second-class status, without self-perception of disabling discrete and insular status, and with ready recourse to redress in the political process, the Cuban–Americans of Miami defy the grounds for judicial intervention into the political process that are critical for both *Gingles* and *Carolene Products*. As increasing numbers of Central Americans, Asians, and other recent immigrants establish themselves in this country and begin to test the political waters, the arguments over what justifies intervention into the ordinary workings of the political process will resurface.

Samuel Issacharoff, *Groups and the Right to Vote*, 44 Emory L.J. 869 (1995). For a discussion of the ways in which the concept of dilution evolved to respond to these more complex situations, see Heather K. Gerken, *Understanding the Right to an Undiluted Vote*, 114 Harv. L. Rev. 1663, 1675–76 (2001).

2.   One of the most notable aspects of *De Grandy* is that, although the majority relies on two of the voting rights cases decided the previous Term, *Voinovich v. Quilter* and *Growe v. Emison*, it entirely ignores the third, and most well-known, *Shaw v. Reno*. Lani Guinier initially suggested that "[i]f *Shaw v. Reno* marks the voting rights precipice, the Court blinked in its

1993 Term" by holding in *De Grandy* "that society's racial and ethnic cleavages sometimes necessitate majority-minority districts to ensure equal political and electoral opportunity". Lani Guinier, *[E]racing Democracy: The Voting Rights Cases*, 108 Harv. L. Rev. 109 (1994). In light of the continued development of the *Shaw* doctrine, discussed in Chapter 9, was this interpretation of *De Grandy* wishful thinking? Has compactness become an even more indispensable element of any claim for majority non-white districts?

3. In *Voinovich*, the Supreme Court unanimously rejected the claim of a group of plaintiffs characterized by the district court as "Democratic electors and state legislators, some of whom are members of a protected class under the Voting Rights Act," who claimed that Ohio's bitterly partisan state legislative apportionment violated section 2 because it unlawfully "packed" black voters into a few overwhelmingly black districts, wasting minority votes in the packed districts and diluting minority voting strength in surrounding areas where black voting strength had concomitantly been diminished.

Justice O'Connor's opinion for the Court observed that the choice between spreading a minority community among several districts or concentrating them in a few is normally left to the political process (a process that her opinion in *Shaw v. Reno* acknowledged was always *aware* of the racial composition of alternative districts). "Section 2 contains no *per se* prohibitions against particular types of districts.... Only if the apportionment scheme has the *effect* of denying a protected class the equal opportunity to elect its candidate of choice does it violate § 2; where such an effect has not been demonstrated § 2 simply does not speak to the matter." Because the district court had found that Ohio politics was not characterized by racial bloc voting, the choice between dispersal and concentration did not implicate section 2.

Professor Karlan has suggested that "the relatively favorable treatment accorded racial vote dilution claims creates an incentive for partisan groups either to recast their claims to fall under the Voting Rights Act or to use plaintiffs protected by the Act as stalking horses to get into federal court." Pamela S. Karlan, *All Over the Map: The Supreme Court's Voting Rights Trilogy*, 1993 Sup. Ct. Rev. 245; *see also* Pamela S. Karlan, *The Rights To Vote: Some Pessimism About Formalism*, 71 Tex. L. Rev. 1705 (1993). To what extent do recent section 2 cases reflect this dynamic? Is this what Professor Issacharoff and Justice Souter mean when they contrast normal interest-group politics with the special case posed by classical voting rights claims?

4. In *United States v. Charleston County*, 365 F.3d 341 (4th Cir. 2004), the Fourth Circuit addressed the relationship between the three *Gingles* factors and the totality of the circumstances approach. The case involved a challenge to at-large elections to the County Council. The parties agreed that the plaintiffs had established the first two *Gingles* preconditions:

minority voters were sufficiently numerous and geographically compact to constitute a majority in a single-member district and were politically cohesive. But they disagreed as to how the third *Gingles* factor should be analyzed. The county's argument was that voting within the county was polarized as a result of partisanship rather than race.

The court of appeals noted that an inquiry into causation with respect to white bloc voting was relevant. But it explained that

> the approach most faithful to the Supreme Court's case law "is one that treats causation as irrelevant in the inquiry into the three *Gingles* preconditions, but relevant in the totality of circumstances inquiry." ... The inquiry into the *Gingles* preconditions is a preliminary one, designed to determine whether an at-large system potentially violates § 2. ...
>
> But simply clearing the *Gingles* hurdles, while necessary to prove a possible violation of § 2, is not sufficient to establish an actual violation ... *DeGrandy*. It is this inclusive examination of the totality of the circumstances that is tailor-made for considering why voting patterns differ along racial lines. ...

With respect to the county's argument that partisanship, not race, explained the voting patterns, the court noted that there was substantial evidence of partisanship, but nonetheless, given the standard of review, affirmed the district court's finding for the plaintiffs. The court noted that "Charleston County voters are racially divided not only over the desirability of particular candidates, but over the desirability of the at-large system itself. In 1989 the County held a referendum on switching from the at-large system for County Council elections to a system of single-member districts: at least 98 percent of minority voters endorsed the change, while at least 75 percent of white voters wanted to retain at-large elections." Moreover, the court found no systematic proof that partisanship better explained voting patterns. In part, this was a product of South Carolina's election system, since the county does not require that voters register by party: "In the end, the district court was faced with inconclusive evidence of partisanship as the determinant of voting, but 'decisive[]' evidence of 'severe voting polarization, minimal minority electoral success, and an uncommonly large voting district.'"

5. To what extent ought the totality of the circumstances inquiry look into post-electoral influence as well as the ability to form winning coalitions? This issue is treated more fully in Chapter 9 in the discussion surrounding *Georgia v. Ashcroft* and in Chapter 6 in the discussion surrounding *Presley v. Etowah County Commission*.

As a purely doctrinal matter, both cases involved section 5 of the Voting Rights Act. Nonetheless, the Court's discussion in *Georgia v. Ashcroft* of what constitutes "effective exercise of the electoral franchise" may shed light on how claims of dilution are to be assessed, particularly since

Justice O'Connor's opinion for the Court rested explicitly on her concurrence in the judgment in *Thornburg v. Gingles*, 478 U.S. 30 (1986), and on the Court's opinion in *DeGrandy*. Justice O'Connor stated that "[i]n assessing the totality of the circumstances, a court should not focus solely on the comparative ability of a minority group to elect a candidate of its choice." Rather, it should be cognizant of the possible tradeoff between the creation of "a smaller number of safe majority-minority districts [that] may virtually guarantee the election of a minority group's preferred candidate in those districts," thereby providing "descriptive representation," and the creation of a larger number of districts in which minority voters will be part of a winning coalition, thereby achieving greater "substantive representation." Moreover, quoting her *Gingles* concurrence, Justice O'Connor continued that "[t]he power to influence the political process is not limited to winning elections," and thus a reviewing court should also a court examine whether the plan before it creates " 'influence districts'—where minority voters may not be able to elect a candidate of choice but can play a substantial, if not decisive, role in the electoral process," and thereby enjoy influence over the official ultimately elected. The Court declared that section 5 "gives States the flexibility to choose one theory of effective representation over the other."

What implications does this view of effective exercise of the franchise have for section 2 cases? Consider two different scenarios in which such issues might play out. First, jurisdictions faced with a conventional *Gingles*-type vote dilution lawsuit in which the plaintiffs are seeking creation of new majority-nonwhite districts might argue that the existing plan does not dilute the plaintiffs' voting strength once coalition or influence districts are taken into account. Second, plaintiffs might argue that section 2 requires the creation of additional coalition or influence districts. Should that argument be foreclosed by their failure to satisfy the first prong of the *Gingles* test, or does *Georgia v. Ashcroft* undermine the view that *Gingles* creates a threshold test?

Consider also the following observation:

[T]he election of representatives represents only an intermediate point along the path to the determination of policies that are voted on within the legislature. And with regard to that determination, the critical question for an individual cannot simply be whether *she* can elect *her* preferred candidate. Rather, it must focus on whether the system for selecting a governmental *body* gives her an effective opportunity to participate in policymaking.

* * *

That larger question embodies a . . . conception of voting rights [as governance]. . . . Because the voter's horizon extends beyond the moment of representative-selection to various opportunities for collective decisionmaking by assembled legislators, she necessarily will be concerned not merely with who serves as the representative(s) of her district, but, just as centrally, with the overall composition of the governing body. She will, in short, be interested in the degree of both her direct and her virtual representation.

Pamela S. Karlan, *The Rights to Vote: Some Pessimism About Formalism,* 71 Tex. L. Rev. 1705 (1993); *see also* Richard H. Pildes, *The Politics of Race,* 108 Harv. L. Rev. 1359, 1381 (1995). Some scholars have gone even further, to claim that "preferences over assemblies, not candidates, are fundamental." Jean–Pierre Benoit & Lewis A. Kornhauser, *Social Choice in a Representative Democracy,* 88 Am. Pol. Sci. Rev. 185 (1994).

6. Should potential remedial concerns inform the totality-of-the-circumstances inquiry? In this light, consider *LULAC v. Clements,* 999 F.2d 831 (5th Cir.) (en banc), *cert. denied,* 510 U.S. 1071 (1994), discussed earlier in this Chapter with respect to the third *Gingles* factor. The case involved a challenge to Texas's method of electing state-court trial judges. Judges were elected at large, in county-wide elections that used a numbered-post system: that is, although each judge was elected by all the voters within a judicial district, each judge ran for a designated position. The en banc opinion concluded that Texas's interest in "linkage"—that is, in having the electoral base of a district judge correspond to the area over which he or she exercises primary jurisdiction—outweighed the evidence that the at-large structure diluted black voting strength in Harris County (Houston).

> The electoral bases of district judges are linked to the area over which they exercise primary jurisdiction. This linkage has been in place throughout the 143 year history of judicial elections in Texas. By making coterminous the electoral and jurisdictional bases of trial courts, Texas advances the effectiveness of its courts by balancing the virtues of accountability with the need for independence. The state attempts to maintain the fact and appearance of judicial fairness that are central to the judicial task, in part, by insuring that judges remain accountable to the range of people within their jurisdiction. A broad base diminishes the semblance of bias and favoritism towards the parochial interests of a narrow constituency. Appearances are critical because "the very perception of impropriety and unfairness undermines the moral authority of the courts." The fear of mixing ward politics and state trial courts of general jurisdiction is widely held. It is not surprising then that states that elect trial judges overwhelmingly share this structure and electoral scheme.

* * *

The totality of circumstances inquiry that occurs after a showing of the *Gingles* prerequisites is not limited to factors listed in the legislative history of the Voting Rights Act. The weight, as well as tenuousness, of the state's interest is a legitimate factor in analyzing the totality of circumstances. As we have explained, the Voting Rights Act largely codifies Fourteenth Amendment jurisprudence embodied in *White v. Regester.* The substantiality of the state's interest has long been the centerpiece of the inquiry into the interpretation of the Civil War Amendments and their interplay with the civil rights statutes.

* * *

[T]he people of Texas have at least a substantial interest in defining the structure and qualifications of their judiciary. Indeed, Texas' Attorney General has submitted to this court that linkage is a "fundamental right" that "serves [a] compelling interest" of the State of Texas. Linking electoral and jurisdictional bases is a key component of the effort to define the office of district judge. That Texas' interest in the linkage of electoral and jurisdictional bases is substantial cannot then be gainsaid.

The decision to make jurisdiction and electoral bases coterminous is more than a decision about how to elect state judges. It is a decision of what constitutes a state court judge. Such a decision is as much a decision about the structure of the judicial office as the office's explicit qualifications such as bar membership or the age of judges. The collective voice of generations by their unswerving adherence to the principle of linkage through times of extraordinary growth and change speaks to us with power. Tradition, of course, does not make right of wrong, but we must be cautious when asked to embrace a new revelation that right has so long been wrong. There is no evidence that linkage was created and consistently maintained to stifle minority votes. Tradition speaks to us about its defining role—imparting its deep running sense that this is what judging is about.

On the other hand, plaintiffs' interests are not well-served by destroying linkage. The inescapable truth is that the result sought by plaintiffs here would diminish minority influence. Minority voters would be marginalized, having virtually no impact on most district court elections. Given that district judges act alone in exercising their power, that use of the Voting Rights Act is perverse. After subdistricting, a handful of judges would be elected from subdistricts with a majority of minority voters. Creating "safe" districts would leave all but a few subdistricts stripped of nearly all minority members. The great majority of judges would be elected entirely by white voters. Minority litigants would not necessarily have their cases assigned to one of the few judges elected by minority voters. Rather, the overwhelming probability would be that the minority litigant would appear "before a judge who has little direct political interest in being responsive to minority concerns." Under the totality of circumstances, we must recognize that breaking the link between the electoral base and the jurisdiction of this single-member office would perversely lessen minority influence on the conduct of most litigation.

* * *

Plaintiffs urge that the linkage interest can be accommodated even if the existing scheme were found to be illegal.... [Linkage] might be accommodated by remedies other than subdistricting. In particular, plaintiffs point to the use of limited voting or cumulative voting. The Supreme Court, of course, "strongly prefers single-member districts for federal court-ordered reapportionment." In any event, we do not agree that this argument undermines the substantiality of the state's interest.

The allegedly illegal facet of the existing electoral scheme is that it employs at-large elections. Both plaintiffs' amended complaint and plaintiff-intervenors' complaint-in-intervention assert that the existing "at large scheme" violates § 2, and pray for a court order "that district judges in the targeted counties be elected in a system which contains single member districts." By employing at-large elections, the people of Texas have linked the electoral and jurisdictional base of the district judge.

Limited and cumulative voting are election mechanisms that preserve at-large elections. Thus, they are not "remedies" for the particular structural problem that the plaintiffs have chosen to attack. At trial, plaintiffs attempted to prove the three *Gingles* prerequisites. This test establishes "that the minority has the potential to elect a representative of its own choice in some single-member district" and "that the challenged districting thwarts a distinctive minority by submerging it in a larger white voting population." Plaintiffs then tried to supplement that evidence with proof of *Zimmer* factors, such as past discrimination and anti-single shot voting rules. The question presented by this lawsuit is whether Texas' at-large election of district judges violates § 2. To answer that question, we must determine the weight of the state's linkage interest. We will not discount that interest based upon purported remedies that preserve the challenged at-large scheme. Plaintiffs cannot attack at-large voting as a violation of § 2, and then ignore the special characteristics of the judicial office by insisting that they will embrace a remedy that preserves that scheme. To do so would completely shunt consideration of the interest to the remedy stage.

* * *

In finding that Texas' interest is substantial, we recognize that it will not always defeat § 2 liability. Substantiality is not quantifiable, and we translate its force in the practical world of trials to the burden required to overcome it. As we see it, plaintiffs cannot overcome a substantial state interest by proving insubstantial dilution. We hold that proof of dilution, considering the totality of the circumstances, must be substantial in order to overcome the state's interest in linkage established here. As a matter of law, Texas' interest cannot be overridden by evidence that sums to a marginal case. It will take more to create a fact issue for trial....

We do not now attempt to define in detail what sort of proof of dilution would be substantial enough to override the state's linkage interest. We do not change the nature or usual means of proof. The *Gingles* prerequisites and *Zimmer* factors remain. Two facts are especially relevant to assessing the substantiality of the plaintiffs' proof of dilution. One is the willingness of the racial or ethnic majority—in this case, white voters—to give their votes to minority candidates. The other critical fact is the ability of minority voters to elect candidates of their choice even when opposed by most voters from the majority. Among the *Zimmer* factors, proof of racial appeals in elections, non-responsiveness of elected officials to minority voters, and persistent lack of electoral success by minority candidates are most important.

To what extent is *LULAC* internally inconsistent in its treatment of the relationship between voters and elected judges? Would *LULAC*'s analysis apply equally to a multimember court, such as a court of appeals or state supreme court?

C. BEYOND DILUTION THROUGH SUBMERGENCE

Most litigation under amended section 2 has challenged districting decisions—either the use of multi-member (and at-large) election systems or the location of district lines. There have, however, been some challenges to other electoral practices, and the courts' treatment of these have illuminated a number of important doctrinal, practical, and theoretical issues.

Holder v. Hall

512 U.S. 874 (1994).

■ JUSTICE KENNEDY announced the judgment of the Court and delivered an opinion, in which THE CHIEF JUSTICE joined, and in all but Part II–B of which JUSTICE O'CONNOR joined.

This case presents the question whether the size of a governing authority is subject to a vote dilution challenge under [section 2.]

* * *

I

The State of Georgia has 159 counties, one of which is Bleckley County, a rural county in central Georgia. Black persons make up nearly 20% of the eligible voting population in Bleckley County. Since its creation in 1912, the county has had a single-commissioner form of government for the exercise of "county governing authority." Under this system, the Bleckley County Commissioner performs all of the executive and legislative functions of the county government, including the levying of general and special taxes, the directing and controlling of all county property, and the settling of all claims. In addition to Bleckley County, about 10 other Georgia counties use the single-commissioner system; the rest have multi-member commissions.

* * *

II

A

[. . .] In a § 2 vote dilution suit, along with determining whether the *Gingles* preconditions are met and whether the totality of the circumstances supports a finding of liability, a court must find a reasonable alternative practice as a benchmark against which to measure the existing voting practice. As Justice O'Connor explained in *Gingles*: "The phrase vote dilution itself suggests a norm with respect to which the fact of dilution may be ascertained. . . . In order to decide whether an electoral system has made it harder for minority voters to elect the candidates they prefer, a court must have an idea in mind of how hard it should be for minority voters to elect their preferred candidates under an acceptable system."

In certain cases, the benchmark for comparison in a § 2 dilution suit is obvious. The effect of an anti-single-shot voting rule, for instance, can be evaluated by comparing the system with that rule to the system without that rule. But where there is no objective and workable standard for choosing a reasonable benchmark by which to evaluate a challenged voting practice, it follows that the voting practice cannot be challenged as dilutive under § 2.

As the facts of this case well illustrate, the search for a benchmark is quite problematic when a § 2 dilution challenge is brought to the size of a government body. There is no principled reason why one size should be picked over another as the benchmark for comparison. Respondents here argue that we should compare Bleckley County's sole commissioner system to a hypothetical five-member commission in order to determine whether the current system is dilutive. Respondents and the United States as amicus curiae give three reasons why the single commissioner structure should be compared to a five-member commission (instead of, say, a 3–, 10–, or 15–member body): (1) because the five-member commission is a common form of governing authority in the State; (2) because the state legislature had authorized Bleckley County to adopt a five-member commission if it so chose (it did not); and (3) because the county had moved from a single superintendent of education to a school board with five members elected from single-member districts.

These referents do not bear upon dilution. It does not matter, for instance, how popular the single-member commission system is in Georgia in determining whether it dilutes the vote of a minority racial group in Bleckley County. That the single-member commission is uncommon in the State of Georgia, or that a five-member commission is quite common, tells us nothing about its effects on a minority group's voting strength. The sole commissioner system has the same impact regardless of whether it is shared by none, or by all, of the other counties in Georgia. It makes little sense to say (as do respondents and the United States) that the sole commissioner system should be subject to a dilution challenge if it is rare— but immune if it is common.

That Bleckley County was authorized by the State to expand its commission, and that it adopted a five-member school board, are likewise irrelevant considerations in the dilution inquiry. At most, those facts indicate that Bleckley County could change the size of its commission with minimal disruption. But the county's failure to do so says nothing about the effects the sole commissioner system has on the voting power of Bleckley County's citizens. Surely a minority group's voting strength would be no more or less diluted had the State not authorized the county to alter the size of its commission, or had the county not enlarged its school board. One gets the sense that respondents and the United States have chosen a benchmark for the sake of having a benchmark. But it is one thing to say that a benchmark can be found, quite another to give a convincing reason for finding it in the first place.

B

To bolster their argument, respondents point out that our § 5 cases may be interpreted to indicate that covered jurisdictions may not change the size of their government bodies without obtaining preclearance from the Attorney General or the federal courts. . . .

Under § 5 . . . [a] proposed voting practice is measured against the existing voting practice to determine whether retrogression would result from the proposed change. The baseline for comparison is present by definition; it is the existing status. While there may be difficulty in determining whether a proposed change would cause retrogression, there is little difficulty in discerning the two voting practices to compare to determine whether retrogression would occur.

Retrogression is not the inquiry in § 2 dilution cases. Unlike in § 5 cases, therefore, a benchmark does not exist by definition in § 2 dilution cases. And as explained above, with some voting practices, there in fact may be no appropriate benchmark to determine if an existing voting practice is dilutive under § 2. For that reason, a voting practice that is subject to the preclearance requirements of § 5 is not necessarily subject to a dilution challenge under § 2.

* * *

Justice O'Connor's opinion, concurring in part and concurring in the judgment, is omitted.

■ JUSTICE THOMAS, with whom JUSTICE SCALIA joins, concurring in the judgment.

* * *

While the practical concerns Justices Kennedy and O'Connor point out can inform a proper construction of the Act, I would explicitly anchor analysis in this case in the statutory text. Only a "voting qualification or prerequisite to voting or standard, practice, or procedure" can be challenged under § 2. I would hold that the size of a governing body is not a "standard, practice, or procedure" within the terms of the Act. In my view, however, the only principle limiting the scope of the terms "standard, practice, or procedure" that can be derived from the text of the Act would exclude, not only the challenge to size advanced today, but also challenges to allegedly dilutive election methods that we have considered within the scope of the Act in the past.

I believe that a systematic reassessment of our interpretation of § 2 is required in this case.... A review of the current state of our cases shows that by construing the Act to cover potentially dilutive electoral mechanisms, we have immersed the federal courts in a hopeless project of weighing questions of political theory—questions judges must confront to establish a benchmark concept of an "undiluted" vote. Worse, in pursuing the ideal measure of voting strength, we have devised a remedial mechanism that encourages federal courts to segregate voters into racially designated districts to ensure minority electoral success. In doing so, we have collaborated in what may aptly be termed the racial "balkanization" of the Nation.

I can no longer adhere to a reading of the Act that does not comport with the terms of the statute and that has produced such a disastrous misadventure in judicial policymaking. I would hold that the size of a government body is not a "standard, practice, or procedure" because, properly understood, those terms reach only state enactments that limit citizens' access to the ballot.

I

If one surveys the history of the Voting Rights Act, one can only be struck by the sea change that has occurred in the application and enforcement of the Act since it was passed in 1965. The statute was originally perceived as a remedial provision directed specifically at eradicating discriminatory practices that restricted blacks' ability to register and vote in the segregated South. Now, the Act has grown into something entirely different. In construing the Act to cover claims of vote dilution, we have converted the Act into a device for regulating, rationing, and apportioning political power among racial and ethnic groups. In the process, we have read the Act essentially as a grant of authority to the federal judiciary to develop theories on basic principles of representative government, for it is only a resort to political theory that can enable a court to determine which electoral systems provide the "fairest" levels of representation or the most "effective" or "undiluted" votes to minorities.

* * *

A

As it was enforced in the years immediately following its enactment, the Voting Rights Act of 1965 was perceived primarily as legislation directed at eliminating literacy tests and similar devices that had been used to prevent black voter registration in the segregated South....

The Act was immediately and notably successful in removing barriers to registration and ensuring access to the ballot. For example, in Mississippi, black registration levels skyrocketed from 6.7% to 59.8% in a mere two years; in Alabama the increase was from 19.3% to 51.6% in the same time period. By the end of 1967, black voter registration had reached at least 50% in every covered State.

The Court's decision in *Allen v. State Bd. of Elections*, 393 U.S. 544 (1969), however, marked a fundamental shift in the focal point of the Act.... [There, t]he Court reasoned that § 5's preclearance provisions should apply, not only to changes in electoral laws that pertain to registration and access to the ballot, but to provisions that might "dilute" the force of minority votes that were duly cast and counted....

As a consequence, *Allen* also ensured that courts would be required to confront a number of complex and essentially political questions in assessing claims of vote dilution under the Voting Rights Act. The central difficulty in any vote dilution case, of course, is determining a point of comparison against which dilution can be measured. As Justice Frankfurter observed several years before *Allen*, "talk of 'debasement' or 'dilution' is circular talk. One cannot speak of 'debasement' or 'dilution' of the value of a vote until there is first defined a standard of reference as to what a vote should be worth." *Baker v. Carr*, 369 U.S. 186, 300 (1962) (Frankfurter, J., dissenting).... But in setting the benchmark of what "undiluted" or fully "effective" voting strength should be, a court must necessarily make some judgments based purely on an assessment of principles of political theory....

Perhaps the most prominent feature of the philosophy that has emerged in vote dilution decisions since *Allen* has been the Court's preference for single-member districting schemes, both as a benchmark for measuring undiluted minority voting strength and as a remedial mechanism for guaranteeing minorities undiluted voting power....

It should be apparent, however, that there is no principle inherent in our constitutional system, or even in the history of the Nation's electoral practices, that makes single-member districts the "proper" mechanism for electing representatives to governmental bodies or for giving "undiluted" effect to the votes of a numerical minority. On the contrary, from the earliest days of the Republic, multimember districts were a common feature of our political systems. The Framers left unanswered in the Constitution the question whether congressional delegations from the several States should be elected on a general ticket from each State as a whole or under a districting scheme and left that matter to be resolved by the States or by Congress. *See* U.S. Const., Art. I, § 4, cl. 1. It was not until 1842 that Congress determined that Representatives should be elected from single-member districts in the States. Single-member districting was no more the rule in the States themselves, for the Constitutions of most of the 13 original States provided that representatives in the state legislatures were to be elected from multimember districts. Today, although they have come under increasing attack under the Voting Rights Act, multimember district systems continue to be a feature on the American political landscape, especially in municipal governments.

The obvious advantage the Court has perceived in single-member districts, of course, is their tendency to enhance the ability of any numerical minority in the electorate to gain control of seats in a representative body. But in choosing single-member districting as a benchmark electoral plan on that basis the Court has made a political decision and, indeed, a decision that itself depends on a prior political choice made in answer to Justice Harlan's question in *Allen*. Justice Harlan asked whether a group's votes should be considered to be more "effective" when they provide influence over a greater number of seats, or control over a lesser number of seats. In answering that query, the Court has determined that the purpose of the vote—or of the fully "effective" vote—is controlling seats. In other words, in an effort to develop standards for assessing claims of dilution, the Court has adopted the view that members of any numerically significant minority are denied a fully effective use of the franchise unless they are able to control seats in an elected body. Under this theory, votes that do not control a representative are essentially wasted; those who cast them go unrepresented and are just as surely disenfranchised as if they had been barred from registering. Such conclusions, of course, depend upon a certain theory of the "effective" vote, a theory that is not inherent in the concept of representative democracy itself.[6]

In fact, it should be clear that the assumptions that have guided the Court reflect only one possible understanding of effective exercise of the

6. Undoubtedly, one factor that has prompted our focus on control of seats has been a desire, when confronted with an abstract question of political theory concerning the measure of effective participation in government, to seize upon an objective standard for deciding cases, however much it may over- ersimplify the issues before us. If using control of seats as our standard does not reflect a very nuanced theory of political participation, it at least has the superficial advantage of appealing to the "most easily measured indicia of political power."

franchise, an understanding based on the view that voters are "represented" only when they choose a delegate who will mirror their views in the legislative halls.[7] But it is certainly possible to construct a theory of effective political participation that would accord greater importance to voters' ability to influence, rather than control, elections. And especially in a two-party system such as ours, the influence of a potential "swing" group of voters composing 10%–20% of the electorate in a given district can be considerable. Even such a focus on practical influence, however, is not a necessary component of the definition of the "effective" vote. Some conceptions of representative government may primarily emphasize the formal value of the vote as a mechanism for participation in the electoral process, whether it results in control of a seat or not. Under such a theory, minorities unable to control elected posts would not be considered essentially without a vote; rather, a vote duly cast and counted would be deemed just as "effective" as any other. If a minority group is unable to control seats, that result may plausibly be attributed to the inescapable fact that, in a majoritarian system, numerical minorities lose elections.

* * *

But the political choices the Court has had to make do not end with the determination that the primary purpose of the "effective" vote is controlling seats or with the selection of single-member districting as the mechanism for providing that control. In one sense, these were not even the most critical decisions to be made in devising standards for assessing claims of dilution, for in itself, the selection of single-member districting as a benchmark election plan will tell a judge little about the number of minority districts to create. Single-member districting tells a court "how" members of a minority are to control seats, but not "how many" seats they should be allowed to control.

But "how many" is the critical issue. Once one accepts the proposition that the effectiveness of votes is measured in terms of the control of seats, the core of any vote dilution claim is an assertion that the group in question is unable to control the "proper" number of seats—that is, the number of seats that the minority's percentage of the population would enable it to control in the benchmark "fair" system. The claim is inherently based on ratios between the numbers of the minority in the population and the numbers of seats controlled.... As a result, only a mathematical

---

7. Indeed, the assumptions underpinning the Court's conclusions largely parallel principles that John Stuart Mill advanced in proposing a system of proportional representation as an electoral reform in Great Britain. *See* J. S. Mill, Considerations on Representative Government (1861). In Mill's view, a just system of representative government required an electoral system that ensured "a minority of the electors would always have a minority of the representatives." To Mill, a system that allowed a portion of the population that constituted a majority in each district to control the election of all representatives and to defeat the minority's choice of candidates was unjust because it operated to produce a "complete disfranchisement of minorities."

calculation can answer the fundamental question posed by a claim of vote dilution. And once again, in selecting the proportion that will be used to define the undiluted strength of a minority—the ratio that will provide the principle for decision in a vote dilution case—a court must make a political choice.

The ratio for which this Court has opted, and thus the mathematical principle driving the results in our cases, is undoubtedly direct proportionality. . . .

B

The dabbling in political theory that dilution cases have prompted, however, is hardly the worst aspect of our vote dilution jurisprudence. Far more pernicious has been the Court's willingness to accept the one underlying premise that must inform every minority vote dilution claim: the assumption that the group asserting dilution is not merely a racial or ethnic group, but a group having distinct political interests as well. Of necessity, in resolving vote dilution actions we have given credence to the view that race defines political interest. We have acted on the implicit assumption that members of racial and ethnic groups must all think alike on important matters of public policy and must have their own "minority preferred" representatives holding seats in elected bodies if they are to be considered represented at all.

* * *

[The Court has adopted] a working assumption that racial groups can be conceived of largely as political interest groups. And operating under that assumption, we have assigned federal courts the task of ensuring that minorities are assured their "just" share of seats in elected bodies throughout the Nation.

To achieve that result through the currently fashionable mechanism of drawing majority-minority single-member districts, we have embarked upon what has been aptly characterized as a process of "creating racially 'safe boroughs.'" We have involved the federal courts, and indeed the Nation, in the enterprise of systematically dividing the country into electoral districts along racial lines—an enterprise of segregating the races into political homelands that amounts, in truth, to nothing short of a system of "political apartheid." . . . Worse still, it is not only the courts that have taken up this project. In response to judicial decisions and the promptings of the Justice Department, the States themselves, in an attempt to avoid costly and disruptive Voting Rights Act litigation, have begun to gerrymander electoral districts according to race. That practice now promises to embroil the courts in a lengthy process of attempting to undo, or at least to minimize, the damage wrought by the system we created.

* * *

As a practical political matter, our drive to segregate political districts by race can only serve to deepen racial divisions by destroying any need for voters or candidates to build bridges between racial groups or to form voting coalitions. "Black-preferred" candidates are assured election in "safe black districts"; white-preferred candidates are assured election in "safe white districts." Neither group needs to draw on support from the other's constituency to win on election day.

* * *

C

While the results we have already achieved under the Voting Rights Act might seem bad enough, we should recognize that our approach to splintering the electorate into racially designated single-member districts does not by any means mark a limit on the authority federal judges may wield to rework electoral systems under our Voting Rights Act jurisprudence. On the contrary, in relying on single-member districting schemes as a touchstone, our cases so far have been somewhat arbitrarily limited to addressing the interests of minority voters who are sufficiently geographically compact to form a majority in a single-member district. There is no reason a priori, however, that our focus should be so constrained. The decision to rely on single-member geographic districts as a mechanism for conducting elections is merely a political choice—and one that we might reconsider in the future. Indeed, it is a choice that has undoubtedly been influenced by the adversary process: in the cases that have come before us, plaintiffs have focused largely upon attacking multimember districts and have offered single-member schemes as the benchmark of an "undiluted" alternative.

But as the destructive effects of our current penchant for majority-minority districts become more apparent, courts will undoubtedly be called upon to reconsider adherence to geographic districting as a method for ensuring minority voting power. Already, some advocates have criticized the current strategy of creating majority-minority districts and have urged the adoption of other voting mechanisms—for example, cumulative voting or a system using transferable votes—that can produce proportional results without requiring division of the electorate into racially segregated districts.

Such changes may seem radical departures from the electoral systems with which we are most familiar. Indeed, they may be unwanted by the people in the several States who purposely have adopted districting systems in their electoral laws. But nothing in our present understanding of the Voting Rights Act places a principled limit on the authority of federal courts that would prevent them from instituting a system of cumulative voting as a remedy under § 2, or even from establishing a more elaborate mechanism for securing proportional representation based on transferable votes.[17] As some Members of the Court have already recognized, geographic districting is not a requirement inherent in our political system. . . . Like other political choices concerning electoral systems and models of representation, it too is presumably subject to a judicial override if it comes into conflict with the theories of representation and effective voting that we may develop under the Voting Rights Act.

Indeed, the unvarnished truth is that all that is required for districting to fall out of favor is for Members of this Court to further develop their political thinking. We should not be surprised if voting rights advocates encourage us to "revive our political imagination," and to consider "innovative and nontraditional remedies" for vote dilution, for under our Voting Rights Act jurisprudence, it is only the limits on our "political imagination" that place restraints on the standards we may select for defining undiluted voting systems. Once we candidly recognize that geographic districting and other aspects of electoral systems that we have so far placed beyond question are merely political choices, those practices, too, may fall under suspicion of having a dilutive effect on minority voting strength. And when the time comes to put the question to the test, it may be difficult indeed for a Court that, under *Gingles*, has been bent on creating roughly proportional representation for geographically compact minorities to find a principled reason for holding that a geographically dispersed minority cannot challenge districting itself as a dilutive electoral practice. In principle, cumulative voting and other non-district-based methods of effecting proportional representation are simply more efficient and straightforward mechanisms for achieving what has already become our tacit objective: roughly proportional allocation of political power according to race.

* * *

II

* * *

[I believe that section 2 covers only] practices that affect minority citizens' access to the ballot. Districting systems and electoral mechanisms that may affect the "weight" given to a ballot duly cast and counted are simply beyond the purview of the Act.

A

In determining the scope of § 2(a), as when interpreting any statute, we should begin with the statutory language. Under the plain terms of the Act, § 2(a) covers only a defined category of state actions. Only "voting

---

17. Such methods of voting cannot be rejected out-of-hand as bizarre concoctions of Voting Rights Act plaintiffs. The system of transferable votes was a widely celebrated, although unsuccessful, proposal for English parliamentary reform in the last century. And while it is an oddity in American political history, cumulative voting in an at-large system has been employed in some American jurisdictions.

qualifications," "prerequisites to voting," or "standards, practices, or procedures" are subject to challenge under the Act. The first two items in this list clearly refer to conditions or tests applied to regulate citizens' access to the ballot. They would cover, for example, any form of test or requirement imposed as a condition on registration or on the process of voting on election day.

* * *

[W]e have already stretched the terms "standard, practice, or procedure" beyond the limits of ordinary meaning. We have concluded, for example, that the choice of a certain set of district lines is a "procedure," or perhaps a "practice," concerning voting subject to challenge under the Act, even though the drawing of a given set of district lines has nothing to do with the basic process of allowing a citizen to vote—that is, the process of registering, casting a ballot, and having it counted.

* * *

[N]othing in the language used in § 2(a) to describe the protection provided by the Act suggests that in protecting the "right to vote," the section was meant to incorporate a concept of voting that encompasses a concern for the "weight" or "influence" of votes. On the contrary, the definition of the terms "vote" and "voting" in § 14(c)(1) of Act focuses precisely on access to the ballot. Thus, § 14(c)(1) provides that the terms "vote" and "voting" shall encompass any measures necessary to ensure "registration" and any "other action required by law prerequisite to voting, casting a ballot, and having such ballot counted properly and included in the appropriate totals of votes cast."

It is true that § 14(c)(1) also states that the term "voting" "includes all action necessary to make a vote effective," and the Court has seized on this language as an indication that Congress intended the Act to reach claims of vote dilution. But if the word "effective" is not plucked out of context, the rest of § 14(c)(1) makes clear that the actions Congress deemed necessary to make a vote "effective" were precisely the actions listed above: registering, satisfying other voting prerequisites, casting a ballot, and having it included in the final tally of votes cast....[20]

* * *

20. ... Contrary to Justice Stevens' suggestions, *Gomillion v. Lightfoot*, 364 U.S. 339 (1960), does not indicate that the Fifteenth Amendment, in protecting the right to vote, incorporates a concern for anything beyond securing access to the ballot. The *Gomillion* plaintiffs' claims centered precisely on access: their complaint was not that the weight of their votes had been diminished in some way, but that the boundaries of a city had been drawn to prevent blacks from voting in municipal elections altogether. *Gomillion* thus "maintains the distinction between an attempt to exclude Negroes totally from the relevant constituency, and a statute that permits Negroes to vote but which uses the gerrymander to contain the impact of Negro suffrage." *Allen v. State Bd. of Elections*, 393 U.S. 544, 589 (Harlan, J., concurring in part and dissenting in part).

Of course, this interpretation of the terms "standard, practice, or procedure" effectively means that § 2(a) does not provide for any claims of what we have called vote "dilution." But that is precisely the result suggested by the text of the statute. Section 2(a) nowhere uses the term "vote dilution" or suggests that its goal is to ensure that votes are given their proper "weight." And an examination of § 2(b) does not suggest any different result. It is true that in construing § 2 to reach vote dilution claims in *Thornburg v. Gingles*, 478 U.S. 30 (1986), the Court relied largely on the gloss on § 2(b) supplied in the legislative history of the 1982 amendments to the Act. But the text of § 2(b) supplies a weak foundation indeed for reading the Act to reach such claims. . . .

[Section] 2(b) incorporates virtually the exact language of the "results test" employed by the Court in *White v. Regester*, and applied in constitutional voting rights cases before our decision in *Bolden*. The section directs courts to consider whether "based on the totality of circumstances," a state practice results in members of a minority group "having less opportunity than other members of the electorate to participate in the political process and to elect representatives of their choice."

But the mere adoption of a "results" test, rather than an "intent" test, says nothing about the type of state laws that may be challenged using that test. On the contrary, the type of state law that may be challenged under § 2 is addressed explicitly in § 2(a). . . . [T]he incorporation of a results test into the amended section does not necessarily suggest that Congress intended to allow claims of vote dilution under § 2. A results test is useful to plaintiffs whether they are challenging laws that restrict access to the ballot or laws that accomplish some diminution in the "proper weight" of a group's vote. Nothing about the test itself suggests that it is inherently tied to vote dilution claims. A law, for example, limiting the times and places at which registration can occur might be adopted with the purpose of limiting black voter registration, but it could be extremely difficult to prove the discriminatory intent behind such a facially neutral law. The results test would allow plaintiffs to mount a successful challenge to the law under § 2 without such proof.

. . . The most natural reading of [§ 2(b)] would suggest that citizens have an equal "opportunity" to participate in the electoral process and an equal "opportunity" to elect representatives when they have been given the same free and open access to the ballot as other citizens and their votes have been properly counted.

* * *

C

"Stare decisis is not an inexorable command[.]" Our interpretation of § 2 has . . . proved unworkable. As I outlined above, it has mired the federal courts in an inherently political task—one that requires answers to questions that are ill-suited to principled judicial resolution. Under § 2, we have assigned the federal judiciary a project that involves, not the application of legal standards to the facts of various cases or even the elaboration of legal principles on a case-by-case basis, but rather the creation of standards from an abstract evaluation of political philosophy.

Worse, our interpretation of § 2 has required us to distort our decisions to obscure the fact that the political choice at the heart of our cases rests on precisely the principle the Act condemns: proportional allocation of political power according to race. Continued adherence to a line of decisions that necessitates such dissembling cannot possibly promote what we have perceived to be one of the central values of the policy of stare decisis: the preservation of "the actual and perceived integrity of the judicial process."

* * *

Few words would be too strong to describe the dissembling that pervades the application of the "totality of circumstances" test under our interpretation of § 2. It is an empty incantation—a mere conjurer's trick that serves to hide the drive for proportionality that animates our decisions. As actions such as that brought in *Shaw v. Reno* have already started to show, what might euphemistically be termed the benign "creation of majority-minority single-member districts to enhance the opportunity of minority groups to elect representatives of their choice" might also more simply and more truthfully be termed "racial gerrymandering.". . . .

In my view, our current practice should not continue. Not for another Term, not until the next case, not for another day. The disastrous implications of the policies we have adopted under the Act are too grave; the dissembling in our approach to the Act too damaging to the credibility of the federal judiciary. . . . I cannot subscribe to the view that in our decisions under the Voting Rights Act it is more important that we have a settled rule than that we have the right rule. When, under our direction, federal courts are engaged in methodically carving the country into racially designated electoral districts, it is imperative that we stop to reconsider whether the course we have charted for the Nation is the one set by the people through their representatives in Congress. I believe it is not.

* * *

■ Justice Blackmun, with whom Justice Stevens, Justice Souter, and Justice Ginsburg join, dissenting.

* * *

II

* * *

By all objective measures, the proposed five-member Bleckley County Commission presents a reasonable, workable benchmark against which to measure the practice of electing a sole commissioner. First, the Georgia Legislature specifically authorized a five-member commission for Bleckley County. Moreover, a five-member commission is the most common form of governing authority in Georgia. Bleckley County, as one of a small and dwindling number of counties in Georgia still employing a sole commissioner, markedly departs from practices elsewhere in Georgia. This marked "departure . . . from practices elsewhere in the jurisdiction . . . bears on the fairness of [the sole commissioner's] impact." Finally, the county itself has moved from a single superintendent of education to a school board with five members elected from single-member districts, providing a workable and readily available model for commission districts. Thus, the proposed five-member baseline is reasonable and workable.

In this case, identifying an appropriate baseline against which to measure dilution is not difficult. In other cases, it may be harder. But the need to make difficult judgments does not "justify a judicially created limitation on the coverage of the broadly worded statute, as enacted and amended by Congress." Vote dilution is inherently a relative concept, requiring a highly "flexible, fact-intensive" inquiry, and calling for an exercise of the "court's overall judgment, based on the totality of the circumstances and guided by those relevant factors in the particular case," as mandated by Congress. Certainly judges who engage in the complex task of evaluating reapportionment plans and examining district lines will be able to determine whether a proposed baseline is an appropriate one against which to measure a claim of vote dilution based on the size of a county commission.

* * *

■ JUSTICE GINSBURG, dissenting.

I join the dissenting opinion by Justice Blackmun and the separate opinion of Justice Stevens, and add a further observation about the responsibility Congress has given to the judiciary. . . .

[As Justice O'Connor observed in her concurrence in *Gingles*, "t]here is an inherent tension between what Congress wished to do and what it wished to avoid"—between Congress' "intent to allow vote dilution claims to be brought under § 2" and its intent to avoid "creating a right to proportional representation for minority voters." Tension of this kind is hardly unique to the Voting Rights Act, for when Congress acts on issues on which its constituents are divided, sometimes bitterly, the give-and-take of legislative compromise can yield statutory language that fails to reconcile conflicting goals and purposes.

* * *

When courts are confronted with congressionally-crafted compromises of this kind, it is "not an easy task" to remain "faithful to the balance Congress struck.".... However difficult this task may prove to be, it is one that courts must undertake because it is their mission to effectuate Congress' multiple purposes as best they can.

■ Separate opinion of Justice Stevens, in which Justice Blackmun, Justice Souter, and Justice Ginsburg join.

Justice Thomas has written a separate opinion proposing that the terms "standard, practice, or procedure" as used in the Voting Rights Act should henceforth be construed to refer only to practices that affect minority citizens' access to the ballot. Specifically, Justice Thomas would no longer interpret the Act to forbid practices that dilute minority voting strength. To the extent that his opinion advances policy arguments in favor of that interpretation of the statute, it should be addressed to Congress, which has ample power to amend the statute. To the extent that the opinion suggests that federal judges have an obligation to subscribe to the proposed narrow reading of statutory language, it is appropriate to supplement Justice Thomas' writing with a few words of history.

I

Justice Thomas notes that the first generation of Voting Rights Act cases focused on access to the ballot. By doing so, he suggests that the early pattern of enforcement is an indication of the original meaning of the statute. In this regard, it is important to note that the Court's first case addressing a voting practice other than access to the ballot arose under the Fifteenth Amendment. In *Gomillion v. Lightfoot*, the Court held that a change in the boundaries of the city of Tuskegee, Alabama, violated the Fifteenth Amendment.

* * *

Because *Gomillion* was decided only a few years before the Voting Rights Act of 1965 was passed, and because coverage under the Voting Rights Act is generally coextensive with or broader than coverage under the Fifteenth Amendment, it is surely not unreasonable to infer that Congress intended the Act to reach the kind of voting practice that was at issue in that case....

During the years between 1965 and 1969 the question whether the Voting Rights Act should be narrowly construed to cover nothing more than impediments to access to the ballot was an unresolved issue. What Justice Thomas describes as "a fundamental shift in the focal point of the Act," occurred in 1969 [in *Allen v. State Board of Elections*,] when the Court unequivocally rejected the narrow reading, relying heavily on a broad definition of the term "voting" as including " 'all action necessary to make a vote effective.' "

Despite *Allen*'s purported deviation from the Act's true meaning, Congress one year later reenacted § 5 without in any way changing the operative words. During the next five years, the Court consistently adhered to *Allen*, and in 1975, Congress again reenacted § 5 without change.

When, in the late seventies, some parties advocated a narrow reading of the Act, the Court pointed to these Congressional reenactments as solid evidence that *Allen*, even if not correctly decided in 1969, would now be clearly correct.

* * *

If the 1970 and 1975 reenactments had left any doubt as to congressional intent, that doubt would be set aside by the 1982 amendments to § 2. Between 1975 and 1982, the Court continued to interpret the Voting Rights Act in the broad manner set out by *Allen*.... In the 1982 amendment to § 2 of the Voting Rights Act, Congress substituted a "results" test for an intent requirement. It is crystal clear that Congress intended the 1982 amendment to cover non-access claims like those in *Bolden* and *Gomillion*.

II

Justice Thomas' narrow interpretation of the words "voting qualification ... standard, practice, or procedure," if adopted, would require us to overrule *Allen* and the cases that have adhered to its reading of the critical statutory language.... The large number of decisions that we would have to overrule or reconsider, as well as the congressional reenactments discussed above, suggests that Justice Thomas' radical reinterpretation of the Voting Rights Act is barred by the well-established principle that stare decisis has special force in the statutory arena.

* * *

Throughout his opinion, Justice Thomas argues that this case is an exception to stare decisis, because *Allen* and its progeny have "immersed the federal courts in a hopeless project of weighing questions of political theory." There is no question that the Voting Rights Act has required the courts to resolve difficult questions, but that is no reason to deviate from an interpretation that Congress has thrice approved. Statutes frequently require courts to make policy judgments. The Sherman Act, for example, requires courts to delve deeply into the theory of economic organization. Similarly, Title VII of the Civil Rights Act has required the courts to formulate a theory of equal opportunity. Our work would certainly be much easier if every case could be resolved by consulting a dictionary, but when Congress has legislated in general terms, judges may not invoke judicial modesty to avoid difficult questions.

III

When a statute has been authoritatively, repeatedly, and consistently construed for more than a quarter century, and when Congress has reenacted and extended the statute several times with full awareness of that construction, judges have an especially clear obligation to obey settled law. Whether Justice Thomas is correct that the Court's settled construction of the Voting Rights Act has been "a disastrous misadventure" should not affect the decision in this case. It is therefore inappropriate for me to comment on the portions of his opinion that are best described as an argument that the statute be repealed or amended in important respects.

NOTES AND QUESTIONS

1. The Supreme Court remanded *Holder* to the lower courts on the question whether, if plaintiffs could show that the jurisdiction intentionally retained the single-commissioner form of government, the scheme would violate the Fourteenth Amendment. If such a showing could be made, what would the injury be? Does that injury shed any light on how to assess whether the scheme violates the Voting Rights Act?

2. The Court distinguished between section 2 and section 5 because section 5 contains its own baseline—the pre-existing practice. Suppose Bleckley County had had a five-member county commission, elected from five single-member districts, one of which was majority black. If the County were to reduce the number of seats to three, and if blacks were now no longer sufficiently numerous to form a majority in a fairly drawn single-member district, then the Justice Department might well refuse to preclear the new plan on the ground that it diluted black voting strength, and in a judicial preclearance proceeding it would likely prevail if there was any substantial evidence of bloc voting. Now consider the Kent County (Michigan) Board of Commissioners. After the 1990 census, the board reduced the number of seats from 21 to 19. If the county had retained a 21–seat plan, it would have been possible to draw two majority-nonwhite districts while under a 19–seat plan, only one could be drawn. *See Nixon v. Kent County*, 76 F.3d 1381 (6th Cir. 1996) (en banc). Is Kent County immune from all scrutiny under the Voting Rights Act because Michigan is not subject to preclearance?

3. Justice Thomas's concurrence in *Holder* is in some ways the most extraordinary voting rights opinion of modern times. Under what theory of statutory interpretation can section 2 be read not to cover vote dilution?

One scholar claims that "Justice Thomas's project—to shrink the statutory meaning of voting to the single act of casting a ballot—was not a conventional attempt at statutory construction, but a radical reconstruction of the law." Lani Guinier, *[E]racing Democracy*, 108 Harv. L. Rev. 109 (1994). Professor Guinier comments:

> The professed jurisprudential virtue of Justice Thomas's formulation is that it avoids "immers[ing] the federal courts" in the "hopeless project" of choosing between competing political theories and limits federal judicial intervention in local election matters. Justice Thomas's

interpretation of the statute, however, itself rests on a particular political theory. Justice Thomas's political theory, or at least the theory he imputed to the Congress that enacted the Voting Rights Act, is that political equality is satisfied by the simple condition of universal suffrage. His position—that the statute should be limited to claims that challenge direct denial of the right to cast a ballot—rests on a political theory of individualized democracy.

Does Justice Thomas's approach go even beyond Justice Frankfurter's views in *Colegrove v. Green* and *Baker v. Carr*, discussed in Chapter 3?

Although she disagreed with most of the factual and philosophical premises of Justice Thomas's opinion, Professor Guinier nonetheless viewed the opinion as pivotal:

> Despite the gaps in its reasoning, Justice Thomas's opinion is important for two reasons. First, Justice Thomas demonstrated the centrality of political theory to an understanding of minority vote dilution. As Justice Thomas argued, vote dilution claims require the federal judiciary to develop theories of the basic principles of democratic self-government. The question of defining minority vote dilution can only be answered by reference to a theory that defines effective participation in representative government. Second, Justice Thomas provided an enduring rationale for future challenges to the Act. Although the dissents in *Holder* and the majority in *De Grandy* recognized the broad remedial goal of the statute, none of the other opinions in those cases took Justice Thomas's challenge to articulate a theory of democratic representation from which a principled and workable strategy for enforcing the Act might emerge.

What might the contours of such a theory be?

4. *Holder* provided little guidance on the question of how to apply the Voting Rights Act to single-member offices. Lower courts have confronted this question in a variety of circumstances challenging aspects of the electoral system other than the choice to have single-member offices in the first place. One such arena involves runoff or majority-vote requirements.

Butts v. City of New York, 779 F.2d 141 (2d Cir. 1985), *cert. denied*, 478 U.S. 1021 (1986), concerned a challenge to a New York statute providing for a runoff primary if no candidate receives 40 percent or more of the votes cast in a party primary for Mayor or other citywide office in New York City. According to the court of appeals, "[p]olitical observers [were] agreed that the adoption of the run-off law was prompted by the unusual results of the 1969 New York City mayoral election. In the Democratic primary that year, two candidates—Herman Badillo and Robert Wagner—split the votes of the party's mainstream (Badillo receiving 28 percent, and Wagner 29 percent); as a result, the nomination went to Mario Proccacino (with 33 percent of the votes), who had run on a 'safe streets' platform.

Proccacino lost in the general election to incumbent John Lindsay, the nominee of the Independent and Liberal parties."

When a bill to require runoff primaries was introduced in the state senate, opponents argued that it could have the effect of preventing blacks and Hispanics from electing their own candidates to the offices covered by the bill, since the 40 percent threshold figure was just above the combined percentage of blacks and Hispanics in New York City at the time.

A class of black and Hispanic plaintiffs brought a challenge against the law. Although the district court ruled in their favor, finding the enactment intentionally discriminatory, the Second Circuit reversed.

> The events leading up to passage of the bill clearly support an inference of legitimate motive. The Proccacino nomination badly hurt the Democratic party in New York City, and such fluke results were likely to recur as the party system further deteriorated and a broader field of candidates emerged. The application of [the law] solely to citywide offices in New York speaks primarily to the ideological diversity within the City and the importance of those offices. The 40% threshold, which [the district court judge] called "diabolic," was obviously chosen because Proccacino received 33% of the vote in 1969, not because of the minority population figures in New York. Finally, the speed with which the bill passed both houses demonstrates its broad-based support rather than any "nefarious" motives; this broad support is also evident from the strong minority legislative vote in favor of the bill.

The Second Circuit also concluded that the runoff could not be challenged under the results test of section 2.

> Our central disagreement with the district court's interpretation of the Voting Rights Act concerns the kind of electoral arrangements that can violate the Act. There are two basic ways in which members of a class of citizens may have "less opportunity . . . to participate in the electoral process." There may either be restrictive practices that deter members of the class from voting, or electoral arrangements that diminish a class's opportunity to elect representatives in proportion to its numbers. Although the Act makes clear that a class has no right to elect its members by numerical proportion, the class does have a right to an opportunity, equal to that of other classes, to obtain such representation.

> In the context of elections for multi-member bodies, equal opportunity can be denied in a variety of ways. . . . A run-off requirement can exacerbate the unfair effect of at-large voting for a multi-member body, and has been invalidated in that context.

> We cannot, however, take the concept of a class's impaired opportunity for equal representation and uncritically transfer it from the context of elections for multi-member bodies to that of elections for single-member offices. These can be no equal opportunity for representation

within an office filled by one person. Whereas, in an election to a multi-member body, a minority class has an opportunity to secure a share of representation equal to that of other classes by electing its members from districts in which it is dominant, there is no such thing as a "share" of a single-member office.... [S]o long as the winner of an election for a single-member office is chosen directly by the votes of all eligible voters, it is unlikely that electoral arrangements for such an election can deny a class an equal opportunity for representation. We need not determine whether such opportunity could ever be denied in the context of an election to a single-member office. It suffices to rule in this case that a run-off election requirement in such an election does not deny any class an opportunity for equal representation and therefore cannot violate the Act. The rule in elections for single-member office has always been that the candidate with the most votes wins, and nothing in the Act alters this basic political principle. Nor does the Act prevent any governmental unit from deciding that the winner must have not a merely a plurality of the votes, but an absolute majority (as where run-offs are required when no candidate in the initial vote secures a majority) or at least a substantial plurality, such as the 40% level required by [this law.]

In contrast to *Butts*, a district court in Arkansas concluded that the state's adoption of runoff primary laws was tainted by a discriminatory purpose. *See Jeffers v. Clinton*, 740 F. Supp. 585 (E.D. Ark. 1990) (three-judge court). According to the court:

Traditionally, municipal offices, including mayor, council member, and municipal judge, were filled by nonpartisan election, conducted at the general election in November. The person receiving the highest number of votes won. A majority was not required. This situation began to change in 1973. In November 1972 P.A. (Les) Hollingsworth, a black lawyer who later served as an Associate Justice of the Supreme Court of Arkansas, was elected to the Little Rock City Board of Directors by a plurality. The General Assembly responded in its next session, enacting Act 168 of 1973, requiring a majority vote for such offices.

In 1975, a vacancy occurred in the office of Mayor of Pine Bluff, and Robert Handley announced his candidacy. The Rev. Mr. Handley, a black man, appeared to be a strong contender. The Legislature acted promptly. In advance of the special election for Mayor of Pine Bluff, it passed Act 269 of 1975, requiring a majority vote. Mr. Handley was defeated in a run-off.

In November of 1982, Leo Chitman became the first black person to be elected Mayor of West Memphis. He ran first among five candidates but did not get a majority of the votes. He unseated a white incumbent. White candidates had won by a plurality in the past, and no legislative reaction occurred. But when Mr. Chitman was elected Mayor in the same way, the Legislature promptly responded. It passed Act 909 of

1983, to require a majority vote for election to both county and municipal offices.

And finally, in 1988 the Rev. Marion Humphrey, a black lawyer, was elected Municipal Judge of Little Rock by a plurality. Little Rock had not been subject to a majority-vote requirement. But after Judge Humphrey's election, the Legislature reacted quickly. It passed Act 905 of 1989, subjecting municipal offices in all cities and towns to a majority-vote requirement.

We cannot ignore the pattern formed by these enactments. Devotion to majority rule for local offices lay dormant as long as the plurality system produced white officeholders. But whenever black candidates used this system successfully—and victory by a plurality has been virtually their only chance at success in at-large elections in majority-white cities—the response was swift and certain. Laws were passed in an attempt to close off this avenue of black political victory. This series of laws represents a systematic and deliberate attempt to reduce black political opportunity. Such an attempt is plainly unconstitutional. It replaces a system in which blacks could and did succeed, with one in which they almost certainly cannot. The inference of racial motivation is inescapable.

Jeffers imposed a novel remedy. Section 3(c) of the Voting Rights Act provides that a court that finds constitutional voting rights violations may impose a kind of preclearance requirement:

> [T]he court, in addition to such relief as it may grant, shall retain jurisdiction for such period as it may deem appropriate and during such period no voting qualification or prerequisite to voting or standard, practice, or procedure with respect to voting different from that in force or effect at the time the proceeding was commenced shall be enforced unless and until the court finds that [the new practice] does not have the purpose and will not have the effect of denying or abridging the right to vote on account of race or color. . . .

Using this provision, the *Jeffers* court required that "any further statutes, ordinances, regulations, practices, or standards imposing or relating to a majority-vote requirement in general elections in this State must be subjected to the preclearance process."

For a more detailed discussion of the so-called single-member office exception, see, Pamela S. Karlan, *Undoing the Right Thing: Single–Member Offices and the Voting Rights Act*, 77 Va. L. Rev. 1 (1991); for discussion of runoff primaries more generally, see *Voting Rights Act: Runoff Primaries and Registration Barriers: Oversight Hearings before the Subcomm. on Civil and Constitutional Rights of the House Comm. on the Judiciary*, 98th Cong., 2d Sess. (1984); Katherine I. Butler, *The Majority Vote Requirement: The Case Against Its Wholesale Elimination*, 17 Urb. Law. 441 (1985); Laughlin McDonald, *The Majority Vote Requirement: Its*

Use and Abuse in the South, 17 Urb. Law. 429 (1985); Matthew G. McGuire, Note, *Assessing the Legality of Runoff Elections Under the Voting Rights Act,* 88 Colum. L. Rev. 876 (1986).

5. A variety of claims involving so-called "first generation" issues of the right to participate—as opposed to the "second-generation" claims of vote dilution involved in *Gingles* and *Holder*—have also been brought under section 2. To what extent are either the *Gingles* framework or the Senate Report factors helpful in considering challenges to practices other than the structure of electoral districts?

In this light, consider *Mississippi State Chapter, Operation PUSH v. Allain,* 674 F.Supp. 1245 (N.D. Miss. 1987), and *Roberts v. Wamser,* 679 F.Supp. 1513 (E.D. Mo. 1987), *rev'd,* 883 F.2d 617 (8th Cir. 1989). *Operation PUSH* involved a successful section 2 challenge to Mississippi's "dual registration" system, in which voters had to register twice, and often in separate venues, to participate in both national and local elections. *Wamser* involved a challenge to St. Louis's use of a punch card voting system and its failure to conduct manual inspections of ballots for which the machine count failed to register a vote.

In each case, on its way to finding section 2 liability (*Wamser* was ultimately reversed on appeal on standing grounds unconnected to the question whether the system had a disparate impact), the district court made findings with respect to the nine Senate Report factors, including such issues as whether voting was racially polarized, whether elected officials were responsive to the minority community's needs, whether there were racial appeals in campaigns, and the level of minority electoral success. Are these factors relevant to determining whether particular registration or balloting practices violate section 2? How should courts think about the legality of particular registration and balloting practices given the fact that socioeconomic disparities may mean that virtually *any* practice that depends on potential voters' educational levels or financial resources will have a disparate impact? Does the question then become the extent to which an alternative system would have a less disparate impact?

6. To what extent can section 2 be used to challenge voting qualifications that are to some extent within individual voters' control. Consider *Ortiz v. City of Philadelphia,* 28 F.3d 306 (3d Cir. 1994). *Ortiz* involved a challenge to a Pennsylvania law that removed voters from the rolls for failing to vote. (After passage of the National Voter Registration Act of 1993 and the Help America Vote Act of 2002, "nonvoter purges" that remove voters from the rolls solely for failure to vote cannot be used to disqualify individuals from voting in federal elections.)

The court of appeals rejected the plaintiffs' claims. Its starting point was the statement in *Gingles* that "the essence of a § 2 claim is that a certain electoral law, practice, or structure interacts with social and historical conditions to cause an inequality in the opportunities enjoyed by black and white voters to elect their preferred representatives." According to the

Third Circuit, this formulation meant that "there must be some causal connection between the challenged electoral practice and the alleged discrimination that results in a denial or abridgement of the right to vote." And no such causal connection had been demonstrated:

> Here, however, it is not the State which prevents citizens from exercising their right to vote, from participating in the political process, and from electing representatives of their own choosing. We are not confronted with an electoral device—such as "race-neutral" literacy tests, grandfather clauses, good-character provisos, racial gerrymandering, and vote dilution—which discriminates against minorities, which has no rational basis, and which is beyond the control of minority voters. Rather, we are faced with the fact that, for a variety of historical reasons, minority citizens have turned out to vote at a statistically lower rate than white voters.

> As we read Ortiz's complaint, the entire document is drawn to allege that Pennsylvania's purge statute "caused" the disparate purge rates between Philadelphia's white and minority communities. Yet, there is nothing before us, not even one iota of evidence introduced at trial or present in the record, which would establish that fact.

* * *

> [T]he individuals to whom the purge law applies apparently have surmounted and overcome [whatever socioeconomic disadvantages they face] and have registered to vote at least once, if not more often. Had they continued to do so, the purge law could not have affected them, inasmuch as the purge law operates against only those who have registered to vote at least once, but then do not vote or register again. Conversely, if individuals have never registered and have never voted, the purge law still could not be applied to them because, as stated, the purge law affects only those who have once registered to vote.

* * *

> [On the other side of the balancing of various relevant factors] review of the record and present reality demonstrates that the City's purge statute meets an important and legitimate civic interest and is needed to prevent electoral fraud.

> Notably, and of recent date, Philadelphia's Senate election, in which the Democratic candidate ostensibly had prevailed, was invalidated on the basis of findings that absentee votes cast by non-residents and deceased voters had been fraudulently obtained and counted.... [A]t least twenty-two individuals were "purged" because they either had died or no longer lived in the district but had, nevertheless, cast votes in the most recent election—the very fraudulent acts which the purge

statute was designed to overcome.[22] . . . . [E]lectoral fraud has been a part of Philadelphia's landscape for over 100 years.

* * *

[A] focus on societal disadvantages might be entitled to somewhat greater weight in a suit challenging, not Philadelphia's purge act, but, perhaps, more generally, Philadelphia's voter registration procedures themselves.

Of what relevance are the following facts: each year, the percentages of the black and Latino electorate to be purged exceeded the percentages of the white electorate, and each year purged white voters were reinstated at higher rates than blacks and Latinos?

How persuasive is the majority's assertion that purge laws differ from constitutionally suspect restrictions such as literacy tests and poll taxes because the latter sort of practice "has no rational basis, and . . . is beyond the control of minority voters"? If the Voting Rights Act had not banned literacy tests nationwide what would distinguish a section 2 challenge to a fairly administered literacy test from *Ortiz*? Isn't literacy equally within the control of individuals?

7.   The application of section 2 to felon disenfranchisement laws has been a source of considerable litigation in recent years. In *Richardson v. Ramirez*, 418 U.S. 24 (1974), reprinted in Chapter 2, the Supreme Court upheld California's then-lifetime ban on voting by persons convicted of a felony, finding that "the exclusion of felons from the vote has an affirmative sanction in § 2 of the Fourteenth Amendment." Following *Ramirez*, the only successful constitutional challenges to criminal disenfranchisement statutes involved claims of impermissible discrimination in the definition of disenfranchisement-triggering offenses. *See, e.g., Hunter v. Underwood*, 471 U.S. 222 (1985); *McLaughlin v. City of Canton*, 947 F.Supp. 954 (S.D. Miss. 1995). Challenges to disenfranchisement statutes under the Voting Rights Act have consistently been unsuccessful.

---

22. [A recent] article recited in part:

The Board of Elections has begun purging the Second Senate District voting rolls of people who no longer live there—including a woman whose vote was recorded after she died and another whose vote was cast while she lived on a Greek island.

Election officials said the 22 names—including an individual who city investigators found living in New Jersey—would immediately be purged from computerized voting rolls and notification would be delivered to the addresses on their voter registration. Among the 22 people being purged in the Sixth Divi-

sion of the 42d Ward is one individual who has been living in Las Vegas for two years, though a vote was cast in her name in the November election without her knowledge, and a second individual who said he did not vote in any of the five Philadelphia elections in which ballots were cast for him since 1988.Between 1988 and 1993, for example, at least 60 improper ballots were cast in the Sixth Division of the 42d Ward, 27 by machine and 33 by absentee ballot.

Mark Fazlollah, *City Purging 2d District Voter Rolls*, Phila. Inquirer, April 13, 1994, at A1, A7.

In *Farrakhan v. Washington*, 338 F.3d 1009 (9th Cir. 2003), *cert. denied*, 543 U.S. 984 (2004), the Ninth Circuit held that plaintiffs can challenge an offender-disenfranchisement provision under section 2, given that "[f]elon disenfranchisement is a voting qualification, and Section 2 is clear that any voting qualification that denies citizens the right to vote in a discriminatory manner violates the VRA." On remand, however, the district court granted summary judgment to the defendants. It held that, under the totality of the circumstances, the plaintiffs had failed to prove a violation of section 2. While the court found that the plaintiffs' evidence showed significant racial disparities within the criminal justice system, the district court concluded that the "remarkable absence of any history of official discrimination in Washington factors heavily in the Court's totality of the circumstances analysis," as did the plaintiffs' failure to provide evidence of either barriers to the election of minority group members or a lack of responsiveness to minority concerns. With respect to the tenuousness inquiry, while the district court noted that "the State here does not explain why disenfranchisement of felons is 'necessary' to vindicate any identified state interest," the practice was so widespread among the states that the state's interest could not be labeled "tenuous."

In contrast to the Ninth Circuit, two other courts of appeals ruled *en banc* that section 2 simply does not reach felon disenfranchisement provisions. In *Johnson v. Governor of Florida*, 405 F.3d 1214 (11th Cir.), *cert. denied*, 126 S.Ct. 650 (2005), an en banc court of appeals upheld the district court's dismissal of a section 2 challenge to Florida's lifetime disenfranchisement of ex-offenders.

> Despite its broad language, Section 2 does not prohibit all voting restrictions that may have a racially disproportionate effect. Felon disenfranchisement laws are unlike other voting qualifications. These laws are deeply rooted in this Nation's history and are a punitive device stemming from criminal law....

> Most important, Florida's discretion to deny the vote to convicted felons is fixed by the text of § 2 of the Fourteenth Amendment....

> It is a long-standing rule of statutory interpretation that federal courts should not construe a statute to create a constitutional question unless there is a clear statement from Congress endorsing this understanding....

> Here, the plaintiffs' interpretation creates a serious constitutional question by interpreting the Voting Rights Act to conflict with the text of the Fourteenth Amendment....

> When Congress enacted the VRA and its subsequent amendments, there was a complete absence of congressional findings that felon disenfranchisement laws were used to discriminate against minority voters. Without a record of constitutional violations, applying Section 2 of the Voting Rights Act to Florida's felon disenfranchisement law

would force us to address whether Congress exceeded its enforcement powers under the Fourteenth and Fifteenth Amendments....

Instead of a clear statement from Congress indicating that the plaintiffs' interpretation is correct, the legislative history indicates just the opposite—that Congress never intended the Voting Rights Act to reach felon disenfranchisement provisions....

Similarly, in *Hayden v. Pataki*, 449 F.3d 305 (2d Cir. 2006), the court of appeals held that although the literal language of section 2 might reach felon disenfranchisement provisions, the Voting Rights Act was "one of the rare cases [in which] the literal application of a statute will produce a result demonstrably at odds with the intentions of its drafters":

> Here, there are persuasive reasons to believe that Congress did not intend to include felon disenfranchisement provisions within the coverage of the Voting Rights Act, and we must therefore look beyond the plain text of the statute in construing the reach of its provisions.... These reasons include (1) the explicit approval given such laws in the Fourteenth Amendment; (2) the long history and continuing prevalence of felon disenfranchisement provisions throughout the United States; (3) the statements in the House and Senate Judiciary Committee Reports and on the Senate floor explicitly excluding felon disenfranchisement laws from provisions of the statute; (4) the absence of any affirmative consideration of felon disenfranchisement laws during either the 1965 passage of the Act or its 1982 revision; (5) the introduction thereafter of bills specifically intended to include felon disenfranchisement provisions within the VRA's coverage; (6) the enactment of a felon disenfranchisement statute for the District of Columbia by Congress soon after the passage of the Voting Rights Act; and (7) the subsequent passage of statutes designed to facilitate the removal of convicted felons from the voting rolls. We therefore conclude that § 1973 was not intended to—and thus does not—encompass felon disenfranchisement provisions.

The Court noted that several subsequent pieces of federal legislation have addressed felon disenfranchisement—for example, the National Voter Registration Act of 1993 provides that voters' names can be removed from the rolls for "criminal conviction," 42 U.S.C. § 1973gg–6(a)(3)(B), and the Help America Vote Act of 2002 directs States to remove disenfranchised felons from their lists of those eligible to vote in federal elections, 42 U.S.C. § 15483(a)(2)(A)(ii)(I)—and thought this legislation would be inconsistent with treating section 2 as reaching felon disenfranchisement.

In one concurrence, Judge Walker suggested that the Act would be unconstitutional if it did reach felon disenfranchisement because it would then exceed congressional enforcement power under the fourteenth amendment. In another, Judge Jacobs expressed a view of section 2 as "unambiguously" a "guarantee of rights for free people, [that] has nothing to do with the voting of persons who are not permitted to make unmonitored phone calls, or to go at large, or to eat their food with knives and forks. Arguments to the contrary demean the Voting Rights Act."

In dissent, Judge Parker emphasized section 2's basis in the enforcement clause of the Fifteenth Amendment, stating that while the Fourteenth Amendment (with its reduction-of-representation clause) might permit states to disenfranchise persons convicted of a crime, the Fifteenth Amendment swept more broadly to forbid racial discrimination in voting. And he suggested that the huge recent rise in incarceration meant that "[t]he relationship between felon disfranchisement and minority voting is fundamentally different now than forty years ago when the VRA was originally passed, or even almost twenty-five years ago when the 1982 amendments were passed." Judge Calabresi also dissented, arguing that the general permissibility of felon disenfranchisement laws said nothing about whether racially discriminatory felon disenfranchisement laws were acceptable.

Does discrimination in the criminal justice system have to rise to the level of an independent constitutional violation for offender disenfranchisement to violate section 2? In this respect, consider the caution raised in the dissent of Judge Kozinski in *Farrakhan*:

> After the panel's decision, plaintiffs could bring a section 2 challenge based on statistical disparities if states adopt Internet voting, which Arizona already tested in the 2000 Democratic presidential primary. *See* Stephen B. Pershing, *The Voting Rights Act in the Internet Age: An Equal Access Theory for Interesting Times*, 34 Loy. L.A. L. Rev. 1171, 1172 (2001); *see also* Eben Moglen & Pamela S. Karlan, *The Soul of a New Political Machine: The Online, the Color Line and Electronic Democracy*, 34 Loy. L.A. L. Rev. 1089, 1089 (2001) ("The digital divide means that minority citizens have less access to web-based sources of political information and may be less able to use voting techniques, such as online voting, that require a computer."). Plaintiffs could show disparities in wealth, leading to disparities in computer ownership and Internet access, leading to disparities in participation on election day. The authors of a study of Arizona's test-drive of Internet voting concluded that "non-white voters did not vote on the Internet as often as whites, so the Internet voting option seems unlikely to improve the voting rights of minorities. Instead, Internet voting seems likely to weaken the voting rights of minorities, as in this particular case minority turnout dropped substantially more than did white turnout." *Alvarez & Nagler, supra,* at 1147.
>
> Holding elections on a Tuesday could be a thing of the past if a plaintiff somewhere can show that minority voters are disproportionately more likely to be hourly wage earners, who are disproportionately less likely to vote because they can't take time off from work....
>
> The permutations are endless. The bottom line is that virtually every decision by a state as to voting practices will be vulnerable, no matter

how unrelated to race. The fallout from the panel's decision will be felt for a long time to come.

Farrakhan v. Washington, 359 F.3d 1116, 1126 (9th Cir.), *cert. denied,* 543 U.S. 984 (2004) (Kozinski, J., dissenting from the denial of rehearing en banc).

8. In recent years, several states have adopted restrictive new voter identification procedures, as prerequisites both to registration and casting a ballot. (These voter ID laws are discussed in detail in Chapter 2.) To what extent can such laws be challenged as violations of section 2 if relatively higher numbers of minority citizens lack such documents as drivers' licenses or passports? The leading academic article on the emerging use of section 2 to challenge vote denial, with analysis of how courts should address such claims, is Dan Tokaji, *The New Vote Denial: Where Election Reform Meets the Voting Rights Act,* 57 S. Car. L. Rev. 689 (2006). Similarly, consider whether the use of electoral technologies that have a disparate impact—or nonuniformity in voting technologies within a state if minority precincts disproportionally use technologies with high error rates—violates section 2. These election machinery issues are discussed in more detail in Chapter 12.

D. THE CONSTITUTIONALITY OF AMENDED SECTION 2

As the cases in this chapter show, amended section 2 has spawned a torrent of litigation that has dramatically reshaped the American electoral landscape. As late as 1982, a sizeable majority of municipal elections were conducted at large and most southern states elected at least some state legislators from multimember districts. But by the mid–1990's, most jurisdictions with substantial minority populations had switched to using at least some single-member districts, and state legislatures were elected almost entirely from single-member districts, at least some of which were majority nonwhite. *See generally* Quiet Revolution in the South: The Impact of the Voting Rights Act, 1965–1990 (Chandler Davidson & Bernard Grofman eds., 1994); Pamela S. Karlan, *The Future of Voting Rights Litigation,* in Census 2000: Considerations and Strategies for State and Local Government (Benjamin E. Griffith ed. 2000).

As we saw in Chapter 7 and in the Supreme Court's decision in *Gingles,* Congress amended section 2 in substantial part because it disagreed with the Court's decision in *City of Mobile v. Bolden.* Section 2 forbids voting practices and procedures that have a discriminatory result, even if the state or political subdivision behaved without a discriminatory purpose. By contrast, the Court has interpreted both the Fourteenth and the Fifteenth Amendments to prohibit only purposefully discriminatory actions. It is therefore striking that the Court has never squarely addressed the question of the constitutionality of amended section 2's results test.

In *Mississippi Republican Executive Committee v. Brooks*, 469 U.S. 1002 (1984), the Court summarily affirmed an appeal from a district court's order redrawing Mississippi's congressional districts to create a majority-black congressional district. The questions presented in the jurisdictional statement included "Whether Section 2 as amended prohibits only those electoral schemes intentionally designed or maintained to discriminate on the basis of race" and "Whether Section 2, if construed to prohibit anything other than intentional discrimination on the basis of race in registration and voting, exceeds the power vested in Congress by the Fifteenth Amendment." Then-Justice Rehnquist and Chief Justice Burger dissented from the summary affirmance, arguing that plenary review of the scope and constitutionality of section 2 was required.

As a general matter, "[s]ummary affirmances ... without doubt reject the specific challenges presented in the statement of jurisdiction," *Mandel v. Bradley*, 432 U.S. 173, 176 (1977); *see also Illinois State Bd. v. Socialist Workers Party*, 440 U.S. 173, 182–83 (1979). While the Supreme Court itself gives less precedential weight to its own prior summary affirmances, lower courts are required to grant summary affirmances the same binding weight they give to other Supreme Court judgments. *See generally* Robert L. Stern et al., Supreme Court Practice § 4.29 (7th ed. 1993). In part, then, as a result of the Supreme Court's decision in *Brooks*, the lower courts have unanimously upheld amended section 2 against constitutional attack.

For one recent example, see *United States v. Blaine County*, 363 F.3d 897 (9th Cir. 2004). In that case, the defendant county raised the unconstitutionality of section 2 as an affirmative defense to a challenge to its at-large system brought by American Indians. (Note that under section 14(b) of the Voting Rights Act, "[n]o court other than the District Court for the District of Columbia shall have jurisdiction to issue ... any restraining order or temporary or permanent injunction against the execution or enforcement of any provision of this Act . . . .").

The court of appeals noted the Supreme Court's decision in *Brooks* and found that there had been "no doctrinal developments that suggest we should ignore the Supreme Court."

"While it is true that the Supreme Court has, in a series of recent cases, adopted a congruence-and-proportionality limitation on Congressional authority, this line of authority strengthens the case for section 2's constitutionality. Indeed, in the Supreme Court's congruence-and-proportionality opinions, the VRA stands out as the prime example of a congruent and proportionate response to well documented violations of the Fourteenth and Fifteenth Amendments."

On the merits, the court of appeals found that section 2 represented an appropriate use of congressional power:

First, legislation enacted under § 5 of the Fourteenth Amendment need not have geographic restrictions. *City of Boerne*, 521 U.S. at 533

("This is not to say, of course, that § 5 legislation requires termination dates, geographic restrictions or egregious predicates."). Such limitations only "tend to ensure" proportionality when Congress "pervasively prohibits constitutional state action."

Unlike section 5 of the VRA, section 2 does not engage in such a pervasive prohibition of constitutional state conduct.... Because section 5 imposes such a significant burden on state and local governments, Congress had reason to limit its application to jurisdictions with a recent history of pervasive voting discrimination.

Section 2 is a far more modest remedy. The burden of proof is on the plaintiff, not the state or locality.... In contrast to section 5, section 2's results test makes no assumptions about a history of discrimination. Because section 2 "avoids the problem of potential overinclusion entirely by its own self-limitation," nationwide application of this provision is undoubtedly constitutional. S. Rep. No. 97–417, at 43 (1982)....

[A]fter the Supreme Court's recent decision in *Nevada v. Hibbs*, it is clear that Congress need not document evidence of constitutional violations in every state to adopt a statute that has nationwide applicability. In *Hibbs*, the Supreme Court recognized that the "important shortcomings of some state policies" provided sufficient evidence of constitutional violations by the states. As Justice Scalia's dissent so vigorously pointed out, however, Congress failed to document evidence of unconstitutional discrimination in all fifty states. Thus, we decline to hold that Congress had to find evidence of unconstitutional voting discrimination by each of the fifty states in order to apply section 2 nationwide.

As the Ninth Circuit notes, the Supreme Court's recent enforcement clause decisions, beginning with *City of Boerne v. Flores*, 521 U.S. 507 (1997), may shed substantial light on the constitutionality of section 2. In *Boerne*, the Court struck down a provision of the Religious Freedom Restoration Act of 1993 (RFRA) that prohibited state and local governments from "substantially burdening" a person's exercise of religion even if the burden resulted from a rule of general applicability—that is a rule that was not intended to burden religious free exercise—unless the government could demonstrate that the burden "(1) is in furtherance of a compelling governmental interest; and (2) is the least restrictive means of furthering that ... interest." 42 U.S.C. § 2000bb–1.

The Federal Government defended RFRA as an appropriate use of Congress' enforcement power under § 5 of the Fourteenth Amendment. It argued that Congress' "decision to dispense with proof of deliberate or overt discrimination and instead concentrate on a law's effects accords with the settled understanding that § 5 includes the power to enact legislation designed to prevent as well as remedy constitutional violations."

The Court, in an opinion by Justice Kennedy, disagreed. While it acknowledged that "[l]egislation which deters or remedies constitutional violations can fall within sweep of Congress' enforcement power even if in the process it prohibits conduct which is not itself unconstitutional and intrudes into legislative spheres of autonomy previously reserved to the States," it declared that "[t]here must be a congruence and proportionality between the injury to be prevented or remedied and the means adopted to that end."

With respect to RFRA, the Court found no such congruity: the record before Congress did not indicate a pervasive practice of intentional discrimination against religious free exercise that would justify the prophylactic step of prohibiting conduct with a discriminatory impact absent a finding of purposeful discrimination. Given that failure, the Court saw Congress' action as an attempt to redefine the substantive scope of First/Fourteenth Amendment protections, rather than an appropriate remedial response.

For present purposes, perhaps the most significant aspects of *Boerne* were, first, its overruling of the so-called "ratchet" theory of congressional enforcement powers advanced by the Court in *Katzenbach v. Morgan*, 384 U.S. 641 (1966), and second, its explicit contrast between the impermissible use of the enforcement power to enact RFRA and Congress' appropriate use of that power to ban literacy tests and impose the preclearance requirement of section 5 of the Voting Rights Act. Notably, the Court's opinion did not mention the results test of amended section 2.

One commentator has identified three potential explanations within *Boerne*'s discussion of prior Voting Rights Act cases for why Congress could reach nonpurposeful discrimination:

First, under the internal model, literacy tests themselves might be the source of invidious discrimination; that is, the unconstitutional discrimination might occur within the electoral system. Congress and the Court had substantial evidence that literacy tests were administered in deliberately discriminatory ways for the purpose of excluding black citizens who possessed the same abilities as white individuals who were permitted to register. Under this view, Congress could ban literacy tests because the available evidence gave it "reason to believe that many of the laws affected by the congressional enactment have a significant likelihood of being unconstitutional." The congressional ban might—and in fact did—reach some literacy tests that could not be proven to be purposefully discriminatory. But as long as there was "congruence and proportionality between the [unconstitutional] injury to be prevented or remedied and the means adopted to that end," the Constitution does not require a perfect fit.

Second, in the external model, purposeful governmental discrimination outside the electoral system might play out within the electoral system, where it would be observed in the disparate impact of otherwise acceptable policies. For example, the inability of minority voters to pass even a fairly administered literacy test might be "the direct consequence of previous governmental discrimination in education." Under this view, Congress could ban literacy tests to reach and remedy the effects of that impermissible prior discrimination. Again, even though some of the beneficiaries of the ban on literacy tests might not be actual victims of the government's unconstitutional provision of an inferior and inadequate education, there was a sufficient connection to justify some level of overbreadth.

Third, under the prospective model, literacy tests might be seen as enabling future invidious action. For example, if literacy tests eliminate a disproportionate number of minority citizens from the electorate, then their diminished voting power might leave minorities vulnerable to discrimination in a wide range of government programs by officials who would be relieved of any practical need to be responsive to the minority's concerns. Under this expansive view, Congress might ban literacy tests "as a remedial measure to deal with . . . discrimination in the provision of public services."

Pamela S. Karlan, *Two Section Twos and Two Section Fives: Voting Rights and Remedies After* Boerne, 39 Wm. & Mary L. Rev. 725, 728–29 (1998).

Karlan argues that amended section 2 can be sustained under all three models: the internal, the external, and the prospective. With respect to the internal model, she argued that:

> The record before Congress in 1982 revealed numerous "modern instances of generally applicable laws passed because of [racial] bigotry." As the Senate Report accompanying the 1982 amendments explained, the very passage of the 1965 Act seems to have prompted a new wave of purposeful discrimination within the electoral system: "a broad array of dilution schemes were employed to cancel the impact of the new black vote." Of particular salience to the question whether the Act's treatment of racial vote dilution represents appropriate congressional action, "election boundaries were gerrymandered" and "at-large elections were substituted for election by single-member districts, or combined with other sophisticated rules to prevent an effective minority vote." Extensive hearings and the record of preclearance objections during the period from 1975 to 1980 showed repeated problems with apparently purposeful racial vote dilution.

Id. at 733–34. In light of this record, she argued that Congress might reasonably prohibit practices with a discriminatory result on the theory that a broader prophylactic rule was necessary to reach all the cases where purposeful discrimination had occurred.

With respect to the external and prospective models, Karlan argued that racial bloc voting—the *sine qua non* of section 2 vote dilution cases—is partially a contemporary manifestation of external discrimination:

To the extent that racially correlated differences in political preferences are the product of socioeconomic disparities produced by inferior access to schools, government services, and the like, state action has caused polarized voting.... Even beyond the material reasons why past discrimination might cause differences in voting behavior, there may be an attitudinal effect too. The broad range of purposeful past governmental discrimination "is likely to have affected white voters' attitudes by communicating the idea that black voters' attempts to gain political power should be resisted."

Id. at 739. Creating single-member districts might be an appropriate remedy to dampen the present effects of past external discrimination, since it would enable black voters to elect candidates despite them.

Finally, the results test might be an appropriate response to the post-electoral nonresponsiveness that racial bloc voting might produce. Submergence in a racially polarized electorate might produce elected officials with no incentive to be responsive to the minority community's distinctive needs. Given the connection between minority political powerlessness and the unequal provision of government services, "Congress might reasonably conclude that such inequality is better combatted on the wholesale level, by providing all citizens with an equal opportunity to participate in the political process and to elect representatives of their choice, than on only the retail level, by laws that impose equal treatment obligations in discrete areas of state government activity such as schools, public employment, or housing." *Id.* at 740.

By contrast, Professor Douglas Laycock argues that *Boerne* casts a serious shadow over section 2's constitutionality:

The political history of the 1982 Act, and the structural relationship of the statutory and constitutional standards, are indistinguishable from RFRA. RFRA was a direct congressional response to *Smith*; the 1982 Voting Rights Act was a direct congressional response to *City of Mobile v. Bolden*. The legislative history of the 1982 Act denounced *Bolden* as often and as vigorously as the legislative history of RFRA denounced *Smith*. RFRA covered nearly the whole scope of the Free Exercise Clause, and the 1982 Act covers the whole scope of the Fifteenth Amendment. Both RFRA and the 1982 Act enacted a broad standard drawn from prior constitutional interpretation. In each case, the Court's new constitutional standard required discrimination that was either deliberate (in the sense of unconstitutional motive) or overt (in the sense of disparate treatment, whatever the motive) and the statutory standard that Congress enacted in response dispensed with that requirement. In each case, there was some evidence that the new statutory standard simplified proof of constitutional violations, and substantial evidence that Congress disagreed with the new court-defined constitutional standard. The Senate Report on the 1982 Act was explicit about which consideration was more important: "During the hearings, there was considerable discussion of the difficulty often encountered in meeting the intent test, but that is not the principal reason why we have rejected it. The main reason is that, simply put, the test asks the wrong question."

The 1982 Voting Rights Act was not aimed at efforts to prevent blacks from voting; those efforts had largely ended by 1982. Instead, it was aimed at second and third generation voting rights problems, especially the inability of minority groups to elect representatives either in at-large elections or in elections in which the minority vote was dispersed across a number of single-member districts. The 1982 Act requires the creation of minority-controlled districts where there is a history of racially polarized voting and where such districts can be drawn without gross racial gerrymandering. Neither element of this threshold showing is plausibly a violation of the Constitution as the Court interprets it. Plaintiffs seem to be able to prove racially polarized voting almost everywhere, but it is hard to imagine the Court holding that the electoral choices of individual voters are unconstitutional, even when cumulated into racial patterns.

The failure to draw minority-controlled districts is not unconstitutional either, nor is it sufficient evidence of likely unconstitutional motive. The Constitution permits any districting scheme not deliberately designed to reduce minority voting strength. State and local governments have myriad legitimate reasons, and also a range of dubious, but clearly nonracial reasons—especially party gerrymanders and incumbent protection—for at-large elections and for drawing single-member districts one way instead of another. It seems unlikely that color-blind districting would reliably create minority-controlled seats outside the largest concentrations of minority population. As with RFRA, the number of statutory violations appears disproportionately large in relation to the number of constitutional violations. The Court summarily upheld the 1982 Act in 1984, but *Flores* implied the opposite result.

Douglas Laycock, *Conceptual Gulfs in* City of Boerne v. Flores, 39 Wm. & Mary L. Rev. 743, 749–52 (1998). *See also* John Matthew Guard, Comment, *"Impotent Figureheads"? State Sovereignty, Federalism, and the Constitutionality of Section 2 of the Voting Rights Act After* Lopez v. Monterey County *and* City of Boerne v. Flores, 74 Tul. L. Rev. 329 (1999) (distinguishing amended § 2's results test from the practices at issue in *South Carolina v. Katzenbach, Katzenbach v. Morgan, Oregon v. Mitchell*, and *City of Rome v. United States*, and suggesting that *Boerne* therefore casts serious doubt on the Act's constitutionality). For an argument that the potential vulnerability of Section 2 to challenge under *City of Boerne* may spark renewed attention to constitutional vote dilution claims, see Luke P. McLoughlin, *Section 2 of the Voting Rights Act and City of Boerne: The*

Continuity, Proximity, and Trajectory of Vote–Dilution Standards, 31 Vt. L. Rev. 39 (2006).

Finally, Professor Gerken has suggested "a second, less obvious ground for questioning the constitutionality of § 2 under *City of Boerne"* that stems from the Court's recent *Shaw* jurisprudence and its reliance on an individualized, rather than a group-based conception of the harm that flows from unconstitutional districting practices:

> *City of Boerne* held that Congress cannot "alter[] the meaning" of the Constitution or "change what the right is." While Congress may adopt prophylactic measures to prevent future deprivations of a constitutional right or offer remedies for past deprivations, the Court has held that the power to identify the underlying right itself rests exclusively with the judiciary. If the Court were to conclude that the Constitution recognizes only the type of conventional individual harm we see in its recent equal protection jurisprudence, then aggregate rights, with their group-based attributes, arguably exceed the scope of the injury that the Constitution recognizes. Congress would thus lack the power to vindicate these rights.

Professor Gerken identifies what she sees as a fundamental problem with such an attack:

> One major problem for those who seek to invalidate § 2 on these grounds is that any such attack would apply equally to intentional dilution claims brought under the Constitution, which the Court itself has endorsed. . . . An attack on the aggregate aspects of dilution claims . . . would go to the injury itself, and that injury is common to both the statutory and constitutional rights. . . .

> In any case, the lack of a conceptual framework for resolving this question certainly increases the risk that the Court will take the extraordinary step of declaring 2 unconstitutional. Without a theory for understanding precisely what makes dilution claims different, the Court might repeat the mistake it made in *Shaw II*: condemning any right that takes groups into account as a group right.

Heather K. Gerken, *Understanding the Right to an Undiluted Vote,* 114 Harv. L. Rev. 1663, 1737 (2001).

To what extent is the difference in Professor Karlan and Professor Laycock's assessment dependent on different empirical predicates about the record before Congress in 1982?

In addition to the specific decision in *Boerne,* consider the potential implications of the Court's recent federalism cases involving the Eleventh Amendment and sovereign immunity. In the initial cases, the Court struck down a number of congressional efforts to abrogate states' immunity from suit. *See, e.g., Board of Trustees v. Garrett,* 531 U.S. 356 (2001) (involving the employment provisions of the Americans With Disabilities Act); *Kimel v. Florida Board of Regents,* 528 U.S. 62 (2000) (involving the Age Discrimination in Employment Act); and *Florida Prepaid Postsecondary Education Expense Board v. College Savings Bank*, 527 U.S. 627 (1999) (involving amendments to patent law). In *Garrett*, *Florida Prepaid*, and *Kimel*, the Court thought Congress had exceeded its Fourteenth Amendment enforcement powers because of the incongruity between the sweeping prohibition and the likely set of constitutional violations.

More recently, however, the Court took a different turn. In *Nevada Dept. of Human Resources v. Hibbs*, 538 U.S. 721 (2003), the Court in a 6–3 decision upheld the Family and Medical Leave Act of 1993 (FMLA) as a valid exercise of Congress's powers to enforce the Fourteenth Amendment. After examining past congressional policies, the testimony before Congress, and the pattern of state laws, the Court concluded that Congress had a sufficient evidentiary basis for concluding that the states' "record of unconstitutional participation in, and fostering of, gender-based discrimination in administration of leave benefits," required the exercise of Congress's section 5 powers. The Court then distinguished recent section 5 cases that had refused to find congressional power legitimate because those statutes had involved discrimination on the basis of factors (such as age or disability) that do not trigger heightened judicial review.

> Here, however, Congress directed its attention to state gender discrimination, which triggers a heightened level of scrutiny. Because the standard for demonstrating the constitutionality of a gender-based classification is more difficult to meet than our rational-basis test—it must "serv[e] important governmental objectives" and be "substantially related to the achievement of those objectives"—it was easier for Congress to show a pattern of state constitutional violations. Congress was similarly successful in *South Carolina v. Katzenbach*, 383 U.S. 301, 308–313, where we upheld the Voting Rights Act of 1965: Because racial classifications are presumptively invalid, most of the States' acts of race discrimination violated the Fourteenth Amendment....

Similarly, in *Tennessee v. Lane*, 541 U.S. 509 (2004), the Supreme Court held that Title II of the Americans with Disabilities Act, which forbids exclusion of disabled individuals from participating in or receiving the benefits of "the services, programs or activities of a public entity," could constitutionally be applied to abrogate states' sovereign immunity with respect to damages actions involving the denial of access to the courts.

Justice Stevens' opinion for the Court observed that Title II, unlike Title I, which had been at issue in *Garrett*, sought not only to enforce the Fourteenth Amendment's prohibition on irrational discrimination against the disabled—a principle enforced by relatively deferential rationality review—but also to enforce a variety of other basic constitutional guarantees, including some, like the right of access to the courts, the infringement of which are subject to heightened judicial scrutiny. Still, the Court declined to address the question whether Title II could be applied to all government programs:

[N]othing in our case law requires us to consider Title II, with its wide variety of applications, as an undifferentiated whole. Whatever might be said about Title II's other applications, the question presented in this case is not whether Congress can validly subject the States to private suits for money damages for failing to provide reasonable access to hockey rinks, or even to voting booths, but whether Congress had the power under § 5 to enforce the constitutional right of access to the courts.

The Chief Justice, joined by Justices Kennedy and Thomas, dissented on the ground that there was insufficient evidence of unconstitutional state-level discrimination against the disabled to justify Title II's sweeping prohibitions under the *Boerne* congruence-and-proportionality test.

In a solo dissent, Justice Scalia went further, and advanced a different understanding of the scope of section 5 with respect to voting and racial discrimination. For the most part, he would reject an understanding of what it means to "enforce" the Fourteenth Amendment that extends to issuing a still broader prohibition directed to the same end.... Nothing in § 5 allows Congress to go beyond the provisions of the Fourteenth Amendment to proscribe, prevent, or "remedy" conduct that does not itself violate any provision of the Fourteenth Amendment. "But with respect to enforcement of the prohibition against racial discrimination, he was prepared to give Congress 'more expansive scope.' "

> Broad interpretation was particularly appropriate with regard to racial discrimination, since that was the principal evil against which the Equal Protection Clause was directed, and the principal constitutional prohibition that some of the States stubbornly ignored. The former is still true, and the latter remained true at least as late as *Morgan*.

> When congressional regulation has not been targeted at racial discrimination, we have given narrower scope to § 5. In *Oregon v. Mitchell*, 400 U.S. 112 (1970), the Court upheld, under § 2 of the Fifteenth Amendment, that provision of the Voting Rights Act Amendments of 1970, which barred literacy tests and similar voter-eligibility requirements— classic tools of the racial discrimination in voting that the Fifteenth Amendment forbids; but found to be beyond the § 5 power of the Fourteenth Amendment the provision that lowered the voting age from 21 to 18 in state elections. A third provision, which forbade States from disqualifying voters by reason of residency requirements, was also upheld—but only a minority of the Justices believed that § 5 was adequate authority. Justice Black's opinion in that case described exactly the line I am drawing here, suggesting that Congress's enforcement power is broadest when directed "to the goal of eliminating discrimination on account of race." And of course the results reached in *Boerne, Florida Prepaid, Kimel, Morrison,* and *Garrett* are consistent with the narrower compass afforded congressional regulation that does not protect against or prevent racial discrimination.

How do *Hibbs* and *Lane* affect analysis of whether section 2 of the Voting Rights Act is a constitutional exercise of Congress's powers? Does *Lane* generally, and Justice Scalia's approach specifically, require revisiting the issue, raised by Justice Marshall in his dissent in *City of Mobile v. Bolden*, 446 U.S. 55 (1980), reprinted in Chapter 7, whether dilution of minority voting strength is prohibited because of the possibility of invidious purposeful discrimination or because a fundamental right is at issue?

Michael Pitts offers another argument regarding the constitutionality of section 2, namely, the similarity between the totality-of-the-circumstances test as articulated by Congress in the 1982 legislative history and the constitutional test "last expounded upon by the Court in *Rogers v. Lodge*," 458 U.S. 613 (1982):

> In *Lodge*, the Court noted "that discriminatory intent … may often be inferred from the totality of the relevant facts." The Court then discussed what sort of evidence might serve as relevant facts, listing: (1) the minority voter registration rate; (2) the extent of racially polarized voting; (3) the electoral success of minority candidates; (4) the existence of past discrimination in the political process; (5) the existence of past discrimination in education and employment; (6) whether elected officials were unresponsive to minority constituents; (7) whether minority citizens suffer from a depressed socio-economic status; (8) the size of the area encompassed by an at-large district; (9) the legitimate state interest in using at-large elections; and (10) whether other discriminatory devices, such as numbered posts and a majority vote requirement, were used in the electoral system.
>
> Meanwhile, the test for proving that an electoral system dilutes minority votes in violation of Section 2 was principally delineated in *Thornburg v. Gingles*. In *Gingles*, the Court listed the following factors as relevant to the totality analysis: (1) a sufficiently large and geographically compact minority group that could form a majority population in a single-member district; (2) a politically cohesive minority group; (3) a majority group that votes as a bloc to usually defeat a minority group's chosen candidates; (4) a history of discrimination in voting; (5) the extent to which discriminatory devices, such as numbered posts, majority-vote requirements, or unusually large election districts, have been used; (6) the exclusion of minority citizens from any candidate slating process; (7) a history of discrimination in education and employment; (8) the use of racial appeals during election campaigns; (9) the success of minority candidates; (10) the unresponsiveness of elected officials to minority constituents; and (11) the policy underlying the use of at large elections.
>
> As is apparent, the evidentiary factors considered under both the constitutional and statutory standards are nearly, though by no means precisely, identical. The main difference is that *Gingles* places a bit more emphasis on certain foundational factors, such as the ability of

minority voters to comprise a majority of the population in a single-member district and racially polarized voting that results in the usual defeat of the preferred candidates of minority voters.

Michael J. Pitts, Georgia v. Ashcroft*: It's the End of Section 5 As We Know It (And I Feel Fine)*, 32 Pepperdine L. Rev. 265, 310–11 (2005).

For additional discussions of the constitutionality of the Voting Rights Act in light of *Hibbs* and *Lane, see, e.g.,* Richard L. Hasen, *Congressional Power to Renew the Preclearance Provisions of the Voting Rights Act after* Tennessee v. Lane, 66 Ohio St. L.J. 177 (2005); Jennifer G. Presto, Note, *The 1982 Amendments to Section 2 of the Voting Rights Act: Constitutionality After* City of Boerne, 59 Ann. Surv. Am. L. 609 (2003); Ellen D. Katz, *Reinforcing Representation: Congressional Power to Enforce the Fourteenth and Fifteenth Amendments in the Rehnquist and Waite Courts*, 101 Mich, L. Rev. 2341 (2003); Paul Winke, *Why the Preclearance and Bailout Provisions of the Voting Rights Act Are Still a Constitutionally Proportional Remedy*, 28 N.Y.U. Rev. L. & Soc. Change 69 (2003).

CHAPTER 9

RACE AND REPRESENTATION: A NEW SYNTHESIS?

The design of American political institutions was dramatically transformed in the two decades after the 1982 amendments to the Voting Rights Act and their interpretation in *Gingles*. The post–1990 round of reapportionment was the first in which states faced, from the beginning, a substantial prospect of liability if they failed to draw majority-black or-Hispanic districts in areas with politically cohesive minority populations and polarized voting. In addition, other institutional actors and factors combined to enhance the pressure to create these new, majority-minority election districts. Over the next two decades, courts and political actors would grapple with a variety of consequences that these changes initiated.

One important actor in this dynamic was the Department of Justice, which in the 1990s often insisted on the creation of majority-black or-Hispanic districts as a condition for preclearing the redistricting plans of jurisdictions covered under section 5 of the Voting Rights Act (this section of the Act is covered extensively in Chapter 6). While the two major parties might have had different motivations, the policy stayed in place despite a change in administrations. For one thing, career lawyers within the Civil Rights Division were often committed to maximizing minority representation through the creation of additional majority-nonwhite districts. In the initial years of the Republican George H.W. Bush administration, the political appointees ultimately in control of the preclearance process had no reason to resist concentrating pro-Democratic minority voters into new majority-minority districts, thereby drawing away from the electoral strength of Democratic incumbents in adjacent districts. By the time the Clinton administration assumed office in the winter of 1993, the newly created districts had elected a crop of minority Democratic representatives and the battles over redistricting were waged in terms of preserving their districts—not an effort a Democratic administration was likely to abandon.

Additionally, in the 1990s, Democrats still controlled (though that control was obviously waning) the redistricting process within many jurisdictions with large minority populations, particularly in the South. These Democratic state legislators faced an exquisitely difficult problem of both preserving the seats of incumbent white representatives and creating new majority-minority districts. As the case study from Alabama we begin with illustrates, one technique for achieving these aims involved surgically carving up populations of black or Hispanic voters so as to create new majority-minority districts while leaving sufficient numbers of reliable minority Democrats in adjacent majority-white, incumbent-protective districts.

One immediate and visible result of this greater focus on creating majority-black (and Hispanic) congressional districts was an increase in the number of black congressional representatives from 25 in 1989 to 38 in 1992. Hispanic representatives increased from 10 to 17 in the same period. But the creation of these safe minority districts had numerous other consequences as well. Among other effects, this creation of new, safe minority districts necessarily required the redrawing of many other congressional districts at the same time.

This process prompted an entirely new series of constitutional, statutory, and policy issues concerning the way the radiations from *Gingles* radically transformed the design of American political institutions. The following materials explore those issues in the order in which they reached the courts and the political arenas from the 1990s through to the present day. We begin with a concrete example of precisely what *Gingles* meant on the ground starting in the 1990s in states like Alabama that had a substantial minority voting population. The situation in Alabama in the 1990s was replicated in numerous other states, particularly southern ones.

The first map and accompanying data show the design and demographics of Alabama's congressional districts in 1990, on the eve of the new Census. The second shows how these districts were dramatically redesigned in the 1992 post-*Gingles* districting.

A. THE TRANSFORMATION OF DISTRICTING

The most significant difference between the two maps is the creation of new District 7 to create a solidly black-majority district. The creation of District 7 required that thousands of black voters be moved from District 2 and District 6 to expand the black population of District 7. For example, the part of Montgomery County that was moved from District 2 to District 7 was 80 percent black.

I. 1980 CONGRESSIONAL DISTRICTS

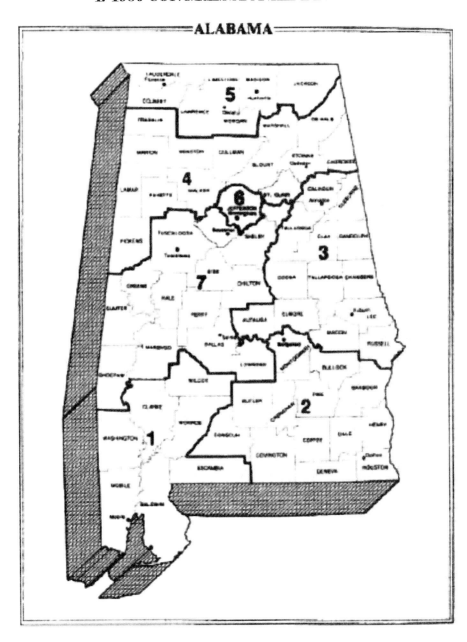

II. 1990 CONGRESSIONAL DISTRICTS

Alabama

Now consider the partisan distribution of Alabama's congressional delegation before and after the post–1990 redistricting, and a comparison of the black percentage of each congressional district. As the Table indicates, the immediate result of the redistricting was the creation of districts that could be expected to elect a different constellation of representatives. In practice, this meant the replacement of two white Democratic congressmen from Districts 6 and 7 with a black Democratic congressman from District 7 and a white Republican congressman from District 6. Notice as well, the near even distribution of black voters prior to 1990 and the concentration of black voters after 1990. Consider whether this result is mandated by the Voting Rights Act after *Gingles* and whether it is constitutionally permissible after *Shaw v. Reno*.

	Party		1990 Black Total Population		Party		1992 Black Total Population
1.	Callahan	R	31%	1.	Callahan	R	28%
2.	Dickinson	R	31%	2.	Everett	R	24%
3.	Browder	D	28%	3.	Browder	D	26%
4.	Bevill	D	7%	4.	Bevill	D	7%
5.	Cramer	D	14%	5.	Cramer	D	15%
6.	**Erdreich**	**D**	**34%**	**6.**	**Bachus**	**R**	**9%**
7.	**Harris**	**D**	**33%**	**7.**	**Hilliard**	**D**	**64%**

The plan adopted was proposed by the State Republican party. As political scientist David Lublin describes:

> Redistricting in Alabama worked exactly as the Republicans hoped. Since the Alabama lines are the product of a plan suggested by the Republicans and imposed by a federal court, this outcome is not altogether surprising.... The net result of these changes was to shift the partisan balance of the Alabama delegation and diminish substantive black representation. Thanks virtually entirely to favorable redistricting, Republicans won one new seat in 1992 and held on to one seat that they otherwise would have lost. Packing black voters into the Seventh District wasted Democratic voting strength and cost Democrats their hold on the Sixth District as well as an opportunity to win the open Second District. Instead of electing three moderate white Democrats, the Second, Sixth, and Seventh Districts now send one liberal black Democrat and two conservative white Republicans to Washington.... After redistricting, Alabama blacks can count on one sure vote on the floor of the House in the form of African American Earl Hilliard, but African Americans will find it exceedingly difficult to gain the vote of Sixth District Republican Spencer Bachus. Having few blacks in his district, Bachus has little reason to worry about black concerns. In effect, redistricting increased the size of the opposition to legislation supported by African Americans by one vote.

David Lublin, *Race, Representation, and Redistricting*, in Classifying By Race 111, 116 (Paul Petersen ed. 1996).

In other work, Professor Lublin has estimated that, nationwide, the creation of new majority-nonwhite congressional districts cost Democrats eleven seats they would otherwise have won. David Lublin, The Paradox of Representation 114 (1997). For a variety of reasons, such estimates depend on a variety of assumptions. Bernard Grofman and Lisa Handley, for example, estimated that the creation of new majority-nonwhite congressional districts might have cost the Democrats anywhere between two and eleven of the seats they lost between 1990 and 1994. See Bernard Grofman & Lisa Handley, *1990s Issues in Voting Rights*, 65 Miss. L.J. 205, 263–65 (1995). By contrast, Professor Engstrom has urged caution in ascribing Democratic losses to the creation of majority-nonwhite districts, noting that "Republican seat gains in the nine Southern states with new black districts have been at essentially the same rate as in the other 41 states" and that in a number of states that created new majority-nonwhite districts and in which the Republicans gained seats, none of the new Republican districts was adjacent to a new black district and "[n]one even contains part of an old district that gave up population to a new black district." Richard L. Engstrom, *Voting Rights Districts: Debunking the Myths*, Campaigns & Elections, Apr. 1995, at 24.

To be sure, there are multiple causes for the political transformation of the South over the last generation. Consider the following observation:

> [T]he Democratic share of the white vote in the South has been dropping for the past thirty years. The decline first appeared in national elections—the 1964 Johnson/Goldwater race was the watershed—but by the 1990s it had reached congressional and statewide contests as well. A majority of the U.S. Senators from the South are Republican (thirteen of twenty-two), as are a majority of the governors (six of eleven). The Republican Party won five of six southern senatorial seats up for election in 1994, as well as four of seven southern gubernatorial races. Neither senatorial nor gubernatorial elections are subject to redistricting. Thus, something beyond districting is clearly at work in producing Republican gains.

Pamela S. Karlan, *Loss and Redemption: Voting Rights at the Turn of a Century*, 50 Vand. L. Rev. 291, 304 (1997). It is possible both that there were long-term forces propelling the rise in the last generation of the Republican Party in the South and, also, that the legally mandated creation of safe minority districts accelerated this trend, at least for districted elections. Note how dramatic the change was for House seats just in the period between 1990, before redistricting, and 1994: in the South, 25 moderate white Democratic representatives lost their seats; there were 12 liberal Democrats elected (most of them minority representatives from newly drawn majority-minority districts); and there were 22 new Republican congressmen elected. David Lublin, Paradox of Representation 110 (1997).

As the Alabama experience illustrates, one consequence of the kind of districting that emerged in the 1990s was the intentional, race-conscious design of election districts, often—as in Alabama—through districts that were highly contorted in shape. These wandering, unusually shaped districts were the product of several factors, including, as in Alabama, the desire to protect incumbent districts and the fact that the black population necessary to constitute a majority district was dispersed across various parts of the state. Are serious constitutional issues raised when government uses racial considerations in this way to design democratic institutions? Based on the following case from the 1970s, the answer seemed to be no. But as you will see subsequently, the redistricting of the 1990s prompted the Supreme Court to reconsider this question.

United Jewish Organizations of Williamsburgh v. Carey

430 U.S. 144 (1977).

■ MR. JUSTICE WHITE announced the judgment of the Court and filed an opinion in which MR. JUSTICE STEVENS joined; Parts I, II, and III of which are joined by MR. JUSTICE BRENNAN and MR. JUSTICE BLACKMUN; and Parts I and IV of which are joined by MR. JUSTICE REHNQUIST.

Section 5 of the Voting Rights Act of 1965 prohibits a State or political subdivision subject to § 4 of the Act from implementing a legislative reapportionment unless it has obtained a declaratory judgment from the District Court for the District of Columbia, or a ruling from the Attorney General of the United States, that the reapportionment "does not have the purpose and will not have the effect of denying or abridging the right to vote on account of race or color . . . ."

The question presented is whether, in the circumstances of this case, the use of racial criteria by the State of New York in its attempt to comply with § 5 of the Voting Rights Act and to secure the approval of the Attorney General violated the Fourteenth or Fifteenth Amendment.

I

Kings County, N.Y. [Brooklyn], together with New York (Manhattan) and Bronx Counties, [are] subject to § 5 of the Act. . . . On January 31, 1974, the provisions of the [1972] statute districting these counties for . . . state senate and state assembly seats were submitted to the Attorney General. . . . On April 1, 1974, the Attorney General concluded that, as to certain districts in Kings County covering the Bedford–Stuyvesant area of Brooklyn, the State had not met the burden placed on it by § 5 and the regulations thereunder to demonstrate that the redistricting had neither the purpose nor the effect of abridging the right to vote by reason of race or color. [The Attorney General had concluded that certain districts had "abnormally high" minority concentrations, while other districts had minority voters diffused across several districts, and that the AG knew "of no necessity for such configuration[s] and believe[d] other rational alternatives" existed].

Under § 5, the State could have challenged the Attorney General's objections to the redistricting plan by filing a declaratory judgment action in a three-judge court in the District of Columbia. Instead, the State sought to meet what it understood to be the Attorney General's objections and to secure his approval. . . . A revised plan, submitted to the Attorney General on May 31, 1974, in its essentials did not change the number of districts with nonwhite majorities, but did change the size of the nonwhite majorities in most of those districts. Under the 1972 plan, Kings County had three state senate districts with nonwhite majorities of approximately 91%, 61%, and 53%; under the revised 1974 plan, there were again three districts with nonwhite majorities, but now all three were between 70% and 75% nonwhite. As for state assembly districts, both the 1972 and the 1974 plans provided for seven districts with nonwhite majorities. However, under the 1972 plan, there were four between 85% and 95% nonwhite, and three were approximately 76%, 61%, and 52%, respectively; under the 1974 plan, the two smallest nonwhite majorities were increased to 65% and 67.5%, and the two largest nonwhite majorities were decreased from greater than 90% to between 80% and 90%.

One of the communities affected by these revisions in the Kings County reapportionment plan was the Williamsburgh area, where about 30,000 Hasidic Jews live. Under the 1972 plan, the Hasidic community was located entirely in one assembly district (61% nonwhite) and one senate district (37% nonwhite); in order to create substantial nonwhite majorities in these districts, the 1974 revisions split the Hasidic community between two senate and two assembly districts. A staff member of the legislative reapportionment committee testified that in the course of meetings and telephone conversations with Justice Department officials, he "got the feeling . . . that 65 percent would be probably an approved figure" for the nonwhite population in the assembly district in which the Hasidic community was located, a district approximately 61% nonwhite under the 1972 plan. To attain the 65% figure, a portion of the white population, including part of the Hasidic community, was reassigned to an adjoining district.

Shortly after the State submitted this revised redistricting plan for Kings County to the Attorney General, petitioners sued on behalf of the Hasidic Jewish community of Williamsburgh, alleging that the 1974 plan "would dilute the value of each plaintiff's franchise by halving its effectiveness," solely for the purpose of achieving a racial quota and therefore in violation of the Fourteenth Amendment. Petitioners also alleged that they were assigned to electoral districts solely on the basis of race, and that this racial assignment diluted their voting power in violation of the Fifteenth Amendment.

* * *

Whether or not the plan was authorized by or was in compliance with § 5 of the Voting Rights Act, New York was free to do what it did as long as it did not violate the Constitution, particularly the Fourteenth and Fifteenth Amendments; and we are convinced that neither Amendment was infringed.

There is no doubt that in preparing the 1974 legislation, the State deliberately used race in a purposeful manner. But its plan represented no racial slur or stigma with respect to whites or any other race, and we discern no discrimination violative of the Fourteenth Amendment nor any abridgment of the right to vote on account of race within the meaning of the Fifteenth Amendment.

It is true that New York deliberately increased the nonwhite majorities in certain districts in order to enhance the opportunity for election of nonwhite representatives from those districts. Nevertheless, there was no fencing out of the white population from participation in the political processes of the county, and the plan did not minimize or unfairly cancel out white voting strength. *Compare White v. Regester,* 412 U.S., at 765–767, and *Gomillion v. Lightfoot,* 364 U.S. 339 (1960), *with Gaffney v. Cummings,* 412 U.S. 735, 751–754 (1973). Petitioners have not objected to the impact of the 1974 plan on the representation of white voters in the county or in the State as a whole. As the Court of Appeals observed, the plan left white majorities in approximately 70% of the assembly and senate districts in Kings County, which had a countywide population that was 65% white. Thus, even if voting in the county occurred strictly according to race, whites would not be underrepresented relative to their share of the population.

In individual districts where nonwhite majorities were increased to approximately 65%, it became more likely, given racial bloc voting, that black candidates would be elected instead of their white opponents, and it became less likely that white voters would be represented by a member of their own race; but as long as whites in Kings County, as a group, were provided with fair representation, we cannot conclude that there was a cognizable discrimination against whites or an abridgment of their right to vote on the grounds of race.... Furthermore, the individual voter in the district with a nonwhite majority has no constitutional complaint merely because his candidate has lost out at the polls and his district is represented by a person for whom he did not vote. Some candidate, along with his supporters, always loses. *See Whitcomb v. Chavis,* 403 U.S., at 153–160.

Where it occurs, voting for or against a candidate because of his race is an unfortunate practice. But it is not rare; and in any district where it regularly happens, it is unlikely that any candidate will be elected who is a member of the race that is in the minority in that district. However disagreeable this result may be, there is no authority for the proposition that the candidates who are found racially unacceptable by the majority, and the minority voters supporting those candidates, have had their Fourteenth or Fifteenth Amendment rights infringed by this process. Their position is similar to that of the Democratic or Republican minority that is submerged year after year by the adherents to the majority party who tend to vote a straight party line.

It does not follow, however, that the State is powerless to minimize the consequences of racial discrimination by voters when it is regularly practiced at the polls. In *Gaffney v. Cummings,* the Court upheld a districting plan "drawn with the conscious intent to . . . achieve a rough approximation of the statewide political strengths of the Democratic and Republican Parties." 412 U.S., at 752. We there recognized that districting plans would be vulnerable under our cases if "racial or political groups have been fenced out of the political process and their voting strength invidiously minimized"; but that was not the case there, and no such purpose or effect may be ascribed to New York's 1974 plan. Rather, that plan can be viewed as seeking to alleviate the consequences of racial voting at the polls and to achieve a fair allocation of political power between white and nonwhite voters in Kings County. . . .

■ MR. JUSTICE BRENNAN, concurring in part.

* * *

[I]t is instructive to consider some of the objections frequently raised to the use of overt preferential race-assignment practices.

First, a purportedly preferential race assignment may in fact disguise a policy that perpetuates disadvantageous treatment of the plan's supposed beneficiaries. Accordingly courts might face considerable difficulty in ascertaining whether a given race classification truly furthers benign rather than illicit objectives. An effort to achieve proportional representation, for example, might be aimed at aiding a group's participation in the political processes by guaranteeing safe political offices, or, on the other hand, might be a "contrivance to segregate" the group, thereby frustrating its potentially successful efforts at coalition building across racial lines. . . . Indeed, even the present case is not entirely free of complaints that the remedial redistricting in Brooklyn is not truly benign. Puerto Rican groups, for example, who have been joined with black groups to establish the "nonwhite" category, protested to the Attorney General that their political strength under the 1974 reapportionment actually is weaker than under the invalidated 1972 districting. A black group similarly complained of the loss of a "safe" seat because of the inadequacy of the 65% target figure. These particular objections, as the Attorney General argued in his memorandum endorsing the 1974 reapportionment, may be ill advised and unpersuasive. Nevertheless, they illustrate the risk that what is presented as an instance of benign race assignment in fact may prove to be otherwise. This concern, of course, does not undercut the theoretical legitimacy or usefulness of preferential policies. At the minimum, however, it does suggest the need for careful consideration of the operation of any racial device, even one cloaked in preferential garb. And if judicial detection of truly benign policies proves impossible or excessively crude, that alone might warrant invalidating any race-drawn line.

Second, even in the pursuit of remedial objectives, an explicit policy of assignment by race may serve to stimulate our society's latent race consciousness, suggesting the utility and propriety of basing decisions on a factor that ideally bears no relationship to an individual's worth or needs. *See, e.g.,* Kaplan, *Equal Justice in an Unequal World: Equality for the Negro—The Problem of Special Treatment,* 61 Nw. U.L. Rev. 363, 379–380 (1966). Furthermore, even preferential treatment may act to stigmatize its recipient groups, for although intended to correct systemic or institutional inequities, such policy may imply to some the recipients' inferiority and especial need for protection. Again, these matters would not necessarily speak against the wisdom or permissibility of selective, benign racial classifications. But they demonstrate that the considerations that historically led us to treat race as a constitutionally "suspect" method of classifying individuals are not entirely vitiated in a preferential context.

Third, especially when interpreting the broad principles embraced by the Equal Protection Clause, we cannot well ignore the social reality that even a benign policy of assignment by race is viewed as unjust by many in our society, especially by those individuals who are adversely affected by a given classification. This impression of injustice may be heightened by the natural consequence of our governing processes that the most "discrete and insular" of whites often will be called upon to bear the immediate, direct costs of benign discrimination. *See, e.g.,* Kaplan, *supra,* at 373–374; *cf.* Ely, *The Constitutionality of Reverse Racial Discrimination,* 41 U. Chi. L. Rev. 723, 737–38 (1974). Perhaps not surprisingly, there are indications that this case affords an example of just such decisionmaking in operation. For example, the respondent-intervenors take pains to emphasize that the mandated 65% rule could have been attained through redistricting strategies that did not slice the Hasidic community in half. State authorities, however, chose to localize the burdens of race reassignment upon the petitioners rather than to redistribute a more varied and diffused range of whites into predominantly nonwhite districts. I am in no position to determine the accuracy of this appraisal, but the impression of unfairness is magnified when a coherent group like the Hasidim disproportionately bears the adverse consequences of a race-assignment policy.

In my view, if and when a decisionmaker embarks on a policy of benign racial sorting, he must weigh the concerns that I have discussed against the need for effective social policies promoting racial justice in a society beset by deep-rooted racial inequities. But I believe that Congress here adequately struck that balance in enacting the carefully conceived remedial scheme embodied in the Voting Rights Act. However the Court ultimately decides the constitutional legitimacy of "reverse discrimination" pure and simple, I am convinced that the application of the Voting Rights Act substantially minimizes the objections to preferential treatment, and legitimates the use of even overt, numerical racial devices in electoral redistricting.

* * *

Moreover, the obvious remedial nature of the Act and its enactment by an elected Congress that hardly can be viewed as dominated by nonwhite representatives belie the possibility that the decisionmaker intended a racial insult or injury to those whites who are adversely affected by the operation of the Act's provisions. Finally, petitioners have not been deprived of their right to vote, a consideration that minimizes the detrimental impact of the remedial racial policies governing the § 5 reapportionment. True, petitioners are denied the opportunity to vote as a group in accordance with the earlier districting configuration, but they do not press any legal claim to a group voice as Hasidim. In terms of their voting interests, then, the burden that they claim to suffer must be attributable solely to their relegation to increased nonwhite-dominated districts. Yet, to the extent that white and nonwhite interests and sentiments are polarized in Brooklyn, the petitioners still are indirectly "protected" by the remaining white assembly and senate districts within the county, carefully preserved in accordance with the white proportion of the total county population. While these considerations obviously do not satisfy petitioners, I am persuaded that they reinforce the legitimacy of this remedy.

Since I find nothing in the first three parts of Mr. Justice White's opinion that is inconsistent with the views expressed herein, I join those parts.

■ Mr. Chief Justice Burger, dissenting.

* * *

The result reached by the Court today in the name of the Voting Rights Act is ironic. The use of a mathematical formula tends to sustain the existence of ghettos by promoting the notion that political clout is to be gained or maintained by marshaling particular racial, ethnic, or religious groups in enclaves. It suggests to the voter that only a candidate of the same race, religion, or ethnic origin can properly represent that voter's interests, and that such candidate can be elected only from a district with a sufficient minority concentration. The device employed by the State of New York, and endorsed by the Court today, moves us one step farther away from a truly homogeneous society. This retreat from the ideal of the American "melting pot" is curiously out of step with recent political history—and indeed with what the Court has said and done for more than a decade. The notion that Americans vote in firm blocs has been repudiated in the election of minority members as mayors and legislators in numerous

American cities and districts overwhelmingly white. Since I cannot square the mechanical racial gerrymandering in this case with the mandate of the Constitution, I respectfully dissent from the affirmance of the judgment of the Court of Appeals.

NOTES AND QUESTIONS

1. The plaintiffs in *UJO,* Hasidic Jews, might themselves be thought of as a discrete and insular minority. Yet Justice White's opinion treats them as part of an undifferentiated white population when it states that "the plan did not minimize or unfairly cancel out white voting strength" in Brooklyn as a whole because the plan left approximately 70% of the senate and assembly districts in Kings County with white majorities although only 65% of the county's population was white. Does this approach make sense? Consider Justice Brennan's observation about the Hasidim's distinctive positions. Cf. James U. Blacksher, *Majority Black Districts*, Kiryas Joel, *and Other Challenges to American Nationalism*, 26 Cumb. L. Rev. 407 (1996); Christopher Eisgruber, *Ethnic Segregation by Religion and Race: Reflections on* Kiryas Joel *and* Shaw v. Reno, 26 Cumb. L. Rev. 515 (1996) (both discussing the Court's later treatment of the deliberate creation of a Hasidic enclave in upstate New York and its relationship to questions of race-conscious districting).

Shaw v. Reno

509 U.S. 630 (1993).

■ JUSTICE O'CONNOR delivered the opinion of the Court.

This case involves two of the most complex and sensitive issues this Court has faced in recent years: the meaning of the constitutional "right" to vote, and the propriety of race-based state legislation designed to benefit members of historically disadvantaged racial minority groups....

I

The voting age population of North Carolina is approximately 78% white, 20% black, and 1% Native American; the remaining 1% is predominantly Asian.... The black population is relatively dispersed; blacks constitute a majority of the general population in only 5 of the State's 100 counties.... The largest concentrations of black citizens live in the [eastern] Coastal Plain, primarily in the northern part.... The General Assembly's first redistricting plan contained one majority-black district centered in that area of the State.

* * *

The Attorney General ... interposed a formal objection [under § 5 of the Voting Rights Act] to the General Assembly's plan. The Attorney

General specifically objected to the configuration of boundary lines drawn in the south-central to southeastern region of the State. In the Attorney General's view, the General Assembly could have created a second majority-minority district "to give effect to black and Native American voting strength in this area" by using boundary lines "no more irregular than [those] found elsewhere in the proposed plan," but failed to do so for "pretextual reasons." . . .

Under § 5, the State remained free to seek a declaratory judgment from the District Court for the District of Columbia notwithstanding the Attorney General's objection. It did not do so. Instead, the General Assembly enacted a revised redistricting plan, . . . that included a second majority-black district. The General Assembly located the second district not in the south-central to southeastern part of the State, but in the north-central region along Interstate 85. . . .

The first of the two majority-black districts contained in the revised plan, District 1, is somewhat hook shaped. Centered in the northeast portion of the State, it moves southward until it tapers to a narrow band; then, with finger-like extensions, it reaches far into the southern-most part of the State near the South Carolina border. District 1 has been compared to a "Rorschach ink-blot test," . . . and a "bug splattered on a windshield". . . .

The second majority-black district, District 12, is even more unusually shaped. It is approximately 160 miles long and, for much of its length, no wider than the I–85 corridor. It winds in snake-like fashion through tobacco country, financial centers, and manufacturing areas "until it gobbles in enough enclaves of black neighborhoods.". . . Northbound and southbound drivers on I–85 sometimes find themselves in separate districts in one county, only to "trade" districts when they enter the next county. Of the 10 counties through which District 12 passes, five are cut into three different districts; even towns are divided. At one point the district remains contiguous only because it intersects at a single point with two other districts before crossing over them. . . . One state legislator has remarked that " 'if you drove down the interstate with both car doors open, you'd kill most of the people in the district.' "

APPENDIX
NORTH CAROLINA CONRESSIONAL PLAN
Chapter 7 of the 1991 Session Laws (1991 Extra Session)

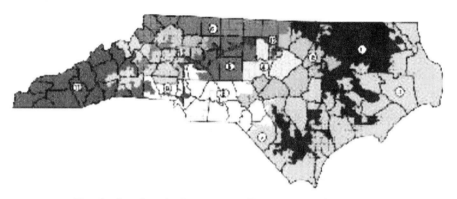

North Carolina's Post–1990 Congressional Districts

(Map Appearing in the Appendix to the Supreme Court's Opinion)

* * *

III

B

Appellants contend that redistricting legislation that is so bizarre on its face that it is "unexplainable on grounds other than race," . . . demands the same close scrutiny that we give other state laws that classify citizens by race. Our voting rights precedents support that conclusion.

In *Guinn v. United States,* the Court invalidated under the Fifteenth Amendment a statute that imposed a literacy requirement on voters but contained a "grandfather clause". . . . The determinative consideration for the Court was that the law, though ostensibly race-neutral, on its face "embodied no exercise of judgment and rested upon no discernible reason" other than to circumvent the prohibitions of the Fifteenth Amendment. . . . In other words, the statute was invalid because, on its face, it could not be explained on grounds other than race.

The Court applied the same reasoning to the "uncouth twenty-eight-sided" municipal boundary line at issue in *Gomillion.* Although the statute that redrew the city limits of Tuskegee was race-neutral on its face, plaintiffs alleged that its effect was impermissibly to remove from the city virtually all black voters and no white voters. The Court reasoned:

If these allegations upon a trial remained uncontradicted or unquali-fied, the conclusion would be irresistible, tantamount for all practical purposes to a mathematical demonstration, that the legislation is solely concerned with segregating white and colored voters by fencing Negro citizens out of town so as to deprive them of their pre-existing municipal vote.

The majority resolved the case under the Fifteenth Amendment.... Justice Whittaker, however, concluded that the "unlawful segregation of races of citizens" into different voting districts was cognizable under the Equal Protection Clause.... This Court's subsequent reliance on *Gomillion* in other Fourteenth Amendment cases suggests the correctness of Justice Whittaker's view.... *Gomillion* thus supports appellants' contention that district lines obviously drawn for the purpose of separating voters by race require careful scrutiny under the Equal Protection Clause regardless of the motivations underlying their adoption.

The Court extended the reasoning of *Gomillion* to congressional districting in *Wright v. Rockefeller*.... Every member of the Court assumed that the plaintiffs' allegation that the statute "segregated eligible voters by race and place of origin" stated a constitutional claim.... The Justices disagreed only as to whether the plaintiffs had carried their burden of proof at trial. The dissenters thought the unusual shape of the district lines could "be explained only in racial terms.".... The majority, however, accepted the District Court's finding that the plaintiffs had failed to establish that the districts were in fact drawn on racial lines. Although the boundary lines were somewhat irregular, the majority reasoned, they were not so bizarre as to permit of no other conclusion. Indeed, because most of the nonwhite voters lived together in one area, it would have been difficult to construct voting districts without concentrations of nonwhite voters....

Wright illustrates the difficulty of determining from the face of a single-member districting plan that it purposefully distinguishes between voters on the basis of race. A reapportionment statute typically does not classify persons at all; it classifies tracts of land, or addresses. Moreover, redistricting differs from other kinds of state decisionmaking in that the legislature always is *aware* of race when it draws district lines, just as it is aware of age, economic status, religious and political persuasion, and a variety of other demographic factors. That sort of race consciousness does not lead inevitably to impermissible race discrimination. As *Wright* demonstrates, when members of a racial group live together in one community, a reapportionment plan that concentrates members of the group in one district and excludes them from others may reflect wholly legitimate purposes. The district lines may be drawn, for example, to provide for compact districts of contiguous territory, or to maintain the integrity of political subdivisions....

The difficulty of proof, of course, does not mean that a racial gerrymander, once established, should receive less scrutiny under the Equal Protection Clause than other state legislation classifying citizens by race. Moreover, it seems clear to us that proof sometimes will not be difficult at all. In some exceptional cases, a reapportionment plan may be so highly irregular that, on its face, it rationally cannot be understood as anything other than an effort to "segregate . . . voters" on the basis of race. *Gomillion,* in which a tortured municipal boundary line was drawn to exclude black voters, was such a case. So, too, would be a case in which a State concentrated a dispersed minority population in a single district by disregarding traditional districting principles such as compactness, contiguity, and respect for political subdivisions. We emphasize that these criteria are important not because they are constitutionally required—they are not, cf. *Gaffney v. Cummings* . . . —but because they are objective factors that may serve to defeat a claim that a district has been gerrymandered on racial lines. *Cf. Karcher v. Daggett,* 462 U.S. 725, 755 (1983) (Stevens, J., concurring) ("One need not use Justice Stewart's classic definition of obscenity—'I know it when I see it'—as an ultimate standard for judging the constitutionality of a gerrymander to recognize that dramatically irregular shapes may have sufficient probative force to call for an explanation"). . . .

Put differently, we believe that reapportionment is one area in which appearances *do* matter. A reapportionment plan that includes in one district individuals who belong to the same race, but who are otherwise widely separated by geographical and political boundaries, and who may have little in common with one another but the color of their skin, bears an uncomfortable resemblance to political apartheid. It reinforces the perception that members of the same racial group—regardless of their age, education, economic status, or the community in which the live—think alike, share the same political interests, and will prefer the same candidates at the polls. We have rejected such perceptions elsewhere as impermissible racial stereotypes. . . . By perpetuating such notions, a racial gerrymander may exacerbate the very patterns of racial bloc voting that majority-minority districting is sometimes said to counteract.

The message that such districting sends to elected representatives is equally pernicious. When a district obviously is created solely to effectuate the perceived common interests of one racial group, elected officials are more likely to believe that their primary obligation is to represent only the members of that group, rather than their constituency as a whole. This is altogether antithetical to our system of representative democracy.

* * *

For these reasons, we conclude that a plaintiff challenging a reapportionment statute under the Equal Protection Clause may state a claim by alleging that the legislation, though race-neutral on its face, rationally cannot be understood as anything other than an effort to separate voters into different districts on the basis of race, and that the separation lacks sufficient justification. It is unnecessary for us to decide whether or how a reapportionment plan that, on its face, can be explained in nonracial terms successfully could be challenged. Thus, we express no view as to whether "the intentional creation of majority-minority districts, without more" always gives rise to an equal protection claim. . . . We hold only that, on the facts of this case, plaintiffs have stated a claim sufficient to defeat the state appellees' motion to dismiss.

* * *

■ Justice White, with whom Justice Blackmun and Justice Stevens join, dissenting.

* * *

[T]he notion that North Carolina's plan, under which whites remain a voting majority in a disproportionate number of congressional districts, and pursuant to which the State has sent its first black representatives since Reconstruction to the United States Congress, might have violated appellants' constitutional rights is both a fiction and a departure from settled equal protection principles. Seeing no good reason to engage in either, I dissent.

I

A

The grounds for my disagreement with the majority are simply stated: Appellants have not presented a cognizable claim, because they have not alleged a cognizable injury. To date, we have held that only two types of state voting practices could give rise to a constitutional claim. The first involves direct and outright deprivation of the right to vote, for example by means of a poll tax or literacy test. *See, e. g., Guinn v. United States,* 238 U.S. 347 (1915). Plainly, this variety is not implicated by appellants' allegations and need not detain us further. The second type of unconstitutional practice is that which "affects the political strength of various groups," *Mobile v. Bolden,* 446 U.S. 55, 83 (1980) (Stevens, J., concurring in judgment), in violation of the Equal Protection Clause. As for this latter category, we have insisted that members of the political or racial group demonstrate that the challenged action have the intent and effect of unduly diminishing their influence on the political process. Although this severe burden has limited the number of successful suits, it was adopted for sound reasons.

The central explanation has to do with the nature of the redistricting process. As the majority recognizes, "redistricting differs from other kinds of state decisionmaking in that the legislature always is aware of race when it draws district lines, just as it is aware of age, economic status, religious and political persuasion, and a variety of other demographic factors." "Being aware," in this context, is shorthand for "taking into account," and it hardly can be doubted that legislators routinely engage in the business of making electoral predictions based on group characteristics—racial, ethnic, and the like.

* * *

With these considerations in mind, we have limited such claims by insisting upon a showing that "the political processes ... were not equally open to participation by the group in question—that its members had less opportunity than did other residents in the district to participate in the political processes and to elect legislators of their choice."... Indeed, as a brief survey of decisions illustrates, the Court's gerrymandering cases all carry this theme—that it is not mere suffering at the polls but discrimination in the polity with which the Constitution is concerned.

In *Whitcomb v. Chavis,* we searched in vain for evidence that black voters "had less opportunity than did other ... residents to participate in the political processes and to elect legislators of their choice." More generally, we remarked:

> The mere fact that one interest group or another concerned with the outcome of [the district's] elections has found itself outvoted and without legislative seats of its own provides no basis for invoking constitutional remedies where ... there is no indication that this segment of the population is being denied access to the political system.

Again, in *White v. Regester,* the same criteria were used to uphold the district court's finding that a redistricting plan was unconstitutional. The "historic and present condition" of the Mexican–American community, a status of cultural and economic marginality, as well as the legislature's unresponsiveness to the group's interests, justified the conclusion that Mexican–Americans were " 'effectively removed from the political process-es,' " and "invidiously excluded ... from effective participation in political life." Other decisions of this Court adhere to the same standards....

I summed up my views on this matter in the plurality opinion in *Davis v. Bandemer....* Because districting inevitably is the expression of interest group politics, and because "the power to influence the political process is not limited to winning elections," the question in gerrymandering cases is "whether a particular group has been unconstitutionally denied its chance to effectively influence the political process." Thus, "an equal protection violation may be found only where the electoral system substantially disadvantages certain voters in their opportunity to influence the political process effectively." ... By this, I meant that the group must exhibit "strong indicia of lack of political power and the denial of fair representa-tion," so that it could be said that it has "essentially been shut out of the political process." ... In short, even assuming that racial (or political) factors were considered in the drawing of district boundaries, a showing of discriminatory effects is a "threshold requirement" in the absence of which there is no equal protection violation, ... and no need to "reach the question of the state interests ... served by the particular districts."

... To distinguish a claim that alleges that the redistricting scheme has discriminatory intent and effect from one that does not has nothing to do with dividing racial classifications between the "benign" and the malicious—an enterprise which, as the majority notes, the Court has treated with skepticism.... Rather, the issue is whether the classification based on race discriminates against anyone by denying equal access to the political process.

* * *

Part of the explanation for the majority's approach has to do, perhaps, with the emotions stirred by words such as "segregation" and "political apartheid." But their loose and imprecise use by today's majority has, I fear, led it astray.... The consideration of race in "segregation" cases is no different than in other race-conscious districting; from the standpoint of the affected groups, moreover, the line-drawings all act in similar fashion. A plan that "segregates" being functionally indistinguishable from any of the other varieties of gerrymandering, we should be consistent in what we require from a claimant: Proof of discriminatory purpose and effect.

The other part of the majority's explanation of its holding is related to its simultaneous discomfort and fascination with irregularly shaped districts. Lack of compactness or contiguity, like uncouth district lines, certainly is a helpful indicator that some form of gerrymandering (racial or other) might have taken place and that "something may be amiss." ... Disregard for geographic divisions and compactness often goes hand in hand with partisan gerrymandering....

But while district irregularities may provide strong indicia of a potential gerrymander, they do no more than that. In particular, they have no bearing on whether the plan ultimately is found to violate the Constitution. Given two districts drawn on similar, race-based grounds, the one does not become more injurious than the other simply by virtue of being snake-like, at least so far as the Constitution is concerned and absent any evidence of differential racial impact. The majority's contrary view is perplexing in light of its concession that "compactness or attractiveness has never been held to constitute an independent federal constitutional requirement for state legislative districts." *Gaffney*.... It is shortsighted as well, for a regularly shaped district can just as effectively effectuate racially discriminatory gerrymandering as an odd-shaped one. By focusing on looks rather than impact, the majority "immediately casts attention in the wrong direction—toward superficialities of shape and size, rather than toward the political realities of district composition." ...

Limited by its own terms to cases involving unusually-shaped districts, the Court's approach nonetheless will unnecessarily hinder to some extent a State's voluntary effort to ensure a modicum of minority representation.

This will be true in areas where the minority population is geographically dispersed. It also will be true where the minority population is not scattered but, for reasons unrelated to race—for example incumbency protection—the State would rather not create the majority-minority district in its most "obvious" location. When, as is the case here, the creation of a majority-minority district does not unfairly minimize the voting power of any other group, the Constitution does not justify, much less mandate, such obstruction. . . .

■ JUSTICE STEVENS, dissenting.

* * *

The duty to govern impartially is abused when a group with power over the electoral process defines electoral boundaries solely to enhance its own political strength at the expense of any weaker group. That duty, however, is not violated when the majority acts to facilitate the election of a member of a group that lacks such power because it remains underrepresented in the state legislature—whether that group is defined by political affiliation, by common economic interests, or by religious, ethnic, or racial characteristics. The difference between constitutional and unconstitutional gerrymanders has nothing to do with whether they are based on assumptions about the groups they affect, but whether their purpose is to enhance the power of the group in control of the districting process at the expense of any minority group, and thereby to strengthen the unequal distribution of electoral power. When the assumption that people in a particular minority group (whether they are defined by the political party, religion, ethnic group, or race to which they belong) will vote in a particular way is used to benefit that group, no constitutional violation occurs. Politicians have always relied on assumptions that people in particular groups are likely to vote in a particular way when they draw new district lines, and I cannot believe that anything in today's opinion will stop them from doing so in the future.

Finally, we must ask whether otherwise permissible redistricting to benefit an underrepresented minority group becomes impermissible when the minority group is defined by its race. The Court today answers this question in the affirmative, and its answer is wrong. If it is permissible to draw boundaries to provide adequate representation for rural voters, for union members, for Hasidic Jews, for Polish Americans, or for Republicans, it necessarily follows that it is permissible to do the same thing for members of the very minority group whose history in the United States gave birth to the Equal Protection Clause.

NOTE ON THE CONSTITUTIONAL INJURY RECOGNIZED IN SHAW

1. *Shaw v. Reno* resembled *Baker v. Carr* in an important way: it recognized a new kind of equal protection claim, but neither resolved the question whether the scheme in front of it violated the Constitution nor set out in any real detail the elements of the new cause of action. And like *Baker v. Carr*, the Court's decision in *Shaw v. Reno* precipitated litigation challenging congressional or state legislative reapportionments in at least a dozen states. Can you envision a *Reynolds v. Sims* waiting in the wings to give easily administered bright-line rules to implement *Shaw*?

2. *Shaw I* held only that a claim of excessive racial gerrymandering stated a cause of action for a Fourteenth Amendment violation. In *Shaw II*, when the merits of this claim returned to the Court, the Court in another 5–4 decision held that North Carolina's district did indeed violate the Constitution.

On remand from *Shaw I*, the state had defended the plan on the ground that its black-majority districts were required under the VRA, either under section 2 or section 5. In *Shaw II*, written by Chief Justice Rehnquist, the Court held that the Twelfth District was not "narrowly tailored" to comply with either section. With respect to the question whether the district was required by section 5, the Court said: "North Carolina's first plan, [to which the Department of Justice had objected,] ... indisputably was ameliorative, having created the first majority-black district in recent history." Thus, that plan, "even if [it] fall[s] short of what might be accomplished in terms of increasing minority representation," had not violated section 5 and the creation of a second majority-black district was not required. *Id.* at 912. As for the claim that the Twelfth District was narrowly tailored to comply with section 2, the Court observed that the first prong of the *Gingles* test requires that the minority group be "geographically compact." *Thornburg v. Gingles*, 478 U.S. 30, 50 (1986). Given the shape of the Twelfth District, the Court doubted that it "contains a 'geographically compact' population of any race." The fact that a section 2 violation might exist somewhere in the state could not justify drawing the Twelfth District, because its residents would not have had a section 2 claim.

3. One of the major issues *Shaw* and its progeny raised was the precise nature of the constitutional harm that the Court recognized. In traditional cases involving the constitutional right to vote, as discussed in Chapter 2, the harm alleged was to the individual voters who were being denied the ability to participate in particular elections. In traditional vote-dilution cases under the Constitution, as discussed in Chapter 8, the harm alleged was to the group of voters whose voting power was being diluted. Precisely who is being injured, and in what specific way, in *Shaw*-type cases? Is it all voters in the state? All voters whose race is taken into account in the redistricting process? Only those voters whose race is used to place them into black-majority districts? Only white voters whose race is used to place them in such districts?

In the wake of *Shaw*, Professors Pildes and Niemi argued that the best understanding of the doctrine was that it did not recognize individualized, material harms to specific voters or even groups of voters. Instead, it recognized what the authors called "expressive harms." In subsequent cases, both majority and dissenting Justices have embraced this characterization of the nature of the constitutional injury in the racial-redistricting cases. Thus, in *Bush v. Vera*, 517 U.S. 952 (1996), Justice O'Connor's opinion described the injury in these cases as an "expressive harm," as did Justice Souter, writing the principal dissent.

Professors Pildes and Niemi characterized the concept of "expressive harms" in the terms of the following excerpt. Consider whether this is the best account of the harms, if there are harms at all, in the racial-redistricting cases. Is it appropriate for constitutional law to acknowledge such non-individualized harms? Would the recognition of such harms be unique to the racial-redistricting context, or does constitutional law already recognize similar injuries elsewhere, such as in cases involving impermissible state "endorsement" of religion under the Establishment Clause?:

> One can only understand *Shaw*, we believe, in terms of a view that what we call *expressive* harms are constitutionally cognizable. An expressive harm is one that results from the ideas or attitudes expressed through a governmental action, rather than from the more tangible or material consequences the action brings about. On this view, the *meaning* of a governmental action is just as important as what that action *does*. Public policies can violate the Constitution not only because they bring about concrete costs, but because the very meaning they convey demonstrates inappropriate respect for relevant public values. On this unusual conception of constitutional harm, when a governmental action expresses disrespect for such values, it can violate the Constitution....

> Indeed, close attention to the language of Justice O'Connor's opinion reveals a constant struggle to articulate exactly these sorts of expressive harms. Thus, the opinion is laden with references to the social perceptions, the messages, and the governmental reinforcement of values that the Court believes North Carolina's districting scheme conveys....

> *Shaw* therefore rests on the principle that, when government appears to use race in the redistricting context in a way that subordinates all other relevant values, the state has impermissibly endorsed too dominant a role for race. The constitutional harm must lie in this endorsement itself: the very expression of this kind of value reductionism becomes the constitutional violation.

Richard Pildes & Richard Niemi, *Expressive Harms, "Bizarre Districts," and Voting Rights: Evaluating Election–District Appearances After* Shaw v. Reno, 92 Mich. L.Rev. 483, 506–09 (1993).

4.   The district designs one sees after 1990 in North Carolina and Alabama are characteristic of those that emerged numerous other places. One study shows that about half the most extravagant district lines were in districts designed to elect a minority representative. *See* Pildes & Niemi, *supra*, at 483 (collecting data on compactness of congressional districts over time). Even in these cases, as in *Shaw*, the ultimate district lines were a product of a complex interaction of desires for minority representation together with partisan and incumbent protection.

In this light, consider the majority-minority state legislative districts drawn after the 1990 Census in California. Because of divided control over the state government, these districts were drawn by special masters under the supervision of the California Supreme Court. The masters were quite explicit about the fact that race came first in drawing their plan. But that fact produced majority-nonwhite districts that were more regular in shape than adjoining majority-white districts because, "[h]aving *first* constructed Latino and African–American congressional and state legislative districts . . . the *remainder* of the districts allocated to Los Angeles County had to be constructed around the periphery; in some instances *they* became rather elongated." *Wilson v. Eu*, 823 P.2d 545, 579–80 (Cal. 1992) (reprinting the report of the special masters) (emphases added). When those districts were subjected to a *Shaw* challenge, the district court upheld them, and the Supreme Court summarily affirmed their constitutionality. *See DeWitt v. Wilson*, 856 F.Supp. 1409 (E.D. Cal. 1994) (three-judge court), *aff'd* 515 U.S. 1170 (1995).

5. The extreme manipulation of election district design that emerged in the 1990s—not just for racial redistricting, but for other purposes, such as partisan and incumbent-protecting ones—was aided greatly by advances in computer technology. In the 1990s, the state of the technology allowed for far more finely calibrated line drawing than had occurred in previous rounds of redistricting, allowing line drawers to perfect the process of equipopulous gerrymandering. In Texas, for example, the state made available to all interested parties a powerful computer program that would automatically readjust district lines to maintain population equality while providing detailed racial and partisan data on each newly created district. The computer program contained all Census data down to the precinct level, and contained racial and ethnic data at the block by block level in many areas. This computer program also contained extensive voting data from past elections, allowing even novices to project the likely electoral outcomes in each new district.

The plan the Texas legislature adopted was soon challenged on *Shaw* grounds. Consider Justice O'Connor's description of the way modern redistricting worked in Texas, from *Bush v. Vera*, 517 U.S. 952 (1996):

> The primary tool used in drawing district lines was a computer program called "REDAPPL." REDAPPL permitted redistricters to manipulate district lines on computer maps, on which racial and other socioeconomic data were superimposed. At each change in configuration of the district lines being drafted, REDAPPL displayed updated

racial composition statistics for the district as drawn. REDAPPL contained racial data at the block-by-block level, whereas other data, such as party registration and past voting statistics, were only available at the level of voter tabulation districts (which approximate election precincts). The availability and use of block-by-block racial data was unprecedented; before the 1990 census, data were not broken down beyond the census tract level.... By providing uniquely detailed racial data, REDAPPL enabled districters to make more intricate refinements on the basis of race than on the basis of other demographic information. The District Court found that the districters availed themselves fully of that opportunity: "In numerous instances, the correlation between race and district boundaries is nearly perfect.... The borders of Districts 18, 29, and 30 [three majority-nonwhite districts that were challenged in the wake of *Shaw v. Reno*] change from block to block, from one side of the street to the other, and traverse streets, bodies of water, and commercially developed areas in seemingly arbitrary fashion until one realizes that those corridors connect minority populations."

In light of these technological advances, should the Court in *Shaw* have imposed a *per se* compactness requirement to constrain the temptation to use ever more elaborate computer-drawn districts? Should it have done so only for highly manipulative districts drawn for racial reasons? For partisan reasons as well? What would the constitutional basis be for the Court's authority to impose such requirements?"

6. If expressive harms are constitutional injuries, can such harms be defined well enough to sustain judicially manageable doctrine? Consider Justice Souter's comments from a later case:

If the Court's first choice is to preserve *Shaw* in some guise with the least revolutionary effect on districting principles and practice, the Court could give primacy to the principle of compactness and define the limits of tolerance for unorthodox district shape by imposing a measurable limitation on the bizarre, presumably chosen by reference to historical practice (adjusted to eliminate the influence of any dilution that very practice may have caused in the past, cf. Pildes & Niemi, 92 Mich. L. Rev., at 573–574, n. 246 (discussing the egregious racial gerrymanders of the 19th century)) and calculated on the basis of a district's dispersion, perimeter, and population. [I]f *Shaw* were defined by measures that identified forbidden shape as the manifestation of unreasonable racial emphasis, we would at least provide the notice and guidance that are missing from the law today.

Bush v. Vera, 517 U.S. 952, 1070–71 (1996) (Souter, J., dissenting).

Should the Court use quantitative measures to define when a district drawn for racial reasons has become "highly irregular?" Note that Justice Souter, a dissenter in *Shaw* and its progeny, argued that unless the Court were to do so, *Shaw* would be unadministrable and should therefore be overruled.

7. *Shaw* lawsuits occupied a significant fraction of the Supreme Court's docket in the 1990s. The Court has issued significant opinions in ten cases elaborating, expanding, contracting, and modifying the principles set out in *Shaw*: *United States v. Hays*, 515 U.S. 737 (1995) (dismissing plaintiffs' claims for lack of standing); *Miller v. Johnson*, 515 U.S. 900 (1995) (striking down Georgia's majority-black Eleventh Congressional District); *Shaw v. Hunt*, 517 U.S. 899 (1996) (*Shaw II*) (striking down North Carolina's majority-black Twelfth Congressional District and dismissing plaintiffs' challenge to the majority-black First Congressional District for lack of standing); *Bush v. Vera*, 517 U.S. 952 (1996) (striking down three majority-minority congressional districts in Texas); *Abrams v. Johnson*, 521 U.S. 74 (1997) (affirming a new congressional redistricting plan drawn by a federal district court following the decision in *Miller v. Johnson*); *Lawyer v. Department of Justice*, 521 U.S. 567 (1997) (upholding a Florida state senate district against a *Shaw* challenge); *Hunt v. Cromartie*, 526 U.S. 541 (1999) (*Cromartie I*) (reversing the district court's grant of summary judgment in a challenge to the North Carolina congressional plan drawn in the wake of *Shaw II*); *Sinkfield v. Kelley*, 531 U.S. 28 (2000) (dismissing, on standing grounds, plaintiffs' challenge to Alabama's state legislative redistricting); *Easley v. Cromartie*, 532 U.S. 234 (2001) (*Cromartie II*) (upholding North Carolina's redrawn plan); *League of United Latin American Citizens v. Perry*, 126 S.Ct. 2594 (2006) (rejecting a *Shaw* challenge on the merits).

In part, the profusion of *Shaw* cases reflects the technical structure of Supreme Court appellate jurisdiction. Most of the time, the Supreme Court has discretion to decide whether to hear a case the process of granting or denying a petition for writ of certiorari. By statute, however, the Court has mandatory appellate jurisdiction over cases heard by three-judge (rather than single-judge) district courts. If a party seeks appellate review of a case tried before a three-judge district court, the case bypasses the courts of appeals and the Supreme Court must decide the merits. Few cases are tried by these special district courts anymore, but federal statutes require them both for cases brought under section 5 of the Voting Rights Act (the preclearance provision discussed in Chapter 7), see 42 U.S.C. § 1973c, and for cases challenging statewide legislative reapportionments, see 28 U.S.C. § 2284. The conventional explanation for why Congress retained three-judge district courts in statewide apportionment cases is that respect for values of federalism in the area of redistricting militated against letting a single district judge overturn a state's decisions. Ironically, though, this structure precludes an intermediate stage of appellate review as well as the opportunity for "percolation" of issues and incremental doctrinal development. For an extensive discussion of the issues raised by the use of three-judge courts, see Michael E. Solimine, *The Three-Judge District Court in Voting Rights Litigation*, 30 U. Mich. J.L. Ref. 79 (1996).

The Court can dispose of these mandatory appeals summarily, by affirming or reversing on the merits without oral argument. *See, e.g., King v. Illinois Board of Elections*, 522 U.S. 1087 (1998) (affirming three-judge court's judgment that Illinois' majority-Hispanic Fourth Congressional District was created to satisfy the state's compelling interest in compliance with § 2 of the Voting Rights Act); *Meadows v. Moon*, 521 U.S. 1113 (1997) (affirming a three-judge court's invalidation of Virginia's majority-black Third Congressional District). But more often, it has noted probable jurisdiction and decided cases after briefing and oral argument.

NOTE ON THE CONSTITUTIONAL INJURY AND ITS RELATIONSHIP TO STANDING

1. The question of the nature of the constitutional harm the Court recognized in the racial gerrymandering cases generated procedural problems related to deciding which plaintiffs had standing to raise *Shaw* claims. In *Shaw v. Reno*, for example, none of the plaintiffs lived in the majority-black First Congressional District and only two of the five lived in the much-maligned majority-black Twelfth. This apparent lack of contact with the districts caused the Court no evident concern. Soon after *Shaw*, however, in *United States v. Hays*, 515 U.S. 737 (1995), the Court overturned a district court's invalidation of Louisiana congressional districting on the grounds that none of the plaintiffs lived in the majority-black district they were challenging.

The Court unanimously held that this precluded them from meeting the "irreducible constitutional minimum" of a concrete, particularized "injury in fact." To establish this, Justice O'Connor writing for the Court held that plaintiffs must show that they "personally [were] denied equal treatment." Plaintiffs who "do not live in the district that is the primary focus of their racial gerrymandering claim, and [who] have not otherwise demonstrated that they, personally, have been subjected to a racial classification" fail that test. Someone who does not live in the district, the Court observed, "assert[s] only a generalized grievance against governmental conduct of which he or she does not approve." By contrast, plaintiffs who allege that they reside within a racially gerrymandered district have "been denied equal treatment because of the legislature's reliance on racial criteria" and they "may suffer the special representational harms racial classifications can cause in the voting context." In light of *Hays*, when the Court next re-confronted the challenge to North Carolina's congressional plan, in *Shaw v. Hunt*, 517 U.S. 899 (1996), it dismissed a *Shaw* challenge to one district because none of the plaintiffs lived there.

2. For a particularly striking example of the post-*Shaw* standing doctrine, consider *Sinkfield v. Kelley*, 531 U.S. 28 (2000). The plaintiffs lived in several majority-white state legislative districts that were adjacent to deliberately-created majority black legislative districts. Taking *Hays* at its word, they challenged the majority-white districts in which they lived: an inevitable consequence of having to redraw those districts would be the need also to redraw the adjacent majority-black districts. The Supreme Court held that these plaintiffs lacked standing:

> Appellees are challenging their own majority-white districts as the product of unconstitutional racial gerrymandering under a redistricting plan whose purpose was the creation of majority-minority districts, some of which border appellees' districts....
>
> The shapes of appellees' districts, however, were necessarily influenced by the shapes of the majority-minority districts upon which they border, and appellees have produced no evidence that anything other than the deliberate creation of those majority-minority districts is responsible for the districting lines of which they complain. Appellees' suggestion thus boils down to the claim that an unconstitutional use of race in drawing the boundaries of majority-minority districts necessarily involves an unconstitutional use of race in drawing the boundaries of neighboring majority-white districts. We rejected that argument in *Hays*, explaining that evidence sufficient to support a *Shaw* claim with respect to a majority-minority district did "not prove anything" with respect to a neighboring majority-white district in which the appellees resided. Accordingly, "an allegation to that effect does not allege a cognizable injury under the Fourteenth Amendment."

What theory of harm underlies this standing doctrine? *See generally* Pamela S. Karlan, *The Fire Next Time: Reapportionment After the 2000 Census*, 50 Stan. L. Rev. 731, 760–62 (1998) (discussing the history of the *Sinkfield* litigation).

3. Does limiting standing to those inside a challenged district match the Court's conception of the substantive harm at stake? For the argument that it does, see John Hart Ely, *Standing to Challenge Pro–Minority Gerrymanders*, 111 Harv. L. Rev. 576 (1997). For the argument that it does not, and a critique of Ely's views, see Samuel Issacharoff & Pamela S. Karlan, *Standing and Misunderstanding in Voting Rights Law*, 111 Harv. L. Rev. 2276, 2279–87 (1998).

4. Perhaps the tension between the substantive harm and the standing rules reflects a more deep-seated tension between constitutional law as the protection of individual rights versus constitutional law as the enforcement of constraints against government acting on the basis of impermissible justifications. Are these problems any different in litigation to enforce the establishment clause of the First Amendment? Compare *Valley Forge Christian College v. Americans United*, 454 U.S. 464 (1982) (sharply divided Court debating standing rules for such claims). The treatment of this issue by the Supreme Court has, to date, been inconclusive.

5. Standing to raise *Shaw* claims largely disappeared as a major litigation concern in the 2000s, in part because so few *Shaw* claims were brought at all. Moreover, in congressional districts of over 600,000 people, finding individual plaintiffs with standing under *Hays* was not difficult.

Standing issues continue to pose doctrinal problems in election-law cases. In a short *per curiam* opinion, the Supreme Court recently held that individual citizens do not have standing to raise challenges under the Elections Clause, Art I., § 4, cl. 2, at least when the claim is that some state institutional actor has unconstitutionally interfered with the powers the clause grants to state "legislatures." In *Lance v. Coffman*, 127 S.Ct. 1194 (2007), plaintiffs argued that the state Supreme Court, by interpreting the state constitution to bar the state legislature from redrawing congressional districts after the state courts had been forced initially to draw them, had interfered with the power the U.S. Constitution grants to state legislatures. The Elections Clause, recall, holds that the "Manner of Holding Elections for Senators and Representatives, shall be prescribed in each state by the legislature thereof; but the Congress may at any time by Law make or alter such Regulations, except as to the places of chusing [sic] Senators." The Court held that individual citizens did not suffer the kind of individualized injury required to ground standing to claim this violation of the clause.

NOTES ON THE SUBSTANTIVE DEVELOPMENT OF SHAW: RACE CONSCIOUSNESS PER SE OR EXCESSIVE RACE CONSCIOUSNESS?

1. In *Miller v. Johnson*, 515 U.S. 900 (1995), which applied *Shaw* to strike down certain congressional districts in Georgia, a five-member majority of the Court, per Justice Kennedy, suggested that *Shaw* stood for the following principles:

> Our observation in *Shaw* of the consequences of racial stereotyping was not meant to suggest that a district must be bizarre on its face before there is a constitutional violation. Nor was our conclusion in *Shaw* that in certain instances a district's appearance (or, to be more precise, its appearance in combination with certain demographic evidence) can give rise to an equal protection claim, ... a holding that bizarreness was a threshold showing, as appellants believe it to be. Our circumspect approach and narrow holding in *Shaw* did not erect an artificial rule barring accepted equal protection analysis in other redistricting cases. Shape is relevant not because bizarreness is a necessary element of the constitutional wrong or a threshold requirement of proof, but because it may be persuasive circumstantial evidence that race for its own sake, and not other districting principles, was the legislature's dominant and controlling rationale in drawing its district lines. The logical implication, as courts applying *Shaw* have recognized,

is that parties may rely on evidence other than bizarreness to establish race-based districting.

Miller thus held that strict scrutiny is triggered when race has served as the "predominant" factor in the drawing of district lines. It is not apparent whether Justice Kennedy's opinion is intended to be consistent with *Shaw*, an extension of it, or a rejection of the Court's earlier focus on the expressive significance of contorted districts. Particularly noteworthy was that Justice O'Connor joined Justice Kennedy's opinion in *Miller*, but then filed a concurrence reinterpreting the majority opinion:

> Application of the Court's standard does not throw into doubt the vast majority of the Nation's 435 congressional districts, where presumably the States have drawn the boundaries in accordance with their customary districting principles. That is so even though race may well have been considered in the redistricting process.... But application of the Court's standard helps achieve *Shaw*'s basic objective of making extreme instances of gerrymandering subject to meaningful judicial review. I therefore join the Court's opinion.

Are Justices Kennedy's and O'Connor's statements reconcilable? Does Justice Kennedy's "predominance" standard provide meaningful guidance for identifying the constitutional harm in a complex fact pattern such as that found in the Texas congressional redistricting case? For the argument that this predominant motive test cannot be implemented intelligibly in the redistricting context, see Richard H. Pildes, *Principled Limitations on Racial and Partisan Redistricting*, 106 Yale L.J. 2505 (1997); Pamela S. Karlan, *Still Hazy After All These Years*: *Voting Rights in the Post–Shaw Era*, 26 Cumb. L. Rev. 287, 288 (1996).

Because race was the "predominant" factor explaining the configuration of the Eleventh District, the Supreme Court applied strict scrutiny. Although the Court assumed, for the sake of argument, that compliance with section 5 of the Voting Rights Act could provide a compelling state interest that would justify reliance on race, it held that the creation of the Eleventh District was not reasonably necessary under a proper interpretation of section 5. The plans the Department of Justice had rejected had each created two majority-black districts; since neither was "retrogressive," the Department's objections were improper.

After the Court in *Miller* invalidated Georgia's initial districting plan, the state legislature was too politically gridlocked to agree on new districts. The federal court thus designed a remedial plan, which the Supreme Court then upheld. *Abrams v. Johnson*, 521 U.S. 74 (1997).

2. After *Shaw I* and *Miller*, it seemed that strict scrutiny could be triggered by either direct or circumstantial evidence of a line drawer's intent, with district shape and adherence to "traditional districting principles" as particularly powerful circumstantial evidence. The second phase of the equal protection inquiry would then concern the question whether a compelling state interest justifies the otherwise unconstitutional plan.

The Court confronted the question of what counts as a compelling state interest most directly in *Bush v. Vera*, 517 U.S. 952 (1996), a challenge to the creation of three majority-minority congressional districts in Texas. First, we offer maps of the three districts—the majority-black Eighteenth and Thirtieth Districts and the majority Hispanic Twenty–Ninth—that the Court struck down.

TEXAS CONGRESSIONAL DISTRICT 29

TEXAS CONGRESSIONAL DISTRICT 18

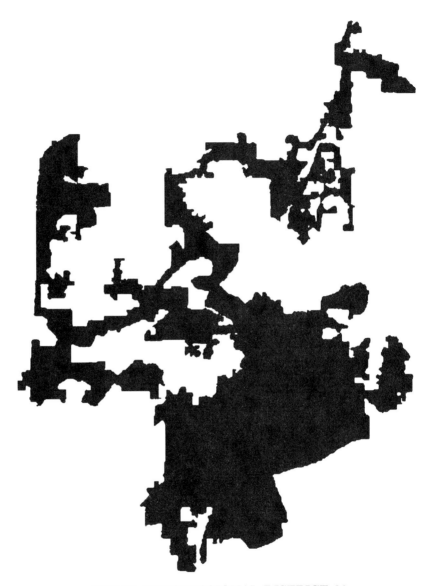

TEXAS CONGRESSIONAL DISTRICT 30

The case produced six different opinions, none garnering a majority. In yet another interesting twist, Justice O'Connor both announced the judgment of the Court and delivered an opinion joined by the Chief Justice and Justice Kennedy, and filed a concurring opinion.

The five justices who agreed that Texas's plan was invalid disagreed as to what triggered strict scrutiny. The Chief Justice, Justice O'Connor, and

Justice Kennedy believed that strict scrutiny was triggered only if race was the most important factor; thus, in a mixed-motive case—where, for example, incumbent protection and other political goals also played a role—strict scrutiny would apply only if the court found that race was "predominant." By contrast, Justice Thomas, joined by Justice Scalia, thought that "all governmental racial classifications must be strictly scrutinized"; thus, *any* use of race rendered a plan constitutionally suspect.

Defenders of the Texas plan—state officials and voters within the challenged districts who intervened to protect them—offered three potential compelling state interests: compliance with the results test of section 2 of the Voting Rights Act, compliance with the discriminatory effects test of section 5 of the Voting Rights Act, and "remedying past and present racial discrimination" more generally.

In response to the first defense, Justice O'Connor's opinion announcing the Court's judgment hedged on the issue of compliance with section 2:

> As we have done in each of our previous cases in which this argument has been raised as a defense to charges of racial gerrymandering, we assume without deciding that compliance with the results test, as interpreted by our precedents, see, e. g., *Growe v. Emison*, 507 U.S. 25, 37–42 (1993), can be a compelling state interest. See *Shaw II*, [517 U.S.] at 915; *Miller*, 515 U.S. at 920–921.... If the State has a "strong basis in evidence," *Shaw I*, 509 U.S. at 656 for concluding that creation of a majority-minority district is reasonably necessary to comply with § 2, and the districting that is based on race "substantially addresses the § 2 violation," *Shaw II*, ante, at 918, it satisfies strict scrutiny.

In her *separate* concurrence, Justice O'Connor was slightly less equivocal. She began by stating that she wrote separately to express her view that "compliance with the results test of § 2 of the Voting Rights Act (VRA) is a compelling state interest," but backpedaled slightly in her discussion:

> In the 14 years since the enactment of § 2(b), we have interpreted and enforced the obligations that it places on States in a succession of cases, assuming but never directly addressing its constitutionality.... Meanwhile, lower courts have unanimously affirmed its constitutionality.... Against this background, it would be irresponsible for a State to disregard the § 2 results test. The Supremacy Clause obliges the States to comply with all constitutional exercises of Congress' power. *See* U.S. Const., Art. VI, cl. 2. Statutes are presumed constitutional, and that presumption appears strong here in light of the weight of authority affirming the results test's constitutionality. In addition, fundamental concerns of federalism mandate that States be given some leeway so that they are not "trapped between the competing hazards of liability." We should allow States to assume the constitutionality of § 2 of the VRA, including the 1982 amendments.

If that is so, the question becomes whether there is a strong basis in evidence for a state's conclusion that the failure to draw a district substantially like the challenged district would subject the state to section 2 liability (see Chapter 9 for the law of section 2). As Justice O'Connor's opinion in *Bush v. Vera* put it:

> A § 2 district that is reasonably compact and regular, taking into account traditional districting principles such as maintaining communities of interest and traditional boundaries, may pass strict scrutiny without having to defeat rival compact districts designed by plaintiffs' experts in endless "beauty contests."

This short passage raises a series of questions. In the first place, should a compact district trigger strict scrutiny in any event? Second, Justice O'Connor's opinion rejected the broad claim that ameliorating racially polarized voting could itself constitute a compelling state interest:

> A State's interest in remedying discrimination is compelling when two conditions are satisfied. First, the discrimination that the State seeks to remedy must be specific, "identified discrimination"; second, the State "must have had a 'strong basis in evidence' to conclude that remedial action was necessary, 'before it embarks on an affirmative action program.'" ... Here, the only current problem that appellants cite as in need of remediation is alleged vote dilution as a consequence of racial bloc voting, the same concern that underlies their VRA § 2 compliance defense.... [S]uch problems will not justify race-based districting unless "the State employ[s] sound districting principles, and ... the affected racial group's residential patterns afford the opportunity of creating districts in which they will be in the majority."

Thus, in the absence of a plausible section 2 claim, the state has no independent compelling interest in dampening the effects of racial bloc voting. Why? Does the three justices' opinion necessarily reflect the assumption that there is a countervailing interest in not using race under any circumstances? Notice Justice O'Connor's use of the phrase "affirmative action program."

Finally, although the three justices agreed that section 5 could provide a compelling state interest for reliance on race, they reiterated that section 5's effects test prohibits only retrogression:

> Nonretrogression is not a license for the State to do whatever it deems necessary to ensure continued electoral success; it merely mandates that the minority's opportunity to elect representatives of its choice not be diminished, directly or indirectly, by the State's actions.

Thus, a plan that goes beyond "maintenance" to afford "substantial augmentation" of the minority's voting strength cannot be justified as necessary or narrowly tailored.

These findings—that the State substantially neglected traditional districting criteria such as compactness, that it was committed from the outset to creating majority-minority districts, and that it manipulated district lines to exploit unprecedentedly detailed racial data—together weighed in favor of the application of strict scrutiny. However, the Court also found that other factors contributed as well to the odd line-drawing in Texas:

> More significantly, the District Court found that incumbency protection influenced the redistricting plan to an unprecedented extent: "[A]s enacted in Texas in 1991, many incumbent protection boundaries sabotaged traditional redistricting principles as they routinely divided counties, cities, neighborhoods, and regions. For the sake of maintaining or winning seats in the House of Representatives, Congressmen or would-be Congressmen shed hostile groups and potential opponents by fencing them out of their districts. The Legislature obligingly carved out districts of apparent supporters of incumbents, as suggested by the incumbents, and then added appendages to connect their residences to those districts. The final result seems not one in which the people select their representatives, but in which the representatives have selected the people"…. This finding receives inferential support from the fact that all but one of Texas' 27 incumbents won in the 1992 elections.

3. In dissent, Justice Stevens attacked the Court by focusing on the design of one majority-white Texas congressional district, the Sixth. A map of this district is below. Justice Stevens described it in these terms:

> District 6 has far less an identifiable core than any of the majority-minority districts struck down by the District Court. To the extent that it "begins" anywhere it is probably near the home of incumbent Rep. Barton in Ennis, located almost 40 miles southwest of Downtown Dallas. From there, the district winds across predominantly rural sections of Ellis County, finally crossing into Tarrant County, the home of Fort Worth. It skips across two arms of Joe Pool Lake, noses its way into Dallas County, and then travels through predominantly republican suburbs of Fort Worth. Nearing the central city, the borders dart into the downtown area, then retreat to curl around the city's northern edge, picking up airport and growing suburbs north of town. Worn from its travels into the far northwestern corner of the county (almost 70 miles, as the crow flies, from Ennis), the district lines plunge south into Eagle Mountain Lake, traveling along the waterline for miles, with occasional detours to collect voters that have built homes along its shores. Refreshed, the district rediscovers its roots in rural Parker county, then flows back toward Fort Worth to the southwest for another bite at Republican voters near the heart of the city. As it does so, the district narrows in places to not much more than a football field in width. Finally, it heads back into the rural regions of its fifth county—Johnson—where it finally exhausts itself only 50 miles from its origin, but hundreds of "miles apart in distance and worlds apart in culture." (quoting *Miller v. Johnson*).

TEXAS CONGRESSIONAL DISTRICT 6

If you were not aware that District 6 was a non-minority district and that Districts 18, 19 and 20 were majority-minority districts, would the differences be apparent to you? Is it true, as Justice Stevens argues in dissent, that "[f]or every geographic atrocity committed by District 30, District 6 commits its own and more"? Would the presence of strangely configured non-minority districts establish a different baseline for defining departures from "traditional districting principles"? For criticism of the way in which the Court uses maps in its racial-redistricting opinions, see Hampton Dellinger, *Words are Enough: The Troublesome Use of Photographs, Maps, and Other Images in Supreme Court Opinions*, 110 Harv. L. Rev. 1704 (1997).

Was District 6 drawn for the purpose of creating a majority-white district or for other reasons? Are there sound constitutional reasons for distinguishing "bizarrely drawn" districts designed for racial purposes rather than political purposes? If not, should *Shaw* be extended to both? Or overruled?

4. Despite *Miller's* apparent rejection of the idea that geographic compactness is the linchpin of *Shaw* claims, compactness has continued to play a central role. First, in deciding whether plaintiffs have shown the predominance of racial considerations, courts rely heavily on the irregularity of district shape: the fact that a district does not adhere to what the courts have viewed as "traditional" standards of compactness raises suspicion. By contrast, if a black community is "geographically compact," then a reapportionment plan that concentrates members of the group in one district should not trigger strict scrutiny in the first place, since a compact majority-black district is fully consonant with traditional apportionment principles.

Second, at the justification stage, in deciding whether section 2 *could* provide a compelling interest for race-conscious districting, a court must again look at compactness. The question here is whether the black community is sufficiently numerous and geographically compact that it would have been able to establish a *prima facie* case under section 2 if no majority-black district had been drawn. Only a reasonable fear of section 2 liability provides the requisite basis in evidence for subordinating other districting principles to racial concerns.

Third, compactness enters the picture again with regard to whether the district that was actually drawn is "narrowly tailored." If it would have been possible to comply with section 2 without doing substantial violence to the traditional principles of districting, including compactness, then a section 2 compliance district that is not compact fails the narrow tailoring test, since it was *unnecessary* to draw a bizarrely shaped district.

Are these three different forms of taking compactness into account three ways of asking essentially the same question? If a district is narrowly tailored, in the sense that it complies with traditional districting principles and provides representation to a geographically compact black community, does *Shaw* require that such a district be subjected to strict scrutiny? Should it be? If so, what is the trigger that alerts a court that strict scrutiny is called for?

At least so far, courts have treated compliance with sections 2 and 5 of the Voting Rights Act as the sole "compelling state interests" that enable districts to survive strict scrutiny. As we point out in Chapter 8, however, the question of amended section 2's constitutionality has not been answered definitively.

B. DENOUEMENT

The course of the litigation over North Carolina's congressional apportionment resulted in a remarkable total of five trips to the United States Supreme Court within the decade. First, before *Shaw*, the plan had been challenged by Republican voters as an unconstitutional political gerrymander. In light of *Davis v. Bandemer*, 478 U.S. 109 (1986), the courts dismissed this complaint; the Supreme Court summarily affirmed in *Pope v. Blue*, 506 U.S. 801 (1992). Then came *Shaw I* and *Shaw II*. After *Shaw II* struck down the state's original districts for the 1990s, the state enacted a new plan in 1997.

Under this new plan, blacks were no longer a majority in District 12; rather, they constituted approximately 47% of the district's total population, 43% of its voting age population, and 46% of registered voters. The 1997 version of the Twelfth District split fewer counties and the distance between its farthest points was substantially reduced. But the district still retained its basic shape along Interstate 85.

Another *Shaw* challenge was brought to the new plan. When the district court ruled in favor of this challenge on summary judgment, a unanimous Supreme Court stepped back in and reversed. The Court found that a full trial was required to decide whether *Shaw* had been violated. *Hunt v. Cromartie*, 526 U.S. 541 (1999). Justice Thomas's opinion for the Court observed that:

> The legislature's motivation is itself a factual question. Appellants asserted that the General Assembly drew its district lines with the intent to make District 12 a strong Democratic district. In support, they presented the after-the-fact affidavit testimony of the two members of the General Assembly responsible for developing the State's 1997 plan. Those legislators further stated that, in crafting their districting law, they attempted to protect incumbents, to adhere to traditional districting criteria, and to preserve the existing partisan balance in the State's congressional delegation, which in 1997 was composed of six Republicans and six Democrats. . . .
>
> Accepting appellants' political motivation explanation as true, as the District Court was required to do in ruling on appellees' motion for summary judgment, appellees were not entitled to judgment as a matter of law. Our prior decisions have made clear that a jurisdiction may engage in constitutional political gerrymandering, even if it so happens that the most loyal Democrats happen to be black Democrats and even if the State were conscious of that fact. Evidence that blacks constitute even a supermajority in one congressional district while amounting to less than a plurality in a neighboring district will not, by itself, suffice to prove that a jurisdiction was motivated by race in drawing its district lines when the evidence also shows a high correlation between race and party preference.

After a full trial, the lower court again found the plan to violate *Shaw*. Just as the entire issue was becoming moot, in light of the new Census, the Supreme Court wrote the final chapter in this saga. By a 5–4 vote, the Court reversed the district court. The majority opinion, written by Justice Breyer, was joined by the other three sitting Justices who had dissented from the Court's earlier *Shaw* cases—Justices Stevens, Souter, and Ginsburg—as well as by Justice O'Connor.

Easley v. Cromartie

532 U.S. 234 (2001).

■ Justice Breyer delivered the opinion of the Court.

In this appeal, we review a three-judge District Court's determination that North Carolina's legislature used race as the "predominant factor" in drawing its 12th Congressional District's 1997 boundaries. The court's findings, in our view, are clearly erroneous. We therefore reverse its conclusion that the State violated the Equal Protection Clause. U.S. Const., Amdt. 14, § 1.

* * *

II

The issue in this case is evidentiary. We must determine whether there is adequate support for the District Court's key findings, particularly the ultimate finding that the legislature's motive was predominantly racial, not political. . . .

We also are aware that we review the District Court's findings only for "clear error." In applying this standard, we, like any reviewing court, will not reverse a lower court's finding of fact simply because we "would have decided the case differently." *Anderson v. Bessemer City*, 470 U.S. 564, 573 (1985). Rather, a reviewing court must ask whether "on the entire evidence," it is "left with the definite and firm conviction that a mistake has been committed." *United States v. United States Gypsum Co.*, 333 U.S. 364, 395 (1948).

. . . That review leaves us "with the definite and firm conviction" that the District Court's key findings are mistaken.

III

* * *

A

The District Court primarily based its "race, not politics," conclusion upon its finding that "the legislators excluded many heavily-Democratic precincts from District 12, even when those precincts immediately border the Twelfth and would have established a far more compact district." . . .

As we said before, the problem with this evidence is that it focuses upon party registration, not upon voting behavior. . . . [W]hite voters registered as Democrats "cross-over" to vote for a Republican candidate more often than do African–Americans, who register and vote Democratic between 95% and 97% of the time. A legislature trying to secure a safe Democratic seat is interested in Democratic voting behavior. Hence, a legislature may, by placing reliable Democratic precincts within a district without regard to race, end up with a district containing more heavily

African–American precincts, but the reasons would be political rather than racial. . . .

B

The District Court wrote that "additionally, plaintiffs' expert, Dr. Weber," showed time and again how race trumped party affiliation in the construction of the 12th District and how political explanations utterly failed to explain the composition of the district.

* * *

The District Court cited two parts of the transcript where Dr. Weber testified about a table he had prepared listing all precincts in the six counties, portions of which make up District 12. Dr. Weber said that District 12 contains between 39% and 56% of the precincts (depending on the county) that are more-than-40% reliably Democratic, but it contains almost every precinct with more-than-40% African–American voters. Why, he essentially asks, if the legislature had had politics primarily in mind, would its effort to place reliably Democratic precincts within District 12 not have produced a greater racial mixture?

Dr. Weber's own testimony provides an answer to this question. As Dr. Weber agreed, the precincts listed in the table were at least 40% reliably Democratic, but virtually all the African–American precincts included in District 12 were more than 40% reliably Democratic. Moreover, none of the excluded white precincts were as reliably Democratic as the African–American precincts that were included in the district. Yet the legislature sought precincts that were reliably Democratic, not precincts that were 40%-reliably Democratic, for obvious political reasons.

Neither does the table specify whether the excluded white reliably-Democratic precincts were located near enough to District 12's boundaries or each other for the legislature as a practical matter to have drawn District 12's boundaries to have included them, without sacrificing other important political goals. The contrary is suggested by the fact that Dr. Weber's own proposed alternative plan would have pitted two incumbents against each other (Sue Myrick, a Republican from former District 9 and Mel Watt, a Democrat from former District 12). Dr. Weber testified that such a result—"a very competitive race with one of them losing their seat"—was desirable. But the legislature, for political, not racial, reasons, believed the opposite. And it drew its plan to protect incumbents—a legitimate political goal recognized by the District Court.

* * *

D

The District Court also relied on two pieces of "direct" evidence of discriminatory intent.

1

The court found that a legislative redistricting leader, Senator Roy Cooper, when testifying before a legislative committee in 1997, had said that the 1997 plan satisfies a "need for 'racial and partisan' balance." The court concluded that the words "racial balance" referred to a 10–to–2 Caucasian/African–American balance in the State's 12–member congressional delegation. Hence, Senator Cooper had admitted that the legislature had drawn the plan with race in mind.

Senator Cooper's full statement reads as follows:

Those of you who dealt with Redistricting before realize that you cannot solve each problem that you encounter and everyone can find a problem with this Plan. However, I think that overall it provides for a fair, geographic, racial and partisan balance throughout the State of North Carolina. I think in order to come to an agreement all sides had to give a little bit, but I think we've reached an agreement that we can live with.

We agree that one can read the statement about "racial ... balance" as the District Court read it—to refer to the current congressional delegation's racial balance. But even as so read, the phrase shows that the legislature considered race, along with other partisan and geographic considerations; and as so read it says little or nothing about whether race played a predominant role comparatively speaking.

2

The second piece of "direct" evidence relied upon by the District Court is a February 10, 1997, e-mail sent from Gerry Cohen, a legislative staff member responsible for drafting districting plans, to Senator Cooper and Senator Leslie Winner. Cohen wrote: "I have moved Greensboro Black community into the 12th, and now need to take [about] 60,000 out of the 12th. I await your direction on this."

The reference to race—i.e., "Black community"—is obvious. But the e-mail does not discuss the point of the reference. It does not discuss why Greensboro's African–American voters were placed in the 12th District; it does not discuss the political consequences of failing to do so; it is addressed only to two members of the legislature; and it suggests that the legislature paid less attention to race in respect to the 12th District than in respect to the 1st District, where the e-mail provides a far more extensive, detailed discussion of racial percentages. It is less persuasive than the kinds of direct evidence we have found significant in other redistricting cases....

IV

We concede the record contains a modicum of evidence offering support for the District Court's conclusion. That evidence includes the Cohen e-mail, Senator Cooper's reference to "racial balance," and to a minor degree, some aspects of Dr. Weber's testimony. The evidence taken together, however, does not show that racial considerations predominated in the drawing of District 12's boundaries. That is because race in this case correlates closely with political behavior. The basic question is whether the legislature drew District 12's boundaries because of race rather than because of political behavior (coupled with traditional, nonracial districting considerations). It is not, as the dissent contends, whether a legislature may defend its districting decisions based on a "stereotype" about African–American voting behavior. . . .

We can put the matter more generally as follows: In a case such as this one where majority-minority districts (or the approximate equivalent) are at issue and where racial identification correlates highly with political affiliation, the party attacking the legislatively drawn boundaries must show at the least that the legislature could have achieved its legitimate political objectives in alternative ways that are comparably consistent with traditional districting principles. That party must also show that those districting alternatives would have brought about significantly greater racial balance. Appellees failed to make any such showing here.

* * *

■ JUSTICE THOMAS, with whom THE CHIEF JUSTICE, JUSTICE SCALIA, and JUSTICE KENNEDY join, dissenting.

* * *

II

Reviewing for clear error, I cannot say that the District Court's view of the evidence was impermissible. First, the court relied on objective measures of compactness, which show that District 12 is the most geographically scattered district in North Carolina, to support its conclusion that the district's design was not dictated by traditional districting concerns. Although this evidence was available when we held that summary judgment was inappropriate, we certainly did not hold that it was irrelevant in determining whether racial gerrymandering occurred. On the contrary, we determined that there was a triable issue of fact. Moreover, although we acknowledged "that a district's unusual shape can give rise to an inference of political motivation," we "doubted that a bizarre shape equally supports a political inference and a racial one." *Hunt*, 526 U.S. at 547, n. 3. As we explained, "some districts . . . are 'so highly irregular that [they] rationally cannot be understood as anything other than an effort to segregate . . . voters' on the basis of race." . . .

[In addition], the court credited Dr. Weber's testimony that the districting decisions could not be explained by political motives. In the first instance, I, like the Court, might well have concluded that District 12 was not significantly "safer" than several other districts in North Carolina merely because its Democratic reliability exceeded the optimum by only 3 percent. And I might have concluded that it would make political sense for incumbents to adopt a "the more reliable the better" policy in districting. However, I certainly cannot say that the court's inference from the facts was impermissible. . . .

Finally, the court found that other evidence demonstrated that race was foremost on the legislative agenda: an e-mail from the drafter of the 1992 and 1997 plans to senators in charge of legislative redistricting, the computer capability to draw the district by race, and statements made by Senator Cooper that the legislature was going to be able to avoid Shaw's majority-minority trigger by ending just short of the majority. The e-mail, in combination with the indirect evidence, is evidence ample enough to support the District Court's finding for purposes of clear error review. . . . Certainly the District Court was entitled to believe that the drafter was targeting voters and shifting district boundaries purely on the basis of race. The Court tries to belittle the import of this evidence by noting that the e-mail does not discuss why blacks were being targeted. However, the District Court was assigned the task of determining whether, not why, race predominated. As I see it, this inquiry is sufficient to answer the constitutional question because racial gerrymandering offends the Constitution whether the motivation is malicious or benign. It is not a defense that the legislature merely may have drawn the district based on the stereotype that blacks are reliable Democratic voters. And regardless of whether the e-mail tended to show that the legislature was operating under an even stronger racial motivation when it was drawing District 1 than when it was drawing District 12, I am convinced that the District Court permissibly could have accorded great weight to this e-mail as direct evidence of a racial motive. Surely, a decision can be racially motivated even if another decision was also racially motivated.

If I were the District Court, I might have reached the same conclusion that the Court does. . . . But I am not the trier of fact, and it is not my role to weigh evidence in the first instance. . . . The only question that this Court should decide is whether the District Court's finding of racial predominance was clearly erroneous. In light of the direct evidence of racial motive and the inferences that may be drawn from the circumstantial evidence, I am satisfied that the District Court's finding was permissible, even if not compelled by the record.

NOTES AND QUESTIONS

1. To what extent is Justice Breyer's account of the Court's prior *Shaw* jurisprudence a recapitulation of the Court's decision and to what extent does it rework those cases? Does *Easley* mark an "exit strategy" designed to allow the Court to step back from the kind of vigorous oversight *Shaw* seemed to foresee? *See* Pamela S. Karlan, *Exit Strategies in Constitutional*

Law: Lessons for Getting the Least Dangerous Branch Out of the Political Thicket, 82 B.U. L. Rev. 667 (2002).

2.   Note that because the Court holds that race was not the predominant factor in the configuration of District 12, the state is never called upon to provide a compelling justification for creating the district.

3.   In a footnote, Justice Thomas "assume[s], because the District Court did, that the goal of protecting incumbents is legitimate, even where, as here, individuals are incumbents by virtue of their election in an unconstitutional racially gerrymandered district." But he states that "this assumption is a questionable proposition." How should the Court treat this issue?

4.   Compare the tenor of Justice Thomas's dissent here with the tone of his discussion of race-conscious districting in *Holder v. Hall*, 512 U.S. 874 (1994), a principal case in the preceding Chapter. Are these opinions consistent with one another in their treatment of the use of race?

5.   Although scholars, politicians, and practitioners had predicted a deluge of *Shaw* litigation following the 2000 census, that particular flood did not eventuate. The overall degree of post-redistricting litigation remained robust. The National Conference of State Legislators website, a major clearinghouse for redistricting-related information—see http://www.senate.leg. state.mn.us/departments/scr/resist/redsum2000/redsum2000.htm— indicated that at least 31 states experienced litigation involving congressional or state legislative redistricting.

In considering why there was not a spate of post–2000 *Shaw* litigation, consider the following issues. First, the *Shaw* "rules" were clearly in place before the post–2000 redistricting began. Thus, plan drawers, legislators, and other interested actors understood from the outset that extensive, explicit discussions of race could trigger strict scrutiny. By contrast, in the post–1990 round of redistricting, actors were operating in a very different legal context: one in which the Voting Rights Act seemed to require race to play an important role. Second, the *Cromartie* Court indicated that protecting incumbents might be a "legitimate political goal" tending to disprove an inference of predominant racial purpose. To the extent that post–2000 majority-minority districts simply reproduced the contours of prior districts, it might be hard to challenge the post–2000 districts as racial gerrymanders rather than incumbent protection. Justice Thomas pointed to this possibility in a footnote in his *Cromartie* dissent:

> I assume, because the District Court did, that the goal of protecting incumbents is legitimate, even where, as here, individuals are incumbents by virtue of their election in an unconstitutional racially gerrymandered district. No doubt this assumption is a questionable proposition. Because the issue was not presented in this action, however, I do not read the Court's opinion as addressing it.

532 U.S. at 262 n.3. Are only newly created districts vulnerable to *Shaw* challenges? Third, consider the interaction of *Shaw* with partisanship. If

minority voters tend to be heavily Democratic (as is true of blacks and many, but not all, Latino groups), then Democrats and Republicans face very different incentives with respect to redistricting. In many cases, Democrats will be tempted to draw less compact districts in minority areas than will Republicans, since Democrats will want to spread, for example, black voters among several districts while Republicans will be happy to "pack" them. Note that many of the states in which successful *Shaw* claims were brought in the 1990s had redistricting controlled, at that time, by the Democratic Party, as in Texas and North Carolina. Does this mean *Shaw* claims are less likely to succeed if Republicans are drawing the districts because district lines will then be less irregular?

Consider the possibility that, from a partisan political perspective, *Shaw* in the 2000 districting and in coming ones might be more of a constraint on Republican-controlled than on Democratic-controlled partisan redistricting. If, as a number of political scientists purport to find, the strategy of setting aside some number of districts to be controlled by African–American voters has, as a byproduct, the effect of making legislative bodies as a whole more Republican, then a purely partisan Republican legislature would prefer to create as many minority districts, with as large minority populations, as possible. The strategy of partisan gerrymandering includes wasting as many votes of the other sides's partisans as possible by concentrating those voters into a few districts. In the South, which has large concentrations of African–American voters, Republicans increasingly control state legislative and executive bodies and hence redistricting. If there are no geographic constraints on the redistricting process, particularly where race is involved, Republicans would be less fettered in pursuit of their optimal partisan strategy, which would appear to include crafting as many districts (baroque or not) to concentrate as many African–American voters as possible.

Might *Shaw* limit not only race-based geographic manipulations of districts, but also the excessive concentration of minority voters in numbers well beyond those needed to ensure minority voters have an equal opportunity to elect candidates of choice? The Voting Rights Act offers only limited protection against such packing; usually, a packing challenge must show that unpacking a district would meet the *Gingles* standard by enabling the creation (in conjunction with other minority voters) of *another* minority-controlled district. Might *Shaw* be applied to mean that race-based excessive concentration of African–American voters beyond levels necessary to ensure effective minority control would violate the Equal Protection clause?

These various interactions of politics and race were illustrated by *Wilkins v. West*, 264 Va. 447 (2002), a challenge to Virginia's 2001 legislative redistricting. *West* was one of a number of cases where plaintiffs chose to bring their challenges in state, rather than federal court. The plaintiffs in *West* chose to bring *only* state-law claims. This had the effect of preventing the defendants from removing the case to federal court. Note that the plaintiffs were not *required* to bring their suit in state court in order to raise state-law claims: a federal court might exercise supplemental jurisdiction under 28 U.S.C. § 1367 over state-law claims and dispose of the case on such grounds. *West* thus illustrates the continued forum shopping that the courts confronted during the post–1990 round of redistricting.

In Virginia, Republicans had been in control of both houses of the state legislature as well as the governorship during the redistricting process. Ostensibly in order to comply with the nonretrogression principle of section 5 of the Voting Rights Act, they passed a plan which continued to contain a significant number of majority-black districts. Democratic members of the state legislature would have preferred a plan that decreased the concentration of black voters in these districts, since the presence of more black voters in adjacent districts might have made those districts more likely to elect Democrats.

The plaintiffs in *West*—Democratic state legislators—relied on two provisions of the Virginia Constitution to challenge the redistricting, including Article I, § 11, which provides in pertinent part that "the right to be free from any governmental discrimination upon the basis of ... race ... shall not be abridged."

With respect to whether the challenged districts reflected excessive reliance on race, the Supreme Court of Virginia noted that the state "readily acknowledged that race was a consideration in drawing the district lines" in order to avoid retrogression under section 5. (Consider whether the use of race to the extent it was used was *required* by section 5 under the subsequent interpretation offered by the U.S. Supreme Court in *Georgia v. Ashcroft*, discussed later in this Chapter). Nonetheless, relying on *Easley v. Cromartie*, the court held that the plaintiffs had failed to show that race was "*the* predominant factor" explaining the challenged districts. The districts followed the outlines of prior districts and were, in several instances, actually more compact than the districts they replaced. In fact, the Court suggested that the fact that particular irregular districts had been in existence for over a decade might actually *create* a community of interest within the district:

> [W]e think it is significant that [the challenged] district's configuration has remained substantially the same for over a decade, allowing development of relationships and communities of interest relative to election of delegates.... Furthermore, House District 74, which was created as a majority black district in 1991, is substantially similar today to its 1991 configuration, and contains 98.3% of the 1991 district which was approved by many of the legislator-plaintiffs in this case.

Finally, the Supreme Court rejected the trial court's determination that the districts contained excessive number of minority voters and thus failed the narrow tailoring prong of the *Shaw* inquiry:

[T]he issue of narrow tailoring is part of the strict scrutiny test, a test not applicable until after a determination is first made that race was the predominant factor in drawing the district. Here, the trial court made no specific factual findings and cited no evidence relative to any of these districts in support of its conclusion that race was the predominant factor in designing each district....

The evidence produced by the defendants showed that these ... districts were all under-populated ..., requiring addition of population, that the redrawn districts were more compact by one or both of the objective tests used, and that the BVAP percentage declined with one exception where the BVAP rose from 56.5% to 58.5%. Finally, the defendants introduced maps and testimony regarding the political voting behavior in the challenged districts which showed a high correlation between race and voting patterns.

6. The Court's heavy reliance on geography in the *Shaw* cases to constrain excessive reliance on race raises a deeper question: To what extent is any individual's conception of political community likely to remain tied to geographic boundaries? For an argument that residency within the geographic territory of local governments has become an outmoded basis for assigning political rights, see Gerald Frug, *Decentering Decentralization,* 60 U. Chi. L. Rev. 253 (1993). Given the nature of contemporary residential, work, social, and commercial patterns, Frug suggests that "[w]e must treat people not as located in one jurisdiction, but as switching center[s] for all the networks of influence within the region that affect their lives."

> Perhaps this emphasis on residency was justifiable when, once upon a time, home, work, family, friends, market, past, present, and future (so we imagine) linked together in one community. But these days some people do not even live at their place of residence: students who spend full-time out-of-state, people who are serving in the military, and business-people who are assigned abroad are residents of the town they are never in. And those people who do live in the area are not found solely at home. Most people spend most of their day in other parts of the region. If the neighborhood where people work deteriorates or their mall closes down, it would affect their lives just as much as an event three blocks away from their residence. In an era when people often do not even know the names of neighbors who live a block away, a person's territorial identity should not be reduced to his or her address.

As a response, Frug offers this novel proposal:

> Consider a plan, for example, in which everyone gets five votes that they can cast in whatever local elections they feel affect their interest ("local" still being defined by the traditional territorial boundaries of city, suburb, or neighborhood). They can define their interests differently in different elections, and any form of connection that they think expresses an aspect of themselves at the moment will be treated as

adequate. Under such an electoral system, mayors, city council members, and neighborhood representatives in the regional legislature would have a constituency made up not only of residents but of workers, shoppers, property owners in neighboring jurisdictions, the homeless, and so forth. People are unlikely to vote in a jurisdiction they do not care about, but there are a host of possible motives for voting (racial integration, racial solidarity, redistribution of wealth, desire for gratification, etc.). Indeed, there is no reason to think that the constituency would be limited solely to those who live in the region.

What do you think of this idea in theory? In practice, what kind of difficulties do you foresee in implementing such a proposal? For a similar analysis of the continuing relevance of geography, see Eben Moglen & Pamela S. Karlan, *The Soul of a New Political Machine: The Online, the Color Line, and Electronic Democracy*, 34 Loy. L.A.L. Rev. 1029 (2001) (suggesting that people's increasing familiarity with "virtual communities" may lead them to think that political aggregation along nongeographic lines may sometimes be appropriate).

7. In addition to *Hunt v. Cromartie II*, the Supreme Court has reached the merits and upheld at least four other plans against *Shaw* claims. *League of United Latin American Citizens v. Perry*, ___ U.S. ___, 126 S.Ct. 2594 (2006); *King v. Illinois Board of Elections*, 522 U.S. 1087 (1998); *Lawyer v. Department of Justice*, 521 U.S. 567 (1997); *DeWitt v. Wilson*, 515 U.S. 1170 (1995), *summarily aff'g* 856 F.Supp. 1409 (E.D. Cal. 1994) (three judge court). In three of these cases, the district lines had not been drawn by overtly political actors: the Florida State Senate district challenged in *Lawyer* was the product of a federal court settlement; the majority-Latino congressional district challenged in *King* had been drawn by a federal court after the state redistricting process deadlocked; and the California state legislative reapportionments challenged in *DeWitt* were the product of three retired California judges appointed by the California Supreme Court as special masters.

Consider the systemic incentives that the Court's decisions in *DeWitt*, *King*, and *Lawyer* might create. If race-conscious districting is effectively permissible when done by courts but not by legislatures, does this turn the Court's original reluctance to enter the political thicket on its head? *Cf.* Samuel Issacharoff, *Judging Politics: The Elusive Quest for Judicial Review of Political Fairness*, 71 Tex. L. Rev. 1643, 1689–90 (1993) (pointing out that roughly one-third of all redistricting after the 1980 census was done either directly by federal courts or under federal supervision but that there were virtually no successful challenges to reapportionments performed by nonpolitical actors, such as distracting commissions); Jeffrey C. Kubin, Note, *The Case for Redistricting Commissions*, 75 Tex. L. Rev. 837, 861–72 (1997) (suggesting that federal courts are more likely to uphold the products of commission-run reapportionments).

8. Does the Supreme Court's deference to judicially created districts extend more generally to districts approved as remedies in section 2 cases? For cases upholding judicially drawn remedial districts against *Shaw* challenges, see *Addy v. Newton County*, 2 F. Supp. 2d 861 (S.D. Miss. 1997), *summarily aff'd*, 184 F.3d 815 (5th Cir. 1999); *cf. Theriot v. Parish of Jefferson*, 966 F.Supp. 1435 (E.D.La.1997).

9. In addition to spurring a deluge of litigation, *Shaw* and its progeny have generated a wealth of scholarship. *See, e.g.*, J. Morgan Kousser, Colorblind Injustice: Minority Voting Rights and the Undoing of the Second Reconstruction 366–455 (1999); T. Alexander Aleinikoff & Samuel Issacharoff, *Race and Redistricting: Drawing Constitutional Lines After Shaw v. Reno*, 92 Mich. L. Rev. 588 (1993); John Hart Ely, *Gerrymanders: The Good, the Bad, and the Ugly*, 50 Stan. L. Rev. 607 (1998); John Hart Ely, *Standing to Challenge Pro–Minority Gerrymanders*, 111 Harv. L. Rev. 576 (1997); Heather K. Gerken, *Understanding the Right to an Undiluted Vote*, 114 Harv. L. Rev. 1663 (2001); Bernard Grofman & Lisa Handley, *1990s Issues in Voting Rights*, 65 Miss. L.J. 205 (1995); Samuel Issacharoff & Pamela S. Karlan, *Standing and Misunderstanding in Voting Rights Law*, 111 Harv. L.Rev. 2276 (1998); Pamela S. Karlan, *The Fire Next Time: Reapportionment After the 2000 Census*, 50 Stan. L. Rev. 731 (1998); Pamela S. Karlan, *Just Politics? Five Not So Easy Pieces of the 1995 Term*, 34 Hous. L. Rev. 289 (1997); Pamela S. Karlan, *Nothing Personal: The Evolution of the Newest Equal Protection from Shaw v. Reno to Bush v. Gore*, 79 N.C.L. Rev. 1345 (2001); Pamela S. Karlan, *Still Hazy After All These Years: Voting Rights in the Post–Shaw Era*, 26 Cumb. L. Rev. 287 (1996); Pamela S. Karlan & Daryl J. Levinson, *Why Voting Is Different*, 84 Calif. L. Rev. 1201 (1996); Daniel Hays Lowenstein, *You Don't Have to Be Liberal to Hate the Racial Gerrymandering Cases*, 50 Stan. L. Rev. 779 (1998); Richard H. Pildes, *The Politics of Race*, 108 Harv. L. Rev. 1359 (1995); Richard H. Pildes, *Principled Limitations on Racial and Partisan Redistricting*, 106 Yale L.J. 2505 (1997); Melissa L. Saunders, *Reconsidering Shaw: The Miranda of Race–Conscious Districting*, 109 Yale L.J. 1603 (2000).

C. A Redistricting Exercise

Imagine yourself in the position of having to redistrict a state in light of the competing concerns of the *Shaw* line of cases and the constraints of the Voting Rights Act. In order to illustrate the difficulties facing well-intentioned redistricting authorities, consider the following problem involving the hypothetical state of New Columbia.

The first map shows the districting of New Columbia after the 2000 Census. This is followed by the revised demographic distributions of the state after the 2004 Census and a map showing the black population concentrations within the state. Your task is to redistrict the state to conform to the applicable law of one-person, one-vote, the Voting Rights Act, and equal protection law. You should be prepared to defend your districting decisions as if they were to be challenged in court.

Keep in mind that this is a streamlined exercise. You are not provided with any data in any form below the county level. Your choices are accordingly constrained to moving around the county building blocks. In the real world, potential redistricters would have information broken down by precincts or census blocks, either of which would dramatically expand the universe of potential districting arrangements. But put yourself in the position of a state legislature in 2004 faced with the problem of redistricting. Further try to keep in mind the added dimension that the *Shaw* line of cases brings to the picture.

© Jerry Wilson
by permission of author

STATE OF NEW COLUMBIA
2000 Plan

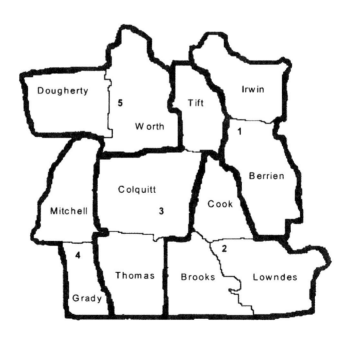

District 1 = Irwin, Berrien = 27.50% Black
District 2 = Cook, Lowndes, Brooks = 24.05% Black
District 3 = Tift, Colquitt, Thomas = 17.38% Black
District 4 = Mitchell, Grady = 30.40% Black
District 5 = Dougherty, Worth = 10.20% Black

STATE OF NEW COLUMBIA
Redistricting Worksheet for 2002

Total Population = 1,000,000

Black Population = 206,500 (20.65%)

White Population = 792,000 (79.2%)

Other Population = 1,500 (.15%)

TVAP (Total Voting Age Population) = 680,850

BVAP (Black Voting Age Population) = 132,773

Number of Seats = 5

Ideal Population = 200,000

STATE OF NEW COLUMBIA

Population

County	TP	BP	TVAP	BVAP
Berrien	75,000	48,750	49,500	32,175
Brooks	135,000	27,000	91,800	17,010
Colquit	50,000	31,500	32,500	21,450
Cook	25,000	13,750	16,250	8,250
Dougherty	25,000	750	17,250	510
Grady	100,000	8,000	70,000	5,280
Irwin	200,000	20,000	138,000	12,800
Lowndes	65,000	9,750	43,550	6,338
Mitchell	50,000	30,000	34,400	18,000
Thomas	100,000	2,000	68,000	13,000
Tift	100,000	3,000	69,000	1,980
Worth	75,000	12,000	51,000	7,680
Total	1,000,000	206,500	680,850	132,773

STATE OF NEW COLUMBIA
Majority Black Areas Shaded

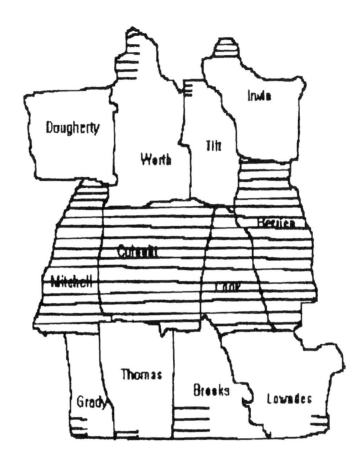

D.   SUBSTANTIVE AND DESCRIPTIVE REPRESENTATION

The Alabama case study at the beginning of this chapter illustrates a second issue that began to emerge in the 1990s and that reached the Supreme Court in the 2000s. In addition to the rise of "bizarrely shaped" districts, the post-*Gingles* districtings had a specific political consequence. As the Alabama example illustrates, a byproduct of concentrating minority voters into "safe" districts is, necessarily, to empty the surrounding districts of minority voters, who typically support the Democratic Party. As a result, those surrounding districts become more white and more conservative, to the point that some previously Democratic districts became Republican ones. Returning to the Alabama example, you will see that while the effect of creating one "safe" black district was, as anticipated, the election of one black member of Congress, a byproduct of this change was that the adjoining district flipped from being held by a moderate white Democratic representative to being controlled by a conservative Republican one, as the district became, at the same time, overwhelming white.

This process, which occurred in many places, raised the issue of what was called the potential tradeoff between "descriptive" and "substantive" representation. Descriptive representation focuses on electing representatives who share certain salient qualities with the electorate they represent—who "look like" their constituents. Substantive representation focuses on electing a legislative body most likely to support the substantive political preferences of some group of voters, such as minority voters. Put concretely, suppose the Alabama experience, repeated throughout many states, helped create a Congress that went from having 24 black members of the House in 1990 to 38 black members in 1994—but that also had the effect of changing the House from being under Democratic to Republican control? (As we noted earlier, the empirical assumptions behind this hypothesis are the subject of debate.) Are minority voters better off with more minority representatives, even if the House overall is less likely to support the substantive policies minority voters prefer? If there is a tradeoff of this sort in city councils, state legislatures, and congressional districts, should substantive or descriptive representation be preferred, and to what extent? And which institutions and actors should make those tradeoffs?

Debates over these issues began in the early 1990s. But they took on greater urgency and intensity after the Republicans gained control of the House in 1994 for the first time in forty years. At that point, analysts sought to determine how much of this change in control might have been affected by the VRA "safe districting" mandate that had been applied for the first time in the 1990s redistrictings. See pages 717 and 786 for some of the relevant studies. The precise numbers continue to be debated. Note that after the 1996 elections, Republicans held a 20-seat majority over the Democrats in the House, but that Democrats recaptured control over the House in the 2006 election.

Was Congress likely to have been aware of these tradeoffs between descriptive and substantive representation when it enacted the 1982 amendments to the Voting Rights Act? Of the magnitude of the tradeoffs?

If Congress had been, would Congress have nonetheless enacted those amendments in the same form? If not, should any of this affect judicial interpretation of the Voting Rights Act?

Entering the 2000 redistricting, there were lively debates about the descriptive-substantive representation tradeoff. The first actors to confront this issue where those with the power to redesign districts, such as state legislatures. In some places, North and South, some legislatures sought to deconcentrate safe minority districts in order to increase the prospects that more Democrats, in the aggregate, would be elected. The Supreme Court then had to confront the legal implications of these tradeoffs, which it did in the following major decision.

Georgia v. Ashcroft

539 U.S. 461 (2003).

■ JUSTICE O'CONNOR delivered the opinion of the Court.

In this case, we decide whether Georgia's State Senate redistricting plan should have been precleared under § 5 of the Voting Rights Act of 1965. . . .

I

A

* * *

All parties here concede that the 1997 plan is the benchmark plan for this litigation because it was in effect at the time of the 2001 redistricting effort. The 1997 plan drew 56 districts, 11 of them with a total black population of over 50%, and 10 of them with a black voting age population of over 50%. The 2000 census revealed that these numbers had increased so that 13 districts had a black population of at least 50%, with the black voting age population exceeding 50% in 12 of those districts.

After the 2000 census, the Georgia General Assembly began the process of redistricting the Senate once again. No party contests that a substantial majority of black voters in Georgia vote Democratic, or that all elected black representatives in the General Assembly are Democrats. The goal of the Democratic leadership—black and white—was to maintain the number of majority-minority districts and also increase the number of Democratic Senate seats. For example, the Director of Georgia's Legislative Redistricting Office, Linda Meggers, testified that the Senate Black Caucus " 'wanted to maintain' the existing majority-minority districts and at the same time 'not waste' " votes.

The Vice Chairman of the Senate Reapportionment Committee, Senator Robert Brown, also testified about the goals of the redistricting effort. Senator Brown, who is black, chaired the subcommittee that developed the Senate plan at issue here. Senator Brown believed when he designed the Senate plan that as the black voting age population in a district increased beyond what was necessary, it would "pus[h] the whole thing more towards [the] Republican[s]." And "correspondingly," Senator Brown stated, "the more you diminish the power of African–Americans overall." Senator Charles Walker was the majority leader of the Senate. Senator Walker testified that it was important to attempt to maintain a Democratic majority in the Senate because "we [African–Americans] have a better chance to participate in the political process under the Democratic majority than we would have under a Republican majority." At least 7 of the 11 black members of the Senate could chair committees.

The plan as designed by Senator Brown's committee kept true to the dual goals of maintaining at least as many majority-minority districts while also attempting to increase Democratic strength in the Senate. Part of the Democrats' strategy was not only to maintain the number of majority-minority districts, but to increase the number of so-called "influence" districts, where black voters would be able to exert a significant—if not decisive—force in the election process. As the majority leader testified, "in the past, you know, what we would end up doing was packing. You put all blacks in one district and all whites in one district, so what you end up with is [a] black Democratic district and [a] white Republican district. That's not a good strategy. That does not bring the people together, it divides the population. But if you put people together on [sic] voting precincts it brings people together."

The plan as designed by the Senate "unpacked" the most heavily concentrated majority-minority districts in the benchmark plan, and created a number of new influence districts. The new plan drew 13 districts with a majority-black voting age population, 13 additional districts with a black voting age population of between 30% and 50%, and 4 other districts with a black voting age population of between 25% and 30%. According to the 2000 census, as compared to the benchmark plan, the new plan reduced by five the number of districts with a black voting age population in excess of 60%. Yet it increased the number of majority-black voting age population districts by one, and it increased the number of districts with a black voting age population of between 25% and 50% by four. As compared to the benchmark plan enacted in 1997, the difference is even larger. Under the old census figures, Georgia had 10 Senate districts with a majority-black voting age population, and 8 Senate districts with a black voting age population of between 30% and 50%. The new plan thus increased the number of districts with a majority black voting age population by three, and increased the number of districts with a black voting age population of between 30% and 50% by another five. The Senate adopted its new districting plan on August 10, 2001, by a vote of 29 to 26. Ten of the eleven black Senators voted for the plan. The Georgia House of Representatives passed the Senate plan by a vote of 101 to 71. Thirty-three of the thirty-four black Representatives voted for the plan. No Republican in either the House or the Senate voted for the plan, making the votes of the black legislators necessary for passage. The Governor signed the Senate plan into law on August 24, 2001, and Georgia subsequently sought to obtain preclearance.

B

* * *

Georgia, which bears the burden of proof in this action attempted to prove that its Senate plan was not retrogressive either in intent or in effect. It submitted detailed [statistical] evidence.... Georgia also submitted testimony from numerous people who had participated in enacting the Senate plan into law, and from United States Congressman John Lewis, who represents the Atlanta area. These witnesses testified that the new Senate plan was designed to increase black voting strength throughout the State as well as to help ensure a continued Democratic majority in the Senate. The State also submitted expert testimony that African–American and non-African–American voters have equal chances of electing their preferred candidate when the black voting age population of a district is at 44.3%. Finally, in response to objections raised by the United States, Georgia submitted more detailed statistical evidence with respect to three proposed Senate districts that the United States found objectionable—Districts 2, 12, and 26—and two districts that the intervenors challenged—Districts 15 and 22....

The United States, through the Attorney General, argued in District Court that Georgia's 2001 Senate redistricting plan should not be precleared.... The United States noted that in District 2, the black voting age population dropped from 60.58% to 50.31%; in District 12, the black voting age population dropped from 55.43% to 50.66%; and in District 26, the black voting age population dropped from 62.45% to 50.80%. Moreover, in all three of these districts, the percentage of black registered voters dropped to just under 50%....

A three-judge panel of the District Court held that Georgia's State Senate apportionment violated § 5, and was therefore not entitled to preclearance ... We noted probable jurisdiction to consider whether the District Court should have precleared the plan as originally enacted by Georgia in 2001, and now vacate the judgment below....

III

A

* * *

Georgia argues that a plan should be precleared under § 5 if the plan would satisfy § 2 of the Voting Rights Act of 1965. We have, however, "consistently understood" § 2 to "combat different evils and, accordingly, to impose very different duties upon the States." *Reno v. Bossier Parish School Bd.,* 520 U.S. 471, 477 (*Bossier Parish I*)…. Georgia here makes the flip side of the argument that failed in *Bossier Parish I*—compliance with § 2 suffices for preclearance under § 5. Yet the argument fails here for the same reasons the argument failed in *Bossier Parish I.* We refuse to equate a § 2 vote dilution inquiry with the § 5 retrogression standard. Georgia's argument, like the argument in *Bossier Parish I,* would "shift the focus of § 5 from nonretrogression to vote dilution, and [would] change the § 5 benchmark from a jurisdiction's existing plan to a hypothetical, undiluted plan." Instead of showing that the Senate plan is nondilutive under § 2, Georgia must prove that its plan is nonretrogressive under § 5.

B

Georgia argues that even if compliance with § 2 does not automatically result in preclearance under § 5, its State Senate plan should be precleared because it does not lead to "a retrogression in the position of racial minorities with respect to their effective exercise of the electoral franchise." *Beer v. United States, supra,* at 141.

While we have never determined the meaning of "effective exercise of the electoral franchise," this case requires us to do so in some detail. First, the United States and the District Court correctly acknowledge that in examining whether the new plan is retrogressive, the inquiry must encompass the entire statewide plan as a whole. Thus, while the diminution of a minority group's effective exercise of the electoral franchise in one or two districts may be sufficient to show a violation of § 5, it is only sufficient if the covered jurisdiction cannot show that the gains in the plan as a whole offset the loss in a particular district.

Second, any assessment of the retrogression of a minority group's effective exercise of the electoral franchise depends on an examination of all the relevant circumstances, such as the ability of minority voters to elect their candidate of choice, the extent of the minority group's opportunity to participate in the political process, and the feasibility of creating a nonretrogressive plan. *See, e.g., Johnson v. De Grandy,* 512 U.S. 997, 1011–1012, 1020–1021, (1994)*; Richmond v. United States,* 422 U.S. 358, 371–372 (1975); *Thornburg v. Gingles, supra,* at 97–100, (O'Connor, J., concurring in judgment). "No single statistic provides courts with a shortcut to determine whether" a voting change retrogresses from the benchmark. *Johnson v. De Grandy, supra,* at 1020–1021.

In assessing the totality of the circumstances, a court should not focus solely on the comparative ability of a minority group to elect a candidate of its choice. While this factor is an important one in the § 5 retrogression inquiry, it cannot be dispositive or exclusive. The standard in § 5 is simple—whether the new plan "would lead to a retrogression in the position of racial minorities with respect to their effective exercise of the electoral franchise." *Beer v. United States,* 425 U.S., at 141.

The ability of minority voters to elect a candidate of their choice is important but often complex in practice to determine. In order to maximize the electoral success of a minority group, a State may choose to create a certain number of "safe" districts, in which it is highly likely that minority voters will be able to elect the candidate of their choice. *See Thornburg v. Gingles,* 478 U.S., at 48–49 (O'Connor, J., concurring in judgment). Alternatively, a State may choose to create a greater number of districts in which it is likely—although perhaps not quite as likely as under the benchmark plan—that minority voters will be able to elect candidates of their choice. *See id.,* at 88–89 (O'Connor, J., concurring in judgment)*; cf.* Pildes, *Is Voting–Rights Law Now at War With Itself? Social Science and Voting Rights in the 2000s,* 80 N.C.L.Rev. 1517 (2002).

Section 5 does not dictate that a State must pick one of these methods of redistricting over another. Either option "will present the minority group with its own array of electoral risks and benefits," and presents "hard choices about what would truly 'maximize' minority electoral success." *Thornburg v. Gingles, supra,* at 89 (O'Connor, J., concurring in judgment). On one hand, a smaller number of safe majority-minority districts may virtually guarantee the election of a minority group's preferred candidate in those districts. Yet ..., such a plan risks isolating minority voters from the rest of the state, and risks narrowing political influence to only a fraction of political districts. *Cf. Shaw v. Reno,* 509 U.S., at 648–650. And while such districts may result in more "descriptive representation" because the representatives of choice are more likely to mirror the race of the majority of voters in that district, the representation may be limited to fewer areas. *See* H. Pitkin, THE CONCEPT OF REPRESENTATION 60–91 (1967).

On the other hand, spreading out minority voters over a greater number of districts creates more districts in which minority voters may have the opportunity to elect a candidate of their choice. Such a strategy has the potential to increase "substantive representation" in more districts, by creating coalitions of voters who together will help to achieve the electoral aspirations of the minority group. It also, however, creates the risk that the minority group's preferred candidate may lose. Yet as we stated in *Johnson v. De Grandy*:

> [T]here are communities in which minority citizens are able to form coalitions with voters from other racial and ethnic groups, having no need to be a majority within a single district in order to elect candidates of their choice. Those candidates may not represent perfection to every minority voter, but minority voters are not immune from the obligation to pull, haul, and trade to find common political ground, the

virtue of which is not to be slighted in applying a statute meant to hasten the waning of racism in American politics.

Section 5 gives States the flexibility to choose one theory of effective representation over the other.

In addition to the comparative ability of a minority group to elect a candidate of its choice, the other highly relevant factor in a retrogression inquiry is the extent to which a new plan changes the minority group's opportunity to participate in the political process. " '[T]he power to influence the political process is not limited to winning elections.' " *Thornburg v. Gingles, supra,* at 99, (O'Connor, J., concurring in judgment) (citations omitted).

Thus, a court must examine whether a new plan adds or subtracts "influence districts"—where minority voters may not be able to elect a candidate of choice but can play a substantial, if not decisive, role in the electoral process. *Cf. Shaw v. Hunt,* 517 U.S. 899, 947, n. 21 (1996) (Stevens, J., dissenting); *Hays v. Louisiana,* 936 F.Supp. 360, 364, n. 17 (W.D.La.1996); *Johnson v. De Grandy, supra,* at 1011–1012; *Thornburg v. Gingles,* 478 U.S., at 98–100 (O'Connor, J., concurring in judgment). In assessing the comparative weight of these influence districts, it is important to consider "the likelihood that candidates elected without decisive minority support would be willing to take the minority's interests into account." *Id.,* at 100 (O'Connor, J., concurring in judgment). In fact, various studies have suggested that the most effective way to maximize minority voting strength may be to create more influence or coalitional districts. [The Court cited numerous of the studies cited in note 7, below.]

Section 5 leaves room for States to use these types of influence and coalitional districts. Indeed, the State's choice ultimately may rest on a political choice of whether substantive or descriptive representation is preferable. *See* Pitkin, *supra,* at 142; Swain, *supra,* at 5. The State may choose, consistent with § 5, that it is better to risk having fewer minority representatives in order to achieve greater overall representation of a minority group by increasing the number of representatives sympathetic to the interests of minority voters. *See Thornburg v. Gingles,* 478 U.S., at 87–89, 99 (O'Connor, J., concurring in judgment); *cf. Johnson v. De Grandy,* 512 U.S. at 1020.

In addition to influence districts, one other method of assessing the minority group's opportunity to participate in the political process is to examine the comparative position of legislative leadership, influence, and power for representatives of the benchmark majority-minority districts. . . . [I]n a representative democracy, the very purpose of voting is to delegate to chosen representatives the power to make and pass laws. The ability to exert more control over that process is at the core of exercising political power. A lawmaker with more legislative influence has more potential to set the agenda, to participate in closed-door meetings, to negotiate from a stronger position, and to shake hands on a deal. Maintaining or increasing legislative positions of power for minority voters' representatives of choice, while not dispositive by itself, can show the lack of retrogressive effect under § 5.

And it is also significant, though not dispositive, whether the representatives elected from the very districts created and protected by the Voting Rights Act support the new districting plan. The District Court held that the support of legislators from benchmark majority-minority districts may show retrogressive purpose, but it is not relevant in assessing retrogressive effect. But we think this evidence is also relevant for retrogressive effect. As the dissent recognizes, the retrogression inquiry asks how "voters will probably act in the circumstances in which they live." The representatives of districts created to ensure continued minority participation in the political process have some knowledge about how "voters will probably act" and whether the proposed change will decrease minority voters' effective exercise of the electoral franchise.

The dissent maintains that standards for determining nonretrogression under § 5 that we announce today create a situation where "[i]t is very hard to see anything left of" § 5. But the dissent ignores that the ability of a minority group to elect a candidate of choice remains an integral feature in any § 5 analysis. *Cf. Thornburg v. Gingles, supra,* at 98 (O'Connor, J., concurring in judgment). And the dissent agrees that the addition or subtraction of coalitional districts is relevant to the § 5 inquiry. Yet assessing whether a plan with coalitional districts is retrogressive is just as fact-intensive as whether a plan with both influence and coalitional districts is retrogressive. As Justice Souter recognized for the Court in the § 2 context, a court or the Department of Justice should assess the totality of circumstances in determining retrogression under § 5. *See Johnson v. De Grandy, supra,* at 1020–1021. And it is of course true that evidence of racial polarization is one of many factors relevant in assessing whether a minority group is able to elect a candidate of choice or to exert a significant influence in a particular district. *See Thornburg v. Gingles,* 478 U.S., at 37 (O'Connor, J., concurring in judgment)*; see also White v. Regester,* 412 U.S., at 755; *Zimmer v. McKeithen,* 485 F.2d 1297 (5th Cir. 1973) (*en banc*).

* * *

C

* * *

Given the evidence submitted in this case, we find that Georgia likely met its burden of showing nonretrogression.... Using the overlay of the 2000 census numbers, Georgia's strategy of "unpacking" minority voters in some districts to create more influence and coalitional districts is apparent. Under the 2000 census numbers, the number of majority black voting age population districts in the new plan increases by one, the number of districts with a black voting age population of between 30% and 50%

increases by two, and the number of districts with a black voting age population of between 25% and 30% increases by another 2.

Using the census numbers in effect at the time the benchmark plan was enacted to assess the benchmark plan, the difference is even more striking. Under those figures, the new plan increases from 10 to 13 the number of districts with a majority-black voting age population and increases from 8 to 13 the number of districts with a black voting age population of between 30% and 50%. Thus, the new plan creates 8 new districts—out of 56—where black voters as a group can play a substantial or decisive role in the electoral process. Indeed, under the census figures in use at the time Georgia enacted its benchmark plan, the black voting age population in Districts 2, 12, and 26 does not decrease to the extent indicated by the District Court.... And regardless of any potential retrogression in some districts, § 5 permits Georgia to offset the decline in those districts with an increase in the black voting age population in other districts. The testimony from those who designed the Senate plan confirms what the statistics suggest—that Georgia's goal was to "unpack" the minority voters from a few districts to increase blacks' effective exercise of the electoral franchise in more districts.

Other evidence supports the implausibility of finding retrogression here. An examination of black voters' opportunities to participate in the political process ... does not indicate retrogression. The 34 districts in the proposed plan with a black voting age population of above 20% consist almost entirely of districts that have an overall percentage of Democratic votes of above 50%. The one exception is proposed District 4, with a black voting age population of 30.51% and an overall Democratic percentage of 48.86%. These statistics make it more likely as a matter of fact that black voters will constitute an effective voting bloc, even if they cannot always elect the candidate of their choice. *See Thornburg v. Gingles*, 478 U.S., at 100 (O'Connor, J., concurring in judgment). These statistics also buttress the testimony of the designers of the plan such as Senator Brown, who stated that the goal of the plan was to maintain or increase black voting strength and relatedly to increase the prospects of Democratic victory.

The testimony of Congressman John Lewis is not so easily dismissed. Congressman Lewis is not a member of the State Senate and thus has less at stake personally in the outcome of this litigation. Congressman Lewis testified that "giving real power to black voters comes from the kind of redistricting efforts the State of Georgia has made," and that the Senate plan "will give real meaning to voting for African Americans" because "you have a greater chance of putting in office people that are going to be responsive." Section 5 gives States the flexibility to implement the type of plan that Georgia has submitted for preclearance—a plan that increases the number of districts with a majority-black voting age population, even if it means that in some of those districts, minority voters will face a somewhat reduced opportunity to elect a candidate of their choice. *Cf. Thornburg v. Gingles, supra,* at 89 (O'Connor, J., concurring in judgment).

The dissent's analysis presumes that we are deciding that Georgia's Senate plan is not retrogressive. To the contrary, we hold only that the District Court did not engage in the correct retrogression analysis because it focused too heavily on the ability of the minority group to elect a candidate of its choice in the majority-minority districts. [W]e must remand the case for the District Court to examine the facts using the standard that we announce today. . . .

The purpose of the Voting Rights Act is to prevent discrimination in the exercise of the electoral franchise and to foster our transformation to a society that is no longer fixated on race. *Cf. Johnson v. De Grandy,* 512 U.S., at 1020*; Shaw v. Reno,* 509 U.S., at 657. As Congressman Lewis stated: "I think that's what the [civil rights] struggle was all about, to create what I like to call a truly interracial democracy in the South. In the movement, we would call it creating the beloved community, an all-inclusive community, where we would be able to forget about race and color and see people as people, as human beings, just as citizens." While courts and the Department of Justice should be vigilant in ensuring that States neither reduce the effective exercise of the electoral franchise nor discriminate against minority voters, the Voting Rights Act, as properly interpreted, should encourage the transition to a society where race no longer matters: a society where integration and color-blindness are not just qualities to be proud of, but are simple facts of life. *See Shaw v. Reno, supra,* at 657.

IV

The District Court is in a better position to reweigh all the facts in the record in the first instance in light of our explication of retrogression. The judgment of the District Court for the District of Columbia, accordingly, is vacated, and the case is remanded for further proceedings consistent with this opinion.

It is so ordered.

■ JUSTICE KENNEDY, concurring.

As is evident from the Court's accurate description of the facts in this case, race was a predominant factor in drawing the lines of Georgia's State Senate redistricting map. If the Court's statement of facts had been written as the preface to consideration of a challenge brought under the Equal Protection Clause or under § 2 of the Voting Rights Act of 1965, a reader of the opinion would have had sound reason to conclude that the challenge would succeed. Race cannot be the predominant factor in redistricting under our decision in *Miller v. Johnson,* 515 U.S. 900, (1995). Yet considerations of race that would doom a redistricting plan under the Fourteenth Amendment or § 2 seem to be what save it under § 5.

I agree that our decisions controlling the § 5 analysis require the Court's ruling here. The discord and inconsistency between §§ 2 and 5 should be noted, however; and in a case where that issue is raised, it should be confronted. There is a fundamental flaw, I should think, in any scheme in which the Department of Justice is permitted or directed to encourage or ratify a course of unconstitutional conduct in order to find compliance with a statutory directive. This serious issue has not been raised here, and, as already observed, the Court is accurate both in its summary of the facts and its application of the controlling precedents. With these observations, I join the opinion of the Court.

■ JUSTICE SOUTER, with whom JUSTICE STEVENS, JUSTICE GINSBURG, and JUSTICE BREYER join, dissenting.

I agree with the Court that reducing the number of majority-minority districts within a State would not necessarily amount to retrogression barring preclearance under § 5 of the Voting Rights Act of 1965. The prudential objective of § 5 is hardly betrayed if a State can show that a new districting plan shifts from supermajority districts, in which minorities can elect their candidates of choice by their own voting power, to coalition districts, in which minorities are in fact shown to have a similar opportunity when joined by predictably supportive nonminority voters.

Before a State shifts from majority-minority to coalition districts, however, the State bears the burden of proving that nonminority voters will reliably vote along with the minority. It must show not merely that minority voters in new districts may have some influence, but that minority voters will have effective influence translatable into probable election results comparable to what they enjoyed under the existing district scheme. And to demonstrate this, a State must do more than produce reports of minority voting age percentages; it must show that the probable voting behavior of nonminority voters will make coalitions with minorities a real prospect. *See, e.g.,* Pildes, *Is Voting–Rights Law Now at War With Itself? Social Science and Voting Rights in the 2000s,* 80 N.C.L. Rev. 1517, 1539 (2002). If the State's evidence fails to convince a factfinder that high racial polarization in voting is unlikely, or that high white crossover voting is likely, or that other political and demographic facts point to probable minority effectiveness, a reduction in supermajority districts must be treated as potentially and fatally retrogressive, the burden of persuasion always being on the State. . . .

II

The Court goes beyond recognizing the possibility of coalition districts as nonretrogressive alternatives to those with majorities of minority voters when it redefines effective voting power in § 5 analysis without the anchoring reference to electing a candidate of choice. It does this by alternatively suggesting that a potentially retrogressive redistricting plan could satisfy § 5 if a sufficient number of so-called "influence districts," in addition to "coalition districts" were created, or if the new plan provided minority groups with an opportunity to elect a particularly powerful candidate. On either alternative, the § 5 requirement that voting changes be nonretrogressive is substantially diminished and left practically unadministrable.

A

The Court holds that a State can carry its burden to show a nonretrogressive degree of minority "influence" by demonstrating that " 'candidates elected without decisive minority support would be willing to take the minority's interests into account.' " But this cannot be right.

The history of § 5 demonstrates that it addresses changes in state law intended to perpetuate the exclusion of minority voters from the exercise of political power. When this Court held that a State must show that any change in voting procedure is free of retrogression it meant that changes must not leave minority voters with less chance to be effective in electing preferred candidates than they were before the change. "[T]he purpose of § 5 has always been to insure that no voting-procedure changes would be made that would lead to a retrogression in the position of racial minorities with respect to their effective exercise of the electoral franchise." *Beer v. United States,* 425 U.S. 130, 141 (1976) (further citations omitted). In addressing the burden to show no retrogression, therefore, "influence" must mean an opportunity to exercise power effectively.

The Court, however, says that influence may be adequate to avoid retrogression from majority-minority districts when it consists not of decisive minority voting power but of sentiment on the part of politicians: influence may be sufficient when it reflects a willingness on the part of politicians to consider the interests of minority voters, even when they do not need the minority votes to be elected. The Court holds, in other words, that there would be no retrogression when the power of a voting majority of minority voters is eliminated, so long as elected politicians can be expected to give some consideration to minority interests.

The power to elect a candidate of choice has been forgotten; voting power has been forgotten. It is very hard to see anything left of the standard of nonretrogression. . . .

Indeed, to see the trouble ahead, one need only ask how on the Court's new understanding, state legislators or federal preclearance reviewers under § 5 are supposed to identify or measure the degree of influence necessary to avoid the retrogression the Court nominally retains as the § 5 touchstone. Is the test purely *ad hominem,* looking merely to the apparent sentiments of incumbents who might run in the new districts? Would it be enough for a State to show that an incumbent had previously promised to consider minority interests before voting on legislative measures? Whatever one looks to, however, how does one put a value on influence that falls short of decisive influence through coalition? . . . The Court gives no guidance for measuring influence that falls short of the voting strength of a coalition member, let alone a majority of minority voters. Nor do I see how the Court could possibly give any such guidance. The Court's "influence" is simply not functional in the political and judicial worlds.

B

Identical problems of comparability and administrability count at least as much against the Court's further gloss on nonretrogression, in its novel holding that a State may trade off minority voters' ability to elect a candidate of their choice against their ability to exert some undefined degree of influence over a candidate likely to occupy a position of official legislative power. The Court implies that one majority-minority district in which minority voters could elect a legislative leader could replace a larger number of majority-minority districts with ordinary candidates, without retrogression of overall minority voting strength. Under this approach to § 5, a State may value minority votes in a district in which a potential committee chairman might be elected differently from minority votes in a district with ordinary candidates.

It is impossible to believe that Congress could ever have imagined § 5 preclearance actually turning on any such distinctions. In any event, if the Court is going to allow a State to weigh minority votes by the ambitiousness of candidates the votes might be cast for, it is hard to see any stopping point. I suppose the Court would not go so far as to give extra points to an incumbent with the charisma to attract a legislative following, but would it value all committee chairmen equally? (The committee chairmen certainly would not.) And what about a legislator with a network of influence that has made him a proven dealmaker? Thus, again, the problem of measurement: is a shift from 10 majority-minority districts to 8 offset by a good chance that one of the 8 may elect a new Speaker of the House?

I do not fault the Court for having no answers to these questions, for there are no answers of any use under § 5. The fault is more fundamental, and the very fact that the Court's interpretation of nonretrogression under § 5 invites unanswerable questions points to the error of a § 5 preclearance regime that defies reviewable administration. We are left with little hope of determining practically whether a districting shift to one party's overall political advantage can be expected to offset a loss of majority-minority voting power in particular districts; there will simply be greater opportunity to reduce minority voting strength in the guise of obtaining party advantage. . . .

III

The District Court never reached the question the Court addresses, of what kind of influence districts (coalition or not) might demonstrate that a decrease in majority-minority districts was not retrogressive. It did not reach this question because it found that . . . the State had not shown the possibility of actual coalitions in the affected districts that would allow any retreat from majority-minority districts without a retrogressive effect. [The dissent then argued that the District Court's findings could be overturned only if clearly erroneous, which the dissent concluded they were not on the record that had been produced in the District Court]....

The reasonableness of the District Court's treatment of the evidence is underscored in its concluding reflection that it was possible Georgia could have shown the plan to be nonretrogressive, but the evidence the State had actually offered simply failed to do that....

The Court's final effort to demonstrate that Georgia's plan is nonretrogressive focuses on statistics about Georgia Democrats. The Court explains that almost all the districts in the proposed plan with a BVAP above 20% have a likely overall Democratic performance above 50%, and from this the Court concludes that "[t]hese statistics make it more likely as a matter of fact that black voters will constitute an effective voting bloc." ...

But ... the Court's argument does not hold up. It proceeds from the faulty premise that even with a low BVAP, if enough of the district is Democratic, the minority Democrats will necessarily have an effect on which candidates are elected. But if the proportion of nonminority Democrats is high enough, the minority group may well have no impact whatever on which Democratic candidate is selected to run and ultimately elected.... Even in a situation where a Democratic candidate needs a substantial fraction of minority voters to win (say the population is 25% minority and 30% nonminority Democrats), the Democratic candidate may still be able to ignore minority interests if there is such ideological polarization as between the major parties that the Republican candidate is entirely unresponsive to minority interests. In that situation, a minority bloc would presumably still prefer the Democrat, who would not need to adjust any political positions to get the minority vote.

All of this reasoning, of course, carries a whiff of the lamp. I do not know how Georgia's voters will actually behave if the percentage of something is x, or maybe y, any more than the Court does. We are arguing about numerical abstractions, and my sole point is that the Court's abstract arguments do not hold up. Much less do they prove the District Court wrong.

NOTES AND QUESTIONS

1. The Court's decision formally addresses only section 5 of the Voting Rights Act. Does the Court's decision also have implications for the kinds of section 2 cases that can be brought?

2. The Court's opinion and the scholarship on which it draws distinguishes among "safe," "coalition," and "influence" districts. What, precisely, do the latter two terms means? How difficult would it be for the administrative preclearance process to depend on these differences? Does the majority give any guidance to the Department of Justice or to three-judge courts in the District of Columbia as to how to assess those tradeoffs? See Samuel Issacharoff, *Is Section 5 of the Voting Rights Act a Victim of Its Own Success?*, 105 Colum. L. Rev. 1710, 1719–20 (2004) ("Overlooked, however, was whether anything like the totality-of-the-circumstances test was feasible in the statutory sixty days for review. The dissent asks caustically about consideration being given to the desire for legislative clout or even the charisma of particular candidates in particular districts. But the key challenge is whether such multifactored inquiries defy 'reviewable administration.' Justice O'Connor does not satisfactorily come to terms with this challenge."). For an account of the Department of Justice preclearance practices arguing that *Ashcroft* could be administered under Section 5, see Meghann E. Donahue, Note, *"The Reports of My Death Are Greatly Exaggerated": Administering Section 5 of the Voting Rights Act After* Georgia v. Ashcroft, 104 Colum. Law Review 1651 (2004).

3. Is there a tension between the Court's decision and its earlier decision in *Presley v. Etowah County Commission*, 502 U.S. 491 (1992) (discussed in Chapter 6)? There, the Court had held that changes "which affect only the distribution of power among officials are not subject to § 5 because such changes have no direct relation to, or impact on, voting." Although "in a real sense every decision taken by government implicates voting," the Court declared that "[a] faithful effort to implement the design of [section 5] must begin by drawing lines between those governmental decisions that involve voting and those that do not." Given *Presley*, a state legislature's decision to strip a representative from a majority-black district of her committee chairmanship would not be subject to section 5 review. But if decreasing or diminishing "legislative positions of power for minority voters' representatives of choice," cannot show the presence of retrogression in minority voters' "effective exercise of the electoral franchise," is there an inconsistency in treating the state's decision to maintain individual legislator's power as evidence of minority voting power?

Later in this Chapter, we discuss the mid-decade Texas congressional reapportionment. Consider whether that plan complied with the section 5 framework laid out in *Georgia v. Ashcroft*.

4. Consider the extent to which the Court's opinion shifts the focus of the section 5 inquiry from the potential results of the new apportionment to the process by which it was produced. Is this shift defensible? In this regard, consider Professor Pildes's argument that it would have been a "perversion" of the Act for the federal government to object to Georgia's plan:

> Here were black and white legislators, willing to make their seats more dependent upon interracial voting coalitions, and yet the Act would have imposed on them more racially homogeneous constituencies. Here was a large contingent of black legislators who, now that they had

entered the halls of legislative power, determined that they and their constituents would have more effective power as part of a Democratic Senate; yet the Act would have required them to become the minority in the senate for the sake of a marginal potential gain in formal black representation. Here was Congressman John Lewis, his life risked in the Selma march to help get the VRA enacted, his seat not at stake, testifying after nearly twenty years in Congress that "giving real power to black voters comes from the kind of redistricting efforts the State of Georgia has made" and that the South has "come a great distance" since a generation ago. And here were black legislators, not demanding safer sinecures for themselves, as officeholders typically do, but taking risks to forge a winning coalition and exercising political agency; yet the Act would have denied these politicians the autonomy to make the hard choices at issue, even with partisan control of government at stake.

Richard H. Pildes, *The Supreme Court, 2003 Term–Foreword: The Constitutionalization of Democratic Politics,* 118 Harv. L. Rev. 28, 92–93 (2004). Note that Representative Lewis strongly supported the 2006 amendment to the Voting Rights Act that was explicitly designed to overturn the Court's ruling in *Georgia v. Ashcroft.* On what basis could Rep. Lewis have supported the Georgia plan, but condemned the Supreme Court's upholding of that plan under the VRA? Was there some more minimal principle available by which the Court could have upheld the plan, other than the principles the Court's decision actually relies on?

In thinking about a process-oriented approach to analyzing retrogression, note that in other contexts, the Supreme Court has occasionally recognized that "[b]ecause of the many facets of human motivation, it would be unwise to presume as a matter of law that human beings of one definable group will not discriminate against other members of that group." *Castaneda v. Partida,* 430 U.S. 482, 499 (1977) (addressing jury selection). Is this view in tension with the very idea of safe minority districting, which assumes that elected minority officials will be the most effective representatives of minority communities? How strong should this concern be when minority elected officeholders are not insisting on making their districts safer, but are agreeing to reduce the minority populations in their districts?

Note that the Court also held in *Georgia v. Ashcroft* that private parties can intervene in a section 5 declaratory judgment action. The district court had permitted four black voters from the objected-to districts to intervene. In granting that motion, the district court found that the intervenors' interests were not adequately represented by the original parties—the state and the United States. Given the fact that the plan the state was seeking to preclear was entirely a product of decisions by Democratic legislators, to say that some black voters objected to the plan raises at least a possibility that the plan was not entirely in the best interest of minority voters—at least as seen by the individual plaintiffs. In a conflict between black elected officials and individual voting rights plaintiffs as to what approach best reflects the interest of the black community in Georgia, how should a court decide? For a discussion of the potential conflict of interest between minority voters and minority elected officials, see Lani Guinier, *The Triumph of Tokenism: The Voting Rights Act and the Theory of Black Electoral Success*, 89 Mich. L. Rev. 1077 (1989).

Predictions about electoral results are inherently *ex ante*. But note that the predictions that underlay black support of the Georgia plan may have been inaccurate along several dimensions:

> The senate majority leader, Charles Walker, who had expressed confidence that the reduction in black population and voting strength in his district would not affect minority voting strength—his district went from being roughly 63 percent in voting age population with a black voter-registration majority to being just slightly over 50 percent in voting age population and minority black in voter registration—was defeated by a white Republican in a racially polarized election. And while Democrats nonetheless retained a 30–26 majority on the basis of the election returns, four white Democratic senators switched in the ensuing fortnight to the Republican Party, giving Republicans control over the Georgia Senate.

Pamela S. Karlan, Georgia v. Ashcroft *and the Retrogression of Retrogression*, 3 Election L. J. 21 (2004).

5. Before *Georgia v. Ashcroft*, similar issues had arisen in lower federal courts. In Tennessee, three of the 33 state senate districts were designed to be majority black in the post–1990 Census redistricting plan. The black voting-age population in Tennessee at the time was 14.4%. Invoking *Gingles*, plaintiffs challenged this plan under § 2, in part on the ground that black voters in six rural counties in west Tennessee had been diluted among several districts, although it would have been possible to concentrate them in a compact 55 percent black district. The state argued that while the creation of a majority black district in west Tennessee would likely increase the number of black state senators, such a change would reduce the overall influence of black voters in the state senate.

In a 1993 opinion, the three-judge federal district court rejected this argument. The court acknowledged that "[c]onceptually it may be true ... that black influence in the legislative process on a statewide basis could be reduced by the creation of one or more additional majority black districts." Nonetheless, the court held that "the language of § 2 and its legislative purposes strongly favor the creation of majority black districts and visible black representation, instead of 'influence' districts ..." *Rural West Tennessee African–American Affairs Council v. McWherter*, 836 F.Supp. 453 (W.D.Tenn.1993) (three-judge court).

While an appeal was pending before the Supreme Court, the Supreme Court decided *Johnson v. De Grandy*, discussed in Chapter 8, and then remanded this case back for reconsideration in light of the decision in *De Grandy*. This time around, the three-judge court reached a diametrically different conclusion. The same panel of judges held that its earlier decision had "deliberately, but improperly, excluded consideration of 'influence districts' when we weighed the 'totality of the circumstances' in deciding whether § 2 had been violated." *Rural West Tennessee African–American Affairs Council v. McWherter,* 877 F.Supp. 1096 (W.D.Tenn.) (three-judge court), *summarily aff'd,* 516 U.S. 801 (1995). The district court reasoned that the *De Grandy* Court's emphasis on the "totality of the circumstances," including its requirement of "a searching practical evaluation of the past and present reality," required courts to conduct a broad inquiry into whether vote dilution was present and to take into account "as many relevant factors as possible," not just those listed in the Senate Report. Relying on the statistical results of the 1992 and 1994 elections, as well as the courtroom testimony of two state senators, the court observed that the large but not majority black populations in the districts in western Tennessee would be able to exert substantial political "influence" in those districts, even if the districts were unlikely to elect a black senator. The district court suggested that any district where a minority group constituted more than 25 percent of the population would be one in which that group possessed legally significant "influence." In light of the three majority-minority districts that existed in the plan, and the likely influence minority voters would have in these other districts, the court held this time that the 1992 Plan did not violate section 2.

Did the Supreme Court's *De Grandy* decision require the lower court's dramatic about face? Does *De Grandy* strongly suggest, if not require, that influence districts can offset "safe" minority election districts? If not, why did the lower court change position? Might the intervening 1994 elections for the United States House have made a difference? In that election, Republicans gained control of the House for the first time in forty years. In the wake of that change, the debates increased regarding whether a necessary byproduct of concentrating minority voters into "safe" districts was to make surrounding districts more conservative by removing more liberal minority voters from those districts.

Consider the following observations about the political dynamic at work in *Rural West*:

> The brooding omnipresence of *Rural West II* is a fact that appears nowhere in the published opinion: the partisan composition of the Tennessee Senate. In February 1995, when *Rural West II* was announced, Democrats enjoyed a one-vote edge. I suspect that the reason Speaker John Wilder, whose district was 21% black, "used his authority to ensure that black senators became chairmen of committees" [as the district court noted] was because those senators were Democrats

and he was too, not because he was responding directly to pressure from constituents. And votes on the Martin Luther King Day bill [a point the district court had emphasized] split largely along party lines as well. Unnoticed by the Rural West II court was a central fact about the passage of the Martin Luther King Day bill: a majority of the senators who voted in favor represented neither majority-black districts nor "influence" districts. The presence of a substantial black community within his district was by no means a necessary determinant of a senator's support, although it might well have been sufficient. Classical logrolling theory—not the concept of black "influence"—is fully adequate to explain the outcome. Black legislators' position as a necessary element of the Democratic majority coalition probably explains more of the affirmative votes than black voters' presence within individual districts. Ironically, within a year after *Rural West II* celebrated black influence within the Tennessee Senate, one of its central preconditions disappeared. In September 1995, two Democratic state senators defected to the Republican Party, and the Republicans gained control of the state senate by a 17–16 margin.

Pamela S. Karlan, *Loss and Redemption: Voting Rights at the Turn of a Century*, 50 Vand. L. Rev., 291, 312 (1997).

A final irony of this saga emerged in 2006. One of the state senators who testified in favor of permitting influence districts to substitute for safe minority districts was Stephen Cohen, a liberal white Democrat who represented one of the districts at issue, a 33% black VAP district. In 2006, Cohen successfully moved up to the United States House, when he was elected from a majority-black congressional district based in Memphis that had been held for over three decades by the most powerful black political family in Tennessee (initially by Harold Ford Sr., then by his son, Harold Ford, Jr., who vacated the seat to run for United States Senate). After Cohen won, he suggested an interest in joining the Congressional Black Caucus, but the Caucus made clear it would not accept a white member.

6. *Implications for the future of the VRA.* Several scholars have argued that *Georgia v. Ashcroft* reflects the Court's conclusion that politics within covered jurisdictions has changed in several fundamental ways that warrant modifying the conventional retrogression analysis, with its focus on the composition of individual districts. But do the changes in politics have broader implications for the continued vitality of section 5?

Consider the following views:

The VRA is a form of national command-and-control regulation for the design of democratic institutions. In the last two decades, the Act mandated an appropriate uniform remedial approach nationwide: safe minority districts for all elections (local, state, and federal) in which voting was racially polarized. That approach made sense when safe districts were essential to the election of black candidates, when the one-party South had no incentive to respond to black voters, and when there were virtually no black elected officials to participate in negotiation over the appropriate structures of democracy itself. Like all command-and-control legislation, the Act did not allow regulated actors latitude to make decisions about how most effectively, in their own diverse contexts, to realize the aims of the Act; those actors were the object of the Act's distrust. And like all regulatory statutes, the VRA must contend with the difficulty of statutory updating as political dynamics change.... [B]ecause the courts have given contemporary social-scientific analysis of voting patterns a central role in the Act's implementation, the Act's interpretation has been more responsive to changing circumstances than many statutes. Nevertheless, courts and policymakers must still interpret facts and make normative judgments about the purposes of democratic representation in constantly changing contexts.

Georgia v. Ashcroft ... can be seen as a form of "democratic experimentalism" in the design of democratic institutions themselves. The decision replaced a single, mandatory remedial regime with one that defines general objectives but leaves representative bodies, with black participation, more flexibility in choosing the means to realize those aims in varied contexts. How much flexibility state and local political bodies should have, and in what circumstances, will be difficult future questions.

Pildes, *supra*, at 95–96. Professor Issacharoff argues that section 5 "is a strong variant of what is often termed the *Carolene Products* view of antidiscrimination law. Although section 5 is obviously a product of congressional rather than court generation, it shares with *Carolene Products'* equal protection law a presumption that a discrete and insular minority group cannot turn to the normal operation of politics to protect its interests." Issacharoff, *supra*, at 1728. If that presumption is no longer true—and Issacharoff expresses significant skepticism that it is, given the critical role black support now plays within the Democratic Party in the South—then the affirmative case for section 5 becomes weaker. Issacharoff then points to another consideration:

[S]o long as the South was solidly Democratic, there was little partisan gain available from controlling the levers of preclearance. The original scope of the VRA was directed primarily to voter eligibility. While in the aggregate bringing black voters into the political process was likely to alter electoral outcomes, my sense is that relatively few preclearance decisions were likely to be directly outcome determinative.... [By contrast, t]he use of preclearance for districting configurations following the decennial census dramatically increases the ability to use preclearance to affect the projected outcomes in terms of partisan representation. I would further suggest, without empirical support as such, that whatever the partisan gain to be had from preclearing or failing to preclear the relocation of voting booths or the change in hours of voting, it is unlikely to be sufficiently obvious or significant as to prompt the intervention of political actors in the normal administrative processes of preclearance. This again raises the question whether the continued application of section 5 might be divided into the administrative side of voting access, where partisan vigilance is likely to be more lax, and matters of extreme partisan concern, such as redistricting, where partisan vigilance is not only likely to be high, but likely to tempt the purported guardians on high in Washington.

Id. at 1730–31.

And another scholar, as well as a former Department of Justice official who enforced § 5, suggests that the Court's recasting of the retrogression test in *Georgia v. Ashcroft* is related to a more general theme:

> [The Court's opinion in *Georgia v. Ashcroft* has] created a substantive standard that helps conform the statute to the Court's recent pronouncements on the scope of Congress's enforcement power as it relates to separation of powers concerns. This is because *Georgia* moves Section 5 away from focusing purely on discriminatory effects, making it possible to persuasively contend that Section 5 no longer represents a wholesale change of the constitutional standard by Congress, but instead involves a standard that more closely approaches the constitutional norm for voting discrimination that has previously been handed down by the Court....

Michael Pitts, Georgia v. Ashcroft: *It's the End of Section 5 As We Know It (And I Feel Fine)*, 32 Pepperdine L. Rev. 265, 269 (2005). By adding a number of additional factors to the retrogression test that go to the motives behind the proposed change,

> *Georgia* does move the Section 5 retrogression test close enough to the constitutional standard to eliminate any separation of powers problem. While nowhere in *Georgia* does the Court explicitly state an intent to move the retrogression standard toward compliance with its recent precedents limiting the scope of Congress's enforcement power, the opinion provides ample evidence for this view....

Id. at 300. Congress's power to enact the Voting Rights Act is considered in greater detail in Chapters 6, 7 and 8. Note that Congress offered findings in the 2006 amendments regarding its views both about changed circumstances and the workability of the *Georgia v. Ashcroft* test.

For a collection of essays by leading legal scholars and political scientists on the issues surrounding whether Section 5 should be renewed, and if so, in what forms and with what modifications to take into account both changing legal requirements and changing factual issues, see The Future of the Voting Rights Act (David Epstein, Richard H. Pildes, Rodolfo de la Garza, and Sharyn O'Halloran eds., 2006). *See also* Pamela S. Karlan, *Section 5 Squared: Congressional Power to Amend and Extend the Voting Rights Act*, 44 Houston L. Rev. 1 (2007); Ellen D. Katz, *Congressional*

Power to Extend Preclearance: A Response to Professor Karlan, 44 Houston L. Rev. 33 (2007).

7. The larger political context: With respect to the partisan political consequences of "safe" minority districting, both political parties wavered on the issue. In the 1980s, the Republican Party, under the leadership of Lee Atwater and Benjamin Ginsburg, at first actively supported the creation of minority districts as a way of undermining the electoral base of Democratic incumbents. In *Shaw*, however, the Republican Party filed an amicus brief urging that the black-majority districts be struck down. What might account for this change in approach? For the argument that the optimal partisan strategy for Republicans is to support minority districts, but to require that they be compact, see David Lublin, The Paradox of Representation 98–119 (1997).

The Democratic Party was divided over the question of majority-minority districts as well. There is substantial evidence that the creation of majority-minority districts was an indispensible element in laying the foundation for significant minority legislative representation. The early studies on the role of minority districting in providing for black and Hispanic representation in Congress are summarized in Richard H. Pildes, *The Politics of Race*, 108 Harv. L. Rev. 1359 (1995) (reviewing Quiet Revolution in the South: The Impact of the Voting Rights Act, 1965–1990 (Chandler Davidson & Bernard Grofman, eds. 1994.)) While the Democratic Party drew considerable support from minority voters and welcomed the expanded minority congressional delegation, there was significant rumbling that the creation of heavily-minority districts was responsible for the Republican rise to power in Congress. Studies of congressional elections through the 1990s largely confirmed that the creation of majority-minority districts continues to be necessary to elect minorities to Congress in all but token numbers. At the same time, recent statewide races raise new questions about these patterns. In the fall 2006 elections, a black Democratic candidate, Harold Ford, Jr., narrowly lost an extremely competitive race for Senator from Tennessee. In the border state of Maryland, another black Senate candidate, this one a Republican, Michael S. Steele, also lost a close contest. But Tennessee has been a consistently Republican state in recent national elections and Maryland, a consistently Democratic one. Ford and Steele, black Democrat and Republican, seemed to have fared as well as white national candidates do today in their states (the black voting-age populations of Tennessee and Maryland are, respectively, 14.8% and 27.1%). Ford ran better than did any white Democrat in Tennessee for the Senate or Presidency in the 2000s, with the exception of Al Gore, who ran almost as well in his home state in 2000 as Ford did in 2006. Similarly, Steele did better in Maryland than any white Republican has for Senate or the Presidency since 1998. At the time this casebook goes to press, even more visible is the enormous attention and enthusiasm for Senator Barack Obama's presidential campaign, whatever the final outcome might be.

In a study of all congressional elections between 1972 and 1994, David Lublin found that in districts without Hispanic voters, the probability of the district electing a black congressperson is 8% when the district is 40% black in total population, 28% when the district is 45% black, 60% when the district is 50% black, and 86% when the district is 55% black. The addition of Hispanic voters typically changed these figures considerably; thus, when a district is 45% black and 20% Hispanic, the probability of electing a black representative goes up to 59%. In terms of the election of Hispanic representatives, a crucial factor was what portion of the Hispanic residents have lived in the state for at least five years; length of residence affected citizenship, registration, and actual turnout to vote. When 95% of the residents have lived in the state for at least five years, a district with 45% Hispanic population had a 61% probability of electing a Hispanic representative. Thus, Hispanics found it easier to get elected than blacks, although polarized voting was significant with respect to both groups, David Lublin, *The Election of African Americans and Latinos to the U.S. House of Representatives, 1972–1994,* 25 Am. Pol. Q. 269 (1997). Another more limited study offered additional insight into racial polarization in voting, but was marred by its failure to separate out Hispanic voters from Anglo voters. *See* Charles Cameron, David Epstein, and Sharyn O'Halloran, *Do Majority–Minority Districts Maximize Substantive Black Representation in Congress,* 90 Am. Pol. Sci. Rev. 794 (1996). This study, which examined only congressional elections in 1992, concluded that to get to the 50 percent probability level of electing a black Democratic congressional candidate, districts in the South needed a black voting age population (BVAP) of 40.3 percent; in the Northwest, a BVAP of 47.3 percent; and in the Northeast, a BVAP of 28.3 percent. These data were consistent with Lublin's, but by grouping Anglo and Hispanic voters together, they fail to signal the crucial role of Hispanic voters in the election prospects of black candidates (note that while blacks and Hispanics have often been coalitional partners in national politics, such as for congressional races, recent developments suggest that in major cities for local elections, Hispanic and black voters now vote antagonistically. Peter Beinart, *New Bedfellows,* The New Republic 22 (Aug. 11/18, 1997)).

Lublin's work from 1997 concludes that there are significant regional variations in the extent to which creating more minority districts leads to electing more conservative representatives in surrounding districts. He finds that "[r]acial redistricting tends to make surrounding districts more conservative and likely to elect Republicans in the South, but not the North"—due to the different geographic dispersion of black voters in the two regions and differing ideology of white voters. He also finds that the net policy effect of replacing two white Democratic congresspersons with one Republican and one minority Democrat is to make the overall representation more conservative; the typically greater liberalism of minority representatives compared to white Democratic ones is more than offset by the greater conservativism of Republicans over white Democrats. Lublin further finds that above a 40% black population, congressional representatives do not become significantly more liberal as the black population is increased further. Therefore, Lublin concludes that "[m]apmakers desiring solely to maximize black substantive representation should give priority to protecting Democratic seats over drawing additional districts greater than 40 percent black ... maximizing the number of Democratic seats, and thus black substantive representation, would entail dismantling many black majority districts." Lublin, *Paradoxes of Representation,* at 99.

However, one study of voting patterns during the later part of the 1990s suggests that that significantly lower black populations, in the 35–40% range, might now have a 50% probability of electing minority-preferred candidates, even in southern jurisdictions, particularly where the black candidate is able to run as an incumbent. *See* Bernard Grofman, Lisa Handley, & David Lublin, *Drawing Effective Minority Districts: A Conceptual Framework and Some Empirical Evidence,* 79 N.C. L. Rev. 1383 (2001) (finding that black voting age populations of 35–40% are often sufficient to give minority voters an equal opportunity to elect candidates of their choice). The reason has to do with the rise of two-party competition in the South. As the Republican Party broke the one-party Democratic Party monopoly that had characterized Southern politics since disfranchisement, many white voters who had been Democrats became Republicans. Many new southern voters, either transplants from other regions of the country or younger individuals, were also Republicans. Moreover, within the Democratic Party, a significant segment of white voters became increasingly willing to support minority candidates. Because black voters now make up such a significant segment of the Democratic Party's support in many Southern jurisdictions, black voters can have meaningful influence over who wins the Democratic primary. If the jurisdiction is more Democratic than Republican on the day of the general election, this means winning the Democratic primary is the key to winning the general election (assuming Democratic Party general election voters do not abandon the Democratic nominee because he or she is a minority candidate). Finally, many of the districts that were 35–40 %black at the end of the 1990s were the product of challenge under *Shaw* and had had a black incumbent run for re-election as an incumbent. The net result, Grofman, Handley, and Lublin find, is that 35–40% minority populations appear sufficient today to enable minority candidates to have a 50–50 chance of being elected in many of the jurisdictions where this had previously been thought not likely.

The study by Cameron and his colleagues also notes the importance of regional variation. That study concludes that, outside the South, the best circumstance for maximizing the political influence of black voters is when black voters are distributed equally across all districts. That is, two districts with 25 percent BVAP will be better, in terms of influence on civil rights legislation, than one district that is 50 percent BVAP and one that is 0 percent BVAP. "Majority-minority districts make little sense in this context, unless they confer significant nonpolicy benefits, as they create greater possibilities for electing Republicans in other districts." Cameron *et al, supra,* at 808. Within the South, this study confirms that the relationship between BVAP and political influence is more complex. While representatives are generally more liberal as the BVAP of their districts goes up, Cameron and his colleagues argue that this responsiveness flattens out when the BVAP is between 25–35 percent. Above those levels, significant improvements in responsiveness do not occur. Thus, in terms of influence on policy, their suggestion is there is no reason to construct districts with BVAP between 25–35 percent. Note though that by 1992, there are few districts with BVAP in this range, particularly in the South, so the analysis here depends less on direct data than statistical inferences. Putting these effects together, the study concludes that in the South, the approach that maximizes the influence of black voters is to construct as many districts as possible that are around 47 percent black, with the remaining black voters distributed as evenly as possible over other districts.

Suppose such districts produced a legislative body whose membership was disproportionately, or even overwhelmingly, white. Is there an important value to having a descriptively representative legislature? Note the extent to which a body's agenda may be influenced by the presence of a few vigorous partisans of a group's position. A few strong partisans may have more influence than a number of lukewarm supporters. How can, or should, the Voting Rights Act take into account these issues?

How should these findings affect one's view about whether the Voting Rights Act is good public policy with respect to its conception of vote dilution? How should these findings affect judicial interpretation of the Act?

8. In 2006, Congress reauthorized section 5 for another 25 years. As part of that process, it decided to "fix" *Georgia v. Ashcroft* by amending section 5 to address the Court's decision. There is considerable dispute, however, about how to interpret the amended version that Congress enacted. For full coverage of these issues, see Chapter 6.

E. Concerns About Racial Essentialism

The Court's opinion in *Georgia v. Ashcroft* also reflected a growing judicial concern with the extent to which the VRA as applied in the 1990s and 2000s involved a kind of "racial essentialism." By this, the Court meant policies based too quickly and without sufficient justification on the view that voters of a certain race or ethnicity vote alike and have common political interests. Concerns of this sort had long animated critics of the VRA, and they might underlie cases like *Shaw* as well. This concern found its most direct judicial expression in the Court's most recent foray into the VRA, a case focused primarily on whether Texas' mid-decade redistricting was an unconstitutional partisan gerrymander. The Court rejected that claim in portions of the opinion reproduced in Chapter 10. But the case also presented important VRA claims, some of which the Court accepted, some of which it rejected, in an opinion that sheds important light on how the Court views the frontiers of the VRA today.

League of United Latin of United Latin American Citizens v. Perry

___ U.S. ___, 126 S.Ct. 2594 (2006).

■ JUSTICE KENNEDY announced the judgment of the Court and delivered the opinion of the Court with respect to Par[t] III, [and] an opinion with respect to Parts I and IV, in which THE CHIEF JUSTICE and JUSTICE ALITO join. . . .

I

To set out a proper framework for the case, we first recount the history of the litigation and recent districting in Texas. An appropriate starting point is not the reapportionment in 2000 but the one from the census in 1990.

The 1990 census resulted in a 30–seat congressional delegation for Texas, an increase of 3 seats over the 27 representatives allotted to the State in the decade before. In 1991 the Texas Legislature drew new district lines. At the time, the Democratic Party controlled both houses in the state legislature, the governorship, and 19 of the State's 27 seats in Congress. Yet change appeared to be on the horizon. In the previous 30 years the Democratic Party's post-Reconstruction dominance over the Republican Party had eroded, and by 1990 the Republicans received 47% of the statewide vote, while the Democrats received 51%.

Faced with a Republican opposition that could be moving toward majority status, the state legislature drew a congressional redistricting plan designed to favor Democratic candidates. Using then-emerging computer technology to draw district lines with artful precision, the legislature enacted a plan later described as the "shrewdest gerrymander of the 1990s.". . .

The 1990's were years of continued growth for the Texas Republican Party, and by the end of the decade it was sweeping elections for statewide office. Nevertheless, despite carrying 59% of the vote in statewide elections in 2000, the Republicans only won 13 congressional seats to the Democrats' 17.

These events likely were not forgotten by either party when it came time to draw congressional districts in conformance with the 2000 census and to incorporate two additional seats for the Texas delegation. The Republican Party controlled the governorship and the State Senate; it did not yet control the State House of Representatives, however. As so constituted, the legislature was unable to pass a redistricting scheme, resulting in litigation and the necessity of a court-ordered plan [Plan 1151C] to comply with the Constitution's one-person, one-vote requirement. . . . [See *Balderas* v. *Texas*, 2001 U.S. Dist. LEXIS 25740 (E.D. Tex. 2001), *aff'd*, 536 U.S. 919 (2002). Because of the criteria the court took into account] "the practical effect of this effort was to leave the 1991 Democratic Party gerrymander largely in place. . . ."

The continuing influence of a court-drawn map that "perpetuated much of [the 1991] gerrymander," was not lost on Texas Republicans when, in 2003, they gained control of the State House of Representatives and, thus, both houses of the legislature. The Republicans in the legislature "set out to increase their representation in the congressional delegation." After a protracted partisan struggle, during which Democratic legislators left the State for a time to frustrate quorum requirements, the legislature enacted a new congressional districting map in October 2003. It is called Plan 1374C. The 2004 congressional elections did not disappoint the plan's drafters. Republicans won 21 seats to the Democrats' 11, while also obtaining 58% of the vote in statewide races against the Democrats' 41%. . . .

* * *

III

Plan 1374C made changes to district lines in south and west Texas that appellants challenge as violations of § 2 of the Voting Rights Act and the Equal Protection Clause of the Fourteenth Amendment. The most significant changes occurred to District 23, which—both before and after the redistricting—covers a large land area in west Texas, and to District 25, which earlier included Houston but now includes a different area, a north-south strip from Austin to the Rio Grande Valley.

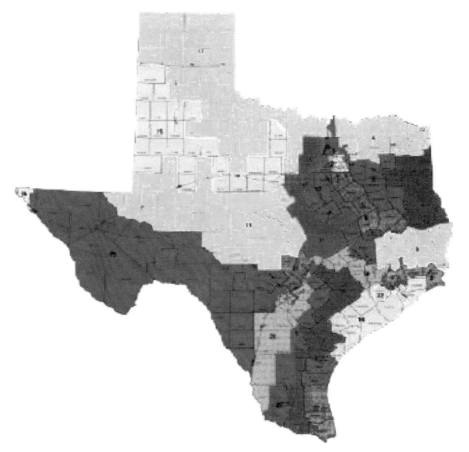

After the 2002 election, it became apparent that District 23 as then drawn had an increasingly powerful Latino population that threatened to oust the incumbent Republican, Henry Bonilla. Before the 2003 redistricting, the Latino share of the citizen voting-age population was 57.5%, and Bonilla's support among Latinos had dropped with each successive election since 1996. In 2002, Bonilla captured only 8% of the Latino vote, and 51.5% of the overall vote. Faced with this loss of voter support, the legislature acted to protect Bonilla's incumbency by changing the lines—and hence the population mix—of the district. To begin with, the new plan divided Webb County and the city of Laredo, on the Mexican border, that formed the county's population base. Webb County, which is 94% Latino, had previously rested entirely within District 23; under the new plan, nearly 100,000 people were shifted into neighboring District 28.... To replace the numbers District 23 lost, the State added voters in counties comprising a largely Anglo, Republican area in central Texas. In the newly drawn district, the Latino share of the citizen voting-age population dropped to 46%, though the Latino share of the total voting-age population remained just over 50%.

These changes required adjustments elsewhere, of course, so the State inserted a third district between the two districts to the east of District 23

... New District 25 is a long, narrow strip that winds its way from McAllen and the Mexican border towns in the south to Austin, in the center of the State and 300 miles away. In between it includes seven full counties, but 77% of its population resides in split counties at the northern and southern ends. Of this 77%, roughly half reside in Hidalgo County, which includes McAllen, and half are in Travis County, which includes parts of Austin. The Latinos in District 25, comprising 55% of the district's citizen voting-age population, are also mostly divided between the two distant areas, north and south. . . .

The District Court summed up the purposes underlying the redistricting in south and west Texas: "The change to Congressional District 23 served the dual goal of increasing Republican seats in general and protecting Bonilla's incumbency in particular, with the additional political nuance that Bonilla would be reelected in a district that had a majority of Latino voting age population—although clearly not a majority of citizen voting age population and certainly not an effective voting majority." The goal in creating District 25 was just as clear: "to avoid retrogression under § 5" of the Voting Rights Act given the reduced Latino voting strength in District 23.

* * *

B

Appellants argue that the changes to District 23 diluted the voting rights of Latinos who remain in the district. . . .

To begin the *Gingles* analysis, it is evident that the second and third *Gingles* preconditions—cohesion among the minority group and bloc voting among the majority population—are present in District 23. The District Court found "racially polarized voting" in south and west Texas, and indeed "throughout the State." The polarization in District 23 was especially severe: 92% of Latinos voted against Bonilla in 2002, while 88% of non-Latinos voted for him. Furthermore, the projected results in new District 23 show that the Anglo citizen voting-age majority will often, if not always, prevent Latinos from electing the candidate of their choice in the district. . . .

The first *Gingles* factor requires that a group be "sufficiently large and geographically compact to constitute a majority in a single-member district." Latinos in District 23 could have constituted a majority of the citizen voting-age population in the district, and in fact did so under Plan 1151C. Though it may be possible for a citizen voting-age majority to lack real electoral opportunity, the Latino majority in old District 23 did possess electoral opportunity protected by § 2.

While the District Court stated that District 23 had not been an effective opportunity district under Plan 1151C, it recognized the district was "moving in that direction." . . . Since the redistricting prevented the immediate success of the emergent Latino majority in District 23 and that "there was a denial of opportunity in the real sense of that term."

Plan 1374C's version of District 23, by contrast, "is unquestionably not a Latino opportunity district." Latinos, to be sure, are a bare majority of the voting-age population in new District 23, but only in a hollow sense, for the parties agree that the relevant numbers must include citizenship. This approach fits the language of § 2 because only eligible voters affect a group's opportunity to elect candidates. In sum, appellants have established that Latinos could have had an opportunity district in District 23 had its lines not been altered and that they do not have one now.

Considering the district in isolation, the three *Gingles* requirements are satisfied. The State argues, nonetheless, that it met its § 2 obligations by creating new District 25 as an offsetting opportunity district. It is true, of course, that "States retain broad discretion in drawing districts to comply with the mandate of § 2." *Shaw* v. *Hunt,* 517 U.S. 899, 917, n. 9 (1996) *(Shaw II)*. This principle has limits, though. The Court has rejected the premise that a State can always make up for the less-than-equal opportunity of some individuals by providing greater opportunity to others. As set out below, these conflicting concerns are resolved by allowing the State to use one majority-minority district to compensate for the absence of another only when the racial group in each area had a § 2 right and both could not be accommodated. . . .

Simply put, the State's creation of an opportunity district for those without a § 2 right offers no excuse for its failure to provide an opportunity district for those with a § 2 right. And since there is no § 2 right to a district that is not reasonably compact, the creation of a noncompact district does not compensate for the dismantling of a compact opportunity district. . . .

The District Court . . . failed to decide whether District 25 was reasonably compact for § 2 purposes. It recognized there was a 300–mile gap between the Latino communities in District 25, and a similarly large gap between the needs and interests of the two groups. After making these observations, however, it did not make any finding about compactness. It ruled instead that, despite these concerns, District 25 would be an effective Latino opportunity district because the combined voting strength of both Latino groups would allow a Latino-preferred candidate to prevail in elections. The District Court's general finding of effectiveness cannot substitute for the lack of a finding on compactness. . . .

The Latinos in the Rio Grande Valley and those in Central Texas, [the district court] found, are "disparate communities of interest," with "differences in socio-economic status, education, employment, health, and other characteristics." The court's conclusion that the relative smoothness of the district lines made the district compact, despite this combining of discrete communities of interest, is inapposite because the court analyzed the issue only for equal protection purposes. In the equal protection context, compactness focuses on the contours of district lines to determine whether race was the predominant factor in drawing those lines. Under § 2, by contrast, the injury is vote dilution, so the compactness inquiry embraces different considerations. "The first *Gingles* condition refers to the compactness of the minority population, not to the compactness of the contested district." *Bush v. Vera*, 517 U.S. 952, 997 (1996)....

While no precise rule has emerged governing § 2 compactness, the "inquiry should take into account 'traditional districting principles such as maintaining communities of interest and traditional boundaries.' " ... [A] State may not "assume from a group of voters' race that they 'think alike, share the same political interests, and will prefer the same candidates at the polls.' " *Miller* (quoting *Shaw* v. *Reno*). In the absence of this prohibited assumption, there is no basis to believe a district that combines two far-flung segments of a racial group with disparate interests provides the opportunity that § 2 requires or that the first *Gingles* condition contemplates....

As witnesses who know the south and west Texas culture and politics testified, the districting in Plan 1374C "could make it more difficult for thinly financed Latino-preferred candidates to achieve electoral success and to provide adequate and responsive representation once elected." We do not question the District Court's finding that the groups' combined voting strength would enable them to elect a candidate each prefers to the Anglos' candidate of choice. We also accept that in some cases members of a racial group in different areas—for example, rural and urban communities—could share similar interests and therefore form a compact district if the areas are in reasonably close proximity. When, however, the only common index is race and the result will be to cause internal friction, the State cannot make this a remedy for a § 2 violation elsewhere. We emphasize it is the enormous geographical distance separating the Austin and Mexican-border communities, coupled with the disparate needs and interests of these populations—not either factor alone—that renders District 25 noncompact for § 2 purposes....

Since District 25 is not reasonably compact, Plan 1374C contains only five reasonably compact Latino opportunity districts. Plan 1151C, by contrast, created six such districts. The District Court did not find, and the State does not contend, that any of the Latino opportunity districts in Plan 1151C are noncompact....

Appellants have thus satisfied all three *Gingles* requirements as to District 23, and the creation of new District 25 does not remedy the problem.

C

We proceed now to the totality of the circumstances, and first to the proportionality inquiry, comparing the percentage of total districts that are Latino opportunity districts with the Latino share of the citizen voting-age population. As explained in *De Grandy*, proportionality is "a relevant fact in the totality of circumstances." 512 U.S., at 1000. It does not, however, act as a "safe harbor" for States in complying with § 2....

We conclude the answer in these cases is to look at proportionality statewide. The State contends that the seven districts in south and west Texas correctly delimit the boundaries for proportionality because that is the only area of the State where reasonably compact Latino opportunity districts can be drawn. This argument, however, misunderstands the role of proportionality. We have already determined, under the first *Gingles* factor, that another reasonably compact Latino district can be drawn. The question now is whether the absence of that additional district constitutes impermissible vote dilution. This inquiry requires an " 'intensely local appraisal' " of the challenged district....

The role of proportionality is not to ... allow the State to trade off the rights of some against the rights of others. Instead, it provides some evidence of whether "the political processes leading to nomination or election in the State or political subdivision are not equally open to participation." 42 U.S.C. § 1973(b).... Particularly given the presence of racially polarized voting—and the possible submergence of minority votes—throughout Texas, it makes sense to use the entire State in assessing proportionality.

[The Court found that only sixteen percent of districts were Latino opportunity districts whereas Latinos made up twenty-two percent of the Texas' citizen voting-age population.] Even if Plan 1374C's disproportionality were deemed insubstantial, that consideration would not overcome the other evidence of vote dilution for Latinos in District 23....

Latinos' diminishing electoral support for Bonilla indicates their belief he was "unresponsive to the particularized needs of the members of the minority group." In essence the State took away the Latinos' opportunity because Latinos were about to exercise it. This bears the mark of intentional discrimination that could give rise to an equal protection violation. Even if we accept the District Court's finding that the State's action was taken primarily for political, not racial, reasons, the redrawing of the district lines was damaging to the Latinos in District 23. The State not only made fruitless the Latinos' mobilization efforts but also acted against those Latinos who were becoming most politically active, dividing them with a district line through the middle of Laredo....

The Court has noted that incumbency protection can be a legitimate factor in districting, see *Karcher* v. *Daggett*, [462 U.S. at 725,] but experience teaches that incumbency protection can take various forms, not all of them in the interests of the constituents. If the justification for incumbency protection is to keep the constituency intact so the officeholder is accountable for promises made or broken, then the protection seems to accord with concern for the voters. If, on the other hand, incumbency protection means excluding some voters from the district simply because they are likely to

vote against the officeholder, the change is to benefit the officeholder, not the voters. By purposely redrawing lines around those who opposed Bonilla, the state legislature took the latter course. . . .

D

Because we hold Plan 1374C violates § 2 in its redrawing of District 23, we do not address appellants' claims that the use of race and politics in drawing that district violates . . . equal protection. We also need not confront appellants' claim of an equal protection violation in the drawing of District 25. The districts in south and west Texas will have to be redrawn to remedy the violation in District 23, and we have no cause to pass on the legitimacy of a district that must be changed. . . . District 25, in particular, was formed to compensate for the loss of District 23 as a Latino opportunity district, and there is no reason to believe District 25 will remain in its current form once District 23 is brought into compliance with § 2. We therefore vacate the District Court's judgment as to these claims.

IV

Appellants also challenge the changes to district lines in the Dallas area, alleging they dilute African–American voting strength in violation of § 2 of the Voting Rights Act. Specifically, appellants contend that an African–American minority effectively controlled District 24 under Plan 1151C, and that § 2 entitles them to this district.

Before Plan 1374C was enacted, District 24 had elected Anglo Democrat Martin Frost to Congress in every election since 1978. Anglos were the largest racial group in the district, with 49.8% of the citizen voting-age population, and third largest were Latinos, with 20.8%. African–Americans were the second-largest group, with 25.7% of the citizen voting-age population, and they voted consistently for Frost. The new plan broke apart this racially diverse district, assigning its pieces into several other districts.

[A]ppellants . . . contend African–Americans had effective control of District 24. As the Court has done several times before, we assume for purposes of this litigation that it is possible to state a § 2 claim for a racial group that makes up less than 50% of the population. Even on the assumption that the first *Gingles* prong can accommodate this claim, however, appellants must show they constitute "a sufficiently large minority to elect their candidate of choice with the assistance of cross-over votes."

The relatively small African–American population can meet this standard, according to appellants, because they constituted 64% of the voters in the Democratic primary. Since a significant number of Anglos and Latinos voted for the Democrat in the general election, the argument goes, African–American control of the primary translated into effective control of the entire election.

The District Court found, however, that African–Americans could not elect their candidate of choice in the primary. . . .

Appellants fail to demonstrate clear error in this finding. In the absence of any contested Democratic primary in District 24 over the last 20 years, no obvious benchmark exists for deciding whether African–Americans could elect their candidate of choice. The fact that African–Americans voted for Frost—in the primary and general elections—could signify he is their candidate of choice. Without a contested primary, however, it could also be interpreted to show (assuming racial bloc voting) that Anglos and Latinos would vote in the Democratic primary in greater numbers if an African–American candidate of choice were to run, especially given Texas' open primary system. The District Court heard trial testimony that would support both explanations, and we cannot say that it erred in crediting the testimony that endorsed the latter interpretation. . . .

That African–Americans had influence in the district, does not suffice to state a § 2 claim. . . . The opportunity "to elect representatives of their choice" requires more than the ability to influence the outcome between some candidates, none of whom is their candidate of choice. There is no doubt African–Americans preferred Martin Frost to the Republicans who opposed him. The fact that African–Americans preferred Frost to some others does not, however, make him their candidate of choice. Accordingly, the ability to aid in Frost's election does not make the old District 24 an African–American opportunity district for purposes of § 2. . . .

Appellants respond by pointing to *Georgia* v. *Ashcroft,* where the Court held that the presence of influence districts is a relevant consideration under § 5 of the Voting Rights Act. The inquiry under § 2, however, concerns the opportunity "to elect representatives of their choice," 42 U.S.C. § 1973(b), not whether a change has the purpose or effect of "denying or abridging the right to vote," § 1973c. *Ashcroft* recognized the differences between these tests, and concluded that the ability of racial groups to elect candidates of their choice is only one factor under § 5. So while the presence of districts "where minority voters may not be able to elect a candidate of choice but can play a substantial, if not decisive, role in the electoral process" is relevant to the § 5 analysis, the lack of such districts cannot establish a § 2 violation. The failure to create an influence district in these cases thus does not run afoul of § 2 of the Voting Rights Act. . . .

■ JUSTICE STEVENS, [dissenting in part.]

* * *

IV

I would hold that the cracking of District 24—which under the *Balderas* Plan was a majority-minority district that consistently elected Democratic Congressman Martin Frost—was unconstitutional. Readily manageable standards enable us to analyze both the purpose and the effect of the "granular" decisions that produced the replacements for District 24. Applying these standards, which I set forth below, I believe it is clear that the manipulation of this district for purely partisan gain violated the First and Fourteenth Amendments. . . .

That an impermissible, predominantly partisan, purpose motivated the cracking of former District 24 is further demonstrated by the fact that, in my judgment, this cracking caused Plan 1374C to violate § 5 of the Voting Rights Act, 42 U.S.C. § 1973c. . . .

By cracking *Balderas* District 24, and by not offsetting the loss in black voters' ability to elect preferred candidates elsewhere, Plan 1374C resulted in impermissible retrogression.

Under the *Balderas* Plan, black Americans constituted a majority of Democratic primary voters in District 24. According to the unanimous report authored by staff attorneys in the Voting Section of the Department of Justice, black voters in District 24 generally voted cohesively, and thus had the ability to elect their candidate of choice in the Democratic primary. Moreover, the black community's candidates of choice could consistently attract sufficient crossover voting from nonblacks to win the general election, even though blacks did not constitute a majority of voters in the general election. Representative Frost, who is white, was clearly the candidate of choice of the black community in District 24, based on election returns, testimony of community leaders, and "scorecards" he received from groups dedicated to advancing the interests of African–Americans. . . .

■ JUSTICE SOUTER, with whom JUSTICE GINSBURG joins, concurring in part and dissenting in part.

* * *

I join Part III of the principal opinion, in which the Court holds that Plan 1374C's Districts 23 and 25 violate § 2 of the Voting Rights Act of 1965, 42 U.S.C. § 1973, in diluting minority voting strength. But I respectfully dissent from Part IV, in which a plurality upholds the District Court's rejection of the claim that Plan 1374C violated § 2 in cracking the black population in the prior District 24 and submerging its fragments in new Districts 6, 12, 24, 26, and 32. On the contrary, I would vacate the judgment and remand for further consideration. . . .

Although both the plurality today and our own prior cases have sidestepped the question whether a statutory dilution claim can prevail without the possibility of a district percentage of minority voters above 50%, the day has come to answer it.

Chief among the reasons that the time has come is the holding in *Georgia* v. *Ashcroft*, 539 U.S. 461 (2003), that replacement of a majority-minority district by a coalition district with minority voters making up fewer than half can survive the prohibition of retrogression under § 5 of the Voting Rights Act. . . . Thus, despite the independence of § § 2 and 5, there is reason to think that the integrity of the minority voting population in a coalition district should be protected much as a majority-minority bloc would be. While protection should begin through the preclearance process, in jurisdictions where that is required, if that process fails a minority voter has no remedy under § 5, because the State and the Attorney General (or the District Court for the District of Columbia) are the only participants in preclearance, see 42 U.S.C. § 1973c. And, of course, vast areas of the country are not covered by § 5. Unless a minority voter is to be left with no recourse whatsoever, then, relief under § 2 must be possible, as by definition it would not be if a numerical majority of minority voters in a reconstituted or putative district is a necessary condition. I would therefore hold that a minority of 50% or less of the voting population might suffice at the *Gingles* gatekeeping stage. To have a clear-edged rule, I would hold it sufficient satisfaction of the first gatekeeping condition to show that minority voters in a reconstituted or putative district constitute a majority of those voting in the primary of the dominant party, that is, the party tending to win in the general election. . . .

The pertinence of minority voters' role in a primary is obvious: a dominant party's primary can determine the representative ultimately elected, as we recognized years ago in evaluating the constitutional importance of primary elections. . . .

I would accordingly not reject this § 2 claim at step one of *Gingles*, nor on this record would I dismiss it by jumping to the ultimate § 2 issue to be decided on a totality of the circumstances, see *De Grandy*, 512 U.S., at 1009–1022, and determine that the black plaintiffs cannot show that submerging them in the five new districts violated their right to equal opportunity to participate in the political process and elect candidates of their choice. The plurality, on the contrary, is willing to accept the conclusion that the minority voters lost nothing cognizable under § 2 because they could not show the degree of control that guaranteed a candidate of their choice in the old District 24. The plurality accepts this conclusion by placing great weight on the fact that Martin Frost, the perennially successful congressional candidate in District 24, was white. . . .

There are at least two responses. First, "under § 2, it is the status of the candidate as the chosen representative of a particular group, not the race of the candidate, that is important." *Gingles*, *supra* (emphasis deleted). Second, Frost was convincingly shown to have been the "chosen representative" of black voters in old District 24. In the absence of a black-white primary contest, the unchallenged evidence is that black voters dominated a primary that consistently nominated the same and ultimately successful candidate; it takes more than speculation to rebut the demonstration that Frost was the candidate of choice of the black voters. . . . [T]he uncontroverted and overwhelming evidence is that Frost was strongly supported by minority voters after more than two decades of sedulously considering minority interests. . . .

■ Chief Justice Roberts, with whom Justice Alito joins, concurring in part, concurring in the judgment in part, and dissenting in part.

I join Parts I and IV of the plurality opinion. . . .

I must, however, dissent from Part III of the Court's opinion. . . .

The majority reaches its surprising result because it finds that Latino voters in one of the State's Latino opportunity districts—District 25—are insufficiently compact, in that they consist of two different groups, one from around the Rio Grande and another from around Austin. According to the majority, this may make it more difficult for certain Latino-preferred candidates to be elected from that district—*even though Latino voters make up 55% of the citizen voting age population in the district and vote as a bloc.* The majority prefers old District 23, despite the District Court determination that new District 25 is "a more effective Latino opportunity district than Congressional District 23 had been."

The majority dismisses the District Court's careful factfinding on the ground that the experienced judges did not properly consider whether District 25 was "compact" for purposes of § 2. But the District Court opinion itself clearly demonstrates that the court carefully considered the compactness of the minority group in District 25, just as the majority says it should have. The District Court recognized the very features of District 25 highlighted by the majority and unambiguously concluded, under the totality of the circumstances, that the district was an effective Latino opportunity district, and that no violation of § 2 in the area had been shown. . . .

Never before has this or any other court struck down a State's redistricting plan under § 2, on the ground that the plan achieves the maximum number of possible majority-minority districts, but loses on style points, in that the minority voters in one of those districts are not as "compact" as the minority voters would be in another district were the lines drawn differently. Such a basis for liability pushes voting rights litigation into a whole new area—an area far removed from the concern of the Voting Rights Act to ensure minority voters an equal opportunity "to elect representatives of their choice." 42 U.S.C. § 1973(b).

I

* * *

The next generation of voting rights litigation [after *Gingles*] confirmed that "manipulation of [single-member] district lines" could also dilute minority voting power if it packed minority voters in a few districts when they might control more, or dispersed them among districts when they might control some. Again the basis for this application of *Gingles* was clear: A configuration of district lines could only dilute minority voting strength if under another configuration minority voters had better electoral prospects. Thus in cases involving single-member districts, the question was whether an *additional* majority-minority district should be created....

We have thus emphasized, since *Gingles* itself, that a § 2 plaintiff must at least show an apportionment that is likely to perform *better* for minority voters, compared to the existing one....

De Grandy confirmed that simply proposing a set of districts that divides up a minority population in a different manner than the State has chosen, without a gain in minority opportunity districts, does not show vote dilution, but "only that lines could have been drawn elsewhere."

Here the District Court found that six majority-Latino districts were all that south and west Texas could support. Plan 1374C provides six such districts, just as its predecessor did. This fact, combined with our precedent making clear that § 2 plaintiffs must show an alternative with *better* prospects for minority success, should have resulted in affirmance of the District Court decision on vote dilution in south and west Texas....

The majority does "not question" the District Court's parsing of the statistical evidence to reach the finding that District 25 was an effective Latino opportunity district. But the majority nonetheless rejects that finding, based on its own theory that "the practical consequence of drawing a district to cover two distant, disparate communities is that one or both groups will be unable to achieve their political goals," and because the finding rests on the "prohibited assumption" that voters of the same race will "think alike, share the same political interests, and will prefer the same candidates at the polls." It is important to be perfectly clear about the following, out of fairness to the District Court if for no other reason: No one has made any "assumptions" about how voters in District 25 will vote based on their ethnic background. Not the District Court; not this dissent. There was a trial. At trials, assumptions and assertions give way to facts. In voting rights cases, that is typically done through regression analyses of past voting records. Here, those analyses showed that the Latino candidate of choice prevailed in every primary and general election examined for District 25....

What is blushingly ironic is that the district preferred by the majority—former District 23—suffers from the same "flaw" the majority ascribes to District 25, except to a greater degree. While the majority decries District 25 because the Latino communities there are separated by "enormous geographical distance," and are "hundreds of miles apart," Latino communities joined to form the voting majority in old District 23 are nearly twice as far apart. Old District 23 runs "from El Paso, over 500 miles, into San Antonio and down into Laredo. It covers a much longer distance than ... the 300 miles from Travis to McAllen [in District 25]." So much for the significance of "enormous geographical distance." ...

II

The majority arrives at the wrong resolution because it begins its analysis in the wrong place.... According to the majority, "§ 2 does not forbid the creation of a noncompact majority-minority district," but "the noncompact district cannot . . . remedy a violation elsewhere in the state."

The issue, however, is not whether a § 2 violation in District 23, viewed "in isolation," can be remedied by the creation of a Latino opportunity district in District 25. When the question is where a fixed number of majority-minority districts should be located, the analysis should never begin by asking whether a *Gingles* violation can be made out in any one district "in isolation." In these circumstances, it is always possible to look at one area of minority population "in isolation" and see a "violation" of § 2 under *Gingles*. For example, if a State drew three districts in a group, with 60% minority voting age population in the first two, and 40% in the third, the 40% can readily claim that their opportunities are being thwarted because *they* were not grouped with an additional 20% of minority voters from one of the other districts. But the remaining minority voters in the other districts would have precisely the same claim if minority voters were shifted from their districts to join the 40%. That is why the Court has explained that no individual minority voter has a right to be included in a majority-minority district. Any other approach would leave the State caught between incompatible claims by different groups of minority voters. . . .

[N]o one disputes that at least the Latino voters in the border area of District 25—the larger concentration—*must* be part of a majority-Latino district if six are to be placed in south and west Texas.

This is not, therefore, a case of the State drawing a majority-minority district "anywhere," once a § 2 violation has been established elsewhere in the State. The question is instead whether the State has some latitude in deciding where to place the maximum possible number of majority-minority districts, when one of those districts contains a substantial proportion of minority voters who *must* be in a majority-minority district if the maximum number is to be created at all.

Until today, no court has ever suggested that lack of compactness under § 2 might invalidate a district that a State has chosen to create in the first instance. . . .

* * *

The State has drawn a redistricting plan that provides six of seven congressional districts with an effective majority of Latino voting-age citizens in south and west Texas, and it is not possible to provide more. The majority nonetheless faults the state plan because of the *particular mix* of Latino voters forming the majority in one of the six districts—a combination of voters from around the Rio Grande and from around Austin, as opposed to what the majority uncritically views as the more monolithic majority assembled (from more farflung communities) in old District 23. This despite the express factual findings, from judges far more familiar with Texas than we are, that the State's new district would be a more effective Latino majority district than old District 23 ever was, and despite the fact that *any* plan would necessarily leave *some* Latino voters outside a Latino-majority district.

Whatever the majority believes it is fighting with its holding, it is not vote dilution on the basis of race or ethnicity. I do not believe it is our role to make judgments about which *mixes* of minority voters should count for purposes of forming a majority in an electoral district, in the face of factual findings that the district is an effective majority-minority district. It is a sordid business, this divvying us up by race. When a State's plan already provides the maximum possible number of majority-minority effective opportunity districts, and the minority enjoys effective political power in the area well in *excess* of its proportion of the population, I would conclude that the courts have no further role to play in rejiggering the district lines under § 2. . . .

■ JUSTICE SCALIA, with whom JUSTICE THOMAS joins, and with whom THE CHIEF JUSTICE and JUSTICE ALITO joins as to Part III, concurring in the judgment in part and dissenting in part.

* * *

II

I would dismiss appellants' vote-dilution claims premised on § 2 of the Voting Rights Act of 1965 for failure to state a claim, for the reasons set forth in JUSTICE THOMAS's opinion, which I joined, in *Holder* v. *Hall*, 512 U.S. 874 (1994) (opinion concurring in judgment). As THE CHIEF JUSTICE makes clear, see *ante*, the Court's § 2 jurisprudence continues to drift ever further from the Act's purpose of ensuring minority voters equal electoral opportunities.

III

Because I find no merit in . . . the claims addressed by the Court, I must consider appellants' race-based equal protection claims. The GI Forum appellants focus on the removal of 100,000 residents, most of whom are Latino, from District 23. They assert that this action constituted intentional vote dilution in violation of the Equal Protection Clause. The Jackson appellants contend that the intentional creation of District 25 as a majority-minority district was an impermissible racial gerrymander. The District Court rejected the equal protection challenges to both districts.

A

[A]ppellants contend in a vote-dilution claim the plaintiff need not show that the racially discriminatory motivation *predominated*, but only that the invidious purpose was *a* motivating factor. Appellants contrast *Easley* v. *Cromartie*, 532 U.S. 234, 241 (2001) (in a racial-gerrymandering claim, "race must not simply have been *a* motivation for the drawing of a majority-minority district, but the *predominant* factor motivating the legislature's districting decision" (citation and internal quotation marks omitted)), with *Arlington Heights* v. *Metropolitan Housing Development Corp.*, 429 U.S. 252, 265–266 (1977), and *Rogers* v. *Lodge*, 458 U.S. 613, 617 (1982). Whatever the validity of this distinction, on the facts of these cases it is irrelevant. The District Court's conclusion that the legislature was not racially motivated when it drew the plan as a whole, and when it split Webb County, dooms appellants' intentional-vote-dilution claim.

We review a district court's factual finding of a legislature's motivation for clear error.... I cannot say that the District Court clearly erred when it found that "the legislative motivation for the division of Webb County between Congressional District 23 and Congressional District 28 in Plan 1374C was political."...

Of the individuals removed from District 23, 90 percent of those of voting age were Latinos, and 87 percent voted for Democrats in 2002. The District Court concluded that these individuals were removed because they voted for Democrats and against Bonilla, not because they were Latino. This finding is entirely in accord with our case law, which has recognized that "a jurisdiction may engage in constitutional political gerrymandering, even if it so happens that the most loyal Democrats happen to be black Democrats and even if the State were *conscious* of that fact." *Hunt* v. *Cromartie*, 526 U.S. 541, 551 (1999)....

B

The District Court's finding with respect to District 25 is another matter. There, too, the District Court applied the approach set forth in *Easley*.... In my view, however, when a legislature intentionally creates a majority-minority district, race is necessarily its predominant motivation and strict scrutiny is therefore triggered.... [T]he State's concession here sufficiently establishes that the legislature classified individuals on the basis of their race when it drew District 25: "To avoid retrogression and achieve compliance with § 5 of the Voting Rights Act ..., the Legislature chose to create a new Hispanic-opportunity district—new CD 25—which would allow Hispanics to actually elect its candidate of choice." Brief for State Appellees 106. Unquestionably, in my view, the drawing of District 25 triggers strict scrutiny.

Texas must therefore show that its use of race was narrowly tailored to further a compelling state interest. Texas asserts that it created District 25 to comply with its obligations under § 5 of the Voting Rights Act.... Since its changes to District 23 had reduced Latino voting power in that district, Texas asserts that it needed to create District 25 as a Latino-opportunity district in order to avoid § 5 liability.

We have in the past left undecided whether compliance with federal antidiscrimination laws can be a compelling state interest. I would hold that compliance with § 5 of the Voting Rights Act can be such an interest.

We long ago upheld the constitutionality of § 5 as a proper exercise of Congress's authority under § 2 of the Fifteenth Amendment to enforce that Amendment's prohibition on the denial or abridgment of the right to vote. See *South Carolina* v. *Katzenbach*, 383 U.S. 301 (1966). If compliance with § 5 were not a compelling state interest, then a State could be placed in the impossible position of having to choose between compliance with § 5 and compliance with the Equal Protection Clause. Moreover, the compelling nature of the State's interest in § 5 compliance is supported by our recognition in previous cases that race may be used where necessary to remedy identified past discrimination. Congress enacted § 5 for just that purpose, and that provision applies only to jurisdictions with a history of official discrimination. In the proper case, therefore, a covered jurisdiction may have a compelling interest in complying with § 5. . . .

Appellants concede . . . that the changes made to District 23 "necessitated creating an additional effective Latino district elsewhere, in an attempt to avoid Voting Rights Act liability." Nor do appellants charge that in creating District 25 the State did more than what was required by § 5. In light of these concessions, I do not believe a remand is necessary, and I would affirm the judgment of the District Court. . . .

NOTES AND QUESTIONS

1. Over the course of the last twenty years, the Court had addressed claims involving race and redistricting in three separate contexts: vote dilution claims under section 2 of the Voting Rights Act—the topic of Chapter 8; preclearance proceedings under section 5, exemplified most recently by *Georgia v. Ashcroft*—covered in Chapter 6; and claims of unconstitutionally excessive reliance on race—the so-called *Shaw* line of cases, discussed earlier in this Chapter.

In *LULAC v. Perry*, the various lines seem to converge. How well do the different opinions use, or integrate, the various strands of existing doctrine? For example, is Justice Kennedy saying merely that new District 25, because it is not *required* by *Gingles*, cannot serve as a substitute for the destruction of old District 23, or do his comments about the district suggest that it violates *Shaw*? Does his discussion of the destruction of old District 23 suggest that the Department of Justice erred in preclearing Texas's plan? Similarly, does Justice Scalia's finding that new district 25 survives strict scrutiny because it was necessary to prevent the retrogression in Latino voting strength that the elimination of old District 23 would cause suggest that he would otherwise have found a violation of section 2 had no new Latino district been created? Can this be squared with his reaffirmation of his agreement with Justice Thomas in *Holder*, where Justice Thomas suggested that section 2 cannot be read to reach claims of vote dilution, rather than outright vote denial? Do the tensions and asymmetries among the doctrines suggest the need for a more fundamental rethinking of judicial constraints on redistricting?

2.   In holding that the dismantling of District 23 violated section 2, the Court accepted such a claim even though the existing district had not been electing a "candidate of choice" of the Hispanic community. How much does Justice Kennedy's opinion concluding, nonetheless, that the new District 23 violated section 2 rest on a conclusion that the dismantling of this district reflected intentional discrimination against Hispanic voters—which would violate the Constitution, just as much as the VRA?

3.   Note that no Justice would have held that House District 25 violated *Shaw*. The majority did not even address the question. Moreover, note that Justice Scalia's opinion concluded that District 25 had to survive strict scrutiny review, but that it did so because it was narrowly tailored to secure section 5 preclearance. Justice Scalia's opinion is the first that, after plenary consideration, would subject a district to strict scrutiny under *Shaw*, but then find the district to meet this standard of review.

4.   In some ways, the most significant aspect of the Court's decision might well be the Court's analysis of the reasons District 25, the Hispanic majority district that ran from Austin to the Rio Grande Valley, was not consistent with or required by the VRA, and thus why it could not be a proper offset district for the dismantling of District 23. In addition to the geographic distances this district spanned, the Court was troubled that the district joined together poor rural Hispanics along the Texas border with more affluent Hispanics living in the urban area around the state capital of Austin. Invoking the lower court's findings of fact, Justice Kennedy noted that these different "Latino communities at the opposite ends of District 25 have divergent 'needs and interests,' owing to 'differences in socio-economic status, education, employment, health, and other characteristics.' " The Court appeared to view the Austin and Rio Grande Hispanic communities as living in worlds far apart, not just physically, but culturally, economically, educationally, and in other ways—differences that were decisive. For Texas to lump these voters together, because they were Hispanic, was to engage in what Justice Kennedy viewed as a troubling and legally problematic "racial essentialism." In the key passage, he concluded that the racial essentialism he saw at work in the Austin–Rio Grande district was inconsistent with the VRA itself. In Justice Kennedy's words: "We do a disservice to these important goals [of the VRA] by failing to account for the differences between people of the same race."

What would the consequences of this view be for application of the VRA more generally? Does this view undermine the concept of racially-polarized voting that has been central to the Act? For one view that it does, see Richard H. Pildes, *The Decline of Legally Mandated Minority Representation*, ___ Ohio St. L.J. ___ (2007). For a different view, see Guy–Uriel Charles, *Race, Representation, and Redistricting*, ___ Ohio St. L.J. ___ (2007).

F.   RACE AND REPRESENTATION UNDER THE FIFTEENTH AMENDMENT

For the most part, contemporary controversies involving race and representation arise under the Fourteenth Amendment, rather than the Fifteenth Amendment. In part, this is a product of the voting rights revolution of the 1960's: formal race-based disenfranchisement is relatively rare, although disputes still persist over the disparate impact of such practices as the felon disenfranchisement laws discussed in Chapter 2. In part, this is also a product of the Supreme Court's constricted reading of the Fifteenth Amendment. In *City of Mobile v. Bolden*, 446 U.S. 55, 65 (1980), a plurality of the Court suggested that the Fifteenth Amendment is satisfied as long as minority citizens are able to "register and vote without hindrance," regardless of whether their votes are purposefully diluted, and a majority of the Court seemed to endorse the *Bolden* plurality's view in *Reno v. Bossier Parish School Board*, 528 U.S. 320 (2000).

As the *Shaw* cases suggest, not every use of race in the reapportionment process violates the equal protection clause. First, some level of race-consciousness seems to be entirely permissible: as long as race is not a predominant factor in drawing district lines, the courts seem prepared to allow it to be part of the pluralist bargaining process. Second, the compelling governmental interest in complying with sections 2 and 5 of the Voting Rights Act also apparently justifies taking race into account.

But can race ever play a role in a case where the Fifteenth Amendment comes into play? Note the apparently categorical language of section 1 of the amendment: "The right of citizens of the United States to vote shall not be denied or abridged by the United States or by any State on account of race, color, or previous condition of servitude." Can restriction of the franchise itself on racial grounds ever be justified? And what does it mean to say that a restriction is "racial," rather than political? The Court confronted these questions in a case involving the election of a special governmental body in Hawaii.

Rice v. Cayetano

528 U.S. 495 (2000).

■ JUSTICE KENNEDY delivered the opinion of the Court.

* * *

The Hawaiian Constitution limits the right to vote for nine trustees chosen in a statewide election. The trustees compose the governing authority of a state agency known as the Office of Hawaiian Affairs, or OHA. The agency administers programs designed for the benefit of two subclasses of the Hawaiian citizenry. The smaller class comprises those designated as "native Hawaiians," defined by statute ... as descendants of not less than one-half part of the races inhabiting the Hawaiian Islands prior to 1778. The second, larger class of persons benefitted by OHA programs is "Hawaiians," defined to be ... those persons who are descendants of people inhabiting the Hawaiian Islands in 1778. The right to vote for trustees is limited to "Hawaiians," the second, larger class of persons, which of course includes the smaller class of "native Hawaiians."

Petitioner Rice, a citizen of Hawaii and thus himself a Hawaiian in a well-accepted sense of the term, does not have the requisite ancestry even for the larger class. He is not, then, a "Hawaiian" in terms of the statute; so he may not vote in the trustee election. The issue presented by this case is whether Rice may be so barred. Rejecting the State's arguments that the classification in question is not racial or that, if it is, it is nevertheless valid for other reasons, we hold Hawaii's denial of petitioner's right to vote to be a clear violation of the Fifteenth Amendment.

II

[Congress was concerned with the condition of native Hawaiian people after the creation of the new Territory and took measures to rehabilitate the population. Congress set aside land in the Hawaiian Homes Commission Act to benefit "native Hawaiians." Upon admission as a state, Hawaii incorporated the Act into its Constitution and Congress granted the State title to public lands and public property covered by the Act and an additional 1.2 million acres in the state.] The legislation authorizing the grant recited that these lands, and the proceeds and income they generated, were to be held "as a public trust" to be "managed and disposed of for one or more of" five purposes:

> [1] for the support of the public schools and other public educational institutions, [2] for the betterment of the conditions of native Hawaiians, as defined in the Hawaiian Homes Commission Act, 1920, as amended, [3] for the development of farm and home ownership on as widespread a basis as possible[,] [4] for the making of public improvements, and [5] for the provision of lands for public use.

In the first decades following admission, the State apparently continued to administer the lands that had been set aside under the Hawaiian Homes Commission Act for the benefit of native Hawaiians. The income from the balance of the public lands is said to have "by and large flowed to the department of education."

In 1978 Hawaii amended its Constitution to establish the Office of Hawaiian Affairs, which has as its mission "the betterment of conditions of native Hawaiians ... [and] Hawaiians." Members of the 1978 constitutional convention, at which the new amendments were drafted and proposed, set forth the purpose of the proposed agency:

Members [of the Committee of the Whole] were impressed by the concept of the Office of Hawaiian Affairs which establishes a public trust entity for the benefit of the people of Hawaiian ancestry. Members foresaw that it will provide Hawaiians the right to determine the priorities which will effectuate the betterment of their condition and welfare and promote the protection and preservation of the Hawaiian race, and that it will unite Hawaiians as a people.

Implementing statutes and their later amendments vested OHA with broad authority to administer two categories of funds: a 20 percent share of the revenue from the 1.2 million acres of lands granted to the State pursuant to ... the Admission Act, which OHA is to administer "for the betterment of the conditions of native Hawaiians," and any state or federal appropriations or private donations that may be made for the benefit of "native Hawaiians" and/or "Hawaiians." (The 200,000 acres set aside under the Hawaiian Homes Commission Act are administered by a separate agency.) The Hawaiian Legislature has charged OHA with the mission of "serving as the principal public agency ... responsible for the performance, development, and coordination of programs and activities relating to native Hawaiians and Hawaiians"....

OHA is overseen by a nine-member board of trustees, the members of which "shall be Hawaiians" and—presenting the precise issue in this case—shall be "elected by qualified voters who are Hawaiians, as provided by law." The term "Hawaiian" is defined by statute:

"Hawaiian" means any descendant of the aboriginal peoples inhabiting the Hawaiian Islands which exercised sovereignty and subsisted in the Hawaiian Islands in 1778, and which peoples thereafter have continued to reside in Hawaii.

The statute defines "native Hawaiian" as follows:

"Native Hawaiian" means any descendant of not less than one-half part of the races inhabiting the Hawaiian Islands previous to 1778, as defined by the Hawaiian Homes Commission Act, 1920, as amended; provided that the term identically refers to the descendants of such blood quantum of such aboriginal peoples which exercised sovereignty and subsisted in the Hawaiian Islands in 1778 and which peoples thereafter continued to reside in Hawaii.

Petitioner Harold Rice is a citizen of Hawaii and a descendant of preannexation residents of the islands. He is not, as we have noted, a descendant of pre-1778 natives, and so he is neither "native Hawaiian" nor "Hawaiian" as defined by the statute. Rice applied in March 1996 to vote in the elections for OHA trustees. To register to vote for the office of trustee he was required to attest: "I am also Hawaiian and desire to register to vote in OHA elections." Rice marked through the words "am also Hawaiian and," then checked the form "yes." The State denied his application.

Rice sued Benjamin Cayetano, the Governor of Hawaii, in the United States District Court for the District of Hawaii. (The Governor was sued in his official capacity, and the Attorney General of Hawaii defends the challenged enactments. We refer to the respondent as "the State.") Rice contested his exclusion from voting in elections for OHA trustees....

III

The purpose and command of the Fifteenth Amendment are set forth in language both explicit and comprehensive. The National Government and the States may not violate a fundamental principle: They may not deny or abridge the right to vote on account of race....

... The State maintains [that the statutory classification] is not a racial category at all but instead a classification limited to those whose ancestors were in Hawaii at a particular time, regardless of their race....

Ancestry can be a proxy for race. It is that proxy here. Even if the residents of Hawaii in 1778 had been of more diverse ethnic backgrounds and cultures, it is far from clear that a voting test favoring their descendants would not be a race-based qualification. But that is not this case. For centuries Hawaii was isolated from migration. The inhabitants shared common physical characteristics, and by 1778 they had a common culture. Indeed, the drafters of the statutory definition in question emphasized the "unique culture of the ancient Hawaiians" in explaining their work. The provisions before us reflect the State's effort to preserve that commonality of people to the present day.... The very object of the statutory definition in question and of its earlier congressional counterpart in the Hawaiian Homes Commission Act is to treat the early Hawaiians as a distinct people, commanding their own recognition and respect. The State, in enacting the legislation before us, has used ancestry as a racial definition and for a racial purpose....

As for the further argument that the restriction differentiates even among Polynesian people and is based simply on the date of an ancestor's residence in Hawaii, this too is insufficient to prove the classification is nonracial in purpose and operation. Simply because a class defined by ancestry does not include all members of the race does not suffice to make the classification race neutral.Here, the State's argument is undermined by its express racial purpose and by its actual effects.

The ancestral inquiry mandated by the State implicates the same grave concerns as a classification specifying a particular race by name. One of the principal reasons race is treated as a forbidden classification is that it demeans the dignity and worth of a person to be judged by ancestry instead of by his or her own merit and essential qualities. An inquiry into ancestral lines is not consistent with respect based on the unique personality each of us possesses, a respect the Constitution itself secures in its concern for persons and citizens.

The ancestral inquiry mandated by the State is forbidden by the Fifteenth Amendment for the further reason that the use of racial classifications is corruptive of the whole legal order democratic elections seek to preserve. The law itself may not become the instrument for generating the prejudice and hostility all too often directed against persons whose particular ancestry is disclosed by their ethnic characteristics and cultural traditions. . . . Ancestral tracing of this sort achieves its purpose by creating a legal category which employs the same mechanisms, and causes the same injuries, as laws or statutes that use race by name. The State's electoral restriction enacts a race-based voting qualification.

IV

The State offers three principal defenses of its voting law, any of which, it contends, allows it to prevail even if the classification is a racial one under the Fifteenth Amendment. We examine, and reject, each of these arguments.

A

[The State argued that the exclusion of non-Hawaiians from voting is permitted under cases allowing for differential treatment of Indian tribes. *Morton v. Mancari*].

If Hawaii's restriction were to be sustained under *Mancari* . . . it would be necessary to conclude that Congress . . . has determined that native Hawaiians have a status like that of Indians in organized tribes, and that it may, and has, delegated to the State a broad authority to preserve that status. These propositions would raise questions of considerable moment and difficulty. . . .

The tribal elections established by the federal statutes the State cites illuminate its error. If a non-Indian lacks a right to vote in tribal elections, it is for the reason that such elections are the internal affair of a quasi-sovereign. The OHA elections, by contrast, are the affair of the State of Hawaii. . . .

Although it is apparent that OHA has a unique position under state law, it is just as apparent that it remains an arm of the State.

The validity of the voting restriction is the only question before us. As the court of appeals did, we assume the validity of the underlying administrative structure and trusts, without intimating any opinion on that point . . . . Nonetheless, the elections for OHA trustee are elections of the State, not of a separate quasi-sovereign, and they are elections to which the Fifteenth Amendment applies. . . .

B

Hawaii further contends that the limited voting franchise is sustainable under a series of cases holding that the rule of one person, one vote does not pertain to certain special purpose districts such as water or irrigation districts. . . .

. . . The question before us is not the one-person, one-vote requirement of the Fourteenth Amendment, but the race neutrality command of the Fifteenth Amendment. Our special purpose district cases have not suggested that compliance with the one-person, one-vote rule of the Fourteenth Amendment somehow excuses compliance with the Fifteenth Amendment. We reject that argument here. . . . The Fifteenth Amendment has independent meaning and force. A State may not deny or abridge the right to vote on account of race, and this law does so.

C

Hawaii's final argument is that the voting restriction does no more than ensure an alignment of interests between the fiduciaries and the beneficiaries of a trust. Thus, the contention goes, the restriction is based on beneficiary status rather than race. . . .

[But] the State's position rests, in the end, on the demeaning premise that citizens of a particular race are somehow more qualified than others to vote on certain matters. That reasoning attacks the central meaning of the Fifteenth Amendment. The Amendment applies to "any election in which public issues are decided or public officials selected." There is no room under the Amendment for the concept that the right to vote in a particular election can be allocated based on race. Race cannot qualify some and disqualify others from full participation in our democracy. All citizens, regardless of race, have an interest in selecting officials who make policies on their behalf, even if those policies will affect some groups more than others. Under the Fifteenth Amendment voters are treated not as members of a distinct race but as members of the whole citizenry. Hawaii may not assume, based on race, that petitioner or any other of its citizens will not cast a principled vote. . . .

* * *

When the culture and way of life of a people are all but engulfed by a history beyond their control, their sense of loss may extend down through generations; and their dismay may be shared by many members of the larger community. As the State of Hawaii attempts to address these realities, it must, as always, seek the political consensus that begins with a sense of shared purpose. One of the necessary beginning points is this principle: The Constitution of the United States, too, has become the heritage of all the citizens of Hawaii.

In this case the Fifteenth Amendment invalidates the electoral qualification based on ancestry. The judgment of the Court of Appeals for the Ninth Circuit is reversed.

■ JUSTICE STEVENS, with whom JUSTICE GINSBURG joins as to Part II, dissenting.

The Court's holding today rests largely on the repetition of glittering generalities that have little, if any, application to the compelling history of the State of Hawaii. When that history is held up against the manifest purpose of the Fourteenth and Fifteenth Amendments, and against two centuries of this Court's federal Indian law, it is clear to me that Hawaii's election scheme should be upheld.

III

. . . Section 1 of the Fifteenth Amendment provides:

The right of citizens of the United States to vote shall not be denied or abridged by the United States or by any State on account of race, color, or previous condition of servitude.

As the majority itself must tacitly admit, the terms of the Amendment itself do not here apply. The OHA voter qualification speaks in terms of ancestry and current residence, not of race or color.... The ability to vote is a function of the lineal descent of a modern-day resident of Hawaii, not the blood-based characteristics of that resident, or of the blood-based proximity of that resident to the "peoples" from whom that descendant arises.

The distinction between ancestry and race is more than simply one of plain language. The ability to trace one's ancestry to a particular progenitor at a single distant point in time may convey no information about one's own apparent or acknowledged race today. Neither does it of necessity imply one's own identification with a particular race, or the exclusion of any others "on account of race." The terms manifestly carry distinct meanings, and ancestry was not included by the framers in the Amendment's prohibitions.

Presumably recognizing this distinction, the majority relies on the fact that "ancestry can be a proxy for race." That is, of course, true, but it by no means follows that ancestry is always a proxy for race. Cases in which ancestry served as such a proxy are dramatically different from this one. For example, the literacy requirement at issue in *Guinn v. United States*, 238 U.S. 347 (1915), relied on such a proxy. As part of a series of blatant efforts to exclude blacks from voting, Oklahoma exempted from its literacy requirement people whose ancestors were entitled to vote prior to the enactment of the Fifteenth Amendment. The *Guinn* scheme patently "served only to perpetuate . . . old [racially discriminatory voting] laws and to effect a transparent racial exclusion." As in *Guinn*, the voting laws held invalid under the Fifteenth Amendment in all of the cases cited by the majority were fairly and properly viewed through a specialized lens—a lens honed in specific detail to reveal the realities of time, place, and history behind the voting restrictions being tested.

That lens not only fails to clarify, it fully obscures the realities of this case, virtually the polar opposite of the Fifteenth Amendment cases on which the Court relies. In *Terry v. Adams*, 345 U.S. 461 (1953), for example, the Court held that the Amendment proscribed the Texas "Jaybird primaries" that used neutral voting qualifications "with a single proviso—Negroes are excluded." Similarly, in *Smith v. Allwright*, 321 U.S. 649 (1944), it was the blatant "discrimination against Negroes" practiced by a political party that was held to be state action within the meaning of the Amendment. Cases such as these that "strike down these voting systems . . . designed to exclude one racial class (at least) from voting," have no application to a system designed to empower politically the remaining members of a class of once sovereign, indigenous people.

Ancestry surely can be a proxy for race, or a pretext for invidious racial discrimination. But it is simply neither proxy nor pretext here. All of the persons who are eligible to vote for the trustees of OHA share two qualifications that no other person old enough to vote possesses: They are beneficiaries of the public trust created by the State and administered by OHA, and they have at least one ancestor who was a resident of Hawaii in 1778. A trust whose terms provide that the trustees shall be elected by a class including beneficiaries is hardly a novel concept. The Committee that drafted the voting qualification explained that the trustees here should be elected by the beneficiaries because "people to whom assets belong should have control over them. . . . The election of the board will enhance representative governance and decision-making accountability and, as a result, strengthen the fiduciary relationship between the board member, as trustee, and the native Hawaiian, as beneficiary." The described purpose of this aspect of the classification thus exists wholly apart from race. It is directly focused on promoting both the delegated federal mandate, and the terms of the State's own trustee responsibilities.

The majority makes much of the fact that the OHA trust—which it assumes is legitimate—should be read as principally intended to benefit the smaller class of "native Hawaiians," who are defined as at least one-half descended from a native islander circa 1778, not the larger class of "Hawaiians," which includes "any descendant" of those aboriginal people who lived in Hawaii in 1778 and "which peoples thereafter have continued to reside in Hawaii." It is, after all, the majority notes, the larger class of Hawaiians that enjoys the suffrage right in OHA elections. There is therefore a mismatch in interest alignment between the trust beneficiaries and the trustee electors, the majority contends, and it thus cannot be said that the class of qualified voters here is defined solely by beneficiary status.

While that may or may not be true depending upon the construction of the terms of the trust, there is surely nothing racially invidious about a decision to enlarge the class of eligible voters to include "any descendant" of a 1778 resident of the Islands. The broader category of eligible voters serves quite practically to ensure that, regardless how "dilute" the race of native Hawaiians becomes—a phenomenon also described in the majority's lavish historical summary—there will remain a voting interest whose ancestors were a part of a political, cultural community, and who have inherited through participation and memory the set of traditions the trust seeks to protect. The putative mismatch only underscores the reality that it cannot be purely a racial interest that either the trust or the election provision seeks to secure; the political and cultural interests served are—unlike racial survival—shared by both native Hawaiians and Hawaiians.

Beyond even this, the majority's own historical account makes clear that the inhabitants of the Hawaiian Islands whose descendants comprise the instant class are identified and remain significant as much because of culture as because of race. . . .

Even if one refuses to recognize the beneficiary status of OHA trustee voters entirely, it cannot be said that the ancestry-based voting qualification here simply stands in the shoes of a classification that would either privilege or penalize "on account of" race. The OHA voting qualification—part of a statutory scheme put in place by democratic vote of a multiracial majority of all state citizens, including those non-"Hawaiians" who are not entitled to vote in OHA trustee elections—appropriately includes every resident of Hawaii having at least one ancestor who lived in the Islands in 1778. That is, among other things, the audience to whom the congressional apology was addressed. Unlike a class including only full-blooded Polynesians—as one would imagine were the class strictly defined in terms of race—the OHA election provision excludes all full-blooded Polynesians currently residing in Hawaii who are not descended from a 1778 resident of Hawaii. Conversely, unlike many of the old southern voting schemes in which any potential voter with a "taint" of non-Hawaiian blood would be excluded, the OHA scheme excludes no descendant of a 1778 resident because he or she is also part European, Asian, or African as a matter of race. The classification here is thus both too inclusive and not inclusive enough to fall strictly along racial lines. . . .

[T]he majority next posits that "one of the principal reasons race is treated as a forbidden classification is that it demeans the dignity and worth of a person to be judged by ancestry instead of by his or her own merit and essential qualities." That is, of course, true when ancestry is the basis for denying or abridging one's right to vote or to share the blessings of freedom. But it is quite wrong to ignore the relevance of ancestry to claims of an interest in trust property, or to a shared interest in a proud heritage. There would be nothing demeaning in a law that established a trust to manage Monticello and provided that the descendants of Thomas Jefferson should elect the trustees. Such a law would be equally benign, regardless of whether those descendants happened to be members of the same race.

In this light, it is easy to understand why the classification here is not "demeaning" at all, for it is simply not based on the "premise that citizens of a particular race are somehow more qualified than others to vote on certain matters." It is based on the permissible assumption in this context that families with "any" ancestor who lived in Hawaii in 1778, and whose ancestors thereafter continued to live in Hawaii, have a claim to compensation and self-determination that others do not. For the multiracial majority of the citizens of the State of Hawaii to recognize that deep reality is not to demean their own interests but to honor those of others.

It thus becomes clear why the majority is likewise wrong to conclude that the OHA voting scheme is likely to "become the instrument for generating the prejudice and hostility all too often directed against persons whose particular ancestry is disclosed by their ethnic characteristics and cultural traditions." The political and cultural concerns that motivated the nonnative majority of Hawaiian voters to establish OHA reflected an interest in preserving through the self-determination of a particular people ancient traditions that they value. The fact that the voting qualification was established by the entire electorate in the State—the vast majority of which is not native Hawaiian—testifies to their judgment concerning the Court's fear of "prejudice and hostility" against the majority of state residents who are not "Hawaiian," such as petitioner.... Indeed, the best insurance against that danger is that the electorate here retains the power to revise its laws....

[Justices Breyer and Souter concurred separately in the result; Justice Ginsburg also authored a separate dissenting opinion]

NOTES AND QUESTIONS

1. For more extensive discussions of the special legal status of native Hawaiians, see Jon Van Dyke, *The Political Status of the Hawaiian People*, 17 Yale L. & Pol'y Rev. 95 (1998); Stuart Benjamin, Note, *Equal Protection and the Special Relationship: The Case of Native Hawaiians*, 106 Yale L. J. 537 (1996).

2. What makes the OHA classification "racial"? Does *Rice* simply offer a mechanical application of *Guinn*—where the state's reliance on the status of one's forebears in 1867 surely reflected a discriminatory racial purpose? Professor Katz suggests a more complex account: while the distribution of employment benefits—the issue in *Mancari*—did not create a racial classification, the definition of an electoral constituency in the same terms would. Ellen Katz, *Race and the Right to Vote After* Rice v. Cayetano, 99 Mich. L. Rev. 491, 503–04 (2000). In other words, what the Court treats as a "racial classification" varies depending on whether the classification operates in the sphere of democratic politics rather than that of employment and other societal benefits. For further discussion of the notion of "double barrelled" heightened scrutiny, where notions of race and fundamental rights intersect, see Pamela S. Karlan, *Just Politics?: Five Not So Easy Pieces of the 1995 Term*, 34 Houston L. Rev. 289, 298–99 (1997) (identifying "a central problem with the Court's political jurisprudence: the conflation of cases involving fundamental rights—in particular, the right to vote—and cases involving suspect classifications—in particular, race. When there is a double-barreled equal protection claim, it is often difficult to discern where the Court is coming from, let alone where it is heading. Double-barreled cases make slippery precedents because they can readily be distinguished by committing them to the alternative doctrinal line. But precisely because they lie at the intersection, they can represent budding doctrinal movement.")

3. Was it necessary for the Court even to reach the question whether the Hawaiian statute involved a racial classification? Or could the Court have reached the same outcome under the fundamental-rights strand of the Fourteenth Amendment?:

> The Court certainly viewed the OHA's voting regime as bestowing a benefit distinct from the types of benefits provided to tribal members under a host of other federal programs, including the job preferences at issue in *Mancari*. Justice Kennedy explained that extending *Mancari* to approve the OHA's electoral regime would allow Hawaii "to fence out whole classes of its citizens from decisionmaking in critical state affairs." Indeed, the Court appears to have understood the OHA's voting regime to implicate a fundamental constitutional right, namely the right to vote, while it saw *Mancari* as involving no correspondingly fundamental right to the benefits at issue there. As a result, the Court could simply have concluded under the Fourteenth Amendment that, *Mancari* notwithstanding, it must apply strict judicial scrutiny to the State of Hawaii's attempt to deny non-native Hawaiians the fundamental right to vote, and further that the restriction failed under such analysis.

Katz, *supra*, at 502. Does the explanation for the Court's choice lie in many of the Justices's current skepticism both about racial classifications and about fundamental rights jurisprudence?

4. The Fifteenth Amendment squarely prohibits race discrimination, but only in a narrow sphere: "[t]he right of citizens of the United States *to vote* shall not be denied or abridged . . . on account of race" (emphasis added). But if the OHA is a special-purpose governmental body, like the office involved in cases like *Salyer Land Company v. Tulare Lake Basin Water Storage* District, 410 U.S. 719 (1973), discussed in Chapter 3, does the determination of its electorate implicate the right to vote? Professor Katz sees a paradox here. Katz, *supra*, at 508. But does *Salyer Land Company* stand for the proposition that the "right to vote" was not implicated by California's restriction of the franchise or only for the more modest proposition that restrictions on *this* aspect of the right to vote, like restrictions of the franchise to resident citizens, as in *Holt Civic Club v. City of Tuscaloosa*, 439 U.S. 60 (1978) (discussed in Chapter 2), does not require strict scrutiny rather than rationality review?

5. Does *Rice* have broader implications for the Court's voting rights jurisprudence? Professor Katz suggests its relationship to the Court's *Shaw* jurisprudence:

> [T]he decision is best explained by a conception of voting's intrinsic values. The Court, in reaching its holding, demonstrates its view that voting has both expressive and constitutive effects and that the use of racially-motivated electoral rules undermines those effects.
>
> The Court communicates its understanding of voting's expressive effect through its conviction that even ostensibly benign racial classifications have a destructive effect on both the individuals who are so classified and those who are left out....
>
> Akin to the expressive harm underlying the Equal Protection Clause violation at issue in the *Shaw* cases, the injury conceived of here rests on the view that the Constitution prohibits a race-based denial of the vote because that denial disseminates the impermissible message that race constitutes a relevant criterion upon which to define the political community. This message itself becomes the harm the Fifteenth Amendment apparently prohibits, and the harm the Court concludes that Mr. Rice suffered as a result of the OHA's voting regime.

Katz, *supra*, at 514–15. If *Rice* is read broadly, for the proposition that the Fifteenth Amendment contains a categorical prohibition on the use of race to define an electorate (without the safety-valve of justification through the compelling state interest test), then does it go beyond *Shaw*?

> Under this reading, a perceived reliance on race, even as one factor among many, imposes a state-approved identity on voters that undermines their ability to constitute themselves freely as citizens through the exercise of the franchise.

* * *

> The broad reading ... suggests that a districting plan that fails to give rise to strict scrutiny under *Shaw* may still be invalid under *Rice*, and, even more dramatically, that most applications of section 2 of the Voting Rights Act are unconstitutional.... The Supreme Court, long divided about how [the results] standard should be implemented, has allowed racially informed decisionmaking under section 2. The strong reading of *Rice* would preclude such consideration of race in the districting process.

Katz, *supra*, at 523–25.

6. In *Office of Hawaiian Affairs v. Cayetano*, 94 Haw. 1 (2000), the Hawaii Supreme Court addressed the implications of *Rice* for the continued tenure in office of the OHA trustees. The state's governor took the position that the elections of the eight OHA Trustees were invalid, that their positions were therefore vacant, and that he had the authority under state law to appoint replacement trustees.

On that limited question, the Hawaii Supreme Court disagreed. It found that the U.S. Supreme Court had neither invalidated the election nor mandated a new election. The governor could not take the extreme remedy of replacing the trustees merely because they were elected by an unconstitutional process. It found that "the State must take further action apart from this proceeding before the positions presently held by the eight OHA trustees, elected in 1996 and 1998, are deemed vacant and ready to be filled" by the Governor.

A fuller discussion of the remedial issues for defective elections follows in Chapter 12.

CHAPTER 10

REDISTRICTING AND REPRESENTATION

In the wake of a new Census each decade, the decennial redistricting process forces a confrontation with fundamental questions concerning the appropriate design of the election process and democratic institutions. Because of the need to conform to new distributions of population, these redistricting battles throw the established political order into disarray and force a reexamination of the aims of representation in each state and subordinate political jurisdiction. This chapter explores the contested right of political opportunity by examining the diverse and competing claims for representation along partisan and incumbent lines. We have already examined the contested terrain of claims for equitable racial and ethnic representation, which overlap heavily with partisan conflicts, as evident in cases such as *Bush v. Vera*, 517 U.S. 952 (1996), and *Easley v. Cromartie*, 532 U.S. 234 (2001) (*Cromartie II*). These competing claims call into question the very purpose of elections in a democratic order, which the Supreme Court has identified as selecting "the free and uncorrupted choice of those who have the right to take part in that choice." *Ex parte Yarbrough*, 110 U.S. 651, 662 (1884).

But districting necessarily imposes a filtering device on the popular choice of the voters. In their aggregate, voters may have a prescribed set of choices. When those votes are broken down into territorially-based sub-units, however, substantially different results may obtain, even with one person, one vote's constraint on districts. The enormous resources devoted to redistricting battles reflect the understanding that different configurations of voters may yield different electoral outcomes, even with the same distribution of total votes. Even the Supreme Court has recognized that districting of necessity entails substantive, outcome-oriented judgments:

> The very essence of districting is to produce a different—a more politically fair—result than would be reached with elections at large, in which the winning party would take 100% of the legislative seats. Politics and political considerations are inseparable from districting and apportionment.

Gaffney v. Cummings, 412 U.S. 735, 752–53 (1973).

This chapter will explore some of the most controversial issues in determining when and under what circumstances districting authorities may seek a "more politically fair" outcome through the manipulation of electoral configurations. The Court has been careful not to treat all ends-oriented districting as constitutionally infirm gerrymandering. However, the Court's attempt to distinguish the permissible from the impermissible has run into grave difficulties. As will become evident, it is not so simple to distinguish the workaday processes of districting from "the deliberate and arbitrary distortion of district boundaries and populations for partisan or personal political purposes." *Kirkpatrick v. Preisler,* 394 U.S. 526, 538 (1969) (Fortas, J. concurring). This chapter addresses these issues in the context of claims that districts are being manipulated for political ends; the preceding chapter explored, in part, analogous claims that districts are being manipulated for racial ends.

A. PARTISAN GERRYMANDERING

Recall that in *Reynolds v. Sims,* 377 U.S. 533, 579 (1964), the Court identified imprecise election rules as "an open invitation to partisan gerrymandering." One of the reasons given for courts to enter the "political thicket" was to provide meaningful constraints on the temptation to engage in gerrymanders of all kinds. Unfortunately, the Court's experiences post-*Baker/Reynolds* showed that one-person, one-vote was itself an insufficient constraint on gerrymandering. We turn now to the threat of the equipopulous gerrymander, a threat that, as we shall see, has become a more powerful one in recent years than when the Court first confronted the issue.

1. THE INCOMPLETE PROTECTION OF ONE PERSON, ONE VOTE AND THE EMERGENCE OF CLAIMS OF POLITICAL VOTE DILUTION

Gaffney v. Cummings
412 U.S. 735 (1973).

■ MR. JUSTICE WHITE delivered the opinion of the Court.

The questions in this case are whether the population variations among the election districts provided by a reapportionment plan for the Connecticut General Assembly, proposed in 1971, made out a prima facie case of invidious discrimination under the Equal Protection Clause and whether an otherwise acceptable reapportionment plan is constitutionally vulnerable where its purpose is to provide districts that would achieve "political fairness" between the political parties.

* * *

[We hold that the deviations in population among the districts fall within permissible limits and thus that the legislature's plan does not violate the principle of one person, one vote.]

The record abounds with evidence, and it is frankly admitted by those who prepared the plan, that virtually every Senate and House district line was drawn with the conscious intent to create a districting plan that would achieve a rough approximation of the statewide political strengths of the Democratic and Republican Parties, the only two parties in the State large enough to elect legislators from discernible geographic areas. Appellant insists that the spirit of "political fairness" underlying this plan is not only permissible, but a desirable consideration in laying out districts that otherwise satisfy the population standard of the reapportionment cases. Appellees, on the other hand, label the plan as nothing less than a gigantic political gerrymander, invidiously discriminatory under the Fourteenth Amendment.[18]

We are quite unconvinced that the reapportionment plan offered by the three-member Board violated the Fourteenth Amendment because it attempted to reflect the relative strength of the parties in locating and defining election districts. It would be idle, we think, to contend that any political consideration taken into account in fashioning a reapportionment plan is sufficient to invalidate it. Our cases indicate quite the contrary. The very essence of districting is to produce a different—a more "politically fair"—result than would be reached with elections at large, in which the winning party would take 100% of the legislative seats. Politics and political considerations are inseparable from districting and apportionment. The political profile of a State, its party registration, and voting records are available precinct by precinct, ward by ward. These subdivisions may not be identical with census tracts, but, when overlaid on a census map, it requires no special genius to recognize the political consequences of drawing a district line along one street rather than another. It is not only obvious, but absolutely unavoidable, that the location and shape of districts may well determine the political complexion of the area. District lines are rarely neutral phenomena. They can well determine what district will be predominantly Democratic or predominantly Republican, or make a close race likely. Redistricting may pit incumbents against one another or make very difficult the election of the most experienced legislator. The reality is that districting inevitably has and is intended to have substantial political consequences.

It may be suggested that those who redistrict and reapportion should work with census, not political, data and achieve population equality without regard for political impact. But this politically mindless approach may produce, whether intended or not, the most grossly gerrymandered results; and, in any event, it is most unlikely that the political impact of

18. Appellees also maintain that the shapes of the districts would not have been so "indecent" had the Board not attempted to "wiggle and joggle" boundary lines to ferret out pockets of each party's strength. That may well be true, although any plan that attempts to follow Connecticut's "oddly shaped" town lines is bound to contain some irregularly shaped districts. But compactness or attractiveness has never been held to constitute an independent federal constitutional requirement for state legislative districts.

such a plan would remain undiscovered by the time it was proposed or adopted, in which event the results would be both known and, if not changed, intended.

It is much more plausible to assume that those who redistrict and reapportion work with both political and census data. Within the limits of the population equality standards of the Equal Protection Clause, they seek, through compromise or otherwise, to achieve the political or other ends of the State, its constituents, and its officeholders. What is done in so arranging for elections, or to achieve political ends or allocate political power, is not wholly exempt from judicial scrutiny under the Fourteenth Amendment. As we have indicated, for example, multimember districts may be vulnerable, if racial or political groups have been fenced out of the political process and their voting strength invidiously minimized. Beyond this, we have not ventured far or attempted the impossible task of extirpating politics from what are the essentially political processes of the sovereign States. Even more plainly, judicial interest should be at its lowest ebb when a State purports fairly to allocate political power to the parties in accordance with their voting strength and, within quite tolerable limits, succeeds in doing so. There is no doubt that there may be other reapportionment plans for Connecticut that would have different political consequences and that would also be constitutional. Perhaps any of appellees' plans would have fallen into this category, as would the court's, had it propounded one. But neither we nor the district courts have a constitutional warrant to invalidate a state plan, otherwise within tolerable population limits, because it undertakes, not to minimize or eliminate the political strength of any group or party, but to recognize it and, through districting, provide a rough sort of proportional representation in the legislative halls of the State.

Reversed.

■ [Dissenting opinion of JUSTICE BRENNAN omitted.]

Karcher v. Daggett

462 U.S. 725 (1983).

[In *Karcher*, the Supreme Court, in an opinion by Justice Brennan, ruled that New Jersey's post–1980 congressional redistricting plan unconstitutionally violated the one-person, one-vote rule. The majority opinion appears as a principal case in Chapter 3. Although the disparity in district size was less than the margin of error of the Census enumeration, the Court nonetheless held that any unjustified departure from exact population equality would doom a congressional election plan. Justice Stevens in concurrence and Justice Powell in dissent invited the Court to reexamine the basis for its ruling.]

■ JUSTICE STEVENS, concurring.

* * *

II

* * *

I am convinced that judicial preoccupation with the goal of perfect population equality is an inadequate method of judging the constitutionality of an apportionment plan. I would not hold that an obvious gerrymander is wholly immune from attack simply because it comes closer to perfect population equality than every competing plan. On the other hand, I do not find any virtue in the proposal to relax the standard set forth in *Wesberry* and subsequent cases, and to ignore population disparities after some arbitrarily defined threshold has been crossed.... Rather, we should supplement the population equality standard with additional criteria that are no less "judicially manageable." In evaluating equal protection challenges to districting plans, just as in resolving such attacks on other forms of discriminatory action, I would consider whether the plan has a significant adverse impact on an identifiable political group, whether the plan has objective indicia of irregularity, and then, whether the State is able to produce convincing evidence that the plan nevertheless serves neutral, legitimate interests of the community as a whole.

* * *

As a threshold matter, plaintiffs must show that they are members of an identifiable political group whose voting strength has been diluted. They must first prove that they belong to a politically salient class, one whose geographical distribution is sufficiently ascertainable that it could have been taken into account in drawing district boundaries.[12] Second, they must prove that in the relevant district or districts or in the State as a whole, their proportionate voting influence has been adversely affected by the challenged scheme.[13] Third, plaintiffs must make a prima facie showing that raises a rebuttable presumption of discrimination.

---

12. Identifiable groups will generally be based on political affiliation, race, ethnic group, national origin, religion,or economic status, but other characteristics may become politically significant in a particular context....

13. The difficulty in making this showing stems from the existence of alternative strategies of vote dilution. Depending on the circumstances, vote dilution may be demonstrated if a population concentration of group members has been fragmented among districts, or if members of the group have been overconcentrated in a single district greatly in excess of the percentage needed to elect a candidate of their choice.

In litigation under the Voting Rights Act, federal courts have developed some familiarity with the problems of identifying and measuring dilution of racial group voting strength. Some of the concepts developed for statutory purposes might be applied in adjudicating constitutional claims by other types of political groups. The threshold showing of harm may be more difficult for adherents of a political party than for members of a racial group, however, because there are a number

One standard method by which members of a disadvantaged political group may establish a dilution of their voting rights is by reliance on the "one person, one vote" principle, which depends on a statewide statistical analysis. But prima facie evidence of gerrymandering can surely be presented in other ways. One obvious type of evidence is the shape of the district configurations themselves. One need not use Justice Stewart's classic definition of obscenity—"I know it when I see it"—as an ultimate standard for judging the constitutionality of a gerrymander to recognize that dramatically irregular shapes may have sufficient probative force to call for an explanation.

Substantial divergences from a mathematical standard of compactness may be symptoms of illegitimate gerrymandering.... To some extent, geographical compactness serves independent values; it facilitates political organization, electoral campaigning, and constituent representation. A number of state statutes and Constitutions require districts to be compact and contiguous. These standards have been of limited utility because they have not been defined and applied with rigor and precision.[18] Yet ... scholars have set forth a number of methods of measuring compactness that can be computed with virtually the same degree of precision as a population count.[19] It is true, of course, that the significance of a particular compactness measure may be difficult to evaluate, but as the figures in this case demonstrate, the same may be said of population disparities. In addition, although some deviations from compactness may be inescapable because of the geographical configuration or uneven population density of a particular State, the relative degrees of compactness of different district maps can always be compared. As with the numerical standard, it seems

of possible base-line measures for a party's strength, including voter registration and past vote-getting performance in one or more election contests.

18. One state statute and 21 State Constitutions explicitly require that districts be compact; two state statutes and 27 Constitutions explicitly provide that districts be formed of contiguous territory.

19. The scholarly literature suggests a number of different mathematical measures of compactness, each focusing on different variables. One relatively simple method is to measure the relationship between the area of the district and the area of the smallest possible circumscribing circle. This calculation is particularly sensitive to the degree of elongation of a given shape. Another simple method is to determine the ratio of a figure's perimeter to the circumference of the smallest possible circumscribing circle, a measurement that is well suited to measuring the degree of indentation. Other measures of compactness are based on the aggregate of the distances from the district's geometrical or population-weighted center of gravity to each of its points; the degree of indentation of the boundaries of a nonconvex district; the aggregate length of district boundaries; and the ratio of the maximum to the minimum diameters in a district. In each case, the smaller the measurement, the more compact the district or districts. *See also* 1980 Iowa Acts, ch. 1021, § 4b(3)c (setting forth alternative geometrical tests for determining relative compactness of alternative districting plans: the absolute value of the difference between the length and width of the district, and the "ratio of the dispersion of population about the population center of the district to the dispersion of population about the geographic center of the district").

fair to conclude that drastic departures from compactness are a signal that something may be amiss.

Extensive deviation from established political boundaries is another possible basis for a prima facie showing of gerrymandering. . . . Subdivision boundaries tend to remain stable over time. Residents of political units such as townships, cities, and counties often develop a community of interest, particularly when the subdivision plays an important role in the provision of governmental services. In addition, legislative districts that do not cross subdivision boundaries are administratively convenient and less likely to confuse the voters. Although the significance of deviations from subdivision boundaries will vary with the number of legislative seats and the number, size, and shape of the State's subdivisions, the number can be counted and alternative plans can be compared.

A procedural standard, although obviously less precise, may also be enlightening. If the process for formulating and adopting a plan excluded divergent viewpoints, openly reflected the use of partisan criteria, and provided no explanation of the reasons for selecting one plan over another, it would seem appropriate to conclude that an adversely affected plaintiff group is entitled to have the majority explain its action. On the other hand, if neutral decisionmakers developed the plan on the basis of neutral criteria, if there was an adequate opportunity for the presentation and consideration of differing points of view, and if the guidelines used in selecting a plan were explained, a strong presumption of validity should attach to whatever plan such a process produced.

* * *

If a State is unable to respond to a plaintiff's prima facie case by showing that its plan is supported by adequate neutral criteria, I believe a court could properly conclude that the challenged scheme is either totally irrational or entirely motivated by a desire to curtail the political strength of the affected political group. This does not mean that federal courts should invalidate or even review every apportionment plan that may have been affected to some extent by partisan legislative maneuvering. But I am convinced that the Judiciary is not powerless to provide a constitutional remedy in egregious cases.[28]

III

In this case it is not necessary to go beyond the reasoning in the Court's opinions in *Wesberry v. Sanders, Kirkpatrick v. Preisler,* and *White v. Weiser,* 412 U.S. 783 (1973), to reach the correct result. None of the

---

28. *See Gomillion v. Lightfoot,* 364 U.S. 339, 341 (1960) (noting that allegations would "abundantly establish that Act 140 was not an ordinary geographic redistricting measure even within familiar abuses of ger- rymandering"). If the Tuskegee map in *Gom- illion* had excluded virtually all Republicans rather than blacks from the city limits, the Constitution would also have been violat- ed . . . .

additional criteria that I have mentioned would cast any doubt on the propriety of the Court's holding in this case. Although I need not decide whether the plan's shortcomings regarding shape and compactness, subdivision boundaries, and neutral decisionmaking would establish a prima facie case, these factors certainly strengthen my conclusion that the New Jersey plan violates the Equal Protection Clause.

A glance at the map shows district configurations well deserving the kind of descriptive adjectives—"uncouth" and "bizarre"—that have traditionally been used to describe acknowledged gerrymanders. I have not applied the mathematical measures of compactness to the New Jersey map, but I think it likely that the plan would not fare well. In addition, while disregarding geographical compactness, the redistricting scheme wantonly disregards county boundaries. For example, in the words of a commentator: "In a flight of cartographic fancy, the Legislature packed North Jersey Republicans into a new district many call 'the Swan.' Its long neck and twisted body stretch from the New York suburbs to the rural upper reaches of the Delaware River." That district, the Fifth, contains segments of at least seven counties. The same commentator described the Seventh District, comprised of parts of five counties, as tracing "a curving partisan path through industrial Elizabeth, liberal, academic Princeton and largely Jewish Marlboro in Monmouth County. The resulting monstrosity was called 'the Fishhook' by detractors."

Such a map prompts an inquiry into the process that led to its adoption. The plan was sponsored by the leadership in the Democratic Party, which controlled both houses of the state legislature as well as the Governor's office, and was signed into law the day before the inauguration of a Republican Governor. The legislators never formally explained the guidelines used in formulating their plan or in selecting it over other available plans. Several of the rejected plans contained districts that were more nearly equal in population, more compact, and more consistent with subdivision boundaries, including one submitted by a recognized expert . . . whose impartiality and academic credentials were not challenged. The District Court found that [that] Plan "was rejected because it did not reflect the leadership's partisan concerns."

[A map of the plan can be found in Chapter 3.]

* * *

NOTES AND QUESTIONS

1. An interesting tangent to *Gaffney* concerns the three-judge district court's effort to draw districts after it had struck down the Connecticut legislature's plan. (The Supreme Court's resolution of the case, which upheld the legislature's plan, meant that the court-drawn redistricting never went into effect.) The district court hired then-Professor Robert Bork to serve as a special master and asked him to draw the districts. Bork had earlier termed one person, one vote a "fiasco," and was later to write that there was "no better example of the Court's . . . disregard for the Constitution in whose name it spoke than the legislative reapportionment cases, which created the principle of one person, one vote." Robert H. Bork, The Tempting of America: The Political Seduction of the Law 84 (1990). But he agreed to serve, and after several interactions with various political actors and experts—the most amusing of which prompted him, after a politician sarcastically pointed at the map and said "That is Connecticut, professor," to reply, "For now"—he started on the task armed only with the map and a set of population figures. He "utterly ignored geographical and demographic facts," and produced a map that maximized population equality. *Id.* at 88. Though a Republican at the time, Professor Bork learned the political consequences of his plan when John Bailey, the chairman of the Connecticut Democratic Party came up to him in a restaurant and thanked him for doing a "fine reapportionment." *Id.* at 89. His experience as a special master further confirmed his view of one person, one vote.

2. Note that in both *Gaffney* and *Karcher* the plaintiffs combined one person, one vote claims—that is "quantitative" vote-dilution claims—with more "qualitative" claims that focus not on arithmetic equality but on the quality of representation different groups of individuals are likely to obtain. Are the one person, one vote claims anything more than a placeholder for these harder-to-articulate qualitative claims? See Pamela S. Karlan, *The Fire Next Time: Reapportionment After the 2000 Census*, 50 Stan. L. Rev. 731, 762 (1998).

3. *Karcher* represents the Court's unresolved confrontation with the purposes of the one-person, one-vote rule of apportionment. As political operatives became more accustomed to the strictures of the equipopulation rule, and as computer technology improved, the one-person, one-vote rule at best inconvenienced would-be gerrymanderers. Recall, however, the difficulties the Court had in articulating the basis for intervening to protect equally-weighted voting. How likely is the Court to develop the foundations for evaluating whether the electoral system has been infected by partisan gerrymandering?

4. How would plaintiffs go about proving a claim of partisan vote dilution? Justice Stevens identifies a three part test: (a) proof of belonging to a politically salient class; (b) proof of less than proportionate voting influence; and (c) prima facie proof that raises the presumption of discrimination. Do any of these factors have readily apparent meaning? Are any of them comparable to the presumptions raised in racial vote-dilution claims? Moreover, is it likely that Justice Stevens' factors will be entirely absent in *any* redistricting conducted by partisan political actors?

2. Equal Protection Constraints on Political Gerrymanders

Davis v. Bandemer and Recognition of a New Constitutional Claim

The question whether partisan manipulation of election districts might violate the Constitution was unresolved in the Court in the first two decades after *Baker v. Carr*. Then, for the first time in *Davis v. Bandemer*, 478 U.S. 109 (1986), the Court held that claims of partisan gerrymandering were justiciable as potential violations of the Equal Protection Clause. The case involved a challenge to the post–1980 redistricting of the Indiana state legislature. Plaintiffs claimed that the state's districting arrangements, including its use of multimember districts, led to a significant under-representation of statewide Democratic voting strength in the state legislature.

In a deeply divided decision, the Court held that a partisan gerrymandering claim of this sort was justiciable. Writing for a plurality of the Court, Justice White identified the elements such a claim would have to establish to prevail. Plaintiffs had to show both "intentional discrimination against an identifiable political group" and "an actual discriminatory effect on that group." After affirming the district court's finding of discriminatory intent, Justice White rejected the lower court's determination that intentional deviation from proportional representation created a discriminatory effect:

> [T]he mere fact that a particular apportionment scheme makes it more difficult for a particular group in a particular district to elect the representatives of its choice does not render that scheme constitutionally infirm.... [T]he power to influence the political process is not limited to winning elections. An individual or a group of individuals who votes for a losing candidate is usually deemed to be adequately represented by the winning candidate and to have as much opportunity to influence that candidate as other voters in the district. We cannot presume in such a situation, without actual proof to the contrary, that the candidate elected will entirely ignore the interests of those voters. This is true even in a safe district where the losing group loses election after election. Thus, a group's electoral power is not unconstitutionally diminished by the simple fact of an apportionment scheme that makes winning elections more difficult, and a failure of proportional representation alone does not constitute impermissible discrimination under the Equal Protection Clause....

Justice White then set out the proper standard:

> [U]nconstitutional discrimination occurs only when the electoral system is arranged in a manner that will consistently degrade a voter's or a group of voters' influence on the political process as a whole.... [T]he question is whether a particular group has been unconstitutionally denied its chance to effectively influence the political process.... [T]he inquiry centers on the voters' direct or indirect influence on the elections of the state legislature as a whole.... In this context, such a finding of unconstitutionality must be supported by evidence of continued frustration of the will of a majority of the voters or effective denial to a minority of voters of a fair chance to influence the political process.

The Court concluded that the plaintiffs had not met this standard.

Justice O'Connor, joined by Chief Justice Burger and then-Justice Rehnquist, concurred in the judgment. But these Justices would have dismissed the claims of partisan gerrymandering altogether, on the view that such claims presented "nonjusticiable political questions." Justice O'Connor's opinion expressed concern that judicial intervention would inevitably lead "toward some form of rough proportional representation for all political groups," a notion inconsistent with "our history, our traditions, or our political instutions." Justice O'Connor also believed that the need for judicial intervention was limited because political gerrymandering is self-limiting:

> In order to gerrymander, the legislative majority must weaken some of its safe seats, thus exposing its own incumbents to greater risks of defeat—risks they may refuse to accept past a certain point. Similarly, an overambitious gerrymander can lead to disaster for the legislative majority: because it has created more seats in which it hopes to win relatively narrow victories, the same swing in overall voting strength will tend to cost the legislative majority more and more seats as the gerrymander becomes more ambitious. More generally, each major party presumably has ample weapons at its disposal to conduct the partisan struggle that often leads to a partisan apportionment, but also often leads to a bipartisan one.

Justice Powell, joined by Justice Stevens, dissented in part. These Justices would have found the Indiana scheme to have violated the Equal Protection clause. They offered a multi-factor test based on Justice Stevens concurrence in *Karcher*:

> The most important of these factors are the shapes of voting districts and adherence to established political subdivision boundaries. Other relevant considerations include the nature of the legislative procedures by which the apportionment law was adopted and legislative history reflecting contemporaneous legislative goals.

Given that "the procedures used in redistricting Indiana were carefully designed to exclude Democrats from participating in the legislative process," that the districts intentionally ignored traditional political subdivisions, and evidence that the districts were drawn for purely partisan reasons without any consideration of the public interest in a fair political process, Justices Powell and Stevens would have found a constitutional violation.

NOTES AND QUESTIONS

1. While upholding the justiciability of partisan gerrymandering claims, the Court rejected the proof in *Bandemer* as insufficient to establish that Indiana's districting scheme "consistently degrade[d] a voter's or a group of voters' influence on the political process as a whole." What evidence would establish such "consistent degradation"? How would a prospective litigant establish the requisite consistency in light of the fact that district lines must be redrawn every ten years to conform to the one-person, one-vote requirement? Could a litigant ever prove that any particular group would have "no hope of doing any better" after the next decennial census?

2. The Court in *Bandemer* appeared uncertain as to how to define the harm in gerrymandering claims. If it is true, as the Court posits, that individuals who vote for winning or losing candidates can equally be presumed to be fairly represented, then why enter this thicket at all? Typically there are two forms of benefits to be obtained from gerrymandered districts. First, parties in power can enhance their electoral opportunities by displacing incumbents of the other party from their established constituents, thus denying those incumbents the benefits obtained from name recognition, past delivery of constituent services, and prior social investment in the district. The second advantage comes with altering the mix of expected partisan votes. By controlling the redistricting process, swing seats can be weakened for the opposing party or strengthened through the addition or subtraction of predictable blocs of voters. Ideally, party strength is maximized by winning each seat with one vote over the minimum required. Control over redistricting allows a party to tailor districts so that a safe cushion is created in districts that can be captured, without wasting loyal votes through the overpacking of those districts. Conversely, the ideal victory for the opponent party comes in districts that are as close to 100 percent packed as possible, thereby "wasting" as many votes as possible. Should constitutional doctrine recognize such harms? If so, how? Alternatively, how persuasive is Justice O'Connor's claim that such gerrymandering is inherently unstable?

3. In her concurrence in the judgment, Justice O'Connor argues that recognizing a claim of partisan vote dilution will accelerate a push toward proportional representation, which in turn, threatens to undermine the current two-party system. Should the privileged position of the Democratic and Republican parties be given constitutional protection? There appears a significant danger of insider manipulation of the political process when the majority political parties are given license to engage in what political scientist Bruce Cain terms a "bipartisan gerrymander." In *Gaffney*, the Court found that such an apportionment of electoral opportunity between the major parties justified oddly drawn district lines. Is there any tension between attacking districting for seeking political ends, as the plaintiffs did in *Bandemer*, and the Court's acceptance in *Gaffney* that the Constitution permits pursuing a "fair partisan balance" through the districting process? For further consideration of the extent to which the current system entrenches the two-party system, see the discussion in Chapter 4.

4. The Court's decision in Bandemer was announced on the same day as its decision in Thornburg v. Gingles, 478 U.S. 30 (1986). That case involved the 1982 amendments to section 2 of the Voting Rights Act, which prohibit, among other things, the use of districting plans that result in the dilution of racial minority groups' voting strength. (Gingles is a principal case in Chapter 9.) Section 2 eliminated the requirement that plaintiffs in constitutional racial vote-dilution cases must satisfy of proving a discriminatory purpose as well as a discriminatory effect.

One of the groups of plaintiffs in Bandemer consisted of black voters in center-city Indianapolis who found themselves placed in multimember, predominantly Republican districts. By a star-crossed fate of history, this turns out to be the same group of minority inner-city plaintiffs who in *Whitcomb v. Chavis*, a principal case in Chapter 7, had unsuccessfully claimed unconstitutional racial vote dilution arising from the state's inclusion of their community in county-wide majority-white multimember districts. This group finally achieved some relief when the state agreed to abandon its multi-member scheme and create several majority-black single-member districts under a Voting Rights Act challenge. See Dickinson v. Indiana State Election Bd., 817 F.Supp. 737 (S.D. Ind. 1992) (recounting the history of the complex litigation); Pamela S. Karlan & Daryl J. Levinson, *Why Voting Is Different*, 84 Cal. L. Rev. 1201, 1221–22 (1996)(recounting the history of the repeated representational challenges).

5. Although constitutional claims of political and racial vote dilution are based on the same constitutional provision–the equal protection clause–and both require proof of discriminatory purpose and discriminatory intent, the Court's treatment of questions of intent and effect differ dramatically in the two kinds of cases. Why? Does this reflect the Court's descriptive view of the world and the likelihood of unfair dilution or does it reflect a more normative notion of when reliance on political factors, as opposed to racial ones, is excessive?

6. *Bandemer* serves as a curious sequel to the reapportionment cases that began with *Baker v. Carr* and *Reynolds v. Sims*. Recall that *Baker* announced only that claims of malapportionment were constitutionally cognizable. It was left to *Reynolds* to provide any operational content to *Baker* by the introduction of the one-person, one-vote rule. In a similar fashion to *Baker*, *Bandemer* established only the justiciability of partisan gerrymandering claims. What would follow? Despite the similarity between the new partisan gerrymandering cause of action and the concept of "fair and effective representation" identified in *Reynolds v. Sims*, *Bandemer* is a decisive step beyond the *Baker/Reynolds* line of cases. In the one-person, one-vote line of cases, the Court attempted to police the electoral processes leading up to the actual casting of ballots. This approach kept the Court at a safe remove from having to assess the propriety of the *outcome* of elections. By contrast, any claim made under *Bandemer* necessarily embroils courts in the messy business of comparing challenged electoral outcomes with a court's conception of what a proper electoral system would have yielded. The Supreme Court provided very little guidance of how this inquiry is to be handled. Indeed, *Bandemer* itself offered only the elliptical language of needing proof of continued frustration of the will of a majority of voters or effective denial to a minority of a fair chance to influence the political process.

After *Bandemer* opened the door to partisan gerrymandering claims, the lower courts struggled for years to make sense of *Bandemer*'s instructions. One of the most noteworthy cases in this saga is the following one, which suggested how little bite *Bandemer* would have as a practical matter, unless the Supreme Court were to give the doctrine more teeth.

Badham v. Eu

694 F.Supp. 664 (N.D.Cal.1988), *aff'd*, 488 U.S. 1024 (1989).

■ POOLE, CIRCUIT JUDGE, with whom ZIRPOLI, DISTRICT JUDGE, concurs:

This case involves a constitutional challenge by plaintiffs, Republican congressional representatives and certain registered Republican voters of California, to Assembly Bill 2X, Chapter 6, 1st Extraordinary Session of the 1983–84 California Legislature ("A.B. 2X"), which effected the redistricting of congressional districts in California following the 1980 Census.

* * *

In the 1984 election, Republicans received 50.1% of the vote statewide, but received only 40% of the congressional seats (18 of 45). This disparity narrowed somewhat in 1986, when Republicans received 46.9% of the vote and retained the same 18 seats. Plaintiffs have alleged that these results are the direct consequence of A.B. 2X and that they are a reliable prediction of future elections.

The parties disagree over whether these allegations are sufficient to satisfy the first prong of *Bandemer*'s "effects" test. Plaintiffs contend that the only deficiency in *Bandemer* was that the plaintiffs there relied solely on the results of a single election, whereas plaintiffs here have alleged that "the 1981 reapportionment would consign the [Republicans] to a minority status throughout the 1980's." Defendants argue that plaintiffs must show much more serious deficiencies, such as those shown in the racial gerrymandering cases, and in addition must show that "the [Republicans] would have no hope of doing any better in the reapportionment that would occur after the 1990 census." We need not resolve this dispute, however, because in any case it is clear that plaintiffs cannot satisfy the second prong of the "effects" test. In order to satisfy the second prong, plaintiffs must show "strong indicia of lack of political power and the denial of fair representation." The *Bandemer* plurality specifically based this requirement on its prior "cases relating to challenges by racial groups to individual multi-member districts," and noted that "[i]n those case, the racial minorities ... had essentially been shut out of the political process."

It is on this second prong of the "effects" threshold that plaintiffs' complaint falters. Specifically, there are no factual allegations regarding California Republicans' role in "the political process as a whole." There are no allegations that California Republicans have been "shut out" of the political process, nor are there allegations that anyone has ever interfered with Republican registration, organizing, voting, fundraising, or campaigning. Republicans remain free to speak out on issues of public concern; plaintiffs do not allege that there are, or have ever been, any impediments to their full participation in the "uninhibited, robust, and wide-open" public debate on which our political system relies.

* * *

[W]e also may take judicial notice of other facts which demonstrate that California Republicans are far from being effectively "shut out" of the political process. Instead, California Republicans represent so potent a political force that it is unnecessary for the judiciary to intervene, as we would be constrained to do to protect the trampled rights of a disadvantaged political or racial minority.

Chief among our observations is our undisputed knowledge that California Republicans still hold 40% of the congressional seats, a sizeable bloc that is far more than mere token representation. It simply would be ludicrous for plaintiffs to allege that their interests are being "entirely ignore[d]" in Congress when they have such a large contingent of representatives who share those interests. We also note that California has a Republican governor, and one of its two senators is a Republican. Given also that a recent former Republican governor of California has for seven years been President of the United States, we see the fulcrum of political power to be such as to belie any attempt of plaintiffs to claim that they are bereft of the ability to exercise potent power in "the political process as a whole" because of the paralysis of an unfair gerrymander.

* * *

NOTES AND QUESTIONS

1. Is *Badham* a proper reading of *Bandemer*? Could either the Democrats or Republicans, in any state, ever make out a claim under the court's test in *Badham*? Many observers believed the California plan was "the most egregious gerrymander of the decade." Bernard Grofman, *An Expert Witness Perspective on Continuing and Emerging Voting Rights Controversies: From One Person, One Vote to Partisan Gerrymandering*, 21 Stetson L. Rev. 783, 816 (1992). If it is invulnerable to constitutional attack, would any plans be likely to be struck down?

The architect of the plan challenged in *Badham*, Representative Phil Burton, described it has "my contribution to modern art." See Frederick K. Lowell & Teresa A. Craigie, *California's Reapportionment Struggle: A*

Classic Clash Between Law and Politics, 2 J.L. & Pol. 245, 246 (1985). According to one account of his activities, "[w]hen Burton finally unveiled his computer-drawn magic . . . politicians were struck dumb by his genius. . . . One district, drawn specifically for Burton's ally Howard Berman, was an incredible 385–sided figure that meandered through most of the San Fernando Valley." John H. Fund, *Beware the Gerrymander, My Son*, Nat'l Rev., Apr. 7, 1989, at 34. For a captivating description of the California state legislative redistricting battles of the 1980s, see Bruce E. Cain, The Reapportionment Puzzle 81–103 (1984).

To get a sense of the political consequences of the plan, consider the following facts. In the 1980 election, using the post–1970 redistricting, which was performed by a special master appointed by the California Supreme Court after a gubernatorial-legislative standoff, Democrats won 22 seats and Republicans won 21. In the 1982 election, after the Democrats had paired three sets of Republican incumbents and split another Republican incumbent's district into six pieces, the Democrats won 26 seats while the Republicans won only 17. The Democrats thus captured 60 percent of the congressional seats with only 52.2 percent of the statewide two-party congressional vote. See Michael E. Lewyn, *How to Limit Gerrymandering*, 45 Fla. L. Rev. 403, 439 (1993).

2.   Throughout its subsequent history, *Bandemer* served almost exclusively as an invitation to litigation without much prospect of redress. Only one case actually found an unconstitutional partisan gerrymander. *See Republican Party of North Carolina v. Martin*, 980 F.2d 943 (4th Cir.1992). In *Martin*, the Court of Appeals, after finding that the complaint alleged the requisite intent to gerrymander, further found that the plaintiff Republican Party had stated a cause of action based on the following alleged facts:

> [I]n order to claim an effect sufficient to state a violation of the Equal Protection Clause, RPNC must allege that the North Carolina voting scheme produces disproportionate results in elections for superior court judges and consistently degrades the influence of Republican voters "on the political process as a whole." Clearly, its complaint alleges disproportionate results. RPNC claims that throughout the twentieth century, it has been, and continues to be, virtually impossible for a qualified candidate for a superior court judgeship to prevail, if running as a Republican. Specifically, RPNC states that only one Republican superior court judge has been elected in the approximately 220 elections held to fill this office since 1968. Yet, registered Republicans comprise approximately 27 percent of the voting population in North Carolina. Moreover, RPNC claims that consistency of voter habits combined with the geographical distribution of party affiliation throughout the state renders it likely that this trend will continue into the foreseeable future. . . .

> RPNC's complaint sets forth data to support its allegations that not only are the election results disproportionate, but also that the nomi-

nation and slating of candidates is affected. Claiming that the method of electing superior court judges inhibits potential Republican candidates from seeking this office, RPNC points to data revealing that in the 1984 and 1986 general elections of 40 judgeships up for election, only four were contested by Republican candidates, and that since 1968, of approximately 220 judgeships up for election, a Republican candidate offered for election in only ten. RPNC maintains that these data demonstrate that few Republicans will offer to run since the chance of success is almost nonexistent. RPNC also asserts that the method of electing superior court judges diminishes campaign contributions for these elections because potential contributors are unwilling to donate money or other resources to a candidate who is perceived to be an almost certain loser. Thus, the complaint does contain allegations of an effect that goes beyond mere disproportionate election results.

Contests for superior court judgeships ... involve statewide elections even though the office is essentially a local one and with very few exceptions, candidates are known only within their local areas. This combination of factors—the status as a statewide candidate for a local office, the requirement to run in a statewide election, and the placement on a ballot with numerous other candidates seeking the same office but from different local districts—encourages, and as history has demonstrated, results in straight-party voting. Voters have little incentive to focus on individual candidates who reside in other districts and thus will discharge their duties in areas of the state distant from the voters' local area.

We recognize that RPNC has not alleged that Republicans have been "excluded from participating in the affairs of their own party or from the processes by which candidates are nominated and elected," *Bandemer,* 478 U.S. at 137, and that to the extent *Bandemer* might be read to require such allegations in order for a political group to allege exclusion from the political process as a whole, RPNC's claims would fail. However, we cannot conclude that a political party that has clearly alleged an effect that amounts to more than disproportionate election results must also allege and ultimately prove this type of exclusion. To do so would hold, in effect, that regardless of the specific allegations of its complaint an identifiable political group could not survive a motion to dismiss or prevail on the merits of its claim. We decline to adopt a construction of *Bandemer* that would render nugatory its holding that political groups may bring claims of partisan gerrymandering.

Subsequently, the Court of Appeals upheld a preliminary injunction ordering computation of votes on both a state-wide and single-district basis. In case of a disparity in electoral outcomes, the court ordered that the sitting judge be held over until the final merits of the case were resolved. *Republican Party of North Carolina v. North Carolina State Board of*

Elections, 27 F.3d 563 (4th Cir.1994). Following a trial on a stipulated record, the district court then ordered that elections be held from judicial districts rather than statewide. Prior to the entry of the final order, however, the political dynamics of the state shifted. In the 1994 election, all eight Republicans seeking statewide election to superior court were elected. This prompted the Court of Appeals to vacate the injunction and order the case remanded for reconsideration of the facts in light of the 1994 elections. *Republican Party of North Carolina v. Hunt,* 77 F.3d 470 (4th Cir.1996).

3. Are the factual allegations accepted in *Martin* sufficient to state a claim under *Bandemer?* Does the 1994 victory of Republican candidates show that a claim of exclusion by one of the two major parties is difficult to maintain? Should such claims be so difficult to maintain?

4. Should the difficulty courts had in applying *Bandemer* call into question the premise of judicial review of political gerrymandering between the major parties? Or should courts accept that redistricting is an inherently political contest for which judicial review is inappropriate? *See* Daniel H. Lowenstein & Jonathan Steinberg, *The Quest for Legislative Districting in the Public Interest: Elusive or Illusory?,* 33 UCLA L. Rev. 1, 74 (1985).

Social scientists have attempted to address the question of how to measure gerrymandering, but have reached no definitive resolution. One approach would use statewide races for secondary state office as a standard for measuring actual partisan support for each party, and then calibrate the results of districted elections against the votes obtained. Another would impose some kind of compactness criterion on redistricting, while yet another would attempt to measure the susceptibility of the political system to change if voters were to shift party allegiances. *See* Charles Backstrom *et al., Establishing a Statewide Electoral Effects Baseline, in* Political Gerrymandering and the Courts 145–62 (Bernard Grofman, ed., 1990) (using bellwether statewide races); Thomas Hofeller & Bernard Grofman, *Comparing the Compactness of California Congressional Districts Under Three Different Plans: 1980, 1982 and 1984, in* Political Gerrymandering, *supra,* at 281–88 (using compactness models); Richard G. Niemi, *The Swing Ratio as a Measure of Partisan Gerrymandering, in* Political Gerrymandering, *supra,* at 171–77 (using the swing ratio as a measure of the immunity from change of a particular electoral arrangement).

Other alternatives would constrain the discretion of redistricting authorities by forcing them to "precommit" to a mechanism to redistrict in advance of the actual redistricting decision. This approach is summarized in Samuel Issacharoff, *Judging Politics: The Elusive Quest for Judicial Review of the Political Process,* 71 Tex. L. Rev. 1643 (1993) (proposing the use of a precommitment to computer modeled redistricting plans before census data are available to partisan actors). Among the possible mechanisms to take redistricting out of partisan hands are either computer models that redistrict automatically or redistricting commissions that operate at one remove from partisan interests. For a discussion of various computer programs that pick an arbitrary point, such as the northwest corner of a state, and then redistrict based on contiguity, compactness, and population equality, as well as more sophisticated approaches, see Michelle H. Browdy, Note, *Computer Models and Post–*Bandemer *Redistricting*, 99 Yale L.J. 1379 (1990). For a discussion of various state experiences with non-partisan redistricting commissions, see Jeffrey C. Kubin, Note, *The Case for Redistricting Commissions*, 75 Tex. L. Rev. 837 (1997).

5. *Political fairness in state courts.* In *Peterson v. Borst*, 786 N.E.2d 668 (Ind. 2003), the Indiana Supreme Court held that a state trial court plan imposed after a political deadlock violated principles of political fairness.

The Indianapolis–Marion County City–County Council, the legislative body for the consolidated city-county government, elects 25 of its 29 members from single-member districts. The applicable redistricting statute requires that the districts be (1) "compact, subject only to natural boundary lines (such as railroads, major highways, rivers, creeks, parks, and major industrial complexes); (2) contain, as nearly as is possible, equal population; and (3) do not cross precinct boundary lines." It also provides that if the council fails to redistrict in a timely manner, the superior court, sitting en banc, can appoint a special master to perform the task.

In 2002, the Council began the redistricting process. A plan proposed by the Republican leader was adopted 15 to 14 with all Republican members voting in favor and all Democratic Members voting against. The Democratic Mayor vetoed the proposal. Among the plans considered were the "Borst Plan" proposed by Phillip C. Borst, Republican leader of the Council, and the "Boyd Plan" proposed by Rozelle Boyd, the Democratic leader of the Council. In October, the Council passed an ordinance approving the Borst Plan. The vote was 15 to 14, with all Republican members voting in favor of the plan and all Democrats voting against it. Indianapolis Mayor Bart Peterson, a Democrat, vetoed the ordinance, asserting among other things that the Borst Plan violated the requirement that districts be compact.

The Council did not attempt to override Mayor Peterson's veto. Instead, Borst filed a lawsuit asking the Marion County Superior Court to declare the Borst Plan valid and order it into effect. The Superior Court is composed of 32 judges, of whom 17 are Republicans and 15 are Democrats. After trial, 16 judges—all Republican—voted in favor of approving the plan Borst, while 13 judges—all Democrats—voted against it.

Democratic council members and the mayor, who had intervened in Borst's lawsuit, appealed to the Indiana Supreme Court.

In a unanimous opinion, the Indiana Supreme Court reversed, holding that "the Superior Court's adoption of a plan that has been uniformly supported by one major political party and uniformly opposed by the other is incompatible with applicable principles of both the appearance and fact of judicial independence and neutrality." The Court noted that while politics plays a legitimate role in legislative and executive districting decisions, it is an illegitimate factor for judicial consideration. Given time pressures created by an impending election, the Indiana Supreme Court drew the district boundaries itself using a process that aimed to be "free of any hint of political partisanship."

In a similar vein, consider *In the Matter of Legislative Districting of the State*, 805 A.2d 292 (Md. 2002) (Maryland redistricting). There, the Maryland Court of Appeals confronted over a dozen federal and state constitutional challenges to the state legislative redistricting challenges that raised federal and state constitutional claims. Article III, § 4 of the Maryland Constitution law required that "[e]ach legislative district shall consist of adjoining territory, be compact in form, and of substantially equal population. Due regard shall be given to natural boundaries and the boundaries of political subdivisions."

The 2002 plan was crafted by the state's Democratic governor. The plan contained 22 inter-jurisdictional, or shared, senatorial districts, an increase of four over the 1992 plan, which had itself contained an unprecedented number of splits. Some counties were split among a striking number of districts. Baltimore County was in twelve senatorial districts. Anne Arundel County was in 5 separate districts, two of which had only minuscule numbers of county residents. Baltimore City and Baltimore County shared five districts drawn so that they were controlled by the City, although it had a smaller population than the adjacent County.

The Court of Appeals concluded that the state's plan, crafted by the Democratic governor, failed the "due regard" prong of Article III, § 4. The court noted that the ultimate power to draw legislative districts lies with the political branches and that political considerations were a legitimate factor in their decisions. Nevertheless, it found that political considerations could not "trump" the districting requirements in the state constitution. The Court of Appeals appointed expert consultants to draw a plan that complied with applicable law "without regard to political considerations."

Do opinions like *Peterson v. Borst* change the political dynamic by creating additional pressure on political actors to reach compromises in the redistricting process, given that the judiciary will be forbidden to consider incumbency in redrawing districts? *Cf.* Daniel R. Ortiz, *Federalism, Reapportionment, and Incumbency: Leading the Legislature to Police Itself*, 4 J.L. & Pol. 653 (1988) (arguing that the prospect of politically neutral federal court reapportionment creates pressure on redistricting authorities to reach political solutions).

For other examples of state-court decisions using state constitutional provisions to strike down reapportionments, *see* Seth Warren Whitaker, Note, *State Redistricting Law: Stephenson v. Bartlett and the Judicial Promotion of Electoral Competition*, 91 Va. L. Rev. 203 (2005). Why are state courts more willing to find partisan gerrymandering violations than federal courts?

B. Redistricting in the **2000's**

In the round of redistricting that followed the 2000 Census, two important consequences emerged that reflected the increasingly powerful technology available to plan drawers and the intensity of the political struggle to capture control of a closely divided House of Representatives. One consequence was that in some states where one party fully controlled the redistricting process, the 2000 round produced some exceptionally aggressive partisan gerrymanders. The second consequence was that the 2000 round saw the proliferation of the "sweetheart" or bipartisan gerrymander, in which the two major parties agreed to carve up seats in a way that protected incumbents of both parties in increasingly safe, non-competitive elections districts—some districts ceded to one party, others to the other party. The result of such sweetheart gerrymanders is that there is no meaningful electoral competition on general election day. Each of these two developments posed challenges to existing constitutional doctrine. We explore each in turn.

1. Partisan Gerrymandering

In the 2000's, lawyers aggressively sought to challenge partisan gerrymandering. The lower courts, however, were no more receptive to *Davis v. Bandemer,* 478 U.S. 109 (1986), than they had been in the 1990s.

Occasionally, some individual judges pressed the courts to take on these claims, but no lower court did. Compare Martinez v. Bush, 234 F. Supp. 2d 1275, 1353 (S.D. Fla. 2002) (three-judge court) (Jordan, J., concurring) ("I urge the Supreme Court to note probable jurisdiction in this case or one of the other political gerrymandering cases arising from this electoral cycle and hear oral argument.") with Duckworth v. State Administration Bd. of Election Laws, 332 F.3d 769 (4th Cir. 2003) (holding that bizarrely drawn districts "are not probative as to the discriminatory effect that must be proven in political gerrymandering cases").

The struggle in Michigan offers an exemplary case study of 2000 redistricting politics and litigation. The account below is taken from an article written by one of the lawyers who represented the Democratic plaintiffs. See Sam Hirsch, *The United States House of Unrepresentatives: What Went Wrong in the Latest Round of Congressional Redistricting*, 2 Election L.J. 179, 205–11 (2003).

Michigan had lost one seat due to reapportionment after the 2000 Census. At the time of the state's redistricting in 2001, Republicans narrowly controlled both houses of the state legislature and the governor's office. In federal elections, however, Michigan voters tend to be more

Democratic than Republican. Democrats held nine of the state's 16 congressional seats. Democrats have won the last three presidential contests, nine of the last ten U.S. Senate elections, and a plurality of votes cast statewide in 14 of 15 of the last U.S. House elections. Democratic presidential candidate Al Gore prevailed by five percentage points in the 2000 presidential election.

On a virtually straight party-line vote, the Michigan legislature adopted a plan that paired six incumbent Democratic congressional representatives against each other in three districts (this gerrymandering technique is known as "kidnapping" existing officeholders). By contrast, the seven incumbent Republican members of Congress were placed in extremely safe districts. The legislature also used "cracking" and "packing" to maximize Republican control; most Democratic voters were heavily concentrated in a small number of districts with the remainder sprinkled throughout the rest of the state. Expert testimony for the challengers purported to demonstrate that this pattern would hold true throughout the decade of the 2000s: competitive Democratic candidates would be likely to win only five of the State's 15 congressional districts, even when on a statewide basis, a majority of voters voted for Democratic House candidates. In addition, 14 of the 15 districts were so safe for one of the two parties that the general election was predicted not to be competitive in all those districts. In addition, the plaintiffs also challenged both the extent to which the plan violated external districting criteria and the process by which the plan had been adopted.

Plaintiffs brought federal constitutional challenges, to a three-judge federal court, under *Bandemer*. In a brief opinion, despite "disproportionality in abundance" and "ample charges of discriminatory motive," the court dismissed for failure even to state a claim upon which relief could be granted. *O'Lear v. Miller*, 222 F. Supp. 2d 850 (E.D. Mich. 2002). As with other *Bandemer* challenges, the court found insufficient proof of the "discriminatory effects" that *Bandemer* required. The Supreme Court summarily affirmed, with Justices Stevens and Breyer noting their dissent. *O'Lear v. Miller*, 537 U.S. 997 (2002). Note that Justice Breyer is perhaps the most vocal advocate on the current Court of the view that the central role of constitutional law is to ensure the openness and integrity of the democratic process. See Stephen Breyer, Our Democratic Constitution, 77 N.Y.U. L. Rev. 245 (2002).

Recall also that, on the eve of the 2000 districting, the Court announced (or clarified what had been implied earlier) that partisan gerrymandering could be a valid defense to a claim of racial gerrymandering. See *Easley v. Cromartie*, 532 U.S. 234 (2001), discussed in Chapter 9. Critics of the Court's failure to put teeth in its partisan gerrymandering doctrine have argued that this only makes the ineffectiveness of the constraints on partisan gerrymandering all the more difficult to justify. See, e.g., John Hart Ely, *Gerrymanders: The Good, the Bad, and the Ugly,* 50 Stan. L. Rev.

607, 621 (1998) ("It is true that by its impossibly high proof requirements the Court in *Bandemer* essentially eliminated political gerrymandering as a meaningful cause of action, but only after it had essentially declared the practice unconstitutional. And yet, a scant decade later, the dissenters in the cases under discussion stand ready to invoke it as an 'innocent' alternative explanation of what appears to be racially motivated gerrymandering. Effectively making a practice nonjusticiable doesn't make it constitutional, especially when the Court has indicated that it isn't. Especially when the Court was right.").

After summarily affirming the Michigan case, the Supreme Court then agreed to hear a case from Pennsylvania that brought the partisan gerrymandering issue back to the Court for the first time since *Bandemer*. (The case had first been litigated as a one-vote, one-person case, and that phase of the litigation is discussed in Chapter 3). The result was a Court as deeply divided on the judicial role in addressing partisan gerrymandering as possible:

Vieth v. Jubelirer

541 U.S. 267 (2004).

■ Justice Scalia announced the judgment of the court and delivered an opinion, in which the Chief Justice, Justice O'Connor, and Justice Thomas join.

* * *

II

Political gerrymanders are not new to the American scene. One scholar traces them back to the Colony of Pennsylvania at the beginning of the 18th century, where several counties conspired to minimize the political power of the city of Philadelphia by refusing to allow it to merge or expand into surrounding jurisdictions, and denying it additional representatives. *See* E. Griffith, The Rise and Development of the Gerrymander 26–28 (1974).... "By 1840 the gerrymander was a recognized force in party politics and was generally attempted in all legislation enacted for the formation of election districts. It was generally conceded that each party would attempt to gain power which was not proportionate to its numerical strength." Griffith 123.

It is significant that the Framers provided a remedy for such practices in the Constitution. Article 1, § 4, while leaving in state legislatures the initial power to draw districts for federal elections, permitted Congress to "make or alter" those districts if it wished. Many objected to the congressional oversight established by this provision. In the course of the debates in the Constitutional Convention, Charles Pinkney and John Rutledge moved to strike the relevant language. James Madison responded in defense of the provision that Congress must be given the power to check partisan manipulation of the election process by the States:

> "Whenever the State Legislatures had a favorite measure to carry, they would take care so to mould their regulations as to favor the candidates they wished to succeed. Besides, the inequality of the Representation in the Legislatures of particular States, would produce a like inequality in their representation in the Natl. Legislature, as it was presumable that the Counties having the power in the former case would secure it to themselves in the latter. What danger could there be in giving a controuling power to the Natl. Legislature?" 2 Records of the Federal Convention of 1787, at 240–241 (1911).

[. . .] The power bestowed on Congress to regulate elections, and in particular to restrain the practice of political gerrymandering, has not lain dormant. In the Apportionment Act of 1842, 5 Stat. 491, Congress provided that Representatives must be elected from single-member districts "composed of contiguous territory." *See* Griffith 12 (noting that the law was "an attempt to forbid the practice of the gerrymander"). Congress again imposed these requirements in the Apportionment Act of 1862, 12 Stat. 572, and in 1872 further required that districts "contai[n] as nearly as practicable an equal number of inhabitants," 17 Stat. 28, § 2. In the Apportionment Act of 1901, Congress imposed a compactness requirement. 31 Stat. 733. The requirements of contiguity, compactness, and equality of population were repeated in the 1911 apportionment legislation, 37 Stat. 13, but were not thereafter continued. Today, only the single-member-district-requirement remains. *See* 2 U.S.C. § 2c. Recent history, however, attests to Congress's awareness of the sort of districting practices appellants protest, and of its power under Article I, § 4 to control them. Since 1980, no fewer than five bills have been introduced to regulate gerrymandering in congressional districting. *See* H.R. 5037, 101st Cong., 2d Sess. (1990); H.R. 1711, 101st Cong., 1st *Sess.* (1989); H.R. 3468, 98th Cong., 1st Sess. (1983); H.R. 5529, 97th Cong., 2d Sess. (1982); H.R. 2349, 97th Cong., 1st Sess. (1981).[29]

Eighteen years ago, we held that the Equal Protection Clause grants judges the power–and duty–to control political gerrymandering, see *Davis v. Bandemer,* 478 U.S. 109 (1986). It is to consideration of this precedent that we now turn.

III

As Chief Justice Marshall proclaimed two centuries ago, "[i]t is emphatically the province and duty of the judicial department to say what the

---

29. The States, of course, have taken their own steps to prevent abusive districting practices. A number have adopted standards for redistricting, and measures designed to insulate the process from politics. *See, e.g.,* Iowa Code § 42.4(5) (2003); N.J. Const., Art. II, § 2; Haw.Rev.Stat. § 25–2 (1993); Idaho Code § 72–1506 (1948–1999); Me.Rev.Stat. Ann., Tit. 21–A, §§ 1206, 1206–A (West Supp.2003); Mont.Code Ann. § 5–1–115 (2003); Wash. Rev.Code § 44.05.090 (1994).

law is." *Marbury v. Madison,* 1 Cranch 137, 177 (1803). Sometimes, however, the law is that the judicial department has no business entertaining the claim of unlawfulness–because the question is entrusted to one of the political branches or involves no judicially enforceable rights ... One of the most obvious limitations imposed by that requirement is that judicial action must be governed by *standard,* by *rule.* Laws promulgated by the Legislative Branch can be inconsistent, illogical, and ad hoc; law pronounced by the courts must be principled, rational, and based upon reasoned distinctions.

Over the dissent of three Justices, the Court held in *Davis v. Bandemer* that, since it was "not persuaded that there are no judicially discernible and manageable standards by which political gerrymander cases are to be decided," 478 U.S. at 123, such cases *were* justiciable. The clumsy shifting of the burden of proof for the premise (the Court was "not persuaded" that standards do not exist, rather than "persuaded" that they do) was necessitated by the uncomfortable fact that the six-Justice majority could not discern what the judicially discernable standards might be. There was no majority on that point ... The lower courts have lived with that assurance of a standard (or more precisely, lack of assurance that there is no standard), coupled with that inability to specify a standard, for the past 18 years. In that time, they have considered numerous political gerrymandering claims; this Court has never revisited the unanswered question of what standard governs.

Nor can it be said that the lower courts have, over 18 years, succeeded in shaping the standard that this Court was initially unable to enunciate. They have simply applied the standard set forth in *Bandemer's* four-Justice plurality opinion. This might be thought to prove that the four-Justice plurality standard has met the test of time–but for the fact that its application has almost invariably produced the same result (except for the incurring of attorney's fees) as would have obtained if the question were nonjusticiable: judicial intervention has been refused. As one commentary has put it, "[t]hroughout its subsequent history, *Bandemer* has served almost exclusively as an invitation to litigation without much prospect of redress." S. Issacharoff, P. Karlan, & R. Pildes, The Law of Democracy 886 (rev. 2d ed. 2002).... To think that this lower-court jurisprudence has brought forth "judicially discernible and manageable standards" would be fantasy.

Eighteen years of judicial effort with virtually nothing to show for it justify us in revisiting the question whether the standard promised by *Bandemer* exists. As the following discussion reveals, no judicially discernible and manageable standards for adjudicating political gerrymandering claims have emerged. Lacking them, we must conclude that political gerrymandering claims are nonjusticiable and that *Bandemer* was wrongly decided.

A

We begin our review of possible standards with that proposed by Justice White's plurality opinion in *Bandemer* because, as the narrowest ground for our decision in that case, it has been the standard employed by the lower courts.

* * *

In the lower courts, the legacy of the plurality's test is one long record of puzzlement and consternation. [citations omitted] Because this standard was misguided when proposed, has not been improved in subsequent application, and is not even defended before us today by the appellants, we decline to affirm it as a constitutional requirement.

B

Appellants take a run at enunciating their own workable standard based on Article I, § 2, and the Equal Protection Clause. We consider it at length not only because it reflects the litigant's view as to the best that can be derived from 18 years of experience, but also because it shares many features with other proposed standards, so that what is said of it may be said of them as well. Appellants' proposed standard retains the two-pronged framework of the *Bandemer* plurality–intent plus effect–but modifies the type of showing sufficient to satisfy each.

To satisfy appellants' intent standard, a plaintiff must "show that the mapmakers acted with a *predominant intent* to achieve partisan advantage," which can be shown "by direct evidence or by circumstantial evidence that other neutral and legitimate redistricting criteria were subordinated to the goal of achieving partisan advantage." Brief for Appellants 19 (emphasis added). As compared with the *Bandemer* plurality's test of mere intent to disadvantage the plaintiff's group, this proposal seemingly makes the standard more difficult to meet—but only at the expense of making the standard more indeterminate.

"Predominant intent" to disadvantage the plaintiff political group refers to the relative importance of that goal as compared with all the other goals that the map seeks to pursue—contiguity of districts, compactness of districts, observance of the lines of political subdivision, protection of incumbents of all parties, cohesion of natural racial and ethnic neighborhoods, compliance with requirements of the Voting Rights Act of 1965 regarding racial distribution, etc. Appellants contend that their intent test *must* be discernible and manageable because it has been borrowed from our racial gerrymandering cases. To begin with, in a very important respect that is not so. In the racial gerrymandering context, the predominant intent test has been applied to the challenged district in which the plaintiffs voted. Here, however, appellants do not assert that an apportionment fails their intent test if any single district does so. Since "it would be quixotic to attempt to bar state legislatures from considering politics as they redraw district lines," Brief for Appellants 3, appellants propose a test that is satisfied only when "partisan advantage was the predominant motivation *behind the entire statewide plan," id.,* at 32 (emphasis added). Vague as the "predominant motivation" test might be when used to evaluate single districts, it all but evaporates when applied statewide. Does it mean, for instance, that partisan intent must outweigh all other goals—contiguity, compactness, preservation of neighborhoods, etc.—*statewide?* And how is the statewide "outweighing" to be determined? If three-fifths of the map's districts forgo the pursuit of partisan ends in favor of strictly observing political-subdivision lines, and only two-fifths ignore those lines to disadvantage the plaintiffs, is the observance of political subdivisions the "predominant" goal between those two? We are sure appellants do not think so.

Even within the narrower compass of challenges to a single district, applying a "predominant intent" test to *racial* gerrymandering is easier and less disruptive. The Constitution clearly contemplates districting by political entities, see Article I, § 4, and unsurprisingly that turns out to be root-and-branch a matter of politics. By contrast, the purpose of segregating voters on the basis of race is not a lawful one, and is much more rarely encountered. Determining whether the shape of a particular district is so substantially affected by the presence of a rare and constitutionally suspect motive as to invalidate it is quite different from determining whether it is so substantially affected by the excess of an ordinary and lawful motive as to invalidate it. Moreover, the fact that partisan districting is a lawful and common practice means that there is almost *always* room for an election-impeding lawsuit contending that partisan advantage was the predominant motivation; not so for claims of racial gerrymandering. Finally, courts might be justified in accepting a modest degree of unmanageability to enforce a constitutional command which (like the Fourteenth Amendment obligation to refrain from racial discrimination) is clear; whereas they are not justified in inferring a judicially enforceable constitutional obligation (the obligation not to apply *too much* partisanship in districting) which is both dubious and severely unmanageable. For these reasons, to the extent that our racial gerrymandering cases represent a model of discernible and manageable standards, they provide no comfort here.

The effects prong of appellants' proposal replaces the *Bandemer* plurality's vague test of "denied its chance to effectively influence the political process," with criteria that are seemingly more specific. The requisite effect is established when "(1) the plaintiffs show that the districts systematically 'pack' and 'crack' the rival party's voters, *and* (2) the court's examination of the 'totality of circumstances' confirms that the map can thwart the plaintiffs' ability to translate a majority of votes into a majority of seats." Brief for Appellants 20 (emphasis and footnote added). This test is loosely based on our cases applying § 2 of the Voting Rights Act, to discrimination by race. But a person's politics is rarely as readily discernible—and *never* as permanently discernible—as a person's race. Political affiliation is not an immutable characteristic, but may shift from one election to the next; and even within a given election, not all voters follow the party line. We dare say (and hope) that the political party which puts forward an utterly incompetent candidate will lose even in its registration stronghold. These facts make it impossible to assess the effects of partisan gerrymandering, to fashion a standard for evaluating a violation, and finally to craft a remedy.

Assuming, however, that the effects of partisan gerrymandering can be determined, appellants' test would invalidate the districting only when it prevents a majority of the electorate from electing a majority of representatives. Before considering whether this particular standard is judicially manageable we question whether it is judicially discernible in the sense of being relevant to some constitutional violation. Deny it as appellants may (and do), this standard rests upon the principle that groups (or at least political-action groups) have a right to proportional representation. But the Constitution contains no such principle. It guarantees equal protection of the law to persons, not equal representation in government to equivalently sized groups. It nowhere says that farmers or urban dwellers, Christian fundamentalists or Jews, Republicans or Democrats, must be accorded political strength proportionate to their numbers.

Even if the standard were relevant, however, it is not judicially manageable. To begin with, how is a party's majority status to be established? Appellants propose using the results of statewide races as the benchmark of party support. But as their own complaint describes, in the 2000 Pennsylvania statewide elections some Republicans won and some Democrats won. Moreover, to think that majority status in statewide races establishes majority status for district contests, one would have to believe that the only factor determining voting behavior at all levels is political affiliation. That is assuredly not true. As one law review comment has put it:

> "There is no statewide vote in this country for the House of Representatives or the state legislature. Rather, there are separate elections between separate candidates in separate districts, and that is all there is. If the districts change, the candidates change, their strengths and weaknesses change, their campaigns change, their ability to raise money changes, the issues change—everything changes. Political parties do not compete for the highest statewide vote totals or the highest mean district vote percentages: They compete for specific seats." Lowenstein & Steinberg, *The Quest for Legislative Districting in the Public Interest: Elusive or Illusory*, 33 UCLA L.Rev. 1, 59–60 (1985).

See also Schuck, Partisan Gerrymandering: A Political Problem Without Judicial Solution, in Political Gerrymandering and the Courts 240, 241 (1990).

But if we could identify a majority party, we would find it impossible to assure that that party wins a majority of seats—unless we radically revise the States' traditional structure for elections. In any winner-take-all district system, there can be no guarantee, no matter how the district lines are drawn, that a majority of party votes statewide will produce a majority of seats for that party. The point is proved by the 2000 congressional elections in Pennsylvania, which, according to appellants' own pleadings, were conducted under a judicially drawn district map "free from partisan gerrymandering." On this "neutral playing fiel[d]," the Democrats' statewide majority of the major-party vote (50.6%) translated into a minority of seats (10, versus 11 for the Republicans). Whether by reason of partisan districting or not, party constituents may always wind up "packed" in some districts and "cracked" throughout others. Consider, for example, a legislature that draws district lines with no objectives in mind except compactness and respect for the lines of political subdivisions. Under that system, political groups that tend to cluster (as is the case with Democratic voters in cities) would be systematically affected by what might be called a "natural" packing effect.

Our one-person, one-vote cases have no bearing upon this question, neither in principle nor in practicality. Not in principle, because to say that each individual must have an equal say in the selection of representatives, and hence that a majority of individuals must have a majority say, is not at all to say that each discernable group, whether farmers or urban dwellers or political parties, must have representation equivalent to its numbers. And not in practicality, because the easily administrable standard of population equality adopted by *Wesberry* and *Reynolds* enables judges to decide whether a violation has occurred (and to remedy it) essentially on the basis of three readily determined factors—where the plaintiff lives, how many voters are in his district, and how many voters are in other districts; whereas requiring judges to decide whether a districting system will produce a statewide majority for a majority party casts them forth upon a sea of imponderables, and asks them to make determinations that not even election experts can agree upon.

For these reasons, we find appellants' proposed standards neither discernible nor manageable.

IV

We turn next to consideration of the standards proposed by today's dissenters. We preface it with the observation that the mere fact that these four dissenters come up with three different standards—all of them different from the two proposed in *Bandemer* and the one proposed here by appellants—goes a long way to establishing that there is no constitutionally discernible standard.

A

Justice Stevens concurs in the judgment that we should not address plaintiffs' statewide political gerrymandering challenges. Though he reaches that result via standing analysis, while we reach it through political-question analysis, our conclusions are the same: these statewide claims are nonjusticiable.

Justice Stevens would, however, require courts to consider political gerrymandering challenges at the individual-district level. Much of his dissent is addressed to the incompatibility of severe partisan gerrymanders with democratic principles. We do not disagree with that judgment, any more than we disagree with the judgment that it would be unconstitutional for the Senate to employ, in impeachment proceedings, procedures that are incompatible with its obligation to "try" impeachments. The issue we have discussed is not whether severe partisan gerrymanders violate the Constitution, but whether it is for the courts to say when a violation has occurred, and to design a remedy. On that point, Justice Stevens's dissent is less helpful, saying, essentially, that if we can do it in the racial gerrymandering context we can do it here.

We have examined the many reasons why that is not so. Only a few of them are challenged by Justice Stevens. He says that we "mistakenly assum[e] that race cannot provide a legitimate basis for making political judgments." But we do not say that race-conscious decisionmaking is always unlawful. Race can be used, for example, as an indicator to achieve the purpose of neighborhood cohesiveness in districting. What we have said is impermissible is "the purpose of segregating voters on the basis of race,"—that is to say, racial gerrymandering for race's sake, which would be the equivalent of political gerrymandering for politics' sake. Justice Stevens says we "er[r] in assuming that politics is 'an ordinary and lawful motive' " in districting, but all he brings forward to contest that is the argument that an *excessive* injection of politics is *un*lawful. So it is, and so does our opinion assume. That does not alter the reality that setting out to segregate voters by race is unlawful and hence rare, and setting out to segregate them by political affiliation is (so long as one doesn't go too far) lawful and hence ordinary.

Justice Stevens's confidence that what courts have done with racial gerrymandering can be done with political gerrymandering rests in part upon his belief that "the same standards should apply." But in fact the standards are quite different. A purpose to discriminate on the basis of race receives the strictest scrutiny under the Equal Protection Clause, while a similar purpose to discriminate on the basis of politics does not. "[N]othing in our case law compels the conclusion that racial and political gerrymanders are subject to precisely the same constitutional scrutiny. In fact, our country's long and persistent history of racial discrimination in voting–as well as our Fourteenth Amendment jurisprudence, which always has reserved the strictest scrutiny for discrimination on the basis of race—would seem to compel the opposite conclusion." *Shaw*, 509 U.S. at 650, (internal citation omitted). That quoted passage was in direct response to (and rejection of) the suggestion made by Justices White and Stevens in dissent that "a racial gerrymander of the sort alleged here is functionally equivalent to gerrymanders for nonracial purposes, such as political gerrymanders." . . .

Having failed to make the case for strict scrutiny of political gerrymandering, Justice Stevens falls back on the argument that scrutiny levels simply do not matter for purposes of justiciability. He asserts that a standard imposing a strong presumption of invalidity (strict scrutiny) is no more discernible and manageable than a standard requiring an evenhanded balancing of all considerations with no thumb on the scales (ordinary scrutiny). To state this is to refute it. As is well known, strict scrutiny readily, and almost always, results in invalidation. Moreover, the mere fact that there exist standards which this Court could apply—the proposition which much of Justice Stevens's opinion is devoted to establishing—does not mean that those standard are discernible in the Constitution. This Court may not willy-nilly apply standards—even manageable standards—having no relation to constitutional harms. Justice Stevens points out that *Bandemer* said differences between racial and political groups "may be relevant to the manner in which the case is adjudicated, but these differences do not justify a refusal to entertain such a case." 478 U.S. at 125. As 18 years have shown, *Bandemer* was wrong.

B

Justice Souter, like Justice Stevens, would restrict these plaintiffs, on the allegations before us, to district-specific political gerrymandering claims. Unlike Justice Stevens, however, Justice Souter recognizes that there is no existing workable standard for adjudicating such claims. He proposes a "fresh start": a newly constructed standard loosely based in form on our Title VII cases, see *McDonnell Douglas Corp. v. Green,* 411 U.S. 792 (1973), and complete with a five-step prima facie test sewn together from parts of, among other things, our Voting Rights Act jurisprudence, law review articles, and apportionment cases. Even if these self-styled "clues" to unconstitutionality could be manageably applied, which we doubt, there is no reason to think they would detect the constitutional crime which Justice Souter is investigating–an "extremity of unfairness" in partisan competition.

Under Justice Souter's proposed standard, in order to challenge a particular district, a plaintiff must show (1) that he is a member of a "cohesive political group"; (2) "that the district of his residence . . . paid little or no heed" to traditional districting principles; (3) that there were "specific correlations between the district's deviations from traditional districting principles and the distribution of the population of his group"; (4) that a hypothetical district exists which includes the plaintiff's residence, remedies the packing or cracking of the plaintiff's group, and deviates less from traditional districting principles; and (5) that "the defendants acted intentionally to manipulate the shape of the district in order to pack or crack his group." When those showings have been made, the burden would shift to the defendants to justify the district "by reference to objectives other than naked partisan advantage."

While this five-part test seems eminently scientific, upon analysis one finds that each of the last four steps requires a quantifying judgment that is unguided and ill suited to the development of judicial standards: *How much* disregard of traditional districting principles? *How many* correlations between deviations and distribution? *How much* remedying of packing or cracking by the hypothetical district? *How many legislators* must have had the intent to pack and crack–and *how efficacious* must that intent have been (must it have been, for example, a *sine qua non* cause of the districting, or a *predominant* cause)? At step two, for example, Justice Souter would require lower courts to assess whether mapmakers paid "little or no heed to . . . traditional districting principles." What is a lower court to do when, as will often be the case, the district adheres to some traditional criteria but not others? Justice Souter's only response to this question is to evade it: "It is not necessary now to say exactly how a district court would balance a good showing on one of these indices against a poor showing on another, for that sort of detail is best worked out case by case." But the devil lurks precisely in such detail. The central problem is determining when political gerrymandering has gone too far. It does not solve that problem to break down the original unanswerable question (How much political motivation and effect is too much?) into four more discrete but equally unanswerable questions.

Justice Souter's proposal is doomed to failure for a more basic reason: No test—yea, not even a five-part test—can possibly be successful unless one knows what he is testing *for*. In the present context, the test ought to identify deprivation of that minimal degree of representation or influence to which a political group is constitutionally entitled. As we have seen, the *Bandemer* test sought (unhelpfully, but at least gamely) to specify what that minimal degree was: "[a] chance to effectively influence the political process." So did the appellants' proposed test: "[the] ability to translate a majority of votes into a majority of seats." Brief for Appellants 20. Justice Souter avoids the difficulties of those formulations by never telling us what his test is looking for, other than the utterly unhelpful "extremity of unfairness." He vaguely describes the harm he is concerned with as vote dilution, a term which usually implies some actual effect on the weight of a vote. But no element of his test looks to the effect of the gerrymander on the electoral success, the electoral opportunity, or even the political influence, of the plaintiff group. We do not know the precise constitutional deprivation his test is designed to identify and prevent. . . .

Like us, Justice Souter acknowledges and accepts that "some intent to gain political advantage is inescapable whenever political bodies devise a district plan, and some effect results from the intent." Thus, again like us, he recognizes that "the issue is one of how much is too much." And once those premises are conceded, the only line that can be drawn must be based, as Justice Souter again candidly admits, upon a substantive "no-tio[n] of fairness." This is the same flabby goal that deprived Justice Powell's test of all determinacy. To be sure, Justice Souter frames it somewhat differently: courts must intervene, he says, when "partisan competition has reached an *extremity* of unfairness." We do not think the problem is solved by adding the modifier.

C

We agree with much of Justice Breyer's dissenting opinion, which convincingly demonstrates that "political considerations will likely play an important, and proper, role in the drawing of district boundaries." This places Justice Breyer, like the other dissenters, in the difficult position of drawing the line between good politics and bad politics. Unlike them, he would tackle this problem at the statewide level.

The criterion Justice Breyer proposes is nothing more precise than "the *unjustified* use of political factors to entrench a minority in power." While he invokes in passing the Equal Protection Clause, it should be clear to any reader that what constitutes *unjustified* entrenchment depends on his own theory of "effective government." While one must agree with Justice Breyer's incredibly abstract starting point that our Constitution sought to create a "basically democratic" form of government, that is a long and impassable distance away from the conclusion that the judiciary may assess whether a group (somehow defined) has achieved a level of political power (somehow defined) commensurate with that to which they would be entitled absent *unjustified* political machinations (whatever that means).

Justice Breyer provides no real guidance for the journey. Despite his promise to do so, he never tells us what he is testing for, beyond the unhelpful "*unjustified* entrenchment." Instead, he "set[s] forth several sets of circumstances that lay out the indicia of abuse," "along a continuum," proceeding (presumably) from the most clearly unconstitutional to the possibly unconstitutional. With regard to the first "scenario," he is willing to assert that the indicia "would be sufficient to support a claim." This seems refreshingly categorical, until one realizes that the indicia consist not merely of the failure of the party receiving the majority of votes to acquire a majority of seats in two successive elections, *but also* of the fact that there is no "neutral" explanation for this phenomenon. But of course there *always is* a neutral explanation–if only the time-honored criterion of incumbent protection. The indicia set forth in Justice Breyer's second scenario "*could* also add up to unconstitutional gerrymandering;" and for those in the third "a court *may* conclude that the map crosses the constitutional line." We find none of this helpful. Each scenario suffers from at least one of the problems we have previously identified, most notably the difficulties of assessing partisan strength statewide and of ascertaining whether an entire statewide plan is motivated by political or neutral justifications. And even at that, the last two scenarios *do not even purport to provide an answer*, presumably leaving it to each district court to determine whether, under those circumstances, *"unjustified* entrenchment" has occurred. In sum, we neither know precisely what Justice Breyer is testing for, nor precisely what fails the test.

But perhaps the most surprising omission from Justice Breyer's dissent, given his views on other matters, is the absence of any cost-benefit analysis. Justice Breyer acknowledges that "a majority normally can work its political will," and well describes the number of actors, from statewide executive officers, to redistricting commissions, to Congress, to the People in ballot initiatives and referenda, that stand ready to make that happen. He gives no instance (and we know none) of permanent frustration of majority will. But where the majority has failed to assert itself for some indeterminate period (two successive elections, if we are to believe his first scenario), Justice Breyer simply assumes that "court action may prove necessary." Why so? In the real world, of course, court action that is available tends to be sought, not just where it is necessary, but where it is in the interest of the seeking party. And the vaguer the test for availability, the more frequently interest rather than necessity will produce litigation. Is the regular insertion of the judiciary into districting, with the delay and uncertainty that brings to the political process and the partisan enmity it brings upon the courts, worth the benefit to be achieved—an accelerated (by some unknown degree) effectuation of the majority will? We think not.

V

Justice Kennedy . . . concludes that courts should continue to adjudicate such claims because a standard *may* one day be discovered.

The first thing to be said about Justice Kennedy's disposition is that it is not legally available. The District Court in this case considered the plaintiffs' claims *justiciable* but dismissed them because the standard for unconstitutionality had not been met. It is logically impossible to affirm that dismissal without either (1) finding that the unconstitutional-districting standard applied by the District Court, or some other standard that it *should* have applied, has not been met, or (2) finding (as we have) that the claim is nonjusticiable. Justice Kennedy seeks to affirm "[b]ecause, in the case before us, we have no standard." But it is *our* job, not the plaintiffs', to explicate the standard that makes the facts alleged by the plaintiffs adequate or inadequate to state a claim. We cannot nonsuit *them* for our failure to do so.

* * *

Justice Kennedy worries that "[a] determination by the Court to deny all hopes of intervention could erode confidence in the courts as much as would a premature decision to intervene." But it is the function of the courts to provide relief, not hope. What we think would erode confidence is the Court's refusal to do its job—announcing that there may well be a valid claim here, but we are not yet prepared to figure it out. Moreover, that course does more than erode confidence; by placing the district courts back in the business of pretending to afford help when they in fact can give none, it deters the political process from affording genuine relief. As was noted by a lower court confronted with a political gerrymandering claim:

> "When the Supreme Court resolves *Vieth,* it may choose to retreat from its decision that the question is justiciable, or it may offer more guidance on the nature of the required effect.... We have learned firsthand what will result if the Court chooses to do neither. Throughout this case we have borne witness to the powerful, conflicting forces nurtured by *Bandemer's* holding that the judiciary is to address 'excessive' partisan line-drawing, while leaving the issue virtually unenforceable. Inevitably, as the political party in power uses district lines to lock in its present advantage, the party out of power attempts to stretch the protective cover of the Voting Rights Act, urging dilution of critical standards that may, if accepted, aid their party in the short-run but work to the detriment of persons now protected by the Act in the long-run. Casting the appearance both that there is a wrong and that the judiciary stands ready with a remedy, *Bandemer* as applied steps on legislative incentives for self-correction." *Session,* 298 F.Supp.2d at 474.

[. . .] Reduced to its essence, Justice Kennedy's opinion boils down to this: "As presently advised, I know of no discernible and manageable standard that can render this claim justiciable. I am unhappy about that, and hope that I will be able to change my opinion in the future." What are the lower courts to make of this pronouncement? We suggest that they must treat it as a reluctant fifth vote against justiciability at district and statewide levels—a vote that may change in some future case but that holds, for the time being, that this matter is nonjusticiable.

VI

We conclude that neither Article I, § 2, nor the Equal Protection Clause, nor (what appellants only fleetingly invoke) Article I, § 4, provides a judicially enforceable limit on the political considerations that the States and Congress may take into account when districting.

Considerations of *stare decisis* do not compel us to allow *Bandemer* to stand. That case involved an interpretation of the Constitution, and the claims of *stare decisis* are at their weakest in that field, where our mistakes cannot be corrected by Congress. *See Payne v. Tennessee,* 501 U.S. 808, 828 (1991). They are doubly weak in *Bandemer* because the majority's inability to enunciate the judicially discernible and manageable standard that it thought existed (or did not think did not exist) presaged the need for reconsideration in light of subsequent experience. And they are triply weak because it is hard to imagine how any action taken in reliance upon

Bandemer could conceivably be frustrated–except the bringing of lawsuits, which is not the sort of primary conduct that is relevant.

While we do not lightly overturn one of our own holdings, "when governing decisions are unworkable or are badly reasoned, 'this Court has never felt constrained to follow precedent.' " *Id.* at 827 (quoting *Smith v. Allwright*, 321 U.S. 649, 665 (1944)). Eighteen years of essentially pointless litigation have persuaded us that *Bandemer* is incapable of principled application. We would therefore overrule that case, and decline to adjudicate these political gerrymandering claims.

The judgment of the District Court is affirmed.

■ JUSTICE KENNEDY, concurring in the judgment.

A decision ordering the correction of all election district lines drawn for partisan reasons would commit federal and state courts to unprecedented intervention in the American political process. The Court is correct to refrain from directing this substantial intrusion into the Nation's political life. While agreeing with the plurality that the complaint the appellants filed in the District Court must be dismissed, and while understanding that great caution is necessary when approaching this subject, I would not foreclose all possibility of judicial relief if some limited and precise rationale were found to correct an established violation of the Constitution in some redistricting cases.

When presented with a claim of injury from partisan gerrymandering, courts confront two obstacles. First is the lack of comprehensive and neutral principles for drawing electoral boundaries. No substantive definition of fairness in districting seems to command general assent. Second is the absence of rules to limit and confine judicial intervention. With uncertain limits, intervening courts—even when proceeding with best intentions—would risk assuming political, not legal, responsibility for a process that often produces ill will and distrust.

. . . I would add two comments to the plurality's analysis. The first is that the parties have not shown us, and I have not been able to discover, helpful discussions on the principles of fair districting discussed in the annals of parliamentary or legislative bodies. Our attention has not been drawn to statements of principled, well-accepted rules of fairness that should govern districting, or to helpful formulations of the legislator's duty in drawing district lines.

Second, even those criteria that might seem promising at the outset (*e.g.*, contiguity and compactness) are not altogether sound as independent judicial standards for measuring a burden on representational rights. They cannot promise political neutrality when used as the basis for relief. Instead, it seems, a decision under these standards would unavoidably have significant political effect, whether intended or not. For example, if we were to demand that congressional districts take a particular shape, we could not assure the parties that this criterion, neutral enough on its face, would not in fact benefit one political party over another.

... There are, then, weighty arguments for holding cases like these to be nonjusticiable; and those arguments may prevail in the long run. In my view, however, the arguments are not so compelling that they require us now to bar all future claims of injury from a partisan gerrymander. It is not in our tradition to foreclose the judicial process from the attempt to define standards and remedies where it is alleged that a constitutional right is burdened or denied. Nor is it alien to the Judiciary to draw or approve election district lines. Courts, after all, already do so in many instances. A determination by the Court to deny all hopes of intervention could erode confidence in the courts as much as would a premature decision to intervene.

Our willingness to enter the political thicket of the apportionment process with respect to one-person, one-vote claims makes it particularly difficult to justify a categorical refusal to entertain claims against this other type of gerrymandering. The plurality's conclusion that absent an "easily administrable standard," the appellants' claim must be nonjusticiable contrasts starkly with the more patient approach of *Baker v. Carr,* 369 U.S. 186 (1962), not to mention the controlling precedent on the question of justiciability of *Davis v. Bandemer, supra,* the case the plurality would overrule.

That no [appropriate] standard has emerged in this case should not be taken to prove that none will emerge in the future. Where important rights are involved, the impossibility of full analytical satisfaction is reason to err on the side of caution.... If a State passed an enactment that declared "All future apportionment shall be drawn so as most to burden Party X's rights to fair and effective representation, though still in accord with one-person, one-vote principles," we would surely conclude the Constitution had been violated. If that is so, we should admit the possibility remains that a legislature might attempt to reach the same result without that express directive. This possibility suggests that in another case a standard might emerge that suitably demonstrates how an apportionment's *de facto* incorporation of partisan classifications burdens rights of fair and effective representation (and so establishes the classification is unrelated to the aims of apportionment and thus is used in an impermissible fashion).

... Technology is both a threat and a promise. On the one hand, if courts refuse to entertain any claims of partisan gerrymandering, the temptation to use partisan favoritism in districting in an unconstitutional manner will grow. On the other hand, these new technologies may produce new methods of analysis that make more evident the precise nature of the burdens gerrymanders impose on the representational rights of voters and parties. That would facilitate court efforts to identify and remedy the burdens, with judicial intervention limited by the derived standards.

If suitable standards with which to measure the burden a gerrymander imposes on representational rights did emerge, hindsight would show that the Court prematurely abandoned the field. That is a risk the Court should not take.... The plurality thinks I resolve this case with reference to no standard, but that is wrong. The Fourteenth Amendment standard governs; and there is no doubt of that. My analysis only notes that if a subsidiary standard could show how an otherwise permissible classification, as applied, burdens representational rights, we could conclude that appellants' evidence states a provable claim under the Fourteenth Amendment standard.

Though in the briefs and at argument the appellants relied on the Equal Protection Clause as the source of their substantive right and as the basis for relief, I note that the complaint in this case also alleged a violation of First Amendment rights. The First Amendment may be the more relevant constitutional provision in future cases that allege unconstitutional partisan gerrymandering. After all, these allegations involve the First Amendment interest of not burdening or penalizing citizens because of their participation in the electoral process, their voting history, their association with a political party, or their expression of political views. Under general First Amendment principles those burdens in other contexts are unconstitutional absent a compelling government interest.... First Amendment concerns arise where a State enacts a law that has the purpose and effect of subjecting a group of voters or their party to disfavored treatment by reason of their views. In the context of partisan gerrymandering, that means that First Amendment concerns arise where an apportionment has the purpose and effect of burdening a group of voters' representational rights....

Where it is alleged that a gerrymander had the purpose and effect of imposing burdens on a disfavored party and its voters, the First Amendment may offer a sounder and more prudential basis for intervention than does the Equal Protection Clause. The equal protection analysis puts its emphasis on the permissibility of an enactment's classifications. This works where race is involved since classifying by race is almost never permissible. It presents a more complicated question when the inquiry is whether a generally permissible classification has been used for an impermissible purpose. That question can only be answered in the affirmative by the subsidiary showing that the classification as applied imposes unlawful burdens. The First Amendment analysis concentrates on whether the legislation burdens the representational rights of the complaining party's voters for reasons of ideology, beliefs, or political association. The analysis allows a pragmatic or functional assessment that accords some latitude to the States.

Finally, I do not understand the plurality to conclude that partisan gerrymandering that disfavors one party is permissible. Indeed, the Court seems to acknowledge it is not. . . . This is all the more reason to admit the possibility of later suits . . .

* * *

The ordered working of our Republic, and of the democratic process, depends on a sense of decorum and restraint in all branches of government, and in the citizenry itself. Here, one has the sense that legislative restraint was abandoned. That should not be thought to serve the interests of our political order. Nor should it be thought to serve our interest in demonstrating to the world how democracy works. Whether spoken with concern or pride, it is unfortunate that our legislators have reached the point of declaring that, when it comes to apportionment, " 'We are in the business of rigging elections.' " *J. Hoeffel, Six Incumbents Are a Week Away from Easy Election*, Winston-Salem Journal, Jan. 27, 1998, p. B1 (quoting a North Carolina state senator).

Still, the Court's own responsibilities require that we refrain from intervention in this instance. The failings of the many proposed standards for measuring the burden a gerrymander imposes on representational rights make our intervention improper. If workable standards do emerge to measure these burdens, however, courts should be prepared to order relief. With these observations, I join the judgment of the plurality.

■ Justice Stevens, dissenting.

* * *

The concept of equal justice under law requires the State to govern impartially. Today's plurality opinion would exempt governing officials from that duty in the context of legislative redistricting and would give license, for the first time, to partisan gerrymanders that are devoid of any rational justification. In my view, when partisanship is the legislature's sole motivation—when any pretense of neutrality is forsaken unabashedly and all traditional districting criteria are subverted for partisan advantage—the governing body cannot be said to have acted impartially.

I

The judicial standards applicable to gerrymandering claims are deeply rooted in decisions that long preceded *Bandemer* and have been refined in later cases. Among those well-settled principles is the understanding that a district's peculiar shape might be a symptom of an illicit purpose in the line-drawing process ... With purpose as the ultimate inquiry, other considerations have supplied ready standards for testing the lawfulness of a gerrymander.

* * *

To begin with, the plurality errs in assuming that politics is "an ordinary and lawful motive." We have squarely rejected the notion that "a purpose to discriminate on the basis of politics," is never subject to strict scrutiny. On the contrary, "political belief and association constitute the core of those activities protected by the First Amendment," *Elrod v. Burns,* 427 U.S. 347 (1976) (plurality opinion), and discriminatory governmental decisions that burden fundamental First Amendment interests are subject to strict scrutiny, *id.* at 363; *cf. Police Dept. of Chicago v. Mosley,* 408 U.S. 92, 94–95 (1972). Thus, unless party affiliation is an appropriate requirement for the position in question, government officials may not base a decision to hire, promote, transfer, recall, discharge, or retaliate against an employee, or to terminate a contract, on the individual's partisan affiliation or speech. *See Board of Comm'rs, Wabaunsee Cty. v. Umbehr,* 518 U.S. 668, 674–675 (1996); *O'Hare Truck Service, Inc. v. City of Northlake,* 518 U.S. 712, 716–717 (1996); *Rutan v. Republican Party of Ill.,* 497 U.S. 62, 64–65 (1990); *Branti v. Finkel,* 445 U.S. 507, 519–520 (1980); *Elrod,* 427 U.S. at 355–363. It follows that political affiliation is not an appropriate standard for excluding voters from a congressional district.

The plurality argues that our patronage cases do not support the proposition that strict scrutiny should be applied in political gerrymandering cases because "[i]t is elementary that scrutiny levels are claim specific." It is also elementary, however, that the level of scrutiny is relevant to the question whether there has been a constitutional violation, not the question of justiciability. The standards outlined above are discernible and judicially manageable regardless of the number of cases in which they must be applied or the level of scrutiny at which the analysis occurs. [T]the relevant lesson of the patronage cases is that partisanship is not always as benign a consideration as the plurality appears to assume.

State action that discriminates against a political minority for the sole and unadorned purpose of maximizing the power of the majority plainly violates the decisionmaker's duty to remain impartial. . . . Thus, the critical issue in both racial and political gerrymandering cases is the same: whether a single non-neutral criterion controlled the districting process to such an extent that the Constitution was offended. This Court has treated that precise question as justiciable in *Gomillion* and in the *Shaw* line of cases, and today's plurality has supplied no persuasive reason for distinguishing the justiciability of partisan gerrymanders. Those cases confirm and reinforce the holding that partisan gerrymandering claims are justiciable.

II

* * *

A challenge to a specific district or districts, on the other hand, alleges a different type of injury entirely—one that our recent racial gerrymandering cases have recognized as cognizable. . . .

Undergirding the *Shaw* cases is the premise that racial gerrymanders effect a constitutional wrong when they disrupt the representational norms that ordinarily tether elected officials to their constituencies as a whole.

"[L]egislatures," we have explained, "should be bodies which are collectively responsive to the popular will," *Reynolds*, 377 U.S. at 565, for "[l]egislators are elected by voters, not farms or cities or economic interests," *id.* at 562. Gerrymanders subvert that representative norm because the winner of an election in a gerrymandered district inevitably will infer that her success is primarily attributable to the architect of the district rather than to a constituency defined by neutral principles. The *Shaw* cases hold that this disruption of the representative process imposes a cognizable "representational har[m]." *Hays*, 515 U.S. at 745.

This [case involves] precisely the harm that the *Shaw* cases treat as cognizable in the context of racial gerrymandering. The same treatment is warranted in this case.... The risk of representational harms identified in the *Shaw* cases is equally great, if not greater, in the context of partisan gerrymanders.... The parallel danger of a partisan gerrymander is that the representative will perceive that the people who put her in power are those who drew the map rather than those who cast ballots, and she will feel beholden not to a subset of her constituency, but to no part of her constituency at all. The problem, simply put, is that the will of the cartographers rather than the will of the people will govern.

III

[W]hile political considerations may properly influence the decisions of our elected officials, when such decisions disadvantage members of a minority group—whether the minority is defined by its members' race, religion, or political affiliation—they must rest on a neutral predicate. Thus, the Equal Protection Clause implements a duty to govern impartially that requires, at the very least, that every decision by the sovereign serve some nonpartisan public purpose.

... Consistent with that principle, our recent racial gerrymandering cases have examined the shape of the district and the purpose of the districting body to determine whether race, above all other criteria, predominated in the line-drawing process.... Just as irrational shape can serve as an objective indicator of an impermissible legislative purpose, other objective features of a districting map can save the plan from invalidation.... In my view, the same standards should apply to claims of political gerrymandering, for the essence of a gerrymander is the same regardless of whether the group is identified as political or racial. Gerrymandering always involves the drawing of district boundaries to maximize the voting strength of the dominant political faction and to minimize the strength of one or more groups of opponents. In seeking the desired result, legislators necessarily make judgments about the probability that the members of identifiable groups—whether economic, religious, ethnic, or racial—will vote in a certain way. The overriding purpose of those predictions is political. It follows that the standards that enable courts to identify and redress a racial gerrymander could also perform the same function for other species of gerrymanders. . . .

The racial gerrymandering cases therefore supply a judicially manageable standard for determining when partisanship, like race, has played too great of a role in the districting process. Just as race can be a factor in, but cannot dictate the outcome of, the districting process, so too can partisanship be a permissible consideration in drawing district lines, so long as it does not predominate. If, as plaintiff-appellant Furey has alleged, the predominant motive of the legislators who designed District 6, and the sole justification for its bizarre shape, was a purpose to discriminate against a political minority, that invidious purpose should invalidate the district.

The plurality reasons that the standards for evaluating racial gerrymanders are not workable in cases such as this because partisan considerations, unlike racial ones, are perfectly legitimate. Until today, however, there has not been the slightest intimation in any opinion written by any Member of this Court that a naked purpose to disadvantage a political minority would provide a rational basis for drawing a district line. On the contrary, our opinions referring to political gerrymanders have consistently assumed that they were at least undesirable, and we always have indicated that political considerations are among those factors that may not dominate districting decisions. Purely partisan motives are "rational" in a literal sense, but there must be a limiting principle. "[T]he word 'rational'—for me at least—includes elements of legitimacy and neutrality that must always characterize the performance of the sovereign's duty to govern impartially." *Cleburne v. Cleburne Living Center, Inc.*, 473 U.S. 432, 452 (1985) (Stevens, J., concurring). A legislature controlled by one party could not, for instance, impose special taxes on members of the minority party, or use tax revenues to pay the majority party's campaign expenses. The rational basis for government decisions must satisfy a standard of legitimacy and neutrality; an acceptable rational basis can be neither purely personal nor purely partisan. *See id.* at 452–453.

[T]he view that the plurality implicitly embraces today—that a gerrymander contrived for the sole purpose of disadvantaging a political minority is less objectionable than one seeking to benefit a racial minority—is doubly flawed. It disregards the obvious distinction between an invidious and a benign purpose, and it mistakenly assumes that race cannot provide a legitimate basis for making political judgments of all races sometimes vote for Democratic candidates, and vice versa. . . .

Under my analysis, if no neutral criterion can be identified to justify the lines drawn, and if the only possible explanation for a district's bizarre shape is a naked desire to increase partisan strength, then no rational basis exists to save the district from an equal protection challenge. Such a narrow test would cover only a few meritorious claims, but it would preclude extreme abuses, such as those disclosed by the record in *Badham v. Eu,* 694 F.Supp. 664 (N.D.Cal.1988), *summarily aff'd,* 488 U.S. 1024

(1989), and it would perhaps shorten the time period in which the pernicious effects of such a gerrymander are felt. This test would mitigate the current trend under which partisan considerations are becoming the be-all and end-all in apportioning representatives.

IV

* * *

Quite obviously, however, several standards for identifying impermissible partisan influence are available to judges who have the will to enforce them. We could hold that every district boundary must have a neutral justification; we could apply Justice Powell's three-factor approach in *Bandemer*; we could apply the predominant motivation standard fashioned by the Court in its racial gerrymandering cases; or we could endorse either of the approaches advocated today by Justice Souter and Justice Breyer. What is clear is that it is not the unavailability of judicially manageable standards that drives today's decision. It is, instead, a failure of judicial will to condemn even the most blatant violations of a state legislature's fundamental duty to govern impartially.

Accordingly, I respectfully dissent.

■ JUSTICE SOUTER, with whom JUSTICE GINSBURG joins, dissenting.

I

* * *

[T]he issue is one of how much is too much, and we can be no more exact in stating a verbal test for too much partisanship than we can be in defining too much race consciousness when some is inevitable and legitimate. Instead of coming up with a verbal formula for too much, then, the Court's job must be to identify clues, as objective as we can make them, indicating that partisan competition has reached an extremity of unfairness.

II

Since this Court has created the problem no one else has been able to solve, it is up to us to make a fresh start. There are a good many voices saying it is high time that we did, for in the years since *Davis,* the increasing efficiency of partisan redistricting has damaged the democratic process to a degree that our predecessors only began to imagine. . . .

I would adopt a political gerrymandering test analogous to the summary judgment standard crafted in *McDonnell Douglas Corp. v. Green,* 411 U.S. 792 (1973), calling for a plaintiff to satisfy elements of a prima facie cause of action, at which point the State would have the opportunity not only to rebut the evidence supporting the plaintiff's case, but to offer an affirmative justification for the districting choices, even assuming the proof of the plaintiff's allegations. My own judgment is that we would have better luck at devising a workable prima facie case if we concentrated as much as possible on suspect characteristics of individual districts instead of statewide patterns. It is not that a statewide view of districting is somehow less important; the usual point of gerrymandering, after all, is to control the greatest number of seats overall. But, as will be seen, we would be able to call more readily on some existing law when we defined what is suspect at the district level, and for now I would conceive of a statewide challenge as itself a function of claims that individual districts are illegitimately drawn. Finally, in the same interest of threshold simplicity, I would stick to problems of single-member districts; if we could not devise a workable scheme for dealing with claims about these, we would have to forget the complications posed by multimember districts.

III

A

For a claim based on a specific single-member district, I would require the plaintiff to make out a *prima facie* case with five elements. First, the resident plaintiff would identify a cohesive political group to which he belonged, which would normally be a major party, as in this case and in *Davis*. There is no reason in principle, however, to rule out a claimant from a minor political party (which might, if it showed strength, become the target of vigorous hostility from one or both major parties in a State) or from a different but politically coherent group whose members engaged in bloc voting, as a large labor union might do. The point is that it must make sense to speak of a candidate of the group's choice, easy to do in the case of a large or small political party, though more difficult when the organization is not defined by politics as such. Second, a plaintiff would need to show that the district of his residence, paid little or no heed to those traditional districting principles whose disregard can be shown straightforwardly: contiguity, compactness, respect for political subdivisions, and conformity with geographic features like rivers and mountains. Because such considerations are already relevant to justifying small deviations from absolute population equality, and because compactness in particular is relevant to demonstrating possible majority-minority districts under the Voting Rights Act of 1965, there is no doubt that a test relying on these standards would fall within judicial competence.

Indeed, although compactness is at first blush the least likely of these principles to yield precision, it can be measured quantitatively in terms of dispersion, perimeter, and population ratios, and the development of standards would thus be possible. It is not necessary now to say exactly how a district court would balance a good showing on one of these indices against a poor showing on another, for that sort of detail is best worked out case by case.

Third, the plaintiff would need to establish specific correlations between the district's deviations from traditional districting principles and the distribution of the population of his group. For example, one of the districts to which appellants object most strongly in this case is District 6, which they say "looms like a dragon descending on Philadelphia from the west, splitting up towns and communities throughout Montgomery and Berks Counties." To make their claim stick, they would need to point to specific protuberances on the draconian shape that reach out to include Democrats, or fissures in it that squirm away from Republicans. They would need to show that when towns and communities were split, Democrats tended to fall on one side and Republicans on the other. Although some counterexamples would no doubt be present in any complex plan, the plaintiff's showing as a whole would need to provide reasonable support for, if not compel, an inference that the district took the shape it did because of the distribution of the plaintiff's group. That would begin, but not complete, the plaintiff's case that the defendant had chosen either to pack the group (drawn a district in order to include a uselessly high number of the group) or to crack it (drawn it so as to include fatally few), the ordinary methods of vote dilution in single-member district systems.

Fourth, a plaintiff would need to present the court with a hypothetical district including his residence, one in which the proportion of the plaintiff's group was lower (in a packing claim) or higher (in a cracking one) and which at the same time deviated less from traditional districting principles than the actual district. Cf. *Thornburg v. Gingles*, 478 U.S. 30, 50 (1986) (requiring a similar showing to demonstrate that a multimember district is "responsible for minority voters' inability to elect [their preferred] candidates"). This hypothetical district would allow the plaintiff to claim credibly that the deviations from traditional districting principles were not only correlated with, but also caused by, the packing or cracking of his group. Drawing the hypothetical district would, of course, necessarily involve redrawing at least one contiguous district, and a plaintiff would have to show that this could be done subject to traditional districting principles without packing or cracking his group (or another) worse than in the district being challenged.

Fifth, and finally, the plaintiff would have to show that the defendants acted intentionally to manipulate the shape of the district in order to pack or crack his group. *See Washington v. Davis*, 426 U.S. 229 (1976). In substantiating claims of political gerrymandering under a plan devised by a single major party, proving intent should not be hard, once the third and fourth (correlation and cause) elements are established, politicians not being politically disinterested or characteristically naive. I would, however, treat any showing of intent in a major-party case as too equivocal to count unless the entire legislature were controlled by the governor's party (or the dominant legislative party were vetoproof).[5] . . .

---

5. *Amici* JoAnn Erfer et al. suggest that a political party strong enough to redistrict without the other's approval is analogous to a firm that exercises monopolistic control over a market, and that the ability to exercise such unilateral control should there-

B

A plaintiff who got this far would have shown that his State intentionally acted to dilute his vote, having ignored reasonable alternatives consistent with traditional districting principles. I would then shift the burden to the defendants to justify their decision by reference to objectives other than naked partisan advantage. They might show by rebuttal evidence that districting objectives could not be served by the plaintiff's hypothetical district better than by the district as drawn, or they might affirmatively establish legitimate objectives better served by the lines drawn than by the plaintiff's hypothetical.

The State might, for example, posit the need to avoid racial vote dilution. It might plead one person, one vote, a standard compatible with gerrymandering but in some places perhaps unattainable without some lopsided proportions. The State might adopt the object of proportional representation among its political parties through its districting process.

This is not, however, the time or place for a comprehensive list of legitimate objectives a State might present. The point here is simply that the Constitution should not petrify traditional districting objectives as exclusive, and it is enough to say that the State would be required to explain itself, to demonstrate that whatever reasons it gave were more than a mere pretext for an old-fashioned gerrymander.

C

As for a statewide claim, I would not attempt an ambitious definition without the benefit of experience with individual district claims, and for now I would limit consideration of a statewide claim to one built upon a number of district-specific ones. Each successful district-specific challenge would necessarily entail redrawing at least one contiguous district, and the more the successful claims, the more surrounding districts to be redefined. At a certain point, the ripples would reach the state boundary, and it would no longer make any sense for a district court to consider the problems piecemeal.

D

. . . The enquiries I am proposing are not, to be sure, as hard-edged as I wish they could be, but neither do they have a degree of subjectivity inconsistent with the judicial function.

fore trigger "heightened constitutional scrutiny." Brief 18–19 (citing *Terry v. Adams,* 345 U.S. 461 (1953), the Texas Jaybird primary case). *See* also Issacharoff, *Gerrymandering and Political Cartels*, 116 Harv. L.Rev. 593 (2002); Issacharoff & Pildes, *Politics as Markets: Partisan Lockups of the Dem-* *ocratic Process,* 50 Stan. L.Rev. 643 (1998). The analogy to antitrust is an intriguing one that may prove fruitful, though I do not embrace it at this point out of caution about a wholesale conceptual transfer from economics to politics.

... The harm from partisan gerrymandering is (as I have said) a species of vote dilution: the point of the gerrymander is to capture seats by manipulating district lines to diminish the weight of the other party's votes in elections. To devise a judicial remedy for that harm, however, it is not necessary to adopt a full-blown theory of fairness, furnishing a precise measure of harm caused by divergence from the ideal in each case. It is sufficient instead to agree that gerrymandering is, indeed, unfair, as the plurality does not dispute; to observe the traditional methods of the gerrymanderer, which the plurality summarizes, *ante*, at 1774–1776; and to adopt a test aimed at detecting and preventing the use of those methods, which, I think, mine is. . . .

■ JUSTICE BREYER, dissenting.

* * *

I

I start with a fundamental principle. "We the People," who "or-dain[ed] and establish[ed]" the American Constitution, sought to create and to protect a workable form of government that is in its " 'principles, structure, and whole mass,' " basically democratic. G. Wood, The Creation of the American Republic, 1776–1787, at 595 (1969) (quoting W. Murray, Political Sketches, Inscribed to His Excellency John Adams 5 (1787)). *See also*, *e.g.*, A. Meiklejohn, Free Speech and Its Relation to Self–Government 14–15 (1948). In a modern Nation of close to 300 million people, the workable democracy that the Constitution foresees must mean more than a guaranteed opportunity to elect legislators representing equally populous electoral districts. There must also be a method for transforming the will of the majority into effective government.

This Court has explained that political parties play a necessary role in that transformation. . . . A party-based political system that satisfies this minimal condition encourages democratic responsibility. It facilitates the transformation of the voters' will into a government that reflects that will.

Why do I refer to these elementary constitutional principles? Because I believe they can help courts identify at least one abuse at issue in this case. To understand how that is so, one should begin by asking why single-member electoral districts are the norm, why the Constitution does not insist that the membership of legislatures better reflect different political views held by different groups of voters. History, of course, is part of the answer, but it does not tell the entire story. The answer also lies in the fact that a single-member-district system helps to assure certain democratic objectives better than many "more representative" (*i.e.*, proportional) electoral systems. Of course, single-member districts mean that only parties with candidates who finish "first past the post" will elect legislators. That fact means in turn that a party with a bare majority of votes or even a plurality of votes will often obtain a large legislative majority, perhaps freezing out smaller parties. But single-member districts thereby diminish the need for coalition governments. And that fact makes it easier for voters to identify which party is responsible for government decisionmaking (and which rascals to throw out), while simultaneously providing greater legislative stability. This is not to say that single-member districts are preferable; it is simply to say that single-member-district systems and more-directly-representational systems reflect different conclusions about the proper balance of different elements of a workable democratic government.

If single-member districts are the norm, however, then political considerations will likely play an important, and proper, role in the drawing of district boundaries. In part, that is because politicians, unlike nonpartisan observers, normally understand how "the location and shape of districts" determine "the political complexion of the area." . . .

More important for present purposes, the role of political considerations reflects a surprising mathematical fact. Given a fairly large state population with a fairly large congressional delegation, districts assigned so as to be perfectly random in respect to politics would translate a small shift in political sentiment, say a shift from 51% Republican to 49% Republican, into a seismic shift in the makeup of the legislative delegation, say from 100% Republican to 100% Democrat. *See* M. Altman, *Modeling the Effect of Mandatory District Compactness on Partisan Gerrymanders*, 17 Pol. Geography 989, 1002 (1998) (suggesting that, where the state population is large enough, even randomly selected compact districts will generally elect *no* politicians from the party that wins fewer votes statewide). Any such exaggeration of tiny electoral changes—virtually wiping out legislative representation of the minority party—would itself seem highly undemocratic.

Given the resulting need for single-member districts with nonrandom boundaries, it is not surprising that "traditional" districting principles have rarely, if ever, been politically neutral. Rather, because, in recent political memory, Democrats have often been concentrated in cities while Republicans have often been concentrated in suburbs and sometimes rural areas, geographically drawn boundaries have tended to "pac[k]" the former. . . . All this is well known to politicians, who use their knowledge about the effects of the "neutral" criteria to partisan advantage when drawing electoral maps. And were it not so, the iron laws of mathematics would have worked their extraordinary volatility-enhancing will.

This is to say that traditional or historically-based boundaries are not, and should not be, "politics free." Rather, those boundaries represent a series of compromises of principle—among the virtues of, for example, close representation of voter views, ease of identifying "government" and "opposition" parties, and stability in government. They also represent an uneasy truce, sanctioned by tradition, among different parties seeking political advantage.

As I have said, reference back to these underying considerations helps to explain why the legislature's use of political boundary drawing considerations ordinarily does *not* violate the Constitution's Equal Protection Clause.... The use of purely political boundary-drawing factors, even where harmful to the members of one party, will often nonetheless find justification in other desirable democratic ends, such as maintaining relatively stable legislatures in which a minority party retains significant representation.

II

At the same time, these considerations can help identify at least one circumstance where use of purely political boundary-drawing factors can amount to a serious, and remediable, abuse, namely the *unjustified* use of political factors to entrench a minority in power. By entrenchment I mean a situation in which a party that enjoys only minority support among the populace has nonetheless contrived to take, and hold, legislative power. By *unjustified* entrenchment I mean that the minority's hold on power is purely the result of partisan manipulation and not other factors. These "other" factors that could lead to "justified" (albeit temporary) minority entrenchment include sheer happenstance, the existence of more than two major parties, the unique constitutional requirements of certain representational bodies such as the Senate, or reliance on traditional (geographic, communities of interest, etc.) districting criteria.

The democratic harm of unjustified entrenchment is obvious.... Where unjustified entrenchment takes place, voters find it far more difficult to remove those responsible for a government they do not want; and these democratic values are dishonored.

The need for legislative stability cannot justify entrenchment, for stability is compatible with a system in which the loss of majority support implies a loss of power. The need to secure minority representation in the legislature cannot justify entrenchment, for minority party representation is also compatible with a system in which the loss of minority support implies a loss of representation. Constitutionally specified principles of representation, such as that of two Senators per State, cannot justify entrenchment where the House of Representatives or similar state legislative body is at issue. Unless some other justification can be found in particular circumstances, political gerrymandering that so entrenches a minority party in power violates basic democratic norms and lacks countervailing justification. For this reason, whether political gerrymandering does, or does not, violate the Constitution in other instances, gerrymandering that leads to entrenchment amounts to an abuse that violates the Constitution's Equal Protection Clause.

III

Courts need not intervene often to prevent the kind of abuse I have described, because those harmed constitute a political majority, and a majority normally can work its political will. Where a State has improperly gerrymandered legislative or congressional districts to the majority's disadvantage, the majority should be able to elect officials in statewide races—particularly the Governor—who may help to undo the harm that districting has caused the majority's party, in the next round of districting if not sooner. And where a State has improperly gerrymandered congressional districts, Congress retains the power to revise the State's districting determinations. *See* U.S. Const., Art. I, § 4; *ante,* at 1775–1776 (plurality opinion) (discussing the history of Congress' "power to check partisan manipulation of the election process by the States").

Moreover, voters in some States, perhaps tiring of the political boundary-drawing rivalry, have found a procedural solution, confiding the task to a commission that is limited in the extent to which it may base districts on partisan concerns. According to the National Conference of State Legislatures, 12 States currently give "first and final authority for [state] legislative redistricting to a group other than the legislature." A number of States use a commission for congressional redistricting: Arizona, Hawaii, Idaho, Montana, New Jersey, and Washington, with Indiana using a commission if the legislature cannot pass a plan and Iowa requiring the district-drawing body not to consider political data. Indeed, where state governments have been unwilling or unable to act, "an informed, civically militant electorate," *Baker v. Carr,* 369 U.S. 186, 270 (1962) (Frankfurter, J., dissenting), has occasionally taken matters into its own hands, through ballot initiatives or referendums. Arizona voters, for example, passed Proposition 106, which amended the State's Constitution and created an independent redistricting commission to draw legislative and congressional districts. Ariz. Const., Art. 4, pt. 2, § 1 (West 2001). Such reforms borrow from the systems used by other countries utilizing single-member districts.

But we cannot always count on a severely gerrymandered legislature itself to find and implement a remedy. The party that controls the process has no incentive to change it. And the political advantages of a gerrymander may become ever greater in the future. The availability of enhanced computer technology allows the parties to redraw boundaries in ways that target individual neighborhoods and homes, carving out safe but slim victory margins in the maximum number of districts, with little risk of cutting their margins too thin. By redrawing districts every 2 years, rather than every 10 years, a party might preserve its political advantages notwithstanding population shifts in the State. The combination of increasingly precise map-drawing technology and increasingly frequent map drawing means that a party may be able to bring about a gerrymander that is not only precise, but virtually impossible to dislodge. Thus, court action may prove necessary.

* * *

The bottom line is that courts should be able to identify the presence of one important gerrymandering evil, the unjustified entrenching in power of a political party that the voters have rejected. They should be able to separate the unjustified abuse of partisan boundary-drawing considerations to achieve that end from their more ordinary and justified use. And they should be able to design a remedy for extreme cases.

IV

I do not claim that the problem of identification and separation is easily solved, even in extreme instances. But courts can identify a number of strong indicia of abuse. The presence of actual entrenchment, while not always unjustified (being perhaps a chance occurrence), is such a sign, particularly when accompanied by the use of partisan boundary drawing criteria in the way that Justice Stevens describes, *i.e.*, a use that both departs from traditional criteria and cannot be explained other than by efforts to achieve partisan advantage. Below, I set forth several sets of circumstances that lay out the indicia of abuse I have in mind. The scenarios fall along a continuum: The more permanently entrenched the minority's hold on power becomes, the less evidence courts will need that the minority engaged in gerrymandering to achieve the desired result.

Consider, for example, the following sets of circumstances. First, suppose that the legislature has proceeded to redraw boundaries in what seem to be ordinary ways, but the entrenchment harm has become obvious. *E.g.*, (a) the legislature has not redrawn district boundaries more than once within the traditional 10–year period; and (b) no radical departure from traditional districting criteria is alleged; but (c) a majority party (as measured by the votes actually cast for all candidates who identify themselves as members of that party in the relevant set of elections; *i.e.*, in congressional elections if a congressional map is being challenged) has *twice* failed to obtain a majority of the relevant legislative seats in elections; and (d) the failure cannot be explained by the existence of multiple parties or in other neutral ways. In my view, these circumstances would be sufficient to support a claim of unconstitutional entrenchment.

Second, suppose that plaintiffs could point to more serious departures from redistricting norms. *E.g.*, (a) the legislature has not redrawn district boundaries more than once within the traditional 10–year period; but (b) the boundary-drawing criteria depart radically from previous or traditional criteria; (c) the departure cannot be justified or explained other than by reference to an effort to obtain partisan political advantage; and (d) a majority party (as defined above) has once failed to obtain a majority of the relevant seats in election using the challenged map (which fact cannot be explained by the existence of multiple parties or in other neutral ways). These circumstances could also add up to unconstitutional gerrymandering.

Third, suppose that the legislature clearly departs from ordinary districting norms, but the entrenchment harm, while seriously threatened, has not yet occurred. *E.g.*, (a) the legislature has redrawn district boundaries more than once within the traditional 10–year census-related period–

either, as here, at the behest of a court that struck down an initial plan as or of its own accord; (b) the boundary-drawing criteria depart radically from previous traditional boundary-drawing criteria; (c) strong, objective, unrefuted statistical evidence demonstrates that a party with a minority of the popular vote within the State in all likelihood will obtain a majority of the seats in the relevant representative delegation; and (d) the jettisoning of traditional districting criteria cannot be justified or explained other than by reference to an effort to obtain partisan political advantage. To my mind, such circumstances could also support a claim, because the presence of midcycle redistricting, for any reason, raises a fair inference that partisan machinations played a major role in the map-drawing process. Where such an inference is accompanied by statistical evidence that entrenchment will be the likely result, a court may conclude that the map crosses the constitutional line we are describing.

The presence of these, or similar, circumstances—where the risk of entrenchment is demonstrated, where partisan considerations render the traditional district-drawing compromises irrelevant, where no justification other than party advantage can be found—seem to me extreme enough to set off a constitutional alarm. The risk of harm to basic democratic principle is serious; identification is possible; and remedies can be found. . . .

NOTES AND QUESTIONS

1. Does the Court unanimously agree that excessive partisan gerrymandering is unconstitutional in principle?

2. Justice Scalia's plurality opinion notes that the original design of the Constitution gave Congress the power to control what we now call partisan gerrymandering. Thus, Justice Scalia can be viewed as taking a political-process approach; the Court should not address the issue because there is a political mechanism by which the problem of partisan gerrymandering, if problem it be, can be cured.

Of what relevance should it be that, at the time of the Constitution's framing, the Constitution did not contemplate the emergence of national political parties, but was affirmatively hostile to them? Indeed, the Constitution was designed to preclude the emergence of political parties. In addition, as parties became established, the fates of national political parties and state parties have, over time, become closely bound together— so much so that, in the 2000 redistricting, several courts have found that national party leaders in the United States House played a central role in the redistricting process in some states. Indeed, in light of the close partisan division in the House, some states were prompted to engage in re-redistricting in the middle of the decade, precisely because national party leaders in the United States House pressed for this. If Congress was originally envisioned as a detached, neutral umpire that might stand above partisan conflicts in the states, Congress is now a self-interested player in the partisan struggles over districting.

Does the rise of national and state parties, with interlocking self-interests in districting questions, suggest a major design defect in the original Constitution? Note that many modern constitutions explicitly create some kind of independent entity to oversee elections. There is no other major country with districted elections in which districts are drawn by politically self-interested actors. Does the rise of modern party politics undermine the appropriateness of relying on the original expectation that Congress would address partisan gerrymandering? Do these changes lead to the view that the Court should take on a role that was originally envisioned for Congress?

3. A second approach to the problem emerges from the opinions of Justices Stevens and Souter. They define partisan gerrymandering at the level of individual districts, and both would apply doctrinal lines from race and redistricting to partisan gerrymandering. Justice Stevens would essentially apply the *Shaw* line of cases to address partisan gerrymandering. Justice Souter would treat the problem as one of vote dilution and would draw on the Voting Rights Act precedents to give content to that idea. Does it make sense to conceive of partisan gerrymandering as a problem that can be coherently addressed at the level of individual districts, as opposed to on a statewide basis?

Note that, in the wake of the uncertain doctrinal rule of *Shaw v. Reno*, many commentators predicted that the 2000 round of redistricting would lead to litigation contests in most states that had significant-sized minority populations. Instead, however, the 2000 round turned out to generate almost no litigation raising *Shaw* claims. Despite the uncertainties surrounding the contours of *Shaw*, redistricters apparently took away the message that they were required and permitted to engage in race-conscious districting where the Voting Rights Act required it, as long as minority-controlled districts did not substantially deviate in design (meaning, most significantly, in shape) from other districts. Thus, *Shaw* established that unclear legal doctrine could nonetheless result in a stable political equilibrium, as redistricters internalized and interpreted for themselves the meaning of *Shaw*. *Shaw* thus reflects the intriguing possibility that, at least in some circumstances, legal doctrines and judicial remedies can produce stable political practices even when those doctrines cannot be specified through necessary and sufficient criteria that would govern their application judicially.

Does the experience with *Shaw* have any implications for how the Court ought to address partisan gerrymandering? Does that experience provide a different kind of answer to the plurality's concerns about the difficulty of constructing clear legal standards to address partisan gerrymandering? Is it possible that, even if constitutional doctrine must necessarily lack bright-line rules in this area, political actors would have strong incentives to internalize boundaries against partisan excessiveness in order to keep districting plans out of court? Can vague law nonetheless yield stable political practices in some contexts? For the argument that the Court in *Vieth*, as in *Shaw*, might have had reason to conclude that even an imprecise doctrinal constraint on excessive partisan districting might come to be internalized by redistricters in a way that would yield clear enough boundaries in practice on partisanship in districting, see Richard H. Pildes, *The Supreme Court, 2003 Term–Foreword: Constitutionalization of Democratic Politics*, 118 Harv. L. Rev. 28, 64–76 (2004).

4. A third approach is that of Justice Breyer, who several times characterizes the constitutional injury from partisan gerrymandering as a "democratic harm." This might be the strongest endorsement by any Justice in any case that the Constitution should be read to directly protect the general, structural or systemic objectives of the system of democratic elections. Are "democratic harms" individualized grievances? Who ought to have standing to raise them? What is the relationship between the "expressive harms" which the Court has been willing to recognize in the *Shaw* cases and the "democratic harms" that Justice Breyer would recognize here? What other regulations of the electoral process might be viewed as creating the kinds of "democratic harms" that Justice Breyer identifies?

How would Justice Breyer define impermissible "entrenchment" of a minority party in power? Notice that some of his examples involve reasoning backward, ex post, from actual election results under the challenged plan. Other examples involve ex ante predictions about how elections are likely to come out under a proposed plan. Are there important differences between the two contexts?

5. Note that amidst all these divergent approaches, Justice Kennedy is the likely decisive vote for any future partisan gerrymandering claims. He suggests that a First Amendment approach, rather than the equal protection one that was pursued in *Vieth*, might be a more appropriate framework for judicial involvement with partisan gerrymandering. In what way would shifting the form of the claim to the First Amendment provide answers to any of the remedial questions that lead Justice Kennedy to agree with the plurality that no administrable standard has yet been generated under the equal protection clause that would permit courts to address partisan gerrymandering? Note that Justice Kennedy says First Amendment concerns would arise "where an apportionment has the purpose and effect of burdening a group of voters' representational rights." But he also says that the difficulty in addressing partisan gerrymandering, at least under the equal protection clause, is precisely that political classifications are generally permissible ones.

Prior to *Vieth*, *Professor* Guy–Uriel Charles had argued that the design of election districts should be seen to implicate First Amendment rights of association. In the context of racial gerrymandering, Charles argued that voters who preferred to be in the same districts as other voters of similar identities and/or values had constitutionally protected rights of association that the state was required to honor. See Guy–Uriel E. Charles, *Racial Identity, Electoral Structures, and the First Amendment Right of Association*, 91 Calif. L. Rev. 1209 (2003). Given the inevitable distributional conflicts in designing districts, could the state possibly honor all the competing "rights of association" claims that various voters might assert? Does Professor Charles' argument provide insight into whether partisan gerrymandering should be unconstitutional and, if so, whether there are judicially manageable standards for addressing such issues?

6. What should be made of note 5 in Justice Souter's dissent, in which he noted the possibility of judicial adoption of approaches from the antitrust context as a means of addressing partisan gerrymandering? Does this suggest the possibility in the future of another approach altogether to partisan gerrymandering? How would this approach compare to that of Justice Breyer? Recently, Judge Richard A. Posner has strongly endorsed the position that constitutional doctrine should be structured around the central aim of ensuring that politics remains robustly competitive; Posner, an economist and judge, argues that antitrust analysis provides useful insight for courts overseeing electoral regulations. Richard A. Posner, Law, Pragmatism, and Democracy 130–213 (2003). On the relationship of competitive theories of politics to deliberative and rights-oriented theories, see Richard H. Pildes, *Competitive, Deliberative, and Rights–Oriented Democracy*, 3 Elec. L. J.685 (2004) (review of Posner).

7. Professor Adam Cox provocatively argues that judicial review of partisan gerrymandering claims concerning congressional districts is even more complex for yet another reason. Adam Cox, *Partisan Gerrymandering and Disaggregated Redistricting*, 2004 Sup. Ct. Rev. 409. The real "baseline" for such claims, Cox argues, should be Congress as a whole, not any one state's individual delegation. Perhaps an aggressive Republican gerrymander in Texas "offsets" an aggressive Democratic gerrymander in California. Can courts evaluate the partisan "fairness" of an individual state's congressional districting plan without considering the "fairness" of the composition of Congress as a whole?

8. *Larios v. Cox.* Precisely because political gerrymandering claims are so difficult to adjudicate, a number of courts have recently used one-person, one-vote as a tool for addressing what they perceive as excessively partisan plans. This has put substantial pressure on the approach, announced by the Supreme Court in cases from *Gaffney* to *Brown v. Thompson*, of permitting population deviations of less than 10 percent in state legislative and local redistricting plans. (For a discussion of this point, see Chapter 3) For one particularly striking example, consider the post–2000 Georgia state legislative redistricting.

At the time of the 2000 redistricting for the state legislature in Georgia, Democrats still controlled both houses of the Georgia legislature and the governorship, though Republican support was growing fast. Based on Supreme Court doctrine, the Democrats were advised that they had a "safe harbor" as long as the total population deviation of a plan did not exceed 10 percent—that no matter what the reasons or motivations for population deviations between districts of + or -5 percent, there were no constitutional constraints. *Larios v. Cox*, 300 F. Supp. 2d 1320 (N.D. Ga.) (three-judge court), *summarily aff'd* 542 U.S. 947 (2004). While creating a plan whose total population deviation was only 9.98 percent, the Democrats used this margin consistently for various partisan purposes; they split counties into numerous parts, drew oddly-shaped districts, placed two incumbent Republicans in the same district, and packed Republican voters into districts.

The district court dismissed the plaintiffs' claims of unconstitutional gerrymandering. But interestingly, the court accepted instead the plaintiffs' one-person, one-vote claim:

> The Supreme Court has specifically detailed a number of state policies that, when applied in a consistent and nondiscriminatory manner, can justify some level of population deviation. In *Karcher v. Daggett*, discussing population deviations, the Court indicated the kind of policies that might permit some deviation from perfect population equality: "Any number of consistently applied legislative policies might justify some variance, including, for instance, making districts compact, respecting municipal boundaries, preserving the cores of prior districts, and avoiding contests between incumbent Representatives." . . .

The court found that the deviation was not motivated by any of these policies. It recounted evidence showing that the redistricting plan was not drawn to make districts compact, respect municipal boundaries, or preserve the core of prior districts:

> The record makes abundantly clear that the population deviations in the Georgia House and Senate were not driven by any traditional redistricting criteria such as compactness, contiguity, and preserving county lines. Instead, the defense has put forth two basic explanations for the population deviations. First, . . . the concerted effort to allow rural and inner-city Atlanta regions of the state to hold on to their legislative influence (at the expense of suburban Atlanta). . . . Second, the deviations were created to protect incumbents in a wholly inconsistent and discriminatory way. On this record, neither explanation can convert a baldly unconstitutional scheme into a lawful one. . . .

The court also noted:

> The population deviations in the Georgia House and Senate Plans are not the result of an effort to further any legitimate, consistently applied state policy. . . . First, forty years of Supreme Court jurisprudence have established that the creation of deviations for the purpose of allowing the people of certain geographic regions of a state to hold legislative power to a degree disproportionate to their population is

plainly unconstitutional. Moreover, the protection of incumbents is a permissible cause of population deviations only when it is limited to the avoidance of contests between incumbents and is applied in a consistent and nondiscriminatory manner. The incumbency protection in the Georgia state legislative plans meets neither criterion. . . .

The court rejected reading *Gaffney* to create a "safe harbor" to one person, one vote claims for population deviations of less than 10 percent. It concluded that any effort to minimize population deviations in this case had ceased once the +/-5 percent level was reached, even though perfect equality was certainly attainable given current technology:

> Such use of a 10% population window as a safe harbor may well violate the fundamental one person, one vote command of *Reynolds*, requiring that states "make an honest and good faith effort to construct districts . . . as nearly of equal population as practicable" and deviate from this principle only where "divergences . . . are based on legitimate consider-ations incident to the effectuation of a rational state policy." . . .

The court declared that the plan was unconstitutional under *Reynolds* because even the relatively small population deviation could not be justified by any interest the Supreme Court recognizes as valid, including the protection of incumbents:

> First, the policy of protecting incumbents was not applied in a consis-tent and neutral way. On the contrary, it was applied in a blatantly partisan and discriminatory manner, taking pains to protect only Democratic incumbents. . . .

> [Second,] the protection was overexpansive. The Supreme Court has said only that an interest in avoiding contests between incumbents may justify deviations from exact population equality, not that general protection of incumbents may also justify deviations. . . .

Even more noteworthy than the lower court decision is that the Supreme Court summarily affirmed in a one-sentence opinion. *Cox v. Larios*, 542 U.S. 947 (2004). Justice Stevens, in a concurrence joined by Justice Breyer, explained that the Court's recent decision in *Vieth* meant that "the equal-population principle remains the only clear limitation on improper districting practices, and we must be careful not to dilute its strength. It bears emphasis, however, that had the Court in *Vieth* adopted a standard for adjudicating partisan gerrymandering claims, the standard likely would have been satisfied in this case. . . . [T]he District Court's detailed factual findings regarding appellees' equal protection claim con-firm that an impermissible partisan gerrymander is visible to the judicial eye and subject to judicially manageable standards."

In particular, Justice Stevens emphasized the challenged plan's "selec-tive incumbent protection" as evidence of its unconstitutionality:

> Drawing district lines that have no neutral justification in order to place two incumbents of the opposite party in the same district is

probative of the same impermissible intent as the "uncouth twenty-eight-sided figure" that defined the boundary of Tuskegee, Alabama, in *Gomillion v. Lightfoot,*364 U.S. 339, 340 (1960), or the "dragon descending on Philadelphia from the west" that defined Pennsylvania's District 6 in *Vieth....*

Justice Scalia, the author of the plurality opinion in *Vieth* that would have held claims of unconstitutional political gerrymandering nonjusticiable, would have set *Cox v. Larios* for oral argument. In a solo dissent, he pointed to the Court's prior decisions that appeared to have created a ten percent safe harbor for state and local legislative plans. He asserted that in *Vieth*, "all but one of the Justices agreed that [taking political considerations into account while districting] *is* a traditional criterion ... so long as it does not go too far." Thus, the population deviation may have been constitutional.

As an aside to remind you of the broader context of Georgia's redistricting, recall that because Georgia is a covered jurisdiction under section 5 of the Voting Rights Act of 1965 (see Chapter 6), the state was required to show that the plan would not cause, and was not intended to cause, a retrogression in minority voting strength. That question produced litigation of its own, including a decision by the United States Supreme Court in *Georgia v. Ashcroft*, 537 U.S. 1151 (2003). In addition, the plaintiffs in *Larios*—Republican voters who lived in overpopulated districts—filed a lawsuit, claiming that the plan was an unconstitutional political gerrymander, an unconstitutional racial gerrymander, and a violation of one-person, one-vote.

In *Larios*, the question was whether partisan gerrymandering is a valid defense that justifies departures from one-vote, one-person even when state districts deviate no more than 10 percent. The interesting question is whether the analysis in *Larios*, of either the district court or Justice Stevens' and Breyer's concurrence, can be used by plaintiffs seeking affirmatively to attack a plan on partisan gerrymandering grounds. In particular, suppose a plan selectively pairs incumbents of one party. Does *Larios* suggest this could be the basis of a successful partisan gerrymandering claim after *Vieth*? Note that judicial doctrine against selective pairing of incumbents, as part of an overall partisan gerrymandering effort, would be a relatively easily manageable standard for the courts, unlike a more general constraint against partisan gerrymandering.

For another example of a district court explicitly using one-person, one-vote as vehicle to address excessive partisanship in the redistricting process, consider *Hulme v. Madison County*, 188 F. Supp. 2d 1041 (S.D. Ill. 2001). According to the district court, the Madison County process "demonstrated the worst of politics. The process fell so far short of representing the electorate that it seems the citizens of Madison County were not so much as an afterthought.... Far from some semblance of bipartisanship, the reapportionment process in Madison County was characterized by threats, coercion, bullying, and a skewed view of the law." Among the more egregious examples the court described were the following: at an early committee meeting, Democrat Wayne Bridgewater, the chair of the redistricting committee, announced that he planned to "cannibalize" Republican districts. At another meeting, when a Republican member of the Board approached him to express objections to the proposed plan, Bridgewater declared, "We are going to shove it [the map] up your f—— ass and you are going to like it, and I'll f—— any Republican I can." And at the final meeting where the Board approved Bridgewater's plan, he tore up a Republican proposed map. The plan the Board adopted split substantially more precincts than alternative plans, took a township that could have supported two whole districts and divided it among three districts diluting its influence, and paired two Republican incumbents.

Ultimately, despite the fact that the plan's total deviation was 9.3 percent, the district court held that the plan violated one-person, one-vote because "the apportionment process had a 'taint of arbitrariness or discrimination.'" Although the vices of the process that had produced the plan had relatively little to do with the size of the population deviation— after all, the alternative plan to which the district court pointed had a deviation of 8.51 percent, rather than 9.3 percent—and much to do with excessive partisanship, the district court used the doctrinal tool at hand to strike down the product of a deeply disturbing process.

Note that in both *Larios* and *Hulme*, the courts recognized that the plaintiffs could not make out a straightforward political gerrymandering claim under prevailing equal protection standards. Does this mean that evidence of political gerrymandering should be usable to rebut the presumption of constitutionality afforded by the 10 percent safe harbor?

Does it make a difference that in cases like *Larios* and *Hulme* courts consider the political motivations of the plan drawers at the justification stage, rather than as part of the plaintiffs' case in chief? Consider the following view:

> [W]hile *Vieth* essentially cuts off first-order political gerrymandering claims—that is, plaintiffs cannot get a plan struck down simply by showing that it constitutes an excessively partisan gerrymander—*Cox v. Larios* restores an opportunity for second-order judicial review of political gerrymanders: if a plan contains any population deviations, a court may decide that the deviations are caused by impermissible partisanship and strike the plan down as a formal matter for failure to comply with one person, one vote. . . .

> Is there some reason to prefer second-order adjudication of political gerrymandering claims to first-order adjudication? If there is, we don't see it. To be sure, once the system reequilibrates to the understanding that all deviations—and not simply those greater than 10%—may require neutral justifications, second-order adjudication may be less frequent than first-order challenges would have been. And perhaps

tightening up the population deviation standards may foreclose some gerrymanders, or at least limit them at the margins. But it seems as if second-order adjudication is more arbitrary, since outcomes turn not primarily on the degree of partisanship—even though partisan considerations drove the plan, prompted the litigation, and explained the courts' intervention—but rather on the fortuity of essentially meaningless deviations among the districts' populations. Whatever the virtues of holding reapportionment to the one person, one vote rule of equal population, the normative foundations of the equipopulosity rule are not sufficiently robust to justify on their own the result in *Larios*. Although there is apparent precision to the strict application of the equipopulation principle in *Larios*, the mathematical exactitude is compromised by the general imprecision of the underlying census enumeration, and the inclusion of children, aliens, and other disenfranchised individuals (such as ex-offenders)—whose numbers can vary dramatically from district to district. Given the fact that the mathematical weight of citizens' votes is likely to vary significantly even in districts with identical populations, it is difficult to see why trivial population disparities should on their own be constitutionally suspect.

Samuel Issacharoff & Pamela S. Karlan, *Where To Draw the Line?: Judicial Review of Political Gerrymandering*, 153 U. Pa. L. Rev. 541, 567–69 (2004).

9. How legitimate or compelling an interest should states having in protecting or favoring incumbent legislators in electoral processes? Note that some state courts have struck down, on federal and state constitutional grounds, laws that required incumbents to be listed first on election ballots. *See Gould v. Grubb*, 536 P.2d 1337 (Cal. 1975).

2. BIPARTISAN GERRYMANDERING

While partisan gerrymandering is as old as the American Republic, the 2000 redistricting brought to the fore the practice of what has come to be known as the sweetheart or bipartisan gerrymander. Bipartisan gerrymanders reflect a non-aggression pact between the two parties, or to focus on the individuals involved, between the incumbents of both parties. Democratic incumbents are put in districts that are safely Democratic; so too for Republicans. The result on the day of the general election can be elections that are simply not competitive at all; safe districts for each party will reliably vote for whatever candidate emerges from the party primary.

First, consider the evidence: the congressional elections in the wake of the 2000 round of redistricting appear to have been among the least competitive in recent American history. This absence of meaningful competition is carefully documented in Sam Hirsch, *The United States House of Unrepresentatives: What Went Wrong in the Latest Round of Congressional Redistricting*, 2 Election L.J. 179, 205–11 (2003). Redistricting typically threatens incumbents and produces more competitive elections than at any time during the rest of the decade; the need to revise districts requires moving longstanding constituents out of districts and adding new ones in. Yet in the 2002 general election, only four challengers managed to beat incumbents. This is a record low for any election year, let alone a redistricting year. Overall, only 38 districts nationwide were won with less than 55 percent of the major-party vote, a standard measure of electoral competitiveness, in the last congressional elections. *See* CQ's Politics in America 2004: The 108th Congress (David Hawkings & Brian Nutting eds., 2003).

In fact, neither party lost more than three seats in any state until the sweeping Democratic Party gains in 2006. Moreover, general elections were even more non-competitive than suggested merely by looking at how much turnover took place in seats held. Reelected incumbents prevailed by even larger margins than in previous decades. For example, 337 incumbents won with more than 60 percent of the major-party vote; over the previous four decades, the average in a post-redistricting year had been 261 of these "landslide" winners. Of course, overall the House is finely balanced between the two parties; but this balance does not result from competitive elections at the individual district level. Contrast the non-competitiveness of House elections, which are based on gerrymandered districts, with elections the same day for state governors and U.S. Senators, both of which are elected statewide and hence without any opportunity for gerrymandering: while one of eleven House elections were decided by 10 percentage points or less, about half of all gubernatorial and U.S. Senate elections were within that margin. Hirsch, *supra*, at 183. On the other hand, recent work suggests that the advantage of incumbency is just as strong for executive offices, where no district gerrymandering can take place, as for House districts. *See* Stephen Ansolabehere & James M. Snyder, Jr., *The Incumbency Advantage in U.S. Elections: An Analysis of State and Federal Offices*, 1942–2000, 1 Election L. J. 315, 328 (2002). Thus, the extent to which non-competitive House elections reflect other attributes of incumbency advantage beyond those associated with gerrymandering is an uncertain question. For a broader picture on the lack of competitiveness in the wake of the 2000 round of redistricting, consider the following table, from Hirsch, *supra*, at 184:

TABLE 1.   COMPARISON OF THE 2002 ELECTION
WITH ELECTIONS FROM 1972 TO 2000

Category	Avg. "Normal" Election (1974–1980) (1984–1900) (1994–2000)	Avg. Post-Reapportion-ment Election (1972, 1982, 1992)	2002 Election
Incumbents reelected	375	348	381

By >20 points	297	261	381
By <20 points	78	87	43
Incumbents defeated	21	35	16
In the primary	3	13	8
In the general	18	22	8
Incumbent retirements	37	48	35
New members	60	87	54

For an account of the difficulties presented by diminished competition in changing partisan control of the House, see Samuel Issacharoff & Jonathan Nagler, *Protected from Politics: Diminishing Margins of Electoral Competition in U.S. Congressional Elections*, ___ Ohio St. L. J. ___ (2007). This article also presents historic data since the end of World War II showing how rare was the voter shift between parties in 2006.

Second, consider whether constitutional law should—or can—do anything to address the triumph of the bipartisan gerrymander. Should *Gaffney v. Cummings*, 412 U.S. 735 (1973), be revisited? Was the Court wrong not to see any harm in bipartisan gerrymanders, and if so, what exactly is that harm? Note that bipartisan gerrymandering might be thought better than one-party partisan gerrymandering; while the raison d'etre of the latter is to bring about great skews between the percentage of votes one party receives statewide and the percentage of legislative seats it actually wins, bipartisan gerrymanders tend to match the votes cast for a party statewide and the percentage of seats that party receives. If 40 percent of voters tend to vote Democratic in a state with 10 congressional districts, a bipartisan gerrymander will likely give that party 4 out of the 10 seats. If, nonetheless, there is a meaningful harm here, what remedies might judicial doctrine be capable of providing for that harm?

Professor Issacharoff argues that there are at least two harms that ought to cause greater judicial concern current doctrine reflects. First, safe districts tend to select more extreme candidates from within each party than more competitive districts would. Primary elections tend to be dominated by the activist wings of the parties; a more competitive district on general election day creates incentives for party voters to choose more moderate candidates likely to prevail in the general election. "Left behind in the 'sweetheart gerrymander' are the droves of median voters increasingly estranged from the polarized parties. Left behind as well are the incentives to provide representation to the community as a whole . . . The result is not only less electoral accountability but also more fractiousness in government and more difficulty in forming legislative coalitions across party lines." Samuel Issacharoff, *Gerrymandering and Political Cartels*, 116 Harv. L. Rev. 593, 628 (2002). Second, Issacharoff argues that if parties were forced to compete more for votes, they would be forced to attempt to educate and influence voters, which might lead to shifts in voter preferences for candidates and keep candidates accountable to these shifts.

Has constitutional law failed to recognize these harms because it has cast legal issues about gerrymandering, and the structure of democratic politics more generally, either into a matter of conventionally understood individual rights or into the model of anti-discrimination under the equal protection clause? Do either of these approaches enable courts to recognize the harms that result from sweetheart gerrymandering? The problems of bipartisan gerrymandering, like many others in the law of politics, involve harms that are more structural and systemic than those addressed through individual rights doctrines or group-based discrimination models that require some unfair treatment of an identifiable group (typically, a minority group). What place should the value of competitive elections have in constitutional doctrine? For elaboration of these questions, see Richard H. Pildes, *The Constitution and Political Competition*, 30 Nova L. Rev. 253 (2006).

Note that the only source for state power to design congressional election districts comes from Art. I, Sec. 4, the Elections Clause. Professor Pildes argues that courts should hold it beyond the scope of the limited, enumerated power that the Elections Clause grants state legislatures for those legislatures to engage in the systematic, intentional, elimination of competitive congressional districts across a state. Should the courts accept this argument? Compare cases holding that Congress has acted beyond other enumerated powers under Art. I and those holding that states have exceeded their power under the Elections Clause in other contexts. On congressional powers, see, e.g., *Board of Trustees v. Garrett*, 531 U.S. 356, 365 (2001); *United States v. Morrison*, 529 U.S. 598, 607, 620–21 (2000); *City of Boerne v. Flores*, 521 U.S. 507, 516 (1997); *United States v. Lopez*, 514 U.S. 549, 553 (1995). On state powers under the Elections Clause, see *Cook v. Gralike*, 531 U.S. 510, 522–23 (2001); *U.S. Term Limits, Inc. v. Thornton*, 514 U.S. 779, 834–35 (1995).

Professor Issacharoff argues that courts should hold that districting done by self-interested political actors should be presumptively unconstitutional per se. On constitutional grounds, is Professor Issacharoff's remedial recommendation appealing? Is there any other judicial remedy for sweetheart gerrymandering that one can imagine? Would a judicial declaration that the method of districting used for nearly 200 years throughout the nation was unconstitutional be an appropriate exercise of judicial power?

Professor Persily has challenged the view that competitive districts are such an essential component of democracy. *See* Nathaniel Persily, *In Defense of Foxes Guarding Henhouses: The Case for Judicial Acquiescence to Incumbent–Protecting Gerrymanders*, 116 Harv. L. Rev. 649 (2002). Professor Persily essentially defends the position in *Gaffney v. Cummings*. As long as representative bodies are fairly representative in partisan makeup, he argues, the system is functioning well. Moreover, Professor

Persily argues that the current system *is* quite competitive, if one shifts focus from the district level to the level of the legislature as a whole. Thus, Professor Persily argues that competition is only one value a democratic system should seek to realize; fair representation and effective governance are other values, and these latter often are in conflict with the values associated with competitive elections.

Is there a difference between the principle that competitiveness of districted elections should be maximized and the principle that legislatures should not have the power to systematically and intentionally eliminate nearly all competitive elections? If so, is one principle more appropriate for judicial enforcement than the other?

As a closing reflection, consider the following comments from a Democratic member of Congress in California, Rep. Loretta Sanchez, regarding Michael Berman, the consultant (and brother of a Democratic member of Congress) the Democratic Party hired to advise it on designing the 2000 redistricting plan for California's congressional districts:

> So Rep. Loretta Sanchez of Santa Ana said she and the rest of the Democratic congressional delegation went to Berman and made their own deal. Thirty of the 32 Democratic incumbents have paid Berman $20,000 each, she said, for an "incumbent-protection plan." "Twenty thousand is nothing to keep your seat," Sanchez said. "I spend $2 million (campaigning) every election. If my colleagues are smart, they'll pay their $20,000, and Michael will draw the district they can win in. Those who have refused to pay? God help them." *See* H. Quach and D. Bunis, *All Bow to Redistrict Architect*, Orange County Register, A1 (Aug. 26, 2001).

3.   ENDLESS REDISTRICTING?

When partisan control of a legislative chamber as a whole, such as the U.S. House, is potentially at stake, the partisan struggles over districting at the individual state level become all the more acute. The intensely competitive context over the House as a whole in the early 2000s manifested itself in a new phenomenon: endless redistricting. When initial elections with new congressional districts after the 2000 census produced results the current state legislature did not like, state legislatures decided to take another shot at redistricting in the middle of the decade. Are there any legal constraints on the prospect of constant, mid-decade redistricting to perfect the partisan aims of sitting legislatures?

1.   One place re-redistricting occurred was Colorado. Colorado gained one congressional seat in 2000 as a result of an increase of 1 million new residents statewide. When the legislature was too politically gridlocked to create a new redistricting plan for the 2002 election, a state judge designed the districts as a remedy in redistricting litigation. After the 2002 elections, Republicans gained full control of the state legislative process and decided to redistrict the congressional seats in the middle of the decade. Republicans had won the newly created district, but by only 121 votes. Under the judicially-drawn plan, that district was a competitive, working-class district of older Denver suburbs right around the city; it contained equal numbers of Republicans, Democrats, and unaffiliated voters. One local political scientist described it as "Colorado in a microcosm ... I thought it was a beautiful district in terms of having a competitive race." J. Martinez, *Remap Boosts GOP's Grip: New Lines Fortify Hold on House, Anger Dems*, Denver Post, A01 (June 16, 2003).

But what is beautiful to a pro-competition academic theorist is not so to political actors. After the 2002 elections, the Republican-dominated state legislature therefore sought to make this district far safer for the Republican incumbent; the district was re-designed so that it become less Hispanic, more Anglo, and more Republican, and blue-collar neighborhoods were moved out to nearby districts that were already overwhelmingly Democratic. In another change designed to make other districts more safely Republican, heavily Democratic and Hispanic Pueblo County was split in two, with both halves being added to districts that would remain overwhelmingly Republican. The link between national politics and state districting practices was evident in reported consultation between White House political advisors and state redistricters in Colorado. *See* J. Eilperin, *GOP'S New Push on Redistricting: House Gains Are At Stake in Colorado, Texas*, Washington Post A04 (May 9, 2003).

The Colorado Supreme Court held that this venture violated the state constitution. That court concluded that, once districts had been lawfully established, they could not be re-drawn, under the Colorado constitution, until a new census. *People ex rel. Salazar v. Davidson*, 79 P.3d 1221 (2003) (en banc).

The United States Supreme Court denied certiorari, but three Justices would have granted the petition to decide whether Art. I, § 4 of the federal Constitution precluded the state courts from playing the role they had played in drawing Colorado's congressional districts. As you recall, Art. I, § 4 specifies that, subject to congressional override, election regulations for the House and Senate "shall be prescribed in each State by the Legislature thereof." These three Justices—Chief Justice Rehnquist and Justices Scalia and Thomas—questioned whether state courts could draw congressional districts, even when the state legislature had been too paralyzed to do so, in light of Art. I, § 4's grant of power to the state "legislature." These Justices accepted that the term "legislature" could be construed broadly enough to include the normal lawmaking process of the state—so that the governor, through the veto power, could participate in legislation regarding House and Senate electoral regulations—but not so broadly as to permit the state courts to draw districts, at least when state law did not expressly make the state courts a part of the normal lawmaking process on these matters. *See Colorado General Assembly v. Salazar*, 541 U.S. 1093 (2004) (Rehnquist, C.J., dissenting). Note that this is the same position on which these three Justices would have decided *Bush v. Gore*. In a later iteration of this litigation, the Supreme Court held that individual citizens do not have standing to enforce the Elections Clause in a context in which plaintiffs argue that the state courts have interfered with the powers the Elections Clause bestows on the state legislature. See *Lance v. Coffman*, 549 U.S. ___ (2007).

2. Texas was another site of re-redistricting. In the first elections after the 2000 redistricting, Democrats held a 17–15 dominance in the state's congressional delegation.

In 2001, Democrats controlled the state House, Republicans the state Senate, and a three-judge federal court drew the districts, which the court based on the prior decade's districts as well as the need to create two new districts, given Texas' population explosion in the 1990s. When the Republicans tried to push the new districting plan through the state legislature in 2003, after the 2002 elections gave Republicans full control, Democratic legislators fled the state (not for the Alamo, but for a motel in Oklahoma) to deprive the legislature of a quorum. The events that followed had the quality of history unfolding as both tragedy and farce. It included efforts by Texas Republicans to have state officials in Oklahoma and New Mexico (where Texas Senators subsequently holed up) arrest the escaped Texas officials and forcibly return them to Texas for a quorum vote. These states both had Democratic governors and the efforts at political extradition failed. Perhaps even more bizarre was the effort to stop some legislators from leaving the state by plane by reporting the suspected tail numbers of the planes to the Federal Aviation Authority, claiming criminal use of the airplanes and asking that they be tracked down—the FAA failed to locate the planes. The entire bizarre tale is told with panache in Steve Bickerstaff, Congressional Redistricting in Texas and the Fall of Tom DeLay (2006). Ultimately the Democratic boycott broke and eventually the state legislature did pass a new redistricting plan. Of what relevance should it be that the 1990s districting plan, on which the three-judge federal court relied, designed when Democrats were in control, was declared the most aggressively partisan gerrymander of that decade by the prestigious Almanac of American Politics: "for its creatively drawn lines in unlikely places; for the convoluted boundaries of its districts ... for the partisan effrontery which enabled the Democrats to protect all but one of their incumbents and to capture the state's three new seats as well." Michael Barone & Grant Ujifusa, The Almanac of American Politics 1209 (1994) (several of these districts were held to be unconstitutional racial gerrymanders in *Bush v. Vera*, 517 U.S. 952 (1996)). Of what relevance should it also be that by 2003, virtually every statewide office in Texas was held by a Republican, which suggests the statewide majority has become Republican? Is the Republican re-redistricting effort, then, a crass partisan ploy or an effort to restore partisan fairness in light of a crass partisan Democratic gerrymander of the 1990s?

In something of a contrast to the Colorado Supreme Court, a three-judge federal district court originally held that nothing in the federal Constitution precluded a state legislature from re-drawing congressional districts after a federal court had already drawn those districts earlier in the decade. The three-judge court reached this decision before *Vieth*, see *Session v. Perry*, 298 F. Supp. 2d 451 (E.D.Tex. 2004), and the Supreme Court then remanded the case after *Vieth* for reconsideration. The three-judge court then had the unenviable task of deciding how to apply the Supreme Court's 4–1–4 decision in *Vieth*. On remand, the three-judge court reached the same conclusion it had previously—namely, that the reredistricting did not violate the Constitution. See *Henderson v. Perry*, 399 F. Supp. 2d 756 (E.D. Tex. 2005).

On appeal, the Supreme Court affirmed, at least with respect to the claims of unconstitutional partisan gerrymandering. *League of United Latin American Citizens (LULAC) v. Perry*, 126 S.Ct. 2594 (2006). The Court did strike down parts of the plan as a violation of the Voting Rights Act; that portion of the Court's opinion is excerpted in Chapter 9.

Justice Scalia, in an opinion joined by Justice Thomas, reiterated his position from *Vieth* that claims of unconstitutional political gerrymandering were simply nonjusticiable. Chief Justice Roberts, in an opinion joined by Justice Alito, both of whom had joined the Court after *Vieth* sidestepped the question of justiciability.

Justice Kennedy's views remained somewhat elusive. He reiterated his refusal to declare political gerrymandering nonjusticiable altogether. In a part of his opinion joined by Justices Souter and Ginsburg, Justice Kennedy rejected the challengers' theory that a partisan-inspired mid-decade re-redistricting would violate one person, one vote because the state would be relying on inevitably out-of-date census figures in crafting the districts. He distinguished *Cox v. Larios*, 542 U.S. 947 (2004) (per curiam), discussed above, by noting that there, the census figures themselves revealed a population deviation (a deviation unjustifiable because explicable only on partisan grounds), whereas here, the census figures themselves revealed no deviation.

In parts of his opinion joined by no other justice, Justice Kennedy expressed a more general preference for redistricting to be regulated by the political branches, state and federal:

> That Congress is the federal body explicitly given constitutional power over elections is also a noteworthy statement of preference for the democratic process. As the Constitution vests redistricting responsibilities foremost in the legislatures of the States and in Congress, a lawful, legislatively enacted plan should be preferable to one drawn by the courts.

> It should follow, too, that if a legislature acts to replace a court-drawn plan with one of its own design, no presumption of impropriety should attach to the legislative decision to act.

Thus, while a rule or presumption of invalidity for mid-decade redistricting would have the virtue of simplicity, and would avoid addressing the drawing of individual district lines by focusing instead on the decision to redistrict itself, Justice Kennedy saw no justification for according different levels of skepticism to "a highly effective partisan gerrymander that coincided with decennial redistricting" and "a bumbling, yet solely partisan, mid-decade redistricting."

The four justices who found partisan gerrymandering claims justiciable in *Vieth*—Justices Stevens, Breyer, Souter, and Ginsburg—adhered to that position. On the merits, Justices Souter and Ginsburg joined Justice Kennedy in rejecting mid decade-specific challenges to the re-redistricting. On the more general question of political gerrymandering, Justice Souter, in an opinion joined by Justice Ginsburg, saw "nothing to be gained by working through these cases on the standard I would have applied in *Vieth*, because here as in *Vieth* we have no majority for any single criterion of impermissible gerrymander." He did reserve the question whether a "test of gerrymander turning on the process followed in redistricting" might have some utility.

In an opinion dissenting in relevant part from the Court's holding that the Texas plan did not constitute an unconstitutional political gerrymander, Justice Stevens, joined by Justice Breyer, distinguished the issue presented from the one presented in *Vieth*:

> Unlike *Vieth*, the narrow question presented by the statewide challenge in this litigation is whether the State's decision to draw the map in the first place, when it was under no legal obligation to do so, was permissible. It is undeniable that identifying the motive for making that basic decision is a readily manageable judicial task. See *Gomillion* v. *Lightfoot*, 364 U.S. 339, 341 (1960) (noting that plaintiffs' allegations, if true, would establish by circumstantial evidence "tantamount for all practical purposes to a mathematical demonstration," that redistricting legislation had been enacted "solely" to segregate voters along racial lines).... Indeed, although the Constitution places no *per se* ban on midcycle redistricting, a legislature's decision to redistrict in the middle of the census cycle, when the legislature is under no legal obligation to do so, makes the judicial task of identifying the legislature's motive simpler than it would otherwise be....

> The requirements of the Federal Constitution that limit the State's power to rely exclusively on partisan preferences in drawing district lines are the Fourteenth Amendment's prohibition against invidious discrimination, and the First Amendment's protection of citizens from official retaliation based on their political affiliation.... These protections embodied in the First and Fourteenth Amendments reflect the fundamental duty of the sovereign to govern impartially.

> The legislature's decision to redistrict at issue in this litigation was entirely inconsistent with these principles. By taking an action for the

sole purpose of advantaging Republicans and disadvantaging Democrats, the State of Texas violated its constitutional obligation to govern impartially.

Justice Breyer also dissented, relying on his analysis in his *Vieth* dissent to conclude that the Texas plan was designed not only to maximize partisan advantage but to entrench Republican representatives even if they lost the support of the voters: "In sum, the risk of entrenchment is demonstrated, partisan considerations [have] rendered the traditional district-drawing compromises irrelevant, and no justification other than party advantage can be found. The record reveals a plan that overwhelmingly relies upon the unjustified use of purely partisan line-drawing considerations and which will likely have seriously harmful electoral consequences. For these reasons, I believe the plan in its entirety violates the Equal Protection Clause."

Does the emergence of re-redistricting shed any light on proposals to turn districting over to independent commissions? If legislative majorities are able to redistrict repeatedly over the decennial cycle, what happens to the view that the process of gerrymandering is self-limiting because of the imprecision of carving districts at the start of a ten-year electoral cycle? The leading article on the emergence of re-redistricting, written before the Supreme Court's decision in the Texas case, is Adam Cox, *Commentary: Partisan Fairness and Redistricting Politics*, 79 N.Y.U. L. Rev. 751 (2004). Cox argues for a per se rule against re-redistricting.

Should the appropriateness or legality of mid-decade redistricting depend on whether a legislature never adopted a valid plan earlier in the decade, as in Texas? Is it a sound result that mid-decade redistricting for congressional districts is legal in some states, as in Texas, and not in others, as in Colorado, by virtue of differences in state law? Should Congress legislate to establish a uniform rule on this subject? Is Congress likely to do so?

CHAPTER 11

DIRECT DEMOCRACY

From the Greek city-states to the Roman plebiscites to the New England town meetings, direct democratic participation in political decisions has served as an alternative to government by elected representatives. In recent years, there has been a revival of direct democratic participation at the state level on major issues of statewide importance. This revival has come in the form of increasing use of the two most prevalent forms of direct democracy in contemporary America: the initiative and the referendum. Professor David Magleby has offered a brief description of the two processes:

> Using the initiative, voters may write statutes, and in some states constitutional amendments, which will go to the ballot if sufficient valid petition signatures are gathered.... Initiatives that meet the signature requirement go either directly to the voters (the direct initiative) or are placed on the state legislature's agenda (the indirect initiative), where, if the legislature does not enact the initiative within a specified time, the proponents have the option to gather additional signatures and place the measure on the ballot. Five states permit both the indirect and direct initiative, and not surprisingly when they do, initiative sponsors prefer taking their issue directly to the voters.

> In contrast, citizens may use the popular referendum to place laws previously enacted by local or state legislative bodies before the voters for approval. As with the initiative, citizen petitions qualify a popular referendum for the ballot. Initiatives are sometimes used as referendums, as in the case of a 1964 California measure that overturned an open-housing law passed by the state legislature.... Referendums can also be called by local or state legislatures. For instance, all states except Delaware require that constitutional changes go before the voters in a referendum, and many state legislatures place measures on the ballot for voter approval.

David B. Magleby, *Governing by Initiative: Let the Voters Decide? An Assessment of the Initiative and Referendum Process*, 66 U. Colo. L. Rev. 13, 13–14 (1995).

This chapter considers several questions that arise from the increasing role of direct popular decisionmaking in democratic government. We begin by asking whether such decisionmaking is consistent with the constitutional structure and the framers' theory of government. We then turn to the

890

way popular decisionmaking interacts with the voting rights system more generally.

A. CONSTITUTIONAL UNDERPINNINGS AND CONCERNS

The constitutional system reflects a Madisonian design of institutional checks and balances to avoid the risk of majority factions having untrammeled power. In The Federalist Papers No. 10, Madison clearly distinguishes between "pure Democracy" in which citizens jointly administer the state, and a "Republic" based on government by representatives:

From this view of the subject it may be concluded that a pure democracy, by which I mean a society consisting of a small number of citizens, who assemble and administer the government in person, can admit of no cure for the mischiefs of faction. A common passion or interest will, in almost every case, be felt by a majority of the whole; a communication and concert result from the form of government itself; and there is nothing to check the inducements to sacrifice the weaker party or an obnoxious individual. Hence it is that such democracies have ever been spectacles of turbulence and contention; have ever been found incompatible with personal security or the rights of property; and have in general been as short in their lives as they have been violent in their deaths. Theoretic politicians who have patronized this species of government, have erroneously supposed that by reducing mankind to a perfect equality in their political rights, they would, at the same time, be perfectly equalized and assimilated in their possessions, their opinions, and their passions.

A republic, by which I mean a government in which the scheme of representation takes place, opens a different prospect, and promises the cure for which we are seeking. Let us examine the points in which it varies from pure democracy, and we shall comprehend both the nature of the cure and the efficacy which it must derive from the Union.

The two great points of difference between a democracy and a republic are: first, the delegation of the government, in the latter to a small number of citizens elected by the rest; secondly, the greater number of citizens, and greater sphere of country over which the latter may be extended.

The effect of the first difference is, on the one hand, to refine and enlarge the public views, by passing them through the medium of a chosen body of citizens, whose wisdom may best discern the true interest of their country, and whose patriotism and love of justice will be least likely to sacrifice it to temporary or partial considerations. Under such a regulation, it may well happen that the public voice, pronounced by the representatives of the people, will be more consonant to the public good than if pronounced by the people themselves, convened for the purpose. . . .

The other point of difference is, the greater number of citizens and extent of territory which may be brought within the compass of republican than of democratic government; and it is this circumstance principally which renders factious combinations less to be dreaded in the former than in the latter. The smaller the society, the fewer probably will be the distinct parties and interests composing it; the fewer the distinct parties and interests, the more frequently will a majority be found of the same party; and the smaller the number of individuals composing a majority, and the smaller the compass within which they are placed, the most easily will they concert and execute their plans of oppression. Extend the sphere, and you take in a greater variety of parties and interests; you make it less probable that a majority of the whole will have a common motive to invade the rights of other citizens; or if such a common motive exists, it will be more difficult for all who feel it to discover their own strength, and to act in unison with each other.

Technological change has made the process of citizen consultation far easier. Some have pointed to recent technological advances as a justification for embracing more direct democratic participation and decisionmaking. *See, e.g.,* Lawrence Grossman, The Electronic Republic (1995). But the key to Madisonian republicanism rested in government at one remove from the direct wishes (and passions) of the populace: a republic is "a government which derives all its powers directly or indirectly from the great body of the people; and is administered by persons holding offices during pleasure, for a limited period, or during good behavior." By contrast, "[l]awmaking by popular vote on an initiated proposal of course bypasses the committee study, hearings, amendments, and compromises of legislative deliberation; that was and is its purpose." Hans A. Linde, *When Initiative Lawmaking Is Not "Republican Government": The Campaign Against Homosexuality,* 72 Or. L. Rev. 19, 34 (1993).

Despite the concerns of the Founders, direct democracy came to be seen as an antidote to the entrenched power of political machines and the powers of moneyed interests at the legislative level. The major expansion of direct democracy in this country occurred in the Progressive period at the turn of the twentieth century. Initiatives and referenda were touted at the time as a means of overcoming the capture of legislatures by special interests, such as the railroads, mining companies, and other industries, and of circumventing the power of ward-based political machines, in much the same way as the system of at-large elections of city and county officials was promoted during that same period. Direct participation was also thought to educate and improve the civic virtue of citizens. In addition, in Oregon itself—the fount of direct decisionmaking—the legislature had become so deadlocked that the normal processes of legislation by representatives had ground to a halt. *See generally* Nathaniel Persily, *The Peculiar Geography of Direct Democracy: Why The Initiative, Referendum and Recall Developed in the American West*, 2 Mich. L. & Pol'y Rev. 11 (1997). One prominent proponent of direct lawmaking, Senator Jonathan Bourne, Jr., of Oregon put his case this way, in speaking to an academic audience:

> Always there are a few intellectual leaders who are in advance of the masses of the people; but the practical workings of delegated government are such that the masses of the people are always in advance of those individuals who secure political but not intellectual leadership. "Practical politics," under a system of delegated government, brings into power men who are guided more by selfish interest than by general welfare. Popular government reverses this condition and gives power to intellectual leaders rather than to men whose success is due to skill as "practical politicians."

XLIII Annals of the American Academy of Political and Social Science 7 (1912).

In response to the arguments of initiative proponents, 23 states enacted the initiative, the referendum, or both between 1898 and 1918. During the early decades of the twentieth century, these new devices were invoked quite frequently; but from the 1940s to the 1960s, direct lawmaking declined. K.K. DuVivier, *By Going Wrong All Things Come Right: Using Alternative Initiatives to Improve Citizen Lawmaking*, 63 U. Cinn. L. Rev. 1185, 1188 (1995). There has recently been a resurgence in use of these devices, however, which began in the late 1960s and then took off with the success in 1978 of California's Proposition 13, the symbol of the "property tax revolt," which capped property taxes. Increasingly, these direct lawmaking devices are being used for statewide lawmaking at rates comparable to when the process was first created early in the century. In California itself, for example, voters passed only two initiatives in the 1950s; three in the 1960s; seven in the 1970s; and then 21 in the 1980s and 15 between 1990 and 1996. Peter Schrag, *Take the Initiative, Please: Referendum Madness in California*, 28 Am. Prospect 61 (1996). For discussion of the use of direct lawmaking for local government issues, see Clayton Gillette, *Plebiscites, Participation, and Collective Action in Local Government Law*, 86 Mich. L. Rev. 930 (1988). The statewide initiative remains largely, though not exclusively, a phenomenon of western politics, where it began: California and Oregon accounted for nearly one-third of all statewide initiatives in the 1980s.

The Supreme Court confronted the question whether direct democracy was constitutionally permissible in a challenge brought by Pacific States Telephone & Telegraph to an Oregon gross revenue tax enacted by initiative in 1906. As with its early forays into reapportionment, discussed in Chapter 3, it declined to address the merits of the challengers' constitutional claims.

Pacific States Telephone & Telegraph Company v. Oregon

223 U.S. 118 (1912).

■ MR. CHIEF JUSTICE WHITE delivered the opinion of the Court:

* * *

The case is this: In 1902 Oregon amended its Constitution. This amendment, while retaining an existing clause vesting the exclusive legislative power in a general assembly consisting of a senate and a house of representatives, added to that provision the following: "But the people reserve to themselves power to propose laws and amendments to the Constitution, and to enact or reject the same at the polls, independent of the legislative assembly, and also reserve power at their own option to approve or reject at the polls any act of the legislative assembly." [Art. 4, sec. 1.] Specific means for the exercise of the power thus reserved was contained in further clauses authorizing both the amendment of the Constitution and the enactment of laws to be accomplished by the method known as the initiative and that commonly referred to as the referendum. As to the first, the initiative, it suffices to say that a stated number of voters were given the right at any time to secure a submission to popular vote for approval of any matter which it was desired to have enacted into law, and providing that the proposition thus submitted, when approved by popular vote, should become the law of the state. The second, the referendum, provided for a reference to a popular vote, for approval or disapproval, of any law passed by the legislature, such reference to take place either as the result of the action of the legislature itself, or of a petition filed for that purpose by a specified number of voters.... By resort to the initiative in 1906, a law taxing certain classes of corporations was submitted, voted on, and promulgated by the governor in 1907 as having been duly adopted....

The Pacific States Telephone & Telegraph Company, an Oregon corporation engaged in business in that state, made a return of its gross receipts, as required by the statute, and was accordingly assessed 2 per cent upon the amount of such return. The suit which is now before us was commenced by the state to enforce payment of this assessment and the statutory penalties for delinquency.... [The corporation's legal challenges] are all based upon the single contention that the creation by a state of the power to legislate by the initiative and referendum causes the prior lawful state government to be bereft of its lawful character as the result of the provisions of Section 4 of article 4 of the Constitution, that "the United States shall guarantee to every state in this Union a republican form of government, and shall protect each of them against invasion; and on application of the legislature, or of the executive (when the legislature cannot be convened), against domestic violence." This being the basis of all the contentions, the case comes to the single issue whether the enforcement of that provision, because of its political character, is exclusively committed to Congress, or is judicial in its character.

* * *

It was long ago settled that the enforcement of [the republican form of government clause in Article IV, Sec. 4] belonged to the political department. In [*Luther v. Borden*, 48 U.S. 1 (1849)], it was held that the question, which of the two opposing governments of Rhode Island, namely, the charter government or the government established by a voluntary convention, was the legitimate one, was a question for the determination of the political department; and when that department had decided, the courts were bound to take notice of the decision and follow it ... [T]he settled distinction which the doctrine just stated points out between judicial authority over justiciable controversies and legislative power as to purely political questions ... distinguish[es] between things which are widely different; that is, the legislative duty to determine the political questions involved in deciding whether a state government republican in form exists, and the judicial power and ever-present duty whenever it becomes necessary, in a controversy properly submitted, to enforce and uphold the applicable provisions of the Constitution as to each and every exercise of governmental power....

As the issues presented, in their very essence, are, and have long since by this court been, definitely determined to be political and governmental, and embraced within the scope of the powers conferred upon Congress, and not, therefore, within the reach of judicial power, it follows that the case presented is not within our jurisdiction, and the writ of error must therefore be, and it is, dismissed for want of jurisdiction.

NOTES AND QUESTIONS

1. State and federal courts have struck down the *results* of many initiatives and referenda on federal constitutional grounds. *See, e.g., U.S. Term Limits v. Thornton,* 514 U.S. 779 (1995) (striking down Arkansas' imposition of term limits on its congressional delegation on Qualifications Clause grounds; discussed later in this Chapter); *Evans v. Romer,* 882 P.2d 1335 (Colo. 1994), *aff'd,* 517 U.S. 620 (1996) (striking down Colorado's anti-gay rights constitutional amendment on equal protection grounds). But they have not seriously revisited the question whether the very *process* of lawmaking through initiative and referendum is constitutional. Perhaps as a result, federal courts have also not considered in any meaningful way important subsidiary questions. For example, should the fact that a law emerges from direct democratic processes as opposed to the ordinary legislative process influence the techniques the courts use to interpret the law? Are there certain kinds of laws whose constitutionality should turn on whether they are enacted by voters rather than legislatures? We pursue this question below. Should the courts develop techniques of working with the products of direct lawmaking that differ from those the courts use to deal with ordinary legislation?

2. What would or should have happened had the Supreme Court reached the merits in *Pacific States*? Is lawmaking by direct democracy consistent with the concerns for "majority faction" so central in The Federalist Papers No. 10? If one "great point of difference between a democracy and a republic" is that in the latter, representative government produces one check on the tendency of popular government to sacrifice to its ruling passion or interest both the public good and the rights of other citizens, should the Court have held the initiative process unconstitutional, or at least applied special scrutiny to policies adopted through initiatives? One answer to these questions might be that *Pacific States* involved the choice at the state level between different forms of lawmaking. Perhaps the Constitution and the Federalist Papers should not be understood to articulate any general conception of self-government, but only one applicable to national lawmaking institutions. In that case, consider whether Congress could by statute create a national initiative referendum mechanism. Could such a mechanism be created only by a constitutional amendment? Consider these two proposals for a national referendum process, the second of which was introduced as a proposed constitutional amendment in the late 1970s with more than 50 congressional supporters:

a) Whenever the president and Congress are in conflict or deadlock on domestic legislation, either or both may submit the question at issue to a referendum vote of the electorate. The people of the United States may petition for referendum on national legislation, after passage by Congress.... When 10 percent of registered voters in more than one-third of all states sign a legal petition for referendum, the proposed law shall be put to majority decision of the electorate at the next regularly scheduled election.

b) A national initiative would be held when advocates of a policy proposal, in an 18–month period, gathered signatures equal to 3% of the ballots cast in the last presidential election, including 3% in each of at least ten states (about 3 million signatures). At the next regularly scheduled national election, if a majority of those voting approved, the measure would take effect in 30 days (or as otherwise specified). Congress could amend or repeal by a two-thirds vote in both houses within two years of adoption and by a simple majority vote after that. The initiative could not be used to amend the Constitution, call up troops, or declare war.

For discussion, see Thomas E. Cronin, Direct Democracy 157–95 (1989).

3. *Pacific States* explicitly distinguishes the question whether a particular state's government is "republican in form"—a question it holds to be nonjusticiable—from the question whether a particular "exercise of governmental power" by a state's government is permissible—the ordinary stuff of constitutional adjudication. Should the state's form of government shed any light on judicial evaluation of the latter sorts of questions? Put more concretely, suppose the Court had reached the merits in *Pacific States* and had upheld the initiative form of lawmaking on the merits. Would that mean that courts faced with federal constitutional challenges to a state law or state constitutional provision should review the challenged measure without regard to its provenance? Or should courts pay particularly close attention to the differences between representative institutions and popular lawmaking in assessing popular lawmaking's use in specific cases and its compliance with constitutional standards—particularly those designed to insure that the *process* of lawmaking facilitates focused and thoughtful deliberation? Compare Julian N. Eule, *Judicial Review of Direct Democracy*, 99 Yale L.J. 1503 (1990) (arguing that judicial review is especially important because the initiative process gives full sway to majority preferences without any Madisonian checks and balances) with Robin Charlow, *Judicial Review, Equal Protection and the Problem with Plebiscites*, 79 Cornell. L. Rev. 527 (1994) (arguing that those pressing for more aggressive judicial review of initiatives are wrong and are more often frustrated with the substantive content of current equal protection doctrine) and Mark Tushnet, *Fear of Voting: Differential Standards of Judicial Review of Direct Legislation*, 1996 N.Y.U. Ann. Surv. Am. L. (1997) (arguing against differential judicial review for popularly enacted laws as compared to ordinary legislation). For a case study of the role of constitutional arguments in initiative processes, see David A. Sklansky, *Proposition 187 and the Ghost of James Bradley Thayer*, 17 Chicano–Latino L. Rev. 24 (1995) (documenting that in the process of adopting California's Proposition 187, which barred aliens from a variety of social services, supporters urged the disregard of constitutional concerns on the assumption that judicial review would take care of any problems). We shall return to these questions below. But consider for the moment some of the purely interpretive problems. As summarized by Professor Jane Schacter:

> The case of direct democracy tests the limits of judicial willingness to deploy intentionalist methodology. There are reasons to suspect that a search for "popular intent" will be even more problematic than the traditional search for legislative intent. Consider, for example, the mass size of the electorate; the absence of legislative hearings, committee reports, or other recorded legislative history; and the inability of citizen lawmakers to deliberate about, or to amend, proposed ballot measures. In addition, voters are not professional lawmakers, so it is problematic to impute to the electorate the same knowledge about law, legal terminology, and legislative context that courts routinely ascribe—if sometimes only as aspiration—to legislators. These structural dynamics of the direct lawmaking process should further burden what is in any circumstance a problematic quest for the single intent underlying a law.

Jane S. Schacter, *The Pursuit of "Popular Intent": Interpretive Dilemmas in Direct Democracy*, 105 Yale L.J. 107 (1995). For a sophisticated argument as to how courts should go about the process of interpreting the products of direct lawmaking, see Philip P. Frickey, *Interpretation on the Borderline: Constitution, Canons, Direct Democracy*, 1996 N.Y.U. Ann. Surv. Am. L. (1997). To the general problems of legal interpretation of texts enacted popularly—rather than through formal legislative means— can be added the problems caused by initiatives whose language is overwhelmingly long or hopelessly obscure. In addition, it is not uncommon for voters to approve two apparently conflicting initiatives in the same election—a process that sometimes results because once one initiative gets underway, others will seek to qualify an "alternative" initiative on the same topic. For endorsement of this process of generating competing, alternative initiatives, see K.K. DuVivier, *By Going Wrong All Things Come Right: Using Alternative Initiatives to Improve Citizen Lawmaking*, 63 U. Cinn. L. Rev. 1185 (1995). Under California law, when such a conflict occurs, the provision that has received the most votes prevails. In *Taxpayers to Limit Campaign Spending v. Fair Political Practices Commission*, 799 P.2d 1220 (1990), this had the ironic effect of leading to invalidation of both of the two campaign finance reform initiatives that voters had approved; the court held the two in conflict, declared the one with the most votes to be the one adopted, but struck that one down as unconstitutional. As a result, voters got no campaign finance reform of any form.

4. Does the Guarantee Clause critique of direct democracy embody an overly romantic notion of the legislative process? Critics of direct democracy argue that it tends to inflame passions on single issues, thereby undermining the processes of reasoned deliberation that should hold sway in a legislative setting. Others, however, argue that the contrast is between direct democracy and "an idealized construct of the legislative process" that fails to take into account the real infirmities of legislative deadlock and interest group capture. *See* Richard Briffault, *Distrust of Democracy*, 63 Tex. L. Rev. 1347, 1350 (1985). Briffault emphasizes that the existence of initiative provisions can serve as an indirect check on legislative policy, even when initiatives are not directly used to make law. The fact that voters can turn to the initiative to overturn legislative policies can cast a shadow over the dynamics of legislative policymaking. For analysis of this possible role of initiatives, see Elisabeth R. Gerber, *Legislative Response to the Threat of Popular Initiatives*, 40 Am. J. Pol. Sci. 99 (1996). One measure of the role of direct democracy as a form of institutional reform, even over the objection of established political power, can be found in the fact that 23% of initiatives and referenda dealing with "government and political process issues" pass, a far higher rate than for other initiatives and referenda. Elizabeth R. Gerber, The Populist Paradox: Interest Group Influence and the Promise of Direct Legislation 118 (1999).

In thinking about the relationship between direct democracy and representative institutions, keep in mind that direct democracy has been structured in a number of different ways in different states. Some states permit only the initiative; some states permit only the referendum; some states permit both. In Michigan, initiatives must first be submitted to the legislature and are voted on only if the legislature fails to enact the measure within a specified time. Florida and North Carolina permit initiatives only for constitutional amendments, while other states permit the initiative also for statutes. Some states prohibit the initiative or referendum for certain subjects, such as appropriations, special legislation, or laws for health and safety. Other states prohibit direct lawmaking on more precisely defined subjects: in Massachusetts, for issues involving religion; in Montana, for issues involving support for state government; in Colorado, for matters dealing with property classifications. For a general overview of state practices, see ABA Task Force on Initiatives and Referenda, *The Challenge of Direct Democracy in a Republic: Report and Recommendations of the Task Force on Initiatives and Referenda* 8–9 (1992).

The effect of the shadow of direct lawmaking processes on legislatures presumably depends on the precise form direct lawmaking is required to take in different states. Should any of the constitutional issues surrounding direct lawmaking depend on which particular form is used? For example, is there less of a "republican form of government" concern with direct lawmaking that involves a specific role for the legislature? Some states permit initiative advocates to choose whether to seek a constitutional amendment or a statutory initiative on the same subject; constitutional amendments can only be changed through subsequent popular vote, but statutory initiatives can be amended either through popular vote or legislative action. Magleby, *supra,* at 13. For an argument that in such states, voters are unlikely to perceive the consequences of the difference, and that therefore courts should adopt strong presumptions that difficult to characterize initiatives will be treated as statutory rather than constitutional, see Elizabeth Garrett, *Who Directs Direct Democracy?*, 4 U. Chi. L. Sch. Roundtable 17 (1997).

5. *Hybrid democracy.* In thinking about the relationship between direct democracy and representative government, we might distinguish between structural and strategic influences. In the former category, consider the wide variety of limitations on representative government that have been enacted through the initiative process. Perhaps the most striking is the imposition of term limits. Term limits are likely to affect legislative behavior both by changing legislators' time horizons and by producing less-experienced legislative bodies. In addition, many initiatives require or forbid certain forms of government spending, thereby limiting elected officials' flexibility. In this respect, consider states which have imposed balanced-budget requirements, restrictions on raising taxes, and the like.

In a recent article discussing aftermath of California's 2003 gubernatorial recall, Professor Garrett describes how direct democracy affects the strategic calculus of elected officials:

Scholars have increasingly studied the effect of the existence of the initiative process on the laws considered and enacted by the legislature.... [L]awmakers in states permitting initiatives enact a different sort of legislation than do legislators in states without initiatives.... [U]nder certain conditions, legislation on issues that are likely to be the subject of popular vote will be closer to the preferences of the median voter. When strategic lawmakers understand that their decisions can be second-guessed by voters if a ballot question is qualified, they take that reality into consideration when determining what laws to pass and the content of those laws. Lawmaking does not occur in a vacuum; it is affected by all parts of the political environment....

Interaction between direct and representative democracy will continue to be seen during Schwarzenegger's term. Schwarzenegger is a Republican facing a Democratic legislature and working on an agenda that runs counter to some legislators' priorities. Schwarzenegger has demonstrated that he is willing to resort to the initiative and referendum to enact his agenda over the next few years. In his first State of the State address, he announced that he would take workers compensation reform to the voters in the fall of 2004 if the legislature did not quickly send him an acceptable bill, which they soon did. He has organized a political committee to raise money for campaigns for ballot measures he supports, as well as for lobbying activities in Sacramento and for coordinating grassroots movements to further his policy agenda.

[s]chwarzenegger will not actually govern entirely by initiative, a strategy that does not allow for coordinated policy or thoughtful legislating on complex issues.... Using ballot questions as a way to circumvent recalcitrant legislators occasionally may improve democratic institutions; using them as the main method of governing is inefficient, unwise, and impossible.

Schwarzenegger's rhetoric about resorting to initiatives if the legislature stands in the way of reform is a political strategy. He is making a credible threat that he will take issues to the people as part of his negotiations with an unfriendly legislature....

Elizabeth Garrett, *Democracy in the Wake of the California Recall*, 153 U. Pa. L. Rev. 239, 278–81 (2004).

6. *"Gerrymandering" Direct Democracy to Disfavor Selected Issues.* With the revitalization of direct democracy in recent years, political struggles over the structure of direct democracy itself have, not surprisingly, increased. A fascinating recent example comes from Utah, whose constitution incorporated the voter initiative in 1900. Since then, voter initiatives became law when a majority of voters endorsed them. In the late 1990s, though, environmental groups, frustrated that the Utah legislature would not enact laws more protective of wildlife, began a ballot-measure campaign to put such proposed laws up for adoption through voter initiative. In turn, Utah's legislature responded by amending the state constitution so that any voter initiative relating to wildlife management, which sought to "allow, limit, or prohibit" the taking of wildlife, or the methods and seasons of doing so, would become law only if two-thirds of voters (rather than a simple majority) approved. As required by the Utah constitution, this constitutional amendment passed the legislature with a two-thirds vote and was then approved with 56% support of the voters.

Environmental groups then sued, resting principally on the argument that the First Amendment to the U.S. Constitution prohibited Utah's constitution from singling out certain subjects of direct democracy for special, more burdensome voting rules. Such singling out, they argued, burdened core political speech by making it more difficult to pass legislation on particular subjects (Query: why did the plaintiffs believe a First Amendment argument was stronger than an equal protection argument in this case?). In an en banc decision, the Tenth Circuit rejected these First Amendment arguments. As that court put it, many structural features of the democratic process are designed to make some outcomes more likely than others. Provisions that do so on specific issues do not, therefore, implicate the First Amendment. While the First Amendment guarantees that all points of view must be heard, it does not guarantee that all must prevail. *Initiative and Referendum Institute v. Walker,* 450 F.3d 1082 (10th Cir. 2006), *cert. denied,* 127 S.Ct. 1254 (2007). Thus, structural features of direct democracy that require greater voter support for some issues than others do not implicate the First Amendment.

Compare this analysis with the Supreme Court's decision in *Jones,* the California blanket-primary case. One justification for changing the structural features of California's primary process was that doing so would encourage more centrist candidates and elected officials. But the Court held that this very purpose and justification itself violated the First Amendment. Is that result consistent with the Tenth Circuit's conclusion? If not, which court has the better of the analysis?

7. The arguments for and against the proposition that direct democracy is inconsistent with the Guarantee Clause are well summarized in *Symposium: Guaranteeing a Republican Form of Government,* 65 Colo. L. Rev. 709 (1994). For a review of litigation in state courts, see Hans A. Linde, *When Initiative Lawmaking Is Not "Republican Government": The Campaign Against Homosexuality,* 72 Or. L. Rev. 19 (1993).

8. To what extent does *Pacific States* resemble *Colegrove v. Green,* 328 U.S. 549 (1946), in which the Court declined to exercise jurisdiction over claims of quantitative malapportionment in Illinois' congressional delegation, or *Giles v. Harris,* 189 U.S. 475 (1903), in which the Court declined to exercise jurisdiction over challenges by black voters to provisions of Alabama's disenfranchising convention? Here, presumably, there would be no major enforcement problem. That is, if the Supreme Court had simply declared initiatives unconstitutional, it is hard to imagine that states would have continued to hold them, whereas administrability problems loomed large in both *Colegrove* and *Giles.* On the other hand, any line drawing short of outright approval or rejection of initiatives and referenda might be very tricky to police. Consider, for example, what would have happened if the Court had upheld initiatives or referenda regarding the enactment or amendment of a state *constitution*, while requiring lawmaking once a constitution is established to be done legislatively. Would this be easily circumvented by constitutionalizing everything? In this light, consider the vast difference between the U.S. Constitution, which is quite short and largely structural in nature, and many state constitutions which are lengthy documents that regulate large substantive areas.

NOTE ON MONEY AND THE INITIATIVE PROCESS

In *Meyer v. Grant*, 486 U.S. 414 (1988), discussed in Chapter 6, the Supreme Court unanimously held unconstitutional on First Amendment grounds state efforts to prohibit the use of paid signature gatherers in the initiative process. Colorado had defended this policy with the argument, among others, that it was necessary to protect "the integrity of the initiative process." The Court construed this defense in an exceedingly narrow way, taking it to mean that the state was concerned that paid signature gatherers were more likely to take fraudulent signatures. Having construed the state's justification this way, the Court held that there was no evidence to support this speculation, and that the state had other means of prohibiting such fraud. Ironically, in the aftermath of *Meyer*, Colorado has found that paid signature collection does result in greater fraud. Richard Collins & Dale Oesterle, *Structuring the Ballot Initiative: Procedures that Do and Don't Work*, 66 U. Colo. L. Rev. 47, 74 (1995); Magleby, *supra*, at 23. Recall also that the Court's decision that corporations have the same First Amendment rights as voters to engage in political campaigning arose in the initiative context, where a Massachusetts statute had made it criminal for corporations to make donations in initiative campaigns (except where the measure material affected corporate property, business, or assets). *First National Bank of Boston et. al. v. Bellotti*, 435 U.S. 765 (1978). Before *Bellotti*, eighteen states had limited corporate spending in initiative campaigns. See also *Citizens Against Rent Control v. Berkeley*, 454 U.S. 290 (1981) (striking down on First Amendment grounds a $250 cap on contributions individuals or corporations could make to committees formed to support or oppose ballot measures).

But was protecting the integrity of direct lawmaking at stake in *Meyer* in only the limited sense of protecting fraud that the Court viewed as relevant? *Meyer* and *First National Bank of Boston* also raise more general questions about the actual and appropriate role of money and interest groups in direct lawmaking processes. *Meyer* enabled the rise of an initiative industry of paid signature gatherers. For a critique of *Meyer*, see Daniel H. Lowenstein & Robert Stern, *The First Amendment and Paid Initiative Circulators: A Dissenting View and a Proposal*, 17 Hast. Const. L.Q. 175 (1989). States vary but typically require valid signatures from about 8 percent of those who voted for governor in the previous election to qualify an initiative for the ballot. In California, this means around one million signatures. Most signatures must be gathered under tight deadline pressures, typically 90–150 days. According to recent studies, professional agencies charge up to $1.50 per name in California, and as low as 30 cents per name in North Dakota. Between signature gathering and the other costs associated simply to qualify a measure for the ballot, the cost of doing so is estimated for California to be around one million dollars. *See, e.g.,* Dan Morain, *1996 Expected to be Boon Year for Initiatives,* L.A. Times, Dec. 9, 1995 at A1; Briffault, *supra,* at 1352.

The cost of the actual campaign on the merits is much greater and has reached stunning levels in recent years. Interest groups hire consultants to poll voters and gauge their response to different words and messages that might be used; they launch advertising and promotion efforts; they seek to line up coalitions to support the initiative and do door-to-door campaigning or use direct-mail and other fund-raising techniques. In 1988, the California ballot contained five different initiatives on automobile insurance; the insurance industry reportedly spent $88 million campaigning on these measures—more than either presidential candidate directly spent that year on his presidential campaign. Peter Schrag, *Take the Initiative, Please: Referendum Madness in California,* 28 Am. Prospect 61 (1996). The average spending for four statewide initiatives in Michigan in 1992 was more than $5 million. Proponents of an initiative in Washington to approve financing for a new football stadium reportedly spent more than $3 million on the campaign, breaking the state's previous record of $2.1 million spent on an unsuccessful initiative to legalize slot machines on tribal reservations. David Scoffer, *Stadium Foes Chide Allen for Not Voting: Campaign to Set Spending Record,* The Seattle Times, May 28, 1997, B1.

Many commentators now believe that the direct lawmaking process is at least as driven by "special interests" as ordinary lawmaking, and that the image of direct lawmaking as a means for citizen control over special-interest captured legislatures is largely an illusion. *See, e.g.,* Elizabeth Garrett, *Who Directs Direct Democracy?, supra;* Daniel H. Lowenstein, *Campaign Spending and Ballot Propositions: Recent Experience, Public Choice Theory and the First Amendment,* 29 UCLA L. Rev. 505 (1982); Randy M. Mastro *et al., Taking the Initiative: Corporate Control of the Referendum Process through Media Spending and What to do About It,* 32 Fed. Comm. L.J. 315 (1981); John S. Shockley, *Direct Democracy, Campaign Finance, and the Courts: Can Corruption, Undue Influence, and Declining Voter Confidence Be Found,* 39 U. Miami L. Rev. 377 (1985). But studies of the relationship between spending and success suggest that the link is complex rather than deterministic. One study found that campaign spending was the decisive factor in about one-eighth of the ballot measures held between 1976–1984. David D. Schmidt, Citizen Lawmakers: The Ballot Initiative Revolution 35 (1989). Several studies conclude that heavy spending is much more effective in defeating measures than in getting them enacted. *See, e.g.,* Lowenstein, *Campaign Spending,* at 511. Consider whether the considerations in favor and against limitations on expenditures in candidate contests discussed in Chapter 6 are the same or different in the context of direct lawmaking.

On the other hand, direct democracy may be the only mechanism for contesting what Professor Klarman has called "legislative entrenchment," that is, the tendency of legislators to act to retain their hold on their offices. *See* Michael Klarman, *Majoritarian Judicial Review: The Entrenchment Problem*, 85 Geo. L.J. 491 (1997). Campaign finance law is especially susceptible to legislative entrenchment, since incumbents are in a good position to pass laws that help them keep their seats and to block laws that would open the process up to more competitive challenges. *See id.* at 522–23, 536–37. Despite concerns about the role of money in the direct lawmaking process, though, many political reforms not capable of being legislatively adopted have succeeded through this alternative route. It is significant how many states have recently approved ballot initiatives dealing with campaign finance. The Maine Clean Election Act, discussed in Chapter 6, is a particularly sweeping example of citizen-initiated campaign finance reform. And voters in five other states also approved ballot measures in 1996 intended to reduce money's influence on the election process. We return at the end of this Chapter to another example of popular lawmaking that responds in part to an entrenchment problem: term limits.

B. DIRECT DEMOCRACY AND RIGHTS OF POLITICAL PARTICIPATION

In recent times, the initiative process has been used to take on some of the most controversial political issues of the day. In this section, we focus on areas where the courts' treatment of the products of direct democracy intersect with judicial regulation of the political process more generally.

Hunter v. Erickson

393 U.S. 385 (1969).

■ MR. JUSTICE WHITE delivered the opinion of the Court.

The question in this case is whether the City of Akron, Ohio, has denied a Negro citizen, Nellie Hunter, the equal protection of its laws by amending the city charter to prevent the city council from implementing any ordinance dealing with racial, religious, or ancestral discrimination in housing without the approval of the majority of the voters of Akron.

The Akron City Council in 1964 enacted a fair housing ordinance premised on a recognition of the social and economic losses to society which flow from substandard, ghetto housing and its tendency to breed discrimination and segregation contrary to the policy of the city to "assure equal opportunity to all persons to live in decent housing facilities regardless of race, color, religion, ancestry or national origin." Akron Ordinance No. 873–1964 § 1.

* * *

[Subsequently, the Akron City Charter was amended to provide that:]

Any ordinance enacted by the Council of The City of Akron which regulates the use, sale, advertisement, transfer, listing assignment, lease, sublease or financing of real property of any kind or of any interest therein on the basis of race, color, religion, national origin or ancestry must first be approved by a majority of the electors voting on the question at a regular or general election before said ordinance shall be effective. Any such ordinance in effect at the time of the adoption of this section shall cease to be effective until approved by the electors as provided herein.

Akron City Charter § 137. The proposal for the charter amendment had been placed on the ballot at a general election upon petition of more than 10% of Akron's voters, and the amendment had been duly passed by a majority.

* * *

Here ... there was an explicitly racial classification treating racial housing matters differently from other racial and housing matters.

By adding § 137 to its Charter the City of Akron ... not only suspended the operation of the existing ordinance forbidding housing discrimination, but also required the approval of the electors before any future ordinance could take effect. Section 137 thus drew a distinction between those groups who sought the law's protection against racial, religious, or ancestral discriminations in the sale and rental of real estate and those who sought to regulate real property transactions in the pursuit of other ends. Those who sought, or would benefit from, most ordinances regulating the real property market remained subject to the general rule: the ordinance would become effective 30 days after passage by the City Council, or immediately if passed as an emergency measure, and would be subject to referendum only if 10% of the electors so requested by filing a proper and timely petition. Passage by the Council sufficed unless the electors themselves invoked the general referendum provisions of the city charter. But for those who sought protection against racial bias, the approval of the City Council was not enough. A referendum was required by charter at a general or regular election, without any provision for use of the expedited special election ordinarily available. The Akron charter obviously made it substantially more difficult to secure enactment of ordinances subject to § 137.

* * *

Like the law requiring specification of candidates' race on the ballot, *Anderson v. Martin,* 375 U.S. 399 (1964), § 137 places special burdens on racial minorities within the governmental process. This is no more permissible than denying them the vote, on an equal basis with others. *Cf. Gomillion v. Lightfoot,* 364 U.S. 339 (1960); *Reynolds v. Sims,* 377 U.S. 533 (1964); *Avery v. Midland County,* 390 U.S. 474 (1968).... Because the core of the Fourteenth Amendment is the prevention of meaningful and unjustified official distinctions based on race, racial classifications are constitutionally suspect, and subject to the most rigid scrutiny. They bear a far heavier burden of justification than other classifications.

We are unimpressed with any of Akron's justifications for its discrimination. Characterizing it simply as a public decision to move slowly in the delicate area of race relations emphasizes the impact and burden of § 137, but does not justify it. The amendment was unnecessary either to implement a decision to go slowly, or to allow the people of Akron to participate in that decision. Likewise, insisting that a State may distribute legislative power as it desires and that the people may retain for themselves the power over certain subjects may generally be true, but these principles furnish no justification for a legislative structure which otherwise would violate the Fourteenth Amendment. Nor does the implementation of this change through popular referendum immunize it. *Lucas v. Colorado General Assembly,* 377 U.S. 713, 736–737 (1964). The sovereignty of the people is itself subject to those constitutional limitations which have been duly adopted and remain unrepealed. Even though Akron might have proceeded by majority vote at town meeting on all its municipal legislation, it has instead chosen a more complex system. Having done so, the State may no more disadvantage any particular group by making it more difficult to enact legislation in its behalf than it may dilute any person's vote or give any group a smaller representation than another of comparable size. *Cf. Reynolds v. Sims,* 377 U.S. 533 (1964); *Avery v. Midland County,* 390 U.S. 474 (1968).

We hold that § 137 discriminates against minorities, and constitutes a real, substantial, and invidious denial of the equal protection of the laws.

* * *

■ MR. JUSTICE BLACK, dissenting.

* * *

[One] argument used by the Court supposedly to support its holding is that we have in a number of our cases supported the right to vote without discrimination. And we have. But in no one of them have we held that a State is without power to repeal its own laws when convinced by experience that a law is not serving a useful purpose. Moreover, it is the Court's opinion here that casts aspersions upon the right of citizens to vote. I say that for this reason. Akron's repealing law here held unconstitutional, provides that an ordinance in the fair housing field in Akron "must first be approved by a majority of the electors voting on the question at a regular or general election before said ordinance shall be effective." The Court uses this granted right of the people to vote on this important legislation as a key argument for holding that the repealer denies equal protection to Negroes. Just consider that for a moment. In this Government, which we boast is "of the people, by the people, and for the people," conditioning the enactment of a law on a majority vote of the people condemns that law as unconstitutional in the eyes of the Court! There may have been other state laws held unconstitutional in the past on grounds that are equally as fallacious and undemocratic as those the Court relies on today, but if so I do not recall such cases at the moment. It is time, I think, to recall that the Equal Protection Clause does not empower this Court to decide what ordinances or laws a State may repeal. I would not strike down this repealing ordinance.

NOTES AND QUESTIONS

1. *Hunter* illustrates some of the difficulties the Court has had in applying "tiers of scrutiny" equal protection analysis to voting rights claims. As Justice Marshall argued in his dissent in *City of Mobile v. Bolden*, 446 U.S. 55 (1980), a case treated more extensively in Chapter 7, strict scrutiny can be triggered either by the use of a racial classification in providing a state benefit, or by state impairment of a fundamental right of citizenship. In *Hunter,* the Court characterized the ordinance as involving "an explicitly racial classification." But in exactly what way was that so? The Akron charter amendment did single out regulation "on the basis of race, color, religion, national origin or ancestry" for different treatment than regulation directed at, for example, discrimination on the basis of age. But a large proportion of contemporary antidiscrimination law does exactly the same thing. For example, Title VII of the 1964 Civil Rights Act forbids discrimination in employment on the basis of race, religion, national origin, and sex, but not on the basis of political affiliation. Is Title VII "an explicitly racial classification" that is presumptively invalid and must be justified under strict scrutiny? If not—and no court has ever subjected standard antidiscrimination ordinances to strict scrutiny—this suggests that it is not the mere mention of race that makes for a racial classification.

In *Hunter,* the Court focused on the effects of the Akron ordinance to explain why it was a racial classification. First, the Court suggested that the charter amendment would have disproportionate effects on racial minorities because "the reality [was] that the law's impact [fell] on the minority." But in contemporary equal protection doctrine, disparate impact alone would not be enough; *Washington v. Davis,* 426 U.S. 229 (1976), would undermine *Hunter* unless plaintiffs could also establish the charter amendment had been adopted for a discriminatory purpose.

Moreover, if *Hunter* is an ordinary disproportionate impact case, why did the Court find it either necessary or desirable to invoke its apportionment decisions as well? This suggests a different theory underlying *Hunter*: that the amendment was unconstitutional because it restructured the political process selectively for different groups. Those who supported certain kinds of regulations of housing could pursue change through the city council; those who sought regulation of housing to protect against racial, religious, or ancestral discriminations had to get the voters of Akron to approve. Perhaps this selective restructuring of the political process for certain groups was the constitutional defect. In a concurring opinion, Justices Harlan and Stewart offered what might be considered a third theory: that the *purpose* of the charter amendment was to make it more difficult for certain racial and religious minorities to achieve legislation in their interest. Is that an alternative rationale for finding that although the Akron charter amendment was facially neutral it had a discriminatory purpose? Is it persuasive?

2. *The problem of issues versus groups.* Any substantive constitutional provision restructures the political process with respect to the issue involved. When abortion is recognized as a constitutional right, those who desire to see abortion restricted or prohibited cannot appeal to the ordinary political process, but are left with only the recourse of seeking constitutional amendment to transform their preferences into policies. Whether the relevant provision explicitly says so or not, any substantive issue dealt with constitutionally is necessarily an issue that can no longer be addressed in the ordinary political process. Does that mean that the equal protection rights of pro-life voters have been violated when the Constitution is read to recognize that pregnant women have a constitutional right to make decisions regarding continuation of their pregnancies? But suppose pro-lifers were to succeed in having the Constitution amended to prohibit abortion. At that point, those who are pro-choice would not be able to resort to the ordinary legislative process; they would have to now seek a constitutional amendment if they were to transform their preferences into policies.

If *Hunter* rests on impermissible restructurings of the political process, the problem then is to distinguish between restructuring that makes it more difficult for one side to achieve success *on an issue* and restructuring that makes it more difficult for *a relevant group* to participate in the political process. Had the charter amendment in Akron permitted black voters to participate only in direct lawmaking but not lobby the city council, that would obviously have been an unconstitutional group-disadvantaging gerrymandering of the political process. But the charter amendment did not classify voters by race; on its face, it classified issues. For what reasons, then, is the amendment to be understood as regulating groups rather than issues? Is it because the Court perceives there to be a strong correlation between one's stance on fair-housing legislation and one's race? But what if a significant number of white voters supported such legislation in Akron, even if not enough to defeat the charter amendment?

Is it because the Court perceives the beneficiaries of such legislation to be overwhelming racial or religious minorities? In that event, would it make any difference to the constitutional issue—to whether the charter amendment was treated as "an explicitly racial classification"—if minorities in Akron were actually somewhat divided over whether fair-housing legislation was in their interest?

3. Is the Court's approach in *Hunter* reminiscent of its perspective in *Gomillion v. Lightfoot*, 364 U.S. 339 (1960), discussed *supra* in Chapter 2? Given the Court's statement that "we do not hold that mere repeal of an existing ordinance violates the Fourteenth Amendment," *Hunter*, 393 U.S. at 390 n.5, does the Court's measure of appropriate political power here depend on its acceptance of the pre-existing baseline of lawmaking authority as fair? *See generally* Pamela S. Karlan, *Just Politics?: Five Not So Easy Pieces of the 1995 Term*, 34 Houston L. Rev. 289 (1997) (discussing this aspect of *Hunter*). Why does the Court mistrust Akron's popular legislation process if the same result could be obtained by getting the city council simply to repeal the fair housing ordinance?

4. The permissibility of popular repeal of pre-existing state policy perceived to involve racial questions, and the restructuring of governmental processes for such questions, was revisited in a pair of Supreme Court decisions in 1982, in which the Court reached diametrically opposite results. In *Crawford v. Board of Education*, 458 U.S. 527 (1982), the Court upheld a voter initiated amendment to the California Constitution (Proposition I) that forbade state courts from ordering busing to achieve desegregation unless a federal court would do so to remedy a violation of the equal protection clause of the Fourteenth Amendment of the United States Constitution. But in *Washington v. Seattle School District No. 1*, 458 U.S. 457 (1982), the Court struck down a Washington State initiative (Initiative 350) that prohibited school boards from requiring any student to attend a school other than the one geographically nearest or next nearest to his home.

Justice Powell's opinion for the Court in *Crawford* rejected, as "destructive of a State's democratic processes and of its ability to experiment" the claim that "once a State chooses to do 'more' than the Fourteenth Amendment requires, it may never recede." *Id.* at 535. *Hunter*, in contrast to Proposition I, "involved more than a 'mere repeal' of the fair housing ordinance; persons seeking antidiscrimination housing laws—presumptively racial minorities—were singled out for mandatory referendums while no other group . . . [faced] that obstacle."

> [Proposition I neither] distorts the political process for racial reasons [nor] allocates governmental or judicial power on the basis of a discriminatory principle. The Constitution does not require things which are different in fact or opinion to be treated in law as though they were the same. . . . Surely it was constitutional for the . . . people of the State to determine that the standard of the Fourteenth Amend-

ment was more appropriate for California courts to apply in desegregation cases than the standard repealed by Proposition I.

By contrast, the *Seattle School District* Court relied heavily on *Hunter* in identifying "a simple but central principle":

> [State action that] explicitly us[es] the racial nature of a decision to determine the decisionmaking process ... places special burdens on racial minorities within the governmental process, thereby making it more difficult for certain racial and religious minorities [than for other members of the community] to achieve legislation that is in their interest. Such a structuring of the political process ... [is] no more permissible than [is] denying [members of a racial minority] the vote, on an equal basis with others ... [T]he practical effect of Initiative 350 is to work a reallocation of power of the kind condemned in *Hunter*. The initiative removes the authority to address a racial problem—and only a racial problem—from the existing decisionmaking body, in such a way as to burden minority interests. Those favoring the elimination of de facto school segregation now must seek relief from the state legislature, or from the statewide electorate. Yet authority over all other student assignment decisions, as well as over most other areas of educational policy, remains vested in the local school board.... As in *Hunter*, then, the community's political mechanisms are modified to place effective decisionmaking authority over a racial issue at a different level of government.

* * *

> [It is true that t]he State might have vested all decisionmaking authority in itself ... [But] until the passage of Initiative 350, Washington law in fact had established the local school board, rather than the State, as the entity charged with making decisions of the type at issue here ... Given this statutory structure, we have little difficulty concluding that Initiative 350 worked a major reordering of the State's educational decisionmaking process. Before adoption of the initiative, the power to determine what programs would most appropriately fill a school district's educational needs—including programs involving student assignment and desegregation—was firmly committed to the local board's discretion. The question whether to provide an integrated learning environment rather than a system of neighborhood schools surely involved a decision of that sort. After passage of Initiative 350, authority over all but one of those areas remained in the hands of the local board. By placing power over desegregative busing at the state level, then, Initiative 350 plainly differentiates between the treatment of problems involving racial matters and that afforded other problems in the same area. The District Court and the Court of Appeals similarly concluded that the initiative restructured the Washington political process, and we see no reason to challenge the determinations of courts familiar with local law.

* * *

[Initiative 350] burdens all future attempts to integrate Washington schools in districts throughout the State, by lodging decisionmaking authority over the question at a new and remote level of government. Indeed, the initiative, like the charter amendment at issue in *Hunter*, has its most pernicious effect on integration programs that do not arouse extraordinary controversy. In such situations the initiative makes the enactment of racially beneficial legislation difficult, though the particular program involved might not have inspired opposition had it been promulgated through the usual legislative processes used for comparable legislation. This imposes direct and undeniable burdens on minority interests.

5. Can *Crawford* and *Seattle School District* be reconciled simply by pointing to the standards for appellate review—in the California case, the lower courts declined to find a racially discriminatory purpose, while in the Washington case, they found such an impermissible intent? In *Crawford*, the Court pointed to Proposition I's statement of purpose:

[The] Legislature and people of the State of California find and declare that this amendment is necessary to serve compelling public interests, including those of making the most effective use of the limited financial resources now and prospectively available to support public education, maximizing the educational opportunities and protecting the health and safety of all public school pupils, enhancing the ability of parents to participate in the educational process, preserving harmony and tranquility in this state and its public schools, preventing the waste of scarce fuel, resources, and protecting the environment.

The Court found that voters might have been motivated by any of these purposes, as well as by a belief that mandatory busing was actually "aggravating rather than ameliorating the desegregation problem," and quoted with approval the California state court's characterization of "petitioners' claim of discriminatory intent on the part of millions of voters as but 'pure speculation.' "

In this case the Proposition was approved by an overwhelming majority of the electorate. It received support from members of all races. The purposes of the Proposition are stated in its text and are legitimate, nondiscriminatory objectives. In these circumstances, we will not dispute the judgment of the Court of Appeal or impugn the motives of the State's electorate.

In *Seattle School District*, however, the lower court had reached a different conclusion about the popular intent behind Initiative 350:

Neither the initiative's sponsors, nor the District Court, nor the Court of Appeals had any difficulty perceiving the racial nature of the issue settled by Initiative 350. Thus, the District Court found that the text of the initiative was carefully tailored to interfere only with desegregative busing. Proponents of the initiative candidly "represented that there would be no loss of school district flexibility other than in busing for desegregation purposes." ... The Washington electorate surely was aware of this, for it was "assured" by CiVIC officials [the people who had drafted the initiative] that "99% of the school districts in the state"—those that lacked mandatory integration programs—"would not be affected by the passage of 350." It is beyond reasonable dispute, then, that the initiative was enacted because of, not merely in spite of, its adverse effects upon busing for integration.

Is this account of *Seattle School District* persuasive? Unlike *Hunter*, the regulation under challenge does not expressly refer to racial or ethnic groups. Even if busing is characterized as an issue of a "racial nature," why is taking a position on that issue tantamount to being motivated by constitutionally discriminatory purposes? Is strict scrutiny necessary to ferret out the underlying racial motive in *Seattle School District*? If so, does the opinion suffer from circular reasoning in that exacting scrutiny is necessary to ferret out an unarticulated racial purpose, which in turn provides the evidence of a racial classification, which in turn justifies the initial application of strict scrutiny?

6. Does the difference between the cases turn on the fact that *Crawford* involved restrictions on the remedial powers of courts, while *Seattle School District* involved school boards, an entity more conventionally conceived as a policymaking body? Note that the *Seattle* Court, as in *Hunter*, invoked the Court's precedents from the apportionment area—precedents that do not apply to courts.

7. Opponents of direct democracy charge that the initiative and referendum processes overreward voting majorities and threaten minority rights. *See* Derrick A. Bell, Jr., *The Referendum: Democracy's Barrier to Racial Equality*, 54 Wash. L. Rev. 1 (1978). Think about the reasons why a majority might be able to enact discriminatory legislation through the popular processes even when such legislation would not be enacted by its representatives. To what extent do anonymity, the lack of any requirement for giving reasons, and the inability to logroll account for the difference in outcomes? On the other hand, an argument can be made that legislators rarely can devote themselves to systematic attention to any particular issue, no matter how pressing, and that deliberation among citizens on an issue of public moment may be of higher quality that legislative debate. *See* Lynn A. Baker, *Direct Democracy and Discrimination: A Public Choice Perspective*, 67 Chi.–Kent L. Rev. 707, 744–52 (1992).

Evans v. Romer

882 P.2d 1335 (Colo. 1994).

■ CHIEF JUSTICE ROVIRA delivered the opinion of the Court.

* * *

["Amendment 2"—a proposal to amend article II, section 30 of the Colorado constitution—was approved by the state's voters in November 1992 by a vote of 813,966 to 710,151 (53.4% to 46.6%).]

Amendment 2 provides:

> No Protected Status Based on Homosexual, Lesbian, or Bisexual Orientation. Neither the State of Colorado, through any of its branches or departments, nor any of its agencies, political subdivisions, municipalities or school districts, shall enact, adopt or enforce any statute, regulation, ordinance or policy whereby homosexual, lesbian or bisexual orientation, conduct, practices or relationships shall constitute or otherwise be the basis of or entitle any person or class of persons to have or claim any minority status, quota preferences, protected status or claim of discrimination. This Section of the Constitution shall be in all respects self-executing.

* * *

[In our decision reviewing the trial court's entry of a preliminary injunction,] we held that the Equal Protection Clause of the United States Constitution protects the fundamental right to participate equally in the political process, and that any legislation or state constitutional amendment which infringes on this right by fencing out an independently identifiable class of persons must be subject to strict judicial scrutiny.

> The right to participate equally in the political process is clearly affected by Amendment 2, because it bars gay men, lesbians, and bisexuals from having an effective voice in governmental affairs insofar as those persons deem it beneficial to seek legislation that would protect them from discrimination based on their sexual orientation. Amendment 2 alters the political process so that a targeted class is prohibited from obtaining legislative, executive, and judicial protection or redress from discrimination absent the consent of a majority of the electorate through the adoption of a constitutional amendment.

> Rather than attempting to withdraw antidiscrimination issues as a whole from state and local control, Amendment 2 singles out one form of discrimination and removes its redress from consideration by the normal political processes.

* * *

A legislative enactment which infringes on a fundamental right or which burdens a suspect class is constitutionally permissible only if it is "necessary to promote a compelling state interest," *Dunn v. Blumstein,* [405 U.S. 330 (1972)], and does so in the least restrictive manner possible.... Defendants ... argue that Amendment 2 "promotes the compelling governmental interest of allowing the people themselves to establish public social and moral norms." In support of this proposition, defendants define two related norms which are promoted by Amendment 2: Amendment 2 preserves heterosexual families and heterosexual marriage and, more generally, it sends the societal message condemning gay men, lesbians, and bisexuals as immoral.... [But d]efendants have cited no authority to support the proposition that the promotion of public morality constitutes a compelling governmental interest, and we are aware of none. At the most, this interest is substantial. However, a substantial governmental interest is not sufficient to render constitutional a law which infringes on a fundamental right—the interest must be compelling.

Furthermore, even recognizing the legitimacy of promoting public morals as a governmental interest, it is clear to us that Amendment 2 is not necessary to preserve heterosexual families, marriage, or to express disapproval of gay men, lesbians, and bisexuals. First, we reject defendants' suggestion that laws prohibiting discrimination against gay men, lesbians, and bisexuals will undermine marriages and heterosexual families because married heterosexuals will "choose" to "become homosexual" if discrimination against homosexuals is prohibited. This assertion flies in the face of the empirical evidence presented at trial on marriage and divorce rates....

Defendants also argue that the "endorsement" of homosexuality undermines marriage and heterosexual families because antidiscrimination laws implicitly endorse that conduct which is deemed an improper basis for discrimination. We are of the opinion, however, that antidiscrimination laws make no assumptions about the morality of protected classes—they simply recognize that certain characteristics, be they moral or immoral—have no relevance in enumerated commercial contexts. For instance, it is difficult to imagine how a law which prohibits employers from discriminating against anyone engaged in off-duty, legal conduct such as smoking tobacco, see § 24–34–402.5, 10A C.R.S. (1994 Supp.), constitutes an endorsement of smoking.

In short, prohibitions on discrimination against gay men, lesbians, and bisexuals do not imply an endorsement of any particular sexual orientation or practices. To the contrary, prohibitions on discrimination imply at most that termination of employment, eviction or denial of rental opportunities, denial of insurance coverage, and other sanctions in commercial contexts based on sexual orientation are not appropriate ways of advancing even valid moral beliefs.

* * *

Defendants contend that Amendment 2 "prevents government from supporting the political objectives of a special interest group." ... [D]efendants offer no authority to support the rather remarkable proposition that the government has a compelling interest in seeing that the state does not support the political objectives of a "special interest group." The state exists for the very purpose of implementing the political objectives of the governed so long as that can be done consistently with the constitution. The fact that some political objectives are promoted by "special interest groups" is utterly inconsequential. Indeed, virtually any law could be regarded as a benefit to a "special interest group." If defendants' argument had any merit at all, the compelling state interest defined would justify striking down almost any legislative enactment imaginable. This is clearly not the law. No citation of authority is needed to make the point.

* * *

Defendants claim that Amendment 2 "serves to deter factionalism through ensuring that decisions regarding special protections for homosexuals and bisexuals are made at the highest level of government." More specifically, they argue that "Amendment 2 is intended, not to restrain the competition of ideas," but "seeks to ensure that the deeply divisive issue of homosexuality's place in our society does not serve to fragment Colorado's body politic." Amendment 2 accomplishes this end by eliminating "city-by-city and county-by-county battles over this issue."

We reject the argument that the interest in deterring factionalism, as defined by defendants, is compelling. Political debate, even if characterized as "factionalism," is not an evil which the state has a legitimate interest in deterring but rather, constitutes the foundation of democracy. "There is no significant state or public interest in curtailing debate or discussion of a ballot measure." *Citizens Against Rent Control v. City of Berkeley*, 454 U.S. 290, 299 (1981). We fail to see how the state, which is charged with serving the will of the people, can have any legitimate interest in preventing one side of a controversial debate from pressing its case before governmental bodies simply because it would prefer to avoid political controversy or "factionalism."

* * *

NOTES AND QUESTIONS

1. We focus on the opinion of the Colorado Supreme Court because it found Amendment 2 unconstitutional on the basis of the "fundamental right to participate in the political process" that had been the rationale for *Hunter*. The United States Supreme Court reached the same result as the Colorado Supreme Court, but on different grounds that made no mention of any right to participate in the political process. In evaluating the Supreme Court's handling of the issue, compare Justice Kennedy's focus on traditional equal protection review to Justice Scalia's efforts to rebut not only the Court majority but the Colorado Supreme Court's process-based striking down of Amendment 2.

Romer v. Evans

517 U.S. 620 (1996).

■ Justice Kennedy delivered the opinion of the Court.

One century ago, the first Justice Harlan admonished this Court that the Constitution "neither knows nor tolerates classes among citizens."

Plessy v. Ferguson, 163 U.S. 537, 559 (1896) (dissenting opinion). Unheeded then, those words now are understood to state a commitment to the law's neutrality where the rights of persons are at stake. The Equal Protection Clause enforces this principle and today requires us to hold invalid a provision of Colorado's Constitution.

* * *

II

[Amendment 2] imposes a special disability upon [homosexuals] alone. Homosexuals are forbidden the safeguards that others enjoy or may seek without constraint. They can obtain specific protection against discrimination only by enlisting the citizenry of Colorado to amend the State Constitution or perhaps, on the State's view, by trying to pass helpful laws of general applicability. This is so no matter how local or discrete the harm, no matter how public and widespread the injury. We find nothing special in the protections Amendment 2 withholds. These are protections taken for granted by most people either because they already have them or do not need them; these are protections against exclusion from an almost limitless number of transactions and endeavors that constitute ordinary civic life in a free society.

III

The Fourteenth Amendment's promise that no person shall be denied the equal protection of the laws must coexist with the practical necessity that most legislation classifies for one purpose or another, with resulting disadvantage to various groups or persons. . . .

Amendment 2 fails, indeed defies, even this conventional inquiry. First, the amendment has the peculiar property of imposing a broad and undifferentiated disability on a single named group, an exceptional and, as we shall explain, invalid form of legislation. Second, its sheer breadth is so discontinuous with the reasons offered for it that the amendment seems inexplicable by anything but animus toward the class it affects; it lacks a rational relationship to legitimate state interests.

Taking the first point, even in the ordinary equal protection case calling for the most deferential of standards, we insist on knowing the relation between the classification adopted and the object to be attained. The search for the link between classification and objective gives substance to the Equal Protection Clause; it provides guidance and discipline for the legislature, which is entitled to know what sorts of laws it can pass; and it marks the limits of our own authority. In the ordinary case, a law will be sustained if it can be said to advance a legitimate government interest, even if the law seems unwise or works to the disadvantage of a particular group, or if the rationale for it seems tenuous. . . . By requiring that the classification bear a rational relationship to an independent and legitimate legislative end, we ensure that classifications are not drawn for the purpose of disadvantaging the group burdened by the law.

.... A law declaring that in general it shall be more difficult for one group of citizens than for all others to seek aid from the government is itself a denial of equal protection of the laws in the most literal sense. "The guaranty of 'equal protection of the laws is a pledge of the protection of equal laws.'" *Skinner v. Oklahoma ex rel. Williamson,* 316 U.S. 535, 541 (1942) (quoting *Yick Wo v. Hopkins,* 118 U.S. 356, 369 (1886))....

A second and related point is that laws of the kind now before us raise the inevitable inference that the disadvantage imposed is born of animosity toward the class of persons affected. "[I]f the constitutional conception of 'equal protection of the laws' means anything, it must at the very least mean that a bare ... desire to harm a politically unpopular group cannot constitute a *legitimate* governmental interest." *Department of Agriculture v. Moreno,* 413 U.S. 528, 534 (1973). Even laws enacted for broad and ambitious purposes often can be explained by reference to legitimate public policies which justify the incidental disadvantages they impose on certain persons. Amendment 2, however, in making a general announcement that gays and lesbians shall not have any particular protections from the law, inflicts on them immediate, continuing, and real injuries that outrun and belie any legitimate justifications that may be claimed for it. We conclude that, in addition to the far-reaching deficiencies of Amendment 2 that we have noted, the principles it offends, in another sense, are conventional and venerable; a law must bear a rational relationship to a legitimate governmental purpose, and Amendment 2 does not.

.... We must conclude that Amendment 2 classifies homosexuals not to further a proper legislative end but to make them unequal to everyone else. This Colorado cannot do. A State cannot so deem a class of persons a stranger to its laws. Amendment 2 violates the Equal Protection Clause, and the judgment of the Supreme Court of Colorado is affirmed.

■ Justice Scalia, with whom The Chief Justice and Justice Thomas join, dissenting.

The Court has mistaken a Kulturkampf for a fit of spite. The constitutional amendment before us here is not the manifestation of a " 'bare ... desire to harm' " homosexuals, but is rather a modest attempt by seemingly tolerant Coloradans to preserve traditional sexual mores against the efforts of a politically powerful minority to revise those mores through use of the laws....

I

* * *

The central thesis of the Court's reasoning is that any group is denied equal protection when, to obtain advantage (or, presumably, to avoid disadvantage), it must have recourse to a more general and hence more difficult level of political decisionmaking than others. The world has never heard of such a principle, which is why the Court's opinion is so long on emotive utterance and so short on relevant legal citation. And it seems to me most unlikely that any multilevel democracy can function under such a principle. For *whenever* a disadvantage is imposed, or conferral of a benefit is prohibited, at one of the higher levels of democratic decisionmaking (*i.e.*, by the state legislature rather than local government, or by the people at large in the state constitution rather than the legislature), the affected group has (under this theory) been denied equal protection. To take the simplest of examples, consider a state law prohibiting the award of municipal contracts to relatives of mayors or city councilmen. Once such a law is passed, the group composed of such relatives must, in order to get the benefit of city contracts, persuade the state legislature-unlike all other citizens, who need only persuade the municipality. It is ridiculous to consider this a denial of equal protection, which is why the Court's theory is unheard of.

The Court might reply that the example I have given is *not* a denial of equal protection only because the same "rational basis" (avoidance of corruption) which renders constitutional the *substantive discrimination* against relatives (*i.e.*, the fact that they alone cannot obtain city contracts) also automatically suffices to sustain what might be called the *electoral-procedural discrimination* against them (*i.e.*, the fact that they must go to the state level to get this changed). This is of course a perfectly reasonable response, and would explain why "electoral-procedural discrimination" has not hitherto been heard of: A law that is valid in its substance is automatically valid in its level of enactment. But the Court cannot afford to make this argument, for as I shall discuss next, there is no doubt of a rational basis for the substance of the prohibition at issue here. The Court's entire novel theory rests upon the proposition that there is something *special*-something that cannot be justified by normal "rational basis" analysis-in making a disadvantaged group (or a nonpreferred group) resort to a higher decisionmaking level. That proposition finds no support in law or logic.

* * *

III

* * *

[Amendment 2] sought to counter both the geographic concentration and the disproportionate political power of homosexuals by (1) resolving the controversy at the statewide level, and (2) making the election a single-issue contest for both sides. It put directly, to all the citizens of the State, the question: Should homosexuality be given special protection? They answered no. The Court today asserts that this most democratic of procedures is unconstitutional. Lacking any cases to establish that facially absurd proposition, it simply asserts that it *must* be unconstitutional, because it has never happened before....

But there is a much closer analogy, one that involves precisely the effort by the majority of citizens to preserve its view of sexual morality statewide, against the efforts of a geographically concentrated and politically powerful minority to undermine it. The Constitutions of the States of Arizona, Idaho, New Mexico, Oklahoma, and Utah *to this day* contain provisions stating that polygamy is "forever prohibited." Polygamists, and those who have a polygamous "orientation," have been "singled out" by these provisions for much more severe treatment than merely denial of favored status; and that treatment can only be changed by achieving amendment of the state constitutions. The Court's disposition today suggests that these provisions are unconstitutional, and that polygamy must be permitted in these States on a state-legislated, or perhaps even local-option, basis—unless, of course, polygamists for some reason have fewer constitutional rights than homosexuals.

The United States Congress, by the way, *required* the inclusion of these antipolygamy provisions in the Constitutions of Arizona, New Mexico, Oklahoma, and Utah, as a condition of their admission to statehood. *See* Arizona Enabling Act, 36 Stat. 569; New Mexico Enabling Act, 36 Stat. 558; Oklahoma Enabling Act, 34 Stat. 269; Utah Enabling Act, 28 Stat. 108. (For Arizona, New Mexico, and Utah, moreover, the Enabling Acts required that the antipolygamy provisions be "irrevocable without the consent of the United States and the people of said State"—so that not only were "each of [the] parts" of these States not "open on impartial terms" to polygamists, but even the States as a whole were not; polygamists would have to persuade the whole country to their way of thinking.) Idaho adopted the constitutional provision on its own, but the 51st Congress, which admitted Idaho into the Union, found its Constitution to be "republican in form *and . . . in conformity with the Constitution of the United States.*" Act of Admission of Idaho, 26 Stat. 215 (emphasis added). Thus, this "singling out" of the sexual practices of a single group for statewide, democratic vote—so utterly alien to our constitutional system, the Court would have us believe—has not only happened, but has received the explicit approval of the United States Congress.

I cannot say that this Court has explicitly approved any of these state constitutional provisions; but it has approved a territorial statutory provision that went even further, depriving polygamists of the ability even to achieve a constitutional amendment, by depriving them of the power to vote. In *Davis v. Beason*, 133 U.S. 333 (1890), Justice Field wrote for a unanimous Court:

> In our judgment, § 501 of the Revised Statutes of Idaho Territory, which provides that "no person . . . who is a bigamist or polygamist or who teaches, advises, counsels, or encourages any person or persons to become bigamists or polygamists, or to commit any other crime defined

by law, or to enter into what is known as plural or celestial marriage, or who is a member of any order, organization or association which teaches, advises, counsels, or encourages its members or devotees or any other persons to commit the crime of bigamy or polygamy, or any other crime defined by law ... is permitted to vote at any election, or to hold any position or office of honor, trust, or profit within this Territory," *is not open to any constitutional or legal objection. Id.,* at 346–347 (emphasis added)....

IV

* * *

I would not myself indulge in such official praise for heterosexual monogamy, because I think it no business of the courts (as opposed to the political branches) to take sides in this culture war.

But the Court today has done so, not only by inventing a novel and extravagant constitutional doctrine to take the victory away from traditional forces, but even by verbally disparaging as bigotry adherence to traditional attitudes. To suggest, for example, that this constitutional amendment springs from nothing more than " 'a bare ... desire to harm a politically unpopular group,' " ... is nothing short of insulting....

When the Court takes sides in the culture wars, it tends to be with the knights rather than the villeins—and more specifically with the Templars, reflecting the views and values of the lawyer class from which the Court's Members are drawn. How that class feels about homosexuality will be evident to anyone who wishes to interview job applicants at virtually any of the Nation's law schools. The interviewer may refuse to offer a job because the applicant is a Republican; because he is an adulterer; because he went to the wrong prep school or belongs to the wrong country club; because he eats snails; because he is a womanizer; because she wears real-animal fur; or even because he hates the Chicago Cubs. But if the interviewer should wish not to be an associate or partner of an applicant because he disapproves of the applicant's homosexuality, *then* he will have violated the pledge which the Association of American Law Schools requires all its member schools to exact from job interviewers....

Today's opinion has no foundation in American constitutional law, and barely pretends to. The people of Colorado have adopted an entirely reasonable provision which does not even disfavor homosexuals in any substantive sense, but merely denies them preferential treatment. Amendment 2 is designed to prevent piecemeal deterioration of the sexual morality favored by a majority of Coloradans, and is not only an appropriate means to that legitimate end, but a means that Americans have employed before. Striking it down is an act, not of judicial judgment, but of political will. I dissent.

NOTES AND QUESTIONS

1.   *Romer* is one of the relatively few examples of statutes struck down under the equal protection clause for not being rationally related to any governmental objective. How successful is that effort? Can Amendment 2 be held unconstitutional without invoking the same concerns about restructuring the political process that the Court invoked in Hunter? Compare the following passages from *Hunter*, which the United States Supreme Court did not rely upon, and *Romer*:

ROMER v. EVANS 517 U.S. 620 (1996)	HUNTER v. ERICKSON 393 U.S. 385 (1968)
"Central both to the idea of the rule of law and to our own Constitution's guarantee of equal protection is the principle that government and each of its parts remain open on impartial terms to all who seek its assistance. . . . A law declaring that in general it shall be more difficult for one group of citizens than for all others to seek aid from the government is itself a denial of equal protection of the laws in the most literal sense."	"A state may no more disadvantage any particular group by making it more difficult to enact legislation in its behalf than it may dilute any person's vote or give any group a smaller representation than another of comparable size."
"[T]he protections Amendment 2 withholds . . . are protections taken for granted by most people either because they already have them or do not need them."	"The majority needs no protection against discrimination and if it did, a referendum might be bothersome but no more than that."

Given these parallels, why did the U.S. Supreme Court so assiduously avoid relying on *Hunter*? Why did the Court not see the case as raising issues about the structure of the political process? For one extensive explanation, see Pamela S. Karlan, *Just Politics?: Five Not So Easy Pieces of the 1995 Term, supra.* Would reliance on *Hunter* have suggested that classifications involving sexual orientation were suspect or quasi-suspect, thus warranting heightened judicial scrutiny?

2.   Justice Scalia's vigorous dissent in *Romer* quite clearly views the case as a political process case by which Amendment 2 was designed to correct a failure in Colorado's political process that had given gay people and their allies disproportionate political power:

> [Amendment 2] sought to counter both the geographic concentration and the disproportionate political power of homosexuals by (1) resolving the controversy at the statewide level, and (2) making the election a single-issue contest for both sides. It put directly, to all the citizens of the State, the question: Should homosexuality be given special protec-

tion? They answered no. The Court today asserts that this most democratic of procedures is unconstitutional.

How might the majority respond to Justice Scalia's attack?

3. It seems implausible that the Colorado Supreme Court would have reached the same decision in *Romer* if the state legislature had simply pre-empted all local anti-discrimination ordinances. Is it the fact that Amendment 2 is a *constitutional* provision or the fact that it was *popularly enacted* more salient? In this regard, consider the possible array of lawmaking. Laws might be enacted either popularly or through representatives; they might be either constitutional provisions or statutes.

4. *Romer* reflects a growing trend toward placing some of the most controversial issues of the day directly before the electorate. Oftentimes, as in *Romer*, the proposed referendum or initiative would remove from governmental consideration certain social programs that are thought to fare better legislatively. Courts have had a difficult time with these "hand-tying" referenda since the object appears to be to prevent the duly elected representatives of the majority of the population from enacting legislation. Beginning with *Lucas v. Colorado* and continuing through *Gordon v. Lance, Hunter, Crawford*, and *Seattle School District No. 1*, the case law has treated with perhaps understandable uncertainty initiatives and referenda that appear both to be intended to place barriers on minority demands on the political process *and* to operate by restricting only the operation of majoritarian processes. One of the most controversial of such recent initiatives was the California Civil Rights Initiative, presented to the voters as Proposition 209. This initiative sought to end all affirmative action programs in California public programs by decreeing that the state and its subdivisions may not grant preferential treatment to any individual or group on the basis of "race, sex, color, ethnicity, or national origin." A district court entered a preliminary injunction against the operation of Proposition 209 on the grounds, *inter alia,* that the statewide effect of the proposition would impose a substantial political burden on minorities and women seeking redress through the political process, a burden apparently condemned by *Hunter* and *Seattle School District No. 1. See Coalition for Economic Equity v. Wilson,* 946 F.Supp. 1480 (N.D. Cal. 1996). On appeal, the Ninth Circuit reversed and held:

> Plaintiffs allege that Proposition 209 places procedural burdens in the path of women and minorities, who together constitute a majority of the California electorate. Is it possible for a majority of voters impermissibly to stack the political deck against itself? The Supreme Court leaves us, quite frankly, a little perplexed as to the answer.
>
> The "political structure" equal protection cases, namely *Hunter* and *Seattle*, addressed the constitutionality of political obstructions that majorities had placed in the way of minorities to achieving protection against unequal treatment. *Hunter*, holding that the Akron amendment denied minorities equal protection of the laws, observed that

"[t]he majority needs no protection against discrimination and if it did, a referendum might be bothersome but no more than that." *Hunter*, 393 U.S. at 391. *Seattle* addressed a political structure held "to place special burdens on the ability of minority groups to achieve beneficial legislation." *Seattle*, 458 U.S. at 467. In *Romer v. Evans*, 116 S.Ct. 1620 (1996), the most recent "political structure" case, Colorado's Amendment 2 left homosexuals to "obtain specific protection against discrimination only by enlisting the citizenry of Colorado." *Id.* at 1627. It would seem to make little sense to apply "political structure" equal protection principles where the group alleged to face special political burdens itself constitutes a majority of the electorate....

When the electorate votes up or down on a referendum alleged to burden a majority of the voters, it is hard to conceive how members of the majority have been denied the vote.

Coalition for Economic Equity v. Wilson, 122 F.3d 692 (9th Cir. 1997). Should majoritarian alterations of political *procedures*, as in *Lucas v. Colorado*, be more suspect than majoritarian alterations of *substantive* rights? Can the procedures and the substantive implications of referenda such as Proposition 209 or Amendment 2 really be kept effectively separate? Are the outcomes in *Coalition of Economic Equity* and *Romer* reconcilable?

5. What explains the increasing recourse to referenda and initiatives to address highly controversial social issues? One theory is suggested by Justice Scalia's public choice critique of the majority in *Romer*. On this view, public referenda serve as healthy antidotes to the ability of highly motivated, self-interested minorities to leverage their political strength either in local governance or in the legislative process. For just the reasons suggested by Madison in Federalist No. 10, popular ballots may provide for greater appeals to inflamed passion than legislative bodies constrained by deliberative processes and subject to institutional checks and balances. At the same time, an argument can be made that such extra-legislative processes may serve as a check on the inherent limitations of elected legislative bodies:

> [An] important function of the substitutive plebescite is the "safety valve" it provides for particularly volatile issues that state legislators, concerned with reelection, might not want to handle. It is noteworthy that many landmark reforms that were highly controversial at the time of enactment began as initiatives in various states: women's suffrage, the abolition of poll taxes, prohibition and antiprohibition measures, the eight-hour work day, campaign finance regulations, and establishment of the nation's first presidential primary system, to name but a few.

Lynn A. Baker, *Direct Democracy and Discrimination: A Public Choice Perspective*, 67 Chi.–Kent L. Rev. 707, 754–55 (1992). Initiatives also serve other political functions than simply seeking to have enacted into law a particular policy in a particular state, and advocates have become increasingly aware of additional aims initiative campaigns can realize. Success in one state often becomes a catalyst for similar ballot propositions elsewhere. Candidates for political office now sponsor or endorse initiatives in an effort to bring more supporters to the polls. Political parties sometimes hope that voters can be more mobilized to turn out for certain highly visible initiative battles, and will then vote for candidates from the party supporting the initiative. For a survey of different motivations underlying the revival of initiatives, see Magleby, *supra*, at 28–29.

6. The exchange over Amendment 2 highlights an unresolved question in both constitutional law and political theory over the right level at which the "demos" has a right to express itself through a majoritarian process. Perhaps the most interesting confrontation with this issue came in *Reference re Secession of Quebec,* 2 S.C.R. 217 (1998), a dramatic presentation to the Supreme Court of Canada of whether Quebec had a right to hold a referendum, in Quebec alone, to determine whether to secede from Canada. One of the main questions presented was whether the decision to secede belonged to the people of Quebec specifically, or to all Canadians:

> By the terms of this Reference, we have been asked to consider whether it would be constitutional in such a circumstance for the National Assembly, legislature or government of Quebec to effect the secession of Quebec from Canada *unilaterally....* [W]hat is claimed by a right to secede "unilaterally" is the right to effectuate secession without prior negotiations with the other provinces and the federal government. At issue is not the legality of the first step but the legality of the final act of purported unilateral secession. The supposed juridical basis for such an act is said to be a clear expression of democratic will in a referendum in the province of Quebec. This claim requires us to examine the possible juridical impact, if any, of such a referendum on the functioning of our Constitution, and on the claimed legality of a unilateral act of secession.

> Although the Constitution does not itself address the use of a referendum procedure, and the results of a referendum have no direct role or legal effect in our constitutional scheme, a referendum undoubtedly may provide a democratic method of ascertaining the views of the electorate on important political questions on a particular occasion. The democratic principle identified above would demand that considerable weight be given to a clear expression by the people of Quebec of their will to secede from Canada, even though a referendum, in itself and without more, has no direct legal effect, and could not in itself bring about unilateral secession. Our political institutions are premised on the democratic principle, and so an expression of the democratic will of the people of a province carries weight, in that it would confer legitimacy on the efforts of the government of Quebec to initiate the

Constitution's amendment process in order to secede by constitutional means. . . .

The federalism principle, in conjunction with the democratic principle, dictates that the clear repudiation of the existing constitutional order and the clear expression of the desire to pursue secession by the population of a province would give rise to a reciprocal obligation on all parties to Confederation to negotiate constitutional changes to respond to that desire. The amendment of the Constitution begins with a political process undertaken pursuant to the Constitution itself. In Canada, the initiative for constitutional amendment is the responsibility of democratically elected representatives of the participants in Confederation. Those representatives may, of course, take their cue from a referendum, but in legal terms, constitution-making in Canada, as in many countries, is undertaken by the democratically elected representatives of the people. The corollary of a legitimate attempt by one participant in Confederation to seek an amendment to the Constitution is an obligation on all parties to come to the negotiating table. The clear repudiation by the people of Quebec of the existing constitutional order would confer legitimacy on demands for secession, and place an obligation on the other provinces and the federal government to acknowledge and respect that expression of democratic will by entering into negotiations and conducting them in accordance with the underlying constitutional principles already discussed.

What is the content of this obligation to negotiate? At this juncture, we confront the difficult inter-relationship between substantive obligations flowing from the Constitution and questions of judicial competence and restraint in supervising or enforcing those obligations. This is mirrored by the distinction between the legality and the legitimacy of actions taken under the Constitution. We propose to focus first on the substantive obligations flowing from this obligation to negotiate; once the nature of those obligations has been described, it is easier to assess the appropriate means of enforcement of those obligations, and to comment on the distinction between legality and legitimacy.

The conduct of the parties in such negotiations would be governed by the same constitutional principles which give rise to the duty to negotiate: federalism, democracy, constitutionalism and the rule of law, and the protection of minorities. Those principles lead us to reject two absolutist propositions. One of those propositions is that there would be a legal obligation on the other provinces and federal government to accede to the secession of a province, subject only to negotiation of the logistical details of secession. This proposition is attributed either to the supposed implications of the democratic principle of the Constitution, or to the international law principle of self-determination of peoples.

For both theoretical and practical reasons, we cannot accept this view. We hold that Quebec could not purport to invoke a right of self-determination such as to dictate the terms of a proposed secession to the other parties: that would not be a negotiation at all. As well, it would be naive to expect that the substantive goal of secession could readily be distinguished from the practical details of secession. The devil would be in the details. The democracy principle, as we have emphasized, cannot be invoked to trump the principles of federalism and rule of law, the rights of individuals and minorities, or the operation of democracy in the other provinces or in Canada as a whole. No negotiations could be effective if their ultimate outcome, secession, is cast as an absolute legal entitlement based upon an obligation to give effect to that act of secession in the Constitution. Such a foregone conclusion would actually undermine the obligation to negotiate and render it hollow.

However, we are equally unable to accept the reverse proposition, that a clear expression of self-determination by the people of Quebec would impose *no* obligations upon the other provinces or the federal government. The continued existence and operation of the Canadian constitutional order cannot remain indifferent to the clear expression of a clear majority of Quebecers that they no longer wish to remain in Canada. This would amount to the assertion that other constitutionally recognized principles necessarily trump the clearly expressed democratic will of the people of Quebec. Such a proposition fails to give sufficient weight to the underlying constitutional principles that must inform the amendment process, including the principles of democracy and federalism. The rights of other provinces and the federal government cannot deny the right of the government of Quebec to pursue secession, should a clear majority of the people of Quebec choose that goal, so long as in doing so, Quebec respects the rights of others. Negotiations would be necessary to address the interests of the federal government, of Quebec and the other provinces, and other participants, as well as the rights of all Canadians both within and outside Quebec.

How does the Canadian ruling on the inability of Quebec to determine unilaterally whether to secede contrast with the decision of the Colorado Supreme Court on the right of political subdivisions to be the source of expanded legal rights? How would Justice Scalia react to the Quebec decision?

NOTE ON IMPROVING THE PROCESSES OF DIRECT LAWMAKING

The language in Colorado Amendment 2 appears exceptionally ambiguous: it bans "any minority status, quota preferences, protected status, or claim of discrimination" on the basis of homosexual, lesbian, or bisexual orientation. Does this Amendment ban protection against discrimination of any sort against people based on their sexual orientation? Or does it only ban the granting of "special preferences" to people on the basis of sexual orientation? As is the case with many initiatives today, a lawsuit was filed seeking to enjoin Amendment 2 immediately after it passed. Thus, both the Colorado Supreme Court and the United States Supreme Court were asked to decide significant constitutional questions involving major social policy issues when the relevant legal provision is ambiguous and vague and has never been applied in any concrete case. Is there anything troubling about substantive constitutional decisions being made in such contexts?

The problem of vague and obscure initiative language might be thought worse than problems of vagueness in ordinary legislation. In the latter case, there are often authoritative sources of interpretive intent to which courts can look to give content to seemingly unclear language: committee report, debates on the floor of the legislature, and the like. But as noted above, the problems of looking outside the text of an initiative to other sources to give the language content is fraught with problems when the process involves several million voters and no sources of authoritative statements analogous to committee reports. In addition, when courts interpret unclear statutes, legislatures can more easily re-enter the process and respond than voters can when they enact constitutional amendments through direct lawmaking. There might also be greater incentives for professionals in the initiative process to deploy vague or even misleading language because voters might be more easily manipulated than professional legislators. Because the courts have not focused much attention on the differences between direct lawmaking and legislative enactments, they have not yet addressed whether they should develop doctrines specifically designed to deal with the process of direct lawmaking and the distinct interpretive problems it raises.

Several possible reforms have, however, been suggested. One already on the books in some states is the "single-subject rule." For example, in California during the 1940s, initiative sponsors began to load them up with an array of diverse subjects; one included provisions relating to pensions, taxes, the right to vote for Indians, gambling, oleomargarine, the health professions, reapportionment of the state Senate, fish and game, and surface mining. In response, the California Constitution was amended in 1948 to limit initiatives to a single subject. For an overview of how courts there have applied this provision, see Daniel H. Lowenstein, *California Initiatives and the Single–Subject Rule*, 30 UCLA L. Rev. 936 (1983). Similar regulations apply to direct lawmaking and have been the subject of judicial interpretation in Arizona, Florida, Massachusetts, and Montana. Single-subject requirements might be considered to serve either of at least two purposes. First, they encourage the use of direct lawmaking as a response to specific failings in the legislature. When direct lawmaking is limited to addressing a single subject, as opposed to a list of unrelated policies, it might be more likely to be invoked only when the legislature has been given an opportunity to address the particular policy. Second, single-subject rules discourage a logrolling sort of strategy in which different provisions are included to appeal to different interest groups.

More broadly, an ABA Task Force completed a detailed study of the initiative process that concluded with several recommendations. ABA Task-force on Initiatives and Referenda, *The Challenge of Direct Democracy in a Republic: Report and Recommendations of the Task Force on Initiatives and Referenda* 8–9 (1992). Some of these focused on the means by which measures qualified to appear on the ballot. The Task Force emphasized the capacity of pre-ballot review by courts or administrative agencies to address misleading or confusing language in ballot titles and propositions. Thus, the Task Force recommended that state officials be available to assist in drafting; that state officials should have the power to draft the title for the measure; and that courts should be permitted to determine before a measure appears on the ballot whether the submitted language was misleading or confusing. With respect to the process of voter decisions on the merits, the Task Force also had recommendations. Thus, to increase voter comprehension of the issues, the Task Force suggested that all states provide voters with a pamphlet at least 30 days before the vote that would include the ballot title of the provision; a summary of it; an explanation of the effects of a vote either way and would include advocacy statements from proponents and opponents. Several states already have such requirements. In addition, the Task Force recommended that states should sponsor and moderate hearings or debates on initiative proposals; no state currently requires such hearings.

Would some or all of these process oriented proposals enhance the deliberative character of direct lawmaking? Or should they be seen as efforts by legal elites to so legalize the process of popular lawmaking that such lawmaking would be drained of its role as a vehicle for popular challenges to professional politics?

In this light, consider political scientist James Morone's argument that the history of democratic reforms shows how they quickly come to reproduce the very problems they were designed to cure. Professor Morone points to direct democracy as one example of this phenomenon:

> The other contrivances of Progressive democracy bore similar consequences. The people were swamped rather than strengthened by the referendum. In Oregon, for example, voters were asked to judge forty-one amendments and sixty-one laws in twelve years. The ostensibly democratic device clearly favored educated voters who could fathom the complex questions being put to them. It took organization and money to organize referenda, launch an initiative, or circulate recall petitions.

James A. Morone, The Democratic Wish 124 (1990).

C. Popular Lawmaking and Problems of Entrenchment

The preceding cases suggested a rationale for more skeptical judicial review of certain products of popular lawmaking: those that target discrete and insular minorities who are particularly unlikely to be able to protect themselves in an unmediated political process. But is there ever an argument that courts should be especially deferential to popular lawmaking, that is, that courts should be especially reluctant to strike down a provision because it was enacted by the people directly? In this regard, consider the term limits controversy.

U.S. Term Limits, Inc. v. Thornton

514 U.S. 779 (1995).

■ Justice Stevens delivered the opinion of the Court.

* * *

Today's cases present a challenge to an amendment to the Arkansas State Constitution that prohibits the name of an otherwise-eligible candidate for Congress from appearing on the general election ballot if that candidate has already served three terms in the House of Representatives or two terms in the Senate. . . . Such a state-imposed restriction is contrary to the "fundamental principle of our representative democracy," embodied in the Constitution, that "the people should choose whom they please to govern them." *Powell v. McCormack*, 395 U.S. 486, 547 (1969). Allowing individual States to adopt their own qualifications for congressional service would be inconsistent with the Framers' vision of a uniform National Legislature representing the people of the United States. If the qualifications set forth in the text of the Constitution are to be changed, that text must be amended.

I

At the general election on November 3, 1992, the voters of Arkansas adopted Amendment 73 to their State Constitution. Proposed as a "Term Limitation Amendment," its preamble stated:

"The people of Arkansas find and declare that elected officials who remain in office too long become preoccupied with reelection and ignore their duties as representatives of the people. Entrenched incumbency has reduced voter participation and has led to an electoral system that is less free, less competitive, and less representative than the system established by the Founding Fathers. Therefore, the people of Arkansas, exercising their reserved powers, herein limit the terms of the elected officials."

The limitations in Amendment 73 apply to three categories of elected officials.... Section 3, the provision at issue in these cases, applies to the Arkansas Congressional Delegation. It provides:

"(a) Any person having been elected to three or more terms as a member of the United States House of Representatives from Arkansas shall not be certified as a candidate and shall not be eligible to have his/her name placed on the ballot for election to the United States House of Representatives from Arkansas.

"(b) Any person having been elected to two or more terms as a member of the United States Senate from Arkansas shall not be certified as a candidate and shall not be eligible to have his/her name placed on the ballot for election to the United States Senate from Arkansas."

* * *

II

[T]he constitutionality of Amendment 73 depends critically on the resolution of two distinct issues. The first is whether the Constitution forbids States from adding to or altering the qualifications specifically enumerated in the Constitution. The second is, if the Constitution does so forbid, whether the fact that Amendment 73 is formulated as a ballot access restriction rather than as an outright disqualification is of constitutional significance....

Twenty-six years ago, in *Powell v. McCormack,* 395 U.S. 486 (1969), we reviewed the history and text of the Qualifications Clauses in a case involving an attempted exclusion of a duly elected Member of Congress. The principal issue was whether the power granted to each House in Art. I, § 5, to judge the "Qualifications of its own Members" includes the power to impose qualifications other than those set forth in the text of the Constitution. In an opinion by Chief Justice Warren for eight Members of the Court, we held that it does not.... In *Powell,* ... [w]e noted that allowing Congress to impose additional qualifications would violate that "fundamental principle of our representative democracy ... 'that the people should choose whom they please to govern them.'"

Our opinion made clear that this broad principle incorporated at least two fundamental ideas.[2] First, we emphasized the egalitarian concept that the opportunity to be elected was open to all. We noted in particular Madison's statement in *The Federalist* that "'under these reasonable limitations [enumerated in the Constitution], the door of this part of the

---

2. The principle also incorporated the more practical concern that reposing the power to adopt qualifications in Congress would lead to a self-perpetuating body to the detriment of the new republic. *See* 2 Farrand 250 (Madison) ("'If the Legislature could regulate [the qualification of electors or elected], it can by degrees subvert the Constitution. A Republic may be converted into an aristocracy or oligarchy as well by limiting the number capable of being elected, as the number authorised to elect'") ...

federal government is open to merit of every description, whether native or adoptive, whether young or old, and without regard to poverty or wealth, or to any particular profession of religious faith.' "

Second, we recognized the critical postulate that sovereignty is vested in the people, and that sovereignty confers on the people the right to choose freely their representatives to the National Government. Thus, in *Powell*, we agreed with the sentiment expressed on behalf of Wilkes' admission to Parliament: " 'That the right of the electors to be represented by men of their own choice, was so essential for the preservation of all their other rights, that it ought to be considered as one of the most sacred parts of our constitution.' "

* * *

III

Our reaffirmation of *Powell* does not necessarily resolve the specific questions presented in these cases. For petitioners argue that whatever the constitutionality of additional qualifications for membership imposed by Congress, the historical and textual materials discussed in Powell do not support the conclusion that the Constitution prohibits additional qualifications imposed by States. In the absence of such a constitutional prohibition, petitioners argue, the Tenth Amendment and the principle of reserved powers require that States be allowed to add such qualifications.... Contrary to petitioners' assertions, the power to add qualifications is not part of the original powers of sovereignty that the Tenth Amendment reserved to the States. Petitioners' Tenth Amendment argument misconceives the nature of the right at issue because that Amendment could only "reserve" that which existed before. As Justice Story recognized, "the states can exercise no powers whatsoever, which exclusively spring out of the existence of the national government, which the constitution does not delegate to them.... No state can say, that it has reserved, what it never possessed."

* * *

With respect to setting qualifications for service in Congress, no such right existed before the Constitution was ratified. The contrary argument overlooks the revolutionary character of the government that the Framers conceived.... [T]he Framers envisioned a uniform national system, rejecting the notion that the Nation was a collection of States, and instead creating a direct link between the National Government and the people of the United States. In that National Government, representatives owe primary allegiance not to the people of a State, but to the people of the Nation.... Our conclusion that States lack the power to impose qualifications vindicates the same "fundamental principle of our representative democracy" that we recognized in Powell, namely that "the people should choose whom they please to govern them."

As we noted earlier, the *Powell* Court recognized that an egalitarian ideal—that election to the National Legislature should be open to all people of merit—provided a critical foundation for the Constitutional structure. This egalitarian theme echoes throughout the constitutional debates. In *The Federalist No. 57*, for example, Madison wrote:

> "Who are to be the objects of popular choice? Every citizen whose merit may recommend him to the esteem and confidence of his country. No qualification of wealth, of birth, of religious faith, or of civil profession is permitted to fetter the judgment or disappoint the inclination of the people."

.... Additional qualifications pose the same obstacle to open elections whatever their source. The egalitarian ideal, so valued by the Framers, is thus compromised to the same degree by additional qualifications imposed by States as by those imposed by Congress.

Similarly, we believe that state-imposed qualifications, as much as congressionally imposed qualifications, would undermine the second critical idea recognized in Powell: that an aspect of sovereignty is the right of the people to vote for whom they wish. Again, the source of the qualification is of little moment in assessing the qualification's restrictive impact.

Finally, state-imposed restrictions, unlike the congressionally imposed restrictions at issue in *Powell*, violate a third idea central to this basic principle: that the right to choose representatives belongs not to the States, but to the people. From the start, the Framers recognized that the "great and radical vice" of the Articles of Confederation was "the principle of LEGISLATION for STATES or GOVERNMENTS, in their CORPORATE or COLLECTIVE CAPACITIES, and as contradistinguished from the INDIVIDUALS of whom they consist." The Federalist No. 15 (Hamilton). Thus the Framers, in perhaps their most important contribution, conceived of a Federal Government directly responsible to the people, possessed of direct power over the people, and chosen directly, not by States, but by the people. The Framers implemented this ideal most clearly in the provision, extant from the beginning of the Republic, that calls for the Members of the House of Representatives to be "chosen every second Year by the People of the several States." Art. I, § 2, cl. 1. Following the adoption of the 17th Amendment in 1913, this ideal was extended to elections for the Senate. The Congress of the United States, therefore, is not a confederation of nations in which separate sovereigns are represented by appointed delegates, but is instead a body composed of representatives of the people.

* * *

Consistent with these views, the constitutional structure provides for a uniform salary to be paid from the national treasury, allows the States but a limited role in federal elections, and maintains strict checks on state interference with the federal election process. The Constitution also provides that the qualifications of the representatives of each State will be judged by the representatives of the entire Nation. The Constitution thus creates a uniform national body representing the interests of a single people.

Permitting individual States to formulate diverse qualifications for their representatives would result in a patchwork of state qualifications, undermining the uniformity and the national character that the Framers envisioned and sought to ensure. Such a patchwork would also sever the direct link that the Framers found so critical between the National Government and the people of the United States.[3]

* * *

V

The merits of term limits, or "rotation," have been the subject of debate since the formation of our Constitution, when the Framers unanimously rejected a proposal to add such limits to the Constitution. The cogent arguments on both sides of the question that were articulated during the process of ratification largely retain their force today. Over half the States have adopted measures that impose such limits on some offices either directly or indirectly, and the Nation as a whole, notably by constitutional amendment, has imposed a limit on the number of terms that the President may serve. Term limits, like any other qualification for office, unquestionably restrict the ability of voters to vote for whom they wish. On the other hand, such limits may provide for the infusion of fresh ideas and new perspectives, and may decrease the likelihood that representatives will lose touch with their constituents. It is not our province to resolve this longstanding debate.

We are, however, firmly convinced that allowing the several States to adopt term limits for congressional service would effect a fundamental change in the constitutional framework. Any such change must come not by legislation adopted either by Congress or by an individual State, but rather—as have other important changes in the electoral process—through the Amendment procedures set forth in Article V. The Framers decided that the qualifications for service in the Congress of the United States be fixed in the Constitution and be uniform throughout the Nation. That decision reflects the Framers' understanding that Members of Congress are chosen by separate constituencies, but that they become, when elected, servants of the people of the United States. They are not merely delegates appointed by separate, sovereign States; they occupy offices that are

---

3. There is little significance to the fact that Amendment 73 was adopted by a popular vote, rather than as an act of the state legislature. In fact, none of the petitioners argues that the constitutionality of a state law would depend on the method of its adoption. This is proper, because the voters of Arkansas, in adopting Amendment 73, were acting as citizens of the State of Arkansas, and not as citizens of the National Government. The people of the State of Arkansas have no more power than does the Arkansas Legislature to supplement the qualifications for service in Congress....

integral and essential components of a single National Government. In the absence of a properly passed constitutional amendment, allowing individual States to craft their own qualifications for Congress would thus erode the structure envisioned by the Framers, a structure that was designed, in the words of the Preamble to our Constitution, to form a "more perfect Union."

* * *

■ JUSTICE THOMAS, with whom THE CHIEF JUSTICE, JUSTICE O'CONNOR, and JUSTICE SCALIA join, dissenting.

It is ironic that the Court bases today's decision on the right of the people to "choose whom they please to govern them." Under our Constitution, there is only one State whose people have the right to "choose whom they please" to represent Arkansas in Congress. The Court holds, however, that neither the elected legislature of that State nor the people themselves (acting by ballot initiative) may prescribe any qualifications for those representatives. The majority therefore defends the right of the people of Arkansas to "choose whom they please to govern them" by invalidating a provision that won nearly 60% of the votes cast in a direct election and that carried every congressional district in the State.

I dissent. Nothing in the Constitution deprives the people of each State of the power to prescribe eligibility requirements for the candidates who seek to represent them in Congress. The Constitution is simply silent on this question. And where the Constitution is silent, it raises no bar to action by the States or the people.

* * *

[T]he majority infers from the Framers' "democratic principles" that the [Constitution] must have been generally understood to preclude the people of the States and their state legislatures from prescribing any additional qualifications for their representatives in Congress. But the majority's evidence on this point establishes only two more modest propositions: (1) the Framers did not want the Federal Constitution itself to impose a broad set of disqualifications for congressional office, and (2) the Framers did not want the Federal Congress to be able to supplement the few disqualifications that the Constitution does set forth. The logical conclusion is simply that the Framers did not want the people of the States and their state legislatures to be constrained by too many qualifications imposed at the national level. The evidence does not support the majority's more sweeping conclusion that the Framers intended to bar the people of the States and their state legislatures from adopting additional eligibility requirements to help narrow their own choices.

* * *

The fact that the Framers did not grant a qualification-setting power to Congress does not imply that they wanted to bar its exercise at the state level. One reason why the Framers decided not to let Congress prescribe the qualifications of its own members was that incumbents could have used this power to perpetuate themselves or their ilk in office. As Madison pointed out at the Philadelphia Convention, Members of Congress would have an obvious conflict of interest if they could determine who may run against them. But neither the people of the States nor the state legislatures would labor under the same conflict of interest when prescribing qualifications for Members of Congress, and so the Framers would have had to use a different calculus in determining whether to deprive them of this power.

As the majority argues, democratic principles also contributed to the Framers' decision to withhold the qualification-setting power from Congress. But the majority is wrong to suggest that the same principles must also have led the Framers to deny this power to the people of the States and the state legislatures. In particular, it simply is not true that "the source of the qualification is of little moment in assessing the qualification's restrictive impact." There is a world of difference between a self-imposed constraint and a constraint imposed from above.

Congressional power over qualifications would have enabled the representatives from some States, acting collectively in the National Legislature, to prevent the people of another State from electing their preferred candidates. The John Wilkes episode in 18th-century England illustrates the problems that might result. As the majority mentions, Wilkes's district repeatedly elected him to the House of Commons, only to have a majority of the representatives of other districts frustrate their will by voting to exclude him. Americans who remembered these events might well have wanted to prevent the National Legislature from fettering the choices of the people of any individual State (for the House of Representatives) or their state legislators (for the Senate).

Yet this is simply to say that qualifications should not be set at the national level for offices whose occupants are selected at the state level.... Indeed, the invocation of democratic principles to invalidate Amendment 73 seems particularly difficult in the present case, because Amendment 73 remains fully within the control of the people of Arkansas. If they wanted to repeal it (despite the 20–point margin by which they enacted it less than three years ago), they could do so by a simple majority vote.

* * *

Amendment 73 is not the act of a state legislature; it is the act of the people of Arkansas, adopted at a direct election and inserted into the state constitution. The majority never explains why giving effect to the people's decision would violate the "democratic principles" that undergird the Constitution. Instead, the majority's discussion of democratic principles is directed entirely to attacking eligibility requirements imposed on the people of a State by an entity other than themselves.

The majority protests that any distinction between the people of the States and the state legislatures is "untenable" and "astonishing." In the limited area of congressional elections, however, the Framers themselves drew this distinction: they specifically provided for Senators to be chosen by the state legislatures and for Representatives to be chosen by the people. In the context of congressional elections, the Framers obviously saw a meaningful difference between direct action by the people of each State and action by their state legislatures.

* * *

III

It is radical enough for the majority to hold that the Constitution implicitly precludes the people of the States from prescribing any eligibility requirements for the congressional candidates who seek their votes. This holding, after all, does not stop with negating the term limits that many States have seen fit to impose on their Senators and Representatives.[4] Today's decision also means that no State may disqualify congressional candidates whom a court has found to be mentally incompetent, see, e.g., Fla. Stat. §§ 97.041(2), 99.021(1)(a) (1991), who are currently in prison, see, e.g., Ill. Comp. Stat. Ann., ch. 10, §§ 5/3–5, 5/7–10, 5/10–5 (1993 and West Supp. 1995), or who have past vote-fraud convictions, see, e.g., Ga. Code Ann. §§ 21–2–2(25), 21–2–8 (1993 and Supp. 1994). Likewise, after today's decision, the people of each State must leave open the possibility that they will trust someone with their vote in Congress even though they do not trust him with a vote in the election for Congress. *See, e.g.*, R. I. Gen. Laws § 17–14–1.2 (1988) (restricting candidacy to people "qualified to vote").

In order to invalidate § 3 of Amendment 73, however, the majority must go farther.... Amendment 73 does not actually [prescribe "genuine, unadulterated, undiluted term limits."].... It says only that if they are to win reelection, they must do so by write-in votes.

* * *

---

4. Going into the November 1994 elections, eight States had adopted "pure" term limits of one sort or another. *See* Colo. Const., Art. XVIII, § 9a; Mich. Const., Art. II, § 10; Mo. Const., Art. III, § 45(a); Mont. Const., Art. IV, § 8; Ohio Const., Art. V, § 8; Ore. Const., Art. II, § 20; S.D. Const., Art. III, § 32; Utah Code Ann. § 20A–10–301. Eight other States had enacted "ballot access" provisions triggered by long-term incumbency or multiple prior terms in Congress. *See* Ariz. Const., Art. VII, § 18; Ark. Const., Amdt. 73, § 3; Calif. Elec. Code Ann. § 25003 (West Supp. 1994); Fla. Const.,Art. VI, § 4(b)(5), (6); N.D. Cent. Code § 16.1–01–13.1 (Supp. 1993); Okla. Const., Art. II, § 12A; Wash. Rev. Code §§ 29.68.015, 29.68.016 (1994); Wyo. Stat. § 22–5–104 (Supp. 1994). In the 1994 elections, six more States—Alaska, Idaho, Maine, Massachusetts, Nebraska, and Nevada—enacted term-limit or ballot-access measures, bringing to 22 the total number of States with such provisions. *See* Pear, *The 1994 Elections*, N. Y. Times, Nov. 10, 1994, p. B7, Col. 4. In 21 of these States, the measures have been enacted by direct vote of the people.

The majority suggests that this does not matter, because Amendment 73 itself says that it has the purpose of "evading the requirements of the Qualifications Clauses." ... [I]nquiries into legislative intent are even more difficult than usual when the legislative body whose unified intent must be determined consists of 825,162 Arkansas voters.

The majority nonetheless thinks it clear that the goal of § 3 is "to prevent the election of incumbents." In reaching this conclusion at the summary-judgment stage, however, the majority has given short shrift to petitioners' contrary claim. Petitioners do not deny that § 3 of Amendment 73 intentionally handicaps a class of candidates, in the sense that it decreases their pre-existing electoral chances. But petitioners do deny that § 3 is intended to (or will in fact) "prevent" the covered candidates from winning reelection, or "disqualify" them from further service. One of petitioners' central arguments is that congressionally conferred advantages have artificially inflated the pre-existing electoral chances of the covered candidates, and that Amendment 73 is merely designed to level the playing field on which challengers compete with them.

To understand this argument requires some background. Current federal law (enacted, of course, by congressional incumbents) confers numerous advantages on incumbents, and these advantages are widely thought to make it "significantly more difficult" for challengers to defeat them. For instance, federal law gives incumbents enormous advantages in building name recognition and good will in their home districts. *See, e.g.*, 39 U.S.C. § 3210 (permitting Members of Congress to send "franked" mail free of charge); 2 U.S.C. §§ 61–1, 72a, 332 (permitting Members to have sizable taxpayer-funded staffs); 2 U.S.C. § 123b (establishing the House Recording Studio and the Senate Recording and Photographic Studios). At the same time that incumbent Members of Congress enjoy these in-kind benefits, Congress imposes spending and contribution limits in congressional campaigns that "can prevent challengers from spending more ... to overcome their disadvantage in name recognition." App. to Brief for State of Washington as Amicus Curiae A–4 (statement of former 10–term Representative William E. Frenzel, referring to 2 U.S.C. § 441a). Many observers believe that the campaign-finance laws also give incumbents an "enormous fund-raising edge" over their challengers by giving a large financing role to entities with incentives to curry favor with incumbents. In addition, the internal rules of Congress put a substantial premium on seniority, with the result that each Member's already plentiful opportunities to distribute benefits to his constituents increase with the length of his tenure. In this manner, Congress effectively "fines" the electorate for voting against incumbents.

Cynics see no accident in any of this. As former Representative Frenzel puts it: "The practice ... is for incumbents to devise institutional structures and systems that favor incumbents." App. to Brief for State of Washington A–3. In fact, despite his service from 1971 to 1989 on the

House Administration Committee (which has jurisdiction over election laws), Representative Frenzel can identify no instance in which Congress "changed election laws in such a way as to lessen the chances of re-election for incumbents or to improve the election opportunities for challengers."

At the same time that incumbents enjoy the electoral advantages that they have conferred upon themselves, they also enjoy astonishingly high reelection rates. As Lloyd Cutler reported in 1989, "over the past thirty years a weighted average of ninety percent of all House and Senate incumbents of both parties who ran for reelection were reelected, even at times when their own party lost control of the Presidency itself." . . . [I]n the 100th Congress, as many Representatives died as were defeated at the polls. Even in the November 1994 elections, which are widely considered to have effected the most sweeping change in Congress in recent memory, 90 percent of the incumbents who sought reelection to the House were successful, and nearly half of the losers were completing only their first terms. Only 2 of the 26 Senate incumbents seeking reelection were defeated, and one of them had been elected for the first time in a special election only a few years earlier.

The voters of Arkansas evidently believe that incumbents would not enjoy such overwhelming success if electoral contests were truly fair—that is, if the government did not put its thumb on either side of the scale. The majority offers no reason to question the accuracy of this belief. Given this context, petitioners portray § 3 of Amendment 73 as an effort at the state level to offset the electoral advantages that congressional incumbents have conferred upon themselves at the federal level.

* * *

I do not mean to suggest that States have unbridled power to handicap particular classes of candidates, even when those candidates enjoy federally conferred advantages that may threaten to skew the electoral process. But laws that allegedly have the purpose and effect of handicapping a particular class of candidates traditionally are reviewed under the First and Fourteenth Amendments rather than the Qualifications Clauses. Term-limit measures have tended to survive such review without difficulty.

To analyze such laws under the Qualifications Clauses may open up whole new vistas for courts. If it is true that "the current congressional campaign finance system . . . has created an electoral system so stacked against challengers that in many elections voters have no real choices," are the Federal Election Campaign Act Amendments of 1974 unconstitutional under (of all things) the Qualifications Clauses? If it can be shown that nonminorities are at a significant disadvantage when they seek election in districts dominated by minority voters, would the intentional creation of "majority-minority districts" violate the Qualifications Clauses even if it were to survive scrutiny under the Fourteenth Amendment? More generally, if "district lines are rarely neutral phenomena" and if "districting inevitably has and is intended to have substantial political consequences," will plausible Qualifications Clause challenges greet virtually every redistricting decision?

* * *

NOTES AND QUESTIONS

1. Virtually every state whose constitution provides for direct democracy passed some form of term limit initiative during the 1990s. What conclusions can we draw from this phenomenon? Consider Professor Klarman's analysis:

> The term limits issue reveals legislative entrenchment at its worst. Contemporary public opinion polls reveal strong support for legislative term limits. Yet state legislatures generally have refused to do their constituents' bidding on this issue. Twenty-two of the twenty-four states that had enacted legislative term limits as of 1994 acted through popular initiative and referendum. By contrast, of those states whose constitutions lack any mechanism for amendment that permits circumvention of the legislature, only one—New Hampshire—has adopted legislative term limits. In other words, the correlation between adoption of term limits and the existence of state constitutional mechanisms for bypassing the legislature is nearly perfect; virtually every state possessing a popular initiative and referendum mechanism has adopted legislative term limits through that process, while every state but one lacking such a mechanism has failed to do so. This could be a coincidence, but I doubt it. More likely, this is legislative entrenchment par excellence.

Michael J. Klarman, *Majoritarian Judicial Review: The Entrenchment Problem*, 85 Geo. L.J. 491, 510 (1997).

2. Conceptions of democratic politics are central to the Court's decision in *Thornton*. The Court found many of the legally relevant sources to which it looked to be ambiguous, but then justified its result by appeal to what it called "the fundamental principle of our representative democracy . . . that the people should choose whom they please to govern them." Indeed, the Court characterized that principle as the "most importan[t] factor" in its decision, more important than "the text and structure of the Constitution" and "the relevant historical materials." *Thornton* thus turns in part on underlying assumptions about how the relationship between representative institutions and popular will should be conceived.

Are the Court's assumptions correct? For the argument that term limits foster democracy and enable more accurate expression of voters' preferences, see Einer Elhauge, *Are Term Limits Undemocratic*, 64 U. Chi. L. Rev. 83, 193 (1997). Elhauge argues that term limits "reduce collective action pressures to vote for a senior incumbent to gain a higher share of legislative clout. And term limits lower entry barriers that keep out challengers. Both effects would likely reduce the ideological divergence between electorates and their representatives." Do term limits undermine or actually further "the fundamental principle of our representative democracy?" For further analysis of the policy and political consequences of term limits, see Matthew Spitzer & Linda Cohen, *Term Limits*, 80 Geo. L.J. 477 (1992). For further discussion of the historical materials, see Polly J. Price, *Term Limits on Original Intent?: An Essay on Legal Debate and Historical Understanding*, 82 Va. L. Rev. 493 (1996).

3. *Thornton* might be thought to address only state efforts to regulate qualifications for service in the federal government, or for those offices the Constitution specifically creates and for which it defines qualifications. For this view, see Kathleen M. Sullivan, *Dueling Sovereignties: U.S. Term Limits, Inc. v. Thornton*, 109 Harv. L. Rev. 78 (1995). But a federal district court relied on *Thornton* to hold unconstitutional a voter initiative in California that imposed lifetime term limits on *state* legislators. *Bates v. Jones*, 958 F.Supp. 1446 (N.D. Cal. 1997). Proposition 140 limited state senators to two four-year terms and state lower-house members to three two-year terms. The district court held that the "fundamental principle of our representative government" the Supreme Court invoked in *Thornton*, as well as the fact that Proposition 140 purportedly burdened "fundamental rights to vote on an equal basis with others" made lifetime state term limits a violation of the Constitution. In reaching this conclusion, the district court relied on the reapportionment cases, see Chapter 3, for the principle that voters must be provided an equal basis for political participation. Is this a correct application of *Thornton*? Of the one-vote, one-person cases?

A divided en banc court of appeals reversed. *Bates v. Jones*, 131 F.3d 843 (9th Cir. 1997), *cert. denied*, 523 U.S. 1021 (1998). The en banc majority held that the burden imposed by Proposition 140 was quite small: incumbents "may enjoy the incumbency of a single office for a number of years, and ... they are not precluded from running for some other state office."

> Most important, the lifetime term limits do not constitute a discriminatory restriction. Proposition 140 makes no distinction on the basis of the content of protected expression, party affiliation, or inherently arbitrary factors such as race, religion, or gender. Nor does the Proposition "limit[] political participation by an identifiable political group whose members share a particular viewpoint, associational preference, or economic status."

In her concurrence, Judge Rymer would have gone further: quoting the Supreme Court's decision in *In re Duncan*, 139 U.S. 449 (1891), to hold that Proposition 140 reflected California citizens' exercise of "the right of the people to choose their own officers for governmental administration, and pass their own laws" protected by the guaranty clause of Art. I, § 4. Consider the interesting relationship this poses in light of *Pacific States*.

4. To what extent is the pressure for term limits the outgrowth either of the Court's campaign finance jurisprudence or its hands-off approach to claims of political gerrymandering? Are these three forms of regulation substitutes for one another? *See generally* Richard L. Hasen, *Clipping Coupons for Democracy: An Egalitarian/Public Choice Defense of Campaign Finance Vouchers*, 84 Cal. L. Rev. 1, 3 (1996) (linking dissatisfactions with incumbency to push for term limits); Kristen Silverberg, Note, *The Illegitimacy of the Incumbent Gerrymander*, 74 Tex. L. Rev. 913 (1996). Could demands for term limits be satisfied if redistricting power were removed from incumbent control and served to genuinely "reshuffle" the political deck every ten years? Would such active redistricting be a less intrusive mechanism for unsettling the incumbent edge identified in Justice Thomas's dissent? Both term limits and more aggressive redistricting policies are examples of "precommitment strategies." Although voters are free to vote incumbents out of office, or free to reject incumbents running from gerrymandered districts, there are credible reasons to believe that these policy preferences might be disregarded when a particular election is held. A precommitment strategy is one by which an actor chooses to restrict options *ex ante* for fear of temptation to yield at a later point of decision. The classic example from literature is the decision of Ulysses to have himself bound to the mast of his ship in order that he not give in to the temptations of the song of the Sirens. *See* Jon Elster, Ulysses and the Sirens: Studies in Rationality and Irrationality 37–47 (1979); *see also* Samuel Issacharoff, *Judging Politics: The Elusive Quest for Judicial Review of Political Fairness*, 71 Tex. L. Rev. 1643, 1664–69 (1993) (providing examples of contemporary uses of precommitment strategies); Michael Fitts, *Can Ignorance Be Bliss? Imperfect Information as a Positive Influence in Political Institutions*, 88 Mich. L. Rev. 917 (1990) (discussing congressional uses of such strategies).

5. *Thornton* relies heavily on *Powell v. McCormack*, both for the latter's historical analysis and its analysis of "democratic principles." Quoting *Powell*, Justice Stevens sums up the Court's holding by stating that state-imposed restrictions on legislative qualifications, such as term limits, are contrary to the "fundamental principle of our representative democracy . . . that the people should choose whom they please to govern them."

Is the context of *Powell* the same as that in *Thornton*? At stake in *Powell* was the desire of voters in Adam Clayton Powell's congressional district to return him to office despite well-known allegations that he had acted improperly and perhaps illegally in his previous term in the House. Thus, when the House of Representatives acted to deprive Powell of his seat, he was being excluded not because the voters in his district imposed a barrier to his continued service, but because a political body, the United States House, sought to exclude him *despite* the manifested desire of his constituents that he represent them.

In this respect, *Powell* is remarkably similar to the famous Wilkes episode, which was so central to the consciousness of the Framing generation regarding democratic elections. Wilkes was expelled from Parliament for taking political positions the majority in the House of Commons opposed; despite being re-elected by his constituents, Parliament again expelled him and barred him from re-election. When Wilkes finally prevailed, the episode came to stand in both England and the United States for the principle that the people had the right to elect members of their choice, free of political control.

By contrast, in *Thornton* no outside political institution imposed constraints on the voters of Arkansas. Instead, the people of Arkansas themselves voted to adopt a general policy judgment concerning whom they would let represent them. Justice Stevens asserts that *Powell* recognized "the critical postulate that sovereignty is vested in the people, and that sovereignty confers on the people the right to choose freely their representatives to the National Government." In what way is this "critical postulate" violated when the people of Arkansas exercise their sovereignty by deciding not to permit anyone to represent them more than a certain number of terms? Note that, as Justice Thomas's dissent points out, a substantial majority of voters in every congressional district in Arkansas voted to endorse term limits. Thus, one cannot even say in this context that a statewide majority was constraining the preferences of the voters in any particular district. On the other hand, consider the extent to which a current majority was tying the hands of future majorities by adding an element beyond periodic elections to the determination of voter choice.

Consider another possible difference between *Powell*, the Wilkes episode, and term limits. In the first two, political bodies were not applying general qualifications policies, established in advance of specific cases; they were making more particularistic, ad hoc decisions about specific cases. In *Thornton*, term limits were being established as a general policy. Are the dangers of political manipulation of purported "qualifications" standards much greater in the former context? Should this matter?

6. Is it realistic to expect a national constitutional amendment for congressional term limits? In this regard, consider the provisions in Article V for proposing a constitutional amendment. Article V sets out two paths: first, Congress can propose such amendments if two thirds of each House agrees; second, the state legislatures of two thirds of the states can call a constitutional convention, which can then propose amendments. In either event, the amendment then goes to the states for ratification. Recent experience suggests that even explicit congressional promises to follow the former path are unlikely to succeed. *See* Klarman, *supra*, at 511–12. As for the latter path, note that no such constitutional convention has ever been called. *See* Ronald D. Rotunda & Stephen J. Safranek, *An Essay on Term Limits and a Call for a Constitutional Convention*, 80 Marq. L. Rev. 227 (1996).

7. Is Justice Stevens' approach a contemporary manifestation of the principles announced in *Lucas v. Forty–Fourth General Assembly of Colorado*, 377 U.S. 713 (1964), regarding a majority's inability to bind itself with regard to political rights? Is Justice Thomas's approach reminiscent of Justice Frankfurter's perspective in *Colegrove v. Green*, 328 U.S. 549 (1946), that Illinois' congressional delegation represents Illinois as a polity rather than individual Illinois citizens? For an interesting discussion of these issues, see Henry P. Monaghan, *We the Peoples, Original Understanding, and Constitutional Amendment*, 96 Colum. L. Rev. 121 (1996).

8. For further discussion of *Thornton*, see, e.g., Elizabeth Garrett, *Term Limitations and the Myth of the Citizen–Legislator*, 81 Cornell L. Rev. 623 (1996); Ronald D. Rotunda, *The Aftermath of Thornton*, 13 Const. Commentary 201 (1996); Harry H. Wellington, *Term Limits: History, Democracy, and Constitutional Interpretation*, 40 N.Y.L. Sch. L. Rev. 833 (1996); Mark R. Killenbech & Steve Sheppard, *Another Such Victory? Term Limits, Section 2 of the Fourteenth Amendment, and the Right to Representation*, 45 Hastings L.J. 1121 (1994).

9. Starting in 1842, Congress required that States elect congressional representatives from single-member districts, rather than at-large from the state as a whole. Before then, some states elected their congressional delegations at-large; other states had already shifted to single-member districts. For the history of congressional districting, see Chapter 13. *Thornton* prohibits both Congress and state legislatures from imposing new "qualifications" for the House and Senate. Is the congressional imposition of districting for House elections arguably a violation of this holding? Before Congress imposed this requirement, were states that voluntarily adopted districted elections in violation of the Qualifications Clauses, as interpreted in *Thornton*? Which is the appropriate baseline, at-large or districted elections, for determining whether congressional elections comply with "the fundamental principle" that the people have a right to choose their representatives? Does a "fundamental principle" put in such sweeping terms make any sense at all in this context; that is, is there a general, universal principle of democracy that should be understood to require *either* districted elections or at-large elections—or should voters be able to impose either upon themselves without violating democracy's "fundamental principles"? If so, how do term limits differ?

10. Through the Twenty–Second Amendment, the people of the United States imposed term limits on their choice of potential Presidents. Does this constraint violate any "fundamental principle" of democracy? If not, is the situation any different when similar limits are imposed on Senators or Representatives?

11. Even if there are good reasons that neither Congress nor state legislatures should be granted the power to impose additional qualifications for representatives, do those reasons apply with the same force when "the people" impose these constraints through direct initiative?

The Court dismisses this possibility with the comment that "We are aware of no case that would even suggest that the validity of a state law under the Federal Constitution would depend at all on whether the state law was passed by the state legislature or by the people directly through amendment of the state constitution." This view that for constitutional analysis, all law is the same, regardless of its source, is as the Court says, a position the Court has generally taken. But does this only show that the Court continues to fail to think carefully about the difference between different lawmaking processes? In terms of either the general philosophy of democracy or constitutional analysis, should the source of additional representative qualifications, such as term limits, be irrelevant?

Consider the alternative view:

Madison made an often-quoted speech in which he . . . opposed . . . the Section [a proposal in the Constitutional Convention that would have given Congress power to add additional qualifications for election to the House or Senate] as vesting an improper and dangerous power in the legislature. The qualifications of the electors and elected were fundamental articles in a Republican Govt . . . and ought to be fixed by the Constitution. If the legislature could regulate those of either, it can by degrees subvert the Constitution. A Republic may be converted into an aristocracy or oligarchy as well as by limiting the number capable of being elected, as the number authorized to elect. In all cases where the representatives of the people will have a personal interest distinct from their Constituents, there was the same reason for being jealous of them. . . .

This passage is worth noting because it shows that Madison, like others at the convention, was opposed to additions of qualifications by the legislature, not to additions of qualifications in general. Madison was not the only delegate to hold this belief: Benjamin Franklin also "did not think the elected had any right in any case to narrow the privileges of the electors," through specifying additional qualifications for either electors or elected. Madison's objection in both cases, which he repeated when participating in Virginia's Constitutional Convention of 1829, was specifically directed against legislatures, for the protection of the electors. Madison felt that the legislature could not be trusted to prescribe qualifications, because such a "fundamental article of Republican gov[ernment]" was beyond the power of a mere agent to alter. . . .

[T]he national people, according to Madison, can delegate powers to the state peoples without delegating that power to the state governments. This distinction between state people and state government is the foundation on which this article's argument rests. The "states"—meaning the state peoples. . . . have powers that no state government possesses. The power of the state peoples can extend to "a fundamental article" of Republican government like electoral and legislators' qualifications. The power of the state governments cannot extend so far.

The text of Article I, Section 2 gives explicit support for such an exclusive delegation to the state peoples alone: the provision specifically refers to the "people of the several states" as choosing representatives. Assuming that the framers of the Constitution meant what they said, the duty of choosing representatives, and the correlative duty of excluding some from being representatives, is delegated exclusively to the people of the several states rather than to the state governments.

It would be a singular perversion of Madison's reasoning to interpret his argument against legislative control of qualifications as a justification for excluding the electors themselves from adding extra qualifications for the elected through state constitutions. Madison's argument was a defense of the elector's power, not a limitation of it. His argument was premised on the power of the electors, the state peoples, to control the elected.

Roderick M. Hills, Jr., *A Defense of State Constitutional Limits on Federal Congressional Terms*, 53 U. Pitt. L. Rev. 97, 120–22 (1991).

12. At the end of its opinion, the Court drew a distinction between permissible state regulation of the conditions a candidate must meet to get onto the ballot and the unconstitutional imposition of new qualifications for officeholding. This distinction might bear on the constitutionality of various preconditions that can be imposed for candidates seeking to get onto the ballot. These conditions are particularly important for candidates seeking to challenge the dominance of the two major political parties— independent candidates or candidates seeking to run under the banner of new parties. Ballot-access restrictions includes requirements that candidates collect a specific number of signatures on nominating petitions; that these signatures be distributed across the relevant jurisdiction in particular ways; that the candidates not have lost in a party primary for the seat in question. We saw in Chapter 5 that in general the Court has permitted a wide variety of restrictive ballot access measures. Could the decision in *Thornton* be used to attack the Court's prior precedents?

Take "sore loser" statutes as an example. In Texas, a candidate who runs for President in the primary of a party and loses cannot run in the general election as an independent candidate for President. Thus, if someone like Colin Powell were to run as a Republican in the Texas primaries and lost, he would not be able to get on the Texas ballot as an independent in the general election for President. Is this Texas statute a permissible regulation of access to the ballot, or an impermissible addition of new qualifications for the office of the Presidency (that the candidate not have lost a party primary) beyond those specified in the Qualifications Clause for that office, Art. II, § 5? What is the difference *Thornton* suggests between new qualifications and legitimate ballot-access restrictions?

13. How does the qualifications clause interact with state laws regarding the *removal* of candidates from the ballot? This question arose after Rep. Tom DeLay, who had won the March 2006 Republican primary election for a House seat from Texas, decided not to seek reelection. Having made that decision, he then registered to vote, obtained a driver's license, and filed a state resident income tax withholding statement in Virginia. DeLay and the Chairperson of the Republican Party of Texas contended that his change in residence made him ineligible to run for the House and thereby entitled the Party, under Texas law, to select a replacement candidate to run as the Republican nominee in the general election.

The Texas Democratic Party (TDP) brought suit, seeking declaratory and injunctive relief. The TDP asserted that the qualifications clause precluded Texas from declaring DeLay ineligible because the inhabitancy provision of the clause—that no person can serve as a representative "who shall not, when elected, be an Inhabitant of that State in which he shall be chosen"—meant that DeLay remained eligible to be elected from Texas regardless of his current residence as long as he was a resident of Texas on Election Day.

Although the TDP had brought its suit in state court, the Republican Party of Texas (RPT) removed the case to federal court, presumably because it believed it was more likely to prevail there. The move was unsuccessful. Both the district court and the court of appeals held that the state's action in removing DeLay violated the qualifications clause. *Texas Democratic Party v. Benkiser*, 2006 WL 1851295 (W.D. Tex.), *aff'd*, 459 F.3d 582 (5th Cir. 2006). The TDP had direct standing to challenge DeLay's removal from the ballot because "DeLay's replacement would cause it economic loss" in that the TDP "would need to raise and expend additional funds and resources to prepare a new and different campaign in a short time frame." Moreover,

> A second basis for the TDP's direct standing is harm to its election prospects. The TDP's witnesses testified below that if the RPT were permitted to replace DeLay with a more viable candidate, then its congressional candidate's chances of victory would be reduced. In addition, according to the TDP, "down-ballot" Democratic candidates, like county commissioners and judges, would suffer due to the change's effect on voter turnout and volunteer efforts. The RPT contends that these harms do not amount to an injury in fact. Voluminous persuasive authority shows otherwise. We find these cases persuasive because a political party's interest in a candidate's success is not merely an ideological interest. Political victory accedes power to the winning party, enabling it to better direct the machinery of government toward the party's interests.

On the merits, the court of appeals found "ample evidence" that the Framers had deliberately chosen the "when elected" language of the qualifications clause. The clause, it said, was designed to avoid unduly restricting electors' choices:

> Our conclusion conforms with the Texas principle that "[a]ny constitutional or statutory provision which restricts the right to hold office must be strictly construed against ineligibility." *Wentworth v. Meyer*, 839 S.W.2d 766, 767, 35 Tex. Sup. Ct. J. 1137 (Tex. 1992). In addition, it is supported by decisions in the Ninth and Tenth Circuits that struck down pre-election day residency requirements. *Schaefer v. Townsend*, 215 F.3d 1031, 1039 (9th Cir. 2000); *Campbell v. Davidson*, 233 F.3d 1229, 1235 (10th Cir. 2000). In *Schaefer*, relying on *U.S. Term Limits* and evidence of the Framers' intent, the Ninth Circuit held that a one-year pre-election residency requirement "violates the Constitution by handicapping the class of nonresident candidates who otherwise satisfy the Qualifications Clause." 215 F.3d at 1037. The Tenth Circuit, in *Campbell*, struck down a Colorado law that, *inter alia*, required candidates to be residents of the state for at least thirty days. 233 F.3d at 1231–35. Like the Ninth Circuit, it relied on *U.S. Term Limits* and evidence of the Framers' intent. *Id.* at 1233 (Citing The Federalist No. 52 (James Madison)).

Ultimately, the Republicans were forced to rally behind a write-in candidate and lost DeLay's seat in the Democratic sweep of 2006. For a definitive account of the relation between campaign finance shenanigans, redistricting, national politics, and the post–2001 Texas re-redistricting, see Steve Bickerstaff, Lines in the Sand: Congressional Redistricting in Texas and the Fall of Tom DeLay (2006).

Contrast the decision in *Benkiser* with an earlier decision by a Texas federal district court in *Jones v. Bush*, 122 F.Supp. 2d 713 (N.D. Tex.), *aff'd*, 244 F.3d 134 (5th Cir. 2000). That case concerned the interpretation of the Twelfth Amendment, which provides in pertinent part that when members of the Electoral College cast their ballots for President and Vice President at least one of the candidates for whom they vote "shall not be an inhabitant of the same state with themselves." In *Jones*, several Texas voters brought suit claiming that the state's electors in the 2000 presidential election could not vote for both George W. Bush for President and Dick Cheney for Vice President because both men were inhabitants of Texas. Although the district court held that the plaintiffs lacked standing to sue, because they failed either to show an individualized injury or to show that they should enjoy third-party standing to vindicate the rights of other candidates, it nonetheless went on to reject their claim on the merits. It found that Cheney had become an inhabitant of Wyoming in July of 2000, beginning sometime during the week in which Bush had chosen Cheney as his running mate, by registering to vote there, obtaining a Wyoming driver's license, selling his Texas residence, and notifying various individuals and entities that he had moved. (Ironically, the Republican defendants in *Jones* had argued that the operative date for determining inhabitance under the Twelfth Amendment was the day the Electoral College votes, the opposite of the position they took in *Texas Democratic Party*.)

The need for the Republican Party to declare DeLay ineligible came from the fact that under Texas law, the party could not otherwise replace him. For an example of a state court that construed its election laws liberally to enable a party to nominate a substitute candidate under analogous circumstances, see *New Jersey Democratic Party v. Sampson*, 814 A.2d 1028 (N.J. Sup. Ct. 2002). Democratic incumbent Senator Robert Torricelli, plagued by ethics charges and behind his Republican challenger in the polls, withdrew thirty-six days before the general election. A New Jersey statute set out procedures for replacing a withdrawing candidate up until 51 days before an election, but provided no procedures for replacing a candidate closer to election day. Arguably, that statute precluded a later substitution for reasons similar to those at issue in *Texas Democratic Party*—namely, fairness to candidates, avoiding voter confusion, efficiency in preparing and distributing ballots, and prevention of last-minute manipulation. The New Jersey Supreme Court nonetheless held that because election laws should be construed "to allow the greatest scope for public participation in the electoral process, to allow candidates to get on the ballot, to allow parties to put their candidates on the ballot, and most importantly, to allow the voters a choice on Election Day," the Democratic Party should be permitted to nominate a substitute and the state should be required to place the substitute's name, on the general election ballot.

Cook v. Gralike

531 U.S. 510 (2001).

■ JUSTICE STEVENS delivered the opinion of the Court.

In *U.S. Term Limits, Inc. v. Thornton*, 514 U.S. 779 (1995), we reviewed a challenge to an Arkansas law that prohibited the name of an otherwise eligible candidate for the United States Congress from appearing on the general election ballot if he or she had already served three terms in the House of Representatives or two terms in the Senate. We held that the ballot restriction was an indirect attempt to impose term limits on congressional incumbents that violated the Qualifications Clauses in Article I of the Constitution rather than a permissible exercise of the State's power to regulate the "Times, Places and Manner of holding Elections for Senators and Representatives" within the meaning of Article I, § 4, cl. 1.

In response to that decision, the voters of Missouri adopted in 1996 an amendment to Article VIII of their State Constitution designed to lead to the adoption of a specified "Congressional Term Limits Amendment" to the Federal Constitution. At issue in this case is the constitutionality of Article VIII.

I

Article VIII "instructs" each Member of Missouri's congressional delegation "to use all of his or her delegated powers to pass the Congressional Term Limits Amendment" set forth in § 16 of the Article. Mo. Const., Art. VIII, § 17(1). That proposed amendment would limit service in the United States Congress to three terms in the House of Representatives and two terms in the Senate.

Three provisions in Article VIII combine to advance its purpose. Section 17 prescribes that the statement "DISREGARDED VOTERs' INSTRUCTION ON TERM LIMITS" be printed on all primary and general ballots adjacent to the name of a Senator or Representative who fails to take any one of eight legislative acts in support of the proposed amendment. Section 18 provides that the statement "DECLINED TO PLEDGE TO SUPPORT TERM LIMITS" be printed on all primary and general election ballots next to the name of every nonincumbent congressional candidate who refuses to take a "Term Limit" pledge that commits the candidate, if elected, to performing the legislative acts enumerated in § 17. And § 19 directs the Missouri Secretary of State to determine and declare, pursuant to § § 17 and 18, whether either statement should be printed alongside the name of each candidate for Congress.

Respondent Don Gralike was a nonincumbent candidate for election in 1998 to the United States House of Representatives from Missouri's Third Congressional District. A month after Article VIII was amended, respondent brought suit in the United States District Court for the Western District of Missouri to enjoin petitioner, the Secretary of State of Missouri, from implementing the Article, which the complaint alleges violates several provisions of the Federal Constitution.

* * *

IV

The federal offices at stake "arise from the Constitution itself." *U.S. Term Limits, Inc.* v. *Thornton*, 514 U.S. at 805. Because any state authority to regulate election to those offices could not precede their very creation by the Constitution, such power "had to be delegated to, rather than reserved by, the States." *Id.* at 804. Cf. 1 Story § 627 ("It is no original prerogative of state power to appoint a representative, a senator, or president for the union"). Through the Elections Clause, the Constitution delegated to the States the power to regulate the "Times, Places and Manner of holding Elections for Senators and Representatives," subject to a grant of authority to Congress to "make or alter such Regulations." Art. I, § 4, cl. 1; *see United States* v. *Classic,* 313 U.S. 299 (1941). No other constitutional provision gives the States authority over congressional elections, and no such authority could be reserved under the Tenth Amendment. By process of elimination, the States may regulate the incidents of such elections, including balloting, only within the exclusive delegation of power under the Election Clause.

With respect to the Elections Clause, petitioner argues that Article VIII "merely regulates the manner in which elections are held by disclosing information about congressional candidates." As such, petitioner concludes, Article VIII is a valid exercise of Missouri's delegated power.

We disagree. To be sure, the Elections Clause grants to the States "broad power" to prescribe the procedural mechanisms for holding congressional elections. *Tashjian v. Republican Party of Conn.*, 479 U.S. 208, 217 (1986); see also *Smiley v. Holm*, 285 U.S. 355, 366 (1932) ("It cannot be doubted that these comprehensive words embrace authority to provide a complete code for congressional elections"). Nevertheless, Article VIII falls outside of that grant of authority. As we made clear in *U.S. Term Limits*, "the Framers understood the Elections Clause as a grant of authority to issue procedural regulations, and not as a source of power to dictate electoral outcomes, to favor or disfavor a class of candidates, or to evade important constitutional restraints." 514 U.S. at 833–834. Article VIII is not a procedural regulation. It does not regulate the time of elections; it does not regulate the place of elections; nor, we believe, does it regulate the manner of elections. As to the last point, Article VIII bears no relation to the "manner" of elections as we understand it, for in our commonsense view that term encompasses matters like "notices, registration, supervision of voting, protection of voters, prevention of fraud and corrupt practices, counting of votes, duties of inspectors and canvassers, and making and publication of election returns." *Smiley*, 285 U.S. at 366; *see also U.S. Term Limits, Inc. v. Thornton,* 514 U.S. at 833. In short, Article VIII is not among "the numerous requirements as to procedure and safeguards which experience shows are necessary in order to enforce the fundamental right involved," *Smiley,* 285 U.S. at 366, ensuring that elections are "fair and honest," and that "some sort of order, rather than chaos, is to accompany the democratic process," *Storer v. Brown*, 415 U.S. 724, 730 (1974).

Rather, Article VIII is plainly designed to favor candidates who are willing to support the particular form of a term limits amendment set forth in its text and to disfavor those who either oppose term limits entirely or would prefer a different proposal. *Cf. Anderson v. Celebrezze,* 460 U.S. 780, 788, n. 9 (1983) ("We have upheld generally applicable and evenhanded [ballot access] restrictions that protect the integrity and reliability of the electoral process itself"). As noted, the state provision does not just "instruct" each member of Missouri's congressional delegation to promote in certain ways the passage of the specified term limits amendment. It also attaches a concrete consequence to noncompliance—the printing of the statement "DISREGARDED VOTERs' INSTRUCTIONS ON TERM LIMITS" by the candidate's name on all primary and general election ballots. Likewise, a nonincumbent candidate who does not pledge to follow the instruction receives the ballot designation "DECLINED TO PLEDGE TO SUPPORT TERM LIMITS."

In describing the two labels, the courts below have employed terms such as "pejorative," "negative," "derogatory," " 'intentionally intimidating,' " "particularly harmful," "politically damaging," "a serious sanction," "a penalty," and "official denunciation." 191 F.3d at 918, 919, 922, 925; 996 F. Supp. at 908; *see id.* at 910, 916. The general counsel to petitioner's office, no less, has denominated the labels as "the Scarlet Letter." App. 34–35. We agree with the sense of these descriptions. They convey the substantial political risk the ballot labels impose on current and prospective congressional members who, for one reason or another, fail to comply with the conditions set forth in Article VIII for passing its term limits amendment. Although petitioner now claims that the labels "merely" inform Missouri voters about a candidate's compliance with Article VIII, she has acknowledged under oath that the ballot designations would handicap candidates for the United States Congress. *Id.* at 66. To us, that is exactly the intended effect of Article VIII.

Indeed, it seems clear that the adverse labels handicap candidates "at the most crucial stage in the election process—the instant before the vote is cast." *Anderson v. Martin,* 375 U.S. 399, 402 (1964). At the same time, "by directing the citizen's attention to the single consideration" of the candidates' fidelity to term limits, the labels imply that the issue "is an important—perhaps paramount—consideration in the citizen's choice, which may decisively influence the citizen to cast his ballot" against candidates branded as unfaithful. *Ibid.* While the precise damage the labels may exact on candidates is disputed between the parties, the labels surely place their targets at a political disadvantage to unmarked candidates for congressional office. Thus, far from regulating the procedural mechanisms of elections, Article VIII attempts to "dictate electoral outcomes." *U.S. Term Limits, Inc. v. Thornton,* 514 U.S. at 833–834. Such "regulation" of congressional elections simply is not authorized by the Elections Clause.

Accordingly, the judgment of the Court of Appeals is affirmed.

■ JUSTICE KENNEDY, concurring.

I join the opinion of the Court, holding § 15 *et seq.* of Article VIII of the Missouri Constitution violative of the Constitution of the United States. It seems appropriate, however, to add these brief observations with respect to Part III of the opinion. The Court does not say the States are disabled from requesting specific action from Congress or from expressing their concerns to it. As the Court holds, however, the mechanism the State seeks to employ here goes well beyond this prerogative.

A State is not permitted to interpose itself between the people and their National Government as it seeks to do here. Whether a State's concern is with the proposed enactment of a constitutional amendment or an ordinary federal statute it simply lacks the power to impose any conditions on the election of Senators and Representatives, save neutral provisions as to the time, place, and manner of elections pursuant to Article I, § 4. As the Court observed in *U.S. Term Limits, Inc. v. Thornton*, 514 U.S. 779 (1995), the Elections Clause is a "grant of authority to issue procedural regulations," and not "a source of power to dictate electoral outcomes, to favor or disfavor a class of candidates, or to evade important constitutional restraints." *Id.* at 833–834. The Elections Clause thus delegates but limited power over federal elections to the States. *Id.* at 804. The Court rules, as it must, that the amendments to Article VIII of the Missouri Constitution do not regulate the time or place of federal elections; rather, those provisions are an attempt to control the actions of the State's congressional delegation.

The dispositive principle in this case is fundamental to the Constitution, to the idea of federalism, and to the theory of representative government. The principle is that Senators and Representatives in the National Government are responsible to the people who elect them, not to the States in which they reside. The Constitution was ratified by Conventions in the several States, not by the States themselves, U.S. Const., Art. VII, a historical fact and a constitutional imperative which underscore the proposition that the Constitution was ordained and established by the people of the United States. U.S. Const., preamble. The idea of federalism is that a National Legislature enacts laws which bind the people as individuals, not as citizens of a State; and, it follows, freedom is most secure if the people themselves, not the States as intermediaries, hold their federal legislators to account for the conduct of their office. If state enactments were allowed to condition or control certain actions of federal legislators, accountability would be blurred, with the legislators having the excuse of saying that they did not act in the exercise of their best judgment but simply in conformance with a state mandate. As noted in the concurring opinion in *Thornton*, "nothing in the Constitution or The Federalist Papers ... supports the idea of state interference with the most basic relation between the National Government and its citizens, the selection of legislative representatives." 514 U.S. at 842. Yet that is just what Missouri seeks to do through its law—to wield the power granted to it by the Elections Clause to handicap those who seek federal office by affixing pejorative labels next to their names on the ballot if they do not pledge to support the State's preferred position on a certain issue. Neither the design of the Constitution nor sound principles of representative government are consistent with the right or power of a State to interfere with the direct line of accountability between the National Legislature and the people who elect it. For these reasons Article VIII is void.

This said, it must be noted that when the Constitution was enacted, respectful petitions to legislators were an accepted mode of urging legislative action. *See* W. Miller, Arguing About Slavery 105–107 (1995). This right is preserved to individuals (the people) in the First Amendment. Even if a State, as an entity, is not itself protected by the Petition Clause, there is no principle prohibiting a state legislature from following a parallel course and by a memorial resolution requesting the Congress of the United States to pay heed to certain state concerns. From the earliest days of our Republic to the present time, States have done so in the context of federal legislation. *See, e.g.,* 22 Annals of Cong. 153–154 (1811) (reprinting a resolution by the General Assembly of the Commonwealth of Pennsylvania requesting that the charter of the Bank of the United States not be renewed); 2000 Ala. Acts 66 (requesting targeted relief for Medicare cuts); 2000 Kan. Sess. Laws ch. 186 (urging Congress to allow state-inspected meat to be shipped in interstate commerce). Indeed, the situation was even more complex in the early days of our Nation, when Senators were appointed by state legislatures rather than directly elected. At that time, it appears that some state legislatures followed a practice of instructing the Senators whom they had appointed to pass legislation, while only requesting that the Representatives, who had been elected by the people, do so. *See* 22 Annals of Cong. 153–154 (1811). I do not believe that the situation should be any different with respect to a proposed constitutional amendment, and indeed history bears this out. *See, e.g.,* 13 Annals of Cong. 95–96 (1803) (reprinting a resolution from the State of Vermont and the Commonwealth of Massachusetts requesting that Congress propose to the legislatures of the States a constitutional amendment akin to the Twelfth Amendment). The fact that the Members of the First Congress decided not to codify a right to instruct legislative representatives does not, in my view, prove that they intended to prohibit nonbinding petitions or memorials by the State as an entity.

If there are to be cases in which a close question exists regarding whether the State has exceeded its constitutional authority in attempting to influence congressional action, this case is not one of them. In today's case the question is not close. Here the State attempts to intrude upon the relationship between the people and their congressional delegates by seeking to control or confine the discretion of those delegates, and the interference is not permissible.

With these observations, I concur in the Court's opinion.

■ JUSTICE THOMAS, concurring in Parts I and IV and concurring in the judgment.

I continue to believe that, because they possess "reserved" powers, "the people of the States need not point to any affirmative grant of power in the Constitution in order to prescribe qualifications for their representatives in Congress, or to authorize their elected state legislators to do so." *U.S. Term Limits, Inc. v. Thornton,* 514 U.S. 779, 846 (1995) (THOMAS, J., dissenting). For this reason, I disagree with the Court's premise, derived from *U.S. Term Limits,* that the States have no authority to regulate congressional elections except for the authority that the Constitution expressly delegates to them. Nonetheless, the parties conceded the validity of this premise and I therefore concur.

■ CHIEF JUSTICE REHNQUIST, with whom JUSTICE O'CONNOR joins, concurring in the judgment.

I would affirm the judgment of the Court of Appeals, but on the ground that Missouri's Article VIII violates the First Amendment to the United States Constitution. Specifically, I believe that Article VIII violates the First Amendment right of a political candidate, once lawfully on the ballot, to have his name appear unaccompanied by pejorative language required by the State. Our ballot access cases based on First Amendment grounds have rarely distinguished between the rights of candidates and the rights of voters. In *Bullock v. Carter,* 405 U.S. 134, 143 (1972), we said: "The rights of voters and the rights of candidates do not lend themselves to neat separation; laws that affect candidates always have at least some theoretical, correlative effect on voters." And in *Anderson v. Celebrezze,* 460 U.S. 780 (1983), we said that "voters can assert their preferences only through candidates or parties or both." Actions such as the present one challenging ballot provisions have in most instances been brought by the candidates themselves, and no one questions the standing of respondents Gralike and Harmon to raise a First Amendment challenge to such laws.*

Article I, § 4, provides that "the Times, Places and Manner of holding Elections for Senators and Representatives, shall be prescribed in each State by the Legislature thereof ..." Missouri justifies Article VIII as a "time, place, and manner" regulation of election. Restrictions of this kind are valid "provided that they are justified without reference to the content of the regulated speech, that they are narrowly tailored to serve a significant governmental interest, and that they leave open ample alternative channels for communication of the information." *Clark v. Community for Creative Non–Violence,* 468 U.S. 288 (1984). Missouri's Article VIII flunks two of these three requirements. Article VIII is not only not content neutral, but it actually discriminates on the basis of viewpoint because only those candidates who fail to conform to the State's position receive derogatory labels. The result is that the State injects itself into the election process at an absolutely critical point—the composition of the ballot, which is the last thing the voter sees before he makes his choice—and does so in a way that is not neutral as to issues or candidates. The candidates who are thus singled out have no means of replying to their designation which would be equally effective with the voter.

In *Anderson v. Martin,* 375 U.S. 399 (1964), we held a Louisiana statute requiring the designation of a candidate's race on the ballot violated

---

* The Court of Appeals upheld their First Amendment claim, but based its reasoning on the view that the ballot statements were "compelled speech" by the candidate, and therefore ran afoul of cases such as *Wooley v. Maynard,* 430 U.S. 705 (1977). I do not agree with the reasoning of the Court of Appeals. I do not believe a reasonable voter, viewing the ballot labeled as Article VIII requires, would think that the candidate in question chose to characterize himself as having "disregarded voters' instructions" or as "having declined to pledge" to support term limits.

the Equal Protection Clause. In describing the effect of such a designation, the Court said: "By directing the citizen's attention to the single consideration of race or color, the State indicates that a candidate's race or color is an important—perhaps paramount—consideration in the citizen's choice, which may decisively influence the citizen to cast his ballot along racial lines." *Id.* at 402. So, too, here the State has chosen one and only one issue to comment on the position of the candidates. During the campaign, they may debate tax reform, Social Security, national security, and a host of other issues; but when it comes to the ballot on which one or the other of them is chosen, the State is saying that the issue of term limits is paramount. Although uttered in a different context, what we said in *Police Department of Chicago v. Mosley,* 408 U.S. 92, 96 (1972) is equally applicable here: "[Government] may not select which issues are worth discussing or debating."

If other Missouri officials feel strongly about the need for term limits, they are free to urge rejection of candidates who do not share their view and refuse to "take the pledge." Such candidates are able to respond to that sort of speech with speech of their own. But the State itself may not skew the ballot listings in this way without violating the First Amendment.

NOTES AND QUESTIONS

1. The majority in *Cook* engaged in a rather formal, structural analysis to strike down the Missouri law because it found that the statute violated the congressional power to regulate the time, place and manner of elections under Article 1, § 4 of the Constitution. If this is the basis for the Court's decision, where does *Cook* leave the states in terms of their ability to regulate federal elections? For example, how does the state now have the authority to designate party identification next to a candidate's name on ballots for federal offices? Taking *Cook* a step further, what are the implications for other state regulations of national campaigns? Would a state now be barred from imposing stricter disclosure laws on the financing of congressional campaigns than are currently in place through the Federal Election Campaign Act?

2. Some have argued in favor of ballot notations as a useful political tool in the democratic struggle to uproot entrenched power structures. That view points to the passage of the Seventeenth Amendment (which established the direct election of United States senators) as a successful operation of ballot notations.

> Throughout the 1890s and early 1900s, the people of various states were devising more or less effective means of limiting state legislators' discretion in their choice of federal senators. What evolved into the most sophisticated approach, the so-called Oregon Plan (or Scheme), began simply enough: State legislative candidates in Oregon were given the opportunity to formally pledge to follow the will of the voters, as

expressed through an advisory election, when it came time to pick the next federal senator. Initially, the pledges were moral only. As other states began to follow Oregon's lead, however, more creative and coercive devices were employed. Nebraska, in fact, pioneered precisely the kind of scarlet letter system under attack today. Other states followed suit, crafting variations on the Oregon and Nebraska devices to suit their local needs. Ultimately, Oregon voters enacted a state constitutional amendment that, as a matter of state law, bound state legislators to select the United States Senate candidates who were most popular among state voters. By 1912, when the Senate approved the Seventeenth Amendment, nearly sixty percent of the senators were already selected by virtual direct election.

Of course, the Nebraska scarlet letters and the Oregon constitutional provision binding state legislators, as well as all the copycat measures from other states, were never litigated in the United States Supreme Court, or lower courts for that matter.... Thus, this history may be strong historical support for modern scarlet letter proponents.

Vikram David Amar, *The People Made Me Do It? Can the People of the States Instruct and Coerce Their State Legislatures in the Article V Constitutional Amendment Process?*, 41 Wm. & Mary L. Rev. 1037 (2000). For further argument that these direct democracy mechanisms can be used as a way of overcoming the entrenched status of incumbents, particularly in the era of incumbent-protecting gerrymanders, see Samuel Issacharoff, *Collateral Damage: The Endangered Center in American Politics*, 46 Wm. & Mary L. Rev. 415 (2004).

3. On the opposing side, there is perhaps a distinct argument against ballot notations apart from the formalistic structuralism put forth by the majority in *Cook*. Both the district and appeals courts in the case relied heavily on a First Amendment argument in invalidating the Missouri ballot notation law. They held that requiring a designation next to candidates who did not come out in support of congressional term limits "infringes on [candidates'] freedom of expression by attempting to compel a candidate to take a specific position in favor of term limits and by limiting the candidate's ability to fully express the candidate's views on term limits." *Gralike v. Cook*, 996 F.Supp. 901, 908 (W. D. Mo. 1998). The district court went on to explain:

The Amendment limits a candidate's speech in several ways.

First, the Amendment punishes candidates for speaking out against term limits by requiring the Secretary of State to place negative words next to their names on the ballot. Thus, the Amendment interferes directly with a candidate's right to speak freely on a matter of public concern in the same way that criminal sanction or fines would.

Second ... the Amendment compels candidates to speak on the term limits issue.... The Amendment uses the threat of being disadvantaged in the election to coerce candidates into taking a position on the term limits issue. A state law infringes on protected First Amendment rights whether it compels an individual to speak by threatening criminal prosecution or rather simply requires an individual to speak as a condition precedent to engaging in an otherwise lawful activity. Thus, the Amendment infringes on a candidate's right to refrain from speaking on an issue.

What is the force of the district court's argument given the wholesale absence of any First Amendment analysis in the Supreme Court's majority opinion?

4. Note that both *U.S. Term Limits v. Thornton* and *Cook v. Gralike* involved state laws that were passed by statewide referendum, a voting mechanism we saw earlier, in Chapter 4, in *California Democratic Party v. Jones*. Recall that in *Jones*, the Supreme Court struck down a California law authorizing the use of blanket primaries on the ground that such a process violated the political parties' First Amendment right to freedom of association—a right that the Court did *not* find candidates possessed in *Cook*. Taken together, what do these cases tell us about the viability of the statewide referendum? Does the fact that the First Amendment did not play a significant role in *Thornton* and *Gralike* make the referendum process in *Jones* seem stronger or weaker?

DOES DIRECT LAWMAKING CONTRIBUTE TO GOOD POLICYMAKING?

We have considered the constitutional questions initiatives raise, as well as certain procedural reforms that some suggest might improve the process, including a more aggressive judicial role. We have also raised questions about whether the same interest group processes that characterize ordinary lawmaking also characterize direct lawmaking in the age of the initiative industry. But even apart from these specific questions and the issues particular initiatives raise, what has been the general and cumulative effect of the recent revival of direct lawmaking? In the state in which the initiative has been invoked the most frequently, California, one estimate is that by 1990, only eight percent of the state budget was controlled by the legislature; voters controlled the remainder through the voter initiative process. DuVivier, *supra*, at 1189 n.23.

But the more important development is the way the initiative, which for a half century was regarded as an extraordinary expedient available in the rare cases of serious legislative failure or abuse, has not just been integrated into the regular governmental-political system, but has begun to replace it. Some students of California government think it's easier to amend the state constitution by initiative than to approve budgets or raise taxes, both of which require two-thirds votes in the legislature. Whether or not that's correct, the initiative has by general agreement become the principal driver of policy in California, some-times for the good, but more often not. The cumulative effect of the plebiscitary reforms of the past two decades has been to strip cities, school districts, and especially counties of their ability to generate their own funds; to divide authority and responsibility uncertainly between state and local government and among scores of agencies; and to make it increasingly unclear who is ultimately accountable for the results of all these changes.

Peter Schrag, *Take the Initiative, Please: Referendum Madness in California*, 28 Am. Prospect 61 (1996). Was Madison right?

For a less grave example, consider the following observation from Professor Collins:

[In the Canadian election campaign of 2000], Stockwell Day led the second strongest party and now heads the opposition in Parliament. Mr. Day likes the initiative process, and during the campaign, he advocated a national initiative right for Canada. His proposal received a lot of attention. On a televised political program, a journalist proposed the following initiative: "We demand that the government of Canada force Stockwell Day to change his first name to Doris." More than a million signatures were quickly obtained on a petition to do just that, more than enough to force a vote under Mr. Day's proposal.

This was an insightful way to highlight one of the problems with initiative lawmaking—its potential use against a targeted minority fueled by dislike rather than substantive policy.

Richard B. Collins, *How Democratic Are Initiatives?*, 72 U. Colo. L. Rev. 983, 985 (2001). If, as the Supreme Court held in *Burdick v. Takushi*, 504 U.S. 428 (1992), "the function of the election process is to winnow out and finally reject all but the chosen candidates, not to provide a means of giving vent to short-range political goals, pique, or personal quarrels" (internal citations and quotation marks omitted), is there something distinctive about initiatives that makes these motivations more appropriate there?

For a contrary view, consider the argument that direct democracy undercuts the power of special interests in legislative settings and results in policies more amenable to the median voters: "When citizens vote their preferences on a single dimension of choice, the median usually prevails. In general, direct democracy factors the issues, so the median voter should prevail. In contrast, members of legislatures bargain, compromise, and roll logs. In general, indirect democracy splices issues, which should result in bargains or cycles." Robert Cooter, The Strategic Constitution 232–33 (1999).

DIRECT DEMOCRACY IN THE AGE OF THE INTERNET

As voting over the internet becomes an imaginable possibility, questions of direct democracy have assumed an additional importance. So-called "cyberpopulists" see the Internet as increasing citizen participation, not merely by making it easier to vote but, more importantly, by increasing the array of voting opportunities. *See generally* Neil Netanel, *Cyberspace Self-Governance: A Skeptical View from Liberal Democratic Theory* 88 Cal. L. Rev. 395 (1999). The standard Internet-based pitch for direct democracy goes something like this. The Internet will enable citizens to become far better informed about public issues. First, they have access to more sources of information overall (and perhaps they can process that information in more useful ways). Second, the decreased (essentially trivial) cost of communication makes it possible to disseminate good ideas even if those ideas are not initially backed by large amount of money. Finally, voters can vote costlessly, without having to go to the polls at inconvenient times. According to the Direct Democracy Online Project, one website promoting the idea, "[r]epresentative democracy, such as we have in the United States" was "originally devised to get around the practical problem of transportation in a large democracy; specifically, that all of the people in a nation could not economically vote on a great number of issues, simply because they could not all be physically present to debate and cast a ballot in one location."

Is this view correct as either a descriptive or normative matter? In this light, consider the following argument:

Even on its own terms, of course, this account has problems. What does it mean to say that it's easier to become well informed? It's rather expensive, actually, not so much in financial terms—on this, the net partisans are right, since it costs very little to gain access to literally millions of information providers—but rather in terms of time and comprehension. Anyone who wants to increase the opportunities for direct democracy should be forced to read through the current official voter information pamphlets in California: more than a hundred pages of densely written statutory text for the two dozen or so propositions already on the ballot. Surely, the minimum that can be expected is knowing the text of a proposition on which one is voting, but even that task seems beyond the competence or interest of most of the eligible electorate. . . .

So what will voters do? Three responses seem particularly likely. The first is not voting on an issue at all unless one feels sufficiently well informed, a response that may leave the field to the less conscientious elements of the electorate or may result in disproportionate influence for single-issue voters who care about that issue. Second, one could vote essentially at random or according to some rule largely unrelated to the merits of specific measures. Consider, for example, the well-documented phenomenon that people tend to vote "no" when they don't understand a ballot proposition—a consideration that might be thought of as essentially conservative or risk-averse until one realizes that framers of ballot language are aware of this point and draft propositions to take advantage of this tendency. Third, voters may spend their scarce comprehension effort looking for shorthand clues that tell them how to vote—for example, looking to see which groups support or oppose a particular measure. This last response seems the most reasonable, ... but note that it reintroduces the idea of relying on mediating institutions. Those institutions may be different in the Internet world, but they're no less useful. Indeed, they may be more so precisely because the costs of sending communication are so reduced.... In deciding how to vote, then, citizens should rely on information generated over the Internet only to the extent that the information is reliable, and that may be a function of its being provided by "brand-name" intermediaries: the political parties, large media outlets, long-established interest groups, and the like.

Eben Moglen & Pamela S. Karlan, *The Soul of a New Political Machine: The Online, the Color Line, and Electronic Democracy*, 34 Loy. L.A.L. Rev. 1089 (2001). After surveying the relatively standard arguments about the differences between direct and representative democracy, particularly with respect to the interests of minority groups, the authors conclude:

Internet voting, then, may often produce outcomes that are quick, certain, and wrong. Ironically, representative government may be even *more* desirable in the age of the Internet precisely because it's sometimes slow and creaky. It may perform its traditional braking function with respect to a new source of what Madison described as factional passion: immediate access and expression, without an opportunity for reflection.

Does modern technology undermine or further reinforce the current validity of Madison's views?

CHAPTER 12

REMEDIAL POSSIBILITIES FOR DEFECTIVE ELECTIONS

It is now time to acknowledge that, yes, there is a large elephant sitting in the corner of the room. The Law of Democracy is not without its points of controversy. At various times, the issues surrounding minority voting rights, or malapportionment, or gerrymandering, or campaign finance have not only presented difficult legal issues, they have even commanded public attention and policy debates of considerable sweep. And yet, none of these issues has brought the legal issues so squarely to the forefront of national and even international debates as the Supreme Court's dramatic intervention into the disputed presidential election of 2000, culminating in *Bush v. Gore*, 531 U.S. 98 (2000).

In some sense, *Bush v. Gore* is the outgrowth of many of the issues left open in the discussion of the substantive law governing the political process. As the preceding chapters show, constitutional and statutory violations can take many forms. In *Giles v. Harris*, for example, discussed in Chapter 2, the plaintiffs claimed that local election officials acted contrary to their statutorily defined duties in refusing to register black voters. Or in *Baker v. Carr*, discussed in Chapter 3, the Tennessee Constitution froze into place an apportionment that resulted in vastly different numbers of citizens in different legislative districts. But finding that there has been some constitutional or statutory violation does not, of itself, necessarily determine what should be done.

Nothing, however, in the years since the reapportionment cases has so hauntingly evoked Justice Frankfurter's warning about the perils of courts entering the political thicket as the Supreme Court's resolution of the 2000 election in favor of George W. Bush. The events in Florida raised long-standing and unresolved issues about the role of courts in remedying election mishaps after the fact. Of necessity, any remedy entered after an election, particularly if it is an injunction involving the vote tabulation, risks bringing courts into the unwelcome role of "deciding" electoral outcomes. At the same time, problems of election administration, as opposed to structural problems such as at-large elections or campaign finance regulations, may become evident only after the election is held. We begin this Chapter with a discussion of the range of remedial options available after an election defect becomes apparent.

Bush v. Gore highlighted a separate set of concerns beyond simply the form remedies might take. Defects in the conduct of elections raise not only the question of *what* may courts do, but also of *which* courts are empowered to act. While the Constitution speaks in broad terms of how federal officials will be elected, the actual administration of elections gets pushed down the ladder to states and then to counties and finally to local election officials. This creates a paradox, as quite apparent in Florida in 2000, that claims of impropriety in the conduct of a national election turn heavily on interpretations of state law to determine whether the challenged activities were proper or not. At the same time, the dramatic expansion of federal law governing state election activity does not allow for a neat divide between state and federal interests. The second part of this Chapter will turn to *Bush v. Gore* itself in the context of the tension between federal and state authority over electoral crises.

Finally, we will turn in Part III to the reforms spawned by the reaction to the Florida events in 2000, as well as to the new landscape of litigation over election administration that has emerged in the wake of *Bush v. Gore*.

Part I: Remedial Options

A.   ORDERING A NEW ELECTION

Bell v. Southwell

376 F.2d 659 (5th Cir. 1967).

■ JOHN R. BROWN, Circuit Judge

A Georgia election was conducted under procedures involving racial discrimination which was gross, state-imposed, and forcibly state-compelled. Nevertheless the District Court by summary judgment held it could not set aside such election or order a new one even though in parallel cases the unconstitutional discriminatory practices were enjoined.... We reverse.

The underlying facts out of which the controversy grew may be quickly stated. The Justice of the Peace for the 789th Militia District in Americus, Sumter County, Georgia, died on June 23, 1965.... [A] special election to fill the vacancy ... was held on July 20, 1965. Mrs. Mary F. Bell, one of the plaintiffs, a Negro, was a candidate as was the winner, J. W. Southwell, a defendant, and four other white men. Following Georgia procedure, the results of the election were canvassed and the defendant J. W. Southwell declared the winner. Of the 2,781 votes cast, Negroes actually voting numbered 403 out of a total of 1,223 registered and qualified Negro voters in the District. On July 29, 1965, and after the expiration of the time for election contest under Georgia laws, this suit was filed. The District Judge by opinion denied relief for [two] reasons.... First, even assuming the admitted racial discrimination intimidated Negroes from voting, if all of the qualified Negroes not voting were added to the ... vote of Southwell's opponents, the result could not have been changed. Second ... Federal Courts simply do not have power to void a state election.

This suit, brought on their own behalf and on behalf of other Negroes and other voters in the District by Mrs. Bell, a qualified elector and candidate, and two other named Negro qualified voters, against the defendants Southwell and Horne, the Ordinary [that is, the local official responsible for running the election], invoked the Civil Rights Acts, 42 U.S.C.A. §§ 1971, 1981, 1983, 1985, 28 U.S.C.A. § 1343(3), (4). The main charge was that the election officials including the Ordinary had conducted the election in violation of the rights established under the Constitution and laws of the United States. The specific allegations fell in two categories, one relating to the election system and the second to specific acts of intimidation. In the first it was alleged that voting lists for the election were segregated on the basis of race. Likewise, voting booths were segregated according to race, with one booth for "white males", another for "white women", and a third for Negroes. During the course of the election, a number of qualified Negro women voters were denied the right to cast their ballots in the "white women's" booth. In the second group were charges that the officials barred representatives of candidate Bell from viewing the voting, another was physically struck by an election official and police allowed a large crowd of white males to gather near the polls thus intimidating Negroes from voting. In addition, the plaintiffs were commanded by a deputy sheriff, acting under directions of the Ordinary, to leave the white women's polling booth and after their respectful refusal to do so on the ground that they had the constitutional right to vote without being subjected to racial discrimination, they were arrested. With precision, through simultaneous motions for temporary restraining order, preliminary injunction, show cause orders, and the immediate release from arrest, the plaintiffs requested that the Court declare the defendant Southwell was not the legally elected Justice of the Peace, that he be enjoined from taking office, and that the Ordinary be ordered to call a new election....

It rounds out the picture to state that ... two parallel companion cases were before the District Court, one by the United States against various officials of Sumter County, the other an identical suit by these appellants-plaintiffs against the same Georgia officials. Hearing them simultaneously with the application for preliminary relief in the instant case, the District Judge in those two cases entered an injunction enjoining the defendants from maintaining racial segregation at the polls, from maintaining segregated voting lists, from arresting or interfering with Negro voters, and from prosecuting the plaintiffs for their conduct leading to their arrest on July 20, 1965....

By the decrees in the companion cases ..., the trial Court in unmistakable terms and action characterized the practices as flagrant violations of the Constitution. These steps were taken, so the Judge said, "to insure that in the future, elections in Sumter County will be free from discrimination." Despite his determination that for the future these glaring racial discriminations could not go on, the trial Judge concluded that a Federal Court was either powerless—or at least ought not to exercise power—to set aside a State election. The Judge was apparently influenced by two factors. The first is one going to the existence of power or the propriety of its exercise. On the basis of *Reynolds v. Sims*, and other reapportionment cases, the trial Court recognizing that a prohibitory decree could look to the future, nevertheless held that it could not rectify the past since, as the Judge put it, "only a few minutes' reflection is needed to realize that the implications of such a decision would be staggering." The second [factor that influenced the district judge was that,] granting the existence of this crude discrimination, there is no way to tell whether the result would have been different in its absence. Hence, no harm or injury is shown by these complainants. Neither of these factors warrant, in our view, the complete denial of relief.

Drastic, if not staggering, as is the Federal voiding of a State election, and therefore a form of relief to be guardedly exercised, this Court [has].... expressly recognized the existence of this power. Of course ... not every unconstitutional racial discrimination necessarily permits or requires a retrospective voiding of the election. But the power is present....

As to the second [factor identified by the district court,] we do not think the Court could justify denial of effective, present relief because of any assumed inability to demonstrate that the outcome would have been different. The appellants seem to suggest that the existence of such flagrant racial discrimination would raise a presumption that the vote of every actual and potential voter was affected. On that approach, it is not Negroes alone who suffer, it is the body politic as a whole, both Negro and white. And this is certainly true at least to the extent that the trial Court legally could not assume—as it evidently did—that all white voters would vote for white candidates, all Negroes for Negroes, or that no whites would vote for Negroes in a free, untainted election.

[W]e think it is a mistake to cast this in terms of presumption. The fact is that there are certain discriminatory practices which, apart from demonstrated injury or the inability to do so, so infect the processes of the law as to be stricken down as invalid. Thus in jury-race exclusion cases, once the evidence, either direct or by inference from statistical percentages, establishes the existence of racial discrimination, the law requires that the indictment (or the petit jury verdict of guilty) be set side even though the accused is unable to demonstrate injury in fact. And at times demonstrated actual discrimination is not even required if the racially conscious system affords a ready opportunity for it in practice. Of course the Court discharging an accused from such indictment or conviction as a legalism finds that the accused was "prejudiced", but it is not in terms of the personal harm suffered or a factual demonstration that things would have turned out better. Rather, it is the law's recognition that in areas of such vital importance, state-imposed racial discrimination cannot be tolerated and to eliminate the practice or the temptation toward it, the law must extinguish the judgment wrought by such a procedure.

Even more directly, in connection with the elective process, the Supreme Court gave full play to this approach in striking down the Louisiana law requiring the designation of the race of each candidate on the ballot. *Anderson v. Martin*, 1964, 375 U.S. 399. It takes little transposition to substitute for the ballot's written racial candidate label the state-supplied racial marker for places and manner of voting. In each situation it is "... placing a racial label ... at the most crucial stage in the electoral process—the instant before the vote is cast...." By each mechanism "the State furnishes a vehicle by which racial prejudice may be so aroused as to operate against one group because of race and for another." And in both situations this "is true because by directing the citizen's attention to the single consideration of race or color, the State indicates that ... race or color is an important—perhaps paramount—consideration in the citizen's choice, which may decisively influence the citizen to cast his ballot along racial lines." And as much for one as for the other, the "vice lies not in the resulting injury but in the placing of the power of the State behind a racial classification that induces racial prejudice at the polls." 375 U.S. 399, 402....

[With respect to the question whether the election should be set aside,] the Georgia authorities ... insist here that the relief sought was properly denied since the injunction was requested after the election was over.

But we certainly inten[d] no such mechanical rule. In *Hamer [v. Campbell*, where we refused to order such relief,] the vice sought to be corrected was the denial of the right to vote to Negroes through operation of the registration procedure. That was known to exist before the election was held. It was also known that the effects could not be eradicated except through equitable court relief. Here, of course, the vice occurred on election day upon the opening of the polls. It might be suggested that the Negro voters should have anticipated that the traditional practice of racially segregated lists and polling places would be maintained. But it was equally permissible for them to think that at this late date and in the atmosphere of that moment and the passage of successive Civil Rights statutes increasing protection against racial discrimination, that these Georgia authorities would measure up to the demands of the Constitution.

There was really no effective relief available before the election. The moment the election process began, there was a protest by these Negro voters and others seeking an eradication of the discrimination and an opportunity for all members of that race, indeed for all voters, to vote without regard to race or color. That this self-help was not successful, indeed resulted in the unwarranted arrest and detention of those who protested, does not fault them for want of diligence. And within but a few days after the result of the election was published, this suit was filed as a part of an attack on many fronts.

Considering the gross, spectacular, completely indefensible nature of this state-imposed, state-enforced racial discrimination and the absence of an effective judicial remedy prior to the holding of the election, this is far removed from a belated effort to set aside retrospectively an election held long before on the ground that re-examination of the circumstances indicates a denial of constitutional rights on the part of candidates or voters, or both. The parties here moved with unusual diligence and ... relief "... if it is to be had, must perforce come from the Court or the voters must simply be told to wait four more years."

In the face of gross, unsophisticated, significant, and obvious racial discriminations in the conduct of the election and the now established power of a Federal Court to extinguish its effects even to the point of setting aside the election, the [state law] reasons relied on by the District Judge warrant but a brief comment. The Court's fundamental mistake was in assuming that this was an election contest as such in which the winner is challenged because of ineligibility, fraud or irregularities in the conduct of the election, the receipt or counting of illegal ballots which would change the result and the like, and which, as a separate special statutory proceeding, must be timely filed by specified persons following statutory procedures and in particular tribunals. Mrs. Bell and her co-plaintiffs alone or as members of the class did not challenge the eligibility of Mr. Southwell or the fact that he received an overwhelming majority. Indeed, Mrs. Bell as a former candidate did not seek to be selected over Southwell or any other opponent. What, and all, she and others sought was an election conducted free of such indefensible, racial distinctions. That being so, it was not the usual simple case of counting votes and denying relief for want of affirmative proof of a different result....

This leaves only a tag end. There is a suggestion that the District Court enjoining Southwell from taking office pursuant to the election would be powerless to grant affirmative relief requiring that the Ordinary call a special election. In this vital area of vindication of precious constitutional rights, we are unfettered by the negative or affirmative character of the words used or the negative or affirmative form in which the coercive order is cast. If affirmative relief is essential, the Court has the power and should employ it.

The cause must therefore be reversed and remanded for the entry of an appropriate order setting aside the election and requiring the calling of a special election.

NOTES AND QUESTIONS

1. For a general discussion of federal courts' power to set aside state elections, see Kenneth W. Starr, *Federal Judicial Invalidation as a Remedy* *for Irregularities in State Elections*, 49 N.Y.U.L. Rev. 1092 (1974). Dean Starr noted that as of 1974, federal intervention in state elections was a relatively new phenomenon, in part as a product of the political question doctrine, which viewed elections generally, and state elections particularly, as not amenable to federal judicial oversight.

Starr emphasized the equitable nature of the invalidation power, and discussed its relative advantages and disadvantages. On the one hand, purely prospective injunctive relief—e.g., an order forbidding the unconstitutional practice in the future—"necessarily leave[s] intact the results achieved under an unlawful scheme ... until a new election is held in the natural course of events." *Id.* at 1103. Invalidation provides a more complete remedy since it returns the voters more nearly to the status quo ante in which a constitutional election can be conducted. At the same time, invalidation seemed to Starr a less intrusive federal remedy than structural reform—for example, the reapportionment decisions that precipitated major reorganization of states' election systems.

On the other hand, Starr noted that invalidation could involve costly new elections which might, among other things, depress voter participation, thereby not actually returning voters to the status quo ante. And the delays necessary to conduct new elections might leave incumbents in office who themselves might lack legitimacy.

Starr identified three theoretical bases for exercising the power to invalidate elections. The first was "invalidation as retribution" for outrageous, intentional, illegal conduct by government officials during the election process. *Id.* at 1115. Starr saw *Bell* as such a case. A second theory would authorize invalidations for the purpose of "ensuring electoral purity," *id.* at 1121, without regard to official intent, but such a per se rule seemed too automatic to him. Finally, a third approach, which Starr found the "most pragmatic," would contemplate invalidation when unconstitutional actions were "outcome-determinative," that is, when they might have affected the actual outcome of an election: "There is no logical correlation between the invalidation remedy and the violation if the violations which have occurred cannot reasonably be viewed as having affected the actual result of an election." *Id.* at 1125.

2. The power exercised in *Bell* is quite rare. To get a sense of how reluctant courts are to order such a drastic remedy, consider the facts in *Hamer v. Ely*, 410 F.2d 152 (5th Cir. 1969). The case involved an election in Sunflower, Mississippi, for mayor and city council. The election was the first in which the majority-black town's black population was able to cast ballots. (Their ability to vote was the product of the Voting Rights Act of 1965 and a prior federal court order.) The election was a cause celebre, in part because of the presence of Fannie Lou Hamer, one of the key heroes of the Civil Rights Movement.

Every one of the black candidates lost. In a lawsuit asking the district court to set aside the election, the plaintiffs alleged that the local Election

Commission refused to appoint any black election workers to help illiterate black voters cast their ballots. Instead, the Commission appointed, among other people, election officials who were employers or creditors of black voters. The plaintiffs argued that many illiterate black voters therefore cast their ballots without aid, rather than disclose how they voted. They pointed to the fact that a majority of the ballots rejected for irregularities contained votes only for black candidates and very few contained votes only for white candidates. Nonetheless, the district judge found it "significant that not one witness was offered, not one witness testified that he or she was illiterate and needed assistance in casting his ballot, but refused to ask for assistance because he did not want a white person to know how his vote was cast." The court of appeals agreed that the election was fundamentally fair:

> Of course, it would be naive to doubt that there must have been some Negroes who were unwilling to ask for aid because of a reluctance to disclose or fear of disclosing how they intended to vote. But this election was held in a fishbowl. The report of the federal observers is in the record. Commenting on the report the district judge said:

> "It speaks clearly and demonstrates that this election was fairly and properly held in every respect, and it is not questioned but that every person who was given assistance was assisted fairly and impartially with the ballot in each instance being marked in exact accord with the voter's wishes."

As for the way in which the local election commission provided assistance, the court of appeals stated:

> The [Voting Rights] Act requires that voters be apprised of their right to assistance, not that they be induced to accept it. In the Sunflower election, voters were apprised of their right and each was informed that he could request a federal observer to be with him in the voting booth to check the quality of assistance rendered by the election official.

> On the cold record before us, the attitude of Sunflower's Election Commissioners may have been shoddy, but it does not justify the "drastic, if not staggering" procedure, *Bell v. Southwell*, of a federal court's voiding a state election. Such "drastic" measures are properly reserved for cases involving serious violations of voting rights.

3. Most of the cases setting aside elections involve claims of racial discrimination. To what extent is the willingness of courts to intervene under these circumstances a product of their sense that race discrimination, as opposed to other explanations for why a particular election went wrong, is an ongoing problem that can be stopped only through drastic measures? For an example of a case not involving claims of racial discrimination in which an election was set aside on purely state-law grounds, consider *Akizaki v. Fong*, 51 Haw. 354 (1969). The case involved an election to the Hawaii state legislature. In the final tabulation of the votes for the sixth and final seat from a multimember district, the Republican candidate, Fong, received two more votes than the Democratic candidate, Akizaki. Akizaki contested the election and proved before the trial court that at least nineteen absentee ballots were invalid because of late postmarks. Due to a mistake by election officials, these ballots were nevertheless opened and counted. Worse, they were "commingled" with validly cast absentee ballots and it could not later be determined for whom the invalid ballots had been cast. The trial court's solution was to discard 174 absentee ballots, among which were the 19 invalid ones. Once these 174 votes were thrown out, Akizaki had more votes than Fong, and the trial court declared him the winner.

The Hawaii Supreme Court reversed:

> The fundamental interest to be protected here is that of the people of the Fifteenth Representative District in choosing whomever they please to represent them in the House of Representatives. The right to vote is perhaps the most basic and fundamental of all the rights guaranteed by our democratic form of government. Implicit in that right is the right to have one's vote count and the right to have as nearly perfect an election proceeding as can be provided. The result we reach must be consistent with these principles.

* * *

> It remains to be decided whether the result reached by the court below was correct. We hold that it was not, and that a new election should have been ordered. Because of the commingling of the valid and invalid absentee ballots, there is simply no way to determine what the actual result of the election was, and who should therefore be declared the winner. In such a situation, HRS § 12–103 directs the court to invalidate the election.

> The trial court's approach was plausible; but to excise the entire absentee vote contained in the 174 ballots excluded by the court, in order to eliminate the nineteen ballots known to be invalid, inflicts too harsh a result on those absentee voters whose votes were validly cast.

> Pursuant to HRS § 12–105, this court may, in election contest cases, enter any judgment the circuit court would have been authorized to enter. Our judgment is, as provided in HRS § 12–103, that the election was invalid for the reason that a correct result cannot be ascertained because of the mistake we have noted on the part of the election officials in opening the late-postmarked envelopes and commingling those ballots with ballots validly cast. Therefore, in accordance with HRS § 12–103, and in order to protect the right of the people of the Fifteenth Representative District to choose their representatives, we invalidate the election as between Fong and Akizaki. As set out in HRS § 12–103, a certified copy of our judgment shall be filed with the

governor, so that he may call a new election as between Fong and Akizaki as provided by the statute.

Many states have similar statutes requiring new elections when the result of an initial election cannot be determined. *See, e.g.*, N.Y. Elect. Law § 16–102 (1999) ("The court may direct . . . the holding of a new primary election . . . where it finds there has been such fraud or irregularity as to render impossible a determination as to who rightfully was nominated or elected.").

B.   ENJOINING AN UPCOMING ELECTION

As the previous section suggested, courts will often refuse to set aside an election if the injured parties could have prevented the violation of their rights by seeking relief before the election. Sometimes pre-election relief will involve simply a declaratory judgment about a particular election practice or an injunction forbidding or requiring a particular action. For example, voters might decide to challenge an unconstitutional apportionment and seek an injunction forbidding the state from conducting an election under the challenged scheme.

Since the plaintiffs in such a lawsuit are seeking equitable relief, doctrines such as laches come into play. Every use of an unconstitutional or illegal election practice involves a new violation of voters' or candidates' rights—in other words, there isn't a statute of limitations that immunizes a practice from challenge. (There almost always is, however, a statute of limitations with regard to challenging the *outcome* of a particular election. For example, in many States, a challenge to the results of an election must be filed within a relatively few days after the election results are certified. But although a plaintiff can challenge an election law or regulation at any time, a court might refuse to afford immediate relief to a plaintiff who waits until the very eve of an election before bringing suit over a practice that she either knew or should have known would be in effect.

Even when plaintiffs do file their lawsuit in a timely manner, however, equitable considerations may play a substantial role in a court's decision whether to stop an upcoming election.

Chisom v. Roemer

853 F.2d 1186 (5th Cir. 1988).

■ HENRY POLITZ, CIRCUIT JUDGE

On August 3, 1988, following an expedited appeal, we vacated the preliminary injunction issued by the district court which had enjoined the election of a justice of the Louisiana Supreme Court from the First

Supreme Court District, and ordered that "said election shall be conducted in accordance with the laws of the State of Louisiana at the times and in the manner specified therein." Consistent with a reservation then made, we now assign our reasons for that decision.

Background

On September 19, 1986 complainants, black registered voters in Orleans Parish, Louisiana, and an organization active in voting-rights issues, filed the instant suit, alleging that the present system of electing two justices to the Louisiana Supreme Court from the First Supreme Court District violates section 2 of the Voting Rights Act of 1965 as amended. Their complaint was met with a motion to dismiss under Rule 12(b)(6) of the Federal Rules of Civil Procedure, which the court granted, essentially based on the conclusion that section 2 did not apply to judicial elections. On appeal we reversed and remanded.

After an application for panel rehearing and for a rehearing en banc was declined, the case was returned to the district court. Thereafter, complainants applied for a preliminary injunction to prevent the election scheduled for October 1, 1988 of a justice from the First Supreme Court District, a position held by Justice Pascal F. Calogero, Jr. since 1972. Based on the evidence presented the district judge concluded that the election should be enjoined. Defendants appealed....

* * *

The trial court concluded that complainants had satisfied the tetrad test for issuance of a preliminary injunction which was synthesized, although not originated, in the oft-cited case of *Canal Authority of State of Florida v. Callaway*, 489 F.2d 567, 572 (5th Cir.1974), by showing:

(1) a substantial likelihood that plaintiff will prevail on the merits;

(2) a substantial threat that plaintiff will suffer irreparable injury if the injunction is not granted;

(3) that the threatened injury to plaintiff outweighs the threatened harm the injunction may do to defendant; and

(4) that granting the preliminary injunction will not disserve the public interest.

Analysis

Inasmuch as our decision is powered by a consideration of the essence and ramifications of the third and fourth factors, we pretermit a discussion of the first two, except for these limited comments. It remains to be seen whether the complainants will prevail on the merits, indeed the Supreme Court has yet to speak on the critical issue whether section 2 of the Voting Rights Act applies to judicial elections. And we can only speculate as to the state of the record in this case after trial on the merits.

As to irreparable injury, complainants urge a black-letter, per se rule to the effect that if an electoral standard, practice, or procedure abridges section 2 of the Voting Rights Act it automatically does irreparable injury to all or a portion of the body politic. Some district courts would agree. *See Dillard v. Crenshaw County*, 640 F. Supp. 1347 (M.D.Ala.1986); *Harris v. Graddick*, 593 F. Supp. 128 (M.D.Ala.1984); *Cook v. Luckett*, 575 F. Supp. 479 (S.D. Miss.1983). We do not. We are not prepared to adopt a per se rule in such a vital area of state-federal relations. We recognize and are in full accord with the teachings of the Supreme Court in *Reynolds v. Sims*, that "the right to vote freely for the candidate of one's choice is of the essence of a democratic society and any restrictions on that right strike at the heart of representative government. And the right of suffrage can be denied by a debasement or dilution of the weight of a citizen's vote just as effectively as by wholly prohibiting the free exercise." We are cognizant, however, that " 'the possibility that . . . other corrective relief will be available at a later date, in the ordinary course of litigation, weighs heavily against a claim of irreparable harm.' " In this we agree with the commentators who suggest that "only when the threatened harm would impair the court's ability to grant an effective remedy is there really a need for preliminary relief." Wright & Miller, Federal Practice and Procedure § 2948 at 431–34 (1973).

Should the election be enjoined?

Assuming per arguendo that there has been a prima facie showing of likelihood of success on the merits, and irreparable injury, our disposition of this appeal turns on a negative response to the question: Does the public interest require that this election be enjoined? Would such an injunction be in the best interests of: all of the citizens of the State of Louisiana; the citizens of the First Supreme Court District; the black citizenry of Louisiana; that of the First Supreme Court District; or the black electorate of Orleans Parish? We are persuaded beyond peradventure that the answer must be a resounding "no" on behalf of all of these groupings of Louisianians.

Our analysis begins with the staunch admonition that a federal court should jealously guard and sparingly use its awesome powers to ignore or brush aside long-standing state constitutional provisions, statutes, and practices. There can be no doubt that under the Supremacy Clause, federal courts do and indeed must have this authority in our unique form of government. It is the use of this power that must be maintained in the balance, a balance which is more delicate than usual when a state's judicial process is involved.

It cannot be gainsaid that federal courts have the power to enjoin state elections. *Watson v. Commissioners Court of Harrison County*, 616 F.2d 105 (5th Cir.1980); *Hamer v. Campbell*, 358 F.2d 215 (5th Cir.), cert. denied, 385 U.S. 851 (1966). But, "intervention by the federal courts in state elections has always been a serious business," *Oden v. Brittain*, 396 U.S. 1210, (1969) (Black, J., opinion in chambers), not to be lightly engaged in.

Indeed, even after an adjudication on the merits that a legislative apportionment plan violated the Constitution, the Supreme Court invited the use of a velvet glove over the mailed fist:

> In awarding or withholding immediate relief, a court is entitled to and should consider the proximity of a forthcoming election and the mechanics and complexities of state election laws, and should act and rely upon general equitable principles. With respect to the timing of relief, a court can reasonably endeavor to avoid a disruption of the election process which might result from requiring precipitate changes that could make unreasonable or embarrassing demands on a State in adjusting to the requirements of the court's decree.

Reynolds v. Sims, 377 U.S. at 585. *Sims* has been the guidon to a number of courts that have refrained from enjoining impending elections. In another instance, the Supreme Court stayed a district court's hand after a three-judge court found Indiana's multi-member districting provisions unconstitutional. *Whitcomb v. Chavis*, 396 U.S. 1055 and 396 U.S. 1064 (1970) (granting a stay pending appeal, 305 F. Supp. 1359, 1364 (S.D.Ind.1969)). *See also Maryland Citizens v. Governor of Maryland*, 429 F.2d 606 (4th Cir.1970); *Dillard v. Crenshaw County; Banks v. Bd. of Ed., City of Peoria*, 659 F. Supp. 394 (C.D.Ill.1987); *Knox v. Milwaukee County*, 581 F. Supp. 399 (E.D.Wis.1984).

We consider significant the Supreme Court's action in *Chavis*. In staying the reapportionment plan ordered by a three-judge court, the Supreme Court permitted the conduct of an election under the old scheme which had been found constitutionally infirm. In dissenting from the refusal to vacate their stay order, Justice Douglas pointedly stated: "The State contends that without a stay it will be forced to conduct the forthcoming election under the reapportionment plan of the District Court. By granting the stay, however, this Court has equally forced the appellees to go through the election under the present scheme which was held unconstitutional by the District Court." Nonetheless the court permitted the election to proceed.

The case at bar

Against this backdrop we consider the realities of the case at bar. The district court concluded that the issuance of an injunction would either be neutral, in ultimate result, or preferable to not enjoining the election. We do not find the court's reasoning persuasive. To the extent this is a factual finding by the trial court, we view it as clearly erroneous; to the extent it is a conclusion of law, we view it as erroneous.

Preventing this judicial election at this late stage is not a passive or neutral act. It is the proverbial gossamer-thin veil which is fraught with difficulties. The consequences to Louisiana's judicial system are as significant as they are uncertain. Indeed, the very uncertainties introduced account in large measure for the significance of the impact.

The core value of the law and its implementing judicial system is stability—the ability reasonably to anticipate the results of actions and proceedings, by individuals and by legal institutions. Staying the election for a justice of the First Supreme Court District casts a cloud over the Louisiana Supreme Court, as staying any judicial election would cast a cloud over the affected court. The Louisiana Constitution provides that the terms of the justices of its supreme court are ten years. The term of Justice Calogero expires on December 31, 1988. If the regularly scheduled election did not go forward, would Louisiana have seven justices on its highest court on January 1, 1989? If the election is enjoined and Justice Calogero continues to serve, will there be any question about the validity of his actions as a justice?

The Louisiana Constitution prescribes that four justices must concur to render judgment. Decisions in both civil and criminal cases decided on a 4–3 basis are not a rarity. The sparse offerings by the state in defense of the application for the preliminary injunction include the affidavit of the Director of the Louisiana Supreme Court's Central Staff of attorneys. He advises that since 1976 the Louisiana Supreme Court has reviewed 82 death penalty appeals. In 30 of those appeals the conviction was reversed or the death sentence was vacated. Twenty percent of those reversals were decided on a 4–3 vote. The record does not contain statistics for 4–3 renditions in civil cases, or in the denial of writs of certiorari or review, which require the agreement of four justices, but the number undoubtedly is very substantial. One need only thumb through a selective sampling of the Southern Reporter Second series for a feel of just how substantial that number is. What is the consequence if Justice Calogero is one of the four? Is an uncertainty introduced?

Does the general statutory provision declaring that public officers hold their offices until their successors are "inducted into office" apply in this instance? Our research reflects no case in which the Louisiana Supreme Court has applied this statute to a justice or judge. Until Louisiana's highest court resolves this question it remains just that, an open question and, as such, it casts a shadow on the functioning of the Louisiana Supreme Court.

Appellees and the trial court refer to the provision of the Louisiana Constitution which addresses the temporary posting of judicial vacancies. Article 5, § 22, provides that until a vacancy in a judicial office is filled "the supreme court shall appoint a person meeting the qualifications for the office . . . to serve at its pleasure. The appointee shall be ineligible as a candidate at the election to fill the vacancy." *Id.* § 22(B). If the election is enjoined, after midnight on December 31, 1988 is the post now held by Justice Calogero to be deemed vacant and subject to an appointment by his former-fellow justices? Because of the involvement of the federal court, and its preventing of the election, would this be a vacancy subject to appointment? If it is deemed such and Justice Calogero accepts an appointment, would he be eligible to seek reelection to the judicial post he has held since 1972 when the federal court did permit an election to proceed? More shadows on the otherwise clear patina of the Louisiana judicial system. Are such warranted? Can they be justified or permitted?

Further, in Article 5, § 6, the Louisiana Constitution establishes that "the judge oldest in point of service on the supreme court shall be chief justice." Justice Calogero currently is second in point of service to the chief justice. If the election is enjoined and his office is deemed vacant, should he not be offered, or should he decline an appointment out of caution for the Article 5, § 22(B) proscription; if he is reelected, would his service have been interrupted so as to cause a forfeiture of his claim to be oldest in point of service?

Finally, what about the litigants during this period? What will be the racial demographics of that group? Will they be affected adversely? Will that effect be significant? Can it be justified?

Appellees suggest that the specter of problems with and for the Louisiana Supreme Court are manageable. The trial court states: "Regardless of the state constitutional provisions, this Court has in any event the power under the Supremacy Clause to fashion both preliminary and final equitable relief that will both provide plaintiffs with a full and adequate remedy and protect other important state interests." Is this a suggestion that the chancellor will appoint a successor to Calogero, perhaps Calogero, and, out of a sense of fair play, decree that all state constitutional questions as to his service are to be taken for naught, that the proscription against his running for the office is nullified, and, further, order that no one may suggest a break in his service for purposes of eligibility for the office of chief justice? Is such necessary? Should the federal court even contemplate that scenario? We are most reluctant to do so.

Were we to countenance such a scenario, other interests would be disserved. As the *Dillard* court recognized, the extension of the terms of incumbents or the court's appointment of replacements, effectively denies "the entire electorate the right to vote and thus seem to offend basic principles . . ."

How long would this disenfranchisement of all of the voters of the First Supreme Court District continue? As discussed *infra*, this case must run its full course, and, thereafter, assuming violations are found, the Louisiana Legislature must be afforded an opportunity to repair the defects the court discloses. Is the electorate to have no say whatever as to the person to serve during that period? Can that conceivably be considered in the best interests of the citizenry?

In addition to the foregoing caution to the use of injunctive powers before trial on the merits, and indeed even after trial on the merits, we are also keenly mindful of another well-established rubric which must be brought to bear in the resolution of the present conundrum. It is now established beyond challenge that upon finding a particular standard, practice, or procedure to be contrary to either a federal constitutional or statutory requirement, the federal court must grant the appropriate state or local authorities an opportunity to correct the deficiencies. In *Reynolds v. Sims* the Supreme Court commended the district court for refraining from enjoining an impending election until the Alabama Legislature had been given an opportunity to remedy the defects in their legislative apportionment scheme. Further, after trial on the merits, and a declaration that an existing election scheme is unlawful, it is "appropriate, whenever practicable, to afford a reasonable opportunity for the legislature to meet constitutional [or federal statutory] requirements by adopting a substitute measure rather than for the federal court to devise and order into effect its own plan." *Wise v. Lipscomb*, 437 U.S. 535, 540 (1978). The court goes on to cite authorities for the proposition that the legislatures should first be given a chance, and quoting *Reynolds v. Sims*, the *Sanchez* court noted that "judicial relief becomes appropriate only when a legislature fails to reapportion according to federal constitutional requisites in a timely fashion after having had an adequate opportunity to do so." 452 U.S. at 150 n. 30; *Connor v. Finch*, 431 U.S. 407 (1977).

As found by the district court, the Louisiana Legislature has signaled no reluctance to address this matter. When this court held that section 2 applied to judicial elections, remedial legislation was offered and seriously considered in the just-recessed legislative session. This legislature gives every indication of promptly responding to a need for action should it occur.

We understand these precedents to mandate that the responsible state or local authorities must be first given an opportunity to correct any constitutional or statutory defect before the court attempts to draft a remedial plan. In the case at bar, that means that should the court rule on the merits that a statutory or constitutional violation exists the Louisiana Legislature should be allowed a reasonable opportunity to address the problem. We have no reason whatsoever to doubt that the governor and legislature will respond promptly....

In the interim, we are convinced that the system in place for the election of the subject judicial officer should be left undisturbed. There are a number of variables and several contingencies. But notwithstanding their final alignment, at the appropriate time, should it become necessary, the federal courts may fashion whatever remedy the law, equity, and justice require.

The preliminary injunction is VACATED and it is ordered that the presently scheduled election for justice of the First Supreme Court District of Louisiana proceed in accordance with the laws of Louisiana.

NOTES AND QUESTIONS

1. The Court of Appeals' decision rests in part on the availability of "other corrective relief ... at a later date, in the ordinary course of litigation." What does this mean? That if the election system is later held invalid a court can order a special election to refill a seat?

2. A major source of injunctive relief barring elections is section 5 of the Voting Rights Act of 1965, 42 U.S.C. § 1973c(a), which is covered extensively in Chapter 6. Section 5 prohibits certain states and political subdivisions that had a history of discrimination and depressed political participation from making any changes with respect to their election systems unless they receive "preclearance," that is, prior approval from the U.S. Department of Justice or a federal district court in Washington, D.C.

In *Clark v. Roemer*, 500 U.S. 646 (1991), another case involving judicial elections in Louisiana, the Supreme Court described the principles that govern injunctions in section 5 cases:

> Section 5 requires States to obtain either judicial or administrative preclearance before implementing a voting change. A voting change in a covered jurisdiction "will not be effective as law until and unless cleared" pursuant to one of these two methods. Failure to obtain either judicial or administrative preclearance "renders the change unenforceable." If voting changes subject to § 5 have not been precleared, § 5 plaintiffs are entitled to an injunction prohibiting the State from implementing the changes.

> The District Court ignored these principles altogether. It presented a number of reasons for not enjoining the election, none of which we find persuasive. The court cited the short time between election day and the most recent request for injunction, the fact that qualifying and absentee voting had begun, and the time and expense of the candidates. But the parties, the District Court, and the candidates had been on notice of the alleged § 5 violations since appellants filed their July 1987 amended complaint. When Louisiana asked the Attorney General for reconsideration of its original preclearance decision in June 1990, it became apparent that the State intended to hold elections for the unprecleared seats in the fall of the same year. Less than a month later, and more than two months before the scheduled October 6, 1990, election, appellants filed a motion to enjoin elections for the unprecleared seats. Appellants displayed no lack of diligence in challenging elections for the unprecleared seats, and every participant in the process knew for over three years that the challenged seats were unprecleared, in violation of § 5. . . .

> Nor did the District Court's vague concerns about voter confusion and low voter turnout in a special election for the unprecleared seats justify its refusal to enjoin the illegal elections. Voters may be more confused and inclined to avoid the polls when an election is held in conceded violation of federal law. Finally, the District Court's stated purpose to avoid possible challenges to criminal and civil judgments does not justify allowing the invalid elections to take place. To the contrary, this

concern counsels in favor of enjoining the illegal elections, thus averting a federal challenge to state judgments.

The three-judge District Court, maintained that its decision to give provisional effect to elections conducted in violation of § 5 "closely paralleled" a number of our decisions, including *Perkins v. Matthews*, 400 U.S. 379 (1971), *NAACP v. Hampton County Election Comm'n*, 470 U.S. 166 (1985), *Berry v. Doles*, 438 U.S. 190 (1978), and *Georgia v. United States*, 411 U.S. 526 (1973). The cases are inapposite. *Perkins* stated that "in certain circumstances ... it might be appropriate to enter an order affording local officials an opportunity to seek federal approval and ordering a new election only if local officials fail to do so or if the required federal approval is not forthcoming." But in *Perkins*, as in *Hampton County, Berry*, and *Georgia*, the elections in question had been held already; the only issue was whether to remove the elected individuals pending preclearance. Here the District Court did not face the ex post question whether to set aside illegal elections; rather, it faced the ex ante question whether to allow illegal elections to be held at all. On these premises, § 5's prohibition against implementation of unprecleared changes required the District Court to enjoin the election. This is especially true because, unlike the circumstance in *Perkins, Hampton County, Berry*, or *Georgia*, the Attorney General interposed objections before the election.

We need not decide today whether there are cases in which a district court may deny a § 5 plaintiff's motion for injunction and allow an election for an unprecleared seat to go forward. An extreme circumstance might be present if a seat's unprecleared status is not drawn to the attention of the State until the eve of the election and there are equitable principles that justify allowing the election to proceed. No such exigency exists here. The State of Louisiana failed to preclear these judgeships as required by § 5. It received official notice of the defect in July 1987, and yet three years later it had still failed to file for judicial preclearance, the "basic mechanism" for preclearance, It scheduled elections for the unprecleared seats in the fall of 1990 even after the Attorney General had interposed objections under § 5. In short, by the fall 1990 election, Louisiana had with consistency ignored the mandate of § 5. The District Court should have enjoined the elections.

An injunction in a section 5 case may prevent elections from occurring for a very long time: in *Beer v. United States*, a principal case in Chapter 6 involving the New Orleans City Council, elections were enjoined for over five years; elections were enjoined in Richmond, Virginia during the pendency of *City of Richmond v. United States* for a similar period of time.

3. In the context of section 5, Florida raises some interesting questions. Five counties within the state are covered jurisdictions, which cannot make any change respecting elections without first establishing that the proposed change will have neither a discriminatory purpose nor a discriminatory effect. On the other hand, the state as a whole is *not* a covered jurisdiction. Suppose in the face of uncertainty over the 2000 presidential vote, the Florida Legislature had decided to appoint its own slate of electors. Would the decision to abolish, at least for the 2000 election, determination of the electors by popular vote have required preclearance? Cf. *Lopez v. Monterey County*, 525 U.S. 266 (1999) (discussing how the preclearance regime applies to partially covered states).

4. The California gubernatorial recall election offers another illustration of the analysis courts perform when asked to postpone an election that is already in some sense underway. In the summer of 2003, a campaign to recall Governor Gray Davis submitted sufficient signatures to trigger a recall election. Under the California Constitution, that recall election had to be conducted not less than 60 and not more than 80 days after certification of the signatures. Accordingly, the recall election was scheduled for October 2003. Pursuant to another provision of the state constitution, this also meant that two initiative measures that had originally been scheduled for the March 2004 election—one of them a controversial measure that would have forbidden the state from collecting any racial information—were moved up to the October 2003 election.

A few years earlier, California had agreed, in settlement of a lawsuit, to decertify the use of punch card voting systems in time for the March 2004 election. But the new machines were not yet in place.

The Southwest Voter Registration Education Project, the Southern Christian Leadership Conference of Greater Los Angeles, and the NAACP and its branches filed a lawsuit alleging that the planned use of punch-card machines in the October 2003 election would violate the equal protection clause and section 2 of the Voting Rights Act.

Ultimately, an en banc court of appeals allowed the election to go forward. The en banc court bypassed the merits of the claims and resolved the issues on matters of timing instead:

> The decision to enjoin an impending election is so serious that the Supreme Court has allowed elections to go forward even in the face of an undisputed constitutional violation. *See, e.g.*, *Ely v. Klahr*, 403 U.S. 108, 113, 115 (1971); *Whitcomb v. Chavis*, 396 U.S. 1055 and 396 U.S. 1064 (1970); *Kilgarlin v. Hill*, 386 U.S. 120, 121 (1967) (per curiam). . . .

> In this case, hardship falls not only upon the putative defendant, the California Secretary of State, but on all the citizens of California, because this case concerns a statewide election. The public interest is significantly affected. For this reason our law recognizes that election cases are different from ordinary injunction cases. Interference with impending elections is extraordinary, and interference with an election after voting has begun [because some absentee ballots had already

been cast] is unprecedented.... Time and money have been spent to prepare voter information pamphlets and sample ballots, mail absentee ballots, and hire and train poll workers. Public officials have been forced to divert their attention from their official duties in order to campaign. Candidates have crafted their message to the voters in light of the originally-announced schedule and calibrated their message to the political and social environment of the time. They have raised funds under current campaign contribution laws and expended them in reliance on the election's taking place on October 7. Potential voters have given their attention to the candidates' messages and prepared themselves to vote. Hundreds of thousands of absentee voters have already cast their votes in similar reliance upon the election going forward on the timetable announced by the state. These investments of time, money, and the exercise of citizenship rights cannot be returned. If the election is postponed, citizens who have already cast a vote will effectively be told that the vote does not count and that they must vote again. In short, the status quo that existed at the time the election was set cannot be restored because this election has already begun....

We must of course also look to the interests represented by the plaintiffs, who are legitimately concerned that use of the punch-card system will deny the right to vote to some voters who must use that system. At this time, it is merely a speculative possibility, however, that any such denial will influence the result of the election.

Is it better to have unresolved legal issues decided before an election takes place, rather than after the fact when it will often be known to all, including judges, which candidates will benefit from legal rulings? If the cost of having the rules settled clearly in advance, however, is to postpone a major election on the eve of voting, was the court right that judicial intervention to postpone the election would be inappropriate, particularly where the risk that any legal errors would actually affect the outcome is unknown?

C. ADJUSTING THE VOTE TOTALS

One issue that frequently arises in challenges to the outcomes of a particular election—as opposed to challenges to the larger structural rules within which elections take place—involves the question whether particular ballots that were counted ought to have been excluded or particular ballots that were not counted ought to have been included. Often, as in the Florida presidential election of 2000, litigation follows some kind of administrative proceeding in which disappointed voters or candidates seek recounts and adjustments of the original totals.

States differ quite dramatically in their standards for deciding what counts as a legal ballot. At one end, Florida's courts have taken a relatively liberal view: in *Palm Beach County Canvassing Board v. Harris*, 772 So.2d 1220 (Fla. 2000), the Court relied on a provision of the then-extant Florida Election Code, § 101.5614(5), which provided that "no vote shall be declared invalid or void if there is a clear indication of the intent of the voter as determined by the canvassing board." It held that as long as a canvassing board could determine a voter's intent in a manual recount, the vote should not be discarded even if it had not been picked up during the machine tabulation because, for example, the voter had not completely dislodged the chad the way he had been instructed to do. On the other, some states have quite specific standards for what counts as a legal vote, and may end up invalidating particular ballots for quite technical reasons. For example, in jurisdictions using paper ballots, the Illinois Election Code expressly required that voters mark their paper ballots by making a cross (x) in the space next to the candidate of their choice. Ill. Election Code, ch. 10, § 17–11. Applying this hard-and-fast rule, Illinois courts held that votes would not be counted "unless two lines intersect in a cross in the appropriate place on the ballot, even if the voter's intent is clear." *Pullen v. Mulligan*, 561 N.E.2d 585, 609 (1990). Thus, in one case, the court refused to count ballots which the voter had marked with a check, rather than a cross, or ballots on which the voter had written the word "yes," rather than marking the box with an "x". *Scribner v. Sachs*, 164 N.E.2d 481 (1960). In other cases, lines that did not actually cross within the box were held not to constitute a legal vote, *Greene v. Bjorseth*, 183 N.E. 464, 481 (Ill.1932), as were circles made within the circle next to a candidate's name. *Isenburg v. Martin*, 127 N.E. 663 (Ill.1920).

In general, cases involving judicial orders to count additional ballots do not raise particularly complex legal issues. The exceptions—like the post–2000 controversy in Florida—revolve, not around whether a particular ballot should have been included, but rather around whether recounts should be conducted at all and, if they should, what the standard ought to be.

Delahunt v. Johnston, 671 N.E.2d 1241 (Mass.1996), is a fairly typical example of an additive case. The case involved the 1996 Democratic primary in the Tenth Congressional District. After the initial tabulation of the votes, Johnston was declared the winner with 266 more votes than Delahunt. After recounts pursuant to petitions in several municipalities, Johnston was again declared the winner, this time with 175 more votes than Delahunt.

Delahunt then filed a judicial challenge. The trial court reviewed 956 contested ballots, and counted as votes for either Delahunt or Johnston many ballots that had previously been recorded as blank. These ballots were cast on punch cards designed to be counted by computer. As in Florida, many of the ballots involved incompletely removed chads. Reflecting the newly identified votes, the judge concluded that Delahunt was the winner.

The question presented on appeal was:

> [W]hether a discernible indentation made on or near a chad should be recorded as a vote for the person to whom the chad is assigned. The trial judge concluded that a vote should be recorded for a candidate if the chad was not removed but an impression was made on or near it. We agree with this conclusion.
>
> We apply the standard that has been expressed in our cases concerning the counting of punch card (and other) ballots. "The cardinal rule for guidance of election officers and courts in cases of this nature is that if the intent of the voter can be determined with reasonable certainty from an inspection of the ballot, in the light of the generally known conditions attendant upon the election, effect must be given to that intent and the vote counted in accordance therewith, provided the voter has substantially complied with the requisites of the election law; if that intent cannot thus be fairly and satisfactorily ascertained, the ballot cannot rightly be counted."

Interestingly, the Supreme Judicial Court took the position that review of a voter's intent is a question of law to be decided de novo and thus it reviewed each of the disputed ballots itself.

On the merits, the Supreme Judicial Court found Johnston's contention that many voters started to express a preference in the congressional contest, pressed the card, but pulled the stylus back because they really did not want to express a choice on that contest to be unpersuasive:

> The large number of ballots with discernible impressions makes such an inference unwarranted, especially in a hotly contested election.
>
> .... Once one accepts, as we have, the presence of a discernible impression made by a stylus as a clear indication of a voter's intent, our task is to assess each of the 956 ballots. We have done so and have agreed with the trial judge's conclusions on all but twenty-eight ballots. Our totals concerning the contested ballots show that Delahunt gained 659 votes, Johnston gained 283 votes, and fourteen ballots were blank. This resulted in a net gain of 376 votes for Delahunt which more than offset Johnston's 175 vote lead before the contested ballots were counted.

The Court added a footnote explaining the disparity in recount results: "On balance, we are slightly more willing to find an intention expressed on ballots where the trial judge ruled there was none. The net effect of our willingness on twenty-three additional ballots to identify voters' intentions (and of our other disagreements with the judge [five ballots]) was insignificant. In the final calculations, Delahunt gained twelve new votes, and Johnston gained ten."

For an example of how searching appellate judicial review can be, consider *Escalante v. City of Hermosa Beach,* 195 Cal.App.3d 1009 (1987). The case involved a ballot proposition in Hermosa Beach. The initial canvass produced a result of 2,397 voters having voted "yes," and 2,398 having voted "no." After a recount, the tally was adjusted to 2,398 "yes" votes and 2,400 "no" votes.

At that point, a voter who supported the ballot measure filed an election contest in state court. He claimed that illegal votes had been cast and that the city clerk and the recount board, in conducting the recount, made errors sufficient to change the result of the election. Voters who opposed the ballot measure filed a cross-statement on the same grounds, claiming the initiative was in fact defeated by a larger majority than that found on recount.

At trial, the Superior Court made eight sets of determinations about contested ballots: (1) the city clerk erroneously failed to count two "yes" votes of absentee voters who marked their punch card ballots with a pen on the chad designated "yes," rather than punching out the chad as directed; (2) the clerk properly counted as a "no" vote a ballot punched "no" with transparent adhesive tape on the reverse side holding the "yes" chad in place; (3) five ballots punched "no" that also had other chads punched out were properly counted as "no" votes; (4) one ballot punched "yes" with an additional chad punched so that it remained attached to the ballot by only one of its four arms was also properly counted; (5) two ballots with neither the "yes" or "no" chads punched out, but with nearby chads punched, were properly not counted; (6) the clerk erred in counting one voter's absentee ballot; and (7) the clerk properly counted the ballot of Anthony C. De Bellis, Jr., who had moved shortly before election day but who voted in his former precinct; and (8) the clerk acted within her discretion in refusing to count the absentee ballot of Jane R. Woods. After making these determinations, the result was 2,400 votes in favor of the ballot measure, and 2,399 against the measure, which then carried.

On appeal, the District Court of Appeal reviewed each of the Superior Court's de terminations and upheld all of them except one: it held that De Bellis—ironically a member of the Hermosa Beach City Council—was not entitled to vote in the election because he had not properly complied with the provisions governing reregistration by voters who moved within a city. Since De Bellis had apparently testified at trial that he had voted in favor of the ballot measure, the Court of Appeal's rejection of the De Bellis "Yes" vote produced a tie: 2,399 votes for, and 2,399 votes against, the ballot measure. Since the contestant had failed to establish precinct board errors, or illegal votes, "sufficient to change the election result," Cal. Elect. Code §§ 20021(e), 20024, the election results were confirmed.

Notice, then, that there are two potential mechanisms for ensuring the kind of equal treatment of ballots. As we shall see, this becomes a central issue in the Supreme Court's decision in *Bush v. Gore,* where the Court suggested that uniformity of treatment is required by the Fourteenth Amendment. Uniformity can be achieved through detailed substantive rules about what counts or does not count as a valid vote. But it can also be pursued "procedurally," rather than substantively, through protest, contest, and appeals processes, which ultimately place disputed ballots before a single arbiter. *See* Pamela S. Karlan, *Equal Protection: Bush v. Gore and the Making of a Precedent* in The Unfinished Election of 2000 (Jack N. Rakove ed. 2001) (discussing various ways of equalizing treatment of ballots). More often, election contests involve not the attempt to have votes counted that were initially omitted, but rather a request to have ballots thrown out that were originally included.

In re the Matter of the Protest of Election Returns

707 So.2d 1170 (Fla. App. 1998).

■ Per Curiam:

This appeal involves an election contest which occurred during the November 4, 1997, Miami Mayoral election. After considering the evidence, the lower tribunal issued a Final Judgment which found that the evidence demonstrated an extensive "pattern of fraudulent, intentional and criminal conduct that resulted in such an extensive abuse of the absentee ballot laws that it can fairly be said that the intent of these laws was totally frustrated." The lower court ordered that the appropriate remedy was to declare the entire Mayoral election void and order that a new election be held within sixty (60) days. While we find that substantial competent evidence existed to support the trial court's findings of massive fraud in the absentee ballots, we disagree as to the appropriateness of the trial court's remedy in ordering a new election.

In July, 1996, Joe Carollo became the Mayor of the City of Miami. On November 4, 1997, a general election was held for the position of Executive Mayor, with Joe Carollo and Xavier Suarez as two of the contenders. Carollo received a majority of the precinct votes (51.41%) and Suarez received a majority of the absentee votes (61.48%), resulting in Carollo receiving 49.65% of the votes and Suarez receiving 46.80% of the votes when the absentee ballot votes were combined with the machine precinct votes.

Since neither of the parties received a majority of the overall votes, a run-off election was held on November 13, 1997. In that election, Suarez defeated Carollo in both precinct votes and the absentee votes. On November 14, 1997, the results of the November 13, 1997, election were certified and Suarez assumed the position of Mayor of the City of Miami. On the same day, Carollo filed a protest to the run-off election pursuant to Section 102.166, Florida Statutes (1997), as well as the November 4th and November 13th election results, under Section 102.168, Florida Statutes (1997). The filings were consolidated. The principal relief sought by Carollo was to be declared the victor of the Mayoral election, having received a majority of the "untainted" precinct votes or, in the alternative, for a new election.

A bench trial was held and, on March 3, 1998, the trial court declared the Mayoral election void. This judgment was based on the trial court's finding of massive absentee voter fraud which affected the electoral process.

The uncontradicted statistical evidence presented by Kevin Hill, Ph.D., a political scientist and expert in research methodology and statistical analysis, indicated that the amount of fraud involved in the absentee ballots was of such consequence so as to have affected the outcome of the election. Dr. Hill analyzed the absentee ballot voting, finding that the absentee ballots cast in Commission District 3 could not be explained by any normal statistical measurement. District 3 is the area which the trial court found "was the center of a massive, well conceived and well orchestrated absentee ballot voter fraud scheme." Dr. Hill referred to the results of the absentee ballots as an "outlier" and an "aberrant case" so unlikely that it was "literally off the charts" of probability tables. The odds of this occurring by chance were 5,000 to 1.

Dr. Hill finally concluded it was "reasonable" that the absentee ballot deviation in favor of Suarez resulted only from voting fraud, ruling "out almost every other conceivable possibility to a high degree of probability."

An expert documents examiner, Linda Hart, concluded that 225 illegal absentee ballots were cast, in contravention of statutory requirements. An FBI agent with 26 years of experience, Hugh Cochran, identified 113 confirmed false voter addresses. There was evidence of 14 stolen ballots, and of 140 ballots that were falsely witnessed. In addition, evidence was presented that more than 480 ballots were procured or witnessed by the 29 so-called "ballot brokers" who invoked their privilege against self-incrimination instead of testifying at trial.

The trial court specifically found that the above described absentee ballot voter fraud scheme, "literally and figuratively, stole the ballot from the hands of every honest voter in the City of Miami". The trial court further found that, as a result thereof, "the integrity of the election was adversely affected." Based on our review of the record, there was certainly ample evidence of fraud to support the findings of the trial court's Final Judgment.

We are confronted with the question of whether the trial court erred in finding that the remedy for the instant absentee voting fraud was to order a new election. We hold that it did.

An important decision concerning the issue of the appropriate remedy to be provided upon a finding that absentee ballot fraud has affected the electorial process is *Bolden v. Potter*, 452 So. 2d 564 (Fla. 1984). In that case, the Supreme Court of Florida held that: "Although the will of the electorate must be protected, so must the sanctity of the ballot and the integrity of the election. Courts cannot ignore fraudulent conduct which is purposefully done to foul the election or corrupt the ballot." The Supreme

Court of Florida went on to expressly approve the trial court's remedy, which was to invalidate all of the absentee ballots and, thereafter, to solely rely on the machine vote to determine the outcome of the election. Similarly, in *Boardman v. Esteva*, 323 So. 2d 259 (Fla. 1975), *app. dism.*, 425 U.S. 967 (1976), the Supreme Court of Florida held that "The general rule is that where the number of invalid absentee ballots is more than enough to change the result of an election, then the election shall be determined solely upon the basis of machine vote."

We are mindful of the fact that the trial court found there was no evidence that Mr. Suarez knew of, or in any way participated in, the absentee voter fraud. However, as the Supreme Court stated in *Bolden v. Potter*:

> We also reject the district court's implication that the burden of proof, with regard to fraud or corruption, is dependent upon the status of the offender. It makes no difference whether the fraud is committed by candidates, election officials, or third parties. The evil to be avoided is the same, irrespective of the source. As long as the fraud, from whatever source, is such that the true result of the election cannot be ascertained with reasonable certainty, the ballots affected should be invalidated.

.... Mr. Suarez contends that to eliminate all of the absentee ballots would effectively disenfranchise those absentee voters who legally voted. We first note that unlike the right to vote, which is assured every citizen by the United States Constitution, the ability to vote by absentee ballot is a privilege. In fact, the Florida Legislature created this privilege by enacting statutory provisions separate from those applicable to voting at the polls....

Consistent with the fact that there is no legal precedent in Florida to support the action of the trial court in ordering a new election as the proper remedy upon a finding of massive absentee voter fraud is the public policy of the State of Florida to not encourage such fraud. Rather, it must be remembered that the sanctity of free and honest elections is the cornerstone of a true democracy. As the Supervisor of Elections, David Leahy, noted during his trial testimony, were we to approve a new election as the proper remedy following extensive absentee voting fraud, we would be sending out the message that the worst that would happen in the face of voter fraud would be another election....

Further, we refuse to disenfranchise the more than 40,000 voters who, on November 4, 1997, exercised their constitutionally guaranteed right to vote in the polling places of Miami. In the absence of any findings of impropriety relating to the machine vote in this election, public policy dictates that we not void those constitutionally protected votes, the majority of which were cast for Mr. Carollo. In addition, a candidate who wins an election by virtue of obtaining a majority of the votes cast is entitled to take office as a result thereof, and not be forced into a second election, whether it is a statutorily mandated run-off election or a court ordered special election, when the said second election only comes about due to absentee ballot fraud, in the first election, that favored one of his or her opponents....

To the extent that the trial court's remedy, to correct the massive absentee ballot fraud that occurred in the November 4, 1997, election involved the holding of a completely new election which, in effect, invalidated all of the machine votes that were cast by the voters in person at the polls, we find that such a remedy is not warranted by Florida legal precedent. As a result, the voiding of the entire election and the ordering of a new election is hereby reversed, and this cause is remanded to the trial court with directions to enter a Final Judgment, forthwith, that voids and vacates the absentee ballots only and, furthermore, provides that the outcome of the November 4, 1997, City of Miami Mayoral election shall be determined solely upon the machine ballots cast at the polls, resulting in the election of Joe Carollo as Mayor of the City of Miami. Consequently, the trial court's Final Judgment shall delete the requirement of the holding of a new election since, by virtue of the foregoing, there is no need for such an election....

NOTES AND QUESTIONS

1.   Following the District Court of Appeals' decision, a group of voters who had cast legal absentee votes in the Miami mayoral election brought suit in federal court, claiming that their right to vote had been unconstitutionally denied. In *Scheer v. City of Miami*, 15 F. Supp. 2d 1338 (S.D. Fla. 1998), the district court rejected their challenge. As a preliminary matter, the district court held that the plaintiffs had standing. The defendants had argued that the plaintiffs lacked standing because even if their votes for Suarez had been counted, Carollo would still have won the election. But Chief Judge Davis found that the state courts had not identified "exactly" how many absentee ballots had been cast illegally:

> If they could, the remedy would have been obvious—invalidate the fraudulent votes and count the lawful ones. However, isolating the number of fraudulent votes is and was impossible. Therefore, it is also impossible to know for sure if Carollo would have won the election even counting the class in this case. Accordingly, Plaintiffs have standing because they have an identifiable harm—their votes were invalidated even though they were lawfully cast.

Leaving aside the remedial question, however, is the question of electoral outcome irrelevant to the issue of standing? That is, suppose a state electoral process threw out even a single legally cast ballot. Given the nature of the right to vote, wouldn't that voter have suffered an injury in fact sufficient to confer standing? Suppose, as we discuss later in this section, a voter sued for damages. It seems unlikely he would be required to prove as an element in his case that his vote would have changed the outcome.

On another preliminary question, Chief Judge Davis rejected the Florida court's right/privilege distinction. Regardless of whether Florida's conferral of the ability to vote by absentee ballot was a pure act of legislative grace, once the state had conferred that ability in a particular election, it could not change the rules after a ballot was cast.

On the merits, Chief Judge Davis refused to find that the state courts had violated a federal constitutional right in their decision to disregard all absentee ballots rather than requiring a special election:

> Our predecessor court in *Gamza v. Aguirre*, 619 F.2d 449, 453 (5th Cir. 1980), recognized a distinction between state laws and patterns of state action that systematically deny equality in voting, and episodic events that, despite non-discriminatory laws, may result in the dilution of an individual's vote. Unlike systematically discriminatory laws, isolated events that adversely affect individuals are not presumed to be a [constitutional violation]. . . .

The Ninth Circuit, in refusing to meddle with a state election, summarized the law in all of these election cases:

A general pattern emerges from all of these cases taken together. Mere fraud or mistake will not render an election invalid. However, a court will strike down an election . . . if two elements are present: (1) likely reliance by voters on an established election procedure and/or official pronouncements about what the procedure will be in the coming election; and (2) significant disenfranchisement that results from a change in the election procedures.

This case is about mere fraud—nothing more. It has nothing to do with reliance on an established procedure or a change in the election procedures. If anything, the voters must be presumed to have known of Florida's procedure of voiding all absentee votes if there was evidence of fraud. . . .

Florida courts have established and followed this policy for good reason. The absentee voting scheme as it now exists in Florida lends itself to fraud, manipulation, and deceit. The state legislature continues to attempt improvements, but to date criminals have found ways to abuse the system. Accordingly, Florida courts for the past sixty years have constructed a means of dealing with absentee voter fraud. It is not this Court's province to upset this remedy as it has been well thought out by the state courts. For example, as the state appellate court in this case noted, "were we to approve a new election as the proper remedy following extensive absentee voting fraud, we would be sending out the message that the worst that would happen in the face of voter fraud would be another election."

"Even if Plaintiffs were able to set forth a constitutional violation, the Court must take into account equitable considerations in fashioning the appropriate remedy in each case.... A federal court reaching into the state political process to invalidate an election necessarily implicates important concerns of federalism and state sovereignty. It should not resort to this intrusive remedy until it has carefully weighed all equitable considerations." *Gjersten v. Board of Election Comm'rs*, 791 F.2d 472, 478 (7th Cir. 1986)....

The almost circus atmosphere surrounding this case makes the remedy Plaintiffs seek even more drastic and staggering.... The City of Miami has been scarred by the events that took place during and after the 1997 Mayoral election. The City and its citizens are finally starting to heal. Equity necessitates that the Court not re-open these wounds....

Note the way in which Chief Judge Davis's treatment of the plaintiffs' claims mirrors the United States Supreme Court's treatment of claims of the denial of procedural due process in *Parratt v. Taylor*, 451 U.S. 527 (1981), and its progeny. In those cases, the Court has held that a state's deprivation of a property or liberty interest—and state actors may perpetrate such deprivations quite often—rises to the level of a Fourteenth Amendment violation only when the state fails to provide adequate procedural protections. In cases where the deprivation is unauthorized or unforeseeable, such protection may be provided by a post-deprivation hearing. For a discussion of the procedural due process issue in the context of voting, see Peter M. Shane, *Disappearing Democracy: How* Bush v. Gore *Undermined the Federal Right to Vote for Presidential Electors*, 29 Fla. St. U. L. Rev. 535 (2001).

2. The 2004 Washington state gubernatorial election involved a similar problem. The initial vote count showed Republican candidate Dino Rossi prevailing over Democratic candidate Christine Gregoire by a mere 261 votes out of more than 2.8 million cast. Rossi's narrow margin of victory triggered a state-law provision mandating a machine recount, although the margin was not so narrow as to trigger a mandatory manual recount. After that machine recount, Rossi was 42 votes ahead of Gregoire. The Democratic party then filed for a manual recount, pursuant to state law. After that manual recount, the outcome switched: Gregoire now prevailed by 130 votes. The state legislature, dominated by Democrats, accepted the election results along a party-line vote, with only one Democrat breaking ranks to vote against acceptance. The Secretary of State certified the result and issued Gregoire the certificate of election, thereby making her Governor.

Rossi's only remaining option was litigation to overturn the election results through an election contest suit. In that suit, Rossi argued that more illegal votes had been cast and counted than the margin by which Gregoire had been certified the winner. He thus sought a court-ordered new election.

The trial court held that 1,678 illegal votes had been cast, more than the margin of victory. But the court also held there was no evidence of election fraud and no evidence of partisan manipulation in the election errors that had occurred. Absent that, the court held that state law permitted an election result to be overturned only when the contestant could show that the illegal results had changed the election's result. Rossi could not do so because there was no way to prove conclusively, after the election, that any of these illegal votes had been cast for Gregoire, if so, how many, or that properly excluding these votes would have changed the outcome. The most interesting aspect of the litigation was Rossi's theory of "proportional deduction," backed up by the testimony of social scientists, as his attempt to deal with the difficult of proving how individual ballots had been cast. The precincts in which various illegal ballots had been cast were known. Rossi argued that the court should take the overall proportions of votes cast for each candidate in a precinct and discount the illegal ballots in that precinct by the same proportion (e.g., if 60% of the votes in a precinct went for Gregoire, 60% of the illegal ballots in a precinct should be assumed to have been cast for her).

In *Borders v. King County*, No. 05–2–00027–3 (Chelen County Super. Ct. 2005), available at http://www.secstate.wa.gov/documentvault/ Final% 20Judgment694.pdf, the court resolutely rejected this theory: "With respect to proportional deduction, the Court concludes that an election such as this should not be overturned because one judge picks a number and applies a proportional deduction analysis. To do so, within the context of the facts of this case, would constitute the ultimate act of judicial egotism and judicial activism which neither the voters for Mr. Rossi or for Ms. Gregoire should condone." The court's decision was delivered orally from the bench and remains unpublished. Rossi chose not to appeal. Had there been fraud, with more fraudulent votes cast than the margin of victory, the court would have overturned the election, but absent fraud, the court would not order a new election or change the outcome without more specific proof regarding for whom specific illegal ballots had been cast. Gregoire now sits as Washington's Governor.

For relevant newspaper coverage, see Angela Galloway, *It's Rossi, by 0.0093%*, Seattle Post–Intelligencer, November 18, 2004; Chris McGain & Angela Galloway, *Recount Gives Rossi a 42–Vote Victory*, Seattle Post–Intelligencer, November 25, 2004; Chris McGann & Kyle Arnold, *Divided Joint Session Certifies Gregoire Governor–Elect*, Seattle Post–Intelligencer, January 12, 2005. See also *Developments in the Law, Voting and Democracyt, Part IV: Deducting Illegal Votes in Contested Elections*, 119 Harv. L. Rev. 1155 (2006) (discussing the *Borders* case); Joaquin G. Avila, *The Washington 2004 Gubernatorial Election Crisis: The Necessity of Restoring Public Confidence in the Electoral Process*, 29 Seattle U.L. Rev. 313 (2005).

3.   The role of statistical evidence in election challenges is an interesting, and perhaps underanalyzed, question. If a reviewing court or administrative body knows that some number of votes have been cast illegally, but does not know for whom those votes were cast, it turns out that courts' intuitions are often misguided.

In *Mathematical Probability In Election Challenges*, 73 Colum. L. Rev. 241 (1973), Michael O. Finkelstein and Herbert E. Robbins set out a formula: $Z = d^* \sqrt{(s-k)/sk}$, where d is the winner's plurality, s is the number of votes cast for the winner or his challenger, and k is the number of invalid votes cast for the winner or his challenger. The value of z—which is a standard normal variate—determines the probability that the outcome would be reversed, and as z increases, this probability declines very quickly. For example, if z is 0.5, the probability of reversal is .81, while if $z=1$, the probability is .16, and if $z=1.5$, the probability is .07. Thus, there is less than a one percent chance of reversal if z is greater than 2.4. A full table of values and associated probabilities can be found in most statistics textbooks. *See, e.g.*, Alan Agresti & Barbara Finley, Statistical Methods for the Social Sciences tbl. A (3d ed. 1997).

Consider a case like *Ippolito v. Power*, 22 N.Y.2d 594 (1968), which involved a primary election for positions in the state Democratic Party. There were 2,827 votes cast, and the winner's plurality was 17 votes. In order to vote, each voter was required to sign in on an individual voter registration card. The courts found 101 votes that were suspect "for some kind of irregularity without any evidence of fraud or intentional misconduct." Six voter sign-in cards had been submitted by registered Conservatives (who could not have voted in the election); seven cards had not been signed; one card was "irregular" in some undescribed way; nineteen cards were submitted without any indication of party enrollment; and there were 68 more votes than there were sign-in cards to begin with. The New York Court of Appeals affirmed a lower court's decision to order a new election because "it does not strain the probabilities to assume a likelihood that the questioned votes produced or could produce a change in the results." Finkelstein and Robbins point out that the probability of there being a different outcome in a case like *Ippolito* is roughly 5 percent. That is, if we imagine all of the votes as pebbles being placed in an urn, with the winner's pebbles being white and the loser's being red, and we were to draw 101 pebbles out of the urn, there is a five percent chance that the number of red pebbles remaining in the urn would exceed the number of white pebbles.

Had the New York Court of Appeals understood this, would they have found a significantly substantial probability to overturn the election? What does this say about margins of error generally?

Note that Finkelstein and Robbins's model presupposes that the illegally cast votes are not systematically biased towards one candidate. In cases where either eyewitness, circumstantial, or statistical evidence suggests that a particular candidate was the disproportionate beneficiary of illegal votes, the likelihood of a changed outcome may be much higher.

Obviously, if *all* of the voters who cast illegal ballots in *Ippolito* had supported the winning candidate, the probability that the outcome would have been different in the absence of improper votes would have been 100 percent.

4. Setting aside all absentee ballots as the remedy in a case where only some absentee ballots were cast illegally may seem a draconian remedy. Of course if it were possible to identify precisely which ballots were invalid, the remedy would be clear: disregard those ballots and only those ballots. Despite the general sanctity of the secret ballot, it may sometimes be possible to do so. Consider, for example, N.J. Stat. § 19:29–7 (2000), and N.J.R. Evid.513, which govern state election contests in New Jersey. Section 19:29–7 provides that in an election contest, "[t]he judge may require any person called as a witness who voted at such election to answer touching his qualification as a voter, and if the court, from his examination, or otherwise, is satisfied that he was not a qualified voter in the election district where he voted, he may compel him to disclose for whom he voted." And Rule 513 provides that "[e]very person has a privilege to refuse to disclose the tenor of his vote at a political election unless the judge finds that the vote was cast illegally." The predecessor versions of these provisions were implicitly approved against federal constitutional attack in *Hoch v. Phelan*, 796 F.Supp. 130 (D.N.J. 1992).

Even in the case where it is impossible to identify and disregard individual illegal ballots, there is a potential compromise position between excluding all potentially tainted ballots or conducting a new election. It may be possible to reduce each candidate's total according to some formula that allocates improperly cast votes among them. For a discussion of this issue, see the wonderfully captioned *In re the Purported Election of Bill Durkin*, 700 N.E.2d 1089 (Ill. App. 1998). Durkin, Finn, and Tenpas were candidates for mayor of Waukegan, Illinois. Durkin, the Democratic candidate, received 4,296 total votes, Finn, an independent, received 4,260 total votes, and Tenpas, whose party affiliation was not noted by the court, received of 1,069.

Finn challenged the results and showed that 71 absentee ballots were invalid, because the voter had failed to provide a reason on his or her application, as required by state law. The absentee ballots in each precinct were commingled with the votes cast in person, so that it was not possible to ascertain the specific candidate for whom the illegal absentee ballots were cast (although it was possible to determine how many absentee votes there were in each precinct).

Finn argued that since 51 of the 71 absentee voters whose votes were determined to be illegal had declared their political party membership as Democrats in a primary election held on February 25, 1997, the "party affiliation method" should be used to allocate those votes. Those 51 votes should be subtracted from Durkin's vote total because Durkin was the Democratic candidate in the general election. The other 20 votes should be deducted from Durkin, Finn, and Tenpas according to the percentages of votes each candidate received in the precincts in which these votes were cast. The net effect of Finn's proposed allocation was a lowering of Durkin's vote total to 4,232 votes and a lowering of Finn's vote total to 4,254 votes. Thus, according to Finn's proposed allocation of the 71 illegal votes, he was the winner of the election.

Not surprisingly, Durkin (and the county canvassing board of which he was a member) proposed using the "proportion method" alone. Durkin's proposal apportioned the 71 illegal votes between Finn and Durkin on the basis of the percentage of votes each candidate received in the precincts where the illegal votes had been cast. According to this proposed allocation, Durkin would lose 49.8675 votes and Finn would lose 17.7329 votes. This would lower Durkin's total votes received to 4,246.1325 votes and Finn's total votes received to 4,242.2671 votes, leaving Durkin still as the winner, albeit now by only four votes.

The courts agreed with Durkin, rejecting the party affiliation method because this contest involved an independent candidate:

> It is well established that a court may use party affiliation to determine the candidate for whom illegal votes were cast and, when such votes have been identified, to allocate such illegal votes against that candidate by deducting them from that candidate's vote total. *See, e.g., Talbott v. Thompson*, 350 Ill. 86, 97–98, 182 N.E. 784 (1932) (party affiliation raises presumption voter cast ballot for nominee of her or his political party, and presumption determines for whom ballot was cast in absence of countervailing evidence); *Leach v. Johnson*, 20 Ill.App.3d 713, 718–19, 313 N.E.2d 636 (1974) (absent better evidence, party affiliation is best evidence for determining candidate for whom illegal vote was cast). This is the party affiliation method of allocating illegal votes.

> It is also well established that, when the evidence does not disclose the recipient of illegal votes, such votes should be eliminated by allocating them to the candidates in the same proportion that each candidate received votes in the precincts where the illegal votes were cast. This is the proportion method of allocating illegal votes. . . .

> Using the party affiliation method in this case would be unfair because, as the trial court noted, only candidates affiliated with a political party can lose votes when this method is applied, while an independent candidate cannot lose votes. Of course, if the party affiliation method reliably determined the candidate for whom the illegal votes were cast, its use would be appropriate. However, we believe that the circumstances of this case cast doubt on the reliability of the party affiliation method in determining the candidate for whom the illegal votes were cast. We believe that determining party affiliation, and therefore how votes were cast, in a general election that includes a strong independent candidate based on the voting records from a previous primary

election in which the independent candidate did not participate, as in this case, is not a reliable method of determining how votes were cast. Because the independent candidate did not participate in the primary election, voters in that election did not have a chance to vote for the independent candidate at that time. Based on the strong showing of petitioner, the independent candidate for mayor in the general election, it is reasonable to conclude that many of the voters who participated in the primary election split their tickets and voted for the independent candidate in the general election. Without evidence of the numbers of such voters, the party affiliation established by the primary election records is unreliable.

5. If there are only two candidates in an election, throwing out illegally cast votes—if they can be identified—may be an entirely adequate remedy. Subtracting votes to which a candidate is not entitled poses no theoretical problem. But what happens if the problem isn't that the votes are illegal, and thus shouldn't be counted at all, but rather than the votes should be reassigned to a different candidate? Is it possible, or desirable, to *add* votes to a candidate's total? The controversy in Florida during the 2000 election over the so-called "butterfly ballot" in Palm Beach County poses this question in a particularly dramatic form.

Palm Beach County, like roughly 20 percent of the counties in the United States, then used a punch card voting system. Voters insert blank cards into machines that list the candidates for office and using a stylus punch out pre-scored holes. In the 2000 presidential election, Palm Beach County used a ballot design in which the holes were placed between two columns of candidates. George W. Bush was the first candidate listed in the left-hand column (because, as a matter of state law, the candidate whose party received the highest number of votes in the previous gubernatorial election received the first spot on the ballot), and Al Gore was the second candidate listed in the left-hand column (because the Democrats had received the second highest number of votes in the last gubernatorial election). Pat Buchanan, a conservative candidate of the Reform Party, was the first candidate listed in the right-hand column.

Given the two columns of candidates, the first hole was that for Bush. But the second hole did not correspond to the second candidate on the ballot, Gore. Rather, it corresponded to the first candidate in the *right-hand* column, namely, Buchanan. The hole for Gore was thus the third hole.

On Election Day itself, voters in Palm Beach County began to complain about the form of the ballot and to claim that they had mistakenly voted for Buchanan when they meant to vote for Gore. A group of voters filed suit in Florida state court, claiming that the ballot had violated various state-law requirements regarding the order of candidates' names on the ballot and the placement of the holes. Ultimately, their claims were rejected by the trial court and the Florida Supreme Court, which held that the ballot did not violate state law. *Fladell v. Palm Beach County Canvassing Board*, 772 So.2d 1240 (Fla. 2000).

Leaving aside the question of the ballot's legality under state law, the possibility that the ballot might have affected the outcome of the election in Florida, and thus across the nation, seems fairly well established. A group of political scientists used a variety of techniques to study the Palm Beach results. In an analysis of returns from 4300 counties across the United States (in every state but Michigan [where Buchanan was not on the ballot], Alaska, Hawaii, and Delaware), they concluded that Palm Beach County produced the second most anomalous result "in terms of having exceptionally high support for Buchanan that deviates from expected patterns." Jonathan N. Wand, Kenneth W. Shotts, Jasjeet S. Sekhon, Walter R. Mebane, Jr. and Michael C. Herron, *Voting Irregularities in Palm Beach County* (2000). The authors analyzed county-by-county data from Florida and concluded, first, that "compared to other Florida counties as measured in a number of ways, the Palm Beach County vote share for Buchanan is extremely large. In fact, what we know about other counties in Florida implies that this vote share is so large as to be practically unbelievable. It is virtually certain that there is something unique about Palm Beach County, and the only obvious factor that is unique to Palm Beach County is its ballot format," and, second, using census data, that "Palm Beach County actually contains relatively few Buchanan supporters." (A later version of the study is published as Jonathan N. Wand et al., *The Butterfly Did It: The Aberrant Vote for Buchanan in Palm Beach County, Florida*, 95 Am. Pol. Sci. Rev. (2001).)

Other social scientists estimated that roughly 2000 of the 3400 votes Buchanan received in Palm Beach County had been cast by voters who thought they were voting for Gore. *See, e.g.*, Henry E. Brady, *Report on Voting and Ballot Form in Palm Beach County* (Nov. 16, 2000) (available from http://elections.fas.harvard.edu/statement/hbrady/).

What sorts of remedies might be available to a court that found the Palm Beach ballot to be illegal? In the special context of the presidential election, a new election was never a realistic possibility. Among other things, the requirement for a uniform national election day seemed to preclude it. But suppose this had been an election for statewide office. Could a court reallocate votes on the basis of statistical evidence regarding the "expected" outcome?

In this context, consider how courts and the public have thought about an analogous issue—how to conduct the decennial census. (We treat this issue more fully in Chapter 3.) Most social scientists agree that it is more accurate to use "adjusted" figures than to rely on the initial count, since statistical techniques can correct predictable under-and over-counts of identifiable groups. Nonetheless, Congress has mandated using the unadjusted figures to apportion congressional seats among the states, and many states also require use of the uncorrected figures. To some extent, this choice may reflect predictions about the partisan political consequences of choosing one set of numbers over the other. But there may also be a visceral preference for using the actual numbers because a sample just doesn't "feel" like an actual enumeration. Consider in this light the pressure for a manual recount in Florida. In an essay in the New York Times, Lawrence M. Krauss, the head of the physics department at Case Western Reserve University wrote that the so-called "law of large numbers suggests that roughly 68 percent of the time, if one performed precisely the same experiment on precisely the same system over and over again," that is, if one counted and recounted Florida's six million ballots repeatedly, "the total number of events [i.e., votes] counted would be expected to vary by at least 2,000 events." *Analyze This: A Physicist on Applied Politics*, N.Y. Times, Nov. 21, 2000, at F4. Thus, there may be no scientific reason to expect one counting method rather than another to produce the most reliable result, especially if the standard for a legally cast ballot is not clear in the first place.

6. In one case, a state trial court did reallocate votes among candidates, but its decision was overturned on appeal. *Bradley v. Perrodin*, 106 Cal. App.4th 1153 (Ct. App. 2nd Dept. 2003), *rev. denied*, 2003 WL 22725661 (Cal. 2003).

The case concerned, among other things a hotly contested city council runoff election in Compton, California. The local election official conceded that he had listed the candidates' names on the ballot in the wrong order. (California law requires placement based on a random alphabetical draw before each election. *See* Cal. Election Code § 13112; *Gould v. Grubb*, 536 P.2d 1337 (Cal. 1975) (striking down a city charter provision that required that any incumbent seeking reelection automatically be given the advantageous top ballot as discriminatory).)

Based on expert testimony about the "primacy" effect—the advantage a first-listed candidate enjoys, presumably because some number of voters simply vote for the first candidate listed—the trial court found that candidate Irving had received 295 extra votes because she had erroneously been listed first. So she shifted the 295 votes to candidate Andrews, which gave Andrews more votes, and declared Andrews the winner.

On appeal, the court of appeal held that Irving should have been disqualified for unrelated election fraud:

> Although we agree Irving's election was properly annulled, we disagree that judgment was properly entered for Andrews, who was judicially declared elected despite her failure to win the highest number of legal votes in the June runoff election. Under [Cal. Election Code §] 16603, having found Irving, the winning candidate, disqualified for having committed misdeeds that failed to change the result of the election, the trial court should have entered judgment "annulling and setting aside the election." The Elections Code does not permit the trial court ... to

declare another candidate elected by shifting legal votes between the two candidates under the primacy effect theory. . . .

[W]e find that by shifting votes from Irving to Andrews based solely on the primacy effect theory the trial court exceeded its authority. Under sections 16203 [and] 16703, only illegal votes may be discarded in an election contest. If the court finds, after discarding the illegal votes given for the winning candidate, that another candidate "has the highest number of legal votes, the court shall declare that person elected." Otherwise, if discarding the illegal votes given for the winning candidate would not change the result of the election, and the winning candidate is disqualified from taking office due to having committed offenses against the elective franchise, the court shall enter judgment "annulling and setting aside the election.". . . .

Instead, in a ruling unprecedented, to our knowledge, in this country, the trial court shifted 295 legal votes from Irving to Andrews based solely on the 3.32% primacy effect assumed to be enjoyed, on average, by those listed first on the ballot. While many courts and legislatures have recognized the advantage afforded to candidates whose names are listed first on the ballot, no judicial or statutory authority exists to reverse the results of an election where, due to unintentional clerical error, the ballot listed the candidates in the wrong alphabetical order. . . . Name-order error occurring in the absence of fraud and resulting purely from unintentional clerical error, as in this case, is not a valid ground for an election contest. . . . The fact that 295 legal votes may have been cast for Irving solely because her name was erroneously listed first on the ballot does not, in itself, impeach the integrity of those 295 votes. Legal votes randomly cast by the least informed or least interested voters are entitled to the same weight as legal votes cast by the most highly educated and informed voters in our society. The legality or illegality of a vote cast by a qualified voter in a lawful manner does not depend upon the voter's motive or purpose in voting a certain way. To shift 295 legal votes to "correct" the votes "randomly" cast for Irving solely as a result of her erroneous advantageous ballot position (and to award those same "random" votes to Andrews based solely on the primacy effect theory) would be, without any lawful justification, to disenfranchise those 295 voters.

What notion of voting and autonomy does *Bradley* evoke? Is there in fact anything different about reallocating votes among candidates on the basis of statistical estimates as opposed to simply invalidating votes?

D. Permanently Enjoining a Particular Election Practice

The remedies discussed in the preceding sections all focus, to one degree or another, on discrete elections. In those kinds of litigation, plaintiffs seek to change election outcomes. But there are other remedies that focus not on the results of a particular election, but rather on more systemic change.

Throughout this book, we have focused on particular constitutional or statutory constraints on electoral practices, ranging from fundamental rights equal protection/due process scrutiny for restrictions on the franchise, to one-person, one-vote's impact on legislative reapportionment, to the Voting Rights Act's protection of minority voting rights, to the First Amendment's constraints on campaign finance regulation. The usual context in which such questions arise is litigation by plaintiffs who seek declaratory judgments or permanent injunctive relief against the use of practices that deny, dilute, or abridge their rights.

The general equitable principles that govern such cases can be stated relatively simply, although in practice they can raise difficult questions. Having found a statutory or constitutional violation, the courts are to order relief that remedies the violation as completely as possible. *See, e.g.,* S. Rep. No. 97–417, p. 31 (1982) (stating, with respect to violations of section 2 of the Voting Rights Act that "[t]he court should exercise its traditional equitable powers to fashion the relief so that it completely remedies the prior dilution of minority voting strength and fully provides equal opportunity for minority citizens to participate and to elect candidates of their choice."). At the same time, precisely because regulation of the political process trenches so intimately on core state decisionmaking, the courts are required to give states a fair opportunity to propose a remedy before imposing one of their own devising. *See, e.g., Reynolds v. Sims,* 377 U.S. 533, 586 (1964) (finding that, even once the district court had found a violation of one-person, one-vote, it "acted wisely in declining to stay the impending primary election," "properly refrained from acting further until the Alabama Legislature had been given an opportunity to remedy the admitted discrepancies in the State's legislative apportionment scheme," and "correctly recognized that legislative reapportionment is primarily a matter for legislative consideration and determination, and that judicial relief becomes appropriate only when a legislature fails to reapportion according to federal constitutional requisites in a timely fashion after having had an adequate opportunity to do so").

Oddly enough, relatively little of the extensive federal case law on equitable remedies and the political process focuses on the nitty-gritty of balloting itself. But in the wake of *Bush v. Gore,* this may well change. There, the Court noted that "[t]his case has shown that punch card balloting machines can produce an unfortunate number of ballots which are not punched in a clean, complete way by the voter. After the current counting, it is likely legislative bodies nationwide will examine ways to improve the mechanisms and machinery for voting." The Court's decision prompted several lawsuits, in Florida and elsewhere, challenging the use of punch card systems. For copies of the pleadings in these cases, see http://

election2000.stanford.edu. Is there also a role for courts in policing voting technologies?

One source of litigation might be section 2 of the Voting Rights Act, whose contours we explore in detail in Chapters 7–9. Essentially, section 2 forbids the use of any voting "qualification or prerequisite to voting or standard, practice, or procedure" that makes it more difficult for minority voters to participate in the political process or elect the candidate of their choice. A different section of the Voting Rights Act, § 14(c)(3), defines "voting" to include "all action necessary to make a vote effective in any primary, special, or general election, including, but not limited to, registration, listing pursuant to this Act, or other action required by law prerequisite to voting, casting a ballot, *and having such ballot counted properly and included in the appropriate totals of votes cast* with respect to candidates for public or party office and propositions for which votes are received in an election." 42 U.S.C. § 1973*l*(c)(3) (emphasis added). Interestingly enough, most litigation under the Act has concentrated on rules for aggregating votes—such as the use of at-large elections or the choice among district boundaries in reapportionment plans—rather than on the nuts and bolts of the actual voting process. In part, this may be a function of a general lack of awareness about problems with electoral technology: since most elections do not appear to be very close, the public generally may not be concerned with how votes are counted. In part, it may also be a function of the major impetus behind voting rights litigation: the desire of politically active minority individuals and organizations to obtain election rules that enable them to elect candidates. At-large elections and districting plans that dilute minority voting strength are more obvious targets for such lawsuits.

There are, however, cases in which the Voting Rights Act has been applied to enjoin the future use of particular election technologies. The leading section 5 coverage case, *Allen v. State Board of Elections*, 393 U.S. 544 (1969), held that Virginia was required to seek preclearance of changes in the way illiterate voters could cast write-in votes and could not implement its new statute unless and until it complied with the Voting Rights Act.

E. DAMAGES

In *Memphis Community School District v. Stachura*, 477 U.S. 299, 312 n.14 (1986), the Supreme Court noted a long series of cases in which plaintiffs who were illegally prevented from voting in state elections suffered compensable injury. These cases extend back at least to *Ashby v. White*, 2 Ld. Raym. 938, 92 Eng. Rep. 126 (1703).

A number of nineteenth century cases involved damages. For example, purely as a matter of state law, the Maine Supreme Judicial Court in *Sanders v. Getchell*, 76 Me. 158 (1884), ordered the award of $25 in damages to a plaintiff whom the Waterville selectmen refused to place on the town's voting rolls because he had moved to the town to attend an educational institution. (The ability of students to register where they attend school remains a live issue today.) The Supreme Judicial Court held that under the circumstances of this case—the plaintiff was 32 years old at the time he sought to register and had lived in Waterville for many years— "[t]o deprive him of his right to vote . . . was not reasonable." At the same time, the court disagreed with the plaintiff that "the damages should be either exemplary or severe. We think the wisest and most just conclusion, in view of all the circumstances, will be to accord to the plaintiff no greater damages than sufficient to carry the costs."

In the early twentieth century, many of the White Primary cases (discussed in Chapter 4) were brought as damages actions. In *Nixon v. Herndon*, 273 U.S. 536 (1927), for example, the plaintiff—a black registered voter from El Paso—sued the Judges of Elections for refusing to permit him to vote in a primary election. He claimed damages of $5,000. Texas had enacted a statute that provided that "in no event shall a negro be eligible to participate in a Democratic party primary election held in the State of Texas. . . ."

The defendants moved to dismiss the complaint on the ground that case raised a nonjusticiable political question. The Supreme Court, in an opinion by Justice Holmes, unanimously disagreed:

> The objection that the subject matter of the suit is political is little more than a play upon words. Of course the petition concerns political action but it alleges and seeks to recover for private damage. That private damage may be caused by such political action and may be recovered for in a suit at law hardly has been doubted for over two hundred years, since *Ashby v. White*, 2 Ld. Raym. 938, 3 id. 320, and has been recognized by this Court. *Wiley v. Sinkler*, 179 U.S. 58, 64, 65. *Giles v. Harris*, 189 U.S. 475, 485. *See also* Judicial Code, § 24 (11), (12), (14). Act of March 3, 1911, c. 231; 36 Stat. 1087, 1092. If the defendants' conduct was a wrong to the plaintiff the same reasons that allow a recovery for denying the plaintiff a vote at a final election allow it for denying a vote at the primary election that may determine the final result.

The Court's citation of *Wiley v. Sinkler*, 179 U.S. 58 (1900), illustrates a practical problem with using damages actions. The plaintiff, a resident of Charleston, South Carolina, sued the city's board of election managers to recover damages in the sum of $2500 for wrongfully and wilfully rejecting his vote in the 1894 congressional elections. The Supreme Court unanimously recognized a qualified voter's right to sue for damages:

> The right to vote for members of the Congress of the United States is not derived merely from the constitution and laws of the State in which they are chosen, but has its foundation in the Constitution of the United States. . . .

This action is brought against election officers to recover damages for their rejection of the plaintiff's vote for a member of the House of Representatives of the United States. The complaint, by alleging that the plaintiff was at the time, under the constitution and laws of the State of South Carolina and the Constitution and laws of the United States, a duly qualified elector of the State, shows that the action is brought under the Constitution and laws of the United States.

The damages are laid at the sum of $2500. What amount of damages the plaintiff shall recover in such an action is peculiarly appropriate for the determination of a jury, and no opinion of the court upon that subject can justify it in holding that the amount in controversy was insufficient to support the jurisdiction of the Circuit Court.

Nonetheless, the Court unanimously affirmed the dismissal of the plaintiff's complaint because he could not show that he had been properly registered to vote under South Carolina's draconian registration scheme (which had been designed essentially to disenfranchise black voters.) As we discuss in Chapter 2 with respect to *Giles v. Harris*, 189 U.S. 475 (1903), and a similar registration scheme in Alabama, the Supreme Court was essentially unwilling at the turn of the century to order injunctive relief against discriminatory registration systems.

By contrast, consider the one reported federal case in which damages were awarded.

Wayne v. Venable

260 F. 64 (8th Cir. 1919).

■ JOHN SANBORN, CIRCUIT JUDGE

[The plaintiffs in this case, J.A. Venable and J.V. Boyd sued the defendants] for $5,000 damages and $10,000 punitive damages, because, as each of the plaintiffs alleged, [the defendants] conspired and combined with each other and others to prevent them ... from casting their votes ... for presidential electors, United States Senator, and a member of Congress at the general election in the [Eagle] township on November 7, 1916.... [T]he two actions were consolidated and tried together, and they resulted in a verdict in favor of each of the plaintiffs against Wayne and Alexander for $2,000. Judgments accordingly were rendered....

The right of qualified electors to vote for a member of Congress at a general state election, which is also an election at which a Congressman is to be lawfully voted for and elected, is a right "fundamentally based upon the Constitution [of the United States], which created the office of member of Congress, and declared it should be elective, and pointed to the means of ascertaining who should be electors." *Ex parte Yarbrough*, 110 U.S. 655, 664, 665 (1884).

An action for damages in the proper federal court lies by a qualified elector for his wrongful deprivation of this right by a defendant or by an effective conspiracy of several defendants who deprive him thereof. . . .

In the eyes of the law this right is so valuable that damages are presumed from the wrongful deprivation of it without evidence of actual loss of money, property, or any other valuable thing, and the amount of the damages is a question peculiarly appropriate for the determination of the jury, because each member of the jury has personal knowledge of the value of the right. . . .

The record in this case convinces that while there was a conflict in the evidence regarding nearly all the material issues of fact, there was at the close of the evidence substantial evidence of these facts. The plaintiffs were qualified electors of Eagle township at the election therein on November 7, 1916, at which election a United States Senator and a member of Congress were lawfully to be voted for and elected. At this election in Eagle township, Harry A. Wayne, Walter Alexander, and T. L. Hughes were the judges of the election. After they met at the polling place on election day they appointed James T. Ritchie a special deputy sheriff to assist in conducting the election, and instructed him how he should admit into a schoolroom, where the voting was conducted, those desiring to vote, and that he should admit them one at a time. . . . Mr. Leach, a qualified voter in Eagle township, had a store 50 or 75 feet from the voting place. He testified that he tried to vote half a dozen times, but Mr. Ritchie was in charge of the door and would not let him in, although automobiles were coming in and the people from them voted in preference to those theretofore at the polling place waiting for an opportunity to vote. . . .

The Statutes of Arkansas (Kirby's Dig. § 2812) provided: "The polls shall be opened at eight o'clock a.m. and shall remain continuously opened until half-past six o'clock p.m." The polls were not opened for voting until about 9:30 a.m., and a recess was taken for lunch. There were about 220 votes usually cast at an election in Eagle township generally, but at this election only about 105 were received. When the polls were opened, and for an hour or more before that time, there were about 100 men waiting for the polls to open so that they could vote. The electors were not admitted in the order of their arrival or their proximity to the polling place, but Mr. Ritchie, by calling or beckoning, selected those who should vote and admitted them, while at the same time he repeatedly refused to admit those nearer the entrance who had been waiting longer. Automobile loads of voters came to the polls from Mr. Swartz's place and Mr. Wilder's place, while many voters who had been waiting to vote and had repeatedly been refused admission to the polling room by Mr. Ritchie were still waiting to vote. Mr. Swartz came out of the polling room to these men as they came up in the automobiles, led them up to the door, and they were admitted by Ritchie and permitted to vote one after the other until they had all voted, before any other voter who had been refused admission was permitted to enter the polling place. The voting was very slow—from 5 to 20 minutes were used to get in a single vote, only one voter was admitted to the polling place at a time, and no other one was admitted until he came out, save in exceptional instances until about 15 minutes before the polls closed, when announcement was made that the polls would close in 15 minutes, the door of the polling room was opened, and during that 15 minutes voters were admitted more rapidly, but it was too late for all those present to vote, and 40 or 50 of them were still there trying to get in and vote when the polls closed, while many others who had repeatedly tried to vote and had been turned back during the day, had become satisfied that they would not be permitted to vote, and had gone away and were in that way deprived of their rights to vote. Each of the plaintiffs waited long, repeatedly advanced towards the door and tried to vote, and was repeatedly prevented by Ritchie from so doing, and in this way each of the plaintiffs was deprived of his vote and of his right to vote for any of the candidates at this election. . . .

The suggestion of counsel for the defendants that the federal court has no jurisdiction over these actions because the plaintiffs produced no direct testimony that they wanted or intended to vote at this election for a candidate for United States Senator, or for a candidate for Congressman, while they proved that they were deeply interested in the election of a candidate for a justice of the peace, is insignificant and negligible. They pleaded in their complaint that they were deprived of their right to vote for a candidate for United States Senator and for a candidate for Congressman by the conspiracy of these defendants which they alleged and the attainment of its object. They proved to the satisfaction of the jury that they were deprived of their right to vote for any one at this election by the conspiracy and the attainment of its object, and as the whole is greater than any of its parts and includes all of them, they proved that they were deprived of their rights to vote for a candidate for United States Senator and for a candidate for Congressman, and that constitutes proof of a cause of action over which the federal court has jurisdiction. . . .

The judgment below must therefore be affirmed and it is so ordered.

NOTES AND QUESTIONS

1. In *Memphis Community School District v. Stachura*, 477 U.S. 299, 312 n.14 (1986), the Supreme Court, after noting the long series of cases in which plaintiffs who were illegally prevented from voting were held to have suffered compensable injury, explained that "the 'value of the right' [to vote] in the context of these decisions is the money value of the particular loss that the plaintiff suffered—a loss of which 'each member of the jury has personal knowledge.' It is not the value of the right to vote as a general, abstract matter, based on its role in our history or system of government." How, then, ought a jury to determine the appropriate measure of damages? Is the way in which a plaintiff's rights have been denied relevant? For example, some denials may inflict greater dignitary interests than others. If the election is close and the vote of the plaintiff (or, more plausibly, a group of similarly situated plaintiffs) might have affected the outcome, are the damages greater? In *Santana v. Registrars of Voters of Worcester*, 398 Mass. 862 (1986), plaintiffs sought $25,000 in compensatory damages and $25,000 in punitive damages, introducing evidence that "the defendants' actions had caused them to become upset, angry, humiliated, distraught, frustrated and embarrassed. One plaintiff complained of a pounding headache while another said she now feels nervous, anxious and fearful when going to vote." Nonetheless, the trial judge found that none of the plaintiffs suffered financial loss or physical or emotional injury. As a result, he awarded only nominal damages and denied the plaintiffs' request for compensatory or punitive damages. The Massachusetts Supreme Judicial Court affirmed, and noted that after *Stachura*, "presumed" damages were no longer appropriate, and a plaintiff could recover for emotional distress only if it was accompanied by physical injury or was the product of willful, rather than negligent government acts.

Note also that damages are decided by juries, or at least either party to a damages lawsuit is entitled to ask for a jury. What effect will this have on a plaintiff's ability to obtain substantial damages, particularly if the plaintiff is a member of an unpopular group?

Finally, there are very few contemporary reported cases involving the award of damages to voters whose rights have been denied. There is dicta in *Palmer v. Board of Education*, 46 F.3d 682, 686 (7th Cir. 1995), suggesting that damages remain available, although voters today normally seek injunctive relief. Compare the Supreme Court's reference in *Stachura* to "whatever the wisdom of th[e] decisions [authorizing damages] in the context of the changing scope of compensatory damages over the course of this century...." Why *don't* plaintiffs seek compensatory (or punitive) damages? Is it because they want to avoid trial before juries? Are there other strategic or tactical reasons?

2. As a matter of federal statutory law, the vehicle for seeking damages is most likely 42 U.S.C. § 1983, which provides for damages whenever a person acting under color of state law "subjects ... any citizen of the United States ... to the deprivation of any rights, privileges, or immunities secured by the Constitution and laws." But there are two significant limitations on a plaintiff's ability to obtain damages (as opposed to prospective, injunctive relief). First, with respect to lawsuits against local governments (section 1983 does not permit lawsuits against states themselves), the plaintiff must show that the deprivation was pursuant to an official custom or policy, and this can be difficult to do if there is no statute involved and the denial was the result of action by a low-level official such as a poll worker. Second, with respect to lawsuits against individual government officials, the question of qualified immunity arises. Plaintiffs can obtain damages only for violations of clearly established law: if the scope of the plaintiff's right is unclear, the official is immune from damages liability. For extensive treatment of the general questions of qualified immunity and governmental liability, see John C. Jeffries, Jr., et al. Civil Rights Actions: Enforcing the Constitution (2d ed. 2007); Martin A. Schwartz & John E. Kirklin, Section 1983 Litigation: Claims and Defenses (3d ed.1997).

3. Although damages actions are apparently available, this does not mean that damages offer a sufficiently complete form of relief so as to obviate the need for injunctive relief. *See, e.g., Dillard v. Crenshaw County*, 640 F.Supp. 1347, 1363 (M.D. Ala. 1986) ("Given the fundamental nature of the right to vote, monetary remedies would obviously be inadequate in this case; it is simply not possible to pay someone for having been denied a right of this importance.").

4. Do disappointed *candidates* have the ability to seek compensatory or punitive damages?

Hutchinson v. Miller

797 F.2d 1279 (4th Cir. 1986).

■ J. HARVIE WILKINSON, CIRCUIT JUDGE

Plaintiffs are three unsuccessful candidates for public office who seek to recover approximately $9 million in damages under 42 U.S.C. § 1983, 18 U.S.C. § 1964 (Racketeer Influenced and Corrupt Organizations Act—RICO), and the common law of West Virginia, for alleged irregularities in the 1980 general election. . . .

We conclude that federal courts are not available for awards of damages to defeated candidates. . . .

I

Plaintiffs were Democratic candidates in the 1980 general election in West Virginia. John Hutchinson sought re-election to the United States House of Representatives in the Third Congressional District of West Virginia. This district included Kanawha and Boone Counties—where the disputed elections occurred—as well as twelve other counties. Plaintiff Leonard Underwood was the incumbent delegate to the state house from Kanawha County, and plaintiff William Reese sought election as a County Commissioner for Kanawha County. Hutchinson and Reese were defeated by wide margins, while Underwood's loss was a narrow one.

Underwood requested a recount of all computer punchcard ballots cast in the election. When the Kanawha County Commission denied this request, Underwood sought a writ of mandamus in the Circuit Court of Kanawha County to compel a hand count of ballots. That action was dismissed, and a similar attempt before the state Supreme Court was found to be time barred. Hutchinson filed a formal election complaint with the

United States Attorney in January, 1981. The resolution of that complaint is not revealed in the record, but apparently was not satisfactory to Hutchinson. Plaintiffs filed their original complaint in this suit in February, 1983.

As amended, the complaint in essence charges that the election night totals were pre-determined by defendants, who then conspired to cover up their activities. Named as defendants in the suit were both local officials and private citizens alleged to have acted in concert with those officials. The officials included Margaret Miller, Clerk of the County Commission of Kanawha County; Carolyn Critchfield, Ann Carroll, Darlene Dotson and Clayton Spangler, employees in the clerk's office; James Roark, the Prosecuting Attorney of Kanawha County in 1980; and Bernard Meadows, employed by the Clerk of the County Commission of Boone County. Private citizens named as defendants included Steven Miller, husband of Margaret Miller; David Staton, the successful Congressional candidate in the 1980 election; and John Cavacini, who in 1980 was associated with the campaign of Governor John D. Rockefeller, IV. Finally, plaintiffs sued Computer Election Systems, Inc. (CES), which provided computer vote tabulating systems in Kanawha County, and four employees of CES–Keith Long, Carl Clough, Cherrie Lloyd, and William Biebel.

Plaintiffs allege that a conspiracy among the defendants began as early as January, 1979, when Kanawha County Commissioners considered the use of electronic voting equipment. They suggest that the Millers' support for the CES system and their role in the bidding process reveals the genesis of a scheme to fix the 1980 election. This purported scheme continued as CES employees helped county officials prepare for the use of CES equipment in the November election. Defendants, by contrast, describe the selection and preparation of CES equipment as legitimate and lawful activity designed to assist them in the efficient conduct of the election.

The CES system provided the county with electronic punch card vote tabulation, in which voters indicated their choices on computer punch cards. After polls were closed, these cards were transported to countywide tabulation centers in locked and sealed ballot boxes. The ballots were removed by teams of workers, who arranged them for feeding into the computer and noted in log books the time when ballot boxes were opened. Plaintiffs cite as evidence of election fraud the fact that the log shows one box was opened after the computer tabulation was printed out.

Plaintiffs' main allegations focus on events at the central tabulation center for Kanawha County. They rely largely on the testimony of Walter Price, incumbent candidate for the House of Delegates who was at the center on election night. Price testified that he observed Margaret Miller manipulating computer toggle switches during the election count, purportedly in an attempt to alter vote counts. He saw an "unknown gentleman"—whom plaintiffs identify as Carl Clough—placing a phone receiver into his briefcase. Plaintiffs suggest that this activity is consistent with the use of a portable modem, perhaps in an effort to change vote totals. Price also testified that Stephen Miller took computer cards from his coat pocket and gave them to his wife, who allegedly fed the cards into the computer.

Finally, plaintiffs assert that numerous irregularities occurred after the election, including improper handling of the ballots and release of exact returns prior to the canvass, and destruction of ballots that violated the terms of W. Va. Code § 3–6–9. Plaintiffs make similar, though less detailed, allegations with respect to the election process in Boone County....

The court considered motions for directed verdicts at the close of plaintiffs' case. It found that plaintiffs' claims failed for several reasons. The court held that plaintiffs had failed to prove a conspiracy, noting that the only evidence the election was rigged was "purely speculative ... mere suspicion." It also found that plaintiffs Reese and Hutchinson had not shown that they were harmed by the alleged actions; there was no evidence that their large losses would have been victories in the absence of the alleged conspiracy. Further, finding only "mere election irregularities" and no evidence to suggest that the election was fundamentally unfair, the court held that plaintiffs had failed to prove a deprivation of a constitutional right essential to a § 1983 action. Finally, the court dismissed plaintiffs' claims under RICO, finding "absolutely no proof" that would allow it to consider the claim.

II

Though our disposition of this dispute rests on the view that damages are unavailable to defeated candidates as a method of post-election relief, we are guided by an awareness of the broader context in which this suit arises. The plaintiffs ask us to arbitrate what is essentially a political dispute over the results of an election. We find it useful, for proper understanding of this case, to discuss the structural characteristics and mechanisms for review of disputed elections. This examination reveals both the proper sphere and the limits of judicial oversight of controversies in the electoral process.

As in any suit under § 1983 the first inquiry is "whether the plaintiff has been deprived of a right 'secured by the Constitution and laws.' " *Baker v. McCollan,* 443 U.S. 137, 140 (1979). In their complaint, plaintiffs alleged that defendants deprived them of "their constitutionally protected right to participate fully and fairly in the electoral process," and "their constitutional right to vote or receive votes," and their Fifth Amendment right to hold property, in this case public office. The district court found that plaintiffs proceeded at trial as "defeated or disenfranchised candidates rather than as ... disenfranchised voters." Thus, plaintiffs essentially assert that they have been deprived of their "right to candidacy."

Courts have recognized that some restrictions on political candidates violate the Constitution because of their derivative effect on the right to vote. We assume, without deciding, that plaintiffs have sufficiently alleged

a deprivation of constitutional rights to meet the basic requirements of a
§ 1983 cause of action. That assumption, however, cannot end the matter. . . .

We first acknowledge and affirm the significant duty of federal courts
to preserve constitutional rights in the electoral process. Our role, however,
primarily addresses the general application of laws and procedures, not the
particulars of election disputes. Federal courts have, for example, invalidated class-based restrictions of the right to vote. The dilution of votes
through malapportionment has also been a major concern of the federal
judiciary. Courts have also acted to further the congressional mandate, as
expressed in the Voting Rights, that race shall not affect the right to vote.
Intervention for reasons other than racial discrimination "has tended, for
the most part, to be limited to striking down state laws or rules of general
application which improperly restrict or constrict the franchise" or otherwise burden the exercise of political rights. By these means, federal courts
have assumed an active role in protecting against dilution of the fundamental right to vote and the denial of this right through class disenfranchisement.

By contrast, "circuit courts have uniformly declined to endorse action
under § 1983 with respect to garden variety election irregularities." *See,
e.g., Welch v. McKenzie,* 765 F.2d 1311 (5th Cir. 1985); *Gamza v. Aguirre,*
619 F.2d 449 (5th Cir. 1980); *Hennings v. Grafton,* 523 F.2d 861 (7th Cir.
1975); *Pettengill v. Putnam County R–1 School District,* 472 F.2d 121 (8th
Cir. 1973); *Powell v. Power,* 436 F.2d 84 (2d Cir. 1970). These courts,
mainly considering disputes involving state elections, have declined to
interfere because of the constitutional recognition that "states are primarily responsible for their own elections," *Welch,* 765 F.2d at 1317, and that
alternative remedies are adequate to guarantee the integrity of the democratic process. The discussion of those alternative means of resolving
electoral disputes is the focus of the following section.

III

We note initially that the Constitution anticipates that the electoral
process is to be largely controlled by the states and reviewed by the
legislature. This control reaches elections for federal and state office.
Article I, sec. 4, cl. 1, grants to the states the power to prescribe, subject to
Congressional preemption, the "Times, Places and Manner of holding
Elections for Senators and Representatives." In addition, states undoubtedly retain primary authority "to regulate the elections of their own officials."

Where state procedures produce contested results, the Constitution
dictates that, for congressional elections, "Each House shall be the Judge of
the Elections, Returns and Qualifications of its own Members." Art. I, Sec.
5, cl. 1. The House accordingly has the authority "to determine the facts
and apply the appropriate rules of law, and, finally, to render a judgment

which is beyond the authority of any other tribunal to review." This plenary power is paralleled at the state level by the power of the West Virginia legislature to review the elections of its own members. Contests for county offices, such as that of plaintiff Reese, are resolved by county courts.

We thus proceed with awareness that the resolution of particular electoral disputes has been primarily committed to others in our system. The express delegation to Congress and the states of shared responsibility for the legitimation of electoral outcomes and the omission of any constitutional mandate for federal judicial intervention suggests the inadvisability of permitting a § 1983 or civil RICO action to confer upon federal judges and juries "a piece of the political action," no matter what relief is sought. Consideration of the various ways in which these other bodies have regulated and monitored the integrity of elections only confirms our hesitation to consider the disputed details of political contests.

Those with primary responsibility have not abandoned their duty to ensure the reliability and fairness of democratic elections. The House of Representatives, for example, has developed a body of guiding precedent regarding election contests, *see* 2 Deschler's Precedents of the United States House of Representatives, 323–888 (1977), and has enacted detailed procedures designed to ensure due process and just consideration of disputes. *See* Federal Contested Elections Act, 2 U.S.C. §§ 381–396. The operation of these procedures was illustrated recently in the review of a close election contest for the House of Representatives in Indiana. *See generally* H. R. Rep. No. 58, 99th Cong., 1st Sess. (1985). The partisan and acrimonious nature of that debate only reaffirms the wisdom of avoiding judicial embroilment and of leaving disputed political outcomes to the legislative branch. Had the framers wished the federal judiciary to umpire election contests, they could have so provided. Instead, they reposed primary trust in popular representatives and in political correctives.

Dissatisfied candidates for office in West Virginia are also presented with numerous avenues by which to challenge election results, some of which parallel the federal model. The legislature is directed by Art. 4, § 11 of the West Virginia Constitution "to prescribe the manner of conducting and making returns of elections, and of determining contested elections . . .," and has accordingly enacted procedures for ballot control and recounts, W. Va. Code §§ 3–6–6 to 3–6–9 and election contests, W. Va. Code §§ 3–7–1 to 3–7–9. Initially, of course, the election returns are counted and certified by a board of canvassers. W. Va. Code § 3–6–9. West Virginia courts have long exercised "election mandamus" powers by which they may "compel any [election] officer . . . to do and perform legally any duty herein required of him." W. Va. Code § 3–1–45. Appellant Underwood, in fact, attempted to employ this very procedure to compel a recount, but his writ was denied as untimely.

State and federal legislatures, moreover, are not concerned solely with election results, but have subjected the entire electoral process to increasing regulation. . . . Thus it seems fair to conclude that the demonstration of judicial restraint under 42 U.S.C. § 1983 will not leave American elections unsupervised or unregulated.

Finally, both state and federal authorities have employed criminal penalties to halt direct intrusions on the election itself. Federal conspiracy laws such as 18 U.S.C. § 241 have been applied to those engaged in corruption of election procedures. *See also* 18 U.S.C. § 594 (prohibiting intimidation of voters); 18 U.S.C. § 600 (prohibiting promise of employment or other benefit for political activity). Criminal sanctions are also available under West Virginia law for those found to have filed false returns, tampered with ballots, bought or sold votes, and the like. *See* W. Va. Code §§ 3–9–1 to 3–9–24. A state grand jury investigated the very allegations at issue here, and issued one indictment, which did not result in a conviction.

IV

Though the presence of even exhaustive alternative remedies does not usually bar an action literally within § 1983 or other statutes, *Patsy v. Board of Regents*, 457 U.S. 496 (1982); *Monroe v. Pape*, 365 U.S. 167 (1961), we are persuaded in this context that we must refrain from considering the particulars of a disputed election, especially in a suit for damages. To do otherwise would be to intrude on the role of the states and the Congress, to raise the possibility of inconsistent judgments concerning elections, to erode the finality of results, to give candidates incentives to bypass the procedures already established, to involve federal courts in the details of state-run elections, and to constitute the jury as well as the electorate as an arbiter of political outcomes. These costs, we believe, would come with very little benefit to the rights fundamentally at issue here—the rights of voters to fair exercise of their franchise. Instead, plaintiffs, who voluntarily entered the political fray, would stand to reap a post-election recovery that might salve feelings of rejection at the polls or help retire debts from the campaign but would bear very little relationship to the larger public interest in partisan debate and competition undeterred by prospects of a post-election suit for damages.

Plaintiffs' theories in this case illustrate the ways in which a lawsuit such as this could intrude on the role of states and Congress to conduct elections and adjudge results. In their complaint, plaintiffs allege damages including, inter alia, loss of income (salary from holding public office), earning capacity, time expended for election purposes and various election expenses, as well as injury to reputation. These losses, of course, would have resulted from election defeat absent any conspiracy by defendants. Injury to reputation, for example, may inhere in any political loss where exposure of opposition blemishes has from the earliest days of the Republic been a part of the quest for public office. Loss of the public official's salary is, ipso facto, an element of each and every political defeat.

Thus, plaintiffs in order to recover damages must perforce rely on the theory that defendants' alleged conspiracy cost them an election they otherwise would have won. In presenting their case plaintiffs would essentially ask a jury to review the outcome of the election. As explained above, however, the task is reserved for states and legislatures, and though the jury's review would not directly impair their primary responsibility to adjudge elections, its re-examination of election results would be inconsistent with proper respect for the role of others whose job it is to canvass the returns and declare a prevailing party. This intrusion, moreover, would not be limited to that of a jury, for the judiciary itself would doubtless be asked to review the jury's judgment of the election in post-trial motions. Principles of separation of powers and federalism, therefore, dictate that both jury and court avoid this inquiry.

Just as the review of electoral results by judge or jury is inconsistent with proper respect for the role of states and Congress, so too the outcomes of these deliberations are potentially inconsistent with the results of the electoral process. Were plaintiffs successful in convincing the jury that they should have won the election or should receive an award of damages, the courts would enter a judgment at odds with the judgment of Congress and of West Virginia, which have seated the apparent victors in these elections. The difficulties inherent in such continuing assaults on political legitimacy would be obvious and might impair the respect to which the enactments of those duly elected are entitled.

Closely related to the problem of inconsistent judgments is the need for finality in elections. Inconsistent judgments, of course, call into question the results of an election in a way that detracts from finality. Even without inconsistent judgments, suits asking federal courts to replay elections cast into limbo contests that should have been long since decided. This case is illustrative. The election at issue occurred in 1980. Plaintiffs did not even bring their suit until 1983, after plaintiff Hutchinson's term would have expired. Now, nearly six years after the election, the parties remain in court essentially to contest the integrity of the election. So long as such avenues are available to defeated candidates, the apparent finality of election outcomes will be illusory.

Maintenance of this action might also provide incentives to losing candidates to ignore the principal routes established to challenge an election and to proceed instead to have the election reviewed in federal courts in hopes of gaining monetary compensation. Plaintiffs in this case, for example, made incomplete use of state and federal procedures yet still seek to recover millions of dollars in this action. Underwood pursued his efforts to secure a recount in an untimely fashion; though Hutchinson filed a complaint with the United States Attorney, there is no evidence that he pursued other avenues available to contest the election; Reese apparently made no attempts to employ available procedures. To allow these plaintiffs access to the federal courts would undermine the processes that are intended to serve as the primary routes to election control: "federal courts would adjudicate every state election dispute, and the elaborate state election contest procedures, designed to assure speedy and orderly disposition of the multitudinous questions that may arise in the electoral process, would be superseded by a section 1983 gloss."

We further believe that federal courts are ill-equipped to monitor the details of elections and resolve factual disputes born of the political process. As one court has noted, "were we to embrace plaintiffs' theory, this court would henceforth be thrust into the details of virtually every election, tinkering with the state's election machinery, reviewing petitions, election cards, vote tallies, and certificates of election for all manner of error and insufficiency under state and federal law." *Powell v. Power*, 436 F.2d 84, 86 (2d Cir. 1970). Elections are, regrettably, not always free from error. Voting machines malfunction, registrars fail to follow instructions, absentee ballots are improperly administered, poll workers become over-zealous, and defeated candidates are, perhaps understandably, inclined to view these multifarious opportunities for human error in a less than charitable light. Quite apart from the serious problems of federalism and separation of powers problems raised by these tasks, we find sifting the minutiae of post-election accusations better suited to the factual review at the administrative and legislative level, where an awareness of the vagaries of politics informs the judgment of those called upon to review the irregularities that are inevitable in elections staffed largely by volunteers.

To ask a jury to undertake such tasks, moreover, is to risk the intrusion of political partisanship into the courtroom, where it has no place. From the exercise of jury strikes to the final rendering of verdict, the spectre of partisanship would intrude and color court proceedings. Such disputes belong, and have been placed, in the political arena, and we cannot accept the substitution of the civil jury for the larger, more diverse, and more representative political electorate that goes to the polls on the day of the election.

These concerns suggest that the federal judiciary should proceed with great caution when asked to consider disputed elections, and have caused many courts to decline the requests to intervene except in extraordinary circumstances. . . . [P]laintiffs' suit for damages strikes us as an inapt means of overseeing the political process. It would provide not so much a correction of electoral ills as a potential windfall to plaintiffs and political advantage through publicity. Those who enter the political fray know the potential risks of their enterprise. If they are defeated by trickery or fraud, they can and should expect the established mechanisms of review—both civil and criminal—to address their grievances, and to take action to insure legitimate electoral results. In this way, they advance the fundamental goal of the electoral process—to determine the will of the people—while also protecting their own interest in the electoral result. A suit for damages, by contrast, may result principally in financial gain for the candidate. We can imagine no scenario in which this gain is the appropriate result of the decision to pursue elected office, and we can find no other case in which a defeated candidate has won such compensation. Nor do we believe, in light of the multitude of alternative remedies, that such a remedy is necessary either to deter misconduct or to provide incentives for enforcement of election laws. . . .

NOTES AND QUESTIONS

1. The Fourth Circuit's opinion makes explicit a distinction that lurks within many of the materials in this chapter. Just whose rights are being vindicated in post-election contests? As Professor Karlan has pointed out in a related context, "[t]he general assumption in contemporary equal protection law, which seems to play out most of the time, is that faced with a finding of unconstitutionality, the state will remedy the inequality by providing the benefit to the previously excluded group (that is, by 'levelling up') rather than by depriving the previously included group ('leveling down'). The few examples in ordinary equal protection of leveling down—the closing of the schools in Prince Edward County, Virginia, or the swimming pools in Jackson, Mississippi—stand out precisely because of their rarity." Pamela S. Karlan, *Race, Rights and Remedies in Criminal Adjudication*, 96 Mich. L. Rev. 2001, 2027 (1998). What is the ultimate remedial theory in damages actions?

F. CRIMINAL PROSECUTION

In addition to the full panoply of civil remedies—preliminary and permanent injunctive relief and damages—violations of state and federal election laws, particularly violations committed by government officials, may often trigger criminal liability. During the 2000 election, for example, Republican election officials in two Florida counties permitted party officials to fill in parts of absentee ballot applications, arguably in violation of Florida law. Nonetheless, in light of the overall thrust of Florida's election code, which is that ballots should not be discarded for technical violations as long as they were cast by qualified voters, the circuit court and the Florida Supreme Court refused to exclude the challenged ballots. But the Florida Supreme Court's opinion states that:

> We find the Supervisor's conduct in this case troubling and we stress that our opinion in this case is not to be read as condoning anything less than strict adherence by election officials to the statutorily mandated election procedures. . . . "[T]his case [does not] concern[] potential sanctions for election officials who fail to faithfully perform their duties. It is for the legislature to specify what sanction should be available for enforcement against election officials who fail to faithfully perform their duties."

Jacobs v. Seminole County Canvassing Board, 773 So.2d 519, 524 (Fla. 2000) (quoting *Beckstrom v. Volusia County Canvassing Board*, 707 So.2d 720, 725–26 (Fla. 1998)). And in a footnote the Florida Supreme Court observed that "chapter 104 of the Florida Election Code provides certain penalties for election officials and others who violate the Code. However, violations of the Code will not necessarily invalidate the votes of innocent electors."

Criminal prosecutions of government officials, or voters themselves, are infrequent, but by no means unheard of. And criminal prosecutions often produce important principles of law that affect future civil cases. For example, consider *Guinn v. United States*, 238 U.S. 347 (1915), discussed in Chapter 2. In *Guinn*, the United States Supreme Court struck down Oklahoma's "grandfather clause," which had effectively disenfranchised African Americans. The case involved a criminal prosecution of Oklahoma election officials under the predecessor to 18 U.S.C. § 241, which provides, in pertinent part that "[i]f two or more persons conspire to injure, oppress, threaten, or intimidate any person . . . in the free exercise or enjoyment of any right or privilege secured to him by the Constitution or laws of the United States, . . . [t]hey shall be fined . . . or imprisoned . . . or both. . . ." The Court held that the grandfather clause violated the Fifteenth Amendment because, although it was neutral on its face, it clearly had been adopted for the purpose of preventing blacks from registering and voting. Having recognized that principle in *Guinn*, the Court and lower courts then applied it to other facially neutral but purposefully discriminatory practices such as literacy tests, at-large elections, and dilutionary redistricting schemes.

Federal law has a number of criminal provisions that have been used to protect the right to vote. Some, like 18 U.S.C. § 241 and 18 U.S.C. § 242, which makes it a crime for a person acting "under color of [state] law" to "willfully subjec[t] any person . . . to the deprivation of any rights, privileges, or immunities secured or protected by the Constitution or laws of the United States," penalize the denial of constitutional rights generally. Other provisions, such as Chapter 29 of Title 18, or section 11 of the Voting Rights Act, are directed specifically at election-related offenses. In light of the discussions throughout the book about the delicate questions of federalism and the distinctive federal interests involved in elections, it is not surprising that federal statutes often use a jurisdictional handle that requires the presence of a candidate for federal office on the ballot. So, for example, 18 U.S.C. § 594 makes it a crime to "intimidat[e], threate[n], coerc[e], or attemp[t] to intimidate, threaten, or coerce, any other person for the purpose of interfering with the right of such other person to vote or to vote as he may choose, or of causing such other person to vote for, or not to vote for, any candidate for the office of President, Vice President, Presidential elector, Member of the Senate, Member of the House of Representatives, Delegate from the District of Columbia, or Resident Commissioner, at any election held solely or in part for the purpose of electing such candidate. . . ." And the provisions of section 11 of the Voting Rights Act that deal with what might be viewed as "retail" fraud also require that the election be held held "solely or in part for the purpose of selecting or electing" candidates to federal office.

States, too, have extensive criminal codes regulating elections. For example, Florida has provisions in Chapter 104 of its election code that parallel the federal criminal provisions regarding vote buying and selling, intimidation and use of force, vote fraud and the like. In addition, Florida law criminalizes various forms of official malfeasance. *See, e.g.,* Fla. Stat. § 104.051 (2000), which provides, in pertinent part:

> (2) Any official who willfully refuses or willfully neglects to perform his or her duties as prescribed by this election code is guilty of a misdemeanor of the first degree, punishable as provided in s. 775.082 or s. 775.083.

> (3) Any official who performs his or her duty as prescribed by this election code fraudulently or corruptly is guilty of a felony of the third degree, punishable as provided in s. 775.082, s. 775.083, or s. 775.084.

> (4) Any supervisor, deputy supervisor, or election employee who attempts to influence or interfere with any elector voting a ballot commits a felony of the third degree, punishable as provided in s. 775.082, s. 775.083, or s. 775.084.

In considering the relative efficacy of criminal prosecutions, think about the deterrence value these pack for individual voters who are inclined to commit what might be called "retail" fraud—that is, to cast a ballot they are not entitled to, or to accept a payment for voting or not voting in a particular way—as opposed to the impact of criminal sanctions on actors within the political system who are more prone to "wholesale" fraud.

There is a rich, and growing, literature on one aspect of the criminal law surrounding elections, namely, vote buying. For representative articles, see, e.g., Richard L. Hasen, *Vote Buying*, 88 Calif. L. Rev. 1323 (2000); Pamela S. Karlan, *Not By Money but by Virtue Won? Vote Trafficking and the Voting Rights System*, 80 Va. L. Rev. 1455 (1994); Pamela S. Karlan, *Politics By Other Means*, 85 Va. L. Rev. 1697 (1999); Saul Levmore, *Voting with Intensity*, 53 Stan. L. Rev. 111 (2000).

Part II: The Election of 2000

The scramble for votes in Florida in 2000 exposed what had long been the dark secret of the entire electoral process: significant inaccuracies and mistakes infect the actual process of recording and tabulating votes. In effect, elections have an unacknowledged "margin of error"—a concept that is readily identified with opinion polls and the Census calculation of the population. The existence of such error in elections rarely rises to the forefront. Most elections are not within the margin of error of the political process, and if they are so close to begin with, there appears not to be a compelling equitable consideration in allowing adjustments to the electoral process to be implemented retrospectively. After all, if the "wrong" candidate is declared the winner, the voters can cure the problem by voting her out of office the next time around. And absent fraud or willful manipulation, the error in any election might be thought random. Even if *ex post* analysis reveals systematic tendencies to make errors involving identifiable groups of voters, such as less experienced voters, as long as those systematic tendencies are not known in advance and not intentionally exploited by state actors who, for example, choose election technologies, there would be little reason to believe that the resulting error rate reflected a calculated political manipulation by those holding political power. In these circumstances, a judicial tendency to let the errors lie where they fall might be most understandable.

Moreover, most election processes are not subject to particularly penetrating public scrutiny. Voters may express concern and even outrage if, for example, tie-ups on election day cause the lines to swell and delays to mount. But rarely will mere inconvenience attract anything beyond the most fleeting attention. Nor is this an area where elected officials are likely to intercede. The one unassailable generalization that can be made about elected officials is that they were all elected. Once elections end and public attention fades, there is rarely any incentive for those who have succeeded in the electoral arena to alter the rules and procedures that put them in office.

But what happens when the consequences of electoral error have implications nationwide? What happens when error threatens to tip the scales of an election for president? What happens if public scrutiny brings to light pervasive inaccuracies in how the electoral process actually functions? What if the public demands accountability for electoral machines that function poorly, or ballots that are confusing, or counting processes that include rather fluid assessments of the now infamous "hanging chads," "pregnant chads," and the like?

A. THE FEDERAL INTEREST IN ELECTION PROCEDURES

Two key questions, one substantive, one procedural, arise regarding whether and when federal courts have a role to play in overseeing contested elections. The procedural question involves the *timing* of any federal oversight that is otherwise justified: at what stage in an election dispute is it proper for federal courts to play a role to enforce the relevant federal interests, if any, that the election dispute implicates. This question of the proper timing of federal intervention is addressed in Section D, below. The substantive question is dealt with in this section: what substantive *reasons* are sufficient to justify federal intervention in election disputes. What exactly are the federal constitutional interests (or, statutory interests, if applicable) in various aspects of the election process, including in potential disputes that arise post-election? To what extent does the federal interest vary, if at all, when what is at stake is national office, such as election to the House, the Senate, or even the Presidency? This became the critical issue for the Supreme Court decision that terminated the 2000 Presidential election dispute. This Section will provide the general legal framework within which courts have addressed these questions.

With respect to national offices, the answer might be thought simple: surely federal constitutional interests are implicated when national offices are at issue. But even here, the legal structure is counterintuitive and hardly simple. The unique legal architecture of American democracy—a product of the original Constitutional design and subsequent legal additions built upon that original structure—envisions a complex interlacing of federal and state interests in matters of voting, elections, and political participation. Many of the issues involving electoral structures are left to be resolved at the state level, even when national offices are at stake. Recall, for example, that the original Constitution only specifies voter eligibility requirements for one national office, the House of Representatives. This is then modified by the Seventeenth Amendment which mandates direct election for senators. And even here, the federal requirements are completely derivative of state-law suffrage requirements. For example, Art. I., § 2 states that electors for the House of Representatives "shall have the Qualifications requisite for Electors of the most numerous branch of the State Legislature." Defining the boundary line, then, between issues left to be resolved as a matter of state law and issues that instead implicate distinct, federal constitutional interests, requires working out the intricate relationship between federal and state law that has long structured the American democratic system—even for national offices.

1. STATE ELECTIONS

We begin with the context of state elections. Before turning to the cases, it is helpful to understand the general structure of the legal problem regarding which aspects of state elections can trigger federal constitutional interests. The central problem is this: every dispute about state election processes implicates, by definition, questions involving voting and democratic processes. In a colloquial sense, then, every dispute about state elections could be said to implicate "the right to vote." But if every dispute implicated "the right to vote" in *a constitutional sense*—under the Fourteenth Amendment, for example—then every issue concerning state elections would be transformed into a federal case. Federal constitutional law would then be turned into a detailed election code for state elections. This would hardly be unprecedented in democratic countries. In France, for example, the Constitutional Court sits as the election overseer for all elections and has broad administrative powers over the conduct of local elections both before they are held and afterwards, in cases of electoral challenges.

This has not, however, been the American experience. Just as the United States Supreme Court has resisted constitutionalizing the vast body of state tort law and has refused to permit the ordinary deprivation of state-law property interests to be transformed into Fourteenth Amendment due process issues where state procedures are adequate, *Parratt v. Taylor*, 451 U.S. 527 (1981), the federal courts have also declined to transform most issues of the regulation of state elections into federal constitutional matters. The question then becomes where, precisely, the boundary line between state and federal interests ought to be drawn.

On the one hand, the courts have recognized a number of discrete, quite specific constitutional interests in the structure of elections. The courts recognized most of these interests only beginning in the 1960s, after *Baker v. Carr*, 369 U.S. 186 (1962). Thus, state election districts must comply with the one-vote, one-person principle. The Constitution imposes some constraints on partisan and racial design of all election districts. Since *Harper v. Virginia State Board of Elections*, 383 U.S. 663 (1966), the Court has also held that definitions of who can participate in what elections, on what terms, are subject to equal protection and due process review. Similarly, the Constitution imposes some constraints on the conditions states can impose upon candidates seeking access to being listed on the ballot. So, too, the First Amendment recognizes some degree of associational rights that protect the integrity and autonomy of political parties from certain types of state regulation. Of course, state election laws that discriminate on their face along racial lines have been unconstitutional since The White Primary Cases (the first of which is *Nixon v. Herndon*, 273 U.S. 536 (1927)), and election laws that reflect an impermissible racial or ethnic purpose are unconstitutional under either the Fourteenth or Fifteenth Amendments. Finally, the most important federal statutes that overlay state elections are the Voting Rights Act, which prohibits electoral structures and practices whose purpose or effect is to dilute the voting power of certain statutorily-protected groups, and the National Voter Registration Act and the Help America Vote Act. These are most of the specific, targeted federal interests that the courts have recognized in election processes.

On the other hand, if there were a more generalized constitutional interest in ensuring "the integrity of the electoral process" or in ensuring "fundamental fairness" in elections, then every dispute over the running of state elections would, indeed, potentially be subject to federal oversight and control. Thus, federal courts have sought to map out the distinction between the discrete areas of federal legal interest in state elections and the rest of the issues that might be disputed about the structure of elections, with the latter being left to be resolved through the ordinary processes of state law. What follows are representative federal court cases that provide content to these general principles.

a. *Lack of Sufficient Federal Interest.*

A typical result, in an opinion written by the highly-respected Judge Alvin Rubin, is provided by the oft-cited *Gamza v. Aguirre*, 619 F.2d 449

(5th Cir. 1980). In a run-off election for a local school board, candidate Gamza discovered that there was a technological misconfiguration in the voting machines in certain precincts; as a result, he alleged that his opponent had been given votes that rightly were intended for Gamza. The trial court found that the machine errors and miscounts had resulted from innocent human error. After failing in state court, Gamza claimed a deprivation of federal voting rights.

In rejecting this claim, the Fifth Circuit acknowledged that the failure to count votes adequately, stated abstractly, could easily sound like a constitutional issue. But the way the legal structure gave content to this abstract right required attending to the functional structure embodied in the Constitution, the nature of the federal court system, the limits of federal jurisdiction, and the role of states in election processes. Because the constitutional framework leaves the conduct of state elections to the states, the Fifth Circuit concluded that federal law must:

> ... recognize a distinction between state laws and patterns of state action that systematically deny equality in voting, and episodic events that, despite non-discriminatory laws, may result in the dilution of an individual's vote. Unlike systematically discriminatory laws, isolated events that adversely affect individuals are not presumed to be a violation of the equal protection clause. The unlawful administration by state officers of a non-discriminatory state law, "resulting in its unequal application to those who are entitled to be treated alike, is not a denial of equal protection unless there is shown to be present in it an element of intentional or purposeful discrimination."

> If every state election irregularity were considered a federal constitutional deprivation, federal courts would adjudicate every state election dispute, and the elaborate state election contest procedures, designed to assure speedy and orderly disposition of the multitudinous questions that may arise in the electoral process, would be superseded by a section 1983 gloss. [Constitutional law does] not authorize federal courts to be state election monitors.

619 F.2d at 453.

In a similar case, voters claimed constitutional voting rights had been denied because electronic voting machines, which allegedly did not meet state-law standards, had malfunctioned and election officials had failed to respond as state law purportedly required. The Seventh Circuit rejected these claims, noting that not every election irregularity rises to the level of a constitutional violation—and that mere violation of a state statute by an election official was not, in itself, such a violation. *Hennings v. Grafton*, 523 F.2d 861 (7th Cir. 1975). As that court put it: "the work of conducting elections in our society is typically carried on by volunteers and recruits for whom it is at most an avocation and whose experience and intelligence vary widely. Given these conditions, errors and irregularities, including the kind of conduct proved here, are inevitable, and no constitutional guarantee exists to remedy them. Rather, state election laws must be relied upon to provide the proper remedy (citations omitted)." *See also Welch v. McKenzie*, 765 F.2d 1311 (5th Cir. 1985) (despite numerous violations of state election laws, no federal constitutional violation in absence of racially discriminatory intent behind those violations or racial vote dilution occurring); *Pettengill v. Putnam County R–1 School District, Unionsville, Missouri*, 472 F.2d 121 (8th Cir. 1973) (federal courts should not become the "arbiter of disputes" which arise in elections and attempt to "oversee the administrative details of a local election" absent aggravating factors such as denial of the vote on grounds of race or fraudulent interference with a free election by stuffing of the ballot box) (holding no federal violation in alleged improper counting of ballots).

Similarly, in an important dispute over the Alabama Democratic gubernatorial primary, the Eleventh Circuit held that the appropriate forums for election disputes involving state offices were the court system of the affected state and, for primaries, the internal machinery of the political parties themselves. *Curry v. Baker*, 802 F.2d 1302 (11th Cir. 1986), involved a dispute over whether one of the Democratic primary candidates, Graddick, had encouraged voters who had already voted in the earlier Republican primary to turn out and vote in the special run-off primary for the Democratic nominee—despite state law precluding such cross-over voting. State law permitted the parties to resolve such contested primary disputes through internal party machinery. The Democratic Party used this machinery and concluded that Graddick had violated state law and party rules; the Party therefore awarded the nomination to his competitor. Graddick then turned to the federal courts and argued that the Democratic Party decision had violated "the fundamental fairness of the electoral process." According to Graddick and his supporters, the Party decision had diluted and debased the constitutionally protected right to vote. The Eleventh Circuit rejected this argument, holding that state processes, including internal party processes, were adequate to deal with the primary-election contest.

In sum, while "federal courts [will] closely scrutinize state laws whose very design infringes on the rights of voters, federal courts will not intervene to examine the validity of individual ballots or supervise the administrative details of a local election." *Id.* at 1314. A "federally protected right 'is implicated where the entire election process—including as part thereof the state's administrative and judicial corrective process—fails on its face to afford fundamental fairness." *Id.* at 1317.

b. *Sufficient Federal Interests.*

At the same time that federal courts seek to avoid becoming enmeshed in election disputes, given that the electoral machinery is overwhelmingly controlled at the state level, federal courts do of course enforce *specific* constitutional and federal statutory guarantees when they are implicated in elections. Most of this casebook addresses what these specific constitutional interests have come to be over the course of American constitutional history. In addition to those interests—ensuring one-person, one-vote, avoiding impermissible restrictions on the franchise, and the like—the further important question that arises in ongoing election disputes is whether there is any more general federal constitutional interest in ensuring that states resolve election disputes "appropriately."

The most aggressive and intriguing finding of just such a federal constitutional interest, which reached a final judgment in the federal Court of Appeals for the Eleventh Circuit, resulted from a trilogy of cases titled *Roe v. Alabama*. The electoral context involved a statewide general election for Chief Justice of the Alabama Supreme Court and the state Treasurer, among other offices. Particularly for the former office, the initial votes were quite close, with the margin of victory appearing to be between 200 to 300 votes. A massive and lengthy dispute then arose over 1000 to 2000 contested absentee ballots not counted in the initial returns. The critical state-law question was whether those ballots were illegal and not validly to be counted because they were either not properly notarized or witnessed. And the further question, which eventually triggered a federal constitutional decision, was whether the answer the Alabama state courts gave to *that* question—whether these absentee ballots could be counted—was *itself* an answer that was consistent with prior state law and practice on absentee ballots with these defects. If not—if the Alabama courts had changed a clearly established rule of state law and/or longstanding established state practices—did the decision of the state judicial system then amount to a federal constitutional violation? What is the federal interest in state elections in ensuring consistency and regularity? If there is such a federal interest, it would presumably apply with even greater force, would it not, in the context of elections for national office, even if the ground rules for those elections are established in the first instance at the state level?

Particularly noteworthy is the fact that these cases come from the Eleventh Circuit. That is the Court that oversees Florida, among other states, and therefore it is the federal court of appeals that would play a key role—if any federal court of appeals would play any role at all—in the 2000 Presidential election dispute that emerged out of the Florida electoral process. In light of the *Roe* cases, it may be easier to understand why lawyers for the Bush campaign pressed so ardently to draw the Eleventh Circuit into the Florida dispute. We will begin with the crucial substantive holding, in *Roe I*, 43 F.3d 574 (11th Cir. 1995), about the nature of the federal substantive interest in state electoral ground rules. After presenting *Roe I*, we will then elaborate upon the procedural interplay between state and federal courts in this contest—returning to the issues of timing of federal intervention discussed in Section D. This procedural aspect of the *Roe* cases will, like the substantive aspect, help explain why the interaction between state and federal courts in the 2000 Presidential election litigation had the structure and sequence of events that it did.

Roe I arose in this context: after the disputed election, absentee voters brought suit in the Alabama Circuit Court in which they sought an order requiring these disqualified absentee ballots to be included in the vote count. The state Circuit Court ordered the Secretary of State to include these ballots in the count. Another group of plaintiffs then turned to the United States District Court with an action that argued the state Circuit Court's order to include the absentee ballots so changed pre-existing state law on absentee ballots as to violate federal constitutional standards under the Fourteenth Amendment. The District Court agreed and issued a preliminary injunction against the state Circuit Court order. *Roe I* addressed whether, at this stage of the litigation, such a claim against state-election decisions by state courts could constitute a federal constitutional violation—and if so, under what circumstances. We include the central holding of *Roe I* on that key point:

Roe v. State of Alabama [Roe I]

43 F.3d 574 (11th Cir. 1995).

■ JUDGES: Before TJOFLAT, CHIEF JUDGE, EDMONDSON and BIRCH, CIRCUIT JUDGES

PER CURIAM:

* * *

II

Appellants contend that the plaintiffs failed to allege, or to demonstrate, the violation of a right "secured by the Constitution" as required under section 1983. We disagree. In this case, Roe, Hooper, and Martin allege that "the actions of the Defendants and the Defendant Class . . . would constitute a retroactive validation of a potentially controlling number of votes in the elections for Chief Justice and Treasurer" that "would result in fundamental unfairness and would violate plaintiffs' right to due process of law" in violation of the Fourteenth Amendment, and that this violation of "the plaintiffs' rights to vote and . . . have their votes properly and honestly counted" constitutes a violation of the First and Fourteenth Amendments.

The right of suffrage is "a fundamental political right, because preservative of all rights." *Yick Wo v. Hopkins*, 118 U.S. 356, 370 (1886). "The right of suffrage can be denied by a debasement or dilution of the weight of a citizen's vote just as effectively as by wholly prohibiting the free exercise of the franchise." *Reynolds v. Sims*, 377 U.S. 533, 554 (1964). Not every state election dispute, however, implicates the Due Process Clause of the Fourteenth Amendment and thus leads to possible federal court intervention. Generally, federal courts do not involve themselves in " 'garden variety' election disputes." If, however, "the election process itself reached the point of patent and fundamental unfairness, a violation of the due process clause may be indicated and relief under § 1983 therefore in order. Such a situation must go well beyond the ordinary dispute over the counting and marking of ballots." We address, then, whether the plaintiffs have demonstrated fundamental unfairness in the November 8 election. We conclude that they have.

The plaintiffs acknowledge that the State of Alabama is free to place reasonable time, place, and manner restrictions on voting, and that Alabama can require that voters be qualified electors. *See generally Burdick v. Takushi*, 504 U.S. 428, 433 (1992) ("Common sense, as well as constitutional law, compels the conclusion that government must play an active role in structuring elections...."). They argue, however, that section 17–10–7 of the Alabama Election Code clearly requires that affidavits accompanying absentee ballots either be notarized or signed by two witnesses; that the statewide practice in Alabama prior to the November 8 general election was to exclude absentee ballots that did not comply with this rule; and that the circuit court's order requiring the state's election officials to perform the ministerial act of counting the contested absentee ballots, if permitted to stand, will constitute a retroactive change in the election laws that will effectively "stuff the ballot box," implicating fundamental fairness issues.

We agree that failing to exclude the contested absentee ballots will constitute a post-election departure from previous practice in Alabama. *See Griffin v. Burns*, 570 F.2d 1065, 1075 (1st Cir. 1978). This departure would have two effects that implicate fundamental fairness and the propriety of the two elections at issue. First, counting ballots that were not previously counted would dilute the votes of those voters who met the requirements of section 17–10–7 as well as those voters who actually went to the polls on election day. Second, the change in the rules after the election would have the effect of disenfranchising those who would have voted but for the inconvenience imposed by the notarization/witness requirement.

Appellants point out that "[a] judicial construction of a statute is an authoritative statement of what the statute meant before as well as after the decision of the case giving rise to that construction." Thus, appellants urge, the Montgomery County Circuit Court's ruling merely articulated in a clearer way what the law has always been in Alabama. This argument, however, ignores the fact that section 17–10–7, on its face, requires notarization or witnessing, that the Secretary and the Attorney General have acknowledged the requirement and that, as the district court found, the practice of the election officials throughout the state has been to exclude absentee ballots that did not meet this requirement. We consider it unreasonable to expect average voters and candidates to question the Secretary's, the Attorney General's, and the election officials' interpretation and application of the statute, especially in light of its plain language.

Appellants also argue that this case presents a case of enfranchisement of those who cast the contested absentee ballots, rather than a disenfranchisement of qualified voters, and thus does not rise to the level of a constitutional violation. They rely heavily on *Partido Nuevo Progresista v. Barreto Perez*, 639 F.2d 825 (1st Cir. 1980), *cert. denied*, 451 U.S. 985 (1981). In that case, the plaintiffs challenged the tallying of ballots in a local election in Puerto Rico. A section of the Electoral Law of Puerto Rico provided that, if a handwritten ballot was used in an election, the Electoral Commission had to guarantee that the elector was qualified to vote by making a mark in a specific place on the ballot. The section stated that if the mark was not made in the correct space, the ballot would be null and void. After the election, the Administrator of the Election Commission and the Commonwealth's Electoral Review Board held that several ballots were invalid because they were not marked correctly. The Supreme Court of Puerto Rico reversed, holding that, despite the section's clear language, the ballots should be counted. The *Barreto Perez* plaintiffs, citing *Griffin*, alleged that the Puerto Rico Supreme Court's ruling constituted a change in the method of counting ballots after the election and, therefore, violated the Constitution. *Id.* at 826.

The First Circuit did not agree for two reasons. First, the court found it significant that "this case does not involve a state court order that disenfranchises voters; rather it involves a ... decision that enfranchises them—plaintiffs claim that votes were 'diluted' by the votes of others, not that they themselves were prevented from voting." *Id.* at 828 (emphasis in original). Second, the court found that "no party or person is likely to have acted to their detriment by relying upon the invalidity of [the contested] ballots...." *Id.* Accordingly, the First Circuit found no constitutional injury. We need not address the court's apparent holding that dilution is not a constitutional injury because the facts of this case differ markedly from those of *Barreto Perez*. We believe that, had the candidates and citizens of Alabama known that something less than the signature of two witnesses or a notary attesting to the signature of absentee voters would suffice, campaign strategies would have taken this into account and supporters of Hooper and Martin who did not vote would have voted absentee.

■ EDMONDSON, CIRCUIT JUDGE, dissenting:

I know of no other case involving disputed ballots in which a federal court has intervened in a state election where the plaintiff failed to show, in fact, either:

1. that plaintiff had "lost" the election but would have won the election if lawful votes only had been counted (that is, the alleged constitutional error changed the election result); or

2. that it was impossible ever to know that his opponent (the apparent winner) had truly won the election because of the nature of the voting irregularities (that is, the alleged constitutional error placed in everlasting doubt what was the true result of the election).

Nothing is known in this case about whether the alleged illegalities have affected or will affect the outcome of the pertinent elections. Yet today we plow into Alabama's election process and uphold a preliminary injunction that, in effect, overrules a pre-existing state court order which had directed that the contested votes be counted. And, instead, the federal courts (basically, stopping short the state election processes) order that the contested votes be not counted at all. This high level of federal activity seems unnecessary and, therefore, improper. So, I conclude that the district court abused its discretion.

For all we or anyone else knows, if the contested absentee votes in this case were counted, plaintiffs' candidates would win the elections, even taking those contested votes into account. In such event, none of the plaintiffs would be aggrieved by the decision to count absentee ballots not strictly complying with the state's statute. I believe everyone involved in this election dispute would understand that a court's allowing the simple adding up of which of the contested absentee votes went to which candidate would not be the same thing as saying that the' contested votes will have value ultimately, as a matter of law, for deciding the final, official outcome of the elections. But instead of letting the votes be counted as an Alabama court has directed and then seeing if there is even a controversy about the election's outcome, the federal courts have jumped into the process and blocked the very step that might show there is no big problem to be dealt with by federal judges. I would not interfere with the counting of the contested ballots, although I agree that all the ballots and envelopes and other election materials pertinent to the contested ballots should be maintained and protected so that additional judicial review, if needed, would be convenient and possible.

This difference with my colleagues is more than just academic bickering about technicalities. Federal courts are not the bosses in state election disputes unless extraordinary circumstances affecting the integrity of the state's election process are clearly present in a high degree. This well-settled principle—that federal courts interfere in state elections as a last resort—is basic to federalism, and we should take it to heart. . . .

As I understand the law, "only in extraordinary circumstances will a challenge to a state election rise to the level of a constitutional deprivation." *Curry v. Baker*, 802 F.2d 1302, 1314 (11th Cir. 1986). To my way of thinking, the federal courts have acted too aggressively too soon and have, as a result, become entangled in Alabama's state election too much. At a time when we do not know whether the contested votes, in fact, will make any difference at all in the outcome of the elections, it is hard for me to say that I am now facing the kind of extraordinary circumstances—patent and fundamental unfairness tied to concrete harm—that will amount to a constitutional deprivation and that will justify immediate significant federal interference in the election processes of a state.

I would dissolve the district court's injunction except to the extent that the injunction requires all election materials in the defendants' control to be preserved and protected in a way (for example, keeping questionable individual absentee ballots and their envelopes together) that a fair review of the election remains, in fact, possible and convenient. This limited relief should be enough to protect plaintiffs until the Alabama law becomes clear, assuming that there is a live controversy about this election after the contested ballots are counted.

NOTES AND QUESTIONS

1. The minuet between state and federal judicial movements in the *Roe* litigation reveals much about the general timing of federal judicial intervention in state-regulated electoral processes, a subject we explore in more detail in Section D. We summarize those steps here to enable readers to appreciate these timing issues. First, after the disputed election results became apparent, certain absentee voters brought an action in the state Circuit Court, in which they sought an order that the contested absentee ballots be counted. That court issued a temporary restraining order (TRO) in which it ordered the Secretary of State to refrain from certifying the election until the county canvassing officials had included the contested absentee ballots in the vote totals they forwarded to the Secretary of State. Second, in response to this decision, other voters and two candidates went to federal District Court to seek an injunction ordering state officials *not* to comply with the state Circuit Court's orders. The federal District Court found from the evidence presented that the state Circuit Court order constituted a "change in the past practice" of Alabama regarding absentee ballots. As a result, the District Court concluded that were state officials to comply with the state Circuit Court's orders, those officials would be in violation of the Fourteenth Amendment to the United States Constitution. The District Court therefore entered a preliminary injunction requiring the Secretary of State to certify the election results *without* the contested absentee ballots.

Roe I was the appeal from the District Court's injunction. As the above excerpts portray, *Roe I* agreed with the District Court's judgment that federal constitutional interests would be implicated were the state courts of Alabama to change the state practice of dealing with the contested ballots in issue. But *Roe I* concluded that it was as yet unclear whether Alabama had indeed changed its pre-existing electoral rules and practices. *Roe I* therefore accommodated the diverse federal and state interests in disputed elections in the following way: having established the relevant substantive constitutional principles, *Roe I* then certified to the Alabama Supreme Court the central question of state law: did Alabama law make the contested absentee ballots legal or illegal votes? At the same time, the Eleventh Circuit ordered the Secretary of State not to certify any election results for Chief Justice and Treasurer, the two offices in question.

The Alabama Supreme Court responded to the Eleventh Circuit by concluding that the ballots in question were indeed legal votes under

Alabama law. The Eleventh Circuit's next move, then, was to remand the proceedings to the federal District Court for extensive findings of fact on 17 specific questions designed to establish whether the state courts had actually changed state election laws that had existed before the fall election. *Roe v. State of Alabama*, 52 F.3d 300 (11th Cir. 1995) (*Roe II*), *cert. denied*, 516 U.S. 908 (1995). After a three-day trial, the District Court then made detailed findings that before the contested election Alabama's practice had "uniformly" been to exclude absentee ballots like those contested. Indeed, the Eleventh Circuit concluded that the facts found in the District Court "were stronger in favor of the Roe class than the prior panel could have expected" and thus that the evidence of a change in state election practices had been firmly established. The District Court had entered a final judgment ordering the Secretary of State to certify the results for the Chief Justice and Treasurer *without* including the contested absentee ballots. In *Roe III*, the 11th Circuit affirmed this final judgment. *Roe v. State of Alabama*, 68 F.3d 404 (11th Cir. 1995). Thus, the federal courts ended up holding that a state court interpretation of state election law, for two state offices, had so changed the pre-existing state law as to constitute impermissible vote dilution under the Due Process clause of the Fourteenth Amendment.

How long did this dance between federal and state courts take? The election was held on November 8, 1994. The state Circuit Court TRO was entered nine days later, on November 17, 1994. The federal district court preliminary injunction was entered on December 5, 1994. *Roe I* was decided January 4, 1995. *Roe III*, which brought the litigation to conclusion, was issued October 13, 1995—nearly a year after the election. In light of the unique time pressures in resolving disputed Presidential elections, driven by the meeting date of the Electoral College, what does the *Roe* litigation suggest about the capacity of federal and state courts jointly to work out adequate judicial solutions to disputed Presidential contests? Would it have improved the resolution of the Presidential election dispute had any of the federal courts involved, such as the Eleventh Circuit, followed the *Roe* practice of certifying questions of state-election law to the Florida Supreme Court?

2. The constitutional violation established in *Roe I* seemingly rests on "two effects" that implicate constitutional due process and equal protection concerns. A crucial question relevant to the *Bush v. Gore* litigation, among others, is whether *both* these effects must be present to generate a federal constitutional violation. The first effect centers on a change in state election law: the conclusion of a federal court that a state-court interpretation of state election laws effectively changes those laws. The second effect focuses on actual detrimental reliance of state voters on what appeared to be existing state election law before the state court interpretation at issue. Is a "change" in state law sufficient to trigger the constitutional violation? Or must it be a "change" that also frustrates concrete and specific reliance interest of voters? Note that in the *Roe* litigation there was not any allegation that state officials had engaged in fraudulent conduct or acted with partisan intent to manipulate outcomes; the claim was that even apparently neutral action could amount to unconstitutional unfairness by its effects on the electoral process.

3. *Vote Dilution and Changes in State Law.* The first effect is unconstitutional vote dilution that occurs when state election rules change in a way to include votes that were previously not treated as legal votes under state law. Those injured would include voters who went to the polls and cast legal votes or who cast legal absentee votes; a change in state law that permits previously illegal votes to be counted then, apparently, dilutes the votes legally cast. Recall that the federal courts must distinguish, as *Roe I* itself recognizes, between ordinary disputes over counting ballots, and state practices that reach the point of "patent and fundamental unfairness." But suppose a federal court simply disagrees with a state court interpretation of the state's election laws, when the consequence of any judicial decision is to include or exclude certain ballots: if the federal court believed state law precluded inclusion of certain ballots, would *Roe I* mean that unconstitutional vote dilution would occur were the state court to interpret state law differently and conclude that those ballots *should* be included? Or, if the state court excludes certain ballots, and the federal courts believe state law requires inclusion of such ballots, is this tantamount to unconstitutional vote dilution against voters whose votes have been excluded? Is there a risk that the principle of *Roe I* would turn every dispute over the interpretation of state election law into a federal constitutional question? Does *Roe I* succeed at its own task of drawing a line between ordinary ballot counting disputes and those that involve patent and fundamental unfairness? Does the answer depend on exactly how overwhelming the evidence must be that a state court interpretation actually changes existing state law? Does the answer also depend on whether detrimental reliance, as well as a change in state law, is required to establish a federal constitutional violation?

4. *Assessing State Judicial Interpretations as Unconstitutional Changes in State Law.* How convinced, and with what evidence, should a federal court be that a state judicial decision changes state election practices, in the midst of an election dispute, so dramatically as to amount to a federal constitutional violation? We can imagine a spectrum of possible contexts. At one end, the prior state law can be embodied not only in written legal texts, but in longstanding judicial and administrative practices consistent with those texts. The more the specific issue has been regularly confronted, particularly in contexts analogous to that at issue, the more possible it becomes to have a firmly anchored set of baseline laws and practices against which federal courts can assess any potential "changes" in state practices. In such a case, a federal court has a wealth of evidence to draw on in assessing whether one particular state judicial ruling is a sharp departure from pre-existing state rules.

That was precisely the situation in the *Roe* litigation. After an extensive trial, the District Court made the following factual findings: (1) every county in Alabama (except one) had consistently and for years excluded absentee ballots like those contested; (2) the Secretary of State had consistently maintained that ballots like those contested were not to be counted and had instructed every voting official in the State to that effect; (3) not one election official testified to the Court that the contested ballots would ordinarily be included; (4) had voters known they could have voted absentee under laxer standards, many more might have voted. In light of this longstanding, unequivocal, consistent state practice, the District Court concluded the state Circuit Court's decision to include the ballots was an "abominable" post-election change of practice that amounted to "ballot-box stuffing" and was hence unconstitutional. *Roe v. Mobile County Appointing Board*, 904 F.Supp. 1315, 1335 (S. D. Ala. 1995).

Now consider the other pole of the spectrum. Suppose a state has an election law on the books that has not been tested or applied with any frequency (if at all) and hence has not been the subject of extensive judicial or administrative elaboration. Indeed, suppose the statute has never been applied to the kind of election context currently before the state courts. When the state courts interpret such a statute in the midst of this kind of election, what possible baseline can the federal courts use to assess whether that state interpretation is a dramatic "change in state law"? If there is no evidence of actual prior state practices on the matter, nor even official positions that the Secretary of State has taken in advance and instructed state officials to follow, what kind of evidence can the federal court possibly look at to determine whether judicial interpretation has become an "abominable" post-election change?

In such a situation, can the federal court possibly be engaging in anything other than simply second-guessing whether the state court has read the statute the same way the federal court would, if the federal court had the power to interpret state law? The only evidence the federal court would have before it would be the text of the state statute itself. Perhaps, in some states, the federal court would also have whatever legislative history was relevant—though the state legislature might well have enacted the statute without any thought at all about its application to the particular kind of election matter now at issue. Yet this set of information, mostly confined to the text of the statute itself, is exactly the same information before the state court. Absent any fuller set of evidence about established state practices implementing the law in question, is not the federal court left with nothing more than the role of deciding whether it, in the first instance, would interpret the bare text of the state law the same way the state court has? If the federal court has no more to draw on than the same state statutory text on which the state court drew, is there a sufficient prior established state-law practice that ought to justify triggering the "extraordinary" federal constitutional intervention that is warranted only when matter of "patent and fundamental unfairness" are involved? Recall that the task of doctrine in this area is to distinguish ordinary state-election disputes from matters that warrant the extraordinary intervention of constitutional law because some "abominable" or comparable change in law has turned the election. If the situation can only involve differences in view between state and federal courts over how state laws ought to be interpreted, where those differences cannot be grounded in anything other than the words of the particular statute itself—because there is no long-standing state practice one way or the other—how can federal courts conclude a constitutional violation has occurred? In this context, is there not a real danger that federal courts will simply substitute their own judgment about the proper meaning of state law—precisely the massive intrusion on state interests the doctrine is designed to guard against—rather than ensure the state acts consistently with its own prior laws and practices? It is only ensuring that consistency that is supposed to trigger any federal constitutional interest.

5.   The Presidential election dispute in Florida arose in this latter context. Florida law provided for the protest and the contest of disputed elections. Fla. Stat. Ann. §§ 102.166 (protest); 102.168 (contest). Yet uncontradicted assertions at oral argument before the Supreme Court stated that the last *statewide* contest of an election had been in 1919—long before the current statutes had been enacted. Thus, there was simply no state law or administrative practice of significance that bore on the question of how Florida applied these disputed-election statutes to a statewide election contest. In addition, there was no evidence that, when these state laws were designed, any legislator had a Presidential election contest in mind one way or the other. These protest and contest statutes make no reference at all to disputed Presidential elections; yet such elections undoubtedly raise distinct concerns of their own, such as the relevance of the Electoral College meeting date—distinct concerns even as compared to disputed statewide races for offices like Governor, to which the statutes had also not previously been applied.

The Florida courts were thus required to apply state laws never before applied to statewide disputed elections, in the even more remote context of a Presidential election whose resolution the Florida legislature had presumably not considered one way or the other when drafting these protest and contest statutes. When the Florida courts then issued their interpretations of these statutes in the midst of the Presidential election dispute, what role should the federal courts have played in determining whether any of those interpretations so changed pre-existing Florida law as to be an "abominable" change in state practice justifying "extraordinary" federal constitutional intervention to ensure no "patent and fundamental unfairness" that rose to the level of a federal constitutional violation? If the Florida courts permitted amended returns, based on manual recounts, or ordered manual recounts to be conducted in certain ways and under certain conditions, against what baseline would federal courts assess whether these interpretations amounted to "changes in state law practices" akin to those in *Roe I*?

In this context, *should* federal courts play any role in overseeing state-election laws? Lacking any firm anchor in a clear set of established prior practices, if the federal courts can do no more than simply issue their own interpretations of how best to read state law, can such a difference of view ever rise to the level of the "patent" unfairness that is required for a federal constitutional interest in the process?

Does or should *Roe I* permit federal courts to find state judicial interpretation an unconstitutional change in law when there is no evidence on which to anchor that judgment other than the very statutes being interpreted? If *Roe I* is extended that far, does the decision succeed in its stated goal of avoiding turning every disputed state election law ruling into a federal constitutional question? Note that in the Presidential election litigation, when decisions of the Florida courts were challenged as having unconstitutionally changed state law, the central evidence of that change was simply the text of the relevant statutes themselves and arguments about how best to interpret them. Thus, the complexity and ferocity of disputes over whether there was any federal constitutional issue posed by the Florida Supreme Court interpretations of state law can be illuminated by recognizing that these disputes arose at one pole of the spectrum of possibilities for federal oversight of state election rulings—the pole at which there is little upon which to base judgment of consistency other than the state statutes themselves whose interpretation is at issue.

6. *Detrimental Reliance, Due Process, and Constitutional Violations.* Recall that *Roe I* identified two constitutional defects that justified constitutional intervention there. Up until now, we have been exploring the first: a profound change in state law in the midst of a disputed election. The second effect rests on detrimental reliance and appears to implicate due process, as opposed to vote dilution, constitutional principles. Here the constitutional question is whether the purportedly "new" state rule—had it been clearly specified in advance—would have led (or might have led) significant numbers of non-voters to vote, had they known that a laxer standard would have been in place. That principle was also implicated in *Roe I* because the disputed judicial interpretation made it easier for voters to cast absentee ballots. Thus, according to the *Roe I* court, the post-election change in interpretation "disenfranchised" those who would have voted but for the more onerous absentee ballot restrictions previous state practice had imposed. Because voters notified in advance of the "new rule" might well have voted, the retroactive adoption of this rule violated the due process rights of such potential voters.

As noted above, a key question about *Roe I* is whether both effects—a change in state law and detrimental reliance leading to non-voting by those who might otherwise have voted—are necessary to establish a constitutional violation. Suppose a state judicial decision that arguably changes state law, but not in a way that could plausibly be said to deny due process by effectively disenfranchising voters who would otherwise have voted had they known of the new rule. For further analysis of these issues, see Richard H. Pildes, *Judging "New Law" in Election Disputes*, 28 Fla. St. U. L. Rev. 691 (2001).

An important predecessor to *Roe I*, which rests heavily on the detrimental reliance, due process principle, is *Griffin v. Burns*, 570 F.2d 1065 (1st Cir. 1978). In the primary for a local city council race, the Secretary of State concluded that ordinary absentee and shut-in ballot laws for the general election should also be applied to primaries. The Secretary and other state officials publicized the availability of such ballots, and almost 10% of the total vote in the primary came from these ballots. The candidate who had won the machine vote, McCormick, but lost the total vote due to these absentee ballots then brought and won an action in the Rhode Island Supreme Court. In a 3–2 decision, the state Supreme Court held that state law did not permit these ballots for primary elections, since the relevant laws did not explicitly so authorize. Four days later, the Rhode Island legislature amended the law to permit expressly the use of such ballots in primaries. Meanwhile, the candidate who had won the total vote, Griffin, but lost in light of the state Supreme Court ruling that the absentee ballots that had provided his margin of victory were illegally cast under state law, then brought an action in federal district court (along with voters who had used the absentee ballots that had been tossed out). The district court found that the Rhode Island Supreme Court decision had violated the constitutional rights of these voters; as a remedy, the district court ordered that a new primary election be held.

The First Circuit affirmed. On the substantive federal interest, the First Circuit noted that states are not constitutionally required to provide for absentee or shut-in voting in primary elections. The First Circuit also noted that, despite the constitutional importance of the right to vote, federal courts tended to intervene in state election disputes only in the most limited circumstances: where state laws of general applicability are unconstitutional on their face, or where overt racial discrimination in limiting the ballot was involved. In contrast, "garden variety" election irregularities—errors in election administration, malfunctioning of voting machines, even some claims of official misconduct—do not typically rise to the level of constitutional violations, especially where the state provides adequate corrective processes. "If every election irregularity or contested vote involved a federal violation, the court would 'be thrust into the details of virtually every election, tinkering with the state's election machinery, reviewing petitions, registration cards, vote tallies, and certificates of election for all manner of error and insufficiency under state and federal law.'" *Id.* at 1977 (citation omitted).

Nonetheless, the First Circuit concluded, federal intervention was warranted here. The general principle justifying such intervention was similar to that in *Roe I*: where "broad-gauged unfairness permeates an election, even if derived from apparently neutral action" an election process can reach "the point of patent and fundamental unfairness" that triggers a due process violation. Due process "is implicated where the entire election process—including as part thereof the state's administrative and judicial corrective process—fails on its face to afford fundamental fairness." *Id.* at 1078. Applying this standard, the First Circuit did *not* hold, as in *Roe I*, that the Rhode Island Supreme Court had unconstitutionally changed state law. Instead, the First Circuit compared the state Supreme Court's decision with longstanding, prior state practice; with the advice the relevant state administrative officials provided before the election; with the actions of the state legislature both before the state Supreme Court decision (acquiescing in regular use of such ballots in primaries) and after the decision (amending the law to expressly permit such ballots in primaries). Thus, the First Circuit concluded that absentee voters had relied reasonably on the advice that they could cast absentee ballots and that the Rhode Island Supreme Court decision had come as such a surprise, that to exclude these ballots— around 10% of those cast—would violate fundamental fairness notions embodied in the Due Process clause. The key fact was the reliance of these voters on longstanding state practice: evidence had been introduced that, had they known absentee balloting was not permitted, at least some of these voters would have gone to the polls and voted in person. The evidence was sufficient to establish that this number could have affected the election outcome. Because Rhode Island's Supreme Court had ruled these illegal votes, the First Circuit concluded that it ought not to order the votes to be treated as legally cast. Instead, the First Circuit affirmed the District Court's use of its equitable powers to order a new primary election. Note that *Griffin* is a case of (1) detrimental reliance without also being a case of (2) a change in state law that, in and of itself, amounted to an unconstitutional departure. That is, if *Roe I* requires both (1) and (2), *Griffin* is a case that turns on the unfair surprise to individual voters of being disenfranchised by a state supreme court interpretation that was inconsistent with longstanding state practice and with official state advice these voters were given in advance of the election.

If detrimental reliance of individual voters is critical to the federal substantive interest in election disputes like those in *Roe I* and *Griffin*, how would that affect what kind of federal substantive interest, if any, existed in the 2000 Presidential election litigation? Recall that one of the key flashpoints for controversy was whether the Florida Supreme Court had changed pre-existing state law through any of that court's important decisions: permitting amended returns from selective hand recounts to be included in the pre-certification vote totals; or permitting a post-certification contest of election which involved extensive hand recounts of "undervoted" ballots across numerous counties. Whatever else might be said about these decisions, if they do constitute a change of law, do they do so in a way that would implicate detrimental reliance on the part of voters comparable to that in *Roe I* and *Griffin*? Would any voters be able to claim, plausibly, that had they known the Florida Supreme Court would authorize hand recounts, those voters would have acted in some different way—somehow changed their voting practices? Wouldn't the claim of detrimental reliance have to amount to voters saying, had they known they could get a vote counted without fully punching out the chad, they would have done so? For voters who did the work required to punch out the actual chad, can they claim any due process violation in having had to do more work than required, had they only known of the hand recount possibility? For voters who did not vote, could they plausibly claim, as in *Griffin*, that they would have turned out at the polls had they only known a partially punched chad would be treated as a valid vote? All readers can agree, we assume, that these claims of detrimental reliance would be fanciful. It is thus important to notice one way in which any challenge to the Florida Supreme Court decisions as "changed law" necessarily differs from the claims in cases like *Roe I* and *Griffin*; such claims depend on the view that a state court change in election law, in itself, can amount to a constitutional violation, even without that change implicating the Due Process interests of individual voters by retroactively changing the election process in a way to which voters would have self-protectively responded *ex ante* had they had notice of the change in advance. In other words, a challenge to the Florida Supreme Court decisions on "changed law" grounds would depend on federal constitutional law prohibiting such changes, even when they do not implicate specific reliance interests of voters (note that in the litigation, the Bush lawyers did point to other federal sources of such a "general" constraint on changes in state law, beyond the fundamental fairness due process principles invoked in *Roe I* and *Griffin*; the Bush campaign argued that in the distinct context of a presidential election, Art.II of the U.S. Constitution and The Electoral Count Act, 3 U.S.C. § 5, did constitute broad, general barriers against judicial interpretations that changed pre-existing law, without the further need to show detrimental reliance of individual voters on the previous interpretation).

7. *The dissent in Roe I.* To protect the boundary between constitutional law and state-election dispute resolution processes for state elections, including state judicial processes, Judge Edmondson re-asserts that federal intervention requires "extraordinary circumstances affecting the integrity of the state's election processes." Note that he fails to find that in *Roe I* because of the *timing* of federal intervention being sought, not because of disagreement with the underlying substantive constitutional principles. Judge Edmondson therefore disagreed with the District Court's grant of a preliminary injunction and the Eleventh Circuit's affirmance of that injunction. Recall that the injunction precluded the Secretary of State, in reliance on the state Circuit Court's order, from including the contested absentee ballots in the certified vote totals. On Judge Edmondson's view, the state system should be allowed to reach finality in addressing the disputed election; only after that point, should federal courts intervene—"as a last resort"—with any kind of relief.

Thus, Judge Edmondson's dissent argues both that the federal court should not intervene until Alabama law becomes clear, through the Alabama Supreme Court, *and until the contested ballots are counted*, should the Alabama courts require their inclusion. This disagreement about the timing of federal court intervention appears to rest on two principles: (1) until the federal courts learn whether the contested ballots would, in fact, change the election outcome if counted, there is no "concrete harm" to any of the plaintiffs. That is, to justify federal intervention, plaintiffs must be able to show as a matter of actual fact that the election outcome has been altered as a result of the state court decision. In addition, Judge Edmondson believes that the federal courts are capable of providing fully adequate relief at the end of the process; that is, should it turn out that state judicial decisions do admit votes to be counted that change the election outcome, and the state courts commit constitutional error in doing so, the federal courts can fully remedy that violation. How? Simply by holding that the Secretary of State must certify the constitutionally valid "winner" as the actual winner of the election. Thus, if candidate A is certified the Chief Justice of the Alabama Supreme Court because the Alabama courts include the contested ballots, and it was constitutional error to include those ballots—and their inclusion changed the election outcome—then the Eleventh Circuit should intervene at that point and order a change in result. Note, then, the second principle included in Judge Edmondson's position on the timing of federal intervention: (2) there is no irreparable harm in letting disputed ballots be counted in the state system, because the federal courts can always repair any wrong simply by ordering a different candidate validly elected. In contrast, the panel majority specifically enjoined anyone from *opening* the contested absentee ballots (needless to say, without opening them, it would have been quite a feat to count them).

These debates about the timing of federal intervention reach a national audience with the question of whether the United States Supreme Court should have *stayed* the ongoing Florida recounts, undertaken pursuant to Florida Supreme Court orders. Note that the question of a stay is a distinct question from that of the proper constitutional rule on the merits, though the questions are related. Should federal courts enjoin the counting of disputed ballots until those courts pass on the merits of the constitutional claims—as the *Roe I* panel majority does? Or should federal courts permit disputed ballots to be counted, with the assurance that if their inclusion is unconstitutional and changes the election outcome, federal courts can order the proper winner to assume office—as the *Roe I* dissent argues? Should federal courts find it irreparable harm to count disputed ballots, which may for the moment change the "winner" of the election, if those courts believe on the merits the process generating those counts is unconstitutional and makes the results a legal nullity? Or should the release of information, whether legally obtained or not, never be considered irreparable harm if the federal courts can intervene at the end and ensure that the correct "winner" assume the office in question?

2. DISTINCT FEDERAL INTERESTS IN NATIONAL ELECTIONS: U.S. HOUSE AND SENATE ELECTIONS

Thus far, we have focused on defining the substantive federal interests implicated in state election disputes. Those interests typically derive from the Constitution, although important federal statutes also govern state electoral practices. When it comes to national offices, the Constitution assigns Congress certain additional powers, or perhaps impose some additional constraints on States, beyond those implicated in state elections. For example, Art. I, § 4 gives Congress a backup power to regulate the time, place, and manner of holding congressional elections. In 1842, Congress first exercised this power to require members of Congress to be elected from single-member districts, rather than at-large. Enforcement of the current version of that federal statute in congressional elections would afford a distinct federal interest for federal court intervention in congressional elections. Additionally, the Seventeenth Amendment provides that citizens shall have the right to vote directly for senators.

But for the most part, apart from a few discrete federal interventions such as the requirement of single-member districts, state law offers the electoral machinery and regulation that determines the conduct of elections—including resolution of disputed elections—for national as well as state offices. Thus, the discussion thus far on the federal judicial role, both procedurally and substantively, for state-election disputes carries over directly to the resolution of election disputes for the United States House and Senate. With one exception about to be mentioned, there is no distinct national regulatory structure for national elections, nor for resolving disputes over such elections. Typically, the ordinary state laws that regulate state election contests and disputes are simply carried over at the state level to national elections. Unless Congress has distinctly legislated special rules for national elections, those elections are governed by whatever laws individual states choose to adopt. As a result, the regulatory framework for national elections in the United States is radically decentralized, not only with individual states free to adopt different regulations, but with individual states free to delegate to their local governments, such as counties, the discretion to adopt diverse rules—such as the appearance of the ballot, the type of voting technology to employ, and the like. That is why, in the 2000 Presidential election dispute, one individual county in Florida–Palm Beach County—was able to design and employ its own distinct ballot, the "Butterfly Ballot," even though the election involved the highest national office. The Constitution has not been thought to require national uniformity in national elections in matters like ballot design, nor has Congress legislated such requirements. Similarly, with one exception, the Constitution also does not impose any uniform procedure for dealing with disputed elections for national office, whether for Congress or the Presidency. To the extent disputes arise, they are left in the first instance to state administrative and judicial processes.

As just suggested, there is one exception, however, when it comes to elections for the House and Senate. The Constitution explicitly makes its each Chamber the exclusive judge of the qualifications of its members. Thus, Art. I, § 5, provides in part: "Each House shall be the Judge of the Elections, Returns and Qualifications of its own Members. . . ." This means that when election disputes arise concerning Senate and House races, the Senate and the House, respectively, are the forums in which such disputes must be resolved. There is no comparable constitutional provision for resolution of disputes over the choice of Presidential electors.

Does Art. I, § 5 therefore oust all ordinary state-law processes for resolving disputed House and Senate elections? Recall that Art. I, § 4 empowers the States to choose the times, places, and manner of holding elections for Senators and Representatives. Put another way, then, what exactly is the line between the state processes through which members of the House and Senate are chosen, and the resolution of any disputes over those choices? When does the "election process" end—the state controlled phase—and a dispute over Elections and Qualifications begin—a process exclusively under the control of the national political branches? That was the question in *Roudebush v. Hartke*, 405 U.S. 15 (1972), the leading case on these issues.

After the closest Senate election in Indiana history in 1970, the Secretary of State certified incumbent Vance Hartke as the winner. The next day, his opponent, Roudebush, filed a petition for a recount in state court. The state court appointed a three-person commission to begin that recount. Hartke then sought an injunction against the recount in federal district court. Hartke argued that any state recount process would interfere with the Senate's Art. I, § 5 powers to judge the qualifications of its own members. While the case was pending in the United States Supreme Court, the Senate administered the oath of office to Hartke, but he was seated without prejudice to the litigation's outcome. The district court had enjoined the recount on the grounds that any judgments about which ballots to count or not could be made only by the Senate, and that permitting any state-run recount might also damage the integrity of the ballots on which the Senate would have to rely.

In a 5-2 decision, the United States Supreme Court reversed and upheld the power of a state to conduct a manual recount, pursuant to ordinary state law, even for disputed Senate elections. The Court held that states had broad powers to regulate elections for national offices, including the use of manual recount processes as the last stage in resolving disputed elections. The Court held that a recount did not prevent the Senate from making an independent evaluation of the election returns any more than the initial count would. The Senate remained free to accept or reject the apparent winner in either count, and to conduct its own recount if it so chose. In response to the concern that a manual recount in the state might compromise the integrity of the ballots, the Court concluded that a court-appointed recount commission could not be supposed to be any less honest or conscientious than the precinct boards that made the initial counts. Thus, *Roudebush* holds that even after the Senate has provisionally seated a member, and even with the Senate's constitutional power to judge the Qualifications of its Members, a state manual recount process does not violate Art. I, § 5.

Given the controversies over recounts in Florida, several references to recount procedures in the Court's opinion are perhaps worth noting. Thus, on manual recounts in general, the Supreme Court wrote:

> Indiana has found, along with many other States, that one procedure necessary to guard against irregularity and error in the tabulation of votes is the availability of a recount. Despite the fact that a certificate of election may be issued to the leading candidate within 30 days after the election, the results are not final if a candidate's option to compel a recount is exercised. A recount is an integral part of the Indiana electoral process and is within the ambit of the broad powers delegated to the States by Art. I, § 4.

Id. at 25. The Court also noted that the United States Senate itself had at times engaged in recounts in close elections when state law did not provide a recount procedure. Finally, the Court pointed out that Indiana law required the Secretary of State to certify to the Governor the winning candidate as soon as the Secretary received certified returns from the counties, which meant within 26 days of the election. Yet as the Court pointed out, any recount could almost certainly not be completed before the Governor was obligated by statute to certify a winner based on the initial count. As the Court noted, however, under Indiana law a recount would supersede the initial count even though the Governor had issued the certificate of election. *Id.* at 25 n.22. The manual recount was then conducted, but did not change the outcome. The disputed election had been on November 17, 1970; the United States Supreme Court decision had been handed down on February 23, 1972; and Hartke was officially seated without reservation on July 24, 1972—close to two years after election day. United States Senate: Election, Expulsion and Censure Cases, 1793–1990, Case 136 (Anne M. Butler & Wendy Wolff, U.S. Senate Historical Office (1995)). Could this same procedure have been followed in a contested elections for the House of Representatives, given that the congressional term of office is two years?

Of perhaps some interest in light of the Florida recount debate, the United States Senate itself has recounted disputed ballots in contested Senate elections. The ballots are shipped under guard from the relevant state to Washington, D.C., where any recount is undertaken by the Senate Committee on Privileges and Elections or individuals appointed by that Committee. A few brief examples, designed to illustrate Senate practices for comparison with the recent Florida debate: in the 1924 elections in Iowa, an insurgent Republican, Brookhart, appeared to defeat narrowly his Democratic challenger, Steck. There was a good deal of ballot confusion, because during the campaign, the Republican Party withdrew its support from Brookhart. A Senate subcommittee (two Republicans, two Democrats) had all 900,000 ballots shipped to D.C. for a recount. Each ballot was examined "in an effort to ascertain what the true intent of the voter had been." *Id.* at Case 105, 313. Interestingly, the disputed ballots included ones that were technically illegal under Iowa law, but that showed a clear intent to vote for Steck. These were ballots that in which voters had attempted to copy exactly a sample newspaper ballot that had shown an arrow pointing to Steck's box; since the arrows were extraneous marks by Iowa law, the ballots had not been counted. The Senate, believing the intent of the voter to vote for Steck was clear, counted these ballots. Under the Senate recount, Steck won and was seated. The Senate has also undertaken only *partial* recounts of the particular ballots put into dispute. Thus, in the closest Senate race in New Hampshire history in 1974, the Democrat, Durkin, seemingly lost to his Republican opponent, Wyman, by 355 votes out of more than 200,000 cast. After a state recount, Durkin was certified the winner by 10 votes, but after a different state body recounted, the Governor certified Wyman the winner by 2 votes. Durkin petitioned the Senate and the relevant Committee agreed to itself recount, but limited to 3,500 disputed ballots. The Committee set up elaborate rules for the counting, but in the end could not resolve internal disagreements about standards and passed the case to the full Senate, which also bogged down and could not reach resolution. In the end, the two candidates agreed to resubmit themselves to the voters in a special election, which Durkin won overwhelmingly by more than 27,000 votes. The process within the Senate took seven months and reached no resolution.

3. DISTINCT FEDERAL INTERESTS IN NATIONAL ELECTIONS: PRESIDENTIAL ELECTIONS

At least three features of the constitutional and federal statutory structure potentially present unique legal issues when it comes to presidential elections and potential disputes over their resolution: (1) the role of the Electoral College in general; (2) the role of Art. II, § 1 of the Constitution, which empowers state legislatures to "direct the manner" of choosing presidential electors; and (3) the Electoral Count Act of 1887, which was passed in an effort to create a mechanism for resolving disputed presidential elections. We will provide historical perspective on the Electoral College here, then briefly note these other potential issues, which will be discussed in detail when we examine the Supreme Court's resolution of the 2000 Presidential election.

a. The Electoral College. There was much debate at the time of the Constitution's adoption over how to select the Nation's Chief Executive. Ultimately, Art. II created the Electoral College, in which each State receives the number of votes equal to its numbers of representatives and Senators; and each State is free to appoint, "in such manner as the Legislature thereof may direct," these electors.

Selection of a President and Vice–President by designated electors from each state was chosen by the delegates to the Constitutional Convention as a compromise between congressional election and direct popular election of the chief executive. Those favoring legislative election argued that the President should be accountable to the legislature; they pointed out that the executives of 8 of 13 states were elected by the legislatures in those states. Advocates of a direct vote, who argued that the President should represent the people and not the states, were a minority that included figures such as James Wilson and James Madison. Most striking about the debate was that "it revolved around the relative *disadvantages* of each mode of election, and few delegates displayed great enthusiasm for any particular choice on its merits." Jack N. Rakove, *The E–College in the E–Age, in* The Unfinished Election of 2000 201–34 (Jack N. Rakove ed., 2001). Legislative election presented separation of powers problems and raised concerns about a weak executive unable to govern; experience with governors elected by state legislatures in the majority of states was thought to bear out this experience. Direct popular vote, on the other hand, would disadvantage the smaller states and slaveholding states, where a significant portion of the population was disenfranchised. The framers were also concerned that no genuinely national figure would emerge after George Washington, and that each state would support only its own candidate. The provision in Art. II explicitly prohibiting both presidential and vice-presidential candidates from residing in the same state was designed to address the latter concern.

The delegates to the Constitutional Convention did not expect that the Electoral College alone—after the inevitable election of George Washington—would often select the President. Instead, the anticipated diffusion of support for Presidential candidates would, it was thought, throw the selection of the President into the House of Representatives. As specified in Art. II, a vote in the House would then take place among the top five candidates (later reduced to three by the Twelfth Amendment). Each state delegation receives one ballot in the case of a House vote for the President. Although both the Electoral College and the House vote clearly favor small states, the combination of the two voting procedures was understood by the Framers as a compromise, in the words of James Madison, "between the larger and smaller states, giving to the latter the advantage of selecting a President from the candidates, in consideration of the former in selecting candidates from the people." Neal R. Peirce & Lawrence D. Longley, The People's President: The Electoral College in American History and the Direct Vote Alternative 17 (1981) (citing Jonathan Elliot, II, The Debates in the Several State Conventions on the Adoption of the Federal Constitution, 495, 464 (2nd ed. 1836)).

As originally formulated, each elector chose two persons, and the runner-up in the voting became Vice–President. The deficiencies in this arrangement became apparent after the election of 1800, in which an equal number of ballots were cast for Thomas Jefferson, the Republican presidential candidate, and Aaron Burr, his running mate, throwing the election into the House for the first of two times (the other was in 1824). In response, the Twelfth Amendment was ratified in 1804, mandating separate ballots for President and Vice–President. If no vice-presidential candidate receives a majority of electoral votes, the vice-president will be chosen by the Senate, with each Senator voting individually from among the two top vote-getters.

The method of selection of state electors was left to the discretion of the states. In the first four Presidential elections, state legislatures picked the electors in the majority of states. States using a popular election to determine their electors were about equally divided up until 1820 between districted elections of Presidential electors and a winner-take-all system. After that date, the winner-take-all system came to dominate. It continues to be used today in every state but for Maine and Nebraska. Among the reasons the winner-take-all system prevailed was that it gave ruling state parties the ability to deliver complete electoral vote blocs to the national candidate (advocates of a return to districting in many states face an uphill battle today, since such a move would reduce the impact of any given state in presidential elections, and would therefore diminish the incentive of candidates to lavish attention on that state).

Before the 2000 election, the candidate receiving a majority of electoral votes had only once failed to capture the popular vote as well. In 1888, Grover Cleveland received 48.6% of the popular vote to Benjamin Harrison's 47.8%, but lost the electoral vote by a margin of 233 to 168. Both before and after 1888, reformers have steadily issued calls to overhaul the Electoral College, or to abandon it altogether. For the debates on the Electoral College and further historical reading, see the following sources: Neal R. Peirce & Lawrence D. Longley, The People's President: The Electoral College in American History and the Direct Vote Alternative, (1981); Peirce & Longley, The Electoral College Primer, (1996); Judith Best, The Choice of the People? Debating the Electoral College (1996); Robert M. Hardaway, The Electoral College and the Constitution: The Case for Preserving Federalism (1994); After the People Vote: Steps in Choosing the President (Walter Berns ed. 1983); Alexander M. Bickel, Reform and Continuity: The Electoral College, the Convention, and the Party System, (1971); Jack N. Rakove, *The E–College in the E–Age, in* The Unfinished Election of 2000 201–34 (Jack N. Rakove ed., 2001); Jack N. Rakove, *The Political Presidency: Discovery and Invention*, in The Revolution of 1800: Democracy, Race, and the New Republic 30–58 (James Horn et. al., eds., 2002); Sanford Levinson, *Presidential Elections and Constitutional Stupidities*, in Constitutional Stupidities, Constitutional Tragedies (Sanford Levinson & William Eskridge, eds.,1998).

b. Art. II and the Role of State Legislatures. Note that Art. II textually commits the manner of choosing presidential electors to the State legislatures. This raises two questions involving the so-called "independent legislature doctrine" under Art. II: (1) when state legislatures enact presidential-elector statutes, are the legislatures freed by virtue of Art. II from any state constitutional limitations to which the legislature would otherwise be bound; (2) when state courts interpret state presidential-elector laws, must state courts treat those statutes differently than other state legislation—in particular, does Art. II require that state courts adhere more closely to the text of the legislative enactments than they otherwise would, were the courts to apply their conventional techniques of statutory interpretation to those laws? Both of these questions became central to the litigation involving the 2000 election; we will discuss these legal issues *infra* when we discuss the litigation itself. The most comprehensive historical treatment to date of these issues, also discussed *infra*, is Hayward H. Smith, *History of the Article II Independent State Legislature Doctrine*, 29 Fla. St. U. L. Rev. 731 (2001). For an account that places *Bush v. Gore* in larger constitutional perspective, see Henry P. Monaghan, *Supreme Court Review of State–Court Determinations of State Law in Constitutional Cases*, 103 Colum. L. Rev. 1919 (2003).

c. The Electoral Count Act of 1887. The Constitution did not create a mechanism through which potential disputes over who the "real" electors of a State were could be resolved. This was long considered one of the major gaps in the Constitution's original design; a disputed choice for Chief Executive could be one of the most explosive issues the country would confront, yet no legal mechanism for resolving such a dispute was established in the Constitution.

Congress debated the issue for years and considered various legislative solutions. But when various disputes arose about the legitimacy of a state's electors, they were resolved in an ad hoc way. Finally, Congress passed the Electoral Count Act in 1887 to establish a uniform system for resolving contested elections. Eleven years earlier, the most serious conflict over who had won the presidential election in United States history had developed over the dispute between Rutherford B. Hayes and Samuel Tilden. Several states had submitted votes from multiple slates of electors; because Congress was divided, with the Republicans controlling the Senate and the Democrats controlling the House, Congress could not easily resolve the issue of which electoral votes to accept. Congress eventually passed a law creating an Electoral Commission composed of five senators, five representatives, and five justices of the Supreme Court which determined what electoral votes to elect and awarded the election to Hayes in a series of 8–7 party line splits.

By 1887, that ad-hoc device of an specially-created Electoral Commission was viewed by Congress as a "contrivance" that could not be repeated in the future. *See* 17 Cong. Rec. 1024 (1886) (Sen. Ingalls). At the same time, Congress needed a binding rule, because the previous approach of counting electoral votes under a joint procedural rule that could be revoked by either house had led to the rule being revoked whenever one house disapproved of the results it would produce. *See* 17 Cong. Rec. 815 (1886) (Sen. Sherman). The Electoral Count Act was passed to resolve these issues definitively without a current election dispute coloring the debate.

The Electoral Count Act has two major provisions. First, it provides that state law procedures in place prior to the election are binding on Congress if they produce a definitive result at least six days prior to the day when the electors are scheduled to meet. 3 U.S.C. § 5. At the very least then, Congress binds itself to accept electoral votes from states that resolve any internal disputes before this six-day window closes. Second, the Electoral Count Act provides a mechanism for resolving disputes over whether to accept votes of electors. 3 U.S.C. § 15. If only one return has been submitted from a state, then that is accepted unless both Houses of Congress, acting separately, agree that it should be rejected because the votes were not "regularly given." *Id.* If multiple returns were submitted, then Congress is to accept the return that conforms to the state determination under section 5. If the Houses of Congress agree upon which of several returns is the proper one, it is counted. If the Houses disagree, then whichever return is "certified by the executive of the State" is counted. *Id.* Because of an awareness that in any serious dispute multiple returns are likely, this procedure has the effect of allowing congressional determinations of which return is proper if both houses agree on which vote is proper. In case of disputes, the slate of electors that the state governor certified wins. These provisions were adopted because of a desire to minimize the circumstances under which a state would be disenfranchised while simultaneously preventing any one house from being able to determine the election. *See* 17 Cong. Rec. 1021 (1886) (Sen. Hoar).

The Electoral Count Act had never been applied or construed by the United States Supreme Court before the *Bush v. Gore* litigation. But the Act came to have critical significance at that point. Section 5, which came to be described as a "safe harbor" provision, was directly involved at several stages of the litigation. Section 15 loomed in the background as the possible final mechanism for resolving the 2000 election, though it never came to be interpreted in the courts or employed in Congress. We explore the specific debates about the meaning and role of the Electoral Count Act *infra* as those debates came up within the actual context of the *Bush v. Gore* litigation.

B. The Federal Interest Potentially Asserted

Bush v. Palm Beach County Canvassing Board (Bush I)

531 U.S. 70 (2000).

■ Per Curiam:

The Supreme Court of the State of Florida interpreted its elections statutes in proceedings brought to require manual recounts of ballots, and the certification of the recount results, for votes cast in the quadrennial Presidential election held on November 7, 2000. Governor George W. Bush, Republican candidate for the Presidency, filed a petition for certiorari to review the Florida Supreme Court decision. We granted certiorari on two of the questions presented by petitioner: whether the decision of the Florida Supreme Court, by effectively changing the State's elector appointment procedures after election day, violated the Due Process Clause or 3 U.S.C. § 5, and whether the decision of that court changed the manner in which the State's electors are to be selected, in violation of the legislature's power to designate the manner for selection under Art. II, § 1, cl. 2 of the United States Constitution.

On November 8, 2000, the day following the Presidential election, the Florida Division of Elections reported that Governor Bush had received 2,909,135 votes, and respondent Democrat Vice President Albert Gore, Jr., had received 2,907,351, a margin of 1,784 in Governor Bush's favor. Under Fla. Stat. § 102.141(4) (2000), because the margin of victory was equal to or less than one-half of one percent of the votes cast, an automatic machine recount occurred. The recount resulted in a much smaller margin of victory for Governor Bush. Vice President Gore then exercised his statutory right to submit written requests for manual recounts to the canvassing board of any county. *See* § 102.166. He requested recounts in four counties: Volusia, Palm Beach, Broward, and Miami–Dade.

The parties urged conflicting interpretations of the Florida Election Code respecting the authority of the canvassing boards, the Secretary of State (hereinafter Secretary), and the Elections Canvassing Commission. On November 14, in an action brought by Volusia County, and joined by the Palm Beach County Canvassing Board, Vice President Gore, and the Florida Democratic Party, the Florida Circuit Court ruled that the statutory 7–day deadline was mandatory, but that the Volusia board could amend its returns at a later date. The court further ruled that the Secretary, after "considering all attendant facts and circumstances," could exercise her discretion in deciding whether to include the late amended returns in the statewide certification.

The Secretary responded by issuing a set of criteria by which she would decide whether to allow a late filing. The Secretary ordered that, by 2 p.m. the following day, November 15, any county desiring to forward late returns submit a written statement of the facts and circumstances justifying a later filing. Four counties submitted statements and, after reviewing the submissions, the Secretary determined that none justified an extension of the filing deadline. On November 16, the Florida Democratic Party and Vice President Gore filed an emergency motion in the state court, arguing that the Secretary had acted arbitrarily and in contempt of the court's earlier ruling. The following day, the court denied the motion, ruling that the Secretary had not acted arbitrarily and had exercised her discretion in a reasonable manner consistent with the court's earlier ruling. The Democratic Party and Vice President Gore appealed to the First District Court of Appeal, which certified the matter to the Florida Supreme Court. That court accepted jurisdiction and sua sponte entered an order enjoining the Secretary and the Elections Canvassing Commission from finally certifying the results of the election and declaring a winner until further order of that court.

The Supreme Court, with the expedition requisite for the controversy, issued its decision on November 21. As the court saw the matter, there were two principal questions: whether a discrepancy between an original machine return and a sample manual recount resulting from the way a ballot has been marked or punched is an "error in vote tabulation" justifying a full manual recount; and how to reconcile what it spoke of as two conflicts in Florida's election laws: (a) between the time frame for conducting a manual recount under Fla. Stat. § 102.166 (2000) and the time frame for submitting county returns under §§ 102.111 and 102.112, and (b) between § 102.111, which provides that the Secretary "shall ... ignor[e]" late election returns, and § 102.112, which provides that she "may ... ignor[e]" such returns.

With regard to the first issue, the court held that, under the plain text of the statute, a discrepancy between a sample manual recount and machine returns due to the way in which a ballot was punched or marked did constitute an "error in vote tabulation" sufficient to trigger the statutory provisions for a full manual recount.

With regard to the second issue, the court held that the "shall ... ignor[e]" provision of § 102.111 conflicts with the "may ... ignor[e]" provision of § 102.112, and that the "may ... ignor[e]" provision controlled. The court turned to the questions whether and when the Secretary may ignore late manual recounts. The court relied in part upon the right to vote set forth in the Declaration of Rights of the Florida Constitution in concluding that late manual recounts could be rejected only under limited circumstances. The court then stated: "[B]ecause of our reluctance to rewrite the Florida Election Code, we conclude that we must invoke the equitable powers of this Court to fashion a remedy...." The court thus imposed a deadline of November 26, at 5 p.m., for a return of ballot counts. The 7–day deadline of § 102.111, assuming it would have applied, was effectively extended by 12 days. The court further directed the Secretary to accept manual counts submitted prior to that deadline.

As a general rule, this Court defers to a state court's interpretation of a state statute. But in the case of a law enacted by a state legislature applicable not only to elections to state offices, but also to the selection of Presidential electors, the legislature is not acting solely under the authority given it by the people of the State, but by virtue of a direct grant of authority made under Art. II, § 1, cl. 2, of the United States Constitution. That provision reads:

> Each State shall appoint, in such Manner as the Legislature thereof may direct, a Number of Electors, equal to the whole Number of Senators and Representatives to which the State may be entitled in the Congress. . . .

Although we did not address the same question petitioner raises here, in *McPherson v. Blacker*, 146 U.S. 1, 25 (1892), we said:

> [Art. II, § 1, cl. 2] does not read that the people or the citizens shall appoint, but that "each State shall"; and if the words "in such manner as the legislature thereof may direct," had been omitted, it would seem that the legislative power of appointment could not have been successfully questioned in the absence of any provision in the state constitution in that regard. Hence the insertion of those words, while operating as a limitation upon the State in respect of any attempt to circumscribe the legislative power, cannot be held to operate as a limitation on that power itself.

There are expressions in the opinion of the Supreme Court of Florida that may be read to indicate that it construed the Florida Election Code without regard to the extent to which the Florida Constitution could, consistent with Art. II, § 1, cl. 2, "circumscribe the legislative power." The opinion states, for example, that "[t]o the extent that the Legislature may enact laws regulating the electoral process, those laws are valid only if they impose no 'unreasonable or unnecessary' restraints on the right of suffrage" guaranteed by the state constitution. The opinion also states that "[b]ecause election laws are intended to facilitate the right of suffrage, such laws must be liberally construed in favor of the citizens' right to vote. . . ."

In addition, 3 U.S.C. § 5 provides in pertinent part:

> If any State shall have provided, by laws enacted prior to the day fixed for the appointment of the electors, for its final determination of any controversy or contest concerning the appointment of all or any of the electors of such State, by judicial or other methods or procedures, and such determination shall have been made at least six days before the time fixed for the meeting of the electors, such determination made pursuant to such law so existing on said day, and made at least six days prior to said time of meeting of the electors, shall be conclusive, and shall govern in the counting of the electoral votes as provided in the Constitution, and as hereinafter regulated, so far as the ascertainment of the electors appointed by such State is concerned.

The parties before us agree that whatever else may be the effect of this section, it creates a "safe harbor" for a State insofar as congressional consideration of its electoral votes is concerned. If the state legislature has provided for final determination of contests or controversies by a law made prior to election day, that determination shall be conclusive if made at least six days prior to said time of meeting of the electors. The Florida Supreme Court cited 3 U.S.C. §§ 1–10 in a footnote of its opinion, but did not discuss § 5. Since § 5 contains a principle of federal law that would assure finality of the State's determination if made pursuant to a state law in effect before the election, a legislative wish to take advantage of the "safe harbor" would counsel against any construction of the Election Code that Congress might deem to be a change in the law.

After reviewing the opinion of the Florida Supreme Court, we find "that there is considerable uncertainty as to the precise grounds for the decision." *Minnesota v. National Tea Co.*, 309 U.S. 551, 555 (1940). This is sufficient reason for us to decline at this time to review the federal questions asserted to be present.

> It is fundamental that state courts be left free and unfettered by us in interpreting their state constitutions. But it is equally important that ambiguous or obscure adjudications by state courts do not stand as barriers to a determination by this Court of the validity under the federal constitution of state action. Intelligent exercise of our appellate powers compels us to ask for the elimination of the obscurities and ambiguities from the opinions in such cases.

Id. at 557.

Specifically, we are unclear as to the extent to which the Florida Supreme Court saw the Florida Constitution as circumscribing the legislature's authority under Art. II, § 1, cl. 2. We are also unclear as to the consideration the Florida Supreme Court accorded to 3 U.S.C. § 5. The judgment of the Supreme Court of Florida is therefore vacated, and the case is remanded for further proceedings not inconsistent with this opinion.

It is so ordered.

NOTES AND QUESTIONS

1. The U.S. Supreme Court's opinion in *Bush I* addresses some fundamental issues of constitutional and statutory voting law that have gone largely unexplored for the past century, even though *Bush II* quickly superseded *Bush I* in importance.

2. The Court places great emphasis on the distinction between the acts of the Florida legislature and the other sources of state law derived either from the State Constitution or the principles of equity. Perhaps not since *Erie v. Tompkins*, 304 U.S. 64 (1938), overruled *Swift v. Tyson*, 41 U.S. (16 Pet.) 1 (1842), has a decision turned so heavily on the question of the source of state law. *Swift* had drawn a sharp distinction between legislative enactments and decisional law of the state courts. For Justice Story, the former were true sources of law that federal courts under the Rules of Decision Act were obligated to follow in construing state law in diversity cases. The latter were merely interpretive guides that could be subsumed under the federal common law without doing violence to state law. *Bush I* suggests that the constitutional delegation of authority in Art. II, § 1 of the Constitution is an exclusive grant of authority to the state legislature to create the procedures for the election of the state's presidential electors. The opinion further raises the possibility that no other state law (including the state constitution) may intercede absent an express delegation of authority from the legislature. If so, the invocation of state constitutional law to cabin the acts of the state legislature would, by extension, violate the supremacy clause of the U.S. Constitution.

3.   The most dramatic suggestion in *Bush I* is the possibility that Art. II, § 1 might immunize state legislatures, when they enact presidential elector statutes, from the state constitutional limitations that would otherwise channel and circumscribe their power. Some commentators have praised *Bush I* as an act of "judicial minimalism," in the sense that the Court did not actually decide any substantive legal issues but rather remanded for clarification from the Florida Supreme Court. *See* Cass Sunstein, *Order Without Law*, 68 U. Chi. L. Rev. 737 (2001). While it is technically true that the Court did not actually decide that Art. II overrides state constitutional law, every actor after *Bush I* appears to have acted as if the Court *had* decided, as a substantive law matter, that state legislatures could indeed not be constrained by their state constitutions when enacting presidential elector statutes. This position is known as the "independent State legislature" doctrine. As a result of *Bush I* and its subsequent interpretation, it thus becomes critical to explore whether the suggestion—which remains a suggestion, not a holding—that Art. II frees state legislatures from their constitutions is a sound understanding of Art. II.

The Court does not point to anything in the history of Art. II's adoption or the political practices that emerged in the wake of Art. II's adoption to support the independent state legislature doctrine. The Court points to two sources: (1) the text of Art. II itself and (2) *McPherson v. Blacker*, 146 U.S. 1 (1892), which the Court appears to treat as essentially the final word on the federal interest in state election matters. To explore the important question of the role of State constitutions in the presidential selection process, we therefore begin with *McPherson*.

1.   ART. II AND "THE INDEPENDENT STATE LEGISLATURE DOCTRINE"

McPherson v. Blacker

146 U.S. 1 (1892).

■ CHIEF JUSTICE FULLER delivered the opinion of the Court.

[McPherson involved a challenge to a statute passed by the Michigan state legislature governing the allocation of Michigan's electoral votes. Previously, Michigan's votes had been distributed on a winner take all, statewide basis. The new legislation required that Michigan electoral votes be awarded on a congressional district basis; the winner in each congressional district in the state would win one elector for that district. The State's remaining two electoral votes (reflecting its two Senate seats) were to go to the winner of the "Eastern" and "Western" halves of the state. Similar district based allocation schemes are used currently in Maine and Nebraska.]

* * *

[I]t is contended that the act is void because in conflict with (1) clause two of section one of Article II of the Constitution of the United States; (2) the Fourteenth and Fifteenth Amendments to the Constitution; and (3) the act of Congress of February 3, 1887.

The second clause of section one of Article II of the Constitution is in these words: "Each State shall appoint, in such Manner as the Legislature thereof may direct, a Number of Electors, equal to the whole Number of Senators and Representatives to which the State may be entitled in the Congress; but no Senator or Representative, or Person holding an Office of Trust or Profit under the United States, shall be appointed an Elector."

The manner of the appointment of electors directed by the act of Michigan is the election of an elector and an alternate elector in each of the twelve Congressional districts into which the State of Michigan is divided, and of an elector and an alternate elector at large in each of two districts defined by the act. It is insisted that it was not competent for the legislature to direct this manner of appointment because the State is to appoint as a body politic and corporate, and so must act as a unit and cannot delegate the authority to subdivisions created for the purpose; and it is argued that the appointment of electors by districts is not an appointment by the State, because all its citizens otherwise qualified are not permitted to vote for all the presidential electors.

"A State in the ordinary sense of the Constitution," said Chief Justice Chase, *Texas v. White*, 7 Wall. 700, 721, "is a political community of free citizens, occupying a territory of defined boundaries, and organized under a government sanctioned and limited by a written constitution, and established by the consent of the governed." The State does not act by its people in their collective capacity, but through such political agencies as are duly constituted and established. The legislative power is the supreme authority except as limited by the constitution of the State, and the sovereignty of the people is exercised through their representatives in the legislature unless by the fundamental law power is elsewhere reposed. The Constitution of the United States frequently refers to the State as a political community, and also in terms to the people of the several States and the citizens of each State. What is forbidden or required to be done by a State is forbidden or required of the legislative power under state constitutions as they exist. The clause under consideration does not read that the people or the citizens shall appoint, but that "each State shall"; and if the words "in such manner as the legislature thereof may direct," had been omitted, it would seem that the legislative power of appointment could not have been successfully questioned in the absence of any provision in the state constitution in that regard. Hence the insertion of those words, while operating as a limitation upon the State in respect of any attempt to circumscribe the legislative power, cannot be held to operate as a limitation on that power itself.

If the legislature possesses plenary authority to direct the manner of appointment, and might itself exercise the appointing power by joint ballot or concurrence of the two houses, or according to such mode as designated, it is difficult to perceive why, if the legislature prescribes as a method of appointment choice by vote, it must necessarily be by general ticket and not by districts. In other words, the act of appointment is none the less the act of the State in its entirety because arrived at by districts, for the act is the act of political agencies duly authorized to speak for the State, and the combined result is the expression of the voice of the State, a result reached by direction of the legislature, to whom the whole subject is committed.

[To further support the constitutionality of electing presidential electors from individual districts, the Court analogized to the congressional mandate that required individual members of Congress to be elected from single-member districts, rather than at-large. That practice, the Court noted, did not contradict the constitutional imperative of Art. I. Sec. 2 that members of Congress be selected by "the People of the several states." Further, the Court suggested that districting is an implicit element of the Twelfth Amendment, as well as its precursor language in Article II. The Twelfth Amendment grants the House of Representatives the authority to resolve Presidential elections not decided by the Electoral College. The House exercises that authority in voting state by state, with each state voting "as a unit, but that vote is arrived at through the votes of its representatives in Congress elected by districts."]

* * *

By the first paragraph of section two, Article I, it is provided: "The House of Representatives shall be composed of Members chosen every second year by the people of the several States, and the Electors in each State shall have the Qualifications requisite for Electors of the most numerous Branch of the State Legislature;" and by the third paragraph "when vacancies happen in the Representation from any State, the Executive Authority thereof shall issue Writs of Election to fill such Vacancies." Section four reads: "The Times, Places and Manner of holding Elections for Senators and Representatives, shall be prescribed in each State by the Legislature thereof; but the Congress may at any time by Law make or alter such Regulations, except as to the Places of choosing Senators."

Although it is thus declared that the people of the several States shall choose the members of Congress, (language which induced the State of New

York to insert a salvo as to the power to divide into districts, in its resolutions of ratification,) the state legislatures, prior to 1842, in prescribing the times, places and manner of holding elections for representatives, had usually apportioned the State into districts, and assigned to each a representative; and by act of Congress of June 25, 1842, 5 Stat. 491, c. 47, (carried forward as Sec. 23 of the Revised Statutes), it was provided that where a State was entitled to more than one representative, the election should be by districts. It has never been doubted that representatives in Congress thus chosen represented the entire people of the State acting in their sovereign capacity.

By original clause three of section one of Article II, and by the Twelfth Amendment which superseded that clause, in case of a failure in the election of President by the people, the House of Representatives is to choose the President; and "the vote shall be taken by States, the representation from each State having one vote." The State acts as a unit and its vote is given as a unit, but that vote is arrived at through the votes of its representatives in Congress elected by districts.

The State also acts individually through its electoral college, although, by reason of the power of its legislature over the manner of appointment, the vote of its electors may be divided.

The Constitution does not provide that the appointment of electors shall be by popular vote, nor that the electors shall be voted for upon a general ticket, nor that the majority of those who exercise the elective franchise can alone choose the electors. It recognizes that the people act through their representatives in the legislature, and leaves it to the legislature exclusively to define the method of effecting the object.

* * *

The Journal of the Convention discloses that propositions that the President should be elected by "the citizens of the United States," or by the "people," or "by electors to be chosen by the people of the several States," instead of by the Congress, were voted down, (Jour. Con. 286, 288; 1 Elliot's Deb. 208, 262,) as was the proposition that the President should be "chosen by electors appointed for that purpose by the legislatures of the States," though at one time adopted. Jour. Con. 190; 1 Elliot's Deb. 208, 211, 217. And a motion to postpone the consideration of the choice "by the national legislature," in order to take up a resolution providing for electors to be elected by the qualified voters in districts, was negatived in Committee of the Whole. Jour. Con. 92; 1 Elliot's Deb. 156. Gerry proposed that the choice should be made by the State executives; Hamilton, that the election be by electors chosen by electors chosen by the people; James Wilson and Gouverneur Morris were strongly in favor of popular vote; Ellsworth and Luther Martin preferred the choice by electors elected by the legislatures; and Roger Sherman, appointment by Congress. The final result seems to have reconciled contrariety of views by leaving it to the state legislatures to appoint directly by joint ballot or concurrent separate action, or through popular election by districts or by general ticket, or as otherwise might be directed.

Therefore, on reference to contemporaneous and subsequent action under the clause, we should expect to find, as we do, that various modes of choosing the electors were pursued, as, by the legislature itself on joint ballot; by the legislature through a concurrent vote of the two houses; by vote of the people for a general ticket; by vote of the people in districts; by choice partly by the people voting in districts and partly by the legislature; by choice by the legislature from candidates voted for by the people in districts; and in other ways, as, notably, by North Carolina in 1792, and Tennessee in 1796 and 1800. No question was raised as to the power of the State to appoint, in any mode its legislature saw fit to adopt, and none that a single method, applicable without exception, must be pursued in the absence of an amendment to the Constitution. The district system was largely considered the most equitable, and Madison wrote that it was that system which was contemplated by the framers of the Constitution, although it was soon seen that its adoption by some States might place them at a disadvantage by a division of their strength, and that a uniform rule was preferable.

[The opinion then goes into an election-by-election summary of the various methods diverse state legislatures used during the 18th and 19th centuries of choosing presidential electors. Among other interesting facts, it notes that Thomas Jefferson advised Virginia for the 1800 election to use the general ticket method "until some uniform mode of choosing a President and Vice–President of the United States shall be prescribed by an amendment to the Constitution." Similarly, the opinion quotes Mr. Justice Story, in the 1st Edition of his Commentaries on the Constitution, as remarking that "it has been thought desirable by many statesmen to have the Constitution amended so as to provide for a uniform mode of choice by the people." The opinion also notes various proposed but failed constitutional amendments requiring that electors be chosen by popular vote on a districted basis.]

* * *

From this review, in which we have been assisted by the laborious research of counsel, and which might have been greatly expanded, it is seen that from the formation of the government until now the practical construction of the clause has conceded plenary power to the state legislatures in the matter of the appointment of electors.

Even in the heated controversy of 1876–1877 the electoral vote of Colorado cast by electors chosen by the legislature passed unchallenged; and our attention has not been drawn to any previous attempt to submit to the courts the determination of the constitutionality of state action.

In short, the appointment and mode of appointment of electors belong exclusively to the States under the Constitution of the United States. They are, as remarked by Mr. Justice Gray in *In re Green*, 134 U.S. 377, 379 (1890) "no more officers or agents of the United States than are the members of the state legislatures when acting as electors of Federal senators, or the people of the States when acting as the electors of representatives in Congress." Congress is empowered to determine the time of choosing the electors and the day on which they are to give their votes, which is required to be the same day throughout the United States, but otherwise the power and jurisdiction of the State is exclusive, with the exception of the provisions as to the number of electors and the ineligibility of certain persons, so framed that Congressional and Federal influence might be excluded.

* * *

It is argued that the district mode of choosing electors, while not obnoxious to constitutional objection, if the operation of the electoral system had conformed to its original object and purpose, had become so in view of the practical working of that system. Doubtless it was supposed that the electors would exercise a reasonable independence and fair judgment in the selection of the Chief Executive, but experience soon demonstrated that, whether chosen by the legislatures or by popular suffrage on general ticket or in districts, they were so chosen simply to register the will of the appointing power in respect of a particular candidate. In relation, then, to the independence of the electors the original expectation may be said to have been frustrated. But we can perceive no reason for holding that the power confided to the States by the Constitution has ceased to exist because the operation of the system has not fully realized the hopes of those by whom it was created. Still less can we recognize the doctrine, that because the Constitution has been found in the march of time sufficiently comprehensive to be applicable to conditions not within the minds of its framers, and not arising in their time, it may, therefore, be wrenched from the subjects expressly embraced within it, and amended by judicial decision without action by the designated organs in the mode by which alone amendments can be made.

Nor are we able to discover any conflict between this act and the Fourteenth and Fifteenth Amendments to the Constitution.... If presidential electors are appointed by the legislatures, no discrimination is made; if they are elected in districts where each citizen has an equal right to vote the same as any other citizen has, no discrimination is made.

We repeat that the main question arising for consideration is one of power and not of policy, and we are unable to arrive at any other conclusion than that the act of the legislature of Michigan of May 1, 1891, is not void as in contravention of the Constitution of the United States for want of power in its enactment.

The judgment of the Supreme Court of Michigan must be affirmed.

NOTES AND QUESTIONS

1. *McPherson* reaffirmed that there could be judicial review of a claim that the state legislature's prerogatives in setting the mechanisms for the selection of electors had been overridden. But *McPherson* stopped at the structural constitutional arrangements governing what body makes the decisions as to how the electors are selected. Much constitutional water has flowed over the dam since *McPherson,* and most of it has addressed an expanded set of constitutional interests in substantive voting rights. It is interesting to speculate how much of the Florida state constitutional doctrine invoked by the Florida Supreme Court could as easily (and unobjectionably) been derived from federal constitutional law found in the breakthrough one-person, one-vote cases and their progeny. Would *Bush I* collapse if the Florida Supreme Court were to turn to federal constitutional authority for the same equitable principles that it derived from state constitutional law? To what extent has the Fourteenth Amendment's guarantee of due process and equal protection impliedly limited the conferral of state legislative authority under Art. II, § 1? For a discussion of this point, see Pamela S. Karlan, *Unduly Partial: The Supreme Court and the Fourteenth Amendment in* Bush v. Gore, 29 Fla. St. U.L. Rev. 587, 594–95 (2001) (arguing that the per curiam "cannot be taken at face value" since surely the Nineteenth Amendment would bar a state from excluding women from participating in the selection of presidential electors and contemporary interpretations of the equal protection clause would prevent states from deliberating picking racially discriminatory systems or otherwise violating equal protection—by, for example, charging individuals to participate).

2. The precise issue that concerned the litigants in *McPherson v. Blacker* was the constitutionality of a Michigan statute that had provided that the state's presidential electors were to be selected from congressional districts, with two floterial districts selecting the electors attributable to the state's senate seats. The plaintiffs claimed that the state had to select its electors at large.

The Court disagreed, holding that the state Legislature's decision to enact a statute providing for popular election by districts was a permissible use of the power conferred by Art. II, § 1's directive that "[e]ach State shall appoint, in such Manner as the Legislature thereof may direct" the electors to which it was entitled. Given that the Legislature could have rejected popular election altogether, there was no problem with its deciding that each voter could essentially vote for only two of the state's twelve electors—the one from his congressional district and a second from the floterial district—rather than for all twelve, the gravamen of plaintiffs' complaint.

3. Note that the first suggestion that Article II's use of the word "Legislature" somehow limits the *states'* ability, through the state constitution or otherwise, to cabin the legislature's decision about how to appoint electors, apparently arises not at the time of the framing but in 1874, in a Senate report proposing that states be required to select their electors from districts. Given that this report was issued eighty years after Article II's enactment and accompanied a piece of legislation that apparently was never enacted, how much weight ought it to be given?

In particular, in *McPherson*, the Michigan Supreme Court had upheld the challenged statute against federal constitutional attack. Thus, the U.S. Supreme Court was not asked to address the question whether, had the Michigan Supreme Court struck down the statute on state constitutional grounds, the Michigan Supreme Court's judgment would have violated Article II. That was roughly the question that engaged the Court in *Bush I*: Assuming that the Florida Legislature had enacted deadlines for certifying presidential elections that violated Florida constitutional law, would the Florida Supreme Court lack its usual power of judicial review? That question conceals some heroic assumptions. It assumes, for example, that Florida's state legislators knowingly enacted a statute contrary to their state's own constitution, despite the oaths they (like all state elected officials) take to uphold the state, as well as the federal, constitution. Isn't the more reasonable assumption that state legislators act against a background commitment to adhering to their state's constitution as well as the United States Constitution and that, absent a clear statement of state constitutional defiance, their acts should be subject to the normal process of judicial review? What does the *McPherson* Court mean when it says: "The State does not act by its people in their collective capacity, but through such political agencies as are duly constituted and established. The legislative power is the supreme authority except as limited by the constitution of the State, and the sovereignty of the people is exercised through their representatives in the legislature unless by the fundamental law power is elsewhere reposed." Does *Bush I* give appropriate consideration to this passage?

4. *The History of Article II.* The most detailed historical examination of Article II and the independent state legislature doctrine is Hayward H. Smith, *History of the Article II Independent State Legislature Doctrine*, 29 Fla. St. U. L. Rev. 731 (2001). In brief, Smith reaches the following conclusions: (1) there was no direct debate one way or the other on whether the Framers or the ratifying conventions meant Article II to create independent state legislatures for this one unique role; (2) however, some state constitutions did restrain state legislatures in their Article II role; for example, Massachusetts and New York contained gubernatorial vetoes in their early constitutions and state legislatures submitted presidential election statutes, like all others, to this veto mechanism; (3) and that there appears to be no historical support for the independent state legislature doctrine before the Civil War. During that War, however, a series of "soldier voter" cases arose in which State constitutions appeared to preclude soldiers, who were out of state at the time, from voting in the pending presidential election. State courts strained to read their constitutions to permit such voting, and in doing so, suggested for the first time the possibility that Article II overrode state constitutions, though these courts did not directly so hold. Thus, in the context of expanding the franchise for soldiers, some judicial basis for the independent state legislature doctrine was recognized for the first time in this era. Some state courts held that Article II required these soldiers to be enfranchised, notwithstanding the state constitutional provisions. Two state courts had directly affirmed the power of state constitutions to regulate the Article II powers of state legislatures before *Bush I;* these decisions, like the rest of the history of Article II, are not mentioned in *Bush I* or *Bush II.*

5. Even the *McPherson* Court recognized that the state legislature's Article II powers are circumscribed by later constitutional provisions, such as the Fourteenth and Fifteenth Amendments, that prohibit discrimination in voting. Thus, for example, although a state legislature might be free to abandon popular voting for electors altogether, it could not deny black citizens the right to vote in a popular election if it should decide to hold one. In light of one-person, one-vote, could Michigan today enact a statute selecting its electors from districts if those districts contained different numbers of people? Indeed, *Bush II*'s central holding will rest, as we shall see, on a rejection of any view that Article II might be unconstrained by later U.S. constitutional amendments: *Bush II* held that state statutes for presidential elections must comply with modern voting rights jurisprudence developed under the Fourteenth Amendment.

6. *The Disappearance of the Issue.* On the same day that the U.S. Supreme Court heard oral argument in *Bush v. Gore (Bush II)*, reprinted below, the Florida Supreme Court issued its opinion on remand from *Bush I.* In *Palm Beach County Canvassing Board v. Harris*, 772 So.2d 1273 (Fla. 2000), the Florida Supreme Court reached precisely the same result that it had reached initially: that is, it held that Secretary of State Harris was required to accept, and include in the certified total, late-arriving returns from counties conducting manual recounts pursuant to Fla. Stat. § 102.166(5). But it reached that result in a different manner. Gone from the Court's opinion was Section II—"Guiding Principles"—in which the Court declared that "the will of the people, not a hyper-technical reliance upon statutory provisions, should be our guiding principle in election cases," and the reliance on the state constitution's recognition of the right to vote. Gone, too, was Section VIII—on "The Right to Vote"—which quoted from the "Florida Constitution and its Declaration of Rights." The Court re-emphasized in its section on "Legislative Intent" that "[l]egislative intent—as always—is the polestar that guides a court's inquiry into the provisions of the Florida Election Code. *See Florida Birth–Related Neurological Injury Compensation Ass'n v. Florida Div. of Admin. Hearings*, 686 So.2d 1349 (Fla. 1997)." The Court furthered repeated that because chapter 102 was ambiguous and contradictory, "the Court must resort to traditional rules of statutory construction to determine legislative intent." Throughout the new opinion, and especially in the conclusion, the Florida Supreme Court restricted its citations of authority to legislative materials and wrapped itself in the mantle of statutory interpretation:

> [T]his Court has at all times been faced with a question of the statutory construction of Florida's election laws in accord with the intent of the Florida Legislature. Our examination of that issue has been limited to a determination of legislative intent as informed by the traditional sources and rules of construction we have long accepted as relevant in determining such intent. Not surprisingly, we have identified the right of Florida's citizens to vote and to have elections determined by the will of Florida's voters as important policy concerns of the Florida Legislature in enacting Florida's election code....
>
> By providing for the popular election of presidential electors, Florida's Legislature has also placed that election under Florida's general statutory election scheme. Hence, there is essentially only one statutory election scheme for all elections whether the elections be for local and state officials or for presidential electors. The Legislature has not chosen to have a separate set of election laws for elections for presidential electors. The Legislature has chosen to have a single election code control all elections. So, we must interpret and apply that single election code here....
>
> It should not be surprising then that this Court's prior opinions that we have relied on for guidance in resolving the pending issue of statutory construction would have little reference to the Legislature's authority in the selecting of presidential electors or the Legislature's decision to grant Florida voters the right to elect presidential electors. In fact, the parties have provided us no citations to court cases in Florida involving disputes over presidential electors under Florida's election laws. This case may be the first.
>
> In sum, Florida's statutory scheme simply makes no provision for applying its rules one way for presidential elector elections and another way for all other elections. That was a legislative decision that we have accepted.... We have construed the provisions providing for a time table as directory in light of what we perceive to be a clear legislative policy of the importance of an elector's right to vote and of having each vote counted. Hopefully, our unbroken line of cases identifying and relying on these legislative policies have not missed the mark. Further, if anything, more recent legislative changes have been crafted not only to be consistent with these policies, but also to ensure adherence to them.
>
> Hence, based upon our perception of legislative intent, we have ruled that election returns must be accepted for filing unless it can clearly be determined that the late filing would prevent an election contest or the

consideration of Florida's vote in a presidential selection. This statutory construction reflects our view that the Legislature would not wish to endanger Florida's vote not being counted in a presidential election. This ruling is not only consistent with our prior interpretation of the entire statutory election scheme, but also with our identification of the important legislative policies underlying that scheme.

For the reasons stated in this opinion, we reverse the orders of the trial court. Based on this Court's status as the ultimate arbiter of conflicting Florida law, we conclude that our construction of the above statutes results in the formation of no new rules of state law but rather results simply in a narrow reading and clarification of those statutes, which were enacted long before the present election took place. We decline to rule more expansively in the present case, for to do so would result in this Court substantially rewriting the Code. We leave that matter to the sound discretion of the body best equipped to address it, the Legislature.

Does the fact that the Florida Supreme Court reached the same result on remand suggest that state constitutional principles had played a role in informing that court's statutory interpretation, but that those principles had not played a decisive role? Or is it a testament to the plasticity of legal reasoning? Why might the Florida Supreme Court have invoked the state constitution and the right to vote in its first opinion? Note that no party had argued to that court that Article II precluded it from relying on its state constitution to interpret state election laws. Had the U.S. Supreme Court's decision the next day in *Bush II* not rendered the Florida Supreme Court's decision essentially moot, how would the U.S. Supreme Court have analyzed the Florida Supreme Court's decision? More generally, what does this inter-court dialogue reveal about the entire subject of "adequate and independent state grounds" and the ability of state courts to insulate their judgments from federal review?

2.   OF "SAFE HARBORS" AND THE ELECTORAL COUNT ACT

1. *Bush I* draws to the center of the dispute the role of 3 U.S.C. § 5, a central provision of the Electoral Count Act of 1887. The history of this Act is provided above. This provision of the U.S. Code speaks to after-the-fact alterations of procedures in state presidential elections. But the Court in *Bush I* appears to accept the argument that 3 U.S.C. § 5 is, in essence, a safe harbor that creates a strong presumption of legitimacy for the state's selection of electors when *Congress* reviews their votes in January. As a general matter, it is difficult to construct out of a safe harbor an obligation that the states must act in conformity with its provisions, as opposed to simply being induced to follow its suggested course of action. Nonetheless, the Court directed the Florida Supreme Court on remand to address what consideration it gave to 3 U.S.C. § 5. This remand set off a chain of invocation of 3 U.S.C. § 5 by every court and every brief filed in the rapidly unfolding Florida cascade. But, if 3 U.S.C. § 5 is truly a guide to congressional evaluation of the credentials of electors from the states, should this statute play any role in judicial oversight of elections? Further, can 3 U.S.C. § 5 be the basis for federal courts overturning the actions of state courts or state legislatures?

2.   Section 5 of Title 3 serves as a "safe harbor" provision for a state determination of who the winning electors are. The design was to ensure that disputes over which electors were the proper electors would always be resolved, but that to the extent possible these determinations would be made by the state government because the Constitution gives responsibility for selecting electors to the states in an effort to isolate Congress from the election of the President. *See* 17 Cong. Rec. 1023 (1886) (Sen. Hoar). At the same time, Congress feared that the process of determining which slate of electors would become too chaotic and subject to state legislatures over-turning the will of the people if legislatures were permitted to change the rules for contests after the election. *See* 18 Cong. Rec. 47 (1886) (Rep. Cooper). Consequently, the Act was designed to balance these concerns by making the decisions of the state government binding, but only if the decisions were controlled by state laws "enacted prior to the day fixed for the appointment of the electors" and only if the final determination was made six days prior to the meeting of the electors. 3 U.S.C. § 5.

3.   Under a robust reading of *McPherson*, is the Electoral Count Act itself unconstitutional? That is, doesn't Article II preclude Congress from intrud-ing into the manner the states have chosen for selecting their presidential electors? Questions about the constitutionality of the Electoral Count Act have been raised but never fully addressed. Various members of Congress argued at the time of passage that the Electoral Count Act was an unconstitutional attempt to remedy "defects in the Constitution . . . by acts of Congress." 17 Cong. Rec. 1058 (1886) (Sen. Wilson). The specifics of the Act were criticized by arguments that the President of the Senate was alone empowered to count the votes of the Electoral College and that both early commentators and the practice of early Congresses showed that Congress's role was purely as witness to the counting by the President of the Senate. *Id.* at 1059.

   For example, does Congress actually have the power it asserts in 3 U.S.C. § 15, to give primacy to the set of electors certified by the "state Executive" in a situation where the two houses of Congress cannot resolve an election contest? What if a state would assign priority in such a situation differently—say, to the electors as determined finally in state judicial proceedings? And what about the "safe harbor" provision, 3 U.S.C. § 5, which played such a central role throughout the litigation? Does Article II preclude Congress from threatening states with the loss of their preferred electors if those electors are not chosen six days before the Electoral College meets? Should not Article II, under the strongest reading, permit states to act independently of Congress up until the actual meeting of the Electoral College?

Indeed, these and other questions regarding the constitutionality of the Electoral Count Act have been longstanding. For example, seven dissenting members of the House committee that reported the Act constitutionally objected precisely to Congress' assertion of power to impose a "safe harbor" on the States:

> In accord with the principles I have mentioned, seven of the committee are of the opinion that, so far as casting the vote is concerned, the State has all the constitutional power conferred, and that Congress can not prescribe that a State shall make its determination within a limited time prior to the day of casting the vote.

> When the Constitution of the United States says that the day on which the electoral votes shall be cast shall be the same throughout the United States, the Constitution thereby imposes a limitation upon the appointing power of the States. The appointment must be made, all determinations concerning it must be made, all disputes concerning it must be settled, prior to that day; but Congress has no power, as is attempted here, to put a statute of limitations other than the limitation imposed by the Constitution on the appointing power of the State, by enacting that the determination of such question must be made six days, or at any other period, before the vote is cast. That is our point of difference [with the committee majority].

18 Cong. Rec. 47 (Dec. 8, 1886) (Rep. Dibble).

Why were these constitutional objections to the imposition of a "safe harbor"—tantamount to an earlier deadline than the meeting of the Electoral College—not raised in the *Bush v. Gore* litigation? None of these arguments have been decided upon by a court; given the structure of the Act, the circumstances under which a court would have the ability to decide whether the Act is constitutional are unclear. A majority of Congress was persuaded by the argument that the Act was permitted under the Necessary and Proper Clause to give substance to the provisions of the Twelfth Amendment.

3.   THE FINAL FLORIDA COURT DECISION AND THE UNITED STATES SUPREME COURT STAY

While *Bush* was pending on remand from the U.S. Supreme Court, the Florida Supreme Court returned to matters of the state's electoral-dispute resolution laws in a second appeal, *Gore v. Harris*, 773 So.2d 524 (Fla. 2000). At issue was an appeal from the denial of a recount by a Leon County trial court. We summarize the result briefly here; the United States Supreme Court decision in *Bush v. Gore* provides a full account of this decision.

The Florida Supreme Court divided 4–3, with the majority reversing the trial court and ordering, *inter alia*, an immediate hand recount of all ballots in the state that were counted by machine and did not register a vote for president—the "undervote" ballots. Unlike the court's earlier opinion in *Palm Beach County Canvassing Board*, the opinion in *Gore* eschewed all reliance on the state constitution in favor of careful invocations of statutory authority for the ordered recount. Similarly, the dissents took pains to challenge the statutory construction of the majority opinion and to claim that the majority had acted beyond the bounds of state legislative action. Although this opinion was ultimately overturned in *Bush II*, a separate interesting question still remains on the remedial front. Because of its determination that the trial court had erred in requiring proof of a "reasonable probability" of an altered election outcome as a precondition to a recount, the *Gore v. Harris* majority fashioned a distinct remedy to address the immediate time pressure created by the rapidly approaching convocation of Electors. This remedy included a recount process for all counties in the state using machine counting mechanisms, but only for the undervote ballots. In addition, the Court ordered that the actions be taken through somewhat altered procedures using, if necessary, court personnel to conduct the recounts. Finally, the majority endorsed a standard that all ballots were to be accepted if the will of the voter could be reasonably ascertained through a visual inspection of the ballot. As support for these remedial actions, the majority pointed to Section 102.168(8) of the state's election contest statute. This provision empowered courts in contest actions to provide "any relief appropriate" to prevent or correct any electoral wrong recognized Section 102.168.

The dissenting opinions argued that such processes were unprecedented in Florida, were not statutorily authorized, and would not work. Does *Bush I* imply anything about the scope of the remedial authority of the Florida Supreme Court? Is it appropriate for the United States Supreme Court to "imply" legal principles without actually announcing those principles as matter of substantive law? It is interesting to note that the Florida Supreme Court acted in *Gore v. Harris* without having actually addressed this issue on remand from the U.S. Supreme Court in *Bush I*. Assuming that the Florida Supreme Court majority is correct in concluding that Florida statutory law compels a recount under the conditions proven at trial in *Gore,* does *Bush I* raise doubts about the range of remedial authority claimed by the *Gore* majority?

Immediately after this second Florida Supreme Court decision, lawyers for the Bush campaign sought a stay from the United States Supreme Court. For part of a Friday evening and Saturday day, the recount process as ordered that Friday by the Florida Supreme Court began to be set into motion. By midday on Saturday, the United States Supreme Court granted the requested stay on a 5–4 vote, treated the request for a stay as a petition for certiorari, granted that requested writ, and ordered oral argument to take place on the merits on that Monday. In an unusual action, the Court's internal disagreements over whether to grant the stay were publicly aired in separate opinions:

Bush v. Gore

531 U.S. 1046 (2000).

■ PER CURIAM:

The application for stay presented to JUSTICE KENNEDY and by him referred to the Court is granted, and it is ordered that the mandate of the Florida Supreme Court, case No. SCOO–2431, is hereby stayed pending further order of the Court. In addition, the application for stay is treated as a petition for writ of certiorari, and the petition for writ of certiorari granted. . . .

■ JUSTICE SCALIA, concurring.

Though it is not customary for the Court to issue an opinion in connection with its grant of a stay, I believe a brief response is necessary to JUSTICE STEVENS' dissent. I will not address the merits of the case, since they will shortly be before us in the petition for certiorari that we have granted. It suffices to say that the issuance of the stay suggests that a majority of the Court, while not deciding the issues presented, believe that the petitioner has a substantial probability of success.

On the question of irreparable harm, however, a few words are appropriate. The issue is not, as the dissent puts it, whether "[c]ounting every legally cast vote ca[n] constitute irreparable harm." One of the principal issues in the appeal we have accepted is precisely whether the votes that have been ordered to be counted are, under a reasonable interpretation of Florida law, "legally cast vote[s]." The counting of votes that are of questionable legality does in my view threaten irreparable harm to petitioner, and to the country, by casting a cloud upon what he claims to be the legitimacy of his election. Count first, and rule upon legality afterwards, is not a recipe for producing election results that have the public acceptance democratic stability requires. Another issue in the case, moreover, is the propriety, indeed the constitutionality, of letting the standard for determination of voters' intent—dimpled chads, hanging chads, etc.—vary from county to county, as the Florida Supreme Court opinion, as interpreted by the Circuit Court, permits. If petitioner is correct that counting in this fashion is unlawful, permitting the count to proceed on that erroneous basis will prevent an accurate recount from being conducted on a proper basis later, since it is generally agreed that each manual recount produces a degradation of the ballots, which renders a subsequent recount inaccurate.

For these reasons I have joined the Court's issuance of stay, with a highly accelerated timetable for resolving this case on the merits.

■ JUSTICE STEVENS, with whom JUSTICE SOUTER, JUSTICE GINSBURG, and JUSTICE BREYER join, dissenting.

To stop the counting of legal votes, the majority today departs from three venerable rules of judicial restraint that have guided the Court throughout its history. On questions of state law, we have consistently respected the opinions of the highest courts of the States. On questions whose resolution is committed at least in large measure to another branch of the Federal Government, we have construed our own jurisdiction narrowly and exercised it cautiously. On federal constitutional questions that were not fairly presented to the court whose judgment is being reviewed, we have prudently declined to express an opinion. The majority has acted unwisely.

Time does not permit a full discussion of the merits. It is clear, however, that a stay should not be granted unless an applicant makes a substantial showing of a likelihood of irreparable harm. In this case, applicants have failed to carry that heavy burden. Counting every legally cast vote cannot constitute irreparable harm. On the other hand, there is a danger that a stay may cause irreparable harm to the respondents—and, more importantly, the public at large—because of the risk that "the entry of the stay would be tantamount to a decision on the merits in favor of the applicants." *National Socialist Party of America v. Skokie*, 434 U.S. 1327, 1328 (1977) (STEVENS, J., in chambers). Preventing the recount from being completed will inevitably cast a cloud on the legitimacy of the election.

It is certainly not clear that the Florida decision violated federal law. The Florida Code provides elaborate procedures for ensuring that every eligible voter has a full and fair opportunity to cast a ballot and that every ballot so cast is counted. *See, e.g.*, Fla. Stat. §§ 101.5614(5), 102.166 (2000). In fact, the statutory provision relating to damaged and defective ballots states that "[n]o vote shall be declared invalid or void if there is a clear indication of the intent of the voter as determined by the canvassing board." Fla. Stat. § 101.5614(5) (2000). In its opinion, the Florida Supreme Court gave weight to that legislative command. Its ruling was consistent with earlier Florida cases that have repeatedly described the interest in correctly ascertaining the will of the voters as paramount. *See State ex rel. Chappell v. Martinez*, 536 So.2d 1007 (Fla.1998); *Boardman v. Esteva*, 323 So.2d 259 (Fla.1976); *McAlpin v. State ex rel. Avriett*, 155 Fla. 33, 19 So.2d 420 (1944); *State ex rel. Peacock v. Latham*, 125 Fla. 69, 169 So. 597, 598 (1936); *State ex rel. Carpenter v. Barber*, 144 Fla. 159, 198 So. 49 (1940). Its ruling also appears to be consistent with the prevailing view in other States. *See, e.g.*, *Pullen v. Mulligan*, 138 Ill.2d 21, 149 Ill.Dec. 215, 561 N.E.2d 585, 611 (1990). As a more fundamental matter, the Florida court's ruling reflects the basic principle, inherent in our Constitution and our democracy, that every legal vote should be counted. *See Reynolds v. Sims*, 377 U.S. 533, 544–555 (1964); *cf. Hartke v. Roudebush*, 321 F.Supp. 1370, 1378–1379 (S.D.Ind.1970) (STEVENS, J., dissenting); *accord Roudebush v. Hartke*, 405 U.S. 15 (1972).

Accordingly, I respectfully dissent.

C. THE FEDERAL INTEREST DECISIVELY ASSERTED

Bush v. Gore

531 U.S. 98 (2000).

■ PER CURIAM:

On December 8, 2000, the Supreme Court of Florida ordered that the Circuit Court of Leon County tabulate by hand 9,000 ballots in Miami–Dade County. It also ordered the inclusion in the certified vote totals of 215 votes identified in Palm Beach County and 168 votes identified in Miami–Dade County for Vice President Albert Gore, Jr., and Senator Joseph Lieberman, Democratic Candidates for President and Vice President. The Supreme Court noted that petitioner, Governor George W. Bush, asserted that the net gain for Vice President Gore in Palm Beach County was 176 votes, and directed the Circuit Court to resolve that dispute on remand. The court further held that relief would require manual recounts in all Florida counties where so-called "undervotes" had not been subject to manual tabulation. The court ordered all manual recounts to begin at once. Governor Bush and Richard Cheney, Republican Candidates for the Presidency and Vice Presidency, filed an emergency application for a stay of this mandate. On December 9, we granted the application, treated the application as a petition for a writ of certiorari, and granted certiorari.

* * *

The petition presents the following questions: whether the Florida Supreme Court established new standards for resolving Presidential election contests, thereby violating Art. II, § 1, cl. 2, of the United States Constitution and failing to comply with 3 U.S.C. § 5, and whether the use of standardless manual recounts violates the Equal Protection and Due Process Clauses. With respect to the equal protection question, we find a violation of the Equal Protection Clause.

II

A

The closeness of this election, and the multitude of legal challenges which have followed in its wake, have brought into sharp focus a common, if heretofore unnoticed, phenomenon. Nationwide statistics reveal that an estimated 2% of ballots cast do not register a vote for President for whatever reason, including deliberately choosing no candidate at all or some voter error, such as voting for two candidates or insufficiently marking a ballot. *See* Ho, More Than 2M Ballots Uncounted, AP Online (Nov. 28, 2000); Kelley, Balloting Problems Not Rare But Only In A Very Close Election Do Mistakes And Mismarking Make A Difference, Omaha

World–Herald (Nov. 15, 2000). In certifying election results, the votes eligible for inclusion in the certification are the votes meeting the properly established legal requirements.

This case has shown that punch card balloting machines can produce an unfortunate number of ballots which are not punched in a clean, complete way by the voter. After the current counting, it is likely legislative bodies nationwide will examine ways to improve the mechanisms and machinery for voting.

B

The individual citizen has no federal constitutional right to vote for electors for the President of the United States unless and until the state legislature chooses a statewide election as the means to implement its power to appoint members of the Electoral College. U.S. Const., Art. II, § 1. This is the source for the statement in *McPherson v. Blacker*, 146 U.S. 1, 35 (1892), that the State legislature's power to select the manner for appointing electors is plenary; it may, if it so chooses, select the electors itself, which indeed was the manner used by State legislatures in several States for many years after the Framing of our Constitution. *Id.*, at 28–33. History has now favored the voter, and in each of the several States the citizens themselves vote for Presidential electors. When the state legislature vests the right to vote for President in its people, the right to vote as the legislature has prescribed is fundamental; and one source of its fundamental nature lies in the equal weight accorded to each vote and the equal dignity owed to each voter. The State, of course, after granting the franchise in the special context of Article II, can take back the power to appoint electors. *See id.*, at 35 ("[T]here is no doubt of the right of the legislature to resume the power at any time, for it can neither be taken away nor abdicated") (quoting S.Rep. No. 395, 43d Cong., 1st Sess.).

The right to vote is protected in more than the initial allocation of the franchise. Equal protection applies as well to the manner of its exercise. Having once granted the right to vote on equal terms, the State may not, by later arbitrary and disparate treatment, value one person's vote over that of another. *See, e.g.*, *Harper v. Virginia Bd. of Elections*, 383 U.S. 663, 665 (1966) ("[O]nce the franchise is granted to the electorate, lines may not be drawn which are inconsistent with the Equal Protection Clause of the Fourteenth Amendment"). It must be remembered that "the right of suffrage can be denied by a debasement or dilution of the weight of a citizen's vote just as effectively as by wholly prohibiting the free exercise of the franchise." *Reynolds v. Sims*, 377 U.S. 533, 555 (1964).

There is no difference between the two sides of the present controversy on these basic propositions. Respondents say that the very purpose of vindicating the right to vote justifies the recount procedures now at issue. The question before us, however, is whether the recount procedures the

Florida Supreme Court has adopted are consistent with its obligation to avoid arbitrary and disparate treatment of the members of its electorate.

Much of the controversy seems to revolve around ballot cards designed to be perforated by a stylus but which, either through error or deliberate omission, have not been perforated with sufficient precision for a machine to count them. In some cases a piece of the card—a chad—is hanging, say by two corners. In other cases there is no separation at all, just an indentation.

The Florida Supreme Court has ordered that the intent of the voter be discerned from such ballots. For purposes of resolving the equal protection challenge, it is not necessary to decide whether the Florida Supreme Court had the authority under the legislative scheme for resolving election disputes to define what a legal vote is and to mandate a manual recount implementing that definition. The recount mechanisms implemented in response to the decisions of the Florida Supreme Court do not satisfy the minimum requirement for non-arbitrary treatment of voters necessary to secure the fundamental right. Florida's basic command for the count of legally cast votes is to consider the "intent of the voter." This is unobjectionable as an abstract proposition and a starting principle. The problem inheres in the absence of specific standards to ensure its equal application. The formulation of uniform rules to determine intent based on these recurring circumstances is practicable and, we conclude, necessary.

The law does not refrain from searching for the intent of the actor in a multitude of circumstances; and in some cases the general command to ascertain intent is not susceptible to much further refinement. In this instance, however, the question is not whether to believe a witness but how to interpret the marks or holes or scratches on an inanimate object, a piece of cardboard or paper which, it is said, might not have registered as a vote during the machine count. The factfinder confronts a thing, not a person. The search for intent can be confined by specific rules designed to ensure uniform treatment.

The want of those rules here has led to unequal evaluation of ballots in various respects. *See Gore v. Harris*, 772 So.2d, at 1267; (Wells, J., dissenting) ("Should a county canvassing board count or not count a 'dimpled chad' where the voter is able to successfully dislodge the chad in every other contest on that ballot? Here, the county canvassing boards disagree"). As seems to have been acknowledged at oral argument, the standards for accepting or rejecting contested ballots might vary not only from county to county but indeed within a single county from one recount team to another.

* * *

An early case in our one person, one vote jurisprudence arose when a State accorded arbitrary and disparate treatment to voters in its different counties. *Gray v. Sanders*, 372 U.S. 368 (1963). The Court found a constitutional violation. We relied on these principles in the context of the Presidential selection process in *Moore v. Ogilvie*, 394 U.S. 814 (1969), where we invalidated a county-based procedure that diluted the influence of citizens in larger counties in the nominating process. There we observed that "[t]he idea that one group can be granted greater voting strength than another is hostile to the one man, one vote basis of our representative government." *Id.*, at 819.

The State Supreme Court ratified this uneven treatment. It mandated that the recount totals from two counties, Miami–Dade and Palm Beach, be included in the certified total. The court also appeared to hold sub silentio that the recount totals from Broward County, which were not completed until after the original November 14 certification by the Secretary of State, were to be considered part of the new certified vote totals even though the county certification was not contested by Vice President Gore. Yet each of the counties used varying standards to determine what was a legal vote. Broward County used a more forgiving standard than Palm Beach County, and uncovered almost three times as many new votes, a result markedly disproportionate to the difference in population between the counties.

In addition, the recounts in these three counties were not limited to so-called undervotes but extended to all of the ballots. The distinction has real consequences. A manual recount of all ballots identifies not only those ballots which show no vote but also those which contain more than one, the so-called overvotes. Neither category will be counted by the machine. This is not a trivial concern. At oral argument, respondents estimated there are as many as 110,000 overvotes statewide. As a result, the citizen whose ballot was not read by a machine because he failed to vote for a candidate in a way readable by a machine may still have his vote counted in a manual recount; on the other hand, the citizen who marks two candidates in a way discernable by the machine will not have the same opportunity to have his vote count, even if a manual examination of the ballot would reveal the requisite indicia of intent. Furthermore, the citizen who marks two candidates, only one of which is discernable by the machine, will have his vote counted even though it should have been read as an invalid ballot. The State Supreme Court's inclusion of vote counts based on these variant standards exemplifies concerns with the remedial processes that were under way.

That brings the analysis to yet a further equal protection problem. The votes certified by the court included a partial total from one county, Miami-Dade. The Florida Supreme Court's decision thus gives no assurance that the recounts included in a final certification must be complete. Indeed, it is respondent's submission that it would be consistent with the rules of the recount procedures to include whatever partial counts are done by the time of final certification, and we interpret the Florida Supreme Court's decision to permit this. *See* 772 So.2d, at 1261, n. 21, (noting "practical difficulties" may control outcome of election, but certifying partial Miami–Dade total nonetheless). This accommodation no doubt results from the truncated contest period established by the Florida Supreme Court in *Bush I*, at respondents' own urging. The press of time does not diminish the constitutional concern. A desire for speed is not a general excuse for ignoring equal protection guarantees.

In addition to these difficulties the actual process by which the votes were to be counted under the Florida Supreme Court's decision raises further concerns. That order did not specify who would recount the ballots. The county canvassing boards were forced to pull together ad hoc teams comprised of judges from various Circuits who had no previous training in handling and interpreting ballots. Furthermore, while others were permitted to observe, they were prohibited from objecting during the recount.

The recount process, in its features here described, is inconsistent with the minimum procedures necessary to protect the fundamental right of each voter in the special instance of a statewide recount under the authority of a single state judicial officer. Our consideration is limited to the present circumstances, for the problem of equal protection in election processes generally presents many complexities.

The question before the Court is not whether local entities, in the exercise of their expertise, may develop different systems for implementing elections. Instead, we are presented with a situation where a state court with the power to assure uniformity has ordered a statewide recount with minimal procedural safeguards. When a court orders a statewide remedy, there must be at least some assurance that the rudimentary requirements of equal treatment and fundamental fairness are satisfied.

Given the Court's assessment that the recount process underway was probably being conducted in an unconstitutional manner, the Court stayed the order directing the recount so it could hear this case and render an expedited decision. The contest provision, as it was mandated by the State Supreme Court, is not well calculated to sustain the confidence that all citizens must have in the outcome of elections. The State has not shown that its procedures include the necessary safeguards. The problem, for instance, of the estimated 110,000 overvotes has not been addressed, although Chief Justice Wells called attention to the concern in his dissenting opinion.

Upon due consideration of the difficulties identified to this point, it is obvious that the recount cannot be conducted in compliance with the requirements of equal protection and due process without substantial additional work. It would require not only the adoption (after opportunity for argument) of adequate statewide standards for determining what is a legal vote, and practicable procedures to implement them, but also orderly judicial review of any disputed matters that might arise. In addition, the Secretary of State has advised that the recount of only a portion of the ballots requires that the vote tabulation equipment be used to screen out undervotes, a function for which the machines were not designed. If a recount of overvotes were also required, perhaps even a second screening would be necessary. Use of the equipment for this purpose, and any new software developed for it, would have to be evaluated for accuracy by the Secretary of State, as required by Fla. Stat. § 101.015 (2000).

The Supreme Court of Florida has said that the legislature intended the State's electors to "participat[e] fully in the federal electoral process," as provided in 3 U.S.C. § 5. 772 So.2d, at 1254; *see also Palm Beach Canvassing Bd. v. Harris*, 772 So.2d 1220, (Fla. 2000). That statute, in turn, requires that any controversy or contest that is designed to lead to a conclusive selection of electors be completed by December 12. That date is upon us, and there is no recount procedure in place under the State Supreme Court's order that comports with minimal constitutional standards. Because it is evident that any recount seeking to meet the December 12 date will be unconstitutional for the reasons we have discussed, we reverse the judgment of the Supreme Court of Florida ordering a recount to proceed.

Seven Justices of the Court agree that there are constitutional problems with the recount ordered by the Florida Supreme Court that demand a remedy. *See post*, at 545 (Souter, J., dissenting); post, at 551, 557–558 (Breyer, J., dissenting). The only disagreement is as to the remedy. Because the Florida Supreme Court has said that the Florida Legislature intended to obtain the safe-harbor benefits of 3 U.S.C. § 5, Justice Breyer's proposed remedy—remanding to the Florida Supreme Court for its ordering of a constitutionally proper contest until December 18—contemplates action in violation of the Florida election code, and hence could not be part of an "appropriate" order authorized by Fla. Stat. § 102.168(8) (2000).

* * *

None are more conscious of the vital limits on judicial authority than are the members of this Court, and none stand more in admiration of the Constitution's design to leave the selection of the President to the people, through their legislatures, and to the political sphere. When contending parties invoke the process of the courts, however, it becomes our unsought responsibility to resolve the federal and constitutional issues the judicial system has been forced to confront.

The judgment of the Supreme Court of Florida is reversed, and the case is remanded for further proceedings not inconsistent with this opinion.

It is so ordered.

* * *

■ Chief Justice Rehnquist, with whom Justice Scalia and Justice Thomas join, concurring.

We join the per curiam opinion. We write separately because we believe there are additional grounds that require us to reverse the Florida Supreme Court's decision.

I

We deal here not with an ordinary election, but with an election for the President of the United States. In *Burroughs v. United States*, 290 U.S. 534, 545 (1934), we said:

> While presidential electors are not officers or agents of the federal government (*In re Green*, 134 U.S. 377, 379), they exercise federal functions under, and discharge duties in virtue of authority conferred by, the Constitution of the United States. The President is vested with the executive power of the nation. The importance of his election and the vital character of its relationship to and effect upon the welfare and safety of the whole people cannot be too strongly stated.

Likewise, in *Anderson v. Celebrezze*, 460 U.S. 780, 794–795 (1983) (footnote omitted), we said: "[I]n the context of a Presidential election, state-imposed restrictions implicate a uniquely important national interest. For the President and the Vice President of the United States are the only elected officials who represent all the voters in the Nation."

In most cases, comity and respect for federalism compel us to defer to the decisions of state courts on issues of state law. That practice reflects our understanding that the decisions of state courts are definitive pronouncements of the will of the States as sovereigns. *Cf. Erie R. Co. v. Tompkins*, 304 U.S. 64 (1938). Of course, in ordinary cases, the distribution of powers among the branches of a State's government raises no questions of federal constitutional law, subject to the requirement that the government be republican in character. *See* U.S. Const., Art. IV, § 4. But there are a few exceptional cases in which the Constitution imposes a duty or confers a power on a particular branch of a State's government. This is one of them. Article II, § 1, cl. 2, provides that "[e]ach State shall appoint, in such Manner as the Legislature thereof may direct," electors for President and Vice President. Thus, the text of the election law itself, and not just its interpretation by the courts of the States, takes on independent significance.

In *McPherson v. Blacker*, 146 U.S. 1 (1892), we explained that Art. II, § 1, cl. 2, "convey[s] the broadest power of determination" and "leaves it to the legislature exclusively to define the method" of appointment. Id., at 27. A significant departure from the legislative scheme for appointing Presidential electors presents a federal constitutional question.

3 U.S.C. § 5 informs our application of Art. II, § 1, cl. 2, to the Florida statutory scheme, which, as the Florida Supreme Court acknowledged, took that statute into account. Section 5 provides that the State's selection of electors "shall be conclusive, and shall govern in the counting of the electoral votes" if the electors are chosen under laws enacted prior to election day, and if the selection process is completed six days prior to the meeting of the electoral college. As we noted in *Bush v. Palm Beach County Canvassing Bd.*,

Since § 5 contains a principle of federal law that would assure finality of the State's determination if made pursuant to a state law in effect before the election, a legislative wish to take advantage of the "safe harbor" would counsel against any construction of the Election Code that Congress might deem to be a change in the law.

If we are to respect the legislature's Article II powers, therefore, we must ensure that postelection state-court actions do not frustrate the legislative desire to attain the "safe harbor" provided by § 5.

* * *

In order to determine whether a state court has infringed upon the legislature's authority, we necessarily must examine the law of the State as it existed prior to the action of the court. Though we generally defer to state courts on the interpretation of state law—*see, e.g., Mullaney v. Wilbur*, 421 U.S. 684 (1975)—there are of course areas in which the Constitution requires this Court to undertake an independent, if still deferential, analysis of state law.

For example, in *NAACP v. Alabama ex rel. Patterson*, 357 U.S. 449, (1958), it was argued that we were without jurisdiction because the petitioner had not pursued the correct appellate remedy in Alabama's state courts. Petitioners had sought a state-law writ of certiorari in the Alabama Supreme Court when a writ of mandamus, according to that court, was proper. We found this state-law ground inadequate to defeat our jurisdiction because we were "unable to reconcile the procedural holding of the Alabama Supreme Court" with prior Alabama precedent. *Id.*, at 456. The purported state-law ground was so novel, in our independent estimation, that "petitioner could not fairly be deemed to have been apprised of its existence." *Id.*, at 457.

Six years later we decided *Bouie v. City of Columbia*, 378 U.S. 347 (1964), in which the state court had held, contrary to precedent, that the state trespass law applied to black sit-in demonstrators who had consent to enter private property but were then asked to leave. Relying upon NAACP, we concluded that the South Carolina Supreme Court's interpretation of a state penal statute had impermissibly broadened the scope of that statute beyond what a fair reading provided, in violation of due process. *See* 378 U.S., at 361–362. What we would do in the present case is precisely parallel: Hold that the Florida Supreme Court's interpretation of the Florida election laws impermissibly distorted them beyond what a fair reading required, in violation of Article II.

This inquiry does not imply a disrespect for state courts but rather a respect for the constitutionally prescribed role of state legislatures. To attach definitive weight to the pronouncement of a state court, when the very question at issue is whether the court has actually departed from the statutory meaning, would be to abdicate our responsibility to enforce the explicit requirements of Article II.

II

* * *

In its first decision, the Florida Supreme Court extended the 7–day statutory certification deadline established by the legislature. This modification of the code, by lengthening the protest period, necessarily shortened the contest period for Presidential elections. Underlying the extension of the certification deadline and the shortchanging of the contest period was, presumably, the clear implication that certification was a matter of significance: The certified winner would enjoy presumptive validity, making a contest proceeding by the losing candidate an uphill battle. In its latest opinion, however, the court empties certification of virtually all legal consequence during the contest, and in doing so departs from the provisions enacted by the Florida Legislature.

The court determined that canvassing boards' decisions regarding whether to recount ballots past the certification deadline (even the certification deadline established by *Harris I*) are to be reviewed de novo, although the election code clearly vests discretion whether to recount in the boards, and sets strict deadlines subject to the Secretary's rejection of late tallies and monetary fines for tardiness. *See* Fla. Stat. § 102.112 (2000). Moreover, the Florida court held that all late vote tallies arriving during the contest period should be automatically included in the certification regardless of the certification deadline (even the certification deadline established by *Harris I*), thus virtually eliminating both the deadline and the Secretary's discretion to disregard recounts that violate it.

Moreover, the court's interpretation of "legal vote," and hence its decision to order a contest-period recount, plainly departed from the legislative scheme. Florida statutory law cannot reasonably be thought to require the counting of improperly marked ballots. Each Florida precinct before election day provides instructions on how properly to cast a vote, § 101.46; each polling place on election day contains a working model of the voting machine it uses, § 101.5611; and each voting booth contains a sample ballot, § 101.46. In precincts using punch-card ballots, voters are instructed to punch out the ballot cleanly:

> AFTER VOTING, CHECK YOUR BALLOT CARD TO BE SURE
> YOUR VOTING SELECTIONS ARE CLEARLY AND CLEANLY
> PUNCHED AND THERE ARE NO CHIPS LEFT HANGING ON
> THE BACK OF THE CARD.

Instructions to Voters, quoted in *Touchston v. McDermott*, 234 F.3d 1133 (11th Cir. 2000) (Tjoflat, J., dissenting). No reasonable person would call it "an error in the vote tabulation," Fla. Stat. § 102.166(5), or a "rejection of legal votes," Fla. Stat. § 102.168(3)(c),[4] when electronic or electromechani-

---

4. It is inconceivable that what constitutes a vote that must be counted under the "error in the vote tabulation" language of the protest phase different from what constitutes a vote that must be counted under the "legal votes" language of the contest phase.

cal equipment performs precisely in the manner designed, and fails to count those ballots that are not marked in the manner that these voting instructions explicitly and prominently specify. The scheme that the Florida Supreme Court's opinion attributes to the legislature is one in which machines are required to be "capable of correctly counting votes," § 101.5606(4), but which nonetheless regularly produces elections in which legal votes are predictably not tabulated, so that in close elections manual recounts are regularly required. This is of course absurd. The Secretary of State, who is authorized by law to issue binding interpretations of the election code, §§ 97.012, 106.23, rejected this peculiar reading of the statutes. See DE 00–13 (opinion of the Division of Elections). The Florida Supreme Court, although it must defer to the Secretary's interpretations, *see Krivanek v. Take Back Tampa Political Committee*, 625 So.2d 840, 844 (Fla. 1993), rejected her reasonable interpretation and embraced the peculiar one. *See Palm Beach County Canvassing Board v. Harris*, 772 So.2d 1273, (Dec. 11, 2000) (*Harris III*).

But as we indicated in our remand of the earlier case, in a Presidential election the clearly expressed intent of the legislature must prevail. And there is no basis for reading the Florida statutes as requiring the counting of improperly marked ballots, as an examination of the Florida Supreme Court's textual analysis shows. We will not parse that analysis here, except to note that the principal provision of the election code on which it relied, § 101.5614(5), was, as THE CHIEF JUSTICE pointed out in his dissent from Harris II, entirely irrelevant. June 18, 2001 *See Gore v. Harris*, 772 So.2d 1243, (Dec. 8, 2000). The State's Attorney General (who was supporting the Gore challenge) confirmed in oral argument here that never before the present election had a manual recount been conducted on the basis of the contention that "undervotes" should have been examined to determine voter intent. Tr. of Oral Arg. in *Bush v. Palm Beach County Canvassing Bd.*, 2000 WL 1763666, at *39–*40 (Dec. 1, 2000); *cf. Broward County Canvassing Board v. Hogan*, 607 So.2d 508, 509 (Fla.Ct.App.1992) (denial of recount for failure to count ballots with "hanging paper chads"). For the court to step away from this established practice, prescribed by the Secretary of State, the state official charged by the legislature with "responsibility to . . . [o]btain and maintain uniformity in the application, operation, and interpretation of the election laws," § 97.012(1), was to depart from the legislative scheme.

III

The scope and nature of the remedy ordered by the Florida Supreme Court jeopardizes the "legislative wish" to take advantage of the safe harbor provided by 3 U.S.C. § 5. *Bush v. Palm Beach County Canvassing Bd.*, *ante*. December 12, 2000, is the last date for a final determination of the Florida electors that will satisfy § 5. Yet in the late afternoon of December 8th–four days before this deadline—the Supreme Court of Florida ordered recounts of tens of thousands of so-called "undervotes" spread through 64 of the State's 67 counties. This was done in a search for elusive—perhaps delusive—certainty as to the exact count of 6 million votes. But no one claims that these ballots have not previously been tabulated; they were initially read by voting machines at the time of the election, and thereafter reread by virtue of Florida's automatic recount provision. No one claims there was any fraud in the election. The Supreme Court of Florida ordered this additional recount under the provision of the election code giving the circuit judge the authority to provide relief that is "appropriate under such circumstances." Fla. Stat. § 102.168(8) (2000).

Surely when the Florida Legislature empowered the courts of the State to grant "appropriate" relief, it must have meant relief that would have become final by the cut-off date of 3 U.S.C. § 5. In light of the inevitable legal challenges and ensuing appeals to the Supreme Court of Florida and petitions for certiorari to this Court, the entire recounting process could not possibly be completed by that date. Whereas the majority in the Supreme Court of Florida stated its confidence that "the remaining under-votes in these counties can be [counted] within the required time frame," 772 So.2d. at 1262, n. 22, it made no assertion that the seemingly inevitable appeals could be disposed of in that time.

* * *

Given all these factors, and in light of the legislative intent identified by the Florida Supreme Court to bring Florida within the "safe harbor" provision of 3 U.S.C. § 5, the remedy prescribed by the Supreme Court of Florida cannot be deemed an "appropriate" one as of December 8. It significantly departed from the statutory framework in place on November 7, and authorized open-ended further proceedings which could not be completed by December 12, thereby preventing a final determination by that date.

For these reasons, in addition to those given in the per curiam, we would reverse.

* * *

■ JUSTICE STEVENS, with whom JUSTICE GINSBURG and JUSTICE BREYER join, dissenting.

The Constitution assigns to the States the primary responsibility for determining the manner of selecting the Presidential electors. *See* Art. II, § 1, cl. 2. When questions arise about the meaning of state laws, including election laws, it is our settled practice to accept the opinions of the highest courts of the States as providing the final answers. On rare occasions, however, either federal statutes or the Federal Constitution may require federal judicial intervention in state elections. This is not such an occasion.

The federal questions that ultimately emerged in this case are not substantial. Article II provides that "[e]ach State shall appoint, in such Manner as the Legislature thereof may direct, a Number of Electors." *Id*. It does not create state legislatures out of whole cloth, but rather takes them as they come—as creatures born of, and constrained by, their state constitutions. Lest there be any doubt, we stated over 100 years ago in *McPherson v. Blacker*, 146 U.S. 1, 25 (1892), that "[w]hat is forbidden or required to be done by a State" in the Article II context "is forbidden or required of the legislative power under state constitutions as they exist." In the same vein, we also observed that "[t]he [State's] legislative power is the supreme authority except as limited by the constitution of the State." *Id.; cf. Smiley v. Holm*, 285 U.S. 355, 367 (1932). The legislative power in Florida is subject to judicial review pursuant to Article V of the Florida Constitution, and nothing in Article II of the Federal Constitution frees the state legislature from the constraints in the state constitution that created it. Moreover, the Florida Legislature's own decision to employ a unitary code for all elections indicates that it intended the Florida Supreme Court to play the same role in Presidential elections that it has historically played in resolving electoral disputes. The Florida Supreme Court's exercise of appellate jurisdiction therefore was wholly consistent with, and indeed contemplated by, the grant of authority in Article II.

It hardly needs stating that Congress, pursuant to 3 U.S.C. § 5, did not impose any affirmative duties upon the States that their governmental branches could "violate." Rather, § 5 provides a safe harbor for States to select electors in contested elections "by judicial or other methods" established by laws prior to the election day. Section 5, like Article II, assumes the involvement of the state judiciary in interpreting state election laws and resolving election disputes under those laws. Neither § 5 nor Article II grants federal judges any special authority to substitute their views for those of the state judiciary on matters of state law.

Nor are petitioners correct in asserting that the failure of the Florida Supreme Court to specify in detail the precise manner in which the "intent of the voter," Fla. Stat. § 101.5614(5) (Supp.2001), is to be determined rises to the level of a constitutional violation.[2] We found such a violation when individual votes within the same State were weighted unequally, *see, e.g., Reynolds v. Sims*, 377 U.S. 533 (1964), but we have never before called into question the substantive standard by which a State determines that a vote has been legally cast. And there is no reason to think that the guidance provided to the factfinders, specifically the various canvassing boards, by the "intent of the voter" standard is any less sufficient—or will lead to results any less uniform—than, for example, the "beyond a reason-

---

2. The Florida statutory standard is consistent with the practice of the majority of States, which apply either an "intent of the voter" standard or an "impossible to determine the elector's choice" standard in ballot recounts. [The footnote goes on to list those states.]

able doubt" standard employed everyday by ordinary citizens in courtrooms across this country.

Admittedly, the use of differing substandards for determining voter intent in different counties employing similar voting systems may raise serious concerns. Those concerns are alleviated—if not eliminated—by the fact that a single impartial magistrate will ultimately adjudicate all objections arising from the recount process. Of course, as a general matter, "[t]he interpretation of constitutional principles must not be too literal. We must remember that the machinery of government would not work if it were not allowed a little play in its joints." *Bain Peanut Co. of Tex. v. Pinson*, 282 U.S. 499, 501 (1931) (Holmes, J.). If it were otherwise, Florida's decision to leave to each county the determination of what balloting system to employ—despite enormous differences in accuracy[4]— might run afoul of equal protection. So, too, might the similar decisions of the vast majority of state legislatures to delegate to local authorities certain decisions with respect to voting systems and ballot design.

* * *

In the interest of finality, however, the majority effectively orders the disenfranchisement of an unknown number of voters whose ballots reveal their intent—and are therefore legal votes under state law—but were for some reason rejected by ballot-counting machines. It does so on the basis of the deadlines set forth in Title 3 of the United States Code. *Ante*, at 532. But, as I have already noted, those provisions merely provide rules of decision for Congress to follow when selecting among conflicting slates of electors. They do not prohibit a State from counting what the majority concedes to be legal votes until a bona fide winner is determined.

Indeed, in 1960, Hawaii appointed two slates of electors and Congress chose to count the one appointed on January 4, 1961, well after the Title 3 deadlines. *See* Josephson & Ross, Repairing the Electoral College, 22 J. Legis. 145, 166, n. 154 (1996). Thus, nothing prevents the majority, even if it properly found an equal protection violation, from ordering relief appropriate to remedy that violation without depriving Florida voters of their right to have their votes counted. As the majority notes, "[a] desire for speed is not a general excuse for ignoring equal protection guarantees."

Finally, neither in this case, nor in its earlier opinion in *Palm Beach County Canvassing Bd. v. Harris*, 772 So.2d 1220 (2000), did the Florida Supreme Court make any substantive change in Florida electoral law. Its decisions were rooted in long-established precedent and were consistent

---

4. The percentage of nonvotes in this election in counties using a punch-card system was 3.92%; in contrast, the rate of error under the more modern optical-scan systems was only 1.43%. *Siegel v. LePore*, 234 F.3d 1163, (charts C and F) (11th Cir., Dec. 6, 2000). Put in other terms, for every 10,000 votes cast, punch-card systems result in 250 more nonvotes than optical-scan systems. A total of 3,718,305 votes were cast under punch-card systems, and 2,353,811 votes were cast under optical-scan systems. *Id.*

with the relevant statutory provisions, taken as a whole. It did what courts do—it decided the case before it in light of the legislature's intent to leave no legally cast vote uncounted. In so doing, it relied on the sufficiency of the general "intent of the voter" standard articulated by the state legislature, coupled with a procedure for ultimate review by an impartial judge, to resolve the concern about disparate evaluations of contested ballots. If we assume—as I do—that the members of that court and the judges who would have carried out its mandate are impartial, its decision does not even raise a colorable federal question.

What must underlie petitioners' entire federal assault on the Florida election procedures is an unstated lack of confidence in the impartiality and capacity of the state judges who would make the critical decisions if the vote count were to proceed. Otherwise, their position is wholly without merit. The endorsement of that position by the majority of this Court can only lend credence to the most cynical appraisal of the work of judges throughout the land. It is confidence in the men and women who administer the judicial system that is the true backbone of the rule of law. Time will one day heal the wound to that confidence that will be inflicted by today's decision. One thing, however, is certain. Although we may never know with complete certainty the identity of the winner of this year's Presidential election, the identity of the loser is perfectly clear. It is the Nation's confidence in the judge as an impartial guardian of the rule of law.

I respectfully dissent.

* * *

■ Justice Souter, with whom Justice Breyer joins and with whom Justice Stevens and Justice Ginsburg join with regard to all but Part C, dissenting.

The Court should not have reviewed either *Bush v. Palm Beach County Canvassing Bd.*, or this case, and should not have stopped Florida's attempt to recount all undervote ballots, by issuing a stay of the Florida Supreme Court's orders during the period of this review. If this Court had allowed the State to follow the course indicated by the opinions of its own Supreme Court, it is entirely possible that there would ultimately have been no issue requiring our review, and political tension could have worked itself out in the Congress following the procedure provided in 3 U.S.C. § 15. The case being before us, however, its resolution by the majority is another erroneous decision.

* * *

C

It is only on the third issue before us [the equal protection claim] that there is a meritorious argument for relief, as this Court's Per Curiam opinion recognizes. It is an issue that might well have been dealt with adequately by the Florida courts if the state proceedings had not been interrupted, and if not disposed of at the state level it could have been considered by the Congress in any electoral vote dispute. But because the course of state proceedings has been interrupted, time is short, and the issue is before us, I think it sensible for the Court to address it.

Petitioners have raised an equal protection claim (or, alternatively, a due process claim), in the charge that unjustifiably disparate standards are applied in different electoral jurisdictions to otherwise identical facts. It is true that the Equal Protection Clause does not forbid the use of a variety of voting mechanisms within a jurisdiction, even though different mechanisms will have different levels of effectiveness in recording voters' intentions; local variety can be justified by concerns about cost, the potential value of innovation, and so on. But evidence in the record here suggests that a different order of disparity obtains under rules for determining a voter's intent that have been applied (and could continue to be applied) to identical types of ballots used in identical brands of machines and exhibiting identical physical characteristics (such as "hanging" or "dimpled" chads). I can conceive of no legitimate state interest served by these differing treatments of the expressions of voters' fundamental rights. The differences appear wholly arbitrary.

In deciding what to do about this, we should take account of the fact that electoral votes are due to be cast in six days. I would therefore remand the case to the courts of Florida with instructions to establish uniform standards for evaluating the several types of ballots that have prompted differing treatments, to be applied within and among counties when passing on such identical ballots in any further recounting (or successive recounting) that the courts might order.

Unlike the majority, I see no warrant for this Court to assume that Florida could not possibly comply with this requirement before the date set for the meeting of electors, December 18.

* * *

To recount these manually would be a tall order, but before this Court stayed the effort to do that the courts of Florida were ready to do their best to get that job done. There is no justification for denying the State the opportunity to try to count all disputed ballots now.

I respectfully dissent.

■ JUSTICE GINSBURG, with whom JUSTICE STEVENS joins, and with whom JUSTICE SOUTER and JUSTICE BREYER join as to Part I, dissenting.

I

THE CHIEF JUSTICE acknowledges that provisions of Florida's Election Code "may well admit of more than one interpretation." *Ante*, at 534. But instead of respecting the state high court's province to say what the State's Election Code means, THE CHIEF JUSTICE maintains that Florida's Supreme

Court has veered so far from the ordinary practice of judicial review that what it did cannot properly be called judging. My colleagues have offered a reasonable construction of Florida's law. Their construction coincides with the view of one of Florida's seven Supreme Court justices. *Gore v. Harris*, 772 So.2d 1243, 1262, (Fla.2000) (Wells, C. J., dissenting); *Palm Beach County Canvassing Bd. v. Harris*, 772 So.2d 1220 (Fla.2000) (on remand) (confirming, 6–1, the construction of Florida law advanced in Gore). I might join THE CHIEF JUSTICE were it my commission to interpret Florida law. But disagreement with the Florida court's interpretation of its own State's law does not warrant the conclusion that the justices of that court have legislated. There is no cause here to believe that the members of Florida's high court have done less than "their mortal best to discharge their oath of office," *Sumner v. Mata*, 449 U.S. 539, 549 (1981), and no cause to upset their reasoned interpretation of Florida law.

* * *

Rarely has this Court rejected outright an interpretation of state law by a state high court. *Fairfax's Devisee v. Hunter's Lessee*, 7 Cranch 603 (1813), *NAACP v. Alabama ex rel. Patterson,* 357 U.S. 449 (1958), and *Bouie v. City of Columbia*, 378 U.S. 347 (1964), cited by THE CHIEF JUSTICE, are three such rare instances. But those cases are embedded in historical contexts hardly comparable to the situation here. *Fairfax's Devisee*, which held that the Virginia Court of Appeals had misconstrued its own forfeiture laws to deprive a British subject of lands secured to him by federal treaties, occurred amidst vociferous States' rights attacks on the Marshall Court. The Virginia court refused to obey this Court's Fairfax's Devisee mandate to enter judgment for the British subject's successor in interest. That refusal led to the Court's pathmarking decision in *Martin v. Hunter's Lessee,* 1 Wheat. 304 (1816). *Patterson*, a case decided three months after *Cooper v. Aaron*, 358 U.S. 1 (1958), in the face of Southern resistance to the civil rights movement, held that the Alabama Supreme Court had irregularly applied its own procedural rules to deny review of a contempt order against the NAACP arising from its refusal to disclose membership lists. We said that "our jurisdiction is not defeated if the nonfederal ground relied on by the state court is without any fair or substantial support." 357 U.S. at 455. *Bouie*, stemming from a lunch counter "sit-in" at the height of the civil rights movement, held that the South Carolina Supreme Court's construction of its trespass laws—criminalizing conduct not covered by the text of an otherwise clear statute—was "unforeseeable" and thus violated due process when applied retroactively to the petitioners. 378 U.S. at 350.

THE CHIEF JUSTICE's casual citation of these cases might lead one to believe they are part of a larger collection of cases in which we said that the Constitution impelled us to train a skeptical eye on a state court's portrayal of state law. But one would be hard pressed, I think, to find additional cases that fit the mold. As JUSTICE BREYER convincingly explains, this case involves nothing close to the kind of recalcitrance by a state high court that warrants extraordinary action by this Court. The Florida Supreme Court concluded that counting every legal vote was the overriding concern of the Florida Legislature when it enacted the State's Election Code. The court surely should not be bracketed with state high courts of the Jim Crow South.

THE CHIEF JUSTICE says that Article II, by providing that state legislatures shall direct the manner of appointing electors, authorizes federal superintendence over the relationship between state courts and state legislatures, and licenses a departure from the usual deference we give to state court interpretations of state law. The Framers of our Constitution, however, understood that in a republican government, the judiciary would construe the legislature's enactments. *See* U.S. Const., Art. III; *The Federalist* No. 78 (A. Hamilton). In light of the constitutional guarantee to States of a "Republican Form of Government," U.S. Const., Art. IV, § 4, Article II can hardly be read to invite this Court to disrupt a State's republican regime. Yet THE CHIEF JUSTICE today would reach out to do just that. By holding that Article II requires our revision of a state court's construction of state laws in order to protect one organ of the State from another, THE CHIEF JUSTICE contradicts the basic principle that a State may organize itself as it sees fit. *See, e.g., Gregory v. Ashcroft*, 501 U.S. 452, 460 (1991) ("Through the structure of its government, and the character of those who exercise government authority, a State defines itself as a sovereign."); *Highland Farms Dairy v. Agnew*, 300 U.S. 608, 612 (1937) ("How power shall be distributed by a state among its governmental organs is commonly, if not always, a question for the state itself.").[2] Article II does not call for the scrutiny undertaken by this Court.

The extraordinary setting of this case has obscured the ordinary principle that dictates its proper resolution: Federal courts defer to state high courts' interpretations of their state's own law. This principle reflects the core of federalism, on which all agree. "The Framers split the atom of sovereignty. It was the genius of their idea that our citizens would have two political capacities, one state and one federal, each protected from incursion by the other." *Saenz v. Roe*, 526 U.S. 489, 504, n. 17 (1999) (*citing U.S. Term Limits, Inc. v. Thornton*, 514 U.S. 779, 838 (1995) (KENNEDY, J., concurring)). THE CHIEF JUSTICE's solicitude for the Florida Legislature comes at the expense of the more fundamental solicitude we owe to the legislature's sovereign. U.S. Const., Art. II, § 1, cl. 2 ("Each State shall appoint, in such Manner as the Legislature thereof may direct," the electors for President and Vice President) (emphasis added). Were the

---

2. Even in the rare case in which a State's "manner" of making and construing laws might implicate a structural constraint, Congress, not this Court, is likely the proper governmental entity to enforce that constraint. *See* U.S. Const., amend. XII; 3 U.S.C. §§ 1–15; *cf. Ohio ex rel. Davis v. Hildebrant,* 241 U.S. 565, 569 (1916) (treating as a nonjusticiable political question whether use of a referendum to override a congressional districting plan enacted by the state legislature violates Art. I, § 4); *Luther v. Borden*, 7 How. 1, 42 (1849).

other members of this Court as mindful as they generally are of our system of dual sovereignty, they would affirm the judgment of the Florida Supreme Court.

II

I agree with Justice STEVENS that petitioners have not presented a substantial equal protection claim. Ideally, perfection would be the appropriate standard for judging the recount. But we live in an imperfect world, one in which thousands of votes have not been counted. I cannot agree that the recount adopted by the Florida court, flawed as it may be, would yield a result any less fair or precise than the certification that preceded that recount.

Even if there were an equal protection violation, I would agree with Justice STEVENS, Justice SOUTER, and Justice BREYER that the Court's concern about "the December 12 deadline" is misplaced. Time is short in part because of the Court's entry of a stay on December 9, several hours after an able circuit judge in Leon County had begun to superintend the recount process. More fundamentally, the Court's reluctance to let the recount go forward—despite its suggestion that "[t]he search for intent can be confined by specific rules designed to ensure uniform treatment" ultimately turns on its own judgment about the practical realities of implementing a recount, not the judgment of those much closer to the process.

Equally important, as Justice BREYER explains, *post*, at 556 (dissenting opinion), the December 12 "deadline" for bringing Florida's electoral votes into 3 U.S.C. § 5's safe harbor lacks the significance the Court assigns it. Were that date to pass, Florida would still be entitled to deliver electoral votes Congress must count unless both Houses find that the votes "ha[d] not been ... regularly given." 3 U.S.C. § 15. The statute identifies other significant dates. *See, e.g.*, § 7 (specifying December 18 as the date electors "shall meet and give their votes"); § 12 (specifying "the fourth Wednesday in December"—this year, December 27—as the date on which Congress, if it has not received a State's electoral votes, shall request the state secretary of state to send a certified return immediately). But none of these dates has ultimate significance in light of Congress' detailed provisions for determining, on "the sixth day of January," the validity of electoral votes. § 15.

The Court assumes that time will not permit "orderly judicial review of any disputed matters that might arise." *Ante*, at 533. But no one has doubted the good faith and diligence with which Florida election officials, attorneys for all sides of this controversy, and the courts of law have performed their duties. Notably, the Florida Supreme Court has produced two substantial opinions within 29 hours of oral argument. In sum, the Court's conclusion that a constitutionally adequate recount is impractical is a prophecy the Court's own judgment will not allow to be tested. Such an untested prophecy should not decide the Presidency of the United States.

I dissent.

■ JUSTICE BREYER, with whom JUSTICE STEVENS and JUSTICE GINSBURG join except as to Part I–A–1, and with whom JUSTICE SOUTER joins as to Part I, dissenting.

The Court was wrong to take this case. It was wrong to grant a stay. It should now vacate that stay and permit the Florida Supreme Court to decide whether the recount should resume.

I

* * *

A

1

The majority raises three Equal Protection problems with the Florida Supreme Court's recount order: first, the failure to include overvotes in the manual recount; second, the fact that all ballots, rather than simply the undervotes, were recounted in some, but not all, counties; and third, the absence of a uniform, specific standard to guide the recounts. As far as the first issue is concerned, petitioners presented no evidence, to this Court or to any Florida court, that a manual recount of overvotes would identify additional legal votes. The same is true of the second, and, in addition, the majority's reasoning would seem to invalidate any state provision for a manual recount of individual counties in a statewide election.

The majority's third concern does implicate principles of fundamental fairness. The majority concludes that the Equal Protection Clause requires that a manual recount be governed not only by the uniform general standard of the "clear intent of the voter," but also by uniform subsidiary standards (for example, a uniform determination whether indented, but not perforated, "undervotes" should count). The opinion points out that the Florida Supreme Court ordered the inclusion of Broward County's under-counted "legal votes" even though those votes included ballots that were not perforated but simply "dimpled," while newly recounted ballots from other counties will likely include only votes determined to be "legal" on the basis of a stricter standard. In light of our previous remand, the Florida Supreme Court may have been reluctant to adopt a more specific standard than that provided for by the legislature for fear of exceeding its authority under Article II. However, since the use of different standards could favor one or the other of the candidates, since time was, and is, too short to permit the lower courts to iron out significant differences through ordinary judicial review, and since the relevant distinction was embodied in the order of the State's highest court, I agree that, in these very special circumstances, basic principles of fairness may well have counseled the adoption of a uniform standard to address the problem. In light of the majority's disposition, I need not decide whether, or the extent to which, as a remedial matter, the Constitution would place limits upon the content of the uniform standard.

2

Nonetheless, there is no justification for the majority's remedy, which is simply to reverse the lower court and halt the recount entirely. An appropriate remedy would be, instead, to remand this case with instructions that, even at this late date, would permit the Florida Supreme Court to require recounting all undercounted votes in Florida, including those from Broward, Volusia, Palm Beach, and Miami–Dade Counties, whether or not previously recounted prior to the end of the protest period, and to do so in accordance with a single-uniform substandard.

* * *

B

The remainder of petitioners' claims, which are the focus of The Chief Justice's concurrence, raise no significant federal questions. I cannot agree that The Chief Justice's unusual review of state law in this case, see ante, at 548–550 (Ginsburg, J., dissenting opinion), is justified by reference either to Art. II, § 1, or to 3 U.S.C. § 5. Moreover, even were such review proper, the conclusion that the Florida Supreme Court's decision contravenes federal law is untenable.

* * *

II

Despite the reminder that this case involves "an election for the President of the United States," *ante*, at 533 (Rehnquist, C. J., concurring), no preeminent legal concern, or practical concern related to legal questions, required this Court to hear this case, let alone to issue a stay that stopped Florida's recount process in its tracks. With one exception, petitioners' claims do not ask us to vindicate a constitutional provision designed to protect a basic human right. *See, e.g., Brown v. Board of Education*, 347 U.S. 483 (1954). Petitioners invoke fundamental fairness, namely, the need for procedural fairness, including finality. But with the one "equal protection" exception, they rely upon law that focuses, not upon that basic need, but upon the constitutional allocation of power. Respondents invoke a competing fundamental consideration—the need to determine the voter's true intent. But they look to state law, not to federal constitutional law, to protect that interest. Neither side claims electoral fraud, dishonesty, or the like. And the more fundamental equal protection claim might have been left to the state court to resolve if and when it was discovered to have mattered. It could still be resolved through a remand conditioned upon issuance of a uniform standard; it does not require reversing the Florida Supreme Court.

Of course, the selection of the President is of fundamental national importance. But that importance is political, not legal. And this Court should resist the temptation unnecessarily to resolve tangential legal disputes, where doing so threatens to determine the outcome of the election.

The Constitution and federal statutes themselves make clear that restraint is appropriate. They set forth a road map of how to resolve disputes about electors, even after an election as close as this one. That road map foresees resolution of electoral disputes by state courts. *See* 3 U.S.C. § 5 (providing that, where a "State shall have provided, by laws enacted prior to [election day], for its final determination of any controversy or contest concerning the appointment of . . . electors . . . by judicial or other methods," the subsequently chosen electors enter a safe harbor free from congressional challenge). But it nowhere provides for involvement by the United States Supreme Court.

To the contrary, the Twelfth Amendment commits to Congress the authority and responsibility to count electoral votes. A federal statute, the Electoral Count Act, enacted after the close 1876 Hayes–Tilden Presidential election, specifies that, after States have tried to resolve disputes (through "judicial" or other means), Congress is the body primarily authorized to resolve remaining disputes. *See* Electoral Count Act of 1887, 24 Stat. 373, 3 U.S.C. §§ 5, 6, and 15.

The legislative history of the Act makes clear its intent to commit the power to resolve such disputes to Congress, rather than the courts:

> "The two Houses are, by the Constitution, authorized to make the count of electoral votes. They can only count legal votes, and in doing so must determine, from the best evidence to be had, what are legal votes. . . . The power to determine rests with the two Houses, and there is no other constitutional tribunal." H. Rep. No. 1638, 49th Cong., 1st Sess., 2 (1886) (report submitted by Rep. Caldwell, Select Committee on the Election of President and Vice–President).

* * *

The Act goes on to set out rules for the congressional determination of disputes about those votes. If, for example, a state submits a single slate of electors, Congress must count those votes unless both Houses agree that the votes "have not been . . . regularly given." 3 U.S.C. § 15. If, as occurred in 1876, one or more states submits two sets of electors, then Congress must determine whether a slate has entered the safe harbor of § 5, in which case its votes will have "conclusive" effect. *Id.* If, as also occurred in 1876, there is controversy about "which of two or more of such State authorities . . . is the lawful tribunal" authorized to appoint electors, then each House shall determine separately which votes are "supported by the decision of such State so authorized by its law." *Id.* If the two Houses of Congress agree, the votes they have approved will be counted. If they disagree, then "the votes of the electors whose appointment shall have been certified by the executive of the State, under the seal thereof, shall be counted." *Id.*

Given this detailed, comprehensive scheme for counting electoral votes, there is no reason to believe that federal law either foresees or requires resolution of such a political issue by this Court. Nor, for that matter, is there any reason to that think the Constitution's Framers would have reached a different conclusion. Madison, at least, believed that allowing the judiciary to choose the presidential electors "was out of the question." Madison, July 25, 1787 (reprinted in 5 Elliot's Debates on the Federal Constitution 363 (2d ed. 1876)).

The decision by both the Constitution's Framers and the 1886 Congress to minimize this Court's role in resolving close federal presidential elections is as wise as it is clear. However awkward or difficult it may be for Congress to resolve difficult electoral disputes, Congress, being a political body, expresses the people's will far more accurately than does an unelected Court. And the people's will is what elections are about.

Moreover, Congress was fully aware of the danger that would arise should it ask judges, unarmed with appropriate legal standards, to resolve a hotly contested Presidential election contest. Just after the 1876 Presidential election, Florida, South Carolina, and Louisiana each sent two slates of electors to Washington. Without these States, Tilden, the Democrat, had 184 electoral votes, one short of the number required to win the Presidency. With those States, Hayes, his Republican opponent, would have had 185. In order to choose between the two slates of electors, Congress decided to appoint an electoral commission composed of five Senators, five Representatives, and five Supreme Court Justices. Initially the Commission was to be evenly divided between Republicans and Democrats, with Justice David Davis, an Independent, to possess the decisive vote. However, when at the last minute the Illinois Legislature elected Justice Davis to the United States Senate, the final position on the Commission was filled by Supreme Court Justice Joseph P. Bradley.

The Commission divided along partisan lines, and the responsibility to cast the deciding vote fell to Justice Bradley. He decided to accept the votes by the Republican electors, and thereby awarded the Presidency to Hayes.

Justice Bradley immediately became the subject of vociferous attacks. Bradley was accused of accepting bribes, of being captured by railroad interests, and of an eleventh-hour change in position after a night in which his house "was surrounded by the carriages" of Republican partisans and railroad officials. C. Woodward, Reunion and Reaction 159–160 (1966). Many years later, Professor Bickel concluded that Bradley was honest and impartial. He thought that " 'the great question' for Bradley was, in fact, whether Congress was entitled to go behind election returns or had to accept them as certified by state authorities," an "issue of principle." The Least Dangerous Branch 185 (1962). Nonetheless, Bickel points out, the legal question upon which Justice Bradley's decision turned was not very important in the contemporaneous political context. He says that "in the circumstances the issue of principle was trivial, it was overwhelmed by all that hung in the balance, and it should not have been decisive." *Id.*

For present purposes, the relevance of this history lies in the fact that the participation in the work of the electoral commission by five Justices, including Justice Bradley, did not lend that process legitimacy. Nor did it assure the public that the process had worked fairly, guided by the law. Rather, it simply embroiled Members of the Court in partisan conflict, thereby undermining respect for the judicial process. And the Congress that later enacted the Electoral Count Act knew it.

This history may help to explain why I think it not only legally wrong, but also most unfortunate, for the Court simply to have terminated the Florida recount. Those who caution judicial restraint in resolving political disputes have described the quintessential case for that restraint as a case marked, among other things, by the "strangeness of the issue," its "intractability to principled resolution," its "sheer momentousness, . . . which tends to unbalance judicial judgment," and "the inner vulnerability, the self-doubt of an institution which is electorally irresponsible and has no earth to draw strength from." Bickel, *supra*, at 184. Those characteristics mark this case.

At the same time, as I have said, the Court is not acting to vindicate a fundamental constitutional principle, such as the need to protect a basic human liberty. No other strong reason to act is present. Congressional statutes tend to obviate the need. And, above all, in this highly politicized matter, the appearance of a split decision runs the risk of undermining the public's confidence in the Court itself. That confidence is a public treasure. It has been built slowly over many years, some of which were marked by a Civil War and the tragedy of segregation. It is a vitally necessary ingredient of any successful effort to protect basic liberty and, indeed, the rule of law itself. We run no risk of returning to the days when a President (responding to this Court's efforts to protect the Cherokee Indians) might have said, "John Marshall has made his decision; now let him enforce it!" Loth, Chief Justice John Marshall and The Growth of the American Republic 365 (1948). But we do risk a self-inflicted wound—a wound that may harm not just the Court, but the Nation.

I fear that in order to bring this agonizingly long election process to a definitive conclusion, we have not adequately attended to that necessary "check upon our own exercise of power," "our own sense of self-restraint." *United States v. Butler*, 297 U.S. 1, 79 (1936) (Stone, J., dissenting). Justice Brandeis once said of the Court, "The most important thing we do is not doing." Bickel, *supra*, at 71. What it does today, the Court should have left undone. I would repair the damage done as best we now can, by permitting the Florida recount to continue under uniform standards.

I respectfully dissent.

NOTES AND QUESTIONS

1. *The constitutional right to vote and the equal protection clause. Bush v. Gore* refers to the evolution of the right to vote in American constitutional law through cases such as *Baker v. Carr* and *Reynolds v. Sims*. Nonetheless, as the Court notes, the constitutional structure does not create an affirmative right to vote for electors of the President—although the last time any state legislature directly chose the electors appears to have been 1860 in South Carolina (Colorado, on the eve of statehood, chose its electors for the 1876 Presidential election by direct action of the territorial legislature). *Bush v. Gore* builds on these precedents and follows the same structure. Article II of the Constitution, which sets up the Electoral College process, does not bestow the right to vote on anyone. Article II permits state legislatures to appoint presidential electors or to choose other manners of choosing electors, such as various forms of popular election (the electors can be elected on a winner-take-all popular vote, as they are in 48 states today, or the legislature can choose to have the electors chosen congressional district by congressional district, as they are in Maine and Nebraska). But once the state legislature chooses popular election for the selection, the Constitution constrains the kind of voting system the state can employ. The principles of *Harper* and *Reynolds* apply to require that any system of electing presidential electors meet the standards of equal protection, including that all votes be weighted equally and that the fundamental rights nature of the right to vote be protected through appropriate procedural and substantive guarantees.

2. *Bush v. Gore* extends to new terrain the Warren Court's constitutionalization of the right to vote. Six members of the Court agreed with this extension, and Justice Breyer agreed that "basic principles of fairness" were implicated by non-uniform recount rules. The first generation cases dealt with the structures of state statutes and the formal conditions on access to the ballot box those statutes—on their face—imposed. The second generation cases dealt with the statutory design of democratic institutions; again, these cases required the Supreme Court to assess state statutes on their face for consistency with equal protection principles. Even then, at the time of *Reynolds* important concerns were expressed about the administrability of the Court's newly announced equal protection principles: what exactly did an undiluted, equally weighted vote mean? But in the *Reynolds* line of cases, the Supreme Court quickly developed a simple and easily administered answer (albeit one some critics consider *too* simple): one person, one vote. *Bush v. Gore* seemed to extend these doctrines to the micro-level of the actual operation of the electoral machinery, literally as well as figuratively, including the ballot-by-ballot counting of votes. What precisely is the content of the equal protection principles that *Bush* announces? How far do or should those principles extend? And as the constitutional ban against unequally weighted votes gets extended to the administration of the voting system, how will or should the courts deal with the administrability concerns that this extension of *Harper* and *Reynolds* inevitably will raise? If the full electoral machinery of the highly decentralized electoral process we currently have must ensure that all votes are, at the end of the day, weighted equally, what precisely does a non-diluted or equally weighted vote mean? Is there any rule-like principle, comparable to that of one vote, one person, looming on the horizon that would provide an answer to these administrability concerns? Note that there is nothing in the Court's opinion that suggests any reason the equal protection concerns it announces are limited to Presidential elections, nor is there any reason to think these concerns should be limited to that one electoral context.

3. Critics of the majority's equal protection holding argued that the Court had focused on one stage of the vote tabulation process—the manual recounts—in isolation from the other stages that had preceded these recounts. In particular, factfinding during the litigation had revealed great disparities in the rates of recorded "undervotes" for the Presidential election depending upon the type of voting technology different counties used to count votes. In Florida, three of every 1,000 optically scanned ballots recorded no presidential vote, while 15 of every 1,000 punch-card ballots were recorded as showing no presidential vote. Under *Bush v. Gore*, does Florida's use of different technologies, with such dramatically different rates of recording votes, violate the equal protection clause? Indeed, can one argue that *Bush v. Gore*'s principles suggest that manual recounts might be constitutionally *required* as a remedy for a voting-rights violation that would otherwise occur were voters in different counties to have differential opportunities of having their "attempted" votes validly counted? If strict scrutiny is the constitutionally required standard, in light of the fundamental right at stake, does a state have a sufficiently compelling justification for permitting such diverse technologies when they have such different consequences for recording votes? Note that the question of the substantive scope of the equal protection doctrine announced in *Bush v. Gore* is a distinct question from the legal significance, under Florida or federal law, of the December 12th and 18th dates for the Electoral College process. That is, there are important questions of equal protection and the right to vote that *Bush v. Gore* now opens up; in that particular case, the Court majority did not pursue the implications of these questions, given the majority's understanding of the finality of the Dec.12th date. But those questions will remain in future cases where similar cutoff dates do not truncate the power of federal courts to provide remedies for equal protection violations.

4. Can one argue that an important constitutional difference exists between differential vote counting that results from different machine technology versus from different human actors applying different standards to evaluate votes in a manual recount? In terms of perceptions of procedural fairness and the legitimacy of election processes, is there a difference between inconsistent technology and inconsistent human judgments about what counts as a vote? Can one argue that the perceived integrity of the electoral process is more compromised when human actors exercise highly discretionary judgments as to what counts as a vote, when those actors know in advance the likely effect on an election outcome? If technology differences do not involve these kind of discretionary and potentially partisan influences, should the equal protection clause be less concerned with technological rather than human differences in vote counting? Should it matter to the equal protection analysis what reasons lie behind different counties in Florida choosing different technologies? Suppose, for example, the choice of machinery reflects variables such as the time at which different counties upgraded their technologies. Suppose, instead, election officials intentionally located less efficient vote-recording technologies in particular precincts or counties for reasons of anticipated partisan advantage. Should intent be crucial here? Or should differential effects alone be enough?

5. Subsequent investigation long after the litigation was complete revealed that the disparities between Florida's counties was greater than had been realized at the time. For example, while there was a threefold difference in rate at which ballots were treated as undervoted between optical-scan and punch-card machines, there was great variation even within those counties that used optical scanners. Optical-scan machines can be programmed to let voters know their ballot is invalid and to give them a second chance to cast a valid vote; that is why the rate of error tends to be lower with optical-scan machines than with punch-card systems. But not all Florida counties with optical scanners had this aspect of the technology available; and not all those that had the equipment used it. Indeed, two counties had the second-chance capabilities on their machines but chose to deactivate it. Thus, there were 24 optical-scan counties that gave voters a second chance; there, only 0.6% of ballots were invalidated. But in 15 optical-scan counties in which the technology was not set up to give voters a second chance, the invalidation rate was 5.7%. This compares with an invalidation rate in the 24 punch-card counties of 3.9%. If optical-scan machines that informed voters that their initial ballot was not valid had been used throughout the State, as many as 120,000 invalidated ballots would, in theory, have been validly corrected and cast.

Other differences across counties also emerged. Voters sometimes filled in an oval—on an optical-scan ballot—or punched a hole—on a punchcard ballot and then also wrote in the same candidate's name on that ballot. Twenty-six counties did not count these ballots; but 34 counties apparently did. Similarly, Florida law requires an automatic recount when the margin of error between candidates in the initial count is less than 0.5%; the 2000 Presidential election triggered this automatic recount process. A 1999 opinion letter from the Division of Elections states that this requires an actual recounting of the ballots. But 18 counties apparently did no recount and instead merely checked the counting mechanisms of their machines to see whether the numbers previously registered matched the numbers they had turned in. The general picture that emerges is that of a radically decentralized electoral system in Florida, with individual county election supervisors exercising a great deal of discretion and little overriding authority or consistency provided through statewide offices, such as the Secretary of State. The information in this note is taken from the detailed investigation reported in John Mintz & Peter Slevin, *Human Factor Was at Core Of Vote Fiasco*, Wash. Post, June 1, 2001, at A1.

Apparently, the more scrutiny applied to Florida's 2000 election processes, the more differing treatment of ballots across counties at all stages of the process comes to be revealed. What light, if any, does this shed on the Court's equal protection holding? What are the implications of that holding for these various other inconsistencies across counties?

6. *Bush v. Gore* not only drew the nation's attention to the problems with election administration but it drew the attention of unprecedented numbers of scholars. Much of the work, like the per curiam's consideration, was "limited to the present circumstances," but some representative pieces that placed *Bush v. Gore* in a larger doctrinal or philosophical framework include essay collections such as A Badly Flawed Election: Debating Bush v. Gore, The Supreme Court, and American Democracy (Ronald Dworkin ed., 2002); Bush v. Gore: The Question of Legitimacy (Bruce Ackerman ed., 2002); The Unfinished Election of 2000 (Jack N. Rakove ed. 2001); The Vote: Bush, Gore and the Supreme Court (Cass R. Sunstein & Richard A. Epstein eds. 2001); Symposium, *The Law of Presidential Elections: Issues in the Wake of Florida 2000*, 29 Fla. St. U.L. Rev. (2001), and articles such as Mary Anne Case, *Are Plain Hamburgers Now Unconstitutional?: The Equal Protection Component of* Bush v. Gore *as a Chapter in the History of Ideas About Law*, 70 U. Chi. L. Rev. 55 (2003); David Cole, *The Liberal Legacy of* Bush v. Gore, 94 Geo. L.J. 1427 (2006); Edward B. Foley, *The Future of* Bush v. Gore, 68 Ohio St. L. J. ___ (2007); Richard L. Hasen, *The Untimely Death of* Bush v. Gore, 60 Stan. L. Rev. ___ (2007); Daniel Lowenstein, *The Meaning of* Bush v. Gore, 68 Oh. St. L. J. (forthcoming 2007); Samuel Issacharoff, Bush v. Gore: *Political Judgments*, 68 U. Chi. L. Rev. 637 (2001); Pamela S. Karlan, *Nothing Personal: The Evolution of the Newest Equal Protection from* Shaw v. Reno *to* Bush v. Gore, 79 N.C.L. Rev. 1346 (2001); Michael J. Klarman, Bush v. Gore *Through the Lens of Constitutional History*, 89 Cal. L. Rev. 721 (2001); Spencer Overton, *Rules, Standards, and* Bush v. Gore: *Form and the Law of Democracy*, 37 Harv. C.R.–C.L.L. Rev. (2002); Richard Pildes, *Democracy and Disorder*, 68 U. Chi. L. Rev. 695 (2001); Edmund P. Sauer, *"Arbitrary and Disparate" Obstacles to Democracy: The Equal Protection Implications of* Bush v. Gore *on Election Administration*, 19 J.L. & Pol. 299 (2003); Mark Tushnet, *Renormalizing* Bush v. Gore: *An Anticipatory Intellectual History*, 90 Geo. L.J. 113 (2001).

D. THE TIMING OF FEDERAL COURT INTERVENTION INTO ELECTORAL AND SIMILAR LITIGATION

In addition to the substantive issue of what federal interests are sufficiently strong to justify a role for federal law—constitutional and statutory—in resolving state and national issues involving democratic processes, there is an important procedural question about the proper timing of federal court intervention, if such intervention is to occur. As has been stressed in earlier sections, the actual conduct of elections is a matter reserved primarily to state law. Nonetheless, there are significant federal interests in the orderly conduct of elections, particularly when the elections in question concern federal office. This tension manifests itself not only in the substantive role of state versus federal law, but in the procedural question of *when* the federal interest arises. Absent a claim of exclusion from the franchise, race discrimination, or an abridgment of some other distinct federal right, the federal interest is primarily in insuring that state procedures are fairly and consistently applied. As a result, the invocation of federal court oversight almost invariably implicates federal review of matters generally thought to be the province of state authority, again reinforcing the importance of the timing question.

To date, the relation of federal and state courts has been most clearly developed in the context of redistricting. As discussed in Chapter 3, there is a distinct federal constitutional interest in guaranteeing equality of voting strength, as reflected in the one-person, one-vote rule of apportionment. However, the cases governing redistricting also point to the right of the states to conduct their own districting practices, subject to the limitations imposed by federal law. An immediate question as to the propriety of federal court action is posed whenever redistricting challenges are filed in both federal and state courts. Such challenges clearly present a constitutionally viable federal claim, but also implicate significant federalism and comity concerns in federal court intervention in ongoing state processes. Although federal court "abstention" doctrines generally dictate caution in invoking federal oversight powers, the fact that there are distinct federal rights at play puts the application of these doctrines in considerable doubt.

Growe v. Emison

507 U.S. 25 (1993).

■ JUSTICE SCALIA delivered the opinion of the Court.

This case raises important issues regarding the propriety of the District Court's pursuing reapportionment of Minnesota's state legislative and federal congressional districts in the face of Minnesota state-court litigation seeking similar relief, and regarding the District Court's conclusion that the state court's legislative plan violated § 2 of the Voting Rights Act of 1965, 42 U.S.C. § 1973.

I

In January 1991, a group of Minnesota voters filed a state-court action against the Minnesota Secretary of State and other officials responsible for administering elections, claiming that the State's congressional and legislative districts were malapportioned, in violation of the Fourteenth Amendment of the Federal Constitution and Article 4, § 2, of the Minnesota Constitution. *Cotlow v. Growe*, [622 N.W. 2d. 561 (Minn. 2001)] The plaintiffs asserted that the 1990 federal census results revealed a significant change in the distribution of the state population, and requested that the court declare the current districts unlawful and draw new districts if the legislature failed to do so. In February, the parties stipulated that, in light of the new census, the challenged districting plans were unconstitutional. The Minnesota Supreme Court appointed a Special Redistricting Panel (composed of one appellate judge and two district judges) to preside over the case.

In March, a second group of plaintiffs filed an action in federal court against essentially the same defendants, raising similar challenges to the congressional and legislative districts. *Emison v. Growe*. The Emison plaintiffs (who include members of various racial minorities) in addition raised objections to the legislative districts under § 2 of the Voting Rights Act, 42 U.S.C. § 1973, alleging that those districts needlessly fragmented two Indian reservations and divided the minority population of Minneapolis. The suit sought declaratory relief and continuing federal jurisdiction over any legislative efforts to develop new districts. A three-judge panel was appointed pursuant to 28 U.S.C. § 2284(a).

While the federal and state actions were getting underway, the Minnesota Legislature was holding public hearings on, and designing, new legislative districts. In May, it adopted a new legislative districting plan, Chapter 246, Minn.Stat. §§ 2.403–2.703 (Supp.1991), and repealed the prior 1983 apportionment. It was soon recognized that Chapter 246 contained many technical errors—mistaken compass directions, incorrect street names, noncontiguous districts, and a few instances of double representation. By August, committees of the legislature had prepared curative legislation, Senate File 1596 and House File 1726 (collectively, Senate File 1596), but the legislature, which had adjourned in late May, was not due to reconvene until January 6, 1992.

* * *

In early December, before the state court issued its final plan, the District Court stayed all proceedings in the Cotlow case, and enjoined parties to that action from "attempting to enforce or implement any order of the ... Minnesota Special Redistricting Panel which has proposed adoption of a reapportionment plan relating to state redistricting or Congressional redistricting." The court explained its action as necessary to prevent the state court from interfering with the legislature's efforts to redistrict and with the District Court's jurisdiction. It mentioned the Emison Voting Rights Act allegations as grounds for issuing the injunction, which it found necessary in aid of its jurisdiction, see 28 U.S.C. § 1651. One judge dissented.

* * *

When the legislature reconvened in January, both Houses approved the corrections to Chapter 246 contained in Senate File 1596 and also adopted a congressional redistricting plan that legislative committees had drafted the previous October. The Governor, however, vetoed the legislation. On January 30, the state court issued a final order adopting its legislative plan and requiring that plan to be used for the 1992 primary and general elections. By February 6, pursuant to an order issued shortly after this Court vacated the injunction, the parties had submitted their proposals for congressional redistricting, and on February 17 the state court held hearings on the competing plans.

Two days later, the District Court issued an order adopting its own legislative and congressional districting plans and permanently enjoining interference with state implementation of those plans. . . .

In early March, the state court indicated that it was "fully prepared to release a congressional plan" but that the federal injunction prevented it from doing so. In its view, the federal plan reached population equality "without sufficient regard for the preservation of municipal and county boundaries."

* * *

II

In their challenge to both of the District Court's redistricting plans, appellants contend that, under the principles of *Scott v. Germano*, 381 U.S. 407 (1965) (per curiam), the court erred in not deferring to the Minnesota Special Redistricting Panel's proceedings. We agree.

The parties do not dispute that both courts had jurisdiction to consider the complaints before them. Of course federal courts and state courts often find themselves exercising concurrent jurisdiction over the same subject matter, and when that happens a federal court generally need neither abstain (i.e., dismiss the case before it) nor defer to the state proceedings (i.e., withhold action until the state proceedings have concluded). *See McClellan v. Carland*, 217 U.S. 268, 282 (1910). In rare circumstances, however, principles of federalism and comity dictate otherwise. We have found abstention necessary, for example, when the federal action raises difficult questions of state law bearing on important matters of state policy, or when federal jurisdiction has been invoked to restrain ongoing state criminal proceedings. *See Colorado River Water Conservation Dist. v. United States*, 424 U.S. 800 (1976). We have required deferral, causing a federal court to "sta[y] its hands," when a constitutional issue in the federal action will be mooted or presented in a different posture following conclusion of the state-court case. *Railroad Comm'n of Texas v. Pullman Co.*, 312 U.S. 496, 501.

In the reapportionment context, the Court has required federal judges to defer consideration of disputes involving redistricting where the State, through its legislative or judicial branch, has begun to address that highly political task itself. In *Germano*, a Federal District Court invalidated Illinois' Senate districts and entered an order requiring the State to submit to the court any revised Senate districting scheme it might adopt. An action had previously been filed in state court attacking the same districting scheme. In that case the Illinois Supreme Court held (subsequent to the federal court's order) that the Senate districting scheme was invalid, but expressed confidence that the General Assembly would enact a lawful plan during its then current session, scheduled to end in July 1965. The Illinois Supreme Court retained jurisdiction to ensure that the upcoming 1966 general elections would be conducted pursuant to a constitutionally valid plan.

This Court disapproved the District Court's action. The District Court "should have stayed its hand," we said, and in failing to do so overlooked this Court's teaching that state courts have a significant role in redistricting. . . .

Today we renew our adherence to the principles expressed in *Germano*, which derive from the recognition that the Constitution leaves with the States primary responsibility for apportionment of their federal congressional and state legislative districts. *See* U.S. Const., Art. I, § 2. "We say once again what has been said on many occasions: reapportionment is primarily the duty and responsibility of the State through its legislature or other body, rather than of a federal court." *Chapman v. Meier*, 420 U.S. 1, 27 (1975). Absent evidence that these state branches will fail timely to perform that duty, a federal court must neither affirmatively obstruct state reapportionment nor permit federal litigation to be used to impede it.

Judged by these principles, the District Court's December injunction of state-court proceedings, vacated by this Court in January, was clear error. It seems to have been based upon the mistaken view that federal judges need defer only to the Minnesota Legislature and not at all to the State's courts. Thus, the January 20 deadline the District Court established was described as a deadline for the legislature, ignoring the possibility and legitimacy of state judicial redistricting. And the injunction itself treated the state court's provisional legislative redistricting plan as "interfering" in the reapportionment process. But the doctrine of *Germano* prefers both state branches to federal courts as agents of apportionment. The Minnesota Special Redistricting Panel's issuance of its plan (conditioned on the legislature's failure to enact a constitutionally acceptable plan in January), far from being a federally enjoinable "interference," was precisely the sort of state judicial supervision of redistricting we have encouraged.

Nor do the reasons offered by the District Court for its actions in December and February support departure from the *Germano* principles. It is true that the Emison plaintiffs alleged that the 1983 legislative districting scheme violated the Voting Rights Act, while the Cotlow complaint never invoked that statute. *Germano*, however, does not require that the federal and state-court complaints be identical; it instead focuses on the nature of the relief requested: reapportionment of election districts. Minnesota can have only one set of legislative districts, and the primacy of the State in designing those districts compels a federal court to defer.

The District Court also expressed concern over the lack of time for orderly appeal, prior to the State's primaries, of any judgment that might issue from the state court, noting that Minnesota allows the losing party 90 days to appeal. We fail to see the relevance of the speed of appellate review. *Germano* requires only that the state agencies adopt a constitutional plan "within ample time . . . to be utilized in the [upcoming] election." It does not require appellate review of the plan prior to the election, and such a requirement would ignore the reality that States must often redistrict in the most exigent circumstances—during the brief interval between completion of the decennial federal census and the primary season for the general elections in the next even-numbered year. Our consideration of this appeal, long after the Minnesota primary and final elections have been held, itself reflects the improbability of completing judicial review before the necessary deadline for a new redistricting scheme.

* * *

The judgment is reversed, and the case is remanded with instructions to dismiss.

So ordered.

NOTES AND QUESTIONS

1. The *Pullman* abstention doctrine identified by the Court in *Growe* is a doctrine that emerges from concern that there should not be premature federal court intervention when ongoing state proceedings might obviate the need for the federal court to act. As a general matter, *Pullman* abstention has been thought a jurisdictional barrier to federal intervention, hence the requirement that federal courts actually abstain from further involvement. Note that in footnote one of *Growe*, the Court recasts the doctrine to dictate "deferral" rather than absention. Presumably the difference is that the presence of ongoing state proceedings should caution federal courts to wait until there is a clear indication that federal interests require immediate action, rather then to dismiss the federal action as essentially preempted by the presence of the state action. Thus, one federal appellate decision has recast *Pullman* abstention as something that "may be a matter of discretion." Under this view, the *Pullman* doctrine should not force federal court abstention when the "timing, outcome and consequences of the state-court proceedings are uncertain" and where there are circumstances requiring immediate determination of the issues before the court. *Public Service of New Hampshire v. Patch*, 167 F.3d 15, 24 (1st Cir. 1998).

2. Federal courts have also refused to defer consideration of overlapping federal and state issues when further state adjudication is unlikely to alter the way in which the federal issues are to be resolved. Thus, the Fifth Circuit has concluded that "deference to state court adjudication only be made where the issue of state law is uncertain. If the state statute in question, although never interpreted by a state tribunal, is not fairly subject to an interpretation which will render unnecessary or substantially modify the federal constitutional question, it is the duty of the federal court to exercise its properly invoked jurisdiction." *Louisiana Debating & Literary Ass'n v. City of New Orleans*, 42 F.3d 1483, 1491–1492 (5th Cir. 1995). *See also Marks v. Stinson*, 19 F.3d 873, 883 n.6 (3d Cir. 1994) (declining to abstain because there the statutes in question were "neither ambiguous nor material to the federal issues presented in this case"); *S & S Pawn Shop Inc. v. City of Del City*, 947 F.2d 432, 442 (10th Cir. 1991) (abstaining because the state law was uncertain and ambiguous and subject to reasonable interpretation by the state court). The Fifth Circuit has further concluded that "abstention is the exception, not the rule." *Louisiana Debating*, 42 F.3d at 1491.

3. Alternatively, courts have interpreted *Growe* to recognize concurrent jurisdiction between state and federal courts. For example:

> The United States Supreme Court in *Growe* made clear that federal courts and state courts have *concurrent jurisdiction* to entertain challenges to redistricting plans and that, as a result, both courts are open to such claims. *Growe* stands only for the proposition that the federal court must "defer" to any state-court redistricting effort; it does not say that the federal court must dismiss its own proceedings. Indeed, in *Growe*, the Supreme Court acknowledged that, after the state court had completed its proceeding, the federal court later rightfully took up the remaining claim under § 2 of the Voting Rights Act of 1965; *Growe* did not require that the plaintiffs there pursue their § 2 claim in state court as well.

Thompson v. Smith, 52 F. Supp. 2d 1364 (M.D. Ala. 1999). On the other hand, federal courts need not be dissuaded from acting by *Pullman* considerations when no state court actions have been filed or are likely to resolve the disputed matters within the relevant period of time. "Once it is apparent that a state court, through no fault of the district court, will not develop a redistricting plan in time for an upcoming election, *Growe* authorizes a federal district court to go ahead and develop a redistricting plan." *Wesch v. Folsom*, 6 F.3d 1465, 1473 (11th Cir. 1993).

4. Once the *Pullman* doctrine is held to require deferral rather than abstention, further options present themselves to the federal courts. In those states that permit federal courts to certify issues of unresolved state law to the highest court of that state, the *Pullman* doctrine may properly be seen as a mechanism to allow further state elaboration of disputed issues of state law, even while the federal courts retain jurisdiction. In

Tunick v. Safir, 209 F.3d 67 (2d Cir. 2000) Judge Calabresi seized upon a statement by the Supreme Court that "[c]ertification today covers territory once dominated by a deferral device called '*Pullman* abstention,' " relying on *Arizonans for Official English v. Arizona*, 520 U.S. 43 (1997). Judge Calabresi noted, "The teaching of *Arizonans*, therefore, is that we should consider certifying in more instances than had previously been thought appropriate, and do so even when the federal courts might think that the meaning of a state law is 'plain.' "

5. Challenged election cases also implicate a second abstention doctrine first identified in *Burford v. Sun Oil Co.*, 319 U.S. 315 (1943). *Burford* abstention is based on considerations of federalism and comity that require federal courts to resist disrupting the customary procedures of state law. In *Burford*, for example, the issue presented was whether a federal court could abstain from exercising jurisdiction when a challenge to the reasonableness of an order of the Texas Railroad Commission would immerse a federal court in the center of the State's complicated oil regulatory apparatus. As a general matter, the *Burford* abstention doctrine is "justified if and only if (1) a state has created a complex regulatory system on a matter of substantial importance to the state, (2) there exist no federal interests in the matter that override the state interests, and (3) the state legislature has made the state courts integral to the administrative scheme by delegating to them broad discretion so that they may participate in the development of regulatory policy." Lewis C. Yelin, Note, *Burford Abstention in Actions for Damages*, 99 Colum. L. Rev. 1871, 1881 (1999). *Pullman* abstention and *Burford* abstention are motivated by different concerns. The former is based in the idea that courts should not decide constitutional issues if they can in any way avoid doing so. Because *Burford* is based in principles of comity and federalism, there is therefore a conspicuous balancing element in *Burford* that is not necessarily present in *Pullman* abstention cases. After *Growe*, however, the lines between the two abstention doctrines has blurred. Thus, in *Quackenbush v. Allstate Insurance Co.*, 517 U.S. 706 (1996), the Court held that there should be "a narrow range of circumstances in which *Burford* can justify dismissal of a federal action." As one court has summarized the state of uncertainty, "In light of the Supreme Court's decision between those circumstances that require dismissal of a suit and those that require postponing consideration of its merits, it may be more appropriate to refer to *Burford* abstention in this case as *Burford* 'deferral.' [citing *Growe*] Nonetheless, after more than a half-century in which courts and commentators have spoken of *Burford* abstention, the court believes that use of the phrase '*Burford* deferral' would be more confusing than clarifying." *In the Matter of Rehabilitation of the Universe Life Insurance Company*, 35 F. Supp. 2d 1297 (D. Kan. 1999).

6. In *Touchston v. McDermott*, 234 F.3d 1161 (11th Cir. 2000), the first federal court appeal in the Florida presidential controversy, the Eleventh Circuit confronted precisely these kind of abstention claims. Although the Court ultimately decided the case on a timing questions (discussed below), it decisively rejected arguments that the abstention doctrines could prove an obstacle to federal oversight:

> Defendants argue that we should abstain from hearing this case under *Burford v. Sun Oil Co.*, 319 U.S. 315 (1943), or under *Railroad Comm'n of Tex. v. Pullman Co.*, 312 U.S. 496 (1941). We conclude that abstention is not appropriate in this case.

The *Burford* abstention doctrine allows a federal court to dismiss a case only if it presents difficult questions of state law bearing on policy problems of substantial public import whose importance transcends the result in the case then at bar, or if its adjudication in a federal forum would disrupt state efforts to establish a coherent policy with respect to a matter of substantial public concern. A central purpose furthered by *Burford* abstention is to protect complex state administrative processes from undue federal interference. The case before us does not threaten to undermine all or a substantial part of Florida's process of conducting elections and resolving election disputes. Rather, Plaintiffs' claims in this case target certain discrete practices set forth in a particular state statute. Further, *Burford* is implicated when federal interference would disrupt a state's effort, through its administrative agencies, to achieve uniformity and consistency in addressing a problem. *See, e.g., Quackenbush v. Allstate Ins. Co.*, 517 U.S. 706, 727–28 (1996). This case does not threaten to undermine Florida's uniform approach to manual recounts; indeed, the crux of Plaintiffs' complaint is the absence of strict and uniform standards for initiating or conducting such recounts. Finally, we note that *Burford* abstention represents an "extraordinary and narrow exception to the duty of a District Court to adjudicate a controversy properly before it." *County of Allegheny v. Frank Mashuda Co.*, 360 U.S. 185, 188 (1959). We do not believe that the concerns raised by Defendants in this case justify our abstention under this narrow doctrine.

Perhaps the most persuasive justification for abstention advanced by Defendants is based on *Pullman*; however, we conclude that abstention under this doctrine would not be appropriate. Under the *Pullman* abstention doctrine, a federal court will defer to "state court resolution of underlying issues of state law." *Harman v. Forssenius*, 380 U.S. 528, 534 (1965). Two elements must be met for *Pullman* abstention to apply: (1) the case must present an unsettled question of state law, and (2) the question of state law must be dispositive of the case or would materially alter the constitutional question presented. The purpose of *Pullman* abstention is to "avoid unnecessary friction in federal-state functions, interference with important state functions, tentative decisions on questions of state law, and premature constitutional adjudication." Because abstention is discretionary, it is only appropriate when the question of state law can be fairly interpreted to avoid adjudication of the constitutional question.

Plaintiffs claim that Florida's manual recount provision is unconstitutional because the statute does not provide sufficient standards to guide the discretion of county canvassing boards in granting a request for a manual recount or in conducting such a recount. There has been no suggestion by Defendants that the statute is appropriately subject to a more limited construction than the statute itself indicates.

Our conclusion that abstention is inappropriate is strengthened by the fact that Plaintiffs allege a constitutional violation of their voting rights. In considering abstention, we must take into account the nature of the controversy and the importance of the right allegedly impaired. Our cases have held that voting rights cases are particularly inappropriate for abstention. In light of this precedent, the importance of the rights asserted by Plaintiffs counsels against our abstention in this case; although, as discussed below, we are mindful of the limited role of the federal courts in assessing a state's electoral process.

We therefore conclude that abstention is not appropriate.

7.   After *Touchston,* what is left of the abstention doctrines? Is there any way to distinguish federal voting claims from all other claims in which a specific federal constitutional or statutory interest is asserted? *Touchston* may be a clear articulation of the transformation of the jurisdictional abstention doctrines into prudential deferral doctrines, spelled out in a context where the federal concern seems particularly palpable. If so, however, it would be an odd development for abstention law to fall in an area where the federal interest, even if substantial, is so heavily defined by the proper use of established state procedures.

8.   Should federal court intervention depend on the availability of other institutional actors capable of redressing the claimed harms? Consider the processes for challenging disputed delegations to the Electoral College in light of the process failure arguments raised in *United States v. Carolene Products,* 304 U.S. 144, 152 n.4 (1938), and in Justice Clark's opinion in *Baker v. Carr,* 369 U.S. 186 (1962)—as discussed more fully in Chapter 3. Both *Carolene Products* and Justice Clark placed great emphasis on the need for federal court intervention when no other actors were capable of redressing a claimed harm through the normal operations of the political process. But consider the elaborate statutory scheme set forth in 3 U.S.C. §§ 2, 5 and 15. For example, section 2 provides that when a state "has failed to make a choice [of electors to the electoral college] on the day prescribed by law, the electors may be appointed on a subsequent day in such a manner as the legislature of such State may direct." In addition, section 5 requires that states make a "final determination of any controversy or contest concerning the appointment" of electors by six days prior to the meeting of the electoral college and deems such state determination to be "conclusive." Finally, section 15 expressly anticipates that there might be unresolved controversies over which electors legitimately represent the state and that there could even be rival sets of electors each claiming to represent their states—as occurred with the Florida, Louisiana and South Carolina delegations in 1876. Resolution of such disputes is entrusted to independent determination by each branch of Congress—with a preference in case of a split between the House and Senate going to the delegation whose certificate of appointment bears the signature of the governor of their state of origin. Given the availability of political organs resolving electoral college disputes, should federal courts refuse to hear contests involving the selection of electors to the electoral college?

9.   Although much of the caselaw on federal intervention into state election practices involves redistricting, there is nonetheless a discrete issue concerning federal oversight of state administration of *federal* elections. The clearest example is, of course, the scramble for judicial relief in the Florida presidential election. Unlike redistricting, presidential elections are subject to direct constitutional and federal statutory commands. The one-person, one-vote command for redistricting is a matter of constitutional construction that is not directly anticipated in the text of the Constitution. By contrast, Article II of the Constitution and the Electoral Count Act directly regulate state conduct of presidential elections. Should that alter the principles of federal oversight?

10.   For a recent example of how the timing of federal jurisdiction plays out, consider the litigation over the 2004 race for Governor of Puerto Rico. With over two million votes cast, the initial vote count showed a margin of only 3,380 votes for the winner. But there was a question about the validity of the way as many as 28,000 ballots had been marked—nearly all of which would go to one candidate. Puerto Rico's Election Commission, which administers elections, ruled these to be valid votes under Puerto Rican law. The candidate who would lose under this ruling then filed a federal court action alleging that the Election Commission's ruling constituted a change in Puerto Rico law and, for that reason, violated the due process clause.

The First Circuit rejected the constitutional claim and held that federal courts should not exercise jurisdiction in circumstances like those at issue. *Rossello–Gonzalez v. Calderon–Serra*, 398 F.3d 1 (1st Cir. 2004). As the court put it:

> There is no doubt that the . . . complaint alleges the violation of a constitutionally guaranteed right, and thus, presents a colorable claim under § 1983 for subject-matter-jurisdiction purposes. The Federal Constitution protects the right of all qualified citizens to vote in local elections. This conclusion, however, does not end our inquiry. Having determined that the District Court could have exercised jurisdiction in this case, we must now inquire whether it should have intervened. . . .

> Here, there is no clearly articulated Commonwealth policy, much less a statute, to indicate the [disputed ballots] were invalid. At most, the decision of the Commission merely clarified previously unsettled law.

Note that the court held that a federal constitutional claim can arise only if the prior law (which an executive or judicial interpretation purportedly is changing) is itself "clearly articulated" and settled in advance of the election at issue. Rulings that "merely clarify previously unsettled law" cannot form a basis for a federal constitutional challenge to state election dispute resolution. This is an important principle not expressly recognized in previous cases.

Is the suggestion tenable that only dramatic "changes in the rules" that disenfranchise voters can ground a due process challenge? Suppose a state court dramatically changes the reading of state election law in a way that leads enough otherwise invalid votes to be treated as valid in a way that tilts the outcome to one candidate. Is there any reason such a ruling should be less subject to due process restrictions merely because the means by which the election outcome was changed involving including votes rather than excluding them?

Note the relationship between the merits of these due process claims and the jurisdictional question of whether the federal courts can hear the case at all. Election disputes increasingly involve complicated boundary disputes, which candidates seek to exploit, between the role of state and federal courts. If one candidate believes she is likely to fare better in state courts, for whatever reason, she will file a complaint there. By definition, that will often mean the other candidate believes he will fare better in the federal courts—and he will file there. These cases therefore often involve simultaneous litigation in both forums, with unclear boundaries on which forum should be in control. That only makes resolution of these high-stakes disputes all the more difficult and contentious. That was the case in the Puerto Rico case; one set of actors sought to have the Puerto Rico Supreme Court resolve the election, while the opposing actors sought to have the federal courts do so.

Also note the unusual way jurisdictional and substantive merits issues are intertwined in the First Circuit's resolution. The court concludes that the due process challenge to a local election dispute does present a colorable basis for federal court jurisdiction. But the court also concludes that the merits of the claim are too weak to justify the actual exercise of the federal court's jurisdiction to decide the dispute. Do you see the difficulties this approach poses to knowing which forum is proper for resolving an election dispute? Is there any other solution to this problem?

Part III: The World After *Bush v. Gore*

Election 2000 and *Bush v. Gore* combined to produce a spate of lawsuits and a flurry of legislative reform on both the state and federal level. The Palm Beach County "butterfly ballot" and the Florida recount were the most notorious problems, but it soon became evident that election administration was beset by a range of problems. The Caltech/MIT Voting Technology Project concluded that somewhere between 4 and 6 million votes had been lost nationwide. While somewhere between 1.5 and 2 million of those lost votes were the result of faulty voting equipment or badly designed ballots, the report concluded that at least as many votes (between 1.5 and 3 million) had been lost because of registration problems and that somewhere between 500,000 and 1.2 million votes had been lost due to problems in polling place operations, such as long lines or untrained poll workers. See Caltech/MIT Voting Tech. Project, Voting: What Is, What Could Be (2001), available at <http://www.vote.caltech.edu/media/ documents/july01/July01_VTP_Voting_Report_Entire.pdf>. A blue-ribbon commission, headed by former Presidents Ford and Carter similarly identified a wide array of problems. *See* Nat'l Comm'n on Fed. Election Reform, To Assure Pride and Confidence in the Electoral Process (2001).

A number of states that permitted punch-card systems were quickly sued. Perhaps the most extensive discussion of the implications of *Bush v. Gore* came in the Ohio punch-card litigation. While the court of appeals ultimately directed that the case be dismissed as moot, after having granted rehearing en banc to review the district court's decision dismissing the plaintiffs' complaint, see *Stewart v. Blackwell*, 473 F.3d 692 (6th Cir. 2007), we include the vacated panel decision because it contains a particularly illuminating discussion of the meaning of *Bush v. Gore*. (We do not include the portions of the opinion dealing with the plaintiffs' claims under the Voting Rights Act.)

Stewart v. Blackwell

444 F.3d 843 (6th Cir. 2006), *vacated by* 473 F.3d 692 (6th Cir. 2006).

■ BOYCE F. MARTIN, JR., CIRCUIT JUDGE.

* * *

[The plaintiffs, Ohio voters, have alleged that] the use of unreliable, deficient voting equipment, including the punch card ballot, in some Ohio counties but not other counties violates the Equal Protection Clause of the Fourteenth Amendment. . . .

Some commentators have suggested that these types of voting rights challenges are taking us into a brave new world. Others suggest that they are simply variations of old challenges. Regardless of the proper characterization, we find ourselves bound by Supreme Court precedent, and therefore, with regard to the plaintiffs' claim under the Equal Protection Clause, we REVERSE the district court's judgment. . . .

I

A. Background Information on Voting Technology

* * *

In the 2000 general election, sixty-nine of eighty-eight Ohio counties used punch card ballots. Eleven counties used optical scan equipment, six used electronic equipment, and two used automatic or "lever" voting machines.... [I]n total, eighty-one of eighty-eight Ohio counties used non-independent-notice equipment—voting technology that does not provide a voter with notice from the voting device that a problem might exist before the ballot is finally cast—in the 2000 general election....

B. The Statistical Evidence

The plaintiffs' expert, Dr. Martha Kropf, testified regarding estimates of intentional and unintentional undervoting based on data collected by National Elections Studies and the Voters News Survey in exit polls and surveys in presidential elections between 1980 and 1996. Kropf testified that intentional undervoting in presidential elections is a relatively rare event that is estimated to involve between .23% and .75% of all residual votes. Dr. Kropf concluded that when levels of undervoting exceed this threshold and vary by equipment it is probable that they resulted from unintentional undervoting that is associated with problems of the punch card ballot.... Kropf reported an overall statewide residual vote rate of 2.29% for punch card systems and 2.14% for central-count optical scans. That is, voters in punch card counties are approximately four times as likely not to have their votes counted as a voter using reliable electronic voting equipment. In some counties specific precincts encountered more severe problems with residual voting. In Akron City Precinct 3–F the residual vote rate was 15% and in Dayton City's 14th Ward Precinct C the residual vote rate was 17%. In addition, the counties in Ohio experiencing the highest percentage of residual votes in the 2000 presidential election were those in which voters used punch card technology while the counties experiencing the lowest percentage of residual votes used other technology. The twenty-nine counties in Ohio with the highest residual vote percentages were all counties that used punch card machines; the seven counties with the lowest residual vote percentages were all counties that did not use punch card machines as their primary voting system....

The Caltech MIT Voting Technology Project report—a joint venture between the two institutions to study, in part, the reliability of existing voting equipment—which is referenced throughout the record, is also informative. As the report notes, that "if voting equipment has no effect on the ability of voters to express their preferences, then the residual vote should be unrelated to machine types." *See* Caltech–MIT Voting Technology Project, *Residual Votes Attributable to Technology: An Assessment of the Reliability of Existing Voting Equipment* (Version 2: March 30, 2001), *available at* http://www.vote.caltech.edu (last accessed April 1, 2006). The report concluded that the error rate from punch cards is 50 percent higher than other technologies and that the pattern holds up when "holding constant turnout, income, racial composition of counties, age distribution of counties, literacy rates, the year of a shift in technology, the number of offices and candidates on the ballot, and other factors that operate in a county or in a particular year." Report at 22. In conclusion, the report stated that "the incidence of such residual votes with punch card methods ... is forty to seventy percent higher than the incidence of residual votes with the other technologies," Report at 17, and cautioned that "if election administrators wish to avoid catastrophic failures, they may heed this warning ... Stop using punch cards," Report at 11.

Defendants' expert Dr. John Lott examined the performance of voting technology across three election cycles, 1992, 1996, and 2000, in the presidential, Congressional, Ohio Senate, and Ohio House elections. His findings for the presidential and U.S. Senate elections mirror Kropf's in the 2000 election. Lott reported an overall statewide residual vote rate of 2.4% for punch card systems....

* * *

III

A.　The Right to Vote

Voting is a fundamental right. *See e.g.*, *Reynolds v. Sims*, 377 U.S. 533, 561–62 (1964) ("Undoubtedly, the right of suffrage is a fundamental matter in a free and democratic society."). For more than a century the Supreme Court has acknowledged the fundamental nature of the right to vote. ... Careful and meticulous scrutiny is necessary because even minor infringements on the franchise can have reverberations in other contexts and throughout democratic society. "A consistent line of decisions by [the Supreme] Court in cases involving attempts to deny or restrict the right of suffrage has made this indelibly clear." *Id.* at 554 ("Undeniably the Constitution of the United States protects the right of all qualified citizens to vote, in state as well as in federal elections."); *see also* U.S. Const. amends. XV, XVII, XIX, XXIV, XXVI.... Dilution of the right to vote may not be accomplished by stuffing the ballot-boxes. *Ex parte Siebold*, 100 U.S. 371, 25 L. Ed. 717 (1879). Nor may the right to vote be diluted by alteration of ballots or improper counting of ballots. *United States v. Classic*, 313 U.S. 299, 315 (1941). In *Classic*, the Court stated that: "Obviously included within the right to choose, secured by the Constitution, is the right of qualified voters within a state to cast their ballots and *have them counted* ... This Court has consistently held that this is a right secured by the Constitution." *Id.* (emphasis added)....

Nearly a year before *Reynolds*, in *Gray v. Sanders*, 372 U.S. 368, 381 (1963), the Supreme Court held unconstitutional Georgia's county unit system in statewide primary elections. The Court found the system to be unconstitutional because it diluted the weight of votes cast by certain Georgia residents based on where they lived. *Id.* at 379–80....

The *Reynolds* Court also favorably cited Justice Douglas's dissent in *South v. Peters*, 339 U.S. 276 (1950), where he stated that:

There is more to the right to vote than the right to mark a piece of paper and drop it in a box or the right to pull a lever in a voting booth.

The right to vote includes the right to have the ballot counted. It also includes the right to have the vote counted at full value without dilution or discount.

* * *

Somewhat more recently decided is *Bush v. Gore*, 531 U.S. 98 (2000),[8] which reiterated long established Equal Protection principles. . . . Echoing long-revered principles, the Court emphasized that states, after granting the right to vote on equal terms, "may not, by later arbitrary and disparate treatment, value one person's vote over that of another."

* * *

IV

* * *

B.   Analysis

Supreme Court precedent . . . instructs that if the Ohio statute permitting localities to use deficient voting technology "infringes on the right to vote," then strict scrutiny applies; if the statute does not "infringe on the right to vote, and merely regulates some tangential aspect of the franchise," then rational basis review applies. This begs the question of what the "right to vote" encompasses. We easily conclude that the right to have one's vote counted on equal terms is part of the right to vote. No other conclusion is possible from the case law and thus, strict scrutiny applies. . . .

Strict scrutiny requires us to determine whether the use of the two challenged technologies in some jurisdictions but not others is a practice "narrowly tailored to further compelling governmental interests." Under this standard, the State's proffered justifications of cost and training are wholly insufficient to sustain its continued certification of the technologies. Administrative convenience is simply not a compelling justification in light of the fundamental nature of the right. *See Frontiero v. Richardson*, 411 U.S. 677, 690 (1973) (plurality) ("When we enter the realm of 'strict judicial scrutiny' there can be no doubt that 'administrative convenience' is

---

8. Of note, *Bush v. Gore* appears to be the first case where a court recognized the developing problem with technology that we confront today. The per curiam opinion noted that the case "brought into sharp focus a common, if heretofore unnoticed, phenomenon"—that nationwide an "estimated 2% of ballots cast do not register a vote for President for whatever reason," and that "punchcard balloting machines can produce an unfortunate number of ballots which are not punched in a clean, complete way by the voter." *Bush*, 531 U.S. at 104. We also note

that the dissent begins by criticizing our "reliance on the Supreme Court's murky decision in *Bush v. Gore*." Dis. Op. at 32. Murky, transparent, illegitimate, right, wrong, big, tall, short or small; regardless of the adjective one might use to describe the decision, the proper noun that precedes it—"Supreme Court"—carries more weight with us. Whatever else *Bush v. Gore* may be, it is first and foremost a decision of the Supreme Court of the United States and we are bound to adhere to it. More on this later.

no shibboleth, the mere recitation of which dictates constitutionality."). Moreover, Ohio's reliance on the cost of upgrading the technology fails in light of the monies already devoted to the process. Additionally, Ohio has used cost as if it were a silver bullet. Any change from the status quo necessarily involves some cost. The State has failed to put forth any evidence indicating that it cannot manage the costs and instead, the evidence indicates that the State has either budgeted for the transition from its own funds or through funds provided by the federal government. The mere fact that there is some cost involved does not make that factor compelling. . . . The continued certification of this technology by the Secretary of State does not provide the minimal adequate procedural safeguards to prevent the unconstitutional dilution of votes based on where a voter resides. *See Bush*, 531 U.S. at 109.[17] . . . .

By maintaining a system in which these two technologies are utilized, voters in Ohio vote under two separate standards. Although voters approach the polls with the opportunity to vote in the same elections for the same candidates, once they step into the voting booth, they have an unequal chance of their vote being counted, *not* as a result of any action on the part of the voter, but because of the different technology utilized. Voters able to utilize notice technology choose candidates and before their vote is turned in and counted, the technology notifies them of any errors that would result in the vote being disregarded. Those voters forced to use non-notice technology are not notified of any errors in their ballot and, should errors exist, their votes are disregarded; moreover, voters using the two challenged technologies have an additional likelihood of disenfranchisement due to the inherent deficiencies of the punch-card and central-count optical scan.[18]

* * *

Although we apply strict scrutiny, we note that the use of this technology would also fail under rational basis review. . . . An individual's vote is the lifeblood of a democracy. To that extent, we find it difficult to

---

17. Additionally, it would be odd indeed for the Supreme Court to have held in *Bush v. Gore* that the Equal Protection Clause protects the right to have one's vote counted properly during a *recount*, but for us to conclude that the Clause does not cover the right to have one's vote counted properly in the first instance.

18. In a glass half-full kind of way, the dissent points out that "we should not, after all, lose sight of the fact that nearly 98% of the votes cast even in the punch-card counties were properly counted in the 2000 presidential election." For comparative purposes, we would simply point out that the 2000 presidential election in Florida was decided by 0.009% of the vote; New Mexico was decided by 0.061% of the vote; Wisconsin, 0.22%; Iowa, 0.31%; Oregon, 0.44%; New Hampshire, 1.27%; Minnesota, 2.4; Missouri, 3.34%; Ohio, 3.51%; Nevada, 3.55%; Tennessee 3.86%; and Pennsylvania, 4.17%. In the 2004 presidential election, Wisconsin was decided by 0.38%; Iowa, 0.67%; New Mexico, 0.79%; New Hampshire, 1.37%; Ohio, 2.11%; Pennsylvania, 2.5%; Nevada, 2.59%; Michigan, 3.42%; and Minnesota, 3.48%. That nearly 98% of the vote was counted seems less deserving of the dissent's accolades in light of the margin of decision in those states.

conjure up what the State's legitimate interest is by the use of technology that dilutes the right to vote. The State says that its interests in failing to decertify non-notice and substandard technology is based on the cost of replacement and training workers on the new machines. We fail to see how the interest is justified or rational at the expense of tens of thousands of votes.

* * *

[T]he main basis for the dissent is some "question [over] the precedential value of *Bush v. Gore*." The dissent answers the question by concluding that *Bush v. Gore* is "a case whose precedential value . . . is at best questionable." The dissent endeavors to explain three "reasons for doubting *Bush v. Gore*'s precedential value: 'The limiting language in the opinion, the lack of seriousness with which the Court undertook its own analysis, and the inconsistency with other jurisprudence by this majority of Justices all point in the direction of assuming that *Bush v. Gore* is not good precedent for an expansive reading of equal protection law in elections.' " (quoting Hasen, Bush v. Gore *and the Future of Equal Protection Law in Elections*, 29 Fla. St. U. L. Rev. at 391). The dissent then focuses on the first two reasons: the lack of the apparent seriousness with which the Court decided the case and the inconsistency with other jurisprudence. It is curious that the dissent bases its analysis on the belief that the Supreme Court decided *Bush v. Gore*, a case that decided the 2000 presidential election, with a "lack of seriousness," and we choose to disagree with that approach. Further, even if the Court was playing fast and loose with the law, we, as an inferior court, are not in a position to disregard Supreme Court precedent because we think they got it wrong. Presumably, if in the dissent's view *Bush v. Gore* had "precedential value"—as we think all Supreme Court opinions do—he would be compelled to join us. . . .

Finally, we reject the dissent's claim that Professor Hasen's article has overruled the Supreme Court's decision in *Bush v. Gore* because "the Supreme Court has had ample opportunity to prove him wrong by explaining, or even citing to, its decision in *Bush v. Gore*." Dis. Op. at 37. If the dissent were correct, perhaps the same must be said about the hundreds of other law review articles discussing the decision's legitimacy and applicability to other factual scenarios. The Court has not sought to debate these other law professors and commentators and under the dissent's reasoning, those articles must also be correct. In fact, taken to its logical extreme, the dissent's reasoning means that every claim in a law review article that the Supreme Court has failed to refute is actually the law of the land. Thus, we find the dissent's claim that *Bush v. Gore* has no precedential value because the Court has not sought to "prove [Professor Hasen] wrong" empty.

* * *

Finally, the dissent criticizes us for not articulating a precise mathematical formula for determining when voting technology is constitutional and when it is not. Precise mathematical formulas, however, have never been a part of voting rights cases or cases involving strict judicial scrutiny. A judicially imposed mathematical formula for evaluating voting rights cases would be purely arbitrary. We simply cannot say that x% error rate raises constitutional concerns but y% error rate does not. Nor has the Supreme Court done so or required us to do so in *any* case applying strict scrutiny. Rather, when confronted with difficult constitutional questions, a reasoned analytical approach is necessary. Once the plaintiffs establish that strict scrutiny applies, the State must put forth a compelling reason for its infringement of a fundamental right and we, as a reviewing court, must evaluate that reasons against the plaintiffs' claims. . . .

We do not review such claims in a vacuum but do so with a focus on the real world justifications and implications of Ohio's decision. Future claims of this sort will be evaluated with these various factors in mind. If, in the dissent's hypothetical example, where one technology yields a 0.1% error rate and another technology has a 0.01% error rate, and a lawsuit is filed similar to this one, the same questions will have to be asked and the context of the challenge studied and evaluated. If switching to the new technology would bankrupt the State, or the technology was in its development phase, or the potential for fraud was high, or for any number of reasons the State did not believe that the technology could properly be implemented, then, even in light of our decision today, the claim may fail. If, however, switching to the new technology provided only minimal inconvenience, then the State's reasons might be found to be less than compelling. In this case, we do not seek to constitutionalize local election procedures, nor do we seek to mandate uniformity and absolute equality in voting procedures, nor do we hold that notice technology is constitutionally mandated; we merely evaluate the right to vote in light of the State's proffered justifications for using the two challenged technologies at issue and hold that the State's reasons are not compelling.

* * *

VII

Violations of the Equal Protection Clause are no less deserving of protection because they are accomplished with a modern machine than with outdated prejudices. The dissent's appeal to caution notwithstanding, "the basic ingredient of [judicial] decision is principle, and it should not be compromised and parceled out a little in one case, a little more in another, until eventually someone receives the full benefit. If the principle is sound and constitutional, it is the birthright of every American, not to be accorded begrudgingly or piecemeal or to special groups only, but to everyone in its entirety whenever it is brought into play." Earl Warren, The Memoirs of Chief Justice Earl Warren 6 (Madison Books 2001) (1977). . . .

■ RONALD LEE GILMAN, CIRCUIT JUDGE, dissenting.

The majority today imposes by judicial decree important changes to the Ohio electoral system, doing so largely in reliance on the Supreme Court's murky decision in *Bush v. Gore*, 531 U.S. 98 (2000) (per curiam), a vacated Ninth Circuit panel opinion in a California recall-election dispute, and two district court cases that never reached a final judgment on the merits. In my view, these sources cannot bear the weight that the majority places on them, and should not form the basis for subjecting an indeterminate number of state and local election decisions to the strictest level of constitutional scrutiny.

I would take a more cautious approach, one that recognizes the primacy of the executive and legislative branches in the electoral process and the significant costs that the majority's holding will place on state and local governments, the entities that are charged with most aspects of election administration.

* * *

I. CONSTITUTIONAL STANDARD OF REVIEW

A reader unfamiliar with the Supreme Court's voting-rights precedents might conclude after reading the majority opinion that federal courts have long dealt with challenges analogous to the one made in the present case, and that strict scrutiny has been universally recognized as the appropriate standard of review. The majority's lengthy exposition of the fundamental nature of the right to vote cites many cases purportedly to that effect, taking quotations out of their factual and legal context. A closer examination of those cases, however, reveals that the challenges upheld in them were significantly different from the one before us in the present case, and that the appropriate standard of review in voting-rights cases is far from settled.

A. Voting-rights precedents

* * *

Stated simply, none of [the] Supreme Court precedents [cited by the majority] resembles the claim made by the plaintiffs in the present case. These plaintiffs do not allege that Ohio has imposed an impermissible voter-qualification requirement, as in *Harper* and *Dunn*. Nor do they argue that the votes in Ohio are "weighted" differently-that is, that a properly marked ballot "is worth more in one district than in another." *Wesberry*, 376 U.S. at 8; *see also Reynolds*, 377 U.S. at 563. Instead, they maintain that voters in counties that employ inferior voting equipment "are subjected to a significantly greater risk that their votes will not be counted." In other words, properly marked ballots are counted and accorded the same value everywhere in the state, but voters in some counties have a reduced chance of turning in a properly marked ballot that will actually be counted because certain voting methods do not catch the voters' own inadvertent mistakes.

This challenge to the nuts-and-bolts of election administration, regardless of its merit, cannot be equated with either discriminatory voter-qualification requirements or generally applicable state laws that deny "equality of voting power," *Gray*, 372 U.S. at 381, which are the principal types of state actions that the Supreme Court has subjected to strict scrutiny. . . .

B.   Rational basis is the proper standard of review

The Supreme Court has never adhered to the view that all legislation or practices that affect the right to vote must be subjected to strict scrutiny. . . . That "flexible framework" was most recently articulated by the Court in *Burdick v. Takushi*, 504 U.S. 428 (1992) [which held that only state laws and regulations that impose "severe restrictions" on the right to vote should be subjected to strict scrutiny.]

* * *

[C]onsistent with *Burdick* is the Ninth Circuit's decision in *Weber v. Shelley*, 347 F.3d 1101 (9th Cir. 2003), a case . . . that I believe is directly on point. In *Weber*, a voter brought an Equal Protection challenge to a California county's decision to replace paper ballots with an electronic-voting system. 347 F.3d at 1102. The computerized system, the voter maintained, was susceptible to manipulation and potential fraud because it lacked a paper audit trail. *Id.* at 1104–1105. Applying the *Burdick* framework, the Ninth Circuit held that the "use of paperless, touchscreen voting systems [did not] severely restrict[] the right to vote," and that the voting procedure was therefore subject only to rational-basis review. *Id.* at 1106. Because the electronic voting machines constituted a reasonable method of ameliorating the problems inherent in paper ballots, the change in voting procedures was rationally related to the state's interest in "ensuring that elections are fair and orderly." *Id.*; *see also id.* at 1107 (opining that the state and the county had "made a reasonable, politically neutral and non-discriminatory choice to certify [and to use] touchscreen systems as an alternative to paper ballots"); *accord Am. Ass'n of People with Disabilities v. Shelley*, 324 F. Supp. 2d 1120, 1127 (C.D. Cal. 2004) (reviewing the California Secretary of State's decision to decertify Direct Recording Electronic (DRE) voting machines under the rational-basis standard of review).

Weber is significant for a number of reasons. First, when faced with an Equal Protection challenge to the type of voting technology certified by the California Secretary of State and utilized by the county, the Ninth Circuit found the appropriate standard of review in Burdick—not in *Reynolds*, *Harper*, *Dunn*, or any other pre-*Burdick* precedents. *See Weber*, 347 F.3d at 1106. The second reason is that, in applying *Burdick*, the Ninth Circuit held that the increased potential for voter fraud with the new voting technology did not constitute a "severe restriction" on the right to vote, so that the decision to implement such electoral changes was subject only to rational-basis review. *Id.*

Finally, and perhaps most importantly, *Weber* is the closest on its facts to the challenge levied by the plaintiffs in the present case. Indeed, *Weber* is the exact converse of the present case. Whereas the plaintiffs here decry the refusal of the counties to utilize improved voting technologies, the voter in *Weber* complained precisely because her county had abandoned traditional paper ballots in favor of the newly available technology. The contrast between the two cases epitomizes the predicament in which election officials find themselves—damned if they upgrade voting machines, damned if they do not—and further supports adopting a constitutional standard of review that affords state and local officials the flexibility necessary to regulate an election system constantly in flux.

* * *

II. EQUAL PROTECTION ANALYSIS AND *BUSH v. GORE*

For the reasons ably articulated by a leading election-law expert-reasons to which I will add a few thoughts of my own—I believe that we should heed the Supreme Court's own warning and limit the reach of *Bush v. Gore* to the peculiar and extraordinary facts of that case. *See* Hasen, Bush v. Gore *and the Future of Equal Protection Law in Elections*, 29 Fla. St. U. L. Rev. at 379.... The majority has chosen a different path, one that unjustifiably expands *Bush v. Gore* into a landmark precedent designed to fundamentally transform federal election law.

A. *Bush v. Gore* should not be given an expansive reading

* * *

In its per curiam opinion, the Court majority cautioned that its analysis was "limited to the present circumstances, for the problem of equal protection in election processes generally presents many complexities." *Bush v. Gore*, 531 U.S. at 109....

In the present case, of course, no state-court order is at issue, and no governmental entity has ordered a "statewide remedy." The allegations of these plaintiffs are a far cry from the lack of uniform rules for discerning the meaning of votes already cast, which is what the Court in *Bush v. Gore* found to be a constitutional violation.

[T]he Supreme Court has had ample opportunity to [explain or even cite] to, its decision in *Bush v. Gore. See, e.g., Clingman v. Beaver*, 544 U.S. 581 (2005); *Vieth v. Jubelirer*, 541 U.S. 267 (2004); *McConnell v. Fed. Election Comm'n*, 540 U.S. 93 (2003); *Georgia v. Ashcroft*, 539 U.S. 461 (2003). But despite taking a steady load of election-related cases, the Court has not cited *Bush v. Gore* even once—not in a majority opinion, in a concurrence, or in a dissent—in the more than five years since that case was decided. The Court, in other words, has adhered to the limiting language that it conspicuously included in the *Bush v. Gore* opinion. I believe that we should follow the same path....

* * *

In the final analysis, I believe that the best course is to understand the Supreme Court's decision in *Bush v. Gore* as a shield to preserve the status quo in an electoral process beset by extraordinary temporal and political pressures. I therefore decline to join the majority in permitting litigants to use that decision as a sword to strike down state election policies that, while ripe for improvement, were previously on solid constitutional ground.

* * *

III. EQUALITY AND VOTING PROCEDURES

The majority holds that the certification and use of non-notice voting technology in one county but not in another violates the Equal Protection Clause because "punch card and central-count optical scan technologies result in a greater likelihood that one's vote will not be counted on the same terms as the vote of someone in a notice county." Notwithstanding its cautionary language to the contrary, the majority is calling for virtually absolute equality in voting methods and procedures across all electoral districts in Ohio.

A closer look at some of the relevant numbers tells much of the story. The key statistic, as the plaintiffs present it, is that the residual-vote rate across the state was 2.29% for punch-card machines, 0.94% for electronic-voting machines, 1.04% for lever machines, and 1.15% for precinct-count optical scanners. In other words, the error rate in punch-card districts is twice that of counties with precinct-count optical scan equipment, and more than twice that of counties using lever or electronic-voting machines. The plaintiffs also rely on direct inter-county comparisons, pointing out that Cuyahoga County, which used punch-cards in the presidential elections at issue, had an error rate four times higher than Franklin County, where electronic-voting machines were used.

What the majority does not indicate, however, is which of these numbers is constitutionally significant. Is the constitutional problem the fact that voters in punch-card districts face an error rate twice as high as voters in precinct-count optical-scan districts? If so, then improvements in technology will not necessarily cure the equal protection problem. This is so because a voter in a county with a much-improved residual vote rate of 0.2% could point to a neighboring county where the rate is 0.1% and say the same thing—namely, that the error rate in her county is twice as high as in the neighboring county. Moreover, as voting technology improves and error rates decline, whatever disparities remain among the different types of voting equipment will be magnified. That is to say, even a technology that yields a negligible error rate of 0.1% might violate the Equal Protection Clause if other jurisdictions within the state employ technology with a rate of 0.01%, which is one-tenth as high. The majority refers to a "greater likelihood" that a vote will not be counted, but fails to articulate a coherent constitutional threshold—a point at which such a likelihood renders state voting practices unconstitutional.

* * *

[M]y reference to a "coherent constitutional threshold" does not require a concrete numerical error rate of x% or y%. Rather, I have criticized the majority for failing to provide a framework for determining when the numerical differences that are unavoidable in the election setting become constitutionally problematic. In responding to this aspect of my dissent, however, the majority does no more than reaffirm its conclusion that the certification and use of non-notice technology *in this case* is unconstitutional. The majority does not explain *why* these particular differences in voting technology are unconstitutional—a failing that exposes its approach as something other than the "reasoned analytical" one that it urges courts to employ "when confronted with difficult constitutional questions." The next court facing the "difficult constitutional questions" inherent in a statistics-based equal protection challenge to state voting practices will therefore know only that, *on these facts and these numbers*, Ohio's use of varied voting methods violated the Equal Protection Clause, but will not know why.

Moreover, I am not the one who has made number-crunching a dominant factor in the equal protection analysis. The plaintiffs themselves did so when they brought a case whose central premise is that statistical differences in voter-error rates suffice to show a constitutional violation. Because these numbers are squarely at issue, I have provided the above hypotheticals in order to highlight the majority's failure to articulate a limiting principle beyond its assurances that it is not announcing a general rule and that "future claims of this sort will be evaluated with [legal, financial, and practical] factors in mind."

* * *

I also believe that the majority fails to grasp that "equality" is not a one-way street. If what the Equal Protection Clause requires is that counties across Ohio utilize voting mechanisms that yield a substantially similar residual-vote rate, then the use of punch-card ballots is presumably permissible so long as *every* county uses punch cards. That this voting method leads to a relatively high percentage of discarded votes statewide should make no difference to the equal protection analysis, since every voter would face the same chance of casting a ballot that is later deemed not to have been properly marked. In other words, while the majority presumes that requiring substantial equivalency in residual-vote rates across districts will prompt local governments to "ratchet up" to notice equipment, those governments would also be free to turn the ratchet down to cheaper non-notice technology.

This all-or-nothing approach carries with it substantial practical concerns....

Beyond the concern that the threat of lawsuits will halt innovation, the all-or-nothing approach increases the risk that technological setbacks could invalidate the electoral results on a statewide basis. Assume, for example, that one or more counties in Ohio want to experiment with Internet voting because such a mechanism might serve to decrease the error rate. If the trail-blazing counties are permitted to implement the new system on their own, security or logistical problems that call into question the validity of election results would affect only those counties, leaving intact the results from the rest of the state. On the other hand, if every county is required to simultaneously adopt a still imperfect system, a widespread technical failure could wipe out the entire state's election results. Instant equality, while fine in theory, does not account for these realities of the electoral system.

* * *

Technology that dilutes voting strength, the majority tells us, "is no less a [constitutional] violation than any other invidious method." But the use of different voting mechanisms has little to do with the type of "invidious discrimination" that the Equal Protection Clause was designed to prevent. That is why I believe that many of the broad statements in the majority opinion, although eloquent, are ultimately hollow. However unpleasant the prospect, human error remains a part of the democratic process, and no constitutional rule is going to change that fact.

* * *

NOTES AND QUESTIONS

1. As *Stewart* illustrates, there are a variety of ways to read *Bush v. Gore*. On one interpretation, the decision recognizes a substantive, individual right to an equally-weighted vote. On another, the case recognizes a procedural right to election systems that limit the risk of partisan manipulation of election outcomes. Consider the following analysis:

> At the risk of opening old wounds, *Bush v. Gore* exemplifies the tension between rights and structural analysis, as well as the ease with which courts invoke familiar frameworks of rights. On the most common reading, *Bush v. Gore* rests on an individual right to an equally weighted vote in a statewide election. This individual right reflects what the Court calls the "equal dignity owed to each voter." Cast in these individual rights terms, that principle requires that various elements of the voting process, such as the technology of voting machines, the standards and methods of voting recounts, and perhaps even the design of ballots, must ensure (individually or cumulatively) that the same weight be given statewide to each vote cast (or validly attempted to be cast). That is a principle of exceptional breadth and administrative expense, but language in *Bush v. Gore* supports it.

On a second reading, perhaps more likely to become the way the decision is absorbed in the courts, Florida's recount process created an unconstitutional risk of partisan manipulation of the recount and hence the election itself. This risk was related to elements seven Justices singled out as procedurally problematic: the lack of sufficiently precise, relatively objective standards specified in advance; the fact that each county was free to devise and then apply its own post hoc standards in a context in which the risks of opportunism were apparent; and the absence of any credible process for ensuring uniformity after the fact. All this in a system to be applied by partisan, elected canvassing boards across sixty-seven counties. These concerns are structural, not matters of individual rights. On this second reading, the constitutional obligation is to design recount processes, and perhaps voting or democratic processes more generally, that sufficiently cabin the risk of partisan, self-interested manipulation. As others have noted, the central elements in *Bush v. Gore* are more consistent with this structural concern for partisan capture of election processes than with any individual right to an equally weighted vote. The stakes in the choice are considerable. If the individual right to equal dignity requires voting technology that yields similar statewide error rates, courts will enjoin or overturn elections more frequently; if the Constitution requires that voting systems be designed to minimize the risk of partisan capture, judicial oversight will be differently and more narrowly targeted.

Richard H. Pildes, *The Supreme Court, 2003 Term–Foreword: Constitutionalization of Democratic Politics*, 118 Harv. L. Rev. 28, 86–99 (2004). *See also* Dan Tokaji, *First Amendment Equal Protection: On Discretion, Inequality, and Participation*, 101 Mich. L. Rev. 2409 (2003) (presenting alternative doctrinal analyses of *Bush v. Gore*). The article by Professor Richard Hasen in the *Stewart* opinions takes yet another tack—suggesting that the case perhaps should not be read to have precedential weight at all. Which reading of *Bush v. Gore* should the courts adopt? For a series of essays exploring the legal and political ramifications thus far of *Bush v. Gore*, see The Final Arbiter: The Consequences of *Bush v. Gore* for Law and Politics (Christopher Banks et. al. eds. 2005).

2. In addition to the equal protection clause theory discussed in the excerpt, *Stewart*, like many other post-*Bush v. Gore* challenges to punch-card systems also involved a challenge under section 2 of the Voting Rights Act of 1965, 42 U.S.C. § 1973, which prohibits the use of voting practices or procedures that have a disparate impact on minority voters. In a number of states with significant minority populations, counties with high minority populations were more likely to use punch-card systems—ironically, often because, as large urban counties, these jurisdictions had adopted machine voting systems earlier than less populous counties and thus had switched technologies before the advent of more accurate systems. (One study, however, concluded that, nationwide, black voters were no more likely than other voters to cast their votes using equipment that notifies voters of errors. *See* Stephen Knack & Martha Kropf, Who Uses Inferior Voting Technology?, 35 PS: Pol. Sci. & Pol. 541 (2002)). Moreover, using punch-card systems, minority voters were disproportionately likely to cast ballots that were not counted. For a comprehensive discussion of the evidence and issues, see Paul Moke & Richard B. Saphire, *The Voting Rights Act and the Racial Gap in Lost Votes*, 58 Hastings L.J. 1 (2006). The one reported pre-*Bush v. Gore* section 2 case involving punch-card ballots was *Roberts v. Wamser*, 679 F.Supp. 1513 (E.D. Mo, 1987), *rev'd on other grounds*, 883 F.2d 617 (8th Cir. 1989).

None of the section 2 cases was litigated to judgment, but two cases produced published opinions refusing to dismiss such claims. *Black v. McGuffage*, 209 F. Supp. 2d 889 (N.D. Ill. 2002), involved a challenge to Illinois' use of punch-card voting systems in a number of counties and the state's use of optical scan systems in several other counties that did not provide in-precinct error notification. (Optical scan ballots can be scanned either at each precinct—in which case it is possible to notify a voter if her ballot contains an error, such as an overvote—or at a central processing facility once the polls close—in which case there is no opportunity for error notification.) The district court denied the defendants' motion to dismiss the complaint. It found that the plaintiffs had stated a claim under both section 2 of the Voting Rights Act, because they had alleged that the use of punch-card systems in predominantly black and Latino precincts resulted in there being a higher error rate in those precincts, thus creating a "greater risk" that the ballots of black and Latino citizens would not be counted, and under the equal protection clause because "voters in some counties [were] statistically less likely to have their votes counted than voters in other counties in the same state in the same election for the same office." The district court also refused to dismiss the plaintiffs' substantive due process claim, stating that "a law that allows significantly inaccurate systems of vote counting to be imposed upon some portions of the electorate and not others without any rational basis runs afoul of the Due Process clause of the U.S. Constitution."

Similarly, in *Common Cause v. Jones*, 213 F. Supp. 2d 1106 (C.D. Cal. 2001), the plaintiffs challenged the decision by the California secretary of state to permit individual counties to use of punch-card systems. The district court denied the motion to dismiss plaintiff's Voting Rights Act and Fourteenth Amendment claims. The case was subsequently rendered moot because the Secretary of State decertified punch card ballots for elections beginning in 2004. *See Common Cause v. Jones*, 213 F. Supp. 2d 1110 (C.D. Cal. 2002). The 2003 gubernatorial recall election, however, was conducted under the old punch-card system in several counties, and the Ninth Circuit, sitting en banc, permitted the election to go forward despite a claim that the continued use of the old system violated the equal protection clause and section 2 of the Voting Rights Act. *See Southwest Voter Registration Education Project v. Shelley*, 344 F.3d 914 (9th Cir. 2003). (That decision is discussed earlier in this Chapter with respect to the question of when courts can enjoin an upcoming election.)

3. Florida adopted a comprehensive electoral reform package in the wake of the 2000 election, but one of its reforms itself spawned *Bush*-inspired litigation.

Pursuant to the new Florida Electronic Voting Systems Act, counties were permitted to use either paperless touchscreen voting machines (which resemble bank ATM machines) or optical scan voting systems. Fifteen of the state's 67 counties, including Palm Beach County, chose to use touchscreens; the other 52 used optical scan.

The new Florida law provided for two kinds of recounts. First, if the margin of victory were 0.5 percent or less, there would be a machine recount, which would retabulate optical scan ballots and check the counters on touchscreen machines. *See* Fla. Stat. § 102.141(6)(a). If that recount were to indicate a margin of victory of 0.25 percent or less, officials would be required to conduct a manual recount of all "residual votes"—both "overvotes" and "undervotes." Fla. Stat. § 102.166—to see if there were a "clear indication on the ballot that the voter has made a definite choice." Fla. Stat. § 102.166(5)(a).

In optical scan counties, the manual recount would be fairly straightforward, since there are individual ballots to examine. But in touchscreen counties, there would be no individual ballot to examine.

Various voters and Democratic elected officials sued state and Palm Beach County election officials, alleging a violation of the equal protection clause because voters in touchscreen counties would be denied the opportunity voters in optical scan counties would have to have their residual votes captured by a manual recount of their actual ballots.

In *Wexler v. Anderson*, 452 F.3d 1226 (11th Cir. 2006), *cert. denied*, 127 S.Ct. 934 (2007), the court of appeals rejected that claim:

> Plaintiffs' fundamental error is one of perspective. By adopting the perspective of the residual voter, they have avoided the question that is of constitutional dimension: Are voters in touchscreen counties less likely to cast an effective vote than voters in optical scan counties? It is this question, and not the question of whether uniform procedures have been followed across a state regardless of differences in voting technology, that the Supreme Court consistently has emphasized in its voting jurisprudence. . . .

> The plaintiffs argue that because voters in touchscreen counties have no opportunity to have their residual votes counted manually whereas voters in optical scan counties have such an opportunity, Florida's disparate treatment of these groups warrants strict scrutiny. The plaintiffs, however, did not plead that voters in touchscreen counties are less likely to cast effective votes due to the alleged lack of a meaningful manual recount procedure in those counties. Thus, if

voters in touchscreen counties are burdened at all, that burden is the mere possibility that should they cast residual ballots, those ballots will receive a different, and allegedly inferior, type of review in the event of a manual recount. Such a burden, borne of a reasonable, non-discriminatory regulation, is not so substantial that strict scrutiny is appropriate.... Thus, we review Florida's manual recount procedures to determine if they are justified by the State's "important regulatory interests." See *Burdick* [*v. Takushi*], 504 U.S. at 434

Here, Florida has important reasons for employing different manual recount procedures according to the type of voting system a county uses. The differences between these procedures are necessary given the differences in the technologies themselves and the types of errors voters are likely to make in utilizing those technologies. Voters casting optical scan ballots can make a variety of mistakes that will cause their ballots not to be counted. For example, a voter casting an optical scan ballot might leave a stray pencil mark or circle a candidate's name rather than filling in the appropriate bubble. Thus, although an optical scan tabulation machine may register an undervote for a particular race on a particular ballot, there may be sufficient indicia on the ballot that the voter actually chose a candidate in that race such that the vote would be counted in a manual recount. In contrast, a voter in a touchscreen county either chooses a candidate for a particular race or does not; the touchscreen machines do not record ambiguous indicia of voter intent that can later be reviewed during a manual recount.

Plaintiffs do not contend that equal protection requires a state to employ a single kind of voting system throughout the state. Indeed, "local variety [in voting systems] can be justified by concerns about cost, the potential value of innovation, and so on." *Bush*, 531 U.S. at 134 (Souter, J., dissenting). Among other things, witnesses for the State testified that touchscreen machines have certain benefits for disabled voters and they prevent some of the voter errors that are characteristic of optical scan voting systems. Accordingly, we hold that Florida's manual recount procedures are justified by the State's important regulatory interests and, therefore, they do not violate equal protection.

4. What does it mean to say that every vote must be counted? Consider the 2004 mayoral election in San Diego. The incumbent, Dick Murphy, appeared to defeat a challenger, Donna Frye, by 2,108 votes out of more than 450,000 cast. But the election registrar had refused to count 5,551 write-in ballots for Frye because on those ballots, voters had failed to shade in a small oval bubble next to the write-in slot, to indicate that they were casting a write-in vote. The relevant optical-scan technology was used for the first time in a general election in San Diego in the election at issue (the technology had also been used in the primary); filling in the bubbles enables the optical scanners to quickly read and tabulate votes. These uncounted votes turned up after the election results were certified when interested actors, including the media, paid for a review of the ballots.

Voters who supported Frye argued that "intent of the voter"—not technical compliance with election law—was the legal standard, at least that it should be the legal standard at the recount stage. At least five lawsuits, in state and federal court, followed to implement this view. But the state trial court ruled that the election laws should be given their "plain meaning." Since the law required the oval to be filled in, the court ruled, the disputed ballots were not valid votes, regardless of what voters might have intended. While appeals were pending, Murphy resigned office for other reasons; a special election was scheduled; and further legal proceedings came to a halt. For coverage, see Greg Moran, *Re-Election of Murphy Will Stand, Judge Rules*, San Diego Union–Tribune (Feb. 3, 2005).

AN INTRODUCTORY NOTE ON THE HELP AMERICA VOTE ACT OF 2002 (HAVA)

In response to the problems illustrated by the 2000 election, Congress enacted a sweeping new federal statute, the Help America Vote Act of 2002 (HAVA), 42 U.S.C. § 15301 et seq. Selected provisions appear in the Documentary Appendix.

HAVA created a new agency, the Electoral Assistance Commission. Among the EAC's responsibilities are conducting research on issues affecting election administration (including providing grants for technology development and pilot programs), developing a national program for certifying voting systems, producing voting system guidelines, maintaining the voter-registration forms developed under the National Voter Registration Act of 1993, and establishing minimum election administration standards for state and local jurisdictions administering federal elections. HAVA also authorized significant federal funding for the replacement of punch-card and lever voting machines and for other improvements in election administration.

Section 301(a) of HAVA sets minimum standards for voting systems used in elections for federal office. It requires that such systems permit a voter to verify her ballot and to correct and change her ballot before it is cast and counted and requires that systems "notify" a voter if she has overvoted. (In many cases, this notification requirement can be met simply by "establishing a voter education program ... that notifies each voter of the effect of casting multiple votes for an office" and tells voters how to correct the ballot.) It also requires that the system produce a record that can be audited. Finally, it provides various protections to disabled and non-English proficient voters and requires, implicitly in response to *Bush v. Gore*, that each state "adopt uniform and nondiscriminatory standards that define what constitutes a vote and what will be counted as a vote for each category of voting system used in the State."

Section 303 sets out various requirements with regard to computerized statewide voter registration databases, designed to ensure accurate voting rolls. The section also sets out new voter identification requirements for individuals who initially register by mail. The various requirements of section 303 reflect a tension that pervaded the legislative history of HAVA between arguments in favor of reforms that would enhance participation by reducing barriers to voting and concerns about vote fraud. *See* Gabrielle B. Ruda, Comment, *Picture Perfect: A Critical Analysis of the Debate on the 2002 Help America Vote Act*, 31 Fordham Urb. L.J. 235 (2003). Compare the discussions surrounding HAVA with those connected to the larger issue of voter identification requirements described in Chapter 2.

Perhaps HAVA's most immediately important innovation came in section 302, which requires states to permit "provisional voting" by individuals who appear at a polling place to vote but whose names do not appear on the official list of eligible voters. Polling officials are required to notify the individual of the right to cast a provisional ballot and if the individual files a written declaration, the poll officials must provide a provision ballot, transmit the ballot cast to the appropriate officials for verification and if the appropriate official "determines that the individual is eligible under State law to vote, the individual's provisional ballot shall be counted as a vote in that election in accordance with State law."

While section 302 thus requires that states provide voters with provisional ballots, it does not specify precisely under what circumstances such ballots should be counted. Needless to say, the varying standards for when provisional ballots should be counted prompted a round of litigation.

Sandusky County Democratic Party v. Blackwell

387 F.3d 565 (6th Cir. 2004).

■ PER CURIAM.

At bottom, this is a case of statutory interpretation. Does the Help America Vote Act require that all states count votes (at least for most federal elections) cast by provisional ballot as legal votes, even if cast in a precinct in which the voter does not reside, so long as they are cast within a "jurisdiction" that may be as large as a city or county of millions of citizens? We hold that neither the statutory text or structure, the legislative history, nor the understanding, until now, of those concerned with voting procedures compels or even permits that conclusion....

To hold otherwise would interpret Congress's reasonably clear procedural language to mean that political parties would now be authorized to marshal their supporters at the last minute from shopping centers, office buildings, or factories, and urge them to vote at whatever polling place happened to be handy, all in an effort to turn out every last vote regardless of state law and historical practice. We do not believe that Congress quietly worked such a revolution in America's voting procedures, and we will not order it.

I

The States long have been primarily responsible for regulating federal, state, and local elections. . . . One aspect common to elections in almost every state is that voters are required to vote in a particular precinct. Indeed, in at least 27 of the states using a precinct voting system, including Ohio, a voter's ballot will only be counted as a valid ballot if it is cast in the correct precinct.

The advantages of the precinct system are significant and numerous: it caps the number of voters attempting to vote in the same place on election day; it allows each precinct ballot to list all of the votes a citizen may cast for all pertinent federal, state, and local elections, referenda, initiatives, and levies; it allows each precinct ballot to list only those votes a citizen may cast, making ballots less confusing; it makes it easier for election officials to monitor votes and prevent election fraud; and it generally puts polling places in closer proximity to voter residences. . . .

HAVA was passed in order to alleviate "a significant problem voters experience[, which] is to arrive at the polling place believing that they are eligible to vote, and then to be turned away because the election workers cannot find their names on the list of qualified voters." H.R. Rep. 107–329 at 38 (2001). HAVA dealt with this problem by creating a system for provisional balloting, that is, a system under which a ballot would be submitted on election day but counted if and only if the person was later determined to have been entitled to vote. . . .

In essence, HAVA's provisional voting section is designed to recognize, and compensate for, the improbability of "perfect knowledge" on the part of local election officials. *See Fla. Democratic Party v. Hood*, 342 F. Supp. 2d 1073, 2004 U.S. Dist. LEXIS 21720, No. 4:04cv395–RH/WCS, at 13 (N.D. Fla. Oct. 21, 2004) (order granting preliminary injunction). "If a person presents at a polling place and seeks to vote, and if that person would be allowed to vote by an honest election worker with perfect knowledge of the facts and law, then the person's vote should count."*Ibid.* But because any given election worker may not in fact have perfect knowledge, the person who claims eligibility to vote, but whose eligibility to vote at that time and place cannot be verified, is entitled under HAVA to cast a provisional ballot. *Ibid.* "On further review—when, one hopes, perfect or at least more perfect knowledge will be available—the vote will be counted or not, depending on whether the person was indeed entitled to vote at that time and place."

* * *

III

HAVA does not itself create a private right of action. Appellees contend that HAVA creates a federal right enforceable against state officials under 42 U.S.C. § 1983. With respect to the right to cast a provisional ballot under the circumstances described in HAVA § 302(a), we agree.

Section 1983 provides a cause of action against any person who, acting under color of state law, abridges rights created by the Constitution or the laws of the United States. *Maine v. Thiboutot*, 448 U.S. 1, 4–8 (1980). Only "unambiguously conferred" rights will support a § 1983 action. *Gonzaga Univ. v. Doe*, 536 U.S. 273, 283 (2002)....

The rights-creating language of HAVA § 302(a)(2) is unambiguous. That section states that upon making the required affirmation, an *"individual shall be permitted* to cast a provisional ballot." 42 U.S.C. § 15482(a)(2) (emphasis added).... HAVA also refers explicitly to the *"right of an individual to cast a provisional ballot,"* 42 U.S.C. § 15482(b)(2)(E) (emphasis added), and requires states to post information at polling places about this right along with "instructions on how to contact the appropriate officials if *these rights* are alleged to have been violated," *ibid.* (emphasis added). The right to cast a provisional ballot is neither vague nor amorphous, and is no less amenable to judicial interpretation and enforcement than any other federal civil right....

Individual enforcement of this right under § 1983 is not precluded by either the explicit language of HAVA, or by a comprehensive enforcement scheme incompatible with individual enforcement. We have reviewed both HAVA's requirement that those States wishing to receive certain types of federal funding must provide administrative procedures by which citizen complaints may be reviewed and resolved, *see* 42 U.S.C. § 15512, and its provision that the U.S. Attorney General may bring a civil action to enforce HAVA's requirements, *see id.* § 15511. We do not find that these provisions, taken together, indicate a congressional intention to "shut the door" to federal judicial review of state actions, which would be otherwise unavailable to citizens whose right to vote provisionally has been denied or abridged.

* * *

V

HAVA requires that any individual affirming that he or she "is a registered voter in the jurisdiction in which the individual desires to vote and that the individual is eligible to vote in an election for Federal office ... shall be permitted to cast a provisional ballot." *See* 42 U.S.C. § 15482(a).

Directive 2004–33 [the interpretive regulation promulgated by the Ohio secretary of state] contravenes this requirement because it requires that a voter's residence in a precinct be determined on the spot by a poll worker, and empowers poll workers to deny a voter a provisional ballot if the voter's residence in the correct precinct cannot be confirmed. ... Under HAVA, the only permissible requirement that may be imposed upon a would-be voter before permitting that voter to cast a provisional ballot is the affirmation contained in § 15482(a): that the voter is a registered voter in the jurisdiction in which he or she desires to vote, and that the voter is eligible to vote in an election for federal office.

Unfortunately, HAVA does not define what "jurisdiction" means in this context, which leaves unclear whether a voter must affirm that he or she is registered to vote in the *precinct* in which he or she desires to vote, the *county* in which he or she desires to vote, or even simply the *state* in which he or she desires to vote. The district court concluded that the term should be given the same meaning as the term "registrar's jurisdiction" is given in the NVRA; namely the geographic reach of the unit of government that maintains the voter registration rolls, *see* 42 U.S.C. § 1973gg–6(j), which in Ohio is each county board of election, *see* Ohio Rev. Code Ann. §§ 3501.11(U), (Y) (West 2004). The district court offered two bases for its conclusion: first, the statement by Senator Dodd on the Senate floor that "it is our intent that the word "jurisdiction" ... has the same meaning as the term "registrar's jurisdiction" in section 8(j) of the National Voter Registration Act, 148 Cong. Rec. S2535 (daily ed. Apr. 11, 2002); and second, the court's belief that permitting provisional ballots to be cast by voters outside their home precincts would further HAVA's purpose of preserving the federal franchise.

We disagree with the district court's interpretation of the term "jurisdiction." Senator Dodd's statement must be weighed against other statements in HAVA's legislative history that suggest quite the contrary—that jurisdiction means the particular state subdivision within which a particular State's laws require votes to be cast. Senator Bond, one of HAVA's floor managers, stated:

> Congress has said only that voters in Federal elections should be given a provisional ballot if they claim to be registered in a particular jurisdiction and that jurisdiction does not have the voter's name on the list of registered voters.... *This provision is in no way intended to require any State or locality to allow voters to vote from any place other than the polling site where the voter is registered.*

148 Cong. Rec. S10488, S10493 (daily ed. Oct. 16, 2002) (emphasis added). Senator Bond also noted:

> Additionally, it is inevitable that voters will mistakenly arrive at the wrong polling place. If it is determined by the poll worker that the voter is registered but has been assigned to a different polling place, it is the intent of the authors of this bill that the poll worker can direct the voter to the correct polling place. *In most states, the law is specific on the polling place where the voter is to cast his ballot. Again, this bill upholds state law on that subject.*

148 Cong. Rec. at S10491 (emphasis added).

Nor can the use of the NVRA's definition of "registrar's jurisdiction" be justified on the ground that doing so will further HAVA's purpose of preserving the franchise. For one thing, permitting voters to cast ballots in any precinct within their county of residence may cause logistical problems at certain favored polling places that outweigh some or all of the benefits expected by the district court. For another, even if importing language from the NVRA will in this case have the effect of expanding the opportunities of Ohioans to vote on election day, so too would ordering that provisional ballots may be cast by any Ohio voter anywhere in the state. Absent an independent reason for turning to the NVRA's definition, the mere fact that equating "jurisdiction" with "county" may have a salutary effect on the franchise cannot suffice to justify reading the language of HAVA in this way.

* * *

HAVA is quintessentially about being able to *cast* a provisional ballot. No one should be "turned away" from the polls, but the ultimate legality of the vote cast provisionally is generally a matter of state law. Any error by the state authorities may be sorted out later, when the provisional ballot is examined, in accordance with subsection (a)(4) of section 15482. But the voter casts a provisional ballot at the peril of not being eligible to vote under state law; if the voter is not eligible, the vote will then not be counted. . . .

VI

In addition to finding that HAVA requires that voters be permitted to cast provisional ballots upon affirming their registration to vote in the county within which they desire to vote, the district court also held that provisional ballots must be counted as valid ballots when cast in the correct county. We disagree.

The only subsection of HAVA that addresses the issue of whether a provisional ballot will be counted as a valid ballot conspicuously leaves that determination to the States. That subsection provides:

> If the appropriate State or local election official to whom the ballot or voter information is transmitted under paragraph (3) determines that the individual is eligible under State law to vote, the individual's provisional ballot shall be counted as a vote in that election in accordance with State law.

42 U.S.C. § 15482(a)(4). The district court interpreted this subsection to require the following procedure after a provisional ballot has been cast: First, an election official determines whether the individual who cast the ballot was eligible to vote in the broadest possible sense of that term. In essence, the district court would have state officials ask only whether a voter was eligible to vote *in some polling place* within the county at the

start of election day. Even someone who has "voted 'improperly' " remains eligible in this sense of eligibility. Second, if the voter is deemed eligible to vote, the provisional ballot is deemed valid, and may then be tallied along with all the other valid ballots in accordance with State rules for tallying votes accurately and promptly. The district court, in other words, interpreted HAVA as leaving to state law only "*how* the ballots are counted" while federal law determines "*whether* they are to be counted." Because the district court found that voters are eligible to vote under Ohio law anywhere in their county of residence, the court held that a provisional ballot cast anywhere in a voter's county of residence must be counted as valid.

The district court's interpretation of this subsection of HAVA is incorrect. To read "eligible understate law to vote" so broadly as to mean not only that a voter must simply be eligible to vote *in some polling place* within the county, but remains eligible even after casting an improper ballot would lead to the untenable conclusion that Ohio must count as valid a provisional ballot cast in the correct county even it is determined that the voter in question had previously voted elsewhere in that county; an impropriety that would not render that voter ineligible based upon the district court's interpretation of HAVA. State law concerning eligibility to vote is not limited to facts about voters as they arise from slumber on election day; they also stipulate, for example, that a voter is eligible to vote only once in each election, and, in Ohio, where a voter is eligible to cast a ballot. In other words, being eligible under State law to vote means eligible to vote *in this specific election in this specific polling place.*

Under Ohio law, a voter is eligible to vote in a particular polling place only if he or she resides in the precinct in which that polling place is located....

* * *

Nor does the legislative history of the statute provide any reason to believe that HAVA requires that ballots cast in the wrong precinct be counted. Senator Bond, for example, stated that "ballots will be counted according to state law.... It is not the intent of the authors to overturn State laws regarding registration or state laws regarding the jurisdiction in which a ballot must be cast to be counted." 148 Cong.Rec. at S10491. Senator Dodd also noted: "Whether a provisional ballot is counted or not depends solely on State law, and the conferees clarified this by adding language in section 302(a)(4) stating that a voter's eligibility to vote is determined under State law." 148 Cong. Rec. at S10510. Moreover, he added that "nothing in this compromise usurps the state or local election official's sole authority to make the final determination with respect to whether or not an applicant is duly registered, whether the voter can cast a regular ballot, or whether that vote is duly counted." *Ibid. See also id.* at S10504 (noting that HAVA does not establish "a Federal definition of when a voter is registered or how a vote is counted").

We therefore hold that HAVA does not require that any particular ballot, whether provisional or "regular," must be counted as valid. States remain free, of course, to count such votes as valid, but remain equally free to mandate, as Ohio does, that only ballots cast in the correct precinct will be counted.

* * *

NOTES AND QUESTIONS

1. The 2004 election was the first to which section 302 applied. According to a report prepared from the Election Day Survey administered by the EAC, jurisdictions reported nearly two million provisional ballots having been cast in 2004, of which 64.5 percent were ultimately counted. Nearly 2.5 percent of people nationwide who voted were given provisional ballots. In Washington state and Alaska, over ten percent of ballots cast on Election Day were provisional.

More than one million of the provisional ballots were cast in so-called "section 203 jurisdictions." These jurisdictions are covered by section 203 of the Voting Rights Act of 1965, which applies to jurisdictions with large numbers of limited English proficiency voters. While section 203 jurisdictions thus accounted for roughly half the provisional ballots cast, they constituted only an eighth of the jurisdictions reporting provisional ballots. The Report noted that "[t]he much higher rate of casting provisional ballots was not offset by the higher rate of counting provisional ballots in these jurisdictions." See http://www.eac.gov/election_survey_2004/html/exec% 20summary.htm. Does the fact that so many provisional ballots may have been cast by limited English proficiency voters suggest that those voters may have been confused about where to show up, or does it suggest that poll workers, perhaps impatient with assisting such voters, simply handed them provisional ballots in order to keep the process moving along?

2. There was a significant variation among states in the percentage of provisional ballots that were ultimately counted. Seventeen states interpreted section 302(a)'s reference to an individual's declaration that she is "a registered voter in the jurisdiction in which the individual desires to vote" as referring to the county. In those jurisdictions, if an individual showed up at the wrong precinct but in the right county, her vote would be counted. Those jurisdictions rejected, on average, 30 percent of the provisional ballots cast. By contrast, the twenty-eight states—like Ohio—and the District of Columbia that rejected provisional ballots unless they were cast in the correct precinct rejected 38 percent of the provisional ballots cast. *See* Gerald M. Feige, Comment, *Refining the Vote: Suggested Amendments to the Help America Vote Act's Provisional Balloting Standards*, 110 Penn. St. L. Rev. 449 (2005).

3. For early assessments of how HAVA has worked, see, e.g., Brandon Fail, Comment, *HAVA's Unintended Consequences: A Lesson for Next Time,*

116 Yale L.J. 493 (2006); Edward P. Foley, *The Promise and Problems of Provisional Voting*, 73 Geo. Wash. L. Rev. 1193 (2005); Glenn D. Magpantay, *Two Steps Forward, One Step Back, and a Side Step: Asian Americans and the Federal Help America Vote Act*, 10 UCLA Asian Pac. Am. L.J. 31 (2005); Daniel P. Tokaji, *Early Returns on Election Reform: Discretion, Disenfranchisement, and the Help America Vote Act*, 73 Geo. Wash. L. Rev. 1206 (2005).

CHAPTER 13

ALTERNATIVE DEMOCRATIC STRUCTURES

At the beginning of this book, in Chapter 1, we asked whether "democracy" could really be said to pre-exist, or remain autonomous from, the specific laws and institutions that construct it in particular contexts. Through historical, legal, and theoretical perspectives, we have tried to show that the democracy we now experience is, indeed, something *constructed*—the outcome of legal rules and institutional frameworks, rather than some entity such as "We the People" that pre-exists these structural choices.

In this Chapter, we turn to dramatically different ways of constructing democratic institutions, particularly voting rules. We examine alternatives to the traditional Anglo–American electoral structure of territorially-based election districts, particularly the single-member district. One possibility is what are called alternative voting systems, which have become of increasing interest recently in the United States: these include cumulative voting, preference voting (or single-transferrable voting, STV), and limited voting. Another option is the kind of electoral system that dominates in European democracies and nearly all Latin American ones, which is one form or another of proportional representation. As material in the previous Chapters shows, controversies today over concepts of representation, the Voting Rights Act, racial redistricting, and the like raise challenges to long taken-for-granted foundations of American democracy. Contemporary struggles in such areas return us to first principles, and the flourishing of interest in alternative democratic structures results from this renewed encounter with the fundamental principles of democratic institutional design.

As you examine these alternative approaches to voting and elections, consider them along several dimensions. First, what is the theory of political representation and democratic politics implied in different electoral structures? Second, to what extent would various problems we have dealt with earlier in the casebook be better addressed, not through the constitutional or policy approaches discussed there, but through wholly different electoral structures such as those presented here? Rather than trying to work within the constraints imposed by a continuing commitment to our current electoral structures, would the problems previous chapters address be more appropriately dealt with through more radical institutional reconfigurations? Finally, the choice of voting systems cannot be debated only in terms of theories of representation and democracy; all voting systems should be seen as packages of potential advantages and disadvantages. From a pragmatic perspective, try to analyze what tradeoffs are presented by the various electoral systems we explore here. What incentives do different systems give candidates? political parties? voters? Even if the current system has the kind of costs exposed throughout this casebook, might that system remain preferable to the plausible alternatives?

In addition to examining alternative voting structures, we will look at the historical development of territorial districting in the United States. How much do current electoral practices reflect, not so much deliberative policy choices among the competing alternatives, but the path dependency of democratic institutions—that is, the fact that particular institutions were chosen at one point in time and then endured in the face of new possibilities primarily because they had already been chosen and were set in place? As a leading scholar of election systems puts it, "one of the best-known generalizations about electoral systems is that they tend to be very stable and to resist change." Arend Lijphart, Democracies 52 (1994). After you understand the alternative possibilities, consider the question posed in Chapter 1 about how a nascent democracy should go about selecting an electoral system. Consider as well whether you think the United States would choose its current electoral structures were that choice being confronted for the first time today, on a clean slate.

We begin with the leading theoretical account of how districted election systems channel politics toward two (and only two) relatively stable, relatively centrist parties.

Duverger's Law, Duverger's Hypothesis

In 1951, the French political scientist, Maurice Duverger, formulated what he called "a true sociological law" concerning the effects of different electoral systems on the structure of politics. This "law" was that systems in which office is awarded to a candidate who receives the most votes (with two candidates, a majority, but with more than two, a plurality) in a single-ballot election will produce a two-party political system, rather than a multi-party one. Maurice Duverger, Political Parties: Their Organization and Activity in the Modern State (1954). This plurality, winner-take-all system is used for nearly all American elections, as it is for British elections. Other political scientists had reached similar conclusions: "single-member district-system-plus-plurality-elections . . . discriminate *moderately* against the second party; but against the third, fourth, and fifth parties the force of this tendency is multiplied to the point of extinguishing their chances of winning seats altogether." Elmer E. Schattschneider, Party Government 75 (1942).

More modern studies essentially confirm this view. *See generally* Douglas Rae, Political Consequences of Electoral Laws (1971). A few qualifications have been added to the general law based on countries, like

Canada and India, that use plurality voting but nonetheless have more than two significant parties. In countries with strong decentralized government, like Canada, local parties can be the main parties in certain provinces, which leads to their ability to capture enough votes at the national level to be viable third parties. But with minor qualifications, most political scientists accept in one form or another Duverger's "law"—particularly if it is viewed as describing a strong tendency, rather than a deterministic view on the influence of institutions on politics. For a good survey of debates between institutionalist and more culturally-oriented explanations of politics, along with a sophisticated reevaluation of Duverger's Law, see Gary Cox, Making Votes Count: Strategic Coordination in the World's Electoral Systems (1997).

Duverger proposed two causal mechanisms to explain this pattern. Both implicitly derive from what today are called rational-choice models for how politicians and voters behave. One mechanism focused on voters: they were assumed not to want to "waste" their votes on candidates who stood little chance of being elected. Rather than voting for a third-party candidate who might be the voter's first choice, a voter in a plurality, winner-take-all system will vote for a candidate from one of the two major parties who has a "realistic" chance to win. Voters do not vote sincerely, but strategically, in the sense that they do not vote their true first preference. Notice that this view, which empirical studies bear out, means that voters are motivated in particular ways when voting—they vote not primarily as a means of expressing their political values, but as a means of influencing the choice between the two candidates with the most likely chance of winning (recall the discussion of whether constitutional doctrine should recognize an expressive dimension of voting in Chapter 4, where we discussed *Burdick v. Takushi*, 504 U.S. 428 (1992)).

The second mechanism focuses on politicians and the way the plurality, winner-take-all system exaggerates the votes of large parties and diminishes the influence of small ones. If candidates from two parties face each other in this system, the one who wins 51 percent of the vote gains office, meaning a candidate with 49 percent of the vote gets nothing. The system has the "balloon effect" of transforming 51 percent of the votes into 100 percent of the political power at issue. Unless a third party can come close to capturing 33 percent of the votes, with the rest evenly divided between the two major parties, it stands little chance of winning office. As a result, Duverger argued that politicians did not consider forming or joining third parties in this system.

Duverger also proposed another generalization about electoral systems, which he termed a "hypothesis" rather than a law. This hypothesis is that systems that use proportional representation will tend to lead to the formation of many independent parties. This, too, stems from the rational-choice model of what motivates voters and politicians; because parties receive seats in proportion to their total votes, votes for smaller parties are not "wasted." While many systems that use proportional representation do have multiple parties, there are notable exceptions: Austria, Ireland, and, until recently, Germany all were countries that were dominated by two principal parties despite using forms of proportional representation. For data correlating the effective number of political parties in different countries with the type of electoral system used, see David M. Farrell, Comparing Electoral Systems 146–47 (1997) (generally showing that countries with plurality, winner-take-all voting have around two effective parties, while those using forms of proportional representation tend to have three to five parties).

Given the strong influence of electoral laws on the shape of democratic politics, re-consider the question posed at the beginning of this book in Chapter 1: how much does law *construct* democracy, rather than democracy pre-exist specific institutional arrangements? How much is the kind of democracy different countries experience a function of cultural and historical differences, and how much is it a function of the technical details of their different electoral institutions? Some historians have famously argued for the proposition of "American exceptionalism," the view that America is distinct from European democracies because there is less ideological disagreement on fundamental questions. *See, e.g.,* Louis Hartz, The Liberal Tradition in America (1955). But how much is America's perceived ideological consensus, either in the 1950s or today, a function of institutions, rather than culture or politics? Would the United States quickly become a Western–European style multi-party democracy if it shifted to proportional representation? *See, e.g.,* Daniel Lazare, The Frozen Republic: How the Constitution is Paralyzing Democracy 295–96 (1995) (arguing that the "Republican–Democratic duopoly" since the mid-nineteenth century reflects "a record of political stagnation without parallel in virtually any other country" and that if House elections were to be based on proportional representation, it would open the door to multi-party political competition).

As with all questions of institutional design, there are gains and losses associated with the choices made. One response to Duverger's observations is to posit that proportional representation systems are a superior form of guaranteeing representation since they allow for a diversity of views to be presented to the electorate. Later in this Chapter we will examine whether that is as true as appears, or if the real difference is between forcing political coalitions to form prior to elections (and running as a broad-tent party) or leaving them to form at the party level after elections in order for non-majority parties to create a government. Additionally, consider the argument that districted election systems have the effect of forcing extreme parties to the margins and hence produce governments that are less vulnerable to parliamentary sabotage by antidemocratic forces that manage to secure parliamentary seats. *See* Samuel Issacharoff, *Fragile Democracies*, 120 Harv. L. Rev. 1405 (2007).

For two interesting perspectives on Duverger's Law, see William H. Riker, *Duverger's Law Revisited* and Maurice Duverger, *Duverger's Law: Forty Years Later*, both in Electoral Laws and Their Political Consequences (Bernard Grofman & Arend Lijphart eds. 1986).

A.   TYPES OF ELECTORAL SYSTEMS

A recent survey, on which this Note draws, suggests there are at least 2,500 works dealing with electoral structures and their consequences. David M. Farrell, Comparing Electoral Systems 1 (1997). Here we provide a brief and simple overview of the basic electoral systems, which we divide into three. Later discussions will provide more detail on several of these different systems.

1. *Majoritarian Systems.* These are the systems used in the United Kingdom and several countries that inherited their institutions from it, including the United States, Canada, Australia, and, until recently, New Zealand. It is also used for some elections in India, Bangladesh, the Philippines, Zambia, Nepal, Thailand, and Chile. There are two common forms of this system, and a third used only in Australia.

The first form is often called "First Past the Post," (FPTP) or the plurality-vote system. Here, the candidate who receives the most votes in a territorial district is elected, regardless of how many votes the candidate receives. In a study of all elections in 27 democracies between 1945–1990, which includes the 24 most durable democracies since 1945, five countries used FPTP in nearly all their elections: Canada, India, New Zealand, the United Kingdom, and the United States. Arend Lijphart, Electoral Systems and Party Systems 18 (1994). Historically, the movement has been away from this system and toward systems of proportional representation. Thus, New Zealand replaced its FPTP system, and none of the newly emerging democracies in the 1970s in Mediterranean Europe (Greece, Portugal, Spain) nor those in eastern and central Europe or the former Soviet Union in the 1980s and 1990s adopted it.

The second form is a more strictly majoritarian one. This is called the second-ballot or runoff system. If no candidate receives an absolute majority in the first round, a second round of elections is held. Rules vary as to how well candidates have to fare in the first round to make it to the second ballot; in some elections, only the top two candidates make it to the second round. The aim of this system is to make it more likely that the candidate elected will have an actual majority of the votes cast in the second round, thus avoiding plurality-elected candidates. This system is used for some elections in the United States, particularly in the South, and has been challenged as a violation of the Voting Rights Act. This system is most commonly associated with France during the Fifth Republic, but it is used for presidential elections in many countries. For extensive discussion of

FPTP and runoff systems in different countries, see Arend Lijphart, Democracies: Patterns of Majoritarian and Consensus Government in Twenty–One Countries 150–169 (1984).

Australia uses what is called the alternative vote system, or "instant run-off," invented in the 1870s by a professor at the Massachusetts Institute of Technology, W.R. Ware. *See* Farrell, *supra*, at 45. The Irish Republic also uses this system for presidential and some other elections, and parts of Canada used it in the 1950s (Ann Arbor, Michigan used it for one mayoral election in the 1970s), but the system is used far more in Australia than anywhere else. Voters rank all the candidates running in order of preference; in Australia, the failure to do so invalidates the ballot. A candidate must receive more than 50 percent of the actual vote to be elected. Thus, if no candidate reaches this level in the initial count, the candidate with the least votes is eliminated, and all his or her votes transferred to the second choice those voters marked. The process continues until a candidate emerges with more than 50 percent of the votes. Notice that this system avoids multiple rounds of elections to generate a majority-supported candidate; voters rank all candidates at once and the vote transfers take place until a winning candidate emerges. This system resembles STV, discussed below, but unlike STV, which is used to elect a representative body as a whole, the instant run-off is used to elect one candidate to represent a district.

The use of single transferable votes was recently at issue in British Columbia, Canada, as a result of a novel experiment in direct citizen participation. A Citizen's Assembly was convened from a random sample of voters who were then allowed to deliberate for a year over voting systems. After presentations by experts, the Assembly favored STV on the grounds that it: (1) is easy to use; (2) is fair, as makes every vote count and results in more proportional representation; (3) gives more powers to voters, which strengthens local bonds between politicians and their constituents, and; (4) provides voters with greater choice. The Citizens' Assembly recommendation was approved by 58 percent of the voters in a public referendum. Although this failed to gain the supermajority necessary to pass the proposal into law, the support spurred British Columbia politicians to publicly consider and support elements of the plan. Professor Heather Gerken has analyzed the experience of the Citizens' Assembly in British Columbia, Canada, and used it as an example of citizen-directed change in electoral systems. Cf. Heather Gerken, Citizens Must Drive Electoral Reform, Roll Call, Nov. 15, 2005. The novelty of the British Columbia experiment was not only the selection of STV—a concept which Professor Gerken says may have limited political sales-appeal—but the use of an open public process which, Gerken recounts, may deflect charges of self-dealing motives that have hampered other reform efforts. Heather K. Gerken, *The Double–Edged Sword of Independence: Inoculating Electoral Reform Commissions Against Everyday Politics*, 6 Elec. L. J. 184 (2007).

2. *Proportional Representation Systems.* Majoritarian systems are based on geographic constituencies (candidates are elected from districts), and voters vote directly for individual candidates. Proportional representation systems come in many forms, but in general, voting tends to focus on parties, not candidates, and the districts involved are much larger—often extending to the entire country. The basic idea of PR is that parties should end up with a number of seats roughly proportional to the number of votes they receive. All European countries other than Great Britain, France, and Ireland use PR.

The origins of PR provide insight into the justifications for it. PR arose in the late nineteenth century, with the extension of the suffrage and the development of mass political parties. Pressure for adopting it was greatest in Belgium and Switzerland; both had sharp cleavages along religious and ethnic lines, which in turn generated pressure for "fairer representation." In 1899, Belgium became the first country to adopt the system of list PR. Finland followed in 1906, Sweden in 1907, and by 1920, most European countries had made the switch.

a.   *List–PR.* In list-PR systems, voters vote for a party, which puts on the ballot a list of candidates. Parties then receive seats in proportion to their votes. To avoid representation of "fringe" parties, most countries establish an electoral threshold, below which a party receives no seats. This threshold ranges from 1.5 percent in Israel to 5 percent in Germany. A few countries, such as the Netherlands and Israel, use the entire nation as the relevant election unit; representation is closest to precise proportionality in these systems. Other countries are divided into regions or constituencies; the smallest of these are found in Greece, where each elects five representatives, and the largest in Portugal, where regions elect 24 candidates. These "districts" are not at all like those in single-member district systems; voters do not vote for individual candidates, and the units are much larger than typical single-member districts. The more regions or constituencies, the greater the likely departure in the national legislature from precise proportionality. Diverse technical formulas are used in various countries for determining exactly how seats should be allocated to parties. For a survey of these formulas, see Arend Lijphart, Electoral Systems and Party Systems (1994).

The most important difference is between *closed list* and *open list* systems. In closed-list PR, the parties decide in which order to list their candidates and voters can only vote for the party list as it is presented to them. Thus, if the region will send 20 candidates to the parliament, the party will list its candidates from 1 to 20. If the party gets 25 percent of the vote, its top 5 candidates would win office. This system of PR is used in many newer democracies, such as Argentina, Colombia, Costa Rica, Israel, Portugal, Spain, Turkey, and Uruguay. Germany also employs it for those seats filled by PR (see below for more on Germany's system). Few countries have dropped this system once they adopted it (Italy and France are exceptions), while several countries have abandoned FPTP for it. Of course, this system grants great power to internal party processes and party elites. But one potential advantage of party control is that it can be used to generate a desired mix of candidates representing the party in office. For example, in the first democratic elections in South Africa, held under closed-list PR, many parties presented ethnically mixed lists that they hoped would appeal to broad constituencies. Woman and minorities can do well under this system, if parties support them, because voters cast ballots for parties not individual candidates, which makes practices like racially-polarized voting more difficult. Farrell, *supra*, at 73.

Open-list PR systems vary in detail and are now used in Austria, Belgium, the Netherlands, Norway, Sweden, France, Luxembourg, and Switzerland. One version allows voters to vote either for a party or one specific candidate; the latter counts as a vote for moving that candidate up in the party's rank-ordering. In the most open systems, voters receive as many votes as there are seats to fill; they can vote for a party; give up to two votes to a candidate; and even cast votes for candidates on different lists.

b. *The Two–Vote System of PR* (also, the German system; or additional-al-member PR; and other names). Many countries seek some hybrid structure that combines the seeming best of PR and majoritarian systems. In this system, voters cast two votes: one goes for a party list, and the other for a candidate elected from a single-member district. Thus, the effort is to capture the benefits both of individual representatives accountable to specific geographic constituencies, as well as the fair representation benefits of a PR system. The longest use of this system has been in Germany, but countries forming democracies today are often drawn to it.

In Germany, half the seats in the Bundestag are filled by election of candidates from single-member districts. The second vote is a closed-list PR ballot, the totals from which are aggregated on a national level to determine the overall proportion of seats each party ought to receive. Candidates from the party lists are then added to that party's candidates elected through the single-member districts up to the point at which the level of proportionality, as measured by the second vote, is attained. Thus, if there were 100 total seats to fill, and Party X elected 20 individual candidates from individual districts in the first vote, and received 40 percent of the vote in the list-PR phase, Party X would then have the first 20 of its candidates on the list also added to office (20 + 20 = 40, which means 40 percent of the seats). The list-PR election is based on geographic regions, analogous to states, known as *Lander*. The system tries to encourage the sense of having individual legislators from districts by calling this phase "the primary vote," but given the electoral structure, the list-PR phase is actually more important in terms of political power. If this system appears a mixture of British and Continental electoral systems, that reflects its origins: after World War II, the British pressed the Germans to adopt districted elections, and to emphasize the role of the *Lander,* in order to enhance the stability of the electoral system. As you will soon learn, in this period, it was widely believed that Germany's pre-war system of PR had fractionalized the government and enhanced its instability by enabling minor parties to gain too great representation. This history of Weimar Germany also explains why the threshold for parties to gain seats is set unusually high in Germany (5 percent or three constituency seats).

Other countries also use hybrids of single-member districts and PR elections, including several that have chosen their electoral systems recently. These mixed systems include Japan, Mexico, Russia, and Italy.

3. *Proportional Representation in the Home of First Past the Post?* First past the post elections (FPTP) originated in the United Kingdom and were inherited in countries, like the United States and other former British colonies, that adopted their electoral systems under strong British influence. What does it say about the continuing appeal of FPTP elections that in the United Kingdom of today, there is now serious political discussion of shifting to a more proportional form of representation? How might it affect debates in the United States were the United Kingdom actually to make this shift—which would leave the United States as the only major Western democracy to use FPTP to elect all its lower house members?

In December, 1997, the Labour Government of the United Kingdom convened an Independent Commission on the British voting system. In October, 1998, the Commission, headed by Lord Jenkins of Hillhead, submitted a report in which it recommended a referendum to consider switching from first past the post single member constituencies to a more proportional system that eliminates some of the problems of multiparty votes. *See* Report of the Independent Commission on the Voting System, available at http://www.archive.official-documents.co.uk/document/cm40/4090/contents.htm (last visited April 2, 2007). The Commission recommended that between 80 and 85 percent of the House of Commons continue to be elected by single member constituencies because of the important constituency service role that Members of Parliament play for all of the residents of their constituency. However, the Commission also recommended switching to what it called Alternative Voting (AV) to select the MPs from the single member districts. AV is known more specifically as Instant Runoff Voting, a system which is described *supra.* AV or Instant Runoff Voting is essentially STV (discussed below) with a single member district; if no candidate has a majority, the candidate with the lowest number of votes is eliminated and the ballots are transferred to the second choices of that candidate's supporters. The process repeats until some candidate has a majority. AV consequently produces at least majority acquiescence to the victor (except in cases where the polity is extremely polarized in more than two directions).

The principal effect of AV is to allow voters to select their preferred candidate out of a three or more party race without having to weigh tactical concerns; the ability to designate a candidate who has a stronger chance as a second choice prevents the vote from being "lost." In addition to implementing AV, the Commission proposed that the remaining 15 to 20 percent of the seats be filled with a regionally based proportional representation system. Each voter would vote for both a candidate and a party; for each of 80 areas within the United Kingdom, the extra seat or seats to be assigned through proportional means would be assigned to the party that is most underrepresented by the single member seats within that area. The system would allow some representation for parties that consistently lose elections in certain areas (such as the Conservative Party invariably losing in major cities and Labour invariably losing in rural areas) while receiving consistent, substantial minority support. The Commission considered extensive reports of alternative voting systems employed in other countries and also highlighted some of the "perverse" results that FPTP can produce, including several elections where minority parties won majorities and where parties with small pluralities won landslide majorities in Parliament. The Commission also extensively considered STV, but concluded that this would require either extremely large districts or enlarging the House of Commons (currently a 659 member body) and that either of those changes was undesirable. The Commission concluded that its proposal would ameliorate these effects, although it warned that AV without a "top-up" provision could accentuate some of the disproportional landslide results based on antipathy towards the ruling party. As with many electoral reforms that threaten to disrupt established political arrangements, this one also continues to await governmental action as this edition goes to press.

4. *Semi–Proportional Representation Systems.* These systems include cumulative voting, preference voting (also known as single-transferrable voting, STV), limited voting, and the instant runoff-voting system. They can be viewed as occupying an intermediate position between majoritarian and proportional representation systems. These semi-proportional systems are discussed in detail in the following material.

B.   CUMULATIVE VOTING

1.   The alternative voting system that has received the most attention in the United States recently is cumulative voting (CV). The reason for this interest is that CV has been offered as an alternative to address the specific problem of racial and ethnic underrepresentation to which so much recent energy has gone under the Voting Rights Act. The approach taken under the Act, the creation of "safe" black and Hispanic election districts, has come under challenge from both constitutional and other directions. In the midst of the intense controversies surrounding this approach, CV has been offered as a means of enhancing minority representation without requiring districts to be set aside on a specific racial or ethnic basis.

2. Cumulative voting received widespread national attention when President Clinton nominated Professor Lani Guinier to be head of the Civil Rights Division of the Department of Justice. Professor Guinier had been a leading advocate for greater use of cumulative voting to address minority representation issues currently addressed through the "safe" districting approach under the Voting Rights Act. Consider some of the arguments she offers for CV in Lani Guinier, The Tyranny of the Majority 16, 152 (1994):

> As a solution that permits voters to self-select their identities, cumulative voting also encourages cross-racial coalition building. No one is locked into a minority identity. Nor is anyone necessarily isolated by the identity they choose. Voters can strengthen their influence by forming coalitions to elect more than one representative.... Women too can use cumulative voting to gain greater representation. Indeed, in other countries with similar, alternative voting systems, women are more likely to be represented in the national legislature ... cumulative voting serves many of the same ends as periodic elections or rotation in office, a solution that Madison and others advocated as a means of protecting against permanent majority factions.... [What CV] does is to transform the unit of representation from a territorial one or racial constituency to a political or psychological one.

For a description of how cumulative voting works, and what its purported advantages might be over the current way of addressing minority underrepresentation, consider the following discussion:

> Cumulative voting is a simple concept: each voter is given as many votes to cast as there are seats to be filled. Voters are free to distribute their votes among candidates in any way they choose. This approach enables voters to express not just their raw preferences, but the intensity with which those preferences are held. In a five-way race, for example, a voter can cast one vote for each candidate, vote three times for one candidate and twice for a second, or cast all his votes for one candidate. In this way, minority groups with common interests and strong preferences for a particular candidate can ensure her election, even in the face of a hostile majority.

> This represents a radically different alternative to the current Voting Rights Act. Rather than breaking up the at-large electoral system into five smaller territorial districts, cumulative voting has the advantage of leaving the original electoral system intact; yet it produces outcomes similar to those under the current laws. Under either approach, a 20 percent black population that chooses to vote cohesively would be able to elect one of the five council members.

> And cumulative voting offers striking advantages. Most obviously, it avoids the drawing of radically defined political districts that so trouble the Act's critics. It might also diminish conflicts between minority groups struggling over district boundary lines, such as between blacks and Hispanics in many places. In fact, cumulative voting reduces

gerrymandering opportunities in general. Because it relies on several candidates competing in at-large elections, it requires geographically broad electoral units. The fewer district lines to be drawn, the fewer the invitations to gerrymander.

But the appeal of cumulative voting runs deeper. It is a way of pursuing the goals of the Voting Rights Act within the framework of political liberalism. Voters voluntarily define their own interests and the voting affiliations that best promote them. Adopting this approach thus avoids any assumption that black or Hispanic voters are monolithic groups with unitary political values and interests. Under the current approach, black voters of widely varying socioeconomic status are sometimes grouped together. Cumulative voting would enable these voters to decide for themselves whether their political values are better defined by what they have in common or by what they do not. The current law, moreover, singles out particular minority groups for distinct legal status. Cumulative voting reduces these moral and political conflicts by minimizing the need for judgments about which minority groups warrant distinct protection. Any group that feels the need to vote cohesively is able to do so. "Redistricting," in effect, is done by voters themselves, not by politicians. Moreover, it takes place with each new election, instead of once a decade in the wake of a new census.

The most common concern about cumulative voting is that it is too confusing. But this reflects an instinctive fear of new voting procedures rather than informed experience. Cumulative voting is already used by some corporations in electing boards of directors. Illinois began using cumulative voting to elect its lower house in the aftermath of the Civil War. (Voters were given several chances to abolish the system, but it lasted until 1980, when the overall structure of the Illinois House was changed.) In New Mexico the city council for Alamogordo was elected in 1987 through cumulative voting, the first such local government election this century. Each voter had three votes to use in filling three city council seats; 70 percent of the voters seized this advantage and cast more than one vote for a particular candidate. Although the city's population was 24 percent Hispanic and 5 percent black, it had been nearly twenty years since either a Hispanic or black politician had been elected at-large. But in the 1987 election, one Hispanic official was elected. She was only fourth in the number of voters who supported her, but because her support was particularly intense, she finished third in total votes. Of Hispanics who voted for her, 80 percent gave her more than one vote. They thus relinquished some influence over two seats in order to ensure the election of the one candidate they strongly preferred. Similarly, in Sisseton, South Dakota, members of the Sisseton Wahpeton Sioux tribe recently used cumulative voting to elect their candidate of choice to the local school board.

Cumulative voting is not a panacea. Voters must be knowledgeable about a larger number of candidates; political campaigns might become more expensive as candidates pursue votes through a larger region; representatives would have ties to a broader constituency, but perhaps not as strong ones to a specific, local political base; political parties might try to influence the results by taking control over the number of candidates they slate for office; and, of greatest concern, political bodies might become more fractured and less effective in governing as more officials come into office with the support of less than 50 percent of voters. These are genuine potential costs that warrant discussion . . . But the status quo has its costs as well. We might therefore begin to test cumulative voting incrementally. The Voting Rights Act could be amended so that courts could consider cumulative voting as one option for redressing violations of existing law. It may turn out that the system is not practical on a large scale. But the Voting Rights Act is here to stay, and we should consider new approaches that protect civil rights while easing political, ideological and racial tensions.

Richard H. Pildes, *Gimme Five: Non-gerrymandering Racial Justice*, The New Republic (March 1, 1993).

3. *Technical properties*: The strategy of choice for a cohesive minority group with intense preferences for a particular candidate is, under cumulative voting, to "plump" all the available votes on one candidate. If five seats on a city council are to be filled, voters would have five votes each to distribute as they saw fit. The pure majoritarianism of traditional single-member districts is constrained because the same majority cannot dominate the election for all five city-council seats. If the voters in a sufficiently large minority group concentrate all their votes on the same candidate, they can assure that candidate's election regardless of how other voters, including a majority of voters, cast their ballots. Even with extensive racially polarized voting, for example, a cohesive minority group that constituted at least one-sixth of the electorate would be able through cumulative voting to control one of the five city-council seats. The concept of the "threshold of exclusion" describes the minimum size a minority group must reach under various voting rules to have effective control over at least one seat. The formula for the threshold of exclusion under cumulative voting is $1/(1+N) + 1$ additional vote, where N is the number of seats to be filled. Thus, with five seats at stake and five votes to cast, a minority that casts one vote more than $1/(1+5)$, or one vote more than one-sixth of the total vote can control the outcome of one seat. This assumes that the minority group votes perfectly cohesively: all members cast all five of their votes for the same minority-preferred candidate. By contrast, the threshold of exclusion of FPTP systems is $\frac{1}{2} + 1$ additional vote.

4. CV has been used as a remedy in voting-rights litigation, particularly in the rural South where it is more difficult to devise districts that concentrate black voters into a majority in particular districts. One of the earliest developments of CV as an alternative remedy came in the massive *Dillard* litigation, which challenged the structure of county commissions and boards of education throughout Alabama. Note that the court here did not impose CV against the preferences of the defendant jurisdiction; the parties entered into a consent decree, which the court approved. After reading the case, you will then read a detailed case study of how CV worked in practice in Chilton County, Alabama.

Dillard v. Chilton County Board of Education and Chilton County Commission

699 F.Supp. 870 (M.D.Ala.1988).

■ Myron H. Thompson, District Judge:

The plaintiffs have brought these two lawsuits on behalf of all black citizens in Chilton County, Alabama. They charge that the "at-large" system used to elect the Chilton County Commission and Board of Education violates § 2 of the Voting Rights Act of 1965. The commission and the school board have admitted that their at-large system violates § 2. The issue before the court is whether a settlement proposed by the parties, incorporating a "cumulative voting" scheme for the county's commission and school board, is acceptable. Several members of the plaintiff class have objected to the settlement, claiming that it does not adequately remedy the § 2 violation. After conducting a hearing, in which the objectors as well as plaintiff class members favoring the settlement testified, the special master in this case, United States Magistrate John L. Carroll, recommended in each of these two cases that the court approve the settlement. For the reasons that follow, the court concludes that the magistrate's recommendations should be adopted.

I

According to the 1980 census, Chilton County has a total population of 30,610. Of that number, 11.86% are black. The black population is dispersed throughout the county.

Chilton County and its school system are currently governed by a five-member commission and a five-member board, respectively.... To remedy the admitted § 2 violation, the plaintiffs, the commission and the school board have proposed a seven-member commission and a seven-member board of education elected by cumulative voting. Under this system, each voter has seven votes to cast among the candidates. However, a voter may distribute his or her votes in any way he or she desires. For example, a voter could vote all seven votes for one candidate, four votes for one candidate and three for another, one vote for each of the seven different candidates, or in various other combinations. There are no majority-vote or numbered-post requirements.

Several members of the plaintiff class argue that the proposed settlement does not cure the § 2 violation, and they have proposed a single-
member districting plan in its place.

II

* * *

[T]he critical issue for the court, in its assessment of the settlement
proposed by the parties, is whether the black voters in the county have
under the settlement the potential to elect representatives of their choice,
even in the face of [severe racial polarization.] In determining whether the
settlement offers such, the court will apply a concept known as "threshold
of exclusion."

The threshold of exclusion "is the percentage of the vote that will
guarantee the winning of a seat even under the most unfavorable circumstances." The worst case scenario that defines the threshold of exclusion is
based on two assumptions. The first is that the majority sponsor only as
many candidates as there are seats to be filled; for example, in a seven-seat
jurisdiction, only seven majority-preferred candidates would run. The second is that the majority spread its votes evenly among its candidates, with
no "crossover voting" for the minority-preferred candidate. If either of
these assumptions is relaxed, then it is entirely possible for the minority
candidate to win even if the minority does not constitute more than the
threshold of exclusion in turnout.

There is a calculable threshold of exclusion for any election scheme.
For example, in an at-large system, such as the one [now] used in Chilton
County, the threshold of exclusion is more than 50%. Any group that
constitutes more than 50% of the electorate in that district—that is, a
group of "50% plus"—is guaranteed that its preferred candidate will win.
Of course, in a plurality-win at-large district, as opposed to a district with a
majority-vote requirement, a group with less than 50% plus of the electorate can elect its preferred candidate in certain cases. For example, a group
constituting 40% of the electorate might elect its candidate in a three-way
contest where the other 60% of the electorate spreads its votes between the
other two candidates, each of whom receives 30%. However, although a
group that constitutes less than 50% plus of the population in an at-large
jurisdiction may, in some cases, elect its preferred candidate, the threshold
of exclusion remains 50% plus; that is, a group of 50% plus, by voting
strategically-sponsoring only as many candidates as there are seats and
voting for the entire majority-sponsored slate—can totally shut out the
minority.

In a cumulative voting system, however, the threshold of exclusion is
dependent on the number of seats to be filled in a given election. It can be
expressed as "1/1 + # of seats plus." Thus, in a jurisdiction with seven
seats, the threshold of exclusion would be 12.5% plus. If 1000 electors vote

for seven positions, and if there is a worst case scenario, only seven candidates preferred by the majority, with an evenly split vote, a minority would need only 876, or 12.51% of the 7000 votes, to elect the candidate of their choice.

The threshold of exclusion concept should not, however, be applied in a vacuum. Section 2 requires that, in evaluating vote dilution claims, a court must engage in "a searching practical evaluation of 'past and present reality.'" *Gingles*. A court must look not to just the worse case scenario or the best scenario, but to the totality of the circumstances, to the social and economic as well as the political circumstances of the jurisdiction in which the election system has been, or will be, used. In actual settings, the above two assumptions will exist in varying degrees; and, more than likely, there will be other factors that impede or facilitate the access of minorities to the political process. Therefore, based on a particular jurisdiction's totality of circumstances, a questioned election system may very well not be adequate for the jurisdiction, even though the percentage of black voters in the jurisdiction exceeds the threshold of exclusion for the system; and, conversely, the system may very well be fully adequate in another jurisdiction, even though the percentage of black voters in that jurisdiction is less than the system's threshold of exclusion. The threshold of exclusion concept is therefore not an automatic cut-off point, but rather is a broad guideline which may be helpful in assessing the impact on minorities of present and proposed election systems.

Under the present at-large system used to elect the Chilton County Commission and Board of Education, the threshold of exclusion is 50% plus. Because the percentage of blacks in the county, 11.86, does not even approach this threshold and because there is extensive racial polarization in the county, black voters in the county do not have a realistic opportunity to participate in the political process and elect candidates of their choice.

In contrast, the cumulative voting system proposed by the parties does offer black voters in the county such an opportunity. Admittedly, the percentage of blacks, 11.86, in the county is less than the threshold and, admittedly, if the black voters cumulate their votes, they will not be able to elect a representative under the worse case scenario. But it also cannot be overlooked that the percentage of black citizens in the county approaches the threshold of exclusion. Looking at the totality of the circumstances in Chilton County, the parties urge, and the court agrees, that the system does offer black voters in the county the potential to elect candidates of their choice to the county commission and school board, even in the face of substantial racially polarized voting.

* * *

IV

Finally, the six members of the plaintiff class, who objected to the cumulative vote proposal, have submitted a single-member districting scheme of their own. The objectors ignore the demographics of Chilton County. As previously noted, black persons comprise only 11.86% of the population of Chilton County, and they are dispersed throughout the county. It is impossible to draw a five or seven single-member district plan which both has a majority black district and satisfies the one-person-one-vote requirement. For example, the objectors presented a five single-member district plan to the court, with most of the black citizens included in one district. However, that district would have a total population of approximately 11,000, making it roughly twice the size of an ideal district. The plan obviously fails to satisfy the one-person-one-vote requirement. *See, e.g., Chapman v. Meier,* 420 U.S. 1, 27 (1975) (court-ordered plans must normally meet the goal of population equality with little more than de minimis variation).

* * *

NOTES AND QUESTIONS

1. More than a decade later, Judge Thompson withdrew his remedial order based, in part, on intervening changes in ability of courts to order this form of injunctive relief without finding discriminatory intent. 222 F. Supp. 2d 1283 (M.D. Ala. 2002). This and subsequent orders are still on appeal.

2. *Case study: Chilton County, Alabama.* The political science literature has thoroughly explored the theoretical advantages and disadvantages of different voting systems. But there are few concrete studies of alternative voting systems in operation, in part because until recently, few American jurisdictions used anything other than the traditional system of plurality, winner-take-all voting rules. Rather than debate the abstract merits of alternative voting systems, however, it is now possible to study local governments in the United States, such as Chilton County, that have quietly been using such systems for nearly a decade.

Does actual experience with cumulative voting raise new issues beyond those identified in the theoretical literature, or does it largely confirm academic predictions? What follows are excerpts from a detailed case study of the aftermath of the *Dillard* litigation in Chilton County:

Richard H. Pildes and Kristen A. Donoghue, Cumulative Voting in the United States

1995 U. Chi. Leg. Forum 241.

* * *

4. *The Chilton County settlement.*

[T]he County stipulated to findings that voting was racially polarized and to substantive liability. On the same day, it filed a proposed settlement agreement that had been reached with the plaintiffs. Conceiving the terms of settlement, however, had proven difficult. The County had been willing to convert to a districted system and to draw a majority-minority district. But, unless the County Commission and Board of Education were increased to at least fifteen members each (an option the County leaders viewed as unwieldy and unduly expensive), the geographic dispersion of black voters in the County made the drawing of a contiguous, relatively compact majority-black district impossible.

In settlement discussions, a private attorney assisting in the settlement process for *Dillard v. Baldwin County Board of Education* proposed moving to an alternative voting system. Alternative voting systems are increasingly common at the local level in Alabama, in part because the leading statewide black political organization understood the concept early and has been a consistent supporter of it. Between twenty and twenty-three jurisdictions in Alabama use limited voting, primarily for municipal elections; indeed, Alabama is the national leader in the use of limited voting.

Chilton County, however, decided instead to opt for cumulative voting. After a "long, long series of discussions" of both cumulative voting and limited voting, the lawyer representing Chilton County, John Hollis Jackson, concluded that cumulative voting would be preferable. Those negotiating the settlement for the County feared that limited voting would be perceived as interfering with principles of equality and fair voting because voters would not be permitted to cast a vote for all the seats being filled. Indeed, when the ADC [the Alabama Democratic Conference, the major black political organization in the State] proposed limited voting, the leading local paper editorialized that "being allowed to vote for only one candidate borders on forbidding residents to have the Constitutionally given right to elect those who govern." In opting for cumulative voting, Chilton County became the only Alabama jurisdiction to do so. The motivating force for the decision to accept an alternative voting system was, without a doubt, the fear of what the federal court might impose instead.

Once Jackson agreed to consider a cumulative-voting remedy, he had to persuade the County's political officials to accept it. Initially, they were incredulous. As Jackson put it, they "acted like I was insane to even bring it to them." Jackson held several meetings with the existing County Commission and Board of Education in which various options, including pursuing the litigation, were discussed. As he put it, one day there would be agreement to accept the cumulative voting solution, the next day, the political leaders would be "totally opposed." Eventually, both bodies became persuaded that, as alien as the idea of cumulative voting had seemed initially, it was the best option. After formally voting to adopt the cumulative voting scheme, the two bodies held a joint press conference to begin the process of persuading the County's citizens to accept it. Once the political leaders endorsed cumulative voting as the best alternative under the circumstances, they remained committed to their decision; thus steadfastness played a considerable role in the eventual, begrudging public acceptance of cumulative voting. The parties drafted a formal settlement agreement and the district court approved it, over the objection of some members of the plaintiff class.

5. *Selling cumulative voting to the citizens of Chilton County.*

One of the most interesting aspects of the Chilton County experience was the self-conscious way public efforts were made to explain and justify the new system. . . .

The official announcement of the settlement came at a news conference led by Jackson in February of 1988, with the first cumulative voting elections to take place in that summer's primaries. Thus, there was little time to prepare for the new system. Both the County Commission and Board of Education, which had been five-member bodies with residency requirements, would become seven-member bodies, elected at large with no residency requirements. The move from five to seven members was necessary for the cumulative voting system to work as intended. . . . With a black population of around 11.8 percent, a five-member body would not ensure Chilton County's black population of control over even one seat in the face of extreme racially polarized voting. With a seven-member board, a cohesive minority just above 12.5 percent would effectively control one seat. . . .

In the news conference explaining the new system, the County's attorney, John Hollis Jackson, told voters, "I can confidently say that not one single member of either board like[d] what he had to do." The same issue of the *Independent Advertiser* that reported the press conference included an editorial entitled "Making the Best of a Bad Situation," indicating that the paper had switched positions and was now reconciled to cumulative voting. While saying that the federal court order would "anger many residents," and that "We are angry too," the editorial also said that cumulative voting was "the better of the evils" and that it was "time to make the best of a bad situation. Learn the new system and exercise your right to vote."

The cumulative voting system apparently was met with contempt and disbelief by the general public. Sue Smith, a Republican elected to the Board of Education in 1988, remembered:

When the idea was first proposed, as far as the public reaction, we thought it was a joke, because the idea that one person could vote seven times in one particular race was just really unheard of at that time, and many people thought it was just something that they were grasping at straws kind of a thing, and it would not ever come into effect here. Once it became the law under the settlement of this court case, a lot of people still didn't believe it.

Nor was this skepticism confined to whites. Bobby Agee, Chilton County's first black County Commissioner, who was elected under cumulative voting, recalled that "I didn't see how it would work.... Everybody kept saying it would work, but in the back of my mind I just could not figure out with the white population being as large as it is and the minority population being as small as it is, I kept thinking we're still going to lose no matter what." As the summer primaries approached, the educational efforts of both local government officials and other, more partisan forces, accelerated....

B. Results to Date under the Cumulative Voting System

* * *

a. *Black representation.*

In fact, cumulative voting has worked just as predicted ex ante with respect to enhancing black representation even in the face of racially polarized voting. In elections for the powerful County Commission in 1988, the first held under cumulative voting, Bobby Agee became the first black representative to be elected to the Chilton County Commission since Reconstruction. Indeed Agee, the only black candidate in the general election, not only was elected, but received more total votes than any other candidate in the fourteen-candidate field.

Statistical analysis of the 1988 election reveals that Agee was not the leading vote getter due to cross-racial support. Instead, black voters effectively used the cumulative voting system to concentrate their support for Agee despite almost no white crossover support. Only 1.5 percent of white voters appear to have cast even a single vote for Agee, while virtually all black voters voted for him. More importantly, most black voters gave Agee multiple votes, including many who cast all seven votes for Agee. One means of testing this is by examining the number of precincts in which various candidates received more votes ("bonus votes") than the number of actual voters. Agee received bonus votes in more precincts than any other candidate, indicating that voters were casting more multiple votes for him than for other candidates.

b. *Representation of other minorities.*

Advocates of cumulative voting assert that, in contrast to race-conscious districting, which enhances the electoral opportunities only of racial minorities, cumulative voting—as a neutral means of enhancing minority representation more generally—ought to enhance minority representation of other groups as well. Cumulative voting has indeed had this effect in Chilton County.

Republicans

Republicans were dramatically underrepresented on the County Commission prior to the 1988 election. In 1988, however, Republicans won three of the seven commission seats. This sudden transformation occurred before the dramatic shift toward the Republican party at the local level in the South. Sue Smith, then Chairperson of the Chilton County Republican Party, believes that cumulative voting contributed to the Republican breakdown of the Democratic monopoly on local political power. In 1992, Republicans again were successful, this time winning two seats on the County Commission. . . .

Women

. . . . In Chilton County, women have been elected to the Board of Education since cumulative voting began. Only one woman was on the Board before 1988, but in the cumulative voting election that year, two women, both Republicans, were elected. A third woman, a Democrat, was nearly elected but placed eighth, one position away from a seat. One of the successful women candidates in the 1988 election commented that she was not sure cumulative voting had played a role in the sudden success of women candidates. She did, however, note that more women were running because more women had decided that they could get elected—which might be associated with the use of cumulative voting. Still, women have not been successful in County Commission elections, even since cumulative voting began. The one woman who has run in a primary or general election for the County Commission was defeated.

In sum, since cumulative voting began, groups that previously had not been represented—blacks, Republicans, and women—have been elected in significant numbers to both the County Commission and the Board of Education.

2.   *Effects on minority representation: substantive representation.*

Descriptive representation—the actual presence of minorities in political office—is the immediate test of alternative voting systems. Descriptive representation might in and of itself bring about several desirable results: among other effects, it might enhance the legitimacy of political bodies within the community as a whole and foster a greater sense of civic inclusion among political minorities. But a major question is whether more minorities in office translates into substantive representation that is more responsive to the minority community. Previous scholarship concludes that verifiable, material changes in local government policy do occur when racial minorities begin to assume public office. Nonetheless, some continue to question the link between descriptive and substantive representation: whether the increased presence of black public officials translates into tangible policy and other benefits for minority voters. Is minority representation of primarily symbolic importance? Do white officials represent the actual substantive interests of black constituents just as effectively? Indeed, white members of the Chilton County Commission questioned whether there was any need for minority representation on the County's various administrative bodies.

In Chilton County, we found at least three significant changes in local government—two policy oriented and one attitudinal—in the wake of the cumulative voting system and the first election of a black County Commissioner. First, the most significant function of the County Commission is to make road-paving decisions. Of the various functions within the Commission's jurisdiction, none occupies more time or matters more to the residents of Chilton County than petitions to have roads paved. The County still has about six hundred miles of unpaved roads, which become muddy in the frequent rains, but financial resources sufficient to pave only eight miles per year.

Before Agee was elected, the County Commission granted road-paving petitions in an *ad hoc* and informal way. At Agee's urging, the Commission adopted a more formal point system with neutral criteria that eliminated the potential for favoritism. The point system depends on the number of houses on a road, whether the mail carrier travels it, if there is a church present, and the like. According to Agee, he was motivated by several problems in the old system and not solely by the aim of ensuring that road-paving services were distributed more equitably in the black community. But one consequence of adopting general, neutral criteria is that more roads now are being paved where black residents live than were under the system that existed before Agee was elected.

Second, Agee's presence has led to the appointment of more minorities to important administrative boards. One of the Commission's principal tasks is appointing, by majority vote, these administrative officials. Agee thus cannot appoint anyone directly, but as he says, "the mere fact of me being there and recommending a minority goes a long way." These administrative boards wield considerable power because they operate independently of the County Commission. Agee has succeeded in appointing a minority to the Hospital Board and the Water Board, both of which previously had not had minority members. . . .

The third benefit observers attributed to Agee's presence was more intangible. Many people, including Agee himself, said that black residents in Chilton County "definitely" took a lot of pride in Agee's presence and felt more connected to local government as a result. As the County's attorney put it, "I do think that the black community is really proud of having elected [black] officials. I think that makes a difference." As the reporter who covers local politics put it, black residents like the cumulative voting system "because it works, and for the longest time they had no voice in government and now they do. . . ."

One of the more dramatic long-term consequences of the emergence of black representation on the County Commission, in the wake of cumulative voting, is that Bobby Agee eventually became Chairperson of the Commission. The Chairperson normally is elected by the other commissioners. An unusual clause in the litigation settlement, however, had entitled Agee to serve as Chairperson. The settlement provided that black officials elected to the County Commission or Board of Education could serve as Chairperson for eight months any time they chose to do so during their initial term in office. Agee, however, did not feel prepared to assume the duties of Chairperson during his first term and did not want to invoke this special clause if unnecessary.

After being in office for one full term, Agee had established enough credibility and expertise that the other commissioners elected him Chairperson for one year and then reelected him for a second year. We found no evidence that the other commissioners were motivated by the specter of Agee invoking his right to serve as Chairperson under the settlement agreement. In any event, even if that motivation played a role in Agee's initial election (in the sense that the settlement was understood to entitle him to serve as Chairperson once), it could not have played any role in his reelection. Instead, the commissioners we interviewed regularly remarked on Agee's judgment, temperament, and ability as the reasons they voted him Chairperson of the Commission. As one put it, "Agee is the most intelligent and most educated man on the commission."

Agee's elevation to Chairperson of the most powerful local government political body in Chilton County illustrates the integrative role cumulative voting can play. Given racially polarized voting patterns, Agee could not have come close to being elected in an at-large election, even after he had served his first term. Yet given the opportunity to serve that cumulative voting created, he earned sufficient respect from his fellow commissioners to be elected Chairperson twice....

3. *Public satisfaction with cumulative voting?*

One of the striking discoveries we made was that cumulative voting was widely disliked in Chilton County. Virtually everyone we interviewed reported this fact. Even more interesting were the reasons for this dislike. The principal reason was the widely shared view that cumulative voting was undemocratic and unconstitutional because it violated the one person, one vote principle. As one observer put it, "they feel it violates their sense of governmental propriety somehow. They keep saying it's unconstitutional, 'I just know it's unconstitutional.' I hear that all the time." Indeed, one person reportedly refused to cast more than one of his seven votes "because the system is unconstitutional." Some attributed this view to the uniqueness of the system: "[I]t goes away from practically the rest of the country and how they vote." Others attributed this view to the fact that "[o]lder people are just stuck in their ways and they don't want to change." ...

Yet more irony emerged when we explored whether dislike of cumulative voting was a cover for resistance to minority political power. We ultimately rejected this explanation. We consistently were told—and came to believe—that, whatever complaints people had about cumulative voting, there was general acceptance of the need for minority representation. Many people stated that they understood the importance of minority representation but would have preferred drawing majority-black districts had that been possible. Indeed, one prominent member of the Board of Education who thought cumulative voting was a terrible system said that he had thought for a long time about what Chilton County could have done instead. He concluded that the County should have set aside one seat on the relevant bodies as a "minority seat," for which all voters would vote but which a minority candidate would have to win. Thus, he preferred a blatantly unconstitutional means—the setting aside of a seat for minority officeholders—to a clearly constitutional one—cumulative voting—because of his strong convictions that the latter violated the fundamental, though relatively recent, principle of one person, one vote. Such is constitutional law in action, rather than on the books.

Nonetheless, the widespread dislike of cumulative voting is not to be interpreted as disapproval of the system. Even people who did not like the system appeared to accept it because "it works." By working, people meant that it did produce the intended result of black elected officials roughly representative of the black population. Based on our interviews, there seemed to be a consensus that cumulative voting was effective, necessary to achieve minority representation, and therefore begrudgingly accepted even while being disliked.

* * *

5. *Statistical analysis of recent cumulative voting elections.*

[F]or the 1992 election, voting was polarized heavily along racial lines: a strong proportional relationship exists between the percentage of black voters and support for black candidates in any given district. Racial voting patterns are more difficult to interpret in the 1994 election, but black candidates continued to poll significantly better in districts with large numbers of black voters.... racial crossover voting appears limited in both elections, especially in 1992....

Our analysis of racial voting patterns in the 1992 County Commission election is confirmed by exit-poll data others have gathered. The validity of these exit polls is confirmed by the close fit between the self-reports of the 702 voters surveyed and the actual election outcomes. Thus, Agee received at least one vote from 67 percent of blacks who voted in this election; among these black voters, 85.4 percent reported casting all seven votes for Agee. On average, then, black voters who supported Agee did so intensely and took advantage of the "plumping" option cumulative voting creates: Agee received an average of 6.28 votes from each black voter who supported him. In contrast, the exit-poll data confirms that Agee received little white crossover support. Among white voters, Agee came in twelfth among all candidates, ranking ahead only of the other black candidate and one white Republican. Only 13.4 percent of whites cast even a single vote for Agee. In other words, only the use of cumulative voting made Agee's election possible. Had the at-large system remained in place, Agee would not have stood a chance....

6. *Partisan side effects and fringe candidates.*

Interestingly, cumulative voting in Chilton County has indirectly weak-ened partisan campaigning in ways we did not see predicted in the literature. In a general election under the cumulative voting system to fill the seven-seat County Commission, each party runs seven candidates. When the parties distribute sample ballots or otherwise provide advice about how their supporters should vote, the major parties recommend casting one vote each for the party's seven candidates.

For any individual candidate, however, the optimal strategy is differ-ent. Each candidate would like to have as many total votes cast for him or her as possible. Thus, the interests of parties and their candidates diverge under cumulative voting. In the first cumulative voting election, most candidates asked for only one vote and followed the party strategy of recommending that voters distribute the remainder of their votes for the party's other candidates. But by subsequent elections, candidates learned the importance of concentrated support. Many candidates therefore began to distribute their own sample ballots in which they asked voters for all seven votes. In turn, political parties have cut back on sample ballots that recommend vote dispersion; in 1994, the Republican party urged voters to pick one Republican candidate and to give that candidate all seven of their votes. Several County leaders reported that in ways like this, cumulative voting has begun to erode traditional party politics. Candidates increasingly tend to run as individuals, rather than as representatives of parties. Those who noticed this effect of cumulative voting viewed it as a benefit at the local-government level; the new system was perceived to be leading voters to elect candidates based more on individual qualities than in previous elections. Of course, in another sense cumulative voting has revitalized party politics by helping Republicans to break the monopoly on local political power that Democrats long held under the traditional majority-rule system.

A longstanding concern about cumulative voting is that it enables the election of extremist or fringe candidates. . . . After seven years, there is no evidence of this problem arising in Chilton County. While the potential for election of fringe candidates exists in theory, it has not occurred in practice. Whether there is any general lesson in Chilton County's failure to elect extremist candidates must be left to speculation. Perhaps political and cultural forces particular to Chilton County make it a generally moderate area; some observers reported that most people, white and black, were "in the middle" and "rather conservative." On the other hand, it might result from structural features concerning the nature of local-government politics and elections, in which case Chilton County's experience might be of greater predictive value for other local governments contemplating alterna-tive voting systems. Local-government elections tend to be pragmatic, rather than ideological, and local office seekers have numerous incentives to fit themselves within the existing party structure—whether for reasons of financial and other support, future political prospects for higher office, or other considerations. Thus, although cumulative voting theoretically does give fringe candidates better electoral prospects, other structural features of local elections might moderate this possibility. . . .

7. *Problems with cumulative voting's at-large feature.*

Before cumulative voting was adopted, Chilton County used at-large elections for the County Commission and Board of Education. This at-large system retained, however, one attribute of a districted system: residency requirements for candidates. Voters throughout the County voted for each seat, but candidates were required to run for specific seats from specific residency districts. Cumulative voting replaces districted elections and necessarily does away with residency districts. As a result, a concern is whether the move toward at-large elections has entailed any significant costs associated with the loss of individual districts.

One specific fear, expressed at the time the system was introduced, was that elected representatives would be disproportionately concentrated in more densely populated parts of the County, such as the city of Clanton. In practice, however, this problem has not materialized. Candidates have continued to be elected from all parts of the County. Perhaps voters in different areas concentrate their votes on candidates from their areas, or perhaps candidates tend to focus their campaigning on different areas. Whatever the dynamics, the different areas of the County all continue to be represented under the cumulative voting system.

A more significant cost, however, has been the decline in specific geographic links between constituents and elected representatives. Legislators often serve an "ombudsman" role in which they serve as intermediaries in conflicts between their constituents and government agencies. The poor and minorities tend to be most dependent on legislators for this role, for they typically lack the traditional alternative mechanisms, such as lobbyists, lawyers, or personal contacts for resolving these conflicts. Political scientists have concluded that constituents more easily identify representatives from single-member districts than at-large systems, although the studies do not examine legislators elected through alternative voting systems, such as cumulative voting. We discovered, however, that cumulative voting does create problems of this sort. The lack of a direct tie between an individual representative and constituents was perhaps the most serious disadvantage of the shift to cumulative voting that we discovered.

Several individuals cited the abandonment of residency requirements as the major problem they had experienced under cumulative voting. A number of people commented that they did not know whom to call on either the County Commission or the Board of Education when they had an issue to discuss. In the former system of residency districts, the representative from a particular "district" was understood to be the person to turn to for local problems. Sue Smith, former member of the Board of Education, remarked:

> [Y]ou lose the feeling of "this is my representative on this Board." And I feel that way on the County Commission now. If I had a problem to speak with the County Commission about I would call two or three of them because I don't really know which one I ought to make contact with. I think that's a sense of frustration for the general population. . . .

Representatives also described some costs in moving to at-large elections. For better or worse, they now feel a general sense of responsibility to citizens of the entire County. When asked about the disadvantages of cumulative voting, Agee cited the at-large feature, because "you've got more people to satisfy . . . where, if you had a district you'd be concerned with just satisfying those people in that district. . . ."

8. *The dynamics of racial politics.*

[O]ur long conversations with Bobby Agee left the impression that cumulative voting has provided a thoughtful advocate for the black community and has begun to decrease racial polarization in politics. Agee reported that in his first campaign, he felt he was considered "the black candidate." He was the only candidate who campaigned in black neighborhoods and when he was elected, the other representatives viewed him as "the black representative." By the second election, however, many white candidates had gained an appreciation for the power of the black vote, and actively campaigned in black neighborhoods. In addition, Agee reported that he now receives more phone calls and requests from white constituents than black constituents, in line with the demographics of Chilton County. Agee's final comment sounds almost quaint in its resonance with the civil-rights discourse of the 1960s: people in Chilton County, he says, are starting to "get away from race, creed[,] and color." They are "[looking] at [the] ability of [the] person."

NOTES AND QUESTIONS

1.   The ideological resistance of Chilton County voters to casting multiple votes, on the ground that doing so violates the principle of one-person, one-vote, suggests an interesting framing question about cumulative voting. Rather than structuring the system so that each voter has seven votes to cast, should each voter be presented as having one vote, *parts* of which they could cast for different candidates? Thus, voters could be told that they could cast one-seventh of a vote for each candidate, or that they could give their one vote to one candidate. Would shifting the frame from "seven votes" to "one vote" that could be parceled out into fractions of one-seventh be likely to reduce the kind of discomfort with multiple voting experienced in Chilton County? If not, is this concern significant enough to suggest that limited voting, discussed *infra*, in which voters cannot cast more than one vote for any one candidate, should be seen as preferable to cumulative voting?

2.   Note that the loss of direct accountability of individual representatives to constituents that some Chilton County residents complain of might be felt most significantly by the poor and the very minorities CV is designed to benefit. One important function local politicians play is to work out conflicts between constituents and various governmental agencies. This role of local representatives, characterized in the excerpt as the function of "ombudsman," is particularly important for those who are least likely to have other resources for resolving these conflicts, such as lawyers, lobbyists, or personal contacts. The demand for constituent services also generally tends to be greatest in districts below average in socioeconomic characteristics.

At least three possible questions are raised by noticing this important ombudsman function of local representation. First, is there reason to think that over time with a CV system, representatives and constituents would find ways to construct similar personal service relationships to those currently existing in the system of districted elections? Recall that many at-large systems for local government elections required candidates to identify specific residency districts from which they were running; would a similar structure be desirable for CV elections? Second, if not, should the effort be to create, if possible, hybrid forms of CV, in which at least some representatives would be elected from districts, and some through CV, in a kind of mixed electoral system? For example, the settlement in *Bencomo v. Phoenix Union High School Dist. No. 10* CV90–0369–PHX–EHC (D. Ariz. July 3, 1990), replaced a pure at-large electoral system with a system using five single-member districts and two seats elected through limited voting. Mixed at-large/districted systems are quite common at the local level in the United States. Third, if CV does compromise the capacity of poor voters to find assistance in negotiating their way through government bureaucracies, should that be a reason sufficient to maintain districted elections? For discussion of this ombudsman function in the context of CV, see Samuel Issacharoff, *Supreme Court Destabilization of Single–Member Districts*, 1995 U. Chi. Legal F. 205, 237–38.

3.   The most important federal court discussion of cumulative voting in recent years arose out of protracted voting-rights litigation in Chicago Heights, Illinois, a Chicago suburb with a longstanding history of racial conflict. The structure of the problem posed reflects a set of factors increasingly likely to arise in voting rights litigation given changes in many jurisdictions' demographic characteristics: a multi-racial and ethnic contest for political power; polarized voting patterns; the constraints of the *Shaw v. Reno* line of cases; and the effort to find alternative remedies to the conventional approach in which single-member districts are nearly always the remedy of choice when at-large local government structures are found to violate the Voting Rights Act. The District Court's opinion appears first, followed by the Seventh Circuit's response to the District Court's efforts.

McCoy v. Chicago Heights

6 F. Supp. 2d 973 (N. D. Ill. 1998).

■ DAVID H. COAR, DISTRICT JUDGE.

The instant case originated in 1987 and 1988 when the plaintiff class ... alleged that the non-partisan, at-large elections in Chicago Heights City Council ... violated Section 2 of the Voting Rights Act of 1965....

[Pursuant to a federal-court approved consent decree in 1994, the City abandoned its at-large election system and substituted a six single-member district plan with a mayor elected at-large. Under this plan, two districts would be majority African–American and a third would have a substantial Hispanic population. In addition, the mayor had the ability to break ties and a veto, as well as substantial appointive powers.

Eventually, voters of Chicago Heights approved this plan in a referendum. But some members of the plaintiff class believed the plan was inadequate. The plaintiff class therefore split. Dissident plaintiffs Perkins and McCoy argued for an aldermanic system, with a seven member council and a weak mayor elected at large].

II. DISCUSSION

The district court need not defer to a state-proposed remedial plan if the plan does not completely remedy the violation or if the plan itself violates Section 2 of the Act. This court finds that the modified strong mayor government is not a complete remedy to the Section 2 violation.... Notably, by granting significant power to the mayor ... who [is] elected at-large, the proposed systems perpetuate the race-based violation of the Voting Rights Act that occurred in the previous at-large voting system....

The City ... and class plaintiffs do not propose any alternate remedy for the voting rights violations. Therefore, this court turns to the remedy proposed by the individual plaintiffs Perkins and McCoy. In terms of the City government, this court is in agreement with the individual plaintiffs that a traditional aldermanic form of government would reduce the power of the mayor, who is necessarily elected at-large. One significant difference between these forms of government is that in the aldermanic form a mayor's veto may be overridden by a two-thirds vote of the aldermen, whereas in the strong mayor format a three-fifths majority is required. While it is true that both the aldermanic government and the strong mayor government allow the mayor to cast tie-breaking votes, the Perkins/McCoy proposal provides for seven aldermen, thus ensuring that tie votes will not result.... Another significant difference is that the modified strong mayor government proposed by the City and the class plaintiffs allows the mayor to appoint the city clerk and city treasurer; however, in the aldermanic form of government these officers would be elected at-large. . . .

In conclusion, this court finds that the remedies proposed by the City . . . and class plaintiffs do not adequately address the Section 2 violation. . . . In contrast, the Perkins/McCoy remedy for governmental structure offers a more complete remedy, yet is not without its own problems. In particular, this court is troubled by the potential of the seven-district structure to be challenged on Equal Protection grounds.

b. Drawing District Lines

Although the Perkins/McCoy proposal is a satisfactory remedy with regards to the governmental structures for the City and the Park District, this court is hesitant to divide Chicago Heights into seven districts. The Supreme Court has held that race must not be a predominant factor in drawing district lines. Voter classifications based upon race are considered suspect and therefore subject to strict scrutiny if they subordinate traditional districting criteria to race. *See, e.g., Bush v. Vera,* 517 U.S. 952 (1996); *Shaw v. Hunt,* 517 U.S. 899 (1996); *Miller v. Johnson,* 515 U.S. 900 (1995); *Shaw v. Reno,* 509 U.S. 630 (1993).

Thus, fashioning a remedy that will draw district lines so as to remedy a voting rights violation, but without making race a predominant factor, is a complicated undertaking. The opponents of the Perkins/McCoy plan have justifiably argued that the creation of seven wards with the predominant intent of racial gerrymandering runs the risk of being challenged on an Equal Protection basis. Creating majority-minority districts as a remedy to voting rights violations inevitably relies on "a quintessentially race-conscious calculus aptly described as the 'politics of second best.' " *Johnson v. De Grandy,* 512 U.S. 997, 1020 (1994) (Souter, concurring) (*citing* B. Grofman, L. Handley & R. Neimi, Minority Representation and the Quest for Voting Equality, 136 (1992)). Thus emerges the paradox of fashioning a voting rights remedy based on districts in voting remedy cases. As one district court has aptly noted, any remedial plan "(even one fashioned solely with race-neutral principles) must be ultimately tested by whether it cures the § 2 violation, . . . race will always be a factor, for the ultimate question is whether the proposed plan provides the complaining racial group (in this case, African–Americans) equal access to the political process within the context of § 2." *Dillard v. City of Greensboro,* 946 F. Supp. 946, 955 (M.D. Ala. 1996) (Thompson, C.J.). Finally, any redistricting plan that this court may approve would be subject to continued constitutional challenges and would require being redrawn after the 2000 census.

5. Cumulative Voting

a. Cumulative Voting Defined

Thus, while this court favors a seven-member structure for the . . . City, seven, single-membered districts would not be an effective remedy for the Section 2 violation in Chicago Heights. However, a drawing of district lines is not required in order to remedy the voting rights violation in Chicago Heights. Rather than dividing the city into seven districts, this court finds that a system of at-large voting that utilizes cumulative voting, in combination with the Perkins/McCoy plan, would successfully remedy the voting rights violation. . . .

If a cumulative voting system were applied to the Perkins/McCoy plan, the seven aldermen . . . would be elected at-large using cumulative voting, rather than electing one alderman . . . from each district as proposed by Perkins and McCoy. Each voter would be allocated seven votes to use as he or she chooses. Thus, the voter could use all seven votes to elect on candidate, or distribute the votes among several candidates. The seven candidates with the highest number of votes would be elected to office.

There are several distinct advantages to a system of regionwide cumulative voting for local office. In particular, rather than using race as a proxy for voting preference, such a system allows voters to "draw their own jurisdictional boundaries, decide which local governments were most important to them, and allocate their votes accordingly." Richard Briffault, *The Local Government Boundary Problem in Metropolitan Areas*, 48 Stan. L. Rev. 1115, 1156 (1996). All minority groups may potentially benefit from such a system—not just racial minorities. For example, in a region where Republicans are in a minority, cumulative voting could allow them to elect a candidate of choice. . . . Relevant to the instant case is the fact that cumulative voting would allow minority voters in Chicago Heights, including the African–Americans and Latinos, to elect candidates of choice without creating race-conscious district lines that would be subject to constitutional challenge. Indeed, cumulative voting does not compartmentalize voters according to their race: "the state does not directly single out any particular minorities for special protection through concentration into 'safe' districts." Pildes & Donoghue, *supra,* at 255.

b.   Federal Court Precedent

The Supreme Court has held that . . . although single-member districts may be preferred, they are not by any means an exclusive remedy to voting rights violations.

Indeed, in a recent Voting Rights Act case, Justices Thomas and Scalia suggested that cumulative voting is a "more efficient and straightforward mechanism[] for achieving what has already become our tacit objective: roughly proportional allocation of power according to race." *Holder v. Hall,* 512 U.S. 874, 912 (1994) (Thomas, J. concurring, joined by Scalia, J.). Although it is by far the most common remedy for a Voting Rights Act violation, geographic districting is not a requirement of our political system:

The decision to rely on single-member geographic districts as a mechanism for conducting elections is merely a political choice—and one that we might reconsider in the future. Indeed, it is a choice that has undoubtedly been influenced by the adversary process: In the cases that have come before us, plaintiffs have focused largely upon attacking multimember districts and have offered single-member schemes as the benchmark of an "undiluted" alternative. But as the destructive effects of our current penchant for majority-minority districts become more apparent, courts will undoubtedly be called upon to reconsider adherence to geographic districting as a method for ensuring minority voting power. Already, some advocates have criticized the current strategy of creating majority-minority districts and have urged the adoption of other voting mechanisms—for example, cumulative voting or a system using transferable votes—that can produce proportional results without requiring division of the electorate into racially segregated districts.

[. . .] Such changes may seem radical departures from the electoral systems with which we are most familiar. Indeed, they may be unwanted by the people in the several States who purposely have adopted districting systems in their electoral laws. But nothing in our present understanding of the Voting Rights Act places a principled limit on the authority of federal courts that would prevent them from instituting a system of cumulative voting as a remedy under § 2, or even from establishing a more elaborate mechanism for securing proportional representation based on transferable votes. As some Members of the Court have already recognized, geographic districting is not a requirement inherent in our political system.

c. One–Person, One–Vote

This court finds that a system of cumulative voting complies with the requirements that the court be mindful of the "one-person, one-vote" requirement of the Equal Protection Clause. . . .

d. Illinois Voting Principles

Cumulative voting also conforms with Illinois' traditional voting principles. The fact that cumulative voting as a remedy has strong roots in Illinois is important given that the Supreme Court has held that district courts should not "intrude upon state policy any more than necessary" in fashioning remedies for voting rights violations.

Illinois was the first state to introduce a cumulative voting system. *See* Henn & Alexander, *supra*, at 495 n.12. Cumulative voting for directors of corporations was introduced in Illinois in 1870. *See id.* In addition, cumulative voting was adopted by the Illinois Constitutional Convention of 1869–70 as a device to assure minority representation in the legislature. *See* Charles Hynerman & Julian Morgan, *Cumulative Voting in Illinois*, 32 Ill. L. Rev. 12, 13 (1937). The main reason for the adoption of the cumulative voting system "was a desire to correct the situation wherein southern Republicans and northern Democrats were going unrepresented in the legislature." *Id.* Under this system, three representatives were elected for two-year terms from 51 different districts. Voters could cast one vote for three candidates, one and one-half votes for two candidates, or one vote for one candidate and two votes for a second candidate. *See id. See also* Ill. Const. of 1870, art. IV, §§ 6, 7, 8. The cumulative voting system in Illinois corporations is still prescribed in some situations; however, cumulative voting for the legislature was repealed in 1980.

Cumulative voting nonetheless remains firmly established as a statutory form of city government in Illinois. As previously noted, the Illinois Municipal Code provides for a form of cumulative voting in a variant of the aldermanic form of government. [Under this State Code, cities are divided into several three-member districts for aldermanic elections].

III. CONCLUSION

In accordance with the Perkins/McCoy plan, the City must adopt an aldermanic form of government, as provided in Article 3.1 of the Illinois Municipal Code. The City will have a total of seven aldermen, who will be elected at-large by cumulative voting for four-year terms. The voting procedure will be as outlined in this opinion—a modified form of the "minority representation plan" provided for by Illinois law in the aldermanic form of government. Each voter will be allocated seven votes to use as he or she chooses, and the seven candidates with the most votes will be elected to office. The mayor, city treasurer, and city clerk will be elected at-large.

Harper v. City of Chicago Heights

223 F.3d 593 (7th Cir. 2000).

■ DIANE P. WOOD, CIRCUIT JUDGE:

* * *

II

A

Standing behind the district court's judgment is the earlier finding— unchallenged, as we said—that the at-large system violated Section 2 of the Voting Rights Act. We think it was correct for the court to ask whether the replacement system eventually approved through referendum would remedy the violation; there was no need for the court to view it as if it had emerged from thin air. When a Section 2 violation has been found, the district court "must, wherever practicable, afford the jurisdiction an opportunity to remedy the violation first, ... with deference afforded the jurisdiction's plan if it provides a full, legally acceptable remedy.... But if the jurisdiction fails to remedy completely the violation or if a proposed remedial plan itself constitutes a § 2 violation, the court must itself take measures to remedy the violation." *Dickinson v. Indiana State Election Bd.*, 933 F.2d 497, 501 n.5 (7th Cir. 1991) (citation and quotations omitted).

* * *

The evidence of the mayor's pattern of voting in tie-breaking situations, taken with the likelihood of ties on an even-numbered council, is enough to support the district court's conclusion that the referendum system did not adequately address the acknowledged problem in the City elections. . . .

B

[But] we are compelled to find here that the remedy for the City crafted by the court cannot stand at this time. . . .

The district court's plan suffers from the same procedural flaw as did the consent decree when it was first presented to this court: the court's plan modifies the election methods set forth in the Illinois Municipal Code without either going through the statutorily required procedures for making such changes to electoral methods or making a judicial finding that it was necessary to make these changes in order to comply with federal law. . . .

The Illinois Municipal Code makes available to cities a variety of election methods. The district court should either have selected one of these methods or found that the Illinois options violate federal law. Instead, as it had done before, it opted for a hybrid system without submitting that plan to the voters, as Illinois law would require, and without explaining why one of the State's authorized systems would not do the job. Although the Municipal Code allows for cumulative voting, it specifies that a city is to be divided into districts (not less than two and not more than six) and that each district is entitled to three aldermen. Without a finding that the Code's cumulative voting method violates federal law, the district court modified the plan to call for the city-wide election of seven council members.

The district court's plan also suffers from a failure to respect the City's preference for single-member districts. The Supreme Court has held that in fashioning an electoral system to remedy a voting rights violation, courts "should follow the policies and preferences of the State, as expressed in statutory and constitutional provisions or in the . . . plans proposed by the state legislature, whenever adherence to state policy does not detract from the Federal Constitution." *White v. Weiser*, 412 U.S. 783, 795 (1973). Accordingly, when a legislative body fails to offer an acceptable remedy, "the court, in exercising its discretion to fashion a remedy that complies with § 2, must to the greatest extent possible give effect to the legislative policy judgments underlying the current electoral scheme or the legally unacceptable remedy offered by the legislative body." *Cane v. Worcester County, Md.*, 35 F.3d 921, 928 (4th Cir. 1994).

Here, the City has demonstrated a clear preference for single-member districts. It proposed a remedial plan that relies on single-member districts and, in doing so, made a policy judgment about which electoral schemes are best suited for the locality. We should defer to the City's plan to the extent possible as long as it does not violate federal law. Although the district court found that the referendum system was inadequate, it did not find that any use of single-member districts violates federal law.

The United States, appearing as amicus curiae, defends the district court's plan on the ground that, under Illinois law, cumulative voting is an accepted electoral practice. Thus, the United States argues, while the district court's plan may have violated the City's preference for single-member districts, the State has no such preference. We find this distinction unconvincing. First, the United States overstates the popularity of cumulative voting in Illinois: although cumulative voting is lawful under the Municipal Code, the use of single-member districts is an equally acceptable electoral practice.... The City proposed and must function under the remedial plan and accordingly its judgments are entitled to deference.

It is somewhat troubling that the City has not articulated why it prefers single-member districts over cumulative voting, but this is not an ironclad requirement for public bodies as long as the entity's actual preference can legitimately be inferred from facts on the record. It is obviously true that deference to legislative policy judgments is predicated on the legislature actually having made a policy judgment rather than an arbitrary choice. But we are satisfied that the City did so. Prior to the district court's order, the parties had never thought of cumulative voting. In the absence of a finding that cumulative voting is the only legally viable remedy, the City should have an opportunity to consider the merits and deficiencies of cumulative voting before that system is imposed upon it. We emphasize that our decision should not be understood as a condemnation of cumulative voting. Cumulative voting is, as the Illinois Municipal Code makes clear, a lawful election method that may be implemented under circumstances demonstrating suitable deference to the legislative body. It also has the virtues the district court identified:

> Rather than using race as a proxy for voting preference, such a system allows voters to draw their own jurisdictional boundaries, decide which local governments were most important to them, and allocate their votes accordingly.... All minority groups may potentially benefit from such a system—not just racial minorities.... Indeed, cumulative voting does not compartmentalize voters according to their race. (citation omitted).

For the reasons discussed above, we AFFIRM the district court's holding that the current election method violates Section 2 of the Voting Rights Act as applied to the City; however, we REVERSE the district court's remedy and REMAND to the court to craft a suitable remedy.

NOTES AND QUESTIONS

1. Does the Seventh Circuit's opinion suggest an attitude of greater acceptance of cumulative voting, at least potentially, than earlier courts of appeals encounters with the issue? Compare this decision with the previously most important court of appeals decision on the issue in the *Worcester County* case, which follows this note and is also cited in the Seventh Circuit's decision. Note the strongly positive comments both courts in *Chicago Heights* appear to make about the virtues of cumulative-voting remedies.

2. Do *Shaw v. Reno* and its progeny put tremendous pressure on district courts that have found Voting Rights Act violations to move toward cumulative voting, as the district court did here? Under what circumstances would a district court be permitted to impose a cumulative-voting remedy over the objections of a recalcitrant jurisdiction? For discussions of this issue, see, e.g., Pamela S. Karlan, *Our Separatism? The Voting Rights Act as an American Nationalities Policy*, 1995 U. Chi. Legal F. 83; Eben Moglen & Pamela S. Karlan, *The Soul of a New Political Machine: The Online, the Color Line, and Electronic Democracy,* 34 Loy. L.A.L. Rev. 1031 (2001); Steven J. Mulroy, *Alternative Ways Out: A Remedial Road Map for the Use of Alternative Electoral Systems as Voting Rights Act Remedies,* 77 N.C.L. Rev. 1867 (1999).

3. Despite *Chicago Heights* and whatever it might be taken to imply about emerging judicial attitudes toward alternative voting systems, questions still remain as to how likely it is that courts will be comfortable accepting novel voting systems, such as cumulative voting, as remedies in litigation. In *Dillard, supra,* the parties agreed upon a CV or limited voting remedy for many of the local government bodies being challenged, and the court approved all the consent decrees that provided for alternative voting systems. But will courts be prepared to impose CV against the objections of defendant jurisdictions? Does the Voting Rights Act give them the power to do so? If the VRA is viewed as not giving judges the power to impose alternative voting, should the statute be amended to expressly authorize CV as one remedial option? If so, under what circumstances should it be appropriate for courts to order CV as a remedy?

4. *Other uses of cumulative voting:*

a. The most significant use of CV in American politics was in Illinois, where in the aftermath of the Civil War, election laws were changed to use CV to elect members of the lower house from three-member election districts. The system was adopted in 1870 and retained until 1980. Illinois had been bitterly riven during the Civil War, and the aim of CV was to provide representation to restore unity in the state by ensuring seats for minority parties within each district, and to help ensure more proportional representation statewide of the different parties. With CV, Republicans would gain some representation in the overwhelmingly Democratic portions of southern Illinois, while Democrats would likewise gain some seats in the Republican northern regions of the state. For House elections, the state was divided in 59 districts, each of which filled three seats, and voters could give one vote each to three candidates; three votes to one candidate; or one and one-half vote to two candidates. In 1970, Illinois voters voted to retain CV in a specific ballot question presented as part of a referendum on a new state constitution, but voted to abolish CV in 1980 when they approved a ballot measure, presented as a cost-saving device, that reduced the size of the state legislature. For the history of the Illinois experience, see Leon Weaver, *Semi–Proportional and Proportional Representation Systems in the United States*, in Choosing an Electoral System: Issues and Alternatives 197 (Arend Lijphart & Bernard Grofman eds., 1984); *see also* Richard Wiste, *Cumulative Voting and Legislative Performance,* in Illinois: Political Processes and Government Performance 119–120 (G. Crane, Jr. ed. 1980); Charles W. Dunn, *Cumulative Voting Problems in Illinois Legislative Elections*, 9 Harv. J. Legis. 627 (1972); George S. Blair, Cumulative Voting: An Effective Device in Illinois Politics (1960); George S. Blair, *Cumulative Voting: Patterns of Party Allegiance and Rational Choice in Illinois State Legislative Contests*, 52 Am. Pol. Sci. Rev. 123 (1958).

The system did achieve its principal goals of reducing geographic divisions between the parties and increasing minority party representation. Only about 1.5 percent of the districts were represented by three figures from the same party from 1920–1980. But a problem was that voters ended up with few actual choices because the political parties would effectively collude; where Democrats were dominant, they would agree to run only two candidates and Republicans one, while where Republicans were dominant, they would agree to run only two candidates and Democrats one. As a result, elections were typically a foregone conclusion. For example, of 1,776 House elections between 1902 and 1969, only 17 districts ever had as many as five candidates run for the three contested seats. Dunn, *supra*, at 646. At the same time, though, CV did increase competition in the primaries, particularly within the minority party because there was much greater incentive to fight for nomination from a minority party. Charles Wiggins & Janice Petty, *Cumulative Voting and Electoral Competition*, 7 Am. Pol. Q. 345, 350–53 (1979).

One possible solution to the problems of diminished competition is to legally mandate that parties run a specified number of candidates in each district. Illinois did modify its rules a bit in this direction in 1970. For a thoughtful assessment of this approach, see Michael E. Lewyn, *When is Cumulative Voting Preferable to Single–Member Districting*, 25 N. Mex. L. Rev. 197, 220–224 (1995).

b. The first adoption of CV this century was in Alamogordo, New Mexico (site of the first test of the atomic bomb) in 1987. Since then, elections there have been the subject of careful study. *See, e.g.*, Richard Engstrom, Delbert A. Taebel, and Richard L. Cole, *Cumulative Voting as a*

Remedy for Minority Vote Dilution: The Case of Alamogordo, New Mexico, V J. Law & Pol. 469 (1989). At the time CV was adopted, although minorities constituted nearly 30 percent of the population, no minority had been elected to the city council since 1970. Under the CV system, to elect the city council, three members were selected at-large by CV and four were elected from districts. An Hispanic woman was elected the first time the system was used, with her election being due to 75 percent of her voters casting more than one vote for her—thus taking advantage of the CV system. Turnout was high in the first election, and nearly all voters used all three of their votes. Despite conclusions of academics that the system had worked well to enhance minority representation, voters in 1997 voted 850–596 to switch to all district elections by 2000.

c.   In Texas, at least twenty-six small cities and school districts now use cumulative voting; one Texas jurisdiction uses limited voting. Robert Brischetto, *Cumulative Voting at Work in Texas: A 1995 Exit Survey of Sixteen Communities*, in Voting and Democracy Report: 1995, at 61, 62 (The Center for Voting and Democracy, 1995). Cumulative voting was introduced first in 1991 in settlement of voting-rights litigation challenging the Lockhart Independent School District. Preliminary studies of these Texas elections reach results similar to those in the Chilton County study: cumulative voting in Texas appears to be working largely as predicted, without significant or unexpected disadvantages.

In what circumstances is CV likely to work best? Lewyn, *supra*, at 226–27 argues that CV is best for small cities, for nonpartisan elections (where political parties cannot control slates as they did in Illinois), and for jurisdictions with a stable, dominant majority faction or party. He argues that CV is not a good approach for big-city or statewide elections, in part because the problems of voter coordination that effective use of the CV option requires are too great in large jurisdictions.

In 2000, Amarillo, Texas, became the largest jurisdiction to switch to cumulative voting. Seats on a four-member school board have been filled through cumulative voting. Thus far, the system has been credited with the first African–American elected to the board and the first election of a Latino candidate since the 1970s. The population of Amarillo is around 10% African American and 20% Latino. *See* Center for Voting and Democracy, *Cumulative Voting Has Major Impact in Amarillo* (last modified Sept. 19, 2000) <http://www.fairvote.org/frames/vra/impact.htm>. The increasing experimentation and apparent success of cumulative voting in Texas and elsewhere has led some newspapers to endorse this voting system. *See, e.g.,* Birmingham News, *Disfranchised Voters*, Aug. 31, 2000. (The Birmingham News, Alabama's largest paper, advocating use of cumulative voting to resolve a Voting Rights Act dispute over council elections in Alabaster).

d.   For other works advocating cumulative voting, particularly as a tool under the Voting Rights Act, see Lani Guinier, The Tyranny of the Majority 99–101 (1994); Pamela S. Karlan, *Maps and Misreadings: The*

Role of Geographic Compactness in Racial Vote Dilution Litigation, 24 Harv. CR–CL L. Rev. 173 (1989). For other studies of cumulative voting in operation, see Richard L. Engstrom, Jason F. Kirksey, & Edward Still, *One Person, Seven Votes: The Cumulative Voting Experience in Chilton County, Alabama*, in Affirmative Action and Representation (Anthony Peacock ed. 1997); Richard L. Engstrom & Charles J. Barrilleaux, *Native–Americans and Cumulative Voting: The Sisseton–Wahpeton Sioux*, 72 Soc. Sci. Q. 389 (1991).

e.   Corporations have a long history of using cumulative voting for shareholder votes, although that practice appears to be waning. For a good history of cumulative voting in the corporate context, see Jeffrey Gordon, *Institutions as Relational Investors: A New Look at Cumulative Voting*, 94 Colum. L. Rev. 124 (1994).

f.   Legislative cumulative voting? Lani Guinier has also proposed that CV might be used, not just in the selection of officeholders, but within governing bodies themselves to vote on policy. She offers this suggestion as a response to situations like that in *Presley v. Etowah County Commission*, 502 U.S. 491 (1992). Consider whether her argument is persuasive:

> Legislative cumulative voting would discourage voting up or down on individual proposals. Rather, over a period of time and a series of legislative proposals, votes on multiple bills would be aggregated or linked. By linking votes on several issues to allow both weighted and split issue voting, the black representatives could more reliably participate in the legislative process, plumping votes to express the intensity of constituent preferences on some issues and trading votes on issues of constituent indifference.

Lani Guinier, The Tyranny of the Majority 108 (1994).

In response, Professor Karlan has argued that "Guinier's procedural solution is a two-edged sword":

> [Guinier's idea] would be impossible to implement: in most legislatures, the form bills take is so subject to manipulation that a minority could be forced to expend all its votes simply to block a few objectionable proposals, thereby both making it impossible for the group to affirmatively enact anything and stripping its members of an effective voice on the remaining items on the agenda. No legislature uses internal cumulative voting, although many engage in the sort of legislative drafting and logrolling that it might resemble.
>
> * * *
>
> [The sorts of changes in legislative voting Guinier suggests] may give a black legislative caucus a "veto" over truly objectionable legislation, but it may do little to fortify an affirmative legislative strategy. Indeed, supermajority rules might actually impede such a strategy by denying progressive majorities the ability to overcome the resistance of a

conservative, or even racist, minority. Supermajority rules tend to favor the status quo by making change difficult to achieve.

Pamela S. Karlan, *Democracy and Dis–Appointment*, 93 Mich. L. Rev. 1273, 1285, 1287 (1995).

C.   PREFERENCE VOTING OR THE SINGLE-TRANSFERRABLE VOTE

Many who are sympathetic to the goals of cumulative voting nonetheless believe that another system better realizes those goals. The more colloquial phrase for this alternative is preference voting, although in the academic literature it is typically called single-transferrable voting (STV). "Many political scientists consider STV the 'best' electoral system because it enables voters to vote for any mix of candidates they prefer, for whatever reason they prefer them." Rein Taagepera and Matthew Shugart, Seats and Votes: The Effects and Determinants of Electoral Systems 27 (1989). The system was invented by an Englishman, Thomas Hare, in 1857, who was worried about rising class antagonisms and sought to promote better political representation. The philosopher and candidate for Parliament, John Stuart Mill, learned of Hare's system and thought it one of the great inventions in democratic government. Mill became the leading advocate for the system, but he was unsuccessful in persuading England to adopt it. For the full historical account, see Jenifer Hart, Proportional Representation: Critics of the British Electoral System 1820–1945 (1992).

STV is thought particularly attractive for countries with traditions of constituents electing individual legislators because, unlike the typical PR system, STV permits voters to vote for individual candidates yet brings about more proportional representation. Thus, STV has been called the "Anglo–Saxon method of securing proportional representation." Vernon Bogdanor, What is Proportional Representation? A Guide to the Issues 76 (1984). The reason is that STV enables a voter "to choose between candidates on personal as well as party grounds, and his choice overrides that of any party organization." Enid Lakeman, How Democracies Vote: A Study of Majority and Proportional Electoral Systems 140 (3d ed. 1970).

The following excerpt provides a lucid summary of how this alternative works and the arguments in favor of it. For those interested in alternatives to districting, would preference voting be better than cumulative voting? As you read, consider whether the choice of voting systems can depend only on their theoretical properties, or whether it must inevitably depend in a democracy on what the social perceptions about different voting systems will likely be. With preference voting, that is a particular concern because while the system is easy to use, explaining how votes are counted in this system is quite difficult. The excerpt comes from a book review of Lani

Guinier, The Tyranny of the Majority (1994), in which Guinier advocates cumulative voting, and the excerpt refers to her work throughout:

Richard Briffault: Lani Guinier and the Dilemmas of American Democracy

95 Colum. L. Rev. 418 (1995).

[T]here is another form of proportional representation, known as single transferable voting (STV), which is well-suited to a nonpartisan setting, and would enhance the proportionate representation of minority interests, would allow voters to form their own constituencies, and in general, would appear likely to perform at least as well as cumulative voting. . . .

Like cumulative voting, STV dispenses with single-member districting and returns to multi-member districts or at-large elections. But instead of allowing voters to cumulate votes behind one candidate, STV provides a preference voting system. The voter casts one ballot but can rank candidates to reflect the voter's relative preferences among them. Ranking candidates in order of preference enables votes that would be "wasted" on one candidate to be transferred to another candidate. A vote can be "wasted" if it is "surplus"—that is, a vote cast for a candidate who would win without it—or if it is cast for a losing candidate. STV saves "wasted" votes by providing for their transfer to the next ranked candidate on a voter's ballot. STV thus increases the proportion of voters who vote for a winning candidate, and increases the likelihood that the voter will be represented by a legislator of his or her choosing.

The vote-transfer feature of STV benefits electoral minorities, even in the face of the firm opposition of the majority.[11] In a jurisdiction with a

---

11. Like cumulative voting, STV relies on the concept of a threshold of exclusion. The threshold for winning a legislative seat in an STV election is $V/(N+1) +1$, where V is the total number of votes and N is the number of seats to be filled. In a jurisdiction with 10,000 voters and five seats, 1,667 votes will be sufficient to elect a candidate, and any candidate receiving that many first-place votes will be deemed elected (no more than five candidates can win 1,667 first-place votes). If one or more candidates (but fewer than five) cross the electoral threshold on first-place votes, their "surplus" votes—that is, the votes above the threshold which were unnecessary to elect them—will be redistributed to the second choices named by those voters, so that additional winners may be determined. If no candidate crosses the threshold on the initial count, the last-place candidate is dropped, and his or her votes are transferred to the candidates listed as the second preference on those ballots which listed the losing candidate as the first preference. If any candidate now has reached the threshold, that candidate is elected. If not, the next lowest candidate is dropped and the process of ballot transfers continues until all the seats are filled.

Transferring the votes of losing candidates is straightforward. All of the ballots of an eliminated candidate are simply transferred to the voters' next choices. The transfer of the surplus votes of winning candidates, however, is more complicated, and several methods are used. One is simply to declare a candidate elected once his or her

five-seat legislature, a candidate with slightly more than one-sixth of the vote will be able to win a seat under either a cumulative voting or STV electoral system. But STV would appear to be superior to cumulative voting [in achieving these goals]: (a) the representation of minority groups in proportion to their numbers; (b) the representation of the greatest diversity of viewpoints; (c) more competitive elections; and (d) the creation of cross-racial alliances.

(a) STV and proportional representation. STV may be more likely than cumulative voting to assure a minority group representation in proportion to its votes. Cumulative voting works best when a group focuses its votes on one candidate. If there are two or more minority candidates, the minority risks the prospect of splitting its vote and failing to elect any of its choices. If the minority constitutes a large proportion of the population and might reasonably seek two or more seats, cumulative voting might result in only one minority seat if minority voters do not divide their votes evenly between the candidates but, instead, give one candidate more votes than she needs for victory while failing to provide the other candidate with sufficient votes to win.

Guinier presents a scenario of a jurisdiction with 1,000 voters, 250 of whom are black, and a ten-member legislative body ... If such a jurisdiction used cumulative voting, the minority would need only 91 votes to win a seat.[12] Guinier assumes that the black electorate would divide itself up into two groups of 91, with 68 voters left over. The two groups of 91 would each take a seat, and the group of 68 would be able to "join with 23 sympathetic whites to elect a third candidate who is also electorally accountable." In this manner, blacks would win their proportionate share of the legislative seats.

But Guinier's example appears to rest on an unduly optimistic appraisal of the ability of a large group of ordinary voters to organize itself and to assign different specific voters to different candidates. It also makes the rosy assumption that an individual black candidate will be content to win just 91 votes and will direct potential supporters to the other black candidate in order to enhance the number of blacks elected. Few candidates are so confident of election or so committed to the advancement of their group in addition to their own success that they believe there are "surplus"

vote crosses the threshold of exclusion and to treat all subsequently counted ballots as surplus, to be applied to the second choices listed on those ballots. A second method, used in Ireland where STV is the basic election system, is to select randomly among the winning candidate's ballots. A third method, probably the preferable one now that computers can be used to count votes, is to distribute a winning candidate's surplus votes according to the percentage of second choice preferences registered on the winning candi-

date's ballots. See generally Richard L. Engstrom, *The Single Transferable Vote: An Alternative Remedy for Minority Vote Dilution*, 27 U.S.F. L. Rev. 781, 790 (1993) (describing alternative versions of STV).

12. Applying the formula of $1/(1+N)$ + 1, with N=10, in a jurisdiction of 1000 voters, the minimum number of votes necessary to win a seat is $1/(1 + 10)$ or 1/11 of 1000, or 90, plus 1, which is 91.

votes that can be given to a potential competitor. Thus, although cumulative voting makes it easier to elect one minority candidate, it is unlikely to produce "full proportional representation" for the minority. That is why political scientists refer to it as a semiproportional system....

STV's vote transfer mechanism may be more likely to produce a proportionate result. Where a group has more than two candidates, and one receives enough first-place votes to be elected, STV would transfer her "surplus" ballots to the next choices on those ballots. If the second-choices are the candidates of the minority group, then the group may elect a second candidate. Moreover, if no minority candidate wins on first-place votes, the vote transfer mechanism could reallocate votes from the weaker minority candidate to the candidates would deny the minority a seat stronger, thus reducing the possibility that competition among minority.[13]

(b) STV and diversity of representation. STV may increase the prospects for minority representation without suppressing divergent points of view within the minority group. With STV, there could be multiple candidates from a group, and the concomitant expression of a variety of viewpoints, without undermining the group's opportunity to elect a candidate of its choice. A conservative black voter, for example, could give her first-place vote to a conservative black candidate and then, if race dominates ideology in her political priorities, give her second-place vote to a more liberal black candidate. In this way, STV could function as both a primary election and a general election in a single ballot, with minority voters participating in an intragroup election without jeopardizing their chances for electoral success in the intergroup election.

Similarly, STV may better advance Guinier's agenda of representing "voluntary constituencies that self-identify their interests" than would cumulative voting. Like districting, cumulative voting rewards only first-place votes. This discourages voters from voting for those candidates who

---

13. For example, assume an election with 1000 voters, 300 minority voters and 700 majority voters; three seats to be filled; two minority-preferred candidates, and three majority-preferred candidates. Assume that the majority votes only for majority-preferred candidates; that it spreads its first-place votes evenly across its candidates (233 or 234 per candidate); and that majority voters' subsequent preferences are also only for majority candidates. Assume that minority voters split, 170 first-place votes for candidate A and 130 first-place votes for candidate B, and that voters for candidate B list candidate A as their second choice. In order to win, a candidate needs $1000/(3+1) + 1$, or 251, votes. On the first first count, candidate B would be eliminated. But B's voters would have listed

A as their second go to A, giving him 300 votes and a seat. Subsequently, the weakest majority candidate would be eliminated and the other two elected.

If this scenario had been played out in a cumulative voting election, all three majority candidates might have been elected if minority voters had split their cumulated votes among two candidates. Alternatively, only one minority candidate might have run, thereby denying the supporters of the other minority candidate the opportunity to express their strongest preference and the opportunity to identify themselves as a political group, and denying the community useful information concerning the existence and strength of candidate B's supporters.

may best represent their views but who, the voters think, are unlikely to garner enough votes to win election. As a result, the ballots cast may understate the real level of support for those candidates among the electorate. This, in turn, serves to discourage candidates who represent groups that do not approach a plurality in a single-member district system or the threshold of exclusion in a cumulative voting jurisdiction from even running. This denies their potential supporters the opportunity to vote for them and denies the community the awareness of the existence and size of such a political group. In practice, much as districting favors local majorities, cumulative voting is likely to help only the largest minority and "not the full range of minority political groups." Like districting, cumulative voting tends to hold down the number of parties or groups that can win representation, even if cumulative voting is less restrictive.

STV can remove this disincentive to vote for candidates perceived to have less chance of winning, since the voter can give her first-choice vote to the long-shot who is her most preferred candidate, while choosing among the perceived front-runners for her second-place selection. If the first-choice candidate fails to win election, and the front-runners have not won enough votes to fill all the seats at issue, the ballot can be counted in the contest among the front-runners. Moreover, if enough voters are no longer discouraged from voting for the long-shot by the fear that their ballots will be wasted, then the long-shot might actually win. Alternatively, the voter could list the long-shot in second place. If the first-place winner wins easily, and a sufficient number of other voters also list the long-shot as a second choice, then the transfer of "surplus" votes could also transform the long-shot into a winner. Even if the long-shot is unable to capture a legislative seat, the existence of the group, and the extent of its political support, will be more clearly known, and the long-shot, and the long-shot's constituency, may become more of a factor in local politics.

(c) STV and competitive elections. For these reasons, STV may also be more likely than cumulative voting to promote competitive elections. Cumulative voting requires group solidarity, discourages intragroup competition, and may lead to de facto deals among the major groups to allocate seats.... Like districting, cumulative voting can produce "safe seats" and uncontested elections. With its built-in incentive to vote for more candidates, STV may be more likely to increase electoral competitiveness.

(d) STV and cross-racial alliances. Finally, STV would appear to be better than cumulative voting in achieving Guinier's other goal—reducing racial polarization in the legislature. By eliminating racially homogeneous black and white districts and using jurisdiction-wide electoral units, both cumulative voting and STV at least make it possible for some candidates to achieve electoral success by putting together a platform that appeals to some blacks and some whites. STV's preferential voting mechanism, however, offers an additional incentive for reducing racial polarization.

Cumulative voting enables minorities to cumulate their votes for one candidate so that the intensity of the group's preference overcomes the group's minority status. Cumulative voting's structural incentive in racially polarized jurisdictions for cumulating votes behind the most intensely preferred candidate is, thus, in deep tension with cumulative voting's potential for cross-racial voting. STV could mute that tension, although not eliminate it, by enabling voters to register several degrees of preference, thus giving them an opportunity to support their own group's candidate and the most attractive candidates of other groups without undermining the prospects of their own-group's first choice. This, in turn, gives candidates an even stronger incentive to campaign across group lines. With STV, candidates might appeal to the voters of groups who would be unlikely to give them first-place votes but might provide them crucial second-place votes. For example, black voters could give their highest preferences to black candidates and their lower-ranked preferences to the white candidates most attractive to them. If the successful black candidate or candidates win more votes than they need to be assured of their seats, their "surplus" would be transferred to the black-preferred white candidates. This could induce some white candidates to campaign for black votes, and ultimately increase the legislature's attention to black political concerns.

It is not clear why Guinier gave no attention to STV and instead focused exclusively on cumulative voting. STV is a more complicated system than cumulative voting, and it works a greater departure from districting. There is relatively little experience with STV in the United States and it could be that its theoretical advantages will fail to materialize in practice. Perhaps Guinier feared that STV is so different from districting that it is, as a practical matter, a nonstarter. On the other hand, STV may have greater potential than cumulative voting to advance Guinier's goals of proportionate minority interest representation, the representation of smaller groups and dissidents within existing groups, and appeals across group lines. Certainly, whatever the strengths and weaknesses of STV, any consideration of the process of electing a democratic legislature ought to examine the full range of options, not just cumulative voting.

NOTES AND QUESTIONS

1. Given the continuing academic enthusiasm for STV, it is particularly noteworthy that relatively few democratic systems or even jurisdictions in democracies have opted to use it. Does that suggest anything about the practicalities or political appeal, as opposed to theoretical advantages, of STV?

STV systems had something of a heyday in municipal elections in the United States from 1915–1945 or so. It was used in about two dozen cities, for city councils, school boards, and local school committees. For a good general survey of this history, see Leon R. Weaver, *The Rise, Decline, and*

Resurrection of Proportional Representation in Local Governments in the United States in Electoral Laws and Their Political Consequences 139 (Bernard Grofman & Arend Lijphart eds. 1986). Between the 1920s and 1940s, 22 local governments adopted STV; but nearly all abandoned these systems in subsequent years, with the exception of Cambridge, Mass., which continues to use it today. In addition, in 1969, mandated by state statute, New York City began using STV to elect its 32 community school boards as part of the theory that devolving authority to local community groups would improve public education.

Weaver concludes that (1) the city councils elected under STV were more diverse, with greater representation of minority parties, significant ethnic groups, and perhaps other segments of the community; (2) that STV affected campaigning style by decreasing the incentives for candidates to engage in personal attacks against others, lest they alienate those candidates' first-choice supporters; (3) that STV even when used with nonpartisan ballots tended to induce the use of parties or party-like groups because programmatic politics and disciplined voting by party was an advantage. As far as the abandonment of these alternative voting systems, Weaver concludes that (1) they were frequently opposed by party organizations and their leaders because they typically lost influence over nominations, since STV was usually accompanied with the right to nominate by petition; (2) party leaders often worked against STV because STV was often enacted by reform forces seeking to bypass party leaders and appeal to the electorate directly; (3) concerns often voiced by skeptics over whether STV would lead to factionalism, extremist candidates, or political paralysis of governing bodies do not appear to have been reasons for the decline of STV; (4) the decline also cannot be attributed to STV not being usable by voters; (5) repeal was made easy by the fact that STV was typically adopted through local referenda, rather than statute, and hence was subject to repeal by the same method. Weaver concludes that more general lessons from this experience are difficult to draw because so much of the political argument pro and con was motivated more by concern for its political consequences than the kinds of questions political scientists debate about STV.

2. From 1937–1945, New York City used preference voting to elect the New York City Council. The system was adopted through a citywide vote, with overwhelming support, in 1936, and used for five elections. Some argue that the system brought about a "golden age" of council politics, because officeholders were formidable challengers to existing party politics who could not have been elected in district system, and because the "system institutionalized the representation of a wide number of political parties with differing viewpoints." Martin Gottlieb, *The "Golden Age" of the City Council*, N.Y. Times, Aug. 11, 1991. In the 1945 elections, in heavily Democratic New York, Democrats won 15 of the 25 seats, with the rest split among Republicans, Liberals, Communists, and American Labor Party members. After the STV system was eliminated, Democrats obtained a virtual monopoly on power, winning 24 of the 25 seats in the 1949 election.

Why did voters repeal the system in 1947? According to a leading study, "the one issue above all others responsible for the repeal of PR in 1947 was Communism." Belle Zeller & Hugh Bone, *The Repeal of P.R. in New York City—Ten Years in Retrospect*, 42 Am. Pol. Sci. Rev. 1127 (1948). One or two Communists were regularly elected, but after World War II, anti-Communist sentiment was easier to mobilize against the system. The Democratic and Republican party organizations fought aggressively against the system because it proved a "real benefit" to independent Democrats and Republicans; the system deprived the party machines of complete control. The black community also fought strongly against repeal, given its success under STV. This study found that turnout was exceptionally high under STV and that, despite fears the system would encourage voting along ethnic and religious lines, political party remained the most important factor in voting patterns.

3. While Cambridge, Massachusetts, continues to use STV, it has become controversial in the one other place STV is used in the United States, for New York community school board elections. On the other hand, in the 1996 elections, voters in San Francisco had on the ballot a proposition to adopt STV to elect the Board of Supervisors, the governing body of San Francisco. The ballot measure was endorsed by many leading political organizations, including the Democratic Party, but it lost 56 percent to 44 percent. Instead, voters opted to return to district-based elections. Since that time, STV has had a couple of adoptions in the U.S. Minneapolis will begin using it for secondary elected office in 2009 and it was adopted in an advisory measure in 2006 in Davis, California, though not yet implemented.

4. Internationally, STV is used for national elections in Australia (the Senate), the Republic of Ireland (for all legislative elections), and Malta (for the unicameral parliament). It is also used for some states in Australia, and for local and European Parliament elections in Ireland. Of the new democracies that formed in recent years in eastern and central Europe and the former Soviet Union, only Estonia, from 1989–1992, used STV. For analyses of the effects of STV on elections in Malta and Ireland, see Arend Lijphart, Electoral Systems and Party Systems, 144–46 (1994). Moreover, all city council elections in Scotland are now to be elected under STV, as are local health board elections in New Zealand.

Notice that all these countries are relatively small in population. Does STV make the most sense only for small jurisdictions? If so, why? Scholars consider there to be a tradeoff with STV systems, as with any electoral system. To achieve the desired level of proportionality, the electoral unit must be large enough to have the requisite number of seats being contested (recall the "threshold of exclusion" analysis). But if the number of seats and candidates grows too large, voters will have to choose between an overwhelming number of candidates. The common view among students of

STV is that the optimal size is a system in which between 5–7 seats are at issue. In general, scholars of electoral systems argue that district magnitude—the number of seats being filled—is perhaps the most important variable in constructing the forms of a country's politics, such as how many parties it has. *See* Rein Taagepera & Matthew Shugart, Seats and Votes: The Effects and Determinants of Electoral Systems Ch.11 (1989).

5.   Consider the incentives STV gives candidates as to how they should conduct their campaigns. Consider the incentives it gives political parties as to how they should choose candidates and structure campaigning. Would these incentives produce better or worse election campaigns?

6.   In addition to the works already cited, for further writings on preference voting or STV, see George H. Hallett, Jr., *Proportional Representation with the Single Transferable Vote: A Basic Requirement for Legislative Elections*, in Choosing an Electoral System: Issues and Alternatives (Arend Lijphart & Bernard Grofman, eds., 1984); Peter Mair, *Districting Choices under the Single–Transferable Vote*, in Electoral Laws and Their Political Consequences 289 (Bernard Grofman & Arend Lijphart eds. 1986).

7.   *Instant Runoff Voting* (IRV). IRV works much as the same as Single Transferrable Voting, but is of potential use within single-member districts. Voters rank candidates in the order they prefer. If no candidate receives a majority, the bottom candidate is eliminated and the ballots for that candidate are transferred to their second choice candidate. The process is repeated until one candidate has a majority. IRV thus produces an actual majority winner without requiring multiple rounds of voting.

IRV is another alternative voting system gaining increasing political support various places. It is particularly attractive in areas with significant third-party politics, because it enables voters to express a preference for such a party without "wasting" the vote in the way that occurs in the conventional First Past the Post (FPTP) voting system. Some states, such as Vermont, have given serious consideration of a shift to IRV, although these remain subjects of discussion only. At the local level, IRV has enjoyed greater success. The list of adoptions includes: Minneapolis beginning with the 2009 municipal elections; North Carolina for judicial vacancies and for municipal pilot programs starting in 2007;Pierce County, Washington for most of its county offices starting in 2008; Takoma Park, Maryland for city council and mayoral elections; Oakland, California for city offices starting in 2008; Burlington, Vermont for mayor, beginning in 2006; San Francisco for its Board of Supervisors and major citywide offices since 2004; Berkeley, California starting in 2008, and a number of others. In addition dozens of American universities use IRV for internal elections, as for their faculty senates. Finally, and perhaps most significantly IRV has been adopted to overcome the difficulty of multiple rounds of balloting for absentee voters. Instant runoff ballots are now being used for all overseas voters in runoff elections in federal and state races in South Carolina and Louisiana and all runoffs of any kind in Arkansas.

D.   LIMITED VOTING

A third alternative voting system also being used more frequently among local governments these days in the United States is limited voting (LV). This is another form of semi-proportional representation. Limited voting works by giving voters fewer votes to cast than the total number of seats at issue. Thus, if five seats on a city council are to be filled, voters throughout the city might each be permitted to cast only three votes. The effect of limiting each voter to three votes is, as with other semi-proportional systems, to prevent the same majority from dominating each and every seat. Well-organized minority groups that are sufficiently large are thereby enabled to control the outcome of at least one seat. In limited voting, the formula for calculating the threshold of exclusion is $V/(V+N) + 1$, where V is the number of votes a voter may cast and N is the number of seats to be filled. Thus, with three votes to cast in a five-member election, the threshold would be $[3/(3+5)]+1$ additional vote, so that any group that gets one vote over 37.5 percent or more of the voting pool could, in principle, effectively control the outcome with respect to at least one seat. Notice that, unlike CV, where minorities must vote cohesively by plumping all or most of their votes for the same candidate, LV requires less strategic coordination among minority voters. With fewer votes to cast, and with only one vote going to any one candidate, LV requires fewer decisions—and hence requires fewer decisions in tandem—from minority voters.

Consider in general the variations between STV, CV, and LV. What distinguishes the systems in terms of their effects on voters, candidates, and parties? In what circumstances might it make most sense to use one or another of these alternatives? For example, CV might require more successful coordination among minority voters than LV does; with CV, the minority group must all concentrate its multiple votes on the same candidate to make most effective use of the system. If members of the minority group do not all follow this path, the candidate most group members prefer might still not be elected. Effective political organizations might thus be required to mobilize minority voters and signal the proper voting strategy. With LV, in contrast, the mechanism by which the majority's power is fragmented is by giving each voter fewer votes to cast than there are seats to fill. LV thus requires less coordination of large numbers of votes among minority voters; voters simply have to decide whether to vote for a candidate, without having to decide as well precisely *how many* votes to give that candidate. As a result, one consideration in deciding whether LV or CV is most appropriate as a means of ensuring minority representation perhaps should be how substantial the difficulties of effective coordination of votes among the relevant minority group might be in particular circumstances. That, in turn, could depend on factors like whether the particular election is a high-visibility or low-visibility one; CV might be well suited to the former, such as city council elections, while LV might be more suited to the latter, such as judicial elections. Another factor might be whether there are existing political organizations with the resources and sophistication to mobilize the relevant minority community to use CV effectively; one reason voting-rights litigators have been willing to endorse CV in Alabama is that the state has a longstanding and effective political organization for black voters that was willing and able to take on the responsibility of educating black voters to make effective use of CV.

There is less discussion in the literature of alternative voting in the United States on LV. As one scholar put it a generation ago, in a remark that remains true today, "LV systems have been more widely adopted and have shown greater capability to survive, but have been written about very little as compared to [CV and STV]." Leon Weaver, *Semi-Proportional and Proportional Representation Systems in the United States*, in Choosing an Electoral System: Issues and Alternatives 191, 201 (Arend Lijphart & Bernard Grofman, eds., 1984). Limited voting has been approved by courts in many states; the Fourth Circuit, for example, has recognized at least four consent decrees in settlement of voting-rights litigation in North Carolina in which limited voting elections were adopted. For discussion of the local jurisdictions that have used LV, and for a survey of the VRA cases that have used LV as a remedy, see Pamela S. Karlan, *Maps and Misreadings: The Role of Geographic Compactness in Racial Vote Dilution Litigation*, 24 Harv. C.R.–C.L. L. Rev. 173, 223–31 (1989); *see also* Richard L. Engstrom, *Modified Multi–Seat Election Systems as Remedies for Minority Vote Dilution*, 31 Stetson L. Rev. 743, 758–60 (1992); Joseph F. Zimmerman, *The Federal Voting Rights Act and Alternative Election Systems*, 19 Wm. & Mary L. Rev. 621, 652–54 (1978).

Most of the limited-voting schemes that have gone into effect at the local level have come in response to actual or potential voting rights litigation. In voluntary settlements, some jurisdictions have agreed to adopt LV. This approach, like that involving CV, typically occurs when geographic constraints prevent effective use of the conventional "safe" minority districting approach as a remedy. And as with CV, the courts of appeals have been reluctant—much more so than district courts, which have been willing to be more experimental—to uphold lower-court decisions imposing LV on a resistant jurisdiction. Does this reluctance reflect a sound appreciation of the policies of the VRA? The limits that should be recognized on the power of federal courts to restructure the basic democratic process of local governments? Apart from those concerns, would LV be a desirable policy tool for dealing with VRA problems, so that Congress should amend the statute to make explicit the power of courts to order it as a remedy? Consider those questions as you study a specific context in which the courts of appeals have overturned a LV alternative:

McGhee v. Granville County Board of Commissioners

860 F.2d 110 (4th Cir. 1988).

■ DICKSON PHILLIPS, CIRCUIT JUDGE:

* * *

I

* * *

The Board [of Commissioners] is the governing body of Granville County. At the time the plaintiffs brought this action, the Board consisted of five members, [elected] on a county-wide at-large basis, but required to reside in particular residence districts. Each member was elected for a four-year term. The terms of the various Board members were staggered, with elections being held in even numbered years. Three of the five incumbent members were serving terms which expired in 1988. The remaining two incumbent members were serving terms which expire in 1990.

Black citizens make up 43.9 percent of the county's total population (1980 data), 40.8 percent of its voting age population (1980 data), and 39.5 percent of its registered voters (1987 data). Despite these population numbers, and despite the fact that a number of black residents have run for election to the Board, no black has ever been elected to the Board.

[After the parties stipulated that the existing electoral structure violated § 2 of the Voting Rights Act, the County proposed as a remedy a single-member districting plan containing seven districts, with members serving staggered terms, thereby both abandoning the at-large election method and expanding Board membership from five to seven. The parties agreed that the best plan of this sort would only be able to create one "safe" black-majority district and one more in which black voters would have "a fighting chance." Because the total black voting-age population in the County was nearly 41 percent, while the single-member districting plan would give blacks no more than 14–28 percent representation on a seven member Board, the plaintiffs objected that the plan would not provide black citizens "a chance to elect a number of commissioners that is commensurate with their portion of the population and with their voting strength." Plaintiffs argued that single member districting was inadequate in Granville County and instead proposed a limited voting plan. The Board would be composed of seven members elected concurrently on a county wide at-large basis, with voters allowed to vote for any three or fewer candidates as they chose. Plaintiffs asserted that this plan would give black voters a fair chance of electing three commissioners, 42 percent of the Board. The district court rejected the County's plan as inadequate. Instead, that court adopted a modified version of the plaintiffs' limited voting plan.]

The [district] court's plan was specific and detailed:

1. The Board shall be expanded to seven members at the 1988 election, and shall remain at that number indefinitely. All terms shall be for four years except as otherwise stated in this order. In all elections, the candidates who receive the highest number of votes shall be deemed elected.

2. The two Commissioners not up for re-election in 1988 shall retain their seats until their terms expire in 1990.

3. In all elections, except as specifically noted herein, voters shall be limited to voting for a maximum of two candidates to fill the available seats.

4. Five Commissioners shall be elected in 1988, with the Commissioner receiving the fewest votes to serve a two-year term to expire in 1990.

5. Starting in 1990, an election shall be had every four years, in even years not divisible by four, to fill the three expiring terms; starting in 1992, an election shall be had every four years in even years divisible by four, to fill the other four expiring terms.

6. Beginning with the election in the year 2000, and in all elections and subsequently in even years divisible by four, voting shall be at large. In subsequent elections, in years not divisible by four, voters shall continue to be limited to voting for a maximum of two candidates to fill the available seats.[14]

[During the one election for which the district court's plan was in effect, black candidates won nomination to three of the five seats being contested, and all the primary winners were running uncontested for the general election at the time of this appeal].

II

The dispositive issue, put in broadest terms, is whether the district court properly could reject the County's remedial single-member district plan and impose instead its own modified version of the plaintiffs' limited voting plan.

[. . . Where] the legislative body does respond with a proposed remedy, a court may not thereupon simply substitute its judgment of a more equitable remedy for that of the legislative body; it may only consider whether the proffered remedial plan is legally unacceptable because it violates anew constitutional or statutory voting rights—that is, whether it

---

14. Within its premises, the district court's plan is an admirably thoughtful and creative one. By rejecting the plaintiffs' concurrent-election proposal and continuing the extant staggered-term feature, the court deliberately sought to guard against massive board turnovers during what inevitably was to be a sensitive transition period. By scaling down the limited voting plan's impact over time, the court sought to take into account an anticipated change in racial polarization voting patterns which the court thought would occur as black representatives allayed traditional white voter concerns about fitness and voting propensities.

fails to meet the same standards applicable to an original challenge of a legislative plan in place. If the remedial plan meets those standards, a reviewing court must then accord great deference to legislative judgments about the exact nature and scope of the proposed remedy, reflecting as it will a variety of political judgments about the dynamics of an overall electoral process that rightly pertain to the legislative prerogative of the state and its subdivisions.

* * *

III

* * *

The judicial and legislative process of putting principled bounds upon the vote dilution concept has now culminated in the Supreme Court's exhaustive analysis of the concept as codified in amended § 2, in *Thornburg v. Gingles* ... Further, and of particular importance to our analysis, the Court noted that the "size and compactness" requirement confines dilution claims to situations where diminution of voting power is "proximately caused by the districting plan," and thus "would not assure racial minorities proportional representation." Finally, in defining the "essence of a § 2 claim," the Court made plain that the adverse "result" for which such a claim seeks a remedy must be traceable ultimately to the impact of "a certain electoral law, practice or structure interact[ing] with social and historical conditions."

IV

* * *

If these principles be accepted—as we do—they of course reveal the fallacy of the plaintiffs' position and the error of the district court's rejection of the County's proposed remedial plan. Within those principles, the plaintiffs' concession that the County plan provided the maximum remedy possible by redistricting establishes the plan as a legally adequate one that should have been accepted in deference to the affected local government's primary jurisdiction to ordain its electoral processes.

The plaintiffs' principal contentions to the contrary deserve some discussion.

A

Their primary contention, expressly accepted by the district court, is that the districting remedy, though concededly maximum by that means, was not the "complete" one legally required. Though not made explicit, it is obvious that this view of "completeness" of remedy has to assume one of two legally erroneous standards against which to measure "completeness."

The first standard necessarily looks to the plight of those minority voters not included within one of the remedial plan's "safe" districts. As to those included within those districts, the remedy is manifestly "complete," both legally and practically. It is only as to those voters not included that the plan might be considered in any sense an incomplete eradication of the "submergence" caused by the at-large voting system. For some, possibly all of these voters, the remedial plan "submerges" their voting power—at least in direct terms—to a greater degree in their new constituencies than did the challenged system in the old. This, of course, is simply an unavoidable mathematical consequence of the demographics that will constrain practically all single-member district remedial plans. It is undoubtedly to some extent an ironic consequence. But it is a consequence that has not been thought to invalidate remedial plans by those courts that have considered the matter directly. Those courts have instead, apparently without exception, simply accepted it as a necessary concomitant of the inevitably rough-hewn, approximate redistricting remedy.

* * *

The other standard implicit in plaintiffs' contention, and in the district court's reasoning, is even more plainly inappropriate. Despite the disavowals of both, it is obvious that ultimately the plaintiffs urged and the district court accepted a proportional representation standard. This directly violates the § 2(b) proviso expressly disclaiming any such "right."

Plaintiffs apparently seek to avoid the proviso's effect, as we understand their position, by insisting that vote dilution violation and vote dilution remedy are to be separately considered in assessing the proviso's intended effect. On this view, the proviso only prohibits finding a violation based solely upon a lack of proportional representation; where a violation properly traceable to a specific voting mechanism is found, the proviso does not then prohibit a court from rejecting a proposed remedy that does not assure approximate proportional representation and imposing one that does. Here the violation established was vote dilution specifically caused by an at-large electoral system, not simply the lack of proportional representation. . . .

This contention seizes upon and seeks to exploit the undoubted logical problem created by Congress' simultaneous allowance of vote dilution claims, which necessarily require some consideration of population proportions, and the disclaimer of any "right" to proportional representation. The problem of statutory interpretation is certainly there, but we are satisfied that to adopt the plaintiffs' position and affirm the district court's reasoning and judgment would simply negate the proviso, and defeat Congress' intention in adopting this disclaimer as the ultimate back-stopping principle of this "compromise" legislation.

The practical consequence of uncoupling violation from remedy in this way would necessarily be to allow proportional representation to become in practical effect the "right" protected by § 2. *Ubi jus, ibi remedium*, and vice versa. Certainly implicit in the *Gingles* Court's analysis of the nature of § 2 vote dilution claims is the notion that, so far as those claims are concerned, right and remedy are inextricably bound together, for to prove vote dilution by districting one must prove the specific way in which dilution may be remedied by redistricting. . . .

Whatever its other effects, we therefore believe that the § 2 proviso prevents a court from rejecting a remedial legislative districting plan which provides the maximum opportunity for representation possible by that means for the sole reason that the representation possible does not sufficiently approximate proportionality.

* * *

NOTES AND QUESTIONS

1. As a matter of either public policy or of the legislative purposes and history of the Voting Rights Act, why should the existing system of territorial districting be the baseline against which claims of minority vote dilution are measured?

2. Does the adoption of alternative voting systems, such as limited voting, for the purpose of enhancing representation of black voters run afoul of the constitutional constraints on the role of race in the design of political institutions that *Shaw v. Reno*, 509 U.S. 630 (1993) and subsequent cases establish? In *Cleveland County Ass'n for Govt. By the People v. Cleveland County Bd. Of Comm'rs*, 965 F.Supp. 72 (D.D.C.1997), Cleveland County, North Carolina entered into a consent decree in which it agreed to move to limited voting to elect its Board of Commissioners. Before litigation began, the Board consisted of five members elected at-large throughout the County, and no black had ever been elected. Plaintiffs and the County agreed to settle a voting-rights lawsuit by increasing the Board to seven members, with each voter to have only four votes to cast. Represented by the same lawyer who filed *Shaw*, another group of plaintiffs then brought an action alleging that this settlement violated the Constitution. They argued that the decision to adopt limited voting was "race conscious" and that race had been "the predominant factor" for the decision. The district court acknowledged that the move to limited voting had been race conscious, but held that strict scrutiny was nonetheless not required because limited voting did not involve any racial classifications or distinguish voters along racial lines. The court of appeals subsequently reversed and remanded the case, holding that the Board lacked power under state law to adopt the remedy; the court did not reach the constitutional question. 142 F.3d 468 (D.C. Cir. 1998).

3. Should the congressional statute that now requires states to use single-member districts to elect members of Congress, 2 U.S.C. § 2 (2000), be amended to give states *the option* of using alternative voting systems, such as CV, preference voting, or limited voting, to elect representatives? The statute currently permits states to use at-large elections only in certain narrowly specified circumstances, such as when the state is entitled to an additional seat in Congress but the state has not yet been redistricted to take account of the increase in representation. In 1995, Rep. Cynthia McKinney (an African American representative whose then-existing majority-black district was declared unconstitutional by the Supreme Court in *Miller v. Johnson*, 515 U.S. 900 (1995)), introduced the "Voters' Choice Act" (H.R. 2545), which provided, in pertinent part:

Sec. 2. Multi-member Districts Permitted for Election of Representatives for States with Certain Voting Systems.

(A) In General.—Notwithstanding Public Law 90–196 (2 U.S.C. 2c), a state that is entitled to more than one representative in Congress may establish a number of districts for election of representatives that is less than the number of representatives to which the state is entitled, if and only if that state uses a system of limited voting, a system of cumulative voting, or a system of preference voting in its multi-member districts.

(B) Limited Voting Described.—Limited voting is a system in which a voter may not cast a number of votes that is more than one-half the number of representatives to be elected.

(C) Cumulative Voting Described.—Cumulative voting is a system in which a voter may cast a number of votes up to the number of representatives to be elected, and the voter may distribute those votes, including fractions of votes, in any combination, including all votes for one candidate.

(D) Preference Voting Described.—Preference voting is a system in which a voter ranks the candidates and candidates win by reaching a required threshold of votes. After totaling first-place votes, all candidates who have reached the threshold are declared elected. Votes in excess of the threshold are transferred to the voters' next-choice candidates: either some votes at full value or all votes at an equally reduced value. When no candidate is above the threshold and all seats have yet to be filled, the candidate with the fewest top-ranked votes is eliminated, and all of the candidate's votes are transferred to the next-choice candidates at full value. Voters may rank candidates equally. When candidates are so ranked, the value of the ballot is divided equally among such candidates. The threshold is calculated as—

(1) votes divided by the number of representatives to be elected;

(2) votes divided by the number of representatives to be elected plus one, plus one vote; or

(3) any number between the number calculated under paragraph (1) and the number calculated under paragraph (2).

(E) Equality Requirement.—In a state that uses districts in a system of limited voting, a system of cumulative voting, or a system of preference voting, the number of residents per representative in a district shall be equal for all representatives elected.

(F) Single–Member Districts Allowed.—A state may use single-member districts alone or in combination with multi-member districts.

Sec. 3. Relation to Voting Rights Act of 1965.

The rights and remedies established by this Act are in addition to all other rights and remedies provided by law, and the rights and remedies established by this Act shall not supersede, restrict, or limit the application of the Voting Rights Act of 1965 (42 U.S.C. 1973 et seq.). Nothing in this Act authorizes or requires conduct that is prohibited by the Voting Rights Act of 1965 (42 U.S.C. 1973 et seq.).

What are the advantages and disadvantages of the Voters' Choice Act? The proposal was referred to the House Judiciary Committee, where no action was taken. Is there any realistic possibility that Congress would voluntarily alter the single-member district requirement?

In Congressional hearings on the proposed Voter's Choice Act for congressional elections, Rep. Tom Campbell, a moderate Republican from California, offered the following noteworthy testimony in favor of the Act and of cumulative voting in particular:

Cumulative voting allows a self-defined minority to achieve representation. . . .

Now, I emphasize the word self-defined minority because that, to me, is essential. I think it is wrong for government to divide us according to race. I believe a color-blind government is the correct constitutional maxim as well as good public policy. And thus whereas the Supreme Court has struck down race conscious drawing of lines in order to create majority-minority-districts, cumulative voting with multi-member districts allows a self-defined minority, whether it be racial or not.

Whether it be economic or political or social or of any particular variety, it is not defined by government. It is, rather, defined by the individuals; and thus it seems to me to escape any condemnation under the fifth or fourteenth amendments and yet account for something very valuable.

I will hopefully humorously and not for any offense purposes explain the plight of a modern Republican in a conservative Republican caucus.

I am routinely outvoted. It would be nice if, for example, of the nine elected leadership positions three of them were moderates. It cannot be so, however, where as each one of them is put up to a majority vote it will always go to a conservative. If, however, we were to elect those nine as we elect a board of directors, cumulative voting, I would have nine votes. So would every other member of my Republican conference, and I would cast all of my nine for three individuals, as opposed to one for each of nine individuals. I would cast three for each, and the three moderates would make it to what I call the board of directors of the Republican Congress of the House of Representatives.

... I define the minority within the majority. And this particular example I used was moderate Republican. It is not done by government, and it is not necessarily done by race. It does strike me as a very farsighted solution. . . .

4. For reliable information about alternative voting systems in the United States, including up-to-date reports on new uses of these systems, the most comprehensive source is an entity named The Center for Voting and Democracy. The Center, a nonpartisan, non-profit organization, studies voting systems and provides support to organizations that advocate changes in voting structures. The Center has been active in promoting redistricting alternatives, proportional and semi-proportional representation systems, and instant runoff voting. Its website is www.fairvote.org.

5. As the materials on the history of territorial districting later in this Chapter suggest, the decision to use geographic districts was a product of a particular set of political, economic, technological, and logistical conditions. Will changes in those dimensions change popular receptivity to alternative voting systems? Consider this recent suggestion along these lines:

But despite the traditionalism, stickiness and convenient manipulability of geographic districting, life in the Internet society accustoms us to a much reduced respect for its factual predicates. As we spend greater and more meaningful portions of our lives in computer-mediated communications with other people, three pervasive changes occur: location doesn't matter, our interests determine our communities, and we don't have to use our feet to vote with them.

In the first place, in the Internet society, everyone is adjacent to everyone else. . . . During any given day we are at least as likely to communicate with people on other continents as in other parts of our county, or to shop with merchants in other time zones as in other neighborhoods of our town. Locality ceases to have a normative significance: our neighborhood pub is less likely to contain our friends than a chat room, the local merchant who charges more than the seller we can find on the net is more likely to gain our resentment than our business, and the sagacity of our local doctor is under constant challenge from the flood of medical information we can find for ourselves online. Being close by is nothing special because everyone's close by. An accessible Congressman is one who gives us a quick substantive answer to our email, not someone who comes home for the weekend and hangs around the mall we don't shop at anymore.

Replacing the normative value of the local is the power of affinity. The network's media allow us to locate others who share our interests and concerns with ease, and thus we increasingly occupy the locality of the like-minded. Nor is our locality in these terms singular: we are simultaneously part of the communities of sea kayakers, gamelon musicians, ex-Bahai atheists, melanoma survivors, lukewarm libertarians (not yet ready to eliminate public libraries and slightly queasy about do-it-yourself howitzer construction) and shiatsu fanciers. A conclave of the people who share all our affinities would be more depopulated than a New Hampshire village meeting on a blizzard evening—in fact it is almost guaranteed to be a solo. But each of the communities comprising our social context will be vibrant, noisy and disputatious. . . .

As geographic proximity assumes less importance in individuals' sense of community, and as people become more connected with one another along dimensions other than physical proximity, they may become more skeptical of the idea that political representation ought to be organized invariably along geographical lines. . . .

Eben Moglen & Pamela S. Karlan, *The Soul of a New Political Machine: The Online, the Color Line, and Electronic Democracy*, 34 Loy. L.A.L. Rev. 1031 (2001).

E.   THE LOT VERSUS THE ELECTION

What about lotteries as an alternative system of election, at least in some contexts? Throughout both the practice and political theory of republican government, until the American and French Revolutions, the lot was considered an integral tool of republican self-government. Indeed, the lot was considered the quintessential democratic selection device, while elections were considered a means of ensuring more aristocratic rule. From today's vantage point, the idea of selecting public officials through some form of lottery likely seems fanciful or absurd, raising the specter of incompetent officeholders and random politics (although lotteries do sometimes play a role in selecting jurors). But in practice, the lot was always used within a broader institutional context that might be thought to have minimized these concerns.

Are there contexts today in which lotteries might be an appropriate alternative voting technique? What values might lottery voting help realize? In what contexts might such a device be a pragmatically useful tool? Consider those questions as you reflect on the theory and practice of lots rather than elections as a means of selecting public officials.

1. *Democratic lotteries, aristocratic elections*: Many leading political theorists of republican government, including Montesquieu, Harrington, Rousseau, and Aristotle, believed the lot was *the* democratic selection device, while elections were intrinsically aristocratic in nature. Indeed, the leading historical study on this issue calls it "a paradox that has hitherto gone unnoticed" that at the same time American and French Revolutions

proclaimed the equality of all citizens, they led to elections becoming the only form of selecting officeholders. Bernard Manin, The Principles of Representative Government 79 (1997).

These thinkers all believed that elections selected for preexisting elites, in part on the view that people will tend to recognize and choose their betters. In contrast, selection by lot had the following advantages: it avoided disgracing those who lost elections; it minimized envy and jealousy of those selected; it reduced the intense factional fighting and intrigue that would surround elections. Most important, the lot would distribute public officeholding in egalitarian and hence democratic terms. Thus, the lot was closely linked to another principle that some republicans considered crucial, that of rotation in office. Rotation both distributed offices in more egalitarian terms and was a check on too great a separation between rulers and ruled. *See* Gordon S. Wood, The Creation of the American Republic 140– 141 (1969) (on rotation being a "cardinal tenet" of republican thought in 1776).

These views about the different social and political effects of different selection systems had their analogues in debates over the Constitution. Anti–Federalists, who opposed ratification, "made the size of the House the leading point in their indictment of the national scheme of representation." Jack N. Rakove, Original Meanings: Politics and Ideas in the Making of the Constitution 228 (1996). They argued that the structure of national elections would ensure that the government would have "the soul of aristocracy," dominated by "the few men of wealth and abilities." The "middle and lower classes" who formed "the democracy" of the American people would not be present. Although the Anti–Federalists did not urge the use of lots, they did endorse a theory of representation that emphasized the need for representatives to mirror their constituencies. Their principal objection was that the proposed ratio between electors and representatives was too small to allow the proper "likeness," "resemblance," and "closeness;" they argued that representation should be a "true picture" of "the people." Manin, *supra*, at 109. As a leading Anti–Federalist put it: "The very term representative, implies, that the person or body chosen for this purpose, should resemble those who appoint them—a representation of the people of America, if it be a true one, must be like the people." II The Complete Anti–Federalist 9, 42 Brutus, Essay III (Herbert J. Storing ed. 1981). This true picture conceived "likeness" in a social or economic sense: "the farmer, merchant, mechanick and other various orders of people, ought to be represented according to their respective weight and numbers." *Id*. Note the similarity to contemporary concerns over descriptive representation discussed in Chapter 9.

The Constitution specifically rejected the Anti–Federalist theory of political representation. Madison and those defending the Constitution justified many of its structural features on grounds that representation should not be a mirror of the constituents. In The Federalist Papers No. 35,

Hamilton rejected as "altogether visionary" the claim that "all classes of citizens should have some of their own number in the representative body, in order that their feelings and interests may be the better understood and attended to." The structural features of the Constitution were designed, essentially, to accentuate the elite effects elections had long been thought to have. Thus, the Constitution was designed to ensure that those with the "most wisdom" and "most virtue" would hold office. The Federalist Papers No. 57. Representative government itself was to be preferred over direct democracy because the "small number of citizens elected by the rest [would] refine and enlarge the public views by passing them through the medium of a chosen body of citizens. . . ." The Federalist Papers No. 10. Most importantly, the Constitution's defenders argued for a large republic and for election from large districts precisely because these devices were thought more likely to select for representatives of a certain type of distinction and character. Thus, "the larger the district of election, the better the representation. . . . Nothing but real weight of character can give a man real influence over a large district." As Madison put it, "large districts are manifestly favorable to the election of persons of general respectability, and of probable attachment to the rights of property, over competitors depending on the personal solicitations practicable on a contracted theatre." *See also* Rakove, *supra*, at 222 (describing the "key hypothesis" of Madison as "that elections held in districts larger than the county and township units used to choose state legislators would encourage a superior class of lawmakers to gain national office, thereby enabling national law to be framed with a deliberation rarely found in the states"). Regular elections, rather than social likeness, would be the link between representatives and constituents.

Consider whether the historical debates over lots versus elections sheds light on the debates over theories of representation underlying the Constitution. Manin concludes his study with this provocative thought: "The fundamental fact about elections is that they are *simultaneously* and indissolubly egalitarian and inegalitarian, aristocratic and democratic." Is that right? Does it shed any light on how to think about the design of democratic institutions?

2. *The historical practice of selection by lot.* The lot was an important element in the earlier democratic systems on which the Framers drew in developing their own political theory. Thus, in the classical democracy of Athens and in the centers of republicanism and civic humanism, the republics of Venice and Florence, lottery selection was used under various circumstances and justified by several considerations. The influence of these systems in so many other areas of the Constitution's design makes the absence of any role for selection by lot all the more intriguing. The following history is taken from Manin, *supra*, at 79–94.

In Athens, the principal political body, the Popular Assembly, was elected. But lots were used to fill numerous other public offices, including important administrative and executive posts. The principal justification seems to have been ensuring rotation in office and widespread political participation. Most interesting, selection by lot was integrated into a much more complex system of institutional arrangements. Thus, for magistrates (who among other things conducted preliminary investigations before lawsuits and presided over courts) the term of office was one year; a citizen could not hold the same position more than once and had to be over 30; and only those who volunteered to be considered were among the pool from which lots were picked. Those selected by lot still had to meet various qualifications: to have paid taxes; performed military service; have behaved properly toward their parents; and to not have had oligarchic sympathies. There was also aggressive ex post monitoring of performance while in office; those selected by lot had to render account on leaving office, and during their terms, any citizen could bring a vote of no confidence against them. These structures might suggest that lottery voting should not be considered in isolation, but in the context of other structures which might surround it.

In Venice and Florence, the justifications for lots were to avoid ruling cliques perpetuating themselves in office and to ensure equal access to public office. The most interesting feature of these experiments is the way Florence combined elections with the lot. Thus, for certain important posts, a nominating committee would first select a large number of citizens deemed potentially qualified for office; the electorate would then vote in secret among those selected. Those who received more than a certain number of votes would then have their names placed in bags, from which the names of those who would assume office were drawn at random. Thus, among those considered qualified and worthy of holding office, the most equitable distribution of office was considered to be by lot.

3. *Contemporary proposals for lottery voting.* Until recently, there have been few proposals to reinvigorate the tradition of using lots as elements in democratic choice. Akhil Amar has suggested consideration of the following structure on the possible benefits of incorporating lots into choosing public representatives. Voters would vote for competing candidates, but the votes would not directly determine outcomes. Instead, the votes would determine the probability that candidate will be elected, but the actual selection would then occur through drawing a single ballot at random. Thus, if A receives 60 percent of the votes and B 40 percent, then A would have a 60 percent probability of being chosen when the random ballot was drawn to determine who would hold office. Among the benefits Amar offers for this proposal is that it would make rotation in office more likely; it would provide a means of enabling minorities to win some of the time; and it would minimize wasted votes because each additional vote a candidate received would increase his or her probability of being elected. *See* Akhil Reed Amar, *Lottery Voting: A Thought Experiment,* 1995 U.Chi.L. Forum 193.

Similarly, Jon Elster suggests the following advantages of lottery voting: it "reconciles honesty with self-interest" in the sense that lottery voting is the only means of ensuring that voters genuinely vote for their most preferred alternative. The reason they have an incentive to do so is related to reasons just noted: because each additional vote increases the likelihood the candidate will be elected, and because even a candidate who only receives 25 percent of the vote still has a 25 percent chance of being elected, voters will vote for the option they genuinely prefer. Elster further argues lottery voting would block the emergence of professional politicians and would ensure that there be no permanently unrepresented minorities. Jon Elster, Solomonic Judgements 78–92 (1989). For the argument that lottery might be an appropriate way to set the legislative agenda, given modern insights into how much the order in which issues are considered can influence substantive outcomes, see Richard H. Pildes & Elizabeth S. Anderson, *Slinging Arrows at Democracy: Social Choice Theory, Value Pluralism, and Democratic Politics*, 90 Colum. L. Rev. 2121, 2196–97 (1990).

Elster notes at least three other contexts in which introducing randomness has been offered as a means to improve the design of political institutions. First, the economist Richard Thaler has suggested that members of Congress might be assigned to committees through a random process; among other aims, the purpose here would be to break up entrenched powers of seniority. Second, Elster proposes that redistricting might be done through random redesign, which he asserts would be "clearly superior to the current American system." Third, elections might be randomly timed; the aim here would be to avoid the tendency of governments to manipulate policy to coincide with election dates known long in advance.

Are the advantages offered on behalf of lottery voting persuasive? In what electoral contexts are they most convincing? A well-known example of weighted selection priorities is the lottery for draft picks conducted by the National Basketball Association each year.

With respect to randomness more generally, would any of these particular uses Elster suggests be attractive? Are there perhaps other contexts in which lots or the features of randomness associated with lots might be a better way of structuring aspects of politics?

F. THE HISTORY OF TERRITORIAL DISTRICTING

To gain perspective on the current system of congressional representation in order to consider alternative possibilities, it is useful to consider the history by which the single-member geographic district came to be the form used for congressional elections. As you analyze the alternative voting systems described above, consider whether the current electoral system in the United States can be said to result from a deliberative choice to reject these alternatives. Instead, are the justifications originally offered for single-member districts ones that would better be realized today by the use of the alternative voting systems described above, or the proportional representation systems described below?

Frequently, it is assumed that the United States has always used single-member districts to elect members of Congress. *See, e.g.,* Steven G. Calabresi, *Beyond the Public/Private Distinction: Political Parties as Mediating Institutions,* 61 U. Chi. L. Rev. 1479, 1507 (1994) ("Today, as in 1789 . . . Representatives represent single-member geographical districts. . . ."). But this is inaccurate. Only after a lengthy struggle did Congress eventually come in 1842 to use its powers under Art. I, § 4 of the Constitution to legislate and require single-member districts. As we examine this history, consider whether the justifications for districts would be better realized today by structures other than geographic districts, such as the alternative voting systems this Chapter explores.

At the time the Constitution was adopted, "[m]ost legislators saw the problem as a choice between two alternatives: at-large or district elections." Rosemarie Zagarri, The Politics of Size 105 (1987). *See also* Andrew Hacker, Congressional Districting: The Issue of Equal Representation 8–10 (1963). Other possibilities, including what we now call alternative voting systems or forms of proportional representation, were not discussed because the mechanics for PR and these other systems had not yet been developed. Both sides in the debates over representation tended to assume that districts would be used. The arguments for districts emphasized that they would protect minority interests within a state, ensuring for example that the "mercantile interest" would not "swallow up the agricultural." Zagarri, *supra,* at 111 (quoting debates in New Jersey). Districts would reflect the heterogeneity of interests within states, and would ensure more connection between local interests and representatives. Writing in The Federalist Papers No. 56, Madison argued that if large states were split into several districts, "it will be found that there will be no peculiar local interest in either, which will not be within the knowledge of the representative of the district." The decision was reached, however, not to resolve the method of election in the Constitution itself, but to leave it to each state to choose its own method of selection—subject to the potential congressional override of Art. I, § 4.

Initially states experimented, some switching back and forth between systems. The majority of states held at-large congressional elections initially; only Massachusetts, New York, Maryland, Virginia, and South Carolina used districts. Pennsylvania's experience is particularly noteworthy. In the east, Federalists dominated, while in the western part of the state, Antifederalist sentiment was strong. Because the Federalists controlled the state legislature, the state adopted at-large congressional elections. In the first federal elections, all eight congressmen elected were Federalists who lived in the eastern part of the state. As one outraged critic put it, "I am sure that Pennsylvania will never again suffer eight representatives to be elected out of a mere corner of the state." Enough pressure was put on the state legislature that by the next elections, it had divided the state into eight congressional districts. In general, most states settled on either districts or at-large elections by this second round of congressional elections and kept that system until Congress intervened in 1842.

The significant fact, though, is the stark pattern regarding which states chose districts. Consistently, the large states employed districted elections while small states used at-large elections. These differences stemmed from both diverse circumstances and distinct conceptions of representation and its relationship to geography.

Small states conceived of representation in traditional geographic terms. "The residents of states with limited territory and relatively small populations continued to think about representation in spatial terms. They presumed that geography represented the most fundamental variable in constructing representative institutions." Zagarri, *supra*, at 147. In their state legislatures, representation was typically by town or county, not population, and they argued that the state was a territorial community that should be represented that way in the House of Representatives.

In the large states, representation was conceived more in demographic than geographic terms. The state was viewed "as an amalgam of diverse interests that an accident of history had united into a single unit." *Id.* at 123. Representation was thought of "in terms of randomly associated individuals rather than communities, in terms of population rather than territory." *Id.* at 143. In these states, geographic boundaries were viewed as malleable, subject to change as population changed. They moved their state capitals to the demographic centers of their states, adopted population-based schemes of representation in their lower houses, and supported districted rather than at-large elections for Congress.

A fascinating set of strategic interactions eventually led to Congress's actions in 1842. Because small states used at-large elections, they tended to elect unified congressional delegations. Within a small state, the representatives tended to come from the same party. But the large-state delegations, elected through individual districts, were more fractured, reflecting the partisan divisions within the state. As a result, congressional delegations from the small states were more effective in the House. As the large states began to recognize this consequence of the different electoral systems, they began to talk about shifting back to at-large elections. This, in turn, prompted the small states to fear that if large states too went to at-large elections, they would soon dominate the small states; unified delegations that would then vote as a bloc would be more likely to represent each of the large states. By 1842, 9 of the 26 states used at-large elections (to get a sense of the magnitude of at-large elections at the time, the largest state using them was Georgia, which was entitled to eight representatives and had a total population of 691,392). But enough of the small states feared the large states switching to at-large elections that there was sufficient support for Congress to step in and require all states to adopt single-member geographic districts. Districting was preferable, in the view of some small states, to universal use of at-large congressional elections.

In 1842, there were enough votes for Congress to pass the Reapportionment Act of 1842, ch. 47, 5 Stat. 491. That Act required, for the first time, that "In every case where a State is entitled to more than one Representative, the number to which each state shall be entitled . . . shall be elected by districts composed of contiguous territory equal in number to the number of Representatives to which said State may be entitled, no one district electing more than one Representative." But despite the Act, New Hampshire, Georgia, Mississippi, and Missouri conducted their 1842 elections under at-large systems; over protests, Congress seated all the members of these states, *Congressional Quarterly Inc., Jigsaw Politics: Shaping the House After the 1990 Census* 18 (1990). The 1842 Act lasted ten years, but it began a regular practice of congressional enactments requiring districted elections for the House.

In 1901, Congress added a compactness requirement to the Act, Reapportionment Act of 1901, ch. 93, § 3, 31 Stat. 733, 734. In 1929, Congress enacted a combined census-reapportionment bill that established a permanent method for apportioning House seats after each Census. Reapportionment Act of 1929, ch. 28, section 22, 46 Stat. 21, 26–27. This legislation contained no statement of whether previous requirements, such as districting, compactness, or contiguity, continued to apply. Three years later, the Supreme Court held that these requirements from earlier legislation had lapsed with the passage of the Reapportionment Act of 1929. *Wood v. Broom*, 287 U.S. 1 (1932). *See also Franklin v. Massachusetts*, 505 U.S. 788, 791 (1992) (discussing the passage of the Reapportionment Act of 1929). Not until 1967 did Congress enact legislation once again requiring that states elect House members from single-member districts. Act of December 14, 1967, Pub. L. No. 90-196, 81 Stat. 581. During the interim period, from 1929–1967, several states, including some large ones, did elect at least some of their delegation at large. Interestingly, a primary motivation for the 1967 legislation reinstituting the requirement of single-member districts was the Voting Rights Act of 1965: Congress feared Southern states might resort to multimember congressional districts to dilute minority voting power. Today, only the seven states that are entitled to a single representative—Alaska, Delaware, Montana, North Dakota, South Dakota, Vermont, and Wyoming—hold at-large congressional elections. Occasionally, states have returned to at-large congressional elections for temporary reasons; Alabama, for example, lost a congressional seat after the 1960 Census and the legislature could not agree on how to redistrict, which led to the state's 1962 and 1964 congressional elections being held on at-large basis. For a good overview of congressional reapportionment acts, see Emanuel Celler, *Congressional Apportionment—Past, Present, and Future,* 17 Law & Contemp. Probs. 268 (1952).

Does this history suggest that the Constitution did not originally resolve the struggle between geographic and demographic views of representation? Does it suggest that by 1842 the demographic conception had become dominant? Consider whether the arguments for districts are best realized today by that system or some alternative system not available or discussed in 1842. Note also the problems with individual states seeking to make independent decisions about how to structure their congressional selection methods. Given that states are not just trying to construct an internally appropriate system, but also to enhance their effectiveness in the House, can congressional election procedures only be effectively regulated at the national level? Does this suggest that if congressional term limits are to be adopted, for example, they should be adopted nationally rather than on a state-by-state basis?

Recall that most alternative voting systems, like CV, were not invented at the time the Constitution was created, nor were they yet recognized when Congress enacted the 1842 districting statute. Would those who supported districting have favored one of these alternative systems had it been known at the time? Consider the views of United States Senator Charles Buckalew of Pennsylvania, at first a leading proponent of districting, who became the leading advocate of cumulative voting and proportional representation by the 1860s. In a speech in Philadelphia in 1867, he described why he would have supported cumulative voting, rather than single-member districts, had the former system been known at the time he campaigned successfully to replace at-large elections with single-member districts:

> I drew the amendment to the Constitution of our State by which your city is broken into districts.... What was the idea of that amendment? ... The idea was to break up the political community, and allow the different political interests which compose it, by choosing in single districts, to be represented in the Legislature of the State. Unfortunately, when that arrangement was made for your city (and for Pittsburgh also, to which it will soon apply), this just, equal, almost perfect system of voting [cumulative voting], which I have spoken of tonight, was unknown; it had not then been announced abroad or considered here, and we did what best we could.

Charles R. Buckalew, Proportional Representation 62–63 (1872).

Does this statement from a leading advocate of districted elections support the view that the United States has not really had a debate between single-member districts and these alternatives?

G.   DEBATE BETWEEN MAJORITARIAN SYSTEMS AND PROPORTIONAL REPRESENTATION

Ever since the well-known debates between John Stuart Mill, an advocate of proportional representation, and the English political writer,

Walter Bagehot, political scientists have debated the merits of Anglo–American majoritarian systems and PR. For a good overview of the debate, see the essays in Choosing an Electoral System: Issues and Alternatives (Arend Lijphart & Bernard Grofman eds. 1984). The central argument for PR is that it produces fairer political representation: representation that more accurately mirrors the range of opinions and party preferences in the political community. The central argument for majoritarian alternatives, which give a candidate who receives 51 percent of the vote 100 percent of the political power by awarding him or her the seat at issue, is that the system enables more effective and stable governance. Representation versus effectiveness are the fundamental lines along which the battle is usually drawn; as the conflict is sometimes cast, "either you can have a representative parliament, or you can have strong and stable government." David M. Farrell, Comparing Electoral Systems 153 (1997). We will examine some of the more specific points of conflict in a moment.

In this country, PR has never been a serious matter of public debate, with the exceptions of the limited local government experiments discussed above. This reluctance was only heightened in the aftermath of World War II, when PR was blamed as one of the causes that enabled the rise of German and Italian fascism. The causal mechanism offered to support this view was that PR led to governments that were so representative that they were unable to govern effectively; the paralysis that resulted generated clamor for effective leadership to address the countries' problems, thus opening the road to dictatorship. In a famous, highly detailed, and widely noticed book published in 1941, Democracy or Anarchy? A Study of Proportional Representation, Professor Ferdinand Hermens of Notre Dame developed this argument. In a chapter entitled "Proportional Representation and the Triumph of Hitler," Hermens began this way: "Nowhere have the consequences of P.R. so demonstrated the utter senselessness of the system as in Germany." Hermens purported to show, through detailed election analyses, that the Nazis' rise to power could be attributed to Weimar Germany's PR system: "P.R. was an essential factor in the breakdown of German democracy." So, too, Hermens argued that fascism had failed in France but succeeded in Italy because the former used majoritarian election systems and the latter used PR. But whether these powerful claims are factually accurate has been disputed. *See, e.g.,* Vernon Bogdanor, What is Proportional Representation 123 (1984). Nonetheless, Hermens' arguments have continued to exert a presence in the limited American debates over PR.

1. *Stability.* A common and powerful charge against PR systems is that they produce unstable governments. But as one leading election-systems scholar puts it: "There is no evidence whatsoever that proportional representation is likely to lead to instability." Vernon Bogdanor, What is Proportional Representation 147 (1984). As another remarks, "the charge of instability is one of the great myths surrounding PR." Douglas Amy, Real Choices, New Voices 159 (1993). For example, in a study of the number of governments various democracies have had between 1945–1992, the United Kingdom predictably fares well, with only 19, compared to countries like France and Italy, which have had 53 and 51. But the United Kingdom is only the sixth most stable on the list, with the five more stable systems all using PR (including Austria, Ireland, and the Netherlands).

The question of stability also depends on what one focuses on. Majoritarian systems can produce great fluctuations in policies even when public opinion shifts only slightly. The system tends to produce two principal parties, for reasons Duverger's Law explains, and small changes in votes from one of the two principal parties to the other can lead to a change in control of the government. If the two parties have widely differing ideologies, this can lead to massive changes in policy with only small shifts in actual voter preferences. Some believe this was manifested in the politics of Great Britain during the 1970s, when the Labour Party was oriented toward more socialist economic approaches and the Conservative Party toward free-market ones. Because the two parties alternated as the majority under the FPTP systems, government policy cycled between more socialist and more free-market systems, with industries being nationalized and de-nationalized. Segments of the business community joined the effort to move Great Britain to a PR system to avoid these dramatic swings in policy that made business planning difficult. The perceived advantage of PR is that governments are typically coalitions, which require greater consensus and compromise for policy changes; that coalitions tend to encourage greater continuity between governments when governments do shift; and that PR systems translate incremental changes in voter preferences into incremental changes in seats allocated to parties, rather than the dramatic shifts that can take place with majoritarian systems.

2. *Coalition Governments and Electoral Mandates.* Critics of PR sometimes argue that it tends to produce coalition governments between several parties, which is viewed as troubling, in part because such governments are said to lack a clear electoral mandate. This is another reason why PR is argued to produce ineffective governments, in addition to purportedly unstable ones. The critique of coalition governments is that voters do not know what policies they are voting for, because coalitions are put together by party leaders after electoral results are in. In addition, because no one party gains majority control, typically, voters cannot as readily hold "the government" responsible for failing to live up to campaign commitments. Majoritarian systems, by contrast, are said to empower one party to govern, which enables voters to hold that party accountable for government policies.

PR elections sometimes lead to one dominant party, but they do tend to produce coalition governments far more often than majoritarian systems. Amy, *supra*, at 157–160. But defenders of PR respond that voters frequently know in advance which coalitions are likely to emerge, either because parties declare so in advance or because it is clear which parties will work together should neither receive a decisive majority. As far as clear mandates go, the assumptions about majoritarian systems are subject to at least two challenges. First, how clear is it in countries like the United States that the party that wins control of the House, the Senate, and/or the Presidency, has a clear electoral mandate? Second, the seeming mandates that dominant parties win is often "manufactured" under majoritarian systems. A manufactured majority is one in which the party that gets a majority of seats does not receive a majority of the actual votes, but becomes a governing majority because of the way majoritarian systems overreward the dominant parties.

Manufactured majorities occur often in majoritarian systems but rarely in PR ones. Lijphart, *Democracies, supra,* at 166–68. As described in the answers to the Voting Quiz in Chapter 1, during the time the Conservative Party governed the United Kingdom from 1979–1996, it never won more than 44 percent of the actual vote. In 1992, it received only 41.9 percent of the vote. Most of the other votes went to the main party on the left, Labour, as well as to the Liberal Democrats, a third party also to the left of the Conservatives. Hence, the "mandate" of the Conservative Party was perhaps rejected by a majority of voters, yet without PR, the Conservative Party was able to control government policy.

The division between proportional and majoritarian systems may be thought of as turning on *when* the voters get to express their preferences: before or after the formation of a government. Proportional systems may be thought of as allowing for the lessening of wasted votes by allowing candidates to run closer to the actual preferences of more voters. By contrast, majoritarian systems may claim to allow better accountability for the actual conduct of governance by forcing one party to run on its record of performance. Consider the following argument made on behalf of non-proportional representation during the reconstitution of Polish parliamentary elections in the post-Soviet era:

> Every system of representation involves some form of aggregation of private preferences into a collective choice, but most participants in the drafting process have not clearly observed this point. In this respect the different electoral systems differ only with respect to the point in time at which the various groups must strike a compromise to produce an effective majority. In the system of proportional representation, this bargain is struck after the elections, when the parties must agree to form a government or pass new legislation. In the majoritarian system, by contrast, the key compromises are made before the election, when various social interests must come together around a party program that can gain a majority of the popular vote. In the majoritarian system, therefore, diverse social interests tend to form two political blocs, each tending toward the center of the political spectrum, and the election itself tends to become a plebiscite on the fate of the bloc in power.

The system of proportional representation, on the other hand, provides no premium for shaping broad coalition programs. On the contrary, the most rational policy is to form narrowly based parties and enter into coalitions only after elections. But then the voters can hold no single party to account for the government's policies each party can still claim to represent the interests of its constituency, and if the government's program does not correspond to the preferences of a party's voters, the party can always attempt to shift the blame to other parties with which it formed a post election coalition. Consequently, the most important political decisions, namely those that aggregate individual (or group) choices into social policies, are never directly subjected to popular approval. The strong theory of representation underlying proportional representation, affirming the identity of the governors and the governed, thus clashes with the strong theory of governmental responsibility, which allows for direct electoral control of the team in power.

Andrzej Rapaczynski, *Constitutional Politics in Poland: A Report on the Constitutional Committee of the Polish Parliament*, 58 U.Chi. L. Rev. 595, 618–19 (1991).

3.   *Extremist and Fringe Parties.* Because PR does enable smaller parties to win seats, the concern arises that extremist parties will gain office, thus legitimating their views through the public platform officeholding provides. Indeed, one of the causes of the demise of PR in local governments in the United States was that during the 1930s and 1940s, some Communists began to win office in PR systems. One response might be that, to the extent marginal viewpoints do have some level of support, they ought to be represented; but that does not address the legitimation point. A somewhat more responsive argument advocates of PR make is that bringing such groups into formal politics actually moderates their views. Raising the threshold of exclusion is one structural way of combating this tendency of PR systems. But perhaps the most significant response is an empirical one: as a practical matter, PR does not appear to have facilitated the rise of extremist parties in post-War European countries. France, for example, now uses a majoritarian system for its direct elections for president, employing a second ballot or runoff system; under this system, the extreme right-wing National Front garnered about 6.5 percent of the vote. Farrell, *supra*, at 157. In a study of such parties in European democracies, the authors found that these parties had achieved comparable levels of support in both majoritarian countries and in PR countries, and that the level of support did not vary with the type of PR system used, thus making it difficult to see a connection between the PR system and the rise of such parties. *See* Michael Gallagher et. al., Representative Government in Modern Europe (2d ed. 1995). Nonetheless, PR systems by their very structure do enable smaller parties to gain office. The potential costs and benefits of that tendency, as well as the other advantages and disadvantages of PR, need to be compared in choosing an electoral structure.

Note also that the concern that PR provides "kingmaker" power to small parties might be of less concern in the United States. PR can produce this kind of result in parliamentary systems "in which not only legislative majorities but also executive power are reconstituted with each shift of electoral preferences." Samuel Issacharoff, *Supreme Court Destabilization of Single–Member Districts*, 1995 U. Chi. Legal F. 205, 237–38. To the extent versions of PR would be adopted in the United States in conjunction with continued direct elections for President or Governors, the power of coalitional partners in the legislature would be diminished.

4. *Election of Women*. PR systems enhance representation of women as compared to majoritarian systems. In a study of the number of women legislators in the lower house of a number of democracies, those using PR averaged 20 percent women, while those using majoritarian systems averaged 10.4 percent. Farrell, *supra*, at 151 (though the most recent elections in Great Britain in 1996 did see a dramatic surge in the number of women MPs). In another study of Western democracies from 1970–1991, those using majoritarian systems elected on average 5.8 percent women, while the comparable figure for PR systems was 14.7 percent women. Amy, *supra*, at 102–03. One confirmation that these differences reflect the differing electoral structures, rather than cultural differences, comes from elections within the same country. Thus, Australia, Japan, and Germany use both PR and single-member or small districts for some elections; the PR elections compared to the districted elections resulted in three times as many women winning office in Australia, ten times as many in Japan, and twice as many female officeholders in Germany between 1987–1993. Wilma Rule, *Why Women Should be Included in the Voting Rights Act*, National Civil Review 355, 363 (1995). For other studies reaching similar conclusions, see Pippa Norris, Politics and Sexual Equality: The Comparative Position of Women in Western Democracies (1987); R. Darcy et al., *Election Systems and the Representation of Black Women in American State Legislatures*, 13 Woman & Politics 73 (1993) (arguing that the problem of black political descriptive underrepresentation is primarily a problem of under-representation of black women officeholders).

The mechanism involved turns on the willingness of parties to nominate and support various candidates. In PR systems, parties do not run individual candidates; they put up a slate of candidates upon whom voters vote as a group (this is particularly true in closed-list PR systems). The parties thus face incentives to offer a slate that represents the diverse constituencies to which the party seeks to appeal. In some PR countries, particular parties have adopted quotas for the percentage of their candidates that should be women. For a survey and critical analysis of this approach, see Anne Phillips, The Politics of Presence 58–83 (1995). In single-member district elections, parties put up the individual candidates they believe are most likely to prevail; this often means candidates who appear uncontroversial, and often the safest candidate is perceived to be a man. Moreover, polarized voting against women or minority candidates can occur in a candidate-based election system, but not as readily in a PR system when voters must choose a party's slate as a whole.

Indeed, so strong is the tendency of alternative voting systems, such as cumulative, limited, and preference voting, as well as PR systems, to enhance descriptive representation of women compared to the tendency of single-member district systems, that some have argued that the Voting Rights Act as amended in 1982 has undermined women's representation. On this view, the very device emphasized in the 1982 amendments—single-member districts to replace at-large and multi-member elections—is precisely the device least likely to enhance women's representation. This argument concludes that the VRA should be amended to emphasize alternative voting systems and PR, and to move away from single-member districts, in order to "include" women in the VRA. Rule, *supra,* at 366.

With respect to the relationship between voting systems and the election of female legislators in the United States, Robert Darcy, Susan Welch, and Janet Clark examined election results from fourteen states and found that women were more likely to run and to be elected from multi-member districts than from single-member ones. Robert Darcy, Susan Welch & Janet Clark, *Women Candidates in Single– and Multi–Member Districts: American State Legislative Races,* 66 Soc. Sci. Q. 945 (1985). This relationship was confirmed by a study of Montana, which changed its electoral system to an exclusively single-member district one following one-person, one-vote litigation arising out of the post–1990 reapportionment. *See* Michael J. Horan & James D. King, *The Demise of the Multi–Member District Sustem and Its Effect Upon the Representation of Women,* 34 Land & Water L. Rev. 407 (1999). Horan and King offer several explanations for women's greater success in multi-member systems:

> First, party elites may exercise a kind of affirmative action, slating women or providing more campaign resources to women in multi-member districts. Pressure to support women candidates is more easily accommodated in multi-member districts than in single-member districts. Also, voters may similarly practice a form of affirmative action. Those with reservations concerning the qualifications of women for public office can cast one ballot for a woman in a multimember district knowing that they will also be represented by a man. Finally, the characteristics and accomplishments of individual candidates are often highlighted more than partisanship, in multimember districts. The typical head-to-head battle between a Republican and Democrat is replaced by something of a free-for-all where each candidate emphasizes his/her own strengths rather than his/her opponent's weaknesses. In this environment, gender gives women a distinctive characteristic, especially in districts where women candidates are novelties.

Id. at 413. Does Horan and King's analysis suggest that there has been a tradeoff between greater representation of minorities through the switch to single-member districts and less representation of women?

5. *Deliberation.* Which electoral system facilitates the appropriate kind of democratic deliberation? Does PR not only bring about fairer representation but also promote more deliberative democracy? Consider whether this view is persuasive:

> Defenders of single-member district representation argue that "government by majority is government by persuasion".... The trouble with these arguments, however, is that they ignore the strong tendency towards vagueness and ambiguity that is generated by these systems. Thus, the persuasion of ordinary citizens is of a superficial sort that leaves much of the decisionmaking to party leaders and leaders of interest groups who are at liberty to bargain with each other in the background. Often this bargaining on the basic points of the legislative agenda is done out of the sight of ordinary citizens and undermines their capacity to control the state. Furthermore, the system of single-member district representation puts a straitjacket on the kinds of issues that are discussed by citizens and parties. In general, the discussion in electoral campaigns tends to take place on a one-dimensional issue space. Discussion in proportional representation elections tends to involve more issues in a number of different dimensions. The single-member district system simplifies unnecessarily the process of social discussion. Some may argue that the multidimensionality of issues for discussion demonstrates that there is greater fragmentation in the public at large than when the issues are very simple. But surely this kind of fragmentation is precisely what we should expect from discussion amongst equals who have very different experiences and roles in the society. And such fragmentation should have the beneficial effect of getting all citizens to understand the diverse interests and points of view that exist in their society and deepening their understanding of how to fairly accommodate these interests.
>
> Overall, a scheme of proportional representation is superior to other electoral schemes in promoting rational social deliberation on the overall aims of society.

Thomas Christiano, The Rule of the Many: Fundamental Issues in Democratic Theory 261 (1996).

6. *Voter Turnout.* Advocates of PR argue that more voters will vote because fewer votes are wasted under PR. Seats are more closely tied to percentages of votes received; hence even voters who prefer a minor party have an incentive to turn out and vote for it. In a comprehensive study, Lijphart appears to confirm this claim: he concludes that average voter turnout is about 9 percent points higher in PR systems than in non-PR ones. Arend Lijphart, *Democracies: Forms, Performance, and Constitutional Engineering,* 26 European J. of Pol. Research 6–7 (1994).

7. *Gerrymandering.* The problems of gerrymandering within a single-member district system are ones that by now should be familiar to readers of this casebook. With PR, the problems of gerrymandering are significantly diminished. If the country as a whole is the electoral unit, no lines need to be drawn; if the country is divided into a few regions, only those lines must be defined. Moreover, the absence of the winner-take-all feature of majoritarian systems makes gerrymandering far less important, even where opportunities exist. Consider, though, whether the same forces that drive gerrymandering would appear elsewhere in the PR systems. Where might those pressures be channeled—into which choices, made by whom?

8. *Examples of PR failings in specific countries.* Critics of PR frequently point to particular countries whose governments are thought to bear out the critics' predictions. That most Western democracies use PR is less salient than that some countries using it are purportedly dominated by small, extremist parties and that effective governing coalitions are difficult to construct. *See, e.g.*, Sanford Levinson, *Gerrymandering and the Brooding Omnipresence of Proportional Representation: Why Won't It Go Away?*, 33 U.C.L.A. L. Rev. 257, 272 (1985) (using example of Israel to raise such concerns about PR). But the examples offered up in this way are frequently distinguished by the extreme versions of PR they use. Whatever their problems, they can be seen not as stemming from PR per se, but the peculiar versions of it they use. Thus, Israel, where small parties do wield exceptional power in the governing coalition, elects all 120 members of its Knesset in one, nationwide election. There are no regions, districts, or states. With 120 seats up for grabs at any one time, a party with as little as 1/120th of the vote (less than 1 percent) could historically have won a seat. In 1992, the threshold of exclusion was raised from 1.0 percent to 1.5 percent, still one of the lowest thresholds for representation in any PR country. Thus, the enormous magnitude of the election district, combined with such low thresholds, has made the Israeli PR system an extreme one— exceptionally prone to the traditional concerns about PR, including the power of small parties and the difficulty of establishing governing coalitions. To enable more decisive government, Israel also subsequently moved to direct elections for its Prime Minister.

Of course, for every country that suffers from political problems that might be associated with PR (Italy was another frequently offered example, before recent reforms in its electoral laws), there are other countries, such as Germany and Austria, that have had strong and stable governments since World War II while using forms of PR.

H. CONSOCIATIONAL DEMOCRACY

A theme through much of the law and theory of democracy has been that of ensuring adequate representation of, and attention to, the interest of minorities within democratic regimes. Proportional representation and alternative voting systems such as cumulative voting, STV, and limited voting are designed to enhance the political representation of such groups. Depending on the particular cultural, historical, and political context, these forms of representation might be sufficient to ensure a well-functioning democratic system when viewed from the vantage point of the different groupings in the society. But if the cleavages between various groups are profound and enduring enough, even these alternatives might be insufficient. The kind of cleavages that have tended to work this way have been at times religious, tribal, ethnic, racial, linguistic, cultural, or some combination of these. After all, even greater presence inside the institutions of political power does not prevent minority groups from still being political minorities, capable of being outvoted by hostile political majorities.

When territories are riven with such conflicts, one possibility is that the relevant groups should be separated and not made to co-exist within the same, single nation-state. Writing in the nineteenth century, the liberal political philosopher John Stuart Mill famously asserted: "Free institutions are next to impossible in a country made up of different nationalities. Among a people without fellow-feeling, especially if they read and speak different languages, the united public opinion, necessary to the working of representative government, cannot exist." John Stuart Mill, Considerations on Representative Government 230 (C. Shields ed. 1958). But another possibility is that creative engineering of democratic institutions might enable stability and a sufficient level of cooperation to emerge even in the midst of these kinds of conflicts. Consociational democracy is the name that has been given to the institutional structures devised in several countries to attempt to sustain democracy in the midst of powerful differences. Are these structures the last frontier in democratic institutional design?

Consider in what circumstances existing or newly forming countries should consider adopting some of these features. Are there any circumstances in the United States today in which it would be worth contemplating using consociational structures?

1. *Theory and Structure.* The basic focus of consociational structures is to foster cooperation among political elites. Countries can adopt one or more element of consociational structures, but the classic work on these systems identifies the four common elements as (1) government by a grand coalition of all significant segments; (2) a mutual veto or concurrent-majority voting rule for some or all issues; (3) proportionality as the principle for allocating political representation, public funds, and civil service positions; (4) considerable autonomy for various segments of the society to govern their internal affairs. Arend Lijphart, Democracy in Plural Societies: A Comparative Exploration 25 (1977).

Grand coalitions aim to replace the model of a governing majority and an opposition that, roughly, take turns in office over time. The stakes in politics are considered too high in the divided societies involved; being part of the government is designed to provide some security and protection. Grand coalitions can take several forms. The four European countries that have used forms of consociationalism and that are the focus of Lijphart's study are Austria, Belgium, the Netherlands, and Switzerland. The apogee of consociationalism in these countries, when they were most divided, was the late 1950s; since then, consociationalism has declined because, according to Lijphart, it succeeded. In Switzerland, the federal executive branch was governed by a seven-member body, according to a "magic formula:" the seats were set aside for the four main parties, 2–2–2–1, roughly proportional to their nationwide support, and the seven members also represented the different regions and languages of the country. Post–World War II Austria was governed from 1945–1966 by a coalition cabinet with balanced delegations from the two dominant parties. Temporary grand coalitions of party leaders were created to resolve the same, exceptionally divisive issue in the Netherlands in 1917 and Belgium in 1958: state aid to religious schools.

Minority vetoes can be formal or informal. They hearken back to John C. Calhoun's unsuccessful pre-Civil War advocacy of a concurrent majority system for the United States Congress, in which a majority from each section of the country, North and South, would have to approve legislation concurrently for it to become law. In contemporary times, an example of a formal minority veto is the Constitution of Belgium, amended in 1970 to require that any bill affecting the "cultural autonomy" of the country's two principal linguistic groups—a Dutch-speaking majority and a French-speaking minority—requires not only the approval of two-thirds majorities in each chamber of the legislature, but also approval of a majority of the legislators from each linguistic group.

The proportionality principle for allocating positions and funds involves group-preference policies and is relatively straightforward; note that in some systems, minority groups get overrepresentation in office or employment or funding. Finally, segmental autonomy seeks to give distinct groups large degrees of autonomous power, particularly over such issues as affect the groups with little spillover to other groups. This autonomy is facilitated by geographical concentration of the relevant groups, in which case autonomy can be territorially based—the strong independent role of the Swiss cantons being one example (federalism can be one form of such autonomy, depending on how it is applied)—but segmental autonomy can also be "personality" based where the segments are too geographically intermingled. In cultural affairs, Belgium, the Netherlands, and Austria all provide substantial decisional autonomy to their different cultural groups, but through power-sharing and voting rules, rather than through territorial allocations of power.

2. *Favorable Conditions.* Austria, Belgium, and the Netherlands are viewed as the most divided of Western democracies, with Switzerland in the middle of the spectrum. In Belgium, for example, about half the population is French speaking, about half Dutch speaking, with strong religious and cultural divides as well.

Consociationalism rests on the hope that elite leaders of the various divided groups can cooperate and compromise. It thus requires that these leaders be committed to maintaining the unity of the country and to democratic politics. Success depends on "the extent to which party leaders are more tolerant than their followers" and "are yet able to carry them along." Hans Daalder, *Parties, Elites, and Political Developments in Western Europe*, in Political Parties and Political Development 69 (Joseph LaPalombara & Myron Weiner eds. 1966). In addition, Lijphart concludes that the following conditions make success more likely with consociational structures for divided societies: (1) a multiple balance of power among three or more groups; (2) small country size; (3) territorial isolation of the various segments; (4) overarching loyalties; (5) prior traditions of elite accommodation; (6) crosscutting cleavages.

The balance of power point is particularly interesting. If one segment has a clear majority, it is likely to seek to govern through majoritarian forms. If there are two principal groups of roughly equal size, they may engage in continual struggle to become the sole, dominant governing power. Thus, consociationalism is thought to work best when there are multiple groups, without the prospect of one becoming dominant (too many groups, however, can make governing more difficult). Note the similarity to Madison's defense in *The Federalist Papers* No. 10 of a large republic precisely because it will contain so many factions that they will cancel each other out. Isolation of the different segments, such as geographic concentration of different groups in specific regions, helps because in societies to which this model extends, closer contact among the different groups has already been judged to increase rather than diminish conflict and hostility. Thus, isolation can facilitate devolution of more autonomy to each group without imposing as many externalities on other groups. Finally, the more that the relevant cleavages are crosscutting—so that religious divides do not map perfectly onto linguistic divides, or ethnic divides onto cultural ones—the more likely accommodation and compromise appear to be. When the same cleavages track each other recurrently, consociationalism is apparently less likely to succeed.

The question whether the consociational forms from these few Western European countries are likely to extend successfully to other divided societies, with a focus on African countries, is comprehensively explored in Donald L. Horowitz, Ethnic Groups in Conflict (1985). He argues that, compared to the group conflicts within modern African states, the ones in the European countries are "less ascriptive in character, less severe in intensity, less exclusive in their command of the loyalty of participants, and less preemptive of other forms of conflict." *Id.* at 572. Thus, he concludes that finding democratic arrangements to stabilize these divisions is both more necessary and more difficult. Horowitz also provides case studies of consociationalism in several other countries, including Lebanon, Nigeria, Sri Lanka, and Guyana. For a critical account of consociationalism, including an account of how recently minted democracies have shied away from formal power-sharing of this sort, see Samuel Issacharoff, *Constitutionalizing Democracy in Fractured Societies*, 82 Tex. L. Rev. 1861 (2004).

3. *Costs.* The most difficult calculus with consociationalism is whether the divisions are so deeply entrenched as to justify this approach. As even defenders of this system acknowledge, in the short run, consociational structures more deeply entrench the relevant divisions. Thus, a prior judgment is required that these divisions are profound enough that efforts to overcome them are less promising than efforts "to recognize them and to turn the segments into constructive elements of stable democracy." Lijphart, *supra,* at 42. Note the parallel with debates over whether race-conscious districting in the United States merely recognizes the reality of racially-polarized voting or accentuates race-consciousness.

Other potential concerns are that government can become paralyzed or unable to act efficiently because consociational structures require such widespread agreement before action is possible. There is also the problem that, these systems focus more on ensuring equality among the relevant groups, rather than a focus on equal treatment of individuals; indeed, to the extent they grant autonomy to specific groups, such systems might enable groups to exert more conformist pressures over their members. In addition, the vision of democracy is more elite oriented than mass oriented. The question must be whether these costs are worth bearing in light of the alternatives in deeply divided societies. Finally, as Horowitz points out, the very question of how to measure whether consociational systems have been effective is uncertain; is mere stability and preservation of the state sufficient, or should success be understood to require more? Absence of violence? Economic prosperity? The reduction of differences? *See* Horowitz, *supra,* at 570–71.

4. *American Consociationalism?* Should any features of consociationalism be brought into American structures for democracy at either the local or national level? Lijphart argues that contrasts between countries using these structures and those that do not are overdrawn: "The fundamental error ... is to exaggerate the degree of homogeneity of the Western democratic states." Lijphart, *supra,* at 21. Are the problems of racial polarization really profound and intractable enough in the United States that features of consociationalism would be appropriate? What about the cultural, religious, and linguistic conflicts between Quebec and other parts of Canada?

Lani Guinier has raised the possibility of employing some consociational features to address problems of race in the United States: " 'A minority veto' for legislation of vital importance to minority interests would respond to evidence of gross 'deliberative gerrymanders.' [These are means majority legislators might use to undermine the power of minority legislators]. Alternatively, depending on the proof of disproportionate majority power, plaintiffs might seek minority assent through other supermajority arrangements, concurrent legislative majorities, consociational arrangements, or rotation in office." *See* Lani Guinier, *The Triumph of Tokenism: The Voting Rights Act and the Theory of Black Electoral Success,* 89 Mich. L.

Rev. 1077, 1140 (1991). Would any of these structural changes be desirable? In what circumstances? There are some examples already in place: after the district court (on remand from the Supreme Court's decision in *City of Mobile v. Bolden* 446 U.S. 55 (1980)) found the at-large electoral structure for city commissioners in Mobile, Alabama, to be unconstitutionally enacted and maintained for discriminatory purposes, the black and white political leaders negotiated a supermajority voting requirement for the reformed City Commission. This provision required affirmative votes from five of the seven commissioners to pass any rules or "transact any business;" three of the seven single-member electoral districts have black voter majorities. For discussion of this provision, see Guinier, Tyranany of the Majority, *supra*, at 17.

Some states routinely use supermajority requirements. For example, California requires a two-thirds vote in each house of the legislature to enact a state budget or approve appropriations. In addition, several of the important initiatives voters have adopted there in recent years impose supermajority voting requirements for certain legislation; for example, Proposition 13, which capped property tax increases, requires a two-third legislative vote to raise most taxes. For the view that California policymaking has become paralyzed as a result of the minority veto these voting requirements give powerful groups, particularly the cumulative effect of all the various supermajority requirements under which the State now operates, see Peter Schrag, *California's Elected Anarchy: A Government Destroyed by Popular Referendum*, Harper's Magazine 50 (Nov. 1994). Schrag notes that tax breaks can be approved through a simple majority vote, but can only be abolished through a supermajority vote because ending a tax break is treated as a "tax increase."

5. For other important works on consociationalism, see Brian Barry, *The Consociational Model and Its Dangers*, 3 European Journal of Political Research 405 (1975); Hans Daalder, *The Consociational Democracy Theme*, 26 World Politics 616 (1974); H. Daalder, *Parties, Elites, and Political Developments in Western Europe*, in Political Parties and Political Development (Jospeph LaPalombara & Myron Weiner eds. 1966); Robert Dahl, Political Oppositions in Western Democracies (1966).

*

THE UNITED STATES CONSTITUTION

We the People of the United States, in order to form a more perfect Union, establish Justice, insure domestic tranquility, provide for common defense, promote the general Welfare, and secure the Blessings of Liberty to ourselves and our Posterity, do ordain and establish this Constitution for the United States of America.

Article I

Section 1.

All legislative Powers herein granted shall be vested in a Congress of the United States, which shall consist of a Senate and House of Representatives.

Section 2.

The House of Representatives shall be composed of Members chosen every second Year by the People of the several States, and the Electors in each State shall have the Qualifications requisite for Electors of the most numerous Branch of the State Legislature.

No Person shall be a Representative who shall not have attained to the Age of twenty five Years, and been seven Years a Citizen of the United States, and who shall not, when elected, be an Inhabitant of that State in which he shall be chosen.

Representatives and direct Taxes shall be apportioned among the several States which may be included within this Union, according to their respective numbers, which shall be determined by adding to the whole Number of free Persons, including those bound to Service for a Term of Years, and excluding Indians not taxed, three fifths of all other Persons. The actual Enumeration shall be made within three Years after the first Meeting of the Congress of the United States, and within every subsequent Term of ten Years, in such Manner as they shall by Law direct. The Number of Representatives shall not exceed one for every thirty Thousand, but each State shall have at Least one Representative; and until such enumeration shall be made, the State of New Hampshire shall be entitled to choose three, Massachusetts eight, Rhode–Island and Providence Plantations one, Connecticut five, New–York six, New Jersey four, Pennsylvania eight, Delaware one, Maryland six, Virginia ten, North Carolina five, South Carolina five, and Georgia three.

The House of Representatives shall chuse their Speaker and other Officers; and shall have the sole Power of Impeachment.

Section 3.

The Senate of the United States shall be composed of two Senators from each State, chosen by the Legislature thereof, for six Years; and each Senator shall have one Vote.

Immediately after they shall be assembled in Consequence of the first Election, they shall be divided as equally as may be into three Classes. The Seats of the Senators of the first Class shall be vacated at the Expiration of the second Year, of the second Class at the Expiration of the fourth Year, and of the third Class at the Expiration of the sixth Year, so that one third may be chosen every second Year; and if Vacancies happen by Resignation, or otherwise, during the Recess of the Legislature of any State, the Executive thereof may make temporary Appointments until the next Meeting of the Legislature, which shall then fill such Vacancies.

No Person shall be a Senator who shall not have attained to the Age of thirty Years, and been nine Years a Citizen of the United States, and who shall not, when elected, be an Inhabitant of that State for which he shall be chosen.

The Vice President of the United States shall be President of the Senate, but shall have no Vote, unless they be equally divided.

The Senate shall choose their other Officers, and also a President pro tempore, in the Absence of the Vice President, or when he shall exercise the Office of President of the United States.

The Senate shall have the sole Power to try all Impeachment's. When sitting for that Purpose, they shall be on Oath or Affirmation. When the President of the United States is tried, the Chief Justice shall preside: And no Person shall be convicted without the Concurrence of two thirds of the Members present.

Judgment in Cases of Impeachment shall not extend further than to removal from Office, and disqualification to hold and enjoy any Office of honor, Trust or Profit under the United States: but the Party convicted shall nevertheless be liable and subject to Indictment, Trial, Judgment and Punishment, according to Law.

Section 4.

The Times, Places and Manner of holding Elections for Senators and Representatives, shall be prescribed in each State by the Legislature thereof; but the Congress may at any time by Law make or alter such Regulations, except as to the Places of choosing Senators.

The Congress shall assemble at least once in every Year, and such Meeting shall be on the first Monday in December, unless they shall by Law appoint a different Day.

Section 5.

Each House shall be the Judge of the Elections, Returns and Qualifications of its own Members, and a Majority of each shall constitute a Quorum to do Business; but a smaller Number may adjourn from day to day, and may be authorized to compel the Attendance of absent Members, in such Manner, and under such Penalties as each House may provide.

Each House may determine the Rules of its Proceedings, punish its Members for disorderly Behaviour, and, with the Concurrence of two thirds, expel a Member.

Each House shall keep a Journal of its Proceedings, and from time to time publish the same, excepting such Parts as may in their Judgment require Secrecy; and the Yeas and Nays of the Members of either House on any question shall, at the Desire of one fifth of those Present, be entered on the Journal.

Neither House, during the Session of Congress, shall, without the Consent of the other, adjourn for more than three days, nor to any other Place than that in which the two Houses shall be sitting.

Section 6.

The Senators and Representatives shall receive a Compensation for their Services, to be ascertained by Law, and paid out of the Treasury of the United States. They shall in all Cases, except Treason, Felony and Breach of the Peace, be privileged from Arrest during their Attendance at the Session of their respective Houses, and in going to and returning from the same; and for any Speech or Debate in either House, they shall not be questioned in any other Place.

No Senator or Representative shall, during the Time for which he was elected, be appointed to any civil Office under the Authority of the United States, which shall have been created, or the Emoluments whereof shall have been encreased during such time; and no Person holding any Office under the United States, shall be a Member of either House during his Continuance in Office.

Section 7.

All Bills for raising Revenue shall originate in the House of Representatives; but the Senate may propose or concur with Amendments as on other Bills.

Every Bill which shall have passed the House of Representatives and the Senate, shall, before it become a Law, be presented to the President of the United States; If he approve he shall sign it, but if not he shall return it, with his Objections to that House in which it shall have originated, who shall enter the Objections at large on their Journal, and proceed to reconsider it. If after such Reconsideration two thirds of that House shall agree to pass the Bill, it shall be sent, together with the Objections, to the other House, by which it shall likewise be reconsidered, and if approved by two thirds of that House, it shall become a Law. But in all such Cases the Votes of both Houses shall be determined by yeas and Nays, and the Names of the Persons voting for and against the Bill shall be entered on the Journal of each House respectively. If any Bill shall not be returned by the President within ten Days (Sundays excepted) after it shall have been presented to him, the Same shall be a Law, in like Manner as if he had signed it, unless the Congress by their Adjournment prevent its Return, in which Case it shall not be a Law.

Every Order, Resolution, or Vote to which the Concurrence of the Senate and House of Representatives may be necessary (except on a question of adjournment) shall be presented to the President of the United States; and before the Same shall take Effect, shall be approved by him, or being disapproved by him, shall be repassed by two thirds of the Senate and House of Representatives, according to the Rules and Limitations prescribed in the Case of a Bill.

Section 8.

The Congress shall have Power To lay and collect Taxes, Duties, Imposts and Excises, to pay the Debts and provide for the common Defense and general Welfare of the United States; but all Duties, Imposts and Excises shall be uniform throughout the United States;

To borrow Money on the credit of the United States;

To regulate Commerce with foreign Nations, and among the several States, and with the Indian Tribes;

To establish an uniform Rule of Naturalization, and uniform Laws on the subject of Bankruptcies throughout the United States;

To coin Money, regulate the Value thereof, and of foreign Coin, and fix the Standard of Weights and Measures;

To provide for the Punishment of counterfeiting the Securities and current Coin of the United States;

To establish Post Offices and post Roads;

To promote the Progress of Science and useful Arts, by securing for limited Times to Authors and Inventors the exclusive Right to their respective Writings and Discoveries;

To constitute Tribunals inferior to the supreme Court;

To define and punish Piracies and Felonies committed on the high Seas, and Offences against the Law of Nations;

To declare War, grant Letters of Marque and Reprisal, and make Rules concerning Captures on Land and Water;

To raise and support Armies, but no Appropriation of Money to that Use shall be for a longer Term than two Years;

To provide and maintain a Navy;

To make Rules for the Government and Regulation of the land and naval Forces;

To provide for calling forth the Militia to execute the Laws of the Union, suppress Insurrections and repel Invasions;

To provide for organizing, arming, and disciplining, the Militia, and for governing such Part of them as may be employed in the Service of the United States, reserving to the States respectively, the Appointment of the Officers, and the Authority of training the Militia according to the discipline prescribed by Congress;

To exercise exclusive Legislation in all Cases whatsoever, over such District (not exceeding ten Miles square) as may, by Cession of particular States, and the Acceptance of Congress, become the Seat of the Government of the United States, and to exercise like Authority over all Places purchased by the Consent of the Legislature of the State in which the Same shall be, for the Erection of Forts, Magazines, Arsenals, dock-Yards, and other needful Buildings;—And

To make all Laws which shall be necessary and proper for carrying into Execution the foregoing Powers, and all other Powers vested by this Constitution in the Government of the United States, or in any Department or Officer thereof.

Section 9.

The Migration or Importation of such Persons as any of the States now existing shall think proper to admit, shall not be prohibited by the Congress prior to the Year one thousand eight hundred and eight, but a Tax or duty may be imposed on such Importation, not exceeding ten dollars for each Person.

The Privilege of the Writ of Habeas Corpus shall not be suspended, unless when in Cases of Rebellion or Invasion the public Safety may require it.

No Bill of Attainder or ex post facto Law shall be passed.

No Capitation, or other direct, Tax shall be laid, unless in Proportion to the Census or Enumeration herein before directed to be taken.

No Tax or Duty shall be laid on Articles exported from any State.

No Preference shall be given by any Regulation of Commerce or Revenue to the Ports of one State over those of another: nor shall Vessels bound to, or from, one State, be obliged to enter, clear, or pay Duties in another.

No Money shall be drawn from the Treasury, but in Consequence of Appropriations made by Law; and a regular Statement and Account of the Receipts and Expenditures of all public Money shall be published from time to time.

No Title of Nobility shall be granted by the United States: And no Person holding any Office of Profit or Trust under them, shall, without the Consent of the Congress, accept of any present, Emolument, Office, or Title, of any kind whatever, from any King, Prince, or foreign State.

Section 10.

No State shall enter into any Treaty, Alliance, or Confederation; grant Letters of Marque and Reprisal; coin Money; emit Bills of Credit; make any Thing but gold and silver Coin a Tender in Payment of Debts; pass any Bill of Attainder, ex post facto Law, or Law impairing the Obligation of Contracts, or grant any Title of Nobility.

No State shall, without the Consent of the Congress, lay any Imposts or Duties on Imports or Exports, except what may be absolutely necessary for executing it's inspection Laws: and the net Produce of all Duties and Imposts, laid by any State on Imports or Exports, shall be for the Use of the Treasury of the United States; and all such Laws shall be subject to the Revision and Control of the Congress.

No State shall, without the Consent of Congress, lay any Duty of Tonnage, keep Troops, or Ships of War in time of Peace, enter into any Agreement or Compact with another State, or with a foreign Power, or engage in War, unless actually invaded, or in such imminent Danger as will not admit of delay.

Article II

Section 1.

The executive Power shall be vested in a President of the United States of America. He shall hold his Office during the Term of four Years, and, together with the Vice President, chosen for the same Term, be elected, as follows

Each State shall appoint, in such Manner as the Legislature thereof may direct, a Number of Electors, equal to the whole Number of Senators and representatives to which the State may be entitled in the Congress: but no Senator or Representative, or Person holding an Office of Trust or Profit under the United States, shall be appointed an Elector.

The Electors shall meet in their respective States, and vote by Ballot for two Persons, of whom one at least shall not be an Inhabitant of the same State with themselves. And they shall make a List of all the Persons voted for, and of the Number of Votes for each; which List they shall sign and certify, and transmit sealed to the Seat of the Government of the United States, directed to the President of the Senate. The President of the Senate shall, in the Presence of the Senate and House of Representatives, open all the Certificates, and the Votes shall then be counted. The Person having the greatest Number of Votes shall be the President, if such Number be a Majority of the whole Number of Electors appointed; and if there be more than one who have such Majority, and have an equal Number of Votes, then the House of Representatives shall immediately chuse by Ballot one of them for President; and if no Person have a Majority, then from the five highest on the List the said House shall in like Manner chuse the President. But in chusing the President, the Votes shall be taken by States, the Representation from each State having one Vote; A quorum for this Purpose shall consist of a Member or Members from two thirds of the States, and a Majority of all the States shall be necessary to a Choice. In every Case, after the Choice of the President, the Person having the greatest Number of Votes of the Electors shall be the Vice President. But if there should remain two or more who have equal Votes, the Senate shall chuse from them by Ballot the Vice President.

The Congress may determine the Time of chusing the Electors, and the Day on which they shall give their Votes; which Day shall be the same throughout the United States.

No Person except a natural born Citizen, or a Citizen of the United States, at the time of the Adoption of this Constitution, shall be eligible to the Office of President; neither shall any Person be eligible to that Office who shall not have attained to the Age of thirty five Years, and been fourteen Years a Resident within the United States.

In Case of the Removal of the President from Office, or of his Death, Resignation, or Inability to discharge the Powers and Duties of the said Office, the Same shall devolve on the Vice President, and the Congress may by Law provide for the Case of Removal, Death, Resignation or Inability, both of the President and Vice President, declaring what Officer shall then act as President, and such Officer shall act accordingly, until the Disability be removed, or a President shall be elected.

The President shall, at stated Times, receive for his Services, a Compensation, which shall neither be encreased nor diminished during the Period for which he shall have been elected, and he shall not receive within that Period any other Emolument from the United States, or any of them.

Before he enter on the Execution of his Office, he shall take the following Oath or Affirmation:—"I do solemnly swear (or affirm) that I will faithfully execute the Office of President of the United States, and will to the best of my Ability, preserve, protect and defend the Constitution of the United States."

Section 2.

The President shall be Commander in Chief of the Army and Navy of the United States, and of the Militia of the several States, when called into the actual Service of the United States; he may require the Opinion, in writing, of the principal Officer in each of the executive Departments, upon any Subject relating to the Duties of their respective Offices, and he shall have Power to grant Reprieves and Pardons for Offences against the United States, except in Cases of Impeachment.

He shall have Power, by and with the Advice and Consent of the Senate, to make Treaties, provided two thirds of the Senators present concur; and he shall nominate, and by and with the Advice and Consent of the Senate, shall appoint Ambassadors, other public Ministers and Consuls, Judges of the supreme Court, and all other Officers of the United States, whose Appointments are not herein otherwise provided for, and which shall be established by Law: but the Congress may by Law vest the Appointment of such inferior Officers, as they think proper, in the President alone, in the Courts of Law, or in the Heads of Departments.

The President shall have Power to fill up all Vacancies that may happen during the Recess of the Senate, by granting Commissions which shall expire at the End of their next Session.

Section 3.

He shall from time to time give to the Congress Information of the State of the Union, and recommend to their Consideration such Measures as he shall judge necessary and expedient; he may, on extraordinary Occasions, convene both Houses, or either of them, and in Case of Disagreement between them, with Respect to the Time of Adjournment, he may adjourn them to such Time as he shall think proper; he shall receive Ambassadors and other public Ministers; he shall take Care that the Laws be faithfully executed, and shall Commission all the Officers of the United States.

Section 4.

The President, Vice President and all civil Officers of the United States, shall be removed from Office on Impeachment for, and Conviction of, Treason, Bribery, or other high Crimes and Misdemeanors.

Article III

Section 1.

The judicial Power of the United States, shall be vested in one supreme Court, and in such inferior Courts as the Congress may from time to time ordain and establish. The Judges, both of the supreme and inferior Courts, shall hold their Offices during good Behaviour, and shall, at stated Times, receive for their Services, a Compensation, which shall not be diminished during their Continuance in Office.

Section 2.

The judicial Power shall extend to all Cases, in Law and Equity, arising under this Constitution, the Laws of the United States, and Treaties made, or which shall be made, under their Authority;—to all Cases affecting Ambassadors, other public Ministers and Consuls;—to all Cases of admiralty and maritime Jurisdiction;—to Controversies to which the United States shall be a Party;—to Controversies between two or more States;—between a State and Citizens of another State; between Citizens of different

States,—between Citizens of the same State claiming Lands under Grants of different States, and between a State, or the Citizens thereof, and foreign States, Citizens or Subjects.

In all Cases affecting Ambassadors, other public Ministers and Consuls, and those in which a State shall be Party, the supreme Court shall have original Jurisdiction. In all the other Cases before mentioned, the supreme Court shall have appellate Jurisdiction, both as to Law and Fact, with such Exceptions, and under such Regulations as the Congress shall make.

The Trial of all Crimes, except in Cases of Impeachment, shall be by Jury; and such Trial shall be held in the State where the said Crimes shall have been committed; but when not committed within any State, the Trial shall be at such Place or Places as the Congress may by Law have directed.

Section 3.

Treason against the United States, shall consist only in levying War against them, or in adhering to their Enemies, giving them Aid and Comfort. No Person shall be convicted of Treason unless on the Testimony of two Witnesses to the same overt Act, or on Confession in open Court.

The Congress shall have Power to declare the Punishment of Treason, but no Attainder of Treason shall work Corruption of Blood, or Forfeiture except during the Life of the Person attainted.

Article IV

Section 1.

Full Faith and Credit shall be given in each State to the public Acts, Records, and judicial Proceedings of every other State. And the Congress may by general laws prescribe the Manner in which such Acts, Records and Proceedings shall be proved, and the Effect thereof.

Section 2.

The Citizens of each State shall be entitled to all Privileges and Immunities of Citizens in the several States.

A Person charged in any State with Treason, Felony, or other Crime, who shall flee from Justice, and be found in another State, shall on Demand of the executive Authority of the State from which he fled, be delivered up, to be removed to the State having Jurisdiction of the Crime.

No Person held to Service or Labour in one State, under the Laws thereof, escaping into another, shall, in Consequence of any Law or Regulation therein, be discharged from such Service or Labour, but shall be delivered up on Claim of the Party to whom such Service or Labour may be due.

Section 3.

New States may be admitted by the Congress into this Union; but no new State shall be formed or erected within the Jurisdiction of any other State;

nor any State be formed by the Junction of two or more States, or Parts of States, without the Consent of the Legislatures of the States concerned as well as of the Congress.

The Congress shall have Power to dispose of and make all needful Rules and Regulations respecting the Territory or other Property belonging to the United States; and nothing in this Constitution shall be so construed as to Prejudice any Claims of the United States, or of any particular State.

Section 4.

The United States shall guarantee to every State in this Union a Republican Form of Government, and shall protect each of them against Invasion; and on Application of the Legislature, or of the Executive (when the Legislature cannot be convened) against domestic Violence.

Article V

The Congress, whenever two thirds of both Houses shall deem it necessary, shall propose Amendments to this Constitution, or, on the Application of the Legislatures of two thirds of the several States, shall call a Convention for proposing Amendments, which, in either Case, shall be valid to all Intents and Purposes, as Part of this Constitution, when ratified by the Legislatures of three fourths of the several States, or by Conventions in three fourths thereof, as the one or the other Mode of Ratification may be proposed by the Congress; Provided that no Amendment which may be made prior to the Year One thousand eight hundred and eight shall in any Manner affect the first and fourth Clauses in the Ninth Section of the first Article; and that no State, without its Consent, shall be deprived of its equal Suffrage in the Senate.

Article VI

All Debts contracted and Engagements entered into, before the Adoption of this Constitution, shall be as valid against the United States under this Constitution, as under the Confederation.

This Constitution, and the Laws of the United States which shall be made in Pursuance thereof; and all Treaties made, or which shall be made, under the Authority of the United States, shall be the supreme Law of the Land; and the Judges in every State shall be bound thereby, any Thing in the Constitution or Laws of any State to the Contrary notwithstanding.

The Senators and Representatives before mentioned, and the Members of the several State Legislatures, and all executive and judicial Officers, both of the United States and of the several States, shall be bound by Oath or Affirmation, to support this Constitution; but no religious Test shall ever be required as a Qualification to any Office or public Trust under the United States.

Article VII

The Ratification of the Conventions of nine States, shall be sufficient for the Establishment of this Constitution between the States so ratifying the Same. done in Convention by the Unanimous Consent of the States present the Seventeenth Day of September in the Year of our Lord one thousand seven hundred and Eighty seven and of the Independence of the United States of America the Twelfth In witness whereof We have hereunto subscribed our Names.

AMENDMENTS

Amendment I

(Ratified in 1791.)

Congress shall make no law respecting an establishment of religion, or prohibiting the free exercise thereof; or abridging the freedom of speech, or of the press; or the right of the people peaceably to assemble, and to petition the Government for a redress of grievances.

Amendment II

(Ratified in 1791.)

A well regulated Militia, being necessary to the security of a free State, the right of the people to keep and bear Arms, shall not be infringed.

Amendment III

(Ratified in 1791.)

No Soldier shall, in time of peace be quartered in any house, without the consent of the Owner, nor in time of war, but in a manner to be prescribed by law.

Amendment IV

(Ratified in 1791.)

The right of the People to be secure in their persons, houses, papers, and effects, against unreasonable searches and seizures, shall not be violated, and no Warrants shall issue, but upon probable cause, supported by Oath or affirmation, and particularity describing the place to be searched, and the persons or things to be seized.

Amendment V

(Ratified in 1791.)

No person shall be held to answer for a capital, or otherwise infamous crime, unless on a presentment or indictment of a Grand Jury, except in cases arising in the land or naval forces, or in the Militia, when in actual service in time of War or public danger; nor shall any person be subject for the same offence to be twice put in jeopardy of life or limb; nor shall be compelled in any criminal case to be a witness against himself, nor be deprived of life, liberty, or property, without due process of law; nor shall private property be taken for public use, without just compensation.

Amendment VI

(Ratified in 1791.)

In all criminal prosecutions, the accused shall enjoy the right to a speedy and public trial, by an impartial jury of the State and district wherein the crime shall have been committed, which district shall have been previously ascertained by law, and to be informed of the nature and cause of the accusation; to be confronted with the witnesses against him; to have compulsory process for obtaining witnesses in his favor, and to have Assistance of Counsel for his defense.

Amendment VII

(Ratified in 1791.)

In Suits at common law, where the value in controversy shall exceed twenty dollars, the right of trial by jury shall be preserved, and no fact tried by a jury, shall be otherwise re-examined in any Court of the United States, than according to the rules of the common law.

Amendment VIII

(Ratified in 1791.)

Excessive bail shall not be required, nor excessive fines imposed, nor cruel and unusual punishments inflicted.

Amendment IX

(Ratified in 1791.)

The enumeration in the Constitution, of certain rights, shall not be construed to deny or disparage others retained by the people.

Amendment X

(Ratified in 1791.)

The powers not delegated to the United States by the Constitution, nor prohibited by it to the States, are reserved to the States respectively, or to the people.

Amendment XI

(Ratified in 1795.)

The Judicial power of the United States shall not be construed to extend to any suit in law or equity, commenced or prosecuted against one of the United States by Citizens of another State, or by Citizens or Subjects of any Foreign State.

Amendment XII

(Ratified in 1804.)

The Electors shall meet in their respective states and vote by ballot for President and Vice–President, one of whom, at least, shall not be an inhabitant of the same state with themselves; they shall name in their ballots the person voted for as President, and in distinct ballots the person voted for as Vice–President, and they shall make distinct lists of all persons voted for as President, and of all persons voted for as Vice–President, and of the number of votes for each, which lists they shall sign and certify, and transmit sealed to the seat of the government of the United States, directed to the President of the Senate;—The President of the Senate shall, in the presence of the Senate and House of Representatives, open all the certificates and the votes shall then be counted;—The person having the greatest number of votes for President, shall be the President, if such number be a majority of the whole number of Electors appointed; and if no person have such majority, then from the persons having the highest numbers not exceeding three on the list of those voted for as President, the House of Representatives shall choose immediately, by ballot, the President. But in choosing the President, the votes shall be taken by states, the representation from each state having one vote; a quorum for this purpose shall consist of a member or members from two-thirds of the states, and a majority of all the states shall be necessary to a choice. And if the House of Representatives shall not choose a President whenever the right of choice shall devolve upon then, before the fourth day of March next following, then the Vice–President shall act as President, as in the case of the death or other constitutional disability of the President.—The person having the greatest number of votes as Vice–President, shall be the Vice–President, if such number be a majority of the whole number of Electors appointed, and if no person have a majority, then from the two highest numbers on the list, the Senate shall choose the Vice–President; a quorum for the purpose shall consist of two-thirds of the whole number of Senators, and a majority of the whole number shall be necessary to a choice. But no person constitutionally ineligible to the office of President shall be eligible to that of Vice–President of the United States.

Amendment XIII

(Ratified in 1865.)

Section 1.

Neither slavery nor involuntary servitude, except as a punishment for crime whereof the party shall have been duly convicted, shall exist within the United States, or any place subject to their jurisdiction.

Section 2.

Congress shall have power to enforce this article by appropriate legislation.

Amendment XIV
(Ratified in 1868.)

Section 1.

All persons born or naturalized in the United States, and subject to the jurisdiction thereof, are citizens of the United States and of the

State wherein they reside. No State shall make or enforce any law which shall abridge the privileges or immunities of citizens of the United States; nor shall any State deprive any person of life, liberty, or property, without due process of law; nor deny to any person within its jurisdiction the equal protection of the laws.

Section 2.

Representatives shall be apportioned among the several States according to their respective numbers, counting the whole number of persons in each State, excluding Indians not taxed. But when the right to vote at any election for the choice of electors for President and Vice President of the United States, Representatives in Congress, the Executive and Judicial officers of a State, or the members of the Legislature thereof, is denied to any of the male inhabitants of such State, being twenty-one years of age, and citizens of the United States, or in any way abridged, except for participation in rebellion, or other crime, the basis of representation therein shall be reduced in the proportion which the number of such male citizens shall bear to the whole number of male citizens twenty-one years of age in such State.

Section 3.

No person shall be a Senator or Representative in Congress, or elector of President and Vice President, or hold any office, civil or military, under the United States, or under any State, who, having previously taken an oath, as a member of Congress, or as an officer of the United States, or as a member of any State legislature, or as an executive or judicial officer of any State, to support the Constitution of the United States, shall have engaged in insurrection or rebellion against the same, or given aid or comfort to the enemies thereof. But Congress may by a vote of two-thirds of each House, remove such disability.

Section 4.

The validity of the public debt of the United States, authorized by law, including debts incurred for payment of pensions and bounties for services in suppressing insurrection or rebellion, shall not be questioned. But neither the United States nor any State shall assume or pay any debt or obligation incurred in aid of insurrection or rebellion against the United States, or any claim for the loss or emancipation of any slave; but all such debts, obligations and claims shall be held illegal and void.

Section 5.

The Congress shall have power to enforce, by appropriate legislation, the provisions of this article.

Amendment XV

(Ratified in 1870.)

Section 1.

The right of citizens of the United States to vote shall not be denied or abridged by the United States or by any State on account of race, color, or previous condition of servitude.

Section 2.

The Congress shall have power to enforce this article by appropriate legislation.

Amendment XVI

(Ratified in 1913.)

The Congress shall have power to lay and collect taxes on incomes, from whatever source derived, without apportionment among the several States, and without regard to any census or enumeration.

Amendment XVII

(Ratified in 1913.)

The Senate of the United States shall be composed of two Senators from each State, elected by the people thereof for six years; and each Senator shall have one vote. The electors in each State shall have the qualifications requisite for electors of the most numerous branch of the State legislatures. When vacancies happen in the representation of any State in the Senate, the executive authority of such State shall issue writs of election to fill such vacancies: Provided, That the legislature of any State may empower the executive thereof to make temporary appointments until the people fill the vacancies by election as the legislature may direct. This amendment shall not be so construed as to affect the election or term of any Senator chosen before it becomes valid as part of the Constitution.

Amendment XVIII

(Ratified in 1919.)

Section 1.

After one year from the ratification of this article the manufacture, sale, or transportation of intoxicating liquors within, the importation thereof into, or the exportation thereof from the United States and all territory subject to the jurisdiction thereof for beverage purposes is hereby prohibited.

Section 2.

The Congress and the several States shall have concurrent power to enforce this article by appropriate legislation.

Section 3. This article shall be inoperative unless it shall have been ratified as an amendment to the Constitution by the legislatures of the several States as provided in the Constitution, within seven years from the date of the submission hereof to the States by the Congress.

Amendment XIX

(Ratified In 1920.)

The right of citizens of the United States to vote shall not be denied or abridged by the United States or by any State on account of sex. Congress shall have power to enforce this article by appropriate legislation.

Amendment XX

(Ratified in 1933.)

Section 1.

The terms of the President and Vice President shall end at noon on the 20th day of January, and the terms of Senators and Representatives at noon on the 3d day of January, of the years in which such terms would have ended if this article had not been ratified; and the terms of their successors shall then begin.

Section 2.

The Congress shall assemble at least once in every year, and such meeting shall begin at noon on the 3d day of January, unless they shall by law appoint a different day.

Section 3.

If, at the time fixed for the beginning of the term of the President, the President elect shall have died, the Vice President elect shall become President. If a President shall not have been chosen before the time fixed for the beginning of his term, or if the President elect shall have failed to qualify, then the Vice President elect shall act as President until a President shall have qualified; and the Congress may by law provide for the case wherein neither a President elect nor a Vice President elect shall have qualified, declaring who shall then act as President, or the manner in which one who is to act shall be selected, and such person shall act accordingly until a President or Vice President shall have qualified.

Section 4.

The Congress may by law provide for the case of the death of any of the persons from whom the House of Representatives may choose a President whenever the right of choice shall have devolved upon them, and for the case of the death of any of the persons from whom the Senate may choose a Vice President whenever the right of choice shall have devolved upon them.

Section 5.

Sections 1 and 2 shall take effect on the 15th day of October following the ratification of this article.

Section 6.

This article shall be inoperative unless it shall have been ratified as an amendment to the Constitution by the legislatures of three-fourths of the several States within seven years from the date of its submission.

Amendment XXI

(Ratified in 1933.)

Section 1.

The eighteenth article of amendment to the Constitution of the United States is hereby repealed.

Section 2.

The transportation or importation into any State, Territory, or possession of the United States for delivery or use therein of intoxicating liquors, in violation of the laws thereof, is hereby prohibited.

Section 3.

This article shall be inoperative unless it shall have been ratified as an amendment to the Constitution by conventions in the several States, as provided in the Constitution, within seven years from the date of the submission hereof to the States by the Congress.

Amendment XXII

(Ratified in 1951.)

Section 1.

No person shall be elected to the office of the President more than twice, and no person who has held the office of President, or acted as President, for more than two years of a term to which some other person was elected President shall be elected to the office of the President more than once. But this Article shall not apply to any person holding the office of President when this Article was proposed by the Congress, and shall not prevent any person who may be holding the office of President, or acting as President, during the term within which this Article becomes operative from holding the office of President or acting as President during the remainder of such term.

Section 2.

This Article shall be inoperative unless it shall have been ratified as an amendment to the Constitution by the legislatures of three-fourths of the several States within seven years from the date of its submission to the States by the Congress.

Amendment XXIII

(Ratified in 1961.)

Section 1.

The District constituting the seat of Government of the United States shall appoint in such manner as the Congress may direct: A number of electors of President and Vice President equal to the whole number of Senators and Representatives in Congress to which the District would be entitled if it were a State, but in no event more than the least populous State; they shall be in addition to those appointed by the States, but they shall be considered, for the purposes of the election of President and Vice President, to be electors appointed by a State; and they shall meet in the District and perform such duties as provided by the twelfth article of amendment.

Section 2.

The Congress shall have power to enforce this article by appropriate legislation.

Amendment XXIV

(Ratified in 1964.)

Section 1.

The right of citizens of the United States to vote in any primary or other election for President or Vice President, for electors for President or Vice President, or for Senator or Representative in Congress, shall not be denied or abridged by the United States or any State by reason of failure to pay any poll tax or other tax.

Section 2.

The Congress shall have power to enforce this article by appropriate legislation.

Amendment XXV

(Ratified in 1967.)

Section 1.

In case of the removal of the President from office or of his death or resignation, the Vice President shall become President.

Section 2.

Whenever there is a vacancy in the office of the Vice President, the President shall nominate a Vice President who shall take office upon confirmation by a majority vote of both Houses of Congress.

Section 3.

Whenever the President transmits to the President pro tempore of the Senate and the Speaker of the House of Representatives his written declaration that he is unable to discharge the powers and duties of his office, and until he transmits to them a written declaration to the contrary, such powers and duties shall be discharged by the Vice President as Acting President.

Section 4.

Whenever the Vice president and a majority of either the principal officers of the executive departments or of such other body as Congress may by law provide, transmit to the President pro tempore of the Senate and the Speaker of the House of Representatives their written declaration that the President is unable to discharge the powers and duties of his office, the Vice President shall immediately assume the powers and duties of the office as Acting President. Thereafter, when the President transmits to the President pro tempore of the Senate and the Speaker of the House of Representatives his written declaration that no inability exists, he shall resume the powers and duties of his office unless the Vice President and a majority of either the principal officers of the executive department or of such other body as Congress may by law provide, transmit within four days to the President pro tempore of the Senate and the Speaker of the House of Representatives their written declaration that the President is unable to discharge the powers and duties of his office. Thereupon Congress shall decide the issue, assembling within forty-eight hours for that purpose if not in session. If the Congress, within twenty-one days after receipt of the latter written declaration, or, if Congress is not in session, within twenty-one days after Congress is required to assemble, determines by two-thirds vote of both Houses that the President is unable to discharge the powers and duties of his office, the Vice President shall continue to discharge the same as Acting President; otherwise, the President shall resume the powers and duties of his office.

Amendment XXVI

(Ratified in 1971.)

Section 1.

The right of citizens of the United States, who are eighteen years of age or older, to vote shall not be denied or abridged by the United States or by any State on account of age.

Section 2.

The Congress shall have power to enforce this article by appropriate legislation.

Amendment XXVII

(Ratified in 1992.)

No law, varying the compensation for the services of the Senators and Representatives, shall take effect, until an election of Representatives shall have intervened.

The Electoral Count Act

(as codified at 3 U.S.C. § 1 et seq.)

§ 1. Time of Appointing Electors

The electors of President and Vice President shall be appointed, in each State, on the Tuesday next after the first Monday in November, in every fourth year succeeding every election of a President and Vice President.

§ 2. Failure to Make Choice on Prescribed Day

Whenever any State has held an election for the purpose of choosing electors, and has failed to make a choice on the day prescribed by law, the electors may be appointed on a subsequent day in such a manner as the legislature of such State may direct.

§ 3. Number of Electors

The number of electors shall be equal to the number of Senators and Representatives to which the several States are by law entitled at the time when the President and Vice President to be chosen come into office; except, that where no apportionment of Representatives has been made after any enumeration, at the time of choosing electors, the number of electors shall be according to the then existing apportionment of Senators and Representatives.

§ 4. Vacancies in Electoral College

Each State may, by law, provide for the filling of any vacancies which may occur in its college of electors when such college meets to give its electoral vote.

§ 5. Determination of Controversy as to Appointment of Electors

If any State shall have provided, by laws enacted prior to the day fixed for the appointment of the electors, for its final determination of any controversy or contest concerning the appointment of all or any of the electors of such State, by judicial or other methods or procedures, and such determination shall have been made at least six days before the time fixed for the meeting of the electors, such determination made pursuant to such law so existing on said day, and made at least six days prior to said time of meeting of the electors, shall be conclusive, and shall govern in the counting of the electoral votes as provided in the Constitution, and as hereinafter regulated, so far as the ascertainment of the electors appointed by such State is concerned.

§ 6. Credentials of Electors; Transmission to Archivist of the United States and to Congress; Public Inspection

It shall be the duty of the executive of each State, as soon as practicable after the conclusion of the appointment of the electors in such State by the final ascertainment, under and in pursuance of the laws of such State providing for such ascertainment, to communicate by registered mail under the seal of the State to the Archivist of the United States a certificate of such ascertainment of the electors appointed, setting forth the names of such electors and the canvass or other ascertainment under the laws of such State of the number of votes given or cast for each person for whose appointment any and all votes have been given or cast; and it shall also thereupon be the duty of the executive of each State to deliver to the electors of such State, on or before the day on which they are required by section 7 of this title to meet, six duplicate-originals of the same certificate under the seal of the State; and if there shall have been any final determination in a State in the manner provided for by law of a controversy or contest concerning the appointment of all or any of the electors of such State, it shall be the duty of the executive of such State, as soon as practicable after such determination, to communicate under the seal of the State to the Archivist of the United States a certificate of such determination in form and manner as the same shall have been made; and the certificate or certificates so received by the Archivist of the United States shall be preserved by him for one year and shall be a part of the public records of his office and shall be open to public inspection; and the Archivist of the United States at the first meeting of Congress thereafter shall transmit to the two Houses of Congress copies in full of each and every such certificate so received at the National Archives and Records Administration.

§ 7. Meeting and Vote of Electors

The electors of President and Vice President of each State shall meet and give their votes on the first Monday after the second Wednesday in December next following their appointment at such place in each State as the legislature of such State shall direct.

§ 8. Manner of Voting

The electors shall vote for President and Vice President, respectively, in the manner directed by the Constitution.

§ 9.   Certificates of Votes for President and Vice President

The electors shall make and sign six certificates of all the votes given by them, each of which certificates shall contain two distinct lists, one of the votes for President and the other of the votes for Vice President, and shall annex to each of the certificates one of the lists of the electors which shall have been furnished to them by direction of the executive of the State.

§ 10.   Sealing and Endorsing Certificates

The electors shall seal up the certificates so made by them, and certify upon each that the lists of all the votes of such State given for President, and of all the votes given for Vice President, are contained therein.

§ 11.   Disposition of Certificates

The electors shall dispose of the certificates so made by them and the lists attached thereto in the following manner:

First. They shall forthwith forward by registered mail one of the same to the President of the Senate at the seat of government.

Second. Two of the same shall be delivered to the secretary of state of the State, one of which shall be held subject to the order of the President of the Senate, the other to be preserved by him for one year and shall be a part of the public records of his office and shall be open to public inspection.

Third. On the day thereafter they shall forward by registered mail two of such certificates and lists to the Archivist of the United States at the seat of government, one of which shall be held subject to the order of the President of the Senate. The other shall be preserved by the Archivist of the United States for one year and shall be a part of the public records of his office and shall be open to public inspection.

Fourth. They shall forthwith cause the other of the certificates and lists to be delivered to the judge of the district in which the electors shall have assembled.

§ 12.   Failure of Certificates of Electors to Reach President of the Senate or Archivist of the United States; Demand on State for Certificate

When no certificate of vote and list mentioned in sections 9 and 11 of this title from any State shall have been received by the President of the Senate or by the Archivist of the United States by the fourth Wednesday in December, after the meeting of the electors shall have been held, the President of the Senate or, if he be absent from the seat of government, the Archivist of the United States shall request, by the most expeditious method available, the secretary of state of the State to send up the certificate and list lodged with him by the electors of such State; and it shall be his duty upon receipt of such request immediately to transmit same by registered mail to the President of the Senate at the seat of government.

§ 13. Same; Demand on District Judge for Certificate

When no certificates of votes from any State shall have been received at the seat of government on the fourth Wednesday in December, after the meeting of the electors shall have been held, the President of the Senate or, if he be absent from the seat of government, the Archivist of the United States shall send a special messenger to the district judge in whose custody one certificate of votes from that State has been lodged, and such judge shall forthwith transmit that list by the hand of such messenger to the seat of government.

§ 14. Forfeiture for Messenger's Neglect of Duty

Every person who, having been appointed, pursuant to section 13 of this title, to deliver the certificates of the votes of the electors to the President of the Senate, and having accepted such appointment, shall neglect to perform the services required from him, shall forfeit the sum of $1,000.

§ 15. Counting Electoral Votes in Congress

Congress shall be in session on the sixth day of January succeeding every meeting of the electors. The Senate and House of Representatives shall meet in the Hall of the House of Representatives at the hour of 1 o'clock in the afternoon on that day, and the President of the Senate shall be their presiding officer. Two tellers shall be previously appointed on the part of the Senate and two on the part of the House of Representatives, to whom shall be handed, as they are opened by the President of the Senate, all the certificates and papers purporting to be certificates of the electoral votes, which certificates and papers shall be opened, presented, and acted upon in the alphabetical order of the States, beginning with the letter A; and said tellers, having then read the same in the presence and hearing of the two Houses, shall make a list of the votes as they shall appear from the said certificates; and the votes having been ascertained and counted according to the rules in this subchapter provided, the result of the same shall be delivered to the President of the Senate, who shall thereupon announce the state of the vote, which announcement shall be deemed a sufficient declaration of the persons, if any, elected President and Vice President of the United States, and, together with a list of the votes, be entered on the Journals of the two Houses. Upon such reading of any such certificate or paper, the President of the Senate shall call for objections, if any. Every objection shall be made in writing, and shall state clearly and concisely, and without argument, the ground thereof, and shall be signed by at least one Senator and one Member of the House of Representatives before the same shall be received. When all objections so made to any vote or paper from a State shall have been received and read, the Senate shall thereupon withdraw, and such objections shall be submitted to the Senate for its decision; and the Speaker of the House of Representatives shall, in like manner, submit such objections to the House of Representatives for its decision; and no electoral vote or votes from any State which shall have been regularly given by electors whose appointment has been lawfully certified to according to section 6 of this title from which but one return has been received shall be rejected, but the two Houses concurrently may reject the vote or votes when they agree that such vote or votes have not been so regularly given by electors whose appointment has been so certified. If more than one return or paper purporting to be a return from a State shall have been received by the President of the Senate, those votes, and those only, shall be counted which shall have been regularly given by the electors who are shown by the determination mentioned in section 5 of this title to have been appointed, if the determination in said section provided for shall have been made, or by such successors or substitutes, in case of a vacancy in the board of electors so ascertained, as have been appointed to fill such vacancy in the mode provided by the laws of the State; but in case there shall arise the question which of two or more of such State authorities determining what electors have been appointed, as mentioned in section 5 of this title, is the lawful tribunal of such state, the votes regularly given of those electors, and those only, of such State shall be counted whose title as electors the two Houses, acting separately, shall concurrently decide is supported by the decision of such State so authorized by its law; and in such case of more than one return or paper purporting to be a return from a State, if there shall have been no such determination of the question in the State aforesaid, then those votes, and those only, shall be counted which the two Houses shall concurrently decide were cast by lawful electors appointed in accordance with the laws of the State, unless the two Houses, acting separately, shall concurrently decide such votes not to be the lawful votes of the legally appointed electors of such State. But if the two Houses shall disagree in respect of the counting of such votes, then, and in that case, the votes of the electors whose appointment shall have been certified by the executive of the State, under the seal thereof, shall be counted. When the two Houses have voted, they shall immediately again meet, and the presiding officer shall then announce the decision of the questions submitted. No votes or papers from any other State shall be acted upon until the objections previously made to the votes or papers from any State shall have been finally disposed of.

§ 16. Same; Seats for Officers and Members of Two Houses in Joint Meeting

At such joint meeting of the two Houses seats shall be provided as follows: For the President of the Senate, the Speaker's chair; for the Speaker, immediately upon his left; the Senators, in the body of the Hall upon the right of the presiding officer; for the Representatives, in the body of the Hall not provided for the Senators; for the tellers, Secretary of the Senate, and Clerk of the House of Representatives, at the Clerk's desk; for the other officers of the two Houses, in front of the Clerk's desk and upon each side of the Speaker's platform. Such joint meeting shall not be dissolved until the count of electoral votes shall be completed and the result declared;

and no recess shall be taken unless a question shall have arisen in regard to counting any such votes, or otherwise under this subchapter, in which case it shall be competent for either House, acting separately, in the manner hereinbefore provided, to direct a recess of such House not beyond the next calendar day, Sunday excepted, at the hour of 10 o'clock in the forenoon. But if the counting of the electoral votes and the declaration of the result shall not have been completed before the fifth calendar day next after such first meeting of the two Houses, no further or other recess shall be taken by either House.

§ 17.   Same; Limit of Debate in Each House

When the two Houses separate to decide upon an objection that may have been made to the counting of any electoral vote or votes from any State, or other question arising in the matter, each Senator and Representative may speak to such objection or question five minutes, and not more than once; but after such debate shall have lasted two hours it shall be the duty of the presiding officer of each House to put the main question without further debate.

§ 18.   Same; Parliamentary Procedure at Joint Meeting

While the two Houses shall be in meeting as provided in this chapter, the President of the Senate shall have power to preserve order; and no debate shall be allowed and no question shall be put by the presiding officer except to either House on a motion to withdraw.

The Voting Rights Act of 1965

(codified at 42 U.S.C. § 1973 et seq.) (selected sections)

§ 2.   Denial or Abridgement of Right to Vote on Account of Race or Color Through Voting Qualifications or Prerequisites; Establishment of Violation

(a) No voting qualification or prerequisite to voting or standard, practice, or procedure shall be imposed or applied by any State or political subdivision in a manner which results in a denial or abridgement of the right of any citizen of the United States to vote on account of race or color, or in contravention of the guarantees set forth in section 4(f)(2) as provided in subsection (b).

(b) A violation of subsection (a) is established if, based on the totality of circumstances, it is shown that the political processes leading to nomination or election in the State or political subdivision are not equally open to participation by members of a class of citizens protected by subsection (a) in that its members have less opportunity than other members of the electorate to participate in the political process and to elect representatives of their choice. The extent to which members of a protected class have been elected to office in the State or political subdivision is one circumstance which may be considered: Provided, That nothing in this section establishes a right to have members of a protected class elected in numbers equal to their proportion in the population.

§ 4. Suspension of the Use of Tests or Devices in Determining Eligibility to Vote

(a) Action by state or political subdivision for declaratory judgment of no denial or abridgement; three-judge district court; appeal to Supreme Court; retention of jurisdiction by three-judge court.

(1) To assure that the right of citizens of the United States to vote is not denied or abridged on account of race or color, no citizen shall be denied the right to vote in any Federal, State, or local election because of his failure to comply with any test or device in any State with respect to which the determinations have been made under the first two sentences of subsection (b) or in any political subdivision of such State (as such subdivision existed on the date such determinations were made with respect to such State), though such determinations were not made with respect to such subdivision as a separate unit, or in any political subdivision with respect to which such determinations have been made as a separate unit, unless the United States District Court for the District of Columbia issues a declaratory judgment under this section. No citizen shall be denied the right to vote in any Federal, State, or local election because of his failure to comply with any test or device in any State with respect to which the determinations have been made under the third sentence of subsection (b) of this section or in any political subdivision of such State (as such subdivision existed on the date such determinations were made with respect to such State), though such determinations were not made with respect to such subdivision as a separate unit, or in any political subdivision with respect to which such determinations have been made as a separate unit, unless the United States District Court for the District of Columbia issues a declaratory judgment under this section. A declaratory judgment under this section shall issue only if such court determines that during the ten years preceding the filing of the action, and during the pendency of such action—

(A) no such test or device has been used within such State or political subdivision for the purpose or with the effect of denying or abridging the right to vote on account of race or color or (in the case of a State or subdivision seeking a declaratory judgment under the second sentence of this subsection) in contravention of the guarantees of subsection (f)(2);

(B) no final judgment of any court of the United States, other than the denial of declaratory judgment under this section, has determined that denials or abridgements of the rights to vote on account of race or color have occurred anywhere in the territory of such State or political subdivision or (in the case of a State or subdivision seeking a declaratory judgment under the second sentence of this subsection) that denials or abridgements of the right to vote in contravention of the guarantees of subsection (f)(2) have occurred anywhere in the territory of such State or subdivision and no consent decree, settlement, or agreement has been entered into resulting in any abandonment of a voting practice challenged on such grounds; and no declaratory judgment under this section shall be entered during the pendency of an action commenced before the filing of an action under this section and alleging such denials or abridgements of the right to vote;

(C) no Federal examiners or observers under this Act have been assigned to such State or political subdivision;

(D) such State or political subdivision and all governmental units within its territory have complied with section 5 of this Act, including compliance with the requirement that no change covered by section 5 has been enforced without preclearance under section 5, and have repealed all changes covered by section 5 to which the Attorney General has successfully objected or as to which the United States District Court for the District of Columbia has denied a declaratory judgment;

(E) the Attorney General has not interposed any objection (that has not been overturned by a final judgment of a court) and no declaratory judgment has been denied under section 5, with respect to any submission by or on behalf of the plaintiff or any governmental unit within its territory under section 5, and no such submissions or declaratory judgment actions are pending; and

(F) such State or political subdivision and all governmental units within its territory–

(i) have eliminated voting procedures and methods of election which inhibit or dilute equal access to the electoral process;

(ii) have engaged in constructive efforts to eliminate intimidation and harassment of persons exercising rights protected under this Act; and

(iii) have engaged in other constructive efforts, such as expanded opportunity for convenient registration and voting for every person of voting age and the appointment of minority persons as election officials throughout the jurisdiction and at all stages of the election and registration process.

(2) To assist the court in determining whether to issue a declaratory judgment under this subsection, the plaintiff shall present evidence of minority participation, including evidence of the levels of minority group registration and voting, changes in such levels over time, and disparities between minority-group and non-minority-group participation.

(3) No declaratory judgment shall issue under this subsection with respect to such State or political subdivision if such plaintiff and governmental units within its territory have, during the period beginning ten years before the date the judgment is issued, engaged in violations of any provision of the Constitution or laws of the United States or any State or

political subdivision with respect to discrimination in voting on account of race or color or (in the case of a State or subdivision seeking a declaratory judgment under the second sentence of this subsection) in contravention of the guarantees of subsection (f)(2) unless the plaintiff establishes that any such violations were trivial, were promptly corrected, and were not repeated.

(4) The State or political subdivision bringing such action shall publicize the intended commencement and any proposed settlement of such action in the media serving such State or political subdivision and in appropriate United States post offices. Any aggrieved party may as of right intervene at any stage in such action.

(5) An action pursuant to this subsection shall be heard and determined by a court of three judges in accordance with the provisions of section 2284 of title 28 of the United States Code and any appeal shall lie to the Supreme Court. The court shall retain jurisdiction of any action pursuant to this subsection for ten years after judgment and shall reopen the action upon motion of the Attorney General or any aggrieved person alleging that conduct has occurred which, had that conduct occurred during the ten-year periods referred to in this subsection, would have precluded the issuance of a declaratory judgment under this subsection. The court, upon such reopening, shall vacate the declaratory judgment issued under this section if, after the issuance of such declaratory judgment, a final judgment against the State or subdivision with respect to which such declaratory judgment was issued, or against any governmental unit within the State or subdivision, determines that denials or abridgements of the right to vote on account of race or color have occurred anywhere in the territory of such State or political subdivision or (in the case of a State or subdivision which sought a declaratory judgment under the second sentence of this subsection) that denials or abridgements of the right to vote in contravention of the guarantees of subsection (f)(2) have occurred anywhere in the territory of such State or subdivision, or if, after the issuance of such declaratory judgment, a consent decree, settlement, or agreement has been entered into resulting in any abandonment of a voting practice challenged on such grounds.

(6) If, after two years from the date of the filing of a declaratory judgment under this subsection, no date has been set for a hearing in such action, and that delay has not been the result of an avoidable delay on the part of counsel for any party, the chief judge of the United States District Court for the District of Columbia may request the Judicial Council for the Circuit of the District of Columbia to provide the necessary judicial resources to expedite any action filed under this section. If such resources are unavailable within the circuit, the chief judge shall file a certificate of necessity in accordance with section 292(d) of title 28 of the United States Code.

(7) The Congress shall reconsider the provisions of this section at the end of the fifteen-year period following the effective date of the amendments made by the Fannie Lou Hamer, Rosa Parks, and Coretta Scott King Voting Rights Act Reauthorization and Amendments Act of 2006 [effective July 27, 2006].

(8) The provisions of this section shall expire at the end of the twenty-five year period following the effective date of the amendments made by the Fannie Lou Hamer, Rosa Parks, and Coretta Scott King Voting Rights Act Reauthorization and Amendments Act of 2006 [effective July 27, 2006].

(9) Nothing in this section shall prohibit the Attorney General from consenting to an entry of judgment if based upon a showing of objective and compelling evidence by the plaintiff, and upon investigation, he is satisfied that the State or political subdivision has complied with the requirements of section 4(a)(1). Any aggrieved party may as of right intervene at any stage in such action.

(b) Required factual determinations necessary to allow suspension of compliance with tests and devices; publication in Federal Register. The provisions of subsection (a) shall apply in any State or in any political subdivision of a state which (1) the Attorney General determines maintained on November 1, 1964, any test or device, and with respect to which (2) the Director of the Census determines that less than 50 per centum of the persons of voting age residing therein were registered on November 1, 1964, or that less than 50 per centum of such persons voted on the presidential election of November 1964. On and after August 6, 1970, in addition to any State or political subdivision of a State determined to be subject to subsection (a) pursuant to the previous sentence, the provisions of subsection (a) shall apply in any State or any political subdivision of a State which (i) the Attorney General determines maintained on November 1, 1968, any test or device, and with respect to which (ii) the Director of the Census determines that less than 50 per centum of the persons of voting age residing therein were registered on November 1, 1968, or that less than 50 per centum of such persons voted in the presidential election of November 1968. On and after August 6, 1975, in addition to any State or political subdivision of a State determined to be subject to subsection (a) pursuant to the previous two sentences, the provisions of a subsection (a) shall apply in any State or any political subdivision of a State which (i) the Attorney General determines maintained on November 1, 1972, any test or device, and with respect to which (ii) the Director of the Census determines that less than 50 per centum of the citizens of voting age were registered on November 1, 1972, or that less than 50 per centum of such persons voted in the Presidential election of November 1972.

A determination or certification of the Attorney General or of the Director of the Census under this section or under section 8 or section 13 shall not be reviewable in any court and shall be effective upon publication in the Federal Register.

(c) "Test or device" defined. The phrase "test or device" shall mean any requirement that a person as a prerequisite for voting or registration for voting (1) demonstrate the ability to read, write, understand, or interpret any matter, (2) demonstrate any educational achievement or his knowledge of any particular subject, (3) possess good moral character, or (4) prove his qualifications by the voucher of registered voters or members of any other class.

(d) Required frequency, continuation and probable recurrence of incidents of denial or abridgement to constitute forbidden use of tests or devices. For purposes of this section no State or political subdivision shall be determined to have engaged in the use of tests or devices for the purpose or with the effect of denying or abridging the right to vote on account of race or color, or in contravention of the guarantees set forth in section 4(f)(2) if (1) incidents of such use have been few in number and have been promptly and effectively corrected by State or local action, (2) the continuing effect of such incidents has been eliminated, and (3) there is no reasonable probability of their recurrence in the future.

(e) Completion of requisite grade level of education in American-flag schools in which the predominant classroom language was other than English.

(1) Congress hereby declares that to secure the rights under the fourteenth amendment of persons educated in American-flag schools in which the predominant classroom language was other than English, it is necessary to prohibit the States from conditioning the right to vote of such persons on ability to read, write, understand, or interpret any matter in the English language.

(2) No person who demonstrates that he has successfully completed the sixth primary grade in a public school in, or a private school accredited by, any State or territory, the District of Columbia, or the Commonwealth of Puerto Rico in which the predominant classroom language was other than English, shall be denied the right to vote in any Federal, State, or local election because of his inability to read, write, understand, or interpret any matter in the English language, except that in States in which State law provides that a different level of education is presumptive of literacy, he shall demonstrate that he has successfully completed an equivalent level of education in a public school in, or a private school accredited by, any State or territory, the District of Columbia, or the Commonwealth of Puerto Rico in which the predominant classroom language was other than English.

(f) Congressional findings of voting discrimination against language minorities; prohibition of English-only elections; other remedial measures.

(1) The Congress finds that voting discrimination against citizens of language minorities is pervasive and national in scope. Such minority citizens are from environments in which the dominant language is other

than English. In addition they have been denied equal educational opportunities by State and local governments, resulting in severe disabilities and continuing illiteracy in the English language. The Congress further finds that, where State and local officials conduct elections only in English, language minority citizens are excluded from participating in the electoral process. In many areas of the country, this exclusion is aggravated by acts of physical, economic, and political intimidation. The Congress declares that, in order to enforce the guarantees of the fourteenth and fifteenth amendments to the United States Constitution, it is necessary to eliminate such discrimination by prohibiting English-only elections, and by prescribing other remedial devices.

(2) No voting qualification or prerequisite to voting, or standard, practice, or procedure shall be imposed or applied by any State or political subdivision to deny or abridge the right of any citizen of the United States to vote because he is a member of a language minority group.

(3) In addition to the meaning given the term under section 4(c), the term "test or device" shall also mean any practice or requirement by which any State or political subdivision provided any registration or voting notices, forms, instructions, assistance, or other materials or information relating to the electoral process, including ballots, only in the English language, where the Director of the Census determines that more than five per centum of the citizens of voting age residing in such State or political subdivision are members of a single language minority. With respect to section 4(b), the term "test or device", as defined in this subsection, shall be employed only in making the determinations under the third sentence of that subsection.

(4) Whenever any State or political subdivision subject to the prohibitions of the second sentence of section 4(a) provides any registration or voting notices, forms, instructions, assistance, or other materials or information relating to the electoral process, including ballots, it shall provide them in the language of the applicable language minority group as well as in the English language: *Provided,* That where the language of the applicable minority group is oral or unwritten or in the case of Alaskan Natives and American Indians, if the predominate language is historically unwritten, the State or political subdivision is only required to furnish oral instructions, assistance, or other information relating to registration and voting.

§ 5. Alteration of Voting Qualifications and Procedures; Action By State or Political Subdivision for Declaratory Judgment of No Denial or Abridgement of Voting Rights; Three–Judge District Court; Appeal to Supreme Court

(a) Whenever a State or political subdivision with respect to which the prohibitions set forth in section 4(a) based upon determinations made under the first sentence of section 4(b) are in effect shall enact or seek to administer any voting qualification or prerequisite to voting, or standard, practice, or procedure with respect to voting different from that in force or effect on November 1, 1964, or whenever a State or political subdivision with respect to which the prohibitions set forth in section 4(a) based upon determinations made under the second sentence of section 4(b) are in effect shall enact or seek to administer any voting qualification or prerequisite to voting, or standard, practice, or procedure with respect to voting different from that in force or effect on November 1, 1968, or whenever a State or political subdivision with respect to which the prohibitions set forth in section 4(a) based upon determinations made under the third sentence of section 4(b) are in effect shall enact or seek to administer any voting qualification or prerequisite to voting, or standard, practice, or procedure with respect to voting different from that in force or effect on November 1, 1972, such State or subdivision may institute an action in the United States District Court for the District of Columbia for a declaratory judgment that such qualification prerequisite, standard, practice, or procedure neither has the purpose nor will have the effect of denying or abridging the right to vote on account of race or color, or in contravention of the guarantees set forth in section 4(f)(2), and unless and until the court enters such judgment no person shall be denied the right to vote for failure to comply with such qualification, prerequisite, standard, practice, or procedure: *Provided,* That such qualification, prerequisite, standard, practice, or procedure may be enforced without such proceeding if the qualification, prerequisite, standard, practice, or procedure has been submitted by the chief legal officer or other appropriate official of such State or subdivision to the Attorney General and the Attorney General has not interposed an objection within sixty days after such submission, or upon good cause shown, to facilitate an expedited approval within sixty days after such submission, the Attorney General has affirmatively indicated that such objection will not be made. Neither an affirmative indication by the Attorney General that no objection will be made, nor the Attorney General's failure to object, nor a declaratory judgment entered under this section shall bar a subsequent action to enjoin enforcement of such qualification, prerequisite, standard, practice, or procedure. In the event the Attorney General affirmatively indicates that no objection will be made within the sixty-day period following receipt of a submission, the Attorney General may reserve the right to reexamine the submission if additional information comes to his attention during the remainder of the sixty-day period which would otherwise require objection in accordance with this section. Any action under this section shall be heard and determined by a court of three judges in accordance with the provisions of section 2284 of title 28 of the United States Code and any appeal shall lie to the Supreme Court.

(b) Any voting qualification or prerequisite to voting, or standard, practice, or procedure with respect to voting that has the purpose of or will have the effect of diminishing the ability of any citizens of the United States on account of race or color, or in contravention of the guarantees set forth in section 4(f)(2), to elect their preferred candidates of choice denies or abridges the right to vote within the meaning of subsection (a) of this section.

(c) The term "purpose" in subsections (a) and (b) of this section shall include any discriminatory purpose.

(d) The purpose of subsection (b) of this section is to protect the ability of such citizens to elect their preferred candidates of choice.

§ 14. Enforcement proceedings.

* * *

(b) Jurisdiction of courts for declaratory judgment, restraining orders, or temporary or permanent injunction. No court other than the District Court for the District of Columbia shall have jurisdiction to issue any declaratory judgment pursuant to section 4 or section 5 or any restraining order or temporary or permanent injunction against the execution or enforcement of any provision of this Act or any action of any Federal officer or employee pursuant hereto.

(c) Definitions.

(1) The terms "vote" or "voting" shall include all action necessary to make a vote effective in any primary, special, or general election, including, but not limited to, registration, listing pursuant to this Act, or other action required by law prerequisite to voting, casting a ballot, and having such ballot counted properly and included in the appropriate totals of votes cast with respect to candidates for public or party office and propositions for which votes are received in an election.

(2) The term "political subdivision" shall mean any county or parish, except that where registration for voting is not conducted under the supervision of a county or parish, the term shall include any other subdivision of a State which conducts registration for voting.

(3) The term "language minorities" or "language minority group" means persons who are American Indian, Asian American, Alaskan Natives or of Spanish heritage.

* * *

(e) Attorney's fees. In any action or proceeding to enforce the voting guarantees of the fourteenth or fifteenth amendment the court, in its discretion, may allow the prevailing party, other than the United States, a reasonable attorney's fee, reasonable expert fees, and other reasonable litigation expenses as part of the costs.

The National Voter Registration Act of 1993

(Codified at 42 U.S.C. § 1973gg et seq.) (selected sections)

§ 2. Findings and Purposes.

(a) Findings. The Congress finds that

(1) the right of citizens of the United States to vote is a fundamental right;

(2) it is the duty of the Federal, State, and local governments to promote the exercise of that right; and

(3) discriminatory and unfair registration laws and procedures can have a direct and damaging effect on voter participation in elections for Federal office and disproportionately harm voter participation by various groups, including racial minorities.

(b) Purposes. The purposes of this Act are—

(1) to establish procedures that will increase the number of eligible citizens who register to vote in elections for Federal office;

(2) to make it possible for Federal, State, and local governments to implement this Act in a manner that enhances the participation of eligible citizens as voters in elections for Federal office;

(3) to protect the integrity of the electoral process; and

(4) to ensure that accurate and current voter registration rolls are maintained.

* * *

§ 4. National Procedures for Voter Registration for Elections for Federal Office.

(a) In General. Except as provided in subsection (b), notwithstanding any other Federal or State law, in addition to any other method of voter registration provided for under State law, each State shall establish procedures to register to vote in elections for Federal office—

(1) by application made simultaneously with an application for a motor vehicle driver's license pursuant to section 5;

(2) by mail application pursuant to section 6; and

(3) by application in person—

(A) at the appropriate registration site designated with respect to the residence of the applicant in accordance with State law; and

(B) at a Federal, State, or nongovernmental office designated under section 7.

(b) Nonapplicability to Certain States. This Act does not apply to a State described in either or both of the following paragraphs:

(1) A State in which, under law that is in effect continuously on and after March 11, 1993, there is no voter registration requirement for any voter in the State with respect to an election for Federal office.

(2) A State in which under law that is in effect continuously on and after March 11, 1993, or that was enacted on or prior to March 11, 1993,

and by its terms is to come into effect upon the enactment of this Act, so long as that law remains in effect, all voters in the State may register to vote at the polling place at the time of voting in a general election for Federal office.

§ 5. Simultaneous Application for Voter Registration and Application for Motor Vehicle Driver's license.

(a) In General. (1) Each State motor vehicle driver's license application (including any renewal application) submitted to the appropriate State motor vehicle authority under State law shall serve as an application for voter registration with respect to elections for Federal office unless the applicant fails to sign the voter registration application.

(2) An application for voter registration submitted under paragraph (1) shall be considered as updating any previous voter registration by the applicant.

(b) Limitation on Use of Information. No information relating to the failure of an applicant for a State motor vehicle driver's license to sign a voter registration application may be used for any purpose other than voter registration.

(c) Forms and Procedures. (1) Each State shall include a voter registration application form for elections for Federal office as part of an application for a State motor vehicle driver's license.

(2) The voter registration application portion of an application for a State motor vehicle driver's license—

(A) may not require any information that duplicates information required in the driver's license portion of the form (other than a second signature or other information necessary under subparagraph (C));

(B) may require only the minimum amount of information necessary to–

(i) prevent duplicate voter registrations; and

(ii) enable State election officials to assess the eligibility of the applicant and to administer voter registration and other parts of the election process;

(C) shall include a statement that—

(i) states each eligibility requirement (including citizenship);

(ii) contains an attestation that the applicant meets each such requirement; and

(iii) requires the signature of the applicant, under penalty of perjury;

(D) shall include, in print that is identical to that used in the attestation portion of the application—

(i) the information required in section 8(a)(5)(A) and (B);

(ii) a statement that, if an applicant declines to register to vote, the fact that the applicant has declined to register will remain confidential and will be used only for voter registration purposes; and

(iii) a statement that if an applicant does register to vote, the office at which the applicant submits a voter registration application will remain confidential and will be used only for voter registration purposes; and

(E) shall be made available (as submitted by the applicant, or in machine readable or other format) to the appropriate State election official as provided by State law.

(d) Change of Address. Any change of address form submitted in accordance with State law for purposes of a State motor vehicle driver's license shall serve as notification of change of address for voter registration with respect to elections for Federal office for the registrant involved unless the registrant states on the form that the change of address is not for voter registration purposes.

(e) Transmittal Deadline. (1) Subject to paragraph (2), a completed voter registration portion of an application for a State motor vehicle driver's license accepted at a State motor vehicle authority shall be transmitted to the appropriate State election official not later than 10 days after the acceptance.

(2) If a registration application is accepted within 5 days before the last day for registration to vote in an election, the application shall be transmitted to the appropriate State election official not later than 5 days after the date of acceptance.

§ 6. Mail Registration.

(a) Form. (1) Each State shall accept and use the mail voter registration application form prescribed by the Federal Election Commission pursuant to section 9(a)(2) for the registration of voters in elections for Federal office.

(2) In addition to accepting and using the form described in paragraph (1), a State may develop and use a mail voter registration form that meets all of the criteria stated in section 9(b) for the registration of voters in elections for Federal office.

(3) A form described in paragraph (1) or (2) shall be accepted and used for notification of a registrant's change of address.

(b) Availability of Forms. The chief State election official of a State shall make the forms described in subsection (a) available for distribution through governmental and private entities, with particular emphasis on making them available for organized voter registration programs.

(c) First–Time Voters. (1) Subject to paragraph (2), a State may by law require a person to vote in person if—

(A) the person was registered to vote in a jurisdiction by mail; and

(B) the person has not previously voted in that jurisdiction.

(2) Paragraph (1) does not apply in the case of a person—

(A) who is entitled to vote by absentee ballot under the Uniformed and Overseas Citizens Absentee Voting Act;

(B) who is provided the right to vote otherwise than in person under section 3(b)(2)(B)(ii) of the Voting Accessibility for the Elderly and Handicapped Act; or

(C) who is entitled to vote otherwise than in person under any other Federal law.

* * *

§ 7. Voter Registration Agencies.

(a) Designation. (1) Each State shall designate agencies for the registration of voters in elections for Federal office.

(2) Each State shall designate as voter registration agencies—

(A) all offices in the State that provide public assistance; and

(B) all offices in the State that provide State-funded programs primarily engaged in providing services to persons with disabilities.

(3)(A) In addition to voter registration agencies designated under paragraph (2), each State shall designate other offices within the State as voter registration agencies.

(B) Voter registration agencies designated under subparagraph (A) may include—

(i) State or local government offices such as public libraries, public schools, offices of city and county clerks (including marriage license bureaus), fishing and hunting license bureaus, government revenue offices, unemployment compensation offices, and offices not described in paragraph (2)(B) that provide services to persons with disabilities; and

(ii) Federal and nongovernmental offices, with the agreement of such offices.

(4)(A) At each voter registration agency, the following services shall be made available:

(i) Distribution of mail voter registration application forms in accordance with paragraph (6).

(ii) Assistance to applicants in completing voter registration application forms, unless the applicant refuses such assistance.

(iii) Acceptance of completed voter registration application forms for transmittal to the appropriate State election official.

(B) If a voter registration agency designated under paragraph (2)(B) provides services to a person with a disability at the person's home, the agency shall provide the services described in subparagraph (A) at the person's home.

(5) A person who provides service described in paragraph (4) shall not—

(A) seek to influence an applicant's political preference or party registration;

(B) display any such political preference or party allegiance;

(C) make any statement to an applicant or take any action the purpose or effect of which is to discourage the applicant from registering to vote; or

(D) make any statement to an applicant or take any action the purpose or effect of which is to lead the applicant to believe that a decision to register or not to register has any bearing on the availability of services or benefits.

(6) A voter registration agency that is an office that provides service or assistance in addition to conducting voter registration shall—

(A) distribute with each application for such service or assistance, and with each recertification, renewal, or change of address form relating to such service or assistance—

(i) the mail voter registration application form described in section 9(a)(2), including a statement that—

(I) specifies each eligibility requirement (including citizenship);

(II) contains an attestation that the applicant meets each such requirement; and

(III) requires the signature of the applicant, under penalty of perjury; or

(ii) the office's own form if it is equivalent to the form described in section 9(a)(2),

unless the applicant, in writing, declines to register to vote;

(B) provide a form that includes—

(i) the question, "If you are not registered to vote where you live now, would you like to apply to register to vote here today?";

(ii) if the agency provides public assistance, the statement, "Applying to register or declining to register to vote will not affect the amount of assistance that you will be provided by this agency.";

(iii) boxes for the applicant to check to indicate whether the applicant would like to register or declines to register to vote (failure to check either box being deemed to constitute a declination to register for purposes of subparagraph (C)), together with the statement (in close proximity to the boxes and in prominent type), "IF YOU DO NOT CHECK EITHER BOX, YOU WILL BE CONSIDERED TO HAVE DECIDED NOT TO REGISTER TO VOTE AT THIS TIME.";

(iv) the statement, "If you would like help in filling out the voter registration application form, we will help you. The decision whether to seek or accept help is yours. You may fill out the application form in private."; and

(v) the statement "If you believe that someone has interfered with your right to register or to decline to register to vote, your right to privacy in deciding whether to register or in applying to register to vote, or your right to choose your own political party or other political preference, you may file a complaint with ___.", the blank being filled by the name, address, and telephone number of the appropriate official to whom such a complaint should be addressed; and

(C) provide to each applicant who does not decline to register to vote the same degree of assistance with regard to the completion of the registration application form as is provided by the office with regard to the completion of its own forms, unless the applicant refuses such assistance.

(7) No information relating to a declination to register to vote in connection with an application made at an office described in paragraph (6) may be used for any purpose other than voter registration.

(b) Federal Government and Private Sector Cooperation. All departments, agencies, and other entitles of the executive branch of the Federal Government shall, to the greatest extent practicable, cooperate with the States in carrying out subsection (a), and all nongovernmental entities are encouraged to do so.

(c) Armed Forces Recruitment Offices. (1) Each State and the Secretary of Defense shall jointly develop and implement procedures for persons to apply to register to vote at recruitment offices of the Armed Forces of the United States.

(2) A recruitment office of the Armed Forces of the United States shall be considered to be a voter registration agency designated under subsection (a)(2) for all purposes of this Act.

(d) Transmittal Deadline. (1) Subject to paragraph (2), a completed registration application accepted at a voter registration agency shall be transmitted to the appropriate State election official not later than 10 days after the date of acceptance.

(2) If a registration application is accepted within 5 days before the last day for registration to vote in an election, the application shall be transmitted to the appropriate State election official not later than 5 days after the date of acceptance.

§ 8. Requirements With Respect to Administration of Voter Registration.

(a) In General. In the administration of voter registration for elections for Federal office, each State shall—

(1) insure that any eligible applicant is registered to vote in an election—

(A) in the case of registration with a motor vehicle application under section 5, if the valid voter registration form of the applicant is submitted to the appropriate State motor vehicle authority not later than the lesser of 30 days, or the period provided by State law, before the date of the election;

(B) in the case of registration by mail under section 6, if the valid voter registration form of the applicant is postmarked not later than the lesser of 30 days, or the period provided by State law, before the date of the election;

(C) in the case of registration at a voter registration agency, if the valid voter registration form of the applicant is accepted at the voter registration agency not later than the lesser of 30 days, or the period provided by State law, before the date of the election; and

(D) in any other case, if the valid voter registration form of the applicant is received by the appropriate State election official not later than the lesser of 30 days, or the period provided by State law, before the date of the election;

(2) require the appropriate State election official to send notice to applicant of the disposition of the application;

(3) provide that the name of a registrant may not be removed from the official list of eligible voters except—

(A) at the request of the registrant;

(B) as provided by State law, by reason of criminal conviction or mental incapacity; or

(C) as provided under paragraph (4);

(4) conduct a general program that makes a reasonable effort to remove the names of ineligible voters from the official lists of eligible voters by reason of—

(A) the death of the registrant; or

(B) a change in the residence of the registrant, in accordance with subsections (b), (c), and (d);

(5) inform applicants under sections 5, 6, and 7 of—

(A) voter eligibility requirements; and

(B) penalties provided by law for submission of a false voter registration application; and

(6) ensure that the identity of the voter registration agency through which any particular voter is registered is not disclosed to the public.

(b) Confirmation of Voter Registration. Any State program or activity to protect the integrity of the electoral process by ensuring the maintenance of an accurate and current voter registration roll for elections for Federal office—

(1) shall be uniform, nondiscriminatory, and in compliance with the Voting Rights Act of 1965; and

(2) shall not result in the removal of the name of any person from the official list of voters registered to vote in an election for Federal office by reason of the person's failure to vote, except that nothing in this paragraph may be construed to prohibit a State from using the procedures described in subsections (c) and (d) to remove an individual from the official list of eligible voters if the individual—

(A) has not either notified the applicable registrar (in person or in writing) or responded during the period described in subparagraph (B) to the notice sent by the applicable registrar; and then

(B) has not voted or appeared to vote in 2 or more consecutive general elections for Federal office.

(c) Voter Removal Programs.

(1) A State may meet the requirement of subsection (a)(4) by establishing a program under which—

(A) change-of-address information supplied by the Postal Service through its licensees is used to identify registrants whose addresses may have changed; and

(B) if it appears from information provided by the Postal Service that—

(i) a registrant has moved to a different residence address in the same registrar's jurisdiction in which the registrant is currently registered, the registrar changes the registration records to show the new address and sends the registrant a notice of the change by forwardable mail and a postage prepaid pre-addressed return form by which the registrant may verify or correct the address information; or

(ii) the registrant has moved to a different residence address not in the same registrar's jurisdiction, the registrar uses the notice procedure described in subsection (d)(2) to confirm the change of address.

(2)(A) A State shall complete, not later than 90 days prior to the date of a primary or general election for Federal office, any program the purpose of which is to systematically remove the names of ineligible voters from the official lists of eligible voters.

(B) Subparagraph (A) shall not be construed to preclude—

(i) the removal of names from official lists of voters on a basis described in paragraph (3)(A) or (B) or (4)(A) of subsection (a); or

(ii) correction of registration records pursuant to this Act.

(d) Removal of Names From Voting Rolls. (1) A State shall not remove the name of a registrant from the official list of eligible voters in elections for Federal office on the ground that the registrant has changed residence unless the registrant—

(A) confirms in writing that the registrant has changed residence to a place outside the registrar's jurisdiction in which the registrant is registered; or

(B)(i) has failed to respond to a notice described in paragraph (2); and

(ii) has not voted or appeared to vote (and, if necessary, correct the registrar's record of the registrant's address) in an election during the period beginning on the date of the notice and ending on the day after the date of the second general election for Federal office that occurs after the date of the notice.

(2) A notice is described in this paragraph if it is a postage prepaid and pre-addressed return card, sent by forwardable mail, on which the registrant may state his or her current address, together with a notice to the following effect:

(A) If the registrant did not change his or her residence, or changed residence but remained in the registrar's jurisdiction, the registrant should return the card not later than the time provided for mail registration under subsection (a)(1)(B). If the card is not returned, affirmation or confirmation of the registrant's address may be required before the registrant is permitted to vote in a Federal election during the period beginning on the date of the notice and ending on the day after the date of the second general election for Federal office that occurs after the date of the notice, and if the registrant does not vote in an election during that period the registrant's name will be removed from the list of eligible voters.

(B) If the registrant has changed residence to a place outside the registrar's jurisdiction in which the registrant is registered, information concerning how the registrant can continue to be eligible to vote.

(3) A voting registrar shall correct an official list of eligible voters in elections for Federal office in accordance with change of residence information obtained in conformance with this subsection.

(e) Procedure for Voting Following Failure To Return Card. (1) A registrant who has moved from an address in the area covered by a polling place to an address in the same area shall, notwithstanding failure to notify the registrar of the change of address prior to the date of an election, be permitted to vote at that polling place upon oral or written affirmation by the registrant of change of address before an election official at that polling place.

(2)(A) A registrant who has moved from an address in the area covered by one polling place to an address in an area covered by a second polling place within the same registrar's jurisdiction and the same congressional district and who has failed to notify the registrar of the change address prior to the date of an election, at the option of the registrant—

(i) shall be permitted to correct the voting records and vote at the registrant's former polling place, upon oral or written affirmation by the registrant of the new address before an election official at that polling place; or

(ii)(I) shall be permitted to correct the voting records and vote at a central location within the same registrar's jurisdiction designated by the registrar where a list of eligible voters is maintained, upon written affirmation by the registrant of the new address on a standard form provided by the registrar at the central location; or

(II) shall be permitted to correct the voting records for purposes of voting in future elections at the appropriate polling place for the current address and, if permitted by State law, shall be permitted to vote in the present election, upon confirmation by the registrant of the new address by such means as are required by law.

(B) If State law permits the registrant to vote in the current election upon oral or written affirmation by the registrant of the new address at a polling place described in subparagraph (A)(i) or (A)(ii)(II), voting at the other locations described in subparagraph (A) need not be provided as options.

(3) If the registration records indicate that a registrant has moved from an address in the area covered by a polling place, the registrant shall upon oral or written affirmation by the registrant before an election official at that polling place that the registrant continues to reside at the address previously made known to the registrar, be permitted to vote at that polling place.

(f) Change of Voting Address Within a Jurisdiction. In the case of a change of address, for voting purposes, of a registrant to another address within the same registrar's jurisdiction, the registrar shall correct the voting registration list accordingly, and the registrant's name may not be removed from the official list of eligible voters by reason of such a change of address except as provided in subsection (d).

(g) Conviction in Federal Court. (1) On the conviction of a person of a felony in a district court of the United States, the United States attorney shall give written notice of the conviction to the chief State election official designated under section 10 of the State of the person's residence.

(2) A notice given pursuant to paragraph (1) shall include—

(A) the name of the offender;

(B) the offender's age and residence address;

(C) the date of entry of the judgment;

(D) a description of the offenses of which the offender was convicted; and

(E) the sentence imposed by the court.

(3) On request of the chief State election official of a State or other State official with responsibility for determining the effect that a conviction may have on an offender's qualification to vote, the United States attorney shall provide such additional information as the United States may have concerning the offender and the offense of which offender was convicted.

(4) If a conviction of which notice was given pursuant to paragraph (1) is overturned, the United States attorney shall give the official to whom the notice was given written notice of the vacation of the judgment.

(5) The chief State election official shall notify the voter registration officials of the local jurisdiction in which an offender resides of the information received under this subsection.

* * *

§ 9. Federal Coordination and Regulations.

* * *

(b) Contents of Mail Voter Registration Form. The mail voter registration form . . .

(1) may require only such identifying information (including the signature of the applicant) and other information (including data relating to previous registration by the applicant), as is necessary to enable the appropriate State election official to assess the eligibility of the applicant and to administer voter registration and other parts of the election process;

(2) shall include a statement that—

(A) specifies each eligibility requirement (including citizenship);

(B) contains an attestation that the applicant meets each such requirement; and

(C) requires the signature of the applicant, under penalty of perjury;

(3) may not include any requirement for notarization or other formal authentication; and

(4) shall include, in print that is identical to that used in the attestation portion of the application—

(i) the information required in section 8(a)(5)(A) and (B);

(ii) a statement that, if an applicant declines to register to vote, the fact that the applicant has declined to register will remain confidential and will be used only for voter registration purposes; and

(iii) a statement that if an applicant does register to vote, the office at which the applicant submits a voter registration application will remain confidential and will be used only for voter registration purposes.

* * *

§ 11.   Civil Enforcement and Private Right of Action.

(a) Attorney General. The Attorney General may bring a civil action in an appropriate district court for such declaratory or injunctive relief as is necessary to carry out this Act.

(b) Private Right of Action.

(1) A person who is aggrieved by a violation of this Act may provide written notice of the violation to the chief election official of the State involved.

(2) If the violation is not corrected within 90 days after receipt of a notice under paragraph (1), or within 20 days after receipt of the notice if the violation occurred within 120 days before the date of an election for Federal office, the aggrieved person may bring a civil action in an appropriate district court for declaratory or injunctive relief with respect to the violation.

(3) If the violation occurred within 30 days before the date of an election for Federal office, the aggrieved person need not provide notice to the chief election official of the State under paragraph (1) before bringing a civil action under paragraph (2).

(c) Attorney's Fees. In a civil action under this section the court may allow the prevailing party (other than the United States) reasonable attorney fees, including litigation expenses, and costs.

(d) Relation to Other Laws. (1) The rights and remedies established by this section are in addition to all other rights and remedies provided by law, and neither the rights and remedies established by this section nor any other provision of this Act shall supersede, restrict, or limit the application of the Voting Rights Act of 1965.

(2) Nothing in this Act authorizes or requires conduct that is prohibited by the Voting Rights Act of 1965.

The Help America Vote Act of 2002

(codified at 42 U.S.C. § 15301 et seq.) (selected sections)

§ 101.   Payments to States for Activities to Improve Administration of Elections.

(a) In General.—Not later than 45 days after the date of the enactment of this Act, the Administrator of General Services (in this title referred to as the "Administrator") shall establish a program under which the Administrator shall make a payment to each State in which the chief executive officer of the State, or designee, in consultation and coordination with the chief State election official, notifies the Administrator not later than 6 months after the date of the enactment of this Act that the State intends to use the payment in accordance with this section.

(b) Use of Payment—

(1) In general.—A State shall use the funds provided under a payment made under this section to carry out one or more of the following activities:

(A) Complying with the requirements under title III.

(B) Improving the administration of elections for Federal office.

(C) Educating voters concerning voting procedures, voting rights, and voting technology.

(D) Training election officials, poll workers, and election volunteers.

(E) Developing the State plan for requirements payments to be submitted under part 1 of subtitle D of title II.

(F) Improving, acquiring, leasing, modifying, or replacing voting systems and technology and methods for casting and counting votes.

(G) Improving the accessibility and quantity of polling places, including providing physical access for individuals with disabilities, providing nonvisual access for individuals with visual impairments, and providing assistance to Native Americans, Alaska Native citizens, and to individuals with limited proficiency in the English language.

(H) Establishing toll-free telephone hotlines that voters may use to report possible voting fraud and voting rights violations, to obtain general election information, and to access detailed automated information on their own voter registration status, specific polling place locations, and other relevant information.

* * *

§ 102.   Replacement of Punch Card or Lever Voting Machines.

(a) Establishment of Program.—

(1) In general.—Not later than 45 days after the date of the enactment of this Act, the Administrator shall establish a program under which the Administrator shall make a payment to each State eligible under subsection (b) in which a precinct within that State used a punch card voting system or a lever voting system to administer the regularly scheduled general election for Federal office held in November 2000 (in this section referred to as a "qualifying precinct").

(2) Use of funds.—A State shall use the funds provided under a payment under this section (either directly or as reimbursement, including as reimbursement for costs incurred on or after January 1, 2001, under

multiyear contracts) to replace punch card voting systems or lever voting systems (as the case may be) in qualifying precincts within that State with a voting system (by purchase, lease, or such other arrangement as may be appropriate) that—

(A) does not use punch cards or levers;

(B) is not inconsistent with the requirements of the laws described in section 906; and

(C) meets the requirements of section 301.

(3) Deadline.—

(A) In general.—Except as provided in subparagraph (B), a State receiving a payment under the program under this section shall ensure that all of the punch card voting systems or lever voting systems in the qualifying precincts within that State have been replaced in time for the regularly scheduled general election for Federal office to be held in November 2004.

(B) Waiver.—If a State certifies to the Administrator not later than January 1, 2004, that the State will not meet the deadline described in subparagraph (A) for good cause and includes in the certification the reasons for the failure to meet such deadline, the State shall ensure that all of the punch card voting systems or lever voting systems in the qualifying precincts within that State will be replaced in time for the first election for Federal office held after January 1, 2006.

* * *

(c) Amount of Payment.—

(1) In general.—Subject to paragraph (2) and section 103(b), the amount of payment made to a State under the program under this section shall be equal to the product of—

(A) the number of the qualifying precincts within the State; and

(B) $4,000.

* * *

§ 201. Establishment.

There is hereby established as an independent entity the Election Assistance Commission (hereafter in this title referred to as the "Commission"), consisting of the members appointed under this part. Additionally, there is established the Election Assistance Commission Standards Board (including the Executive Board of such Board) and the Election Assistance Commission Board of Advisors under part 2 (hereafter in this part referred to as the "Standards Board" and the "Board of Advisors", respectively) and the Technical Guidelines Development Committee under part 3.

§ 202.   Duties.

The Commission shall serve as a national clearinghouse and resource for the compilation of information and review of procedures with respect to the administration of Federal elections by—

(1) carrying out the duties described in part 3 (relating to the adoption of voluntary voting system guidelines), including the maintenance of a clearinghouse of information on the experiences of State and local governments in implementing the guidelines and in operating voting systems in general;

(2) carrying out the duties described in subtitle B (relating to the testing, certification, decertification, and recertification of voting system hardware and software);

(3) carrying out the duties described in subtitle C (relating to conducting studies and carrying out other activities to promote the effective administration of Federal elections);

(4) carrying out the duties described in subtitle D (relating to election assistance), and providing information and training on the management of the payments and grants provided under such subtitle;

(5) carrying out the duties described in subtitle B of title III (relating to the adoption of voluntary guidance); and

(6) developing and carrying out the Help America Vote College Program under title V.

§ 203.   Membership and Appointment.

(a) Membership.—

(1) In general.—The Commission shall have four members appointed by the President, by and with the advice and consent of the Senate.

(2) Recommendations.—Before the initial appointment of the members of the Commission and before the appointment of any individual to fill a vacancy on the Commission, the Majority Leader of the Senate, the Speaker of the House of Representatives, the Minority Leader of the Senate, and the Minority Leader of the House of Representatives shall each submit to the President a candidate recommendation with respect to each vacancy on the Commission affiliated with the political party of the Member of Congress involved.

(3) Qualifications.—Each member of the Commission shall have experience with or expertise in election administration or the study of elections.

(4) Date of appointment.—The appointments of the members of the Commission shall be made not later than 120 days after the date of the enactment of this Act.

(b) Term of Service.—

(1) In general.—Except as provided in paragraphs (2) and (3), members shall serve for a term of 4 years and may be reappointed for not more than one additional term.

(2) Terms of initial appointees.—As designated by the President at the time of nomination, of the members first appointed—

(A) two of the members (not more than one of whom may be affiliated with the same political party) shall be appointed for a term of 2 years; and

(B) two of the members (not more than one of whom may be affiliated with the same political party) shall be appointed for a term of 4 years.

(3) Vacancies.—

(A) In general.—A vacancy on the Commission shall be filled in the manner in which the original appointment was made and shall be subject to any conditions which applied with respect to the original appointment.

(B) Expired terms.—A member of the Commission shall serve on the Commission after the expiration of the member's term until the successor of such member has taken office as a member of the Commission.

(C) Unexpired terms.—An individual appointed to fill a vacancy shall be appointed for the unexpired term of the member replaced.

(c) Chair and Vice Chair.—

(1) In general.—The Commission shall select a chair and vice chair from among its members for a term of 1 year, except that the chair and vice chair may not be affiliated with the same political party.

(2) Number of terms.—A member of the Commission may serve as the chairperson and vice chairperson for only 1 term each during the term of office to which such member is appointed.

* * *

§ 231.   Certification and Testing of Voting Systems.

(a) Certification and Testing.—

(1) In general.—The Commission shall provide for the testing, certification, decertification, and recertification of voting system hardware and software by accredited laboratories.

(2) Optional use by states.—At the option of a State, the State may provide for the testing, certification, decertification, or recertification of its voting system hardware and software by the laboratories accredited by the Commission under this section.

(b) Laboratory Accreditation.—

(1) Recommendations by National Institute of Standards and Technology.—Not later than 6 months after the Commission first adopts voluntary voting system guidelines under part 3 of subtitle A, the Director of the National Institute of Standards and Technology shall conduct an evaluation

of independent, non-Federal laboratories and shall submit to the Commission a list of those laboratories the Director proposes to be accredited to carry out the testing, certification, decertification, and recertification provided for under this section.

* * *

§ 241. Periodic Studies of Election Administration Issues.

(a) In General.—On such periodic basis as the Commission may determine, the Commission shall conduct and make available to the public studies regarding the election administration issues described in subsection (b), with the goal of promoting methods of voting and administering elections which—

(1) will be the most convenient, accessible, and easy to use for voters, including members of the uniformed services and overseas voters, individuals with disabilities, including the blind and visually impaired, and voters with limited proficiency in the English language;

(2) will yield the most accurate, secure, and expeditious system for voting and tabulating election results;

(3) will be nondiscriminatory and afford each registered and eligible voter an equal opportunity to vote and to have that vote counted; and

(4) will be efficient and cost-effective for use.

(b) Election Administration Issues Described.—For purposes of subsection (a), the election administration issues described in this subsection are as follows:

(1) Methods and mechanisms of election technology and voting systems used in voting and counting votes in elections for Federal office, including the over-vote and under-vote notification capabilities of such technology and systems.

(2) Ballot designs for elections for Federal office.

(3) Methods of voter registration, maintaining secure and accurate lists of registered voters (including the establishment of a centralized, interactive, statewide voter registration list linked to relevant agencies and all polling sites), and ensuring that registered voters appear on the voter registration list at the appropriate polling site.

(4) Methods of conducting provisional voting.

(5) Methods of ensuring the accessibility of voting, registration, polling places, and voting equipment to all voters, including individuals with disabilities (including the blind and visually impaired), Native American or Alaska Native citizens, and voters with limited proficiency in the English language.

(6) Nationwide statistics and methods of identifying, deterring, and investigating voting fraud in elections for Federal office.

(7) Identifying, deterring, and investigating methods of voter intimidation.

(8) Methods of recruiting, training, and improving the performance of poll workers.

(9) Methods of educating voters about the process of registering to vote and voting, the operation of voting mechanisms, the location of polling places, and all other aspects of participating in elections.

(10) The feasibility and advisability of conducting elections for Federal office on different days, at different places, and during different hours, including the advisability of establishing a uniform poll closing time and establishing—

(A) a legal public holiday under section 6103 of title 5, United States Code, as the date on which general elections for Federal office are held;

(B) the Tuesday next after the 1st Monday in November, in every even numbered year, as a legal public holiday under such section;

(C) a date other than the Tuesday next after the 1st Monday in November, in every even numbered year as the date on which general elections for Federal office are held; and

(D) any date described in subparagraph (C) as a legal public holiday under such section.

(11) Federal and State laws governing the eligibility of persons to vote.

(12) Ways that the Federal Government can best assist State and local authorities to improve the administration of elections for Federal office and what levels of funding would be necessary to provide such assistance.

(13)(A) The laws and procedures used by each State that govern—

(i) recounts of ballots cast in elections for Federal office;

(ii) contests of determinations regarding whether votes are counted in such elections; and

(iii) standards that define what will constitute a vote on each type of voting equipment used in the State to conduct elections for Federal office.

(B) The best practices (as identified by the Commission) that are used by States with respect to the recounts and contests described in clause (i).

(C) Whether or not there is a need for more consistency among State recount and contest procedures used with respect to elections for Federal office.

(14) The technical feasibility of providing voting materials in eight or more languages for voters who speak those languages and who have limited English proficiency.

(15) Matters particularly relevant to voting and administering elections in rural and urban areas.

(16) Methods of voter registration for members of the uniformed services and overseas voters, and methods of ensuring that such voters receive timely ballots that will be properly and expeditiously handled and counted.

(17) The best methods for establishing voting system performance benchmarks, expressed as a percentage of residual vote in the Federal contest at the top of the ballot.

(18) Broadcasting practices that may result in the broadcast of false information concerning the location or time of operation of a polling place.

(19) Such other matters as the Commission determines are appropriate.

(c) Reports.—The Commission shall submit to the President and to the Committee on House Administration of the House of Representatives and the Committee on Rules and Administration of the Senate a report on each study conducted under subsection (a) together with such recommendations for administrative and legislative action as the Commission determines is appropriate.

* * *

§ 271.   Grants for Research on Voting Technology Improvements.

(a) In General.—The Commission shall make grants to assist entities in carrying out research and development to improve the quality, reliability, accuracy, accessibility, affordability, and security of voting equipment, election systems, and voting technology.

* * *

§ 301.   Voting System Standards.

(a) Requirements.—Each voting system used in an election for Federal office shall meet the following requirements:

(1) In general.—

(A) Except as provided in subparagraph (B), the voting system (including any lever voting system, optical scanning voting system, or direct recording electronic system) shall—

(i) permit the voter to verify (in a private and independent manner) the votes selected by the voter on the ballot before the ballot is cast and counted;

(ii) provide the voter with the opportunity (in a private and independent manner) to change the ballot or correct any error before the ballot is cast and counted (including the opportunity to correct the error through the issuance of a replacement ballot if the voter was otherwise unable to change the ballot or correct any error); and

(iii) if the voter selects votes for more than one candidate for a single office—

(I) notify the voter that the voter has selected more than one candidate for a single office on the ballot;

(II) notify the voter before the ballot is cast and counted of the effect of casting multiple votes for the office; and

(III) provide the voter with the opportunity to correct the ballot before the ballot is cast and counted.

(B) A State or jurisdiction that uses a paper ballot voting system, a punch card voting system, or a central count voting system (including mail-in absentee ballots and mail-in ballots), may meet the requirements of subparagraph (A)(iii) by—

(i) establishing a voter education program specific to that voting system that notifies each voter of the effect of casting multiple votes for an office; and

(ii) providing the voter with instructions on how to correct the ballot before it is cast and counted (including instructions on how to correct the error through the issuance of a replacement ballot if the voter was otherwise unable to change the ballot or correct any error).

(C) The voting system shall ensure that any notification required under this paragraph preserves the privacy of the voter and the confidentiality of the ballot.

(2) Audit capacity.—

(A) In general.—The voting system shall produce a record with an audit capacity for such system.

(B) Manual audit capacity.—

(i) The voting system shall produce a permanent paper record with a manual audit capacity for such system.

(ii) The voting system shall provide the voter with an opportunity to change the ballot or correct any error before the permanent paper record is produced.

(iii) The paper record produced under subparagraph (A) shall be available as an official record for any recount conducted with respect to any election in which the system is used.

(3) Accessibility for individuals with disabilities.—The voting system shall—

(A) be accessible for individuals with disabilities, including nonvisual accessibility for the blind and visually impaired, in a manner that provides the same opportunity for access and participation (including privacy and independence) as for other voters;

(B) satisfy the requirement of subparagraph (A) through the use of at least one direct recording electronic voting system or other voting system equipped for individuals with disabilities at each polling place; and

(C) if purchased with funds made available under title II on or after January 1, 2007, meet the voting system standards for disability access (as outlined in this paragraph).

(4) Alternative language accessibility.—The voting system shall provide alternative language accessibility pursuant to the requirements of section 203 of the Voting Rights Act of 1965 (42 U.S.C. 1973aa–1a).

(5) Error rates.—The error rate of the voting system in counting ballots (determined by taking into account only those errors which are attributable to the voting system and not attributable to an act of the voter) shall comply with the error rate standards established under section 3.2.1 of the voting systems standards issued by the Federal Election Commission which are in effect on the date of the enactment of this Act.

(6) Uniform definition of what constitutes a vote.—Each State shall adopt uniform and nondiscriminatory standards that define what constitutes a vote and what will be counted as a vote for each category of voting system used in the State.

(b) Voting System Defined.—In this section, the term "voting system" means—

(1) the total combination of mechanical, electromechanical, or electronic equipment (including the software, firmware, and documentation required to program, control, and support the equipment) that is used—

(A) to define ballots;

(B) to cast and count votes;

(C) to report or display election results; and

(D) to maintain and produce any audit trail information; and

(2) the practices and associated documentation used—

(A) to identify system components and versions of such components;

(B) to test the system during its development and maintenance;

(C) to maintain records of system errors and defects;

(D) to determine specific system changes to be made to a system after the initial qualification of the system; and

(E) to make available any materials to the voter (such as notices, instructions, forms, or paper ballots).

(c) Construction.—

(1) In general.—Nothing in this section shall be construed to prohibit a State or jurisdiction which used a particular type of voting system in the elections for Federal office held in November 2000 from using the same

type of system after the effective date of this section, so long as the system meets or is modified to meet the requirements of this section.

(2) Protection of paper ballot voting systems.—For purposes of subsection (a)(1)(A)(i), the term "verify" may not be defined in a manner that makes it impossible for a paper ballot voting system to meet the requirements of such subsection or to be modified to meet such requirements.

(d) Effective Date.—Each State and jurisdiction shall be required to comply with the requirements of this section on and after January 1, 2006.

§ 302. Provisional Voting and Voting Information Requirements.

(a) Provisional Voting Requirements.—If an individual declares that such individual is a registered voter in the jurisdiction in which the individual desires to vote and that the individual is eligible to vote in an election for Federal office, but the name of the individual does not appear on the official list of eligible voters for the polling place or an election official asserts that the individual is not eligible to vote, such individual shall be permitted to cast a provisional ballot as follows:

(1) An election official at the polling place shall notify the individual that the individual may cast a provisional ballot in that election.

(2) The individual shall be permitted to cast a provisional ballot at that polling place upon the execution of a written affirmation by the individual before an election official at the polling place stating that the individual is—

(A) a registered voter in the jurisdiction in which the individual desires to vote; and

(B) eligible to vote in that election.

(3) An election official at the polling place shall transmit the ballot cast by the individual or the voter information contained in the written affirmation executed by the individual under paragraph (2) to an appropriate State or local election official for prompt verification under paragraph (4).

(4) If the appropriate State or local election official to whom the ballot or voter information is transmitted under paragraph (3) determines that the individual is eligible under State law to vote, the individual's provisional ballot shall be counted as a vote in that election in accordance with State law.

(5)(A) At the time that an individual casts a provisional ballot, the appropriate State or local election official shall give the individual written information that states that any individual who casts a provisional ballot will be able to ascertain under the system established under subparagraph (B) whether the vote was counted, and, if the vote was not counted, the reason that the vote was not counted.

(B) The appropriate State or local election official shall establish a free access system (such as a toll-free telephone number or an Internet website) that any individual who casts a provisional ballot may access to discover whether the vote of that individual was counted, and, if the vote was not counted, the reason that the vote was not counted.

States described in section 4(b) of the National Voter Registration Act of 1993 (42 U.S.C. 1973gg–2(b)) may meet the requirements of this subsection using voter registration procedures established under applicable State law. The appropriate State or local official shall establish and maintain reasonable procedures necessary to protect the security, confidentiality, and integrity of personal information collected, stored, or otherwise used by the free access system established under paragraph (5)(B). Access to information about an individual provisional ballot shall be restricted to the individual who cast the ballot.

(b) Voting Information Requirements.—

(1) Public posting on election day.—The appropriate State or local election official shall cause voting information to be publicly posted at each polling place on the day of each election for Federal office.

(2) Voting information defined.—In this section, the term "voting information" means—

(A) a sample version of the ballot that will be used for that election;

(B) information regarding the date of the election and the hours during which polling places will be open;

(C) instructions on how to vote, including how to cast a vote and how to cast a provisional ballot;

(D) instructions for mail-in registrants and first-time voters under section 303(b);

(E) general information on voting rights under applicable Federal and State laws, including information on the right of an individual to cast a provisional ballot and instructions on how to contact the appropriate officials if these rights are alleged to have been violated; and

(F) general information on Federal and State laws regarding prohibitions on acts of fraud and misrepresentation.

(c) Voters Who Vote After the Polls Close.—Any individual who votes in an election for Federal office as a result of a Federal or State court order or any other order extending the time established for closing the polls by a State law in effect 10 days before the date of that election may only vote in that election by casting a provisional ballot under subsection (a). Any such ballot cast under the preceding sentence shall be separated and held apart from other provisional ballots cast by those not affected by the order.

(d) Effective Date for Provisional Voting and Voting Information.—Each State and jurisdiction shall be required to comply with the requirements of this section on and after January 1, 2004.

§ 303.   Computerized Statewide Voter Registration List Requirements and Requirements for Voters Who Register by Mail.

(a) Computerized Statewide Voter Registration List Requirements.—

(1) Implementation.—

(A) In general.—Except as provided in subparagraph (B), each State, acting through the chief State election official, shall implement, in a uniform and nondiscriminatory manner, a single, uniform, official, centralized, interactive computerized statewide voter registration list defined, maintained, and administered at the State level that contains the name and registration information of every legally registered voter in the State and assigns a unique identifier to each legally registered voter in the State (in this subsection referred to as the "computerized list"), and includes the following:

(i) The computerized list shall serve as the single system for storing and managing the official list of registered voters throughout the State.

(ii) The computerized list contains the name and registration information of every legally registered voter in the State.

(iii) Under the computerized list, a unique identifier is assigned to each legally registered voter in the State.

(iv) The computerized list shall be coordinated with other agency databases within the State.

(v) Any election official in the State, including any local election official, may obtain immediate electronic access to the information contained in the computerized list.

(vi) All voter registration information obtained by any local election official in the State shall be electronically entered into the computerized list on an expedited basis at the time the information is provided to the local official.

(vii) The chief State election official shall provide such support as may be required so that local election officials are able to enter information as described in clause (vi).

(viii) The computerized list shall serve as the official voter registration list for the conduct of all elections for Federal office in the State.

(B) Exception.—The requirement under subparagraph (A) shall not apply to a State in which, under a State law in effect continuously on and after the date of the enactment of this Act, there is no voter registration requirement for individuals in the State with respect to elections for Federal office.

(2) Computerized list maintenance.—

(A) In general.—The appropriate State or local election official shall perform list maintenance with respect to the computerized list on a regular basis as follows:

(i) If an individual is to be removed from the computerized list, such individual shall be removed in accordance with the provisions of the National Voter Registration Act of 1993 (42 U.S.C. 1973gg et seq.), including subsections (a)(4), (c)(2), (d), and (e) of section 8 of such Act (42 U.S.C. 1973gg–6).

(ii) For purposes of removing names of ineligible voters from the official list of eligible voters—

(I) under section 8(a)(3)(B) of such Act (42 U.S.C. 1973gg–6(a)(3)(B)), the State shall coordinate the computerized list with State agency records on felony status; and

(II) by reason of the death of the registrant under section 8(a)(4)(A) of such Act (42 U.S.C. 1973gg–6(a)(4)(A)), the State shall coordinate the computerized list with State agency records on death.

(iii) Notwithstanding the preceding provisions of this subparagraph, if a State is described in section 4(b) of the National Voter Registration Act of 1993 (42 U.S.C. 1973gg–2(b)), that State shall remove the names of ineligible voters from the computerized list in accordance with State law.

(B) Conduct.—The list maintenance performed under subparagraph (A) shall be conducted in a manner that ensures that—

(i) the name of each registered voter appears in the computerized list;

(ii) only voters who are not registered or who are not eligible to vote are removed from the computerized list; and

(iii) duplicate names are eliminated from the computerized list.

(3) Technological security of computerized list.—The appropriate State or local official shall provide adequate technological security measures to prevent the unauthorized access to the computerized list established under this section.

(4) Minimum standard for accuracy of state voter registration records.—The State election system shall include provisions to ensure that voter registration records in the State are accurate and are updated regularly, including the following:

(A) A system of file maintenance that makes a reasonable effort to remove registrants who are ineligible to vote from the official list of eligible voters. Under such system, consistent with the National Voter Registration Act of 1993 (42 U.S.C. 1973gg et seq.), registrants who have not responded to a notice and who have not voted in 2 consecutive general elections for Federal office shall be removed from the official list of eligible voters, except that no registrant may be removed solely by reason of a failure to vote.

(B) Safeguards to ensure that eligible voters are not removed in error from the official list of eligible voters.

(5) Verification of voter registration information.—

(A) Requiring provision of certain information by applicants.—

(i) In general.—Except as provided in clause (ii), notwithstanding any other provision of law, an application for voter registration for an election for Federal office may not be accepted or processed by a State unless the application includes—

(I) in the case of an applicant who has been issued a current and valid driver's license, the applicant's driver's license number; or

(II) in the case of any other applicant (other than an applicant to whom clause (ii) applies), the last 4 digits of the applicant's social security number.

(ii) Special rule for applicants without driver's license or social security number.—If an applicant for voter registration for an election for Federal office has not been issued a current and valid driver's license or a social security number, the State shall assign the applicant a number which will serve to identify the applicant for voter registration purposes. To the extent that the State has a computerized list in effect under this subsection and the list assigns unique identifying numbers to registrants, the number assigned under this clause shall be the unique identifying number assigned under the list.

(iii) Determination of validity of numbers provided.—The State shall determine whether the information provided by an individual is sufficient to meet the requirements of this subparagraph, in accordance with State law.

(B) Requirements for state officials.—

(i) Sharing information in databases.—The chief State election official and the official responsible for the State motor vehicle authority of a State shall enter into an agreement to match information in the database of the statewide voter registration system with information in the database of the motor vehicle authority to the extent required to enable each such official to verify the accuracy of the information provided on applications for voter registration.

(ii) Agreements with commissioner of social security.—The official responsible for the State motor vehicle authority shall enter into an agreement with the Commissioner of Social Security under section 205(r)(8) of the Social Security Act (as added by subparagraph (C)).

(C) Access to federal information.—Section 205(r) of the Social Security Act (42 U.S.C. 405(r)) is amended by adding at the end the following new paragraph:

"(8)(A) The Commissioner of Social Security shall, upon the request of the official responsible for a State driver's license agency pursuant to the Help America Vote Act of 2002—

"(i) enter into an agreement with such official for the purpose of verifying applicable information, so long as the requirements of subparagraphs (A) and (B) of paragraph (3) are met; and

"(ii) include in such agreement safeguards to assure the maintenance of the confidentiality of any applicable information disclosed and procedures to permit such agency to use the applicable information for the purpose of maintaining its records.

"(B) Information provided pursuant to an agreement under this paragraph shall be provided at such time, in such place, and in such manner as the Commissioner determines appropriate.

"(C) The Commissioner shall develop methods to verify the accuracy of information provided by the agency with respect to applications for voter registration, for whom the last 4 digits of a social security number are provided instead of a driver's license number.

"(D) For purposes of this paragraph—

"(i) the term 'applicable information' means information regarding whether—

"(I) the name (including the first name and any family forename or surname), the date of birth (including the month, day, and year), and social security number of an individual provided to the Commissioner match the information contained in the Commissioner's records, and

"(II) such individual is shown on the records of the Commissioner as being deceased; and

"(ii) the term 'State driver's license agency' means the State agency which issues driver's licenses to individuals within the State and maintains records relating to such licensure.

"(E) Nothing in this paragraph may be construed to require the provision of applicable information with regard to a request for a record of an individual if the Commissioner determines there are exceptional circumstances warranting an exception (such as safety of the individual or interference with an investigation).

"(F) Applicable information provided by the Commission pursuant to an agreement under this paragraph or by an individual to any agency that has entered into an agreement under this paragraph shall be considered as strictly confidential and shall be used only for the purposes described in this paragraph and for carrying out an agreement under this paragraph.

Any officer or employee or former officer or employee of a State, or any officer or employee or former officer or employee of a contractor of a State who, without the written authority of the Commissioner, publishes or communicates any applicable information in such individual's possession by reason of such employment or position as such an officer, shall be guilty of a felony and upon conviction thereof shall be fined or imprisoned, or both, as described in section 208.''

(D) Special rule for certain states.—In the case of a State which is permitted to use social security numbers, and provides for the use of social security numbers, on applications for voter registration, in accordance with section 7 of the Privacy Act of 1974 (5 U.S.C. 552a note), the provisions of this paragraph shall be optional.

(b) Requirements for Voters Who Register by Mail.—

(1) In general.—Notwithstanding section 6(c) of the National Voter Registration Act of 1993 (42 U.S.C. 1973gg–4(c)) and subject to paragraph (3), a State shall, in a uniform and nondiscriminatory manner, require an individual to meet the requirements of paragraph (2) if—

(A) the individual registered to vote in a jurisdiction by mail; and(B)

(i) the individual has not previously voted in an election for Federal office in the State; or

(ii) the individual has not previously voted in such an election in the jurisdiction and the jurisdiction is located in a State that does not have a computerized list that complies with the requirements of subsection (a).

(2) Requirements.—

(A) In general.—An individual meets the requirements of this paragraph if the individual—

(i) in the case of an individual who votes in person—

(I) presents to the appropriate State or local election official a current and valid photo identification; or

(II) presents to the appropriate State or local election official a copy of a current utility bill, bank statement, government check, paycheck, or other government document that shows the name and address of the voter; or

(ii) in the case of an individual who votes by mail, submits with the ballot—

(I) a copy of a current and valid photo identification; or

(II) a copy of a current utility bill, bank statement, government check, paycheck, or other government document that shows the name and address of the voter.

(B) Fail-safe voting.—

(i) In person.—An individual who desires to vote in person, but who does not meet the requirements of subparagraph (A)(i), may cast a provisional ballot under section 302(a).

(ii) By mail.—An individual who desires to vote by mail but who does not meet the requirements of subparagraph (A)(ii) may cast such a ballot by mail and the ballot shall be counted as a provisional ballot in accordance with section 302(a).

(3) Inapplicability.—Paragraph (1) shall not apply in the case of a person—

(A) who registers to vote by mail under section 6 of the National Voter Registration Act of 1993 (42 U.S.C. 1973gg–4) and submits as part of such registration either—

(i) a copy of a current and valid photo identification; or

(ii) a copy of a current utility bill, bank statement, government check, paycheck, or government document that shows the name and address of the voter;

(B)

(i) who registers to vote by mail under section 6 of the National Voter Registration Act of 1993 (42 U.S.C. 1973gg–4) and submits with such registration either—

(I) a driver's license number; or

(II) at least the last 4 digits of the individual's social security number; and

(ii) with respect to whom a State or local election official matches the information submitted under clause (i) with an existing State identification record bearing the same number, name and date of birth as provided in such registration; or

(C) who is—

(i) entitled to vote by absentee ballot under the Uniformed and Overseas Citizens Absentee Voting Act (42 U.S.C. 1973ff–1 et seq.);

(ii) provided the right to vote otherwise than in person under section 3(b)(2)(B)(ii) of the Voting Accessibility for the Elderly and Handicapped Act (42 U.S.C. 1973ee–1(b)(2)(B)(ii)); or

(iii) entitled to vote otherwise than in person under any other Federal law.

(4) Contents of mail-in registration form.—

(A) In general.—The mail voter registration form developed under section 6 of the National Voter Registration Act of 1993 (42 U.S.C. 1973gg–4) shall include the following:

(i) The question "Are you a citizen of the United States of America?" and boxes for the applicant to check to indicate whether the applicant is or is not a citizen of the United States.

(ii) The question "Will you be 18 years of age on or before election day?" and boxes for the applicant to check to indicate whether or not the applicant will be 18 years of age or older on election day.

(iii) The statement "If you checked 'no' in response to either of these questions, do not complete this form.".

(iv) A statement informing the individual that if the form is submitted by mail and the individual is registering for the first time, the appropriate information required under this section must be submitted with the mail-in registration form in order to avoid the additional identification requirements upon voting for the first time.

(B) Incomplete forms.—If an applicant for voter registration fails to answer the question included on the mail voter registration form pursuant to subparagraph (A)(i), the registrar shall notify the applicant of the failure and provide the applicant with an opportunity to complete the form in a timely manner to allow for the completion of the registration form prior to the next election for Federal office (subject to State law).

(5) Construction.—Nothing in this subsection shall be construed to require a State that was not required to comply with a provision of the National Voter Registration Act of 1993 (42 U.S.C. 1973gg et seq.) before the date of the enactment of this Act to comply with such a provision after such date.

(c) Permitted Use of Last 4 Digits of Social Security Numbers.—The last 4 digits of a social security number described in subsections (a)(5)(A)(i)(II) and (b)(3)(B)(i)(II) shall not be considered to be a social security number for purposes of section 7 of the Privacy Act of 1974 (5 U.S.C. 552a note).

(d) Effective Date.—

(1) Computerized statewide voter registration list requirements.—

(A) In general.—Except as provided in subparagraph (B), each State and jurisdiction shall be required to comply with the requirements of subsection (a) on and after January 1, 2004.

(B) Waiver.—If a State or jurisdiction certifies to the Commission not later than January 1, 2004, that the State or jurisdiction will not meet the deadline described in subparagraph (A) for good cause and includes in the certification the reasons for the failure to meet such deadline, subparagraph (A) shall apply to the State or jurisdiction as if the reference in such subparagraph to "January 1, 2004" were a reference to "January 1, 2006".

(2) Requirement for voters who register by mail.—

(A) In general.—Each State and jurisdiction shall be required to comply with the requirements of subsection (b) on and after January 1, 2004, and shall be prepared to receive registration materials submitted by individuals described in subparagraph (B) on and after the date described in such subparagraph.

(B) Applicability with respect to individuals.—The provisions of subsection (b) shall apply to any individual who registers to vote on or after January 1, 2003.

§ 304. Minimum Requirements.

The requirements established by this title are minimum requirements and nothing in this title shall be construed to prevent a State from establishing election technology and administration requirements that are more strict than the requirements established under this title so long as such State requirements are not inconsistent with the Federal requirements under this title or any law described in section 906.

§ 305. Methods of Implementation Left to Discretion of State.

The specific choices on the methods of complying with the requirements of this title shall be left to the discretion of the State.

* * *

§ 401. Actions by the Attorney General for Declaratory and Injunctive Relief.

The Attorney General may bring a civil action against any State or jurisdiction in an appropriate United States District Court for such declaratory and injunctive relief (including a temporary restraining order, a permanent or temporary injunction, or other order) as may be necessary to carry out the uniform and nondiscriminatory election technology and administration requirements under sections 301, 302, and 303.

§ 402. Establishment of State–Based Administrative Complaint Procedures to Remedy Grievances.

(a) Establishment of State–Based Administrative Complaint Procedures to Remedy Grievances.—

(1) Establishment of procedures as condition of receiving funds.—If a State receives any payment under a program under this Act, the State shall be required to establish and maintain State-based administrative complaint procedures which meet the requirements of paragraph (2).

(2) Requirements for procedures.—The requirements of this paragraph are as follows:

(A) The procedures shall be uniform and nondiscriminatory.

(B) Under the procedures, any person who believes that there is a violation of any provision of title III (including a violation which has occurred, is occurring, or is about to occur) may file a complaint.

(C) Any complaint filed under the procedures shall be in writing and notarized, and signed and sworn by the person filing the complaint.

(D) The State may consolidate complaints filed under subparagraph (B).

(E) At the request of the complainant, there shall be a hearing on the record.

(F) If, under the procedures, the State determines that there is a violation of any provision of title III, the State shall provide the appropriate remedy.

(G) If, under the procedures, the State determines that there is no violation, the State shall dismiss the complaint and publish the results of the procedures.

(H) The State shall make a final determination with respect to a complaint prior to the expiration of the 90–day period which begins on the date the complaint is filed, unless the complainant consents to a longer period for making such a determination.

(I) If the State fails to meet the deadline applicable under subparagraph (H), the complaint shall be resolved within 60 days under alternative dispute resolution procedures established for purposes of this section. The record and other materials from any proceedings conducted under the complaint procedures established under this section shall be made available for use under the alternative dispute resolution procedures.

* * *

§ 904.   Review and Report on Adequacy of Existing Electoral Fraud Statutes and Penalties.

(a) Review.—The Attorney General shall conduct a review of existing criminal statutes concerning election offenses to determine—

(1) whether additional statutory offenses are needed to secure the use of the Internet for election purposes; and

(2) whether existing penalties provide adequate punishment and deterrence with respect to such offenses.

(b) Report.—The Attorney General shall submit a report to the Committees on the Judiciary of the Senate and House of Representatives, the Committee on Rules and Administration of the Senate, and the Committee on House Administration of the House of Representatives on the review conducted under subsection (a) together with such recommendations for legislative and administrative action as the Attorney General determines appropriate.

§ 905.   Other Criminal Penalties.

(a) Conspiracy To Deprive Voters of a Fair Election.—Any individual who knowingly and willfully gives false information in registering or voting in violation of section 11(c) of the National Voting Rights Act of 1965 (42 U.S.C. 1973i(c)), or conspires with another to violate such section, shall be fined or imprisoned, or both, in accordance with such section.

(b) False Information in Registering and Voting.—Any individual who knowingly commits fraud or knowingly makes a false statement with respect to the naturalization, citizenry, or alien registry of such individual in violation of section 1015 of title 18, United States Code, shall be fined or imprisoned, or both, in accordance with such section.

§ 906.   No Effect on Other Laws.

(a) In General.—Except as specifically provided in section 303(b) of this Act with regard to the National Voter Registration Act of 1993 (42 U.S.C. 1973gg et seq.), nothing in this Act may be construed to authorize or require conduct prohibited under any of the following laws, or to supersede, restrict, or limit the application of such laws:

(1) The Voting Rights Act of 1965 (42 U.S.C. 1973 et seq.).

(2) The Voting Accessibility for the Elderly and Handicapped Act (42 U.S.C. 1973ee et seq.).

(3) The Uniformed and Overseas Citizens Absentee Voting Act (42 U.S.C. 1973ff et seq.).

(4) The National Voter Registration Act of 1993 (42 U.S.C. 1973gg et seq.).

(5) The Americans with Disabilities Act of 1990 (42 U.S.C. 12101 et seq.).

(6) The Rehabilitation Act of 1973 (29 U.S.C. 701 et seq.).

(b) No Effect on Preclearance or Other Requirements Under Voting Rights Act.—The approval by the Administrator or the Commission of a payment or grant application under title I or title II, or any other action taken by the Commission or a State under such title, shall not be considered to have any effect on requirements for preclearance under section 5 of the Voting Rights Act of 1965 (42 U.S.C. 1973c) or any other requirements of such Act.

Procedures for the Administration of Section 5 of the Voting Rights Act

28 C.F.R. Part 51 (2006) (selected sections)

Subpart A—General Provisions

§ 51.1   Purpose.

(a) Section 5 of the Voting Rights Act of 1965, as amended, 42 U.S.C. 1973c, prohibits the enforcement in any jurisdiction covered by section 4(b) of the Act, 42 U.S.C. 1973b(b), of any voting qualification or prerequisite to voting, or standard, practice, or procedure with respect to voting different from that in force or effect on the date used to determine coverage, until either:

(1) A declaratory judgment is obtained from the U.S. District Court for the District of Columbia that such qualification, prerequisite, standard, practice, or procedure does not have the purpose and will not have the effect of denying or abridging the right to vote on account of race, color, or membership in a language minority group, or

(2) It has been submitted to the Attorney General and the Attorney General has interposed no objection within a 60–day period following submission.

(b) In order to make clear the responsibilities of the Attorney General under section 5 and the interpretation of the Attorney General of the responsibility imposed on others under this section, the procedures in this part have been established to govern the administration of section 5.

§ 51.2   Definitions.

As used in this part—

Act means the Voting Rights Act of 1965, 79 Stat. 437, as amended by the Civil Rights Act of 1968, 82 Stat. 73, the Voting Rights Act Amendments of 1970, 84 Stat. 314, the District of Columbia Delegate Act, 84 Stat. 853, the Voting Rights Act Amendments of 1975, 89 Stat. 400, and the Voting Rights Act Amendments of 1982, 96 Stat. 131, 42 U.S.C. 1973 et seq. Section numbers, such as "section 14(c)(3)," refer to sections of the Act.

Attorney General means the Attorney General of the United States or the delegate of the Attorney General.

Change affecting voting means any voting qualification, prerequisite to voting, or standard, practice, or procedure with respect to voting different from that in force or effect on the date used to determine coverage under section 4(b) and includes, inter alia, the examples given in Sec. 51.13.

Covered jurisdiction is used to refer to a State, where the determination referred to in Sec. 51.4 has been made on a statewide basis, and to a political subdivision, where the determination has not been made on a statewide basis.

Language minorities or language minority group is used, as defined in the Act, to refer to persons who are American Indian, Asian American, Alaskan Natives, or of Spanish heritage. (Sections 14(c)(3) and 203(e)). See 28 CFR part 55, Interpretative Guidelines: Implementation of the Provisions of the Voting Rights Act Regarding Language Minority Groups.

Political subdivision is used, as defined in the Act, to refer to "any county or parish, except that where registration for voting is not conducted under the supervision of a county or parish, the term shall include any other subdivision of a State which conducts registration for voting." (Section 14(c)(2)).

Preclearance is used to refer to the obtaining of the declaratory judgment described in section 5, to the failure of the Attorney General to interpose an objection pursuant to section 5, or to the withdrawal of an objection by the Attorney General pursuant to Sec. 51.48(b).

Submission is used to refer to the written presentation to the Attorney General by an appropriate official of any change affecting voting.

Submitting authority means the jurisdiction on whose behalf a submission is made.

Vote and voting are used, as defined in the Act, to include "all action necessary to make a vote effective in any primary, special, or general election, including, but not limited to, registration, listing pursuant to this Act, or other action required by law prerequisite to voting, casting a ballot, and having such ballot counted properly and included in the appropriate totals of votes cast with respect to candidates for public or party office and propositions for which votes are received in an election." (Section 14(c)(1)).

§ 51.3 Delegation of Authority.

The responsibility and authority for determinations under section 5 have been delegated by the Attorney General to the Assistant Attorney General, Civil Rights Division. With the exception of objections and decisions following the reconsideration of objections, the Chief of the Voting Section is authorized to act on behalf of the Assistant Attorney General.

* * *

§ 51.7 Political Parties.

Certain activities of political parties are subject to the preclearance requirement of section 5. A change affecting voting effected by a political party is subject to the preclearance requirement:

(a) If the change relates to a public electoral function of the party and

(b) If the party is acting under authority explicitly or implicitly granted by a covered jurisdiction or political subunit subject to the preclearance requirement of section 5.

For example, changes with respect to the recruitment of party members, the conduct of political campaigns, and the drafting of party platforms are not subject to the preclearance requirement. Changes with respect to the conduct of primary elections at which party nominees, delegates to party conventions, or party officials are chosen are subject to the preclearance requirement of section 5. Where appropriate the term "jurisdiction" (but not "covered jurisdiction") includes political parties.

* * *

§ 51.11   Right to Bring Suit.

Submission to the Attorney General does not affect the right of the submitting authority to bring an action in the U.S. District Court for the District of Columbia for a declaratory judgment that the change affecting voting does not have the prohibited discriminatory purpose or effect.

§ 51.12   Scope of Requirement.

Any change affecting voting, even though it appears to be minor or indirect, returns to a prior practice or procedure, ostensibly expands voting rights, or is designed to remove the elements that caused objection by the Attorney General to a prior submitted change, must meet the section 5 preclearance requirement.

§ 51.13   Examples of Changes.

Changes affecting voting include, but are not limited to, the following examples:

(a) Any change in qualifications or eligibility for voting.

(b) Any change concerning registration, balloting, and the counting of votes and any change concerning publicity for or assistance in registration or voting.

(c) Any change with respect to the use of a language other than English in any aspect of the electoral process.

(d) Any change in the boundaries of voting precincts or in the location of polling places.

(e) Any change in the constituency of an official or the boundaries of a voting unit (e.g., through redistricting, annexation, deannexation, incorporation, reapportionment, changing to at-large elections from district elections, or changing to district elections from at-large elections).

(f) Any change in the method of determining the outcome of an election (e.g., by requiring a majority vote for election or the use of a designated post or place system).

(g) Any change affecting the eligibility of persons to become or remain candidates, to obtain a position on the ballot in primary or general elections, or to become or remain holders of elective offices.

(h) Any change in the eligibility and qualification procedures for independent candidates.

(i) Any change in the term of an elective office or an elected official or in the offices that are elective (e.g., by shortening the term of an office, changing from election to appointment or staggering the terms of offices).

(j) Any change affecting the necessity of or methods for offering issues and propositions for approval by referendum.

(k) Any change affecting the right or ability of persons to participate in political campaigns which is effected by a jurisdiction subject to the requirement of section 5.

* * *

§ 51.18 Court–Ordered Changes.

(a) In general. Changes affecting voting that are ordered by a Federal court are subject to the preclearance requirement of section 5 to the extent that they reflect the policy choices of the submitting authority.

(b) Subsequent changes. Where a court-ordered change is not itself subject to the preclearance requirement, subsequent changes necessitated by the court order but decided upon by the jurisdiction remain subject to preclearance. For example, voting precinct and polling place changes made necessary by a court-ordered redistricting plan are subject to section 5 review.

(c) In emergencies. A Federal court's authorization of the emergency interim use without preclearance of a voting change does not exempt from section 5 review any use of the practice not explicitly authorized by the court.

* * *

Subpart B—Procedures for Submission to the Attorney General

* * *

§ 51.23 Party And Jurisdiction Responsible For Making submissions.

(a) Changes affecting voting shall be submitted by the chief legal officer or other appropriate official of the submitting authority or by any other authorized person on behalf of the submitting authority. When one or more counties or other political subunits within a State will be affected, the State may make a submission on their behalf. Where a State is covered as a whole, State legislation (except legislation of local applicability) or other changes undertaken or required by the State shall be submitted by the State.

(b) A change effected by a political party (see Sec. 51.7) may be submitted by an appropriate official of the political party.

Subpart C—Contents of Submissions

* * *

§ 51.27 Required contents.

Each submission should contain the following information or documents to enable the Attorney General to make the required determination pursuant to section 5 with respect to the submitted change affecting voting:

(a) A copy of any ordinance, enactment, order, or regulation embodying a change affecting voting.

(b) A copy of any ordinance, enactment, order, or regulation embodying the voting practice that is proposed to be repealed, amended, or otherwise changed.

(c) If the change affecting voting either is not readily apparent on the face of the documents provided under paragraphs (a) and (b) of this section or is not embodied in a document, a clear statement of the change explaining the difference between the submitted change and the prior law or practice, or explanatory materials adequate to disclose to the Attorney General the difference between the prior and proposed situation with respect to voting.

(d) The name, title, address, and telephone number of the person making the submission.

(e) The name of the submitting authority and the name of the jurisdiction responsible for the change, if different.

(f) If the submission is not from a State or county, the name of the county and State in which the submitting authority is located.

(g) Identification of the person or body responsible for making the change and the mode of decision (e.g., act of State legislature, ordinance of city council, administrative decision by registrar).

(h) A statement identifying the statutory or other authority under which the jurisdiction undertakes the change and a description of the procedures the jurisdiction was required to follow in deciding to undertake the change.

(i) The date of adoption of the change affecting voting.

(j) The date on which the change is to take effect.

(k) A statement that the change has not yet been enforced or administered, or an explanation of why such a statement cannot be made.

(*l*) Where the change will affect less than the entire jurisdiction, an explanation of the scope of the change.

(m) A statement of the reasons for the change.

(n) A statement of the anticipated effect of the change on members of racial or language minority groups.

(*o*) A statement identifying any past or pending litigation concerning the change or related voting practices.

(p) A statement that the prior practice has been precleared (with the date) or is not subject to the preclearance requirement and a statement that the procedure for the adoption of the change has been precleared (with the date) or is not subject to the preclearance requirement, or an explanation of why such statements cannot be made.

* * *

(r) Other information that the Attorney General determines is required for an evaluation of the purpose or effect of the change ...

Such information may include items listed in Sec. 51.28 and is most likely to be needed with respect to redistrictings, annexations, and other complex changes. In the interest of time such information should be furnished with the initial submission relating to voting changes of this type. When such information is required, but not provided, the Attorney General shall notify the submitting authority in the manner provided in Sec. 51.37.

§ 51.28   Supplemental Contents.

Review by the Attorney General will be facilitated if the following information, where pertinent, is provided in addition to that required by Sec. 51.27.

* * *

(f) Publicity and participation. For submissions involving controversial or potentially controversial changes, evidence of public notice, of the opportunity for the public to be heard, and of the opportunity for interested parties to participate in the decision to adopt the proposed change and an account of the extent to which such participation, especially by minority group members, in fact took place.

* * *

(h) Minority group contacts. For submissions from jurisdictions having a significant minority population, the names, addresses, telephone numbers, and organizational affiliation (if any) of racial or language minority group members residing in the jurisdiction who can be expected to be familiar with the proposed change or who have been active in the political process.

* * *

Subpart E—Processing of Submissions

* * *

§ 51.34   Expedited Consideration.

(a) When a submitting authority is required under State law or local ordinance or otherwise finds it necessary to implement a change within the 60–day period following submission, it may request that the submission be given expedited consideration. The submission should explain why such consideration is needed and provide the date by which a determination is required.

(b) Jurisdictions should endeavor to plan for changes in advance so that expedited consideration will not be required and should not routinely request such consideration. When a submitting authority demonstrates good cause for expedited consideration the Attorney General will attempt to make a decision by the date requested. However, the Attorney General cannot guarantee that such consideration can be given.

§ 51.37   Obtaining Information from the Submitting Authority.

(a) If a submission does not satisfy the requirements of Sec. 51.27, the Attorney General may request from the submitting authority any omitted information considered necessary for the evaluation of the submission. The request shall be made by letter and shall be made within the 60–day period and as promptly as possible after receipt of the original submission. See also Sec. 51.26(d).

(b) A copy of the request shall be sent to any party who has commented on the submission or has requested notice of the Attorney General's action thereon.

(c) The Attorney General shall notify the submitting authority that a new 60–day period in which the Attorney General may interpose an objection shall commence upon the receipt of a response from the submitting authority that provides the information requested or states that the information is unavailable. The Attorney General can request further information within the new 60–day period, but such a further request shall not suspend the running of the 60–day period, nor shall the receipt of a response to such a request operate to begin a new 60–day period.

* * *

§ 51.41   Notification of Decision Not to Object.

(a) The Attorney General shall within the 60–day period allowed notify the submitting authority of a decision to interpose no objection to a submitted change affecting voting.

(b) The notification shall state that the failure of the Attorney General to object does not bar subsequent litigation to enjoin the enforcement of the change.

(c) A copy of the notification shall be sent to any party who has commented on the submission or has requested notice of the Attorney General's action thereon.

§ 51.42   Failure of the Attorney General to Respond.

It is the practice and intention of the Attorney General to respond to each submission within the 60–day period. However, the failure of the Attorney General to make a written response within the 60–day period constitutes preclearance of the submitted change, provided the submission is addressed as specified in Sec. 51.24 and is appropriate for a response on the merits as described in Sec. 51.35.

§ 51.43 Reexamination of Decision Not to Object.

After notification to the submitting authority of a decision to interpose no objection to a submitted change affecting voting has been given, the Attorney General may reexamine the submission if, prior to the expiration of the 60–day period, information indicating the possibility of the prohibited discriminatory purpose or effect is received. In this event, the Attorney General may interpose an objection provisionally and advise the submitting authority that examination of the change in light of the newly raised issues will continue and that a final decision will be rendered as soon as possible.

§ 51.44 Notification of Decision to Object.

(a) The Attorney General shall within the 60–day period allowed notify the submitting authority of a decision to interpose an objection. The reasons for the decision shall be stated.

(b) The submitting authority shall be advised that the Attorney General will reconsider an objection upon a request by the submitting authority.

(c) The submitting authority shall be advised further that notwithstanding the objection it may institute an action in the U.S. District Court for the District of Columbia for a declaratory judgment that the change objected to by the Attorney General does not have the prohibited discriminatory purpose or effect.

* * *

§ 51.48 Decision After Reconsideration.

(a) The Attorney General shall within the 60–day period following the receipt of a reconsideration request or following notice given under Sec. 51.46(b) notify the submitting authority of the decision to continue or withdraw the objection, provided that the Attorney General shall have at least 15 days following any conference that is held in which to decide. (See also Sec. 51.39(a).) The reasons for the decision shall be stated.

(b) The objection shall be withdrawn if the Attorney General is satisfied that the change does not have the purpose and will not have the effect of discriminating on account of race, color, or membership in a language minority group.

(c) If the objection is not withdrawn, the submitting authority shall be advised that notwithstanding the objection it may institute an action in the U.S. District Court for the District of Columbia for a declaratory judgment that the change objected to by the Attorney General does not have the prohibited purpose or effect.

(d) An objection remains in effect until either it is withdrawn by the Attorney General or a declaratory judgment with respect to the change in question is entered by the U.S. District Court for the District of Columbia.

* * *

Subpart F—Determinations by the Attorney General

§ 51.51 Purpose of the Subpart.

The purpose of this subpart is to inform submitting authorities and other interested parties of the factors that the Attorney General considers relevant and of the standards by which the Attorney General will be guided in making substantive determinations under section 5 and in defending section 5 declaratory judgment actions.

§ 51.52 Basic Standard.

(a) Surrogate for the court. Section 5 provides for submission of a voting change to the Attorney General as an alternative to the seeking of a declaratory judgment from the U.S. District Court for the District of Columbia. Therefore, the Attorney General shall make the same determination that would be made by the court in an action for a declaratory judgment under section 5: Whether the submitted change has the purpose or will have the effect of denying or abridging the right to vote on account of race, color, or membership in a language minority group. The burden of proof is on a submitting authority when it submits a change to the Attorney General for preclearance, as it would be if the proposed change were the subject of a declaratory judgment action in the U.S. District Court for the District of Columbia. See South Carolina v. Katzenbach, 383 U.S. 301, 328, 335 (1966).

(b) No objection. If the Attorney General determines that the submitted change does not have the prohibited purpose or effect, no objection shall be interposed to the change.

(c) Objection. An objection shall be interposed to a submitted change if the Attorney General is unable to determine that the change is free of discriminatory purpose and effect. This includes those situations where the evidence as to the purpose or effect of the change is conflicting and the Attorney General is unable to determine that the change is free of discriminatory purpose and effect.

* * *

§ 51.54 Discriminatory Effect.

(a) Retrogression. A change affecting voting is considered to have a discriminatory effect under section 5 if it will lead to a retrogression in the position of members of a racial or language minority group (i.e., will make members of such a group worse off than they had been before the change) with respect to their opportunity to exercise the electoral franchise effectively. See Beer v. United States, 425 U.S. 130, 140–42 (1976).

(b) Benchmark.

(1) In determining whether a submitted change is retrogressive the Attorney General will normally compare the submitted change to the voting practice or procedure in effect at the time of the submission. If the existing practice or procedure upon submission was not in effect on the jurisdiction's applicable date for coverage (specified in the appendix) and is not otherwise legally enforceable under section 5, it cannot serve as a benchmark, and, except as provided in paragraph (b)(4) of this section, the comparison shall be with the last legally enforceable practice or procedure used by the jurisdiction.

(2) The Attorney General will make the comparison based on the conditions existing at the time of the submission.

(3) The implementation and use of an unprecleared voting change subject to section 5 review under Sec. 51.18(a) does not operate to make that unprecleared change a benchmark for any subsequent change submitted by the jurisdiction. See Sec. 51.18(c).

(4) Where at the time of submission of a change for section 5 review there exists no other lawful practice or procedure for use as a benchmark (e.g., where a newly incorporated college district selects a method of election) the Attorney General's preclearance determination will necessarily center on whether the submitted change was designed or adopted for the purpose of discriminating against members of racial or language minority groups.

§ 51.55 Consistency With Constitutional and Statutory Requirements.

(a) Consideration in general. In making a determination the Attorney General will consider whether the change is free of discriminatory purpose and retrogressive effect in light of, and with particular attention being given to, the requirements of the 14th, 15th, and 24th amendments to the Constitution, 42 U.S.C. 1971(a) and (b), sections 2, 4(a), 4(f)(2), 4(f)(4), 201, 203(c), and 208 of the Act, and other constitutional and statutory provisions designed to safeguard the right to vote from denial or abridgment on account of race, color, or membership in a language minority group.

(b) Section 2. Preclearance under section 5 of a voting change will not preclude any legal action under section 2 by the Attorney General if implementation of the change demonstrates that such action is appropriate.

§ 51.56 Guidance from the Courts.

In making determinations the Attorney General will be guided by the relevant decisions of the Supreme Court of the United States and of other Federal courts.

§ 51.57   Relevant Factors.

Among the factors the Attorney General will consider in making determinations with respect to the submitted changes affecting voting are the following:

(a) The extent to which a reasonable and legitimate justification for the change exists.

(b) The extent to which the jurisdiction followed objective guidelines and fair and conventional procedures in adopting the change.

(c) The extent to which the jurisdiction afforded members of racial and language minority groups an opportunity to participate in the decision to make the change.

(d) The extent to which the jurisdiction took the concerns of members of racial and language minority groups into account in making the change.

* * *

Alabama Constitution of 1901

(excerpts)

ARTICLE I: Declaration of Rights

§ 1

Equality and rights of men.

That all men are equally free and independent; that they are endowed by their Creator with certain inalienable rights; that among these are life, liberty and the pursuit of happiness.

§ 2

People source of power.

That all political power is inherent in the people, and all free governments are founded on their authority, and instituted for their benefit; and that, therefore, they have at all times an inalienable and indefeasible right to change their form of government in such manner as they may deem expedient.

* * *

ARTICLE VIII: Suffrage and Elections

§ 177

Age and citizenship qualifications of electors.

Every male citizen of this state who is a citizen of the United States, and every male resident of foreign birth, who, before the ratification of this Constitution, shall have legally declared his intention to become a citizen of the United States, twenty-one years old or upwards, not laboring under any of the disabilities named in this article, and possessing the qualifications required by it, shall be an elector, and shall be entitled to vote at any election by the people; provided, that all foreigners who have legally declared their intention to become citizens of the United States, shall, if they fail to become citizens thereof at the time they are entitled to become such, cease to have the right to vote until they become such citizens.

§ 178

Residency, registration and poll tax requirements for electors.

To entitle a person to vote at any election by the people, he shall have resided in the state at least two years, in the county one year, and in the precinct or ward three months, immediately preceding the election at which he offers to vote, and he shall have been duly registered as an elector, and shall have paid on or before the first day of February next preceding the date of the election at which he offers to vote, all poll taxes due from him for the year nineteen hundred and one, and for each subsequent year; provided, that any elector who, within three months next preceding the date of the election at which he offers to vote, has removed from one precinct or ward to another precinct or ward in the same county, incorporated town, or city, shall have the right to vote in the precinct or ward from which he has so removed, if he would have been entitled to vote in such precinct or ward but for such removal.

§ 179

Method of voting.

All elections by the people shall be by ballot, and all elections by persons in a representative capacity shall be viva voce.

§ 180

Persons qualified to register as electors—Prior to December 20, 1902.

The following male citizens of this state, who are citizens of the United States, and every male resident of foreign birth who, before the ratification of this Constitution, shall have legally declared his intention to become a citizen of the United States, and who shall not have had an opportunity to perfect his citizenship prior to the twentieth day of December, nineteen hundred and two, twenty-one years old or upwards, who, if their place of residence shall remain unchanged, will have, at the date of the next general election the qualifications as to residence prescribed in section 178 of this Constitution, and who are not disqualified under section 182 of this Constitution, shall, upon application, be entitled to register as electors prior to the twentieth day of December, nineteen hundred and two, namely:

First.—All who have honorably served in the land or naval forces of the United States in the war of 1812, or in the war with Mexico, or in any war with the Indians, or in the war between the states, or in the war with Spain, or who honorably served in the land or naval forces of the Confederate States, or of the State of Alabama in the war between the states; or,

Second.—The lawful descendants of persons who honorably served in the land or naval forces of the United States in the war of the American Revolution, or in the war of 1812, or in the war with Mexico, or in any war with the Indians, or in the war between the states, or in the land or naval forces of the Confederate States, or of the State of Alabama in the war between the states; or,

Third.—All persons who are of good character and who understand the duties and obligations of citizenship under a republican form of government.

§ 181

Same—After January 1, 1903.

After the first day of January, nineteen hundred and three, the following persons, and no others, who, if their place of residence shall remain unchanged, will have, at the date of the next general election, the qualifications as to residence prescribed in section 178 of this article, shall be qualified to register as electors; provided, they shall not be disqualified under section 182 of this Constitution.

First.—Those who can read and write any article of the Constitution of the United States in the English language, and who are physically unable to work; and those who can read and write any article of the Constitution of the United States in the English language, and who have worked or been regularly engaged in some lawful employment, business, or occupation, trade or calling, for the greater part of the twelve months next preceding the time they offer to register; and those who are unable to read and write, if such inability is due solely to physical disability; or,

Second.—The owner in good faith in his own right, or the husband of a woman who is the owner in good faith, in her own right, of forty acres of land situate in this state, upon which they reside; or the owner in good faith in his own right, or the husband of any woman who is the owner in good faith, in her own right, of real estate situate in this state, assessed for taxation at the value of three hundred dollars or more, or the owner in good faith, in his own right, or the husband of a woman who is the owner in good faith, in her own right, of personal property in this state assessed for taxation at three hundred dollars or more; provided, that the taxes due upon such real or personal property for the year next preceding the year in which he offers to register shall have been paid, unless the assessment shall have been legally contested and is undetermined.

§ 182

Certain persons disqualified from registering and voting.

The following persons shall be disqualified both from registering, and from voting, namely:

All idiots and insane persons; those who shall by reason of conviction of crime be disqualified from voting at the time of the ratification of this Constitution; those who shall be convicted of treason, murder, arson, embezzlement, malfeasance in office, larceny, receiving stolen property, obtaining property or money under false pretenses, perjury, subornation of perjury, robbery, assault with intent to rob, burglary, forgery, bribery, assault and battery on the wife, bigamy, living in adultery, sodomy, incest, rape, miscegenation, crime against nature, or any crime punishable by imprisonment in the penitentiary, or of any infamous crime or crime involving moral turpitude; also, any person who shall be convicted as a vagrant or tramp, or of selling or offering to sell his vote or the vote of another, or of buying or offering to buy the vote of another, or of making or offering to make a false return in any election by the people or in any primary election to procure the nomination or election of any person to any office, or of suborning any witness or registrar to secure the registration of any person as an elector.

§ 183

Qualifications as elector required to participate in primary elections, party conventions, mass meetings or other methods of political party action.

No person shall be qualified to vote, or participate in any primary election, party convention, mass meeting, or other method of party action of any political party or faction, who shall not possess the qualifications prescribed in this article for an elector, or who shall be disqualified from voting under the provisions of this article.

§ 184

Applicability of article as to elections held after 1902 general election.

No person, not registered and qualified as an elector under the provisions of this article, shall vote at the general election in nineteen hundred and two, or at any subsequent state, county, or municipal election, general, local, or special; but the provisions of this article shall not apply to any election held prior to the general election in the year nineteen hundred and two.

§ 185

Oath or affirmation when vote challenged; false oath or affirmation constitutes perjury.

Any elector whose right to vote shall be challenged for any legal cause before an election officer, shall be required to swear or affirm that the matter of the challenge is untrue before his vote shall be received, and anyone who willfully swears or affirms falsely thereto, shall be guilty of perjury, and upon conviction thereof shall be imprisoned in the penitentiary for not less than one nor more than five years.

§ 186

Legislature to provide for registration procedure after January 1, 1903; procedure for registration prior to January 1, 1903.

The legislature shall provide by law for the registration, after the first day of January, nineteen hundred and three, of all qualified electors. Until the first day of January, nineteen hundred and three, all electors shall be registered under and in accordance with the requirements of this section, as follows:

First—Registration shall be conducted in each county by a board of three reputable and suitable persons resident in the county, who shall not hold any elective office during their term, to be appointed, within sixty days after the ratification of this Constitution, by the governor, auditor, and commissioner of agriculture and industries, or by a majority of them acting as a board of appointment. If one or more of the persons appointed on such a board of registration shall refuse, neglect, or be unable to qualify or serve, or if a vacancy or vacancies occur in the membership of the board of registrars from any cause, the governor, auditor, and commissioner of agriculture and industries, or a majority of them, acting as a board of appointment, shall make other appointments to fill such board. Each registrar shall receive two dollars per day, to be paid by the state, and disbursed by the several judges of probate, for each entire day's attendance upon the session of the board. Before entering upon the performance of the duties of his office, each registrar shall take the same oath required of the judicial officers of the state, which oath may be administered by any person authorized by law to administer oaths. The oath shall be in writing and subscribed by the registrar, and filed in the office of the judge of probate of the county.

Second—Prior to the first day of August, nineteen hundred and two, the board of registrars in each county shall visit each precinct at least once, and oftener if necessary, to make a complete registration of all persons entitled to register, and shall remain there at least one day from eight o'clock in the morning until sunset. They shall give at least twenty days' notice of the time when, and the place in the precinct where, they will attend to register applicants for registration, by bills posted at five or more public places in each election precinct, and by advertisement once a week for three successive weeks in a newspaper, if there be one published in the county. Upon failure to give such notice, or to attend any appointment made by them in any precinct, they shall, after like notice, fill new appointments therein; but the time consumed by the board in completing such registration shall not exceed sixty working days in any county, except that in counties of more than nine hundred square miles in area, such board may consume seventy-five working days in completing the registration, and except that in counties in which there is any city of eight thousand or more inhabitants, the board may remain in session, in addition to the time hereinbefore prescribed, for not more than three successive weeks in each of such cities; and thereafter the board may sit from time to time in each of such cities not more than one week in each month, and except that in the county of Jefferson the board may hold an additional session of not exceeding five consecutive days' duration for each session, in each town or city of more than one thousand and less than eight thousand inhabitants. No person shall be registered except at the county site or in the precinct in which he resides. The registrars shall issue to each person registered a certificate of registration.

Third—The board of registrars shall not register any person between the first day of August, nineteen hundred and two, and the Friday next preceding the day of election in November, nineteen hundred and two. On Friday and Saturday next preceding the day of election in November, nineteen hundred and two, they shall sit in the courthouse of each county during such days, and shall register all applicants having the qualifications prescribed by section 180 of this Constitution and not disqualified under section 182, who shall have reached the age of twenty-one years after the first day of August, nineteen hundred and two, or who shall prove to the reasonable satisfaction of the board that, by reason of physical disability or unavoidable absence from the county, they had no opportunity to register prior to the first day of August, nineteen hundred and two, and they shall not on such days register any other persons. When there are two or more courthouses in a county, the registrars may sit during such two days at the courthouse they may select, but shall give ten days' notice, by bills posted at each of the courthouses, designating the courthouse at which they will sit.

Fourth—The board of registrars shall hold sessions at the courthouse of their respective counties during the entire third week in November, nineteen hundred and two, and for six working days next prior to the twentieth day of December, nineteen hundred and two, during which sessions they shall register all persons applying who possess the qualifications prescribed in section 180 of this Constitution, and who shall not be disqualified under section 182. In counties where there are two or more courthouses the board of registrars shall divide the time equally between them. The board of registrars shall give notice of the time and place of such sessions by posting notices at each courthouse in their respective counties, and at each voting place and at three other public places in the county, and by publication once a week for two consecutive weeks in a newspaper, if one be published in the county; such notices to be posted and such publications to be commenced as early as practicable in the first week of November, nineteen hundred and two. Failure on the part of the registrars to conform to the provisions of this article as to the giving of the required notices shall not invalidate any registration made by them.

Fifth—The board of registrars shall have power to examine, under oath or affirmation, all applicants for registration, and to take testimony touching the qualifications of such applicants. Each member of such board is authorized to administer the oath to be taken by the applicants and witnesses, which shall be in the following form, and subscribed by the person making it, and preserved by the board, namely: "I solemnly swear (or affirm) that in the matter of the application of ____ for registration as an elector, I will speak the truth, the whole truth, and nothing but the truth, so help me God." Any person who upon such examination makes any willfully false statement in reference to any material matter touching the qualification of any applicant for registration shall be guilty of perjury, and upon conviction thereof, shall be imprisoned in the penitentiary for not less than one nor more than five years.

Sixth—The action of the majority of the board of registrars shall be the action of the board, and a majority of the board shall constitute a quorum for the transaction of all business. Any person to whom registration is denied shall have the right of appeal, without giving security for costs, within thirty days after such denial, by filing a petition in the circuit court or court of like jurisdiction held for the county in which he seeks to register, to have his qualifications as an elector determined. Upon the filing of the petition the clerk of the court shall give notice thereof to any solicitor authorized to represent the state in said county, whose duty it shall be to appear and defend against the petition on behalf of the state. Upon such trial the court shall charge the jury only as to what constituted the qualifications that entitled the applicant to become an elector at the time he applied for registration, and the jury shall determine the weight and effect of the evidence and return a verdict. From the judgment rendered an appeal will lie to the supreme court in favor of the petitioner, to be taken within thirty days. Final judgment in favor of the petitioner shall entitle him to registration as of the date of his application to the registrars.

Seventh—The secretary of state shall, at the expense of the state, have prepared and shall furnish to the registrars and judges of probate of the several counties, a sufficient number of registration books and of blank forms of the oath, certificates of registration and notices required to be given by the registrars. The cost of the publication in newspapers of the notices required to be given by the registrars shall be paid by the state, the bills therefor to be rendered to the secretary of state and approved by him.

Eighth—Any person who registers for another, or who registers more than once, and any registrar who enters the name of any person on the list of registered voters, without such person having made application in person under oath on a form provided for that purpose, or who knowingly registers any person more than once, or who knowingly enters a name upon the registration list as the name of a voter, without any one of that name applying to register, shall be guilty of a felony, and upon conviction thereof shall be imprisoned in the penitentiary for not less than one nor more than five years.

§ 187

County board of registrars to furnish list of registered voters to judges of probate by February 1, 1903; judges of probate to file list with secretary of state by March 1, 1903; term for which registration valid; certificate of registration.

The board of registrars in each county shall, on or before the first day of February, nineteen hundred and three, or as soon thereafter as practicable, file in the office of the judge of probate in their county, a complete list sworn to by them of all persons registered in their county, showing the age of such persons so registered, with the precinct or ward in which each of such persons resides set opposite the name of such persons, and shall also file a like list in the office of the secretary of state. The judge of probate shall, on or before the first day of March, nineteen hundred and three, or as soon thereafter as practicable, cause to be made from such list in duplicate, in the books furnished by the secretary of state, an alphabetical list by precincts of the persons shown by the list of the registrars to have been registered in the county, and shall file one of such alphabetical lists in the office of the secretary of state; for which services by the judges of probate compensation shall be provided by the legislature. The judges of probate shall keep both the original list filed by the registrars and the alphabetical list made therefrom as records in the office of the judge of probate of the county. Unless he shall become disqualified under the provisions of this article, any one who shall register prior to the first day of January, nineteen hundred and three, shall remain an elector during life, and shall not be required to register again unless he changes his residence, in which event he may register again on production of his certificate. The certificate of the registrars or of the judge of probate or of the secretary of state shall be sufficient evidence to establish the fact of such life registration. Such certificate shall be issued free of charge to the elector, and the legislature shall provide by law for the renewal of such certificate when lost, mutilated, or destroyed.

§ 188

Certain information to be furnished prior to registration.

From and after the first day of January, nineteen hundred and three, any applicant for registration may be required to state under oath, to be administered by the registrar or by any person authorized by law to administer oaths, where he lived during the five years next preceding the time at which he applies to register, and the name or names by which he was known during that period, and the name of his employer or employers, if any, during such period. Any applicant for registration who refuses to state such facts, or any of them, shall not be entitled to register, and any person so offering to register, who willfully makes a false statement in regard to such matters or any of them, shall be guilty of perjury, and upon conviction thereof shall be imprisoned in the penitentiary for not less than one nor more than five years.

§ 189

Testimony may be required of any person other than defendant in trials of contested elections, proceedings to investigate elections and criminal prosecutions under election laws; immunity from prosecution due to testimony given.

In the trial of any contested election, and in proceedings to investigate any election and in criminal prosecutions for violations of the election laws, no person other than a defendant in such criminal prosecutions shall be allowed to withhold his testimony on the ground that he may criminate himself or subject himself to public infamy; but such person shall not be prosecuted for any offense arising out of the transactions concerning which he testified, but may be prosecuted for perjury committed on such examination.

§ 190

Duty of legislature to pass laws regulating elections, primary elections and purging of registration lists.

The legislature shall pass laws not inconsistent with this Constitution to regulate and govern elections and all such laws shall be uniform throughout the state; and shall provide by law for the manner of holding elections and of ascertaining the result of the same, and shall provide general registration laws not inconsistent with the provisions of this article for the registration of all qualified electors from and after the first day of January, nineteen hundred and three. The legislature shall also make provision by law, not inconsistent with this article, for the regulation of primary elections, and for punishing frauds at the same, but shall not make primary elections compulsory. The legislature shall by law provide for purging the registration list of the names of those who die, become insane, or convicted of crime, or otherwise disqualified as electors under the provisions of this Constitution, and of any names which may have been fraudulently entered on such list by the registrars; provided, that a trial by jury may be had on the demand of any person whose name is proposed to be stricken from the list.

§ 191

Protection against evils of intoxicating liquors at elections.

It shall be the duty of the legislature to pass adequate laws giving protection against the evils arising from the use of intoxicating liquors at all elections.

§ 192

Electors immune from arrest going to, attending and returning from elections.

Electors shall in all cases, except treason, felony, or breach of the peace, be privileged from arrest during their attendance at elections, or while going to or returning therefrom.

§ 193

Returns of elections for certain officials to be made to secretary of state.

Returns of elections for members of the legislature and for all civil officers who are to be commissioned by the governor, except the attorney-general, state auditor, secretary of state, state treasurer, superintendent of education, and commissioner of agriculture and industries, shall be made to the secretary of state.

§ 194

Poll tax—Amount; maximum age for payment; when due and payable; when delinquent; returns of collections to be separate from other collections.

The poll tax mentioned in this article shall be one dollar and fifty cents upon each male inhabitant of the state, over the age of twenty-one years, and under the age of forty-five years, who would not now be exempt by law; but the legislature is authorized to increase the maximum age fixed in this section to not more than sixty years. Such poll tax shall become due and payable on the first day of October in each year, and become delinquent on the first day of the next succeeding February, but no legal process, nor any fee or commission shall be allowed for the collection thereof. The tax collector shall make returns of poll tax collections separate from other collections.

§ 195

Same—Payment of tax of another; advance of money for payment in order to influence vote.

Any person who shall pay the poll tax of another, or advance him money for that purpose in order to influence his vote, shall be guilty of bribery, and upon conviction therefor shall be imprisoned in the penitentiary for not less than one nor more than five years.

§ 196

Severability of article.

If any section or subdivision of this article shall, for any reason, be or be held by any court of competent jurisdiction and of final resort to be invalid, inoperative, or void, the residue of this article shall not be thereby invalidated or affected.

CAMPAIGN FINANCE IN FLUX, AGAIN

Following *McConnell v. Federal Election Commission,* 540 U.S. 93 (2003), the Court appeared to have backed off an increasingly particularized review of efforts by Congress to alter the form of campaign financing in the U.S. The Court's willingness to accept the appearance of corruption, even the perception of such an appearance, appeared to auger in a newer, more deferential posture toward the awkward relation between the unequal distribution of wealth and the political commitment to equality.

The first indication that this new deference was unlikely to hold came in *Wisconsin Right to Life, Inc. v. FEC,* 126 S.Ct. 1016 (2006), in which a unanimous Court indicated its willingness to entertain specific, as-applied challenges to the new strictures of the Bipartisan Campaign Reform Act. No sooner did *WRTL* return to the Court than a new jurisprudential realignment, under the stewardship of Chief Justice Roberts, began to assert itself. Issued as this edition is in press, *WRTL II* shows how deep the divisions on the Court remain and exposes once again the critical fault lines inherited from *Buckley v. Valeo.*

Federal Election Commission v. Wisconsin Right to Life (*WRTL II*)

127 S.C.T. 2652 (2007).

■ CHIEF JUSTICE ROBERTS announced the judgment of the Court and delivered the opinion of the Court with respect to Parts I and II, in which JUSTICES SCALIA, KENNEDY, THOMAS AND ALITO joined, and an opinion with respect to Parts III and IV, in which JUSTICE ALITO, joined.

Section 203 of the Bipartisan Campaign Reform Act of 2002 (BCRA) makes it a federal crime for any corporation to broadcast, shortly before an election, any communication that names a federal candidate for elected office and is targeted to the electorate. In *McConnell v. Federal Election Comm'n,* 540 U.S. 93 (2003), this Court considered whether § 203 was facially overbroad under the First Amendment because it captured within its reach not only campaign speech, or "express advocacy," but also speech about public issues more generally, or "issue advocacy," that mentions a candidate for federal office. The Court concluded that there was no overbreadth concern to the extent the speech in question was the "functional equivalent" of express campaign speech. On the other hand, the Court "assume[d]" that the interests it had found to "justify the regulation of campaign speech might not apply to the regulation of genuine issue ads."

The Court nonetheless determined that § 203 was not facially overbroad. Even assuming § 203 "inhibit[ed] some constitutionally protected corporate and union speech," the Court concluded that those challenging the law on its face had failed to carry their "heavy burden" of establishing that *all* enforcement of the law should therefore be prohibited....

We now confront such an as-applied challenge. Resolving it requires us first to determine whether the speech at issue is the "functional equivalent" of speech expressly advocating the election or defeat of a candidate for federal office, or instead a "genuine issue a[d]." We have long recognized that the distinction between campaign advocacy and issue advocacy "may often dissolve in practical application. Candidates, especially incumbents, are intimately tied to public issues involving legislative proposals and governmental actions." *Buckley v. Valeo,* 424 U.S. 1, 42 (1976) (*per curiam*). Our development of the law in this area requires us, however, to draw such a line, because we have recognized that the interests held to justify the regulation of campaign speech and its "functional equivalent" "might not apply" to the regulation of issue advocacy.

In drawing that line, the First Amendment requires us to err on the side of protecting political speech rather than suppressing it. We conclude that the speech at issue in this as-applied challenge is not the "functional equivalent" of express campaign speech. We further conclude that the interests held to justify restricting corporate campaign speech or its functional equivalent do not justify restricting issue advocacy, and accordingly we hold that BCRA § 203 is unconstitutional as applied to the advertisements at issue in these cases.

I

Prior to BCRA, corporations were free under federal law to use independent expenditures to engage in political speech so long as that speech did not expressly advocate the election or defeat of a clearly identified federal candidate....

BCRA significantly cut back on corporations' ability to engage in political speech. BCRA § 203, at issue in these cases, makes it a crime for any labor union or incorporated entity-whether the United Steelworkers, the American Civil Liberties Union, or General Motors-to use its general treasury funds to pay for any "electioneering communication." BCRA's definition of "electioneering communication" is clear and expansive. It encompasses any broadcast, cable, or satellite communication that refers to a candidate for federal office and that is aired within 30 days of a federal primary election or 60 days of a federal general election in the jurisdiction in which that candidate is running for office.

Appellee Wisconsin Right to Life, Inc. (WRTL), is a nonprofit, nonstock, ideological advocacy corporation recognized by the Internal Revenue Service as tax exempt under § 501(c)(4) of the Internal Revenue Code. On July 26, 2004, as part of what it calls a "grassroots lobbying campaign,"

Brief for Appellee 8, WRTL began broadcasting a radio advertisement entitled "Wedding." The transcript of "Wedding" reads as follows:

" 'PASTOR: And who gives this woman to be married to this man?

" 'BRIDE'S FATHER: Well, as father of the bride, I certainly could. But instead, I'd like to share a few tips on how to properly install drywall. Now you put the drywall up . . .

" 'VOICE–OVER: Sometimes it's just not fair to delay an important decision.

" 'But in Washington it's happening. A group of Senators is using the filibuster delay tactic to block federal judicial nominees from a simple 'yes' or 'no' vote. So qualified candidates don't get a chance to serve.

" 'It's politics at work, causing gridlock and backing up some of our courts to a state of emergency.

" 'Contact Senators Feingold and Kohl and tell them to oppose the filibuster.

" 'Visit: BeFair.org

" 'Paid for by Wisconsin Right to Life (befair.org), which is responsible for the content of this advertising and not authorized by any candidate or candidate's committee.' "

On the same day, WRTL aired a similar radio ad entitled "Loan." It had also invested treasury funds in producing a television ad entitled "Waiting," which is similar in substance and format to "Wedding" and "Loan."

WRTL planned on running "Wedding," "Waiting," and "Loan" throughout August 2004 and financing the ads with funds from its general treasury. It recognized, however, that as of August 15, 30 days prior to the Wisconsin primary, the ads would be illegal "electioneering communication[s]" under BCRA § 203.

Believing that it nonetheless possessed a First Amendment right to broadcast these ads, WRTL filed suit against the Federal Election Commission (FEC) on July 28, 2004, seeking declaratory and injunctive relief before a three-judge District Court.

* * *

III

WRTL rightly concedes that its ads are prohibited by BCRA § 203. Each ad clearly identifies Senator Feingold, who was running (unopposed) in the Wisconsin Democratic primary on September 14, 2004, and each ad would have been "targeted to the relevant electorate," see 2 U.S.C. § 434(f)(3)(C), during the BCRA blackout period. WRTL further concedes that its ads do not fit under any of BCRA's exceptions to the term "electioneering communication." The only question, then, is whether it is consistent with the First Amendment for BCRA § 203 to prohibit WRTL from running these three ads.

* * *

B

For the reasons regarded as sufficient in *Buckley,* we decline to adopt a test for as-applied challenges turning on the speaker's intent to affect an election. The test to distinguish constitutionally protected political speech from speech that BCRA may proscribe should provide a safe harbor for those who wish to exercise First Amendment rights. The test should also "reflec[t] our 'profound national commitment to the principle that debate on public issues should be uninhibited, robust, and wide-open.'" *Buckley, supra,* at 14 (quoting *New York Times Co. v. Sullivan,* 376 U.S. 54 (1964)). A test turning on the intent of the speaker does not remotely fit the bill.

Far from serving the values the First Amendment is meant to protect, an intent-based test would chill core political speech by opening the door to a trial on every ad within the terms of § 203, on the theory that the speaker actually intended to affect an election, no matter how compelling the indications that the ad concerned a pending legislative or policy issue. No reasonable speaker would choose to run an ad covered by BCRA if its only defense to a criminal prosecution would be that its motives were pure. An intent-based standard "blankets with uncertainty whatever may be said," and "offers no security for free discussion." *Buckley, supra,* at 43 (internal quotation marks omitted).

* * *

C

"The freedom of speech ... guaranteed by the Constitution embraces at the least the liberty to discuss publicly and truthfully all matters of public concern without previous restraint or fear of subsequent punishment." *Bellotti,* 435 U.S. at 776 (internal quotation marks omitted). To safeguard this liberty, the proper standard for an as-applied challenge to BCRA § 203 must be objective, focusing on the substance of the communication rather than amorphous considerations of intent and effect....

In light of these considerations, a court should find that an ad is the functional equivalent of express advocacy only if the ad is susceptible of no reasonable interpretation other than as an appeal to vote for or against a specific candidate. Under this test, WRTL's three ads are plainly not the functional equivalent of express advocacy. First, their content is consistent with that of a genuine issue ad: The ads focus on a legislative issue, take a position on the issue, exhort the public to adopt that position, and urge the public to contact public officials with respect to the matter. Second, their content lacks indicia of express advocacy: The ads do not mention an election, candidacy, political party, or challenger; and they do not take a position on a candidate's character, qualifications, or fitness for office.

Despite these characteristics, appellants assert that the content of WRTL's ads alone betrays their electioneering nature. Indeed, the FEC suggests that *any* ad covered by § 203 that includes "an appeal to citizens to contact their elected representative" is the "functional equivalent" of an ad saying defeat or elect that candidate. Brief for Appellant FEC 31; see Brief for Appellant Sen. John McCain et al. in No. 06–970, pp. 21–23 (hereinafter McCain Brief). We do not agree. To take just one example, during a blackout period the House considered the proposed Universal National Service Act. See App. to Brief for American Center for Law and Justice et al. as *Amicus Curiae* B–3. There would be no reason to regard an ad supporting or opposing that Act, and urging citizens to contact their Representative about it, as the equivalent of an ad saying vote for or against the Representative. Issue advocacy conveys information and educates. An issue ad's impact on an election, if it exists at all, will come only after the voters hear the information and choose-uninvited by the ad-to factor it into their voting decisions. . . .

The FEC and intervenors try to turn this difference to their advantage, citing *McConnell's* statements "that the most effective campaign ads, like the most effective commercials for products . . . avoid the [*Buckley*] magic words [expressly advocating the election or defeat of a candidate]," 540 U.S., at 127, and that advertisers "would seldom choose to use such words even if permitted," *id.*, at 193. An expert for the FEC in these cases relied on those observations to argue that WRTL's ads are especially effective electioneering ads because they are "subtl[e]," focusing on issues rather than simply exhorting the electorate to vote against Senator Feingold. Rephrased a bit, the argument perversely maintains that the *less* an issue ad resembles express advocacy, the more likely it is to be the functional equivalent of express advocacy. This "heads I win, tails you lose" approach cannot be correct. It would effectively eliminate First Amendment protection for genuine issue ads, contrary to our conclusion in *WRTL I* that as-applied challenges to § 203 are available, and our assumption in *McConnell* that "the interests that justify the regulation of campaign speech might not apply to the regulation of genuine issue ads," 540 U.S., at 206, n. 88. Under appellants' view, there can be no such thing as a genuine issue ad during the blackout period-it is simply a very effective electioneering ad.

Looking beyond the content of WRTL's ads, the FEC and intervenors argue that several "contextual" factors prove that the ads are the equivalent of express advocacy. First, appellants cite evidence that during the same election cycle, WRTL and its Political Action Committee (PAC) actively opposed Senator Feingold's reelection and identified filibusters as a campaign issue. This evidence goes to WRTL's subjective intent in running the ads, and we have already explained that WRTL's intent is irrelevant in an as-applied challenge. Evidence of this sort is therefore beside the point, as it should be-WRTL does not forfeit its right to speak on issues simply because in other aspects of its work it also opposes candidates who are involved with those issues.

Next, the FEC and intervenors seize on the timing of WRTL's ads. They observe that the ads were to be aired near elections but not near actual Senate votes on judicial nominees, and that WRTL did not run the ads after the elections. To the extent this evidence goes to WRTL's subjective intent, it is again irrelevant. To the extent it nonetheless suggests that the ads should be interpreted as express advocacy, it falls short. That the ads were run close to an election is unremarkable in a challenge like this. *Every* ad covered by BCRA § 203 will by definition air just before a primary or general election. If this were enough to prove that an ad is the functional equivalent of express advocacy, then BCRA would be constitutional in all of its applications. This Court unanimously rejected this contention in *WRTL I*. . . .

Because WRTL's ads may reasonably be interpreted as something other than as an appeal to vote for or against a specific candidate, we hold they are not the functional equivalent of express advocacy, and therefore fall outside the scope of *McConnell's* holding.

* * *

IV

BCRA § 203 can be constitutionally applied to WRTL's ads only if it is narrowly tailored to further a compelling interest. *McConnell*, 540 U.S., at 205; *Buckley, supra,* at 44–45. This Court has never recognized a compelling interest in regulating ads, like WRTL's, that are neither express advocacy nor its functional equivalent. The District Court below considered interests that might justify regulating WRTL's ads here, and found none sufficiently compelling. We reach the same conclusion. . . .

This Court has long recognized "the governmental interest in preventing corruption and the appearance of corruption" in election campaigns. *Buckley,* 424 U.S., at 45. This interest has been invoked as a reason for upholding *contribution* limits. As *Buckley* explained, "[t]o the extent that large contributions are given to secure a political *quid pro quo* from current and potential office holders, the integrity of our system of representative democracy is undermined." We have suggested that this interest might also justify limits on electioneering *expenditures* because it may be that, in some circumstances, "large independent expenditures pose the same dangers of actual or apparent *quid pro quo* arrangements as do large contributions." *Id.,* at 45.

McConnell arguably applied this interest-which this Court had only assumed could justify regulation of express advocacy-to ads that were the "functional equivalent" of express advocacy. But to justify regulation of WRTL's ads, this interest must be stretched yet another step to ads that are *not* the functional equivalent of express advocacy. Enough is enough. Issue ads like WRTL's are by no means equivalent to contributions, and the *quid-pro-quo* corruption interest cannot justify regulating them. To equate WRTL's ads with contributions is to ignore their value as political speech.

Appellants argue that an expansive definition of "functional equivalent" is needed to ensure that issue advocacy does not circumvent the rule against express advocacy, which in turn helps protect against circumvention of the rule against contributions.... But such a prophylaxis-upon-prophylaxis approach to regulating expression is not consistent with strict scrutiny. "[T]he desire for a bright-line rule ... hardly constitutes the *compelling* state interest necessary to justify any infringement on First Amendment freedom." *MCFL,* 479 U.S., at 263....

A second possible compelling interest recognized by this Court lies in addressing a "different type of corruption in the political arena: the corrosive and distorting effects of immense aggregations of wealth that are accumulated with the help of the corporate form and that have little or no correlation to the public's support for the corporation's political ideas." *Austin,* 494 U.S., at 660. *Austin* invoked this interest to uphold a state statute making it a felony for corporations to use treasury funds for independent expenditures on express election advocacy. *McConnell* also relied on this interest in upholding regulation not just of express advocacy, but also its "functional equivalent." 540 U.S., at 205–206.

These cases did not suggest, however, that the interest in combating "a different type of corruption" extended beyond campaign speech. Quite the contrary....

Accepting the notion that a ban on campaign speech could also embrace issue advocacy would call into question our holding in *Bellotti* that the corporate identity of a speaker does not strip corporations of all free speech rights. It would be a constitutional "bait and switch" to conclude that corporate campaign speech may be banned in part *because* corporate issue advocacy is not, and then assert that corporate issue advocacy may be banned as well, pursuant to the same asserted compelling interest, through a broad conception of what constitutes the functional equivalent of campaign speech, or by relying on the inability to distinguish campaign speech from issue advocacy....

Because WRTL's ads are not express advocacy or its functional equivalent, and because appellants identify no interest sufficiently compelling to justify burdening WRTL's speech, we hold that BCRA § 203 is unconstitutional as applied to WRTL's "Wedding," "Loan," and "Waiting" ads.

* * *

These cases are about political speech. The importance of the cases to speech and debate on public policy issues is reflected in the number of diverse organizations that have joined in supporting WRTL before this Court: the American Civil Liberties Union, the National Rifle Association, the American Federation of Labor and Congress of Industrial Organizations, the Chamber of Commerce of the United States of America, Focus on the Family, the Coalition of Public Charities, the Cato Institute, and many others.

Yet, as is often the case in this Court's First Amendment opinions, we have gotten this far in the analysis without quoting the Amendment itself: "Congress shall make no law ... abridging the freedom of speech." The Framers' actual words put these cases in proper perspective. Our jurisprudence over the past 216 years has rejected an absolutist interpretation of those words, but when it comes to drawing difficult lines in the area of pure political speech-between what is protected and what the Government may ban-it is worth recalling the language we are applying. *McConnell* held that express advocacy of a candidate or his opponent by a corporation shortly before an election may be prohibited, along with the functional equivalent of such express advocacy. We have no occasion to revisit that determination today. But when it comes to defining what speech qualifies as the functional equivalent of express advocacy subject to such a ban-the issue we *do* have to decide-we give the benefit of the doubt to speech, not censorship. The First Amendment's command that "Congress shall make no law ... abridging the freedom of speech" demands at least that.

The judgment of the United States District Court for the District of Columbia is affirmed.

■ JUSTICE ALITO, concurring.

I join the principal opinion because I conclude (a) that § 203 of the Bipartisan Campaign Reform Act of 2002, as applied, cannot constitutionally ban any advertisement that may reasonably be interpreted as anything other than an appeal to vote for or against a candidate, (b) that the ads at issue here may reasonably be interpreted as something other than such an appeal, and (c) that because § 203 is unconstitutional as applied to the advertisements before us, it is unnecessary to go further and decide whether § 203 is unconstitutional on its face. If it turns out that the implementation of the as-applied standard set out in the principal opinion impermissibly chills political speech ..., we will presumably be asked in a future case to reconsider the holding in *McConnell v. Federal Election Comm'n* that § 203 is facially constitutional.

■ JUSTICE SCALIA, with whom JUSTICES KENNEDY and THOMAS join, concurring in part and concurring in the judgment.

A Moroccan cartoonist once defended his criticism of the Moroccan monarch (*lèse majesté* being a serious crime in Morocco) as follows: " 'I'm not a revolutionary, I'm just defending freedom of speech.... I never said we had to change the king-no, no, no, no! But I said that some things the king is doing, I do not like. Is that a crime?' "Well, in the United States (making due allowance for the fact that we have elected representatives instead of a king) it *is* a crime, at least if the speaker is a union or a corporation (including not-for-profit public-interest corporations) and if the representative is identified by name within a certain period before a primary or congressional election in which he is running. That is the import of § 203 of the Bipartisan Campaign Reform Act of 2002 (BCRA), the constitutionality of which we upheld three Terms ago in *McConnell v. Federal Election* Comm'n. As an element essential to that determination of constitutionality, our opinion left open the possibility that a corporation or union could establish that, in the particular circumstances of its case, the ban was unconstitutional because it was (to pursue the analogy) *only* the king's policies and not his tenure in office that was criticized. Today's cases present the question of what sort of showing is necessary for that purpose. For the reasons I set forth below, it is my view that no test for such a showing can both (1) comport with the requirement of clarity that un-chilled freedom of political speech demands, and (2) be compatible with the facial validity of § 203 (as pronounced in *McConnell*). I would therefore reconsider the decision that sets us the unsavory task of separating issue-speech from election-speech with no clear criterion.

* * *

■ JUSTICE SOUTER, with whom JUSTICES STEVENS, GINSBURG, and BREYER join, dissenting.

The significance and effect of today's judgment, from which I respectfully dissent, turn on three things: the demand for campaign money in huge amounts from large contributors, whose power has produced a cynical electorate; the congressional recognition of the ensuing threat to democratic integrity as reflected in a century of legislation restricting the electoral leverage of concentrations of money in corporate and union treasuries; and *McConnell v. Federal Election Comm'n,* declaring the facial validity of the most recent Act of Congress in that tradition, a decision that is effectively, and unjustifiably, overruled today.

* * *

III

In *McConnell,* we found this definition to be "easily understood and objectiv[e]," raising "none of the vagueness concerns that drove our analysis" of the statutory language at issue in *Buckley* and *MCFL,* and we held that the resulting line separating regulated election speech from general political discourse does not, on its face, violate the First Amendment. We rejected any suggestion "that *Buckley* drew a constitutionally mandated line between express advocacy [with magic words] and so-called issue advocacy [without them], and that speakers possess an inviolable First Amendment right to engage in the latter category of speech." *Id.,* at 190. To the contrary, we held that "our decisions in *Buckley* and *MCFL* were specific to the statutory language before us; they in no way drew a constitutional boundary that forever fixed the permissible scope of provisions regulating campaign-related speech." *Id.,* at 192–193. "[T]he presence or absence of magic words cannot meaningfully distinguish electioneering speech," which is prohibitable, "from a true issue ad," we said, since ads that "esche[w] the use of magic words ... are no less clearly intended to influence the election." *Id.*, at 193. We thus found "[l]ittle difference ... between an ad that urged viewers to 'vote against Jane Doe' and one that condemned Jane Doe's record on a particular issue before exhorting viewers to 'call Jane Doe and tell her what you think.'"

We understood that Congress had a compelling interest in limiting this sort of electioneering by corporations and unions, for § 203 exemplified a tradition of "repeatedly sustained legislation aimed at 'the corrosive and distorting effects of immense aggregations of wealth that are accumulated with the help of the corporate form and that have little or no correlation to the public's support for the corporation's political ideas.'" *Id.* at 205 (quoting *Austin,* 494 U.S., at 660). Nor did we see any plausible claim of substantial overbreadth from incidentally prohibiting ads genuinely focused on issues rather than elections, given the limitation of "electioneering communication" by time, geographical coverage, and clear reference to candidate. "Far from establishing that BCRA's application to pure issue ads is substantial, either in an absolute sense or relative to its application to election-related advertising, the record strongly supports the contrary conclusion." 540 U.S., at 207. Finally, we underscored the reasonableness of the § 203 line by emphasizing that it defined a category of limited, but not prohibited, corporate and union speech: "Because corporations can still fund electioneering communications with PAC money, it is 'simply wrong' to view [§ 203] as a 'complete ban' on expression rather than a regulation." *Id.*, at 204 (quoting *Federal Election Comm'n v. Beaumont,* 539 U.S. 146, 162 (2003)). Thus "corporations and unions may finance genuine issue ads [in the runup period] by simply avoiding any specific reference to federal candidates, or in doubtful cases by paying for the ad from a segregated [PAC] fund." 540 U.S. at 206.

* * *

This century-long tradition of legislation and judicial precedent rests on facing undeniable facts and testifies to an equally undeniable value. Campaign finance reform has been a series of reactions to documented threats to electoral integrity obvious to any voter, posed by large sums of money from corporate or union treasuries, with no redolence of "grassroots" about them. Neither Congress's decisions nor our own have understood the corrupting influence of money in politics as being limited to outright bribery or discrete *quid pro quo;* campaign finance reform has instead consistently focused on the more pervasive distortion of electoral institutions by concentrated wealth, on the special access and guaranteed favor that sap the representative integrity of American government and defy public confidence in its institutions. From early in the 20th century through the decision in *McConnell,* we have acknowledged that the value of democratic integrity justifies a realistic response when corporations and labor organizations commit the concentrated moneys in their treasuries to electioneering.

* * *

NOTES AND QUESTIONS

1. Invariably, the immediate effect of *WRTL II* is to announce a realignment of the Court following the addition of two new members. Neither Chief Justice Roberts nor Justice Alito has yet to declare himself fully on the continuing vitality of the post-*Buckley* state of the law, nor on the conceptual validity of the core divide between the regulation of contributions and expenditures. Nonetheless, the opinions of these two Justices evince at least skepticism—if not outright hostility—to the central regulatory enterprise. Also significant is the mild realignment of the former centers of the Court on campaign finance, Justices Breyer and Kennedy. In a series of opinions, each of these Justices had sought to calibrate finely the forms of regulation that would be permissible. Yet, each joins a more sweeping critique of the core post-*Buckley* divide. For Justice Kennedy, this means joining the sweeping critique of Justice Scalia for all regulation, regardless of the categorization as contribution or expenditure. Similarly, Justice Breyer endorses a far broader view of regulatory authority in Justice Souter's dissenting opinion. Indeed, Justice Souter's opinion appears to reach considerably further than Justice Breyer's opinion only one Term earlier in *Randall v. Sorrell*. Moreover, the only Justice to join fully Justice Breyer's opinion in *Sorrell* was Chief Justice Roberts, an alliance on campaign finance that seems particularly short-lived. If *WRTL II* does signal a stable set of views increasingly hostile to campaign finance regulation, this may auger the end of the precarious *Buckley* balance between two poles of the Court, each wanting to overturn *Buckley,* but each unable to topple it in the desired direction.

2. Chief Justice Roberts tries to walk a fine line in not appearing to overrule *McConnell*. Nonetheless, his caustic remark that "enough is enough" likely signals an impatience with the facile use of the corruption rationale to shore up campaign finance reform. How persuasive is the attempt to ground the *WRTL II* holding in a narrow as-applied extension of *McConnell*? Notice that there are only two votes on the Court for this proposition, both by Justices who were not on the Court at the time of *McConnell*. Clearly, the rest of the Court was unpersuaded by the effort to limit the sweep of *WRTL II*. In footnote 7 of his separate opinion, Justice Scalia searingly writes: "The claim that § 203 on its face does not reach a substantial amount of speech protected under the principal opinion's test-and that the test is therefore compatible with *McConnell*-seems to me indefensible. Indeed, the principal opinion's attempt at distinguishing *McConnell* is unpersuasive enough, and the change in the law it works is substantial enough, that seven Justices of this Court, having widely divergent views concerning the constitutionality of the restrictions at issue, agree that the opinion effectively overrules *McConnell* without saying so. This faux judicial restraint is judicial obfuscation." Assuming the seven Justices to be correct, is there any gain to be had from eviscerating precedents slowly as opposed to confronting their continued vitality directly?

3. The issues presented in *WRTL II* concerned independent expenditures and electioneering communications under Title II of BCRA. From the moment the opinion was announced, commentators and reform advocates were decrying the death of BCRA and a potential opening of the floodgates for sham issue advertisements. Certainly the new standard of protection for any communication that could reasonably be construed as something other than express advocacy could be seen as opening the door to new forms of spending by corporations and unions, assuming the desire to do so. One possible effect of *WRTL II* is to create a new form of regulatory misalignment, much as had occurred after *Buckley* truncated the original FECA regulatory design. The one group whose capacity to engage in issue advocacy had not been *sub judice* in *WRTL II* are political parties, who face a distinct set of prohibitions on their capacity to raise and spend soft money under Title I of BCRA. If *WRTL II* does indeed open the prospect of a new round of soft money spending through issue ads that steer clear of the new legal standard, the question resurfaces as to why as a matter of policy political parties should be a disfavored set of potential political speakers? If *WRTL II* proves to alter significantly the BCRA regulatory framework, the question of the special and disfavored treatment of political parties could well resurface as the next constitutional challenge.

INDEX

References are to pages

†